DICTIONARY

OF

ARTS, MANUFACTURES, AND MINES.

VOL. I.

LONDON : PRINTED BY
SPOTTISWOODE AND CO., NEW-STREET SQUARE
AND PARLIAMENT STREET

URE'S DICTIONARY

OF

ARTS, MANUFACTURES, AND MINES

CONTAINING

A CLEAR EXPOSITION OF THEIR PRINCIPLES AND PRACTICE

BY

ROBERT HUNT, F.R.S.

KEEPER OF MINING RECORDS
FORMERLY PROFESSOR OF PHYSICS, ROYAL SCHOOL OF MINES, ETC.
AUTHOR OF 'RESEARCHES ON LIGHT' 'THE POETRY OF SCIENCE' ETC.

assisted by

F. W. RUDLER, F.G.S.

and by numerous Contributors eminent in Science and familiar with Manufactures

Illustrated with upwards of Twenty-one Hundred Engravings on Wood

SEVENTH EDITION

COMPLETELY REVISED AND GREATLY ENLARGED

IN THREE VOLUMES

VOL. I.

LONDON

LONGMANS, GREEN, AND CO.

1875

Another Quality Reprint of a Classic Book
by

The Apple Manor Press

2017

Markham, Virginia

Thousands of titles available at:
www.AppleManorPress.com

Book pages have been individually reproduced and processed by trained
Aritisans using uncompressed high resolution scanned images of the
original pages. Manually processing of the images allows proper attention to detail
not possible through inexpensive automated software.
Most low cost competitors use automated software with no human quality control
to process low quality compressed PDF files intended for internet viewing.

Manual processing each page allows for much better image and print quality

ISBN numbers:
Volume Ia: 978-1-5421-0235-3   Volume IIIa: 978-1-5421-0239-1
Volume Ib: 978-1-5421-0236-0   Volume IIIb: 978-1-5421-0240-7
Volume IIa: 978-1-5421-0237-7   Volume IVa: 978-1-5421-0241-4
Volume IIb: 978-1-5421-0238-4   Volume IVb: 978-1-5421-0242-1

PREFACE

TO

THE SEVENTH EDITION.

——◆◇◆——

THIS DICTIONARY OF ARTS, MANUFACTURES, AND MINES passed through four Editions during the lifetime of Dr. ANDREW URE ; and this is the third Edition which has been required by the public, since, in 1858, it was committed to my care.

These volumes have received the same unrelaxing attention, to every detail, which was bestowed upon the previous Editions, and which secured for them the confidence of the manufacturer, the miner, the metallurgist, and the general public.

Every division of the Arts, each special process of Manufacture, and all the branches of Mining, have been most cautiously examined, and such improvements, as have been proved to be of real utility, have been recorded in all necessary detail. This has led to an increase in the size of the volumes, to the rejection of many articles which had, with the progress of advancing knowledge, become obsolete, and to the curtailing of others which were of less importance than the new ones which it was necessary to introduce. The more important articles have been, for the most part, rewritten, and all of them subjected to a critical revision, while many entirely new articles have been introduced. It is needless to particularise these, since the most hasty comparison between the volumes of the last Edition, and those of the present one, will at once render the new and the amended articles sufficiently obvious.

The type for the whole of the work has been entirely reset, and nearly two hundred woodcut illustrations have been added.

The list of contributors will show to whom we are indebted for the technical articles which distinguish this Dictionary; and the articles themselves will give evidence of their having been treated, in all cases, by men who are thoroughly experienced in the processes which they have described. When the initial letters at the end of the articles do not indicate the authors of them, I am directly responsible for them. In a work treating of the useful applications of Science, it became necessary to introduce such portions of those sciences, which have been economically useful to man, as would render the processes described sufficiently intelligible to all readers, and show the aid which has been rendered by scientific enquiry. Therefore, several divisions of Physics, Chemistry, Geology, and Mineralogy, are succinctly dealt with. Of Chemistry, it should be remarked, that the very rapid advances of discovery in that science, have involved a revolution in the mode of viewing the constitution of bodies, and necessitated the construction of a new mode of expressing that constitution. During the transition period, there naturally arises much difficulty in determining with exactness the formulæ which shall correctly express the composition of a compound. This natural difficulty has been aggravated by the unfortunate introduction of hypothetical views respecting the constitution of compounds, and the creation of systems of notation which are constantly liable to somewhat capricious alteration. As this Dictionary is for the use of a public which cannot be expected to be acquainted with each change in the views entertained by the different schools of Chemistry, it has been thought desirable to retain the formulæ with which they have been long familiar, and to give in another (black) type the formulæ which have been adopted by most modern chemists.

It will be observed that in some cases the Imports and Exports of productions used in the Arts or Manufactures, which were given in the former Editions, do not appear in the present one. This arises from the impossibility of obtaining them: the Custom House authorities now entering a large number of articles under the head of 'Unenumerated,' which were formerly given in detail. This is much to be regretted, since it removes the power of tracing the progress of the special use, or industry, to which the article in question belongs.

To all those gentlemen who have favoured me with contributions my best thanks are due. I have, however, to express my obligations more especially—to Mr. HIGGIN, whose article on 'Calico Printing' gives a more satisfactory description of that industry than any other to be found in any language ; to Mr. HILARY BAUERMAN, who has brought the articles ' Iron ' and ' Steel' up to the most recent date, and to a condition of great completeness; and to Mr. JOHN DARLINGTON, who has submitted to a complete revision all the articles connected with Mining. Of the latter it may be safely said, that they, taken collectively, form a description of the modes of obtaining and of preparing the useful minerals for the market such as is not to be found in any other work in the English language.

My obligations to Mr. F. W. RUDLER, who has assisted me in my heavy labours of producing these volumes, are great. During a period, when the disturbed condition of my health rendered it even dangerous for me to give any prolonged fixed attention to the Dictionary, that gentleman, with almost enthusiastic zeal, devoted his best energies to the tedious details of the work, and gave me all the advantages of his general and exact knowledge.

With the aid that has been received, and the attention which has been bestowed on this work, I feel that it may with confidence be commited to the public, believing that it will be found a useful guide in all those industries which are connected with the Arts, Manufactures, and Mines.

ROBERT HUNT, F.R.S.

April 27, 1875.

LIST OF THE CONTRIBUTORS.

———◦◦———

General Editor—ROBERT HUNT, F.R.S.
KEEPER OF MINING RECORDS, ETC.

Assistant Editor—F. W. RUDLER, F.G.S.

W. C. AITKIN, Esq.
Birmingham.

GEORGE F. ANSELL, Esq.

EMERSON BAINBRIDGE, Esq.
Mining Engineer, Sheffield.

H. K. BAMBER, Esq., F.C.S., &c.

H. BAUERMAN, Esq., F.G.S.
Author of 'A Treatise on the Metallurgy of Iron.'

E. W. BINNEY, Esq., F.G.S., &c.
Manchester.

(*The late*) H. W. BONE, Esq.
Enameller.

HENRY W. BRISTOW, Esq., F.R.S., F.G.S. Author of 'Glossary of Mineralogy.' Director of the Geological Survey of England and Wales.

R. J. COURTNEY, Esq.

JAMES DAFFORNE, Esq.
Assistant Editor of the 'Art Journal.'

JOHN DARLINGTON, Esq.
Mining Engineer. Author of 'Miner's Handbook.'

M. DARTON, Esq.
Bookbinder, London.

(*The late*) F. W. FAIRHOLT, Esq., F.R.A.S. Author of 'Costume in England,' 'Dictionary of Terms in Art,' &c.

E. FRANKLAND, Esq., Ph.D., F.R.S., F.C.S. Professor of Chemistry, Royal School of Mines.

ALFRED FRYER, Esq.
Sugar Refiner, Manchester.

(*The late*) T. H. HENRY, Esq., F.R.S., F.C.S.

E. HELM, Esq.
Manchester. Author of papers on 'Cotton Manufacture.'

(*The late*) W. HERAPATH, Esq., M.D., &c.

R. HERRING, Esq.
Author of 'History of Paper Manufacture.'

JAMES HIGGIN, Esq., F.C.S.
Manchester.

SAMUEL HOCKING, Esq., C.E.
Camborne, Cornwall.

G. MANLEY HOPWOOD, Esq.
Chemist, Manchester.

GEORGE HUNT, Esq.
Brewer, Oldham.

T. B. JORDAN, Esq.
Engineer; Inventor of Wood-carving Machinery.

JAMES B. JORDAN, Esq.
Assistant in Mining Record Office, Museum of Practical Geology.

WILLIAM LINTON, Esq.
Artist. Author of 'Ancient and Modern Colours.'

(*The late*) JAMES McADAM, Jun., Esq. Late Secretary of the Royal Society for the Cultivation of Flax in Ireland.

H. McCALL, Esq.
Lisburn, Ireland. Author of Essays on 'Linen and Flax.'

(*The late*) HERBERT MACKWORTH, Esq., C.E., F.G.S. One of H.M.'s Inspectors of Coal Mines.

HENRY MARLES, Esq., L.R.C.P.

(*The late*) DAVID MORRIS, Esq.
Manchester. Author of 'Cottonopolis.' &c.

x LIST OF THE CONTRIBUTORS.

D. NAPIER, Esq., C.E., &c.

JAMES NAPIER, Esq., F.C.S.
Author of 'Manual of Dyeing,' 'Electro-Metallurgy,' 'Ancient Works in Metal,' &c.

HENRY M. NOAD, Esq., Ph.D., F.R.S.
Author of 'A Manual of Electricity,' &c.

(The late) A. NORMANDY, Esq., M.D.,
F.C.S. Author of 'Handbook of Commercial Chemistry.'

AUGST. B. NORTHCOTE, Esq., F.C.S.
Chemist, University of Oxford.

ROBERT OXLAND, Esq., F.C.S.
One of the Authors of 'Metals and their Alloys.'

THOMAS JOHN PEARSALL, Esq.,
F.C.S., &c., &c.

JOHN ARTHUR PHILIPS, Esq.,
Mem. Inst. C.E., F.G.S., F.C.S. Graduate of the Imperial School of Mines, Paris. Author of 'Elements of Metallurgy,' and 'The Mining Metallurgy of Gold and Silver.'

SEPTIMUS PIESSE, Esq., F.C.S.
Author of 'Treatise on Art of Perfumery,' &c.

ANDREW CROMBIE RAMSAY,
Esq., LL.D., F.R.S., F.G.S. Professor of Geology, Royal School of Mines; Director-General of the Geological Survey of the United Kingdom.

T. A. READWIN, Esq., F.G.S.
Manchester.

(The late) EBENEZER ROGERS, C.E.,
F.G.S.

CHARLES SANDERSON, Esq.
Sheffield. Author of Papers on 'Steel and Iron.'

E. SCHUNK, Esq., Ph.D., F.R.S.
F.C.S.

R. ANGUS SMITH, Esq., Ph.D., F.R.S.
Author of various Papers on 'Air and Water,' 'Life of Dalton,' and 'History of Atomic Theory,' &c.

RICHARD SMITH, Esq.
Superintendent of Metallurgical Laboratory, Royal School of Mines.

WARINGTON W. SMYTH, Esq.,
M.A., F.R.S., F.G.S. Professor of Mining and Mineralogy, Royal School of Mines, and Inspector of Crown Mines.

THOMAS SOPWITH, Esq., M.A.,
F.R.S., F.G.S. Author of 'Isometrical Drawing,' &c.

JOHN SPILLER, Esq., F.C.S.
President of the Photographic Society.

ANDREW TAYLOR, Esq., F.C.S.
Chemist, Edinburgh.

(The late) ROBERT DUNDAS THOMSON, Esq., M.D., F.R.S. Professor of Chemistry in St. Thomas's Hospital College.

JOHN W. TURNER, Esq.
Bradford. Author of Papers on 'Wool and Woollen Manufacture.'

ALFRED TYLOR, Esq., F.G.S.
Author of 'Treatise on Metal Work.'

A. VOELCKER, Esq., Ph.D., F.R.S.,
F.C.S. Consulting Chemist to the Royal Agricultural Society of England.

CHARLES V. WALKER, Esq., F.R.S.
F.R.A.S. Engineer of Telegraphs and Time to the South-Eastern Railway Company. Author of 'Electrotype Manipulation'; Translator of 'Kæmtz's Meteorology,' 'De la Rive's Electricity,' &c.

W. J. WARD, Esq.,
Metallurgical Laboratory, School of Mines.

C. GREVILLE WILLIAMS, Esq.,
F.R.S. Author of 'A Handbook of Chemical Manipulation,' &c.

WM. MATTIEU WILLIAMS, Esq.,
F.C.S.

(The late) HENRY M. WITT, Esq.,
F.C.S. Assistant Chemist, Government School of Mines.

With special assistance and information from the late Sir WM. REID, C.B.; Sir WM. ARMSTRONG, C.B., &c.; ROBERT MALLET, Esq., F.R.S., &c.; Captain DRAYSON, R.A.; GEORGE W. LENOX, Esq.; and many others.

Omissions.

Page 157 *insert* **AMYLAMINE.** See Watts's 'Dictionary of Chemistry.'
  „ 203 „ **ARACEÆ.** A natural order of monocotyledonous plants, to which
                the genus *Arum* gives the name.
  „ 1008 „ **COW TREE.** The milk tree of Demerara.
  „ „ „ **CRAB OIL.** An oil obtained in South America, from the seed of
                the *Carapa Guinanensis.*

A DICTIONARY

OF

ARTS, MANUFACTURES, AND MINES.

———∘∘⦂◦⦂∘∘———

A

AAL. A red dye used in Central India for imparting a permanent colour to the native cotton cloth. It is yielded by the roots of the *Morinda citrifolia*, a small tree belonging to the *Rubiaceæ*, or madder order. Professor T. Anderson has obtained from the aal root a pale yellow crystalline substance which he calls *morindin*, and this when subjected to distillation yields a crystalline sublimate termed *morindone*. It has been found that this morindone is identical with alizarine, one of the colouring principles of madder; and it is conjectured that the morindin may correspond with ruberythric acid.

ABA. A woollen stuff manufactured in Turkey.

ABACA. A species of fibre obtained in the Philippine Islands in abundance. Some authorities refer those fibres to the palm-tree known as the Abaca, or *Anisa textilis*. There seem, indeed, to be several well-known varieties of fibre included under this name, some so fine that they are used in the most delicate and costly textures, mixed with fibres of the pine-apple, forming Pina muslins and textures equal to the best muslins of Bengal. Of the coarser fibres, mats, cordage, and sail-cloth are made. M. Duchesne states that the well-known fibrous manufactures of Manilla have led to the manufacture of the fibres themselves, at Paris, into many articles of furniture and dress. Their brilliancy and strength give remarkable fitness for bonnets, tapestry, carpets, network, hammocks, &c. The only manufactured articles exported from the Philippine Islands, enumerated by Thomas de Comyn, Madrid, 1820 (transl. by Walton), besides a few tanned buffalo hides and skins, are 8,000 to 12,000 pieces of light sail-cloth, and 200,000 lbs. of assorted abaca cordage.

ABICHITE. An arsenate of copper found occasionally in the copper mines of Cornwall and of the Hartz. It usually consists of 54 per cent. of protoxide of copper and 30 per cent. of arsenic acid, with water.

ABIES (*in Botany*). The fir; a genus of trees which belong to the coniferous order. These trees are well known from their ornamental character, and for the valuable timber which they produce. They yield several resins or gum-resins, which are useful in the arts.

ABIES BALSAMEA. The Balm of Gilead fir. It is a native of Canada and Nova Scotia; it produces the Canada Balsam. This elegant tree grows most abundantly in the colder regions of North America. (See CANADA BALSAM).

ABIES CEDRUS (*Cedrus Libani*,. The Cedar. It is a native of Mount Lebanon and the range of Mount Taurus. Cedar wood is said to be very indestructible, and its wood is used in the manufacture of ornamental boxes, on account of its odour. See CEDAR WOOD.

ABIES EXCELSA of De Candolle (*Pinus abies* of Linnæus). The Norway Spruce fir, or Dantzic Deal, a native of Germany, Russia, Norway, and other parts of Northern Europe. It yields a resinous exudation known as Frankincense or Thus, while the wood forms the 'White Deal' of the carpenter. The well-known Burgundy Pitch is prepared from the resin obtained from this tree. See BURGUNDY PITCH; FRANK-INCENSE.

ABIES LARIX (*Larix europæa*). The Common Larch, producing the Venice Turpentine, and a manna called Briançon Manna which exudes from the leaves. See VENICE TURPENTINE.

ABIES NIGRA. The Black Spruce fir, indigenous to the most inclement regions of North America. A considerable quantity of the essence of spruce is extracted from the young branches of this tree; it is, however, also obtained from other varieties of the spruce fir. See SPRUCE ESSENCE.

ABIES PICEA of Linnæus (*Abies pectinata* of De Candolle). The Silver fir, producing the true Strasburg turpentine. See TURPENTINE.

Of the woods of these trees the following quantities were imported in 1871 :—

Hewn Fir.

	Loads	Value £
From Russia	187,619	378,676
„ Sweden . . .	228,980	398,326
„ Norway . . .	226,197	352,837
„ Germany . . .	297,533	682,489
„ France . . .	57,641	60,121
„ United States of America .	109,630	364,437
„ British North America	343,271	1,319,174
„ Other Countries . .	2,700	5,732
Total . . .	1,453,571	3,561,792

Sawn or Split, Planed or Dressed, Fir.

	Loads	Value £
From Russia . . .	479,575	1,155,870
„ Sweden . . .	906,280	1,913,357
„ Norway . . .	435,408	924,757
„ Germany . .	59,757	137,383
„ United States of America .	37,847	121,909
„ British North America	692,824	1,809,199
„ Other countries . .	4,172	8,777
Total . . .	2,615,863	6,071,252

ABIETENE. This hydrocarbon is the product of distillation of the terebinthinate exudation of a coniferous tree indigenous to California, viz., the *Pinus sabiniana*, a tree met with in the dry sides of the foot hills of the Sierra Nevada mountains, and locally known as the nut-pine or digger-pine, on account of the edible quality of its fruit. A gum resin, or rather balsam, is obtained from this tree by incisions made in its wood, and the balsam is submitted to distillation almost immediately after it has been collected, owing to the great volatility of the hydrocarbon (or essential oil, because abietene really stands in the same relation to the balsam alluded to, as oil of turpentine stands to the exudation derived from other species of *Pinus*). The crude oil, as usually met with for sale at San Francisco, is a colourless limpid fluid, requiring only to be redistilled to obtain it quite pure. The commercial article is used under different names, abietene, erasine, theoline, &c., for the removal of grease and paint from clothing and woven fabrics, and likewise as an efficient substitute for petroleum-benzine. Pure abietene is a colourless fluid, possessing a strongly penetrating odour, bearing some resemblance to oil of oranges; sp. gr. at $16 \cdot 5° = 0 \cdot 694$: it is very volatile, highly combustible, burning with a brilliant white smokeless flame, almost insoluble in water, and soluble in 5 parts of alcohol at 95 per cent. Abietene is not acted upon by dry hydrochloric acid gas nor by nitric acid (sp. gr. $= 1 \cdot 43$) in the cold, but heat being applied, a slight reaction takes place; neither concentrated sulphuric acid nor potassium acts upon this hydrocarbon; when treated with chlorine, abietene is converted into fluid of the consistency of glycerine, insoluble in water, colourless, soluble in warm alcohol, and having a sp. gr. $= 1 \cdot 666$. Abietene readily dissolves iodine and bromine, and is a powerful solvent for fixed and volatile oils, castor oil excepted, and also Peruvian balsam and Canada balsam; castor oil is absolutely insoluble in abietene, while, curiously enough, the last-named substance is dissolved by castor oil to some extent. When burned in an ordinary spirit-lamp with not too large a flame, a brilliant white light is obtained without smoke: the vapour of abietene is a powerful anæsthetic when inhaled, and it has been used with success as an insecticide against moths, &c., when sprinkled in closed receptacles.

ABIETIN. A pale yellow, transparent, viscid exudation from the *Abies picea*. It contains 35 per cent. of a volatile oil of an agreeable smell, combined with a resin, and a small quantity of the acid of amber, as well as the peculiar body called *abietin.*

ABLETTE, or **ABLE,** is a name given to several species of fish, but particularly to the Bleak, the scales of which are employed for making the *pearl essence* which is used in the manufacture of artificial pearls. See PEARLS, ARTIFICIAL.

ABRASION. The figuration of materials by wearing down the surface. In general, the abrasive tool or grinder is exactly a counterpart of the form to be produced; thus, for plane surfaces a flat grinder is employed, and for concave surfaces a convex grinder.

ABRAUM SALTS ((*Abraumsalze,* Ger., 'Salts to be removed'). Towards the upper part of the great salt deposits now extensively worked at Stassfurt, in Prussia, the chloride of sodium becomes largely mixed with certain salts of potassium and magnesium, representing the more soluble compounds which remained dissolved in the mother liquor after the greater part of the chloride of sodium had been separated by crystallisation. These mixed salts were formerly regarded as worthless, and were hence termed *Abraumsalze.* Indeed the workings at Stassfurt having been originally undertaken with the view of procuring common rock-salt, it was naturally considered unprofitable to bore through the thick beds of impure salt before reaching the underlying deposit of purer chloride of sodium. The high commercial value of these so-called *Abraumsalze* is now, however, fully recognised; and at the present time they are employed on a very large scale for the production of chloride of potassium. In addition to the rock salt, the chief constituents of the *Abraumsalze* are the minerals known as *Carnallite,* a double chloride of potassium and magnesium; *Sylvine,* or chloride of potassium; and *Kieserite,* or sulphate of magnesia. Similar deposits of salts are worked at Kalucz, in Hungary. See POTASSIUM, CHLORIDE OF.

ABRUS PRECATORIA. The seeds, often strung together as rosaries and necklaces, are well known as 'Prayer Beads.' They are of a brilliant scarlet colour, with a black spot on one side, and are hence termed 'Crabs' Eyes.' In India, they are used by druggists and jewellers as weights, the seeds weighing uniformly about one grain each. The *Abrus* belongs to the *Leguminosæ,* or Pea-order.

ABSINTH. A liquor flavoured with wormwood (*Artemesia absinthium,* Natural Order *Compositæ*) and other species containing the bitter principle termed *absinthine.* To prepare absinth the leaves and flower-heads of the wormwood are steeped in spirit somewhat above 'proof' for several days, with other aromatic and stimulant herbs—such as angelica root, *Calamus aromaticus,* aniseed, dittany leaves and wild marjoram. The liquid is then distilled, and the green essence thus obtained is mixed with certain aromatic extracts. A brilliant tint is obtained by the use of indigo and other vegetable colouring matters: sulphate of copper is said to have been employed for this purpose; and it is also asserted that the liquor is occasionally adulterated with chloride of antimony in order to produce a characteristic milkiness.

Absinth is largely prepared in Switzerland, especially in the canton of Neufchâtel; and indeed the strongest liquor is often known in trade as 'Swiss absinth,' though it may not have been prepared in Switzerland. Of late years, it has been drunk immoderately in France, and large quantities are also consumed in America. Certain French physiologists have alleged that the essential oils in absinth act as an energetic poison, especially affecting the nervous system; other authorities attribute the injurious effects of absinth-drinking to the *Calamus aromaticus* said to be used in its preparation; whilst others again maintain that the effects are merely those which follow the long-continued use of any strong alcoholic liquor—excepting, of course, the poisonous action of any copper-salts which may be present in adulterated absinth.

ABYSSINIAN GOLD. A yellow metal of a fine colour if properly prepared. It is an alloy of 90·74 parts of copper and 8·33 of zinc. The ingot is plated on one side with a thin plate of gold, and it is then rolled out into sheets, from which articles of jewellery are formed in the usual way. The gold on the articles as sold varies from 0·03 to 1·03 per cent. This is also known as *Talmi gold.* The term Abyssinian Gold is sometimes applied in trade to Aluminium Bronze. See ALUMINIUM BRONZE.

ACACIA. (Lat. *acacia,* a thorn; Gr. ἀκή, a point). The acacia is a very extensive genus of trees, or shrubby plants belonging to the *Leguminosæ* or Pea-order. The acacias inhabit the tropical regions generally, but extend in some instances into the temperate zone; being found, for example, in Australia and the neighbouring islands. Botanists are acquainted with nearly 300 species of the acacia, some of them yielding *gum arabic* and other gums known in commerce; while others give a large quantity of *tannin,* especially a species which grows in Van Diemen's Land or Tasmania. The *Acacia vera* is a native of Arabia and of Africa from Senegal to Egypt; the *A. Arabica* is found in the same countries and in India; the *A. Karoo* belongs to the Cape of Good Hope, producing the Cape gum; *A. gummifera* is chiefly found in Africa near Mogador *A. Seyal* in Senegambia; *A. tortilis* grows in the

Desert, as does also *A. Ehrenbergii*, their gums being collected by the Bedouin Arabs; and *A. Senegal* grows in Arabia and Africa, from Senegal to the Cape of Good Hope. See ARABIC, GUM; GUM.

ACACIA CATECHU. The catechu acacia (*Mimosa catechu* of Linnæus) is a tree with a moderately high and stout stem, growing in mountainous places in various parts of India. Its unripe pods and wood, by decoction, yield the catechu. This kind of catechu is known under the name of Kutch or Cutch, and must not be confounded with the official catechu (*Catechu pallidum*). This catechu is imported in large masses of 1 cwt. and upwards. It is used in the preparation of some leathers and by dyers. See CATECHU.

ACACIN. A name for common Gum Arabic.

ACAJOU (BOIS D'). The French name for mahogany. See MAHOGANY.

ACAROID RESIN. A resin sometimes called Botany Bay resin, produced by a liliaceous tree growing in New Holland. It contains benzoic and cinnamic acids, which give it, especially when burnt, a grateful odour.

ACESCENT. Substances which have a *tendency* to pass into an acid state; as an infusion of malt, &c.

ACETAL. $C^{12}H^{14}O^4$. ($C^6H^{14}O^2$). One of the products of the oxidation of alcohol under the influence of oxygen condensed in platinum-black. Pieces of well-cleaned pumice-stone are moistened with nearly absolute alcohol, and placed at the bottom of a wide-mouthed flask, which is then filled with capsules containing platinum-black, and exposed to a temperature of 20° Cent. (67° Fahr.), till the whole of the alcohol is acidified. It is a colourless, mobile, ethereal liquid, boiling at 221° F. Its density in the fluid state is 0·821 at 72°. The specific gravity of its vapour 4·138 *Stas.* (mean of three experiments): calculation gives 4·083 for four volumes of vapour. The researches of Wurtz render it evident that the construction o. acetal is quite different from what has generally been supposed, and that it is in fact glycole in which two atoms of hydrogen are replaced by two of ethyle. —C. G. W.

ACETATE. (*Acétate*, Fr.; *Essigsäure*, Ger.) Any saline compound in which the acid constituent is acetic acid. All acetates are soluble in water; the least soluble being the acetates of tungsten, molybdenum, silver, and mercury. The acetates, especially those of lead and alumina, are of great importance in the arts. The acetates are all described under their respective bases;—a rule which will be adopted with all the acids. See ACID.

ACETIC ACID. (*Acide acétique*, Fr.; *Essigsäure*, Ger.; *Acidum aceticum*, Lat.; *Eisel*, Sax.) The word 'acetic' is derived from the Latin *acetum*, applied to vinegar; probably the earliest known body possessing the sour taste and other properties which characterize acids; hence the term ACID, now become generic; both the Latin word, and also the Saxon *acid*, being from the root *acies* (Greek ἀκή), an edge or point, in reference to the *sharpness* of the taste.

Vinegar must have been known from the most remote periods of antiquity. It is mentioned by Moses.[1] Hippocrates employed it in medicine under the name ὀξὺς.[2] Hannibal, in his passage over the Alps, is said to have softened the rocks by fire and vinegar.[3] It was known to the alchemists in the more concentrated state in which it is obtained by the distillation of acetate of copper (verdigris); being mentioned both by Geber[4] and Stahl.

Crystallised acetic acid was first obtained by Westendorff[5] and Lowitz.[6]

Acetic acid exists in nature only in the organised kingdoms, or as a product of the oxidation of organic bodies. According to Vauquelin and Morin it is found in the juices of certain plants, and it probably exists in certain animal fluids.

Gmelin and Geiger state that it has been found in mineral waters, which is quite possible, having been derived from the decay of organic matter originally present.

Acetic acid is produced either by the oxidation, or the destructive distillation of organic bodies containing its elements—carbon, hydrogen, and oxygen.

The oxidation of organic bodies, in order to convert them into acetic acid, may be effected either—1, by exposing them in a finely divided state to the action of air or oxygen gas; 2, by submitting them to the action of ferments in the presence of a free supply of atmospheric air; or, 3, by the action of chemical oxidising agents.

When acetic acid is procured by the *oxidation* of organic bodies, it is generally alcohol that is employed; but by whatever process alcohol is transformed into acetic acid, it is always first converted into an intermediate compound, aldehyde; and this

[1] Numbers, vi. 3.   [2] De Natura Muliebri.
[3] Livy.   [4] Investigation of Perfection.
       [5] Westendorff, Diss. de Opt. Acet. Conc. Gottenburg, 1772.
            [6] Lowitz, Allgem. Journal von Likerer, III. 600.

being a very volatile body, it is desirable always to effect the oxidation as completely and rapidly as possible, to avoid the loss of alcohol by the evaporation of this aldehyde.

Alcohol contains	$C^4H^6O^2$ (**C^2H^6O**)
Aldehyde „	$C^4H^4O^2$ (**C^2H^4O**)
Acetic acid „	$C^4H^4O^4$ (**$C^2H^4O^2$**)

The process, therefore, consists first in the removal of two atoms of hydrogen from alcohol, which are converted into water—aldehyde being produced—and then the further union of this aldehyde with two atoms of oxygen to convert it into acetic acid. See ALDEHYDE.

By the oxidation of alcohol, pure acetic acid is obtained: but the vinegars of commerce are mixtures of the pure acetic acid with water; with saccharine, gummy, and colouring matters; with certain ethers (especially the acetic ether), upon which their agreeable aromatic flavour depends; with empyreumatic oils, &c.

The pure acetic acid (free from water and other impurities) may be obtained most advantageously, according to Melsens,[1] by distilling pure acetate of potash with an excess of acetic acid (which has been obtained by the redistillation of ordinary acetic acid, procured either by oxidising alcohol, or by the destructive distillation of wood): the acid which first passes over contains water; but finally it is obtained free.

Properties of pure Acetic Acid.—When absolutely pure, acetic acid is a colourless liquid of specific gravity 1·064, which at temperatures below 62° F. (17° C.) solidifies into a colourless crystalline mass. It has strongly acid properties, being as powerfully corrosive as many mineral acids, causing vesication when applied to the skin; and it possesses a peculiarly pungent, though not a disagreeable smell.

The vapour of the boiling acid is highly combustible, and burns with a blue flame. Hydrated acetic acid dissolves camphor, gliadine, resins, the fibrine of blood, and several organic compounds. When its vapour is conducted through a slightly ignited porcelain tube, it is converted entirely into carbonic acid and acetone, an atom of the acid being resolved into an atom of each of the resultants. At a white heat the acid vapour is converted into carbonic acid, carburetted hydrogen, and water.

It attracts water with great avidity, mixing with it in all proportions. Its solution in water increases in density with the increase of acetic acid up to a certain point; but beyond this point its density again diminishes. Its maximum density being 1·073, and corresponding to an acid containing $C^4H^4O^4+2Aq$, which may be extemporaneously produced by mixing 77·2 parts of crystallised acetic acid with 22·8 parts of water. This hydrate boils at 104° C. (219° F.), whilst the crystallised acid boils only at 120° C. (248° F.)[2]

The proportion of acetic acid in aqueous mixtures may therefore be ascertained, within certain limits, by determination of the specific gravity. See ACETIMETRY.

The following Table, by Mohr, indicates the per-centage of acetic acid in mixtures of different specific gravities; but of course this is only applicable in cases where no sugar or other bodies are present which increase the specific gravity :—

Abstract of Mohr's Table of the Specific Gravity of Mixtures of Acetic Acid and Water.[3]

Per-centage of Acetic Acid, $C^4H^4O^4$	Density	Per-centage of Acetic Acid, $C^4H^4O^4$	Density
100	1·0635	45	1·055
95	1·070	40	1·051
90	1·073	35	1·046
85	1·073	30	1·040
80	1·0735	25	1·034
75	1·072	20	1·027
70	1·070	15	1·022
65	1·068	10	1·015
60	1·067	5	1·0067
55	1·064	1	1·001
50	1·060		

[1] Comptes Rendus, xix. 611.　　　[2] Gerhardt, Chimie Organique, i. 718.
[3] Mohr, Ann. der Chem. und Phar. xxxi. 227.

Which numbers closely agree with those obtained by Dr. Ure .—

Acid	Sp. Gr.	Acid	Sp. Gr.	Acid	Sp. Gr.
100	1·0620	76	1·0743	52	1·0617
98	1·0650	74	1·0740	50	1·0603
96	1·0680	72	1·0733	45	1·0558
94	1·0700	70	1·0725	40	1·0512
92	1·0715	68	1·0716	35	1·0459
90	1·0728	66	1·0712	30	1·0405
88	1·0730	64	1·0701	25	1·0342
86	1·0735	62	1·0687	20	1·0282
84	1·0738	60	1·0675	15	1·0213
82	1·0740	58	1·0665	10	1·0147
80	1·0750	56	1·0647	5	1·0075
78	1·0748	54	1·0634		

Acetic acid was formerly (and is still by some chemists) viewed as the hydrated teroxide of a radical, Acetyl. $\underbrace{(C^4 H^3) O^3}_{\text{Acetyl.}}$, HO

And therefore an anhydrous acetic acid, $C^4 H^3 O^3$, was supposed to exist. Many attempts have been made to isolate this anhydrous acetic acid $C^4 H^3 O^3$; and a body which has received this name has been obtained by Gerhardt,[1] by the double decomposition of chloride of acetyl and an alkaline acetate, thus—

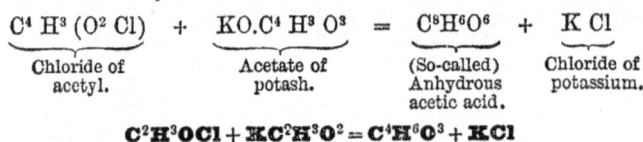

$$\underbrace{C^4 H^3 (O^2 Cl)}_{\substack{\text{Chloride of}\\\text{acetyl.}}} + \underbrace{KO.C^4 H^3 O^3}_{\substack{\text{Acetate of}\\\text{potash.}}} = \underbrace{C^8H^6O^6}_{\substack{\text{(So-called)}\\\text{Anhydrous}\\\text{acetic acid.}}} + \underbrace{K Cl}_{\substack{\text{Chloride of}\\\text{potassium.}}}$$

$$\mathbf{C^2H^3OCl + KC^2H^3O^2 = C^4H^6O^3 + KCl}$$

This body Gerhardt describes as a colourless liquid having a strong smell of acetic acid, but associated with the flavour of hawthorn blossom, having a specific gravity of 1·073, and boiling at 137° C. (278° F.); falling in water in the form of oily drops, only dissolving on gently heating that fluid. It is, however, not anhydrous acetic acid, but a compound isomeric with the hypothetical anhydrous acetic acid $C^4 H^3 O^3$, containing, in fact, double the amount of matter, its formula being $C^8 H^6 O^6$. See ISOMERISM.

The impure varieties of acetic acid known as vinegar, pyroligneous acid, &c., are the products met with in commerce, and therefore those require more minute description in this work.

Before describing the manufacture of these commercial articles, it may be interesting to allude to a method of oxidising alcohol by means of spongy platinum; which may yet meet with extensive practical application. It is a well-known fact that spongy platinum (e.g. platinum black), from its minute state of division, condenses the oxygen of the air within its pores; consequently, when the vapour of alcohol comes in contact with this body, a supply of oxygen in a concentrated state is presented to it, and the platinum, without losing any of its properties, effects the combination between the oxygen and the alcohol, converting the latter into acetic acid.

This may be illustrated by a very simple experiment. Place recently ignited spongy platinum, loosely distributed on a platinum-gauze, at a short distance over a saucer containing warm alcohol, the whole standing under a bell-glass supported by wedges on a glass dish, so that on removing the stopper from the bell-glass a slow current of air circulates through the apparatus; the spongy platinum soon begins to glow, in consequence of the combustion going on upon its surface, and acetic acid vapours are abundantly produced, which condense and run down the sides of the glass. The simultaneous formation of aldehyde is, at the same time, abundantly proved by its peculiar odour.

In Germany this method has been actually carried out on the large scale, and, if it were not for the high price of platinum and the heavy duty on alcohol, it might be extensively employed in this country on account of its elegance and extreme simplicity. See ACETAL.

[1] Comptes Rendus, xxxiv. 755.

The processes employed for the manufacture of Acetic Acid, which is principally used in the arts, and those for the production of Vinegar, which is chiefly for domestic use, are widely different and carried on in separate works; they will, therefore, be best described under their respective heads.

MANUFACTURE OF ACETIC ACID (PYROLIGNEOUS ACID).

A.—*By destructive distillation of Wood.*

The general nature of the process of destructive distillation will be found detailed under the head of DISTILLATION, DESTRUCTIVE; as well as a list of products of the rearrangement of the molecules of organic bodies under the influence of heat in closed vessels. We shall, therefore, at once proceed to the details of the process as specially applied in the manufacture of acetic acid from wood.

The forms of apparatus very generally employed on the Continent for obtaining at the same time crude acetic acid, charcoal, and tar, are those of Schwartz and Reichenbach; but in France the process is carried out with special reference to the production of acetic acid alone.

The following is a description of that in use at Nuits and Rouen:—

Into large cylindrical vessels (*fig.* 1) made of rivetted sheet iron, and having at their top and side a small sheet-iron cylinder, the wood intended for making charcoal is introduced. To the upper part of this vessel a cover of sheet iron, B, is adapted, which is fixed with bolts. This vessel, thus closed, represents, as we see, a vast retort. When it is prepared, as we have said, it is lifted by means of a swing crane, C, and placed in a furnace, D (*fig.* 2), of a form relative to that of the vessel, and the opening of the furnace is covered with a dome, E, made of masonry or brickwork. The whole being thus arranged, heat is applied in the furnace at the bottom. The moisture of the wood is first dissipated, but by degrees the liquor ceases to be transparent, and becomes sooty. An adapter tube, A, is then fitted to the lateral cylinder. This adapter enters into another tube at the same degree of inclination, which commences the condensing apparatus. The means of condensation vary according

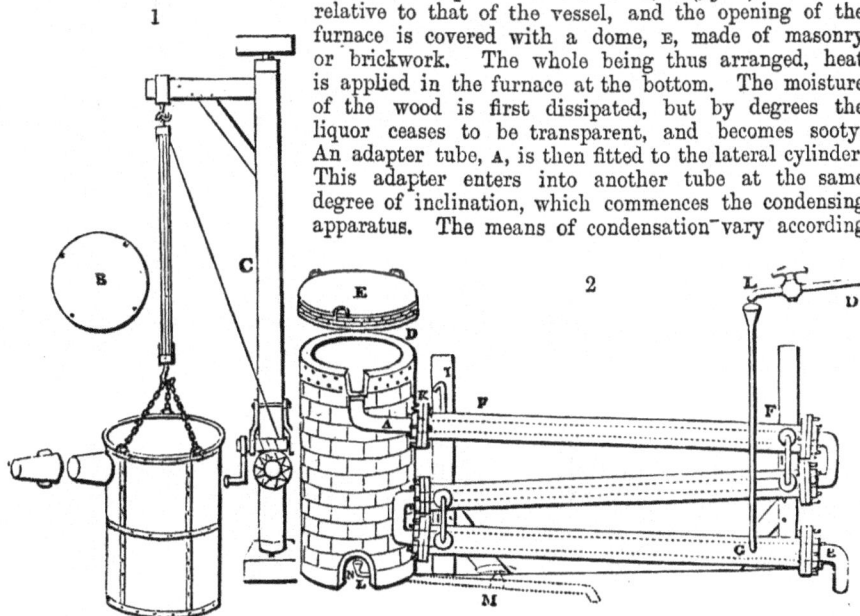

to the localities. In certain works they cool by means of air, by making the vapour pass through a long series of cylinders, or sometimes, even, through a series of casks connected together; but most usually water is used for condensing, when it can be easily procured in abundance. The most simple apparatus employed for this purpose consists of two cylinders, F F (*fig.* 2), the one within the other, and which leave between them a sufficient space to allow a considerable body of water to circulate along and cool the vapours. This double cylinder is adapted to the distilling vessel, and placed at a certain inclination. To the first double tube, F F, a second, and sometimes a third, entirely similar, are connected, which, to save space, return upon themselves in a zigzag fashion. The water is set in circulation by an ingenious means now adopted in many different manufactories. From the lower extremity, G, of the system of condensers, a perpendicular tube rises, whose length should be a little more than the most elevated point of the system. The water, furnished by a reservoir L, enters by means of the perpendicular tube through the lower part of the system, and fills the whole space between the double cylinders. When the apparatus is in action, the vapours, as they condense, raise the temperature of the water, which, by the column in L G, is pressed to the upper part of the cylinders, and runs over by the spout K. To this point a very short tube is attached, which is bent towards the ground, and serves as an overflow.

The condensing apparatus is terminated by a conduit in bricks covered and sunk in the ground. At the extremity of this species of gutter is a bent tube, E, which discharges the liquid product into the first cistern. When it is full, it empties itself, by means of an overflow pipe, into a great reservoir; the tube which terminates the gutter plunges into the liquid, and thus intercepts communication with the inside of the apparatus. The disengaged gas is brought back, by means of pipes M L, from one of the sides of the conduit to the under part of the ashpit of the furnace. These pipes are furnished with stopcocks, M, at some distance in front of the furnace, for the purpose of regulating the jet of the gas, and interrupting, at pleasure, communication with the inside of the apparatus. The part of the pipes which terminates in the furnace rises perpendicularly several inches above the ground, and is expanded like the rose of a watering-can, N. The gas, by means of this disposition, can distribute itself uniformly under the vessel, without suffering the pipe which conducts it to be obstructed by the fuel or the ashes.

3

4

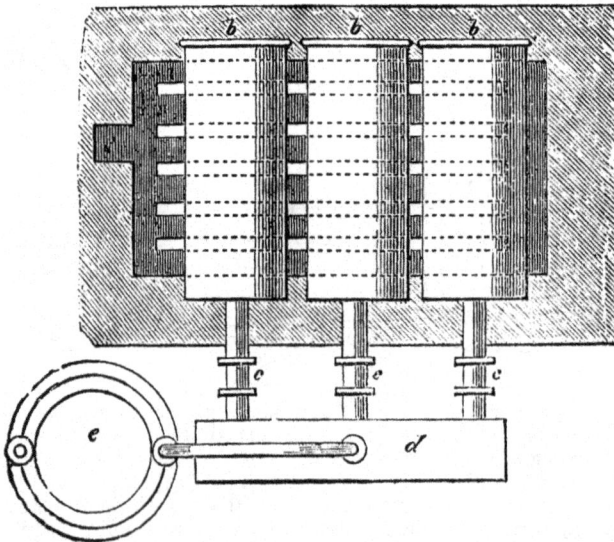

The temperature necessary to effect the carbonisation is not at first considerable: however, at the last, it is raised so high as to make the vessels red hot; and the duration of the process is necessarily proportional to the quantity of wood carbonised. For a vessel which shall contain about 5 meters cube (nearly 6 cubic yards), 8 hours of fire is sufficient. It is known that the carbonisation is complete by the colour of the flame of the gas: it is first of a yellowish red; it becomes afterwards blue, when more carbonic oxide than carburetted hydrogen is evolved; and towards the end it becomes entirely white,—a circumstance owing, probably, to the furnace being more heated at this period, and the combustion therefore more complete. There is still another means of knowing the state of the process, to which recourse is more frequently had: that is the cooling of the first tubes, which are not surrounded with water: a few drops of this fluid are thrown upon their surface, and if they evaporate quietly, it is judged that the calcination is sufficient. The adapter tube is then unluted, and is slid into its junction pipe; the orifices are immediately stopped with plates of iron and plaster loam. The brick cover, E, of the furnace is first removed

by means of the swing crane, then the cylinder itself is lifted out and replaced immediately by another one previously charged. When the cylinder which has been
taken out of the furnace is entirely cooled, its cover is removed, and the charcoal
is emptied. Five cubic meters of wood furnish about 7 chaldrons and a half of
charcoal.

The carbonisers of Reichenbach and Schwartz are usually employed with special
reference to the manufacture of wood-charcoal, the condensation of the volatile
products being only a secondary consideration.

In England the distillation of wood, with especial reference to the manufacture
of pyroligneous acid, is generally carried out in large iron retorts, placed horizontally in the furnace; the process, in fact, closely resembling the distillation of
coal in the manufacture of coal gas, excepting that the retorts are generally larger,
being sometimes 4 feet in diameter, and 6 or 8 feet long. Generally two, or even
three, are placed in each furnace, as shown in *fig.* 3, so that the fire of the single
furnace, *a*, plays all round them. The doors for charging the retorts are at one end, *b*
(*fig.* 4), and the pipe for carrying off the volatile products at the other, *c*, by which
they are conducted, first to the tar-condenser, *d*, and finally through a worm in a
large tub, *e*, where the crude acetic acid is collected.

Of course, in different localities an endless variety of modifications of the process
are employed.

In the Forest of Dean, instead of cylindrical retorts, square sheet-iron boxes are
used, 4 ft. 6 in. by 2 ft. 9 in., which are heated in large square ovens.

Dr. Ure gives the following description of special works in Glasgow :—

The cylinders here employed are 6 feet long, and both ends project a little beyond
the brickwork. One end has a disk, or round plate of cast-iron, well fitted and

5

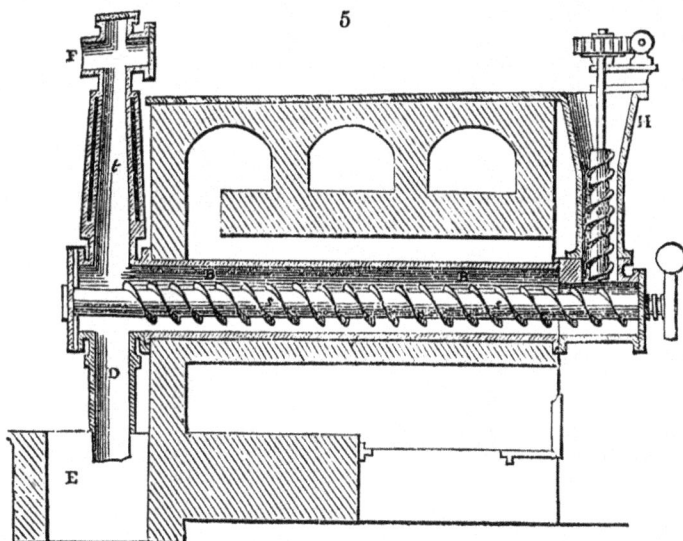

firmly bolted to it, from the centre of which an iron tube, about 6 inches in diameter,
proceeds, and enters at a right angle the main tube of refrigeration. The diameter
of this tube may be from 9 to 14 inches, according to the number of cylinders. The
other end of the cylinder is called the mouth of the retort; this is closed by a disc of
iron, smeared round its edge with clay-lute, and secured in its place by iron wedges.
The charge of wood for such a cylinder is about 8 cwt. The hard woods—oak,
ash, birch, and beech—are alone used in this manufactory—fir not being found to
answer. The heat is kept up during the day, and the furnace allowed to cool during
the night. Next morning the door is opened, the charcoal removed, and a new
charge of wood introduced. The average product of crude vinegar is 35 gallons.
It is much contaminated with tar, is of a deep brown colour, and has a specific gravity of 1·025. Its total weight is therefore about 300 lbs. ; but the residuary charcoal
is found to weigh no more than one-fifth of the wood employed; hence nearly one-
half of the ponderable matter of the wood is dissipated in incondensable gases.

With regard to the relative advantages of cylindrical retorts or square boxes,
it should be remarked, that the cylinders are more adapted for the distillation of the
large billets of Gloucestershire and the refuse ship timber of Glasgow, Newcastle,

and Liverpool; but, on the other hand, where light wood is used, such as that generally carbonised in the Welsh factories, the square ovens answer better.

An ingenious improvement in the manufacture of pyroligneous acid was patented some years ago by the late Mr. A. G. Halliday, of Manchester, and adopted by several large manufacturers. The process consists in effecting the destructive distillation of waste materials, such as sawdust and spent dyewoods, by causing them to pass in continuous motion through heated retorts. For this purpose the materials, which are almost in a state of powder, are introduced into a hopper, H (*fig.* 5), whence they descend into the retort, B, being kept all the while in constant agitation, and at the same time moved forward to the other end of the retort by means of an endless screw, *s*. By the time they arrive there the charge has been completely carbonised, and all the pyroligneous acid evolved at the exit tube, *t*. The residuary charcoal falls through the pipe D into a vessel of water, E, whilst the volatile products escape at F, and are condensed in the usual way.

Several of these retorts are generally set in a furnace side by side; the retorts are only 14 inches in diameter, and eight of these retorts produce in 24 hours as much acid as 16 retorts 3 feet in diameter upon the old system. In the manufacturing districts of Lancashire and Yorkshire, where such immense quantities of spent dyewoods accumulate, and have proved a source of annoyance and expense for their removal, this process has afforded a most important means of economically converting them into valuable products—charcoal and acetic acid.

Mention should also be made of Messrs. Solomons and Azulay's patent for employing superheated steam to effect the carbonisation of the wood, which is passed directly into the mass of materials. Since the steam accompanies the volatile products, it necessarily dilutes the acid; but this is in a great degree compensated for by employing these vapours to concentrate the distilled products, by causing them to traverse a coil of tubing placed in a pan of the distillates.

As regards the yield of acetic acid from the different kinds of wood, some valuable facts have been collected and tabulated by Stolze, in his work on Pyroligneous Acid:—

One Pound of Wood		Weight of Acid	Carbonate of Potassa neutralised by One Ounce of Acid	Weight of Charcoal
		ozs.	grs.	ozs.
White birch	Betula alba	7 1/8	55	3 7/8
Red beech	Fagus sylvatica	7	54	3 7/8
Large-leaved linden	Tilia pataphylla	6 7/8	52	3 5/8
Oak	Quercus robur	6 7/8	50	4 1/8
Ash	Fraxinus excelsior	7 1/2	44	3 3/4
Horse chestnut	Æsculus hippocastanus	7 3/8	41	3 1/2
Lombardy poplar	Populus dilatata	7 3/8	40	3 3/4
White poplar	Populus alba	7 3/8	39	3 3/4
Bird cherry	Prunus padus	7	37	3 1/2
Basket willow	Salix	7 3/8	35	3 1/2
Buckthorn	Rhamnus	7 1/2	34	3 1/2
Logwood	Hæmatoxylon campechianum	7 1/8	35	2
Alder	Alnus	7 3/8	30	3 1/8
Juniper	Juniperus communis	7 1/4	29	3 5/8
White fir	Pinus abies	6 7/8	29	3 3/8
Common pine	Pinus sylvestris	6 3/4	28	3 1/2
Common savine	Juniperus sabina	7	27	3 5/8
Red fir	Abies pectinata	6 3/8	25	3 3/4

Properties of the crude Pyroligneous Acid.

The crude pyroligneous acid possesses the properties of acetic acid, combined with those of the pyrogenous bodies with which it is associated. As first obtained, it is black, from the large quantity of tar which it holds in solution; and although certain resins are removed by redistillation, yet it is impossible to remove some of the empyreumatic oils by this process, and a special purification is necessary.

In consequence of the presence of creosote, and other antiseptic hydrocarbons, in the crude pyroligneous acid, it possesses, in a very eminent degree, anti-putrescent properties. Flesh steeped in it for a few hours may be afterwards dried in the air without corrupting; but it becomes hard, and somewhat leather-like; so that this mode of preservation does not answer well for butcher's meat. Fish are sometimes cured with it.

Purification of Pyroligneous Acid.

This is effected either, 1st, by converting it into an acetate—acetate of lime or soda—and then, after the purification of these salts by exposure to heat sufficient to destroy the tar, and repeated recrystallisation, liberating the acid again by distilling with a stronger acid, e.g. sulphuric.

Or, 2ndly, by destroying the pyrogenous impurities by oxidising agents, such as binoxide of manganese in the presence of sulphuric acid, &c.

The former is the method generally adopted.

After the naphtha has been expelled, the acid liquor is run off into tanks to deposit part of its impurities; it is then syphoned off into another vessel, in which is either milk of lime, quicklime, or chalk; the mixture is boiled for a short time, and then allowed to stand for 24 hours to deposit the excess of lime with any impurities which the latter will carry down with it. The supernatant liquor is then pumped into the evaporating pans.

The evaporation is effected either by the heat of a fire applied beneath the evaporating pans, or more frequently by a coil of pipe in the liquor through which steam is passed—the liquor being kept constantly stirred, and the impurities which rise to the surface during the process carefully skimmed off.

From time to time, as the evaporation advances, the acetate of lime which separates is removed by ladles, and placed in baskets to drain; and the residual mother-liquor is evaporated to dryness. This mass, by ignition, is converted into carbonate of lime and acetone.

If the acetate of lime have been procured by directly saturating the crude acid, it is called *brown acetate;* if from the acid once purified by redistillation, it is called *grey acetate.*

From this grey acetate of lime acetate of soda is now prepared, by adding sulphate of soda to the filtered solution of the acetate of lime. In performing this operation, it is highly important to remember that, for every equivalent of acetate of lime, it is necessary to add two equivalents of sulphate of soda, on account of the formation of a double sulphate of soda and lime. The equation representing the change being :—

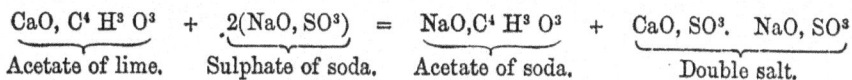

$$\underbrace{CaO, C^4 H^3 O^3}_{\text{Acetate of lime.}} + \underbrace{.2(NaO, SO^3)}_{\text{Sulphate of soda.}} = \underbrace{NaO, C^4 H^3 O^3}_{\text{Acetate of soda.}} + \underbrace{CaO, SO^3. \ NaO, SO^3}_{\text{Double salt.}}$$

$$Ca(C^2H^3O^2)^2 \ + \ 2Na^2SO^4 \ = \ 2NaC^2H^3O^2 \ + \ CaSO^4. \ Na^2SO^4.$$

Or, if sulphuric acid be considered as a bibasic acid, which this very reaction so strongly justifies—

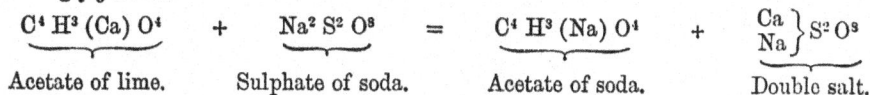

$$\underbrace{C^4 H^3 (Ca) O^4}_{\text{Acetate of lime.}} \ + \ \underbrace{Na^2 S^2 O^8}_{\text{Sulphate of soda.}} \ = \ \underbrace{C^4 H^3 (Na) O^4}_{\text{Acetate of soda.}} \ + \ \underbrace{\left.\begin{matrix} Ca \\ Na \end{matrix}\right\} S^2 O^8}_{\text{Double salt.}}$$

If this point be neglected, and only one equivalent of sulphate of soda be used, one-half of the acetate of lime may escape decomposition, and thus be lost.

After the separation of the double salt, the solution of acetate of soda is drawn off, any impurities allowed to subside, and then concentrated by evaporation until it has a density of 4·3—when the acetate of soda crystallises out, and may be further purified, if requisite, by another re-solution and re-crystallisation. The contents of the mother liquors are converted into acetone and carbonate of soda, as before.

The crystallised acetate of soda is now fused in an iron pot, at a temperature of about 400°, to drive off the water of crystallisation, the mass being kept constantly stirred. A stronger heat must not be applied, or we should effect the decomposition of the salt.

For the production of the acetic acid from this salt, a quantity of it is put into a stout copper still, and a deep cavity made in the centre of the mass, into which sulphuric acid of specific gravity 1·84 is poured in the proportion of 35 per cent. of the weight of the salt; the walls of the cavity are thrown in upon the acid, and the whole briskly agitated with a wooden spatula. The head of the still is then luted, and connected with the condensing worm, and the distillation carried on at a very gentle heat. The worm should be of silver or porcelain, as also the still-head; and even silver solder should be used to connect the joinings in the body of the still. The still is now generally heated by a steam 'jacket.' See DISTILLATION.

The acid which passes over is nearly colourless, and has a specific gravity of 1·05. That which collects at the latter part of the operation is liable to be somewhat empyreumatic, and therefore before this point is reached the receiver should be changed ; and throughout the entire operation, care should be taken to avoid applying too high a temperature, as the flavour and purity of the acid will invariably suffer.

Any trace of empyreuma may be removed from the acid by digestion with animal charcoal and redistillation.

A considerable portion of this acid crystallises at a temperature of from 40° to 50° F., constituting what is called *glacial acetic acid*, which is the compound $C^4 H^4 O^4$, or $C^4 H^3 O^3$, HO ($C^2H^4O^2$).

For culinary purposes, pickling, &c., the acid of specific gravity 1·05 is diluted with five times its weight of water, which renders it of the same strength as Revenue proof vinegar.

Several modifications and improvements of this process have recently been introduced, which require to be noticed.

The following process depends upon the difficult solubility of sulphate of soda in strong acetic acids :—100 lbs. of the pulverised salt being put into a hard glazed stoneware receiver, or deep pan, from 35 to 36 lbs. of concentrated sulphuric acid are poured in one stream upon the powder, so as to flow under it. The mixture of the salt and acid is to be made very slowly, in order to moderate the action and the heat generated, as much as possible. After the materials have been in intimate contact for a few hours, the decomposition is effected ; sulphate of soda in crystalline grains will occupy the bottom of the vessel, and acetic acid the upper portion, partly liquid and partly in crystals. A small portion of pure acetate of lime added to the acid will free it from any remainder of sulphate of soda, leaving only a little acetate in its place ; and though a small portion of sulphate of soda may still remain, it is unimportant, whereas the presence of any free sulphuric acid would be very injurious. This is easily detected by evaporating a little of the liquid, at a moderate heat, to dryness, when that mineral acid can be distinguished from the neutral soda sulphate. This plan of superseding a troublesome distillation, which is due to M. Mollerat, is one of the greatest improvements in this process, and depends upon the insolubility of the sulphate of soda in acetic acid. The sulphate of soda thus recovered, and well drained, serves anew to decompose acetate of lime ; so that nothing but this cheap earth is consumed in carrying on the manufacture. To obtain absolutely pure acetic acid, the above acid has to be distilled in a glass retort.

Völckel recommends the use of hydrochloric instead of sulphuric acid for decomposing the acetate.

The following is his description of the details of the process :—

' The crude acetate of lime is separated from the tarry bodies which are deposited on neutralisation, and evaporated to about one-half its bulk in an iron pan. Hydrochloric acid is then added until a distinctly acid reaction is produced on cooling ; by this means the resinous bodies are separated, and come to the surface of the boiling liquid in a melted state, whence they can be removed by skimming, while the compounds of lime, with creosote, and other volatile bodies, are likewise decomposed, and expelled on further evaporation. From 4 to 6 lbs. of hydrochloric acid for every 33 gallons of wood vinegar is the average quantity required for this purpose. The acetate having been dried at a high temperature on iron plates, to char and drive off the remainder of the tar and resinous bodies, is then decomposed, by hydrochloric acid, in a still with a copper head and leaden condensing tube. To every 100 lbs. of salt about 90 to 95 lbs. of hydrochloric acid of specific gravity 1·16 are required. The acid comes over at a temperature of from 100° to 120° C. (212° to 248° F.), and is very slightly impregnated with empyreumatic products, while a mere cloud is produced in it by nitrate of silver. The specific gravity of the product varies from 1·058 to 1·061, and contains more than 40 per cent. of real acid ; but as it is seldom required of this strength, it is well to dilute the 90 parts of hydrochloric acid with 25 parts of water. These proportions then yield from 95 to 100 parts of acetic acid of specific gravity 1·015.

This process is recommended on the score of economy and greater purity of product. The volatile empyreumatic bodies are said to be more easily separated by the use of hydrochloric than sulphuric acid ; moreover, the chloride of calcium being a more easily fusible salt than the sulphate of lime, or even than the double sulphate of lime and soda, the acetic acid is more freely evolved from the mixture. The resinous bodies also decompose sulphuric acid towards the end of the operation, giving rise to sulphurous acid, sulphuretted hydrogen, &c., which contaminate the product.

The decomposition of acetate of lime or lead by means of sulphuric acid has many inconveniences, and there is danger of the product being contaminated with sulphuric acid. Christl[1] was therefore induced to employ hydrochloric acid as a decomposing agent, and has found that when this acid is not used in excess, the distillate contains scarcely an appreciable trace of chlorine. A mixture of 100 lbs. of raw acetate of lime, obtained from the distillation of wood, and containing 90 per cent. of neutral acetate, with 120 lbs. of hydrochloric acid (20° Baumé) is allowed to stand during a night, and then distilled in a copper vessel. The application of heat requires to be gradual, in order to prevent the somewhat thick liquor from running over. The product of acetic acid amounts to about 100 lbs. of 8° B.; it has a faint yellow colour and empyreumatic odour, which may be perfectly removed by treatment with wood charcoal and subsequent rectification.

In order to obtain the acetate of lime sufficiently pure, Völckel[2] adopts the following process:—The raw pyroligneous acid is saturated with lime without previous distillation. A part of the resinous substances dissolved in the acid are thus separated in combination with lime. The solution of impure acetate of lime is allowed to stand until it becomes clear, or it is filtered, then evaporated in an iron pan to about one-half, and hydrochloric acid added until a drop of the cooled liquid distinctly reddens litmus-paper. A part is sometimes distilled off in a copper still, in order to obtain wood-spirit. The addition of acid serves to separate a great part of the resin still held in solution, which collects together in the boiling liquid, and may be skimmed off, and likewise decomposes the compounds of lime with creosote, and some other imperfectly-known volatile substances which are driven off by further evaporation. As these volatile substances have little or no action upon litmus-paper, its being reddened by the liquor is a sign, that not only are the lime compounds of these substances decomposed, but also a small quantity of acetate of lime. The quantity of acid necessary for this purpose varies, and depends upon the nature of the pyroligneous acid, which is again dependent upon the quantity of the water in the wood from which it is obtained. Three hundred pints of wood-liquor will require from 4 to 6 lbs. of hydrochloric acid.

The solution of acetate of lime is evaporated to dryness, and a tolerably strong heat applied at last, in order to remove all volatile substances. Both operations may be performed in the same iron pans; but when the quantity of salt is large, the latter may be more advantageously effected upon cast-iron plates. The drying of the salt requires very great care, for the empyreumatic substances adhere very strongly to the acetate of lime, as well as to the compound of resin and acetic acid mixed with it, and when not perfectly separated, pass over with the acetic acid in the subsequent distillation with an acid, communicating to it a disagreeable odour. The drying must therefore be continued until, upon cooling, the acetate does not smell at all, or but very slightly. It then has a dirty brown colour. The acetic acid is obtained by distillation with hydrochloric acid, in a still with a copper head and leaden condenser; and when proper precautions are taken, the acetic acid does not contain a trace of either metal. The quantity of hydrochloric acid required cannot be exactly stated, because the acetate of lime is mixed with resin, and already formed chloride of calcium. In most instances 90 or 95 parts by weight of acid, 1·16 specific gravity, are sufficient to decompose completely 100 parts of the salt, without introducing much hydrochloric acid into the distillate.

The distilled acetic acid possesses only a very faint empyreumatic odour, very different from that of the raw pyroligneous acid; it is perfectly colourless, and should only become slightly turbid on the addition of nitrate of silver. If the acid has a yellowish colour, this is owing to resin having been spirted over in the distillation. It is therefore advisable to remove the resin,—which is separated on the addition of hydrochloric acid, and floats upon the surface of the liquid,—either by skimming or filtration through a linen cloth. The distilled acid has a specific gravity ranging between 1·058 and 1·061, containing upwards of 40 per cent. of anhydrous acetic acid. It is rarely that acid of this strength is required; and as the distillation is easier when the mixture is less concentrated, water may be added before or towards the end of the distillation. Völckel recommends as convenient proportions—

100 parts of acetate of lime,
90 to 95 hydrochloric acid,
25 parts water,

which yield from 95 to 100 parts of acetic acid of 1·105 specific gravity; 150 litres of raw pyroligneous acid yield about 50 lbs. of acetic acid of the above specific gravity.

The acid prepared in this way may be still further purified by adding a small

[1] Dingler's Polytech. Journ.   [2] Ann. der Chem. und Pharm.

quantity of carbonate of soda and redistilling; it is thus rendered quite free from chlorine, and any remaining trace of colour is likewise removed. The slight empyreumatic smell may be removed by distilling the acid with about 2 or 3 per cent. of acid chromate of potash. Oxide of manganese is less efficacious as a purifying agent.

Although pure acetic acid may be procured by the distillation of vinegar, the whole of the acid cannot be obtained except by distilling to dryness, by which means the extractive substances are burnt, and the distillate rendered impure. In order to obviate this difficulty, Stein [1] proposes to add 30 lbs. of salt to every 100 lbs. of vinegar; the boiling point is thus raised, and the acid passes over completely.

B.—*Manufacture of Acetic Acid from Acetate of Copper.*

Before the process for pyroligneous acid, or wood vinegar, was known, there was only one method of obtaining strong vinegar practised by chemists; and it is still followed by some operators, to prepare what is called radical or aromatic vinegar. This consists in decomposing, by heat alone, the crystallised binacetate of copper, commonly, but improperly, called distilled verdigris. With this view, we take a stoneware retort (*fig.* 6), of a size suited to the quantity we wish to operate upon, and coat it with a mixture of fireclay and horsedung, to make it stand the heat better. When this coating is dry, we introduce into the retort the crystallised acetate slightly bruised, but very dry; we fill it as far as it will hold without spilling when the beak is considerably inclined. We then set it in a proper furnace. We attach to its neck an adapter pipe, and two or three globes with opposite tubulures, and a last globe with a vertical tubulure. The apparatus is terminated by a Welter's tube, with a double branch; the shorter issues from the last globe, and the other dips into a flask filled with distilled vinegar. Everything being thus arranged, we lute the joinings with a putty made of pipeclay and linseed oil, and cover them with glue paper.

6

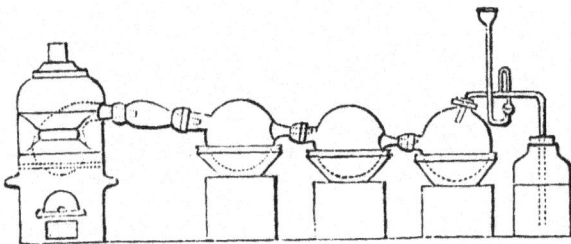

Each globe is placed in a separate basin of cold water, or the whole may be put into an oblong trough, through which a constant stream of cold water is made to flow. The tubes must be allowed a day to dry. Next day we proceed to the distillation, tempering the heat very nicely at the beginning, and increasing it by very slow degrees till we see the drops follow each other pretty rapidly from the neck of the retort, or the end of the adapter tube. The vapours which pass over are very hot, whence a series of globes are necessary to condense them. We should renew, from time to time, the water of the basins, and keep moist pieces of cloth upon the globes; but this demands great care, especially if the fire be a little too brisk, for the vessels become, in that case, so hot, that they would infallibly be broken if touched suddenly with cold water. It is always easy for us to regulate this operation according to the emission of gas from the extremity of the apparatus. When the air-bubbles succeed each other with great rapidity, we must damp the fire.

The liquor which passes in the first half hour is weakest; it proceeds, in some measure, from a little water sometimes left in the crystals, which, when well made, however, ought to be anhydrous. A period arrives towards the middle of the process when we see the extremity of the beak of the retort, and of the adapter, covered with crystals of a lamellar or needle shape, and of a pale green tint. By degrees these crystals are carried into the condensed liquid by the acid vapours, and give a colour to the product. These crystals are merely some of the cupreous salt forced over by the heat. As the process approaches its conclusion, we find more difficulty in raising the vapours; and we must then augment the intensity of the heat, in order to continue their disengagement. Finally, we judge that the process is altogether finished, when the globes become cold, notwithstanding the furnace is at the hottest, and when no more vapours are evolved. The fire may then be allowed to go out, and the retort to cool.

As the acid thus obtained is slightly tinged with copper, it must be rectified before bringing it into the market. For this purpose we may make use of the same apparatus, only substituting for the stoneware retort a glass one, placed in a sand-bath.

---

[1] Polytech. Centralblatt, 1852, p. 395.

All the globes ought to be perfectly clean and dry. The distillation is to be conducted in the usual way. If we divide the product into thirds, the first yields the feeblest acid, and the third the strongest. We could not push the process quite to dryness, because there remain in the last portions certain impurities which would injure the flavour of the acid.

The total acid thus obtained forms nearly one-half of the weight of the acetate employed, and the residuum forms three-tenths; so that about two-tenths of the acid have been decomposed by the heat, and are lost.—*Ure.*

Other metallic acetates may be used instead of the acetate of copper, but with variable results as to the amount of acetic acid which they yield. Acetates which have easily reducible oxides—as those of copper, silver, mercury, lead, &c.—afford a larger proportion of acetic acid; but acetone and marsh gas, as well as carbonic oxide and carbonic acid, invariably accompany it. The acetate of silver gives no acetone; whilst those of the alkaline earths yield chiefly acetone or marsh gas, and are converted into carbonates. See ACETONE.

Anhydrous Acetic Acid, as made by Gerhardt, is obtained by mixing perfectly dry fused acetate of potash with about half its weight of chloride of benzoyle, and applying a gentle heat; when a liquid distils over, which, after being rectified, has a constant boiling point of 279° F., and is heavier than water, with which it does not mix until after it has been agitated with it for some time. It dissolves at once in hot water, forming acetic acid.

Uses of Acetic Acid.

Acetic acid is extensively employed in the arts, in the manufacture of the various acetates, especially those of alumina and iron, so extensively employed in calico-printing as mordants, sugar of lead, &c. It is likewise used in the preparation of varnishes, for dissolving gums and albuminous bodies; in the culinary arts, especially in the manufacture of pickles and other condiments; in medicine, externally, as a local irritant, and internally, to allay fever, &c.

For the treatment in cases of poisoning, we refer to Taylor, Pereira, and other medical authorities.

For the Manufacture of Vinegar, see VINEGAR.

ACETIC ETHERS. (*Acetate of Ethyl. Essigäther. Essignaphtha. Essigsäures Æthyloxyd.*) These are compounds of acetic acid with the alcohol radicals. See RADICALS, ALCOHOL, and RADICALS, CHEMICAL.

ACETIMETER. An apparatus used in the processes for determining the strength of vinegar. Consult WATTS's *Dictionary of Chemistry.*

ACETIMETRY. *Determination of the Strength of Vinegar.*—If in vinegars, we were dealing with mixtures of pure acetic acid and water, the determination of the density might to a certain extent afford a criterion of the strength of the solution; but vinegar, especially that obtained from wine and malt, invariably contains gluten, saccharine, and mucilaginous matters, which increase its density and render this method altogether fallacious.

An accurate means of determining the strength of vinegar is by ascertaining the quantity of carbonate of soda or potash neutralised by a given weight of the vinegar under examination. This is performed by adding to the vinegar a standard solution of the alkaline carbonate of known strength from a burette, until, after boiling to expel the carbonic acid, a solution of litmus previously introduced into the liquid is rendered distinctly blue.

The details of this process, which is equally applicable to mineral and other organic acids, will be found fully described under the head of ACIDIMETRY.

Roughly, it may be stated that every 53 grains of the pure anhydrous carbonate of soda, or every 69 grains of carbonate of potassa (*i.e.* one equivalent), correspond to 60 grains of acetic acid ($C^4 H^4 O^4$).

It is obvious that preliminary examinations should be made to ascertain if sulphuric, hydrochloric, or other mineral acids are present; and, if so, their amount determined; otherwise they will be reckoned as acetic acid.

The British malt vinegar is stated in the 'London Pharmacopœia' to require a drachm (60 grains) of crystallised carbonate of soda (which contains 10 equivalents of water of crystallisation), for saturating a fluid ounce, or 4·46 grains; it contains, in fact, from 4·6 to 5 per cent. of real acetic acid.

The same authorities consider that the purified pyroligneous acid should require 87 grains of carbonate of soda for saturating 100 grains of the acid.

Dr. Ure suggests the use of the bicarbonate of potash. Its atomic weight, referred to hydrogen as unity, is 100·584, while the atomic weight of acetic acid is 51·563; if we estimate 2 grains of the bicarbonate as equivalent to 1 of the real acid, we shall commit no appreciable error. Hence a solution of the carbonate containing 200 grains in 100 measures will form an acetimeter of the most perfect and convenient kind; for the measures of test liquid expended in saturating any measure—for instance, an ounce or 1,000 grains of acid—will indicate the number of grains of real acetic acid in that quantity. Thus 1,000 grains of the above proof would require 50 measures of the acetimetrical alkaline solution, showing that it contains 50 grains of real acetic acid in 1,000, or 5 per cent.

Although the bicarbonate of potash of the shops is not absolutely constant in composition, yet the method is no doubt accurate enough for all practical purposes.

The acetimetrical method employed by the Excise is that recommended by Messrs. J. and P. Taylor, and consists in estimating the strength of the acid by the specific gravity which it acquires when saturated by hydrate of lime. Acid which contains 5 per cent. of real acid is equal in strength to the best malt vinegar, called by the makers No. 24, and is assumed as the standard of vinegar strength, under the denomination of 'proof vinegar.' Acid which contains 40 per cent. of real acetic acid, is therefore, in the language of the Revenue, 35 per cent. *over proof ;* it is the strongest acid on which duty is charged by the acetimeter. In the case of vinegars which have not been distilled, an allowance is made for the increase of weight due to the mucilage present; hence, in the acetimeter sold by Bate, a weight, marked м. is provided, and is used in trying such vinegars. As the hydrate of lime employed causes the precipitation of part of the mucilaginous matter in the vinegar, it serves to remove this difficulty to a certain extent. (*Pereira.*)

As the colour of malt vinegar or impure acetic acid sometimes obscures the exact termination of the reaction, when a standard solution of carbonate of soda is used, with litmus as an indicator, it is better to use the ammoniacal solution of copper recommended by Kiefer. This is made by dissolving sulphate of copper in water and adding solution of ammonia till the precipitate of basic salt, which forms at first, just redissolves. The strength of the copper solution is then ascertained by means of a standard solution of sulphuric acid. To use it a certain quantity of the vinegar to be tested is measured with a pipette and placed in a beaker or other suitable vessel and the copper solution gradually run into it from a burette. The bluish green precipitate formed disappears on stirring as long as any free acid remains, but as soon as it is completely neutralised a permanent turbidity is produced. A sheet of dark-coloured paper placed under the beaker enables the end of the experiment to be distinguished with greater facility. It is necessary that the acid should be so dilute that the precipitate, which is seen on adding the first drop of copper solution, only disappears on agitating the mixture; it is then of a suitable strength.

An excellent method, equally applicable to every description of acetic acid, has been proposed by Mohr. Pure precipitated carbonate of lime or baryta is added in excess to a known quantity of the acid to be tested. When the effervescence has ceased the mixture is heated, to complete the saturation of the acid and to expel the carbonic acid gas. The excess of the earthy carbonate employed is then filtered off, washed with hot water, and its amount ascertained by means of a standard acid and an alkaline solution, as described in the article on alkalimetry. The result thus obtained is subtracted from the weight of the carbonate added, and gives the quantity which has been consumed in saturating the acid. 100 parts of carbonate of lime dissolved, represent 102 of acetic acid, viewed as anhydrous, or 120 of the hydrated acid.

ACETONE. A volatile spirit obtained by the distillation of the acetates of the alkaline earths. It may also be prepared by the destructive distillation of citric acid, or by distilling starch, sugar, or gum with quicklime. The formula of acetone is $C^6H^6O^2$ (**C^3H^6O**). See PYROACETIC SPIRIT.

ACETYL. Some chemists (following Berzelius, who denied the existence of oxidised radicals) regard acetyl as a radical, the teroxide of which constituted acetic acid. The followers of Gerhardt, on the other hand, consider acetic acid to contain a radical of the formula $C^4H^3O^2$ (**C^2H^3O**). The latter is generally known as acetyl. Dr. Williamson proposes to call it othyl.

ACETYLAMINE. C^4H^5N (**C^2H^5N**). An oily alkaloid, produced by acting with the oil of olefiant gas (Dutch liquid, or chloride of ethylene) on an alcoholic solution of ammonia.

ACETYLENE. A hydrocarbon containing C_4H_2 (**C_2H_2**). By passing a voltaic current through carbon points in an atmosphere of hydrogen, acetylene is formed by the direct union of its elements. It may also be produced by the incomplete combustion of certain hydrocarbons, and indeed by the imperfect oxidation of most organic compounds. Acetylene is a colourless gas, possessing a peculiar odour, and burning with an intensely luminous flame. A highly characteristic reaction of acetylene, by which its presence may readily be determined, is the formation of a red precipitate when brought in contact with an ammoniacal solution of subchloride of copper. This red compound explodes either by percussion, or on being suddenly heated to a temperature a little above that of boiling water. It has been suggested that this is probably the cause of certain gas explosions which have occurred in unscrewing the brass fittings of gas-meters. Acetylene is one of the constituents of coal gas, and the red explosive compound is liable to be formed by contact of the gas with the brass-work.

ACHROMATIC, *destitute of colour.* White light consists, as is shown by its decomposition by a prism, of several coloured rays, having different degrees of refrangibility. When, therefore, white light passes through any transparent body, such as a lens, it is liable to this decomposition to a greater or a less extent, and hence colour is produced. This is termed *chromatic aberration.* Many, especially old-fashioned, telescopes exhibit objects surrounded by beautifully coloured fringes. Now the means which have been devised to prevent this are termed achromatic, signifying the *deprivation of colour.* See LIGHT.

ACHROMATIC LENS. Hale, in 1733, constructed lenses which did not produce chromatic dispersion. In 1757 Dollond arrived, by a perfectly independent examination, at the same discovery, and published it.

A lens may be regarded as a number of prisms united round a centre; therefore a ray of light falling on a lenticular glass is decomposed, and the rays being of unequal refrangibility, they have on its axis as many foci as there are colours. The images, therefore, of objects which are produced at these points are superimposed, more or less, and the edges fringed with indistinct colours. The least refrangible rays unite at foci further away than the more refrangible; and the object sought for, and attained, by both Hale and Dollond, was the means of uniting these rays at one focal point. They combined flint-glass with crown-glass, and found that, by a suitable curvature given to the object-glasses, the images seen through them were distinct, and free from these adventitious colours.

Telescopes, microscopes, &c., fitted up with such combinations of lenses as those described, are called achromatic telescopes.

ACICULITE. A name applied to Aikenite (a native sulphide of bismuth, copper and lead), in allusion to its occurrence in acicular, or needle-like crystals. See AIKENITE.

ACID. (*Acidus,* sour, *L.*) The term acid was formerly applied to bodies which were sour to the taste, and in popular language the word is still so used. It is to be regretted that the necessities of science have led to the extension of this word to any bodies combining with bases to form salts, whether such combining body is sour or otherwise. Had not the term *acid* been established in language as expressing a sour body, there would have been no objection to its use; but chemists now apply the term to substances which are not sour, and which do not change blue vegetable colours; and consequently they fail to convey a correct idea to the *popular* mind.

Hobbes, in his ' Computation or Logic,' says, ' A name is a word taken at pleasure to serve for a mark which may raise in our mind a thought like to some thought we had before, and which, being pronounced to others, may be to them a sign of what thought the speaker had, or had not, before in his mind.' This philosopher thus truly expresses the purpose of a name; and this purpose is not fulfilled by the term *acid,* as now employed.

Mr. John Stuart Mill, in his ' System of Logic,' thus, as it appears not very happily, endeavours to show that the word *acid,* as a scientific term, is not inappropriate or incorrect.

' Scientific definitions, whether they are definitions of scientific terms, *or of common terms used in a scientific sense,* are almost always of the kind last spoken of: their main purpose is to serve as the landmarks of scientific classification. And, since the classifications in any science are continually modified as scientific knowledge advances, the definitions in the sciences are also constantly varying. A striking instance is afforded by the words acid and alkali, especially the former. As experimental discovery advanced, the substances classed with acids have been constantly multiplying; and, by a natural consequence, the attributes connoted by the word have receded and become fewer. At first it connoted the attributes of combining with an alkali to form a neutral substance (called a salt), being compounded of a base and oxygen, causticity to the taste and touch, fluidity, &c. The true analysis of muriatic acid into chlorine and hydrogen caused the second property, composition from a base and oxygen, to be excluded from the connotation. The same discovery fixed the attention of chemists upon hydrogen as an important element in acids; and more recent discoveries having led to the recognition of its presence in sulphuric, nitric, and many other acids, where its existence was not previously suspected, there is now a tendency to include the presence of this element in the connotation of the word. But carbonic acid, silica, and sulphurous acid, have no hydrogen in their composition; that property cannot, therefore, be connoted by the term, unless those substances are no longer to be considered acids. Causticity and fluidity have long since been excluded from the characteristics of the class by the inclusion of silica and many other substances in it; and the formation of neutral bodies by combination with alkalis, together with such electro-chemical peculiarities as this is supposed to imply, are now the only *differentia* which form the fixed connotation of the word acid as a term of chemical science.'

The term ALKALI, though it is included by Mr. J. S. Mill in connection with *acid* in his remarks, does not stand, even as a scientific term, in the objectional position in which we find acid. *Alkali* is not, strictly speaking, a common name to which any definite idea is attached. *Acid*, on the contrary, is a word *commonly* employed to signify sour. The highest chemical authorities, following Gerhardt, now define ACIDS to be *Salts of Hydrogen*, or compounds in which the hydrogen may be readily replaced by a metal so as to form an ordinary salt.

An acid must now be defined to be a body which has the power of destroying more or less completely the characteristic properties of alkalis—at the same time losing its own distinguishing peculiarities. See ALKALI; ANHYDRIDES.

In this Dictionary all the acids named will be found under their respective heads, as ACETIC, NITRIC, SULPHURIC Acids, &c.

ACIDIFIER. Any body whose presence appears to be necessary for the production of an acid.

ACIDIMETER. An instrument for measuring the strength or quantity of real acid contained in a free state in liquids. The construction of that instrument is founded on the principle that the quantity of real acid present in any sample is proportional to the quantity of alkali which a given weight of it can neutralise. The instrument, like the alkalimeter (see ALKALIMETER), is made to contain 1,000 grains in weight of pure distilled water, and is divided accurately into 100 divisions, each of which therefore represents 10 grains of pure distilled water; but as the specific gravity of the liquids which it serves to measure may be heavier or lighter than pure water, 100 divisions of such liquids are often called 1,000 grains' measure, irrespectively of their weight (specific gravity), and accordingly 10–20 &c. divisions of the acidimeter are spoken of as 100–200 &c. grains' measure; that is to say, as a quantity or measure which, if filled with pure water, would have weighed that number of grains.

ACIDIMETRY. Acidimetry is the name of a chemical process of analysis by means of which the strength of acids—that is to say, the quantity of pure free acid contained in a liquid—can be ascertained or estimated. The principle of the method is based upon Dalton's law of chemical combinations; or, in other words, upon the fact that, in order to produce a complete reaction, a certain definite weight of reagent is required.

If, for example, we take 1 equivalent, or 49 parts in weight, of pure oil of vitriol of specific gravity 1·8485, dilute it (of course within limits) with no matter what quantity of water, and add thereto either soda, potash, magnesia, ammonia, or their carbonates, or in fact any other base, until the acid is neutralised—that is to say, until blue litmus-paper is no longer, or only very faintly, reddened when moistened with a drop of the acid liquid under examination—it will be found that the respective weights of each base required to produce that effect will greatly differ, and that with respect to the bases just mentioned these weights will be as follows:—

Soda (caustic)	1 equiv.	= 31 parts in weight ⎤	Saturate or neutralise 1
Potash (caustic)	,,	= 47	,,	eqv. = 49 parts in weight
Ammonia	,,	= 17	,,	of pure oil of vitriol (sp.
Carbonate of soda	,,	= 53	,,	gr. 1·8485), or 1 equiv.
Carbonate of potash	,,	= 69	,, ⎦	of any other acid.

This being the case, it is evident that if we wish to ascertain by such a method the quantity of sulphuric acid or of any other acid contained in a liquid, it will be necessary, on the one hand, to weigh or measure accurately a given quantity of that liquid to be examined, and, on the other hand, to dissolve in a known *volume* of water the *weight* above mentioned of any one of the bases just alluded to, and to pour that solution gradually into that of the acid until neutralisation is obtained; the number of volumes of the basic solution which will have been required for the purpose will evidently indicate the amount in weight of acid which existed in the liquid under examination. Acidimetry is therefore exactly the reverse of alkalimetry, since in principle it depends on the number of volumes of a solution of a base diluted with water to a definite strength, which are required to neutralise a known weight or measure of the different samples of acids.

The solution containing the *known weight* of base, and capable therefore of saturating a *known weight* of acid, is called a 'test-liquor;' and an aqueous solution of ammonia, of a standard strength, as first proposed by Dr. Ure, affords a most exact and convenient means of effecting the purpose, when gradually poured from a graduated dropping-tube or acidimeter into the sample of acid to be examined.

The strength of the water of ammonia used for the experiment should be so adjusted that 1,000 grains' measure of it (that is, 100 divisions of the alkalimeter) really contain one equivalent (17 grains) of ammonia, and consequently neutralise one equivalent of any one real acid. The specific gravity of the pure water of ammonia employed as a test for that purpose should be exactly 0·992, and when so adjusted, 1,000 grains' measure (100 divisions of the acidimeter) will then neutralise exactly

40 grains, or one equivalent, of			sulphuric acid (dry).
49 "	"	"	oil of vitriol, sp. gr. 1·8485.
37·5 "	"	"	hydrochloric acid (gas, dry).
54 "	"	"	nitric acid (dry).
60 "	"	"	crystallised acetic acid.
45 "	"	"	oxalic acid.
150 "	"	"	tartaric acid.
51 "	"	"	acetic acid.

And so forth with the other acids.

A standard liquor of ammonia of that strength becomes, therefore, a universal acidimeter, since the number of measures or divisions used to effect the neutralisation of 10 or of 100 grains of any one acid, being multiplied by the atomic weight or equivalent number of the acid under examination, the product, divided by 10 or by 100, will indicate the per-centage of real acid contained in the sample; the proportion of free acid being thus determined with precision, even to $\frac{1}{50}$th of a grain, in the course of five minutes, as will be shown presently.

The most convenient method of preparing the standard liquor of ammonia of that specific gravity is by means of a glass bead, not but that specific-gravity bottles and hydrometers may, of course, be employed; but Dr. Ure remarks, with reason, that they furnish incomparably more tedious and less delicate means of adjustment. The glass bead, of the gravity which the test-liquor of ammonia should have, floats, of course, in the middle of such a liquor at the temperature of 60° F.; but if the strength of the liquor becomes attenuated by evaporation, or its temperature increased, the attention of the operator is immediately called to the fact, since the difference of a single degree of heat, or the loss of a single hundredth part of a grain of ammonia per cent., will cause the bead to sink to the bottom—a degree of precision which no hydrometer can rival, and which could not otherwise be obtained, except by the troublesome operation of accurate weighing. Whether the solution remains uniform in strength is best ascertained by introducing into the bottle containing the ammonia test-liquor two glass beads, so adjusted that one, being very slightly heavier than the liquid, may remain at the bottom; whilst the other, being very slightly lighter, reaches the top, and remains just under the surface as long as the liquor is in the normal state; but when, by the evaporation of some ammonia, the liquor becomes weaker, and consequently its specific gravity greater, the bead at the bottom rises towards the surface, in which case a few drops of strong ammonia should be added to restore the balance.

An aqueous solution of ammonia, of the above strength and gravity, being prepared, the acidimetrical process is in every way similar to that practised in alkalimetry; that is to say, a known weight, for example, 10 or 100 grains of the sample of acid to be examined, are poured into a sufficiently large glass vessel, and diluted, if need be, with water, and a little tincture of litmus is poured into it, in order to impart a distinct red colour to it; 100 divisions, or 1,000 grains' measure, of the standard ammonia test-liquor above alluded to, are then poured into an alkalimeter (which, in the present case, is used as an acidimeter), and the operator proceeds to pour the ammonia test-liquor from the alkalimeter into the vessel containing the acid under examination, in the same manner, and with the same precautions used in alkalimetry (see ALKALIMETRY), until the change of colour, from red to blue, of the acid liquor in the vessel indicates that the neutralisation is complete and the operation finished.

Let us suppose that 100 grains in weight of a sample of sulphuric acid, for example, have required 61 divisions (610 water-grains' measure) of the acidimeter for their complete neutralisation, since 100 divisions (that is to say, a whole acidimeter full) of the test-liquor of ammonia is capable of neutralising exactly 49 grains—one equivalent—of oil of vitriol, of specific gravity 1·8485, it is clear that the 61 divisions employed will have neutralised 29·89 of that acid, and, consequently, the sample of sulphuric acid examined contained that quantity per cent. of pure oil of vitriol, representing 24·4 per cent. of pure anhydrous sulphuric acid: thus—

$$\text{Divisions.} \quad \text{Oil of Vitriol}$$
$$100 \quad : \quad 49 \quad :: \quad 61 \quad : \quad x \quad = \quad 29\text{·}89.$$

$$\text{Anhydrous Acid.}$$
$$100 \quad : \quad 40 \quad :: \quad 61 \quad : \quad z \quad = \quad 24\text{·}4.$$

The specific gravity of an acid of that strength is 1·2178.

In the same manner, suppose that 100 grains in weight of hydrochloric acid have required 90 divisions (900 grains' measure) of the acidimeter for their complete neutralisation, the equivalent of dry hydrochloric acid gas being 36·5, it is clear that since 90 divisions only of the ammonia test-liquor have been employed, the sample operated upon must have contained per cent. a quantity of acid equal to 33·30 of dry hydrochloric acid gas, in solution, as shown by the proportion:—

$$\text{Divis.} \quad \text{Hydrochloric acid.}$$
$$100 \quad : \quad 36\text{·}5 \quad :: \quad 90 \quad : \quad x \quad = \quad 32\text{·}85.$$

The specific gravity of such a sample would be 1·1646.

Instead of the ammonia test-liquor just alluded to, it is clear that a solution containing one equivalent of any other base—such as, for example, carbonate of soda, or carbonate of potash, caustic lime, &c.—may be used for the purpose of neutralising the acid under examination. The quantity of these salts required for saturation will of course indicate the quantity of real acid, and, by calculation, the per-centage thereof in the sample, thus:—The equivalent of pure carbonate of soda being 53, and that of carbonate of potash 69, either of these weights will represent one equivalent, and consequently 49 grains of pure oil of vitriol, 36·5 of dry hydrochloric acid, 60 of crystallised, or 51 of anhydrous acetic acid, and so on. The acidimetrical assay is performed as follows:—

If with *carbonate of soda*, take 530 grains of pure and dry carbonate of soda, obtained by igniting the bicarbonate of that base (see ALKALIMETRY), and dissolve them in 10,000 water-grains' measure (1,000 acidimetrical divisions) of distilled water. It is evident that each acidimeter full (100 divisions) of such a solution will then correspond to one equivalent of any acid, and accordingly if the test-liquor of carbonate of soda be poured from the acidimeter into a weighed quantity of any acid, with the same precautions as before, until the neutralisation is complete, the number of divisions employed in the operation will, by a simple rule of proportion, indicate the quantity of acid present in the sample as before. Pure carbonate of soda is easily obtained by recrystallising once or twice the crystals of carbonate of soda of commerce, and carefully washing them. By heating them gradually they melt, and at a very low red heat entirely lose their water of crystallisation and become converted into pulverulent anhydrous neutral carbonate of soda, which should be kept in well-closed bottles.

When *carbonate of potash* is used, then, since the equivalent of carbonate of potash is 69, the operator should dissolve 690 grains of it in the 10,000 grains of pure distilled water, and the acidimeter being now filled with this test-liquor, the assay is carried on again precisely in the same manner as before. Neutral carbonate of potash for acidimetrical use is prepared by heating the bicarbonate of that base to redness, in order to expel one equivalent of its carbonic acid; the residue left is pure neutral carbonate of potash; and in order to prevent its absorbing moisture, it should be put, whilst still hot, on a slab placed over concentrated sulphuric acid, or chloride of calcium, under a glass bell, and, when sufficiently cool to be handled, transferred to bottles carefully closed.

To adapt the above methods to the French weights and measures, now used also generally by the German chemist, we need only substitute 100 decigrammes for 100 grains, and proceed with the graduations as already described.

A solution of *caustic lime* in cane sugar has likewise been proposed by M. Peligot for acidimetrical purposes. To prepare such a solution, take pure caustic lime, obtained by heating Carrara marble with charcoal in a furnace; when sufficiently roasted to convert it into quicklime, slake it with water, and pour upon the slaked lime as much water as is necessary to produce a milky liquor; put this milky liquor in a bottle, and add thereto, *in the cold*, a certain quantity of pulverised sugar-candy; close the bottle with a good cork, and shake the whole mass well. After a certain time it will be observed that the milky liquid has become very much clearer, and perhaps quite limpid; filter it, and the filtrate will be found to contain about 50 parts of lime for every 100 of sugar employed. The liquor should not be heated, because saccharate of lime is much more soluble in cold than in hot water, and if heat were applied it would become turbid or thick, though on cooling it would become clear again.[1]

A concentrated solution of lime in sugar being thus obtained, it should now be diluted to such a degree that 1,000 water-grains' measure of it may be capable of saturating exactly one equivalent of any acid, which is done as follows:—Take 100 grains of hydrochloric acid of specific gravity 1·1812, that weight of acid contains exactly one equivalent = 36·5 of pure hydrochloric acid gas; on the other hand, fill the acidimeter up to 0 (zero) with the solution of caustic lime in sugar prepared as abovesaid, and pour the contents into the acid until exact neutralisation is obtained, which is known by testing with litmus-paper in the usual manner already described. If the whole of the 100 divisions of the acidimeter had been required exactly to neutralise the 100 grains' weight of hydrochloric acid of the specific gravity mentioned, it would have been a proof that it was of the right strength; but suppose, on the contrary, that only 50 divisions of the lime solution in the acidimeter have been sufficient for the purpose, it is evident that it is half too strong, or, in other words, one equivalent of lime (= 28) is contained in those 50 divisions instead of in 100. Pour, therefore, at once, 50 divisions or measures of that lime-liquor into a glass cylinder accurately divided into 100 divisions, and fill up the remaining 50 divisions with water; stir the whole well, and 100 divisions of the lime-liquor will, of course, now contain as much lime as was contained before in the 50; or, in other words, 100 acidimetrical divisions will now contain 1 equivalent of lime, and therefore will be capable of exactly neutralising 1 equivalent of any acid.

When, however, saccharate of lime is used for the determination of sulphuric acid, it is necessary to dilute it considerably, for otherwise a precipitate of sulphate of lime would be produced. This reagent, moreover, is evidently applicable only to the determination of such acids the lime salts of which are soluble in water.

Instead of a solution of caustic lime in sugar, a clean dry piece of white Carrara marble may be used. Suppose, for example, that the acid to be assayed is acetic acid, the instructions given by Brande are as follows:—A clean dry piece of marble is selected and accurately weighed; it is then suspended by a silk thread in a known quantity of the vinegar or acetic acid to be examined, and which is cautiously stirred with a glass rod, so as to mix its parts, but without detaching any splinters from the weighed marble, till the whole of the acid is saturated, and no further action on the marble is observed. The marble is then taken out, washed with distilled water, and weighed; the loss in weight which it has sustained may be considered as equal to the quantity of acetic acid present, since the atomic weight of carbonate of lime (= 50) is very nearly the same as that of acetic acid (= 51). Such a process, however, is obviously less exact than those already described.

But, whichever base is employed to prepare the test-liquor, it is clear that the acid tested with it must be so far pure as not to contain any other free acid than that for which it is tested, for in that case the results arrived at would be perfectly fallacious. Unless, therefore, the operator has reason to know that the acid, the strength of which has to be examined by that process, is genuine of its kind, he must make a qualitative analysis to satisfy himself that it is so; for in the contrary case the acid would not be in a fit state to be submitted to an acidimetrical assay.

The strength of acids may also be ascertained by determining either the *volumes* or the *weight* of carbonic acid gas disengaged from pure bicarbonate of soda by a given weight of any acid.

For *measuring* exactly the volumes of carbonic acid thus expelled, Dr. Ure's apparatus, represented in *fig.* 7, may be used. As it is absolutely requisite, for the success of the experiment, that the whole of the acid taken for examination should be completely saturated, the operator must accordingly take care to use a little more bicarbonate than is necessary for the purpose.

Now the equivalent number of bicarbonate of soda is 75, and the carbonic acid contained therein = 44; that of oil of vitriol is 49; wherefore by mixing together 75 grains of pure bicarbonate of soda with 49 grains of pure oil of vitriol, 44 grains of carbonic acid gas will be expelled, equal in bulk or volume to 2,381 acidimetrical divisions (23,810 water-grains' measure). These proportions, however, would be inconvenient, the more especially as the acidimeter in question should contain exactly 10,000 water-grains' measure, marked in series of 10 divisions from 0 (zero) at the top down to 100, such an arrangement at once enabling the operator to read off the amount of real acid *per cent.*; and accordingly a weight, or proportion of acid capable of disengaging exactly 10,000 water-grains' measure of carbonic acid from a quantity of

---

[1] The directions given by M. Violette for the preparation of Saccharate of Lime are as follow:— Digest in the cold 50 grammes of slaked caustic lime in 1 litre of water containing 100 grammes of sugar.

bicarbonate more than sufficient to supersaturate it is used. That weight or portion varies, of course, with each kind of acid, thus :—

For anhydrous sulphuric acid it is	. .	16·80 grains.
,, Oil of vitriol	. . . . .	20·58 ,,
,, Anhydrous nitric acid	. . .	22·67 ,,
,, ,, hydrochloric acid	. .	15·33 ,,
,, ,, acetic acid	. . .	21·42 ,,
,, Crystallised citric acid	. . .	80·64 ,,
,, ,, tartaric acid	. . .	63·00 ,,

Therefore by taking, of any sample of acid to be examined, the exact number of grains corresponding to each of the above-mentioned acids, we shall obtain a volume of carbonic acid gas proportioned to the strength and purity of the sample of each of them respectively. The *modus operandi* is as follows :—Charge the glass cylinder A with water, and pour upon the surface of the latter a layer of olive oil, about 1 inch in thickness, so that the level corresponds exactly to the 0 (zero) of the graduated scale etched on the glass cylinder. Through the cork in the mouth of the cylinder, push the taper tail of the flask c, air-tight; introduce into this flask c about 50 grains of bicarbonate of soda, in powder, and pour upon them a little more water than is sufficient to cover the powder; and if, for example, the object is to determine the amount of pure oil of vitriol contained in a given sample of that acid, weigh now accurately 20·58 grains of that sample, dilute it with water, and suck it up into the taper dropping glass tube, D; shut the stopcock, introduce the dropping-tube, pushing it air-tight through the perforated cork until its extremity plunges into the mixture of bicarbonate of soda and water in the flask, c. On opening now slightly the stopcock of the dropping-tube, the acid contained therein coming in contact with the bicarbonate will cause the evolution of a volume of carbonic acid proportioned to its strength. Supposing the same sample of sulphuric acid which was found by the acidimetrical process first described to contain 29·89 of oil of vitriol, or 24·4 of anhydrous sulphuric acid, per cent., to be now examined by the present method, it will be found that the 20·58 grains of that acid taken for the experiment have disengaged a volume of carbonic acid gas corresponding nearly to the number 30 of the graduated scale of the glass cylinder, thereby indicating nearly 30 per cent. of pure oil of vitriol in the sample under consideration.

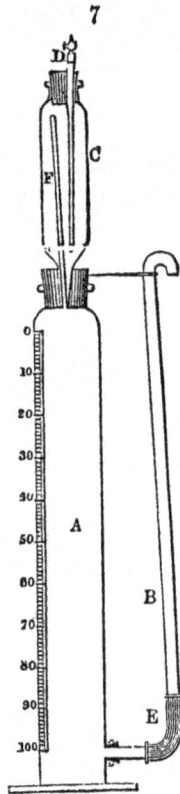

In the same manner the sample of hydrochloric acid, which by the former process was found to contain 32·85 per cent. of pure hydrochloric acid, would now disengage a volume of carbonic acid gas which would depress the level of the water in the glass cylinder nearly to the point marked 33, and therefore the operator would at once know that the quantity of pure hydrochloric acid gas contained in the sample was a little less than 33 per cent., a degree of accuracy quite sufficient for all commercial purposes, and which might besides be rendered still more accurate by lengthening the glass cylinder and diminishing its bore, so that the divisions may be sufficiently distant as to admit of being subdivided into fractions.

The principal objection to this form of acidimeter, however, is its expense, and also the difficulty or trouble of introducing into it *the whole* of the accurately weighed quantity of acid, a circumstance which renders it less applicable to acidimetry than to alkalimetry. By suppressing, however, the top flask, c, and using instead of it a common Florence flask, connected with the cylinder, the cost is considerably reduced, and the operator is at once enabled to secure the complete reaction of the whole of the accurately weighed acid upon the bicarbonate of soda. The arrangement has, besides, several other advantages, which the simple inspection of *fig.* 8 renders apparent. It consists of a 10,000 water-grains'-measure glass cylinder, A, graduated in the same manner, and provided with a discharge-tube, B, as before; but the mouth of the cylinder need not be larger than that of an ordinary wine-bottle, which allows of its being corked air-tight with greater ease and certainty. This cork is perforated, and provided with a tube passing air-tight through it, and connected—by a length of vulcanised india-rubber, c—with the disengagement tube of an ordinary Florence flask, into which the bicarbonate of soda and a certain quantity of water has been previously introduced, and likewise a small test-tube, E, containing the exactly weighed quantity of acid to be examined. All the joints being perfectly air-tight, if the Florence flask be now carefully tilted on one side, a portion of the acid in the test-tube will, of course, flow down upon the bicarbonate of soda, and a corresponding quantity of carbonic acid gas being evolved will depress the water in the glass cylinder, causing an overflow from the tube B, which should be held over a basin, and progressively lowered so as to keep the discharging aperture on a level with the descending water in the cylinder. The operation is terminated when, all the acid in the test-tube having been completely upset and all effervescence being entirely at an end, the level of the water in the cylinder A remains stationary; the number of divisions of the scale corresponding to that level are then read off; they indicate the per-centage strength of the sample.

The bicarbonate of soda of commerce frequently contains some neutral carbonate of soda, which should be removed before using it for that and for the following process; this is easily done by washing it with a moderate quantity of *cold* water, which dissolves the neutral carbonate, but leaves the greater portion of the bicarbonate in an undissolved state; it should then be dried spontaneously by spreading it in the air, and then kept in stoppered bottles; for though bicarbonate of soda does not undergo decomposition by exposure to dry air, a moist atmosphere converts a portion of it into a neutral carbonate, with 5 equivalents of water ($NaO, CO^2, 5HO$).

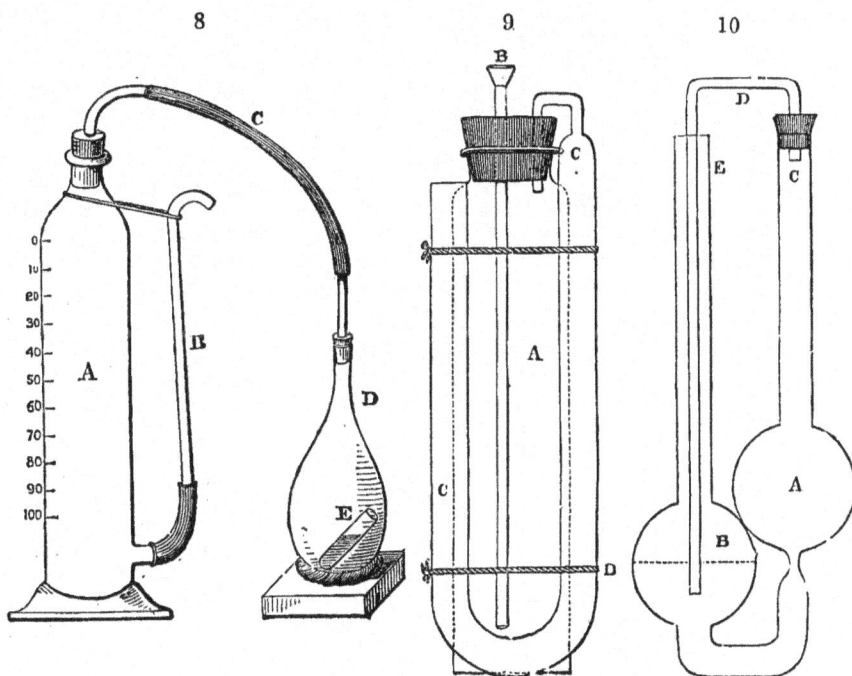

Acidimetrical operations may likewise be performed by determining the *weight* instead of the volumes of the carbonic acid expelled from bicarbonate of potash, or of soda, by a given quantity of acid. For this purpose either of the apparatus contrived by Dr. Ure, and represented above, may be used. The details of their construction are given in ALKALIMETRY, to which the reader is referred.

Since 1 equivalent of any acid will disengage 2 equivalents ($=44$) of carbonic acid from 1 equivalent ($=75$) of *bicarbonate* of soda, it is evident that by determining what quantity of any pure acid is capable of disengaging or expelling 10 grains of carbonic acid gas, then taking that quantity of the acid to be examined, and causing it to react upon a mass of bicarbonate of soda more than sufficient to saturate or neutralise it (in order to make sure that the acid has produced all its effect), the loss sustained after the operation from the carbonic gas expelled, multiplied by ten, will at once indicate the exact per-centage of real acid contained in the sample examined. Of course the weight of acid capable of disengaging exactly 10 grains of carbonic acid gas varies with each kind of acid; and that weight is found by dividing 10 times the atomic weight of the acid, whatever it may be, by 44; that is to say, by the atomic weight of the two equivalents of carbonic acid gas contained in the bicarbonate of soda.

For sulphuric acid, for example, the proportion would be as follows :—

$$2\ CO^2 \qquad SO^3$$
$$44 \quad : \quad 40 \quad :: \quad 10 \quad : \quad x$$
$$x = 9\cdot09 \text{ (or more correctly, } 9\cdot1\text{).}$$

Applying this rule, the weights to be taken are as follows, in reference to—

Dry sulphuric acid	9·1
„ nitric acid	12·27
„ hydrochloric acid	8·29
„ acetic (dry)	11·59
Crystallised tartaric acid	34·09
„ citric acid	43·64

Each of these quantities of real acid, with 25 or 26 grains of bicarbonate of soda, will give off 10 grains of carbonic acid gas; and hence, by adding a cypher, that is, multiplying by ten, whatever weight the apparatus loses denotes the per-centage of acid in the sample under trial, without the necessity of any arithmetical reduction. Let us suppose, for example, that the apparatus, being charged with 9·1 grains of a sample of sulphuric acid, is found, after the experiment, to have lost 7·5 grains; this multiplied by $10 = 75 \cdot 0$; therefore the sample contained 75 per cent. of dry sulphuric acid. If the apparatus had lost 2·44 grains thus, it would have indicated 24·4 per cent. of dry or anhydrous acid. Persons accustomed to the French metrical system may use decigrammes instead of grains, and they will arrive at the same per-centage results.

11

Another apparatus for ascertaining the weight of carbonic expelled for the purposes of either acidimetry or alkalimetry, and which the operator himself may readily construct, is represented in *fig.* 11.

A is a small matrass, with a somewhat wide mouth, capable, however, of being hermetically closed by a cork perforated with two holes, through one of which a bulbed tube, B, passes filled with fragments of chloride of calcium; through the other hole a tube, c, is introduced, sufficiently long to reach the bottom of the matrass A.

A certain quantity (say 25 grains) of bicarbonate of soda, greater than is required for saturation, is then introduced into the matrass A, and likewise enough water to cover it. A small glass test-tube is next charged with the proper quantity of the acid to be examined, namely, 9·1 if for sulphuric acid, 12·27 if for nitric acid, &c. &c., as before mentioned, and it is carefully introduced into the matrass A, taking care that the acid does not come in contact with the bicarbonate of soda, which is easily avoided by lowering the tube containing the acid into the matrass with a thread, or by carefully sliding it down, and keeping it nearly in an upright position, leaning against the sides of the matrass, as shown by the letter *b*. The matrass is then to be closed with the cork provided with its tubes, as above directed, and the whole is accurately weighed. This done, the apparatus is gently jerked, or tilted, on one side, so as to cause a portion of the acid in the tube *b* to flow among the bicarbonate of soda on which it is resting. A disengagement of carbonic acid gas immediately takes place from the decomposition of the carbonate of soda by the acid. When the violent effervescence has subsided, a fresh quantity of acid is again jerked, or spilled, out of the tube, until the whole of the acid is emptied, the tube occupying now a horizontal position, as represented by letter *a*. The water, which is mechanically carried off by the carbonic acid, is arrested by the chloride of calcium of the bulbed tube B. When all disengagement of carbonic acid gas has ceased, even after shaking the apparatus, the residuary gas is sucked up through the bulbed tube B, while the atmospheric air enters at the orifice, *d*, of the bent tube, *c*, to replace it. If the apparatus has become warm during the reaction, it should be allowed to cool completely, and it is then weighed again accurately. The difference between the first and second weighing, the loss, represents, of course, the weight of the carbonic acid gas expelled, and consequently the per-centage of real acid contained in the sample.

Instead of the preceding arrangement, the apparatus contrived by Drs. Fresenius and Will may be used. The annexed figure at once renders the construction of that apparatus intelligible, and as a full description of it is given in the article on ALKALIMETRY, the reader is accordingly referred thereto. When that contrivance is used for acidimetrical purposes, proceed as follows:—Fill bottle A with ordinary oil of vitriol to about one-half of its capacity, and pour into bottle B the accurately weighed quantity of acid to be examined, namely, 9·1 grains for sulphuric acid, 12·27 for nitric acid, &c. &c., according to the rule and table given (page 24), and dilute it with water, so that bottle B may be one-third full. Put now into a test-tube a quantity of bicarbonate of soda sufficient to saturate the weight of acid contained in bottle B, and suspend it into that bottle by means of a thread, kept tight by the pressure of the cork. Weigh now the whole apparatus accurately; this done, carefully loosen the thread, so that the test-tube charged with bicarbonate of soda may fall into the acid, and the cork being instantly adjusted air-tight, the whole of the carbonic acid gas disengaged is led by tube c into the concentrated sulphuric acid of bottle A, which absorbs all its moisture before it finally escapes through the tube a. When all effervescence has ceased, the operator, by applying his lips to that tube a, sucks out all the residuary carbonic acid gas contained in the apparatus, and replaces it by atmospheric air, which enters at d. The apparatus,

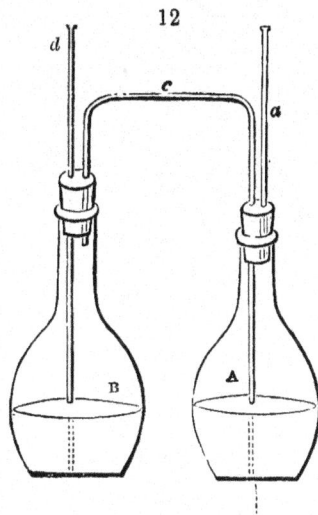

if it have become warm, should be allowed to cool completely, and on weighing it again the loss indicates the per-centage of real acid present in the sample.

The balance used in these methods should, of course, be sufficiently delicate to indicate small weights when heavily laden.

We shall terminate this article by a description of Liebig's acidimetrical method of determining the amount of prussic acid contained in solutions; for example, in medicinal prussic acid, in laurel and bitter-almond water, essence of bitter almonds, and cyanide of potassium. The process is based upon the following reaction:—When an excess of caustic potash is poured into a solution which contains prussic acid, cyanide of potassium is, of course, formed; and if nitrate of silver be then poured into such a liquor, a precipitate of cyanide of silver is produced, but it is immediately redissolved by shaking, because a double cyanide of silver and of potassium (Ag Cy + K Cy) is formed, which dissolves, without alteration, in the excess of potash employed. The addition of a fresh quantity of nitrate of silver produces again a precipitate which agitation causes to disappear as before; and this reaction goes on until *half* the amount of prussic acid present in the liquor has been taken up to produce cyanide of silver, the other *half* being engaged with the potassium in the formation of a double cyanide of silver and of potassium, as just said. As soon, however, as this point is reached, any new quantity of nitrate of silver poured in the liquor causes the cyanide of potassium to react upon the silver of the nitrate, to produce a *permanent* precipitate of cyanide of silver, which indicates that the reaction is complete, and that the assay is terminated. The presence of chlorides, far from interfering, is desirable, and a certain quantity of common salt is accordingly added, the reaction of chloride of silver being analogous to that of the cyanide of the same metal.

To determine the strength of prussic acid according to the above process, a test or normal solution should be first prepared, which is as follows:—

Since 1 equivalent of nitrate of silver (=170) represents, as we have seen, 2 equivalents of prussic acid (=54), dissolve, therefore, 170 grains of pure fused nitrate of silver in 10,000 water-grains' measure of pure water; 1,000 water-grains' measure (1 acidimeter full) of such solution will therefore contain 17 grains of nitrate of silver, and will therefore represent 5·4 grains of prussic acid; and consequently each acidimetrical division 0·054 grain of pure prussic acid.

ACIPENSER. A genus of cartilaginous ganoid fishes, to which the Sturgeon belongs, and from which isinglass is obtained. The roe of the sturgeon yields caviaire. There are at least eight species; four, however, appear to yield the Isinglass of commerce. The Beluga or large Sturgeon, *Acipenser Huso.* The Osseter, *A. Güldenstadtii.* The Sterlet, *A. Ruthenus,* and the Sewraga, *A. Stellatus.* These inhabit the Black and Caspian Sea, and the great rivers flowing into them. See CAVIAIRE; ISINGLASS.

ACONITINE. C^{60} H^{47} NO^{14} ($C^{30}H^{47}NO^7$). A poisonous alkaloid constituting the active principle of the Monkshood (*Aconitum Napellus*) and other species of Aconite.

ACONITUM. (ἀκόνιτον.) The Greek name for the Hemlock. See CONIUM.

ACONITUM is now the name of a genus of plants belonging to the *Ranunculaceæ,* nearly all the species being remarkable for their poisonous properties. *A. Napellus* is the Monkshood or Wolf's-bane, commonly cultivated in gardens as a showy flower, but the leaves and root are highly poisonous, and death has resulted from eating the root by mistake for horse-radish. The Bikh, Bish, or Nabee poison, used by the hill-tribes of Northern India for poisoning arrows, is obtained from *A. ferox*, which is said to be a more powerful poison than either of the other species; the quantity of the poisonous alkaloid *Aconitine* depending on the temperature in which the plant has grown. The root of the Aconite or Monkshood having been very frequently mistaken for the horse-radish root, and several deaths having been produced by eating it, a few of the distinctions between them are given. The aconite root, as shown in *fig.* 13, is conical and tapering rapidly to a point. The horse-radish is slightly conical at the crown, then of almost the same thickness for several inches. Aconite is coloured more or less brown, the horse-radish is externally white. The odour of the aconite is

13

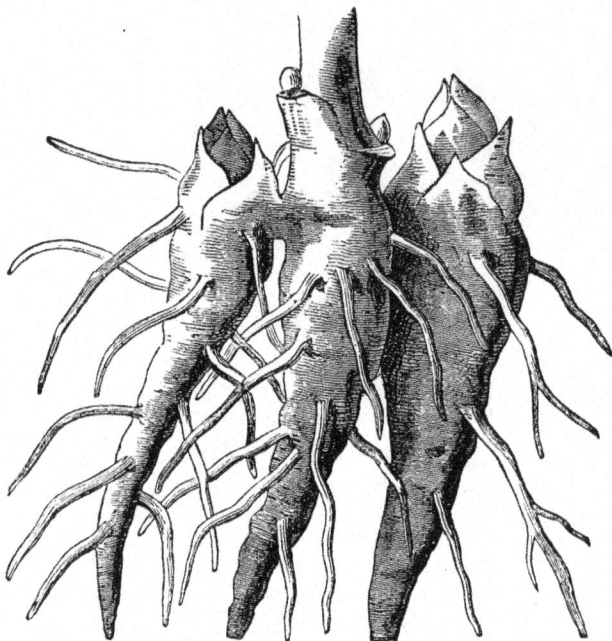

merely earthy, that of horse-radish pungent and irritating. Aconite root is the most virulent in the winter months and early spring, when the leaves are absent.

ACORNS. The fruit of the oak (*Quercus*). These possess some of the properties of the bark, but in a very diluted degree. Acorns are now rarely used. Pigs are sometimes fed upon them. The acorn-cups of *Quercus Ægilops* are used in tanning and dyeing, and are imported under the name of Valonia. See VALONIA.

ACORUS CALAMUS. The common sweet flag. This plant is a native of England, growing abundantly in the rivers of Norfolk, from which county the London market is chiefly supplied. The *radix calami aromatica* of the shops occurs in flattened pieces about one inch wide and four or five inches long. It is employed medicinally as an aromatic, and it is said to be used by some distillers to flavour gin. The essential oil (*oleum acori calami*) of the sweet flag is used by snuff-makers for scenting snuff, and it sometimes enters as one of the aromatic ingredients of aromatic vinegar. The Acorus belongs to the *Araceæ* or arum-order. See ARACEÆ.

ACROSPIRE. (*Plumule*, Fr.; *Blattkeim*, Ger.). The sprout at the end of seeds when they begin to germinate. Maltsters use the name to express the growing of the barley. 'The first leaves that appear when corn sprouts.'—*Lindley*.

ACRYLAMINE, or **ALLYLAMINE.** $C^6 H^7 N$ ($C^3 H^7 N$). An alkaloid obtained by Hofmann and Cahours, by boiling cyanate of allyle with a strong solution of potash. It boils at about 365°.—C. G. W.

ACTINISM. (From ἀκτὶν, a ray; signifying merely the *power* of a ray, without defining what character of ray is intended.)

As early as 1812, M. Berard (in a communication to the Academy of Sciences, on some observations made by him of the phenomena of solar action) drew attention to the fact, that three very distinct sets of physical phenomena were manifested: Light, Heat, and Chemical action. Chaptal, Berthollet, and Biot reported on this paper by M. Berard; and, as showing the extent to which this very important inquiry had proceeded in the hands of this philosopher, the following quotation is given from their report:

'M. Berard found that the chemical intensity was greatest at the violet end of the spectrum, and that it extended, as Ritter and Wollaston had observed, a little beyond that extremity. When he left substances exposed for a certain time to the action of each ray, he observed sensible effects, though with an intensity continually decreasing, in the indigo and blue rays. Hence we must consider it as extremely probable, that if he had been able to employ reactions still more sensible, he would have observed analogous effects, but still more feeble, even in the other rays. To show clearly the great disproportion which exists in this respect between the energies of different rays, M. Berard concentrated, by means of a lens, all that part of the spectrum which extends from *the green to the extreme violet*, and he concentrated, by another lens, all that portion which extends from the *green to the extremity of the red ray.* This last pencil formed a white point, so brilliant that the eyes were scarcely able to endure it, yet the muriate of silver remained exposed more than two hours to this brilliant point of light, without undergoing any sensible alteration. On the other hand, when exposed to the other pencil, which was much less bright, and less hot, it was blackened in less than six minutes. . . . . If we wish to consider solar light as composed of three distinct substances, one which occasions *light*, another *heat*, and the third *chemical combinations*, it will follow that each of those substances is separable by the prism into an infinity of different modifications, like Light itself; since we find, by experiment, that each of the three properties, *chemical, calorific,* and *colourific*, is spread, though unequally, over a certain extent of the spectrum. Hence we must suppose, on that hypothesis, that there exists *three spectrums*, one above another; namely, a calorific, a colourific, and a chemical spectrum.'

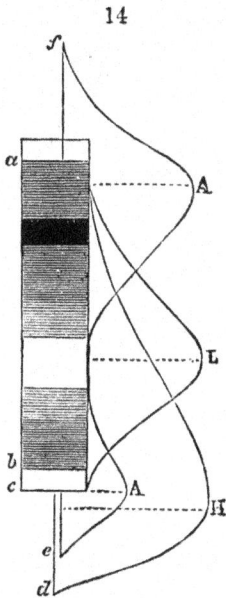

This was the earliest indication of the probable existence of a physical influence, in the solar rays, distinct from Light and Heat. A large number of philosophers still hold to the idea that the chemical changes produced by the sunbeam are due to *light*, and this idea is confirmed in the public mind by the universal adoption of the term *photography* (light-drawings) to indicate the production of pictures by the agency of the sunbeam. See PHOTOGRAPHY.

The actual conditions of the sunbeam will be understood by reference to the annexed woodcut, *fig.* 14, and attention to the following description: *a b* represents the prismatic spectrum—as obtained by the decomposition of white light by the prism—or Newtonian luminous spectrum, consisting of certain bands of colour. Newton determined those rays to be seven in number; red, orange, yellow, green, blue, indigo, and violet; recent researches, by Sir John Herschel and others, have proved the existence of two other rays; one, the extreme red or crimson ray *c*, found at the least refrangible end of the spectrum, the other occurring at the most frangible end, or beyond the violet rays, which is a lavender or grey ray. Beyond this point up to *f*, Professor Stokes has discovered a new set of rays, which are only brought into view when the light is received upon the surfaces of bodies which possess the property of altering the refrangibility of the rays. Those rays have been called the *fluorescent rays*, from the circumstance that some of the varieties of Fluor Spar exhibit this phenomenon in a remarkable manner. (See FLUORESCENCE.) The curved line L from *a* to *c* indicates the full extent of the luminous spectrum, the point marked L showing the maximum of illuminating power, which exists in the yellow ray.

Sir William Herschel and Sir Henry Englefield determined, in the first instance, the maximum point for the calorific rays, and Sir John Herschel subsequently confirmed their results, proving that the greatest heat was found below the red ray, and that it gradually diminished in power with the increase of refrangibility in the rays, ceasing entirely in the violet ray. Heat rays have been detected down to the point *d*, and the curved line H indicates the extent of their action.

Now, if any substance capable of undergoing chemical change be exposed to this spectrum, the result will be found to be such as is represented in the accompanying drawing, *fig.* 15. Over the space upon which the greatest amount of light falls, *i.e.*, the region of the yellow and orange rays L, no chemical change is effected: by prolonged action a slight change is brought about where the red ray falls, *r*, but from the mean green ray *g* up to the point *f*, a certain amount of chemical action is maintained; the maximum of action being in the blue and violet rays A. Thus the curved line (*fig.* 14) from *e* to *f* represents the extent and degree of chemical power as manifested in the solar spectrum. Two maxima are marked A A, differing widely, however, in their degree.

Here, as in Berard's experiments, we see that where the *light* is the strongest, there is no chemical action, and that as the luminous power diminishes the chemical force is more decidedly manifested.

Again, we find that if we take a piece of yellow glass, stained with oxide of silver, we have a medium which entirely prevents the permeation of the chemical rays, though it obstructs no Light. But, if a very dark blue glass is taken, we find that ninety per cent. of the luminous rays are obstructed, while the chemical rays permeate it most freely. Numerous experiments of an analogous character appear to prove that the chemical and luminous powers of the sunbeam are balanced against each other (see Hunt's 'Researches on Light'), that they are indeed antagonistic principles or powers. That there are three very distinct sets of phenomena, every one admits.

LIGHT (*luminous power*), to which belongs the phenomena of vision and the production of colour.

HEAT (*calorific power*), the function of which appears to be the determining the physical condition of all matter, as regards its solid, fluid, or gaseous condition.

ACTINISM (*chemical power*), to which all the phenomena of photography are due, and many of the more remarkable changes observed in the vegetable kingdom.

ACTINO-CHEMISTRY was a term first applied by Sir John Herschel, and has been generally adopted to indicate the phenomena of chemical change by the action of the solar rays. *Actinism* was first proposed to express the chemical *principle* of the sunbeam by the Editor of this Dictionary at the meeting of the British Association at York.

ACTINOGRAPH. A name given to an instrument for recording the variations in the chemical (*actinic*) power of the solar beams. The name signifies *ray writer*.

ACTINOLITE. A variety of Hornblende   See HORNBLENDE.

ACTINOMETER. (*Ray measurer.*) The name of various forms of instuments, the objects of which are to measure the direct heat radiations from the sun. The term has also been applied to instruments employed to measure the varying intensities of Light.

ADAMANTINE SPAR. An old name for Corundum.   See CORUNDUM.

ADAMITE. A native hydrous arsenate of zinc, occurring in the silver-mines of Chañarcillo in Chili, and in the Dép. du Var, France.

ADAM'S NEEDLE. A name commonly given to the *Yucca gloriosa*, a plant belonging to the *Liliaceæ* or Lily-order, the fibres of which have been used in the manufacture of paper.

ADANSONIA DIGITATA. The Baobab tree, a native of Western Africa. It yields a fibre which has lately been used in paper-making.

ADDITIONS. Such articles as are added to the fermenting wash of the distiller, were of old distinguished by this trivial name.

ADHESION (*sticking together*). The union of two surfaces. With the phenomena which are dependent upon bringing two surfaces so closely together that the influence of *cohesion* is exerted, we have not to deal. In arts and manufactures, adhesion is effected by interposing between the surfaces to be united some body possessing peculiar properties, such as gum, plaster, resin, marine or ordinary glue, and various kinds of cement. *Adhesion* should be restricted to mean, sticking together by means of some interposed substance; *cohesion*, the state of union effected by natural attraction.

Not only is adhesion exhibited in works of art or manufacture; we find it very strikingly displayed in nature. Fragments of rocks which have been shattered by convulsion are found to be cemented together by silica, lime, oxide of iron, and the like ; and broken parts of mineral lodes are frequently reunited by the earthy minerals.

ADIPIC ACID. $C^{12} H^{10} O^8$. ($C^6 H^{10} O^4$.) One of the fixed fatty acids produced by the action of nitric acid on oleic acid, suet, spermaceti, and other fatty bodies. See Watts's 'Dictionary of Chemistry.'

ADIPOCIRE. From *adeps*, fat; *cera*, wax. (*Adipocire*, Fr.; *Fettwachs*, Ger.) The fatty matter supposed to be generated in dead bodies buried under peculiar circumstances. It is chiefly *margarate of ammonia*. In 1786 and 1787, when the churchyard of the *Innocents*, at Paris, was cleaned out, and the bones transported to the Catacombs, it was discovered that not a few of the *cadavres* were converted into a saponaceous white substance, more especially many of those which had been interred for fifteen years in one pit, to the amount of 1,500, in coffins closely packed together. These bodies were flattened in consequence of their mutual pressure ; and though they generally retained their shape, there was deposited round the bones of several of them a greyish white, somewhat soft, flexible substance. Fourcroy presented to the Academy of Sciences, in 1789, a memoir which appeared to prove that the fatty body was an ammoniacal soap containing phosphate of lime ; that the fat was similar to spermaceti, as it assumed, on slow cooling, a foliated crystalline structure ; as also to wax, as, when rapidly cooled, it became granular ; hence he called it *adipocire*. Its melting point was 52·5° C. (126·5° F.)

This substance was again examined by Chevreul, in 1812, and was found by him to contain margaric acid, oleic acid, combined with a yellow colouring odorous matter, besides ammonia, a little lime, potash, oxide of iron, salts of lactic acid, an azotised substance ; and was therefore considered as a combination of margaric and oleic acids, in variable proportions. These fat acids are obviously generated by the reaction of the ammonia upon the margarine and oleïne, though they eventually lose the greater part of that volatile alkali. It is sometimes confounded with chlorestine. Bog butter is said to be a similar substance. See Fat and Fatty Bodies.

ADIPOSE SUBSTANCE or **ADIPOSE TISSUE**. (*Tissu graisseux*, Fr.) An animal oil, resembling in its essential properties the vegetable oils. During life, it appears to exist in a fluid or semi-fluid state ; but, in the dead animal, it is frequently found in a solid form, constituting *suet*, which, when divested of the membrane in which it is contained, is called *tallow*. See Tallow, Oils, &c.

ADIT or **ADIT LEVEL**. The horizontal entrance to a mine ; a passage or level driven into the hill-side. The accompanying section gives, for the purpose of distinctness, an exaggerated section of a portion of the subterranean workings of a metalliferous mine. It should be understood that *d* represents a mineral-lode, upon which the *shaft*, *a*, has been sunk. At a certain depth from the surface of the hill the miners would be inconvenienced by water, consequently a level is *driven* in from the side of the hill, *b*, through which the water flows off, and through which also the miner can bring out the broken rock, or any ores which he may obtain. Proceeding still deeper, supposing the workings to have commenced, as is commonly the case, at a certain elevation above the sea-level, similar conditions to those described again arising, another level is driven so as to intersect the shaft or shafts, as shown at *c*. In this case, *b* would be called the *shallow*, and *c* the *deep* adit. The economy of such works as these is great, saving the cost of expensive pumping machinery, and also of considerable labour in the removal of ores or other matter from the mine.

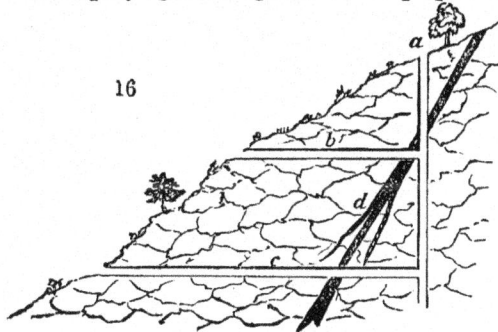

The great Gwennap Adit, in Cornwall, with its branches, was cut through the solid rock for nearly 30 miles ; through it, numerous mines are drained to a certain depth, and the water pumped from greater depths discharged. The Nentforce Level, or Adit, in Alston Moor, has been wrought under the course of the River Nent, and it extends about 3¼ miles into that important mining district, serving to drain a considerable number of the Nenthead mines. Many of the mines in Cumberland and in Derbyshire are worked by the Adit called a *Day-level* only ; the adit, as at *c*, being carried into the hill until it reaches the lode. The ore is obtained by working up into the hill. It falls into the level, and is carried out in tram-wagons. See Mining.

ADULARIA. A variety of orthoclase. See Felspar.

ADULTERATION. The practice of debasing any product of manufacture by the introduction of cheap and often injurious materials. The extent to which the adulteration of almost every useful article is carried, is at once a disgrace to the trading community, and a standing reflection on an age and country which boasts of its high moral character and its devotion to Christianity.

ADZE. A cutting instrument ; differing from the axe by the edge being placed at nearly right angles to the handle, and being slightly curved up or inflected towards it. The instrument is held in both hands, whilst the operator stands upon his work in a stooping position; the handle being from twenty-four to thirty inches long, and the weight of the blade from two to four pounds. The adze is swung in a circular path almost of the same curvature as the blade, the shoulder joint being the centre of motion, and the entire arm and tool forming, as it were, one inflexible radius; the tool, therefore, makes a succession of small arcs, and in each blow the arm of the workman is brought in contact with the thigh, which serves as a stop to prevent accident. In coarse preparatory works, the workman directs his adze through the space between his two feet; he thus surprises us by the quantity of wood removed; in fine works he frequently places his toes over the spot to be wrought, and the adze penetrates two or three inches beneath the sole of the shoe; and he thus surprises us by the apparent danger, yet perfect working of the instrument, which, in the hands of a shipwright in particular, almost rivals the joiner's plane; it is with him the nearly universal paring instrument, and is used upon works in all positions.—*Holtzapffel.*

ÆOLIAN HARP. A musical instrument; the invention of Kircher; although it was probably indicated by Hero of Alexandria. The musical sounds are produced by the action of a current of air upon strings placed above a long box of thin deal. The wires of the electric telegraph on the sides of our railroads are frequently set in such a state of vibration by the wind, that they become gigantic Æolian harps.

AERATED WATER. The common commercial name of water artificially impregnated with carbonic acid or oxygen.

AEROLITES. Meteoric stones. It has long been well established that masses of solid matter have fallen from the atmosphere upon this earth. Various hypotheses have been proposed to account for them; amongst others the following may be named :—

1. That they are aggregations of solid matter which take place in the higher regions of the air. It is known, however, that our atmosphere does not contain the chemical elements of meteorites; and, moreover, the large size of many of these meteoric masses—some weighing several tons each—renders it extremely improbable that they should be formed by condensation or aggregation in a highly attenuated atmosphere.

2. That they are projected from volcanoes in the moon. The researches of Nasmyth, Smyth, and others appear to show that our satellite, whatever may have been her condition at one period, is now in a state of comparative, if not of perfect, repose. Some astronomers think they have observed changes in some parts of the moon's surface, but there are no indications sufficiently clear to warrant the assumption of there being any volcanoes in a state of activity.

3. That belts composed of fragments of matter circulate in certain fixed orbits around the sun, and that these fragments, sometimes entering our atmosphere, are involved in the earth's influences, and fall in obedience to the law of gravitation. The flights of 'shooting stars' which are observed at particular periods appear to favour this view.

It has not been proved, however, that meteorites move in circumsolar orbits; and indeed evidence may be adduced tending to show that they have probably come from regions of space beyond the limits of the solar system.

It is usual to distinguish between *aerolites*, or meteoric *stones*, and *siderites*, or masses of meteoric *iron*; but the two classes pass into each other through certain meteorites, termed *siderolites*, which are partly metallic and partly stony. An aerolite, or meteoric stone, is composed of a number of crystalline minerals, usually loosely aggregated, and presenting a peculiar spherular structure. The surface of the stone is invariably coated with an incrustation, in most cases lustrous and of a black colour. This crust seems to be the result of superficial fusion consequent upon the great development of heat due to the resistance which the stone suddenly encounters on entering the earth's atmosphere.

Among the minerals found in aerolites may be noticed—olivine and augite (two silicates of magnesia), several alloys of iron and nickel, troilite (sulphide of iron), schreibersite (phosphide of iron and nickel), graphite, and certain hydrocarbons similar to what are commonly regarded as organic compounds. The following average per-centage composition of an aerolite has been calculated, by Reichenbach, from a very large number of trustworthy analyses : silica, 40; iron, 25; magnesia, 20; alumina, 2; sulphur, 2; nickel, 1·5; lime, 1·5; chromium, 0·5; manganese, 0·33; sodium, 0·33; other elements, 1·34; oxygen, hydrogen, and loss, 5·5.

Some interesting experiments on the artificial formation of meteorites have been carried out, within the last few years, by M. Daubrée. This chemist has been successful in producing, on a small scale, certain products strongly resembling meteorites, both in structure and composition. The artificial aerolites were produced by fusing a rock called Lherzolite, the fusion being effected either alone or in the presence of certain reducing agents. Other experiments have been made by heating iron, silicon, and magnesium, in an imperfectly oxidising atmosphere.

It is perhaps unnecessary in this place to do more than refer to Dr. Mayer's theory, which seeks to explain the source of solar heat by the impact of meteorites falling into the mass of the sun—a subject on which Mr. Waterston and Sir W. Thomson have also written. It has even been suggested that the zodiacal light may be a luminous crowd of meteoric stones showered down upon the sun. This hypothesis has not, however, received the support it claimed, and the whole question remains in a state of considerable uncertainty.

AEROSTATION; AERONAUTICS. The ascent into the atmosphere by means of balloons, which are either filled with hot air—FIRE-BALLOONS, or a light gas—AIR-BALLOONS.

The Montgolfier balloon is a bag filled with air, which is rarefied by the action of fire, which is kept burning under the mouth of the bag; and thus the whole mass is rendered specifically lighter than the surrounding medium.

The investigations of Cavendish led to the use of hydrogen gas—the lightest of known bodies—to inflate silken bags; and since his time our balloons have been inflated with either pure hydrogen, or with common coal gas—carburetted hydrogen.

Notwithstanding the numerous attempts which have been made to navigate the air, nothing has yet been done to enable the aeronaut to steer his balloon. In whatever current of air he may be, with that current he moves; and, until this difficulty is overcome, we cannot expect any satisfactory results from aeronautics. The great use of balloons during the siege of Paris led to considerable improvements in the art of aerostation. They were largely employed during the siege of Paris in enabling the besieged to communicate outside the city. A balloon-post (*Poste aérienne*) was thus established, and no fewer than 54 ascents were made between October 1870 and January 1871. M. Dupuy de Lôme has constructed balloons characterized by remarkable stability of the car, and furnished with screws and rudder, whereby the speed and direction of the balloon are brought, to a certain extent, under the control of the aeronaut; nevertheless, the great problem of aerostation yet remains unsolved. Some interesting and useful experiments have been made by using captive balloons, by which we have arrived at some facts connected with the upper regions of the air, which could not be obtained by any other means. By means of balloons, valuable meteorological observations have been made at great altitudes in the atmosphere by Mr. Glaisher and other scientific aeronauts.

ÆRUGO. (*Verdigris. Acetate and carbonate of copper.*) The name formerly given to the bright green rust, produced by the oxygen of the air and carbonic acid, upon copper, and its alloys, bronze and brass. The Romans gave this name; they considered that the *ærugo* added much to the beauty of their statues; and adjusted the composition of their alloys with the view of producing the finest green colour. This was frequently effected artificially; and to distinguish the real from the artificial they used for the former the term *ærugo nobilis*. This is the *patina* of the Italians; it is a form of verdigris. See VERDIGRIS; COPPER, ACETATE and CARBONATE.

ÆTHER. See ETHER.

ÆTHIOPS MINERAL. The black sulphide of mercury prepared by rubbing mercury and sulphur together. The term *Æthiops* was applied by the old pharmaceutical chemists to several mineral preparations of a black or dark colour.

ÆTHIOPS ANTIMONIALIS was a sulphide of antimony and mercury.

ÆTHIOPS MARTIALIS. Black oxide of iron.

ÆTHIOPS NARCOTICUS. Sulphide of mercury obtained by precipitation.

ÆTHIOPS PER SE. The grey powder obtained by exposing impure mercury to the air.

AFFINITY. The term used by chemists to denote the peculiar attractive force which produces the combination of dissimilar substances—as an acid with an alkali, or of sulphur with a metal. See CHEMICAL AFFINITY.

AFRICAN HEMP. A fibre prepared from the leaves of *Sansevieria Zeylanica*, a member of the lily order extensively distributed through tropical Africa and India.

AFRICAN TEAK. A valuable wood for ship-building, the produce of *Oldfieldia Africana*, Bth., a tree belonging to the spurge order. This wood is to be carefully distinguished from the true teak. See TEAK.

AGALMATOLITE. The 'Figure-stone,' or Pagodite, of China; a soft mineral in which carvings are commonly executed by the Chinese. Under the common name of agalmatolite, are included several minerals similar in physical characters, but essentially distinct in chemical composition. The true agalmatolite is a hydrous silicate of alumina and potash, closely allied to pinite. Professor Brush has shown that certain specimens of so-called agalmatolite are really a compact form of pyrophyllite (hydrous silicate of alumina), whilst others are silicates of magnesia, either hydrous or anhydrous.

AGAR-AGAR. A seaweed forming a large article of commerce in the East. It is frequently called Bengal Isinglass, from the fact of its being found largely in the Bengal market. It is used for making jellies and for stiffening purposes. See ALGÆ.

AGARICUS. A genus of the class Fungi, so numerous that 4,000 species have been enumerated. The mushrooms are of this order. The *Agaricus campestris* is the one commonly used in this country as food, and from which the sauce called ketchup is made. In Italy this species is considered poisonous, while many species used there and in France are unused here. The truffle is a mushroom, *Tuber cibarium*, and its commercial value is so great that in Rome the yearly average of taxed mushrooms from 1837 to 1847 was between 60,000 and 30,000 lbs. weight. The *Agaricus muscaria* is a poisonous species, though used by the natives of Kamtschatka and Korea to produce intoxication; the Russian name is monchomore, and an infusion of this taken with some liquor produces raving delirium and not unfrequently a desire to commit suicide or assassination. Another variety is beautifully phosphorescent. The Agarici grow in decaying animal or vegetable matter; they are cellular plants, with a rounded *thallus* on a stalk; the spores or seeds occur underneath the cup in the *gills* or *hymenium.* Their growth is remarkably rapid, and there is often great difficulty in distinguishing between the edible and poisonous varieties.

All the fungi of this genus contain a larger amount of nitrogen than either peas or beans. The following are a few of the analyses given in Watts's 'Chemical Dictionary:'

	Nitrogen.
Agaricus deliciosus . .	4·68.
,, arvensis . .	7·26.
,, muscarius . .	6·34.
Lycoperdon echinatum . .	6·16.

Upon this depends their nutritive properties.

AGATE. (*Agate*, Fr.; *Achat*, Ger.) The term *Agate* is not employed to denote any distinct mineral of uniform composition, but is applied rather to certain mixtures of siliceous minerals, consisting of different varieties of chalcedony usually associated with jasper, quartz, amethyst, and other natural forms of silica. The agate is the ἀχάτης of the Greeks, by whom it was so called after the river in Sicily of that name (now the Drillo), whence, according to Theophrastus, agates were first procured. Bochart, with much probability, deduces the name from the Punic and Hebrew, *nakad*, spotted.

In some agates, as in certain varieties from Saxony and Bohemia, the chalcedony and other component minerals have been deposited in fissures, thus forming true veins; but in by far the greater number of cases the materials of the agate have been formed, layer after layer, in the cavities of a vesicular rock. When the formation of the agate has proceeded with regularity, a transverse section of the stone exhibits a number of concentric lines representing the edges of the successive deposits—these deposits differing one from another in colour, density, and other physical characters, and thus producing the variegated patterns exhibited by most agates. As the component minerals are formed in regular sequence, the successive layers being deposited *from without inwards,* it follows that the innermost portion of an agate must always be the most recent.

Agates are usually found either embedded in a rock called *melaphyre,* or in the form of free nodules, liberated by decomposition of the matrix. Although the term melaphyre has been somewhat loosely applied, it is now generally used to designate a fine-grained eruptive rock, composed mainly of a felspar—either oligoclase or labradorite—and augite, with more or less magnetic iron-ore: it is chiefly associated with stratified rocks of palæozoic age. When fresh, the melaphyre, as its name implies, (μέλas, black) is usually of a black or very dark colour, but on weathering it often becomes green or brown; it is the altered varieties of melaphyre that most commonly contain agates. Some varieties are porphyritic, and were formerly called *augitic porphyry.*

Unwilling to admit the igneous origin of the agate-bearing melaphyres, some authorities, as Bischof, have maintained that the cavities now occupied by siliceous minerals have been formed by the removal of crystals in the porphyritic rock—these cavities having been enlarged and their angles rounded off by subsequent solution. Although such an explanation may be admissible in certain cases, it seems much more probable that in by far the larger number of rocks the cavities were originally formed by the disengagement of gas or steam at a time when the melaphyre was in a molten or partially molten state. The formation of such vesicles in a plastic mass may be well illustrated by the spongy texture of a loaf of bread. Originally the form of the bubbles in the viscid rock would be more or less globular, but by movement of the pasty mass the hollows might become elongated, or, as often happens, pointed at one extremity; if the mass were slowly moving upwards the point would be directed downwards. In many cases the cavities have been much extended and laterally compressed; and hence the agates now occupying such hollows are elongated, flattened and pointed, thus resembling almonds, and the rock containing them is consequently termed *amygdaloidal* melaphyre. Evidence of the movement of the viscous rock-mass is further afforded by the parallelism often observable in the amygdaloidal agates as they lie in the rock—the longer axes of these agates being all arranged in one direction. The smaller agates are often perfectly amygdaloidal, but the larger specimens are usually distorted. It is likely that the cavities of the large amygdaloids may have been produced by the coalescence of several smaller vesicles.

On the cooling of the igneous mass, water charged with carbonic acid would percolate through the rock, and effect the decomposition of some of the mineral constituents—the chemical changes being perhaps aided by the heat still lingering in the rock. The products of this decomposition might be carried into the vesicular cavities, and thrown down as a lining on their inner walls. Among the first formed of such products are the minerals called *delessite*, or ferruginous chlorite, and the somewhat similar substance termed '*green earth;*' many vesicular cavities exhibit nothing more than a layer of such green minerals, derived probably from the decomposition of the augite in the rock, whilst most agates—especially the smaller ones—when freed from their matrix present a green external coating of a like nature. In other cases a hydrous peroxide of iron appears to have been formed, perhaps by further alteration of the green earth; and hence many large agates present a rusty exterior or exhibit a pitted surface due to the former presence of a coating of this mineral. The smaller cavities in amygdaloidal rocks are commonly filled with carbonate of lime, and the solid nodules removed from such rocks consequently appear as small green-coated masses of calcite. But in most cases silica has been separated from the silicates decomposed in the rock, and has been thrown down in a gelatinous state on the walls of the cavity as a coating of chalcedony. This coating may be nothing more than a thin rind, thus forming a hollow agate or *geode*. It generally happens that crystalline silica is deposited on the inner surface of the chalcedonic layer, which thus bears a crop of crystals of quartz—the free pointed ends of these crystals being all directed towards the centre of the geode. Fine amethysts are often found seated in such situations. In other cases the cavity may contain stalactitic deposits of chalcedony, or crystals of calcite, or of various hydrated silicates called *zeolites*, and rarely of certain metallic minerals—as iron-glance, copper-pyrites, native copper, &c.

By continued deposition of chalcedony, or of alternate layers of chalcedony and crystalline quartz, the cavity may become completely filled, and a solid agate thus formed.

Many agates exhibit, on section, tubular orifices, which are commonly supposed to have served as inlets through which the agate-forming materials have been introduced by infiltration. In some specimens these inlets have become choked up at an early period in the history of the stone, and the introduction of fresh matter was thus prevented; in other cases the tubes have remained open until the cavity was completely filled, and connexion has thus been maintained between the very heart of the agate and the exterior. This 'infiltration theory' has been staunchly supported by Von Buch and Nöggerath. On the other hand, Haidinger supposed that the silica, instead of being introduced through special apertures, exuded through the general walls of the cavity. After a lining had been laid down uniformly over the interior, more silica in solution might pass from the exterior through this layer by a kind of osmosis, and thus gain access to the interior. But in describing the modern method of colouring agates, it will be shown that certain layers of chalcedony are quite impermeable to fluids, at least under ordinary conditions of temperature and pressure. As soon, then, as a dense impervious layer was deposited, it would seem at first sight that all action must cease; but it has been suggested that siliceous solutions might still find their way to the interior through the cracks with which agates are almost invariably rent.

A different theory of agate formation has been advanced by Reusch. He supposes that warm siliceous solutions were from time to time introduced into the cavities by the action of intermittent thermal springs, the cavities being thus alternately filled and emptied. The intermission of the action may account for the definite succession of the deposits, and the sharp lines of separation between the several strata. This theory has been ingeniously extended by Lange, who seeks to explain the formation of

both concentric and horizontal layers in the same stone, an association often observed
in the South American agates, and always difficult of explanation. Lange maintains
that when the gelatinous silica, deposited in a warm state, had choked up the entrance,
the tension of the steam confined in this closed cavity would cause the siliceous jelly
to be pressed equally in all directions against the inner surface of the cavity, thus
forming a continuous lining, until the steam finally burst the coating at its weakest
point, and so effected its egress : the so-called inlets of infiltration may therefore be really
canals of eruption. If the cavity were large, the elasticity of the vapour might be
insufficient to press the gelatinous matter against the sides of the hollow, and the
contents would then be precipitated, in obedience to the force of gravity, in horizontal
strata on the floor of the cavity : hence the co-existence of concentric and horizontal
layers in a single agate.

According to the varying conditions under which the successive strata of an agate
have been formed, different varieties of the mineral are produced, and many of these
are sufficiently well characterized to receive special names. Thus, when the cavity in
which the stone has been formed presents angular contours, the layers naturally adapt
themselves to these angles, and the cut stone thus exhibits a zigzag pattern, whence
it is termed *fortification agate*. If the deposits form concentric rings the stone is
called *eye agate*. Such trivial names as *ribbon agate*, *landscape agate*, *clouded agate*,
and the like, sufficiently explain themselves. A beautiful *brecciated agate*, in which
angular fragments of a banded variety are cemented together, chiefly by amethyst, is
well known from Schlottwitz in Saxony.

The colours of agate are arranged in parallel or concentric bands, or assume
the form of clouds or spots, or arborescent and moss-like stains. These colours are
due to the presence of metallic oxides. When black and white strata alternate, the
stone is called an *onyx*; when the layers are brown, or red and white, it becomes a
sardonyx. If the white stratum of an onyx be so thin as to appear bluish white, the
stone is termed by jewellers a *nicolo*. The *mocha stone* is a variety containing
dendritic markings due to the presence of oxide of manganese, or of iron, whilst the
moss agate is a chalcedony, containing green moss-like markings, referable to included
inorganic colouring-matter disposed in these patterns.

The chief localities which yield agates to any extent are the melaphyre rocks in
the Galgenberg and elsewhere in the neighbourhood of Oberstein in Rhenish
Bavaria, and the beds of the Rio Pardo, the Taquarie, and other rivers in Uruguay,
which yield the nodules commonly called 'Brazilian agates.' Fine Oriental agates
are imported from India, chiefly from Cambay, where they are largely cut and
polished. The well-known 'Scotch pebbles' are true agates found in various localities
in Scotland, especially in the amygdaloidal rocks of Kinnoul Hill in Perthshire; near
Montrose in Forfarshire; at Dunbar; at Dunglass in Haddingtonshire, and elsewhere.
The pebbles found on the south coast of England are not true agates, but are simply
flints derived from the upper chalk, and often exhibit patterns due to the presence of
choanites, ventriculites, and other organic remains. At the same time large numbers
of agates are also sold, at low prices, at most English watering-places, but these, so
far from being local 'pebbles,' are generally South American agates, cut and polished
in Germany, whence they are largely imported. Fine pebbles of agate and other
siliceous stones are found in the Vaal River in South Africa, and also in the Nile.
Mr. Daintree has recently described a local eruption of melaphyre, parts of which
contain fine agates, at Agate Creek, a tributary of the Gilbert River in Queensland.
Some beautiful polished examples of Queensland agates were exhibited in the International Exhibition of 1872.

Agates are used in the arts for a variety of purposes, such as knife-edges of delicate
balances, small mortars for chemical purposes, burnishers for gold and silver, styles
for writing, seal-handles, brooches, bracelets, beads, and an endless variety of small
ornamental objects.

These hard stones are cut and polished almost exclusively in a small district at the
foot of the Southern Hundsrück in Western Germany. The works are chiefly situated
along the Valley of the Idar, a small stream which flows into the Nahe. At a distance
of about 40 miles from Bingen, where the Nahe empties itself into the Rhine, the
small town of Oberstein is situated. Oberstein and Idar—about two miles distant—
are the chief centres of the agate trade. Although it is true that there are many
other localities where agate-working is carried on to a limited extent, it is only in
this district—at least in Western countries—that the trade is systematically pursued,
and forms the staple industry. From the low value of labour, the agates are there
cut and polished at incredibly low prices, and vast quantities of the cut stones are
sent thence to all the continental fairs and watering-places. A large trade is also
carried on with London, Birmingham, Paris, New York, and other distant localities ;
considerable quantities, too, are exported to the interior of Africa.

The localisation of the agate industry in the neighbourhood of Oberstein and Idar, at a very early date—certainly more than 400 years ago—may be traced to the plentiful occurrence of agates in the surrounding hills, especially in the hill called the Galgenberg or Steinkaulenberg. These hills consist of a melaphyre, more or less amygdaloidal, which has burst through the sandstones of the Saarbrück coal-field. Adits were formerly driven into the hill-side, and the agate-bearing rocks were systematically quarried. The workings in these quarries have for several years past been almost, if not entirely, abandoned, chiefly through the large importations constantly being received from South America.

In 1827 some Idar polishers who had emigrated to Uruguay accidentally discovered some fine agates, used at that time as paving-stones. Large quantities of the amygdaloidal nodules were easily collected, as loose pebbles, from the bed of the River Taquarie, and were despatched to Oberstein by way of Hamburg. The South American agates are evidently derived from decomposed melaphyre rocks, for although never found actually embedded in the matrix, portions of the mother-stone are occasionally seen adhering to the pebbles. As the agate-nodules are obtained without the expense of quarrying, the cost is confined to that of collecting them from the surface of the ground, or separating them from the superficial detritus. The stones are brought down to the coast on mules, or in waggons drawn by oxen, and are received at Porto Alegre, or at Salto, whence they are taken to Monte Video and Buenos Ayres, and shipped from these ports to Europe. Formerly they left the country free of duty, and were brought over as ballast, but an export duty has now to be paid, amounting in Uruguay to six per cent. of their value, and in Brazil to ten per cent. Arrived at Hamburg, Antwerp, or Havre, the agates are conveyed by rail to Oberstein—the rough stones travelling in open trucks, while the choicer carnelians are packed in cases. The total cost of transport by sea and land amounts to from 3s. to 6s. per cwt. Large parcels of the agates are displayed in the courtyards of the inns, and after due advertisement are sold by public auction. Prior to the sale the polishers inspect the lots, and break off samples of the stones, which are taken home and tested as to their power of taking colour by methods to be presently described. From forty to fifty auctions take place annually, and though the prices of the stones vary greatly according to their quality, it may be said that ordinary agates may be bought on an average for about 15s. per cwt. In 1867, the auction sales for the year realised a gross sum of nearly 16,000l.

The agates are first roughly dressed with chisel and hammer. From the texture of the stone the experienced workman is able to judge in what directions the stone will most readily split, and hence by a few skilfully-directed blows he manages to trim the agate rudely into the shape which it is intended to assume. The more valuable stones are, however, sawn into shape with emery and water. The grinding is effected on large red grindstones, mounted on a horizontal axis, and rotating in a vertical plane. Each axle carries from three to five stones, and communicates on the outside with a water-wheel. These wheels vary from 10 to 18 feet in diameter, and are usually undershot. Most of the mills are situated on the Idar, a stream which rises in one of the highest parts of the Hochwald. At the village of Idar it is about 1,012 feet above the sea-level, and at Oberstein, where it debouches into the Nahe, it is 905 feet high. It is in the Idar valley, between these two villages, that most of the agate-mills are situated. In consequence of the want of water during a dry season, the mills often stand idle, and hence in a few of the larger works steam-power has of late years been introduced. The grindstones, to which the water-wheel or steam-engine gives motion, are made of new red sandstone, quarried at the Kaiserslautern near Mannheim, and are about 5 feet in diameter and one foot in width. They usually make three revolutions per minute. When the stones have been badly selected, or used too soon after having left the quarry, they have been known to fly to pieces with great violence, and in this way several fatal accidents formerly occurred. The wheels revolve in a well, the horizontal shaft being nearly on a level with the floor, below which the lower half of the wheel is concealed. A small stream of water is introduced by a launder above, and by constantly trickling over the stones keeps them moist. Two workmen are generally employed, side by side, at each stone. The workman lies in an almost horizontal position, resting his chest and stomach on a bare wooden grinding-stool, adapted to the shape of his body, while he presses his feet against a block of wood fastened to the floor: the reaction of this fixed block enables him to apply any object with great force to the moving grindstone. The specimen to be ground is either held directly in the hand or applied to the stone by means of a short piece of soft wood. The form is given to the object by holding it in certain channels cut on the circumference of the stone. During grinding, the friction causes the agate to glow with a beautiful reddish phosphorescent light, visible even in the daytime, and quite distinct from sparks elicited by friction. After having been ground, the stones are polished with tripoli on a cylinder of hard wood, or on a plate of tin or lead.

An important branch of the agate trade is that of artificially colouring the stones—an art which has attained great perfection in recent times, but is far from being a modern invention. Pliny states (bk. xxxvii. cap. 75) that in Arabia agates are found which are purified and prepared for the cutter by being heated in honey for seven days and seven nights. Evidently the mere absorption of this saccharine matter into the pores of the stones would be insufficient to materially alter the appearance of the agate; but if the absorbed honey could have been carbonized by the action of sulphuric acid—as at present practised—the dark colour of the brownish layers would have been considerably heightened, and the stones improved for the cameo-worker. Believing that this was really the process described by Pliny, though he was ignorant of the entire secret, some authorities have argued in favour of the knowledge of oil of vitriol by the ancient Romans, while others have suggested that the native sulphuric acid from volcanic emanations was probably employed; others, again, have maintained that the honey was merely charred by exposure to heat, as is said to be still practised in the East. Be that as it may, it appears that the secret of artificially producing a black colour in agates was for ages handed down traditionally by the Italian cameo-workers. From time to time, Italian travellers visited Idar, and purchased stones, which were taken to Rome and there coloured. At length the secret of this art oozed out under peculiar circumstances, and, being once known in Idar, rapidly spread, and has not only been the means of greatly developing the agate-industry, but has, to a large extent, caused the removal of the seat of stone-engraving from Italy to Germany.

All artificial colouration of these hard stones depends for its success on variations in texture and density presented by the different layers. Sections of agate under the microscope often exhibit distinct pores, and the unequal texture of the several layers is well seen by the action of hydrofluoric acid, which readily attracts certain strata while it is resisted by others, thus producing an uneven surface, from which an impression of the agate may be naturally printed—a process which has been beautifully carried out by Dr. Leydolt. Not only do the component layers of an agate absorb liquids with different degrees of facility, but the stones as a whole exhibit like differences; some stones absorbing the colour rapidly, others requiring months to do so, and others, again, entirely refusing to take colour. The South American agates, as a rule, lend themselves with peculiar facility to this artificial colouration, and are much more porous than the true German agates.

Black or dark brown colours are those commonly developed in agates—these dark strata, when alternating with dense white layers, forming beautiful onyxes well fitted for cameo-work. To produce the dark colour, the stones, having been well washed and dried, are placed in honey, thinned with water, and are exposed in a warm place for several days, in some cases as long as three weeks. The vessel containing them is heated by being placed in hot ashes or on a stove, but the syrup is never allowed to boil. After having lain in the warm honey for a sufficient time, depending on the texture of the stone, they are removed, well washed, and placed in a vessel with sufficient commercial oil of vitriol to cover them; the vessel being covered with a slate, and exposed to a moderate temperature. The sulphuric acid carbonises the saccharine matter previously absorbed by the porous layers of the agate, and produces a black or a deep brown colour according as the action is more or less intense. Olive oil is used by the Italians instead of honey, but the chemical reactions are, of course, essentially the same in the two cases. Some stones blacken in a few hours, others require several days, while bad stones never take colour. When sufficiently tinted the stones are removed from the acid, washed, dried, and polished; they are then generally laid in oil to improve the lustre, and are finally dried in bran. Whilst the charring of the syrup or oil gives a dark colour to the porous layers, it is said that the white colour of the denser strata is also heightened; but this is probably merely the effect of contrast. If the darker parts of the stone should be too deep, the colour can be 'drawn,' or made lighter by the action of nitric acid.

The art of agate-colouration has reached so advanced a state that stones can now be tinted to almost any desired hue; some of the processes are, however, still kept secret by the polishers. In 1845 the method of colouring agate *blue* was first introduced. This is now effected in various ways. One of the best modes is to submit the stone successively to the action of solutions of yellow prussiate of potash (ferrocyanide of potassium), and of a per-salt of iron, thus causing a precipitate of Prussian blue to be thrown down in the pores of the stone. Or, red prussiate of potash and common green vitriol may be used; or an ammoniacal sulphate of copper may be formed, by placing the stone in a solution of blue vitriol and then in ammonia. A *green* colour was formerly produced by nitrate of nickel, but it is now obtained by using chromic acid,

The green stones are largely used as artificial chrysoprase, and the colour is more intense and said to be more durable than that of the natural chrysoprase. A *yellow* tint is obtained by prolonged digestion in warm hydrochloric acid, the acid acting on the oxide of iron normally present in the stone, and thus forming a yellow perchloride. One of the commonest and at the same time most easily developed colours is the *red* tint of the carnelian. It was long ago observed that yellow and grey chalcedony might be caused to assume a bright red colour by mere exposure to sunshine, the heat being sufficient to expel the water more or less completely from the hydrated peroxide of iron normally present in the stone. In India it has long been the practice to convert yellowish chalcedony into red carnelian by solar heat. The Idar workers generally expose the agates to the heat of an oven, gradually raised until all hygroscopic water is expelled. The stones are then moistened with sulphuric acid, and raised to a red heat, whereby an anhydrous peroxide of iron, of fine red colour, is developed. Or a pernitrate of iron may be formed by throwing a handful of old nails into half-a-pint of aquafortis mixed with a pint of water, and the stones having been soaked in this solution are heated so as to decompose the absorbed salt, and cause a precipitate of ferric oxide in the pores of the agate. Several *organic* colours have been introduced by the agate-worker, but they are generally fugitive : mauve and magenta agates, and other equally unnatural stones, are common in the market. The ingenuity of the Idar workmen also enables them to imitate successfully the dendritic markings in mocha-stones.

Another important branch of industry connected with the agate-trade is that of mounting the finished objects. Though dignified by the name of *Goldschmiede*, the mounters usually work in gilt tomback ; some of the better kinds of agate-ware are now, however, set in silver. Drilling, engraving, cameo-cutting, and etching with hydrofluoric acid, are also extensively practised in Idar ; and, in addition to agates, large quantities of Oriental blood-stones and other semi-precious stones, and even pastes, are largely cut and mounted in this district.

In 1867 there were in Birkenfeld and the neighbourhood 724 grindstones working in 153 mills. The number of grinders and polishers in Birkenfeld was 1,129, but in addition to this number about 300 workmen dwelt beyond the limits of the Principality. There were also about 258 persons engaged in drilling and boring the agates, and about 700 so-called goldsmiths. Including those employed in the sale of the stones, in making paper cases, and otherwise connected with the trade, it may be said that upwards of 3,000 persons depend for their support on the agate-industry in the neighbourhood of Idar and Oberstein.

[For further information on the subject of this Article the reader may consult the following works :—Billing's 'The Science of Gems,' 1867, p. 48 *et seq.;* Kluge, 'Edelsteinkunde,' 1860, p. 401 ; Lange, 'Die Halbedelsteine aus der Familie der Quarze und die Geschichte der Achatindustrie,' 1868 ; Nöggerath, 'Die Kunst, Onyxe, Carneole, Chalcedone u. andere verwandte Steinarten zu färben,' Karsten's 'Archiv. xxii.' 1848, p. 262, and 'Edin. New Phil. Journ.', xlviii. 1850, p. 166 ; Nöggerath, 'Ueber die Achatmandeln in den Melaphyren,' Haidinger's 'Naturwissentschaftliche Abhandlungen,' iii. 1850, p. 93 ; Kenngott, 'Ueber die Achatmandeln in den Melaphyren, namentlich über die von Thesis in Tirol,' *Op. cit.* iv. 1851, p. 72 ; Haidinger's 'Berichte,' vi. 1850, p. 62 ; Bischof, 'Lehrbuch d. Chem. u. Phys. Geologie,' ed. 2, ii. p. 853 ; iii. p. 457, 464, 623 *et seq.;* Reusch, 'Ueber den Agat' ; Poggendorff's 'Annalen,' cxxiii. 1864, p. 94].—F. W. R.

AGATE. An instrument used by gold-wire drawers, so called from the agate fixed in the middle of it.

AICH METAL. An alloy patented in 1860 by Johann Aich, and recommended for use in ship-building and sheathing. In composition it approaches close to Keir's metal. The following are found to be the best proportions: copper, 60 lbs. ; zinc, 38 lbs. 2 ozs. ; and iron, 1 lb. 8 ozs. The proportion of zinc may, however, be increased to 40 per cent., and that of iron may vary between 0·5 and 3 per cent.

AIKENITE. A native sulphide of bismuth, lead, and copper, crystallising in needle-shaped crystals belonging to the prismatic or orthorhombic system. It is found at Bersow in the Urals, and is believed to occur in Georgia and North Carolina in the United States.

AIR. The gaseous envelope which surrounds this earth is emphatically so called ; it consists of the gases nitrogen and oxygen.

About 79 measures of nitrogen, or azote, and 21 of oxygen, with $\frac{1}{100}$th of carbonic acid, constitute the air we breathe. The term *air* is applied to any permanently gaseous body. And we express different conditions of the air, as *good air, bad air, foul air,* &c. See ATMOSPHERE.

AIR-BRICK. A brick of the ordinary size and kind, but perforated so as to admit the passage of air through the openings when built into the walls.

AIR, COMPRESSED. For its employment in some mining operations, see MINING.

AIR-ENGINE. The considerable expansibility of air by heat naturally suggested its use as a motive power long before theoretical investigation demonstrated its actual value. The great advance made during the last few years in our knowledge of the mechanical action of heat has enabled us to determine with certainty the practical result which may be obtained by the use of any contrivance for employing heat as a prime mover of machinery. We are indebted to Sir Wm. Thomson for the fundamental theorem which decides the economy of any thermo-dynamic engine. It is—that in any perfectly constructed engine the fraction of heat converted into work is equal to the range of temperature from the highest to the lowest point, divided by the highest temperature reckoned from the zero of absolute temperature. Thus, if we have a perfect engine in which the highest temperature is 280° and the lowest 80° F., the fraction of heat converted into force will be $\dfrac{280-80}{280+460}$, or rather more than one quarter. So that, if we use a coal of which one pound in combustion gives out heat equivalent to 10,380,000 foot-pounds, such an engine as we have just described would produce work equal to 2,805,405 foot-pounds for each pound of coal consumed in the furnace. From the above formula of Sir Wm. Thomson, it will appear that the economy of any perfect thermo-dynamic engine depends upon the range of temperature we can obtain in it. And as the lowest temperature is generally nearly constant, being ruled by the temperature of the surface of the earth, it follows that the higher we can raise the highest temperature, the more economical will be the engine. The question is thus reduced to this:—In what class of engine can we practically use the highest temperature? In the steam-engine worked with saturated vapour, the limit is obviously determined by the amount of pressure which can be safely employed. In the steam-engine worked with super-heated vapour—*i.e.* in which the vapour, after passing from the boiler, receives an additional charge of heat without being allowed to take up more water—and also in the air-engine, the limit will depend upon the temperature at which steam or air acts chemically upon the metals employed, as well as upon the power of the metals themselves to resist the destructive action of heat. It thus appears that the steam-engine worked with super-heated steam possesses most of the economical advantages of the air engine. But when we consider that an air-engine may be made available where a plentiful supply of water cannot be readily obtained, the importance of this kind of thermo-dynamic engine is incontestable. The merit of first constructing a practical air-engine belongs to Mr. Stirling. Mr. Ericsson has subsequently introduced various refinements, such as the respirator—a reticulated mass of metal, which, by its extensive conducting surface, is able, almost instantaneously, to give its own temperature to the air which passes through it. But various practical difficulties attend these refinements, which, at best, only apply to engines worked between particular temperatures. The least complex engine, and that which would probably prove most effectual in practice, is that described in the 'Philosophical Transactions,' 1852, Part I. It consists of a pump, which compresses air into a receiver, in which it receives an additional charge of heat; and a cylinder, the piston of which is worked by the heated air as it escapes. The difference between the work produced by the cylinder and that absorbed by the pump constitutes the force of the engine; which, being compared with the heat communicated to the receiver, gives results exactly conformable with the law of Sir Wm. Thomson above described.—J. P. J.

Dr. Joule has proposed various engines to be worked at temperatures below redness, which, if no loss occurred by friction or radiation, would realise about one-half the work due to the heat of combustion, or about four times the economical duty which has, as yet, been attained by the most perfect steam-engine.

A detailed account of Ericsson's Calorific Engine may be useful, especially as a certain amount of success has attended his efforts in applying the expansive power of heat to move machinery. Ericsson's engines have been for some years at work in the foundry of Messrs. Hogg and Delamater, in New York; one engine being of five and another of sixty horse-power. The latter has four cylinders. Two, of seventy-two inches diameter, stand side by side. Over each of these is placed one much smaller. Within these are pistons exactly fitting their respective cylinders, and so connected, that those within the lower and upper cylinders move together. Under the bottom of each of the lower cylinders a fire is applied, no other furnaces being employed. Neither boilers nor water are used. The lower is called the working cylinder; the upper, the supply cylinder. As the piston in the supply cylinder moves down, valves placed in its top open, and it becomes filled with cold air. As the piston rises within it, these valves close, and the air within, unable to escape as it came, passes through another set of valves into a receiver, from whence it has to pass into the working cylinder, to force up the working piston within it. As it leaves the receiver to perform this duty, it passes through what is called *the regenerator*, where it becomes heated to about 450°; and upon entering the working cylinder, it is further heated by the supply underneath. For the sake of illustration, merely, let us suppose that the working cylinder contains double the area of the supply cylinder; the cold air which entered the upper cylinder will, therefore, but only half fill the lower one. In the course of its passage to the latter, however, it passes through *the regenerator ;* and as it enters the working cylinder, we will suppose that it has become heated to about 480°, by which it is expanded to double its volume, and with this increased capacity it enters the working cylinder. We will further suppose the area of the piston within this cylinder to contain 1,000 square inches, and the area of the piston in the supply cylinder above to contain but 500. The air presses upon this with a mean force, we will suppose, of about eleven pounds to each square inch; or, in other words, with a weight of 5,500 pounds. Upon the surface of the lower piston the heated air is, however, pressing upwards with a like force upon each of its 1,000 square inches; or, in other words, with a force which, after overcoming the weight above, leaves a surplus of 5,500 pounds, if we make no allowance for friction. This surplus furnishes the working power of the engine. It will be seen that after one stroke of its pistons is made, it will continue to work with this force so long as sufficient heat is supplied to expand the air in the working cylinder to the extent stated; for, so long as the area of the lower piston is greater than that of the upper, and a like pressure is upon every square inch of each, so long will the greater piston push forward the smaller, as a two-pound weight upon one end of a balance will be sure to bear down a one-pound weight placed upon the other. We need hardly say, that after the air in the working cylinder has forced up the piston within it, a valve opens; and as it passes out, the pistons, by the force of gravity, descend, and cold air again rushes into and fills the supply cylinder. In this manner the two cylinders are alternately supplied and discharged, causing the pistons in each to play up and down substantially as they do in the steam-engine.

The regenerator must now be described. It has been stated that atmospheric air is first drawn into the supply cylinder, and that it passes through the regenerator into the working cylinder. The regenerator is composed of wire net, like that used in the manufacture of sieves, placed side by side, until the series attains a thickness of about 12 inches. Through the almost innumerable cells formed by the intersections of the wire, the air must pass on its way to the working cylinder. In passing through these it is so minutely divided that all parts are brought into contact with the wires. Supposing the side of the regenerator nearest the working cylinder is heated to a high temperature, the air, in passing through it, takes up, as we have said, about 450° of the 480° of heat required to double the volume of the air; the additional 30° are communicated by the fire beneath the cylinder.

The air has thus become expanded, it forces the piston upwards; it has done its work—valves open, and the imprisoned air, heated at 480°, passes from the cylinder and again enters the regenerator, through which it must pass before leaving the machine. It has been said that the side of this instrument nearest the cylinder is kept hot; the other side is kept cool by the action upon it of the air entering in the opposite direction at each up-stroke of the pistons; consequently, as the air from the working cylinder passes out, the wires absorb the heat so effectually, that when it leaves the regenerator it has been robbed of it all, except about 30°.

The regenerator in the 60-horse engine measures 26 inches in height and width internally. Each disc of wire composing it contains 676 superficial inches, and the net has ten meshes to the inch. Each superficial inch, therefore, contains 100 meshes, which, multiplied by 676, gives 67,600 meshes in each disc; and, as 200 discs are employed, it follows that the regenerator contains 13,520,000 meshes ; and consequently as there are as many spaces between the discs as there are meshes, we find that the air within it is distributed in about 27,000,000 minute cells. Thence every particle of air, in passing through the regenerator, is brought into very close contact with a surface of metal which heats and cools it alternately. Upon this action of the regenerator, Ericsson's Calorific Engine depends. In its application on the large scale, contemplated in the great Atlantic steamer called 'The Ericsson,' the result was not satisfactory. We may, however, notwithstanding this result, safely predicate, from the investigation of Messrs. Thomson and Joule, that the expansion of air by heat will eventually, under some conditions, take the place of steam as a motive power.

AIR-GRATING. A kind of air-brick built into walls to admit air under the floors or into close places. Air-gratings are often made of iron.

AIR-GUN. This is a weapon in which the elastic force of air is made use of to project the ball. It is so arranged, that in a cavity in the stock of the gun, air can be, by means of a piston, powerfully condensed. Here is a reserved force, which, upon its being relieved from pressure, is at once exerted. When air has been condensed to about $\frac{1}{40}$th of its bulk, it exerts a force which is still very inferior to that of gunpowder. In many other respects the air-gun is but an imperfect weapon, consequently it is rarely employed.

AIR-HOLES. The cavities in a metal casting—produced by the escape of air through the liquid metal.

AIR-PUMP. A machine by which the air can be exhausted from any vessel containing it. It is employed in scientific investigations for exhibiting many very interesting phenomena in connection with the pressure of air, and its presence or absence; and it is connected with, and forms an important part of, the improved modern steam-engine. Similar machines are also used for condensing atmospheric air; these have been employed on a large scale in some civil engineering purposes. For a description of the Sprengel pump, see ASPIRATOR.

AIR-SHAFT. In Mining, a shaft devoted to the purpose of maintaining the circulation of air in a colliery or metalliferous mine. (See MINING, VENTILATION.)

AIRO-HYDROGEN BLOWPIPE. A blowpipe in which air is used in the place of oxygen, to combine with and give intensity of heat to a hydrogen flame for the purposes of soldering. See AUTOGENOUS SOLDERING.

AJUTAGE. A tube through which water is discharged—as in a fountain.

ALABASTER. *Gypsum* (*Albâtre*, Fr.; *Alabaster*, Ger.), a sulphate of lime. (See ALABASTER, ORIENTAL.) When massive, it is called indifferently *alabaster* or *gypsum*; and when in distinct and separate crystals, it is termed *selenite*. Massive alabaster occurs in Britain in the new red or keuper marl: in Glamorganshire, on the Bristol Channel; in Leicestershire, at Syston; at Tutbury and near Burton-on-Trent, in Staffordshire; at Chellaston, in Derbyshire; near Droitwich it is associated in the marl with rock salt, in strata respectively 40 and 75 feet in thickness; and at Northwich and elsewhere the red marl is intersected with frequent veins of gypsum. At Tutbury it is quarried in the open air, and at Chellaston in caverns, where it is blasted by gunpowder: at both places it is burned in kilns, and otherwise prepared for the market. It lies in irregular beds in the marl, that at Chellaston being about 30 feet thick. There is, however, reason to suppose that it was not originally deposited along with the marl as sulphate of lime, but rather that calcareous strata, by the access of sulphuric acid and water, have been converted into sulphate of lime— a circumstance quite consistent with the bulging of the beds of marl with which the gypsum is associated, the lime, as a sulphate, occupying more space than it did in its original state as a carbonate. At Tutbury, and elsewhere, though it lies on a given general horizon, yet it can scarcely be said to be truly bedded, but ramifies among the beds and joints of the marl in numerous films, veins, and layers of fibrous gypsum. A thick bed of white crystalline alabaster, or gypsum, has been discovered during the Sub-Wealden Exploration in Sussex. It occurs in beds which are probably of Purbeck age.

A snow-white alabaster occurs at Volterra, in Tuscany, much used in works of art in Florence and Leghorn. In the Paris basin it occurs as a granular crystalline rock, in the lower Tertiary rocks, known to geologists as the upper part of the Middle Eocene freshwater strata. It is associated with beds of white and green marls; but in the Thüringerwald there is a great mass of sulphate of lime in the Permian strata. It has been sunk through to a depth of 70 feet, and is believed to be metamorphosed magnesian limestone or Zechstein. In the United States this calcareous salt occurs in numerous lenticular masses in marly and sand strata of that part of the Upper Silurian strata known as the Onondaga salt group. It is excavated for agricultural purposes. For mineralogical character, &c., see GYPSUM.—A. C. R.

The fineness of the grain of alabaster, the uniformity of its texture, the beauty of its polished surface, and its semi-transparency, are the qualities which render it valuable to the sculptor and to the manufacturer of ornamental articles.

The alabaster is worked with the same tools as marble; and as it is many degrees softer, it is so much the more easily cut; but it is more difficult to polish, from its little solidity. After it has been fashioned into the desired form, and smoothed down with pumice-stone, it is polished with a pap-like mixture of chalk, soap, and milk; and, last of all, finished by friction with flannel. It is apt to acquire a yellowish tinge.

Besides the harder kinds, employed for the sculpture of large figures, there is a softer alabaster, pure white and semi-transparent, from which small ornamental objects are made, such as boxes, vases, lamps, stands of timepieces, &c. This branch of business is much prosecuted in Florence, Leghorn, Milan, &c., and employs a great many turning-lathes. Of all the alabasters, the Florentine merits the preference, on account of its beauty and uniformity. Other sorts of gypsum, such as that of Salzburg and Austria, contain sand veins and hard nodules, and require to be quarried by cleaving and blasting operations, which are apt to crack it and render it unfit for all delicate objects of sculpture. It is, besides, of a grey shade, and often stained with darker colours.

The alabaster best adapted for the fine arts is white when newly broken, and becomes yet whiter on the surface by drying. It may be easily cut with the knife or chisel, and formed into many pleasing shapes by suitable steel tools. It is worked either by the hand alone, or with the aid of a turning-lathe. The turning tools should not be too thin or sharp-edged; but such as are employed for ivory and brass are most suitable for alabaster, and are chiefly used to shave and to scratch the surface. The objects which cannot be turned may be fashioned by the rasping tools, or with minute files. Fine chisels and graving tools are also used for the better pieces of statuary.

For polishing such works, a peculiar process is required: pumice-stone, in fine powder, serves to smooth down the surfaces very well, but it soils the whiteness of the alabaster. To take away the unevenness and roughness, dried shave-grass (*equisetum*) answers best. Friction with this plant and water polishes down the asperities left by the chisel: the fine streaks left by the grass may be removed by rubbing the pieces with slaked lime, finely pulverised, sifted, and made into a paste; or with putty-powder (oxide of tin) and water. The polish and satin-lustre of the surface are communicated by friction, first with soap-water and lime, and finally with powdered and elutriated talc or French chalk.

Such articles as consist of several pieces are joined by a cement composed of quick-lime and white of egg, or of well-calcined and well-sifted Paris plaster, mixed with the least possible quantity of water.

Alabaster objects are liable to become yellow by keeping, and are especially injured by smoke, dust, &c. They may be in some measure restored by washing with soap and water, then with clear water, and again polished with shave-grass. Grease-spots may be removed either by rubbing with talc powder, or with oil of turpentine.

The surface of alabaster may be etched by covering over the parts that are not to be touched with a solution of wax in oil of turpentine, thickened with white lead, and immersing the articles in pure water after the varnish has set. The action of the water is continued from 20 to 50 hours, more or less, according to the depth to which the etching is to be cut. After removing the varnish with oil of turpentine, the etched places, which are necessarily deprived of their polish, should be rubbed with a brush dipped in finely-powdered gypsum, which gives a kind of opacity, contrasting well with the rest of the surface.

Alabaster may be stained either with metallic solutions, with spirituous tinctures of dyeing plants, or with coloured oils, in the same way as marbles.

ALABASTER, ORIENTAL. Oriental alabaster is a form of stalagmitic or stalactitic carbonate of lime, an Egyptian variety of which is highly esteemed. It is also procured from the Pyrenees, from Chili, and from parts of the United States of America. Ancient quarries are still in existence in the province of Oran, in Algeria. The well-known 'Gibraltar stone' and the Californian marble are similar stalagmitic forms of carbonate of lime. This Oriental alabaster, or alabaster of the ancients, is to be carefully distinguished from the mineral now commonly known as alabaster; the former is a *carbonate*, the latter a *sulphate* of lime. See ONYX, ALGERIAN.

ALBAN. A white resinous substance extracted from gutta-percha by either alcohol or ether. See GUTTA-PERCHA.

ALBANI STONE. (*Lapis albanus*). The Peperino of modern geologists. A dark volcanic tufa found in Italy, much used at Rome before building with marble became common. The Italian name *peperino* is derived from *pepe*, pepper, which it somewhat resembles.

ALBATA PLATE, a name given to one of the varieties of white metal now so commonly employed. See COPPER and ALLOYS.

ALBERTITE. A jet-black mineral substance resembling asphalt, discovered in 1849 at Hillsborough, in Albert Co., New Brunswick. It occurs in irregular fissures in Lower Carboniferous rocks, and is now usually regarded as the residue left on the drying-up of a great body of petroleum. 'The deposit of the Albert mine would thus be a vein or fissure constituting an ancient reservoir of petroleum, which, by the loss of its more volatile parts and partial oxidation, has been hardened into a coaly substance.' (*Dawson*). Albertite has been largely used in the United States for the distillation of oil and coke. The yield per ton is said to be 100 (crude) gallons of oil, and 14,500 cubic feet of illuminating gas, while a residue of good coke remains in the retorts.

ALBITE. A soda felspar. See FELSPAR.

ALBOLITH. A cement prepared by calcining native carbonate of magnesia (magnesite) and mixing the magnesia thus obtained with silica.

ALBUM GRÆCUM. The white fæces of dogs, hyænas, &c. After the hair has been removed from skins, this is used to preserve the softness of them, and prepare them for the tan-pit. Fowls' dung is considered by practical tanners as superior to the dung of dogs, and this is obtained as largely as possible. These excreta may be said to be essentially phosphate of lime and mucus. We are informed that various artificial compounds which represent, chemically, the conditions of those natural ones, have been tried without producing the same good results. It is a reflection on our science, if this is really the case. Album Græcum is frequently found fossilised in bone-caverns which have been used as hyæna dens.

ALBUMEN or **ALBUMIN.** (*Album Ovi.*) Albumen is a substance which forms a constituent part of the animal fluids and solids, and which is also found in the vegetable kingdom. It exists nearly pure in the white of egg. Albumen according to several analyses consists of :—

Carbon	53·4
Hydrogen	7·1
Nitrogen	15·7
Sulphur	1·3
Oxygen (according to *Lieberkuhn*)	22·1

The coagulation of albumen by heat is illustrated in the boiling of an egg. The salts of tin, bismuth, lead, silver, and mercury form with albumen white insoluble precipitates; therefore, in cases of poisoning by corrosive sublimate, nitrate of silver, or sugar of lead, the white of egg is the best antidote which can be administered.

Albumen is employed for clarifying vinous and syrupy liquids; when boiled with them it coagulates and entangles the colouring matter, either falling to the bottom or floating on the surface of the fluid, according to its specific gravity. In this way it is employed, especially as it is found in the serum of blood, in sugar-refining. It is also used in fixing the colours in calico-printing. It is employed in photography, and mixed with recently slaked lime it forms a very useful cement, becoming in a short time as hard as stone.

VEGETABLE ALBUMEN is identical in composition with that of the white of egg. It is abundant in nearly all the roots used for food, as the potato, turnip, carrot, &c. It is found in large quantity in wheat-flour, and in most oleaginous seeds. See Watts's ' Dictionary of Chemistry.'

ALBUMENISED PAPER. A paper prepared with the white of egg for photographic purposes. See PHOTOGRAPHY.

ALBUMINOIDS. A term applied to compounds which play an important part in the economy of both animal and vegetable life. The more important are ALBUMEN, FIBRIN, and CASEIN.

ALCARAZZAS. Porous earthenware vessels made in Spain from a sandy marl, and but slightly fired. They are used for cooling liquors. These vessels are made in France under the name of *hydrocérames;* similar kinds of earthenware are also manufactured in Staffordshire and Derbyshire.

ALCIDÆ. A family of sea-birds, to which the Guillemots and Penguins belong. The Patagonian Penguin is larger than a goose, slate-coloured on the back, and white with a black mark on the breast, encircled by a citron-yellow cravat. The plumage is very close, and the breast is used as tippets and for trimming ladies' dresses. The black Guillemot (*Uria grylle*) also yields its feathers to meet the requirements of fashion.

ALCOHOL. (*Alcool,* Fr.; *Alkohol,* or *Weingeist,* Ger.) The word *alcohol* is derived from the Hebrew word ' *kohol,*' כחל *to paint.* The Oriental females were and are still in the habit of painting the eyebrows with various pigments; the one generally employed was a preparation of antimony, and to this the term was generally applied. It became, however, gradually extended to all substances used for the purpose, and ultimately to strong spirits, which were employed, probably, as solvents for certain colouring principles. The term was subsequently exclusively used to designate ardent spirits, and ultimately the radical or principle upon which their strength depends.

As chemistry advanced, *alcohol* was found to be a member only of a class of bodies agreeing with it in general characters; and hence the term is now generic, and we speak of the various *alcohols.* Of these, common or vinous alcohol is the best known; and, in common life, by ' alcoholic liquors,' we invariably mean those containing the original or vinous alcohol.

When the characters of ordinary alcohol have been stated, allusion will be made to the class of bodies of which this is the type.

Fermented liquors were known in the most remote ages of antiquity. We read (Genesis ix.) that after the flood 'Noah planted a vineyard, and he drank of the wine and was drunken.' Homer, who certainly lived 900 years before the Christian era, also frequently mentions wine, and notices its effects on the body and mind (Odyssey IX. and XXI.); and Herodotus tells us that the Egyptians drank a liquor fermented from barley. The period when fermented liquors were submitted to distillation, so as to obtain 'ardent spirits,' is shrouded in much obscurity. Raymond Lully[1] was acquainted with 'spirits of wine,' which he called *aqua ardens*. The separation of absolute alcohol would appear to have been first effected about this period (1300), by Arnauld de Villeneuve, a celebrated physician residing in Montpellier (*Gerhardt*), and its analysis was first performed by Th. de Saussure.[2]

The preparation of alcohol may be divided into three stages :—

1. The production of a fermented vinous liquor—the Fermentation.
2. The preparation from this of an ardent spirit—the Distillation.
3. The separation from this ardent spirit of the last traces of water—the Rectification.

1. *Fermentation.* The term 'fermentation' is now applied to those mysterious changes which vegetable (and animal) substances undergo when exposed, at a certain temperature, to contact with organic or even organised bodies in a state of change.

There are several bodies which suffer these metamorphoses, and under the influence of a great number of different exciting substances, which are termed the 'ferments;' moreover, the resulting products depend greatly upon the temperature at which the change takes place.

The earliest known and best studied of these processes is the one commonly recognised as the *vinous* or *alcoholic fermentation*.

In this process solutions containing *sugar*—either the juice of the grape (see Wine) or an infusion of germinated barley, malt (see Beer)—are mixed with a suitable quantity of a ferment; beer or wine yeast is usually employed (see Yeast), and the whole maintained at a temperature of between 70° and 80° F. (21° to 26° C.)

Other bodies in a state of putrefactive decomposition will effect the same result as the yeast, such as putrid blood, white of egg, &c.

The liquid swells up, a considerable quantity of froth collects on the surface, and an abundance of gas is disengaged, which is ordinary carbonic acid (CO^2). The composition of (pure) alcohol is expressed by the formula $C^4 H^6 O^2$ ($C^2 H^6 O$), and it is produced in this process by the breaking up of *grape sugar*, $C^{12} H^{12} O^{12}. 2HO$ ($C^6 H^{12} O^6. H^2 O$) into alcohol, carbonic acid, and water, thus :—

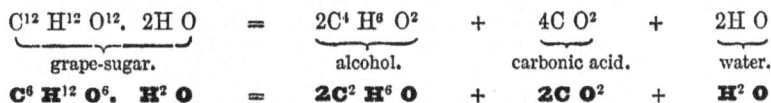

$$C^{12} H^{12} O^{12}. 2H O = 2C^4 H^6 O^2 + 4C O^2 + 2H O$$
grape-sugar.   alcohol.   carbonic acid.   water.
$$C^6 H^{12} O^6. H^2 O = 2C^2 H^6 O + 2C O^2 + H^2 O$$

It is invariably the *grape sugar* which undergoes this change; if the solution contains cane sugar, the cane sugar is first converted into grape sugar under the influence of the ferment. See Sugar.

Much diversity of opinion exists with respect to the office which the ferment performs in this process, since it does not itself yield any of the products. See Fermentation.

The liquid obtained by the vinous fermentation has received different names, according to the source whence the saccharine solution was derived. When procured from the expressed juice of fruits—such as grapes, currants, gooseberries, &c.—the product is denominated *wine;* from a decoction of malt, *ale* or *beer;* from a mixture of honey and water, *mead;* from apples, *cider;* from the leaves and small branches of spruce-fir (*Abies excelsa*, &c.), together with sugar or treacle, *spruce;* from rice, *rice beer* (which yields the spirit *arrack*); from cocoa-nut juice, *palm wine*.

It is an interesting fact that alcohol is produced in very considerable quantities (in the aggregate) during the raising of bread. The carbonic acid which is generated in the dough, and which during its expulsion raises the bread, is one of the products of the fermentation of the sugar in the flour, under the influence of the yeast added; and of course at the same time the complementary product, alcohol, is generated. As

[1] Thomson's History of Chemistry, i. 41. (1830).   [2] Annales de Chimie, xlii. 225.

Messrs. Ronalds and Richardson remark:[1] 'the enormous amount of bread that is baked in large towns—in London, for instance, 8·8 millions of cwts. yearly—would render the small amount of alcohol contained in it of sufficient importance to be worth collecting, provided this could be done sufficiently cheaply.' In London it has been estimated that in this way about 300,000 gallons of spirit are annually lost; but the cost of collecting it would far exceed its value.

2. *Distillation.* By the process of *distillation*, *ardent spirits* are obtained, which have likewise received different names according to the sources whence the fermented liquor has been derived: viz. that produced by the distillation of wine being called *brandy*, and in France *cognac*, or *eau de vie;* that produced by the distillation of the fermented liquor from sugar and molasses, *rum.* There are several varieties of spirits made from the fermented liquor produced from the cereals (and especially barley), known according to their peculiar methods of manufacture, flavour, &c.—as *whisky*, *gin*, *Hollands*—the various *compounds* and *liqueurs.* In India, the spirit obtained from a fermented infusion of rice is called *arrack.*

3. *Rectification;* preparation of *absolute alcohol.* It is impossible by distillation alone to deprive spirit of the whole of the water and other impurities—to obtain, in fact, *pure* or *absolute* alcohol.

This is effected by mixing with the liquid obtained after one or two distillations, certain bodies which have a powerful attraction for water. The agents commonly employed for this purpose are quicklime, carbonate of potash, anhydrous sulphate of copper, or chloride of calcium. Perhaps the best adapted for the purpose, especially where large quantities are required, is quicklime; it is powdered, mixed in the retort with the spirit (previously twice distilled), and the neck of the retort being securely closed, the whole is left for 24 hours, with occasional shaking; during this period the lime combines with the water, and then on carefully distilling, avoiding to continue the process until the last portions come over, an alcohol is obtained which is free from water. If not quite free, the same process may be again repeated.

In experiments on a small scale, an ordinary glass retort may be employed, heated by a water-bath, and fitted to a Liebig's condenser cooled by ice-water, which passes lastly into a glass receiver, similarly cooled.

Although alcohol of sufficient purity for most practical purposes can be readily obtained, yet the task of procuring absolute alcohol entirely free from a trace of water, is by no means an easy one.

Mr. Drinkwater[2] effected this by digesting ordinary alcohol of specific gravity ·850 at 60° F. for 24 hours with carbonate of potash previously exposed to a red heat; the alcohol was then carefully poured off and mixed in a retort with as much fresh-burnt quicklime as was sufficient to absorb the whole of the alcohol; after digesting for 48 hours, it was slowly distilled in a water-bath at a temperature of about 180° F. This alcohol was carefully redistilled, and its specific gravity at 60° F. found to be ·7947, which closely agrees with that given by Gay-Lussac as the specific gravity of absolute alcohol. He found, moreover, that recently ignited anhydrous sulphate of copper was a less efficient dehydrating agent than quicklime.

Graham recommends that the quantity of lime employed should never exceed three times the weight of the alcohol.

Chloride of calcium is not so well adapted for the purification of alcohol, since the alcohol forms a compound with this salt.

Many other processes have been suggested for depriving alcohol of its water.

A curious process was proposed many years ago by Soemmering,[3] which is dependent upon the peculiar fact, that whilst water moistens animal tissues, alcohol does not, but tends rather to abstract water from them. If a mixture of alcohol and water be enclosed in an ox bladder, the water gradually traverses the membrane and evaporates, whilst the alcohol does not, and consequently by the loss of water the spirituous solution becomes concentrated.

This process, though an interesting illustration of exosmose, is not practically applicable to the production of anhydrous alcohol; it is, however, an economical method, and well suited for obtaining alcohol for the preparation of varnishes. Smugglers, who bring spirits into France in bladders hid about their persons, have long known, that although the liquor decreased in bulk, yet it increased in strength; hence the people preferred the article conveyed clandestinely. Professor Graham ingeniously proposed to concentrate alcohol as follows:—

'A large shallow basin is covered, to a small depth, with recently burnt quicklime, in coarse powder, and a smaller basin, containing three or four ounces of com-

[1] Chemical Technology, by Dr. F. Knapp: edited by Messrs. Ronalds and Richardson. Vol. iii. 199.
[2] On the Preparation of Absolute Alcohol, and the Composition of Proof Spirit. See Memoirs of the Chemical Society, vol. iii. p. 447.
[3] Soemmering: 'Denkschriften d. k. Akad. d. Wissenschaften zu München,' 1711 to 1824.

mercial alcohol, is made to rest upon the lime; the whole is placed under the low receiver of an air-pump, and the exhaustion continued till the alcohol evinces signs of ebullition. Of the mingled vapours of alcohol and water which now fill the receiver, the quicklime is capable of uniting with the aqueous only, which is therefore rapidly withdrawn, while the alcohol vapour is unaffected; and as water cannot remain in the alcohol as long as the superincumbent atmosphere is devoid of moisture, more aqueous vapour rises, which is likewise abstracted by the lime, and thus the process goes on till the whole of the water in the alcohol is removed. Several days are always required for this purpose.'

Properties of Alcohol (Absolute).

In the state of purity, alcohol is a colourless liquid, highly inflammable, burning with a pale blue flame, very volatile, and having a density of 0·792 at 15·5° C. (60° F.) (*Drinkwater*). It boils at 78·4° C. (173° F.) It has never yet been solidified, and the density of its vapour is 1·6133.

Anhydrous alcohol is composed by weight of 52·18 carbon, 13·04 hydrogen, and 34·78 of oxygen. It has for its formula $C^4 H^6 O^2 = C^4 H^5 O + HO$, or hydrated oxide of ethyle. It has a powerful affinity for water, removing the water from moist substances with which it is brought in contact. In consequence of this property, it attracts water from the air, and rapidly becomes weaker, unless kept in very well-stopped vessels. In virtue of its attraction for water, alcohol is very valuable for the preservation of organic substances, and especially of anatomical preparations, in consequence of its causing the coagulation of albuminous substances; and for the same reason it causes death when injected into the veins.

When mixed with water a considerable amount of heat is evolved, and a remarkable contraction of volume is observed, these effects being greatest with 54 per cent. of alcohol and 46 of water, and thence decreasing with a greater proportion of water. For alcohol which contains 90 per cent. of water, this condensation amounts to 1·94 per cent. of the volume; for 80 per cent., 2·87; for 70 per cent., 3·44; for 60 per cent., 3·73; for 40 per cent., 3·44; for 30 per cent., 2·72; for 20 per cent., 1·72; for 10 per cent., 0·72.

Alcohol is prepared absolute for certain purposes, but the mixtures of alcohol and water commonly met with in commerce are of an inferior strength. Those commonly sold are 'Rectified Spirit' and 'Proof Spirit.'

'Proof Spirit' is defined by Act of Parliament, 58 Geo. III. c. 28, to be 'such as shall, at the temperature of fifty-one degrees of Fahrenheit's thermometer, weigh exactly twelve-thirteenth parts of an equal measure of distilled water.' And by very careful experiment, Mr. Drinkwater has determined that this proof spirit has the following composition :—

Alcohol and Water			Specific Gravity at 60° F.	Bulk of the mixture of 100 measures of Alcohol, and 81·82 of Water
By weight		By measure		
Alcohol Water 100 + 103·09 49·24 + 50·76		Alcohol Water 100 + 81·82	·919	175·25

Spirit which is weaker is called 'under proof;' and that stronger, 'above proof.' The origin of these terms is as follows :—Formerly a very rude mode of ascertaining the strength of spirits was practised, called the *proof;* the spirit was poured upon gunpowder and inflamed. If, at the end of the combustion, the gunpowder took fire, the spirit was said to be *above* or *over proof.* But if the spirit contained much water, the powder was rendered so moist that it did not take fire: in which case the spirit was said to be *under* or *below proof.*

Rectified spirit contains from 54 to 64 per cent. of absolute alcohol; and its specific gravity is fixed by the London and Edinburgh Colleges of Physicians at 0·838, whilst the Dublin College fixes it at 0·840.

In commerce the strength of mixtures of alcohol and water are stated at so many *degrees, according to Sykes's hydrometer*, above or below proof. This instrument will be explained under the head of ALCOHOLOMETRY.

As will have been understood by the preceding remarks, the specific gravity or density of mixtures of alcohol and water rises with the diminution of the quantity of alcohol present; or, in other words, with the amount of water. And since the strength of spirits is determined by ascertaining their density, it becomes highly important to determine the precise ratio of this increase. This increase in density with the amount of water, or diminution with the quantity of alcohol, is, however, not directly proportional, in consequence of the contraction of volume which mixtures of alcohol and water suffer.

It therefore became necessary to determine the density of mixtures of known composition, prepared artificially. This has been done with great care by Mr. Drinkwater;[1] and the following Table by him is recommended as one of the most accurate :—

Table of the Quantity of Alcohol, BY WEIGHT, contained in Mixtures of Alcohol and Water of the following Specific Gravities :—

Specific Gravity at 60° F.	Alcohol per cent. by weight.	Specific Gravity at 60° F.	Alcohol per cent. by weight.	Specific Gravity at 60° F.	Alcohol per cent. by weight.	Specific Gravity at 60° F.	Alcohol per cent. by weight.	Specific Gravity at 60° F.	Alcohol per cent. by weight.
1·0000	0·00	·9967	1·78	·9934	3·67	·9901	5·70	·9869	7·85
·9999	0·05	·9966	1·83	·9933	3·73	·9900	5·77	·9868	7·92
·9998	0·11	·9965	1·89	·9932	3·78	·9899	5·83	·9867	7·99
·9997	0·16	·9964	1·94	·9931	3·84	·9898	5·89	·9866	8·06
·9996	0·21	·9963	1·99	·9930	3·90	·9897	5·96	·9865	8·13
·9995	0·26	·9962	2·05	·9929	3·96	·9896	6·02	·9864	8·20
·9994	0·32	·9961	2·11	·9928	4·02	·9895	6·09	·9863	8·27
·9993	0·37	·9960	2·17	·9927	4·08	·9894	6·15	·9862	8·34
·9992	0·42	·9959	2·22	·9926	4·14	·9893	6·22	·9861	8·41
·9991	0·47	·9958	2·28	·9925	4·20	·9892	6·29	·9860	8·48
·9990	0·53	·9957	2·34	·9924	4·27	·9891	6·35	·9859	8·55
·9989	0·58	·9956	2·39	·9923	4·33	·9890	6·42	·9858	8·62
·9988	0·64	·9955	2·45	·9922	4·39	·9889	6·49	·9857	8·70
·9987	0·69	·9954	2·51	·9921	4·45	·9888	6·55	·9856	8·77
·9986	0·74	·9953	2·57	·9920	4·51	·9887	6·62	·9855	8·84
·9985	0·80	·9952	2·62	·9919	4·57	·9886	6·69	·9854	8·91
·9984	0·85	·9951	2·68	·9918	4·64	·9885	6·75	·9853	8·98
·9983	0·91	·9950	2·74	·9917	4·70	·9884	6·82	·9852	9·05
·9982	0·96	·9949	2·79	·9916	4·76	·9883	6·89	·9851	9·12
·9981	1·02	·9948	2·85	·9915	4·82	·9882	6·95	·9850	9·20
·9980	1·07	·9947	2·91	·9914	4·88	·9881	7·02	·9849	9·27
·9979	1·12	·9946	2·97	·9913	4·94	·9880	7·09	·9848	9·34
·9978	1·18	·9945	3·02	·9912	5·01	·9879	7·16	·9847	9·41
·9977	1·23	·9944	3·08	·9911	5·07	·9878	7·23	·9846	9·49
·9976	1·29	·9943	3·14	·9910	5·13	·9877	7·30	·9845	9·56
·9975	1·34	·9942	3·20	·9909	5·20	·9876	7·37	·9844	9·63
·9974	1·40	·9941	3·26	·9908	5·26	·9875	7·43	·9843	9·70
·9973	1·45	·9940	3·32	·9907	5·32	·9874	7·50	·9842	9·78
·9972	1·51	·9939	3·37	·9906	5·39	·9873	7·57	·9841	9·85
·9971	1·56	·9938	3·43	·9905	5·45	·9872	7·64	·9840	9·92
·9970	1·61	·9937	3·49	·9904	5·51	·9871	7·71	·9839	9·99
·9969	1·67	·9936	3·55	·9903	5·58	·9870	7·78	·9838	10·07
·9968	1·73	·9935	3·61	·9902	5·64				

The preceding Table, though very accurate as far as it goes, is not sufficiently extensive for practical purposes, only going, in fact, from 6 to 10 per cent. of alcohol; the Table of Tralle's (page 50) extends to 50 per cent. of absolute alcohol.

Moreover, Drinkwater's Table has the (practical) disadvantage (though scientifically more correct and useful) of stating the per-centage *by weight;* whereas in Tralle's Table it is given by *volume.* And since liquors are vended by measure, and not by weight, the centesimal amount by volume is usually preferred. But as the bulk of liquids generally, and particularly that of alcohol, is increased by heat, it is necessary that the statement of the density in a certain volume should have reference to some normal temperature. In the construction of Tralle's Table the temperature of the

[1] Memoirs of the Chemical Society, vol. iii. p. 454.

liquids was 60° F.; and of course, in using it, it is necessary that the density should be observed at that temperature.

In order to convert the statement of the composition *by volume* into the content by weight, it is only necessary to multiply the per-centage of alcohol by volume by the specific gravity of absolute alcohol, and then divide by the specific gravity of the liquid.

It has been thought desirable to retain the following remarks by Dr. Ure, and to give Mr. Gilpin's Tables in addition to the others.

The importance of extreme accuracy in determining the density of alcoholic mixtures in the United Kingdom, on account of the great revenue derived from them to the State, and their consequent high price in commerce, induced the Lords of the Treasury a few years ago to request the Royal Society to examine the construction and mode of applying the instrument now in use for ascertaining and charging the duty on spirits. This instrument, which is known and described in the law as Sikes's hydrometer, possesses, in many respects, decided advantages over those formerly in use. The committee of the Royal Society state, that a definite mixture of alcohol and water is as invariable in its value as absolute alcohol can be; and can be more readily, and with equal accuracy, identified by that only quality or condition to which recourse can be had in practice, namely, specific gravity. The committee further proposed, that the standard spirit be that which, consisting of alcohol and water alone, shall have a specific gravity of 0·92 at the temperature of 62° F., water being unity at the same temperature; or, in other words, that it shall at 62° weigh $\frac{92}{100}$ths or $\frac{23}{25}$ths of an equal bulk of water at the same temperature.

This standard is rather stronger than the old proof, which was $\frac{12}{13}$ths or 0·923; or in the proportion of nearly 1·1 gallon of the present proof spirit per cent. The proposed standard will contain nearly one-half by weight of absolute alcohol. The hydrometer ought to be so graduated as to give the indication of strength; not upon an arbitrary scale, but in terms of specific gravity at the temperature of 62°.

The committee recommend the construction of an equation table, which shall indicate the same strength of spirit at every temperature. Thus in standard spirit at 62° the hydrometer would indicate 920, which in this table would give proof spirit. If that same spirit were cooled to 40°, the hydrometer would indicate some higher number; but which, being combined in the table with the temperature as indicated by the thermometer, should still give proof or standard spirit as the result.

It is considered advisable, in this and the other tables, not to express the quality of the spirit by any number over or under proof, but to indicate at once the number of gallons of standard spirit contained in, or equivalent to, 100 gallons of the spirit under examination. Thus, instead of saying 23 over proof, it is proposed to insert 123; and in place of 35·4 under proof, to insert its difference to 100, or 64·6.

It has been considered expedient to recommend a second table to be constructed, so as to show the bulk of spirit of any strength at any temperature, relative to a standard bulk of 100 gallons at 62°. In this table a spirit which had diminished in volume, at any given temperature, 0·7 per cent., for example,. would be expressed by 99·3; and a spirit which had increased at any given temperature 0·7 per cent., by 100·7.

When a sample of spirit, therefore, has been examined by the hydrometer and thermometer, these tables will give first the proportion of standard spirit at the observed temperature, and next the change of bulk of such spirit from what it would be at the standard temperature. Thus at the temperature of 51°, and with an indication (specific gravity) of 8,240, 100 gallons of the spirit under examination would be shown by the first table to be equal to 164·8 gallons of standard spirit of that temperature; and by the second table it would appear that 99·3 gallons of the same spirit would become 100 at 62°, or in reality contain the 164·8 gallons of spirit in that state only in which it is to be taxed.

But as it is considered that neither of these tables can alone be used for charging the duty (for neither can express the actual quantity of spirit of a specific gravity of 0·92 at 62° in 100 gallons of stronger or weaker spirit at temperatures above or below 62°), it is considered essential to have a third table, combining the two former, and expressing this relation directly, so that upon mere inspection it shall indicate the proportion of standard spirit in 100 gallons of that under examination in its then present state. In this table the quantities should be set down in the actual number of gallons of standard spirit at 62°, equivalent to 100 of the spirit under examination; and the column of quantities may be expressed by the term *value*, as it in reality expresses the proportion of the only valuable substance present.

The following specimen Table has been given by the committee :—

Temperature 45°			Temperature 75°		
Indication [1]	Strength	Value	Indication	Strength	Value
9074	114·5		8941	114·5	
7	114·3		4	114·3	
9	114·2		5	114·2	
81	114·0		8	114·0	
3	113·9		9	113·9	
5	113·7		52	113·7	
6	113·6		3	113·6	
9	113·4		6	113·4	
90	113·3		7	113·3	
3	113·1		9	113·1	

The mixture of alcohol and water, taken as spirit in Mr. Gilpin's Tables, is that of which the specific gravity is 0·825 at 60° F., water being unity at the same temperature. The specific gravity of water at 60° being 1,000, at 62° it is 99,981. Hence, in order to compare the specific gravities given by Mr. Gilpin with those which would result when the specific gravity of water at 62° is taken at unity, all the former numbers must be divided by 99,981.

Table of the Specific Gravities of different Mixtures, BY WEIGHT, of Alcohol and Water, at different Temperatures; constructed by Mr. Gilpin, for the use of the British Revenue on Spirits.

Temperature. Fahr.	Pure Alcohol	100 Alcohol 5 Water	100 Alcohol 10 Water	100 Alcohol 15 Water	100 Alcohol 20 Water	100 Alcohol 25 Water	100 Alcohol 30 Water	100 Alcohol 35 Water	100 Alcohol 40 Water	100 Alcohol 45 Water	100 Alcohol 50 Water
Deg.											
30	0·83896	0·84995	0·85957	0·86825	0·87585	0·88282	0·88921	0·89511	0·90054	0·90558	0·91023
35	·83672	·84769	·85729	·86587	·87357	·88059	·88701	·89294	·89839	·90345	·90811
40	·83445	·84539	·85507	·86361	·87184	·87838	·88481	·89073	·89617	·90127	·90596
45	·83214	·84310	·85277	·86131	·86905	·87613	·88255	·88849	·89396	·89909	·90380
50	·82977	·84076	·85042	·85902	·86676	·87984	·88030	·88626	·89174	·89684	·90160
55	·82736	·83834	·84802	·85664	·86441	·87150	·87796	·88393	·88945	·89458	·89933
60	·82500	·83599	·84568	·85430	·86208	·86918	·87569	·88169	·88720	·89232	·89707
65	·82262	·83362	·84334	·85193	·85976	·86686	·87337	·87938	·88490	·89006	·89479
70	·82023	·83124	·84092	·84951	·85736	·86451	·87105	·87705	·88254	·88773	·89252
75	·81780	·82878	·83851	·84710	·85496	·86212	·86864	·87466	·88018	·88538	·89018
80	·81530	·82631	·83603	·84467	·85248	·85966	·86622	·87228	·87776	·88301	·88781
85	·81291	·82396	·83371	·84243	·85036	·85757	·86411	·87021	·87590	·88120	·88609
90	·81044	·82150	·83126	·84001	·84797	·85518	·86172	·86787	·87360	·87889	·88376
95	·80794	·81900	·82877	·83753	·84550	·85272	·85928	·86542	·87114	·87654	·88146
100	·80548	·81657	·82639	·83513	·84038	·85031	·85688	·86302	·86879	·87421	·87915

Temperature, Fahr.	100 Alcohol 55 Water	100 Alcohol 60 Water	100 Alcohol 65 Water	100 Alcohol 70 Water	100 Alcohol 75 Water	100 Alcohol 80 Water	100 Alcohol 85 Water	100 Alcohol 90 Water	100 Alcohol 95 Water	100 Alcohol 100 Water
Deg.										
30	0·91449	0·91847	0·92217	0·92563	0·92889	0·93191	0·93474	0·93741	0·93991	0·94222
35	·91241	·91640	·92009	·92355	·92680	·92986	·93274	·93541	·93790	·94025
40	·91026	·91428	·91799	·92151	·92476	·92783	·93072	·93341	·93592	·93827
45	·90812	·91211	·91584	·91937	·92264	·92570	·92859	·93131	·93382	·93621
50	·90596	·90997	·91370	·91723	·92051	·92358	·92647	·92919	·93177	·93419
55	·90367	·90768	·91144	·91502	·91837	·92145	·92436	·92707	·92963	·93208
60	·90144	·90549	·90927	·91287	·91622	·91933	·92225	·92499	·92758	·93002
65	·89920	·90328	·90707	·91066	·91400	·91715	·92010	·92283	·92546	·92794
70	·89695	·90104	·90484	·90847	·91181	·91493	·91793	·92069	·92333	·92580
75	·89464	·89872	·90252	·90617	·90952	·91270	·91569	·91849	·92111	·92364
80	·89225	·89639	·90021	·90385	·90723	·91046	·91340	·91622	·91891	·92142
85	·89043	·89460	·89843	·90209	·90558	·90882	·91186	·91465	·91729	·91969
90	·88817	·89230	·89617	·89988	·90342	·90688	·90967	·91248	·91511	·91751
95	·88588	·89003	·89390	·89763	·90119	·90443	·90747	·91029	·91290	·91531
100	·883571	·88769	·89158	·89536	·89889	·90215	·90522	·90805	·91066	·91310

[1] By specific gravity.

Table of the Specific Gravities of different Mixtures, &c. (continued.)

Temperature, Fahr.	95 Alcohol 100 Water	90 Alcohol 100 Water	85 Alcohol 100 Water	80 Alcohol 100 Water	75 Alcohol 100 Water	70 Alcohol 100 Water	65 Alcohol 100 Water	60 Alcohol 100 Water	55 Alcohol 100 Water	50 Alcohol 100 Water
Deg.										
30	0·94447	0·94675	0·94920	0·95173	0·95429	0·95681	0·95944	0·96209	0·96470	0·96719
35	·94249	·94484	·94734	·94988	·95246	·95502	·95772	·96048	·96315	·96579
40	·94058	·94295	·94547	·94802	·95060	·95328	·95602	·95879	·96159	·96434
45	·93860	·94096	·94348	·94605	·94871	·95143	·95423	·95703	·95993	·96280
50	·93658	·93897	·94149	·94414	·94683	·94958	·95243	·95534	·95831	·96126
55	·93452	·93696	·93948	·94213	·94486	·94767	·95057	·95357	·95662	·95966
60	·93247	·93493	·93749	·94018	·94296	·94579	·94876	·95181	·95493	·95804
65	·93040	·93285	·93546	·93822	·94099	·94388	·94689	·95000	·85318	·95635
70	·92828	·93076	·93337	·93616	·93898	·94193	·94500	·94813	·95139	·95469
75	·92613	·92865	·93132	·93413	·93695	·93989	·94301	·94623	·94957	·95292
80	·92393	·92646	·92917	·93201	·93488	·93785	·94102	·94431	·94768	·95111

Temperature, Fahr.	45 Alcohol 100 Water	40 Alcohol 100 Water	35 Alcohol 100 Water	30 Alcohol 100 Water	25 Alcohol 100 Water	20 Alcohol 100 Water	15 Alcohol 100 Water	10 Alcohol 100 Water	5 Alcohol 100 Water
Deg.									
30	0·96967	0·97200	0·97418	0·97635	0·97860	0·98108	0·98412	0·98804	0·99334
35	·96840	·97086	·97319	·97556	·97801	·98076	·98397	·98804	·99344
40	·96706	·96967	·97220	·97472	·97737	·98033	·98373	·98795	·99345
45	·96563	·96840	·97110	·97384	·97666	·97980	·98338	·98774	·99338
50	·96420	·96708	·96995	·97284	·97589	·97920	·98293	·98745	·99316
55	·96272	·96575	·96877	·97181	·97500	·97847	·98239	·98702	·99284
60	·96122	·96437	·96752	·97074	·97410	·97771	·98176	·98654	·99244
65	·95962	·96288	·96620	·96959	·97309	·97688	·98106	·98494	·99194
70	·95802	·96143	·96484	·96836	·97203	·97596	·98028	·98527	·99134
75	·95638	·95987	·96344	·96708	·97086	·97495	·97943	·98454	·99066
80	·95467	·95826	·96192	·96568	·96963	·97385	·97845	·98367	·98991

Experiments were made, by direction of the committee, to verify Gilpin's Tables, which showed that the error introduced in ascertaining the strength of spirits by Tables founded on Gilpin's numbers must be quite insensible in the practice of the Revenue. The discrepancies thus detected, on a mixture of a given strength, did not amount in any one instance to unity in the fourth place of decimals. From a careful inspection of such documents the committee are of opinion that Gilpin's Tables possess a degree of accuracy far surpassing what could be expected, and sufficiently perfect for all practical or scientific purposes.

The following Table is given by Mr. Lubbock, for converting the *apparent* specific gravity, or *indication*, into true specific gravity:—

Indication	− Temperature							62°	+				Indication
	30°	32°	37°	42°	47°	52°	57°		67°	72°	77°	80°	
·82	·00083	·00078	·00065	·00052	·00039	·00025	·00012		·00011	·00024	·00035	·00042	·82
·83	·00084	·00079	·00066	·00052	·00039	·00026	·00012		·00012	·00024	·00036	·00042	·83
·84	·00085	·00080	·00066	·00053	·00039	·00026	·00013		·00012	·00024	·00036	·00043	·84
·85	·00086	·00081	·00067	·00054	·00040	·00026	·00013		·00012	·00025	·00037	·00043	·85
·86	·00087	·00082	·00068	·00054	·00040	·00027	·00013		·00012	·00025	·00037	·00044	·86
·87	·00088	·00083	·00069	·00055	·00041	·00027	·00013		·00012	·00025	·00037	·00044	·87
·88	·00089	·00084	·00070	·00055	·00041	·00027	·00013		·00012	·00026	·00038	·00045	·88
·89	·00090	·00085	·00070	·00055	·00042	·00028	·00013		·00012	·00026	·00038	·00045	·89
·90	·00091	·00085	·00071	·00056	·00042	·00028	·00014		·00013	·00026	·00039	·00046	·90
·91	·00092	·00086	·00072	·00057	·00043	·00028	·00014		·00013	·00026	·00039	·00046	·91
·92	·00093	·00087	·00073	·00058	·00043	·00029	·00014		·00013	·00027	·00040	·00047	·92
·93	·00094	·00088	·00073	·00059	·00044	·00029	·00014		·00013	·00027	·00040	·00047	·93
·94	·00095	·00089	·00074	·00059	·00044	·00029	·00014		·00013	·00027	·00040	·00048	·94
·95	·00096	·00090	·00075	·00060	·00045	·00029	·00014		·00013	·00028	·00041	·00048	·95
·96	·00097	·00091	·00076	·00060	·00045	·00030	·00014		·00013	·00028	·00041	·00049	·96
·97	·00098	·00092	·00077	·00061	·00046	·00030	·00015		·00014	·00028	·00042	·00049	·97
·98	·00099	·00093	·00077	·00062	·00046	·00030	·00015		·00014	·00028	·00042	·00050	·98
·99	·00100	·00094	·00078	·00062	·00047	·00031	·00015		·00014	·00029	·00043	·00050	·99
·100	·00101	·00095	·00079	·00063	·00047	·00031	·00015						100

Tralle's Table of the Composition BY VOLUME *of Mixtures of Alcohol and Water of different Densities.*

Per-centage of Alcohol by volume	Specific Gravity at 60° F.	Differ-ence of the spe-cific gra-vities	Per-centage of Alcohol by volume	Specific Gravity at 60ᵇ F.	Differ-ence of the spe-cific gra-vities	Per-centage of Alcohol by volume	Specific Gravity at 60° F.	Differ-ence of the spe-cific gra-vities
0	0·9991		34	0·9596	13	68	0·8941	24
1	0·9976	15	35	0·9583	13	69	0·8917	24
2	0·9961	15	36	0·9570	13	70	0·8892	25
3	0·9947	14	37	0·9556	14	71	0·8867	25
4	0·9933	14	38	0·9541	15	72	0·8842	25
5	0·9919	14	39	0·9526	15	73	0·8817	25
6	0·9906	13	40	0·9510	16	74	0·8791	26
7	0·9893	13	41	0·9494	16	75	0·8765	26
8	0·9881	12	42	0·9478	16	76	0·8739	26
9	0·9869	12	43	0·9461	17	77	0·8712	27
10	0·9857	12	44	0·9444	17	78	0·8685	27
11	0·9845	12	45	0·9427	17	79	0·8658	27
12	0·9834	11	46	0·9409	18	80	0·8631	27
13	0·9823	11	47	0·9391	18	81	0·8603	28
14	0·8912	11	48	0·9373	18	82	0·8575	28
15	0·9802	10	49	0·9354	19	83	0·8547	28
16	0·9791	11	50	0·9335	19	84	0·8518	29
17	0·9781	10	51	0·9315	20	85	0.8488	30
18	0·9771	10	52	0·9295	20	86	0·8458	30
19	0·9761	10	53	0·9275	20	87	0·8428	30
20	0·9751	10	54	0·9254	21	88	0·8397	31
21	0·9741	10	55	0·9234	20	89	0·8365	32
22	0·9731	10	56	0·9213	21	90	0·8332	33
23	0·9720	11	57	0·9192	21	91	0·8299	33
24	0·9710	10	58	0·9170	22	92	0·8265	34
25	0·9700	10	59	0·9148	22	93	0·8230	35
26	0·9689	11	60	0·9126	22	94	0·8194	36
27	0·9679	10	61	0·9104	22	95	0·8157	37
28	0·9668	11	62	0·9082	22	96	0·8118	39
29	0·9657	11	63	0·9059	23	97	0·8077	41
30	0·9646	11	64	0·9036	23	98	0·8034	43
31	0·9634	12	65	0·9013	23	99	0·7988	46
32	0·9622	12	66	0·8989	24	100	0·7939	49
33	0·9609	13	67	0·8965	24			

In order, however, to employ this Table for ascertaining the strength of mixtures of alcohol and water of different densities (which is the practical use of such Tables), it is absolutely necessary that the determination of the density should be performed at an invariable temperature,—viz. 60° F. The methods of determining the density will be hereafter described; but it is obvious that practically the experiment cannot be conveniently made at any fixed temperature, but must be performed at that of the atmosphere.

M. Gay-Lussac has constructed a most valuable Table, of which the following is an abstract, which is supplied with his 'Alcoomètre.' (See ALCOHOLOMETRY.) It enables one to ascertain, from the observed density at any given temperature, the density at the normal temperature 15·5° C. (60° F.), and hence the strength; or, *vice versâ*, from the observed density at 60° F. to find the density at any other temperature.

The first vertical column of this Table contains the temperatures, from 0° to 30° C.; and the first horizontal line the indications of the alcoomètre. In the same Table he has most ingeniously inserted a correction of the volume of the spirits when the temperature differs from 15·5° C. (60° F.). All the numbers printed in small characters, under each *real strength*, i.e. per-centage of absolute alcohol, indicate the volume which 1,000 *litres (the litre being* 1·760773 *pints)* of a spirituous liquor would have when measured at the temperature at which its apparent strength is given.

Alcoömetrical Table of real Strength, by M. Gay-Lussac.

Temp. C.	31c	32c	33c	34c	35c	36c	37c	38c	39c	40c
Deg. 10	33·0 1002	34 1002	35 1003	36 1003	37 1003	38 1003	39 1003	40 1003	41 1003	42 1003
11	32·6 1002	33·6 1002	34·6 1002	35·6 1002	36·6 1002	37·6 1002	38·6 1002	39·6 1002	40·6 1003	41·6 1003
12	32·2 1001	33·2 1001	34·2 1002	35·2 1002	36·2 1002	37·2 1002	38·2 1002	39·2 1002	40·2 1002	41·2 1002
13	31·8 1001	32·8 1001	33·8 1001	34·8 1001	35·8 1001	36·8 1001	37·8 1001	38·8 1001	39·8 1001	40·8 1001
14	31·4 1001	32·4 1001	33·4 1001	34·4 1001	35·4 1001	36·4 1001	37·4 1001	38·4 1001	39·4 1001	40·4 1001
15	31 1000	32 1000	33 1000	34 1000	35 1000	36 1000	37 1000	38 1000	39 1000	40 1000
16	30·6 1000	31·6 1000	32·5 999	33·5 999	34·5 999	35·5 999	36·5 999	37·5 999	38·5 999	39·5 999
17	30·2 999	31·2 999	32·1 999	33·1 999	34·1 999	35·1 999	36·1 999	37·1 999	38·1 999	39·1 999
18	29·8 999	30·8 999	31·7 998	32·7 998	33·7 998	34·7 998	35·7 998	36·7 998	37·7 998	38·7 998
19	29·4 998	30·4 998	31·3 998	32·3 998	33·3 998	34·3 998	35·3 998	36·3 998	37·3 997	38·3 997
20	29 998	30 998	30·9 997	31·9 997	32·9 997	33·9 997	34·9 997	35·9 997	36·9 997	37·9 997
21	28·6 997	29·6 997	30·5 997	31·5 997	32·5 997	33·5 997	34·5 997	35·5 996	36·5 996	37·5 996
22	28·2 997	29·2 997	30·1 996	31·1 996	32·1 996	33·1 996	34·1 996	35·1 996	36·1 996	37·1 996
23	27·8 996	28·8 996	29·7 996	30·7 996	31·7 996	32·7 996	33·7 996	34·7 995	35·7 995	36·7 995
24	27·4 996	28·4 996	29·3 995	30·3 995	31·3 995	32·3 995	33·3 995	34·3 995	35·3 995	36·3 994
25	27 995	28 995	28·9 995	29·9 995	30·9 995	31·9 994	32·9 994	33·9 994	34·9 994	35·9 994

Temp. C.	41c	42c	43c	44c	45c	46c	47c	48c	49c	50c
Deg. 10	43 1003	44 1004	45 1004	46 1004	46·9 1004	47·9 1004	48·9 1004	49·9 1004	50·9 1004	51·8 1004
11	42·6 1003	43·6 1003	44·6 1003	45·6 1003	46·6 1003	47·6 1003	48·6 1003	49·5 1003	50·5 1003	51·5 1003
12	42·2 1002	43·2 1002	44·2 1002	45·2 1002	46·2 1002	47·2 1002	48·2 1002	49·2 1002	50·2 1002	51·1 1002
13	41·8 1001	42·8 1001	43·8 1001	44·8 1002	45·8 1002	46·8 1002	47·8 1002	48·8 1002	49·8 1002	50·8 1002
14	41·4 1001	42·4 1001	43·4 1001	44·4 1001	45·4 1001	46·4 1001	47·4 1001	48·4 1001	49·4 1001	50·4 1000
15	41 1000	42 1000	43 1000	44 1000	45 1000	46 1000	47 1000	48 1000	49 1000	50 1000
16	40·6 999	41·6 999	42·6 999	43·6 999	44·6 999	45·6 999	46·6 999	47·6 999	48·6 999	49·6 999
17	40·2 999	41·2 999	42·2 999	43·2 998	44·2 998	45·2 998	46·2 998	47·2 998	48·2 998	49·2 998
18	39·8 998	40·8 998	41·8 998	42·8 998	43·8 998	44·9 998	45·9 998	46·9 998	47·9 998	48·9 998
19	39·4 997	40·4 997	41·4 997	42·5 997	43·5 997	44·5 997	45·5 997	46·5 997	47·5 997	48·5 997
20	39 997	40 997	41 997	42·1 997	43·1 996	44·1 996	45·1 996	46·1 996	47·2 996	48·2 996
21	38·6 996	39·6 996	40·6 996	41·7 996	42·7 996	43·7 996	44·8 996	45·8 996	46·8 995	47·8 995

Alcoömetrical Table of real Strength, by M. Gay-Lussac (continued).

Temp. C.	41c	42c	43c	44c	45c	46c	47c	48c	49c	50c
Deg. 22	38·2 996	39·2 995	40·2 995	41·3 995	42·3 995	43·3 995	44·3 995	45·3 995	46·4 995	47·4 995
23	37·8 995	38·8 995	39·8 995	40·9 994	41·9 994	42·9 994	43·9 994	44·9 994	46 994	47 994
24	37·4 994	38·4 994	39·4 994	40·5 994	41·5 994	42·5 994	43·6 994	44·6 994	45·6 993	46·6 993
25	37 994	38 994	39 993	40·1 993	42·1 993	42·2 993	43·2 993	44·2 993	45·2 993	46·3 993

Temp. C.	51c	52c	53c	54c	55c	56c	57c	58c	59c	60c
Deg. 10	52·9 1004	53·8 1004	54·8 1004	55·8 1004	56·8 1004	57·8 1004	58·8 1004	59·7 1004	60·7 1004	61·7 1004
11	52·5 1003	53·5 1003	54·4 1003	55·4 1003	56·4 1003	57·4 1003	58·4 1003	59·4 1003	60·4 1003	61·4 1003
12	52·1 1002	53·1 1002	54·1 1002	55 1002	56 1002	57 1002	58 1002	59 1002	60 1002	61 1002
13	51·8 1002	52·7 1002	53·7 1002	54·7 1002	55·7 1002	56·7 1002	57·7 1002	58·7 1002	59·7 1002	60·7 1002
14	51·4 1001	52·3 1001	53·3 1001	54·3 1001	55·3 1001	56·3 1001	57·3 1001	58·3 1001	59·3 1001	60·3 1001
15	51 1000	52 1000	53 1000	54 1000	55 1000	56 1000	57 1000	58 1000	59 1000	60 1000
16	50·6 999	51·6 999	52·6 999	53·6 999	54·6 999	55·6 999	56·6 999	57·6 999	58·6 999	59·6 999
17	50·3 998	51·3 998	52·3 998	53·3 998	54·3 998	55·3 998	56·3 998	57·3 998	58·3 998	59·3 998
18	49·9 998	50·9 998	51·9 998	52·9 998	53·9 998	54·9 998	55·9 998	56·9 997	57·9 997	58·9 997
19	49·5 997	50·6 997	51·6 997	52·6 997	53·6 997	54·6 997	55·6 997	56·6 997	57·6 997	58·6 997
20	49·2 996	50·2 996	51·2 996	52·2 996	53·2 996	54·2 996	55·2 996	56·2 996	57·2 996	58·2 996
21	48·8 995	49·8 995	50·8 995	51·8 995	52·9 995	53·9 995	54·9 995	55·9 995	56·9 995	57·9 995
22	48·4 995	49·4 995	50·4 995	51·4 994	52·5 994	53·5 994	54·5 994	55·5 994	56·5 994	57·5 995
23	48 994	49·1 994	50·1 994	51·1 994	52·1 994	53·1 994	54·1 994	55·1 993	56·1 993	57·1 993
24	47·6 993	48·7 993	49·7 993	50·7 993	51·8 993	52·8 993	53·8 993	54·8 993	55·8 993	56·8 992
25	47·3 993	48·3 993	49·3 993	50·3 992	51·4 992	52·4 992	53·4 992	54·4 992	55·5 992	56·6 992

Temp. C.	61c	62c	63c	64c	65c	66c	67c	68c	69c	70c
Deg. 10	62·7 1004	63·7 1004	64·7 1004	65·7 1004	66·7 1004	67·6 1004	68·6 1004	69·6 1004	70·6 1004	71·6 1004
11	62·4 1003	63·4 1003	64·4 1003	65·4 1003	66·4 1003	67·3 1003	68·3 1003	69·3 1004	70·3 1004	71·3 1004
12	62 1002	63 1002	64 1002	65 1002	66 1002	67 1002	68 1003	69 1003	70 1003	71 1003
13	61·7 1002	62·7 1002	63·7 1002	64·7 1002	65·7 1002	66·7 1002	67·7 1002	68·7 1002	69·6 1002	70·6 1002
14	61·3 1001	62·3 1001	63·3 1001	64·3 1001	65·3 1001	66·3 1001	67·3 1001	68·3 1001	69·3 1001	70·3 1001
15	61 1000	62 1000	63 1000	64 1000	65 1000	66 1000	67 1000	68 1000	69 1000	70 1000

Alcöometrical Table of real Strength, by M. Gay-Lussac (continued).

Temp. C.	61c	62c	63c	64c	65c	66c	67c	68c	69c	70c
Deg. 16	60·6 (999)	61·7 (999)	62·7 (999)	63·7 (999)	64·7 (999)	65·7 (999)	66·7 (999)	67·7 (999)	68·7 (990)	69·7 (999)
17	60·3 (998)	61·3 (998)	62·3 (998)	63·3 (998)	64·3 (998)	65·3 (998)	66·3 (998)	67·3 (998)	68·3 (998)	69·3 (998)
18	59·9 (997)	61 (997)	62 (997)	63 (997)	64 (997)	65 (997)	66 (997)	67 (997)	68 (997)	69 (997)
19	59·6 (997)	60·6 (997)	61·6 (997)	62·7 (997)	63·7 (997)	64·7 (997)	65·7 (997)	66·7 (997)	67·7 (996)	68·7 (996)
20	59·2 (996)	60·3 (996)	61·3 (996)	62·3 (996)	63·3 (996)	64·3 (996)	65·4 (996)	66·4 (996)	67·4 (996)	68·4 (996)
21	58·9 (995)	59·9 (995)	61 (995)	62 (995)	63 (995)	64 (995)	65 (995)	66 (995)	67 (995)	68·1 (995)
22	58·5 (994)	59·5 (994)	60·6 (994)	61·6 (994)	62·7 (994)	63·7 (994)	64·7 (994)	65·7 (994)	66·7 (994)	67·8 (994)
23	58·1 (993)	59·2 (993)	60·2 (993)	61·3 (993)	62·3 (993)	63·3 (993)	64·3 (993)	65·4 (993)	66·3 (993)	67·4 (993)
24	57·8 (992)	58·9 (992)	59·9 (992)	61 (992)	62 (992)	63 (992)	64 (992)	65 (992)	66 (992)	67·1 (992)
25	57·5 (992)	58·5 (992)	59·5 (992)	60·6 (991)	61·6 (991)	62·6 (991)	63·7 (991)	64·7 (991)	65·7 (991)	66·7 (991)

Temp. C.	71c	72c	73c	74c	75c	76c	77c	78c	79c	80c
Deg. 10	72·6 (1004)	73·5 (1004)	74·5 (1005)	75·5 (1005)	76·5 (1005)	77·5 (1005)	78·5 (1005)	79·5 (1005)	80·5 (1005)	81·5 (1005)
11	72·3 (1004)	73·2 (1004)	74·2 (1004)	75·2 (1004)	76·2 (1004)	77·2 (1004)	78·2 (1004)	79·2 (1004)	80·2 (1004)	81·2 (1004)
12	72 (1003)	72·9 (1003)	73·9 (1003)	74·9 (1003)	75·9 (1003)	76·9 (1003)	77·9 (1003)	78·9 (1003)	79·9 (1003)	80·9 (1003)
13	71·6 (1002)	72·6 (1002)	73·6 (1002)	74·6 (1002)	75·6 (1002)	76·6 (1002)	77·6 (1002)	78·6 (1002)	79·6 (1002)	80·6 (1002)
14	71·3 (1001)	72·3 (1001)	73·3 (1001)	74·3 (1001)	75·3 (1001)	76·3 (1001)	77·3 (1001)	78·3 (1001)	79·3 (1001)	80·3 (1001)
15	71 (1000)	72 (1000)	73 (1000)	74 (1000)	75 (1000)	76 (1000)	77 (1000)	78 (1000)	79 (1000)	80 (1000)
16	70·7 (999)	71·7 (999)	72·7 (999)	73·7 (999)	74·7 (999)	75·7 (999)	76·7 (999)	77·7 (999)	78·7 (999)	79·7 (999)
17	70·3 (998)	71·3 (998)	72·3 (998)	73·3 (998)	74·3 (998)	75·4 (998)	76·4 (998)	77·4 (998)	78·4 (998)	79·4 (998)
18	70 (997)	71 (997)	72 (997)	73 (997)	74 (997)	75·1 (997)	76·1 (997)	77·1 (997)	78·1 (997)	79·1 (997)
19	69·7 (996)	70·7 (996)	71·7 (996)	72·7 (996)	73·7 (996)	74·7 (996)	75·8 (996)	76·8 (996)	77·8 (996)	78·8 (996)
20	69·4 (996)	70·4 (996)	71·4 (995)	72·4 (995)	73·4 (995)	74·4 (995)	75·5 (995)	76·5 (995)	77·5 (995)	78·5 (995)
21	69·1 (995)	70·1 (995)	71·1 (995)	72·1 (994)	73·1 (994)	74·1 (994)	75·2 (994)	76·2 (994)	77·2 (994)	78·2 (994)
22	68·8 (994)	69·8 (994)	70·8 (994)	71·8 (994)	72·8 (993)	73·8 (993)	74·8 (993)	75·9 (993)	76·9 (993)	77·9 (993)
23	68·4 (993)	69·4 (993)	70·5 (993)	71·5 (993)	72·5 (992)	73·5 (992)	74·5 (992)	75·5 (992)	76·6 (992)	77·6 (992)
24	68·1 (992)	69·1 (992)	70·1 (992)	71·2 (992)	72·2 (992)	73·2 (992)	74·2 (992)	75·2 (991)	76·3 (991)	77·3 (991)
25	67·8 (991)	68·8 (991)	69·8 (991)	70·8 (991)	71·8 (991)	72·8 (991)	73·9 (991)	74·9 (991)	76 (991)	77 (991)

Alcoömetrical Table of real Strength, by M. Gay-Lussac (continued).

Temp. C.	81c	82c	83c	84c	85c	86c	87c	88c	89c	90c
Deg. 10	82·4 / 1005	83·4 / 1005	84·4 / 1005	85·4 / 1005	86·4 / 1005	87·4 / 1005	88·3 / 1005	89·3 / 1005	90·2 / 1005	91·2 / 1005
11	82·2 / 1004	83·1 / 1004	84·1 / 1004	85·1 / 1004	86·1 / 1004	87·1 / 1004	88 / 1004	89 / 1004	90 / 1004	91 / 1004
12	81·9 / 1003	82·9 / 1003	83·9 / 1003	84·8 / 1003	85·8 / 1003	86·8 / 1003	87·8 / 1003	88·7 / 1003	89·7 / 1003	90·7 / 1003
13	81·6 / 1002	82·6 / 1002	83·6 / 1002	84·6 / 1002	85·5 / 1002	86·5 / 1002	87·5 / 1002	88·5 / 1002	89·5 / 1002	90·5 / 1002
14	81·3 / 1001	82·3 / 1001	83·3 / 1001	84·3 / 1001	85·3 / 1001	86·3 / 1001	87·3 / 1001	88·2 / 1001	89·2 / 1001	90·2 / 1001
15	81 / 1000	82 / 1000	83 / 1000	84 / 1000	85 / 1000	86 / 1000	87 / 1000	88 / 1000	89 / 1000	90 / 1000
16	80·7 / 999	81·7 / 999	82·7 / 999	83·7 / 999	84·7 / 999	85·7 / 999	86·7 / 999	87·7 / 999	88·7 / 999	89·7 / 999
17	80·4 / 998	81·4 / 998	82·4 / 998	83·4 / 998	84·4 / 998	85·4 / 998	86·4 / 998	87·4 / 998	88·4 / 998	89·5 / 998
18	80·1 / 997	81·1 / 997	82·1 / 997	83·1 / 997	84·1 / 997	85·2 / 997	86·2 / 997	87·2 / 997	88·2 / 997	89·2 / 997
19	79·8 / 996	80·8 / 996	81·9 / 996	82·9 / 996	83·9 / 996	84·9 / 996	85·9 / 996	86·9 / 996	87·9 / 996	88·9 / 996
20	79·5 / 995	80·5 / 995	81·6 / 995	82·6 / 995	83·6 / 995	84·6 / 995	85·6 / 995	86·6 / 995	87·7 / 995	88·7 / 995
21	79·2 / 994	80·2 / 994	81·3 / 994	82·3 / 994	83·3 / 994	84·3 / 994	85·3 / 994	86·4 / 994	87·4 / 994	88·4 / 994
22	78·9 / 993	79·9 / 993	81 / 993	82 / 993	83 / 993	84 / 993	85 / 993	86·1 / 993	87·1 / 993	88·2 / 993
23	78·6 / 992	79·6 / 992	80·7 / 992	81·7 / 992	82·7 / 992	83·8 / 992	84·8 / 992	85·8 / 992	86·8 / 992	87·9 / 992
24	78·3 / 991	79·3 / 991	80·4 / 991	81·4 / 991	82·4 / 991	83·5 / 991	84·5 / 991	85·5 / 991	86·5 / 991	87·6 / 991
25	78 / 991	79 / 991	80·1 / 990	81·1 / 990	82·1 / 990	83·2 / 990	84·2 / 990	85·2 / 990	86·3 / 990	87·4 / 990

The *boiling point* of mixtures of alcohol and water likewise differs with the strength of such mixtures.

According to Gay-Lussac, absolute alcohol boils at 78·4° C. (173° F.) under a pressure of 760 *millimetres* (*the millimetre being* 0·03937 *English inches*). When mixed with water, of course its boiling point rises in proportion to the quantity of water present, as is the case in general with mixtures of two fluids of greater and less volatility. A mixture of alcohol and water, however, presents this anomaly, according to Soemmering: when the mixture contains less than six per cent. of alcohol, those portions which first pass off are saturated with water, and the alcoholic solution in the retort becomes richer, till absolute alcohol passes over; but when the mixture contains more than six per cent. of water the boiling point rises, and the quantity of alcohol in the distillate steadily diminishes as the distillation proceeds.

Temperature	Alcoholic content of the vapour	Alcoholic content of the boiling liquid	Temperature	Alcoholic content of the vapour	Alcoholic content of the boiling liquid
Fahr. 170·0	93	92	Fahr. 189·8	71	20
171·8	92	90	192·0	68	18
172	91	85	164	66	15
172·8	90½	80	196·4	61	12
174	90	70	198·6	55	10
174·6	89	70	201	50	7
176	87	65	203	42	5
178·3	85	50	205·4	36	3
180·8	82	40	207·7	28	2
183	80	35	210	13	1
185	78	30	212	0	0
187·4	76	25			

According to Gröning's researches, the preceding temperatures of the alcoholic vapours correspond to the accompanying contents of alcohol in per-centage of volume which are disengaged in the boiling of the spirituous liquid.

Gröning undertook this investigation in order to employ the thermometer as an alcoholometer in the distillation of spirits; for which purpose he thrust the bulb of the thermometer through a cork inserted into a tube fixed in the capital of the still. The state of the barometer ought also to be considered in making comparative experiments of this kind. Since, by this method, the alcoholic content may be compared with the temperature of the vapour that passes over at any time, so also the contents of the whole distillation may be found approximately; and the method serves as a convenient means of making continual observations on the progress of the distillation.

From the mean of a great many experiments, Dr. Ure drew up the following Table, which shows the boiling point of alcohol of various specific gravities:—

Boiling Point	Specific Gravity	Boiling Point	Specific Gravity
178·5 F.	0·9200	185·6 F.	0·9665
179·75 „	0·9321	189·0 „	0·9729
180·4 „	0·9420	191·8 „	0·9786
182·01 „	0·9516	196·4 „	0·9850
183·40 „	0·960	202·0 „	0·992

Density of the Vapour.—One volume of alcohol yields 488·3 volumes of vapour at 212° F. The specific gravity of the vapour, taking air as unity, was found by Gay-Lussac to be 1·6133. [Its vapour-density, referred to hydrogen as unity, is 13·3605?]

Spirituous vapour passed through an ignited tube of glass or porcelain is converted into carbonic oxide, water, hydrogen, carburetted hydrogen, olefiant gas, naphthaline, empyreumatic oil, and carbon; according to the degree of heat and nature of the tube, these products vary. Anhydrous alcohol is a non-conductor of electricity, but is decomposed by a powerful voltaic battery. Alcohol burns in the air with a blue flame into carbonic acid and water; the water being heavier than the spirit, because 46 parts of alcohol contain 6 of hydrogen, which form 54 of water. In oxygen the combustion is accompanied with great heat, and this flame, directed through a small tube, powerfully ignites bodies exposed to it.

Platinum in a finely divided state has the property of determining the combination of alcohol with the oxygen of the air in a remarkable manner. A ball of spongy platinum, placed slightly above the wick of a lamp fed by spirit and communicating with the wick by a platinum wire, when once heated, keeps at a red heat, gradually burning the spirit. This has been applied in the construction of the so-called 'philosophical pastilles;' eau-de-cologne or other perfumed spirit being thus made to diffuse itself in a room.

Mr. Gill has also practically applied this in the construction of an alcohol lamp without flame.

A coil of platinum wire, of about the one-hundredth part of an inch in thickness, is coiled partly round the cotton wick of a spirit-lamp, and partly above it, and the lamp lighted to heat the wire to redness; on the flame being extinguished, the alcohol vapour keeps the wire red hot for any length of time, so as to be in constant readiness to ignite a match, for example. This lamp affords sufficient light to show the hour by a watch in the night, with a very small consumption of spirit.

This property of condensing oxygen, and thus causing the union of it with combustible bodies, is not confined to platinum, but is possessed, though in a less degree, by other porous bodies. If we moisten sand in a capsule with absolute alcohol, and cover it with previously heated nickel powder, protoxide of nickel, cobalt powder, protoxide of cobalt, protoxide of uranium, or oxide of tin (these six bodies being procured by ignition of their oxalates in a crucible), or finely powdered peroxide of manganese, combustion takes place, and continues so long as the spirituous vapour lasts.

Solvent Power.—One of the properties of alcohol most valuable in the arts is its *solvent power.*

It dissolves gases to a very considerable extent, which gases, if they do not enter into combination with the alcohol, or act chemically upon it, are expelled again on boiling the alcohol.

Several salts, especially the deliquescent, are dissolved by it, and some of them give a colour to its flame; thus the solutions of the salts of strontia in alcohol burn with a *crimson flame*, those of copper and borax with a *green* one, lime a *reddish*, and baryta with a *yellow* flame.

This solvent power is, however, most remarkable in its action upon resins, ethers, essential oils, fatty bodies, alkaloids, as well as many organic acids. In a similar way it dissolves iodine, bromine, and in small quantities sulphur and phosphorus. In general it may be said to be an excellent solvent for most hydrogenised organic substances.

Uses.—In consequence of this property it is most extensively used in the chemical arts: *e.g.* for the solution of gum-resins, &c., in the manufacture of varnishes; in pharmacy, for the separating of the active principles of plants, in the preparation of tinctures. It is also employed in the formation of chloroform, ether, spirits of nitre, &c.

The great use of alcohol, in its various states of mixture, is, and has been from time immemorial, as a *beverage.* There cannot be a doubt that alcoholic liquors are beneficial to most healthy persons when *moderately* enjoyed; and the man who advocates their rational *use* cannot be held answerable for their *abuse.*

Absolute alcohol (or strong spirits) acts locally as an irritant, contracting the tissues; but its effects on the organism, when taken internally, arises from its action, by the nerves, on the brain. Dr. Pereira has graphically described three stages of their effects :—

> 1. First or mildest degree   . Excitement.
> 2. Second degree   .   .   . Intoxication, or drunkenness.
> 3. Third degree   .   .   . Coma, or true apoplexy.

These effects are tolerably familiar, and for a more minute description of them we must refer to Dr. Pereira [1] and other medical authors.

The important applications of alcohol in the arts, as a solvent for resins, &c., have been before alluded to. To the chemist it is a most valuable agent of separation. By its means he is enabled, in complicated organic mixtures, to separate those substances which are soluble from those which are insoluble in this menstruum. It may likewise be employed for separating certain salts—*e.g.* the chloride of strontium from that of barium, &c. &c.

From it are also manufactured ether, chloroform, chloral, and, indirectly, acetic acid; and in pharmacy, sweet spirits of nitre, the various tinctures, &c. &c.

The Spirits *imported* and retained for *Home Consumption* were as follows :—

IMPORTS						
Spirits	1870		1871		1872	
	Quantity	Value	Quantity	Value	Quantity	Value
	Proof gallons	£	Proof gallons	£	Proof gallons	£
Rum . .	6,915,117	808,809	7,557,422	771,598	6,586,257	675,820
Brandy .	7,942,965	2,153,699	5,373,486	1,905,276	3,519,413	1,329,644
Other Sorts	2,332,049	184,869	1,877,390	186,825	1,558,166	187,160

These Spirits were chiefly imported :—Rum, from British West India Islands, British Guiana, Mauritius, Spanish West India Islands; and Brandy, from France, Holland, Germany.

The quantities retained for HOME CONSUMPTION were :—

Rum . .	3,851,863	4,168,905	4,405,192
Brandy .	3,526,132	3,715,675	3,944,725
Other Sorts	1,027,857	1,010,929	680,918

[1] Pereira, Materia Medica, vol. ii. p. 1948.

Spirits Exported.

Spirits	1867	1868	1869	1870	1871	1872
	Gallons	Gallons	Gallons	Gallons	Gallons	Gallons
British and Irish	1,286,598	1,364,155	1,673,773	1,457,265	1,607,061	1,795,868
Foreign :						
Brandy . .	365,316	459,857	415,546	847,492	420,324	
Rum . .	2,468,478	2,507,175	1,396,157	1,334,358	1,680,289	
Unenumerated .	883,050	999,705	1,743,469	1,762,894	1,832,455	

Total quantities of Spirits distilled and charged with Excise Duty for consumption in England and Wales, Scotland and Ireland, in each of the years ending 31st of March, 1866, 1867, 1868.

Places	Distilled			Charged with duty for consumption		
	1865–66	1866–67	1867–68	1865–66	1866–67	1867–68
	Gallons	Gallons	Gallons	Gallons	Gallons	Gallons
England and Wales	7,705,679	7,513,520	7,008,052	9,214,529	9,285,645	9,170,561
Scotland .	13,097,101	11,805,841	11,084,595	7,421,421	7,783,945	7,144,144
Ireland .	5,746,680	5,486,050	5,851,574	5,403,266	6,057,261	6,377,648
United Kingdom	26,549,460	24,805,411	23,944,221	22,039,216	23,126,851	22,692,353

The following are the quantities of spirits charged with duties of excise in each of the years named :—

	Gallons.			Gallons.			Gallons.
1842 .	. 18,841,890		1850 .	. 23,919,432		1858 .	. 23,686,751
1844 .	. 20,608,525		1852 .	. 25,270,262		1860 .	. 21,873,369
1846 .	. 24,106,697		1854 .	. 26,148,511		1862 .	. 19,700,250
1848 .	. 22,234,379		1856 .	. 23,922,453		1864 .	. 21,039,582

Every English distiller has now to pay a licence-duty of ten guineas before he can lawfully conduct operations, and afterwards a duty of 7s. 10d. per imperial gallon of spirits, proof strength, which he produces.

The Scotch and Irish distillers had to pay the same licence-fee as the English; and in addition to this, the Scotch distiller paid a duty of 4s. 8d. per imperial gallon of proof strength, and the Irish a duty of 3s. 4d.; but the duties are now equalized.

ALCOHOL, METHYLATED. It was for a long time a great desideratum for the manufacturer to obtain spirit free from duty. The Government, feeling the necessity for this, have sanctioned the sale of spirit which has been flavoured with methyl-alcohol, so as to render it unpalatable, *free of duty*, under the name of '*methylated spirit.*' This methylated spirit can now be obtained, in large quantities by giving suitable security to the Board of Inland Revenue of its employment for manufacturing purposes only, and must prove of great value to those manufacturers who are large consumers.

Professors Graham, Hofmann, and Redwood, in their 'Report on the Supply of Spirit of Wine, free of duty, for use in the Arts and Manufactures,' addressed to the Chairman of the Board of Inland Revenue, came to the following conclusions :—

'From the results of this inquiry it has appeared that means exist by which spirit of wine, produced in the usual way, may be rendered unfit for human consumption, as a beverage, without materially impairing it for the greater number of the more valuable purposes in the arts to which spirit is usually applied. To spirit of wine, of not less strength than corresponds to density 0·830, it is proposed to make an addition of 10 per cent. of purified wood-naphtha (*wood or methylic spirit*), and to issue this mixed spirit for consumption, duty-free, under the name of *Methylated Spirit.* It has been shown that methylated spirit resists any process for its purification; the removal of the substance added to the spirit of wine being not only difficult, but, to all appearance, impossible; and further, that no danger is to be apprehended of the methylated spirit being ever compounded so as to make it palatable. . . . . It may be found safe to reduce eventually the proportion of the mixing ingredient to 5 per cent., or even a smaller proportion, although it has been recommended to begin with the larger proportion of 10 per cent.'

And further, the authors justly remark :—' The command of alcohol at a low price is sure to suggest a multitude of improved processes, and of novel applications, which can scarcely be anticipated at the present moment. It will be felt far beyond the limited range of the trades now more immediately concerned in the consumption of spirits; like the repeal of the duty on salt, it will at once most vitally affect the chemical arts, and cannot fail, ultimately, to exert a beneficial influence upon many branches of industry.'

And in additional observations, added subsequently to their original Report, the chemists above named recommend the following restriction upon the sale of the methylated spirit :—' That the methylated spirit should be issued, by agents duly authorised by the Board of Inland Revenue, to none but manufacturers, who should themselves consume it : and that application should always be made for it according to a recognised form, in which, besides the quantity wanted, the applicant should state the use to which it is to be applied, and undertake that it should be applied for that purpose only. The manufacturer might be permitted to retail varnishes and other products containing the methylated spirit, but not the methylated spirit itself in an unaltered state.' They recommend that the methylated spirit should not be made with the ordinary crude, very impure wood-naphtha, since this could not be advantageously used as a solvent for resins by hatters and varnish-makers, as the less volatile parts of the naphtha would be retained by the resins after the spirit had evaporated, and the quality of the resin would be thus impaired. If, however, the methylated spirit be originally prepared with the crude wood-naphtha, it may be purified by a simple distillation from 10 per cent. of potash.

It appears that the boon thus afforded to the manufacturing community of obtaining spirit *duty free* has been acknowledged and appreciated; and now for most purposes, where the small quantity of wood-spirit does not interfere, the methylated spirit is generally used.

It appears that even ether and chloroform, which one would expect to derive an unpleasant flavour from the wood-spirit, are now made of a quality quite unobjectionable from the methylated spirit; but care should be taken, especially in the preparation of medicinal compounds, not to extend the employment of the methylated spirit beyond its justifiable limits, lest so useful an article should get into disrepute.[1] Methylated spirit can be procured also in small quantities from the wholesale dealers, containing in solution 1oz. to the gallon of shellac, under the name of ' finish.'

ALCOHOLATES, or **ALCOATES**. Graham has shown that alcohol forms crystallisable compounds with several salts. These bodies, which he called ' *Alcoholates*,' are in general rather unstable combinations, and almost always decomposed by water. Among the best known are the following :—

Alcoholate of chloride of calcium	.	$2\,C^4H^6O^2, Ca\,Cl,$	$4C^2H^6O.\ Ca\ Cl^2$
„ „ of zinc	.	$C^4H^6O^2, Zn\,Cl,$	$2C^2H^6O.\ Zn\ Cl^2$
„ bichloride of tin .	.	$C^4H^6O^2, Sn\,Cl^2,$	$2C^2H^6O.\ Sn\ Cl^4$
„ nitrate of magnesia	.	$3\,C^4H^6O^2, MgO,N\,O^5,$	$6C^2H^6O.\ Mg2(NO^3)$

ALCOHOLOMETRY, or **ALCOÖMETRY**. *Determination of the Strength of Mixtures of Alcohol and Water.* Since the commercial value of the alcoholic liquors, commonly called ' spirits,' is determined by the amount of pure or absolute alcohol present in them, it is evident that a ready and accurate means of determining this point is of the highest importance to all persons engaged in trade in such articles.

If the mixture contain nothing but alcohol and water, it is only necessary to determine the *density* or *specific gravity* of such a mixture; if, however, it contain saccharine matters, colouring principles, &c., as is the case with wine, beer, &c., other processes become necessary, which will be fully discussed hereafter.

The determination of the specific gravity of spirit, as of most other liquids, may be effected, with perhaps greater accuracy than by any other process, by means of a stoppered specific-gravity bottle. If the bottle be of such a size as exactly to hold 1,000 grains of distilled water at 60° F., it is only necessary to weigh it full of the spirit at the same temperature, when (the weight of the bottle being known) the specific gravity is obtained by a very simple calculation. See SPECIFIC GRAVITY.

---

[1] Some difference of opinion appears to exist whether *Chloroform* can be obtained *pure* from methylated spirit. See METHYL.

This process, though very accurate, is somewhat troublesome, especially to persons unaccustomed to accurate chemical experiments, and it involves the possession of a delicate balance. The necessity for this is, however, obviated by the employment of one of the many modifications of the common *hydrometer*. This is a floating instrument, the use of which depends upon the principle, that a solid body immersed into a fluid is buoyed upwards with a force equal to the weight of the fluid which it displaces, *i.e.* to its own bulk of the fluid; consequently, the denser the spirituous mixture, or the less alcohol it contains, the higher will the instrument stand in the liquid; and the less dense, or the more spirit it contains, the lower will the apparatus sink into it.

There are two classes of hydrometers. 1st. Those which are always immersed in the fluid to the same depth, and to which weights are added to adjust the instrument to the density of any particular fluid. Of this kind are Fahrenheit's, Nicholson's, and Guyton de Morveau's hydrometers.

2nd. Those which are always used with the same weight, but which sink into the liquids to be tried, to different depths, according to the density of the fluid. Of this class are most of the common glass hydrometers, such as Baumé's, Curteis's, Gay-Lussac's, Twaddle's, &c.

Sykes's and Dicas's combine both principles. See HYDRO-METERS.

Sykes's hydrometer, or alcoholometer, is the one employed by the Board of Excise, and therefore the one most extensively used in this country.

This instrument does not immediately indicate the density or the per-centage of absolute alcohol, *but the degree above or below proof*—the meaning of which has been before detailed (p. 45.)

It consists of a spherical ball or float, *a*, with an upper and lower stem of brass, *b* and *c*. The upper stem is graduated into ten principal divisions, which are each subdivided into five parts. The lower stem, *c*, is made conical, and has a loaded bulb at its extremity. There are nine moveable weights, numbered respectively by tens from 10 to 90. Each of these circular weights has a slit in it, so that it can be placed on the conical stem, *c*. The instrument is adjusted so that it floats with the surface of the fluid coincident with zero on the scale, in a spirit of specific gravity ·825 at 60° F., this being accounted by the Excise as '*standard alcohol.*' In weaker spirit, which has therefore a greater density, the hydrometer will not sink so low; and if the density be much greater, it will be necessary to add one of the weights to cause the entire immersion of the bulb of the instrument. Each weight represents so many principal divisions of the stem, as its number indicates; thus, the heaviest weight, marked 90, is equivalent to 90 divisions of the stem, and the instrument, with the weight added, floats at 0 in distilled water. As each principal division on the stem is divided into five subdivisions, the instrument has a range of 500 degrees between the standard alcohol (specific gravity ·825) and water. There is a line on one of the side faces of the stem *b*, near division 1 of the drawing, at which line the instrument with the weight 60 attached to it floats in spirit exactly of the strength of *proof*, at a temperature of 51° F.

In using this instrument, it is immersed in the spirit, and pressed down by the hand until the whole of the graduated portion of the upper stem is wet. The force of the hand required to sink it will be a guide to the selection of the proper weight. Having taken one of the circular weights necessary for the purpose, it is slipped on to the lower conical stem. The instrument is again immersed, and pressed down as before to 0, and then allowed to rise and settle at any point. The eye is then brought to the level of the surface of the spirit, and the part of the stem cut by the surface, *as seen from below*, is marked. The number thus indicated by the stem is added to the number of the weight, and the sum of these, together with the *temperature* of the spirit, observed at the same time by means of a thermometer, enables the operator, by reference to a Table which is sold to accompany the instrument, to find the strength of the spirit tested.

These Tables are far too voluminous to be quoted here; and this is unnecessary, since the instrument is never sold without them.

A modification of Sykes's hydrometer has been adopted for testing alcoholic liquors which is perhaps more convenient, as the necessity for the loading weights is done away with, the stem being sufficiently long not to require them. It is

constructed of glass, and is in the shape of a common hydrometer, the stem being divided into degrees ; it carries a small spirit thermometer in the bulb, to which a scale is fixed, ranging from 30° to 82° F. (0 to 12° C.) There are Tables supplied with the hydrometer, which are headed by the degrees and half degrees of the thermometric scale ; and the corresponding content of spirit, over or under proof at the respective degree of the Table, is placed opposite each degree of the hydrometer.

By means of either of these instruments, and by the use of the Tables accompanying them, we learn the strength, in degrees, *above or below proof ;* and the following Table by Dr. Ure will be found most useful in converting these numbers into specific gravities :—

Per cent. over Proof	Specific Gravity	Per cent. over Proof	Specific Gravity	Per cent. over Proof	Specific Gravity	Per cent. over Proof	Specific Gravity	Per cent. over Proof	Specific Gravity
67·0	0·8156	43·1	0·8597	19·3	0·8948	7·0	0·9282	53·3	0·9693
66·5	0·8166	42·6	0·8604	19·1	0·8951	8·0	0·9295	54·8	0·9701
66·1	0·8174	42·0	0·8615	18·6	0·8959	9·0	0·9306	56·2	0·9709
65·5	0·8188	41·5	0·8622	18·0	0·8966	10·0	0·9318	57·6	0·9718
65·0	0·8199	41·1	0·8629	17·5	0·8974	11·0	0·9329	58·3	0·9722
64·5	0·8210	40·6	0·8636	16·9	0·8981	12·1	0·9341	59·0	0·9726
64·0	0·8221	40·0	0·8646	16·4	0·8989	13·1	0·9353	60·4	0·9734
63·6	0·8227	39·6	0·8653	15·9	0·8996	14·2	0·9364	61·1	0·9738
63·1	0·8238	39·1	0·8660	15·6	0·9000	15·3	0·9376	61·8	0·9742
62·5	0·8249	38·4	0·8671	15·0	0·9008	16·0	0·8384	63·2	0·9750
62·0	0·8259	38·0	0·8678	14·5	0·9015	17·1	0·9396	63·9	0·9754
61·6	0·8266	37·6	0·8685	13·9	0·9023	18·2	0·9407	65·3	0·9762
61·1	0·8277	37·1	0·8692	13·4	0·9030	19·3	0·9419	66·0	0·9766
60·5	0·8287	36·4	0·8702	13·1	0·9034	20·0	0·9426	67·4	0·9774
60·0	0·8298	35·9	0·8709	12·5	0·9041	21·2	0·9437	68·0	0·9778
59·5	0·8308	35·5	0·8716	12·0	0·9049	22·2	0·9448	69·4	0·9786
59·1	0·8315	35·0	0·8723	11·4	0·9056	23·1	0·9456	70·1	0·9790
58·6	0·8326	34·5	0·8730	11·1	0·9060	23·9	0·9464	71·4	0·9798
58·0	0·8336	34·1	0·8737	10·6	0·9067	24·3	0·9468	72·1	0·9802
57·5	0·8347	33·6	0·8744	10·0	0·9075	25·1	0·9476	73·5	0·9810
57·1	0·8354	32·9	0·8755	9·4	0·9082	26·3	0·9488	74·1	0·9814
56·6	0·8365	32·4	0·8762	8·9	0·9089	27·1	0·9496	75·4	0·9822
56·0	0·8376	32·0	0·8769	8·3	0·9097	28·0	0·9503	76·1	0·9826
55·5	0·8386	31·5	0·8776	8·0	0·9100	29·2	0·9515	77·3	0·9834
55·0	0·8366	31·0	0·8783	7·4	0·9107	30·1	0·9522	78·0	0·9838
54·6	0·8343	30·5	0·8790	7·1	0·9111	31·0	0·9530	79·2	0·9846
54·1	0·8413	30·0	0·8797	6·5	0·9118	32·3	0·9542	80·4	0·9854
53·5	0·8424	29·5	0·8804	5·9	0·9126	33·2	0·9550	81·1	0·9858
53·1	0·8431	29·0	0·8811	5·6	0·9130	34·2	0·9557	82·3	0·9866
52·5	0·8441	28·5	0·8818	5·0	0·9137	35·1	0·9565	83·5	0·9874
52·1	0·8448	28·0	0·8825	4·5	0·9145	36·1	0·9573	84·0	0·9878
51·5	0·8459	27·5	0·8832	3·9	0·9152	37·1	0·9580	85·2	0·9886
51·1	0·8465	27·0	0·8840	3·3	0·9159	38·1	0·9588	86·3	0·9894
50·5	0·8476	26·5	0·8847	3·0	0·9163	39·1	0·9596	87·4	0·9902
50·1	0·8482	26·0	0·8854	2·4	0·9170	40·1	0·9603	88·0	0·9906
49·5	0·8493	25·5	0·8861	1·9	0·9178	41·1	0·9611	89·1	0·9914
49·1	0·8499	25·0	0·8869	1·6	0·9182	42·2	0·9619	90·2	0·9922
48·5	0·8510	24·5	0·8876	1·0	0·9189	43·3	0·9627	91·2	0·9930
48·0	0·8516	24·0	0·8883	0·3	0·9196	44·4	0·9635	92·3	0·9938
47·6	0·8523	23·5	0·8890	proof	0·9200	45·0	0·9638	93·3	0·9946
47·0	0·8533	23·0	0·8897	under proof		46·1	0·9646	94·3	0·9954
46·6	0·8540	22·5	0·8904	1·3	0·9214	47·3	0·9654	95·4	0·9962
46·0	0·8550	21·9	0·8912	2·2	0·9226	47·9	0·9657	96·4	0·9970
45·6	0·8556	21·4	0·8919	3·1	0·9237	49·1	0·9665	97·3	0·9978
45·0	0·8566	20·9	0·8926	4·0	0·9248	50·3	0·9674	98·2	0·9986
44·6	0·8573	20·4	0·8933	5·0	0·9259	51·0	0·9677	99·1	0·9993
43·9	0·8583	19·9	0·8940	6·0	0·9270	52·2	0·9685	100·0	1·0000
43·5	0·8590								

And now, by reference either to Drinkwater's, Tralle's, or Gay-Lussac's Tables, the operator will be enabled to find, by the knowledge of the density or specific gravity, at the temperature at which the operation was performed, the per-centage of real alcohol, either by weight or by volume.

In France, Gay-Lussac's *alcoölomètre* is usually employed. It is a common glass hydrometer, with the scale on the stem divided into 100 parts or degrees. The lowest division, marked 0, denotes the specific gravity of pure water; and 100, that of absolute alcohol, both at 15° C. (59° F.) The intermediate degrees, of course, show the per-centage of absolute alcohol by volume at 15° C.; and the instrument is accompanied by the Tables already given for ascertaining the per-centage at any other temperature.

Alcoholometry of Liquids containing besides Alcohol, Saccharine Matters, Colouring Principles, &c., such as Wines, Beer, Liqueurs, &c.

In order to determine the proportion of absolute alcohol contained in wines, or other mixtures of alcohol and water with saccharine and other non-volatile substances, the most accurate method consists in submitting a known volume of the liquid to distillation (in a glass retort, for instance); then, by determining the specific gravity of the distilled product, to ascertain the per-centage of alcohol in this distillate, which may be regarded as essentially a mixture of pure alcohol and water. The distillation is carried on until the last portions have the gravity of distilled water; by then ascertaining the total volume of the distillate, and with the knowledge of its per-centage of alcohol and the volume of the original liquor used, the method of calculating the quantity of alcohol present in the wine, or other liquor, is sufficiently obvious.

In carrying out these distillations care must be taken to prevent the evaporation of the spirit from the distillate, by keeping the condenser cool. And Professor Mulder recommends the use of a refrigerator, consisting of a glass tube fixed in the centre of a jar, so that it may be kept filled with cold water. The tube must be bent at a right angle, and terminate in a cylindrical graduated measure-glass, shaped like a bottle.[1]

It is well to continue the distillation until about two-thirds of the liquid has passed over.

This process, though the most accurate for the estimation of the strength of alcoholic liquors, is still liable to error. The volatile acids and ethers pass over with the alcohol into the distillate, and, to a slight extent, affect the specific gravity. This error may be, to a great extent, overcome by mixing a little chalk with the wine, or other liquor, previous to distillation.

By this method Professor Brande made, some years ago, determinations of the strength of the following wines, and other liquors:[2]—

Proportion of Spirit per Cent. by Measure.

Lissa	. . . . average	25·41	Orange . . . . average 11·26
Raisin	. . . „	25·12	Elder . . . . „ 8·79
Marsala	. . . „	25·09	
Port (of 7 samples)	. „	22·96	Cider . . average 5·21 to 9·87
Madeira	. . „	22·27	Perry . . . „ 7·26
Sherry (of 4 samples)	. „	19·17	Mead . . . „ 7·32
Teneriffe	. . .	19·79	Ale, Burton 8·88
Lisbon	. . .	18·94	Ale, Edinburgh } average 6·87 { 6·20
Malaga	. . .	18·94	Ale, Dorchester } { 5·55
Bucellas	. . .	18·49	Brown Stout . . 6·80
Cape Madeira	. average	20·51	London Porter . . average 4·20
Roussillon	. . . „	19·00	London Small Beer . „ 1·28
Claret	. . . „	15·10	
Sauterne	. . . „	14·22	Brandy . . . „ 53·39
Burgundy	. . . „	14·57	Rum . . . . „ 53·68
Hock	. . . „	12·08	Gin . . . . „ 57·60
Tent	. . . „	13·30	Scotch Whisky . . „ 54·32
Champagne	. . . „	12·61	Irish Whisky . . . „ 53·90
Gooseberry	. . . „	11·84	

[1] The Chemistry of Wine, by G. J. Mulder, edited by H. Bence Jones, M.D.
[2] Brande's Manual of Chemistry; also Philosophical Trans. 1811.

The following results were obtained by the same chemist more recently by this process (1854) :—

Per-centage of Alcohol by Volume.

Port (1834) . . .	22·46	Port (best) . . .	20·2
Sherry (Montilla) . .	19·95	Marcobrunner . .	8·3
Madeira . . .	22·40	Champagne (1st) . .	12·12
Claret (Haut Brion) .	10·0	Champagne (2nd) . .	10·85
Chambertin . .	11·7	Home Ale . . .	6·4
Sherry (low quality) .	20·7	Export Ale . . .	6·4
Sherry (brown) . .	23·1	Strong Ale . . .	9·0
Amontillado . . .	20·5	Stout	5·7
Mansanilla . . .	14·4	Porter	4·18

Dr. Christison determined the Alcoholic Strength of Wines as follows :—

	Per-centage of absolute alcohol by weight in the wine	Per-centage of proof spirit by volume
Port, weakest	14·97	30·56
mean of 7 wines . . .	16·20	33·91
strongest	17·10	37·27
White Port	14·97	31·31
Sherry, weakest	13·98	30·84
mean of 13 wines, excluding those very } long kept in cask . . .	15·37	33·59
Sherry, strongest	16·17	35·12
mean of 9 wines, very long kept in cask } in the East Indies . . .	14·72	32·39
Madre de Xeres . . .	16·90	37·06
Madeira { all long } strongest . . .	16·90	36·81
{ in cask } weakest . .	14·09	30·80
Teneriffe, long in cask at Calcutta . .	13·84	30·21
Cercial	15·45	83·65
Dry Lisbon	16·14	34·71
Chiraz	12·95	28·30
Amontillado	12·63	27·60
Claret, a 1st growth of 1811 . .	7·72	16·95
Château Latour, 1st growth, 1825 .	7·78	17·06
Rosan, 2nd growth, 1825 . . .	7·61	16·74
Ordinary Claret, a superior 'Vin ordinaire' .	8·9	18·96
Rives Altes	·31	22·35
Malmsey	12·86	28·37
Rudesheimer, superior quality . .	8·40	18·44
Rudesheimer, inferior quality . .	6·90	15·19
Hambacher, superior quality . .	7·35	16·15
Giles' Edinburgh Ale, before bottling .	5·70	12·60
Same Ale, two years in bottle . .	86·06	13·40
Superior London Porter, 4 mo. in bottle .	5·36	11·91

Dr. Bence Jones states that the different fermented liquids which he has examined might, in regard to their strength, or stimulating power, be arranged thus :—

Cider	100	Champagne . . .	241
Porter	109	Madeira . . .	325
Stout	133	Marsala . . .	341
Ale	141	Port . . .	358
Moselle	158	Sherry . . .	358
Claret	166	Geneva . . .	811
Burgundy . . .	191	Brandy . . .	986
Hock	191	Rum . . .	1,213

Thus, ten glasses of cider or porter, six glasses of claret, five glasses of Burgundy, four glasses of champagne, three glasses of port, sherry, or Marsala, are equivalent to one glass of brandy.

M. l'Abbé Brossard-Vidal, of Toulon,[1] has proposed to estimate the strength of alcoholic liquors by determining their boiling point. Since water boils at 100° C. (212° F.), and absolute alcohol at 78·4° (173° F.), it is evident that a mixture of water and alcohol will have a higher boiling point the larger the quantity of water present in it. This method is even applicable to mixtures containing other bodies in solution besides spirit and water, since it has been shown that sugar and salts, when present (in moderate quantities), have only a very trifling effect in raising the boiling point, and the process has the great advantage of facility and rapidity of execution, though of course not comparable to the method by distillation, for accuracy.

Mr. Field's patent (1847) alcoholometer is likewise founded upon the same principle. The instrument was subsequently improved by Dr. Ure.

The apparatus consists simply of a spirit-lamp placed under a little boiler containing the alcoholic liquor, into which fits a thermometer of very fine bore.

When the liquor is stronger than proof spirit, the variation in the boiling point is so small that an accurate result cannot possibly be obtained; and, in fact, spirit approaching this strength should be diluted with an equal volume of water before submitting it to ebullition, and then the result doubled.

Another source of error is the elevation of the boiling point, when the liquor is kept heated for any length of time; it is, however, nearly obviated by the addition of common salt to the solution in the boiler of the apparatus, in the proportion of 35 or 40 grains. In order to correct the difference arising from higher or lower pressure of the atmosphere, the scale on which the thermometric and other divisions are marked is made moveable up and down the thermometer tube; and every time, before commencing a set of experiments, a preliminary experiment is made of boiling some pure distilled water in the apparatus, and the zero point on the scale (which indicates the boiling point of water) is adjusted at the level of the surface of the mercury. On p. 55 will be found a Table showing the boiling point of alcohol of different specific gravities.

But even when performed with the utmost care, this process is still liable to very considerable errors, for it is extremely difficult to observe the boiling point to within a degree; and after all, the fixed ingredients present undoubtedly do seriously raise the boiling point of the mixture—in fact, to the extent of from half to a whole degree, according to the amount present.

Silbermann's Method.—M. Silbermann[2] has proposed another method of estimating the strength of alcoholic liquors based upon their expansion by heat. It is well known that, between zero and 100° C. (212° F.), the dilatation of alcohol is triple that of water, and this difference of expansion is even greater between 25° C. (77° F.) and 50° C. (122° F.); it is evident, therefore, that the expansion between these two temperatures becomes a measure of the amount of alcohol present in any mixture. The presence of salts and organic substances, such as sugar, colouring, and extractive matters, in solution or suspension in the liquid, is said not materially to affect the accuracy of the result; and M. Silbermann has devised an apparatus for applying this principle, in a ready and expeditious manner, to the estimation of the strength of alcoholic liquors. The instrument may be obtained of the philosophical instrument makers of London and of Liverpool.

It consists of a brass plate, on which are fixed—1st, an ordinary mercurial thermometer graduated from 22° to 50° C. (77° to 122° F.), these being the working temperatures of the *dilatometer*; and 2ndly, the dilatometer itself, which consists of a glass pipette, open at both ends, and of the shape shown in the figure. A valve of cork or india-rubber closes the tapering end A, which valve is attached to a rod, *b b*, fastened to the supporting plate, and connected with a spring, *n*, by which the lower orifice of the pipette can be opened or closed at will. The pipette is filled, exactly up to the zero point, with the mixture to be examined—this being accomplished by the aid of a piston working tightly in the long and wide limb of the pipette; the action of which serves also another valuable purpose—viz. that of drawing any

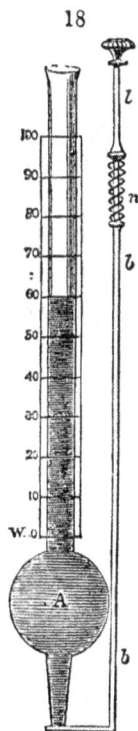

---

[1] *Comptes Rendus*, xxvii. 374.   [2] *Ibid.* xxvii. 418.

bubbles of air out of the liquid. By now observing the dilatation of the column of liquid when the temperature of the whole apparatus is raised, by immersion in a water-bath, from 25° to 50°, the co-efficient of expansion of the liquid is obtained, and hence the proportion of alcohol — the instrument being, in fact, so graduated, by experiments previously made upon mixtures of known composition, as to give at once the per-centage of alcohol.

Another alcoholometer, which, like the former, is more remarkable for the great facility and expedition with which approximative results can be obtained than for a high degree of accuracy, was invented by M. Geisler, of Bonn, and depends upon the measurement of the tension of the vapour of the liquid, as indicated by the height to which it raises a column of mercury.

Geisler's Alcoholometer. It consists of a closed vessel in which the alcoholic mixture is raised to the boiling point, and the tension of the vapour observed by the depression of a column of mercury in one limb of a tube, the indication being rendered more manifest by the elevation of the other end of the column.

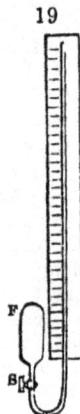

The wine or other liquor of which it is desired to ascertain the strength, is put into the little flask, F, which, when completely filled, is screwed on to the glass which contains mercury, and is closed by a stopcock at s. The entire apparatus, which at present is in an inverted position, is now stood erect, the flask and lower extremity of the tube being immersed in a water-bath. The vinous liquid is thus heated to the boiling point, and its vapour forces the mercury up into the long limb of the tube. The instrument having been graduated, once for all, by actual experiment, the per-centage of alcohol is read off at once on the stem by the height to which the mercurial column rises.

To show how nearly the results obtained by this instrument agree with those obtained by the distillation process, comparative experiments were made on the same wines by Dr. Bence Jones.[1]

	By Distillation (Mr. Witt) per cent. by measure.	By Alcoholometer per cent. by measure.
Port, 1834	22·46	23·2 / 23·5
Sherry, Montilla	19·95	20·7 / 20·6 / 20·6
Madeira	22·40	23·5 / 23·2
Haut Brion claret	10·0	11·1 / 11·1
Chambertin	11·7	13·2 / 13·0
Low-quality sherry	20·7	21·1 / 20·9
Brown sherry	23·1	23·0 / 23·3
Amontillado	20·5	21·0 / 21·0
Mansanilla	14·4	15·4 / 15·4
Port, best	20·2	21·1 / 21·0
Marcobrunner	8·3	9·7 / 9·5
Home ale	6·4	7·0 / 7·1
Export ale	6·4	7·0 / 6·9
Strong ale	2·0	10·7 / 10·8

Tabarié's Method.—There is another method of determining the alcoholic contents of mixtures, which especially recommends itself on account of its simplicity. The

[1] On the Acidity, Sweetness, and Strength of different Wines, by H. Bence Jones, M.D., F.R.S. Proceedings of the Royal Institution, February, 1854.

specific gravity of the liquor is first determined, half its volume is next evaporated in the open air, sufficient water is then added to the remainder to restore its original volume, and the specific gravity again ascertained. By deducting the specific gravity before the expulsion of the alcohol from that obtained afterwards, the difference gives a specific gravity indicating the per-centage of alcohol, which may be found by referring to Gay-Lussac's or one of the other Tables. Tabarié has constructed a peculiar instrument for determining these specific gravities, which he calls an œnometer; but they may be performed either by a specific-gravity bottle or by a hydrometer in the usual way.

Of course this method cannot be absolutely accurate; nevertheless, Prof. Mulder's experience with it has led him to prefer it to any of the methods before described, especially where a large number of samples have to be examined. He states that the results are almost as accurate as those obtained by distillation. The evaporation of the solution may be accelerated by conducting hot steam through it.

Adulterations.—Absolute alcohol should be entirely free from water. This may be recognised by digesting the spirit with pure anhydrous sulphate of copper. If the spirit contain any water, the white salt becomes tinged blue, from the formation of the blue hydrated sulphate of copper.

Rectified spirit, proof spirit, and the other mixtures of pure alcohol and water, should be colourless, free from odour and taste. If containing methylic or amylic alcohols, they are immediately recognised by one or other of these simple tests.

Dr. Ure states that if wood-spirit be contained in alcohol, it may be detected to the greatest minuteness by the test of caustic potash, a little of which, in powder, causing wood-spirit to become speedily yellow and brown, while it gives no tint to alcohol. Thus 1 per cent. of wood-spirit may be discovered in any sample of spirits of wine.

The admixture with a larger proportion than the due amount of water is of course determined by estimating the per-centage of absolute alcohol by one or other of the several methods just described in detail.

The adulterations and sophistications to which the various spirits known as rum, brandy, whisky, gin, &c. are subjected, will be best described under these respective heads, since these liquors are themselves mixtures of alcohol and water with sugar, colouring matters, flavouring ethers, &c.

ALDEHYDE. Aldehyde was first obtained by Döbereiner, who named it *Light Oxygen Ether.* The name is an abbreviation of *Alcohol dehydrogenatum.* It is the fluid obtained from alcohol by the removal of two atoms of hydrogen. Thus, alcohol being represented by the formula $C^4 H^6 O^2$ ($\mathbf{C^2 H^6 O}$), aldehyde becomes $C^4 H^4 O^2$ ($\mathbf{C^2 H^4 O}$). See LAMPIC ACID.

Preparation.—Aldehyde is prepared by various processes of oxidation. Liebig has published several methods, of which the following is perhaps the best. Three parts of peroxide of manganese, three of sulphuric acid, two of water, and two of alcohol of 80 per cent., are well mixed and carefully distilled in a spacious retort. The extreme volatility of aldehyde renders good condensation absolutely necessary. The contents of the retort are to be distilled over a gentle and manageable fire until frothing commences, or the distillate becomes acid. This generally takes place when about one-third has passed over. The fluid in the receiver is to have about its own weight of chloride of calcium added, and, after slight digestion, is to be carefully distilled on the water-bath. The distillate is again to be treated in the same way. By these processes a fluid will be obtained entirely free from water, but containing several impurities. To obtain the aldehyde in a state of purity it is necessary, in the first place, to obtain aldehyde-ammonia; this may be accomplished in the following manner:—The last distillate is to be mixed in a flask with twice its volume of ether, and, the flask being placed in a vessel surrounded by a freezing mixture, dry ammoniacal gas is passed in until the fluid is saturated. In a short time crystals of the compound sought separate in considerable quantity. The aldehyde-ammonia, being collected on a filter, or in the neck of a funnel, is to be washed with ether, and dried by pressure between folds of filtering paper, followed by exposure to the air. It now becomes necessary to obtain the pure aldehyde from the compound with ammonia. For this purpose two parts are to be dissolved in an equal quantity of water, and three parts of sulphuric acid, mixed with four of water, are to be added. The whole is to be distilled on the water-bath, the temperature, at first, being very low, and the operation being stopped as soon as the water boils. The distillate is to be placed in a retort connected with a good condensing apparatus, and, as soon as all the joints are known to be tight, chloride of calcium, in fragments, is to be added. The heat arising from the hydration of the chloride causes the distillation to commence, but it is carried on by a water-bath. The distillate, after one more rectification over chloride of calcium, at a temperature not exceeding 80° F., will consist of pure aldehyde. Aldehyde is a colourless, very volatile, and mobile fluid, having the density 0·800 at 32°. It boils, under ordinary atmospheric pressure, at 70° F. Its vapour density is 1·532. Its formula corresponds to four volumes of vapour; we consequently obtain the theoretical vapour density by multiplying its atomic weight = 44 by half the density of hydrogen, or ·0346. The number thus found is 1·5224, corresponding as nearly as could be desired to the experimental result.

Aldehyde is produced in a great number of processes, particularly during the destructive distillation of various organic matters, and in processes of oxidation. From alcohol aldehyde may be procured by oxidation with platinum black, nitric acid, chromic acid, chlorine (in presence of water); or, as we have seen, a mixture of peroxide of manganese and sulphuric acid. Certain oils, by destructive distillation, yield it. Wood vinegar in the crude state contains aldehyde as well as wood-spirit. Lactic acid, when in combination with weak bases, yields it on destructive distillation. Various animal and vegetable products afford aldehyde by distillation with oxidizing agents, such as sulphuric acid and peroxide of manganese, or bichromate of potash.

The word aldehyde, like that of alcohol, is gradually becoming used in a much more extended sense than it was formerly. By the term is now understood any organic substance which, by assimilating two atoms of hydrogen, yields a substance having the properties of an alcohol, or, by taking up two atoms of oxygen, yields an acid. It is this latter property which has induced certain chemists to say that there is the same relation between an aldehyde and its acid as between inorganic acids ending in *ous* and *ic*. Several very interesting and important substances are now known to belong to the class of aldehydes. The essential oils are, in several instances, composed principally of bodies having the properties of aldehydes. Among the most prominent may be mentioned the oils of bitter almonds, cumin, cinnamon, rue, &c. Now that the character of the aldehydes is becoming better understood, the chances of artificially producing the essential oils above alluded to in the commercial scale become greatly increased. A substitute for one of them has been for some years known under the very incorrect name of artificial oil of bitter almonds. See NITROBENZOLE.—C. G. W.

ALDEHYDE GREEN, *Aniline Green,* or *Emeraldine.* This dye was discovered in 1863 by M. Cherpin, of Saint Ouen, and is employed for dyeing silk; the colour is especially brilliant by candle-light. It may be conveniently prepared by adding one-half part of aldehyde to a cold solution of one part of magenta in three of strong sulphuric acid, and one of water. This mixture, when heated, yields an unstable blue substance known as *aldehyde blue.* By pouring this into a large bulk of boiling water containing about three or four times as much hyposulphite of soda as magenta originally employed, and then boiling and filtering the product, the aldehyde green will be obtained in the filtrate. See ANILINE.

ALDER. (*Aune,* Fr.; *Erle,* Ger.; *Alnus glutinosa,* Lin.) A tree, different species of which are indigenous to Europe, Asia, and America. The common alder seldom grows to a height of more than 40 feet. The wood is stated to be very durable under water. The piles at Venice, and those of Old London Bridge, are stated to have been of alder; and it was much used for pipes, pumps, and sluices. The charcoal of this wood is used for gunpowder.

ALE. The fermented infusion of pale malted barley, combined with infusion of hops. See BEER.

20

ALEMBIC. A Still. See DISTILLATION. The term is, however, applied to a still of peculiar construction, in which the *head,* or *capital,* is a separate piece, fitted and ground to the neck of the boiler, or cucurbit, or otherwise carefully united with a lute. The alembic has this advantage over the common retort, that the residue of distillation may be easily cleared out of the body. It is likewise capable, when skilfully managed, of distilling a much larger quantity of liquor in a given time than a retort of equal capacity. In France the term alembic, or rather *alambic,* is used to designate a glass still.

ALEMBROTH, SALT OF. (*Sal Alembroth.*) The *salt of wisdom* of the alchemists; a compound of bichloride of mercury and sal ammoniac. If two atoms of bichloride of mercury are mixed with one atom of sal ammoniac and eight atoms of water, at 140° this mixture is fluid, but the salt of alembroth crystallises on cooling.

ALENÇON LACE. A French lace, of which it is one of the richest, finest, strongest, and most expensive. It has a six-sided mesh of two threads wove with pure hand-spun linen thread. See LACE.

ALEXANDRITE. A variety of Chrysoberyl occurring in large twin crystals, which are usually arranged in six-rayed star-shaped groups. The mineral presents an emerald-green colour, due probably to the presence of chromium; but by transmitted light the colour is columbine-red. It is found in the emerald-mines of Takowaja, 180 versts east of Katerinburg, in the Ural Mountains; but is not sufficiently clear and free from flaws to be used as a precious stone.

ALGÆ. (*Varech*, Fr.; *Seegras*, or *Alge*, Ger.) An order of cryptogamous plants, including the seaweeds (*fucus*) and the lavers (*ulva*) growing in salt water, and the freshwater confervas. We have only to deal with those seaweeds which are of any commercial value.

Dr. Pereira gives the following list of esculent seaweeds:

Rhodomenia palmata (or Dulse)	*Iridæa edulis.*
Rhodomenia ciliata.	*Alaria esculenta.*
Laminaria saccharina.	*Ulva latissima.*

Rhodomenia palmata passes under a variety of names, dulse, dylish, or dellish, and amongst the Highlanders it is called *dulling*, or waterleaf. It is employed as food by the poor of many nations; when well washed, it is chewed by the peasantry of Ireland without being dressed. It is nutritious, but sudorific, has the smell of violets, imparts a mucilaginous feel to the mouth, leaving a slightly acrid taste. In Iceland the dulse is thoroughly washed in fresh water and dried in the air. When thus treated it becomes covered with a white powdery substance, which is sweet and palatable; this is *mannite* (see MANNA), which Dr. Stenhouse proposes to obtain from seaweeds. 'In the dried state it is used in Iceland with fish and butter, or else, by the higher classes, boiled in milk, with the addition of rye flour. It is preserved packed in close casks: a fermented liquor is produced in Kamtschatka from this seaweed, and in the North of Europe and in the Grecian Archipelago cattle are fed upon it.'—*Stenhouse.*

Laminaria saccharina yields 12·15 per cent. of mannite, while the *Rhodomenia palmata* contains not more than 2 or 3 per cent.

Iridæa edulis.—The fronds of this weed are of a dull purple colour, flat, and succulent. It is employed as food by fishermen, either raw or pinched between hot irons, and its taste is then said to resemble roasted oysters.

Alaria esculenta.—Mr. Drummond informs us that on the coast of Antrim, 'it is often gathered for eating, but the part used is the leaflets, and not the midrib, as is commonly stated. These have a very pleasant taste and flavour, but soon cover the mouth with a tenacious greenish crust, which causes a sensation somewhat like that of the fat of a heart or kidney.'

Ulva latissima (Broad green laver).—This is rarely used, being considered inferior to the *Porphyra laciniata* (Laciniated purple laver). This alga is abundant on all our shores. It is pickled with salt, and sold in England as *laver*, in Ireland as *sloke*, and in Scotland as *slaak*. The London shops are mostly supplied with laver from the coasts of Devonshire. When stewed, it is brought to the table and eaten with pepper, butter or oil, and lemon-juice or vinegar. Some persons stew it with leeks and onions. The pepper dulse (*Laurencia pinnatifida*), distinguished for its pungent taste, is often used as a condiment when other seaweeds are eaten. 'Tangle' (*Laminaria digitata*), so called in Scotland, is termed 'red-ware' in the Orkneys, 'sea-wand' in the Highlands, and 'sea-girdles' in England. The flat leathery fronds of this weed, when young, are employed as food. Mr. Simmonds tells us, 'There was a time when the cry of "Buy dulse and tangle" was as common in the streets of Edinburgh and Glasgow, as is that of "water-cresses" now in our metropolis.'— *Society of Arts' Journal.*

Laminaria potatorum.—The large sea tangle is used abundantly by the inhabitants of the Straits of Magellan and by the Fuegians. Under the name of 'Bull Kelp' it is used as food in New Zealand and Van Diemen's land. It is stated to be exceedingly nutritive and fattening.

Chondrus crispus (chondrus, from χόνδρος, cartilage).—Carrageen, Irish, or pearl moss. For purposes of diet and for medicinal uses, this alga is collected on the west coast of Ireland, washed, bleached by exposure to the sun, and dried. It is not unfrequently used in Ireland by painters and plasterers as a substitute for size. It has also been successfully applied, instead of isinglass, in making blanc-mange and jellies; and in addition to its use in medicine, for which purpose it was introduced by Dr. Todhunter, of Dublin, about 1831, a thick mucilage of carrageen, scented with some prepared spirit, is sold as *bandoline*, *fixature*, or *clysphitique*, and it is employed for stiffening silks. According to Dr. Davy, carrageen consists of

Gummy matter	28·5
Gelatinous matter	49·0
Insoluble matter	22·5
	100·0

The following results, obtained by Dr. Apjohn and Dr. Davy, show, in a satisfactory manner, the value of the algæ. The amount of water is less than that which belongs to the algæ when fresh from the sea, all these having undergone a partial drying in the progress of carriage from the coast :—

Specimens supplied by Dr. Davy, and dried at 212°—

	Nitrogen per cent.
Chondrus crispus, bleached	2·152
Fucus vesiculosus	2·397
Rhodomenia palmata (Dylish). . . .	3·776

Kinds of Algæ	Water	Dry Matter	Per Cent. of Nitrogen in Dry Matter	Protein contained in Dry Matter
Chondrus crispus, bleached . . .	17·92	82·08	1·534	9·587
Chondrus crispus, unbleached, Ballycastle	21·47	78·53	2·142	13·387
Gigartina mammillosa, Ballycastle .	21·55	78·45	2·198	13·737
Chondrus crispus, bleached, (2nd experiment)	19·79	80·21	1·485	9·281
Chondrus crispus, unbleached, Ballycastle, (2nd experiment) . .	19·96	80·04	2·510	15·687
Laminaria digitata, or Dulse tangle, Ballycastle	21·38	78·62	1·588	9·925
Laminaria digitata, or Black tangle, Ballycastle	31·05	68·95	1·396	8·725
Rhodomenia palmata, or Dylish, Ballycastle	16·56	83·44	3·465	21·656
Porphyra laciniata, Ballycastle . .	17·41	82·59	4·650	29·062
Iridæa edulis, Ballycastle . . .	19·61	80·39	3·088	19·300
Alaria esculenta, or Murlins, Ballycastle	17·91	82·09	2·424	15·150
Mean composition of these Algæ .	20·42	79·58	2·407	15·045

The quantity of nitrogen contained in some of these plants is remarkably large, and will, of course, with the proteinaceous substances detected in all the Algæ, account for the high nutritive value ascribed to them.

Plocaria candida.—Ceylon moss; Edible moss. This moss is exported from the islands of the Indian Archipelago, forming a portion of the cargoes of nearly all the junks. It is stated by Mr. Crawford, in his 'History of the Indian Archipelago,' that on the spots where it is collected, the prices seldom exceed from 5s. 8d. to 7s. 6d. per cwt. The Chinese use it in the form of a jelly with sugar, as a sweetmeat, and apply it in the arts as an excellent paste. The gummy matter which they employ for covering lanterns, varnishing paper, &c., is made chiefly from this moss.

As ordinarily sold in Ceylon, it appears to consist of several varieties of marine productions, with the *Plocaria* intermixed.

The *Agar-Agar* of Malacca belongs to this variety; and probably seaweeds of this character are used by the Salangana or esculent swallow in constructing their nests, which are esteemed so great a delicacy by the Chinese. The plant is found on the rocks of Pulo Ticoos and on the shores of the neighbouring islands. It is blanched in the sun for two days, or until it is quite white. It is obtained on submerged banks in the neighbourhood of Macassar, Celebes, by the Bajow-laut, or sea-gipsies, who send it to China. It is also collected on the reefs and rocky submerged ledges in the neighbourhood of Singapore. Mr. Montgomery Martin informs us that Agar-Agar, produces in China from six to eight dollars per pecul in its dry and bulky state. From 6,000 to 12,000 peculs are produced annually, the pecul being equal to 100 catties of 1·333 lbs. each.

Similar to this, perhaps the same in character, is the *Agal-Agal*, another species of seaweed. It dissolves into a glutinous substance, and its principal use is for gumming silks and paper, as nothing equals it for paste, nor is it liable to be eaten by insects. The Chinese make a beautiful kind of lantern formed of netted thread washed over with this gum, and which is extremely light and transparent.

Dr. Macgowan, of Ningpo, forwarded to the Society of Arts, through Sir John Bowring, the following algæ, which he thus names and describes :—

Tan-shwin grass, so named from the place, on the coast of Formosa, whence it is procured. It is used for making *yang-tsai* (ocean-vegetable).

Nin-mau (ox-hair) grass. Made into an iced jelly, and sold in the streets, in hot weather, sugared.

Hâi-tâi (sea-tape). Sent into the interior, wherever fossil coal is used. It is considered corrective of the deleterious exhalations of that fuel. It is usually boiled with pork. This kind comes from Shantung province.

Tsz-tsai (purple vegetable). Often eaten as it is, to give a relish to rice, or cooked.

Fah-tsai (hair vegetable). Boiled, either with animal or vegetable articles, forms a broth. Also the gills eaten with sugar.

Ki-tsai (hen-foot vegetable). Cooked with soy or vinegar. Used by women to make the hair glossy, and to strengthen it. A kind of Bandoline.

Sea-tape, from Japan. It is preferred to the former.

Within the last few years considerable improvements have been effected in the economic applications of algæ or seaweeds. Mr. E. C. C. Stanford's method of utilising the marine algæ is carried out at the works of the British Seaweed Company in the Hebrides. The seaweed is collected during the winter, and the Company is thus enabled to employ a large number of hands at a time when they would otherwise be unoccupied. The dried and compressed weed is distilled in retorts at a low red heat ; a larger quantity of iodine is thus obtained than would be yielded by burning the weed for kelp in the ordinary way, whilst the alkaline salts are obtained more easily and economically. Further, a number of volatile organic products—such as tar, ammonia, and acetic acid—are collected from the distillation, and an illuminating gas is also obtained : indeed, the Company's works are lighted by seaweed gas. Finally, the carbonaceous residue in the retort, known as seaweed charcoal, is recommended for use as a valuable deodorizer instead of earth in the dry-closet system. A collection of products obtained from seaweed by Stanford's process was exhibited in the International Exhibition of 1871. See KELP ; IODINE.

ALGAROBA. See ALGAROVILLA.

ALGAROTH, POWDER OF. *Powder of Algarotti,—English Powder.* This salt was discovered by Algarotti, a physician of Verona. Chloride of antimony is formed by boiling black sulphide of antimony with hydrochloric acid : on pouring the solution into water, a white flocky precipitate falls, which is an oxychloride of antimony. If the water be hot, the precipitate is distinctly crystalline ; this is the powder of algaroth. This oxychloride is used to furnish oxide of antimony in the preparation of tartar emetic.

ALGAROVILLA. This substance is called by the Spaniards *Algaroba*, from the resemblance it bears to the fruit of the Carob (*Ceratonia siliqua*), which is a native of Europe, in the southern countries of Spain and Portugal. It is the fruit of a tree which grows in Chili, of which the botanical name is *Prosopis pallida*, according to Captain Bagnald, R.N., who first brought a sample of it to this country in the year 1832. It consists of pods bruised and agglutinated more or less with the extractive exudation of the seeds and husks. According to a more recent determination, algarovilla is said to be the product of the tree Juga Marthæ of Santa Martha, a province of New Carthagena.

It is an astringent substance replete with tannin, capable, by its infusion in water, of tanning leather, for which purpose it possesses more than four times the power of good oak-bark. Its active matter is very soluble in water at a boiling temperature. The seeds are merely nutritive and demulcent, but contain no astringent property. This resides in the husks. The seeds in the entire pod constitute about one-fifth of the weight, and they are three or four in number in each oblong pod. Alcohol of 60 per cent. over proof dissolves 64 parts in 100 of this substance. The solution consists chiefly of tannin, with a very little resinous matter. Water dissolves somewhat more of it, and affords a very styptic-tasted solution, which precipitates solution of isinglass very copiously, like infusion of galls and catechu. Its solution forms with sulphate of iron a black precipitate.

ALGERIAN ONYX, or ONYX MARBLE. A stalagmitic carbonate of lime, resembling the alabaster of the ancients. The chief quarries are at Ain-Tekbalet in the province of Oran, in Algeria. The deposit there forms regular beds, nearly horizontal, presenting a thickness of from 6 to 10 mètres, and extending over an area of more than 100 hectares. Originally the quarries were worked by the Romans, and subsequently by the Moors of Tlemcen. A few years ago they were re-discovered, and are now actively worked; the marble being highly prized as an ornamental stone. A similar material has been found in the Caucasus, and is worked at Tiflis.

ALIMENT. (*Alimentum*, from *alo*, to feed). The food necessary for the human body, and capable of maintaining it in a state of health.

1. Nitrogenous substances are required to deposit, from the blood, the organised tissue and solid muscle.

2. And carbonaceous, non-nitrogenous bodies, to aid in the processes of respiration, and in the supply of carbonaceous elements, as fat, &c., for the due support of animal heat.

For information on these substances, consult Liebig's 'Animal Chemistry,' the investigations of Dr. Lyon Playfair, and Dr. Robert Dundas Thompson's 'Experimental Researches on Food,' 1846. See FOOD.

ALIMENTARY SUBSTANCES. See NUTRITION.

ALIZARINE. $C^{28}H^8O^8$ ($C^{14}H^8O^4$). One of the red colouring principles of Madder. See MADDER.

In 1869 Messrs. Graebe and Liebermann made the important discovery that alizarine might be produced artificially from anthracene, one of the heavy products of coal-tar distillation. Both scientifically and commercially, the discovery was one of unusual interest: it furnished the first instance of the synthetical formation of an organic colouring matter, and at the same time opened up a new branch of industry.

According to Messrs. Graebe and Liebermann's original process, the anthracene was first subjected to the action of certain oxidising agents, and thus converted into a compound called *anthraquinone* or *oxanthracene*. This conversion may be effected by heating one part of anthracene with two parts of bichromate of potash and sulphuric acid, or by heating one part of anthracene with two parts of bichromate of potash together with one part of glacial acetic acid. The anthraquinone thus obtained is then converted into a bibromide by being heated with bromine. Finally, this *dibromanthraquine* is heated to about 356° F. with caustic potash or soda, and thus yields a blue product, which when cold is treated with water; an excess of acid is then added to the filtered solution, and the yellow precipitate thus thrown down is washed and dried at a gentle heat. This precipitate is identical in chemical composition and in its properties with the alizarine of the madder-root.

Valuable as these researches were in a scientific point of view, it remained for Mr. Perkin to render the process economically available to the manufacturer by introducing important modifications, whereby the use of an expensive agent like bromine was dispensed with. Mr. Perkin showed that when anthraquinone is strongly heated with sulphuric acid of specific gravity 1·84, it is converted into disulphoanthroquinonic acid, and that this acid, when heated with hydrate of potash to a temperature of 356° F., ultimately yields sulphite and alizarate of potash, from which the alizarine may be thrown down, as a bright yellow precipitate, by addition of hydrochloric acid.

ALKALI. A term derived from the Arabians, and introduced into Europe when the Mahometan conquerors pushed their conquests westward. Al, el, or ul, as an Arabic noun, denotes 'God—Heaven—Divine.' As an Arabic particle, it is prefixed to words to give them a more emphatic signification, much the same as our particle *the;* as in *Alcoran*, the Koran, *alchymist*, the chemist.

Kali was the old name for the plant producing potash (the glasswort, so called from its use in the manufacture of glass), and *alkali* signified no more than the kali plant. Potash and soda were for some time confounded together, and were hence called alkalis. Ammonia, which much resembles them when dissolved in water, was also called an alkali. Ammonia was subsequently distinguished as the *volatile alkali*, potash and soda being called *fixed alkalis*. Ammonia was also called the animal alkali; soda was the mineral alkali, being derived from rock-salt, or from the ocean; and potash received the name of vegetable alkali, from its source being the ashes of plants growing upon the land. Alkalis are characterized by being very soluble in water, by neutralising the strongest acids, by turning to brown the vegetable yellows, and to green the vegetable reds and blues.

Some chemists classify all salifiable bases under this name.

In commercial language, the term has been hitherto applied to an impure soda, but now it is understood to comprehend both soda and potash. The imports and exports of the alkalis are given on the opposite page. See POTASH and SODA.

Of Alkali manufactured in the United Kingdom the following quantities were EXPORTED :—

	1870		1871		1872	
	Quantity	Value	Quantity	Value	Quantity	Value
	cwts	£	cwts	£	cwts	£
To Russia	256,210	129,427	241,692	131,994	264,129	177,017
„ Germany	485,454	155,258	682,627	249,138	677,594	332,829
„ Holland	217,892	57,212	266,846	81,283	260,085	104,244
„ France	146,027	53,657	195,777	64,493	88,924	44,878
„ United States . .	1,903,640	755,838	1,924,510	827,051	2,190,559	1,250,591
„ Other Countries . .	844,170	334,653	865,215	393,310	976,754	579,804
Total . .	3,853,393	1,486,045	4,176,667	1,747,269	4,458,045	2,489,363

The IMPORTS of alkali were as follows:—

	cwts	£	cwts	£	cwts	£
Alkali Imported . . .	92,497	153,041	101,560	144,995	88,921	164,530

These quantities were from Germany, Spain, the United States, and other parts of America, and small quantities from a few other places.

ALKALI, ORGANIC, or **ALKALOID.** During the last few years the organic alkaloids have so greatly increased in number, that a considerable volume might be devoted to their history. In Watts's 'Chemical Dictionary' will be found a long list of the most important nitrogen-alkaloids, natural and artificial, with a statement of the sources from which they are derived, or a description of their mode of formation. There are, however, only a few which have become articles of commerce. The principal sources from whence they are obtained are the following: —1. The animal kingdom. 2. The vegetable kingdom. 3. Destructive distillation. 4. The action of potash on the cyanic and cyanuric ethers. 5. The action of ammonia on the iodides, &c. of the alcohol radicals. 6. The action of reducing agents on nitro-compounds. The principal bases existing in the animal kingdom are creatine and sarcosine. The vegetable kingdom is much richer in them, and yields a great number of organic alkalis, of which several are of extreme value in medicine. Modern chemists regard all organic alkalis as derived from the types ammonia or oxide of ammonium. Their study has led to results of the most startling character. It has been found that not only may the hydrogen in ammonia and oxide of ammonium be replaced by metals and compound radicals without destruction of the alkaline character, but even the nitrogen may be replaced by phosphorus or arsenic, and yet the resulting compounds remain powerfully basic. In studying the organic bases, chemists have constantly had in view the artificial production of the bases of cinchona bark. It is true that this result has not as yet been attained; but, on the other hand, bodies have been formed having so many analogies, both in constitution and properties, with the substances sought, that it cannot be doubted the question is merely one of time. The part performed by the bases existing in the juice of flesh has not been ascertained, and no special remedial virtues have been detected in them; but this is not the case with those found in vegetables; it is, in fact, among them that the most potent of all medicines are found—such, for example, as quinine and morphia. It is, moreover, among vegetable alkaloids that we find the substances most inimical to life, for aconitine, atropine, brucine, coniine, curarine, nicotine, solanine, strychnine, &c. &c., are among their number. It must not be forgotten, however, that, used with proper precaution, even the most virulent are valuable medicines. The fearfully poisonous nature of some of the organic bases, together with an idea that they are difficult to detect, has unhappily led to their use by the poisoner; strychnine, especially, has acquired a painful notoriety, in consequence of its employment by a medical man to destroy persons whose lives he had insured. Fortunately for society, the skill of the analyst has more than kept pace with that of the poisoner; and without regarding the extravagant assertions made by some chemists as to the minute quantities of vegetable poisons they are able to detect, it may safely be asserted that it would be very difficult to administer a fatal dose of any ordinary vegetable poison without its being discovered. Another check upon the poisoner is found in the fact that those most difficult of isolation from complex mixtures are those which cause such distinct symptoms of poisoning in the victim, that the medical attendant, if moderately observant, can scarcely fail to have his suspicions aroused.

Under the heads of the various alkaloids will be found (where deemed of sufficient importance), not merely the mode of preparation, but also the easiest method of detection.—C. G. W.

ALKALIMETER. There are various kinds of alkalimeters, but it will be more convenient to explain their construction and use in the article on ALKALIMETRY, to which the reader is referred.

ALKALIMETRY. 1. The object of alkalimetry is to determine the quantity of caustic alkali or of carbonate of alkali contained in the potash or soda of commerce. The principle of the method is, as in acidimetry, based upon Dalton's law of chemical combining ratios—that is, on the fact that in order to produce a complete reaction a certain definite weight of reagent is required, or, in other words, in order to saturate or completely neutralise, for example, one equivalent of a base, exactly one equivalent of acid must be employed, and *vice versâ*. This having been thoroughly explained in the article on ACIDIMETRY, the reader is referred thereto.

2. The composition of the potash and of the soda met with in commerce presents very great variations; and the value of these substances being, of course, in proportion to the quantity of real alkali which they contain, an easy and rapid method of determining that quantity is obviously of the greatest importance both to the manufacturer and to the buyer. The process by which this object is attained, though originally contrived exclusively for the determination of the intrinsic value of these two alkalies (whence its name Alkalimetry), has since been extended to that of ammonia and of earthy bases and their carbonates, as will be shown presently.

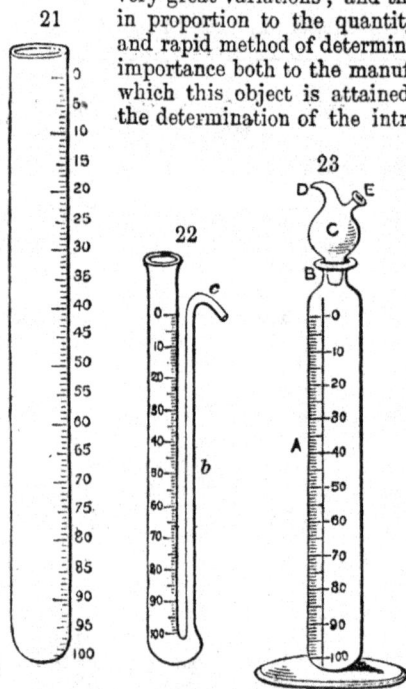

3. Before, however, entering into a description of the process itself, we will give that of the instrument employed in this method of analysis, which instrument is called an *alkalimeter*.

4. The common alkalimeter is a tube closed at one end (see *fig.* 21), of about $\frac{3}{4}$ths of an inch internal diameter, about $9\frac{1}{2}$ inches long, and is thus capable of containing 1,000 grains of pure distilled water. The space occupied by the water is divided accurately into 100 divisions, numbering from above downwards, each of which, therefore, represents 10 grains of distilled water.

5. When this alkalimeter is used, the operator must carefully pour the acid from it by closing the tube with his thumb, so as to allow the acid to trickle in drops as occasion may require; and it is well also to smear the edge of the tube with tallow, in order to prevent any portion of the test acid from being wasted by running over the outside after pouring, which accident would, of course, render the analysis altogether inaccurate and worthless; and, for the same reason, after having once begun to pour the acid from the alkalimeter by allowing it to trickle between the thumb and the edge of the tube, as above mentioned, the thumb must not be removed from the tube till the end of the experiment, for otherwise the portion of acid which adheres to it would, of course, be wasted and vitiate the result. This uncomfortable precaution is obviated in the other forms of alkalimeter now to be described.

6. That represented in *fig.* 22 is Gay-Lussac's alkalimeter; it is a glass tube about 14 inches high, and $\frac{1}{2}$ an inch in diameter, capable of holding more than 1,000 grains of distilled water; it is accurately graduated from the top downwards into 100 divisions in such a way that each division may contain exactly 10 grains of water. It has a small tube, *b*, communicating with the larger one, which small tube is bent and bevelled at the top, *c*. This very ingenious instrument, known also under the names of '*burette*' and '*pouret*,' was contrived by Gay-Lussac, and is by far more convenient than the common alkalimeter, as by it the test acid can be unerringly poured drop by drop, as wanted. The only drawback is the fragility of the small side-tube, *b*, on which account the common alkalimeter, represented in *fig.* 21, was generally used, especially by workmen, because, as it has no side-tube, it is less liable to be broken; but it gives less accurate results, a portion of the acid being wasted in various ways, and it is besides less manageable. Gay-Lussac's '*burette*' is therefore preferable; and if melted wax be run between the space of the large and of the small tube, the

instrument is rendered much less liable to injury; it is generally sold with a separate wooden foot or socket, in which it may stand vertically.

7. The preceding form of alkalimeter (*fig.* 23), which I contrived several years ago, will, I think, be found equally delicate, but more convenient still than that of Gay-Lussac. It consists of a glass tube A, of the same dimensions and graduated in the same manner as that of Gay-Lussac; but it is provided with a glass foot, and the upper part, B, is shaped like the neck of an ordinary glass bottle; c is a bulb blown from a glass tube, one end of which is ground to fit the neck, B, of the alkalimeter, like an ordinary glass stopper. This bulb is drawn to a capillary point at D, and has a somewhat large opening at E. With this instrument the acid is perfectly under the control of the operator, for the globular joint at the top enables him to see the liquor before it actually begins to drop out, and he can then regulate the pouring to the greatest nicety, whilst its more substantial form renders it much less liable to accidents than that of Gay-Lussac; the glass foot is extremely convenient, and is at the same time a great additional security. The manner of using it will be described further on.

8. Another alkalimeter of the same form as that which I have just described,

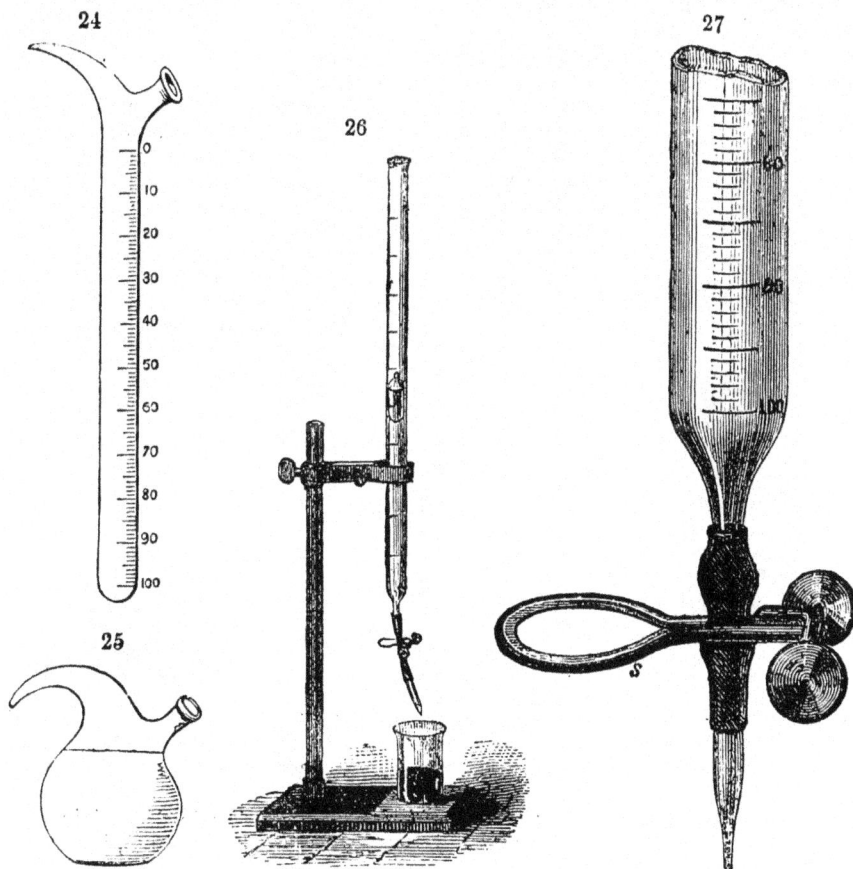

except that it is all in one piece, and has no globular enlargement, is represented in *fig.* 24. Its construction is otherwise the same, and the results obtained are equally delicate; but it is less under perfect control, and the test acid is very liable to run down the tube outside: this defect might be easily remedied by drawing the tube into a finer and more delicate point, instead of in a thick blunted projection, from which the last drop cannot be detached, or only with difficulty and imperfectly. A glass foot would moreover be an improvement.

9. With Schüster's alkalimeter (represented in *fig.* 25), the strength of alkalis is determined by the *weight*, not by the *measure*, of the acid employed to neutralise the alkali: it is, as may be seen, a small bottle of thin glass, having the form of the head of the alkalimeter represented in *fig.* 23. We shall describe further on the process of analysis with this alkalimeter.

10. The alkalimeter most used now is that known as Mohr's (*fig.* 26). It consists of a straight graduated tube, having its lower extremity contracted and drawn out so as

to form a short narrow tube, over which is secured a piece of caoutchouc tubing. This is terminated by a fine glass jet made by drawing out a piece of quill tubing, so as to deliver the solution contained in the alkalimeter in a fine stream, or by single drops, as required. A spring clamp s (*fig.* 27) is used to regulate the flow of the liquid. A screw clamp, with one end attached to the support of the burette, is still better, as it enables the operator to deliver the test liquor at any desired rate, and leaves both hands free. Instead of a clamp a short piece of glass rod, of a diameter slightly greater than the bore of the caoutchouc tube, may be introduced between the end of the alkalimeter and the jet. By slightly pinching the rod between the thumb and forefinger, the caoutchouc tube is expanded laterally, and allows the liquid to escape between the glass rod and its inner surface, effectually closing again the moment the pressure is relieved. A float (*fig.* 28) may be used with advantage with these burettes. It consists of a short glass tube, closed at both ends, and weighted with mercury, so as to float upright and rise but little out of the liquid. A line is etched round the middle of the float, and from this all readings off are made, without regard to the upper surface of the fluid. The float should fit pretty closely, but easily, and the line round it should be perfectly horizontal, or inaccuracies will be introduced into the readings. There are several other forms of alkalimeter, but whichever of them is employed the process is the same—namely, pouring carefully an acid of a known strength into a known weight of the alkali under examination, until the neutralising point is obtained, as will be fully explained presently.

11. Blue litmus-paper being immediately reddened by acids is the reagent used for ascertaining the exact point of the neutralisation of the alkali to be tested. It is prepared by pulverising one part of commercial litmus, and digesting it in six parts of cold water, filtering, and dividing the blue liquid into two equal portions, adding carefully to one of the portions, and *one drop* at a time, as much very dilute sulphuric acid as is sufficient to impart to it a slight red colour, and pouring the portion so treated into the second portion, which is intensely blue, and stirring the whole together. The mixture so obtained is neutral, and by immersing slips of white

28

29

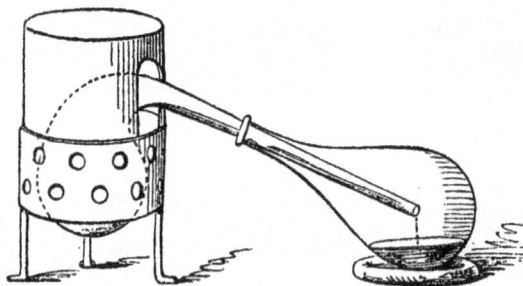

blotting-paper into it, and carefully drying them by hanging them on a stretched piece of thread, an exceedingly sensitive test paper of a light blue colour is obtained, which should be kept in a wide-mouth glass-stoppered bottle, and sheltered from the air and light.

12. Since the principle on which alkalimetry is based consists in determining the amount of acid which a known weight of alkali can saturate or neutralise, it is clear that any acid having this power can be employed.

13. The test acid, however, generally preferred for the purpose, is sulphuric acid, because the normal solution of that acid is more easily prepared, is less liable to change its strength by keeping, and has a stronger reaction on litmus-paper than any other acid. It is true that other acids—tartaric acid, for example—can be procured of greater purity, and that as it is dry and not caustic, the quantities required can be more comfortably and accurately weighed off; and on this account some chemists, after Buchner, recommended its use, but the facility with which its aqueous solution becomes mouldy is so serious a drawback, that it is hardly ever resorted to for that object.

14. When sulphuric acid is employed, the *pure* acid in the maximum state of concentration, or, as it is called by chemists, the *pure* hydrate of sulphuric acid, specific gravity 1·8485, is preferable. Such an acid, however, is never met with in commerce, for the ordinary English oil of vitriol is seldom pure, and never to the maximum state of concentration; the operator, however, may prepare it by distilling ordinary oil of vitriol, but as the specific heat of the vapour of sulphuric acid is very small, the

distillation is a somewhat hazardous operation, unless peculiar precaution be taken. The following apparatus, however, allows of the acid being distilled in a perfectly safe and convenient manner; it consists of a plain glass retort, charged with oil of vitriol : a little protosulphate of iron is added, for the purpose of destroying any nitrous products which the acid may evolve, and it is then placed into a cylinder of iron, the bottom of which is perforated with holes about three-quarters of an inch in diameter, except in the middle, where a large hole is cut of a suitable size for the retort to rest upon ; the sides of the cylinder are likewise perforated, as represented in *fig.* 29. Ignited charcoal is then placed all round the retort, the bottom of which protruding out of the influence of the heat, allows the ebullition to proceed from the sides only. It is well to put into the retort a few fragments of quartz or a few lengths of platinum wire, the effect of which is to render the ebullition more regular.

15. In order to prevent the acid fumes from condensing in the neck of the retort, it should be covered with a cover of sheet iron, as represented in *fig.* 29.

16. The first fourth part which distils over should be rejected, because it is too weak ; the next two-fourths are kept, and the operation is then stopped, leaving the last fourth part of the acid in the retort. The neck of the retort should be about four feet long and about one and a half inches in the bore, and be connected with a large receiver ; and as the necks of retorts are generally much too short for the purpose, an adapter tube should be adjusted to it and to the receiver, but very loosely ; this precaution is absolutely necessary, for otherwise the hot acid falling on the sides of the receiver would crack it ; things, in fact, should be so arranged that the hot drops of the distilling acid may fall into the acid which has already distilled over. Do not surround the receiver with cold water, for the hot acid dropping on the refrigerated surface would also certainly crack it. The acid so obtained is pure oil of vitriol, or monohydrated sulphuric acid, SO^3, HO, and it should be kept in a well-stoppered and dry flask.

17. For commercial assays, however, and, indeed, for every purpose, the ordinary concentrated sulphuric acid answers very well : when used for the determination of the value of potashes, it is made of such a strength that each division (or 10 water-grains' measure) of the alkalimeter saturates exactly one grain of pure potash ; an acid of that particular strength is prepared as follows :—

18. Take 112·76 grains of pure neutral and anhydrous carbonate of soda, and dissolve them in about 5 fluid ounces of hot water.[1] This quantity, namely, 112·76 grains, of neutral carbonate of soda will exactly saturate the same quantity of pure sulphuric acid (SO^3) that 100 grains of pure potash would. It is advisable, however, to prepare at once a larger quantity of test solution of carbonate of soda, which is of course easily done, as will be shown presently.

19. Mix, now, 1 part, by measure, of concentrated sulphuric acid with 10 parts of water, or rather—as it is advisable, where alkalimetrical assays have frequently to be made, to keep a stock of test acid—mix 1,000 water-grains' measure of concentrated sulphuric acid with 10,000 grains of water, or any other larger proportions of concentrated sulphuric acid and water, in the above respective proportions ; stir the whole well, and allow it to cool. The mixture of the acid with the water should be made by first putting a certain quantity of the water into a glass beaker or matrass of a suitable size, then pouring the concentrated acid slowly therein, while a gyratory motion is imparted to the liquid. The vessel containing the acid is then rinsed with the water, and both the rinsing and the rest of the water are then added to the whole mass. When quite cold, fill the graduated alkalimeter with a portion of it up to the point marked 0°, taking the under line of the liquid as the true level ; and whilst stirring briskly with a glass rod the aqueous solution of the 112·76 grains of neutral carbonate of soda above alluded to, drop the test acid from the alkalimeter into the vortex produced by stirring, until, by testing the alkaline solution with a strip of reddened litmus-paper after every addition of acid, it is found that it no longer shows an alkaline reaction (which is known by the slip of reddened litmus-paper not being rendered blue), but, on the contrary, indicates that a very slight excess of acid is present (which is known by testing with a slip of blue litmus-paper, which will then turn slightly red).

20. If, after having exhausted the whole of the 100 divisions (1,000 water-grains' measure) of the diluted acid in the alkalimeter, the neutralisation is found to be *exactly* attained, it is a proof that the test acid is right.

21. But suppose, on the contrary (and this is a much more probable case)—suppose that only 80 divisions of the acid in the alkalimeter have been required to neutralise the alkaline solution, it is then a proof that the test acid is too strong, and accord-

---

[1] Anhydrous, or dry, neutral carbonate of soda may be obtained by keeping a certain quantity of pure bicarbonate of soda for a short time at a dull red heat, in a platinum crucible : the bicarbonate is converted into its neutral carbonate, of course free from water.

ingly it must be further diluted with water, to bring it to the standard strength; and this may at once be done, in the present instance, by adding 20 measures of water to every 80 measures of the acid. This is best accomplished by pouring the whole of the acid into a large glass cylinder, divided into 100 equal parts, until it reaches the mark or scratch corresponding to 80 measures; the rest of the glass, up to 100, is then filled up with water, so that the same quantity of real acid will now be in the 100 measures as was contained before in 80 measures.

22. The acid adjusted as just mentioned should be labelled ' *Test Sulphuric Acid for Potash,*' and kept in well-stoppered bottles, otherwise evaporation taking place would render the remaining bulk more concentrated, consequently richer in acid than it should be, and it would thus, of course, become valueless as a test acid until re-adjusted. Each degree or division of the alkalimeter of such an acid represents 1 grain of pure potash.

23. The alkalimetrical *assay of soda* is also made with sulphuric acid, in preference to other acids, but it must be so adjusted that 100 alkalimetrical divisions (1,000 water-grains' measure) of acid will exactly neutralise 170·98 of pure anhydrous carbonate of soda, that quantity containing 100 grains of pure soda.

24. Dissolve, therefore, 171 grains of pure anhydrous neutral carbonate of soda, obtained as indicated before, in five or six ounces of hot water, and prepare in the meantime the test sulphuric acid, by mixing 1 part, by measure, of ordinary concentrated sulphuric acid with about 9 parts by measure of water, exactly as described before; stir the whole thoroughly, let the mixture stand until it has become quite cold, then pour 1,000 water-grains' measure of the dilute acid so prepared into an alkalimeter—that is to say, fill that instrument up to 0°, taking the under line as the true level, and then, whilst stirring briskly the aqueous solution of the 171 grains of carbonate of soda with a glass rod, pour the acid, with increased precaution as the saturating point is approaching, into the vortex produced, until by testing the liquor alternately with reddened and with blue litmus-paper, or with grey litmus-paper, as before mentioned, the exactly neutralised point is hit.

25. If the whole of the 100 alkalimetrical divisions (1,000 water-grains' measure) have been required to effect the neutralisation, it is a proof that the acid is of the right strength, but if this be not the case, it must be adjusted as described before—that is to say:—

26. Suppose, for example, that only 75 alkalimetrical divisions or measures of the acid in the alkalimeter have been required to neutralise the 171 grains of neutral carbonate of soda operated upon, then 75 measures of the acid should be poured at once into a glass cylinder accurately divided into 100 parts; the remaining 25 divisions should then be filled with water, and the whole being now stirred up, 100 parts of the liquor will of course contain as much real acid as 75 parts contained before, and accordingly the acid may now be used as a test acid for the alkalimetrical assay of soda, each degree or division of the alkalimeter representing one grain of pure soda.

27. The stock of test acid should be kept in well-stoppered flasks, that it may not vary in strength by evaporation, and be labelled ' *Test Sulphuric Acid for Soda.*'

28. Instead, however, of keeping two kinds of ' test sulphuric acid,' of different saturating powers as described, the one for *potash*, the other for *soda*, one kind only may be prepared so as to serve for both alkalis, by constructing, as is very often done, an alkalimeter adjusted so as to indicate the quantities of the acid of a given strength required for the saturation or neutralisation of both potash or soda, or of their respective carbonates; and this, in fact, is the alkalimeter most in use in the factory.

It should be in shape similar to that of Gay-Lussac's (see *fig.* 22), or that described in *figs.* 23 and 24; but, like that represented by *fig.* 21, it generally consists of a tube closed at one end, about three-fourths of an inch internal diameter and about 9½ inches in length; it is graduated into 100 equal parts, and every division is numbered from above downwards (see *fig.* 30).

The following directions for their construction are given by Professor Faraday. 'Let the tube represented in the margin have 1000 grains of water weighed into it; then let the space it occupies be graduated into 100 equal parts, and every ten divisions numbered from above downwards. At 22·1 parts, or 77·99 parts from the bottom, make an extra line, a little on one side or even on the opposite side of the graduation, and write at it with a scratching diamond, *soda*; lower down,

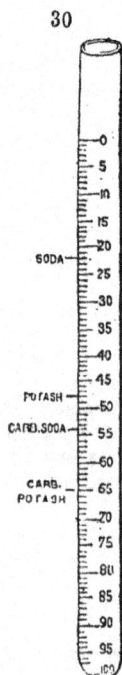

at 48·62 parts, make another line, and write *potash* ; still lower, at 54·43 parts, a third line marked *carb. soda*, and at 65 parts a fourth, marked *carb. potash*. It will be observed that portions are measured off beneath these marks in the inverse order of the equivalent number of these substances, and consequently directly proportionate to the quantities of any particular acid which will neutralise equal weights of the alkalis and their carbonates. As these points are of great importance, it will be proper to verify them by weighing into the tubes first 350, then 513·8, and lastly 779·9 grains of water, which will correspond with the marks if they are correct, or the graduation may be laid down from the surface of the four portions of fluid when weighed in, without reference to where they fall upon the general scale. The tube is now completed, except that it should be observed whether the aperture can be perfectly and securely covered by the thumb of the left hand, and if not, or if there be reason to think it not ultimately secure, then it should be heated and contracted until sufficiently small.'

· 29. The test acid for this alkalimeter should have a specific gravity of 1·1268 ; and such an acid may be prepared by mixing one part, by weight, of sulphuric acid, specific gravity 1·82, with four parts of water, and allowing the mixture to cool. In the meantime, 100 grains of pure anhydrous carbonate of soda, obtained as indicated before, should be dissolved in water, and the test sulphuric acid, of specific gravity 1·1268, prepared as above said, having become quite cold, is poured into the alkalimeter up to the point marked carbonate of soda ; the remaining divisions are filled up with water, and the whole should be well mixed by shaking.

30. If the whole of the sulphuric acid, adjusted as was said, being poured carefully into the solution of the 100 grains of the neutral carbonate of soda, neutralise them exactly—which is ascertained, as usual, by testing the solution with litmus-paper, which should not be either reddened or rendered bluer by it—it is of course a sign that the test is as it should be—that is to say, is of the proper strength ; in the contrary case it must be finally adjusted in the manner already indicated, and which need not be repeated. See §§ 20, 21.

· 31. The best and most convenient process for the analyst, however, consists in preparing a test acid of such a strength that it may serve not only for all alkalis, but indeed for every base ; that is to say, by adjusting the test acid so that 100 alkalimetrical divisions of it (1,000 water-grains' measure) may exactly saturate or neutralise one equivalent of every base. This method, which was first proposed by Dr. Ure, is exceedingly convenient, and the possession of two reciprocal test liquids, namely, the ammonia test liquor of a standard strength, of which we gave a description in the article on Acidimetry, and the standard test acid of which we are now speaking, affords, as Dr. Ure observes, ready and rigid means of verification. For microscopic analysis of alkaline and of acid matter, a graduated tube of a small bore, mounted in a frame, with a valve apparatus at top, so as to let fall drops of any size and at any interval, is desirable ; and such an instrument Dr. Ure employed for many years ; but instead of a tube with a valve apparatus at top, the operator may use a graduated tube of a small bore, terminated by a small length of vulcanised india-rubber tube pinched in a clamp, which may be relaxed in such a way as to permit also the escape of drops of any size at any interval of time, the little apparatus being under perfect command.

32. The test sulphuric acid, of such a strength that 100 alkalimetrical divisions of it can saturate one equivalent of every base, should have a specific gravity of 1·032, and is prepared as follows :—

Take 53 grains (one equivalent) of pure anhydrous neutral carbonate of soda, obtained in the manner indicated before (see § 18), and dissolve them in about one fluid ounce of water. Prepare in the meantime the test sulphuric acid by mixing one part, by measure, of concentrated sulphuric acid with about 11 or 12 parts of water, and stir the whole well. The mixture having become quite cold, fill the alkalimeter with the cold diluted acid up to the point marked 0°, taking the under line of the liquid as the true level, and whilst stirring briskly the aqueous solution of the 53 grains of carbonate of soda above alluded to, pour the acid carefully from the alkalimeter into the vortex produced by stirring, until, by testing the liquor alternately with reddened and with blue litmus-paper, or, more conveniently still, with grey litmus-paper, the neutralising point is exactly hit.

33. If the whole of the 100 divisions of the alkalimeter had been required to neutralise exactly the 53 grains of pure anhydrous carbonate of soda, it would be a proof that the acid is of the right strength ; but if this is not the case, it must be adjusted in the manner described before, that is to say :—

· 34. Let us suppose, for example, that only 50 measures in the alkalimeter have been required to saturate or neutralise the 53 grains of carbonate of soda, then 50 measures should be poured at once into a glass cylinder accurately divided into 100 parts, the remaining 50 divisions should be filled up with water, and the whole being well stirred, 100 parts of the acid liquor will now contain as much real acid as was contained before in the 50 parts.

35. The acid may now be labelled simply, ' *Test or Normal Sulphuric Acid.*' Each one hundred alkalimetrical divisions, or 1,000 water-grains' measure of it, contain one equivalent, or 40 grains of real sulphuric acid; and, consequently, each 100 alkalimetrical divisions of it will neutralise one equivalent, or 31 grains of soda, 47 of potash, 17 of ammonia, 28 of lime, and so forth, with respect to any other base.

36. The stock of test or normal sulphuric acid should, as usual, be kept in well-stoppered bottles, in order to prevent concentration by evaporation. By keeping in the flask containing it a glass bead, exactly adjusted to the specific gravity of 1·032, the operator may always ascertain, at a glance, whether the acid requires readjusting.

37. With a Schüster's alkalimeter, it is convenient to prepare the test acid of such a strength that, according as it has been adjusted for potash or for soda, 10 grains of it will exactly saturate one grain of one or the other of these bases in a pure state. It is considered that the alkalimeter may be charged with a known weight of any of the other sulphuric test acids of a known strength. Suppose, for example, that the test sulphuric acid taken have a specific gravity of 1·032, we know, as we have just shown, that 1·032 grains weight of that acid contains exactly one equivalent of pure sulphuric acid=40, and is capable, therefore, of neutralising one equivalent of any base; and, consequently, by taking a certain weight of this acid before beginning the assay, and weighing what is left of it after the assay, it is very easy to calculate, from the quantity of acid consumed in the experiment, what quantity of base has been neutralised. Thus a loss of 21·96, 60·70, 33·29 grains' weight of this test acid represents one grain of potash, of ammonia, of soda respectively, and so on with the other bases.

38. The operator being thus provided with an appropriate test acid, we shall now describe how he should proceed with each of them in making an alkalimetrical assay with potash.

In order to obtain a reliable result, a fair average sample must be operated upon. To secure this the sample should be taken from various parts of the mass and at once put in a wide-mouth bottle, and well corked up until wanted; when the assay has to be made, the contents of the bottle must be reduced to powder, so as to obtain a fair mixture of the whole; of this weigh out 1,000 grains exactly—or less, if that quantity cannot be spared—and dissolve them in a porcelain capsule, in about 8 fluid ounces of distilled hot water, or in that proportion; and if there be left anything like an insoluble residue, filter, in order to separate it, and wash it on the filter with small quantities of distilled water, and pour the whole solution, with the washings and rinsings, into a measure divided into 10,000 water-grains' measure. If the water used for washing the insoluble residue on the filter has increased the bulk of the solution beyond 10,000 water-grains' measure, it must be reduced by evaporation to that quantity; if, on the contrary, the solution poured in the measure stands below the mark 10,000 water-grains' measure, then as much water must be added thereto as will bring the whole mass exactly to that point. In order to do this correctly, the cylindrical measure should stand well on a table, and the under or lower line formed by the liquid, as it reaches the scratch 10,000, is taken as the true level.

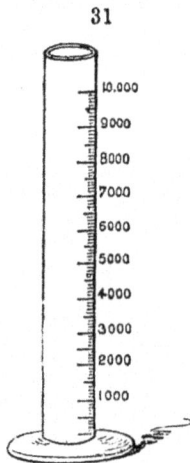

31

39. This being done, 1,000 grains' measure of the filtrate, that is to say, *one-tenth* part of the whole solution, is transferred to a glass beaker, in which the saturation or neutralisation is to be effected, which is best done by means of a pipette capable of containing exactly that quantity when filled up to the scratch, *a*. In order to fill such a pipette it is sufficient to dip it into the alkaline solution and to suck up the liquor a little above the scratch, *a*; the upper orifice should then be stopped with the first finger, and by momentarily lifting it up, the liquor is allowed slowly to fall from the pipette back again into the 10,000 grains' measure until its level reaches exactly the scratch, *a*. The last drop which remains hanging from the point of the pipette may be readily detached by touching the sides of the glass measure with it. The 1,000 grains being thus rigorously measured in the pipette should then be transferred to the glass beaker, in which the neutralisation is to take place, by removing the finger altogether, blowing into it to detach the last drop, and rinsing it with a little water,

32

40. Or, instead of the pipette just described, the operator may measure 1,000 grains by taking an alkalimeter full of the alkaline solution, and emptying it into the glass beaker in which the neutralisation is to take place, rinsing it with a little water, and of course adding the rinsing to the mass in the said glass beaker.

41. Whichever way is adopted, a slight blue colour should be imparted to the 1,000 grains' measure of the alkaline solution, by pouring into it a small quantity of tincture of litmus. The glass beaker should then be placed upon a sheet of white paper, or a slab of white porcelain, in order that the change of colour produced by the gradual addition of the test acid may be better observed.

42. This being done, if the operator have decided upon using the *test sulphuric acid for potash* (§§ 17–22), he should take one of the alkalimeters represented in *figs.* 21, 22, 23, or 24, and fill it up to 0° (taking the under line of the liquid as the true level); then taking the alkalimeter thus charged in his right hand, and in his left the glass beaker containing the alkaline solution coloured blue by tincture of litmus, he should gradually and carefully pour the acid liquor into the alkaline solution in the glass beaker, to which a circular motion should be given whilst pouring the acid, or which should be briskly stirred, in order to insure the rapid and thorough mixing of the two liquors, and therefore their complete reaction; moreover, in order at once to detect any change of colour from blue to red, the glass beaker should be kept over the white sheet of paper or the white porcelain slab, as before stated.

43. At first no effervescence is produced, because the carbonic acid expelled, instead of escaping, combines with the portion of the alkaline carbonate as yet undecomposed, which it converts into bicarbonate of potash, and accordingly no sensible change of colour is perceived; but as soon as a little more than half the quantity of the potash present is saturated, the liquor begins to effervesce, and the blue colour of the solution is changed into one of a vinous, that is, of a purple or bluish-red hue, which is due to the action of the carbonic acid upon the blue colour of the litmus. More acid should be still added, but from this moment with very great care and with increased caution, gradually as the point of neutralisation is approached, which is ascertained by drawing the glass rod used for stirring the liquor across a slip of blue litmus-paper. If the paper remains blue, or if a red or reddish streak is thereby produced which disappears on drying the paper and leaves the latter blue, it is a proof that the neutralisation is not yet complete, and that the reddish streak was due only to the action of the carbonic acid; more acid must accordingly be poured from the alkalimeter, but one drop only at a time, stirring after each addition, until at last the liquor assumes a distinct red or pink colour, which happens as soon as it contains an extremely slight excess of acid; the streaks made now upon the litmus-paper will remain permanently red, even after drying, and this indicates that the reaction is complete and that the assay is finished.

44. If the potash under examination were perfectly caustic, the solution would suddenly change from blue to pink, because there would be no evolution of carbonic acid at all, and consequently no vinous or purple colour produced; if, on the other hand, the potash was altogether in the state of bicarbonate, the first drops of test acid would at once decompose part of it and liberate carbonic acid, and impart a vinous colour to the solution at the very outset, which vinous colour would persist as long as any portion of the bicarbonate would remain undecomposed.

45. The neutralising point being attained, the operator allows the sides of the alkalimeter to drain, and he then reads off the number of divisions which have been employed. If, for example, 50 divisions have been used, then the potash examined contained 50 per cent. of real potash. See observ., § 48–49.

46. Yet it is advisable to repeat the assay a second time, and to look upon this first determination only as an approximation which enables the operator, now that he knows about where the point of neutralisation lies, to arrive, if need be, by increased caution as he reaches that point, at a much greater degree of precision. He should accordingly take again an alkalimeter full (1,000 water-grains' measure)—that is to say, another tenth part of the liquor left in the 10,000 grains' measure—and add thereto at once 48 or 49 alkalimetrical divisions of the test acid, and after having thoroughly agitated the mixture, proceed to pour the acid carefully, two drops only at a time, stirring after such addition, and touching a strip of litmus-paper with the end of the glass rod used for stirring; and so he should go on adding two drops, stirring, and making a streak on the litmus-paper until the liquor assumes suddenly a pink or onion-red colour, and the streak made on the litmus-paper is red also. The alkalimeter is then allowed to drain as before, and the operator reads off the number of divisions employed, from which number 2 drops (or $\frac{2}{10}$ths of a division) should be deducted; Gay-Lussac having shown that, in alkalimetrical assays, the sulphates of alkalis produced *retard* the manifestation of the red colour in that proportion. One alkalimetrical division generally consists of 10 drops, but as this is not always the case, the operator should determine for himself how many drops are necessary to make up one division, and take account of them in the assay according to the ratio thus found. In the example given before, and supposing 10 drops to form one alkalimetrical division, then the per-centage value of the sample of potash under examination, would probably be as follows :—

Number of divisions of acid employed   .   .   50·0
— 2 drops acid in excess .   .   .   .   0·2

Real per-centage of potash   .   .   .   49·8

47. When the alkalimeter described in *fig.* 23 is employed, the test acid may, at the beginning of the experiment, be poured from the larger opening, E; but towards the end—that is, when the neutralising point is approaching—the acid should be carefully poured from the point, D, *in single drops, or only two drops at a time,* until the saturating point is hit, as we have just said. If the operator wishes to pour only one drop, he should close the larger opening, E, of the bulb with the thumb, and then fill the bulb with the test acid by inclining the alkalimeter; putting now the alkalimeter in an upright position, and removing the thumb, a certain quantity of acid will be retained in the capillary point, D; and if the thumb be now pressed somewhat forcibly against the opening, E, the acid contained in the capillary point will be forced out and form one drop, which will then fall into the alkaline solution if it be held over it. If the saturation be complete, the operator, without removing the bulb stopper, may, by applying his lips to the large opening, E, suck the acid engaged in the capillary point back into the alkalimeter.

48. If there should be in the mind of the operator any doubt as to what is meant by the onion-red colour which the liquor tinged blue with tincture of litmus acquires when slightly supersaturated, he may pour into a glass beaker a quantity of pure water equal to, or even larger than, the alkaline solution operated upon, and tinge it blue with a little tincture of litmus, to about the same degree of intensity as the alkaline liquor under examination. If he now pour into the pure water coloured blue with litmus, *one single drop* of the test acid, it will acquire at once, by stirring, the onion-red colour alluded to, and which he may now use as a standard of comparison.

49. Considering the rapidity with which these alkalimetrical operations can be performed, the operator, unless he have acquired sufficient practice, or unless a great degree of accuracy be not required, should repeat the assay two or three times, looking upon the first determination only as an approximation, and as a sort of guide as to the quantity of acid which will be required in the subsequent experiments, whereby he will now be enabled to proceed with increased caution as he approaches the point of saturation; but, at any rate, if he will not take the little extra trouble of a repetition, he should, before he begins to pour the acid, take a little of the filtered alkaline solution out of the glass beaker, as a *corps de réserve,* which he adds to the rest after the saturating point has been approximated, and from that moment he may proceed, but with great care, to complete the neutralisation of the whole.

50. Do not forget that as the test sulphuric acid *must always be added in slight excess* to obtain a distinct red streak on the litmus-paper, a correction is absolutely necessary; that is to say, the excess of sulphuric acid employed must be deducted if a strictly accurate result is sought.

51. If, instead of the special alkalimeter for potash above described, the operator prefers using that prepared of such a strength that 100 divisions of the alkalimeter (1,000 water-grains' measure) contain exactly one equivalent of each alkali or base, which test sulphuric acid, as we have seen, has a specific gravity of 1·032 (*see* §§ 31–36), he should proceed exactly as indicated in § 38 and following; and the alkalimeter being filled with that test acid, of specific gravity 1·032, up to 0°, it (the acid) should be poured carefully into the aqueous solution of the alkali tinged blue with litmus, until exact neutralisation is attained, precisely in the same manner as in § 38 and following.

52. The neutralising point being hit, let us suppose that the whole of the contents of the alkalimeter have been employed, that the aqueous solution tinged blue with litmus is not yet saturated, and that, after having refilled the alkalimeter, the 4 divisions more (altogether 104 divisions) have been required to neutralise the alkali in the aqueous solution; then, since 100 divisions (1,000 water-grains' measure) of the test acid now employed saturate exactly one equivalent, that is, 47 of potash, the question is now, What quantity of potash will have been saturated by the 104 divisions of acid employed? The answer is found, by a simple rule of proportion, to b, nearly 49.

$$100 : 47 :: 104 : x = 48·88.$$

The sample of potash examined contained, therefore, nearly 49 per cent. of pure potash.

53. If instead of the special test sulphuric acid for potash (§ 17), or of the test sulphuric acid for potash, soda, and other bases (§ 28), the operator uses the potash and soda alkalimeter (§§ 31–36), the method to be followed is exactly similar to that described in § 42 and following. Some of the test sulphuric acid, of specific gravity 1·1268, is to be poured into the alkalimeter until it reaches the point marked '*potash*' (that is to say, 48·62 divisions of the alkalimeter), taking the under line of the liquid as the true level, and the remaining divisions up to 0° are carefully filled with water. The operator then closes the aperture of the alkalimeter with the thumb of his left hand, and the whole is violently shaken so as to obtain a perfect mixture.

54. The acid so mixed must now be carefully poured from the alkalimeter into the alkaline solution of the potash under examination until neutralisation is attained, precisely as described in § 42 and following.

55. The neutralising point being hit, the operator allows the sides of the alkalimeter to drain, and he then reads off the number of divisions employed in the experiment, which number indicates the per-centage of real potash contained in the sample.

Had the operator wished to estimate the quantity of potash as carbonate of potash, he should have poured the test acid into the alkalimeter up to the point marked '*carbonate of potash*,' filled the remaining divisions of the alkalimeter up to 0° with water, and proceeding exactly as just mentioned, the number of divisions of acid employed would indicate the per-centage of potash contained in the sample as carbonate of potash.

56. The most accurate and expeditious method of determining the value of a sample of an alkali is by means of a standard acid and a solution of a caustic alkali of corresponding strength contained in two burettes (*fig.* 26). The solution of soda ash, for instance, having been prepared as directed in § 38–40, is tinted with litmus solution, and a quantity of the standard acid more than sufficient to saturate the whole of the alkali is run into it, and the mixture boiled till the carbonic acid is entirely expelled from it and the clear red of the litmus solution is seen. The number of divisions of acid added is then noted and the neutral tint restored by the careful addition of the solution of caustic alkali. From the absence of carbonic acid the reaction is very sharp and decided, and even if the neutral point be overshot, the addition of a few drops of acid followed by the more cautious use of the alkaline solution will enable a correct result to be obtained. If the two standard solutions are of exactly equal strength, it is only necessary to subtract the number of divisions of the alkaline solution used, from that of the acid one, to give at once the number of those of the latter required for the neutralisation of the substance tested, and hence by a simple calculation the per-centage of real alkali.

57. If a *Schüster's alkalimeter* (*fig.* 25) be used, and supposing, for example, that the acid to be employed therewith is so adjusted that 10 grains *weight* of it neutralise exactly 1 grain in weight of potash, proceed as follows :—Take 100 grains in weight of a fair average of the sample, previously reduced to powder, dissolve them in water, filter with the precautions which have already been described before (§ 38 and following), and pour this solution into a glass cylinder graduated into 100 parts, and capable of containing 10,000 water-grains; fill it up with water exactly as described before; of this take now 100 alkalimetrical divisions, that is to say, $\frac{1}{10}$th of the whole solution, and pour it in a glass beaker. On the other hand, charge the Schüster's alkalimeter with a certain quantity of the test acid, and weigh it, along with the alkalimeter itself, in a good balance. This done, proceed with the neutralisation of the solution in the glass beaker, by pouring the acid from the alkalimeter in the usual way, and with the usual precautions, until the saturation is completed. Replace the alkalimeter, with the quantity of unconsumed acid, in the scale of the balance, weigh accurately, and since every grain of acid represents $\frac{1}{10}$th of a grain of potash, the number of grains of acid used in the experiment indicates at once the per-centage of real potash present in the sample.

58. When, however, potash is mixed with soda, as is frequently the case with the potash of commerce, either accidentally or for fraudulent purposes, the determination of the amount of the cheaper alkali could not, until a comparatively recent period, be estimated, except by the expensive and tedious process of a regular chemical analysis. In 1844, however, M. Edmund Pesier, professor of Chemistry at Valenciennes, published an easy and commercial method for the estimation of the quantity of soda which potash may contain, by means of an areometer of a peculiar construction, to which the name of 'Natrometer' has been given by the talented professor.

59. The rationale of the method is grounded upon the increase of specific gravity which sulphate of soda produces in a solution saturated with pure sulphate of potash, and is deduced from the fact that a solution saturated with neutral sulphate of potash possesses a uniform and constant density when the saturation is made at the same temperature, and that the density of such a solution increases progressively in propor-

tion to the quantity of sulphate of soda present; an increase of density so much the more readily observable, that the solubility of the sulphate of potash is greatly augmented by the presence of sulphate of soda. It had at first been thought that, in order to obtain anything like accuracy, it would be necessary to combine all the potash with one same acid, preferably sulphuric acid; and, consequently, that as the potash of commerce always contains a little, and sometimes a rather considerable quantity, of chloride of potassium, the latter salt should first be decomposed. Further experiments, however, established the fact that in dissolving chloride of potassium in a saturated solution of sulphate of potash, the specific gravity of the liquor is not materially increased, since the introduction of as much as 50 per cent. of chloride of potassium does not increase that density more than 3 per cent. of soda would do when examined by the natrometer—a degree of accuracy quite sufficient for commercial purposes. When soda is added to a saturated solution of sulphate of potash, the further addition of chloride of potassium thereto renders the specific gravity of the liquor *less* than it would have been without that addition—an apparent anomaly due to the fact that chlorine, in presence of sulphuric acid, of potash, and of soda, combines with the latter base to form chloride of sodium; and it is this salt which increases the solubility of sulphate of potash, though in a somewhat less degree than sulphate of soda. Thus, if to a saturated solution of sulphate of potash 0.14 of soda be added along with 0.20 of chloride of potassium, the natrometer indicates only 0.125 of soda. Seeing, therefore, that in such an exceptional case the error does not amount to more than 0.015 of error, it will probably be found unnecessary in most cases to decompose the chloride contained in the potashes of commerce, that quantity being too small to materially affect the result. Yet, as the accurate determination of soda in potash was a great desideratum, M. Pesier contrived two processes, one of which, in the hands of the practised chemist, is as perfect as, but much more rapid than, those ordinarily resorted to; the other, which is a simplification of the first, yields results of sufficient accuracy for all commercial purposes.

60. *First process.*—Take 500 grains of a fair average sample of the potash to be examined, dissolve them in as little water as possible, filter, and wash the filter until the washings are no longer alkaline. This filtering, however, may be dispensed with when the potash is of good quality and leaves but a small residue, or when an extreme degree of accuracy is not required.

61. The potash being thus dissolved, a slight excess of sulphuric acid is added thereto; the excess is necessary to decompose the chlorides and expel the muriatic acid. The liquor so treated is then evaporated in a porcelain capsule, about six inches in diameter; and when it begins to thicken, it should be stirred with a glass rod, in order to avoid projections. When dry, the fire must be urged until the residue fuses, and it is then kept in a state of tranquil fusion for a few minutes. The capsule should then be placed upon, and surrounded with, hot sand, and allowed to cool down slowly, to prevent its cracking, which would happen without this precaution.

62. The fused mass in the capsule having become quite cold should now be treated with as little hot water as possible, that is to say, with less than 3,000 grains of hot water; and this is best done by treating it with successive portions of fresh water. All the liquors thus successively obtained should then be poured into a flask capable of holding about 10,000 grains of water, and the excess of sulphuric acid *must be accurately neutralised* by a concentrated solution of pure carbonate of potash—that is to say, until the colour of litmus-paper is no longer affected by the liquor, just as in ordinary alkalimetrical or acidimetrical assays. During this operation, a pretty considerable precipitate of sulphate of potash is, of course, produced.

63. The neutralising point being exactly hit, a *saturated* solution of sulphate of potash is prepared, and brought to the atmospheric temperature; a condition which is expedited by plunging the vessel which contains the solution into a basin full of cold water, and stirring it until the thermometer plunged in the liquor indicates that the temperature of the latter is about the same as, and preferably less than, that of the air, because in the latter case it may be quite correctly adjusted by grasping the vessel with a warm hand. In order, however, to secure exactly the proper temperature, the whole should be left at rest for a few minutes after having withdrawn the vessel from the basin of cold water used for refrigerating it, taking care simply to stir it from time to time, and to ascertain that the thermometer remains at the same degree of temperature. This done, the liquor is filtered into a glass cylinder, c, on which a scratch, H—I, has been made, corresponding to 3,000 water-grains' measure. If the directions given have been exactly followed, it will be found that the filtrate is not sufficient to fill it up to that mark; the necessary volume, however, should be completed by washing the deposit of sulphate of potash in the filter, B, with a saturated solution of the same salt (sulphate of potash) *previously prepared*. It is advisable to use a saturated solution of sulphate of potash which has been kept for some

time, and not one immediately prepared for the purpose, because sulphate of potash in dissolving produces a certain amount of cold, which would create delay, since it would be necessary to wait until the temperature of the mass had become the same as that of the air.

64. The liquor occupying 3,000 water-grains' measure in the cylinder should be next rendered homogeneous by stirring it well, after which the natrometer may be immersed in it. The natrometer is simply an areometer of a peculiar construction, provided with two scales: the one of a pink colour shows the degrees of temperature, and indicates, for each degree of the Centigrade thermometer, the level at which a solution saturated with pure sulphate of potash would stand; on the other scale, each degree represents 1 per cent. of soda (oxide of sodium), as represented in *fig.* 34.

65. The 0° of the two scales coincide with each other. If the experiment take place at the temperature of 0°, the quantity of soda will be directly determined by observing the number of degrees on the soda scale; but if the experiment be performed at 25°, for example, it will be seen that the point at which the instrument would sink in a liquor saturated with pure sulphate of potash corresponds to $\frac{8}{100}$th of soda, and, in this case, it is from *this point* that the 0° of the soda scale should be supposed to begin, which is easily accomplished by a simple subtraction, as will be seen presently.

66. Experiment having shown that the degrees of soda cannot be equidistant, but that, on the contrary, they become smaller and smaller as the quantity of soda increases, the number of degrees of soda are obtained as follows:— From the number of degrees of temperature now indicated *on the pink scale* of the natrometer, subtract the number of degrees of temperature indicated by an ordinary thermometer at starting; then look at the soda scale for the number of soda degrees which correspond to the number of degrees of temperature left after subtraction, and each of the soda degrees, beginning from the 0° of the natrometer, represents 1 per cent.

67. For example:—Suppose the experiment to have been made at starting, and as indicated by an ordinary thermometer, at + 20° Centigrade, and that the level of the solution is now found to stand at 59° on the pink scale of temperature of the natrometer, then by deducting 20 (the original temperature) from 59 (number of degrees indicated by the floating point on the pink scale of temperatures of the natrometer), there remains, of course, 39. Draw the instrument out, and looking now on the said pink scale for 39°, there will be found exactly opposite, on the soda scale, the number 13, which number signifies that the potash under examination contains 13 per cent. of soda (oxide of sodium).

68. As the deposit of sulphate of potash separated by filtering might retain some sulphate of soda, it is advisable, in order to avoid all chance of error, to wash it with a saturated solution of sulphate of potash, adding as much of it as is necessary to bring the whole mass of the liquor up to the mark 3,000 water-grains' measure, in which the natrometer being again immersed, the minute quantity of soda indicated should be added to the per-centage found by the first operation.

69. If a great degree of accuracy is required, the fractions of degree of the instrument must be taken account of; otherwise they may be neglected without the result being materially affected, since 3 degrees of the scale of temperature correspond only to about 1 per cent. of soda.

70. For commercial purposes, the process may be slightly varied, as follows :— Take 500 grains of a fair average sample of the potash to be examined, previously reduced to powder, and throw them into a flask, A (*fig.* 35), capable of containing

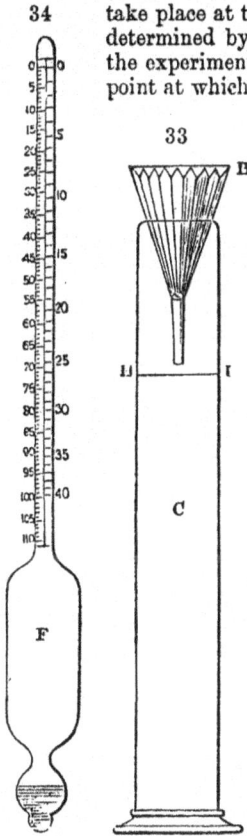

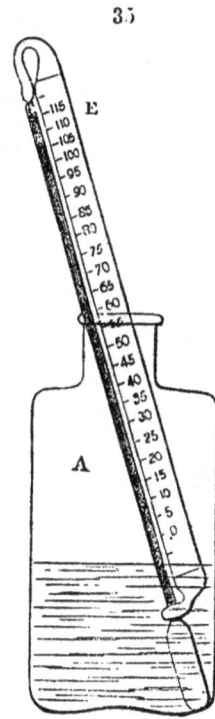

about 6,000 grains of water; pour upon them about 2,000 grains of water, and shake until dissolved. Add now sulphuric acid thereto; this will produce a smart effervescence, and in all probability a deposit of sulphate of potash. We say in all probability, because it is clear that if the potash in question is largely adulterated with soda, or was altogether nothing else than carbonate of soda, as has occasionally happened, it is evident that no deposit of sulphate of potash would take place; and yet, as it is necessary to the success of the operation that the liquor should contain an excess of this latter salt, a certain quantity of it previously reduced to fine powder must in that case be purposely added to the solution.

71. After the disengagement of gas has ceased, it is necessary to pour the dilute acid cautiously, and only drop by drop, until the neutralising point is correctly hit, which will be known as usual by testing with litmus-paper. But if, by accident, too much acid have been used, which is known by the reddening of the litmus-paper, the slight overdose may be neutralised by adding a small quantity of weak solution of potash.

72. As this reaction produces heat, it is necessary to lower the liquor down to the temperature of the atmosphere, decant in a filter placed over the glass cylinder, and fill it up to the scratch 3,000, by washing the residue on the filter with a saturated solution of sulphate of potash, exactly as described in § 63.

73. The glass cylinder being properly filled up to the scratch, remove the funnel, close the orifice of the glass cylinder with the palm of the hand, and shake the whole violently; holding the natrometer, which should be perfectly clean, by its upper extremity, slowly immerse it in the solution. If the potash under examination be pure, the pink scale will indicate the degree of temperature at which the experiment has been made, taking the under line as the true level of the liquid; but if, on the contrary, it contains soda, the pink scale of temperatures will indicate a few degrees more than the real temperature, and this *surplus* number of degrees, being compared with those of the soda scale contiguous to it, on the opposite side, will express the per-centage of soda present in the sample.

74. For example:—Suppose the experiment to have been made at + 12° Centigrade, and to have given a solution marking 25° on the pink scale of temperatures of the natrometer, that is 13° more than the real temperature;—looking, therefore, at number 13 on the pink scale of temperature, it will be seen that the number exactly opposite on the soda scale, and corresponding to it, is 4, which indicates that the sample of potash examined contains 4 per cent. of soda.

It is important to bear in mind that all commercial potashes contain naturally a small quantity of soda, which quantity, in certain varieties, may even be considerable; it is only when the proportion of soda is more considerable than that which is naturally contained *in the species* of potash submitted to analysis, that it should be considered as fraudulently added. The following Table, published by M. Pesier, shows the average composition of the principal varieties of potash found in commerce, when in an unadulterated state:—

Average Composition of Potashes.

	Tuscan Potash	Russian Potash	American Potash	Pearlash	Potash of the Vosges	Potashes obtained in the Laboratory by calcining		Salts of Ivray dissolved and calcined	1851 Potash purified, from Valenciennes	1855 Potash purified, from Valenciennes
						A Mixture of pure Molasses	Molasses obtained from the Cistern of a Distillery			
Sulphate of potash . .	13·47	14·11	15·32	14·38	38·84	4·27	2·98	16·19	1·50	0·70
Chloride of potassium . .	0·95	2·09	8·15	3·64	9·16	18·17	19·69	33·89	1·60	1·70
Carbonate of potash . .	74·10	69·61	68·07[1]	71·38	38·63	51·83	53·90	26·64	89·95	95·24
Carbonate of soda (dry) .	3·01	3·09	5·85	2·31	4·17	24·17	23·17	19·60	5·12	2·12
Insoluble residue . .	0·65	1·21	3·35	0·44	2·66	.	.	.	.	.
Moisture . . .	7·28	8·82	undetermined	4·56	5·34	.	.	.	.	0·50
Phosphoric acid, lime, silica, &c.	0·54	1·07	ditto	3·29	1·20	1·56	0·26	3·68	1·33	0·24
	100·00	100·00		100·00	100·00	100·00	100·00	100·00	100·00	100·00
Alkalimetric degrees .	56	53·1	55	54·4	31·6	60	59·7	36·5	68·5	69·5

[1] In the impossibility of estimating exactly the loss by calcination, and the quantity of oxide of potassium in the caustic state (hydrate of potash), we have reduced the potash to the state of carbonate, to make comparison more easy.

75. *The alkalimetrical assay of soda* is performed exactly in the same manner as that of potash—that is to say: From a fair average sample of the soda to be examined, take 1,000 grains' weight (or less if that quantity cannot be spared), and boil it five or six minutes in about eight fluid ounces of water, filter in order to separate the insoluble portion, and wash the residue on the filter with boiling water until it no longer drops from the filter with an alkaline reaction, and the bulk of the filtered liquid and the washings received in a graduated glass cylinder form 10,000 grains' measure. Should the water which may have been required to wash the residue have increased the bulk of the solution beyond that quantity, it should be evaporated to reduce it to the bulk mentioned.

76. This being done, 1,000 water-grains' measure—that is to say, $\frac{1}{10}$th part of the aqueous solution of the soda ash above mentioned (§ 75)—are transferred to the glass beaker or vessel in which the saturation is intended to take place: it is tinged distinctly blue with tincture of litmus, and the operation is performed in the same manner and with the same precautions as for potash, the glass beaker containing the blue alkaline solution being placed upon a sheet of white paper, or a slab of white porcelain, the better to observe the change of colour which takes place when the saturating point is approaching.

77. Having put into a glass beaker the 1,000 grains' measure of the aqueous solution of soda ash to be examined (§ 75), and if the *test sulphuric acid for soda*, described before (§§ 23–27), the alkalimeter, *fig.* 22, 23, or 24, should be filled with that test acid up to the point marked 0° (taking the under line of the liquid as the true level), and poured therefrom with the precaution already indicated, stirring briskly, at the same time, the liquid in the beaker. As is the case with the alkalimetrical assay of potash, the carbonic acid expelled by the test acid reacting upon the as yet undecomposed portion of the soda ash, converts it into bicarbonate of soda, so that at first no effervescence is produced; but as soon as half the quantity of the soda in the solution is saturated, a brisk effervescence takes place. At first, therefore, the operator may pour at once, without fear, a pretty large quantity of the test acid into the alkaline solution, but as soon as this effervescence makes its appearance he should proceed with increased precaution gradually as the saturating point is approached. The *modus operandi* is, in fact, precisely as already detailed for the assay of potash, precisely the same kind and amount of care is requisite, and the assay is known to be terminated when the streaks made upon the litmus-paper with the stirring rod remain distinctly and permanently of a pink colour.

78. After saturation, and after having allowed the sides of the alkalimeter to drain, the number of divisions at which the test acid stands in the alkalimeter indicate at once the per-centage of the soda assayed, since, as we said, each division of this particular test acid represents one grain of pure soda. If, therefore, the test acid stands at 52 in the alkalimeter, then the soda assayed contained 52 per cent. of real soda. See, besides, the observations of § 48 and following, and also § 81.

79. If, instead of the special test acid for soda just alluded to, the operator employs that which has a specific gravity of 1·032, and 100 alkalimetrical divisions of which saturate one equivalent of each base, the *modus operandi* is the same—that is to say, the alkalimeter is filled with it up to 0°, and it is poured therefrom carefully into the alkaline solution; but as the equivalent of soda is 31, and 100 alkalimetrical divisions of the test sulphuric acid now employed are capable of saturating only that quantity of soda, it is clear that with the soda ash taken as an example in the preceding case, and containing 52 per cent. of real soda, the operator will have to refill his alkalimeter with the same test acid, and that a certain number of divisions of this second filling will have to be employed to perfect the saturation. In this instance the operator will find that nearly 68 divisions more, altogether 168 divisions (correctly, 167°·74) have been required to effect the saturation.

80. If, instead of the special test sulphuric acid for soda (§§ 23–27), or the test sulphuric acid for potash, soda, and other bases (§§ 31–34), the operator uses the potash and soda alkalimeter (§§ 28–35), the method is always the same (§§ 74, 75)—that is to say, the aqueous solution of the soda ash is poured into the glass beaker, the difference being merely, that instead of the alkalimeter being quite filled up with the test sulphuric acid, which, in the present instance, has a specific gravity of 1·268 (§ 29), the said test acid is poured into the alkalimeter only up to the point marked 'soda' (taking the under-line of the liquid as the true level), and the remaining divisions of the alkalimeter are carefully filled up with water. The mouth of the tube should then be thoroughly closed with the thumb of the left hand, and the whole violently shaken until perfectly mixed, taking great care, of course, not to squirt any of the acid out of the tube, which evidently would cause an amount of error proportionate to the quantity of the test acid which would have thus been lost. The acid should then be poured from the alkalimeter with the usual precaution

(§ 76) into the glass beaker containing the aqueous solution of the soda ash under examination, until complete neutralisation is attained, stirring briskly all the time, or after each addition of the test acid. The neutralisation point being hit, the sides of the alkalimeter are allowed to drain, and the operator then reads off the number of divisions employed, which number indicates the per-centage of real soda contained in the sample assayed. Thus, if the sample operated upon be the same as that alluded to before, the number of divisions employed being 52 would indicate 52 per cent. of real soda.

81. If the operator wishes to estimate the amount of soda in the sample as *carbonate of soda*, he should fill the alkalimeter with the test acid in question (specific gravity 1·268) up to the point marked *carbonate of soda*, and fill the remaining divisions with water, shake the whole well, and proceed with the neutralisation of the aqueous solution of the sample in the glass beaker as just described. Supposing, as before, that the sample in question contains 52 per cent. of real soda, it will now be found that the number of divisions employed altogether to saturate the sample completely are very nearly 89, for 52 of caustic soda correspond to 88·90 of the carbonate of that alkali.

82. If the soda ash is very poor, instead of operating upon 1,000 water-grains' measure, or one-tenth part of the whole solution (=100 grains' weight of the soda ash, §§ 76–77), it is advisable to take three or four thousand water-grains' measure of the alkaline solution, and to divide, by three or four, the result obtained by saturation. Suppose, for example, that the quantity of real soda found is 46 ; this, if only 1,000 grains' measure had been taken, would, of course, indicate 46 per cent. ; but as 4,000 water-grains' measure of solution have been taken instead, that number 46 must, accordingly, be divided by 4, which gives 11½ per cent. only of real soda contained in the sample under examination.

83. The soda ash of commerce contains generally a per-centage of insoluble substances, which are removed by filtering, as we said, and a greater or less quantity of chloride of sodium (common salt) and of sulphate of soda, which, however, do not in the slightest degree interfere with the accuracy of the result. But there is a source of error resulting from the presence in the soda ash of sulphide of calcium, of sulphite, and sometimes also, though more rarely, of hyposulphite, of soda. When sulphuret of calcium is present in the ash, on heating the latter by hot water, a double decomposition takes place : the sulphuret of calcium, reacting upon the carbonate of soda, forms sulphuret of sodium and carbonate of lime. Now sulphuret of sodium saturates the test acid just as carbonate of soda ; but as it has no commercial value, it is clear that if the ash contains a quantity of the useless sulphuret at all considerable, a very serious damage may be sustained by the purchaser if the per-centage of that substance present in the ash be taken account of as being soda. Sulphite of soda is produced from the oxidation of this sulphuret of sodium, and is objectionable inasmuch that when the test acid is added slowly to the aqueous solution of the ash, the effect is to convert the sulphite into bisulphite of soda, before any evolution of sulphurous acid, and consequently before the pink reaction on litmus-paper is produced.

84. In order to obviate the inaccuracies resulting from the neutralisation of a portion of the test acid by these substances, it is necessary to convert them into sulphates of soda, which is easily done by calcining a quantity of the sample with five or six per cent. of chlorate of potash, as recommended by Gay-Lussac and Welter. The operator, therefore, should intimately mix 50 or 60 grains' weight of pulverised chlorate of potash with 1,000 grains of the pulverised sample, and fuse the mixture in a platinum crucible, for which purpose a blowpipe gas-furnace will be found exceedingly convenient. The fused mass should be washed, and the filtrate being received into a 10,000 water-grains' measure, and made up with water to occupy that bulk, may then be assayed in every respect as described before with one or other of the test acids mentioned.

85. When, however, the soda ash contains some hyposulphite of soda—which fortunately is seldom the case, for this salt is very difficultly produced in presence of a very large excess of alkali—it should not be calcined with chlorate of potash, because in that case one equivalent of hyposulphite becomes transformed, *not into one equivalent of sulphate*, but, reacting upon one equivalent of carbonate of soda, expels its carbonic acid, and forms with the soda of the decomposed carbonate a *second equivalent* of sulphate of soda, each equivalent of hyposulphite becoming thus converted into two equivalents of sulphate, and therefore creating an error proportionate to the quantity of the hyposulphite present, each equivalent of which would thus destroy one equivalent of real and available alkali, and thus render the estimation of the sample inaccurate, and possibly to a very considerable extent.

86. When this is the case, it is therefore advisable, according to Messrs. Fordos and Gelis, to change the condition of the sulphurets, sulphites, and hyposulphites, by add-

ing a little neutral chromate of potash to the alkaline solution, whence results sul-phate of chromium, water, and a separation of sulphur, which will not affect the accu-racy of the alkalimetrical process.

87. Whether the sample to be analysed contains any sulphuret, sulphite, or hypo-sulphite, is easily ascertained as follows :—If, on pouring sulphuric acid upon a por-tion of the sample of soda ash under examination, an odour of sulphuretted hydrogen —that is, an odour of rotten eggs—is evolved, or if a portion of the soda ash, being dissolved in water, and then filtered, produces a *black* precipitate (sulphuret of lead) when solution of acetate of lead is poured into it, then the sample contains a sulphuret.

88. And if, after adding to some dilute sulphuric acid as much bichromate of potash as is necessary to impart to it a distinct reddish-yellow tinge, and a certain quantity of the solution of the soda ash under examination being poured into it. but not in sufficient quantity to neutralise the acid, the reddish-yellow colour becomes green, it is a proof that the sample contains either sulphite or hyposulphite of soda, the green tinge being due to the transformation of the chromic acid into sesquioxide of chromium.

89. And if, muriatic acid being poured into the *clear* solution of the soda ash, a turbidness supervenes after some time if left at rest, or at once if heat is applied, it is due to a deposit of sulphur, an odour of sulphurous acid being evolved, and hy-posulphite of soda is probably present. We say 'probably,' because if sulphurets and sulphites are present, the action of muriatic acid would decompose both, and liberate sulphuretted hydrogen and sulphurous acid; but as these two gases decompose each other, a turbidness due to a separation of sulphur is also formed; thus $2HS + SO^2 = 2HO + 2S$.

90. As we have already had occasion to remark, the soda ash of commerce frequently contains some, and occasionally a large quantity of caustic soda, the pro-portion of which it is at times important to determine. This may be done, according to Mr. Barreswill, by adding a solution of chloride of barium to the aqueous solution of the soda ash, by which the carbonate of soda is converted into carbonate of baryta, whilst the caustic soda, reacting upon the chloride of barium, liberates a quantity of caustic baryta proportionate to that of the caustic soda in the soda ash. After this addition of chloride of barium, the liquor is filtered in order to separate the precipitated carbonate of baryta produced, and which remains on the filter, on which it should be washed with pure water. A few lumps of chalk are then put into a Florence flask, *a*, and some muriatic acid being poured upon it, an effervescence due to a disengagement of carbonic acid is produced; the flask is then closed with a good cork, provided with a bent tube, *b*, reaching to the bottom of the vessel *c*, and the stream of carbonic acid produced is then passed through the liquor *c*, filtered from the carbonate of baryta above mentioned. The stream of carbonic acid produces a precipitate of car-bonate of baryta, which should be also collected on a

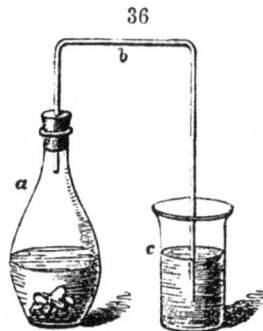

separate filter, washed, dried, and weighed. Each grain of this second precipitate of carbonate of baryta corresponds to 0·3157 of caustic soda.

91. As the soda ash of commerce almost invariably contains earthy carbonates, the sample operated upon should always be dissolved in hot water, and filtered in order to separate the carbonate of lime which otherwise would saturate a proportionate quantity of the test acid, and thus render the analysis worthless.

92. The quantity of water contained in either potash or soda ash is ascertained by heating a weighed quantity of the sample to redness in a covered platinum capsule or crucible. The loss after ignition indicates the proportion of water. If any caustic alkali is present, 1 equivalent = 9 of water, is retained, which cannot be thus elimi-nated, but which may, of course, be determined by calculation after the proportion of caustic soda has been found, as shown before, each 31 grains of caustic soda contain-ing 9 grains of water.

93. Besides the alkalimetrical processes which have been explained in the preceding pages, the proportion of available alkali contained in the sample may be estimated from the amount of carbonic acid which can be expelled by supersaturating the alkali with an acid. The determination of the value of alkalis from the quantity of car-bonic acid thus evolved by the supersaturation of the carbonate acted upon has long been known. Dr. Ure, in the 'Annals of Philosophy,' for October, 1817, and then in his 'Dictionary of Chemistry,' 1821, and more recently in his pamphlet 'Che-mistry Simplified,' described several instruments for analysing earthy and alkaline

carbonates, and for a description of which the reader is referred to the article on ACIDIMETRY. The ingenious little apparatus of Drs. Fresenius and Will for the same purpose, and to which we have already alluded in the same article, gives accurate results; but it should be observed that when the potash or soda of commerce contains any caustic alkali, or bicarbonate, or earthy carbonates, or sulphuret of alkali—which, as we have seen, is frequently, and, indeed, almost invariably, the case, the process is no longer applicable without first submitting the sample to several operations—which render this process troublesome and unsuited to unpractised hands. Thus, if caustic potash is present, the sample must be first mixed and triturated with its own weight of pure quartzose sand and about one-third of its weight of carbonate of ammonia. The mass is then moistened with aqueous ammonia, and then put into a small iron capsule

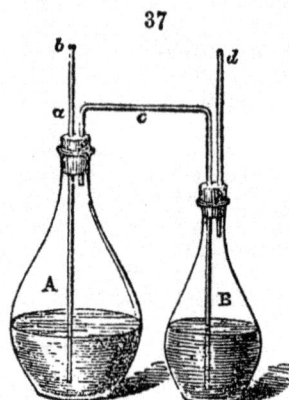

and evaporated to dryness, so as to expel completely the ammonia and carbonate of ammonia. The mass is then treated by water, filtered, washed, and concentrated to a proper bulk by evaporation, transferred to the apparatus, and treated as will be seen presently. If the sample contains caustic soda, instead of one-third, at least half of its weight of carbonate of ammonia should be employed. But for the estimation of *pure* carbonates, Drs. Fresenius and Will's method is both accurate and easy. The apparatus consists of two flasks, A and B; the first should have a capacity of from two to two ounces and a half; the second, or flask B, should be of a somewhat smaller size, and hold about one and a half or two ounces. Both should be provided with perfectly sound corks, each perforated with two holes, through which the tubes *a, c, d* are passing. The lower extremity of the tube *a* must be adjusted so as to reach nearly to the bottom of the flask A, and its upper extremity is closed by means of a small pellet of wax, *b*; *c* is a tube bent twice at right angles, one end of which merely protrudes through the cork into the flask A, but the other end reaches nearly to the bottom of the flask B. The tube *d* of the flask B merely protrudes through the cork into the flask.

94. The apparatus being so constructed, a certain quantity—100 grains, for example—of the potash or soda ash under examination (and which may have been previously dried) is weighed and introduced into the flask A, and water is next poured into this flask to about one-third of its capacity. Into the other flask, or flask B, concentrated ordinary sulphuric acid is poured, and the corks are firmly put in the flasks, which thus become connected, so as to form a twin-apparatus, which is then carried to a delicate balance, and accurately weighed. This done, the operator removes the apparatus from the balance, and applying his lips to the extremity of the tube *d*, sucks out a few air-bubbles, which, as the other tube, *a*, is closed by the wax pellet, rarefies the air in the flask A, and consequently causes the sulphuric acid of flask B to ascend a certain height (after the suction) into the tube *c*; and if, after a short time, the column of sulphuric acid maintains its height in the tube *c*, it is a proof that the apparatus is air-tight, and therefore as it should be. This being ascertained, suction is again applied to the extremity of the tube *d*, so that a portion of the sulphuric acid of the flask B ascends into the tube *c*, and presently falls into the flask A, the quantity which thus passes over being, of course, proportionate to the vacuum produced by the suction. As soon as the acid thus falls in the water containing the alkaline carbonate in the flask A, an effervescence is immediately produced, and as the carbonic acid disengaged must, in order to escape, pass, by the tube *c*, through the concentrated sulphuric acid of the flask B, it is thereby completely dried before it can finally make its exit through the tube *d*. The effervescence having subsided, suction is again applied to the tube *d*, in order to cause a fresh quantity of sulphuric acid to flow over into the flask A, as before; and so on, till the last portion of sulphuric acid sucked over produces no effervescence, which indicates, of course, that all the carbonate is decomposed, and that, consequently, the operation is at an end. A powerful suction is now applied to the tube *d*, in order to cause a tolerably large quantity of sulphuric acid, but not all, to flow into the flask A, which thus becomes very hot, from the combination of the concentrated acid with the water, so that the carbonic acid is thereby thoroughly expelled from the solution. The little wax pellet which served as a stopper is now removed from the tube *d*, and suction applied for some time, in order to sweep the flasks with atmospheric air, and thus displace all the carbonic acid in the apparatus, which is allowed to become *quite cold*, and weighed again, together with the wax pellet, the difference between the first and the second weighings—that is to say, the loss—indicating the quantity of carbonic acid which was contained in the

carbonate, which has escaped, and from which, of course, the quantity of the carbonated alkali acted upon may be calculated. Suppose in effect, that the loss is 19 grains: taking the

$$\text{Equivalent of soda} \quad . \quad . \quad . \quad . \quad . \quad . \quad . = 31$$
$$\text{do} \quad \text{carbonic acid} \quad . \quad . \quad . \quad . \quad . \quad . = 22$$
$$\text{1 equivalent of carbonate of soda} \quad . \quad . \quad . = 53,$$

it is clear that the 19 grains of carbonic acid which have been expelled represent 45·77 grains of carbonate of soda, or, in other words, 100 grains of soda ash operated upon contained 45·77 of real carbonate of soda, thus:—

$$CO_2 \quad NaO.CO_2 \quad CO_2 \qquad NaO. \quad CO_2$$
$$22 \quad : \quad 53 \quad :: \quad 19 \quad : \quad x \quad = \quad 45\text{·}77$$

95. As the soda ash of commerce always contains earthy carbonates, and very frequently sulphurets, sulphites, and occasionally hyposulphites, instead of putting the 100 grains to be operated upon directly into the flask A, it is absolutely necessary first to dissolve them in boiling water, to filter the solution, and to wash the precipitate which may be left on the filter with boiling water. The solution and the washings being mixed together, should then be reduced by evaporation to a proper volume for introduction into the flask A, and the process is then carried on as described. If sulphurets, sulphites, or hyposulphites are present, the ash should be treated exactly as mentioned in §§ 83–91, previous to pouring the solution into the flask A, since otherwise the sulphuretted hydrogen and sulphurous acid, which would be disengaged along with the carbonic acid, would apparently augment the proportion of the latter, and render the result quite erroneous.

96. The balance used for this mode of analysis should be capable of indicating small weights when heavily laden.

ALKALINE EARTHS—Baryta, Lime, and Strontia. These earths are so called to distinguish them from the earths Magnesia and Alumina. They are soluble in water, but to a much less extent than the alkalies. Their solutions impart a brown colour to turmeric paper, and neutralise acids. They are, however, distinguished from the alkalies, by their combination with carbonic acid being nearly insoluble in water.

ALKALI WASTE. A by-product obtained in the manufacture of soda-ash. By heating sulphate of soda with chalk and carbonaceous matter, a mixture of carbonate of soda and sulphide of calcium is obtained. The former salt is dissolved out on lixiviation, whilst the latter remains as an insoluble residue. It is this residue which constitutes 'alkali waste.' The accumulation of this material is often a source of great annoyance to the manufacturer, especially by the evolution of sulphuretted hydrogen. Several methods have, of late years, been introduced for the utilisation of this product, and the recovery of the sulphur which it contains. For a description of these processes see SODA.

ALKANET. (*Orcanette*, Fr.; *Orkanet*, Ger.) *Anchusa tinctoria*. A species of bugloss, or boragewort, cultivated in the neighbourhood of Montpellier and in the Levant. It is sometimes called the bugloss of Languedoc, or the dyer's bugloss. The anchusa is a rough plant, with downy and spear-shaped leaves, and clusters of small purple or reddish flowers, the stamens of which are shorter than the corolla. It affords a fine red colour to alcohol and oils, but a dirty red to water. Its principal use is for colouring ointments, oils, and pomades. The spirituous tincture gives to white marble a beautiful deep stain; but, usually, wax is coloured with the anchusa, and then applied to the surface of warm marble. It stains it flesh-colour, and the stain sinks deep into the stone. Oil coloured by alkanet is used for staining wood in imitation of rosewood.

Alkanet root was analysed by Dr. John, who found the constituents to be a *peculiar colouring* matter (*pseudo-alkanium*), 5·50; extractive, 1·00; gum, 6·25; matters extracted by caustic potash, 65·00; woody fibre, 18·00.

The colouring matter resides in the cortical part of the root, and was regarded by Pelletier as a kind of fatty acid (*anchusic acid*); but it is now usually considered to be a resinoid (*anchusine*), whose composition is $C_{33} H_{20} O_8$ (C_{33} H_{40} O_8). This root is sometimes termed the spurious *alkanet root* (*radix alkannæ spuriæ*), to distinguish it from the Al-kenna.

AL-KENNA, or **AL-HENNA,** is the name of the roots and leaves of *Lawsonia inermis*, which have been long employed in the East to dye the nails, teeth, hair, garments, &c. The leaves, ground and mixed with a little limewater, serve for dyeing the tails of horses in Persia and Turkey.

It is the same as the herb *Henna* frequently referred to by the Oriental poets. The powder of the leaves, being wet, forms a paste, which is bound on the nails for a night, and the colour thus given will last for several weeks.

This plant is distinguished as the true alkanet root (*radix alkannæ vera*).

ALLEMONTITE. A native alloy of arsenic and antimony, containing Sb As³. It is found at Allemont, in Dauphiny (whence the name); at Przibram, in Bohemia; and at Andreasberg, in the Hartz.

ALLIGATION. An arithmetical formula, useful on many occasions for ascertaining the proportion of constituents in a mixture, when they have undergone no change of volume by chemical action, or for finding the price or value of compounds consisting of ingredients of different values. Thus, if a quantity of sugar worth 8*d*. the pound, and another quantity worth 10*d*., are mixed, the question to be solved by alligation is, what is the value of the mixture by the pound? Alligation is of two kinds—*medial*, and *alternate; medial*, when the rate of mixture is sought from the rates and quantities of the simples; *alternate*, when the quantities of the simples are sought from the rates of the simples and the rate of the mixture.—*Webster.*

ALLIOLE. *Alliole* is obtained by distilling crude naphtha, and collecting all that leaves the still in the first distillation before the boiling temperature reaches 194° F.; and on the second distillation, all below 176° F. It boils, when nearly free from *benzole*, at a temperature of from 140° to 158° F., and possesses an alliaceous odour somewhat resembling that of bi-sulphide of carbon.

ALLIUM. A genus of plants belonging to the *Liliaceæ* or lily-order. The bulbs of many species are esculent. *Allium Cepa* is the onion; *A. sativum*, garlic; *A. porrum*, the leek; *A. Ascalonicum*, the shallot; *A. Schœnoprasum*, the chive. The so-called 'Spanish onions,' imported from Spain, Portugal, and Egypt, are merely the large bulbs of varieties of the common onion, which, cultivated in warm dry countries, lose much of their pungency.

ALLOCLASE. A mineral found in the Bannat—once regarded as a Cobalt-glance. It appears to be of a very complex and variable composition. Essentially it is a compound of sulphur, arsenic, iron, zinc, and cobalt.

ALLOPHANE—from ἄλλος *other*, and φαίνω *to appear*, in allusion to the change of appearance which this mineral undergoes before the blowpipe flame. This mineral, which is a hydrated silicate of alumina, consists essentially of silica 24·22, alumina 40·39, and water 35·39. It is generally found lining small cavities, and in veins in marl or chalk. Allophanes have been found containing from 14 to 19 per cent. of oxide of copper, which give them a green colour.

ALLOTROPY. *Allotropic Condition.* A name introduced by Berzelius to signify *another form* of the same substance, derived from ἄλλος, *another*, and τρόπος, *habit*. Carbon, for example, exists as the diamond, a brilliant gem, with difficulty combustible; as graphite, a dark, opaque mass, often crystalline, also of great infusibility; and as charcoal, a dark porous body, which burns with facility.

Sulphur, when melted, is at 230° F. perfectly liquid. Being heated to 430° F., it becomes thick and so tenacious that it can scarcely be poured out of the vessel in which it is melted. When heated to 480° it again becomes liquid, and continues so until it boils. These examples are sufficient to explain the meaning of this term. An extensive series of bodies appears to assume similar allotropic modifications. The probability is that, with the advance of physical and chemical science, many of the substances now supposed to be elementary will be proved to be but allotropic states of some one form of matter. See ISOMERISM.

ALLOY. (*Alliage*, Fr.; *Legirung*, Ger.) From the French *allier*, to unite or mix; or the Latin *alligo*, to bind. This term formerly signified mixing some baser metal with gold and silver, and this meaning is still preserved in reference to coinage; but, in chemistry, it now means any compound of any two or more metals whatever. Thus, bronze is an alloy of copper and tin; brass, an alloy of copper and zinc; and type metal, an alloy of lead and antimony. All the alloys possess metallic lustre, even when cut or broken to pieces; they are opaque; are excellent conductors of heat and electricity; are frequently susceptible of crystallising; are more or less ductile, malleable, elastic, and sonorous. An alloy which consists of metals differently fusible is usually malleable when cold, and brittle when hot, as is exemplified with brass and gong metal.

Many alloys consist of definite or atomic proportions of the simple component metals, though some alloys seem to form in any proportion, like combinations of salt or sugar with water. It is probable that peculiar properties belong to the atomic ratio, as is exemplified in the superior quality of brass made in that proportion.

The experiments of Crookewitt upon amalgams appear to prove that the combination of metals in alloys obeys some laws of a similar character to those which prevail between combining bodies in solution; *i.e.* that a true combining proportion existed.

By amalgamation and straining through chamois leather, he obtained crystalline metallic compounds of gold, bismuth, lead, and cadmium, with mercury, which appeared to exist in true definite proportions. With potassium he obtained two amalgams, KHg^{20} and KHg^{25}. With silver, by bringing mercury in contact with a solution of nitrate of silver, according to the quantity of mercury employed, he obtained such amalgams as Ag^3Hg^{16}, $AgHg^2$, $AgHg^3$, $AgHg^4$.

Beyond those there are many experiments which appear to prove that alloys are true chemical compounds; but, at the same time, it is highly probable that the true chemical alloy is very often *dissolved* (mechanically disseminated) in that metal which is largely in excess. In some cases, however, the alloy appears to be nothing more than a mechanical mixture of the component metals.

Some years since, the Editor, at the request of Sir Henry De la Beche, and guided by the advice of Professor Graham, carried out a series of experiments in the laboratory of the Museum of Practical Geology, with the view of obtaining a good alloy for soldiers' medals, and the results confirmed the views respecting the laws of definite proportional combination among the metals. Many of those alloys were struck at the Mint, and yielded beautiful impressions; but there were many objections urged against the use of any alloy for a medal of honour.

One metal does not alloy indifferently with every other metal, but it is governed in this respect by peculiar affinities; thus, silver will hardly unite with iron, but it combines readily with gold, copper, and lead. In comparing the alloys with their constituent metals, the following differences may be noted. In general, the ductility of the alloy is less than that of the separate metals, and sometimes in a very remarkable degree; on the contrary, the alloy is usually harder than the mean hardness of its constituents. The mercurial alloys or amalgams are, perhaps, exceptions to this rule.

The specific gravity is rarely the mean between that of each of its constituents, but is sometimes greater and sometimes less; indicating, in the former case, a closer cohesion, and, in the latter, a recedure, of the particles from each other in the act of their union. The alloys of the following metals have been examined by Crookewitt, and he has given their specific gravities as in the following Table; the specific gravity of the unalloyed metals being—

Copper	.	.	. 8·794	Zinc.	.	. 6·860
Tin	.	.	. 7·305	Lead	.	. 11·354

That of the alloys was—

$Cu^2 Sn^5$	.	. 7·652	$Cu\ Pb$	.	. 10·375
$Cu\ Sn$	.	. 8·072	$Sn\ Zn^2$	.	. 7·096
$Cu^2 Sn$	.	. 8·512	$Sn\ Zn$	.	. 7·115
$Cu^3 Zn^5$	.	. 7·939	$Sn^3 Zn$	.	. 7·235
$Cu^3 Zn^2$	.	. 8·224	$Sn\ Pb^2$	.	. 9·965
$Cu^2 Zn$	.	. 8·392	$Sn\ Pb$	.	. 9·394
$Cu^2 Pb^3$	.	. 10·753	$Sn^3 Pb$	.	. 9·025

The following Tables of binary alloys exhibit this circumstance in experimental detail :—

Alloys having a density greater than the mean of their constituents.	Alloys having a density less than the mean of their constituents.
Gold and zinc	Gold and silver
Gold and tin	Gold and iron
Gold and bismuth	Gold and lead
Gold and antimony	Gold and copper
Gold and cobalt	Gold and iridium
Silver and zinc	Gold and nickel
Silver and lead	Silver and copper
Silver and tin	Iron and bismuth
Silver and bismuth	Iron and antimony
Silver and antimony	Iron and lead
Copper and zinc	Tin and lead
Copper and tin	Tin and palladium
Copper and palladium	Tin and antimony
Copper and bismuth	Nickel and arsenic
Lead and antimony	Zinc and antimony
Platinum and molybdenum	
Palladium and bismuth	

There are many points of great physical as well as chemical interest in connection with alloys, which require a closer study than they have yet received. There are some striking facts, brought forward by M. Wertheim, deduced from experiments carried on upon fifty-four binary alloys and nine ternary alloys of simple and known composition, which will be found in the 'Journal of the French Institute,' to which the reader desiring information on this point is referred.

It is hardly possible to infer the melting point of an alloy from that of each of its constituent metals; but, in general, the fusibility is increased by mutual affinity in their state of combination. Of this a remarkable instance is afforded in the fusible metal consisting of 8 parts of bismuth, 5 of lead, and 3 of tin, which melts at the heat of boiling water, or 212° F., though the melting point deduced from the mean of its components should be 514° F. This alloy may be rendered still more fusible by adding a little mercury to it, when it forms an excellent material for anatomical injections. See FUSIBLE METAL.

On the Melting Point of Certain Alloys.

	Centigrade Thermometer.		Centigrade Thermometer.
Lead	334°	Tin, 2 atoms; lead, 1 atom .	196°
Tin	230°	„ 1 „ „ 1 „ .	241°
Tin, 5 atoms; lead, 1 atom .	194°	„ 1 „ „ 3 „ .	289°
„ 4 „ „ 1 „ .	189°	„ 2 vols.; „ 1 vol. .	194°
„ 3 „ „ 1 „ .	186°		

In these experiments of M. Kupffer, the temperatures were determined with thermometers of great delicacy, and the weighings were carefully carried out.—*Ann. de Chimie*, xl. 285–302; *Brewster's Edin. Jour. Sci.* i. N.S. p. 299.

The colours of alloys do not depend in any considerable degree upon those of the separate metals; thus, the colour of copper, instead of being rendered paler by a large addition of zinc, is thereby converted into a rich-looking yellow metal, brass.

By means of alloys, we multiply, as it were, the number of useful metals, and sometimes give usefulness to such as are separately of little value. Since these compounds can be formed only by fusion, and that many metals are apt to oxidise readily at their melting temperature, proper precautions must be taken in making alloys to prevent this occurrence. Thus, in combining tin and lead, resin or grease is usually put on the surface of the melting metals, the carbon produced by the decomposition of which protects them, in most cases, sufficiently from oxidation. When we wish to combine tin and iron, as in the tinning of cast-iron tea-kettles, we rub sal-ammoniac upon the surfaces of the hot metals in contact with each other, and thus exclude the atmospheric oxygen by means of its fumes. When there is a notable difference in the specific gravities of the metals which we wish to combine, we often find great difficulties in obtaining homogeneous alloys; for each metal may tend to assume the level due to its density, as is remarkably exemplified in alloys of gold and silver made without adequate stirring of the melting metals. If the mass be large and slow of cooling, after it is cast in an upright cylindrical form, the metals sometimes separate, to a certain degree, in the order of their densities. Thus, in casting large bells and cannon with copper alloys, the bottom of the casting is apt to contain too much copper and the top too much tin, unless very dexterous manipulation in mixing the fused materials has been employed immediately before the pouring out of the melted mass. When such inequalities are observed, the objects are broken and re-melted, after which they form a much more homogeneous alloy. This artifice of a double melting is often had recourse to, and especially in casting the alloys for the specula of telescopes.

When we wish to alloy three or more metals, we often experience difficulties, either because one of the metals is more oxidisable, or denser, or more fusible, than the others, or because there is no direct affinity between two of the metals. In the latter predicament, we shall succeed better by combining the three metals first in pairs, for example, and then melting the two pairs together. Thus, it is difficult to unite iron with bronze directly; but if, instead of iron, we use tin plate, we shall immediately succeed, and the bronze, in this manner, acquires valuable qualities from the iron. Thus, also, to render brass better adapted for some purposes, a small quantity of lead is sometimes added to it, but this cannot be done directly with advantage; it is better to melt the lead first along with the zinc, and then to add this alloy to the melting copper, or the copper to that alloy, and fuse them together.

One of the alloys most useful to the arts is brass; it is more ductile and less easily oxidised than even its copper constituent, notwithstanding the opposite nature of the zinc. (See BRASS.) This alloy may exist in many different proportions, under which it has different names, as tombac, similor, pinchbeck, &c. Copper and tin form compounds of remarkable utility, known under the name of *hard brass*, for the bushes, steps, and bearings of the axles, arbours, and spindles in machinery; and of *bronze, bell-metal*, &c. (See BRONZE, &c.) Gold and silver, in their pure state, are too soft and flexible to form either vessels or coins of sufficient strength and durability; but when alloyed with a little copper, they acquire the requisite hardness and stiffness for these and other purposes. Aluminium has been found by Dr. Percy to possess the same hardening property. See ALUMINIUM BRONZE.

When we have occasion to unite several pieces of the same or of different metals, we employ the process called *soldering*, which consists in fixing together the surfaces by means of an interposed alloy, which must be necessarily more fusible than the metal or metals to be joined. That alloy must also consist of metals which possess a strong affinity for the substances to be soldered together. Hence each metal would seem to require a particular kind of solder, which is, to a certain extent, true. Thus, the solder for gold trinkets and plate is an alloy of gold and silver, or gold and copper; that for silver trinkets is an alloy of silver and copper; that for copper is either fine tin, for pieces that must not be exposed to the fire, or a brass alloy called hard solder, of which the zinc forms a considerable proportion. The solder of lead and tin plate is an alloy of lead and tin, and that of tin is the same alloy with a little bismuth. Tinning, gilding, and silvering may also be reckoned as species of alloys, since the tin, gold, and silver are superficially united in these cases to other metals.

Metallic alloys possess usually more tenacity than could be inferred from their constituents; thus, an alloy of 12 parts of lead with 1 of zinc has a tenacity double that of zinc.

The cohesive force of alloys is well shown in the annexed Table (p. 94), in which the results are mostly those obtained by Muschenbroek.[1]

Metallic alloys are generally much more easily oxidised than the separate metals, a phenomenon which may be ascribed to the increased affinity for oxygen which results from the tendency of the one of the oxides to combine with the other. An alloy of tin and lead heated to redness takes fire, and continues to burn for some time like a piece of bad turf.

Every alloy is, in reference to the arts and manufactures, a new metal, on account of its chemical and physical properties. A vast field here remains to be explored. Not above 60 alloys have been studied by the chemists out of many hundreds which may be made; and of these but few have been yet practically employed. Very slight modifications often constitute valuable improvements upon metallic bodies. Thus, the brass most esteemed by turners at the lathe contains from 2 to 3 per cent. of lead; but such brass does not work well under the hammer; and, reciprocally, the brass which is best under the hammer is too tough for turning.

M. Chaudet has made some experiments on the means of detecting the metals of alloys by the cupelling furnace, and they promise useful applications. The testing depends upon the appearance exhibited by the metals and their alloys when heated on a cupel. The following were Chaudet's results:—

Metals.—Pure tin, when heated this way, fuses, becomes of a greyish-black colour, fumes a little, exhibits incandescent points on its surface, and leaves an oxide which, when withdrawn from the fire, is at first lemon-yellow, but, when cold, white. Antimony melts, preserves its brilliancy, fumes, and leaves the vessel coloured lemon-yellow when hot, but colourless when cold, except a few spots of a rose tint. Zinc burns brilliantly, forming a cone of oxide; and the oxide, much increased in volume, is, when hot, greenish, but, when cold, perfectly white. Bismuth fumes, becomes covered with a coat of melted oxide, part of which sublimes, and the rest enters the pores of the cupel; when cold, the cupel is of a fine yellow colour, with spots of a greenish hue. Lead resembles bismuth very much; the cold cupel is of a lemon-yellow colour. Copper melts, and becomes covered with a coat of black oxide; sometimes spots of a rose tint remain on the cupel.

Alloys.—Tin 75, antimony 25, melt, become covered with a coat of black oxide, have very few incandescent points; when cold, the oxide is nearly black, in consequence of the action of antimony; a $\frac{1}{400}$th part of antimony may be ascertained, in this way, in the alloy. An alloy of antimony containing tin leaves oxide of tin in the cupel; a $\frac{1}{100}$th part of tin may be thus detected. An alloy of tin and zinc gives an oxide which, whilst hot, is of a green tint, and resembles philosopher's wool in appearance. An alloy containing 99 tin 1 zinc did not present the incandescent points of pure tin, and gave an oxide of greenish tint when cold. Tin 95, bismuth 5 parts, gave an oxide of a grey colour. Tin and lead give an oxide of a rusty brown colour. An alloy of lead and tin, containing only 1 per cent. of the latter metal, when

---

[1] Encyclopedia Britannica, Art. STRENGTH, and introduction ad Philoso. Naturæ.

ALLOY OF						Specific Cohesion	Cohesion of square inch in lbs. Avoirdupois	Specific Gravity
	PARTS				PARTS			
Gold .	.	. 2	Silver .	.	. 1	2·972	28,000	
ditto .	.	. 5	Copper	.	. 1	5·307	50,000	
Silver .	.	. 5	ditto .	.	. 1	5·148	48,500	
ditto .	.	. 4	Tin	.	. 1	4·352	41,000	
Brass .	.	.	.	.	.	4·870	45,882	
Copper	.	. 10	Tin	.	. 1	3·407	32,093	
ditto .	.	. 8	ditto .	.	. 1	3·831	36,088	
ditto .	.	. 4	ditto .	.	. 1	4·687	44,071	
ditto .	.	. 6	ditto .	.	. 1	3·794	35,739	
ditto .	.	. 2	ditto .	.	. 1	0·108	1,017	
ditto .	.	. 1	ditto .	.	. 1	0·077	725	
Tin (English)	. 10		Lead	.	. 1	0·733	6,904	
ditto .	.	. 8	ditto .	.	. 1	0·841	7,922	
ditto .	.	. 6	ditto .	.	. 1	0·849	7,997	
ditto .	.	. 4	ditto .	.	. 1	1·126	10,607	
ditto .	.	. 2	ditto .	.	. 1	0·793	7,470	
ditto .	.	. 1	ditto .	.	. 1	0·751	7,074	
Tin (Banca)	. 10		Antimony .		. 1	1·187	11,181	7·359
ditto .	.	. 8	ditto .	.	. 1	1·049	9,881	7·276
ditto .	.	. 6	ditto .	.	. 1	1·341	12,632	7·228
ditto .	.	. 4	ditto .	.	. 1	1·431	13,480	7·192
ditto .	.	. 2	ditto .	.	. 1	1·277	12,092	7·105
ditto .	.	. 1	ditto .	.	. 1	0·338	3,184	7·060
ditto .	.	. 10	Bismuth	.	. 1	1·347	12,688	7·576
ditto .	.	. 4	ditto .	.	. 1	1·772	16,692	7·613
ditto .	.	. 2	ditto .	.	. 1	1·488	14,017	8·076
ditto .	.	. 1	ditto .	.	. 1	1·276	12,020	8·146
ditto .	.	. 1	ditto .	.	. 2	1·063	10,013	8·58
ditto .	.	. 1	ditto .	.	. 4	0·836	7,875	9·009
ditto .	.	. 1	ditto .	.	. 10	0·411	3,871	9·439
Tin (English) .		. 1	Zinc	.	. 1	0·958	9,024	
ditto .	.	. 2	ditto .	.	. 1	1·164	10,964	
ditto .	.	. 4	ditto .	.	. 1	1·089	10,258	
ditto .	.	. 8	ditto .	.	. 1	1·126	10,607	
ditto .	.	. 1	Antimony .		. 1	0·154	1,450	7·000
ditto .	.	. 3	ditto .	.	. 2	0·338	3,184	
ditto .	.	. 4	ditto .	.	. 1	1·202	11,323	
Lead (Scotch)	. 1		Bismuth	.	. 1	0·777	7,319	10·931
ditto .	.	. 2	ditto .	.	. 1	0·620	5,840	11·090
ditto .	.	. 10	ditto .	.	. 1	0·300	2,826	10·827

heated, does not expose a clean surface, like lead, but is covered at times with oxide of tin. Tin 75 and copper 25 gave a black oxide: if the heat be much elevated, the underpart of the oxide is white, which is oxide of tin; the upper part is black, being the oxide of copper, and the cupel becomes of a rose colour. If the tin be impure from iron, the oxide produced by it is marked with spots of a rust colour.

The degree of affinity between metals may be in some measure estimated by the greater or less facility with which, when of different degrees of fusibility or volatility, they unite, or with which they can, after union, be separated by heat. The greater or less tendency to separate into differently proportioned alloys, by long-continued fusion, may also give some information upon this subject. Mr. Hatchett remarked, in his elaborate researches on metallic alloys, that gold made standard with the usual precautions, by silver, copper, lead, antimony, &c., and then cast, after long fusion, into vertical bars, was by no means an uniform compound; but that the top of the bar, corresponding to the metal at the bottom of the crucible, contained the larger proportion of gold. Hence, for a more thorough combination, two red-hot crucibles should be employed, and the liquefied metals should be alternately poured from the one into the other. To prevent unnecessary oxidisation from the air, the crucibles should contain, besides the metal, a mixture of common salt and pounded charcoal. The metallic alloy should also be occasionally stirred up with a rod of earthenware.

When there is a strong affinity between the two metals, their alloy is generally denser than the mean, and *vice versâ*. This is exemplified, as previously shown, in the alloys of copper with zinc and tin, on the one hand, and with copper and lead on the other. When one of the metals, however, is added in excess, there result an atomic compound and an indefinite combination, as would appear from Muschenbroek's experiments. Thus:—

1 of lead with 4 of silver give a density of 10·480
1	do	2	do	11·032
1	do	3	do	10·831

The proportion of the constituents is on this principle estimated in France by the *test of the ball* applied to pewter; in which the weight of the alloyed ball is compared with that of a ball of pure tin or standard pewter cast in the same mould. Alloys possess the elasticity belonging to the mean of their constituents, and also the specific heat.

According to M. Rudberg, while lead solidifies at 325° C., and tin at 228°, their atomic alloy solidifies at 187°, which he calls the fixed point, for a compound Pb Sn³.

An alloy too slowly cooled is often apt to favour the crystallisation of one or more of its components, and thus to render it brittle; and hence an iron mould is preferable to one of sand when there is danger of such a result.

It is not a matter of indifference in what order the metals are melted together in making an alloy. Thus, if we combine 90 parts of tin and 10 of copper, and to this alloy add 10 of antimony; or if we combine 10 parts of antimony with 10 of copper, and add to that alloy 90 parts of tin, we shall have two alloys chemically the same; and still it will be easy to discover that, in other respects—fusibility, tenacity, &c.—they totally differ. Whence this result? Obviously from the nature of their combination, dependent upon the order pursued in the preparation, and which continues after the mixture. In the alloys of lead and antimony also, if the heat be raised in combining the two metals together much above their fusing points, the alloy becomes harsh and brittle; probably because some alloy formed at that high temperature is not soluble in the mass.

In common cases the specific gravity affords a good criterion whereby to judge of the proportion of two metals in an alloy. But a very fallacious rule has been given in some respectable works for computing the specific gravity that should result from the alloying of given quantities of two metals of known densities, supposing no chemical condensation or expansion of volume to take place. Thus, it has been taught, that if gold and copper be united in equal weights, the computed specific gravity is merely the arithmetical mean between the numbers denoting the two specific gravities. Whereas, the specific gravity of any alloy must be computed by dividing the sum of the two weights by the sum of the two volumes, compared, for convenience sake, to water reckoned unity. Or, in another form, the rule may be stated thus:—Multiply the sum of the weights into the products of the two specific-gravity numbers for a numerator; and multiply each specific-gravity number into the weight of the other body, and add the two products together for a denominator. The quotient obtained by dividing the said numerator by the denominator is the truly computed mean specific gravity of the alloy. On comparing with that density the density found by experiment, we shall see whether expansion or condensation of volume has attended the metallic combination. Gold having a specific gravity of 19·36, and copper of 8·87, when they are alloyed in equal weights, give, by the fallacious rule of the arithmetical mean of the densities $\frac{19\cdot36 + 8\cdot87}{2} = 14\cdot11$; whereas the rightly computed density is only 12·16. It is evident that, on comparing the first result with experiment, we should be led to infer that there had been a prodigious condensation of volume, though expansion has actually taken place. Let W, w be the two weights; P, p the two specific gravities, then M, the mean specific gravity, is given by the formula

$$M = \frac{(W + w)\,Pp}{Pw + pW} \quad \therefore \quad 2\,\Delta = -\frac{(P-p)^2}{P+p}$$

= twice the error of the arithmetical mean; which is therefore always in excess.

Alloys of a somewhat complex character are made by Mr. Alexander Parkes, of Birmingham, of a white or pale colour, by melting together 33½ lbs. of foreign zinc, 64 of tin, 1¼ of iron, and 3 of copper; or 50 zinc, 48 tin, 1 iron, and 3 copper; or any intermediate proportion of zinc and copper may be used. The iron and copper are first melted together in a crucible, the tin is next introduced, in such quantities at a time as not to solidify the iron and copper; the zinc is added lastly, and the whole mixed by stirring. The flux recommended for this alloy is, 1 part of lime, 1 part of Cumberland iron ore, and 3 parts of sal-ammoniac.

Another of his alloys is composed of 66 lbs. of foreign zinc, 33½ tin, 3¼ antimony; or 70¾ zinc, 19½ tin, and 2¾ antimony; or any intermediate proportions, and with or without arsenic. He uses black flux. When to be applied to the sheathing of ships, from 8 to 16 oz. of metallic arsenic are added to every 100 lbs. of alloy. A third class of alloys consists of equal parts of iron and nickel; the copper is next added, and lastly the zinc, or the copper and zinc may be added as an alloy. 100 lbs. may consist of 45½ lbs. of iron and nickel (*partes æquales*), and 10½ lbs. of foreign zinc; or 30¾ lbs. of alloy of iron and nickel (*p. æ.*), 46 copper, and 26½ zinc; or any intermediate proportions of zinc and copper. He uses also an alloy of 60 lbs. of copper, 20 of zinc, and 20 of silver; or 60 copper, 10 nickel, 10 silver, and 20 zinc; the copper and nickel being first fused together. His fifth alloy is called by him a non-conductor of heat! It is made of 25 nickel, 25 iron, and 50 copper; or 15 nickel, 25 iron, and 60 copper; the last being added after the fusion of the others.

It may prove convenient to give a general statement of the more striking peculiarities of the important alloys. More detailed information will be found under the heads of the respective metals.

GOLD AND SILVER ALLOYS.—The British standard for gold coin is 22 parts pure gold and 2 parts alloy, and for silver, 222 parts pure silver to 18 parts of alloy.

The alloy for the gold is an indefinite proportion of silver and copper: some coin has a dark red colour from the alloy being chiefly copper; the lighter the colour a larger portion of silver is indicated, sometimes even (when no copper is present) it approaches to a greenish tinge, but the proportion of pure gold is the same in either case.

The alloy for silver coinage is always copper; and a very pure quality of this metal is used for alloying, both for the gold and silver coinage, as almost any other metal being present, even in very small quantities, would make the metals unfit for coinage, from rendering the gold, silver, and copper brittle, or not sufficiently malleable.

The standard for plate (silver) is the same as the coin, and requires the same quantity of copper, and carefully melting with two or three bits of charcoal on the surface while in fusion, to prevent the oxidation of the copper by heat and exposure to the atmosphere.

The gold standard for plate and jewellery varies, by an Act of Parliament, from the 22 carats pure, to 18, 12, and 9: the alloys are gold and silver, in various proportions according to the taste of the workmen; the colour of the articles manufactured depending, as with the coin, on the proportions; if no copper is used in qualities under 22 carats fine gold, the colour varies from a soft green to a greenish white, but a proportion of copper may be used so as to bring the colour to nearly that of 22 fine, 1 silver, and 1 copper.

Wire of either gold or silver may be drawn of any quality, but the ordinary wire for fine purposes, such as lace, contains from 5 to 9 pennyweights of copper in the pound of 240 pennyweights, to render it not so soft as it would be with pure silver.

Gold, silver, and copper may be mixed in any proportions without injury to the ductility, but no reliable scale of tenacity appears to have been constructed, although gold and silver in almost any proportions may be drawn to the very finest wire.

The alloys of silver and palladium may be made in any proportions; it has been found that even 3 per cent. of palladium prevents silver tarnishing so soon as without it; 10 per cent. very considerably protects the silver, and 30 per cent. of palladium will prevent the silver being affected by fumes of sulphuretted hydrogen unless very long exposed: the latter alloy has been found useful for dental purposes, and the alloy with less proportions—say 10 to 15 per cent.—has been used for graduated scales of mathematical instruments.

The alloy of platinum and silver is made for the same purposes as those of palladium, and, by proper care in fusion, are nearly equally useful, but the platinum does not seem to so perfectly combine with the silver as the palladium. Any proportion of palladium with gold injures the colour, and even 1 per cent. may be detected by sight, and 5 per cent. renders it a silver colour, while about 10 per cent. destroys it; but the ductility of the alloy is not much injured.

Gold leaf for gilding contains from 3 to 12 grains of alloy to the ounce. The gold used by respectable dentists is nearly pure, but necessarily contains about 6 grains of copper to the ounce troy, or $\frac{1}{80}$th part.

Antimony in the proportion of $\frac{1}{1920}$ quite destroys the ductility of gold.

Gold and platinum alloy forms a somewhat elastic metal. Hermstadt's imitation of gold consists of 16 parts of platinum, 7 parts of copper, and 1 of zinc, put in a crucible, covered with charcoal powder, and melted into a mass.—P. J.

Dentist's Alloy. For the ordinary purposes of mounting artificial teeth a peculiar metal is required. It must be sufficiently hard and tough, and it must not be liable to corrosion by either acid or acrid fluids. Experience has shown that an alloy of gold, silver, and copper most nearly meets all the required conditions. Dentists use 16-carat gold, which is $\frac{2}{3}$ fine gold and $\frac{1}{3}$ alloy, the alloy being always nearly equal portions of silver and copper, which is not, for these purposes, in the slightest degree injurious.—See AMALGAM.

COPPER ALLOYS.—Copper alloyed with zinc forms BRASS, and with tin we have BRONZE. (See those articles.) The best *Kingston's Metal* is an alloy of copper, tin, and mercury; it is much used for bearings. (See KINGSTON'S METAL.) The alloys of the ancients were usually either brasses or bronzes. The following analyses of ancient coins, &c., by Mr. John Arthur Phillips, are of great value :—

	B.C.	A.D.	Copper	Tin	Lead	Iron	Zinc	Silver	Sulph.	Nickel	Cobalt
Æs	500	..	69·69	7·16	21·82	·47	..	..	trace	trace	·?7
Semis	500	..	62·04	7·66	29·32	·18	..	..	trace	·19	·23
Quadrans	500	..	72·22	7·17	19·56	·40	..	..	trace	·20	·29
Hiero I.	470	..	94·15	5·49	..	·32					
Alexander the Great	335	..	86·77	12·99	..	..	..	..	·06		
Philippus III.	323	..	90·27	9·43							
Philippus V.	200	..	85·15	11·12	2·85	·42	..	..	trace		
Copper coin of Athens	?	..	88·34	9·95	·63	·26	..	..	..	trace	trace
Egyptian, Ptolemy IX.	70	..	84·21	15·64	..	trace	..	..	trace	..	trace
Pompey, First Brass	53	..	74·17	8·47	16·15	·29					
Coin of the Atilia Family	45	..	68·69	4·86	25·43	·11	..	..	..	trace	trace
Julius and Augustus	42	..	79·13	8·00	12·81	trace	..	..	trace		
Augustus and Agrippa	30	..	78·45	12·96	8·62	trace	..	..	trace		
Large Brass of the Cassia Family	20	..	82·26	..	..	·35	17·31	..	trace		
Sword-blade	..	..	89·69	9·58	..	·33	..	..	trace		
Broken sword-blade	..	..	85·62	10·02	..	·44					
Fragment of a sword-blade	..	..	91·79	8·17	..	trace	..	..	trace		
Broken spear-head	..	..	99·71	..	..	..	..	..	·28		
Celt	..	..	90·68	7·43	1·28	trace	..	..	trace		
Celt	..	..	90·18	9·81	..	trace					
Celt	..	..	89·33	9·19	..	·33	..	..	·24		
Celt	..	..	83·61	10·79	3·20	·58	..	..	.	trace	·34
Large Brass of Nero	..	60	81·07	1·05	..	..	17·81				
Titus	..	79	83·04	..	..	·50	15·84				
Hadrian	..	120	85·67	1·14	1·73	·74	10·85				
Faustina, Jun.	..	165	79·14	4·97	9·18	·23	6·27				
Greek Imperial Samosata	..	212	70·91	6·75	21·96	trace					
Victorinus, Sen. (No. 1)	..	262	95·37	·99	trace	trace	..	1·60			
Victorinus, Sen. (No. 2)	..	262	97·13	·10	trace	1·01	..	1·76			
Tetrius, Sen. (No. 1)	..	267	98·50	·37	trace	·46	..	·76			
Tetrius, Sen. (No. 2)	..	268	98·00	·51	..	·05	..	1·15			
Claudius Gothicus, (No. 1)	..	268	81·60	7·41	8·11	..	..	1·86			
Claudius Gothicus, (No. 2)	..		84·70	3·01	2·67	·31	trace	7·93			
Tacitus (No. 1)	..	275	86·08	3·63	4·87	..	..	4·42			
Tacitus (No. 2)	..		91·46	..	..	2·31	..	5·92			
Probus (No. 1)	..	275	90·68	200	2·33	·61	1·39	2·24			
Probus (No. 2)	..		94·65	·45	·45	·80	..	3·22			

Copper, when united with half its weight of lead, forms an inferior alloy, resembling gun-metal in colour, but it is softer and cheaper. This alloy is called *pot-metal* and *cock-metal*, because it is used for large measures and in the manufacture of taps and cocks of all descriptions.

Sometimes a small quantity of zinc is added to pot-metal; but when this is considerable the copper seizes the zinc to form brass, and leaves the lead at liberty, a large portion of which separates on cooling. Zinc and lead are not disposed to unite; but a little arsenic occasions them to combine.

It is not a little curious to find that some of the coins of high antiquity contain zinc: this must have been introduced by the use of calamine, since it does not appear that zinc was known as a metal before 1280 A.D., when Albertus Magnus speaks of it as a *semi-metal*, and calls the alloy of copper and zinc *golden marcasite ;* or rather, perhaps, he means to apply that name to zinc, from its power of imparting a golden colour to copper. The probability is that calamine was known from the earliest times as a peculiar earth, although it was not thought to be an ore of zinc or of any other metal.—See 'Watson's Chemical Essays.'

LEAD ALLOYS.—Of the alloys of copper and lead, Mr. Holtzapffel gives the following description:—Two ounces lead to one pound copper produces a red-coloured and ductile alloy.

Four ounces lead to 1 pound copper gives an alloy less red and ductile. Neither of these is so much used as those following (p. 100), as the object is to employ as much lead as possible.

Tabular Statement of the Physical Peculiarities of the Principal Alloys, adopted, with some alterations, from the ' Encyclopédie Technologique.'

BRITTLE METALS		
ARSENIC	ANTIMONY	BISMUTH
With ZINC, rendering it brittle.	This alloy is very brittle.	Unknown.
With IRON and STEEL, hardening, whitening, and rendering those metals susceptible of a fine polish: much used for steel chains and other ornaments.	30 of iron and 70 of antimony are fusible; very hard, and white. An alloy of two of iron and one of antimony is very hard and brilliant.	Doubtful.
With GOLD, a grey metal, very brittle.	Forms readily a pale yellow alloy, breaking with a fracture like porcelain.	Similar to antimony; of a yellow-green colour.
With COPPER. Composed of 62 parts of copper and 32 arsenic, a grey, brilliant, brittle metal. Increasing the quantity of copper, the alloy becomes white and slightly ductile: used in the manufacture of buttons under the name of white copper, or TOMBAC.	Alloys readily: the alloys are brittle. Those formed with equal parts of the two metals are of a fine violet colour.	Pale-red brittle metal.
With SILVER. 23 of silver and 14 arsenic form a greyish-white brittle metal.	These have a strong affinity; their alloys are always brittle.	Alloys brittle and lamellated.
With LEAD. Arsenic renders lead brittle. The combination is very intimate; not decomposed by heat.	Antimony gives hardness to lead. 24 parts of antimony and 76 of lead, corresponding to Pb^3Sb, appear the point of saturation of the two metals.	The alloys of bismuth and lead are less brittle and more ductile than those with antimony; but the alloy of 3 parts of lead and 2 of bismuth is harder than lead. These alloys are very fusible.
With TIN. Brittle, grey lamellated; less fusible than tin.	The alloys of antimony and tin are very white. They become brittle when the arsenic is in large quantity.	Tin and bismuth unite in all proportions by fusion. All the alloys are more fusible than tin.
With MERCURY. Without interest.	A gritty white alloy.	Mercury dissolves a large quantity of bismuth without losing its fluidity; but drops of the alloy elongate, and form a tail.

DUCTILE METALS.			
IRON	GOLD	COPPER	SILVER
With ZINC. See GALVANISED IRON.	A greenish-yellow alloy, which will take a fine polish.	See BRASS.	Silver and zinc combine easily, forming a somewhat brittle alloy.
With IRON or STEEL.	Gold and iron alloy with ease, and form yellowish alloys, varying in colour with the proportions of the metals. Three or four parts of iron united with one of gold is very hard, and is used in the manufacture of cutting instruments.	Iron and copper do not form true alloys. When fused together, the iron, however, retains a little copper.—Several methods for coating iron with copper and brass will be described.	When 1 of silver and 500 of steel are fused, a very perfect button is formed.— *Stodart and Faraday.*
With GOLD	... ...	Copper and gold alloy in all proportions, the copper giving hardness to the gold. This alloy is much used in coin and in the metal employed in the manufacture of jewellery.	Gold and silver mix easily together; but they do not appear to form a true combination. Jewellers often employ *l'or vert*, which is composed of 70 parts of gold and 30 of silver, which corresponds very nearly to the alloy possessing the maximum hardness.
With COPPER ...	... ...	... ...	Silver and copper alloy in all proportions. These alloys are much used in the arts. The maximum hardness appears to be produced when the alloy contains a fifth of copper.
With LEAD, does not appear to form any alloy.	A very brittle alloy. A thousandth pt. of lead is sufficient to alter the ductility of gold.	Do not appear to form a true alloy.	Unite in all proportions; but a very small quantity of lead will greatly diminish the ductility of silver.
With TIN. A very little iron diminishes the malleability of tin, and gives it hardness.	The alloys of gold and tin are brittle; they preserve, however, some ductility when the proportion of tin does not exceed $\frac{1}{12}$.	Of great importance. See BRONZE.	Alloys readily. A very small quantity of tin destroys the ductility of silver.
With MERCURY. Mercury has no action on iron.	Mercury has a most powerful action on gold. See AMALGAM.	An amalgam which is formed with difficulty, and without interest.	The amalgamation of these two metals is a little less energetic than between mercury and gold. See AMALGAMATION.

Six ounces lead to one pound copper is the ordinary pot-metal, called *dry pot-metal*, as this quantity of lead will be taken up without separating on cooling; this alloy is brittle when warmed.

Seven ounces lead to one pound copper forms an alloy which is rather short, or disposed to break.

Eight ounces lead to one pound copper is an inferior pot-metal, called *wet* pot-metal, as the lead partly oozes out in cooling, especially when the new metals are mixed; it is therefore always usual to fill the crucible in part with old metal, and to add new for the remainder. This alloy is very brittle when slightly warmed. More lead can scarcely be used as it separates on cooling.

Antimony twenty parts and lead eighty parts form the printing-type of France; and lead and antimony are united in various proportions to form the type-metal of our printers. See Type-metal.

Mr. James Nasmyth, in a letter to the 'Athenæum' (No. 1176, p. 511), directed attention to the employment of lead, and its fitness as a substitute for all works of art hitherto executed in bronze or marble. He says the addition of about 5 per cent. of antimony to the lead will give it, not only great hardness, but enhance its capability to run into the most delicate details of the work.

Baron Wetterstedt's patent sheathing for ships consists of lead, with 2 to 8 per cent. of antimony; about 3 per cent. is the usual quantity. The alloy is rolled out into sheets. We are not aware that this alloy has ever been employed.

Emery wheels and grinding tools for the lapidary are formed of an alloy of antimony and lead.

Organ pipes are sometimes made of lead and tin, the latter metal being employed to harden the lead. The pipes, however, of the great organ in the Town Hall a Birmingham are principally made of sheet zinc.

Lead and arsenic form shot-metal. The usual proportions are said to be 40lbs. of metallic arsenic to one ton of lead.

In addition to these, the alloys of iron appear of sufficient importance to require some further notice.

Iron and Manganese. Mr. Mushet concludes, from his experiments, that the maximum combinations of manganese and iron is 40 of the former to 100 of the latter. The alloy 71·4 of tin and 28·6 of manganese is indifferent to the magnet.

Iron and Silver; Steel and Silver.—Various experiments have been made upon alloys of iron and steel with other metals. The only alloys to which sufficient importance has been given are those of iron and silver and steel and silver. M. Guyton states, in the 'Annales de Chimie,' that he found iron to alloy with silver in greater quantity than the silver with the iron. 'Iron can,' he says, 'therefore no longer be said to refuse to mix with silver; it must, on the contrary, be acknowledged that those two metals, brought into perfect fusion, contract an actual chemical union; that, whilst cooling, the heaviest metal *separates for the greatest part;* that notwithstanding each of the two metals retains a portion of the other, as is the case in every liquation, that the part that remains is not simply mixed or interlaid, but chemically united; lastly, that the alloy in these proportions possesses peculiar properties, particularly a degree of hardness that may render it extremely useful for various purposes.'

The experiments of Faraday and Stodart on the alloys of iron and steel are of great value; the most interesting being the alloy with silver. The words of these experimentalists are quoted:—

'In making the silver alloys, the proportion first tried was 1 silver to 160 steel; the resulting buttons were uniformly steel and silver in fibres, the silver being likewise given out in globules during solidifying, and adhering to the surface of the fused button; some of these, when forged, gave out more globules of silver. In this state of mechanical mixture the little bars, when exposed to a damp atmosphere, evidently produced voltaic action; and to this we are disposed to attribute the rapid destruction of the metal by oxidation, no such destructive action taking place when the two metals are chemically combined. These results indicated the necessity of diminishing the quantity of silver, and 1 silver to 200 steel was tried. Here, again, were fibres and globules in abundance; with 1 to 300 the fibres diminished, but still were present; they were detected even when 1 to 400 was used. The successful experiment remains to be named. When 1 of silver to 500 steel were properly fused, a very perfect button was produced; no silver appeared on its surface; when forged and dissected by an acid, no fibres were seen, although examined by a high magnifying power. The specimen forged remarkably well, although very hard; it had in every respect the most favourable appearance. By a delicate test every part of the bar gave silver. This alloy is decidedly superior to the very best steel; and this excellence is unquestionably owing to a combination with a minute quantity of silver. It has been repeatedly made, and always with equal success. Various cutting tools have been made from it of the best quality. This alloy is, perhaps, only inferior to that of steel and rhodium, and it may be procured at small expense; the value of silver, where the proportion is so small, is not worth naming; it will probably be applied to many important purposes in the arts.'

Messrs. Faraday and Stodart show from their researches that not only silver, but platinum, rhodium, gold, nickel, copper, and even tin, have an affinity for steel sufficiently strong to make them combine chemically.

IRON and NICKEL unite in all proportions, producing soft and tenacious alloys. Some few years since, Mr. Nasmyth drew attention to the combination of silicon with steel. Fresh interest has been excited in this direction by the investigations of a French chemist, M. St. Claire Deville, who has examined many of the alloys of silicon. For other alloys of iron, see IRON.

IRON and SILICON combine to form an alloy, which is a sort of fusible steel in which carbon is replaced by silicon. The siliciurets are all of them quite homogeneous, and are not capable of being separated by liquation.

COPPER and SILICON united in various proportions, according to the same chemist. A very hard, brittle, and white alloy, containing 12 per cent. of silicon, is obtained by melting together three parts silico-fluoride of potassium, one part sodium, and one part of copper, at such a temperature that the fused mass remains covered with a very liquid scoria. The copper takes up the whole of the silicon, and remains as a white substance less fusible than silicon, which may serve as a base for other alloys. An alloy with 5 per cent. silicon has a beautiful bronze colour, and will probably receive important applications.

Mr. Oxland and Mr. Truran have given, in 'Metals and their Alloys,' the following useful tabular view of the composition of the alloys of copper. In addition to those given, the alloy of copper and aluminium is now most important. See ALUMINIUM BRONZE.

The principal alloys of copper with other metals are as follows :—

	Copper	Zinc	Tin	Nickel	Antimony	Lead
Antique bronze sword .	87·000	...	13,000			
„ springs . .	97·000	...	3,000			
Bronze for statues . .	91·400	5·530	1·700	...	...	1·370
„ for medals . .	90·000	...	10·000			
„ for cannon . .	90·000	...	10·000			
„ for cymbals . .	78·000	...	22·000			
„ for gilding . .	82·257	17·481	0·238	...	...	0·024
„ „ .	80·000	16·500	2·500	...	...	1·000
Speculum metal . .	66·000	...	33·000			
Brass for sheet . .	84·700	15·300				
Gilding metal . . .	73·730	27·270				
Pinchbeck . . .	80·200	20·000				
Prince's metal . . .	75·000	25·000				
„ „ . .	50·000	50·000				
Dutch metal . . .	84·700	15·300				
English wire . . .	70·290	29·260	0·17	...	...	0·28
Mosaic gold . . .	66·000	33·000				
Gun metal for bearings, stocks, &c. . . .	90·300	9·670	0·03			
Muntz's metal . . .	60·000	40·000				
Good yellow brass . .	66·000	33·000				
Babbitt's metal for bushing	8·300	...	83·00	...	8·3	
Bell metal for large bells .	80·000	...	20·00			
Britannia metal . .	1·000	2·00	81·00	...	16·00	
Nickel silver, English .	60·000	17·8	...	22·2		
„ „ Parisian .	50·000	13·6	...	19·3		
German silver . . .	50·000	25·0	...	25·0		

Some valuable researches on the nature of alloys were undertaken by the late Dr. Matthiessen, the results of which are embodied in his ' Report on the Chemical Nature of Alloys' (*Report of the British Association for the Advancement of Science,* 1863, p. 37), and in a discourse ' On Alloys ' delivered before the Chemical Society (*Journal of the Chem. Soc.,* 1867, p. 201).

ALLOY, NATIVE. Osmium and Iridium, in the proportions of 72·9 of the former and 24·5 of the latter. See OSMIUM, IRIDIUM.

ALLSPICE. Pimento, or Jamaica pepper, so called because its flavour is thought to comprehend the flavour of cinnamon, cloves, and nutmegs. The tree producing this spice (*Eugenia pimenta*) is cultivated in Jamaica in what are called Pimento walks. It is imported in bags, almost entirely from Jamaica. Mr. Montgomery Martin informs us that pimento was exported in one year (1837) from the different districts of Jamaica as follows. (See PIMENTO, PEPPER.)

Kingston and Old Harbour	6,027 bags.
Morant Bay and Port Morant	141 „
Port Antonio	1,259 „
Port Marva and Annotto Bay	3,194 „
Falmouth, Rio Bueno, and St. Ann's Bay . .	28,188 „
Montego Bay and Lucca	3,106 „
Sav-la-Mar and Black River	3,622 „

ALLUVIUM. (*Alluo*, to wash upon; or *alluvio*, an inundation.) Earth, sand, gravel, stones, and other transported matter which has been washed away, and thrown down—by rivers, floods, or other causes—upon land not *permanently* submerged beneath the waters of lakes or seas.—*Lyell.*

ALLYL. $C^{12} H^{10}$ ($C^6 H^{10}$). This radical exists in the oils of mustard and garlic, but is usually obtained by the decomposition of the iodide of allyl, which is obtained by acting on glycerine with iodine and phosphorus.

ALLYL, SULPHIDE OF. This compound is contained in the essential oils produced by distilling with water the leaves and seeds of various plants of the liliaceous and cruciferous orders. It forms the principal constituent of the oil obtained from the bulbs of garlic (*Allium Cepa*). It is also found with oil of mustard in the leaves and seed of *Thlaspi arvense*. The *Alliaria officinalis* distilled yields 90 per cent. of oil of mustard and 10 per cent. of oil of garlic; small quantities are also obtained from the Shepherd's purse, *Capsella Bursa pastoris*, and other plants. The power of the sulphide of Allyl to precipitate some of the metals appears likely to render it of use in the arts. The following are some of the more important:—

Gold precipitate, a beautiful yellow, and films of gold. *Platinum precipitate*, a yellowish-brown precipitate, which forms a *Kermes brown* with hydrosulphide of ammonium. *Silver precipitate*, a dark brown, becoming eventually sulphide of silver.

ALLYLAMINE. See ACRYLAMINE.

ALMAGRERITE. An anhydrous sulphate of zinc, described by Breithaupt. It occurs in crystals belonging to the rhombic system, at the Barranca Jarosa Mine, in the Sierra Almagrera, in Southern Spain.

ALMANDINE, or iron-alumina-garnet, is a silicate of alumina and iron, combined in the following proportions: silica 36·3, alumina 20·56, protoxide of iron 43·2.

It occurs in Greenland, Ceylon, and the Brazils; when cut and polished, it forms a beautiful gem.

The name is probably derived from the Alabandic carbuncles of Pliny, which were cut and polished at Alabanda. Several localities for garnets in Devonshire and Cornwall are given by Mr. Collins in his excellent 'Handbook to the Mineralogy' of these counties; but it is doubtful if the specimens found in Cornwall are true almandine— therefore those localities are given under Garnet. See GARNET.

ALMOND. (*Amande*, Fr.; *Mandel*, Ger.; *Amygdalus communis*.) De Candolle admits five varieties of this species. *A. amara*, bitter almond; *A. dulcis*, sweet almond; *A. fragilis*, tender-shelled almond; *A. macrocarpa*, large-fruited almond; *A. persicoides*, peach almond. There are two kinds of almond usually employed, which do not differ in chemical composition, only that the bitter, by a curious chemical reaction of its constituents, generates in the act of distillation a quantity of volatile oil which contains hydrocyanic acid. Vogel obtained from bitter almonds 8·5 per cent. of husks. After pounding the kernels, and heating them to coagulate the albumen, he procured, by expression, 28 parts of an unctuous oil, which did not contain the smallest particle of hydrocyanic acid. The whole of the oil could not be extracted in this way. The expressed mass, treated with boiling water, afforded sugar and gum, and, in consequence of the heat, some of that acid. The sugar constitutes 6·5 per cent. and the gum 3. The vegetable albumen extracted, by means of caustic potash, amounted to 30 parts: the vegetable fibre to only 5. The poisonous aromatic oil, according to Robiquet and Boutron-Charlard, does not exist ready-formed in the bitter almond, but seems to be produced under the influence of ebullition with water. These chemists have shown—

1st. That neither bitter almonds nor their residuary cake yield any volatile oil by pressure.

2nd. They yield no oil when digested in alcohol or in ether, though the volatile oil is soluble in both these liquids.

3rd. Alcohol extracts from bitter-almond cake, sugar, resin, and *amygdalin*; when the latter substance has been removed, the cake is no longer capable of furnishing the volatile oil by distillation.

4th. Ether extracts no amygdalin, and the cake left, after digestion in ether, yields the volatile oil by distillation with water; but alcohol dissolves out a peculiar white crystalline body, without smell, of a sweetish taste at first, and afterwards bitter, to which they gave the name of *amygdalin*. This substance does not seem convertible into volatile oil.—*Pereira.* See Watts's 'Dictionary of Chemistry.'

Sweet almonds, by the analysis of Boullay, consist of 54 parts of the bland almond oil, 6 of uncrystallisable sugar, 3 of gum, 24 of vegetable albumen, 24 of woody fibre, 5 of husks, 3·5 of water, 0·5 of acetic acid, including loss. We thus see that sweet almonds contain nearly twice as much oil as bitter almonds do.

Three varieties are known in commerce.

1. *Jordan Almonds*, which are the finest, come from Malaga. Of these there are two kinds: the one above an inch in length, flat, with a clear brown cuticle, sweet, mucilaginous, and rather tough; the other more plump and pointed at one end, brittle, but equally sweet with the former.

2. *Valentia almonds* are about three-eighths of an inch broad, not quite an inch long, round at one end, and obtusely pointed at the other, flat, of a dingy brown colour and dusty cuticle.

3. *Barbary and Italian almonds* resemble the latter, but are generally smaller and less flattened.—*Brande, Dictionary of Pharmacy.*

Our *importation* and *exportation* of ALMONDS in 1871 were as follows:—

IMPORTS. 1871.

Countries from which imported	Quantity	Value
	Cwts.	£
France	4,428	15,261
Portugal and Azores	5,156	15,882
Spain and Canary Islands . . .	18,309	76,395
Italy	7,943	26,564
Austrian Territories	1,788	7,932
Morocco	33,934	92,279
Gibraltar	266	550
Other Countries	1,075	3,210
Total . . .	72,899	238,073

EXPORTS.

Countries to which exported	Quantity	Value
	Cwts.	£
Russia	5,594	16,489
Germany	10,821	36,429
Holland	4,848	14,806
Belgium	1,609	4,645
Other Countries	5,820	19,717
Total . . .	28,692	92,086

ALMOND OIL, BITTER. *Oil of bitter almonds. Essential oil of bitter almonds.* (*Oleum Amygdalæ Amaræ.*)

After the fixed oil has been expressed from the bitter almonds, the residual cake is mixed with water and distilled. A volatile oil comes over. It has been convincingly proved that this fine-flavoured essential oil is produced during the process, by some decomposition of the amygdalin and the emulsion of the seeds. It is highly poisonous, owing to the presence of hydrocyanic acid. See BENZOIC ACID, BENZOLE, &c.

ALMOND OIL, SWEET. A bland fixed oil, obtained by expression from bitter or sweet almonds—usually from the former, on account of their cheapness as well as the greater value of the residual cake. The average produce is from 48 to 52 lbs. from 1 cwt. of almonds.

This is commonly known as *Oil of sweet almonds*, the *Oleum Amygdalæ* of the Pharmacopœia. When first obtained it is opaque, and of a yellow colour; but it speedily becomes quite transparent, and is bleached by exposure to light. This oil has a bland taste, and does not congeal at a temperature which solidifies olive-oil. It is often sold for nut-oil, which is supposed to possess this property of remaining fluid in an eminent degree.

ALMOND POWDER (*farina amygdalæ*) is the ground almond cake after the oil has been expressed; it is employed for washing the hands, and it is used by chemists as a lute to connect the parts of their distillatory apparatus together.

ALOE. (*Aloès*, Fr.; *Aloe*, Ger.) In botany a genus of the order *Liliaceæ*. There are many species, all natives of warm climates.

In Africa the leaves of the Guinea aloe are made into durable ropes. Of one species are made lines, bowstrings, stockings, and hammocks; the leaves of another species are used to hold rain-water. A series of trials has been made, within a few years, in Paris, to ascertain the comparative strength of cables made of hemp and of the aloe from Algiers; and they are said to have all turned to the advantage of the aloe. Of cables of equal size, that made of aloe raised a weight of 2,000 kilogrammes (2 tons nearly), that made of hemp a weight of only 400 kilogrammes. The fibre of the aloe is used extensively in Belgium for the ropes used for winding the coal from the very deep coal-pits of Charleroi. The Belgium engineers state that they could not raise the coal with equal facility and safety with any other kind of rope.

The following varieties of the inspissated juices of the Aloe—called ALOES, and often BITTER ALOES—are known in commerce: *Socotrine, Hepatic, Barbadoes, Cape, Mocha, Catalline, and Indian.* The Socotrine Aloes are regarded as the best kind, but that from Barbadoes is the most abundant, and much of it is sold as Socotrine. The Barbadoes Aloes are imported from Barbadoes or Jamaica, usually in gourds weighing from 60 to 70 pounds, but sometimes in boxes holding about half a hundred-weight.

It is believed that Socotrine aloes are obtained from *Aloe Socotrina*, Barbadoes aloes from *A. vulgaris*, Cape aloes from *A. spicata* and its allies, and Indian aloes from *A. Indica*; but the botanical source of some of the commercial varieties of aloes is not definitely known.

A patent was taken (January 27, 1847) for certain applications of aloes to dyeing. Although it has not been employed, the colouring matter so obtained promising to be very permanent and intense, it is thought advisable to describe the process by which it was proposed to prepare the dye. It is as follows:—

Into a boiler or vessel capable of holding about 100 gallons, the patentee puts 10 gallons of water, and 132 lbs. of aloes, and heats the same until the aloes are dissolved; he then adds 80 lbs. of nitric or nitrous acid in small proportions at a time, to prevent the disengagement of such a quantity of nitrous gas as would throw part of the contents out of the boiler. When the whole of the acid has been introduced, and the disengagement of gas has ceased, 10 lbs. of liquid caustic soda, or potash of commerce, of about 30°, are added to neutralise any undecomposed acid remaining in the mixture, and to facilitate the use of the mixture in dyeing and printing. If the colouring matter is required to be in a dry state, the mixture may be incorporated with 100 lbs. of china-clay, and dried in stoves, or by means of a current of air. The colouring matter is used in dyeing by dissolving a sufficient quantity of water, according to the shade required, and adding as much hydrochloric acid or tartar of commerce as will neutralise the alkali contained in the mixture, and leave the dye-bath slightly acidulated. The articles to be dyed are introduced into the bath, which is kept boiling until the desired shade is obtained.

When the colouring matter is to be used in printing, a sufficient quantity is to be dissolved in water, according to the shade required to be produced; this solution is to be thickened with gum, or other common thickening agent, and hydrochloric acid, or tartar of commerce, or any other suitable supersalt, is to be added thereto. After the fabrics have been printed with the colouring matter, they should be subjected to the ordinary process of steaming, to fix the colour.—*Napier.*

ALOETIC ACID. The colouring matter of the aloes depends on this acid, which has been examined by Schunck and Mulder. Aloetic acid is deposited from nitric acid, which has been heated with aloes, as a yellow powder: it dissolves in ammonia with a violet colour; when treated with protochloride of tin it forms a dark-violet heavy powder; and this again, when treated with potash, evolves ammonia, and assumes a violet-blue colour. This solution of aloetic acid in ammonia is violet.

ALPACA. (*Alpaga*, Fr.) An animal of Peru, of the Llama species; also the name given to a woollen fabric woven from the wool of this animal, or a mixture of silky goat's hair with the harsher fibre of sheep's wool. See LLAMA.

ALSTONITE. A double carbonate of lime and baryta, crystallising in the prismatic or orthorhombic system. It occurs at Fallowfield, near Hexham, in Northumberland; and at Bromley Hill, near Alston, in Cumberland.

ALUDEL. The aludels of the earlier chemists were a series of pear-shaped pots, generally made of earthenware, but sometimes of glass, open at both ends. Each aludel had a short neck at top and bottom, so that a series of them could be fitted together, by means of the neck, in succession. The earthenware pear-shaped vessels in which the mercurial vapours are condensed, at Almaden, in Spain, are also known as aludels. See MERCURY.

ALUM. (*Alun*, Fr.; *Alaun*, Ger.) A saline body or salt, consisting of alumina, or the peculiar earth of clay, united with sulphuric acid, and these again united with sulphate of potash or of ammonia. In other words, it is a double salt, consisting of sulphate of alumina and sulphate of potash, or sulphate of alumina and sulphate of ammonia. The common alum crystallises in octahedrons, but there is a kind which takes the form of cubes. It has a sour or rather subacid taste, and is peculiarly astringent. It reddens the blue colour of litmus or red cabbage, and acts like an acid on many substances. Other alkalis may take the place of the ammonia or potash, and other metals that of the aluminium.

Alum was known to the ancients, who used it in medicine, as it is now used, and also as a mordant in dyeing and calico-printing, as at the present day. Old historians do not describe correctly, either the mode of obtaining it or its exact characteristics, so that it is confounded with sulphate of iron, with which it seems generally to have been mixed. But that some qualities were made with very little iron in it, is clear from the fact that it was employed when white for dyeing bright colours. (*Pliny*, xxxv. 15.) It is said by Pliny that the purchasers tested it with tannin (pomegranate juice), in order to see if it blackened. He says that the white kind blackened as well as the black; but in all probability this was a test applied by the dyers to see which blackened least, so as to obtain a good mordant for reds. Pliny's description, although confused, leaves this fact perfectly clear—that there were men in whose minds the knowledge was much clearer than in his, or a manufacture of such magnitude could not have existed. There is mention of some being made from stone, and crystallising in fine hairs, but the characteristics given do not enable us to decide that this was either alum or the peculiar sulphate of alumina which takes that form. The alum was sometimes boiled down to dryness, and heated till it was spongy or like pumice-stone. It was used as burnt alum.

The ancients used it also for preventing the combustibility of wood and wooden buildings. But although the knowledge of it was very accurate, their writers always imagine that sulphate of iron was a kind of alum, because it is said that the black alum was used for dyeing dark colours. They used iron as a mordant, and found its character by galls or by pomegranate juice, which contains tannin. Their alum was chiefly a natural production, and they removed the fine efflorescing crystals which first appeared, or which gradually are raised above the rest, as the finest kind. 'It was produced in Spain, Egypt, Armenia, Macedonia, Pontus, and Africa; the islands Sardinia, Melos, Lipari, and Stromboli. The best was got in Egypt, the next in Melos.' The word is probably Egyptian, as it was best and most abundantly obtained in Egypt. It is not probable that it was the double salt in all cases, but simply a sulphate of alumina. Pliny, indeed, says that a substance called in Greek ὑγρά, or watery, probably from its very soluble nature, and which was milk-white, was used for dyeing wool of bright colours. This may have been the *mountain butter* of the German mineralogists, which is a native sulphate of alumina, iron, &c., of a soft texture, waxy lustre, and unctuous to the touch. The *stypteria* of Dioscorides and the *alumen* of Pliny comprehended, no doubt, a variety of saline substances besides sulphate of iron and alum.

It seems to have come to Europe in later times as *alum of Rocca*, the name of Edessa, or that place where the Italians first learnt the art; but it is not impossible that this name was an Italian prefix, which has remained to this day under the form of *Rock alum, Allume di rocca*. The East has always had some manufactures of it, and Phocis, Lesbos, and other places, were able to supply the Turks with alum for their magnificent Turkey red. It was also made at Foya Nova, near Smyrna, and at Constantinople. The Genoese and other trading people of Italy imported alum into Western Europe for the use of the dyers of red cloth.

A Genoese merchant, Bartholomew Perdix, who had been in Syria, observed a stone suitable for alum in the island Ischia ; he burnt it, and obtained a good result, being the first who introduced the manufacture into Europe. This was in the year 1459 ; about the same time John di Castro learnt the method at Constantinople, and manufactured alum at Tolfa. This discovery of the mineral near Civita Vecchia was considered so important by John di Castro, that he announced it to the Pope as a great victory over the Turks, who annually took from the Christians 300,000 pieces of gold for their dyed wool. A statue was erected to the 'Discoverer of Alum.'— *Beckman.*

The manufacture of alum was then made a monopoly of the Papal Powers, and instead of buying it as before from the East, it was considered Christian to obtain it only from the States of the Church, and, as such, was made compulsory in the West. The manufacture then went to Spain, to a spot near Carthagena. Germany began so early as 1554 to make alum, although Basil Valentine seems to have known of its existence there somewhat sooner. The first establishment known was at Oberkaufungen in Hesse-Cassel, where it still exists. It was not introduced as a manufacture into England until the year 1600, when Sir Thomas Chaloner, the son of Queen Elizabeth's minister of that name, found that his own estate of Guisborough, in Yorkshire, contained alum. This he is said first to have observed from the vegetation, which had a very weak green. Di Castro had first been led to it by the appearance of the holly, but neither can be said to be decisive tests of its presence, nor are the geological features of Tolfa and Guisborough at all alike. The violent denunciations of the Pope did not prevent the manufacture from growing to unexpected magnitude in England. The mines of the same district have ever since sent out alum, which is now known as Whitby alum, and even those at Guisborough itself are now at work, although for seventy years of the period since their discovery they were disused. The manufacture was begun at Hurlet, in Scotland, by Nicholson and Lightbody, in 1766, abandoned, and resumed by Macintosh and Wilson in 1797.

The chemical composition of alum varies with the nature of the bases present, but all alums are constructed on a common type, expressed by the general formula $MO. SO^3. M^2O^3. 3SO^3 + 24HO$. They are, therefore, double sulphates, containing both a protoxide and a sesquioxide, combined with a constant number of molecules of water. The protoxide is generally an alkali—usually potash or ammonia—but other alums are known, though at present of no importance in the arts, in which the metal of the protoxide is silver, thallium, cæsium, or rubidium. On the other hand, the sesquioxide, though generally alumina, may take the form of sesquioxide of iron, of manganese, or of chromium. It is desirable to exhibit this relation between some of the more important alums ; and, as the formulæ representing these double salts are somewhat complex, it may be useful to compare their symbolic expressions constructed with both the old and the new atomic weights :—

	Old formulæ	New formulæ
Potash alum . .	$KO.SO^3.Al^2O^3.3SO^3 + 24HO$	$KAl2(SO^4) + 12H^2O$
Soda alum . .	$NaO.SO^3.Al^2O^3.3SO^3 + 24HO$	$NaAl2(SO^4) + 12H^2O$
Ammonia alum .	$NH^4O.SO^3.Al^2O^3.3SO^3 + 24HO$	$NH^4Al2(SO^4) + 12H^2O$
Iron alum . .	$KO.SO^3.Fe^2O^3.3SO^3 + 24HO$	$KFe2(SO^4) + 12H^2O$
Chrome alum . .	$KO.SO^3.Cr^2O^3.3SO^3 + 24HO$	$KCr2(SO^4) + 12H^2O$
Manganese alum .	$KO.SO^3.Mn^2O^3.3SO^3 + 24HO$	$KMn2(SO^4) + 12H^2O$

The composition of pure *potash-alum* may be represented centesimally and atomically as follows :—

	Per Cent.					Per Cent.		
Potash . .	9·89 or 1 atom 47			Sulphate of potash .	18·32 or 1 atom	27
Alumina .	10·94 ,, 1 ,, 52		or	Sulphate of alumina .	36·21 ,, 1 ,,	172
Sulphuric acid	33·68 ,, 4 ,, 160			Water . . .	45·48 ,, 1 ,,	216
Water . .	45·49 ,, 24 ,, 216					

Its specific gravity is 1·724.

100 parts of water dissolve, at 32 degrees Fahrenheit,	3·29 alum
,, ,, 50 ,, ,,	9·52 ,,
,, ,, 86 ,, ,,	22·01 ,,
,, ,, 122 ,, ,,	30·92 ,,
,, ,, 158 ,, ,,	90·67 ,,
,, ,, 212 ,, ,,	357·48 ,,

These Tables of Poggiale should be re-examined, and gradations made more useful for this country.

One part of crystallised potash alum is soluble—

At 54 degrees Fahrenheit in 13·3 parts of water.				
„ 70	„	„	8·2	„
„ 77	„	„	4·5	„
„ 100	„	„	2·2	„
„ 122	„	„	2·0	„
„ 145	„	„	0·4	„
„ 167	„	„	0·1	„
„ 189·5	„	„	0·06	··

A solution saturated at 46° is 1·045 specific gravity. This difference in the rate of solubility in hot and cold water renders it easily separated from many other salts. The crystals are permanent in the air, or nearly so, unless the air be very dry; if kept at 180° they lose 18 atoms of water, but alum deprived of its water, and exposed to the air of summer, took up 18 atoms in 47 days. It melts at a low temperature in its water of crystallisation. At 356° it loses 43·5 per cent. of water, or 23 atoms; the last atom is only lost when approaching red heat. At a red heat the sulphate of alumina loses its acid, and the alumina seems then able to remove some acid from the potash, losing it again by heat. Alum, when heated with common salt, acts like sulphuric acid, and gives off muriatic acid; the same with chlorides of potassium and ammonium. If boiled with a saturated solution of chloride of potassium, hydrochloric acid is formed and a subsulphate of alumina falls down; this occurs only to a small extent with chloride of sodium, and still less with sal-ammoniac.

Ammonia-Alum, which is now very extensively prepared, contains:—

Ammonia	.	.	.	.	.	3·75 per cent.
Alumina	.	.	.	.	.	11·34 „
Sulphuric acid	.	.	.	.	.	35·29 „
Water .	.	.	.	.	.	49·62 „
						100·00

This salt also occurs in octahedrons, and can only be known from potash-alum by trial. The addition of caustic lime, soda, or potash gives out the ammonia, easily distinguished by the smell. Ammonia-alum readily loses all its ammonia when heated, and the sulphuric acid may be driven off from the remaining sulphate of alumina, so that the pure earth, alumina, will remain.

The greater proportion of the alum at present used in this country is ammonia-alum —an abundant and convenient source of ammonia being furnished by the ammoniacal liquor obtained in the manufacture of coal-gas. In commerce ammonia and potash-alums are sometimes found mixed.

Soda-alum is not an article of commerce, nor is it used in the arts. Nevertheless, the great commercial value of compounds of potash or of ammonia renders it obviously desirable to replace them, if possible, by the cheaper compounds of soda. The cost of sulphate of soda, for example, is trifling compared with that of sulphate of potash or of ammonia—the latter salts being especially in demand by the agriculturist as fertilising agents. Some experiments on the formation and crystallisation of soda-alum were undertaken a few years ago by Mr. J. Carter Bell. Up to the present time, however, there appear to have been great difficulties in the manufacture of this kind of alum, especially in respect to its crystallisation, but these difficulties may not be altogether insuperable. Mr. J. Berger Spence, who has studied the preparation of soda-alum, remarks that 'it may ultimately, now that the practicability of producing soda-alum on the commercial scale has been demonstrated, even with all the difficulty of crystallisation, be a more economical way of producing this double salt.'[1]

For the composition of potash-, soda- and ammonia-alums found ready formed in nature, *see* ALUM, NATIVE.

Applications of Alum.—Alum is an astringent. Its immediate effect on man is to corrugate the fibres and contract the small vessels. It precipitates albuminous liquids and combines with gelatine. It causes dryness of the mouth and throat, and checks the secretions of the alimentary canal, producing constipation—in large quantities, nausea, vomiting, and purging. It is given in lead colic, to convert the lead into sulphate of lead, and is used externally. Its principal use is in dyeing; calico-printers print it as a mordant; the cloth is then put into the dye, and the printed parts absorb the colour.

It is largely employed by the calico-printer in the preparation of acetate of alumina

[1] On the Phenomena of the Crystallisation of a Double Salt, by J. Berger Spence, F.C.S.—'Chemical News,' vol. xxii. 1870, p. 181.

by precipitating a solution of alum with sugar of lead. Paper-makers use alum in their size, and bookbinders in their paste. It is used in tanning leather, and sometimes, both in Asia and Europe, it is used for precipitating rapidly the impurities of water. This is a dangerous process, unless there be a great amount of alkaline salts, such as carbonate of lime or soda, to neutralise the acid. It is extensively used in correcting the baking qualities of bad flour, for which the experience of many has decided that it is a valuable remedy; unfortunately, it is also used to make excellent flour whiter, when there is no need of its presence. Liebig says that lime is equally good, and of course much safer. It is also used in the adulteration of beer. From time immemorial it has been used to prevent the combustibility of wood and cloth. Milner's fire-proof safes are said to be lined with a mixture of alum and sulphate of lime.

Alum heated with charcoal or carbonaceous substances forms Homberg's phosphorus, which inflames spontaneously. It is composed of alumina, sulphide of potassium, and charcoal.

Burnt Alum, or dried alum, is made by gently heating alum till the water is driven off. The alum first melts in its water of crystallisation, and is then dried. It has a stronger action than the hydrated crystals, and is a mild escharotic. It reabsorbs water.

Neutral Alum is a name sometimes given erroneously to alum which has had some of its acid neutralised by an alkali. It is in fact a basic salt of alumina, which may also be made by dissolving alumina in ordinary alum. It deposits a basic salt more readily than ordinary alum, and may be of service in some cases of printing. Properly speaking, the common alum is the neutral salt.

Testing of Alum.—Alum being generally in large crystals, any impurity is more readily seen; this is said to be the reason for keeping up the practice of making this substance instead of the sulphate of alumina alone, which is less bulky and fitted for nearly every purpose for which alum is used. But probably the ancient accidental discovery of the potash form has determined its use to the present day. Iron is readily found in it, by adding to a dilute solution ferrocyanide of potassium or yellow prussiate of potash, which throws down Prussian-blue. A very delicate test is sulphide of ammonium, which throws down both the alumina and iron, but the blacking of the precipitate depends on the amount of iron. The total amount of iron is got by adding pure caustic potash or soda till the solution is strongly alkaline, washing and filtering off the oxide. To look for lime, precipitate the alumina and iron by ammonia, boil and filter—the lime and magnesia are in the solution—add oxalate of ammonia; add tartaric acid to keep up the iron and alumina, make alkaline by ammonia, then precipitate the lime by oxalate of ammonia, filter, and precipitate the magnesia by a phosphate. Silica and insoluble basic sulphates are obtained by simply dissolving the alum in water and filtering. If silica, it is insoluble in acids; if a basic sulphate, it will dissolve in sulphuric acid, and the addition of sulphate of potash or ammonia will convert it into potash- or ammonia-alum.

Pure alum gives a white precipitate with ammonia, no precipitate with sulphuretted hydrogen gas, and no precipitate with oxalate of ammonia and ammonia, if tartaric acid be previously added.

The addition of ammonia to a solution of alum, or the addition of any other alkali, in insufficient quantity, causes a precipitate, not of pure alumina, as one might suppose, but of a subsulphate of alumina. Even an excess of alkali will not remove all the sulphuric acid without heat being applied; an excess, on the other hand, is apt to dissolve some of the alumina, especially if few salts are present, and the solution not much boiled. Sulphide of ammonium precipitates it thoroughly.

In a saturated solution of tersulphate of alumina, the crystals of alum are almost insoluble.

If we dissolve alum in 20 parts of water, and drop this solution slowly into water of caustic ammonia till this be nearly, but not entirely, saturated, a bulky white precipitate will fall down, which, when properly washed with water, is pure aluminous earth or hydrate of alumina; and, dried, forms 10·94 per cent. of the weight of the alum. If this earth, while still moist, be dissolved in dilute sulphuric acid, it will constitute, when as neutral as possible, simple sulphate of alumina, which requires only two parts of cold water for its solution. If we now decompose this solution, by pouring into it water of ammonia, there appears an insoluble white powder, which is subsulphate of alumina, or basic alum, and contains three times as much earth as exists in the neutral sulphate. If, however, we pour into the solution of the neutral sulphate of alumina a solution of sulphate of potash, a white powder will fall if the solutions be concentrated, which is true *alum*; if the solutions be dilute, by evaporating their mixture, and cooling it, crystals of alum will be obtained.

When newly precipitated alumina is boiled in a solution of alum, a portion of the earth enters into combination with the salt, constituting an insoluble compound which falls in the form of a white powder. The same combination takes place, if we decompose a boiling hot solution of alum with a solution of potash, till the mixture appears nearly neutral by litmus-paper. This insoluble or basic alum exists native in the alum-stone of Tolfa, near Civita Vecchia. (*See below.*)

Ores or Raw Material.—The chief difficulty in manufacturing alum has been the solution of the alumina. This substance is generally combined with silica in such a strong combination, that even powerful acids cannot remove it without assistance. The older methods, however, took no notice of these difficulties, and obtained the alum more or less directly from nature. The method now practised at the Solfatara di Pozzuoli and in the island Vulcano is simply to take the efflorescence and the earth containing it, wash it with water, and concentrate. But it very seldom contains a sufficient amount of potash to form alum. A salt of potash is then added, chiefly a carbonate. To transform this into a sulphate, a portion of the sulphate of alumina is decomposed. The use of a carbonate is a wasteful method of modern times; the ancients would have felt no difficulty, but boiled all down, and so obtained the whole alumina there. Their product, therefore, would have been basic sulphate of alumina, which it evidently was when this practice was resorted to. When they merely concentrated and then crystallised, they got pure alum; but they lost a great deal of their alumina.

Alum occurs ready formed in nature in the alum-stones of Italy, &c., as an efflorescence on stones, and in certain mineral waters in the East Indies. (See ALUM, NATIVE.) The alum of European commerce is manufactured artificially, either from the alum-schists or stones, or from clay. The mode of manufacture differs according to the nature of these earthy compounds. Some of them, such as the alum-stone, contain all the elements of the salt, but mixed with other matters, from which it must be freed. The schists contain only the elements of two of the constituents, namely, clay and sulphur, which are convertible into sulphate of alumina, and this may be then made into alum by adding the alkaline ingredient. To this class belong the alum-slates, and other analogous schists, containing brown coal. Alum has of late years been very extensively prepared by Spence's process, in which the raw material is a carbonaceous shale from the coal-measures. Quite recently a new method of alum manufacture has been introduced, in which the raw material is a siliceous phosphate of alumina and iron from Redonda in the West Indies. Each of these methods of manufacturing alum will now be separately described.

I. *Manufacture of Alum from the Alum-Stone.*—The alum-stone or alunite is a mineral of limited occurrence, being found in moderate quantity at Tolfa (near Civita Vecchia, in the Roman States), and in larger quantity in Hungary, at Beregszaz and Muszay, where it forms entire beds in a hard substance, partly characterized by numerous cavities, containing drusy crystallisations of pure alum-stone or basic alum. It is also found in the Isle of Milo and elsewhere in the Grecian Archipelago. The alum-stone appears to be confined to volcanic districts, where it is formed by the action of sulphurous acid gas and steam on trachytic and other felspathic rocks. The ordinary alum-stone is a massive rock, often cellular in texture, and sometimes sufficiently hard to be employed as a millstone.

The composition of ordinary alum-stone is fairly represented by the following selection of analyses :—

	Klaproth	Rammelsberg	Klaproth	Descotils	Cordier
	Tolfa, Italy	Tolfa, Italy	Beregszaz, Hungary	Montione, Tuscany	Mont d'Or, France
Silica . . .	56·5	1·94	62·3	...	28·4
Alumina . . .	19·0	34·02	17·5	40·0	31·8
Sulphuric acid . .	16·5	36·94	12·5	35·6	27·0
Potash . . .	4·0	10·38	1·0	13·8	5·8
Water . . .	3·0	16·72	5·0	10·0	3·7
Peroxide of iron .	...	...	...	...	1·4

The older analysts examined the rock as a whole, including all impurities, and hence the proportion of silica in their determinations appears much higher than in the more recent analyses, which relate to the alunite alone, separated as far as possible from mechanically-associated quartzose matter.

The purest specimens of alunite, which exhibit the mineral in rhombohedral crystals, consist of a basic sulphate of alumina with sulphate of potash, referable to the formula: $KO.SO^3 + 3(Al^2 O^3. SO^3) + 6 HO$ (**KAl^3 S^2 O^{11} + 3H^2 O**).

In preparing alum from the alum-stone, the ore is first sorted. The larger lumps contain more or fewer flints disseminated through them, and are, according to their quality, either picked out to make alum, or thrown away. The sorted pieces are roasted or calcined, by which operation apparently the hydrate of alumina, associated with the sulphate of alumina, loses its water and its affinity for alum. It becomes, therefore, free; and during the subsequent exposure to the weather the stone gets disintegrated, and the alum becomes soluble in water.

The calcination is performed in common limekilns in the ordinary way. In the regulation of the fire it is requisite, here, as with gypsum, to prevent any fusion or running together of the stones, or even any disengagement of sulphuric or sulphurous acids, which would cause a corresponding diminution in the produce of alum. For this reason the contact of the ignited stones with carbonaceous matter ought to be avoided.

The calcined alum-stones, piled in heaps from 2 to 3 feet high, are to be exposed to the weather, and meanwhile they must be continually kept moist by sprinkling them with water. As the water combines with the alum the stones crumble down, and fall, eventually, into a pasty mass, which must be lixiviated with warm water, and allowed to settle in a large cistern. The clear supernatant liquor, being drawn off, is to be evaporated, and then crystallised. A second crystallisation finishes the process, and furnishes a marketable alum. Thus the Roman alum is made, which is covered with a fine red film of peroxide of iron.

Roman Alum crystallises—partly in octahedrons, like other alums, partly in cubes. If these cubes are dissolved in water of about 110° F., the evaporated liquid gives crystals of common or octahedral alum. It was said that on heating, it deposited subsulphate of alumina; but Loewel says that such crystals were impure, and he finds no real difference of composition. All that seems to be known with certainty is, that it is formed when there is a salt of alumina in solution with the alum containing more alumina than the neutral or common alum. This can very readily occur in the Roman alum, where there is a great excess of alumina in the alum-stone. The Roman alum is prized for its great freedom from iron; it was said by MM. Thenard and Roard to contain only $\frac{1}{2200}$th of sulphate of iron, whilst the ordinary alum contained $\frac{1}{1000}$th.

II. *Alum Manufacture from Alum-Schist.*—The greater portion of the alum found in British commerce was until recently made from alum-slate and analogous substances. This slate contains more or less iron pyrites, mixed with coaly or bituminous matter, which is occasionally so abundant as to render the schist somewhat combustible. In the strata of brown coal and bituminous wood, where the upper layers lie immediately under clay beds, they consist of the coaly substance rendered impure with clay and pyrites. This triple mixture constitutes the essence of all good alum-schists, and it operates spontaneously towards the production of sulphate of alumina. The coal, besides burning, serves to make the texture open, and to allow the air and moisture to penetrate freely, so as to change the sulphur and iron present into acid and oxide. When these schists are exposed to a high temperature in contact with air, the pyrites loses one-half of its sulphur, in the form of sublimed sulphur or of sulphurous acid, and becomes a black sulphide of iron, which speedily attracts oxygen, and changes to sulphate of iron, or green vitriol. The brown-coal schists contain, commonly, some green vitriol crystals spontaneously formed in them. The sulphate of iron transfers its acid to the clay, progressively, as the iron, by the action of the air with a little eleva-tion of temperature, becomes peroxidised; whereby sulphate of alumina is produced. A portion of the green vitriol remains, however, undecomposed, and so much the more as there may happen to be less of other salifiable bases present in the clay-slate. Should a little magnesia or lime be present, the vitriol gets more completely decom-posed, and a portion of Epsom salt and gypsum is produced.

The production of alum from alum-stone, in which the whole ingredients have been found, has been far from enough for the supply of the world, and recourse has been had to substances very different in composition,—alum-shale, or schist, and clay. Until within a few years the only supply of alum in Britain has been from the lias shales of Whitby, and the lower coal-measures of Campsie and Hurlet, near Glasgow, and they are still the only places where it is manufactured from the 'ore,' as it is called.

The manufacture of alum from alum-schists may be described under the six follow-ing heads:—1. The preparation of the alum-shale. 2. The lixiviation of the shale. 3. The evaporation of the lixivium. 4. The addition of the saline ingredients, or the precipitation of the alum. 5. The washing of the aluminous salts; and, 6. The crystallisation.

1. *Preparation of the Alum-Shale.*—Some alum-shales are of such a nature that, being piled in heaps in the open air, and moistened from time to time, they get spon-taneously hot, and by degrees fall into a pulverulent mass, ready to be lixiviated. The

greater part, however, require the process of ustulation, from which they derive many advantages. The cohesion of the dense shale is thereby so much impaired that its decomposition becomes more rapid; the decomposition of the pyrites is quickened by the expulsion of a portion of the sulphur; and the ready-formed green vitriol is partly decomposed by the heat, with a transference of its sulphuric acid to the clay, and the production of sulphate of alumina.

Such alum-shales as contain too little bitumen or coal for the roasting process must be interstratified with layers of small coal or brushwood over an extensive surface. At Whitby the alum-rock, broken into small pieces, is laid upon a horizontal bed of fuel, composed of brushwood; but at Hurlet small coal is chiefly used for the lower bed. When about four feet of rock is piled on, fire is set to the bottom in various parts; and whenever the mass is fairly kindled, more rock is placed over the top. At Whitby this piling process is continued till the calcining heap is raised to the height of 90 or 100 feet. The horizontal area is also augmented at the same time till it forms a great bed nearly 200 feet square, having therefore about 100,000 yards of solid measurement. The rapidity of the combustion is tempered by plastering up the crevices with small schist moistened. When such an immense mass is inflamed, the heat is sure to rise too high, and an immense waste of sulphur and sulphuric acid must ensue. This evil has been noticed at the Whitby works. At Hurlet the height to which the heap is piled is only a few feet, while the horizontal area is expanded: which is a much more judicious arrangement. At Whitby 130 tons of calcined schist produces on an average 1 ton of alum. In this humid climate it would be advisable to pile up on the top of the horizontal strata of brushwood or coal and schist, a pyramidal mass of schist, which, having its surface plastered smooth, with only a few air-holes, will protect the mass from the rains, and at the same time prevent the combustion from becoming too vehement. Should heavy rains supervene, a gutter must be scooped out round the pile for receiving the aluminous lixivium, and conducting it into the reservoir.

It may be observed, that certain alum-schists contain abundance of combustible matter, to keep up a suitable calcining heat after the fire is once kindled; and therefore nothing is needed but the first layer of brushwood, which, in this case, may be laid over the first bed of the bituminous schist.

A continual but very slow heat, with a smothered fire, is most beneficial for the ustulation of alum-slate. When the fire is too brisk, the sulphide of iron may run with the earthy matters into a species of slag, or the sulphur will be dissipated in vapour, by both of which accidents the product of alum will be impaired. Those bituminous alum-schists which have been used as fuel under steam boilers have suffered such a violent combustion that their ashes yield almost no alum. Even the best regulated calcining pipes are apt to burn too briskly in high winds, and should have their draught-holes carefully stopped under such circumstances. It may be laid down as a general rule, that the slower the combustion the richer the roasted ore will be in sulphate of alumina. When the calcination is complete, the heap diminishes to one-half its original bulk; it is covered with a light reddish ash, and is open and porous in the interior, so that the air can circulate freely throughout the mass. To favour this access of air, the masses should not be too lofty; and in dry weather a little water should be occasionally sprinkled on them, which, by dissolving away some of the saline matter, will make the interior more open to the atmosphere.

The following analyses of shales are by G. Kersten :—

	Hermann-schachte	Glückauf-gang	Blücher-schachte
Carbonaceous matter	41·10	27·92	34·20
Silica	44·02	51·32	50·21
Peroxide of iron	6·23	8·40	0·42
Alumina	5·60	7·62	5·21
Magnesia	0·32	0·26	0·53
Sulphur	1·25	2·89	1·72
Oxide of manganese	0·12	traces	traces
Sulphate of lime	traces	traces	traces
	98·64	98·41	98·39

Messrs. Richardson and Ronalds have given some very detailed analyses of the Whitby and Campsie shales :—

	Whitby		Campsie		
	Top Rock	Bottom Rock	Top Rock	Top Rock	Bottom Rock
Sulphur	...	...	22·36	23·44 ⎫	
Iron	...	...	18·16	15·04 ⎭	9·63
Sulphuret of iron . . .	4·20	8·50			
Silica	52·25	51·16	15·40	15·40	0·47
Protoxide of iron . . .	8·49	6·11	...	...	2·18
Alumina	18·75	18·30	11·35	11·64	18·91
Lime	1·25	2·15	1·40	2·22	0·40
Magnesia	0·91	0·90	0·50	0·32	2·17
Oxide of manganese . .	traces	traces	0·15	...	0·55
Sulphuric acid	1·37	2·50	...	...	0·05
Potash	0·13	traces	0·90	...	1·26
Soda	0·20	traces	...	...	0·21
Chlorine	traces	traces			
Carbon and loss . . .	...	...	29·78		
Carbon	...	...	...	28·80	
Coal	4·97	8·29	...	...	8·51
Loss	...	...	...	3·13	0·59
Water	2·88	2·00	...	...	8·54
	95·40	91·91	100·00	99·99	100·00

As the Top rock contains a larger excess of iron pyrites than the Bottom, they are mixed so as to diffuse the sulphuric acid equally.

Erdmann has thus analysed his German specimens :—

		Garnsdorff	Wezelstein
Soluble in acid	Sulphuret of iron	7·533	10·166
	Silica	0·060	0·100
	Peroxide of iron	0·966	2·466
	Alumina	1·833	3·166
	Lime	0·400	1·000
	Magnesia	trace	1·022
Insoluble in acid	Silica	50·066	52·200
	Alumina	8·900	17·900
	Peroxide of iron	1·300	3·566
	Magnesia	1·000	1·133
	Lime	trace	trace
	Coal	22·833	0·805
	Water	2·208	5·080

	Shales from Freienwalde, by Klaproth.	Shales from Pützberg, by Bergemann.
Alumina	16·000	10·80
Silica	40·00	45·30
Magnesia	0·25	
Sulphur	2·85	3·94
Carbon	19·65	5·95
Protoxide of iron . .	6·40	5·50
Oxide of manganese . .	—	0·60
Sulphate of protoxide of iron .	1·80	5·73
„ „ alumina . .	—	1·20
„ „ lime . .	1·50	1·71
„ „ potash . .	1·50	1·75
Chloride of potassium . .	0·50	0·35
Sulphuric acid . . .	—	0·47
Water	10·75	16·50
	101·20	99·70

Here the sulphur has evidently existed in combination with iron, which has been united to oxygen by the analysts. The amount of sulphate shows a partial disintegration and other changes.

Lampadius gives another analysis with much more sulphur:—

Alum-Shale from Siehda.

Sulphate of alumina	2·68
Potash-alum	0·47
Sulphate of iron	0·95
Sulphate of lime	1·70
Silica	10·32
Alumina	9·21
Magnesia	traces
Oxide of iron	2·30
Oxide of manganese	0·31
Sulphur	7·13
Water	33·90
Carbon	31·03
	100·00

When alum is made of such shale, the object is first of all to oxidise the sulphur, forming sulphuric acid. This acid then dissolves the alumina. The result may be accomplished by allowing the shale to disintegrate spontaneously in the air, the sulphur oxidising and dissolving the alumina. But in general, as at Whitby and Campsie, combustion must be resorted to. This can be accomplished without the use of coal, further than is needful simply to set fire to that portion which exists in the shale itself. Indeed, the Campsie shale, having more coal than is desirable for slow combustion, is mixed with some spent material, in order to diminish the force of the heat.

The sulphur is united with the iron, forming a bisulphide, each atom of which must, therefore, take up seven atoms of oxygen, $FeS^2 + 7O = FeO. SO^3 + SO^3$. When combustion takes place, the sulphur oxidises: if rapid combustion is permitted, sulphurous acid gas escapes; if slow combustion, the sulphurous acid penetrates the mass slowly, receives another atom of oxygen, unites to a base, and a sulphate is the consequence. Sulphate of iron is formed, and free sulphuric acid. In the process it is probable that the oxidation is completed by means of the iron. Protoxide of iron readily becomes peroxide; the sulphurous acid readily decomposes peroxide, forming sulphuric acid and protoxide of iron. This protoxide of iron is again converted into peroxide, and if not dissolved is rendered, to a great extent, difficult to dissolve, by reason of the heat of the mass. For this reason partly, there is less sulphate of iron in the alum than might be expected. To effect these changes it is desirable to burn very slowly, so as to allow no loss of sulphurous acid, and, in washing, to allow the water to stand a long time on the burnt ore. Another method, by which the sulphuric acid is transferred to the alumina, is the peroxidation of the protoxide in the sulphate of iron; acid is by this means set free and begins to act on the alumina.

The protosulphate of iron being formed, it is removed by boiling down the liquor until the protosulphate of iron crystallises out, at the same time the solution becoming saturated with the aluminous salt. The sulphate of iron is soluble in 0·3 of hot water, the alum in 0·06. The liquid around the crystals on the remaining mother-liquor contains iron also; this is washed off by adding pure liquors.

The presence of lime or magnesia in the ores is, of course, a means of abstracting acid, preventing the alumina being dissolved, and even precipitating it when dissolved.

Knapp says that at Salzweiler, near Duttweiler, in Rhenish Prussia, the roasting of the ore takes place in the pit or mine. The stratum of brown coal which lies under it, having been accidentally set fire to in 1660, has smouldered till the present time without intermission.

When the ores are roasted, one-half of the sulphur is freed and sent into the mass, or escapes as sulphurous acid; and the remaining protosulphide of iron is afterwards converted into green vitriol.

When the calcined mineral becomes thoroughly cold, we may proceed to the lixiviation. But as, from the first construction of the piles or beds till their complete calcination, many weeks, or even months, may elapse, care ought to be taken to provide a sufficient number or extent of them, so as to have an adequate supply of material for carrying on the lixiviating and crystallising processes during the course of the year, or at least during the severity of the winter season, when the calcination may be suspended, and the lixiviation becomes unsatisfactory. The beds are known to be sufficiently decomposed by the efflorescence of the salt which appears upon the stones, from the strong aluminous taste of the ashes, and from the appropriate chemical test of lixiviating an aliquot average portion of the mass, and seeing how much alum it will yield with solution of sulphate of potash or chloride of potassium.

2. *The Lixiviation.*—The lixiviation is best performed in stone-built cisterns; those of wood, however strong at first, are soon decomposed, and need repairs. They ought to be erected in the neighbourhood of the calcining heaps, to save the labour of transport, and so arranged that the solutions from the higher cisterns may spontaneously flow into the lower. In this point of view, a sloping terrace is the best situation for an alum work. In the lowest part of this terrace, and in the neighbourhood of the boiling-house, there ought to be two or more large tanks, for holding the crude lixivium, and they should be protected from the rain by a proper shed. Upon a somewhat higher level the cisterns of the clear lixivium may be placed. Into the highest range of cisterns the calcined mineral is to be put, taking care to lay the largest lumps at the bottom, and to cover them with lighter ashes. A sufficient quantity of water is now to be run over it, and allowed to rest for some time. The lixivium may then be drawn off, by a stopcock connected with a pipe at the bottom of the cistern, and run into another cistern at a somewhat lower level. Fresh water must now be poured on the partly exhausted schist, and allowed to remain for a sufficient time. This lixivium, being weak, should be run off into a separate tank. In some cases a third addition of fresh water may be requisite, and the weak lixivium which is drawn off may be reserved for a fresh portion of calcined mineral. In order to save evaporation, it is always requisite to strengthen weak leys by employing them instead of water for fresh portions of calcined schist. Upon the ingenious disposition and form of these lixiviating cisterns, much of the economy and success of an alum work depends. The hydrometer should be always used to determine the degree of concentration which the solutions acquire.

The lixiviated stone, being thus exhausted of its soluble ingredients, is to be removed from the cisterns, and piled up in a heap in any convenient place, where it may be left, either spontaneously to decompose, or, after drying, subjected to another calcination.

After calcining and washing the Campsie ores, the residue had the following composition :—

Silica	38·40
Alumina	12·70
Peroxide of iron	20·80
Oxide of manganese	traces
Lime	2·07
Magnesia	2·00
Potash	1·00
Sulphuric acid	10·76
Water	12·27
	100·00

It is, therefore, very far from being a complete process; but it is not considered profitable to remove the whole of the alumina. In some places the exhausted ore is burnt a second time with fresh ore, as at Campsie, but we are not told the estimated exhaustion.

The density of the solution may be brought, upon an average, up to the specific gravity of from 1·09 to 1·15. The latter density may always be obtained by pumping up the weaker solutions upon fresh calcined *mine*. This strong liquor is then drawn off, when the sulphate of lime, the oxide of iron, and the earths are deposited. It is of advantage to leave the liquor exposed to air for some time, whereby the green vitriol may pass into a persulphate of iron with the deposition of some oxide, when the acid will act better on the clay present, so as to increase the quantity of sulphate of alumina. The manufacture of alum is the more imperfect, as the quantity of sulphate of iron left undecomposed is greater, and therefore every expedient ought to be tried to convert the sulphate of iron into sulphate of alumina.

3. *The Evaporation of the Schist Lixivium.*—As the aluminous liquors, however well settled at first, are apt, on the great scale, to deposit earthy matters in the course of their concentration by heat, they are best evaporated by a surface fire, such as that employed at Hurlet and Campsie. A water-tight stone cistern must be built, having a layer of well-rammed clay behind the flags or tiles which line its bottom and sides.

The cistern may be 4 or 6 feet wide, 2 or 3 feet deep, and 30 or 40 feet long, and it is covered in by an arch of stone or brickwork. At one extremity of this tunnel, or covered canal, a fire-grate is set, and at the other a lofty chimney is erected. The cistern being filled to the brim with the alum ley, a strong fire is kindled in the reverberatory grate, and the flame and hot air are forced to sweep along the surface of the liquor, so as to keep it in constant ebullition, and to carry off the aqueous parts in vapour. The soot which is condensed in the process falls to the bottom and leaves the body of the liquor clear. As the concentration goes on, more of the rough lixivium is run in from the settling cistern, placed on a somewhat higher level, till the whole gets charged with a clear liquor of a specific gravity sufficiently high for transferring into the proper lead boilers.

At Whitby, the lead pans are 10 feet long, 4 feet 9 inches wide, 2 feet 2 inches deep at the one end, and 2 feet 8 inches deep at the other. This increase of depth and corresponding slope facilitates the decantation of the concentrated lixivium by means of a syphon applied at the lower end. The bottom of the pan is supported by a series of parallel iron bars placed very near each other. In these lead pans the liquor is concentrated, at a brisk boiling heat, by means of the flame of a flue beneath them. Every morning the pans are emptied into a settling cistern of stone or lead. The specific gravity of the liquor should be about 1·4 or 1·5, being a saturated solution of the saline matters present. The proper degree of density must vary, however, with different kinds of lixivia, and according to the different views of the manufacturer. For a liquor which consists of two parts of sulphate of alumina, and one part of sulphate of iron, a specific gravity of 1·25 may be sufficient; but for a solution which contains two parts of sulphate of iron to one of sulphate of alumina, so that the green vitriol must be withdrawn first of all by crystallisation, a specific gravity of 1·4 may be requisite.

The construction of an evaporating furnace well adapted to the concentration of aluminous and other crude lixivia is described under Soda. The liquor basin may be made of tiles or flags puddled in clay, and secured at the seams with a good *hydraulic* cement. A mortar made of quicklime mixed with the exhausted schist in powder, and iron turnings, is said to answer well for this purpose. Sometimes over the reverberatory furnace a flat pan is laid, instead of the arched top, into which the crude liquor is put for neutralisation and partial concentration. In Germany, such a pan is made of copper, because iron would waste too fast, and lead would be apt to melt. From this preparation-basin the under evaporating trough is gradually supplied with hot liquor. At one side of this lower trough, there is sometimes a door, through which the sediment may be raked out as it accumulates upon the bottom. Such a contrivance is convenient for this mode of evaporation, and it permits, also, any repairs to be readily made; but, indeed, an apparatus of this kind, well mounted at first, will serve for many years.

In the course of the final concentration of the liquors, it is customary to add some of the mother-waters of a former process, the quantity of which must be regulated by a proper analysis and knowledge of their contents. If these mother-waters contain much free sulphuric acid, they may prove useful in dissolving a portion of the alumina of the sediment which is always present in greater or less quantity.

4. *The Precipitation of the Alum by adding Alkaline Salts.*—As a general rule, it is most advantageous to separate, first of all, from the concentrated clear liquors, the alum in the state of powder or small crystals, by addition of the proper alkaline matters, and to leave the mingled foreign salts, such as the sulphate of iron or magnesia, in solution, instead of trying to abstract those salts by a previous crystallisation. In this way we not only simplify and accelerate the manufacture of alum, and leave the mother-waters to be worked up at any convenient season, but we also avoid the risk of withdrawing any of the sulphate of alumina with the sulphate of iron or magnesia. On this account the concentration of the liquor ought not to be pushed so far as that, when it gets cold, it should throw out crystals, but merely to the verge of this point. This density may be determined by suitable experiments. The powder of alum is also called *flour*.

The clear liquor should now be run off into the precipitation cistern, and have the sulphate of potash or chloride of potassium, or impure sulphate or carbonate of ammonia, added to it. The sulphate of potash, which is the most direct, forms 18·34 parts out of 100 of crystallised alum; and therefore that quantity, or an equivalent in chloride of potassium, or other potash, or ammoniacal salts, must be introduced into the aluminous liquor. Since sulphate of potash takes 10 parts of cold water to dissolve it, but is much more soluble in boiling water, and since the precipitation of alum is more abundant the more concentrated the mingled solutions are, it would be prudent to add the sulphate solution as hot as may be convenient: but, as chloride of potassium is fully three times more soluble in cold water, it is to be preferred as a precipitant, when it can be procured at a cheap rate. It has, also, the advantage of decomposing the sulphate of iron present into a chloride, a salt very difficult of crystallisation, and, therefore, less apt to contaminate the crystals of alum. Of late years chloride of potassium has been largely obtained from carnallite, and sulphate of potash has been procured from kainite, two minerals found in great abundance in the salt-mines of Stassfurt, in Prussia. The quantity of alkaline salts requisite to precipitate the alum, in a granular powder, from the lixivium, depends on their richness in potash or ammonia, on the one hand, and on the richness of the liquors in sulphate of alumina on the other; and this must be ascertained, for each large quantity of product, by a preliminary experiment in a precipitation glass. Here, an aliquot measure of the aluminous liquor being taken, the liquid precipitant must be added in successive portions, as long as it causes any cloud, when the quantity added will be indicated by the graduation of the vessel. A very exact approximation is not practicable upon the great scale; but, as the mother-waters are afterwards mixed together in one cistern, any excess of the precipitant at one time is corrected by excess of aluminous sulphate at another, and the resulting alum-meal is collected at the bottom. When the precipitated saline powder is thoroughly settled and cooled, the supernatant mother-water must be drawn off by a pump, or rather a syphon or stopcock, into a lower cistern. The more completely this drainage is effected, the more easily and completely will the alum be purified.

100 parts of alum are formed from the sulphate of alumina liquor,

> by 18·32 of sulphate of potash,
> „ 13·86 of sulphate of ammonia,
> or 15·69 of chloride of potassium.

Sulphate of ammonia is soluble in 1 of hot and 2 of cold water; sulphate of potash in nearly 10, and chloride of potassium in 3, of water of ordinary temperature; alum, in 13 parts of water. A portion of the alum formed will remain in solution; this will depend on the quantity of liquid; the rest falls as a powder.

This mother-liquor has generally a specific gravity of 1·4 at a medium temperature of the atmosphere, and consists of a saturated solution of sulphate or muriate of black and red oxide of iron with sulphate of magnesia, in certain localities, and chloride of sodium, when kelp salts have been used as a precipitant, as also a saturated solution of sulphate of alumina. By adding some of it, from time to time, to the fresh lixivia, a portion of that sulphate is converted into alum; but, eventually, the mother-water must be evaporated, so as to obtain from it a crop of ferruginous crystals; after which it becomes capable, once more, of giving up its alum to the alkaline precipitants.

When the aluminous lixivia contain a great deal of sulphate of iron, it may be good policy to withdraw a portion of it by crystallisation before precipitating the alum. With this view the liquors must be evaporated to the density of 1·4, and then run off into crystallising stone cisterns. After the green vitriol has crystallised, the liquor should be pumped back into the evaporating pan, and again brought to the density of 1·4. On adding to it, now, the alkalino-saline precipitants, the alum will fall down from this concentrated solution, in a very minute crystalline powder, easy to wash and purify. But this method requires more vessels and manipulation than the preceding, and should only be had recourse to from necessity; since it compels us to carry on the manufacture of both the valuable alum and the lower-priced salts at the same time; moreover, the copperas extracted at first from the schist liquors carries with it, as we have said, a portion of the sulphate of alumina, and acquires thereby a dull aspect; whereas the copperas obtained after the separation of the alum is of a brilliant appearance.

5. *The Washing, or Edulcoration, of the Alum Powder.*—This crystalline pulverulent matter has a brownish colour, from the admixture of the ferruginous liquors; but it may be freed from it by washing with very cold water, which dissolves not more than one-eighteenth of its weight of alum. After stirring the powder and the water well together, the former must be allowed to settle, and then the washing must be drawn off. A second washing will render the alum nearly pure. The less water is employed and the more effectually it is drained off, the more complete is the process. The second water may be used in the first washing of another portion of alum powder, in the place of pure water. These washings may be added to the schist lixivia. This powder is now extensively sold without further manipulation.

6. *The Crystallisation.*—The washed alum is put into a lead pan, with just enough water to dissolve it at a boiling heat; fire is applied, and the solution is promoted by stirring. Whenever it is dissolved in a saturated state, it is run off into the crystallising vessels, which are called *roching* casks. These casks are about five

feet high, three feet wide at the top, and somewhat wider at the bottom; they are made of very strong staves, nicely fitted to each other, and held together by strong iron hoops, which are driven on *pro tempore*, so that they may be easily knocked off again, in order to take the staves asunder. The concentrated solution, during its slow cooling in these close vessels, forms large regular crystals, which hang down from the top, and project from the sides, while a thick layer or cake lines the whole interior of the cask. At the end of eight or ten days, more or less according to the weather, the hoops and staves are removed, when a cask of apparently solid alum is disclosed to view. The workman now pierces this mass with a pickaxe at the side near the bottom, and allows the mother-water of the interior to run off on the sloping stone floor into a proper cistern, whence it is taken and added to another quantity of washed powder to be crystallised with it. The alum is next broken into lumps, exposed in a proper place to dry, and is then put into the finished bing for market. There is sometimes a little insoluble basic alum (sub-sulphate) left at the bottom of the cask. This, being mixed with the former mother-liquors, gets sulphuric acid from them; or, being mixed with a little sulphuric acid, it is equally converted into alum.

Alum Liquors.—In the alum works on the Yorkshire coast, eight different liquors are met with:

1st. 'Raw Liquor.' The calcined alum-shale is steeped in water till the liquor has acquired a specific gravity of 9 or 10 pennyweights, according to the language of the alum-maker.

2nd. 'Clarified Liquor.' The raw liquor is brought to the boiling point in lead pans, and suffered to stand in a cistern till it has cleared; it is then called clarified liquor. Its gravity is raised to 10 or 11 pennyweights.

3rd. 'Concentrated Liquor.' Clarified liquor is boiled down to about 20 pennyweights. This is kept merely as a test of the comparative value of the potash salts used by the alum-maker.

4th. 'Alum Mother-Liquor.' The alum pans are fed with clarified liquor, which is boiled down to about 25 or 30 pennyweights, when a proper quantity of potash salt in solution is mixed with it, and the whole run into coolers to crystallise. The liquor pumped from these rough crystals is called 'alum mothers.'

5th. 'Salts Mothers.' The alum mothers are boiled down to a crystallising point, and afford a crop of 'Rough Epsom,' which is a sulphate of magnesia and protoxide of iron.

6th and 7th. 'Alum Washings.' The rough crystals of alum (No. 4) are washed twice in water, the first washing being about 4 pennyweights, the second about 2½, the difference in gravity being due to mother-liquor clinging to the crystals.

8th. 'Tun Liquor.' The washed crystals are now dissolved in boiling water, and run into the 'roching tuns' (wood vessels lined with lead) to crystallise. The mother-liquor of the 'roch alum' is called 'tun liquor:' it is, of course, not quite so pure as a solution of roch alum in water.

The alum-maker's specific-gravity bottle holds 80 pennyweights of water, and by 10 pennyweights he means 10 more than water, or 90.

The numbers on Twaddle's hydrometer, divided by 2·5, give alum-makers' pennyweights.

The alum-maker tests his samples of potash salts comparatively by dissolving equal weights of the different samples in equal measures of alum liquor at 20 pennyweights, heated up to the boiling-point, and weighing the quantity of alum crystals produced on cooling.

For the above information we are indebted to Mr. Maurice Scanlan, who superintended for some time the Mulgrave Alum Works.

According to him 6½ tons of the alum rock at the Mulgrave Works, to the north of Whitby, yield, after calcination, &c., one ton of alum.

The true value of the Whitby alums consists in the amount of soluble alumina which they contain, and for calico-printing also in their freedom from iron.

The alum-shales not being very generally found over the country, and nature having interposed certain limits to the amount manufactured and the speed of the process, many attempts have been made to obtain alum and sulphate of alumina from other sources.

A number of these processes will be afterwards described in chronological order, but the following are those only which are at present largely applied in this country. One of the great advantages of the modern processes is the rapidity with which the alum can be manufactured; thus, an order can now be executed in three weeks which formerly would have occupied many months. For certain purposes, however, the old-fashioned Whitby alum is still preferred.

III. *Alum Manufacture from Coal-Measure Shales.*—The manufacture of alum has of late years taken an entirely new shape, and the two processes of Mr. Spence and Mr. Pochin have absorbed the whole of the manufacture in the north-west.

Mr. Spence, who has a manufactory of ammonia-alum at Newton Heath, near Manchester, called the Pendleton Alum Works, has now become the largest maker of this substance in the world, as his regular production amounts to upwards of 150 tons per week. His method of manufacture is also largely carried on at Goole, in Yorkshire. In Spence's process, which he patented fifteen years ago, he uses for the production of his sulphate-of-alumina solution the carbonaceous shale of the coal-measures.[1] This substance contains from 5 to 10 per cent. of carbonaceous matter, and, when ignited by a small quantity of burning coal, the combustion continues of itself. The raw shale is piled in heaps about 20 feet long, 4 or 5 feet high, and 2 or 3 feet broad. To supply air during the calcination of the shale, a brick drain is constructed under each heap. The calcination occupies about ten days, and must be conducted below a red heat; at higher temperatures, the material has a tendency to vitrify, and the alumina thus becomes insoluble in sulphuric acid. After calcination, the shale is removed to the pans, in which it is treated with oil of vitriol. These pans are each about 40 feet long, 10 feet wide, and 3 feet deep. They are constructed of sheets of cast iron, screwed together, and lined with lead, and the bottom of each pan before use is covered with earthen tiles about 9 inches square. A charge of 20 tons of calcined shale is introduced into each pan, and digested with about 10 tons of oil of vitriol, of specific gravity 1·25, which dissolves out the alumina of the shale. The digestion is conducted at a temperature of 220° F., this temperature being maintained partly by fires under the pans, and partly by the introduction of hot gaseous ammonia evolved from the gas-liquor evaporated in boilers. A double sulphate of alumina and ammonia, or ammonia-alum, is thus formed. After being heated for four or five days, the liquor is drawn off into the coolers, which are large shallow rectangular vessels of lead, each about 29 feet long, 17 feet wide, and $1\frac{3}{4}$ feet deep. In these vessels the liquid is kept in constant agitation by means of a long wooden arm, worked by steam. The formation of large crystals is thus prevented; but, after the lapse of about fourteen hours, the small crystals, which then form a bed several inches thick at the bottom of the vessel, are removed, and thrown into a large square box, lined with lead, in which they are washed with the mother-liquor, and having drained are thrown upon an iron grating formed of bars set about half-an-inch apart. The masses of crystals are thus broken, and the mother-liquor washed out. The crystals are then transferred to a cylindrical vessel, two or three feet high, and about 2 feet in diameter. This vessel has two divisions, one open and the other closed. The alum is placed in the open compartment, and dissolved by means of steam, introduced at a pressure of about 20 lbs. per square inch, through holes in a coil of leaden pipe at the bottom of this division of the vessel. A pipe leads from the top of the cylinder to a wooden vessel, called the dissolving box, which receives the solution of alum before it is drawn off into the roching pans. This box is 3 feet deep, 14 feet long, and 8 feet broad; it is covered with boards, the joints between which are closely packed with cotton waste. After the solution has remained for some hours in this vessel, a quantity of size—about 4 quarts—is poured in, and the suspended impurities are thus caused to settle. The clear solution is tapped off from the dissolving box into the crystallising tubs; each tub is about 6 feet high, and wider below than above. At the bottom of each tub is a round flagstone, upon which the staves of the tub, lined with lead, are built up and kept in place by strong iron hoops screwed together. The hot solution is run into these tubs, and protected by a wooden cover. After standing for about forty days, a sufficient thickness of alum will have crystallised to allow the sides of the tub to be taken down. The block is allowed to stand for about a fortnight longer, and a hole is then made in the lower part of the block, through which the mother-liquor runs out, and is received in tanks. On breaking open the block, the sides of the internal cavity are found to be studded with fine octahedral crystals, presenting a slightly violet tinge. These blocks weigh about 4 tons each.

IV. *Alum Manufacture from Mineral Phosphates.*—In 1870 Mr. Peter Spence patented a novel process for manufacturing alum, using as his raw material a phosphate of alumina and iron obtained from the Island of Redonda, near Antigua, in the West Indies; other mineral phosphates containing alumina may, however, be employed.[2] The process has special value, since not only is the alumina of the

---

[1] This description of Spence's process is taken from a paper on 'The Past and Present History of Alum,' by J. Carter Bell, Esq. F.C.S., Associate of the Royal School of Mines. 'Chemical News,' vol. xii. 1865, pp. 221, 234.

[2] Specification of Patents, A.D. 1870, No. 1676.

mineral dissolved out by sulphuric acid, and used in the manufacture of alum, but the phosphoric acid set free forms a highly valuable by-product.

The following analysis may be cited as that of a good sample of the Redonda phosphate :—

Phosphoric acid	42·6
Alumina	26·1
Peroxide of Iron	3·5
Silica	2·1
Water	25·2
	99·5

The mineral is first calcined at a red heat, whereby the water is expelled, and the material rendered porous, so as to be more freely acted on by sulphuric acid. If desirable, the calcination may be dispensed with, and the raw material merely prepared by grinding. In either case the phosphate is digested in leaden vessels with sulphuric acid of specific gravity 1·6.

The proportion of sulphuric acid varies with the richness of the mineral in alumina ; thus, if it contain 20 per cent. of alumina, an equal weight of acid will be used ; if only 12 per cent. of alumina, about three-fifths its weight of acid ; and so forth. To facilitate solution of the mineral by the acid, heat is applied—most conveniently by blowing steam into the vessel. As solution proceeds, the density of the liquid rises, and the strength of the liquor is then reduced by adding water, or weak liquors from subsequent stages of the process, and the liquid is boiled until its specific gravity ultimately reaches 1·45, or 90° Twaddle. This liquid is then transferred to a closed leaden vessel, and ammoniacal vapour from gas-liquor is distilled into it. The sulphate of ammonia thus formed combines with the sulphate of alumina to form ammonia-alum. From 600 to 900 gallons of gas-liquor are used to each ton of phosphate. After introduction of ammonia, the liquor is allowed to settle, and the clear solution, which has now a specific gravity of 1·4, or 80° Twaddle, is run into leaden coolers, where the alum crystallises. When the phosphate contains 20 per cent. of alumina, it yields about a ton-and-a-half of alum per ton. One of the great difficulties in this process consists in completely freeing the alum from the associated phosphoric acid.

Whilst the alumina of the phosphate is thus utilised for the production of alum, the phosphoric acid, which is at the same time eliminated, forms a product of high value to the agriculturist. Indeed the mother-liquor from which the alum is deposited consists chiefly of a solution of phosphoric acid, with a small proportion of sulphate of alumina, iron, and sulphate or phosphate of ammonia. This liquid may be used as a fertilising agent either directly or made into an artificial manure by being absorbed in sawdust and dried at a low heat.

We believe that Mr. Spence's new process is now carried out on a large scale at the Pendleton Alum Works.

Other Methods of Alum Manufacture.—In addition to the four principal processes of manufacture already described, numerous other methods have from time to time been proposed, and in some cases worked to a limited extent. The more important of these suggested improvements are included in the following notices, which are arranged in chronological order.

In 1743, Ambrose Newton wished to economise the manufacture by boiling the scum of the alum works, the muddy deposit in Yorkshire, and adding to the concentrated solution of 45 pennyweights, stale urine, which is ammonia, until the solution became 27 pennyweights. The liquor stands 'for four days, and strikes out into small allom, and afterwards melted and roached into casks, which stand 14 days, and are taken down and the allom is finished.'

Another patent in 1765, by Holme, Cropper, and two Nicholsons, uses stale urine and kelp liquor. They seem to use, by a mistake in names, iron pyrites only for their alum, but no doubt it contained both iron and alumina. They took advantage of the potash, and perhaps also of the soda, of the kelp.

In 1780, Matthew Sanderson patented a plan for making alum by burning the metallic sulphurets, obtaining the sulphuric acid, and uniting it with aluminous earth —a far-seeing plan, not till long after adopted.

In 1794 Lord Dundonald patented a process for 'washing aluminous, vitriolic, or pyritous schist or materials with sea-water or solutions of salts containing muriate of soda,' or mixing muriate of soda with aluminous or vitriolated salts or pyritous substances. He also proposed the use of muriatic acid. It is probable, then, that both a soda- and an ammonia-alum have been manufactured when the whole method was not very clearly understood.

Macquer, Fourcroy, and Vauquelin having discovered the component parts of alum, Chaptal made it from its elements, using clay. He says, 'Pure clay upon which the sulphuric acid is digested is dissolved with difficulty.' He then says, 'I calcine my clays, and reduce them into small pieces, which I spread on the floor of my leaden chambers. The sulphuric acid, which is formed by combustion of a mixture of sulphur and saltpetre, expands itself in the cavity of these chambers, and exists for a certain time in the vaporous form. In this form it has a stronger action than when it has been weakened by the mixture of a quantity of water more or less considerable, so that it seizes the earths, combines with them, causes them to increase in bulk by the effervescence which takes place, and at the end of several days the whole surface exposed to the vapour is converted into alum. Care is taken to stir these earths from time to time, that they may successively present all their surfaces to the action of the acid.' 'But whatever process may be used to combine the acid with clay, it is necessary to expose the aluminised earths to the air during a greater or less space of time, in order that the combination may be more accurate, and the saturation more complete.' This is, in fact, the mode of making the sulphate of alumina. It was then dissolved in water, drawn off clear, to free it from the silica and undissolved matter, mixed with sulphate of potash, evaporated, and crystallised.

The manufacture of the alum from clay seems to have been a good deal used in France. Their method at present, according to Regnault, is as follows:—'They choose clays, such as kaolins, which contain little iron. The clays are then calcined at a low red heat in a furnace; they are ground to powder in a mill, and mixed with half their weight of sulphuric acid of 1·45 specific gravity. The mixture is then heated in another furnace until the sulphuric acid begins to evaporate. It is then taken out, and left to stand for several days.' After some time the combination becomes intimate, and the usual method of removing the sulphate of alumina from the insoluble matter is resorted to, and the potash, or ammonia-salt, is added, to convert it into alum.

The most usual method has been to allow it to stand some weeks, or months, until the combination has been effected. This has partially arisen from a supposition of the necessity of giving it as much time as is needful with the shales, as it was not known until lately how completely the acid may decompose the clays.

A patent was obtained in November, 1839, by Mr. William Wiesmann, of Duesburg, for improvements in the manufacture of alum. He subjects potters' clay to a moderate red heat, grinds it, and subjects the powder, in leaden pans, to the action of concentrated sulphuric acid (66° B.), taking care to use excess of clay and a moderate heat. The mixture is to be stirred till it is dry, then treated with boiling water, in order to dissolve the sulphate of alumina formed. So far the process is old and well known. The novelty consists in freeing the saline solution from iron by ferrocyanide of potassium (prussiate of potash). When the iron has been all thrown down in the form of Prussian-blue, the liquor is allowed to settle, the supernatant pure sulphate is drawn off, and evaporated till it forms, on cooling, a concrete mass, which may be moulded into the shape of bricks, &c., for the convenience of packing. This was manufactured at Lee-Moor, near Plympton, on a small scale; but it is no longer made in this country. Dr. Muspratt's analysis made it a basic sulphate = $2Al^2O^3$. $5SO^3 + 33$ Aq.; and he adds that manufacturers objected to it because it was impossible to judge of its purity by its merely physical appearance. Mohr's analysis gave—

Alumina	13·91
Sulphuric acid	36·24
Water	49·60
Sulphate of potash	1·50

By having an excess of clay, Wiesmann intended to have all his acid saturated. He found that he could not dissolve all the alumina by using only its equivalent of acid; he preferred, therefore, to lose some of the alumina, as in the other processes.

Hervey's patent of 1839.—Clay is dried, ground, and sieved; it is then mixed with sulphuric acid of from 10° to 80° Twad., and from ½ to an equal quantity of clay, used according to its quality. The mixture is then well stirred; a great ebullition ensues, and after ebullition it is again stirred. This is the formation of the sulphate of alumina, which is washed out, and made into alum in the ordinary way.

In 1842 Mr. Turner patented a method, said to be originally Sprengel's proposal, of extracting the alumina and potash from felspar to make alum. The felspar is heated with sulphate of potash to melting, then carbonate of potash is added. This gives a soluble glass, which, in boiling water, takes up two-thirds of the silica and as much potash as was added to the felspar. This being heated with carbonic acid, gives a gelatinous mass of silica. When dried, the carbonate of potash may be washed out.

The insoluble portion of the glass contains the original felspar, minus two-thirds of its silica—a light, porous substance, similar in composition to elæolite. This is boiled with sulphuric acid of 1·2 specific gravity. The intense heat needed has prevented the success of this process.

In 1842 Kagenbusch proposed to cover the schist over with a plastering of clay, or mud, for several months, and wash with water; then to have it burnt in kilns fitted with air-holes. In this process turf is used, on which the schist rests. The air-holes regulate the combustion, which lasts three days. He uses kelp to obtain the alkali.

In 1850 J. T. Wilson proposed a method of collecting the ammonia from smoke, and using it in making ammonia-alum. What is wanting, he supplements by potash salts, causing a mixed potash- and ammonia-alum to be manufactured.

In 1854 Richardson adds iron pyrites, to increase the amount of sulphur, and, consequently, of sulphuric acid, in the shale; but it does not seem to have been used.

In 1855 Dr. Frankland precipitated the subsulphate of alumina, and added sulphuric acid, thus obtaining the base by a small expenditure of precipitant.

In 1856 J. Metcalf makes a cake similar to the alum-cake described at p. 122; but he uses coarse clay.

In 1856 Henry Pease and Thomas Richardson mix clay with chloride of potassium or with common salt; they convert both into sulphates; the muriatic acid set free dissolves the alumina, and the chloride of aluminium formed is used as alum.

In 1856 Spilsburg's patent purposed to make alum from cryolite.

The Boghead Cannel-coal ash contains about 30 per cent. of alumina, which it has been proposed to dissolve for making alum; but it has not hitherto been found a convenient material.

Among the modern methods adopted for manufacturing alum on the Continent, some of the more interesting are those in which cryolite is the raw material (see CRYOLITE). According to Thomson's method the cryolite is ignited with carbonate of lime, whereby aluminate of soda and fluoride of calcium are produced; the former being soluble and the latter insoluble in water. The aluminate is, therefore, dissolved out, and a current of carbonic acid gas transmitted through the solution. A gelatinous precipitate of alumina is thus thrown down, while carbonate of soda remains in solution. Or bicarbonate of soda may be added to the solution of the aluminate, and the alumina thus precipitated in a compact form. The alumina obtained by either of these methods is dissolved in dilute sulphuric acid, and the sulphate of alumina thus formed is converted into alum.

In another process, introduced by Sauerwein, the cryolite having been powdered, is boiled with water and lime; and, as before, aluminate of soda and fluoride of calcium are obtained. The solution of aluminate is mixed with an excess of finely-powdered cryolite, whereby alumina and fluoride of sodium are produced. The alumina is then converted into sulphate, and this into alum, as previously described.

Sulphate of alumina may also be obtained from cryolite by treating it directly with sulphuric acid.

Alum has likewise been prepared from the mineral called Bauxite, which, on ignition with sulphate of soda and charcoal, yields sulphate of alumina. Again, blast-furnace slag may be employed as the raw material; the slag, treated with hydrochloric acid, yields chloride of aluminium, from which alumina may readily be precipitated.

Alum has been made extensively in England and France from an artificial sulphate of alumina, prepared from clays which are chosen as free as possible from carbonate of lime and oxide of iron. They are calcined in a reverberatory furnace, in order to expel the water, to peroxidise the iron, and to render the alumina more easily acted on by the acid. The expulsion of the water renders the clay porous and capable of absorbing the sulphuric acid by capillary attraction. The peroxidation of the iron renders it less soluble in the sulphuric acid; and the silica of the clay, by reacting on the alumina, impairs its aggregation, and makes it more readily attracted by the acid. The clay should therefore be moderately calcined; but not so as to indurate it like pottery-ware, for certain combinations would then be effected which would make it resist the action of acids. The clay is usually calcined in a reverberatory furnace, the flame of which serves afterwards to heat two evaporating pans and a basin for containing a mixture of the calcined clay and sulphuric acid. As soon as the clay has become friable in the furnace it is taken out, reduced to powder, and passed through a fine sieve. With 100 parts of the pulverised clay, 45 parts of sulphuric acid, of specific gravity 1·45, are well mixed, in a stone basin, arched over with brickwork. The flame and hot air of the reverberatory furnace are made to play along the mixture, in the same way as described for evaporating alum-schist liquors. (See SODA.) The mixture, being stirred from time to time, is at the end of a few days to be raked out, and to be set aside in a warm place, for the acid to work on the clay, during six or eight weeks. At the end of this time, it must be washed, to extract the sulphate of alumina. With this view, it may be treated like the roasted alum ores previously described. If potash-alum is to be formed, this sulphate of alumina is evaporated to the specific gravity of 1·38; but if ammonia-alum, to the specific gravity of only 1·24; because the sulphate of ammonia, being soluble in twice its weight of water, will cause a precipitation of pulverulent alum from a weaker solution of sulphate of alumina than the less soluble sulphate of potash could do.

In preparing alum from clay or shale, it is of infinite importance that so much and no more heat be applied to the clay or shale, in the first instance, as will just expel the water of combination without inducing contraction. A temperature of 600° F. is well adapted to effect this object, provided it be maintained for a sufficient period. When this has been carefully done, the silicate of alumina remaining is easily enough acted upon by sulphuric acid, either slightly diluted or of the ordinary commercial strength. The best form of apparatus is a leaden boiler, divided into two parts by a perforated septum or partition, also in lead; though on a very large scale, brickwork set in clay might be employed. Into one of the compartments the roasted clay or shale should be put, and diluted sulphuric acid being added, the bottom of the other compartment may be exposed to the action of a well-regulated fire, or, what is better, heated by means of steam through the agency of a coil of leaden pipe. In this way a circulation of the fluid takes place throughout the mass of shale; and, as the alumina dissolves, the dense fluid it produces, falling continually towards the bottom of the boiler, is replaced by dilute acid, which, becoming in its turn saturated, falls like the first; and so on in succession, until either the whole of the alumina is taken up, or the acid in great part neutralised. The solution of sulphate of alumina thus obtained is sometimes evaporated to dryness, and sold under the name of 'concentrated alum;' but more generally it is boiled down until of the specific gravity of about 1·35; then one or other of the carbonates or sulphates of potash or ammonia, or chloride of either base, or a mixture of these, is added to the boiling fluid, and as soon as the solution is complete, the whole is run out into a cooler to crystallise. The rough alum thus made is sometimes purified by a subsequent recrystallisation, after which it is 'roched' for the market—a process intended merely to give it the ordinary commercial aspect, but of no real value in a chemical point of view.

Alum Cake.—This substance owes its value to the amount of sulphate of alumina it contains, and is in fact another means of making soluble alumina accessible. We have already seen the many attempts to obtain alumina from clay, and the tedious nature of the operation of solution in acid, as well as the long after-processes of lixiviation and conversion into sulphate of alumina, or into alum, by reboiling or crystallising. Mr. Pochin, of Manchester, has found a method of removing all the difficulties, both of the first and after processes. He uses very fine china clay, free from iron, heats it in a furnace, mixes it thoroughly with acid, and finds that, when the process is managed carefully, the combination of the alumina and sulphuric acid is not only complete, but so violent that he is obliged to dilute his acid considerably, in order to calm the action. When mixed, it is passed into cisterns with moveable sides, where, in a few minutes, it heats violently and boils. The thick liquid gradually becomes thicker, until it is converted into a solid porous mass—the pores being made by the bubbles of steam which rise in the mass, which is not fluid enough to contract to its original volume. The porous mass is perfectly dry, although retaining a large amount of combined water. It retains, of course, all the silica of the original clay, but this is in such fine division that every particle appears homogeneous. The silica gives it a dryness to the touch not easily gained by the sulphate only.

When pure sulphate of alumina is wanted in solution, the silica is allowed to precipitate before using it, but, in many cases, the fine silica is no hindrance; then the solution is made use of at once.

Some quantity of alum has been exported from China, chiefly to India, within a short period. The Chinese use alum very largely in their cements. The alum mines are in the neighbourhood of Peh-kwan harbour, 2° 9' 10" N., 12° 32' 6" E. Ten alum-making establishments appear to exist there, and the process, as described in the *North China Mail*, is similar to that employed where, in this country, the alum-shale is used.

ALUM EARTH. A variety of aluminous schist found associated with the lignites of the tertiary beds, especially on the Rhine.

ALUM, FEATHER. A hydrated sulphate of protoxide and sesquioxide of iron, called by Dana *Halotrichite*. The name 'feather alum' is also sometimes applied to a hydrated sulphate of alumina, known also as *Alunogen*. The latter is found crystallised in a close mass of fine, white, flexible needles, of a feather or hair form, and has been, like a few other substances, called *hair-salt*. It is also found with various degrees of impurity, sometimes with a smaller amount of water. Knapp has collected the list of analyses shown in the Table :—

Analyses of Natural Sulphate of Alumina or Feather Alum.

	Boussin-gault	Hartwell	H. Rose				Göbel	Ber-thier	Th. Thomson		Hera-path
	Saldanho Pasto	Pyroment, Island Mile	Coquimbe, Chili	Friedorf, Bonn	Potschoppel, Dresden	Freienwalde	Ararat	Huelgoet, Britany	Andes	Campsie, Scotland	Adelaide, N.S. Wales
Sulphuric acid .	36·400	40·31	36·97	37·380	35·710	35·637	58·58	12·9	35·872	40·425	35·63
Alumina	16·000	14·98	14·63	14·867	12·778	11·227	38·75	41·5	14·645	10·485	17·09
Peroxide of iron.	0·004	..	2·58	..	..	..	..	..	0·500	8·530	0·04
Protoxide of iron.	..	..	..	2·463	0·667	0·718	+SO²2·78	..	..	..	{ Oxide ofCopper
Protoxide Manganese	..	..	..	..	1·018	0·307					
Potash .	..	0·26	..	0·215	0·324	0·430	..	..	..	1·172	
Soda . .	..	1·13	..	..	..	..			2·262		
Lime . .	0·002	..	..	0·149	0·640	0·449	..	..			
Magnesia	0·004	0·85	0·14	..	0·273	1·912					
Muriatic acid. .	..	0·40									
Silica. .	..	1·13	1·37	..	..	0·430	..	3·5	0·100	..	0·50
Water .	46·600	40·94	44·64	45·164	47·022	48·847	..	42·1	46·375	36·295	46·70
	99·010	100·00	100·33	100·238	98·432	100·000	100·11	100·0	99·754	96·904	99·96

ALUM, NATIVE. This term includes several compounds of sulphate of alumina with the sulphate of some other base, as magnesia, potash, soda, the protoxides of iron, manganese, &c. They occur generally as efflorescences, or in fibrous masses ; when crystallised they assume octahedral forms ; they are soluble in water, and have an astringent taste. The following species are the chief native alums, but it should be understood that the proportion of water of crystallisation is not the same in all, and hence in some cases they cannot be brought within the general formula given under the article ALUM.

Kalinite, or Potash Alum, found as an efflorescence on alum-slate at Whitby, Hurlet and Campsie.

Mendozite, or Soda-alum, found in South America. The following analyses may be cited :—

Soda-alum from Peru, by T. Thomson.

Sulphate of soda	.	.	.	6·50
Alumina	.	.	.	22·55
Sulphuric acid	.	.	.	32·95
Water .	.	.	.	39·20
				101·20

Soda-alum from the Andes.

Sulphuric acid	.	.	.	36·199
Alumina	.	.	.	11·511
Soda .	.	.	.	7·259
Water .	.	.	.	43·819
Silica .	.	.	.	0·180
Lime .	.	.	.	0·255
Peroxide of iron .		.	.	0·199
Protoxide of iron .		.	.	0·760
				100·162

Tschermigite, or Ammonia-alum, found at Tschermig in Bohemia. Analyses have been made of specimens from Tschermig, by Stromeyer :—

Alumina	.	.	.	.	11·602	Sulphate of alumina .	. 38·688
Ammonia	.	.	.	.	3·721	Sulphate of ammonia .	. 12·478
Magnesia	.	.	.	.	0·115	Sulphate of magnesia .	. 0·337
Sulphuric acid	.	.	.	36·065	Water	. 48·390
Water .	.	.	.	.	48·390		
					99·893		99·893

Pickeringite, or Magnesia-alum, found near Iquique in Peru, and in Nova Scotia.
Apjohnite, or Manganese-alum, from Lagos Bay in South Africa.

Bosjemanite, a Manganese-alum, found near the Bosjeman River in South Africa, and at Alum Point, near the Salt Lake, Utah.

ALUM, ROMAN (*Alumen Romanum. Allume di rocca*, It.), called sometimes *Roch* or *Rock Alum*. See ALUM.

ALUM ROOT. The root of the *Geranium maculatum*, a North American plant. It contains a large proportion of tannin, and is used as a powerful astringent.

ALUM-SHALE. The chief natural source from which the alum of commerce is derived in this country. It occurs in a remarkable manner near Whitby, in Yorkshire, and at Hurlet and Campsie, near Glasgow. A full description of the alum-shale, and of the processes by which the crystallisable alum is separated, will be found under ALUM.

ALUM-SLATE. A clay-slate containing bitumen and sulphide of iron, found in the North of England, in Scotland, in Scandinavia, and other places. The *common* variety effloresces and acquires the taste of alum. *The glossy Alum-slate* is of a bluish-black colour, with a semi-metallic lustre. It swells upon exposure to the air, owing to the saline efflorescence formed between the foliations, and is eventually disintegrated.

ALUM-STONE or **ALUNITE.** (*Alun*, Fr.; *Alaunstein*, Ger.)—This mineral, in its purest form, is composed of alumina 37·13, sulphuric acid 38·53, potash 11·34, water 13·00. Silica is also frequently present as an impurity, sometimes to the extent of 60 per cent. It is a white, greyish, or reddish mineral, affording a white streak, and an uneven, flat, conchoidal fracture, which is splintery in the massive varieties. It is transparent or subtranslucent.

Alum-stone is one of the sources of the alum of commerce, which is obtained from it in crystals after frequent roasting, and lixiviation in water. See ALUM.

Alum-stone is found at Tolfa, near Civita Vecchia, in the Roman States (sometimes in crystals); at Muszaly in Hungary; at Pic de Sancy, in France, and in the Grecian Archipelago. The compact varieties from Hungary are so hard as to be used for millstones.

ALUMINA. (Al^2O^3, *atomic weight* 51·4). This is the only oxide which the metal aluminium forms, and it is assumed to be a sesquioxide on account of its isomorphism with sesquioxide of iron.

Alumina occurs in a native state, forming the gems known as the *sapphire* and the *ruby*, and in a less pure form as the minerals *corundum* and *emery*. In a state of hydrate, or in chemical combination with water, alumina constitutes the species known as *diaspore, gibbsite*, and *hydrargyllite*. Such of these minerals as are of economic value will be noticed under their respective heads.

Alumina is obtained in the state of hydrate from common alum (KO, SO^3; Al^2O^3, $3SO^3 + 24HO$) by adding a solution of ammonia (or better, carbonate of ammonia) to the latter salt and boiling. The precipitate is white, and gelatinous in a high degree, and retains the salts, in the presence of which it has been formed, with remarkable pertinacity, so that it is very difficult to wash.

By drying and igniting this hydrate, the anhydrous alumina is produced; but it may be obtained more readily by heating ammonia-alum (NH^4O, SO^3; $Al^2O^33SO^3 + 24HO$). All the constituents of this salt are volatile, with the exception of the alumina.

Alumina is insoluble in water, but soluble both in acids and alkalis. Towards the former it plays the part of a base, producing the ordinary alumina salts; whilst, with the latter, it also enters into combination, but in this case it is an acid, forming a series of compounds which may be called aluminates.

The important application of alumina and its compounds in the arts of dyeing and calico-printing depends upon a peculiar attraction which it possesses for organic bodies. This affinity is so strong, that when digested in solutions of vegetable colouring matters the alumina combines with and carries down the colouring matter, removing it entirely from the solution. Pigments thus obtained, which are combinations of alumina with the vegetable colouring matters, are called ' *lakes*.'

Alumina has not only an affinity for the colouring matters, but at the same time also for the vegetable fibres, cotton, silk, wool, &c.; and hence, if alumina be precipitated upon cloth in the presence of a colouring matter, a most intimate union is effected between the cloth and the colour. Alumina, when employed in this way, is called a ' mordant.'

Other bodies have a similar attraction for colouring matters, *e.g.* binoxide of tin and sesquioxide of iron: each of these gives its peculiar shade to the colour or combination, alumina changing it least.

Mr. Walter Crum[1] has discovered a peculiar soluble modification of alumina. The binacetate of alumina has been found by Mr. Crum to possess the very curious property of parting with its acetic acid until the whole is expelled, by the long-continued application of heat to a solution of this salt; the alumina remains in the solution, in a soluble allotropic condition, forming what has been called *metalumina*. Its coagulum with dyewoods is translucent, and entirely different from the opaque cakes formed by ordinary alumina; hence this solution cannot act as a mordant. But this solution of alumina, which is perfectly colourless and transparent, has the alumina separated from it by the slightest causes. A minute quantity of either an acid, an alkali, even of a neutral salt, or of a vegetable colouring matter, effects the change. The precipitated alumina is insoluble in acids, even boiling sulphuric; this shows another allotropic condition. But it is dissolved by caustic alkalis, by which it is restored to its common state.

ALUMINA, ACETATE OF. The acetates of alumina are extensively used in the arts on account of the property which they possess of being readily decomposed with deposition of their alumina on the fibre of cloth; hence they are used as mordants, in the manner described under CALICO-PRINTING; and sometimes in dyeing they are mixed with the solution of a colouring matter; in this the textile fabric is immersed, whilst, on heating, the alumina is precipitated upon the fabric, which, in consequence of its affinities before alluded to, carries down the colouring matter with it, and fixes it on the cloth.

The acetate of alumina thus employed is obtained by treating sulphate of alumina with neutral acetate of lead, and filtering off the solution from the precipitate of sulphate of lead. Acetate of lime is also used; but the sulphate in this case does not leave the solution so clear or so rapidly.

According to Mr. Walter Crum,[1] the solution resulting from the decomposition of sulphate of alumina Al^2O^3, $3SO^3$ (**Al² 3SO⁴**) by monobasic acetate of lead contains the salt Al^2O^3, $2(C^4H^3O^3. HO)$ [**Al²O³. 4C²H⁴O²**] (binacetate of alumina), together with one equivalent of free acetic acid, the compound Al^2O^3, $3C^4H^3O^3$ (**Al²6C²H³O²**) not appearing to exist. By evaporating this solution at low temperatures, *e.g.* in a very thin layer of fluid below 38° C. (100° F.), Crum obtained a fixed residue completely soluble in water, the composition of which, in the dry state, approached Al^2O^3, $2C^4H^3O^3 + 4HO$ (**Al²O³. 4C²H⁴O² + 2H²O**).

ALUMINA, SILICATES OF. Silicate of alumina is the chief constituent of common clay; it occurs also associated with the silicates of iron, magnesia, lime, and the alkalis in a great variety of minerals, which will be found described elsewhere. The most interesting of these are the felspars and the zeolites. See CLAY, FELSPAR, ZEOLITE.

Of course, being present in clay, silicate of alumina is the essential constituent of porcelain and earthenware. See EARTHENWARE and PORCELAIN.

ALUMINA, SULPHATE OF. The neutral sulphate of alumina, Al^2O^3, $3SO^3 + 18HO$ (**Al²3SO⁴ + 18H²O**), which is obtained by dissolving alumina in sulphuric acid, crystallises in needles and plates; but sulphuric acid and alumina combine in other proportions, *e.g.* a salt of the formula Al^2O^3, $3SO^3 + Al^2O^3$ (**Al²3SO⁴ + Al²O³**) was obtained by Mons, and the solution of this salt, when largely diluted with water, splits into the neutral sulphate and an insoluble powder containing Al^2O^3, $3SO^3 + 2Al^2O^3 + 9HO$ (**Al²3SO⁴ + 2Al²O³ + 9H²O**). This subsalt forms the mineral *aluminite*, or *Websterite*, found near Newhaven, and was found by Humboldt in the schists of the Andes.

The sulphate of alumina is now extensively used in the arts instead of alum, under the name of 'concentrated alum' (see p. 122). For most of the purposes for which alum is employed, the sulphate of potash is an unnecessary constituent, being only added in order to facilitate the purification of the compound from iron; for in consequence of the ready crystallisability of alum, this salt is easily purified. Nevertheless, Wiesmann has succeeded in removing the iron from the crude solution of sulphate of alumina obtained by treating clay with sulphuric acid, by adding ferrocyanide of potassium, which throws down the iron as Prussian-blue; the solution, when evaporated to dryness, is found to consist of sulphate of alumina, containing about 7 per cent. of potash-alum. About 1750 tons of this article were produced at Newcastle-on-Tyne alone in the year 1872. See also ALUM.

ALUMINATE OF SODA. 3 NaO. Al^2O^3 (**3Na²O. Al²O³**). This salt is now manufactured on a large scale for use as a mordant in dyeing and calico-printing; in the preparation of lakes for pigments; in the manufacture of certain forms of artificial stone; and in candle and soap manufacture. The salt is generally obtained by heating Bauxite with carbonate of soda in a reverberatory furnace. The alumina present in the Bauxite combines with the soda, while carbonic acid is expelled. On lixiviating the product, the aluminate of soda is dissolved out; the solution is then filtered, and the filtrate evaporated to dryness. The salt is thus obtained as a whitish powder. See BAUXITE.

ALUMINITE. See WEBSTERITE.

ALUMINIUM. (*Sym.* Al., *at. wt.* 13·7.) The name Aluminium is derived from the Latin *alumen*, for alum, of which salt this metal is the notable constituent.

Aluminium, though never found in the free state, occurs extensively diffused in nature in alumina and certain of its salts, especially the silicates.

The native varieties of *anhydrous* alumina are, the sapphire, ruby, and corundum, whilst the hydrate occurs in nature in the minerals, diaspore and gibbsite. But the chief quantity of aluminium is found in the endless varieties of the mineral silicates of alumina with other bases, such as the felspars, micas, many kinds of clay, the zeolites, &c.

Alumina was first decomposed by Davy, who discovered the metal soon after decomposing the other earths and alkalis; but he never seems to have obtained it without some mixture of potassium. It is evident, however, that the earth was completely reduced to the metallic state by him.

Wöhler obtained aluminium pure in 1827[1] by the reduction of the chloride of aluminium in the form of a grey powder. Later (1845),[2] he succeeded by the same process in obtaining it in globules, which he describes as tin white, tolerably malleable and ductile, not materially oxidised by exposure to the air, of a specific gravity of 2·5, but, when hammered, of 2·67; unacted upon by water at the common temperature, but slowly disengaging hydrogen from water at the boiling point.

In 1854[3] Deville's first experiments on the preparation and properties of aluminium were published. The method he adopted for the liberation of the metal was essentially the same as that originally employed by Wöhler. But, by dint of improvements in the details of the process, he succeeded in procuring the metal in larger globules, which were silver-white, having a fusing point nearly approaching that of silver, which were unoxidised when exposed to the air, even in a fused state, and remaining bright *even in boiling water*, unattacked by either dilute or concentrated nitric or sulphuric acid in the cold; but dissolved by hydrochloric acid with evolution of hydrogen.

Oersted was undoubtedly the first to prepare the chloride of aluminium,[4] and it is even stated that he also procured the metal by the following method:—'Pure alumina, intimately mixed with powdered charcoal, was introduced into a porcelain tube; through this, when strongly heated, a stream of chlorine was directed, and the chloride of aluminium formed was collected in a separate vessel. By mixing this compound with an amalgam of potassium, containing a large proportion of the latter body, and immediately heating the mixture, chloride of potassium was found, and the aluminium combined with the mercury. This, on being distilled out of contact with the air, gave off the mercury, whilst aluminium remained in the form of a metallic button, closely resembling tin.'[5]

Deville's researches raised the hope that the metal might be obtained in sufficient quantity to become of high technical importance, since it was probable that the chloride of aluminium might be decomposed by cheaper metals at a higher temperature; and he obtained a grant from the late Emperor of the French for the purpose of prosecuting his investigations on a sufficient scale.

Bunsen also showed in 1854[6] that aluminium could be obtained in reguline masses by submitting the double chloride of aluminium and sodium or potassium to electrolysis in a fused state.

By fusing the chloride of aluminium (obtained by the process which will be found described under the head of the chloride) with an equal equivalent of common salt, he obtained a double chloride, which fused below 200° C. (360° F.), and from which the metal is readily reduced by the same electrolytic process previously employed by Bunsen in the case of magnesium. See MAGNESIUM.

Bunsen pointed out that the discrepancy existing in the properties of the metal in the two states, as obtained respectively by Wöhler and Deville, arose from its physical condition; for Bunsen found that it was only the massive metal which possessed the properties ascribed to it by Deville, that in fact the pulverulent modification does decompose water at 100° C., as stated by Wöhler.

Almost at the same time Deville published the results of his experiments upon the production of aluminium on a larger scale.[7] He quite gave up the hope of succeeding

[1] Poggendorff's Annalen, xi. 146. [2] Ann. Ch. et. Pharm. liii. 422.
[3] Comptes Rendus, xxxviii. 279.
[4] Ferussai, Bul. des. Sc. Mathémat. &c. 1826, 275.
[5] Record of Mining and Metallurgy, Phillips and Darlington.
[6] Pogg. Ann. xcii. 648. [7] Comptes Rendus, xxxix. 321.

in effecting the reduction of the chlorides by any of the common metals. He adhered to Wöhler's and Bunsen's methods, carrying them out on a larger scale, with modifications and improvements in the details, which enabled him to obtain the metal in such quantities, and thus to study its properties with so much success, as to suggest numerous applications, the probability of which never entered the minds of the original discoverers. Very great credit is therefore due to M. Deville, although it is the practice amongst the German chemists to detract from, or even deny, his merit.

The following is the method described by M. Deville for the preparation of this interesting metal :—

Having obtained the chloride of aluminium, he introduces into a wide glass (or porcelain) tube 200 or 300 grammes of this salt between two plugs of asbestos (or in a boat of porcelain or even copper), allows a current of hydrogen to pass from the generator through a desiccating bottle containing sulphuric acid and tubes containing chloride of calcium, and finally through the tube containing the chloride ; at the same time applying a gentle heat to the chloride, to drive off any free hydrochloric acid which might be formed by the action of the air upon it. He now introduces at the other extremity of the tube a porcelain boat containing sodium ; and when the sodium is fused the chloride of aluminium is heated, until its vapour comes in contact with the fused sodium. A powerful reaction ensues, considerable heat is evolved, and by continuing to pass the vapour of the chloride over the sodium until the latter is all consumed, a mass is obtained in the boat of the double chloride of aluminium and sodium NaCl, $Al^2 Cl^3$ (**2NaCl. Al^2Cl^6**), in which globules of the newly-reduced metal are suspended. It is allowed to cool in the hydrogen, and then the mass is treated with water, in which the double chloride is soluble, the globules of metal being unacted upon.

These small globules are finally fused together in a porcelain crucible, by heating them strongly under the fused double chloride of aluminium and sodium, or even under common salt.

This process, which succeeds without much difficulty on a small scale, is performed far more successfully as a manufacturing operation. Two cast-iron cylinders are now employed instead of the glass or porcelain tube, the anterior one of which contains the chloride of aluminium, whilst in the posterior one is placed the sodium in a tray, about 10 lbs. being employed in a single operation. A smaller iron cylinder intermediate between the two former is filled with scraps of iron, which serve to separate iron from the vapour of chloride of aluminium, by converting the perchloride of iron into the much less volatile protochloride. They also separate free hydrochloric acid and chloride of sulphur.

During the progress of the operation the connecting tube is kept at a temperature of about 400° to 600° F. ; but both the cylinders are but very gently heated, since the chloride of aluminium is volatile at a comparatively low temperature, and the reaction between it and the sodium when once commenced generates so much heat that frequently no external aid is required.

Preparation of Aluminium by Electrolysis.—Mr. Gore has succeeded in obtaining plates of copper coated with aluminium by the electrolysis of solutions of chloride of aluminium, acetate of alumina, and even common alum ;[1] but the unalloyed metal cannot be obtained by the electrolysis of solutions. Deville, however, produced it in considerable quantities by the method originally suggested by Bunsen, viz. by the electrolysis of the fused double chloride of aluminium and sodium Na Cl, $Al^2 Cl^3$ (**2NaCl. Al^2Cl^6**); but since this process is far more troublesome and expensive than its reduction by sodium, it has been altogether superseded.

Preparation of Aluminium from Cryolite. So early as March 30, 1855, a specimen of aluminium was exhibited at one of the Friday-evening meetings of the Royal Institution, which had been obtained in Dr. Percy's laboratory by Mr. Allan Dick, by a process entirely different from that of Deville, which promised, on account of its great simplicity, to supersede all others.[2] It consisted in heating small pieces of sodium, placed in alternate layers with powdered cryolite, a mineral now found in considerable abundance in Greenland, which is a double fluoride of aluminium and sodium, analogous to the double chloride of aluminium and sodium, its formula being 3Na F, $Al^2 F^3$ (**6Na F. Al^2F^6**). The process has the advantage that one of the materials is furnished ready formed by nature.

The experiment was only performed on a small scale by Mr. Dick in a platinum crucible lined with magnesia ; the small globules of metal, which were obtained at the bottom of the mass of fused salt, being subsequently fused together under chloride of potassium or common salt.

Before the description of these experiments was published, M. Rose, of Berlin,

[1] Phil. Mag. vii. 207.   [2] Ibid. x. 364.

published a paper in September, 1855, on the same subject.[1] In Rose's experiments he employed cast-iron crucibles, in which was heated ten parts of a mixture of equal weights of cryolite and chloride of potassium with 2 parts of sodium. The aluminium was obtained in small globules, which were fused together under chloride of potassium, as in Mr. Dick's experiments.

Rose experienced a slight loss of aluminium by fusion under chloride of potassium, and found it more advantageous to perform this fusion under a stratum of the double chloride of aluminium and sodium, as Deville had done.

He never succeeded in extracting the whole quantity of aluminium present in the cryolite (13 per cent.), chiefly on account of the ready oxidisability of the metal when existing in a very finely divided state, as some of it invariably does.

It does not appear that any attempt has since been made to obtain aluminium on the large scale from cryolite, probably from the supply of the mineral not proving so abundant as was at one time anticipated.

In all the processes which have been found practicable on any considerable scale, for the manufacture of aluminium, the powerful affinities of sodium are employed for the purpose of eliminating it from its compounds. The problem of the diminution of the price of aluminium therefore resolves itself into the improvement of the methods for procuring sodium, so as to diminish the cost of the latter metal. M. Deville's attention was therefore directed, in the early steps of the inquiry, to this point; and very considerable improvements have been made by him, which will be found fully described under the head of SODIUM.

Deville[2] has since suggested the employment at once of the double salt of chloride of aluminium and chloride of sodium ($NaCl, Al^2 Cl^3$), instead of the simple chloride of aluminium, so as to obtain the metal by means of sodium. He uses 400 parts of this double salt, 200 of common salt, 200 of fluor spar, and 75 to 80 of sodium. The above-mentioned salts are dried, powdered, and mixed together; then with these the sodium, in small pieces, is mixed, and the whole heated in a crucible under a layer of common salt. After the reaction is complete, the heat is raised so as to promote the separation of the aluminium in the form of a button. It was found, however, that cryolite was, with advantage, substituted for the fluor spar.

C. Brunner[3] employs artificially prepared fluoride of aluminium; but this method cannot offer any advantage over the employment of the chloride, which is cheaper, or the cryolite, which nature affords.

The following remarks on the manufacture of aluminium are from the pen of Mr. Isaac Lowthian Bell of Newcastle, at whose works at Washington this metal was, until lately, produced :—

'Upon the introduction of its manufacture at Washington, the source of the alumina was the ordinary ammonia-alum of commerce—a nearly pure sulphate of alumina and ammonia. Exposure to heat drove off the water, sulphuric acid, and ammonia, leaving the alumina behind. This was converted into the double chloride of aluminium and sodium, by the process described by the French chemist, and practised in France, and the double chloride was subsequently decomposed by fusion with sodium. Faint, however, as the traces might be of impurity in the alum itself, they to a great extent, if not entirely (being of a fixed character when exposed to heat), were to be found in the alumina. From the alumina, by the action of chlorine on a heated mixture consisting of this earth, common salt, and charcoal, these impurities, or a large proportion thereof, found their way into the sublimed double chloride; and once there, it is unnecessary to say that, under the influence of the sodium in the process of reduction, any silica, iron, or phosphorus found their way into the aluminium sought to be obtained. Now, it happens that the presence of foreign matters, in a degree so small as almost to be infinitesimal, interferes so largely with the colour as well as with the malleability of the aluminium, that the use of any substance containing them is of a fatal character. Nor is this all, for the nature of that compound which hitherto has constituted the most important application of this metal—aluminium-bronze—is so completely changed by using aluminium containing the impurities referred to, that it ceases to possess any of those properties which render it valuable. As an example of the amount of interference exercised by very minute quantities of impurity, it is perhaps worthy of notice that very few varieties of copper have been found susceptible of being employed for the manufacture of aluminium-bronze; and hitherto we have not at Washington, nor have they in France, been able to establish in what the difference consists between copper fit for the production of aluminium-bronze, and that which is usually unsuitable for the purpose. These considerations have led us, both here and in France, to adopt the use of another raw material for the production of aluminium, which either does

---

[1] Poggendorff's Annalen, and Phil. Mag. x. 233.   [2] Ann. de Chim. et Phys. xlvi. 415.
[3] Chemical Gazette, 1856, 338.

not contain the impurities referred to as so prejudicial, or contains them in such a form as to admit of their easy separation. This material is Bauxite, so called from the name of the locality where it is found in France. The Bauxite is ground and mixed with the ordinary soda-ash of commerce, and then heated in a furnace. The soda combines with the alumina, and the aluminate of soda so formed is separated from the insoluble portions—viz., peroxide of iron, silico-aluminate of soda, &c.—by lixiviation. Muriatic acid or carbonic acid is then added to the solution, which throws down pure alumina. The remainder of the process is precisely that which is described by Mons. St. Claire Deville. The alumina is mixed with common salt and charcoal, made into balls the size of an orange, and dried. These balls are placed in vertical earthen retorts, kept at a red heat, and through the heated contents chlorine gas is passed. The elements of the earth, under the joint influence of carbon and chlorine at that temperature, are separated, the carbon taking the oxygen and the chlorine the aluminium. The latter substance accompanied by chloride of sodium (common salt) sublimes over, and is collected as a double chloride of aluminium and sodium. Sodium,—being required to effect the decomposition of this compound,—is thus prepared. In small iron retorts kept at as high a temperature as iron can bear, a mixture of soda (carbonate of soda) and carbonaceous matter with a little ground chalk is placed. The metallic base of the alkali distils over, and is collected in coal oil. A portion of the double chloride of aluminium and sodium, and the metallic sodium, along with fluxes, is exposed to a full red heat in a reverberating furnace. The sodium seizes the chlorine combined with the aluminium, and thus liberates the latter metal, which falls to the bottom of the fixed mass. Aluminium is used in sufficient quantity to keep the only work in England—viz., that at Washington—pretty actively employed. As a substance for works of art, when whitened by means of hydrofluoric and phosphoric acid, it appears well adapted, as it runs into the most complicated patterns, and has the advantage of preserving its colour, from the absence of all tendency to unite with sulphur, or to become affected by sulphuretted hydrogen, as happens with silver.' Aluminium has been used in the manufacture of weights and scale-beams for chemists, and for opera- and field-glasses, for which purposes it is exceedingly valuable, by reason of its lightness and its not being liable to tarnish. A greatly increased activity has been given to the manufacture of aluminium by its use in the manufacture of aluminium-bronze—a compound of exceeding beauty, so much like gold that it can scarcely be distinguished from that precious metal.

Properties.—The metal is white, but with a bluish tinge, and even when pure has a lustre far inferior to silver.

Specific gravity, 2·56, and when hammered, 2·67.

Conducts electricity eight times better than iron, and is feebly magnetic. It is highly sonorous.

Its fusing-point is between the melting-points of zinc and silver.

By electrolysis it is obtained in forms which Deville believes to be regular octahedra; but Rose, who has also occasionally obtained aluminium in a crystalline state (from cryolite), denies that they belong to the regular system.

When pure, it is unoxidised even in moist air; but most of the commercial specimens (probably from impurities present in the metal) become covered with a bluish-grey tarnish.

It is unaffected by cold or boiling water; even steam at a red heat is but slowly decomposed by it.

It is not acted upon by cold nitric acid, and only very slowly dissolved even by the boiling acid; scarcely attacked by dilute sulphuric acid, but readily dissolved by hydrochloric acid, with evolution of hydrogen.

Sulphuretted hydrogen and sulphides have no action upon it; and it is not even attacked by fused hydrated alkalis. Professor Wheatstone[1] has shown that in the voltaic series, aluminium, although having so small an atomic number, and so low a specific gravity, is more electro-negative than zinc; but it is positive to cadmium, tin, lead, iron, copper, and platinum.

Impurities in Aluminium.—Many of the discrepancies in the properties of aluminium, as obtained by different experimenters, are due to the impurities which are present in it.

If the naphtha be not carefully removed from the sodium, the aluminium is liable to contain carbon.

Frequently, in preparing aluminium, by the action of the chloride on sodium, by Deville's original process, copper boats have been used for holding the sodium; in this case the metal becomes contaminated, not only with copper, but also with any

---

[1] Phil. Mag. x. 143.

other metals which may be present in the copper—*e.g.* Salm-Horstmar[1] found copper in the aluminium sold in Paris, and Erdmann detected zinc;[2] and in every case the metal is very liable to become mixed with silicon, either from the earthenware tubes, boats, or crucibles; hence Salvétat found, even in the aluminium prepared by Deville himself, 2·87 per cent. of silicon, 2·40 of iron, 6·38 of copper, and traces of lead.

The following analyses of commercial aluminium were communicated to the British Association, at its meeting in 1857, by Professor Mallet:—

	Made in Paris	Made in Berlin
Aluminium	92·969	96·253
Iron	4·882	3·293
Silicon·	2·149	0·454
Titanium	trace	trace
	100·00	100·00

Alloys of Aluminium.—Very small quantities of other metals suffice to destroy the malleability and ductility of aluminium. An alloy containing only $\frac{1}{20}$th of iron or copper cannot be worked, and the presence of $\frac{1}{10}$th copper renders it as brittle as glass. Silver and gold produce brittleness in a less degree. An alloy of 5 parts of silver with 100 of aluminium is capable of being worked like the pure metal, but it is harder, and therefore susceptible of a finer polish; whilst the alloy, containing 10 per cent. of gold, is softer, but, nevertheless, not so malleable as the pure metal. The presence of even $\frac{1}{1000}$th part of bismuth renders aluminium brittle in a high degree.

These statements by Tissier,[3] however, require confirmation; for Debray states that aluminium remains malleable and tough when containing as much as 8 per cent. of iron, or 10 per cent. of copper, but that a larger quantity of either of these metals renders it brittle.

It is curious that only 3 per cent. of silver are sufficient to give aluminium *the brilliance and colour of pure silver, over which the alloy has the great advantage* of not being blackened by sulphuretted hydrogen.

On the other hand, small quantities of aluminium combined with other metals change their properties in a remarkable manner. Thus copper alloyed with only $\frac{1}{10}$th of its weight of aluminium has the colour and brilliance of gold, and is still very malleable (*Tissier*); and when the aluminium amounts only to $\frac{1}{5}$th (*i.e.* 20 per cent.) the alloy is quite white (*Debray*). See ALUMINIUM BRONZE.

An alloy of 90 parts of copper and 10 of aluminium is harder than common bronze, and is capable of being worked at high temperatures easier than the best varieties of iron. Larger quantities of aluminium render the metal harder and brittle.—*Debray.*[4]

An alloy of 100 parts of silver with 5 of aluminium is as hard as the alloy employed in the silver coinage, although the other properties of the silver remain unchanged (*Tissier*). Similar alloys have likewise been prepared by Dr. Percy.[5]

Messrs Calvert and Johnson describe[6] an alloy of 25 parts aluminium to 75 of iron, which has the valuable property of *not oxidising by exposure to moist air.*

Uses of Aluminium.—No very important application of aluminium has yet been made: although, at the time M. Deville's experiments were commenced, sanguine hopes were entertained that aluminium might be produced at a price sufficiently low to admit of its practical application on a large scale, these anticipations have not been realised; and as yet, on account chiefly of its high price, the applications which have been made of this interesting metal are but few.

Its low specific gravity, combined with sufficient tenacity, recommends it for many interesting uses. The fractional weights used by chemists, which are made of platinum, are so extremely small that they are constantly being lost; their much greater volume in aluminium renders this metal peculiarly suitable. In the construction of the beams of balances, strength combined with lightness are desiderata; and M. Deville has had very beautiful balance-beams made of this metal; but at present its high price has prevented their extensive adoption.

These same qualities render this metal suitable for the construction of helmets and other armour; but at present these are but curiosities, and are likely to remain so,

[1] Journal pr. Chem. lxvii. 493.   [2] Journal pr. Chem. lxvii. 494.
[3] C. and J. Tissier, Comptes Rendus, xliii. 885.   [4] Comptes Rendus, xliii. 925.
[5] Proceedings of the Royal Institution, March 14, 1856.   [6] Phil. Mag. x. 245.

unless some cheaper method of eliminating the metal than by the agency of sodium be discovered.

Mr. Gordon has shown that the amount of tension which aluminium wire was capable of resisting will be found to be between that of the best iron and the best steel wire.

Probably one of the most interesting of the applications of aluminium (at least in a scientific point of view) that has been made, is that by Deville and Wöhler, of employing it in the production of crystalline allotropic modifications of certain other elements previously unknown in that state—*e.g.* boron, silicon, and titanium. It depends upon the fact that these elements, in the amorphous state, dissolve in fused aluminium, and on cooling the molten solution, they slowly separate from the aluminium in the crystalline state.

Aluminium may be gilded by being dipped into a solution of the hyposulphite of gold after it has been well cleaned by the successive use of potash, nitric acid, and water. Aluminium is soldered with difficulty. The most successful method is to coat the aluminium with copper by the electrotype process, after which soldering can be effected in the usual way.

ALUMINIUM-BRONZE. This alloy was a discovery of Dr. John Percy, F.R.S., and it appears to be a true chemical compound. Mr. I. L. Bell, who manufactured this beautiful metallic compound on a large scale, thus describes its manufacture:—' Copper is melted in a plumbago crucible, and, after being removed from the furnace, the solid aluminium is added. The union of the two metals is attended with such an increase of temperature, that the whole becomes white hot, and unless the crucible containing the mixture is of a refractory material, it is fused by the intensity of the heat. A vessel which has resisted a heat sufficient to effect the fusion of copper has been melted when the aluminium has been added.'

The value of aluminium-bronze will be gathered from the following statement of results obtained by Lieut.-Colonel A. Strange, F.R.A.S., and communicated by him to the Astronomical Society. Lieut.-Colonel Strange recommended this metal as a valuable material for the construction of astronomical and other philosophical instruments. Regarding the most important qualities as—1. Tensile strength; 2. Resistance to compression; 3. Malleability; 4. Transverse strength or rigidity; 5. Expansive ratio; 6. Founding qualities; 7. Behaviour under files, cutting tools, &c.; 8. Resistance to atmospheric influences; 9. Fitness to receive graduation; 10. Elasticity; 11. Fitness for being made into tubes; 12. Specific gravity—experiments were made to determine each of those conditions.

Tensile strength.—The result of trials by Mr. Anderson of Woolwich was—the average tenacity of this metal proved to be 22 tons 12 cwt. (50,624 lbs.) breaking weight per square inch. Elongations did not take place until 4,300 lbs. in the one case, and 3,600 lbs. in the other had been applied, when a permanent elongation was noticed of ·009 of an inch in the first specimen and ·034 of an inch in the last.

Resistance to compression.—The ultimate amount of compression applied was 59 tons 2 cwt. 1 qr. 4 lbs. (132,416 lbs.), under which the specimen became much distorted. 'The specimen subjected to this enormous pressure, distorted though it is, does not exhibit the trace of a fissure. The cohesion of its particles is inviolate.' Compression was not perceptible until 9 tons 2 cwt. per square inch (20,384 lbs.) was applied, when the specimen gave way to the extent of ·006 of an inch; and on the weight being removed an elasticity of ·001 was observed, which gives the first permanent compression as ·005 of an inch.

Malleability.—The quality of this metal for forging purposes would appear to be excellent. There were specimens in the International Exhibition of 1862, showing that the alloy could be drawn out under the hammer almost to a needle-point.

Transverse strength.—These experiments were made by Messrs. Simms. The same weight applied to these bars altered the index of the instrument as under :—

Brass	2·22 divisions
Gun-metal	0·15 ,,
Aluminium-bronze	0·05 ,,

Hence aluminium-bronze is 3 times more rigid than gun-metal, and 44 times more rigid than brass.

Expansive ratio.—Aluminium-bronze is affected by change of temperature a little less than gun-metal, and much less than brass.

Founding qualities.—The alloy produces admirable castings of any size.

Behaviour under files, cutting tools, &c.—' In this respect it leaves nothing to be desired. It does not clog the file; and in the lathe and planing-machine the tool removes long elastic shavings, leaving a fine, bright, smooth surface.'

Resistance to atmospheric influences.—This alloy tarnishes much less readily than any metal usually employed—viz. gun-metal, brass, silver, cast-iron, or steel.

Fitness to receive graduation. — The lines are remarkably pure and equable, and very distinct under the microscope, notwithstanding the yellow colour of the metal.

Elasticity.—No wires tried for the suspension of Foucault's pendulum for illustrating the rotation of the earth were so durable—not even those of steel—under that severe ordeal, as wires of aluminium-bronze.

Fitness for being made into tubes.—It admits of every process necessary for this purpose.

Specific Gravity.—The specific gravities of alloys of aluminium and copper are :—

3 per cent. of aluminium	. . . . .	8·691
4 „ „	. . . . .	8·621
5 „ „	. . . . .	8·369
10 „ „	. . . . .	7·689

At the Elswick Works Captain Noble, R.A., confirmed previous experiments on the capability of aluminium-bronze to resist longitudinal and transverse fracture; and in addition to this he ascertained that its position to withstand compression stood halfway between that of the finest steel and the best iron.

The bronze, containing 10 parts of aluminium and 90 of copper, affords an alloy endowed with the greatest strength, malleability, and ductility. The colour of the copper is affected by a very trifling addition of the other constituent, and the alloy gradually improves in these valuable qualities just mentioned, until the proportions given above are reached. After this—*i.e.* when more than 10 per cent. of aluminium enters into the composition of the bronze—the alloy gradually becomes weaker and less malleable, and at length so brittle that it is easily pounded in a mortar.

ALUMINIUM, CHLORIDE OF. $Al^2Cl^3 = 133·9$ **(Al^2Cl^6).** *Preparation.*— Chloride of aluminium cannot be prepared by treating alumina with hydrochloric acid, as in the case of most chlorides; for on evaporating the solution to dryness, hydrochloric acid is evolved and alumina alone remains.

The method at present used is, in principle, the same as that originally suggested by Oersted, which has since found numerous other applications. It is impossible to convert alumina into the chloride by the direct action of chlorine alone; at any temperature the chlorine is as incapable of displacing the oxygen from the alumina as it would from lime. But if the attraction of the chlorine for the metal be supported by the affinity of carbon for the oxygen, then the compound is, as it were, torn asunder—carbonic acid or carbonic oxide resulting on the one hand, and the chloride of aluminium on the other.

On the large scale the chlorine is passed over a previously ignited mixture of clay and coal-tar, contained in retorts like those used in the manufacture of coal-gas, which are heated in a furnace; the chloride, which on account of its volatility is carried off, being condensed in a chamber lined with plates of earthenware, where it is deposited in a crystalline mass.

Properties.—It is a yellowish crystalline solid, readily decomposed by the moisture of the air into hydrochloric acid and alumina, and volatile at a dull red heat. It is very soluble in water, but cannot be recovered by evaporating the solution.—H.M.W.

Chloride of aluminium has been brought into use as a disinfectant under the name of *Chloralum.*

ALUMINIUM, FLUORIDE OF. Al^2F^3 **(Al^2F^6).** The existence of the fluoride of aluminium in nature, in the form of the double fluoride of sodium and aluminium, namely, $3Na F, Al^2F^3$ **($6NaF. Al^2F^6$),** as cryolite, and the use of this mineral in the manufacture of aluminium, have been already alluded to. The fluoride of aluminium likewise exists in several other minerals, namely, the topaz, pycnite, fluellite, chiolite, pachnolite, gearksutite, &c.

The pure fluoride can only be obtained artificially by dissolving pure aluminium in hydrofluoric acid. It has a great tendency to form double salts with the fluorides of potassium and sodium.—H. M. W.

ALUMOCALCITE. A milk-white mineral, from Eibenstock, in Saxony. It appears to be an impure form of opal, containing—in addition to the hydrous silica—a notable proportion of lime and alumina.

ALVA or ALFA. See Esparto Grass.

ALVITE. A Norwegian mineral, described by Mr. David Forbes and Mr. T.

Dahll. It is a hydrous silicate of complex constitution, containing yttria, thoria, zirconia, glucina, alumina, and sesquioxide of iron.

AMADOU. (*Amadou*, Fr.; *Zunderschwamm*, Ger.) The name of a spongy combustible substance, prepared from a species of fungus, the *Boletus igniarius*, which grows on the trunks of cherry-trees, ashes, beeches, &c.; it is sometimes known as *spunk*, and as touchwood, but commonly in this country it is called *German tinder*. It must be plucked in the months of August and September. This plant grows horizontally on the several trees on which it is indigenous; when it makes its first appearance it is a little round wart-like body, not larger than a pea; it gradually increases in size and hardness till it becomes of a darkish brown, and is as large as an apple. It afterwards takes a horizontal direction, forms a border, and becomes covered with numerous closely-packed tubes on its under surface. The *Boletus fomentarius* is another indigenous fungus, found on the oak and birch. This is also used in preparing *Amadou*. It was formerly used in surgery, and has hence been called Surgeon's Agaric. Amadou is prepared by removing the outer bark with a knife, and separating carefully the spongy substance—of a yellow brown colour, which lies within it—from the ligneous matter below. This substance is cut into thin slices, and beaten with a mallet to soften it, till it can be easily pulled asunder between the fingers. In this state the *boletus* is a valuable substance for stopping oozing hæmorrhages, and some other surgical purposes. To convert it into tinder it must receive a finishing preparation, which consists in boiling it in a strong solution of nitre, drying it, beating it anew, and putting it a second time into the solution. Sometimes, indeed, to render it very inflammable, it is imbued with gunpowder, whence the distinction of black and brown amadou.

All the puff-balls of the *lycopodium* genus of plants, which have a fleshy or filamentous structure, yield a tinder by soaking in gunpowder-water. The Hindoos employ a leguminous plant, which they call *solu*, for the same purpose. Its thick spongy stem, being reduced to charcoal, takes fire like amadou. See AGARIC.

AMALGAM. When mercury is alloyed with any metal, the compound is called an amalgam of that metal; as, for example, an amalgam of tin, bismuth, &c.

Some amalgams are solids and others fluids; the former are often crystalline, and the latter may be probably regarded as the solid amalgam dissolved in mercury.

Silver Amalgam may be formed by mixing finely-divided silver with mercury. The best process is to precipitate silver from its solution by copper, when we obtain it in a state of fine powder, and then to mix it with the mercury.

A native amalgam of mercury and silver occurs in fine crystals in the mines of Moschellandsberg, in the Palatinate: it is said to be found where the veins of copper and silver intersect each other. Its existence is also recorded in Hungary and Sweden; at Allemont, in Dauphiné; Almaden, in Spain; Kongsberg, in Norway; and in Chili; and the following analyses have been quoted:—

	Silver	Mercury	
Moschellandsberg	36·0	64·0	by Klaproth.
Ditto	25·0	73·3	„ Heyer.
Allemont	27·5	72·5	„ Cordier.

If six parts of a saturated solution of nitrate of silver with two parts of a saturated solution of the protonitrate of mercury are mixed with an amalgam of silver one part and mercury seven, the solution is speedily filled with beautiful arborescent crystals —the *Arbor Dianæ*, the tree of Diana,—or the silver tree.

Gold Amalgam is made by heating together mercury with grains of gold, or gold-foil; when the amalgam of gold is heated, the mercury is volatilised and the gold left. This amalgam is employed in the process known as that of fire-gilding, although, since electro-gilding has been introduced, it is not so frequently employed. A gold amalgam is obtained from the platinum region of Columbia; and it has been reported from California, especially from near Mariposa. Schneider gives its composition, mercury, 57·40; gold, 38·89; silver, 5·0.

Tin Amalgam.—By bringing tinfoil and mercury together, this amalgam is formed, and is used for silvering looking-glasses. If melted tin and mercury are brought together in the proportion of three parts mercury and one part tin, the tin amalgam is obtained in cubic crystals. See SILVERING GLASS.

Electric Machine Amalgam.—Melt equal parts of tin and zinc together, and add three parts of mercury; the mass must be shaken until it is cold, and rubbed down with some lard to give it the proper consistence.

Sodium Amalgam, used for separating gold from its ores. See GOLD, SILVER.

Copper Amalgam.—The French dentists have long made use of this for stopping teeth. It is sold in small rolls of about a drachm and a half in weight; it is covered with a greyish tarnish, has a hardness much greater than that of bone, and its cohesion and solidity are considerable. When heated nearly to the point of boiling water this amalgam swells up, drops of mercury exuding, which disappear again on the cooling of the substance. If a piece, thus heated, be rubbed up in a mortar, a plastic mouldable mass, like poor clay, is obtained, the consistence of which may, by continued kneading, be increased to that of fat clay. If the moulded mass be left for ten or twelve hours, it hardens, acquiring again its former properties, without altering its specific gravity. Hence the stopping, after it has hardened, remains tightly fixed in the hollow of the tooth. The softening and hardening may be repeated many times with the same sample. Pettenkofer ascribes these phenomena to a state of amorphism, into which the amalgam passes from the crystalline condition in the process of softening. All copper amalgams containing between 0·25 to 0·30 of copper exhibit the same behaviour. The above chemist recommends, as the best mode of preparing this amalgam, that a crystalline paste of sulphate of suboxide of mercury (prepared by dissolving mercury in hydrated sulphuric acid at a gentle heat) be saturated under water at a temperature of from 60° to 70°, with finely divided reguline copper (prepared by precipitation from sulphate of copper with iron). One portion of the copper precipitates the mercury, with formation of sulphate of copper; the other portion yields with mercury an amalgam: 100 parts of dissolved mercury require the copper precipitated, by iron, from 232·5 parts of sulphate of copper. As in dissolving the mercury the protoxide is easily formed instead of the suboxide, particularly if too high a temperature be maintained, it is advisable, in order to avoid an excess of mercury in the amalgam, to take 223 parts of sulphate of copper, and to add to the washed amalgam, which is kept stirred, a quantity of mercury in minute portions, corresponding to the amount of suboxide contained in the mercury salt, until the whole has become sufficiently plastic. This amalgam may be obtained by moistening finely-divided copper with a few drops of a solution of nitrate of suboxide of mercury, and then triturating the metal with mercury in a warmed mortar. The rubbing may be continued for some time, and may be carried on under hot water, mercury being added until the required consistence is attained.

A remarkable depression of temperature during the combination of amalgams has been observed by several chemists.

Döbereiner states that when 816 grains of amalgam of lead (404 mercury and 412 lead) were mixed, at a temperature of 68°, with 688 grains of the amalgam of bismuth (404 mercury and 284 bismuth) the temperature suddenly fell to 30°, and by the addition of 808 grains of mercury (also at 68°), it became as low as 17°; the total depression amounting to 51°.

In certain proportions of mixture of the constituents of fusible metal (tin, lead, and bismuth) with mercury, Döbereiner formed surprising depressions of temperature; the temperature, he records of one experiment, sank instantly from 65° to 14°.

AMALGAMATION. See GOLD and SILVER.

AMALIC ACID. A feeble acid obtained by decomposing caffeine with chlorine.

AMANDINE. An albuminous compound, said to exist in sweet almonds.

AMANITA MUSCARIA. A poisonous fungus used in Kamtschatka and Siberia as a narcotic and intoxicating agent. The specific name has reference to its use, when steeped in milk, as a fly-poison. An organic base, called *amanitine*, has been separated from this fungus. By some authorities the poisonous properties are referred to the presence of a peculiar acid called *muscaric acid*.

AMARINE, or *Benzoline.* $C^{42}H^{18}N^2$ ($C^{21}H^{18}N^2$). An organic base obtained by boiling hydrobenzamide with solution of caustic potash. The hydrobenzamide is prepared by the action of ammonia on pure oil of bitter almonds.

AMAZON STONE. A bluish-green variety of Felspar (Orthoclase). It is found at Lake Ilmen in Russia, of a verdigris-green variety. That from Baikal in Siberia is composed of silvery spangles in a green base, of which small vases and other ornaments are made. See FELSPAR.

AMBAR, LIQUID. (*Ambre Liquide,* Fr.) In former editions of this Dictionary, the liquid-ambar, as it was called, was confounded with liquid storax or styrax. It is obtained from the *Liquidambar styraciflua* of Linnæus, growing in Louisiana and Mexico, whereas the *storax* is procured chiefly—it is now entirely—from Trieste; storax was originally extracted from the *Styrax officinalis*, which grows in various parts of Greece, but this resin is lost to commerce, and the present commercial liquid storax appears to be obtained from *Liquidambar orientale* (Müller). Pereira, quoting Buchner's 'Repertorium,' informs us that the storax is known in the East as *buchuri-jag.* Liquid-ambar is rarely used in any art or manufacture. It is brownish ash-grey, of the consistence of turpentine, dries up readily, smells agreeably, like benzoin, has a bitterish, sharp, burning taste; is soluble in 4 parts of alcohol, and contains only 1·4 per cent. of benzoic acid.

AMBER. (*Succin*, Fr.; *Bernstein*, Ger.) The *Electron* of the Greeks, to whom this substance appears to have been well known. From its peculiar property of manifesting electrical phenomena, we have derived our word *electricity*. It appears to have been known to the Romans under the names of *lyncurium* (a name also applied by Theophrastus to a gem-stone, perhaps either tourmaline or zircon), and, because of its supposed vegetable origin, *succinum*. The ancients also gave the name *electrum* to a yellow metal containing gold and silver. See ELECTRUM.

Amber is a mineral solid, of a yellow colour of various shades, which burns entirely away with flame, and consists of carbon, hydrogen, and oxygen, in nearly the same proportions, and in the same state of combination, as in vegetable resin. The chemical composition of amber, according to Schrötter, is—

Carbon	78·82
Hydrogen	10·23
Oxygen	10·9

Its specific gravity varies, by Dr. Ure's trials, from 1·080 to 1·085. It becomes negatively and powerfully electrical by friction. When applied to a lighted candle it takes fire, swells considerably, and exhales a white smoke of a pungent odour; but does not run into drops. Copal, which resembles it in several respects, differs in being softer, and in melting into drops at the flame; and mellite, or honey-stone, which is a mineral of a similar colour, becomes white when laid on a red-hot coal.

The texture of amber is resino-vitreous, its fracture conchoidal, and lustre glassy. It is perfectly homogeneous; sufficiently hard to scratch gypsum, and to take a fine polish. It is, however, scratched by calcareous spar. When amber is distilled in a retort, crystalline needles of succinic acid sublime into the dome, and oil of amber drops from the beak into the receiver. Fossil resins, such as that of Highgate, found in the London-clay formation, do not afford succinic acid by heat; nor does copal.

It is now admitted that amber is not a simple resin. For the most part it consists of a peculiar resin, which is said to resist the action of all known solvents; and it is to this substance that Dana has applied the term *succinite*, as a definite mineral species. But in addition to this resin—which forms from 85 to 90 per cent. of amber—there are two other resins soluble in alcohol and ether, together with the oil and succinic acid above mentioned. It would appear that several distinct resinous substances, occurring in a fossil state, have been classed together under the common name of amber, while in commerce copal and gum anime are occasionally sold for true amber.

When amber is found embedded in its original position, it is usually in beds of the brown-coal formation of lower tertiary age; but fossil resins, apparently identical with amber, also occur in upper cretaceous rocks, and in strata of even greater age. As a rule, the amber is found almost uniformly in separate nodules, disseminated in the sand, clay, or fragments of lignite of the plastic-clay formation. The size of these nodules varies from that of a nut to a man's head; but this magnitude is very rare in true amber. It does not occur either in continuous beds, like the chalk-flints, or in veins; but it lies at one time in the earthy or friable strata which accompany or include the lignites; at another entangled in the lignites themselves. The pieces of amber found in the sands, and other formations evidently alluvial, those met with on the sea-coasts of certain countries, and especially Pomerania, come undoubtedly from the above geological formation; for the organic matters found still adhering to the amber leave no doubt as to its primitive place.

The vegetable origin of amber is satisfactorily determined by its chemical composition, its optical properties,—as shown by Sir David Brewster,—and by the condition in which insects and the remains of insects are found in this resin, along with fragments of leaves and stalks. Certain families of insects occur more abundantly than others. Thus the *hymenoptera*, or insects with four marked membranaceous wings, as the bee and wasp, are not abundant. The *diptera*, or insects with two wings, as gnats and flies, are more numerous. Then come the spider tribe, some *coleoptera* (insects with crustaceous shells or elytra, which shut together and form a longitudinal suture down the back), or beetles—principally those which live on trees, as the *elaterides*, or leapers, and the *chrysomelida*. The insects appear evidently to have struggled after being entangled in the then viscous fluid, and occasionally a leg or a wing is found at some distance from the body, which had been detached in the efforts of the insect to escape from the resin. Göppert has named the tree supposed to have yielded most of the amber, *Pinites succinifer*, but he has shown that several other coniferous trees, of older tertiary age, have also yielded this product.

Germar and Schweiger state that the insects enveloped in amber are in general such as sit on the trunks of trees, or live in the fissures of their bark. These naturalists have not been able to refer them to any living species; but it has been observed that they resemble more the insects of hot climates than those of the temperate zones. The Rev. F. W. Hope, F.R.S., in his paper on the ' Succinic Insects,' states them to be altogether extra-European. D. T. Tessler sent to the Exhibition, in 1851, a piece of amber containing the leg of a toad.

Amber is found abundantly on the Prussian coast of the Baltic, occurring from Dantzic to Memel, especially between Pillau and Dorfe Gross-Hubnicken. It is also found in many of the lignite workings opened in the great plain of North Germany. A rich and unexpected locality was discovered a few years ago in Kurland. It occurs also on the coast of Denmark and Sweden; in Gallicia, near Lemberg; and at Missan, in Poland; in Moravia, at Boskowitz; in the Uralian Mountains, Russia; near Christiania, Norway; in Switzerland, near Basle, and other places. Small quantities are occasionally found in the clay of the Paris and the London basins. ' Amber is occasionally met with in the gravel-pits near London, and I have seen specimens which were found in Hyde Park. At Aldborough after a raking tide it is thrown on the beach in considerable quantities, along with masses of jet.'— *Rev. F. W. Hope*, Trans. Ent. Soc. On the Sicilian coast amber is sometimes found having a peculiar blue tinge. Large discoveries of amber have been reported from Australia.

Amber is collected on the coast of Prussia in several ways. It is found in the beds of streams; in the sand-banks of rivers; in pieces thrown up by the sea and rounded by the waves; it is sought for in the cliffs, and in some places mining operations for it are carried on.

The amber-fishers, clothed in leather dresses, wade into the sea, and seek to discover the amber floating on its surface, which they secure with bag-nets hung at the ends of long poles. They conclude that much amber has been detached from its bed, when they discover many pieces of lignite floating about. Mining is carried on by sinking through the sand and superficial strata to the beds containing the amber and lignite; many of these pits are sunk to the depth of 130 feet. The faces of the precipitous cliffs are explored in boats, and masses of loose earth or rock supposed to contain the object of search are detached with long poles having iron hooks at their ends.

The most extensive use of amber is for the construction of mouth-pieces to pipes; these form an essential constituent of the genuine meerschaum and the Turkish pipe. There is a current belief in Turkey that amber is incapable of transmitting infection, and as it is a great mark of politeness to offer the pipe to a stranger, this supposed negative property of amber accounts in some measure for the estimation in which it is held. Amber necklaces are not uncommon: the Russian peasant girls adorn themselves with double and treble rows of amber beads, but it not unfrequently happens that copal is substituted for the genuine article.

The Prussian Government is said to draw a considerable annual revenue from amber. A good piece of a pound weight fetches 50 dollars. A mass weighing 13 pounds has been found, the value of which at Constantinople was said to be not less than 30,000 dollars.

When amber is to be worked into trinkets, it is first split on a leaden plate at a lathe, and then smoothed into shape on a Swedish whetstone. It is polished on the lathe with chalk and water, or vegetable oil, and finished by friction with flannel.

Amber, after having been filed, may be polished with Trent sand, or scraped Flanders brick on flannel with water, or with rotten-stone with oil on flannel, or the same material dry on the hand. Turned works are, however, generally polished first with glass-paper and then with rotten-stone and oil. Necklaces and other ornaments in amber are frequently cut into facets by the gold-cutters, those artisans who cut and polish facetted works.—*Holtzapffel.*

From the electrical character of amber, it frequently during the process of polishing becomes so excited as to crack and fly to pieces. The workmen, therefore, take several pieces, and work them each for a short time and in regular order. These men are said to be seized with nervous tremors in their wrists and arms from the electricity thus developed.

Pieces of amber may be neatly joined by smearing their edges with linseed oil and pressing them strongly together while they are held over a charcoal fire.

AMBER, ACID OF. See Succinic Acid.

AMBER, OIL OF. (*Oleum succini*). This is obtained by distilling amber, for which purpose chippings of amber and inferior pieces are used. When it is distilled with charcoal, the first product is the *rectified oil of amber*. The oil of amber has a composition of $C^{20} H^{16}$ (**$C^{10}H^{16}$**). When 1 part of rectified oil of amber is dissolved in

24 parts of alcohol of ·830, and 96 of caustic ammonia of ·916, *eau de luce* is formed. Eau de luce was a celebrated old perfume, but it is now rarely made.

If nitric acid is poured into *eau de luce* a viscid resinous mass is formed, which has the smell of musk, and is known as *artificial musk.* Formerly this preparation, dissolved in alcohol, was considered as a specific in whooping-cough, and it was frequently administered in spasmodic diseases.

AMBER VARNISH. A strong and durable varnish is made by dissolving amber in drying linseed oil. The amber is, however, previously heated in an iron pot, over a clear red fire, till it softens and assumes a semi-fluid form. The oil, which has been also made hot, is to be poured on the melted amber, and the mixture diligently stirred.

The following proportions are stated to be the best:—16 ounces of amber and 10 ounces of linseed oil. When these are, by the above method, thoroughly incorporated, and the liquid is somewhat cooled, a pound of oil of turpentine must be added.

Black coachmaker's varnish is prepared by melting 16 ounces of amber and adding thereto about half a pint of boiling-hot drying linseed oil, 3 ounces of asphaltum, and the same quantity of resin. After these have been thoroughly mixed over the fire, the vessel containing the varnish is removed, and, after cooling, a pint of warm oil of turpentine is added.

Amber is composed of a mixture of resins, two of which are soluble in alcohol ether, and in certain hydrocarbons; whilst the third, which forms by far the greater part of the amber, is insoluble in all known solvents. Varnishes are prepared from the soluble portions, and sold under the name of *amber spirit varnishes;* but these are frequently composed of either copal or mastic. They have been much used for varnishing collodion pictures.

AMBERGRIS. (*Ambregris*, Fr.; *Ambra*, Ger.) A morbid secretion from the liver and intestines of the spermaceti whale (*Physeter macrocephalus*). It is found usually swimming on the sea upon the coasts of Coromandel, Japan, the Moluccas, and Madagascar, and also on various parts of the east coast of Africa. Ambergris has not been found in any whales but such as have been dead or sick; its production has therefore been attributed to disease. As portions of the food of the whale are invariably found in any large pieces of ambergris, there is little doubt that it originates in the intestines of that animal.

The best ambergris is ash-coloured, with yellow or blackish veins or spots, scarcely any taste, and very little smell unless heated or much handled, when it yields an agreeable odour. Exposed in a silver spoon it melts without bubble or scum, and on the heated point of a knife it vaporises completely away.

The Chinese try the genuineness of ambergris by scraping it fine upon boiling tea; it should dissolve and diffuse itself generally. Black or white is bad; the smooth and uniform is generally factitious. It has often a black streak, or is marbled yellow and black; has a fatty taste, is lighter than water, melts at 60° C. (140° F.), dissolves readily in absolute alcohol, in ether, and in both fat and volatile oils.

The chemical composition of ambergris is represented by the following formula, $C^{33} H^{32} O$ ($C^{33} H^{64} O$). True ambergris is very rarely met with, by far the largest proportion of that which is sold as ambergris being a preparation scented with *civet* or *musk.* The alcoholic tincture of ambergris is highly fluorescent in sunlight, exhibiting a characteristic yellow green rim on the surface of the solution. This is a test by which genuine ambergris may be distinguished from such as is spurious.

Capt. Alex. Hamilton, in his 'Thirty Years' Experience,' says, 'Sometimes, in the south-west monsoons, they find ambergrease floating on the sea. I saw a piece in Adda Rajah's possession as big as a bushel; and he valued it at 10,000 rupees, or 1,250*l.* sterling.' This was at the Laccadive Islands, 170 miles from the Malabar Coast.—*New Account of the East Indies,* 1688 *to* 1730.

In France the duty upon ambergris is 62 francs per kilogramme when imported in French vessels, and 67 francs when imported in foreign vessels.

Mr. Temple, of British Honduras, speaks of an odorous substance thrown off by the alligator, which appears to resemble ambergris.

AMBOYNA WOOD. A beautiful wood much used for inlaid work. Several varieties are imported, but probably all are produced by one species—the *Pterospermum Indicum,* a tree belonging to the *Byttneriaceæ,* or chocolate order.

AMBREINE. The fragrant substance of ambergris, which may be obtained by digesting ambergris in hot alcohol, from which, on cooling, it is deposited in a crystalline form. It is composed of C 88·37, H 3·32, O 3·31.

AMBRITE. A fossil resin occurring in large masses in New Zealand, and much resembling the common resin of the *Dammara Australis,* with which it is often exported.

AMBROSINE. A resinous mineral found in the phosphatic beds near Charleston, South Carolina, U.S.

AMETHYST. (*Améthyste occidentale*, Fr.; *Amethyst*, Ger.) One of the vitreous varieties of quartz, of a clear purple or bluish-violet tint; but the colour is frequently irregularly diffused, and gradually fades into white. The colour is supposed to be due to the presence of a small per-centage-of manganese, but Heintz attributes it to a compound of iron and soda. The amethyst, from the beauty of its colour, has always been esteemed and used in jewellery. It was one of the stones called by the ancients ἀμέθυστος, a name which they conferred on it from its supposed power of preserving the wearer from intoxication. The most beautiful specimens are procured from India, Ceylon, and Persia, where they occur in geodes and pebbles: it is also found at Oberstein, in the Palatinate; in Transylvania; near Cork, and in the Island of May, in Ireland.—H. W. B.

AMETHYST, ORIENTAL. (*Améthyste orientale*, Fr.; *Demantspath*, Ger.) This term is applied to those varieties of corundum which are of a violet colour. See CORUNDUM.—H. W. B.

AMIANTHUS is the name given to the whiter and more delicate varieties of asbestos, which possess a satin-like lustre, in consequence of the greater separation of the fibres of which they are composed. A variety of amianthus (the *amianthoïde* of Haüy) is found at Oisans, in France, the fibres of which are in some degree elastic. The word amianthus (from ἀμίαντος, undefiled) is expressive of the easy manner by which, when soiled, it may be cleansed and restored to its original purity, by being heated to redness in a fire. See ASBESTOS.

AMIDE. This term and *amidogen* are applied to a class of substances which contain ammonia deprived of an atom of hydrogen.

AMIDINE. A name given to the soluble portion of starch.

AMIDON. The name for starch on the Continent.

AMINES. Chemical substances resembling *Amides*, but containing basic radicals. See Watts's 'Dictionary of Chemistry.'

AMMONIA. NH^3. *at. wt.* 17. (*Ammoniaque*, Fr.; *Ammoniak*, Ger.) The name given by Bergman in 1782 to the gas prepared by treating sal-ammoniac with lime or a caustic alkali. It was first isolated by Dr. Black in 1756, and distinguished by him from its carbonate, with which it had been previously confounded. The aqueous solution had been long known, and is mentioned by Raymond Lully in the thirteenth century. Ammonia being a product of the putrefactive decay, as well as of the destructive distillation of organic substances containing nitrogen, is widely diffused in nature, but, from the very circumstances of its formation, is rarely, if ever, evolved in a free or uncombined state. It exists in the atmosphere, though the relative quantity is small; according to Liebig, if all the ammonia were collected at the level of the sea and had a density corresponding to the atmospheric pressure there, it would form a stratum less than a quarter of an inch in depth; yet he believes that the nitrogen of plants is derived entirely from this source. The opinions of chemists are, however, divided upon this point; Liebig's view is supported by Boussingault and opposed by Mulder and Ville. The ammonia present in the air is carried down by rain, sometimes partly in the form of nitrite or nitrate; the maximum amount of combined nitrogen found in numerous analyses by Lawes, and Gilbert, and Way, being 0·032 part in 100,000 parts of rain-water. Recent experiments by Dr. R. Angus Smith have shown that the proportion of ready-formed ammonia varies with the locality; thus, at Valentia, on the west coast of Ireland, it was as low as 0·018, whilst from the burning of coals and other causes, and the diminished area of absorbent soil and vegetation, it rises in large towns, London giving 0·345 and Glasgow even 0·910 in 100,000. In addition there are certain nitrogenous bodies capable of yielding ammonia, designated by Dr. Smith 'albumenoid ammonia,' since it is formed when these bodies are treated with the same chemical reagents which evolve ammonia from albumen.

Ammonia is found in many mineral and brine springs, some kinds of rock salt, in deep well-water, river-, and sea-water. In volcanic districts its salts are at times exhaled in such quantity as to form an article of commerce. The eruption of Vesuvius in 1794 produced so much sal-ammoniac that the peasants collected it by hundredweights; in an eruption of Hecla in 1845 a similar phenomenon was observed; also at Etna it is sometimes found in sufficient abundance to create a profitable trade. Dr. Daubeny is of opinion that the volcanic ammonia is produced by the action of water upon mineral nitrides (perhaps the nitrides of silicon), similar in properties to the nitrides of titanium and boron, which have been recently more carefully examined by M. St. Claire Deville. The *suffioni* of Tuscany yield, besides boracic acid and several different salts, sulphate of ammonia as an important by-product. All cultivable soils, especially those of ferruginous or argillaceous nature, contain an appreciable quantity of ammonia, and a considerable evolution of its salts has been observed recently on meadow-land being overflowed by a stream of lava. The chloride has also been found as a sublimate arising from the combustion of coal strata. Salts of ammonia exist in plants, but to a much greater extent in the liquid and solid excrements of some animals. As a urate it forms the chief constituent of the excrement of the boa, as well as that of many birds : hence the large quantity of ammoniacal salts in guano. See GUANO.

In the guano deposits of South America large quantities of bicarbonate have been met with and exported to Europe. In several manufacturing processes ammonia is generated as in the purification of caustic soda, by heating it with nitrate of soda, and possibly in this process in sufficient quantity to pay for condensation ; but of all sources of supply the so-called 'ammoniacal liquor' of the gas-works is the most important. This is produced during the dry distillation of coal for the manufacture of illuminating gas, and consists mainly of an aqueous solution of sesquicarbonate of ammonia with some sulphide and sulphocyanide of ammonium, &c.

Formation of Ammonia.—No process has yet been devised for inducing the direct combination of nitrogen and hydrogen to produce ammonia ; but under the disposing influence of the production of other compounds, in the presence of these elements, as well as when these gases are presented to each other in the nascent state, their union is effected.

Thus, when electric sparks are passed through a mixture of nitrogen and oxygen in the presence of hydrogen and aqueous vapour, nitrate of ammonia is generated. If, while zinc is being dissolved in sulphuric acid, nitric acid be added, much ammonia is formed (*Nesbit*); so again, if hydrogen and binoxide of nitrogen be passed over spongy platinum, torrents of ammonia are produced, the hydrogen converting the oxygen of the binoxide into water, when the nitrogen, at the moment of its liberation, combines with the hydrogen to form ammonia.

It has even been proposed to carry out this last method on a manufacturing scale.

Messrs. Crane and Jullien, in their patent of January 18, 1848, describe a method of manufacturing ammonia in the state of carbonate, hydrocyanate, or free ammonia, by passing any of the oxygen compounds of nitrogen, together with any compound of hydrogen and carbon, or any mixture of hydrogen with a compound of carbon or even free hydrogen, through a tube or pipe containing any *catalytic* or contact substance, as follows :—Oxides of nitrogen (such, for instance, as the gases liberated in the manufacture of oxalic acid), however procured, are to be mixed in such proportion with any compound of carbon and hydrogen, or such mixture of hydrogen and carbonic oxide or acid as results from the contact of the vapour of water with ignited carbonaceous matters, and the hydrogen compound or mixture containing hydrogen may be in slight excess, so as to ensure the conversion of the whole of the nitrogen contained in the oxide so employed into either ammonia or hydrocyanic acid, which may be known by the absence of the characteristic red fumes on allowing some of the gaseous matter to come in contact with atmospheric air. The catalytic substance which Messrs. Crane and Jullien prefer is platinum, which may be in the state of sponge, or it may be asbestos coated with platinum. This catalytic substance is to be placed in a tube, and heated to about 600° F., so as to increase the temperature of the product, and at the same time prevent the deposition of carbonate of ammonia, which passes onwards into a vessel of the description well known and employed for the purpose of condensing carbonate of ammonia. The condenser for this purpose must be furnished with a safety pipe, to allow of the escape of uncondensed matter, and made to dip into a solution of any substance capable of combining with hydrocyanic acid or ammonia where they would be condensed. A solution of salt of iron is preferable for this purpose.[1]

Chemical Characters.—The gaseous ammonia liberated from its salts by lime (in a manner to be afterwards described) is a colourless gas of a peculiar pungent odour. It is composed, by weight, of 1 atom of nitrogen and 3 of hydrogen ; or, by volume, of 2 measures of nitrogen and 6 of hydrogen, condensed to four ; and may be resolved into these constituent gases by passing over spongy platinum heated to redness, or by a current of electric sparks. By a pressure of 6·5 atmospheres at 50° F., it is condensed into a colourless liquid. It is combustible, but less so than hydrogen on account of the incombustible nitrogen which it contains ; but its inflammability may be readily seen by passing it into an argand gas flame reduced to a minimum.

Ammonia is very soluble in water, water at 32° F. absorbing no less than 1,149 times its volume of this gas, and at 68° 681·8 times its volume ; and the solution has a less density and a lower boiling point than pure water. The following Table of the density of solutions of ammonia in water, of different strengths, is by Dr. Ure :—

Ammonia in 100	Water in 100	Specific Gravity by Experiment	Ammonia in 100	Water in 100	Specific Gravity by Experiment
26·500	73·500	0·9000	13·250	86·750	0·9455
25·175	74·825	0·9045	11·925	88·075	0·9510
23·850	76·150	0·9090	10·600	19·400	0·9564
22·525	77·475	0·9133	9·275	90·725	0·9614
21·200	78·800	0·9177	7·950	92·050	0·9662
19·875	80·125	0·9227	6·625	93·375	0·9716
18·550	81·450	0·9275	5·300	94·700	0·9768
17·225	82·775	0·9320	3·975	96·025	0·9828
15·900	84·100	0·9363	2·650	97·350	0·9887
14·575	85·425	0·9410	1·325	98·675	0·9945

Upon this variation in density of solutions of ammonia in proportion to their strength, Mr. J. J. Griffin has constructed a useful instrument called an *Ammonia-meter*. It is founded upon the following facts :—That mixtures of liquid ammonia with water possess a specific gravity which is the mean of the specific gravities of their components ; that in all solutions of ammonia, a quantity of anhydrous ammonia, weighing 212½ grains, which he calls a *test-atom*, displaces 300 grains of water, and reduces the specific gravity of the solution to the extent of ·00125 ; and, finally, that the strongest solution of ammonia which it is possible to prepare at the temperature of 62° F. contains in an imperial gallon of solution 100 test-atoms of ammonia.

We extract the following paragraph from Mr. Griffin's paper in the Transactions of the Chemical Society, explanatory of the accompanying Table :—

' The first column shows the *specific gravity* of the solutions ; the second column the *weight* of an imperial gallon in pounds and ounces ; the third column the *per-centage* of ammonia by weight ; the fourth column the *degree* of the solution, as indicated by the instrument, corresponding with the number of *test-atoms* of ammonia present in a gallon of the liquor ; the fifth column shows the number of *grains* of ammonia contained in a gallon ; and the sixth column the *atomic volume* of the solution, or that *measure* of it which contains one test-atom of ammonia. For instance, one gallon of liquid ammonia, specific gravity 880, weighs 8 lbs. or 128 oz. avoirdupois ; its percentage of ammonia, by weight, is 33·117 ; it contains 96 test-atoms of ammonia in one gallon, and 20400·0 grains of ammonia in one gallon ; and, lastly, 104·16 septems containing one test-atom of ammonia. Although no hydrometer, however accurately constructed, is at all equal to the Centigrade mode of chemical testing, yet the Ammonia-meter, and the Table accompanying it, will be found very useful to the manufacturer, enabling him not only to determine the actual strength of any given liquor, but the precise amount of dilution necessary to convert it into a liquor of any other desired strength, whilst the direct quotation of the number of grains of real ammonia contained in a gallon of solution of any specific gravity will enable him to judge at a glance of the money-value of any given sample of ammonia.'

Table of Liquid Ammonia (Griffin).

One Test-Atom of Anhydrous Ammonia$=NH^3$ weighs 212·5 grains. Specific Gravity of Water$=1·00000$. One Gallon of Water weighs 10 lbs., and contains 10,000 Septems. Temperature 62° F.

Specific Gravity of the Liquid Ammonia	Weight of an Imperial Gallon in Avoirdupois lbs. and ozs.		Per-centage of Ammonia by Weight	Test-atoms of Ammonia in one Gallon	Grains of Ammonia in one Gallon	Septems containing one Test-atom of Ammonia
	lbs.	ozs.				
·87500	8	12·0	34·694	100	21250·9	100·00
·87625	8	12·2	34·298	99	21037·5	101·01
·87750	8	12·4	33·903	98	20825·0	102·04
·87875	8	12·6	33·509	97	20612·5	103·09
·88000	8	12·8	33·117	96	20400·0	104·16
·88125	8	13·0	32·725	95	20187·5	105·26
·88250	8	13·2	32·335	94	19975·0	106·38
·88375	8	13·4	31·946	93	19762·5	107·53
·88500	8	13·6	31·558	92	19550·0	108·70
·88625	8	13·8	31·172	91	19337·5	109·89
·88750	8	14·0	30·785	90	19125·0	111·11

Table of Liquid Ammonia (continued).

Specific Gravity of the Liquid Ammonia	Weight of an Imperial Gallon in Avoirdupois lbs. and ozs.		Per-centage of Ammonia by Weight	Test-atoms of Ammonia in one Gallon	Grains of Ammonia in one Gallon	Septems containing one Test-atom of Ammonia
	lbs.	ozs.				
·88875	8	14·2	30·400	89	18912·5	112·36
·89000	8	14·4	30·016	88	18700·0	113·64
·89125	8	14·6	29·633	87	18487·5	114·94
·89250	8	14·8	29·252	86	18275·0	116·28
·89375	8	15·0	28·871	85	18062·5	117·65
·89500	8	15·2	28·492	84	17850·0	119·05
·89625	8	15·4	28·113	83	17637·5	120·48
·89750	8	15·6	27·736	82	17425·0	121·95
·89875	8	15·8	27·359	81	17212·5	123·46
·90000	9	0·0	26·984	80	17000·0	125·00
·90125	9	0·2	26·610	79	16787·5	126·58
·90250	9	0·4	26·237	78	16575·0	128·21
·90375	9	0·6	25·865	77	16362·5	129·87
·90500	9	0·8	25·493	76	16150·0	131·58
·90625	9	1·0	25·123	75	15937·5	133·33
·90750	9	1·2	24·754	74	15725·0	135·13
·90875	9	1·4	24·386	73	15512·5	136·98
·91000	9	1·6	24·019	72	15300·0	138·99
·91125	9	1·8	23·653	71	15087·5	140·85
·91250	9	2·0	23·288	70	14875·0	142·86
·91375	9	2·2	22·924	69	14662·5	144·93
·91500	9	2·4	22·561	68	14450·0	147·06
·91625	9	2·6	22·198	67	14237·5	149·25
·91750	9	2·8	21·837	66	14025·0	151·51
·91875	9	3·0	21·477	65	13812·5	153·85
·92000	9	3·2	21·118	64	13600·0	156·25
·92125	9	3·4	20·760	63	13387·5	158·73
·92250	9	3·6	20·403	62	13175·0	161·29
·92375	9	3·8	20·046	61	12962·5	163·93
·92500	9	4·0	19·691	60	12750·0	166·67
·92625	9	4·2	19·337	59	12537·5	169·49
·92750	9	4·4	18·983	58	12325·0	172·41
·92875	9	4·6	18·631	57	12112·5	175·44
·93000	9	4·8	18·280	56	11900·0	178·57
·93125	9	5·0	17·929	55	11687·5	181·82
·93250	9	5·2	17·579	54	11475·0	185·18
·93375	9	5·4	17·231	53	11262·5	188·68
·93500	9	5·6	16·883	52	11050·0	192·31
·93625	9	5·8	16·536	51	10837·5	196·08
·93750	9	6·0	16·190	50	10625·0	200·00
·93875	9	6·2	15·846	49	10412·5	204·08
·94000	9	6·4	15·502	48	10200·0	208·33
·94125	9	6·6	15·158	47	9987·5	212·77
·94250	9	6·8	14·816	46	9775·0	217·39
·94375	9	7·0	14·475	45	9562·5	222·22
·94500	9	7·2	14·135	44	9350·0	227·27
·94625	9	7·4	13·795	43	9137·5	232·56
·94750	9	7·6	13·456	42	8925·0	238·09
·94875	9	7·8	13·119	41	8712·5	243·90
·95000	9	8·0	12·782	40	8500·0	250·00
·95125	9	8·2	12·446	39	8287·5	256·41
·95250	9	8·4	12·111	38	8075·0	263·16
·94375	9	8·6	11·777	37	7862·5	270·27
·95500	9	8·8	11·444	36	7650·0	277·78
·95625	9	9·0	11·111	35	7437·5	285·71
·95750	9	9·2	10·780	34	7225·0	294·12
·95875	9	9·4	10·4490	33	7012·5	303·03
·96000	9	9·6	10·1190	32	6800·0	312·50
·96125	9	9·8	9·7901	31	6587·5	322·58

Table of Liquid Ammonia (continued).

Specific Gravity of the Liquid Ammonia	Weight of an Imperial Gallon in Avoirdupois lbs. and ozs.		Per-centage of Ammonia by Weight	Test-atoms of Ammonia in one Gallon	Grains of Ammonia in one Gallon	Septems containing one Test-atom of Ammonia
	lbs.	ozs.				
·96250	9	10·0	9·4620	30	6375·0	333·33
·96375	9	10·2	9·1347	29	6162·5	344·83
·96500	9	10·4	8·8083	28	5950·0	357·14
·96625	9	10·6	8·4827	27	5737·5	370·37
·96750	9	10·8	8·1580	26	5525·0	384·62
·96875	9	11·0	7·8341	25	5312·5	400·00
·97000	9	11·2	7·5111	24	5100·0	416·67
·97125	9	11·4	7·1888	23	4887·5	434·78
·97250	9	11·6	6·8674	22	4675·0	454·54
·97375	9	11·8	6·5469	21	4462·5	476·19
·97500	9	12·0	6·2271	20	4250·0	500·00
·97625	9	12·2	5·9082	19	4037·5	526·32
·97750	9	12·4	5·5901	18	3825·0	555·56
·97875	9	12·6	5·2728	17	3612·5	588·24
·98000	9	12·8	4·9563	16	3400·0	625·00
·98125	9	13·0	4·6406	15	3187·5	666·67
·98250	9	13·2	4·3255	14	2975·0	714·29
·98375	9	13·4	4·0111	13	2762·5	769·23
·98500	9	13·6	3·6983	12	2550·0	833·33
·98625	9	13·8	3·3858	11	2337·5	909·09
·98750	9	14·0	3·0741	10	2125·0	1000·00
·98875	9	14·2	2·7632	9	1912·5	1111·10
·99000	9	14·4	2·4531	8	1700·0	1250·00
·99125	9	14·6	2·1438	7	1487·5	1428·60
99250	9	14·8	1·8352	6	1275·0	1666·70
·99375	9	15·0	1·5274	5	1062·5	2000·00
·99500	9	15·2	1·2204	4	850·0	2500·00
·99625	9	15·4	0·9141	3	637·5	3333·30
·99750	9	15·6	0·6087	2	425·0	5000·00
·99875	9	15·8	0·3040	1	212·5	10000·00
1·0000	10 lbs. Water			0		

Ammoniacal gas combines directly with hydrated acids, forming a series of salts, the constitution of which is peculiar, and must be here briefly discussed, that the formulæ hereafter employed in describing them may be understood.

These compounds may be viewed as direct combinations of the ammonia with the hydrated acids; thus, the compound with

Hydrochloric acid   as the Hydrochlorate (NH^3, HCl) (**NH^3. HCl**).
Hydrosulphuric acid   ,,   Hydrosulphate (NH^3, HS) (**$2NH^3$. H^2S**).
Sulphuric acid   ,,   Hydrated sulphate (NH^3; HO,SO^3) (**$2NH^3$. H^2SO^4**).
Nitric acid   ,,   Hydrated nitrate (NH^3; HO,NO^5) (**NH^3. HNO^3**).
Carbonic acid   ,,   Hydrated carbonate (NH^3; HO, CO^2). (**$2NH^3$, H^2O. CO^2**).

But the close analogy of these compounds, in all their properties, to the corresponding salts of potash and soda has led chemists to the assumption of the existence of a group of elements possessing the characters of a metal, of a basyl or hypothetical metallic radical, called ammonium (NH^4), in these salts; which theory of their constitution brings out the resemblance to the potash and soda salts more clearly, thus:—

Chloride   contains   And chloride   contains
of potassium . KCl. (**KCl**)   of ammonium .   . NH^4Cl (**NH^4Cl**)
sulphide ,,   . KS. (**K^2S**)   sulphide ,, .   . NH^4S [(**NH^4**), ^2S].
sulphate of potassa KO,SO^3 (**K^2SO^4**) sulphate of ammonia NH^4O,SO^3 [(**NH^4**)$^2SO^4$].
nitrate   ,, . KO, NO^5 (**KNO^3**) nitrate   ,,   . NH^4O,NO^5 (**NH^4NO^3**).
carbonate ,, . KO, CO^2 (**K^2CO^3**) carbonate   ,,   . NH^4O,CO^2 [(**NH^4**)$^2CO^3$].

Although it may be objected to this view that the metal ammonium is not known, yet a curious metallic compound of this metal with mercury has been obtained; and, after all, it is by no means necessary that the metal should be isolated, for the existence of numerous basic radicals has been assumed in organic chemistry which have never been isolated.

It is true, also, that the oxide of ammonium is unknown, but substitution-products of it have been produced, which are solid bodies, soluble in water, exhibiting all the characters of potash solution, being as powerfully caustic and alkaline. In fact, ammonia is in reality but the type of a vast number of compounds. It is capable of having its hydrogen replaced by metals (as copper, mercury, calcium, &c.), as well as by metallic or basic compound radicals, producing the endless number of artificial organic bases, which are primary, secondary, or tertiary nitrides, according as one, two, or three equivalents of the ammonia is replaced. When the substitution of the hydrogen in ammonia is effected by acid radicals, the compounds are called amides.

Preparation of Ammonia.—Ammonia is obtained by the decomposition of one of the salts of ammonia, either the chloride of ammonium, NH⁴ Cl (sal-ammoniac), or the sulphate, by a metallic oxide, *e.g.* lime.

$$NH^4Cl \quad + \quad CaO,HO \quad = \quad CaCl \quad + \quad NH^3 \quad + \quad 2HO.$$

$$2(NH^4Cl) \quad + \quad CaH^2O^2 \quad = \quad CaCl^2 \quad + \quad 2NH^3 \quad + \quad 2H^2O.$$

On the small scale in the laboratory the powdered ammoniacal salt is mixed with slaked lime, in a Florence flask or a small iron retort, and gently heated; the ammoniacal gas being dried by passing it through a bottle containing lime. Chloride of calcium must not be employed in the desiccation of ammonia, since the ammonia is absorbed by this salt, producing a curious compound, the chloride of caliammonium.

It has been proposed by Knab to make use of the property of chloride of calcium to absorb ammonia and give it up again when heated, for the purpose of storing and transporting it. Solution of ammonia of the usual commercial strength, specific gravity 0·880, contains only 33·12 per cent., whilst the chloride of calcium compound is said to retain 50 per cent.

The gaseous ammonia must be collected over mercury, on account of its solubility in water.

This operation is carried out on the large scale for the purpose of making the aqueous solution of ammonia (*liquor ammoniæ*, or *spirits of hartshorn*).

Solution of Ammonia.

Preparation.—In preparing the aqueous solution, the gas is passed into water contained in Woolfe's bottles, which on the small scale are of glass, whilst on the large scale they are made of earthenware.

A sufficiently capacious still or retort of iron or lead should be employed, which is provided with a moveable neck; and it is desirable to pass the gas through a worm, to cool it, before it enters the first Woolfe's bottle. Each of the series of Woolfe's bottles should be furnished with a safety-funnel in the third neck, to avoid accidents by absorption. The whole of the condensing arrangements should be kept cool by ice or cold water.

Properties.—In the London and in the Edinburgh 'Pharmacopœia' two solutions of ammonia are directed to be prepared, the stronger having the specific gravity 0·882, and containing about 32·5 per cent. of ammonia; the weaker of specific gravity 0·960, containing, therefore, about 10 per cent. of the gas.

Sometimes the commercial solution of ammonia is made by treating impure ammoniacal salts with lime, and it then contains empyreumatic oils; in fact, the various volatile products of the distillation of coal which are soluble in or miscible with water.

Pyrrol may be detected in ammonia by the purple colour which it strikes with an excess of nitric or sulphuric acid. If the residue of its distillation be mixed with potash, Picoline is detected by its peculiar odour. Naphthaline is discovered not only by its odour, but may also be separated by sublimation or heating, after converting the ammonia in the solution into a salt by sulphuric or hydrochloric acid.— Dr. Maclogan.

We *imported* into England of sulphate and liquor of ammonia as follows :—

Ammonia, sulphate of	. . 1856 .	. lbs.	23,904
" "	. . 1855 .	. "	343,609
Ammonia, liquor	. . 1855 .	. "	22,400

Since, for the purpose of purification on the large scale, ammonia is invariably

converted into chloride or sulphate, the details of the manufacture of the ammoniacal salts will be given under those heads.   For the determination of ammonia, see
NITROGEN.—H. M. W.

AMMONIA, CARBONATE OF.   [*The sesquicarbonate* of commerce,
2NH³, 3CO², 2HO (**4NH³, 3CO², 2H²O**), *at. wt.* 118.]   This salt was probably
known to Raymond Lully and Basil Valentine, as the chief constituent of putrid
urine.   The real distinction between ammonia and its carbonate was pointed out by
Dr. Black.

Carbonate of ammonia is formed during the putrefaction of animal substances,
and by their destructive distillation.   Its presence in rain-water has been before
alluded to.

The carbonate of ammonia of commerce is obtained by submitting to sublimation
a mixture either of sal-ammoniac or sulphate of ammonia with chalk.

This is generally carried out in cast-iron retorts, similar in size and shape to those
used in the manufacture of coal gas.   The retorts are charged through a door at one
end, and at the other they communicate with large square leaden chambers, supported
by a wooden frame, in which the sublimed salt is condensed. *Fig.* 38.

38

The product of this first process is impure, being especially discoloured by the
presence of carbonaceous matter, and has to be submitted to resublimation.   This is
carried out in iron pots surmounted by moveable leaden caps.   These pots are either
set in brickwork, and heated by the flue of the retort furnace, or are placed in a water-
bath, as shown in *fig.* 39.   In fact, a temperature not exceeding 150° F. is found
sufficient.

39

The charge of a retort consists usually of about 65 lbs. of sulphate of ammonia (or
an equivalent quantity of the chloride) to 100 lbs. of chalk, which yield about 40 lbs.
of crude carbonate of ammonia.

Modifications of the Process.—Mr. Laming has suggested to bring ammonia and
carbonic acid gases into mutual contact in a leaden chamber having at the lower part
a layer of water, and then to crystallise the salt by evaporating this aqueous solution.

He also proposes to prepare carbonate of ammonia from the sulphide of ammonium of gas liquors, by passing carbonic acid gas into the liquor, which carbonic gas is generated by heating a mixture of oxide of copper and charcoal, in the proportion of twelve parts of the former to one of the latter.

Mr. Hills has described his mode of obtaining sesquicarbonate of ammonia from guano. To effect this, the guano is first mixed with charcoal or powdered coke; the mixture is then heated, and the sesquicarbonate of ammonia obtained by sublimation. The process does not appear to be much employed.

Manufacture of Ammonia from Peat and Shale.—Mr. Hills, in his patent of August 11th, 1846, specified the following method of obtaining ammonia from peat. The peat is placed in an upright furnace and ignited; the air passes through the bars as usual, and the ammonia is collected by passing the products of combustion through a suitable arrangement of apparatus to effect its condensation. This plan of obtaining ammonia from peat appears to be precisely similar to that patented by Mr. Rees Reece (January 23rd, 1849), and made to form an important feature in the operations of the British and Irish Peat Company. The first part of Mr. Reece's patent is for an invention for causing peat to be burned in a furnace by the aid of a blast, so as to obtain inflammable gases and tarry and other products from peat. For this purpose, a blast furnace with suitable condensing apparatus is used. The gases, on their exit from the condensing apparatus, may be collected for use as fuel or otherwise; and the tarry and other products pass into a suitable receiver. The tarry products may be employed to obtain paraffine and oils for lubricating machinery, &c.; and the other products may be made available for evolving ammonia, wood-spirit, and other matters by any of the existing processes. Dr. Hodges, of Belfast, states that in his experiments he obtained nearly 22¾lbs. of sulphate of ammonia from a ton of peat. Sir Robert Kane, who was employed by Government to institute a series of experimental researches on the products obtainable from peat, states that he obtained sulphate of ammonia at the rate of 24$\frac{8}{10}$lbs. per ton of peat. Messrs. Drew and Stocken patented, in 1846, the obtaining ammonia from peat by distillation in close vessels, as practised in the carbonisation of wood. It will thus be seen that the peat is a source of ammonia, but whether this source is a profitable or economical one, in a commercial point of view, is a problem which has not yet received solution.

Ammonia from Schist.—Another source of ammonia is bituminous schist, which, when submitted to destructive distillation, gives off an ammoniacal liquor which may be employed in the manufacture of ammoniacal salts by any of the usual processes. The obtaining of ammonia from schist forms part of a patent granted to Count de Hompesch, September 4, 1841.

Chemical Composition and Constitution.—The true neutral carbonate of ammonia, NH^4O, CO^2 [$(NH^4)^2CO^3$], does not appear to exist. The sesquicarbonate of ammonia of the shops was found by Rose to have the composition assigned to it by Mr. Philips, as given at the head of this article; and it may be viewed as a compound of the true bicarbonate (*i.e.* the double carbonate of ammonia and water), NH^4O, CO^2; HO, CO^2 [$(NH^4)^2CO^3$; H^2CO^3]; with a peculiar compound of anhydrous carbonic acid with ammonia itself, NH^3, CO^2 [$(NH^3)^2CO^2$].

It is invariably found that a certain quantity of water and ammonia are liberated during the distillation, and hence the anomalous character of the compound. In fact, in operating upon 3 equivalents of the sulphate or chloride of the 3 equivalents of the true carbonate of ammonia (NH^4O, CO^2) which may be supposed to be generated, two are decomposed, one losing an equivalent of ammonia, the other an equivalent of water; of course, the ammonia thus liberated, amounting to 14 parts for each 100 of carbonate of ammonia obtained, is not lost; it is passed into water to be saturated with acid, and thus again converted into sulphate or chloride.

Properties.—Sesquicarbonate of ammonia (as it is commonly called) is met with in commerce in the form of fibrous white translucent cakes, about two inches thick.

When exposed to the air the constituents of the less stable compound NH^3, CO^2 are volatilised, and a white opaque mass of the true bicarbonate remains. Hence the odour of ammonia always emitted by the commercial carbonate. Mr. Scanlan has also shown that by treatment with a small quantity of water, the carbonate is dissolved, leaving the bicarbonate. It is soluble in four times its weight of cold water, but boiling water decomposes it.

Impurities.—The commercial salt is sometimes contaminated with empyreumatic oil, which is recognised by its yielding a brownish coloured solution on treatment with water.

It may contain sulphate and chloride of ammonium. For the recognition of the presence of these acids, see SULPHURIC and HYDROCHLORIC acids.

Sulphide and hyposulphite of ammonia are sometimes present, and likewise lead, from the chambers into which the salt has been sublimed.

Other Carbonates of Ammonia.—Besides the neutral or monocarbonate of ammonia before alluded to, the true bicarbonate NH^4O, CO^2; HO, CO^2 [$(NH^4)^2CO^3$; H^2CO^3] and the sesquicarbonate of the shops, Rose has described about a dozen other definite compounds; but, for their description, we must refer to Watts's 'Dictionary of Chemistry.'

AMMONIACUM, GUM. Gum-resin. (*Gomme Ammoniaque*, Fr.; *Ammoniak*, Ger.) This is the inspissated juice of an umbelliferous plant (the *Dorema ammoniacum*), the gum-bearing heracleum, which grows in Persia, the East Indies, and Africa. In the French colony of Algiers this plant grows naturally, and it appears likely to become an object of cultivation. It comes to us either in small white tears clustered together, or in brownish lumps, containing many impurities. It possesses a peculiar smell, somewhat like that of assafœtida, and a bitterish taste. It is employed in medicine. Its only use in the arts is for forming a cement to join broken pieces of china and glass, which may be prepared as follows : ' Take isinglass 1 ounce, distilled water 6 ounces, boil together down to 3 ounces, and add $1\frac{1}{2}$ ounce of strong spirit of wine ;—boil this mixture for a minute or two; strain it; add while hot; first, half an ounce of milky emulsion of gum ammoniac, and then 5 drachms of an alcoholic solution of resin mastic.'

AMMONIA, NITRATE OF.—This salt is not made on an extensive scale ; but as it has a certain consumption for making the protoxide of nitrogen (laughing gas), now largely used by dentists as an anæsthetic, a few remarks respecting it may not be out of place here.

It is obtained by saturating solution of ammonia, or the carbonate, with nitric acid, and then evaporating the solution till crystallisation takes place. It ought to be perfectly free from chloride of ammonium.

This salt crystallises in six-sided prisms, being isomorphous with nitrate of potash.

Its composition is NH^4O, NO^5 [$(NH^4)NO^3$.] It is incapable of existing without the presence of an equivalent of water, in addition to NH^3 and NO^5. If heat be applied, the salt is entirely decomposed into protoxide of nitrogen and water ; thus—

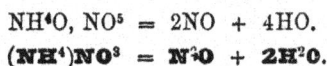

$$NH^4O, NO^5 = 2NO + 4HO.$$

$$(NH^4)NO^3 = N^3O + 2H^2O.$$

Besides its use in the laboratory for making protoxide of nitrogen, it is a constituent of frigorific mixtures, on account of the cold which it produces on dissolving in water.

Lastly, it is very convenient for promoting the deflagration of organic bodies, both its constituents being volatile on heating.

AMMONIA, SULPHATE OF. NH^4O, SO^3 [$(NH^4)^2SO^4$]. This salt is found native in fissures near volcanoes, under the name of *Mascagnin*, associated with sal-ammoniac. It also forms in ignited coal-beds—as at Bradley, in Staffordshire—with chloride of ammonium.

This salt is prepared by saturating the solution of ammonia, obtained by any of the processes before described (either from animal refuse, from coal, in the manufacture of coal gas, from guano, or from any other source), with sulphuric acid, and then evaporating the solution till the salt crystallises out.

Frequently, instead of adding the acid to the ammoniacal liquor, the crude ammoniacal liquor is distilled in a boiler, either alone or with lime, and the evolved ammonia is passed into the sulphuric acid, contained in a large tun or in a series of Woolfe's bottles ; or a modification of Coffey's still may be used with advantage, as in the case of the saturation of hydrochloric acid by ammonia.

If Coffey's still be employed, a considerable concentration of the liquor is effected during the process of saturation, which is subsequently completed generally in iron pans; but great care has to be taken not to carry the evaporation too far, to avoid decomposition of the sulphate by the organic matter invariably present, which reduces it to the state of sulphite, hyposulphite, and even to sulphide, of ammonium.

The salt obtained by this first crystallisation is much purer than the chloride produced under similar circumstances, and one or two recrystallisations effect its purification sufficiently for all commercial purposes.

It is on account of the greater facility of purification which the sulphate affords by crystallisation than the chloride of ammonium, that the former is often produced as a preliminary stage in the manufacture of the latter compound, the purified sulphate being then converted into sal-ammoniac by sublimation with common salt. The acid mother-liquor left in the first crystallisation is returned to be again treated, together with some additional acid, with a fresh quantity of ammonia.

Preparation. Modifications in details and patents.—Since it is in the production of the sulphate of ammonia that the modification of Coffey's still, called the *ammonia still*, is generally employed, it may be well to introduce here a detailed account of its arrangement.

This apparatus is an upright vessel, divided by horizontal diaphragms or partitions into a number of chambers. It is proposed to construct the vessel of wood, lined with lead, and the diaphragms of sheet iron. Each diaphragm is perforated with many small holes, so regulated, both with regard to number and size, as to afford, under some pressure, passage for the elastic vapours which ascend, during the use of the apparatus, to make their exit by a pipe opening from the upper chamber. Fitted to each diaphragm are several small valves, so weighted as to rise whenever elastic vapours accumulate under them in such quantity as to exert more than a certain amount of pressure on the diaphragm. A pipe also is attached to each diaphragm, passing from about an inch above its upper surface to near the bottom of a cup or small reservoir, fixed to the upper surface of the diaphragms next underneath. This pipe is sufficiently large to transmit freely downwards the whole of the liquid which enters for distillation at the upper part of the upright vessel ; and the cup or reservoir into which the pipe dips forms, when full of liquid, a trap by which the upward passage of elastic vapours by the pipe is prevented. The vessel may rest on a close cistern, contrived to receive the descending liquid as it leaves the lowest chamber, and from this cistern it may be run off, by a valve or cock, whenever expedient. The cistern, or in its absence the lowest chamber, contains the orifice of a pipe which supplies the steam for working the apparatus. The exact number of chambers into which the upright vessel is divided is not of essential importance ; but the quantity of liquid and the surface of each diaphragm being given, the distillation, within certain limits, will be more complete the greater the number of chambers used in the process. The liquid undergoing distillation in this apparatus necessarily covers the upper surface of each diaphragm to the depth of about an inch, being prevented from passing downward through the small perforations by the upward pressure of the rising steam and other elastic vapours ; and, on the other hand, the steam being prevented, by the traps, from passing upwards by the pipes, is forced to ascend by the perforations in the diaphragms ; so that the liquid lying on them becomes heated, and in consequence gives off its volatile matters. When the ammoniacal liquid accumulates on one of the diaphragms to the depth of an inch, it flows over one of the short pipes into the trap below, and overflows into the next diaphragm, and so on. See DISTILLATION.

The management of the apparatus varies in some measure with the form in which it is desirable to obtain the ammonia. When the ammonia is required to leave the upper chamber in the form of gas, either pure or impure, it is necessary that the steam which ascends and the current of ammoniacal liquid which descends, should be in such relative proportions that the latter remains at or near the atmospheric temperature during its passage through some of the upper chambers, becoming progressively hotter as it descends, until it reaches the boiling temperature ; in which state it passes through the lower chambers, either to make its escape, or to enter a cistern provided to receive it, and in which it may for some time be maintained at a boiling heat. On the contrary, if the ammonia, either pure or impure, be required to leave the upper chamber in combination with the vapour of water, the supply of steam entering below must bear such proportion to that of the ammoniacal liquid supplied above, that the latter may be at a boiling temperature in the upper part of the apparatus.[1]

The use of this apparatus was patented in the name of Mr. W. E. Newton, Nov. 9, 1841.

Mr. Hills' process, patented Oct. 19, 1848, for concentrating ammoniacal solutions by causing them to descend through a tower of coke through which steam is ascending, is, in fact, nothing more than a rough mode of carrying out the same principle, which is more effectually and elegantly performed by the modification of Coffey's still above described. The concentrated ammonia liquor is then treated with acid and evaporated in the usual way.

Mr. Wilson patented, Dec. 7, 1850, another method of saturating the ammonia with the acid by passing the crude ammonia vapour, obtained by heating the ammoniacal liquor of the gas-works, in at the bottom of a high tower filled with coke, whilst the sulphuric acid descends in a continuous current from the top ; in this manner the acid and ammonia are exposed to each other over a greatly extended surface.

Dr. Richardson (patent, Jan. 26, 1850) mixes the crude ammonia liquors with sulphate of magnesia, then evaporates the solution, and submits the double sulphate of magnesia and ammonia, which separates, to sublimation; but it would not appear that any great advantage is derived from proceeding in this way, either pecuniary or otherwise.

Mr. Laming passes sulphurous acid through the gas liquor, and finally oxidises the sulphite thus obtained to the state of sulphate, by exposure to the air. (Patent. Aug. 12, 1852.)

Michiel's mode of obtaining sulphate of ammonia, patented April 30, 1850, is as follows:—The ammoniacal liquors of the gas-works are combined with sulphate and oxide of lead, which is obtained and prepared in the following way:—Sulphuret of lead in its natural state is taken and reduced to small fragments by any convenient crushing apparatus. It is then submitted to a roasting process, in a suitably arranged reverberatory furnace of the following construction:—The furnace is formed of two shelves, or rather the bottom of the furnace, and one shelf, and there is a communication from the lower to the upper. The galena or sulphuret of lead, previously ground, is then spread over the surface of the upper shelf, to a thickness of about 2 or 2½ inches, and there it is submitted to the heat of the furnace. It remains thus for about two hours, at which time it is drawn off the upper shelf, and spread over the lower shelf or bottom of the furnace, where it is exposed to a greater heat for a certain time, during which it is well stirred, for the purpose of exposing all the parts equally to the action of the heat, and at the same time the fusion of any portion of it is prevented. By this process the sulphuret of lead becomes converted partly into sulphate and partly into oxide of lead. This product of sulphate and oxide of lead is to be crushed by any ordinary means, and reduced to about the same degree of fineness as coarse sand. It is now to be combined with the ammoniacal liquors, when sulphate of ammonia and sulphuret and carbonate of lead will be produced.

The sulphate of ammonia is separated by treatment with water, and the residuary mixture of sulphide and carbonate of lead is used for the manufacture of lead compounds.

Properties.—The sulphate of ammonia obtained by either of the methods above described is a colourless salt, containing, according to Mitscherlich, one atom of water of crystallisation. It is isomorphous with sulphate of potash.

It deliquesces by exposure to the air; 1 part dissolves in 2 parts of cold water, and 1 of boiling water. It fuses at 140° C. (284° F.), but at 280° C. (536° F.) it is decomposed, being volatilised in the form of free ammonia, sulphite, water, and nitrogen.

For the other sulphates, the sulphites, and those salts which are but little used in the arts and manufactures—we refer to Watts's 'Dictionary of Chemistry.'

Uses.—The chief consumption of ammoniacal salts in the arts is in the form of sal-ammoniac, the sulphate of ammonia being principally used as a material for the manufacture of the chloride of ammonium. It may, however, be employed directly in making ammonia-alum, or in the production of free ammonia by treatment with lime.

AMMONIUM. (NH⁴) The radical supposed to exist in the various salts of ammonia. Thus NH⁴O [(**NH⁴**)²O] is the oxide, NH⁴Cl the chloride, of ammonium. Ammonium constitutes one of the best established chemical types. See FORMULÆ, CHEMICAL.

AMMONIUM, CHLORIDE OF. Commonly called SAL-AMMONIAC. (*Sal ammoniac*, Fr.; *Salmiak*, Ger.) The early history of this salt is involved in much uncertainty. It would appear that the *sal ammoniacus* (ἄλς ἀμμωνιακός) of the ancients was, in fact, rock salt. The earliest knowledge of the compound has been claimed both for the Arabians and the Egyptians; but the late Dr. Royle remarked, that 'the salt must have been familiar to the Hindoos ever since they have burnt bricks, as they now do, with the manure of animals, for some may usually be found crystallised at the unburnt extremity of the kiln.'

This salt is formed in the solid state by bringing in contact its two gaseous constituents, hydrochloric acid and ammonia. The gases combine with such force as to generate, not only heat, but sometimes even light. It may also be prepared by mixing the aqueous solutions of these gases, and evaporating till crystallisation takes place.

When ammoniacal gas is brought into contact with dry chlorine, a violent reaction ensues, attended by the evolution of heat and even light. The chlorine combines with the hydrogen to produce hydrochloric acid, which unites with the remainder of the ammonia, forming chloride of ammonium, the nitrogen being liberated. The same reaction takes place on passing chlorine gas into the saturated aqueous solution of ammonia.

Manufacture of Chloride of Ammonium from Camels' Dung.—In Egypt—which undoubtedly was the great seat of the manufacture of this salt from the beginning of the thirteenth to the middle of the seventeenth century, and whence all the European markets were supplied—the following is the process by which it is obtained :—

The original source was the urine and dung of the camel, which are dried by plastering them upon the walls, and burning, other fuel being very scarce in that country. A fire of this material evolves a thick smoke, charged with chloride of ammonium, part of which is condensed with the soot.

In every part of Egypt, but especially in the Delta, peasants are seen driving asses loaded with bags of that soot, on their way to the sal-ammoniac works.

Here it is extracted in the following manner :—Glass globes, coated with loam, are filled with the soot, pressed down by wooden rammers, a space of only two or three inches being left vacant, near their mouths. These globes are set in round orifices formed in the ridge of a long vault or large horizontal furnace flue. Heat is gradually applied by a fire of dry camels' dung, and it is eventually increased till the globes become obscurely red. As the chloride of ammonium is volatile at a temperature much below ignition, it rises out of the soot in vapour, and gets condensed into a cake upon the inner surface of the top of the globe. A considerable portion, however, escapes into the air ; and another portion concretes in the mouth, which must be cleared from time to time by an iron rod. Towards the end, the obstruction becomes very troublesome and must be most carefully attended to and obviated, otherwise the globes would explode by the uncondensed vapours. In all cases when the subliming process approaches to a conclusion, the globes crack or split ; and when they come to be removed, after the heat has subsided, they usually fall to pieces. The upper portion of the mass is separated, because to it the white salt adheres ; and, on detaching the pieces of glass with a hatchet, it is ready for the market. At the bottom of each balloon a nucleus of salt remains, surrounded with fixed pulverulent matter. This is reserved, and, after being bruised, is put in along with the charge of soot in a fresh operation.

The sal-ammoniac obtained by this process is dull, spongy, and of a greyish hue ; but nothing better was for a long period known in commerce. Fifty years ago, it fetched 2s. 6d. a pound ; whereas now, perfectly pure sal-ammoniac may be had at one-fifth of that price,

Manufacture of Sal-Ammoniac from Bones and other Animal Matter.—Various animal offals develop, during their spontaneous putrefactive fermentation, or their decomposition by heat, a large quantity of free or carbonated ammonia among their volatile products. Upon this principle many sal-ammoniac works have been established.—Watts's ' Dictionary of Chemistry.'

The first attempts made in France to obtain sal-ammoniac profitably in this manner failed. A very extensive factory of the kind, which experienced the same fate, was under the superintendence of the celebrated Baumé. It was established at Gravelle, near Charenton, and caused a loss to the shareholders in the speculation of upwards of 400,000 francs, which result closed the concern in 1787. For 10 years after that event, all the sal-ammoniac consumed in France was imported from foreign countries. Since then the two works of MM. Payen and Pluvinet were mounted, and seem to have been tolerably successful. Coal soot was, prior to the introduction of the gasworks, a good deal used in Great Britain for obtaining sal-ammoniac.

In France, bones and other animal matters are distilled in large iron retorts for the manufacture of both animal charcoal and sal-ammoniac.

' The annexed numbers show the produce of a French manufactory of ammonia and its salts, from the distillation of bones and other matters.

' The materials were—

46,754 tons of bones of various kinds.
  30 „   silk waste and old leather.
  11½ „   sulphuric acid.
  80 „   chloride of sodium.
  2¾ „   sulphate of lime.

and the produce was—

2,400 tons of animal charcoal.
  44 „   chloride of ammonium.
  100 „   sulphate of soda.
  4 „   liquor ammonia.
and 25 „   sulphate of ammonia.

—*Muspratt.*

These retorts are iron cylinders, two or three feet in diameter and six feet long. *Figs.* 40 and 41 show the form of the furnace, and the manner in which the cylinders are arranged, the first being a longitudinal, the second a transverse section of it. A, the ashpits under the grates ; B, the fire-places, arched over at top ; C, the vault or bench of fire-bricks, perforated inside with eight flues for distributing the flame; D, a great arch, with a triple voissoir D, d'', d''', under which the retorts are set. The first arch, D, is perforated with twenty vent-holes, the second with four vent-holes, through

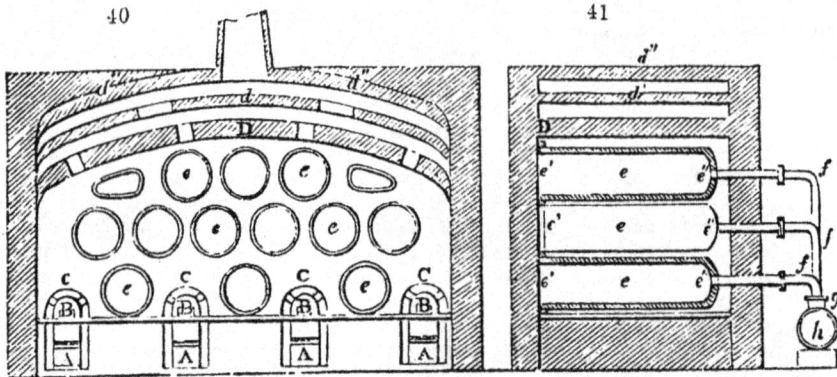

40   41

which the flame passes to the third arch, and thence to the common chimney-stalks. The retorts are shut by the door e' (fig. 41), luted, and made fast with screw-bolts. Their other ends e'', terminate in tubes, f, f, f, which all enter the main pipe h. The condensing pipe proceeds slantingly downwards from the further end of h, and dips into a large sloping iron cylinder immersed in cold water.

The filters used in the large sal-ammoniac works in France are represented in fig. 42. The apparatus consists—1, of a wooden chest, a, lined with lead, and which is

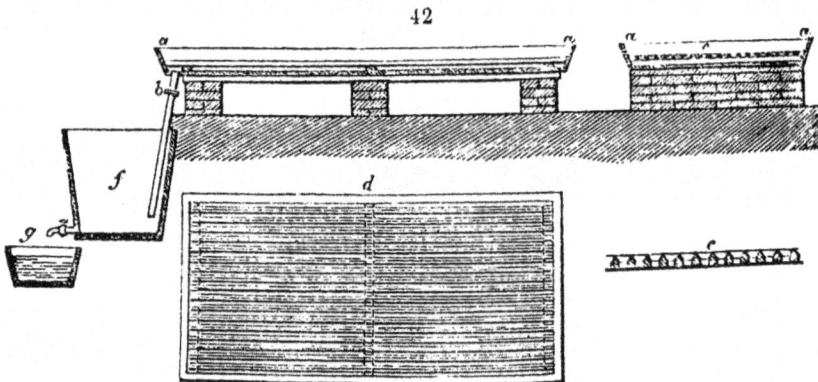

42

turned over at the edges; a socket of lead, b, soldered into the lowest part of the bottom serves to discharge the liquid; 2, of a wooden crib or grating, formed of rounded rods, as shown in the section c, c, and the plan d; this grating is supported one inch at least above the bottom, and set truly horizontal, by a series of wedges; 3, of an open fabric of canvas or strong calico, laid on the grating, and secured over the edges so as to keep it tense. A large wooden reservoir, f, lined with lead, furnished with a cover, is placed under each of the filters; a pump throws back once or twice upon the filters what has already passed through. A common reservoir, g, below the others, may be made to communicate at pleasure with one of them by means of intermediate stopcocks.

The two boilers for evaporating and decomposing are made of lead, about one quarter of an inch thick, set upon a fire-brick vault, to protect them from the direct action of the flame. Through the whole extent of their bottoms above the vault, horizontal cast-iron plates, supported by ledges and brick compartments, compel the flame and burned air, as they issue from the arch, to take a sinuous course before they pass up the chimney. This floor of cast-iron is intended to support the bottom of the boiler, and to diffuse the heat more equably. The leaden boilers are surrounded with brickwork, and supported at their edges with a wooden frame. They may be emptied at pleasure into lower receivers, called crystallisers, by means of leaden syphons and long-necked funnels.

The crystallisers are wooden chests lined with lead, 15 inches deep, 3 or 4 feet broad, and from 6 to 8 feet long, and may be inclined to one side at pleasure. A round cistern receives the drainings of the mother-waters. The pump is made of lead hardened with antimony and tin.

The subliming furnace is shown in *figs*. 43 and 44, by a transverse and longitudinal section; *a* is the ashpit; *b*, the grate and fireplace; *c*, the arch above them. This arch, destined to protect the bottles from the direct action of the fire, is perforated with vent-holes, to give a passage to the products of combustion between the subliming vessels; *d, d*, are bars of iron, upon which the bottom of the bottles rests; *e*, stoneware bottles, protected by a coating of loam from the flame.

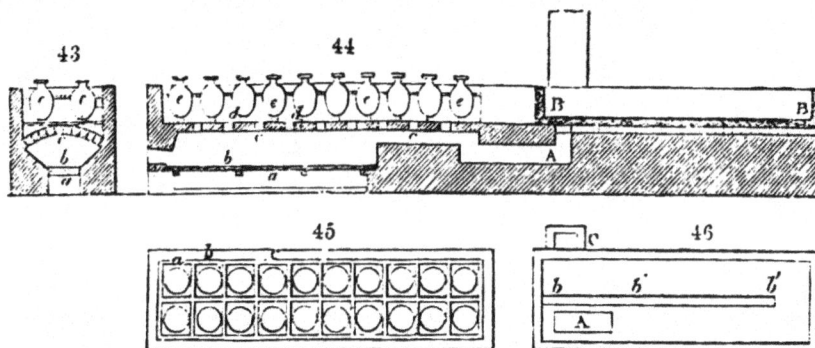

Fig. 45 shows the cast-iron plates, *a, b, c*, which, placed above the vaults, receive each two bottles in a double circular opening.

At the extremity of the above furnace, a second one, called the drier, receives the products of the combustion of the first at ʌ, under horizontal cast-iron plates, and upon which the bottom of a rather shallow boiler, ʙ, rests. After passing twice under these plates, round a longitudinal brick partition, *b, b′, b″*, the products of combustion enter the smoke chimney, c. See plan, *fig*. 46.

The boiler set over this furnace should have no soldered joints. It may be 3½ feet broad, 9 or 10 feet long, and 1 foot deep. The concrete sal-ammoniac may be crushed under a pair of edge millstones, when it is to be sold in powder.

Bones, blood, flesh, horns, hoofs, woollen rags, silk, hair, scrapings of hides and leather, &c., may be distilled for procuring ammonia. When bones are used, the residuum in the retort is bone-black. The charcoal from the other substances will serve for the manufacture of Prussian blue. The bones should undergo a degree of calcination beyond what the ammoniacal process requires, in order to convert them into the best bone-black; but the other animal matters should not be calcined up to that point, otherwise they are of little use in the Prussian blue works. If the bones be calcined, however, so highly as to become glazed, their decolorising power on syrups is nearly destroyed. The other substances should not be charred beyond a red-brown heat.

The condensed vapours from the cylinder-retorts afford a compound liquor holding carbonate of ammonia in solution, mixed with a large quantity of empyreumatic oil, which floats at top. Lest incrustations of salt should at any time tend to obstruct the tubes, a pipe should be inserted within them, and connected with a steam-boiler, so as to blow steam through them occasionally.

The whole liquors mixed have usually a density of 8° or 9° Baumé (1·060). The simplest process for converting their carbonate of ammonia into the chloride of ammonium is to saturate them with hydrochloric acid, to evaporate the solution in a leaden boiler till a pellicle appears, to run it off into crystallisers, and to drain the crystals. Another process is, to decompose the carbonate of ammonia, by passing its crude liquor through a layer of sulphate of lime, 3 or 4 inches thick, spread upon the filters, *fig*. 42. The liquor may be laid on with a pump; it should never stand higher than 1 or 2 inches above the surface of the bruised gypsum, and it should be closely covered with boards, to prevent the dissipation of the volatile alkali in the air. When the liquor has passed through the first filter, it must be pumped up on to the second; or the filters being placed in a terrace-form, the liquor from the first may flow down upon the second, and thus in succession. The last filter should be formed of nearly fresh gypsum, so as to insure the thorough conversion of the carbonate into sulphate. The resulting layers of carbonate of lime should be washed with a little water, to extract the sulphate of ammonia interposed among its particles. The ammoniacal liquor thus obtained must be completely saturated, by adding the requisite quantity of sulphuric acid; even a slight excess of acid can do no harm. It is then to be evaporated, and the oil must be skimmed off in the course of the concentration.

When the liquid sulphate has acquired the density of about 1·160, sea-salt should be added, with constant stirring, till the whole quantity equivalent to the double decomposition is introduced into the lead boiler.

The fluid part must now be drawn off by a syphon into a somewhat deep reservoir, where the impurities are allowed to subside; it is then evaporated by boiling till the sulphate of soda falls down in granular crystals, as the result of the mutual reaction of the sulphate of ammonia and chloride of sodium; while the more soluble chloride of ammonium remains in the liquor. During this precipitation, the whole must be occasionally agitated with wooden paddles; the precipitate being in the intervals removed to the cooler portion of the pan, in order to be taken out by copper rakes and shovels, and thrown into draining-hoppers, placed near the edges of the pan. The drained sulphate of soda must be afterwards washed with cold water, to extract all the adhering sal-ammoniac.

The liquor thus freed from the greater part of the sulphate, when sufficiently concentrated, is to be drawn off by a lead syphon into the crystallisers, where, at the end of 20 or 30 hours, it affords an abundant crop of crystals of sal-ammoniac. The mother-water may then be run off, the crystallisers set aslope to drain the salt, and the salt itself must be washed, first by a weak solution of sal-ammoniac, and lastly with water. It must be next desiccated, by the apparatus *fig.* 46, into a perfectly dry powder, then put into the subliming stoneware balloons, by means of a funnel, and well rammed down. The mouth of the bottle is to be closed with a plate or inverted pot of any kind. The fire must be nicely regulated, so as to effect the sublimation of the pure salt from the under part of the bottle, with due regularity, into a white cake in the upper part. The neck of the bottle should be cleared from time to time with a long steel skewer, to prevent the risk of choking, and consequent bursting; but in spite of every precaution, several of the bottles crack almost in every operation.—*Ure.*

The pots are of variable dimensions, but those most frequently employed are about 18 inches in height in the body, and the cups about 10 or 12 inches, with a breadth of 16 inches at the widest part.

In Scotland a process somewhat similar is pursued, the salt being sublimed in cast-iron pots lined with fire tiles; the condensation being effected in globular heads of green glass, with which each of the iron pots is capped.

Manufacture of Sal-Ammoniac from Gas-Liquor.—By far the largest quantity of the ammoniacal salts now met with in commerce is prepared from 'gas-liquor,' the quantity of which annually produced in the metropolis alone is quite extraordinary— *one* of the London gas-works producing in one year 224,800 gallons of gas-liquor, by the distillation of 51,100 tons of coal; and the total consumption of coal in London for gas-making is estimated at about 840,000 tons.

The principle of the conversion of the nitrogen of coal into ammonia by destructive distillation, as in the manufacture of coal gas, will be found described in connection with the processes of gas manufacture and the products produced by the destructive distillation of coal.

In the purification of the coal gas, the bodies soluble in water are all contained in the 'gas-liquor' (see COAL GAS), together with a certain quantity of tarry matter. The ammonia is chiefly present in the form of carbonate, together with certain quantities of chloride, sulphide, cyanide, and sulphocyanide of ammonium, as well as the salts of the compound ammonias.

For the purpose of preparing the chloride, if hydrochloric acid be not too costly, the liquor is saturated with hydrochloric acid—the solution evaporated to cause the salt to crystallise, and then, finally, the crude sal-ammoniac is purified by sublimation.

Before treatment with the acid, the liquor is frequently distilled.

This is generally effected in a wrought-iron boiler, the liquors passing into a modification of the Coffey's still, by which the solution of ammonia is obtained freer from tar and more concentrated.

The Saturation of the Ammoniacal Liquor with the acid is generally effected by allowing the acid to flow, from a large leaden vessel in which it is held, into an underground tank (*fig.* 47) containing the liquor, which is furnished with an exit tube, passing into a chimney, to carry off the sulphuretted hydrogen and other offensive gases which are disengaged.

Or, in other works, the gas-liquor is put into large tuns, and the acid lifted in gutta-percha carboys by cranes, thrown into the liquor and stirred with it by means of an agitator; the offensive gases being in this case made to traverse the fire of the steam-engine.

Sometimes the vapours produced in the distillation of the crude gas-liquor are passed in at the lower extremity of a column filled with coke, down which the acid trickles,

The *Evaporation of the crude Saline Solution* is generally performed in square or rectangular cast-iron vats, capable of holding from 800 to 1,500 gallons. They are

47

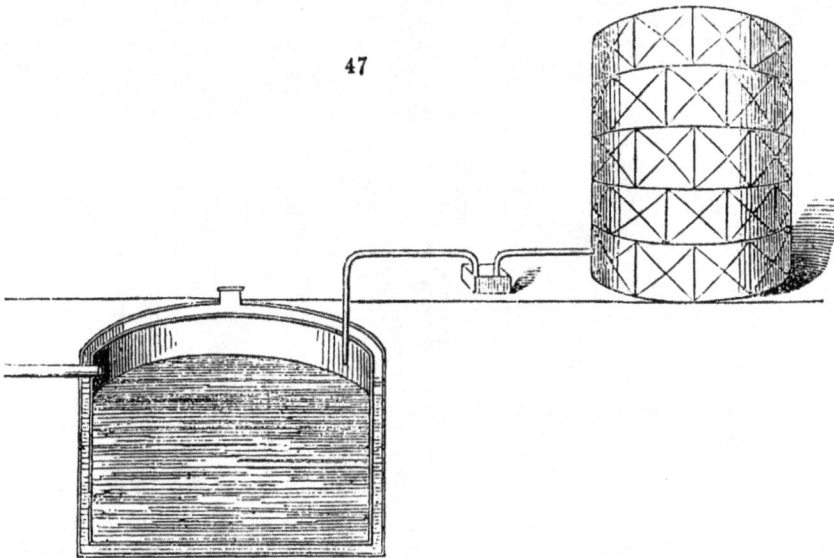

encased in brickwork, the heat being applied by a fire, the flue of which takes a sinuous course beneath the lining of brickwork on which the pan rests, as shown in *fig.* 48.

When the liquor is evaporated to a specific gravity of 1·25, it is transferred to the crystallising pans; but during the process of concentration a considerable quantity of

48

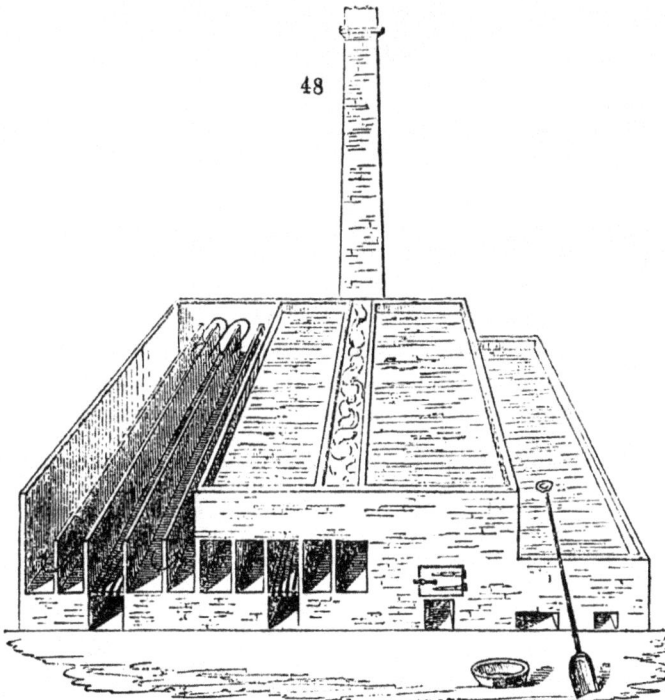

tar separates on the surface, which must be removed, from time to time, by skimming, since it seriously impedes evaporation.

The *crystallisation*, which takes place on cooling, is performed in circular tubs, from 7 to 8 feet wide, and 2 to 3 deep, which are generally embedded entirely or partially in the ground. To prevent the formation of large crystals, which would be inconvenient in the subsequent process of sublimation, the liquor is agitated from time to time. The crude mass obtained, which is contaminated with tarry matter, free acid, and water, is next dried, by gently heating it on a cast-iron plate under a dome. The greyish-white mass remaining is now ready to be transferred to the sublimers.

The method of *sublimation* generally adopted in this country consists in beating down into the metal pots, shown in *fig.* 49, the charge of dry coarsely crystallised sal-

49

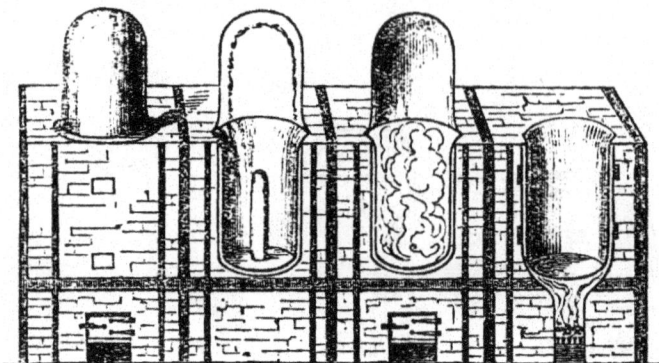

ammoniac. These pots are heated from below and by flues round the sides. The body of the subliming vessel is of cast-iron, and the lid usually of lead, or, less frequently, iron. There is a small hole at the top, to permit the escape of steam, sometimes loosely closed by a plug of sal-ammoniac, which is removed from time to time to observe the progress of the sublimation; great attention is requisite in the management of the heat, for if it be applied too rapidly a large quantity of sal-ammoniac is carried off with the steam, or even the whole apparatus may be blown up; whilst, if the temperature be too low, the cake of sal-ammoniac is apt to be soft and yellow.

The sublimation is never continued until the whole of the salt has been volatilised, since the heat required would decompose the carbonaceous impurities, and they, emitting volatile oily hydrocarbons, diminish the purity of the product. In consequence of this incomplete sublimation, a conical mass (shown in the *fig.* 49) is left behind, called the 'yolk.' After cooling, the dome of the pot is taken off and the attached cake carefully removed. This cake, which is from 3 to 5 inches thick, is nearly pure, only requiring a little scraping, where it was in contact with the dome, to fit it for the market.

Modifications of the Process.—If, as is often the case, sulphuric acid is cheaper or more accessible than hydrochloric, the gas liquor is neutralised with sulphuric acid, and then the sulphate of ammonia thus obtained is sublimed with common salt (chloride of sodium), and thus converted into sal-ammoniac.

$$NH^4O. SO^3 + NaCl = NH^4 Cl + NaO. SO^3.$$

$$(NH^4)2SO^4 + NaCl = 2NH^4Cl + Na^2SO^4.$$

Mr. Croll has taken out a patent for converting crude ammonia into the chloride, by passing the vapours evolved in the first distillation through the crude chloride of manganese, obtained, as a by-product in the preparation of chlorine, for the manufacture of chloride of lime: crude chloride of iron may be used in the same way.

Mr. Laming patented in July, 1843, the substitution of a solution of chloride of calcium for treating the crude gas-liquor, instead of the mineral acids. Mr. Hills, August, 1846, proposed chloride of magnesium for use in the same way; and several other patents have been taken out by both these gentlemen, for the use of various salts in this way.

Manufacture of Sal-Ammoniac from Guano.—Mr. Young took out a patent, November 11th, 1841, in which he describes his method of obtaining ammonia and its salts from guano. He fills a retort, placed vertically, with a mixture of two parts by weight of guano, and one part by weight of hydrate of lime. These substances are thoroughly mixed by giving a reciprocating motion to the agitator placed in the retort; a moderate degree of heat is then applied, which is gradually increased until the bottom of the retort becomes red-hot. The ammoniacal gas thus given off is absorbed by water in a condenser, whilst other gases, which are given off at the same time, being insoluble in water, pass off. Solutions of carbonate, bicarbonate, or sesquicarbonate of ammonia are produced, by filling the condenser with a solution of ammonia, and passing carbonic acid through it. A solution of chloride of ammonium or sulphate of ammonia is obtained by filling the condenser with diluted hydrochloric or sulphuric acid, and passing the ammonia through it as it issues from the retort.

Dr. Wilton Turner obtained a patent, March 11th, 1844, for obtaining salts of ammonia from guano. The following is his method of obtaining chloride of ammonium in conjunction with cyanogen compounds:—The guano is subjected to destructive distillation in close vessels, at a low red heat during the greater part of the operation; but this temperature is increased towards the end. The products of distillation are collected in a series of Woolfe's bottles, by means of which the gases evolved during the operation may be made to pass two or three times through water, before escaping into the air. These products consist of carbonate of ammonia, hydrocyanic acid, and carburetted hydrogen, the first two of which are rapidly absorbed by the water, with the formation of a strong solution of cyanide of ammonium and carbonate of ammonia. After the ammoniacal solution has been removed from the Woolfe's apparatus, a solution of protochloride of iron is added to it, in such quantities as will yield sufficient iron to convert the latter into Prussian blue, which is formed on the addition of hydrochloric acid in sufficient quantity to neutralise the free ammonia; the precipitate thus formed is now allowed to subside, and is carefully separated from the solution, and by being boiled with a solution of potash or soda, will yield the alkaline ferrocyanide, which is obtained by crystallising in the usual way. The solution (after the removal of the precipitate) should be freed from any excess of iron it may contain, by the careful addition of a fresh portion of the ammoniacal liquor, by which means the oxide of iron will be precipitated, and a neutral solution of ammonia obtained. When the precipitated oxide and cyanide of iron have subsided, the solution of chloride of ammonium is drawn off by a syphon, and the sal-ammoniac obtained from it by the usual processes; the oxide of iron is added to the ammoniacal solution next operated upon.

If sulphate of iron and sulphuric acid are used, sulphate of ammonia is the ammoniacal salt produced, the chemical changes and operations being similar to the above.

Since the greater part of the nitrogen present in guano exists in the state of ammoniacal salts, which are decomposed at a red heat, nearly the whole of the ammonia which it is capable of yielding is obtained by this method; still there cannot be a doubt that the conversion of the urea, uric acid, and other nitrogenised organic bodies into ammonia, is greatly facilitated by mixing the guano with lime before heating it, as in Mr. Young's process.

Manufacture of Sal-Ammoniac from Urine.—The urea in the urine of man and other animals is extremely liable to undergo a fermentative decomposition in the presence of the putrefiable nitrogenous matters always present in this excrement, by which it is converted into carbonate of ammonia.

By treating stale urine with hydrochloric acid, sal-ammoniac separates on evaporation.

Properties.—Chloride of ammonium (or sal-ammoniac) usually occurs in commerce, in fibrous masses of the form of large hemispherical cakes, with a round hole in the centre, having, in fact, the shape of the domes in which it has been sublimed. By slowly evaporating its aqueous solution, the salt may occasionally be obtained in cakes nearly an inch in height; but it generally forms feathery crystals, which are composed of rows of minute octahedra, attached by their extremities. Its specific gravity is 1·45, and by heating it sublimes without undergoing fusion. It has a sharp and acrid taste, and one part dissolves in 2·72 parts of water at 65° F., or in an equal weight of water at 212° F.

It is recognised by its being completely volatile on heating, giving a white curdy precipitate of chloride of silver on the addition of nitrate of silver to its aqueous solution, and by the copious evolution of ammonia on mixing it with lime, as well as the production of the yellow precipitate of the double chloride of ammonium and platinum $NH^4Cl, PtCl^2$ (**$2NH^4Cl. PtCl^4$**) on the addition of bichloride of platinum.

Impurities.—In the manufacture of chloride of ammonium, if the purification of the liquor be not effected before crystallising the salt, some traces of protochloride of iron are generally present, and frequently a considerable proportion. Even when the salt is sublimed, the chloride of iron is volatilised together with the chloride of ammonium, and appears to exist in the salt in the form of a double compound (probably of $FeCl, NH^4Cl$, analogous to the compound which chloride of ammonium forms with zinc and tin); and this not only in the brown seams of the cake, but likewise in the colourless portion. This accounts for the observation so often made in the laboratory, that a solution of sal-ammoniac, which, when recently prepared, was perfectly transparent and colourless, becomes gradually red from the peroxidation of the iron and its precipitation in the form of sesquioxide.

It is in consequence of the existence of the iron in the state of this double salt, that Wurtz found that chloride of ammonium containing iron in this form gave no indications of its presence by the usual reagents until after the addition of nitric acid; and it is curious that there likewise exists a red compound of this class in which the iron exists in the state of perchloride similarly marked, in fact as NH^4Cl, Fe^2Cl^3.

A very simple method of removing the iron, suggested by Mr. Brewer, consists in passing a few bubbles of chlorine gas through the hot concentrated solution of the salt, by which the protochloride of iron is converted into the perchloride.

$$2Fe\ Cl^6\quad +\quad Cl\quad =\quad Fe^2Cl^3.$$
$$\mathbf{2FeCl^2\ +\ Cl^2\ =\ Fe^2Cl^6.}$$

The free ammonia always present in the solution decomposes this perchloride with precipitation of sesquioxide, and formation of an additional quantity of sal-ammoniac.

$$Fe^2Cl^3\ +\ 3NH^4O\quad =\ Fe^2\ O^3\ +\ 3NH^4\ Cl.$$
$$\mathbf{Fe^2Cl^6\ +\ 3(NH^4)^2O\ =\ Fe^2\ O^3\ +\ 6NH^4Cl.}$$

The sesquioxide of iron, which is of course present in the form of a brown hydrate, is filtered off or separated by decantation, and a perfectly pure solution is obtained.

The only precaution necessary is to avoid passing more chlorine than is requisite to peroxidise the iron, since the ammonia salt itself will be decomposed with evolution of nitrogen, and the dangerously explosive body, chloride of nitrogen, may result from the union of the liberated nitrogen with chlorine.

Uses.—The most important use of sal-ammoniac in the arts is in joining iron and other metals, in tinning, &c. It is also extensively used in the manufacture of ammonia-alum, which is now largely employed in the manufacture of mordants instead of potash-alum. A considerable quantity is also consumed in pharmacy.

Sal-ammoniac is one of those salts which possesses, in a high degree, the property of producing cold whilst dissolving in water; it is, therefore, a common constituent of frigorific mixtures. See FREEZING MIXTURES.

AMMONIUM, SULPHIDES OF. When sulphuretted hydrogen gas is passed into a solution of ammonia in excess, it is converted into the double sulphide of ammonium and hydrogen—or, as it is frequently called, the hydrosulphate of sulphide of ammonium.—NH^4S, HS (**NH⁴, HS**).

This solution is extensively employed as a re-agent in the chemical laboratory, for the separation of those metals the sulphides of which are soluble in acids—viz. nickel, cobalt, manganese, zinc, and iron, which are precipitated by this reagent in alkaline solutions.

By exposure to the air, the hydrosulphuric acid which it contains is decomposed, the hydrogen being oxidised and converted into water, whilst the liberated sulphur is dissolved by the sulphide of ammonium, forming the bisulphide, or even higher sulphide.

This solution of the polysulphide of ammonium is a valuable reagent for dissolving the sulphides of certain metals, such as tin, antimony, and arsenic, the sulphides of which play the part of acids and form salts with the sulphide of ammonium.

By this deportment with sulphide of ammonium, these metals are separated, both on the small scale in the laboratory, and also on the large scale, from the sulphides of those metals—such as lead, copper, mercury, &c.—the sulphides of which are insoluble in sulphide of ammonium.

The higher sulphides, viz. the tersulphide and the pentasulphide, are bodies of purely scientific interest. They are obtained by distilling the corresponding sulphides of potassium with sal-ammoniac.

All the sulphides of ammonium are soluble in water without decomposition.

Ammonia combines with all the inorganic and organic acids, but for an account of these compound bodies we must refer to Watts's 'Dictionary of Chemistry,' as they have but few applications in the arts and manufactures.

AMORPHOUS. (*Privative* à, destitute of; μορφή, shape: *without shape*). Said of mineral and other substances which occur in forms not easy to be defined. This term may be regarded as the opposite of crystalline. Some elements exist in both the crystalline and the amorphous states, as carbon, which is amorphous in charcoal, but crystalline in the diamond.

The peculiarities which give rise to these conditions—evidently depending upon molecular forces which have not yet been defined—present one of the most fertile fields for study in the range of modern science.

AMYGDALIN. $C^{40}\ H^{27}\ NO^{22}+6\ HO$. (**C²⁰ H²⁷ NO¹¹ + 3H² O.**) A peculiar substance, existing ready-formed in bitter almonds, the leaves of the cherry-laurel, the kernels of the plum, cherry, peach, and the leaves and bark of *Prunus padus*, and in the young sprouts of the *P. domestica*. It is also found in the sprouts of several species of *Sorbus*, such as *S. aucuparia*, *S. torminalis*, and others of the same order. To prepare it, the bitter almonds are subjected to strong pressure between hot plates of metal. This has the effect of removing the bland oil known in commerce as almond-oil. The residue, when powdered, forms almond-meal. To obtain amygdalin from the meal, the latter is extracted with boiling alcohol of 90 or 95 per cent. The tincture is to be passed through a cloth and the residue pressed, to obtain the fluid mechanically adherent to it. The liquids will be milky, owing to the presence of some of the oil. On keeping the fluid for a few hours, it may be separated by pouring off, or by means of a funnel, and so obtained clear. The alcohol is now to be removed by distillation, the latter being continued until five-sixths have come over. The fluid in the retort, when cold, is to have the amygdalin precipitated from it by the addition of half its volume of ether. The crystals are to be pressed between folds of filtering paper, and recrystallised from concentrated boiling alcohol. As thus prepared, it forms pearly scales, very soluble in hot alcohol, but sparingly when cold; it is insoluble in ether, but water dissolves it readily and in large quantity. The crystals contain six atoms of water of crystallisation. Most persons engaged in chemical operations have noticed, when using almond-meal for the purpose of luting, that, before being moistened with water, it has little odour, and what it has is of an oily kind; but, after moistening, it soon acquires the powerful and pleasant perfume of bitter-almond oil. This arises from a singular reaction taking place between the amygdalin and the vegetable albumen or emulsin. The latter merely acts as a ferment, and its elements in no way enter into the products formed. The decomposition, in fact, takes place between one atom of amygdalin and four atoms of water; the product being one atom of bitter-almond oil, two atoms of grape-sugar, and one of prussic acid.

In preparing amygdalin, some chemists add water to the residue of the distillation of the tincture, and then yeast, in order to remove the sugar present, by fermentation, previous to precipitating with ether: the process thus becomes much more complex, because it is necessary to filter the fermented liquid, and concentrate it again by evaporation, before precipitating the amygdalin.

The proof that the decomposition which is experienced by the bitter-almond cake, when digested with water, is owing to the presence of the two principles mentioned, rests upon the following considerations. If the marc, or pressed residue of the bitter almond, be treated with boiling water, the emulsin—or vegetable albumen—will become coagulated, and incapable of inducing the decomposition of the amygdalin. It is only the bitter almond which contains amygdalin; the sweet variety is, therefore, incapable of yielding the essence by fermentation. But sweet almonds resemble the bitter in containing emulsin; and it is exceedingly interesting—as illustrating the truth of the explanation given above—that if a little amygdalin be added to an emulsion of sweet almonds, the bitter-almond essence is immediately formed. A temperature of 100° is the most favourable for the digestion.—C. G. W.

AMYLENE. This hydrocarbon, $C^{10} H^{10}$ ($C^5 H^{10}$), is produced by the dehydration of amylic alcohol by sulphuric acid; also by the dry distillation of amyl-sulphate of calcium. It is a colourless thin liquid, with a faint offensive odour. It has been tried as a substitute for chloroform without success.

AMYLUM MANDIOCÆ. Mandioca or Cassava starch. See CASSAVA and MANDIOCA.

ANACARDIUM NUT. Dr. Bottyer, in the 'Bayerisches Industrie- und Gewerbe-Blatt,' states that the juice of the Anacardium nut, *Anacardium Orientale*, contains an oily matter, which, by exposure to the air, assumes a fine black colour, which is quite permanent against the influences of acids or alkalies, chlorine or cyanide of potassium. It is recommended for use as a marking ink; and if the linen be moistened with a little ammonia, the black is very intense and quite permanent.

ANALYSIS. In chemistry, a term which is employed to signify the art of resolving a compound substance into its constituent parts. Every manufacturer should so study this art, in the proper treatises and schools of chemistry, as to enable him properly to understand and regulate his business.—See Watts's 'Dictionary of Chemistry.' See also SPECTRUM ANALYSIS.

ANATASE. An oxide of titanium, of the same composition as Brookite and Rutile. It occurs in Dauphiny with felspar and ilmenite, in Devonshire in chlorite, and in North Wales with Brookite. It is said to be found in the slags from the iron furnaces of Orange County, United States.

ANCHOR. (*Ancre*, Fr.; *Anker*, Ger.) An iron hook, of peculiar construction and of considerable weight and strength, for enabling a ship to lay hold of the ground, and fix itself in a certain situation by means of a rope called the cable. The necessity for securing boats, canoes, or ships in a certain position, has led to the adoption of anchors, of some description, amongst every nation dwelling upon the shores of seas, lakes, or rivers. They were often of the rudest description. We are informed that the Greeks at first used stone anchors, but that they subsequently employed instruments of iron, having one, two, and three teeth, which were not apparently very different from those we now employ. The anchors which are used by many of the races inhabiting the shores of the Indian Ocean are made of the so-called 'iron-wood,' which is so dense that it sinks in sea-water. The anchor is an instrument of the greatest importance to the navigator, since upon its taking and keeping hold depends his safety upon many occasions, especially near a lee shore, where he might be otherwise stranded or shipwrecked. Anchors are generally made of wrought iron, except among nations who cannot work this metal well, and who therefore use copper. The mode in which an anchor operates will be understood from inspection of *fig*. 50, where,

50

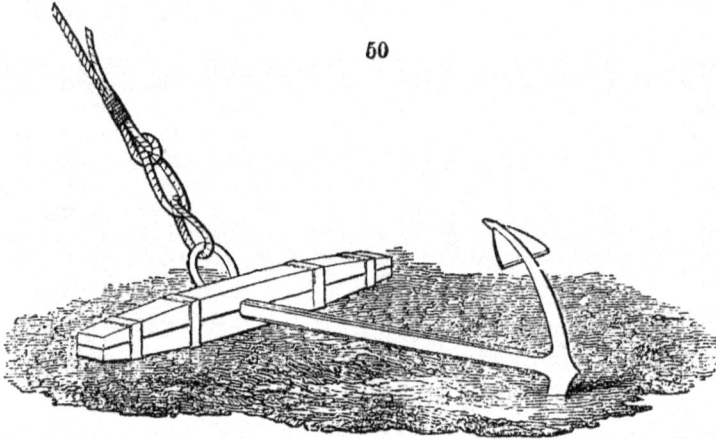

from the direction of the strain, it is obvious that the anchor cannot move without ploughing up the ground in which its hook or fluke is sunk. When this, however, unluckily takes place, from the nature of the ground, from the mode of insertion of the anchor, or from the violence of the winds or currents, it is called *dragging the anchor*. When the hold is good, the cable or the buried arm will sooner break than the ship will drive. Anchors are of different sizes, and have different names, according to the purposes they serve; thus there are *bower, stream*, and *kedge anchors*. Ships of the first class have seven anchors, and smaller vessels, such as brigs and schooners, three.

The metal employed for anchors of wrought iron is known as 'scrap iron,' and for the best anchors, such as Lenox's, they also use good 'Welsh mine iron.'

It is not practical, without occupying more space than can be afforded, to describe in detail the manufacture of an anchor. It does not, indeed, appear desirable that we should do so, since it is so special a form of mechanical industry, that few will consult this volume for the sake of learning to make anchors. The following will therefore suffice. The anchor-smith's forge consists of a hearth of brickwork, raised about 9 inches above the ground, and generally about 7 feet square. In the centre of this is a cavity for containing the fire. A vertical brick wall is built on one side of the hearth, which supports the dome, and a low chimney to carry off the smoke. Behind this wall are placed the bellows, with which the fire is urged; the bellows being so placed that they blow to the centre of the fire. The anvil and the crane by which the heavy masses of metal are moved from and to the fire are adjusted near the hearth. The *Hercules*, a kind of stamping machine, or the steam hammer, need not be described in this place.

To make the anchor, bars of good iron are brought together to be faggoted; the number varying with the size of the anchor. The faggot is kept together by hoops of iron, and the whole is placed upon the properly arranged hearth, and covered up by small coals, which are thrown upon a kind of oven made of cinders. Great care and good management is required to keep this temporary oven sound during the combustion;—a smith strictly attends to this. When all is arranged, the bellows are set to work, and a blast urged on the fire; this is continued for about an hour, when a good welding heat is obtained. The mass is now brought from the fire to the anvil, and the iron welded by the hammers. One portion having been welded, the iron is returned to fire, and the operation is repeated until the whole is welded into one mass.

This will be understood by referring to the annexed figures (*fig*. 51), in which the bars for the shanks, A A, and the arms, B B, are shown, in plan and sections, as bound together, and their shapes after being welded before union; and c c represents the palm.

The different parts of the anchor being made, the arms are united to the end of the shank. This must be done with great care, as the goodness of the anchor depends entirely upon this process being effectively performed. The arms being welded on,

51

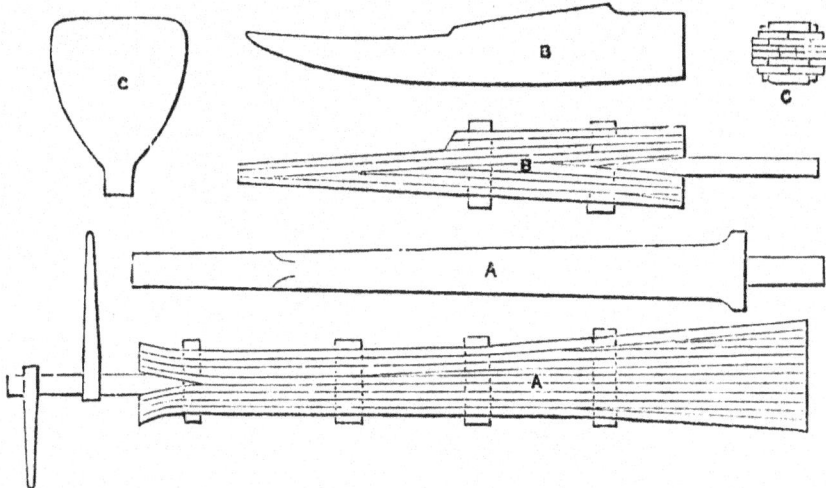

the ring has to be formed and welded. The ring consists of several bars welded together, drawn out into a round rod, passed through a hole in the shank, bent into a circle, and the ends welded together. When all the parts are adjusted, the whole anchor is brought to a red heat, and hammered with lighter hammers than those used for welding, the object being to give a finish and evenness to the surface.

The toughest iron which can be procured should be used in the manufacture of an anchor, upon the strength of which both the security of valuable lives and much property depends.

The manufacture of anchors requires great knowledge of the structure of iron, and skill in the art of working it. The various parts of an anchor are thus named :— In *fig.* 52, A is the *shank*; B, the *arm* or *fluke*; C, the *palm*; D, the *blade*; E, the *square*; F, the *nut*; G, the *ring*; H, the *crown*,—the proportional weights of the several parts being as follows :—

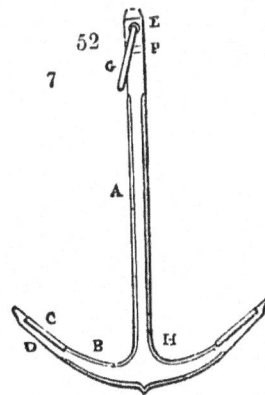

The shank	.	.	.	$\frac{5}{10}$ths of the whole.
Each arm	.	.	.	$\frac{2}{10}$ths	,,
Two palms	.	.	.	$\frac{1}{10}$th	,,
Stock	.	.	.	$\frac{1}{5}$th	,,
Shackle	.	.	.	$\frac{1}{15}$th	,,

The drawings on next page (*fig.* 53) show an anchor on the old plan and the dissected parts of which it is composed; and (*fig.* 54), the patent anchor as invented by Mr. Perring, with its several parts dissected as before.

Perring's improved anchor was a very ingenious one. The bars and half the breadth of the anchor are first welded separately, and then placed side by side, when the upper half is worked into one mass, while the lower part is left disunited, but it has carrier iron bars, or *porters*, as the prolongation rods (3, 3, *fig.* 53), are commonly called, welded to the extremity of each portion. The lower part is now heated and placed in the clamping machine, which is merely an iron plate firmly bolted to a mass of timber, and bearing upon its surface four iron pins. One end of the crown is placed between the first of these pins, and passed under an iron strap; the other end is brought between the other pins, and is bent by the leverage power of the elongated rods or porters.

Thus a part of the arm being formed out of the crown gives much greater security, when a true union of fibres is effected, than when the junction was made merely by a short scarf.

The angular opening upon the side opposite is filled with the *chock*, formed of short iron bars placed upright. When this has been firmly welded, the truss-piece is brought over it. This piece is made of plates similar to the above, except that their edges are here horizontal. The truss-piece is half the breadth of the arm; so that, when united to the crown, it constitutes, with the other parts, the total breadth of the arms at those places.

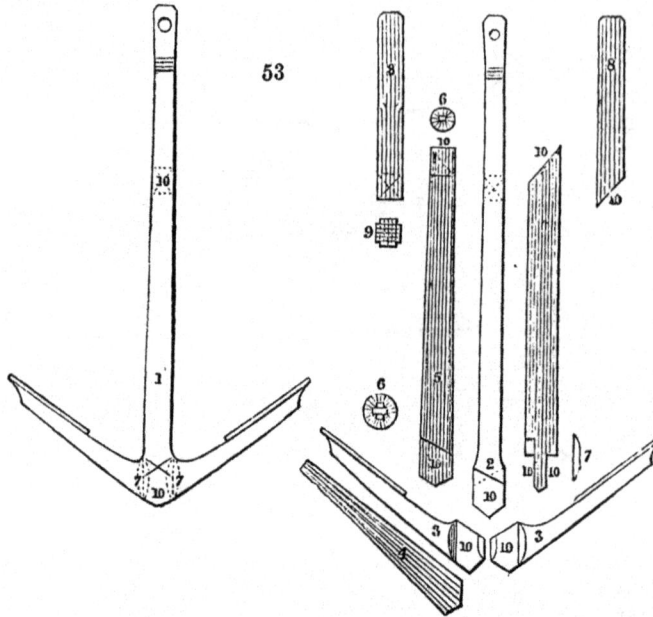

The shank is now shut upon the crown; the square is formed, and the nuts welded to it; the hole is punched out for the ring, and the shank is then fashioned.

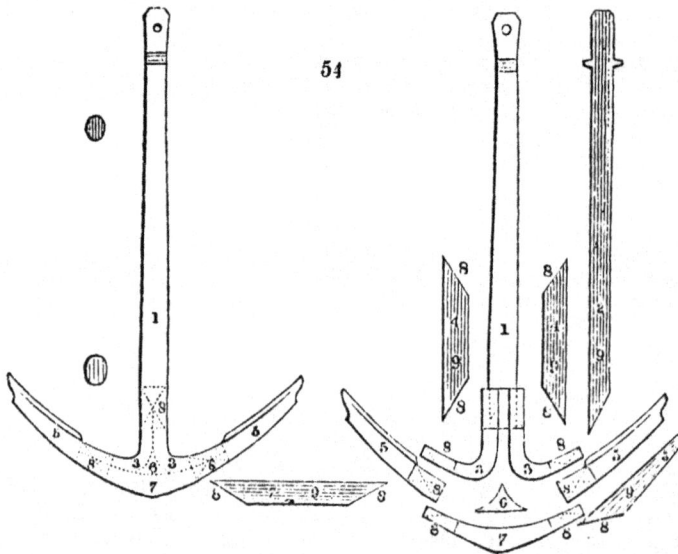

The blade is made much in the way above described. In making the palm, an iron rod is first bent into the approximate form, notching it so that it may more readily take the desired shape. To one end a *porter* rod is fastened, by which the palm is carried and turned round in the fire during the progress of the fabrication. Iron plates are next laid side by side upon the rod, and the joint at the middle is broken by another plate laid over it. When the mass is worked, its under side is filled up by similar plates, and the whole is completely welded; pieces being added to the sides, if necessary, to form the angles of the palm. The blade is then shut on to the palm, after which the part of the arm attached to the blade is united to that which constitutes the crown. The smith-work of the anchor is now finished.

The junction—or shutting-on, as the workmen call it—of the several members of an anchor is effected by an instrument called a Hercules, which is merely a mass of iron raised to a certain height, between parallel uprights, as in the pile-engine or vertical ram, and let fall upon the metal previously brought to a welding heat.

The end of the shank is squared to receive and hold the stock steadily and keep it from turning. To prevent it shifting along, there are two knobs or tenon-like projections. The point of the angle H, between the arms and the shank, is sometimes called the *throat*. The arm, B C, generally makes an angle of 56° with the shank A; it is either round or polygonal, and about half the length of the shank.

The *stock* of the anchor (*fig.* 50) is made of oak. It consists of two beams which embrace the *square*, and are firmly united by iron bolts and hoops, as shown in the figure. The stock is usually somewhat longer than the shank, has in the middle a thickness about one-twelfth of its length, but tapers at its under-side to nearly one-half this thickness at the extremities.

An ingenious form of anchor was made the subject of a patent, by Lieutenant Rodger, of the Royal Navy, in 1828, and was afterwards modified by him in a second patent, obtained in August, 1829. The whole of the parts of the anchor are to be bound together by means of iron bands or hoops, in place of bolts or pins.

Fig. 55 is a side view of a complete anchor, formed upon his improved construction, and *fig.* 56 a plan of the same; *fig.* 57, an end view of the crown and flukes, or arms; *fig.* 56 represents the two principal iron plates, *a a*, of which the shank is constructed, but so as to form parts of the stump-arms to which the flukes are to be connected.

The crown-piece is to be welded to the stump-piece, *c c, fig.* 58, as well as to the end, *l*, of the centre-piece, *h h*, and the scarfs, *m m*, are to be cut to receive the arms or flukes. Previously, however, to uniting the arms or flukes to the stump-arms, the crown and throat of the anchor are to be strengthened by the application of the crown slabs, *n, fig.* 58, which are to be welded upon each side of the crown, overlapping the end of the pillar, *h*, and the throat or knees of the stump-arms and the crown-piece. The stump-arms are then to be strengthened in a similar manner, by the thin flat pieces, *p p*, which are to be welded upon each side. The palms are united to the flukes in the usual way, and the flukes are also united to the stump-arms by means of the long scarfs, *m m*. When the shank of the anchor has been thus formed, and united with the flukes, the anchor-smith's work may be said to be complete.

Another of the improvements in the construction of anchors, claimed under this patent, consists in a new method of affixing the stock upon the shank of the anchor, which is effected in the following manner: in *fig.* 55 the stock is shown affixed to the anchor; in *fig.* 58 it is shown detached. It may be made either of one or two pieces of timber, as shall be found most convenient. It is, however, to be observed that the stock is to be completed before fitting on to the shank. After the stock is shaped, a hole is to be made through the middle of it, to fit that part of the shank to which it is to be affixed. Two stock plates are then to be let in, one on each side of the stock, and made fast by counter-sunk nails and straps, or hoops; other straps or hoops of iron are also to be placed round the stock, as usual.

In place of nuts, formed upon the shank of the anchor, it is proposed to secure the stock by means of a hoop and a key, shown above and below J, in *fig.* 56. By this contrivance the stock is prevented from going nearer to the crown of the anchor than it ought to do, and the key prevents it from sliding towards the shackle.

Since fitting the stock to the shank of an anchor by this method prevents the use of a ring, as in the ordinary manner, the patentee says that he in all cases substitutes a shackle for the ring, and which is all that is required for a chain cable; but when a hempen cable is to be used, he connects a ring to the usual shackle, by means of a joining shackle, as in *figs.* 55 and 56. The stock is shown in *fig.* 59.

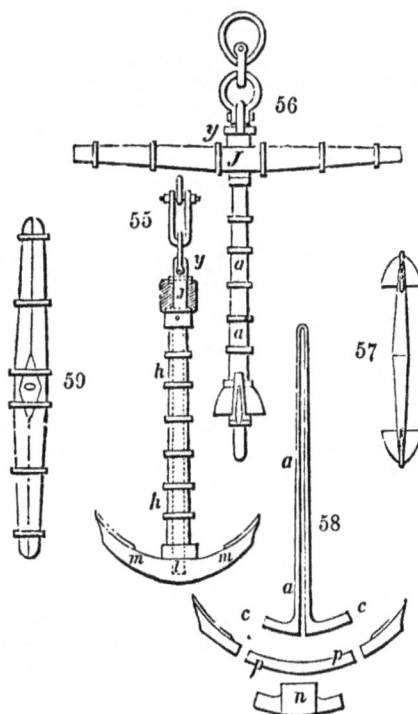

Mr. Rodger proposes, under another patent, dated July, 1833, to alter the size and form of the palms; having found from experience that anchors with small palms will not only hold better than with large ones, but that the arms of the anchor, even without any palms, have been found to take more secure hold of the ground than anchors of the old construction of similar weight and length. He has accordingly fixed upon one-fifth of the length of the arm, as a suitable proportion for the length or depth of the palm. He makes the palms, also, broader than they are long or deep.

Previously to the introduction of Lieutenant Rodger's small-palmed anchor, ships were supplied with heavy, cumbersome contrivances with long shanks and broad palms extending half-way up the flukes. So badly were they proportioned, that it was no uncommon thing for them to break in falling on the bottom, particularly if the ground was rocky. But, if once firmly imbedded in stiff holding ground, there was considerable difficulty in breaking them out. The introduction of the small palm, therefore, forms an important era in the history of anchors.

The next important introduction was Porter's anchor, with moveable flukes or arms. One grand object sought to be attained here, was the prevention of fouling by the cable. It was considered, also, that as great injury was frequently occasioned by a ship grounding on her anchor, the closed upper arm would remedy the evil. It was found, however, that the anchor would not take the ground properly as at first constructed, and hence the 'shark's fin' upon the outside of each fluke.

Rodger's invention was for some time viewed with distrust; but, from time to time, improvements were introduced, until the patent, which gained the Exhibition prize, was brought out. On this the jurors reported as follows :—

'Many remarkable improvements have been recently made by Lieutenant Rodger, R.N., insuring a better distribution of the metal in the direction of the greatest strains. The palm of the anchor, instead of being flat, presents two inclined planes, calculated for cutting the sand or mud instead of resisting perpendicularly; and the consequence is, that these new anchors hold much better in the ground. The committee of Lloyd's—so competent to judge of every contrivance likely to preserve ships—have resolved to allow for the anchors of the ships they insure a sixth less weight if made according to the plan of Lieutenant Rodger.'

The original Porter's anchor has also undergone considerable modification; and, under the name of 'Trotman's anchor,' has now a conspicuous place.

Another invention is that of Mitcheson's, which, in form and proportions, strongly resembles Rodger's; but the palm is that adopted in Trotman's, or Porter's anchor. It is a trifle longer in the shank than Rodger's, and has a peculiar stock, which—although original in its form—lacks originality in its design, since Rodger had previously introduced a plan for an iron stock to obviate the weakness caused by making a hole for the stock to pass through. Mr. Lenox was the inventor of an anchor which differed somewhat from the Admiralty's anchor—a modification of Rodger's—in being shorter in the shank and thicker in the flukes, the palms being spade-shaped. Mr. J. Aylen, the Master-Attendant of Sheerness Dockyard, modified the Admiralty's anchor. Instead of the inner part of the fluke, from the crown to the pea, being rounded, as in the Admiralty plan, or squared as in Rodger's and Mitcheson's, it is hollowed. An American anchor, known as Isaac's, has a flat bar of iron from palm to palm, passing the shank elliptically on both sides; and from the end of the stock to the centre of the shank two other bars are fixed to prevent its fouling.

With the anchors thus briefly described the Admiralty ordered trials to be made at Woolwich, and at the Nore. The results of those trials—the particulars of which need not be given here—were, that Mitcheson's, Trotman's, Lenox's, and Rodger's were selected as the best.

A competent authority, writing in the *United Service Gazette*, says :—' The general opinion deduced from the series of experiments is, that although Mitcheson's has been so successful, the stock is not at present seaworthy. Trotman's has come out of the trial very successfully, but the construction is too complicated to render it a good working anchor. When once in the ground, its holding properties are very superior; in fact, a glance at its grasp will show that it has the capabilities of an anchor of another construction one-fifth larger. There are, however, drawbacks not easily to be overcome. Its taking the ground is more precarious than with other anchors; and if a ship should part her cable, it would scarcely be possible to sweep the anchor. It is also an awkward anchor to fish and to stow. Yet there are other merits which render it, upon the whole, a most valuable invention, and no ship should go to sea without one. *Of Lenox's it is sufficient to say that it has been found equal to, and that it has gained an advantage over, Rodger's;* but so strong is the professional feeling in favour of the latter, that it will ever remain a favourite. Our recommendation would be thus :—Lenox and Rodger for bower anchors, Mitcheson for a sheet, and Trotman for a spare anchor.'

The following Table gives at one view the results of the experiments made by the Admiralty upon breaking the trial-anchors, and the time occupied upon each experiment:—

Anchors	Weight			Proof-strain	First Crack	Broke	Time in Breaking
	Cwts.	qrs.	lbs.	Tons	Tons	Tons	Minutes
Lieut. Rodger's . .	19	0	8	$19\frac{7}{8}$	45	$73\frac{1}{4}$	21
Brown and Lenox's . .	20	3	14	$21\frac{1}{2}$	$44\frac{1}{2}$	47	7
Isaac's	21	0	14	$21\frac{3}{4}$	58	63	10
Trotman's . . .	21	1	10	$21\frac{7}{8}$	51	$53\frac{1}{2}$	18
Honiball's . . .	20	3	7	$21\frac{1}{4}$	54	$75\frac{1}{2}$	42
Admiralty's . . .	20	2	6	$21\frac{1}{4}$	40	$56\frac{1}{2}$	26
Aylen's	21	1	0	$21\frac{3}{4}$	44	$47\frac{1}{2}$	6

The history of the introduction of Lenox's anchors to the British navy was as follows:

After sundry attempts to induce the Admiralty to give up entirely the use of hempen cable anchors, in consequence of their breaking when applied to chain cables, Mr. Lenox, in 1832, was permitted to alter some of the old anchors to such proportions and shape as would enable them to stand a proof-strain upon the machine in Woolwich Dockyard. It was found, as previously apprehended and asserted, that from the inequality of material in the old anchors, not above one in three was successfully altered, and Mr. Lenox was ordered to supply new anchors, which were proved, and then approved of. This state of things continued until 1838, when Mr. Lenox was requested to reconsider and complete the shape and proportions of anchors for the navy, with a view to a contract being given out for the supply of such anchors to the service. Then was constructed the shape called the 'Admiralty,' or 'Sir William Parker's Anchor' (Sir William being then Store Lord). Mr. Lenox suggested to Sir William the doing away with every sharp edge and line in an anchor, and adopting the smooth long-oval (in the section) for the general shape of shank and arm. This was approved of by Sir William, and he brought it out as his anchor. An entire Table of proportions was furnished; but that it might meet with no opposition from the influence of dockyard authority, it was sent to the officers of Portsmouth Yard for their approval. They returned it after a few months, with some slight alterations in the proportions of some of the sizes, and recommended the construction to be on 'Perring's principle' of the cushioned, or made-up, crown.

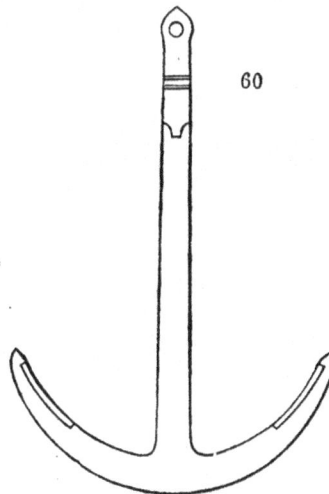

60

It was so adopted, and continued to be made by Brown and Lenox for about a year or two, when the great and unnecessary expense incurred by the plan was pointed out. It was contended it was without any good; because, if the crown of the anchor, or any shut or weld, was made sound and perfect, the amalgamation of the grain of the iron would be complete, and assume its full power or strength, whatever way it might be put together; and the strongest form was that which exposed the least surface of iron to the welding heat, and consequently to injury. About the latter end of 1839, the subject was again opened. Mr. Lenox renewed his objections, by letter to Sir William Parker, to 'Perring's plan' of shutting-up, and the consequence was—a contract, with specification, &c. &c. appeared, and an improved or modified plan of shutting-up (as it is called) was proposed by Mr. Tyler, master-smith of Portsmouth Yard, which was adopted; and Mr. Lenox's shape and proportions (slightly altered, as before said) came out as 'Sir William Parker's,' or the 'Admiralty Anchor,' and continued, until after the trials in 1852, with *every success in actual service that a good anchor could maintain*, and they were made and sold in quantities to all the world.

In the navy of England, and in nearly all foreign navies, this anchor, of which *fig*. 60 represents the form, was adopted. They are also largely employed in the merchant service; but these are not so nicely proportioned as the anchors made for the Government, nor are they so highly finished. Many merchant captains, however, take Rodger's anchor, and our steamers almost invariably take Porter's or Trotman's anchor.

Trotman's Anchor is represented in *fig.* 61, under its various positions. Although for convenience Trotman's anchor is, as we have already stated, largely used by the

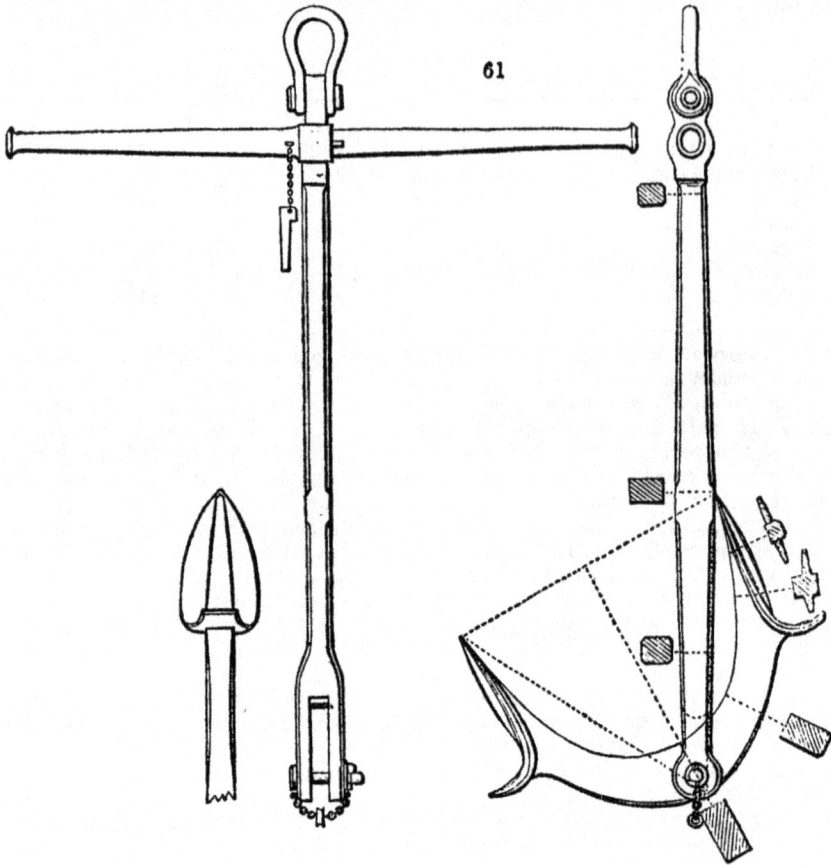

61

merchant steamers, we cannot but feel that the separation of the fluke from the shaft, although it may be in many cases unobjectionable, is attended with the risk that when, in an emergency, the anchor is required, the means of connexion may be at fault.

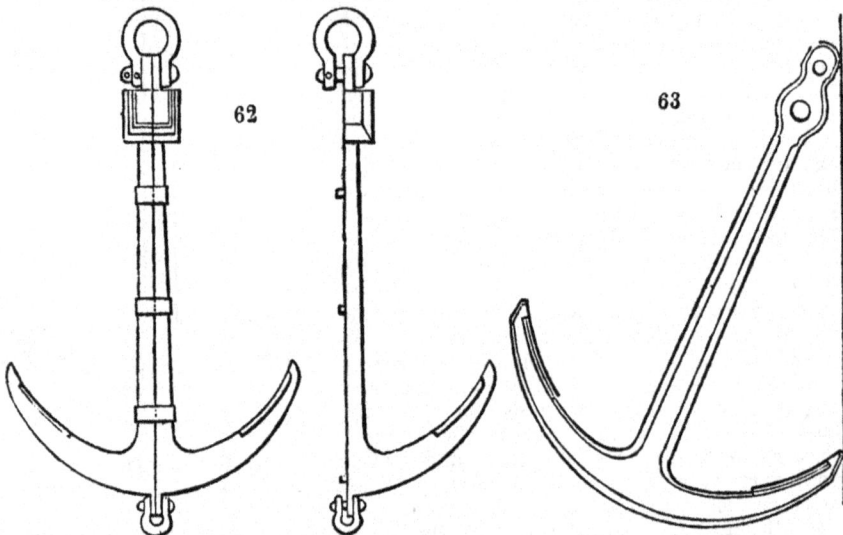

62

63

Captain Hall's anchor is a very valuable one, from the circumstance that it' is capable of division, as shown in *fig.* 62, so that it can be taken out in boats.

There are various other shapes of anchors; but attention has been confined to those generally employed.

We are not in a position to offer any opinion upon the value of the several anchors which have been named. Having described their peculiarities, there remains but little to be said. The solidity of Lenox's anchors—as shown in *fig.* 63, and again in their more recent modifications, in plan and section, with the new form of iron stock, *fig.* 64—has recommended them strongly, and hence their general use.

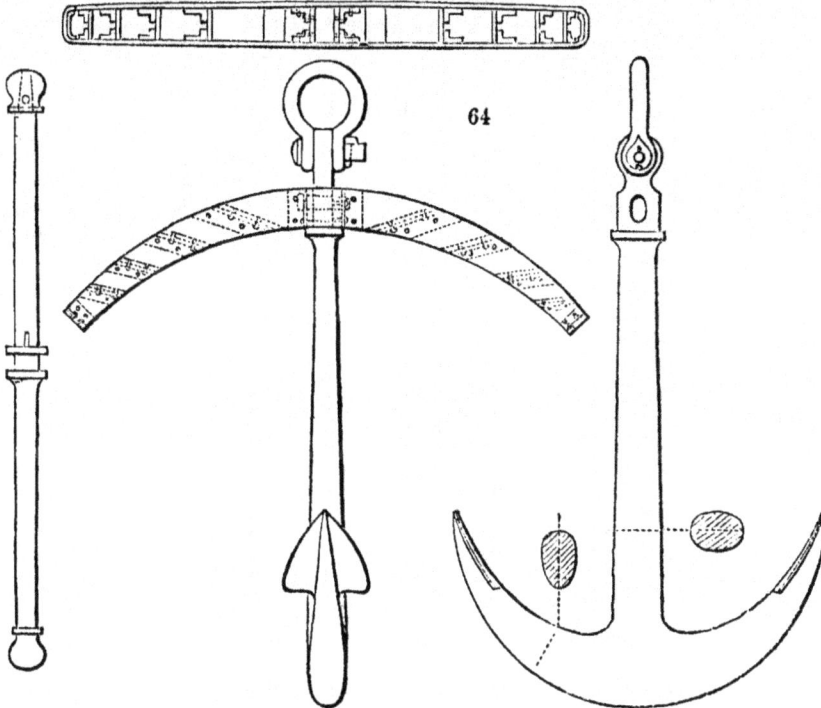

64

The weight of anchors for different vessels is proportioned to the tonnage. The following Tables show the number of anchors now carried, and the weights of each anchor, by the ships of the Navy, under the Admiralty regulations, and by merchant vessels by the regulation of Lloyd's :—

ADMIRALTY REGULATIONS.
Sailing Vessels.

Name of Ship	Tonnage	Number			Weight		
		Bower	Stream	Kedge	Bower	Stream	Kedge
	Tons				Cwt.	Cwt.	Cwt.
Queen	3099	4	1	2	99	25	12
Camperdown	2404	4	1	2	94	23	12
Albion	3082	4	1	2	92	23	12
Vanguard	2609	4	1	2	85	21	10
Cambridge	2139	4	1	2	81	20	10
Revenge	1954	4	1	2	77	19	9
Edinburgh	1772	4	1	2	73	18	9
Southampton	1476	4	1	2	61	15	8
Endymion	1277	4	1	2	53	14	7
Stag	1218	4	1	2	50	13	6
Thalia	1082	4	1	2	47	12	6
Vestal	913	4	1	2	38	10	5
Dido	731	4	1	2	31	9	5
Volage	516	4	1	2	27	8	4
Columbine	492	4	1	2	23	7	4
Cygnet	350	4	1	2	18	6	3
Nautilus	233	4	1	2	13	5	3
Small brigs	...	3	1	1	11	4	2
Cutters	...	2	1	1	9	3	2

Steam Frigates.

Name of Ship	Tonnage	Number			Weight		
		Bower	Stream	Kedge	Bower	Stream	Kedge
	Tons				Cwt.	Cwt.	Cwt.
Terrible	1847	4	1	3	56	14	7
Retribution . . .	1641	4	1	3	52	13	6
Penelope	1616	4	1	3	52	13	6
Avenger	1444	4	1	3	35	11	6
Sampson	1297	4	1	3	35	11	6
Cyclops	1195	4	1	.3	33	10	5

Steam Sloops.

Inflexible . . .	1124	4	1	3	32	10	5
Virago	1059	4	1	3	30	10	5
Medea	835	3	1	3	28	9	5
Hecla	817	3	1	3	26	8	5
Ardent	801	3	1	3	23	7	4
Volcano	720	3	1	3	21	7	4

Steam Gun-Vessels.

Sydenham . . .	596	3	1	3	20	6	4
Spitfire	430	3	1	3	16	6	4
Porcupine . . .	382	3	1	3	13	5	$2\frac{1}{2}$
Harp	345	3	1	3	11	$4\frac{1}{2}$	$2\frac{1}{2}$

For the following Tables I am indebted to the kindness of the Chief Constructor of her Majesty's Navy :—

Screw Frigates, Ironclad.

Name	Tonnage	Number			Weight		
		Bower	Stream	Kedge	Bower	Stream	Kedge
	No.	No.	No.	No.	Cwt.	Cwt.	Cwt.
Achilles . . .	6121	4	1	2	112	35	7 and 5
Warrior . . .	6109	4	1	2	112	35	7 and 5
Bellerophon . .	4270	4	1	2	70 [1]	35	7 and 5
Hector . . .	4089	4	1	2	95	35	7 and 5
Lord Warden .	4080	4	1	2	70 [1]	35	7 and 5
ʏ Prince Consort . .	4045	4	1	2	94	24	13 and 7
Defence . . .	3720	4	1	2	95	35	7 and 5
Pallas . . .	2372	4	1	2	55 [1]	20	7 and 5

Screw Corvette, Ironclad.

Favorite . . .	2094	4	1	2	70	20	9 and 5

Screw Sloops, Ironclad.

Research . . .	1253	3	1	1	38	12	7
Enterprise . .	993	3	1	1	30	9	5

(For *Screw Frigates, not Ironclads*, see Table on p. 169.)

[1] Rodger's anchors.

Chains and Anchors for Sailing Vessels.

Minimum Weights of Anchors, ex. Stock; Sizes and Lengths of Chain Cables, and the proof-strain to which they are to be tested; also Sizes and Lengths of Hawsers and Warps. The Anchors and the Links of the Chains to be of unexceptionable form and proportions.

Numbers for Iron Vessels, per Rules 1871 (See Foot Note)	Ship's Tonnage	Anchors								Stud-Chain Cables †			Ship's Tonnage	Numbers for Iron Vessels	Hawsers and Warps				
		Number			Weight										Stream				
					Bowers *		Including Stock												
		Bowers	Stream	Kedges	Ex. Stock	Admiralty Test	Stream	Kedge	2nd Kedge	Minimum Size	Proved to Admiralty Test, &c.	Length			Chain	Rope	Hawser	Warp	Length
	Tons				Cwts.	Tons	Cwts.	Cwts.	Cwts.	Inches ‡	Tons	Fathoms	Tons		Inches	Inches	Inches	Inches	
2600	50	2	1	1	$3\frac{1}{2}$	$5\frac{18}{20}$	1	$\frac{1}{2}$	..	$\frac{11}{16}$	$8\frac{10}{20}$	120	50	2600	$\frac{7}{16}$	5	3	..	The Length of them to be 90 fathoms each.
3200	75	2	1	1	$4\frac{1}{4}$	$6\frac{12}{20}$	$1\frac{1}{2}$	$\frac{3}{4}$	..	$\frac{12}{16}$	$10\frac{2}{20}$	120	75	3200	$\frac{8}{16}$	5	3	..	
3400	100	2	1	1	5	$7\frac{7}{20}$	$1\frac{3}{4}$	1	..	$\frac{13}{16}$	$11\frac{17}{20}$	150	100	3400	$\frac{9}{16}$	$5\frac{1}{2}$	3	..	
3810	125	2	1	1	$5\frac{3}{4}$	8	2	1	..	$\frac{14}{16}$	$13\frac{15}{20}$	180	125	3810	$\frac{8}{16}$	$5\frac{1}{2}$	$3\frac{1}{2}$	..	
4140	150	2	1	1	$6\frac{1}{2}$	$8\frac{15}{20}$	$2\frac{1}{2}$	$1\frac{1}{4}$	..	$\frac{15}{16}$	$15\frac{18}{20}$	180	150	4140	$\frac{9}{16}$	6	4	..	
4610	175	2	1	1	$7\frac{1}{4}$	$9\frac{9}{20}$	$2\frac{3}{4}$	$1\frac{1}{4}$	..	1	18	180	175	4610	$\frac{9}{16}$	6	4	..	
5020	200	3	1	1	$8\frac{1}{4}$	$10\frac{7}{20}$	3	$1\frac{1}{2}$	..	$1\frac{1}{16}$	$20\frac{6}{20}$	180	200	5020	$\frac{10}{16}$	$6\frac{1}{2}$	4	..	
6070	250	3	1	2	10	12	$4\frac{3}{4}$	$2\frac{1}{4}$	1	$1\frac{2}{16}$	$22\frac{15}{20}$	210	250	6070	$\frac{10}{16}$	7	5	..	
6920	300	3	1	2	12	$13\frac{17}{20}$	5	$2\frac{1}{2}$	$1\frac{1}{4}$	$1\frac{3}{16}$	$25\frac{7}{20}$	210	300	6920	$\frac{11}{16}$	$7\frac{1}{2}$	$5\frac{1}{2}$	..	
7880	350	3	1	2	$13\frac{1}{2}$	$15\frac{3}{20}$	6	3	$1\frac{1}{2}$	$1\frac{4}{16}$	$28\frac{2}{20}$	240	350	7880	$\frac{11}{16}$	$7\frac{1}{2}$	$5\frac{1}{2}$	..	
8600	400	3	1	2	$15\frac{1}{4}$	$16\frac{14}{20}$	$6\frac{1}{2}$	$3\frac{1}{4}$	$1\frac{3}{4}$	$1\frac{5}{16}$	31	240	400	8600	$\frac{12}{16}$	8	6	..	
9420	450	3	1	2	$16\frac{3}{4}$	18	7	$3\frac{1}{2}$	$1\frac{3}{4}$	$1\frac{6}{16}$	34	270	450	9420	$\frac{12}{16}$	$8\frac{1}{2}$	$6\frac{1}{2}$	..	
10030	500	3	1	2	18	19	8	4	2	$1\frac{7}{16}$	$37\frac{3}{20}$	270	500	10030	$\frac{13}{16}$	9	7	..	
11300	600	3	1	2	21	$28\frac{12}{20}$	9	$4\frac{1}{2}$	$2\frac{1}{4}$	$1\frac{8}{16}$	$40\frac{12}{20}$	270	600	11300	$\frac{13}{16}$	$9\frac{1}{2}$	7	4	
12500	700	3	1	2	$23\frac{1}{2}$	$23\frac{10}{20}$	10	5	$2\frac{1}{2}$	$1\frac{9}{16}$	$43\frac{18}{20}$	300	700	12500	$\frac{14}{16}$	10	8	5	
13580	800	3	1	2	$25\frac{1}{2}$	$25\frac{3}{20}$	$10\frac{1}{2}$	$5\frac{1}{4}$	$2\frac{3}{4}$	$1\frac{10}{16}$	$47\frac{10}{20}$	300	800	13580	$\frac{14}{16}$	10	8	5	
14620	900	3	1	2	$27\frac{3}{4}$	$26\frac{18}{20}$	11	$5\frac{1}{2}$	$2\frac{3}{4}$	$1\frac{11}{16}$	$51\frac{5}{20}$	300	900	14620	$\frac{15}{16}$	10	9	$5\frac{1}{2}$	
15600	1000	3	1	2	30	$28\frac{12}{20}$	12	6	3	$1\frac{12}{16}$	$55\frac{2}{20}$	300	1000	15600	$\frac{15}{16}$	10	9	$5\frac{1}{2}$	
17500	1200	3	1	2	32	$30\frac{2}{20}$	13	$6\frac{1}{2}$	$3\frac{1}{4}$	$1\frac{13}{16}$	$59\frac{9}{20}$	300	1200	17500	1	10	$9\frac{1}{2}$	6	
19320	1400	3	1	2	34	$31\frac{12}{20}$	$13\frac{1}{2}$	$6\frac{3}{4}$	$3\frac{1}{4}$	$1\frac{14}{16}$	$63\frac{5}{20}$	300	1400	19320	1	10	10	6	
21100	1600	3	1	2	$36\frac{1}{2}$	$33\frac{8}{20}$	14	7	$3\frac{1}{2}$	$1\frac{15}{16}$	$67\frac{11}{20}$	300	1600	21100	$1\frac{1}{16}$	11	$10\frac{1}{2}$	$6\frac{1}{2}$	
22720	1800	3	1	2	38	$34\frac{10}{20}$	$14\frac{1}{2}$	$7\frac{1}{4}$	$3\frac{1}{2}$	2	72	300	1800	22720	$1\frac{1}{16}$	11	11	7	
24400	2000	3	1	2	40	$35\frac{13}{20}$	15	$7\frac{1}{2}$	$3\frac{3}{4}$	$2\frac{1}{16}$	$76\frac{11}{20}$	300	2000	24400	$1\frac{2}{16}$	11	11	7	
28300	2500	3	1	2	42	$37\frac{2}{20}$	17	$8\frac{1}{2}$	$4\frac{1}{4}$	$2\frac{2}{16}$	$81\frac{5}{20}$	330	2500	28300	$1\frac{2}{16}$	12	12	8	
32100	3000	3	1	2	45	$39\frac{5}{20}$	19	$9\frac{1}{2}$	$4\frac{3}{4}$	$2\frac{3}{16}$	$91\frac{2}{20}$	360	3000	32100	$1\frac{3}{16}$	12	12	8	

Stream (only one required) may be either of Chain or Rope.

All Anchor Stocks must be of acknowledged and approved description.

* Two of the Bower Anchors must not be less than the weight set forth above, but in the third a reduction of 15 per cent will be allowed.

† Unstudded close-link Chains will be admitted as Cables, if proved to *two-thirds* the test required for Stud-Chains. But in all such cases a short length, not less than twelve links, must be tested up to the full strain for Stud-link chains.

‡ In cases where parties are desirous of using or supplying *new* Chains of smaller size than is set forth above, a reduction will be allowed not exceeding one-sixteenth of an inch in Chains of 1 inch to $1\frac{1}{2}$ inch diameter, and one-eighth of an inch in Chains above $1\frac{1}{2}$ inch diameter, provided they be subjected to the Admiralty strain for the size for which they are to be substituted, and further, that a few links, not less than twelve, to be selected by the tester, shall be proved to the breaking-strain, and show a margin of at least 10 per cent. beyond the Admiralty Proof for a chain of the full size required by the Table.

By Section 27 of the Rules, dated February 24, 1870, for the Building and Classification of *Iron Ships*, it is provided that 'Their equipment is to be regulated by the *Number* produced by the sum of the addition of the half moulded breadth of the vessel amidships, her depth from the upper part of keel to the top of the upper deck beam, and the girth of her half midship section to the same height, multiplied by the vessel's length, for one, two, and three-decked vessels, and for spar-decked steam-vessels.'

For a vessel with an awning-deck, the equipment number to be increased one-sixth beyond that which it would be if she were flush decked and without an awning-deck.

For a vessel with a partial awning-deck, poop, topgallant forecastle, or a raised quarter-deck, the equipment number to be increased one-tenth beyond that which it would be if she were flush decked.

CHAINS AND ANCHORS FOR STEAM VESSELS.

Minimum Weights of Anchors, ex. Stock; Sizes and Lengths of Chain Cables, and the proof-strain to which they are to be tested; also Sizes and Lengths of Hawsers and Warps. The Anchors and the Chains to be of unexceptionable form and proportions.

Numbers for Iron Vessels, per Rules 1871 (See Foot Note)	Ship's Tonnage	ANCHORS — Number			ANCHORS — Weight					STUD-CHAIN CABLES †			Ship's Tonnage	Numbers for Iron Vessels	Stream (only one required) may be either of Chain or Rope		HAWSERS AND WARPS	
		Bowers	Stream	Kedges	Bowers* Ex. Stock (Cwts)	Bowers* Admiralty Test (Tons)	Stream (Cwts)	Kedge (Cwts)	2nd Kedge (Cwts)	Minimum Size (Inches)	Proved to Admiralty Test, &c. (Tons)	Length (Fathoms)			Chain (In.)	Rope (In.)	Hawser (In.)	Warp (In.)
	Tons				Cwts	Tons	Cwts	Cwts	Cwts		Tons	Fathoms	Tons				Inches	Inches
2750	75	2	1	1	4	5	1¼	1		13/16	8	120	75	2750	11/16	5½	4	
3750	112	2	1	1	4½	6	1½	1		13/16	10½	120	112	3750	11/16	6	4	
4670	150	2	1	1	5	7	1¾	1		7/8	11	150	150	4670	3/4	6	4	
5420	188	2	1	1	5½	8	2	1¼		15/16	13	180	188	5420	13/16	6½	5	
6170	225	2	1	1	6½	8½	2½	1½		15/16	15	180	225	6170	13/16	7	5½	
6840	262	2	1	1	7¼	9½	2¾	1¾		1	18	180	262	6840	7/8	7½	6	
7500	300	3	1	1	8¾	10½	3	2	1½	1	20	210	300	7500	7/8	7½	6½	
8750	375	3	1	2	10	12	4½	2½	1½	1 1/16	22	210	375	8750	15/16	8½	7	
9800	450	3	1	2	12	13½	5	3	1¾	1 1/8	25	210	450	9800	1	9	7	
10800	525	3	1	2	13½	15½	6	3½	1¾	1 3/16	28	240	525	10800	1 1/16	9½	8	
11830	600	3	1	2	16¼	16½	6½	4	2	1¼	31	240	600	11830	1 1/8	10	8	
12750	675	3	1	2	18	18	7	4½	2	1 5/16	34	270	675	12750	1 3/16	10	9	
13670	750	3	1	2	21	19	8	5	2¼	1 7/16	37	270	750	13670	1¼	10	9	
15400	900	3	1	2	23¼	21	9	5½	2¼	1 9/16	40	270	900	15400	1 5/16	10	9½	
17000	1050	3	1	2	25¼	23	10	6	2½	1 5/8	43	300	1050	17000	1 3/8	11	10	4½
18580	1200	3	1	2	27½	25	11	6½	2½	1 11/16	47	300	1200	18580	1 7/16	11	10½	5
20160	1350	3	1	2	30	26	12	7	3	1 3/4	51	300	1350	20160	1½	11	11	5½
21660	1500	3	1	2	32	28	13	7	3	1 13/16	55	300	1500	21660	1 9/16	11	11	5½
24580	1800	3	1	2	34	30	13½	7	3¼	1 7/8	59	300	1800	24580	1 5/8	12	11	6
27500	2100	3	1	2	36½	31	14	7	3½	1 15/16	63	300	2100	27500	1 11/16	12	11	6½
30330	2400	3	1	2	38	33	14½	7½	3½	2	67	300	2400	30330	1 3/4	12	12	7
33100	2700	3	1	2	38	34	14½	7½	3¼	2	72	300	2700	33100	1 3/4	12	12	7½
35750	{3000 to 3750}	3	1	2	40	35⅜	15	7½	3¾	2 1/16	76½	300	{3000 to 3750}	35750	1 13/16	12	12	8

The Length of them to be 90 fathoms each.

All Anchor Stocks must be of acknowledged and approved description.

* Two of the Bower Anchors must not be less than the weight set forth above, but in the third a reduction of 15 per cent. will be allowed.

† Unstudded close-link Chains will be admitted as Cables, if proved to *two-thirds* the Test required for Stud-Chains. But in all cases such a short length, not less than twelve links, must be tested up to the full strain for Stud-link Chains.

‡ In cases where parties are desirous of using or supplying *new* Chains of smaller size than is set forth above, a reduction will be allowed not exceeding one-sixteenth of an inch in Chains of 1 inch to 1¼ inch diameter, and one-eighth of an inch in Chains above 1¼ inch diameter, provided they be subjected to the Admiralty Strain for the size for which they are to be substituted, and further, that a few links, not less than twelve, to be selected by the tester, shall be proved to the breaking strain, and show a margin of at least 10 per cent. beyond the Admiralty Proof for a Chain of the full size required by the Table.

By Section 27 of the Rules, dated February 24, 1870, for the Building and Classification of *Iron Ships*, it is provided that 'Their equipment is to be regulated by the *Number* produced by the sum of the addition of the half moulded breadth of the vessel amidships, her depth from the upper part of keel to the top of the upper deck beam, and the girth of her half midship section to the same height, multiplied by the vessel's length, for one, two, and three-decked vessels, and for spar-decked steam vessels.'

For a vessel with an awning-deck, the equipment number to be increased one-sixth beyond that which it would be if she were flush decked and without an awning-deck.

For a vessel with a partial awning-deck, poop, topgallant forecastle, or a raised quarter-deck, the equipment number to be increased one-tenth beyond that which it would be if she were flush-decked.

Screw Frigates, not Ironclad.							
Name	Tonnage	Number			Weight		
		Bower	Stream	Kedge	Bower	Stream	Kedge
	No.	No.	No.	No.	Cwt.	Cwt.	Cwt.
Mersey . . .	3733	4	1	3	78	20	9 and 5
Emerald . .	2913	4	1	3	57 [1]	24	9 and 5
Liffey . . .	2654	4	1	2	70	18	9 and 5
Doris . . .	2483	4	1	2	70 and 67	19	9 and 5
Impérieuse . .	2358	4	1	2	70	18	9 and 5
Curaçoa . .	1571	4	1	2	54	18	8 and 4
Screw Sloops, not Ironclad.							
Niger . . .	1072	4	1	2	48	12	7 and 3
Greyhound . .	880	3	1	2	33	8	5 and 3
Intrepid . .	862	3	1	2	23	9	5 and 3
Fawn . . .	751	4	1	2	30	9	5 and 3
Cormorant . .	695	3	1	2	20	6	6 each
Petrel . . .	669	3	1	2	25	6	3 each
Cordelia . .	579	3	1	2	18	7	3 and 1
Syria . . .	488	3	1	2	20	6	4 and 1
Screw Gun-Vessels, not Ironclad.							
Wrangler . .	477	3	1	1	Two of 15 and one of 14	8	3
Espoir . . .	428	3	1	1	14½	6	3

ANCHOVY. (*Anchois*, Fr.; *Acciughe*, It. ; *Anschove*, Ger.) The *Clupea encrasicolus* of Linnæus (*Engraulis encrasicolus*), a small fish, common in the Mediterranean Sea. Anchovies are preserved as a delicacy, and used in the manufacture of anchovy sauce. The Gorgona anchovy is considered the best. They are abundant off the coasts of Cornwall and Wales, but the fishery is entirely neglected. See SARDINES.

ANCHUSIC ACID or ANCHUSIN. The colouring principle of the Alkanet root (*Anchusa tinctoria*). See ALKANET.

ANDAQUIES WAX. A wax produced by a species of bee found on the banks of the Amazon and Orinoco rivers. It is used as a substitute for ordinary bees'-wax in the manufacture of candles.

ANDIRONS, or HAND-IRONS, also called Firedogs. Before the introduction of raised and close fireplaces, these articles were in general use. Strutt, in 1775, says, 'These *awndirons* are used at this day, and are called "*cob-irons;*" they stand on the hearth, where they burn wood, to lay it upon; their fronts are usually carved, with a round knob at the top; some of them are kept polished and bright: anciently many of them were embellished with a variety of ornaments.'

ANEMOMETER. (ἄνεμος wind; μετρέω to measure). An instrument or machine to measure the wind, its *direction* and *force*. Three descriptions of anemometers are now usually employed—1, Dr. Whewell's; 2, Mr. Follett Osler's; 3, Dr. Robinson's. This is not the place to describe either of those most ingenious instruments, a full account of which will be found in the 'Transactions of the British Association' and of the 'Royal Irish Academy.' It is also an instrument designed for measuring the force and velocity of currents of air in mines; and our description of those instruments will be confined to such as are so employed.

It has not been unusual to determine the rate at which the air travels in the gallery or in the shaft of a mine, by the smoke of gunpowder, or by floating light bodies, such as thistle-down, in the air. There is, however, but little accuracy in those methods. The primitive mode of ascertaining the velocity of currents of air in mines was that of choosing a part of the gallery forming the air-way, having as uniform sectional

[1] Rodger's anchors.

dimensions as could be found, and after measuring off a distance of 100 to 150 yards in length, taking a lighted candle and walking in the direction of the current, holding the flame in such a position as to be fully exposed to the influence of the current, but taking care to walk at the particular rate required, to cause the flame to burn in an upright position, without being deflected from the vertical, either by the current or by the progress of the person carrying it. The time required to traverse the distance measured off, being noted by a seconds-watch, enabled the average rate of walking to be determined; and the average rate so found, from three or four trials, was assumed to be the velocity of the air-current; and this, multiplied by the average sectional area of the part of the air-way selected for the experiment, was taken to represent the quantity of air passing in the unit of time. Formerly, when this mode of measuring the air in mines was in use, it would afford a close approximation to the truth; but, with the ventilation now existing in many of our large mines, it would not be practicable to walk as quickly as the currents travel in the principal splits; and running is not a sufficiently steady pace. One of the objections to this, as well as to all other methods that require a considerable distance to be traversed, over which to observe the velocity, is the difficulty of obtaining a gallery of equal area throughout over a sufficient distance; but in cases where this is attainable, this method admits of great accuracy for velocities up to 400 feet per minute.

One of the principal of the second modes employed for the measurement of air, consists in observing the velocity of the smoke from an exploded charge of gunpowder in a part of the gallery, of nearly uniform sectional area; and this, until recently, was the means most generally adopted in the coal mines of this country, for ascertaining the velocity of air-currents; and although it has of late been largely superseded by the use of the anemometer, the practice is still in considerable use, and, so far as regards shaft-velocities, remains the only method. It is, therefore, desirable to ascertain how far the results obtained by this, and similar methods of measuring air-currents, can be relied upon for accuracy; and to investigate the various sources of error connected with them, with a view of either avoiding or making proper allowances for their effects, so far as may be practicable.

The sudden explosion of gunpowder in the confined passages of mines produces several effects, which tend to cause inaccuracies in the results obtained by noting the passage of the smoke, as an index of the velocity of the current.

Experiments prove (as, indeed, might have been anticipated, considering the small quantities of gunpowder used), that in general neither the increase of bulk due to the introduction into the current of the *products of combustion*, nor that due to the *elevation of temperature*, have any appreciable effect on its velocity. But other experiments show that the *force of the explosion*, when a considerable quantity of gunpowder is used in a feeble current, gives an impulse to the current, and creates a velocity in excess of the normal one. A revolving anemometer was placed in an air-passage traversed by a feeble current, so regulated as to be just strong enough to produce thirty revolutions of the instrument per minute. The explosion of a cubic inch of gunpowder, at a distance of seventy feet, did not in any way affect the instrument; but when the charge of gunpowder was increased to twenty cubic inches, the explosion caused a sudden and violent increase of its rate of revolving, acting as a temporary impulse, the revolutions very quickly decreasing to the original number again. The amount of error arising from this source, and which tends to *increase* the apparent velocity, depends on the quantity of gunpowder used, the sectional area of the air-way, and the velocity of the current, increasing with the quantity of gunpowder employed.

These errors may be overcome by using anemometers, or apparatus of various forms; and these may be divided into three classes:—(*a*) Anemometers having vanes or wands, made to *revolve* by the current of air impinging upon them, the rate at which they revolve being indicated by pointers on dials forming a part of the instrument—the pointers being made to revolve by means of wheels connecting them with the axis of the vanes or wands. The anemometers of Combes, Biram, Whewell, Osler, and Robinson, are instances of this class of instruments now in use in this country, all of which require a correction for friction. (*b*) Instruments which are affected by the *force* or impulse of the wind, without being subjected to any continuous revolving motion, such as Dr. Lind's, Henaut's, Bongui's, and Dickinson's anemometers. (*c*) Anemometers of a more complex character, such as Leslie's.

One of the most common forms of anemometer is that devised by Mr. Combes. This consists of a delicately mounted axle turning with the utmost freedom, upon which are mounted four rectangular plane wings, equally inclined as to a plane perpendicular to the axis. In the middle of the axle is an endless screw which drives a wheel with a hundred teeth: this is adjusted so that it advances one tooth for each revolution of the axle. The first wheel carries a cam, which acts upon the teeth of a second wheel which has fifty teeth. At each revolution of the first wheel with the hundred teeth, the cam starts the second wheel with fifty teeth by one tooth. The method of using this instrument will be understood from this concise description. The wings and first wheel are adjusted at zero, and kept immovable until the moment of commencing the observation. Then for every complete revolution of the wings the first wheel is advanced one tooth, and when this wheel has completed its revolution, or advanced a hundred teeth, one tooth is moved forward on the wheel of fifty teeth. An index-pointer fixed upon light uprights indicates the number of revolutions of the axle of the wings. The manner of using this instrument is easily understood. The limbs are placed at zero, and the instrument in the axis of the air-tubes, keeping the limbs immovable by means of a catch, which is loosened at the moment of commencing the observations, and fastened at the end of the same. The division of the limbs does not admit of counting over 5,000 turns, which for a velocity of air at 9·84 feet per second, would correspond with a duration of nearly 3 minutes.

The anemometer of Dr. Robinson is constructed on the assumption that the force of impact of the air against hollow hemispherical cups is twice as great on the concave as on the convex side of the cups, and that the vanes revolve at the rate of one-third the velocity of the current, except in so far as the velocity of revolution is modified by friction.

The mechanism of this instrument is very strong, and allows of the revolutions being recorded throughout the whole day; it would, therefore, be a very suitable anemometer to have near a furnace, or in the principal intake or return of a mine.

Pressure Anemometer.—Perhaps the best known of the pressure anemometers are M. Bongui's, Dr. Lind's, that of Henaut, described by Ponson, and Dickinson's, one of her Majesty's Inspectors of Mines. The anemometer of Bongui consists of an apparatus like a spring balance, furnished with a float-board, or plain surface of given area, and the pressure or impulse is indicated by marks on the sliding-rod of the spring; it is figured and described in the 'Edinburgh Encyclopædia.'

The anemometer most generally used in the coal mines of England is that introduced by the late Mr. Biram. It consists of a series of vanes, which revolve with the action of the air-current—the number of revolutions, or, rather, numbers proportional to the revolutions, being registered by pointers on the face of a dial forming a part of the instrument itself. It is made of three sizes, 4, 6, and 12 inches; is very portable; and is not, with proper care, liable to get out of order, especially the smaller size. A certain force of current is required to overcome the friction, and put the instrument into motion. Some of these instruments will continue to revolve in a current as low as 30 feet per minute, but with the most of them a velocity of about 50 feet is required.

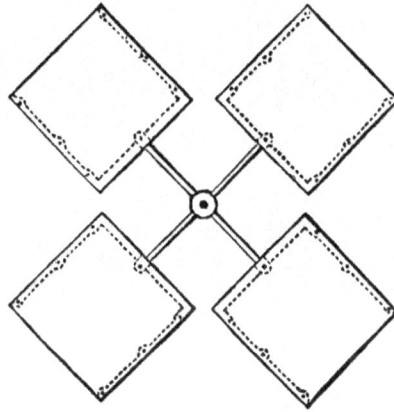

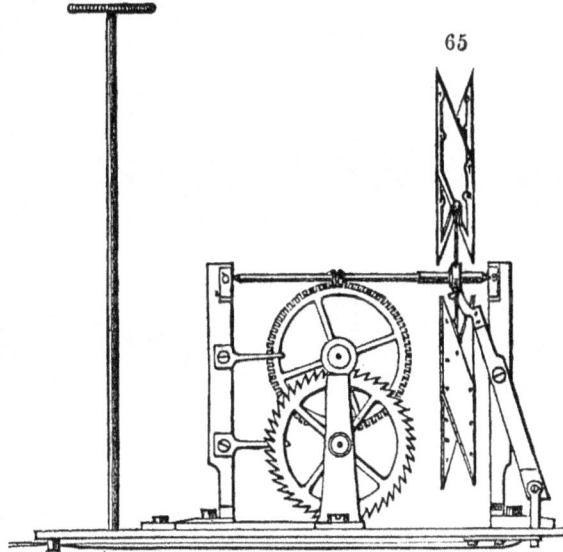

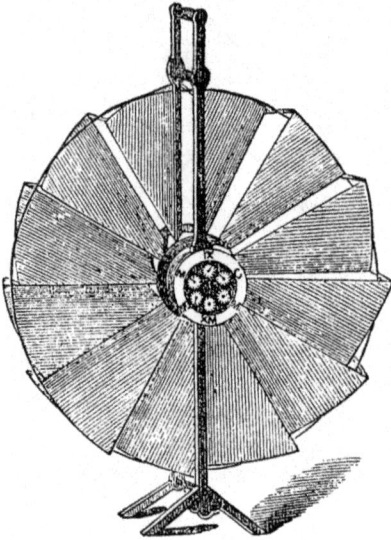

Every one who has occasion to use this anemometer should be aware that it does not register the actual velocity of the air, especially in feeble air-currents; nor yet the number of revolutions of the wands, but only a number proportional to the latter; and although it is of great value, as indicating an increase or decrease in the velocity from time to time, such as the periodical variations in any particular current, it is of comparatively little value, *as generally used*, for ascertaining real velocities, such, for instance, as occur in changing or splitting air-currents, when it is of great importance to know the actual quantities. To obtain, with this instrument, accurate results, available for all purposes, it is necessary, as with Combes' anemometer, to apply a formula to its recorded revolutions, or, rather, to the number indicated by the index, in order to ascertain the actual velocity of any current; each particular instrument requiring special experiments to be made with it, in order to determine the value of the constants required to be employed in the formula. These constants, however, remain the same for the same instrument, so long as it remains in the same condition, and are independent of the velocities of the currents of air in which it is employed.

66

To obtain the constants of this formula, as applicable to any particular instrument, it is absolutely necessary, in making the experiments, to know correctly the true velocity, as a standard of comparison. As before explained, none of the ordinary modes employed for ascertaining the real velocities are reliable; the investigators,

67

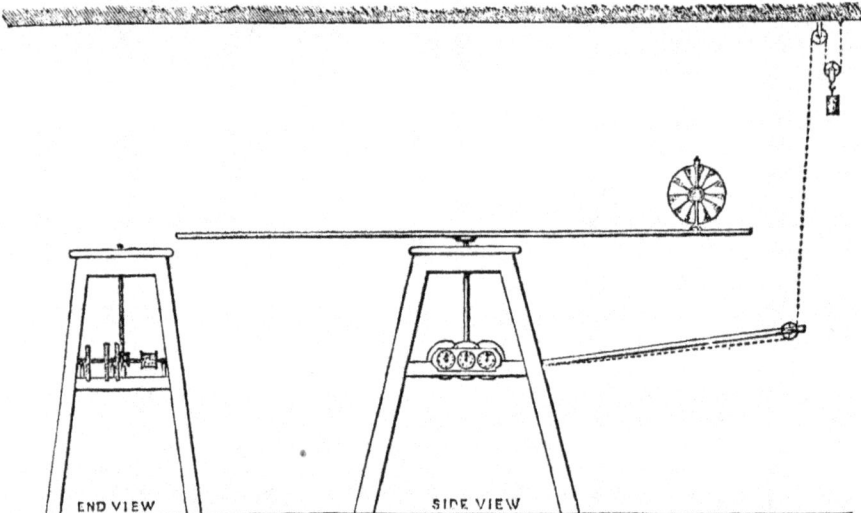

therefore, had a Whirling Machine constructed, the wand of which, in revolving, described a circle of 25 feet in circumference; the number of its revolutions being indicated by a pointer on a dial.

In the first instance, this Whirling Machine was turned by the hand, but as this did not give a sufficiently uniform velocity, a small drum, and a rope with a descending weight attached to it, was employed, to give motion to the machine; and worked thus, it gave extremely accurate results, so far, at least, as regards the uniformity of its own velocity. By fixing the anemometer on the end of the wand, the velocity with which it passes through the air can be ascertained and compared with the revolutions of the anemometer, as indicated on its dial. Fig. 67 represents this machine.

It has been stated by some writers that there is a difference between the force or impulse of air moving upon a body at rest, and the resistance which a body moving through a still atmosphere meets with in its passage, supposing the velocity to be the same in each case ; and besides this, the effect of a body moving in a circle, in a still atmosphere, may not be the same as when moving in a straight line. The experiments of Hutton and others appear, however, to indicate that the force of impact of a wind against a stationary body is always proportional to the resistance which a solid, moved through a still atmosphere, meets with at the same velocity.

A valuable series of experiments were made with this instrument by the late Mr. Atkinson, one of her Majesty's Coal Inspectors, and Mr. John Daglish, for which we must refer to the *Transactions of the North of England Institute of Mining Engineers*. The Tables that are given in connection with the Memoir there published are of the highest possible value.

Water-gauges are sometimes used in determining the rate at which air passes through the shafts or galleries of a mine. They are ordinarily ∪-shaped tubes with a measured quantity of water, one limb of the tube being bent down, so as to be presented to the current of air.

The anemometer of Dr. Lind resembles the photometer of Pitôt ; it determines the velocity of the wind by its action on a small quantity of water in a ∪-shaped tube. As the same instrument is much used in coal mines as a water-gauge for indicating the difference of pressure between the down-cast and up-cast air-column, it will not be at all necessary to give a detailed description of it. From numerous experiments, Dr. Lind considered that the pressure of the wind in direct impulse is nearly proportional to the square of its *velocity*.

Mr. John Daglish, F.G.S. introduced certain improvements in the construction of the water-gauge, which he communicated to the Manchester meeting of the North of England Institute of Mining Engineers, July 14th, 1865.

This communication was made in the following words :—

'Every one who has been much occupied in conducting experiments on the ventilation of mines will have probably felt the inconveniences attending the use of the ordinary form of water-gauge.

'The form of water-gauge introduced by Mr. Daglish, and now extensively in use in the North of England, is constructed with special regard to portability, accuracy, and endurance.

'As the maximum pressure seldom exceeds three inches of water-column, it is not necessary that the travel of the index-scale should exceed this; the scale is divided simply on either side into inches and tenths, the pressure-markings on the scale of the ordinary water-gauge being not only useless but confusing, and prevent the accurate determination of the difference of the level of the water in each tube. The upper end of one of the tubes is bent over, and open to the external air only by a contracted aperture. This prevents the passage of dust into the tube, which is a fruitful source of annoyance in the ordinary water-gauge when placed permanently in exposed situations in dusty mines. The scale is moved by a threaded rod working through a female screw attached to the scale: this insures not only the accurate adjustment of the scale in the first instance, but its retention *in situ*, when adjusted. In the ordinary form, if the brass spring-clips, which attach the scale to the tubes, be too strong, the scale cannot be accurately adjusted, especially when the water column vibrates much ; if, on the other hand, they are too weak, the scale will not remain *in situ*, but falls when released, and this latter is always the tendency after much use ; and unless the tubes are perfectly parallel, the scale will be too stiff in one position, and fall in another. The upper end of the other tube is bent at right angles and fitted up with a short piece of flexible tubing, to the other end of which is attached a short brass tube to be inserted into the aperture to which it is required to attach the water-gauge; this short piece of interposed flexible tubing between the rigid brass and glass prevents the liability to fracture of the tubes, in fixing the

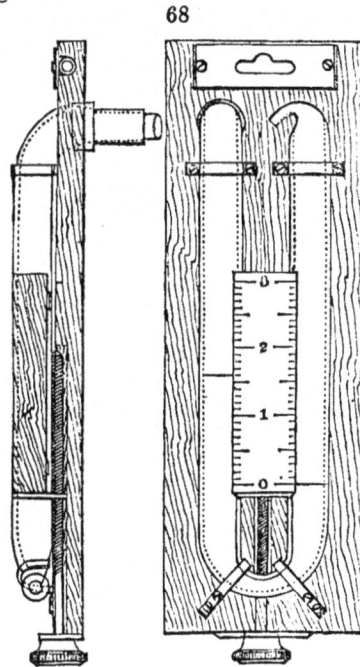

68

apparatus, which is of such frequent occurrence with the ordinary form of water-gauge. The tube is contracted at the bottom bend to prevent the oscillations of the water-column, especially when used near the ventilating shafts; in the original ane-mometer of Dr. Lind, which was similar in principle to the water-gauge, this contraction was used.

'The tubes are fitted to the surface of a flat piece of wood, which entirely prevents liability to fracture, and the apparatus can safely be carried in the pocket; a small bulb-tube is fixed to the wood to allow of it being adjusted perfectly level when in use, and this is of considerable importance, for any deviation from the perpendicular is attended with an alteration in the level of the liquid in each tube. When in use, the writer generally mixes a drop of tincture of rosaniline in the water: with this the position of the surface of the water in each tube is clearly distinguished, and the specific gravity of the fluid not appreciably altered.

'Where any great accuracy is required, a vernier, worked by another threaded screw, could readily be attached to the present scale.'

A new application of the water-gauge for ascertaining the pressure of the ventilating column in mines was made by Mr. John Daglish:—

'The ordinary mode of using the water-gauge in mines, for ascertaining the ventilating pressure, is to place it between the intake and return currents, as near as possible to the bottom of the shaft in the mine. The water-gauge, however, placed in this position, does not give the actual difference of pressure due to the differences of the weight of the downcast and upcast columns of air at their different temperatures, but only the excess of this amount of pressure over the pressure absorbed by the friction of the currents in the shafts.

'This loss of pressure from shaft-friction in deep pits, especially where large quantities of air are moving at high velocities in the shafts, reaches a considerable amount, and very sensibly reduces the indications of the water-gauge as ordinarily employed. By placing in the downcast shaft, however, a range of pipes closed at the lower end by being connected to one leg of a water-gauge, the other leg being open to the upcast shaft, the loss of pressure due to the friction of the air passing down the *downcast shaft* is avoided, and thus not only is the advantage gained of a greater difference in the level of the water in the two tubes than exists under ordinary circumstances, and thereby enabling the existing state of the ventilating pressure to be more easily observed and recorded; but inasmuch as the velocity in the downcast shaft diminishes with a diminished temperature of the upcast shaft, the increased difference of level referred to above is not a constant quantity, but also varies with the heat of the upcast shaft; hence, a water-gauge so fixed, not only gives a greater *extent* of scale under the ordinary state of the ventilation of the mine, but also a greater *range* of scale under variation of temperature.

'Another advantage gained by this mode of using a water-gauge is its freedom from the momentary oscillations which are so objectionable in the water-gauge as ordinarily used, and which prevent very accurate readings.

'But the chief benefit to be derived from the application of a long range of tubes in the downcast shaft, is that of being able to place the water-gauge *on the surface* in any position that may be most desirable, as its action is not interfered with by extending the pipes to any length or in any direction, inasmuch as the column of air in the pipe is dormant and its pressure consequently not reduced by friction.

'At Seaton Colliery, belonging to Earl Vane, the depth of the shaft is 254 fathoms to the furnace in the Hutton-seam; the upcast shaft is 14 feet in diameter, and the quantity of air going down the downcast shaft is 200,000 cubic feet per minute, and

69

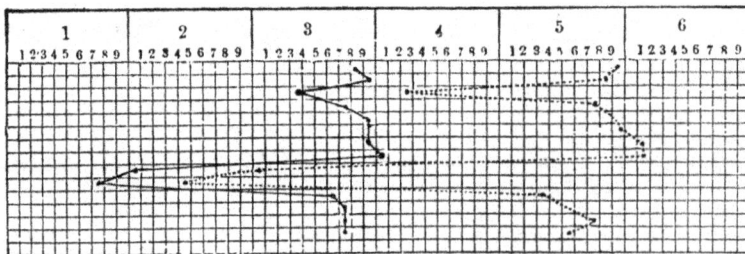

this quantity becomes increased to 300,000 cubic feet per minute in the upcast shaft by expansion due to the high temperature. The ordinary ventilating pressure of the mine, as indicated by a water-gauge fixed in the mine in the usual way, is 3 inches, and becomes as low as 0·7 inches when the furnaces are out for repairs to the shaft.

'The *dotted* line on the preceding diagram (*fig.* 69) exhibits the range of the water-gauge readings, placed in the ordinary position in the mine between the upcast and downcast shafts, taken one each day for a fortnight. The *black* line exhibits the readings of the water-gauge placed in the colliery office, by means of a pipe from the bottom of the downcast shaft, on the principle previously explained.

'The office is 200 yards distant from the top of the pit, which is 508 yards deep; there is, therefore, 708 yards of pipe (in this case the ordinary half-inch gas-pipe).

'It will be observed that in the customary application of the water-gauge, the height of the water-column due to the ventilating pressure is 3 inches, falling to 0·7 inches when the furnaces are out, being a range of little more than 2 inches; whilst in the new application, the ordinary reading is 5 inches, falling to a minimum of 1·5 inches, having, therefore, a range of 3·5 inches, or nearly double.

'By the addition of a galvanic battery the instrument could be made, if this be considered advisable, to ring a bell when the pressure became reduced below a fixed point.'

ANEROID BAROMETER. This instrument was invented by M. Vidi, of Paris. In its latest form it consists of a cylindrical case, about 4 or 6 inches in diameter, and $2\frac{1}{4}$ inches deep, in which lies a thin metal box, near to, and parallel with, the curved boundary of the case, its two ends being distant about half an inch from each other. From this box the air has been partially exhausted, and the pressure of the external atmosphere on it causes it to alter its form. The accompanying figure (70) shows a section of this box. It is made of thin corrugated plates of metal, so that its elasticity is great. By means of the tube F, the air is partially exhausted, when the box takes the form shown by the dotted lines. A small quantity of gas is introduced after exhaustion, the object of which is to compensate for the varying elasticity of the metal at different temperatures. The pressure of the air on the box in ordinary instruments is between 40 and 50 lbs., and it will easily be understood that any variation in this pressure will occasion the distances between the two plates to vary, and consequently the stalk will have a free motion in or out. This is, by an ingenious contrivance, changed from a vertical motion to a motion parallel to the face of the dial, and this is converted into a rotatory one by the application of a watch-chain to a small cylinder or drum. The original very slight motion is augmented by the aid of levers. This is so effectually done, that when the corrugated surfaces move through only the 250th part of an inch, the index-hand on the face turns over a space of three inches. The extreme portability of this little instrument, and its comparative freedom from risk of injury, render it exceedingly useful to the traveller. Its accuracy is proved by the experiments of Professor Lloyd, who placed one under the receiver of an air-pump, and found that its indications corresponded with those of the mercurial gauge to less than 0·01 of an inch; and within ordinary variations of atmospheric pressure the coincidences are very remarkable.—*Lloyd, Nichol, Drew.* See BAROMETER.

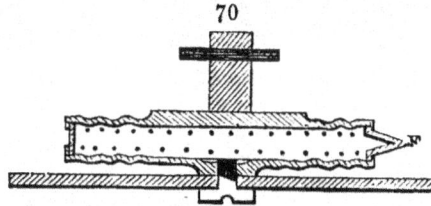

ANETHUM GRAVEOLENS. The common garden *Dill.* This plant is cultivated in England and imported from the South of Europe. It is used medicinally—chiefly on account of its hot and sweetish taste, and for flavouring spirituous cordials.

ANGELICA. (*Angélique*, Fr.; *Angelika*, Ger.) The *Archangelica officinalis.* The dried angelica root is imported from Hamburg in casks. The tender stems, stalks, and the midribs of the leaves, are made, with sugar, into a sweetmeat (candied angelica). The angelica root and seeds are used by rectifiers and compounders in the preparation of gin, and as an aromatic flavouring for ' bitters.' The quantity cultivated in some moist places in this country is sufficient to meet our requirements.

ANGLE-IRON. A piece of iron rolled out in the shape of L to form joints.

ANGLE-RAFTER or HIP-RAFTER. A piece of timber which runs from the angle of the building to the ridge of the roof, into which it is framed.

ANGLE-STAFF. Strips of wood placed upon the vertical angles to protect the plastering.

ANGLESITE. A sulphate of lead found native, generally produced by the decomposition of galena (*sulphide of lead*). It was first found at Pary's mine in Anglesea, whence the name.

ANGORA WOOL. (*Poil de chevron d'Angora*, Fr.) Called also *angola* and *angona*. The wool of the Angora goat (*Capra Angorensis*), employed in the manufacture of shawls, camlets, and fine cloth, &c., is obtained from the long-haired goat of Angora, to which province this animal is peculiar. Lieutenant Conolly has given an account of this goat and some other varieties, *Capra lanigera*, the Cashmere goat, and *Changra* or the shawl-goat of Thibet.—

'The country where it is found was thus described to us—"Take Angora as a centre, then Kizzil Ermak (or Haly's) Chomgere, and from eight to ten hours' march (say thirty miles) beyond; Beybazar, and the same distance beyond, to near Nalaban: Sevree, Hissar, Yoorrook, Tosiah, Costambool, Geredeh, and Cherkesh, from the whole of which tract the common bristly goat is excluded, and the white-haired goat alone is found." The fleece of the white Angora goat is called *tiftik* (the Turkish for goat's hair), in distinction to *yun*, or *yapak*, sheep's wool. After the goats have completed their first year, they are clipped annually, in April or May, and yield progressively, until they attain full growth, from 150 drachms to 1½ *oke* of *tiftik* (from 1 lb. to 4 lbs. English). The hair of the tiftik goat is exported from its native districts raw, in yarn, and woven in the delicate stuffs for which Angora has been long celebrated. The last are chiefly consumed in Turkey, while the yarn and raw material are sent to France and England. It appears that the first parcels of Angora wool were shipped from Constantinople for England in 1820, and it was so little appreciated that it fetched only 10*d.* the pound.

'Within the last two or three years, a new texture made of goats' wool has, however, been introduced both into France and this country, which calls for particular attention. This texture consists of stripes and checks expressly manufactured for ladies' dresses, and having a soft feel and silky appearance. The wool of which this article is made is chiefly the wool of the Angora goat. This wool reaches us through the Mediterranean, and is chiefly shipped at Smyrna and Constantinople. In colour it is the whitest known in the trade, and now more generally used in the manufacture of fine goods than any other. There are, however, other parts of Asiatic Turkey from which limited supplies are received; but in quality not so good as that produced in Angora. After the manufacture of shawls with goats' wool declined in France, this raw material remained neglected for a long while. About two or three years ago, however, the French made another attempt, and brought out a texture for ladies' dresses, in checks and stripes, which they call '*poil de chèvre*.' The warp is a fine spun silk, coloured, and the weft Angora or Syrian white wool, which was thus thrown on the surface. This article has a soft feel, and looks pretty, but in wearing is apt to cut. The price of a dress of French manufacture has been from 2*l.* 10*s.* to 3*l.*; but by adopting a cotton warp, the same article is now made in England and sold for 15*s.*; and it is found that the cotton warp, as a mixture, suits the goats' hair best.'—*Southey on Colonial Sheep and Wools*, London, 1852.

The principal manufactures of '*poil de chèvre*' in France are at Paris, Cronyen, Thelle (Oise), Ecrus (Oise), Montataire (Oise), and Ledau. In England, the wool is chiefly spun at Bradford, and partly manufactured there; at Norwich, and also in Scotland; part of the yarn is exported. Mr. Southey informs us, that the quantity of goats' wool imported into the United Kingdom in 1848 was 896,865 lbs.; in 1849 the quantity rose to 2,536,039 lbs.

The quantity of goats' wool or hair, in which the alpaca wool is included, was:—

Countries	1871		1872 [1]	
	lbs.	£	lbs.	£
From France	253,638	11,977	—	—
„ Austrian Territories .	72,357	6,813	—	—
„ Turkey	7,882,359	1,005,922	—	—
„ British Possessions in South Africa . .	235,860	13,322	—	—
„ Other Countries . .	371,150	17,214	—	—
Total . . .	8,815,364	1,055,248	6,495,482	757,089

In France this article is now applied to the manufacture of a new kind of lace, which in a great measure supersedes the costly fabrics of Valenciennes and Chantilly. The Angora-wool lace is more brilliant than that made from silk, and costing only half the price, it has come into very general wear among the middle classes. The same material is also manufactured into shawls, which sell from 4*l.* to 16*l.* each. See MOHAIR and CASHMERE.

---

[1] The details not obtainable for 1872.

ANHYDRIDES. A name now given by chemists to the so-called oxygen acids, or those which are clearly results of a combination of an element with oxygen.

Thus, the gaseous compound of sulphur and oxygen, commonly called sulphurous acid (SO^2), is now termed sulphurous *anhydride*; indeed, in its anhydrous state, the gas does not exhibit any of the characteristic reactions of an acid, and hence in modern chemistry the term sulphurous *acid* is restricted to the combination of the anhydride with water ($SO^2 . HO$, or H^2SO^3).

ANHYDRITE. A mineral consisting of anhydrous sulphate of lime. It occurs in granular masses; in crystals belonging to the orthorhombic system; in crystalline masses presenting cleavage in three rectangular directions, and hence termed *dice-spar;* and in certain curiously contorted forms known as *tripe-stone.* Anhydrite is frequently found in beds of rock-salt, where it is often associated with gypsum, or hydrous sulphate of lime; indeed, anhydrite may readily pass into gypsum by combination with water, and in certain localities—as at Bex, in Switzerland—extensive beds of anhydrite have been thus hydrated. The compact and granular varieties of anhydrite are often worked into ornamental forms, and the coarser kinds, when occurring in sufficient quantity, have been used for building purposes. The mineral is also useful to the agriculturist, like gypsum, for improving certain soils.

ANIL. The name of the American species of the Indigo plant (*Indigofera*). It is a shrubby plant, growing from $2\frac{1}{2}$ to 3 feet high. From it the name *Aniline* is derived. See ANILINE and INDIGO.

ANILEINE. See ANILINE-VIOLET.

ANILINE. ($C^{12} H^7 N$, or *Unitary System*, $C^6 H^5$, HHN,* Phenylamine.) This organic base having of late years met with an important application in the arts, in the production of beautiful dye-colours, a description of the methods of preparing it, and of some of its characters, becomes necessary; though for details of its more interesting relations in scientific chemistry, we must refer to Watts's 'Dictionary of Chemistry.'

Preparation.—There are few bodies which admit of being prepared in a greater variety of ways—all of them interesting in tracing the chemical history of this most curious body; and we proceed to describe Dr. Hofmann's original mode of procuring it from the basic oil of coal-tar, although this method is no longer resorted to for the manufacture of aniline.

The oil is agitated with hydrochloric acid, which seizes upon the basic oils; after decanting the clear liquor, which contains the hydrochlorates of these oils, it is evaporated over an open fire until it begins to disengage acrid fumes, which indicate a commencement of decomposition, and is then filtered, to separate any adhering neutral compounds. The clear liquor is then decomposed with potash or milk of lime, which liberates the bases themselves in the form of a brown oil, consisting chiefly of a mixture of aniline ($C^6 H^7 N$), and leucol or quinoleine ($C^9 H^8 N$). This mixture is submitted to distillation, and the aniline is chiefly found in that portion which passes over at or about 360° F. (182° C.) : repeated rectification and collection of the product distilling at this temperature purifies the aniline; but to complete the purification, it is well to treat the partially purified aniline once more with hydrochloric acid, to separate the bases again by an alkali, and then to rectify carefully.

The violet reaction of aniline with solution of bleaching-powder enables the operator to test the distillate from time to time, to ascertain when aniline ceases to pass over, since leucol does not possess this property.—*Hofmann.*

Aniline may also be obtained from indigo.

When indigo-blue is dissolved by the aid of heat in a strong solution of potash, and the mass, after evaporation to dryness, submitted to destructive distillation, it intumesces considerably, and aniline is liberated, which condenses in the receiver in the form of a brown oil, together with a little water and ammonia disengaged with it. The aniline is purified by rectification, as in the method before described. By this process, the quantity of aniline obtained is about 18 to 20 per cent. of the indigo used.—*Fritzsche.* (See INDIGO.)

By treatment with potash, the indigo-blue ($C^8 H^5 NO$) is converted into chrysanilic acid and anthranilic acid ($C^7 H^7 NO^2$), and it is this latter body which, by destructive distillation, yields carbonic acid and aniline.

$$C^7 H^7 NO^2 = C^6 H^7 N + CO^2.$$

Nitrobenzol may be converted into aniline, either by the action of sulphuretted hydrogen, or, more conveniently, as has been shown by M. Béchamp, by the action of a basic acetate of iron.

* The formulæ employed throughout this article, and in the following articles on aniline colours, are constructed with the modern atomic weights, although not printed in black type.

For this purpose, the following proportions have been found convenient by the writer; mix in a retort $\frac{1}{4}$ lb. of iron filings, with about 2 ounces of acetic acid, then add about an equal volume of nitrobenzol. After a few minutes a brisk effervescence sets in, and the aniline distils over together with water. The reaction may require to be aided by the application of a very gentle heat; but it takes place with the greatest ease, and an ordinary condensing arrangement should be employed. The aniline having so nearly the density of water, does not readily separate on the surface, but the addition of a small quantity of salt, which dissolves in the water, brings it to the surface. It may then be decanted off, dried by standing for a short time over chloride of calcium, and then purified by rectification, as before described.

Properties.—Aniline is one of the organic basic derivatives of ammonia. In fact, it may be viewed as ammonia in which one equivalent of hydrogen is replaced by the compound radical *Phenyl* ($C^6 H^5$), thus :—

$$N \begin{cases} C^6\ H^5 \\ H \\ H \end{cases}$$

Just as phenyl is one of a series of homologous radicals, so aniline is the first of a series of homologous bases, in which the one equivalent of hydrogen is replaced by these radicals respectively, thus :—

Homologous Radicals.			Homologous Bases.	
Phenyl	. . . $C^6\ H^5$	—	Aniline . . .	$N \begin{cases} C^6\ H^5 \\ H^2 \end{cases}$
Toluyl	. . . $C^7\ H^7$	—	Toluidine . .	$N \begin{cases} C^7\ H^7 \\ H^2 \end{cases}$
Xylyl .	. . . $C^8\ H^9$	—	Xylidine . .	$N \begin{cases} C^8\ H^9 \\ H^2 \end{cases}$
Cumyl	. . . $C^9\ H^{11}$	—	Cumidine . .	$N \begin{cases} C^9\ H^{11} \\ H^2 \end{cases}$
Cymyl	. . . $C^{10}\ H^{13}$	—	Cymidine . .	$N \begin{cases} C^{10}\ H^{13} \\ H^2 \end{cases}$

When pure, it is a colourless liquid of a high refractive power, density 1·028, and of an aromatic odour. It is slightly soluble in water, and mixes in all proportions with alcohol and ether. It boils at 360° F. (182° C.). It dissolves sulphur and phosphorus when cold and coagulates albumen. It has no action on litmus-paper, but turns delicate vegetable colours, such as dahlia-petal infusion, blue.

Its basic characters are well developed; thus it precipitates the oxides from the salts of iron, zinc, and alumina, just like ammonia, and yields, with chloride of platinum, a double salt similar to ammonia, the chloro-platinate of aniline ($2C^6\ H^8$ NCl, PtCl⁴), which on ignition is entirely decomposed, leaving only a residue of platinum. These characters, together with the beautiful blue colour which it strikes with solution of bleaching-powder, or the alkaline hypochlorites generally, are sufficient for the recognition and distinction of this body. (See PHENYL, &c. &c.)

SALTS OF ANILINE.—Aniline combines with acids, forming a long series of salts which are in every respect analogous to the corresponding salts of ammonia. They are nearly all soluble and crystallisable, and are decomposed by the mineral alkalies with liberation of aniline. They are generally colourless, but become red by exposure to the air.

Sulphate of Aniline. ($C^6\ H^7\ N$; $H^2\ SO^4$.)—This salt is employed in the manufacture of Mr. Perkins' aniline colours. It is prepared by treating aniline with dilute sulphuric acid, and evaporating gently till the salt separates. It crystallises from boiling alcohol in the form of beautiful colourless plates of a silvery lustre, for the salt is scarcely at all soluble in cold alcohol. It is very soluble in water, but insoluble in ether.

The crystals redden by exposure to the air ; they can be heated to the boiling point of water without change, but when ignited they are charred with disengagement of aniline and sulphurous acid.

Oxalate of Aniline. ($2C^6\ H^7\ N$; $C^2\ H^2\ O^4$.)—This is one of the best defined salts of aniline : it separates as a crystalline mass on treating an alcoholic solution of oxalic acid with aniline. It is very soluble in hot water, much less so in cold, only slightly soluble in alcohol, and insoluble in ether.

A large number of other salts are known : the hydrochlorate, hydrobromate, hydriodate, nitrate, several phosphates, citrate, tartrate, &c. &c.; but they are of purely scientific interest. The same remark applies to the various products of the decomposition of aniline, which have been so ably investigated by Fritzsche, Zinin, Hofmann, Gerhardt, and other chemists.

Since this was written, the aniline dyes have received such an important development, that it is necessary to give a more detailed description of these beautiful colours.

It appears desirable that a Dictionary of the Arts should comprehend a succinct history of the discovery of a body which has performed so important a part in the advancement of a special industry as Aniline has done.

In 1826 Unverdorben, a German chemist, when exposing indigo to destructive distillation, discovered an oily substance which formed crystalline compounds with acids, to which he gave the name of *Crystalline*. Runge, also a German, subsequently observed in coal-tar oil a substance capable of forming saline compounds, and of striking a violet-blue colour with chloride of lime. To this he gave the name of *Kyanol*, blue oil. At a later period, Fritzsche, when investigating the action of potash on indigo, obtained a quantity of a basic oil, which he analysed, and to which he gave the name of *Aniline*. Zinin, about the same time, found that *Nitrobenzol*, when submitted to the action of sulphuretted hydrogen, was converted into a peculiar and, as he thought, a new substance, to which he gave the name of *Benzidam* (an ammonia derived from Benzol). Hofmann was the first who submitted crystalline, kyanol, aniline, and benzidam to careful experimental comparison, and proved them to be identically the same substance, which now took its place in chemistry under the name of aniline.

In 1825 Michael Faraday, during an examination of the oily products separated in the compressed oil-gas holders—then largely used—discovered *Benzol*, which he then described as a bicarburetted hydrogen. On this important discovery, Dr. Hofmann remarks: 'In this investigation, as indeed throughout the whole series of his immortal researches, Faraday's object was the elaboration of truth for its own intrinsic value and beauty; and in the same spirit has the work been continued by those, who, after Faraday, engaged in the further scientific examination of this subject. Nobody in those early days of benzol, when the substance simply existed as a laboratory curiosity, dreamed of the brilliant career looming in the distance for this body, nor of the marvellous transformation it was destined to undergo. But the experience of the last few years in this matter has only corroborated the old axiom, which cannot be too often repeated, that the search after the true, for its own sake, leads on to the discovery of its natural corollaries, the useful and the beautiful. For those, indeed, lie folded up in truth, to be in due time evolved therefrom, even as the great tree unfolds itself from out the little seed.'

Mitscherlich, some years later, found that benzoic acid, distilled with caustic potash, gave a colourless volatile liquid, identical with the hydrocarbon discovered by Faraday; and hence the name this substance now retains—Benzol. Dr. Hofmann, in 1845, proved the presence of benzol in coal-tar oil, and in 1848 Mansfield showed that an inexhaustible quantity of it could be procured from that source. See BENZOL.

Now, the crude tar of the gas-works is subjected to regulated distillation. Thus is obtained separately *naphtha* or *light oil* (oily liquid lighter than water), and then *dead oil* or *heavy oil* (oily liquid heavier than water), and finally remaining in the retort pitch. From the light oil, benzol is separated by further fractional distillation. Mitscherlich showed, if this benzol is dissolved in fuming nitric acid, and the clear liquid mixed with water, a compound (nitrobenzol) is precipitated as a dense yellow liquid. This is the well-known artificial oil of bitter almonds, which is now prepared easily and economically on a large scale. It was Zinin, already named, who discovered that sulphuretted hydrogen converted this nitrobenzol into aniline, and who, believing the substance thus produced to be a new one, described it under the name of benzidam, or an ammonia derived from benzol. (See NITROBENZOL.)

The successive changes of benzol are thus expressed in chemical symbols.

First change.

Transformation of benzol into nitrobenzol.

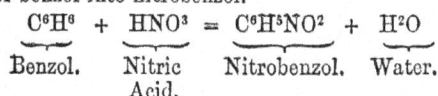

$$C^6H^6 \; + \; HNO^3 \; = \; C^6H^5NO^2 \; + \; H^2O$$

Benzol.   Nitric   Nitrobenzol.   Water.
         Acid.

Second change.

Transformation of nitrobenzol into aniline.

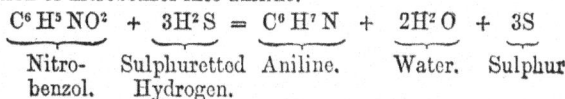

$$C^6H^5NO^2 \; + \; 3H^2S \; = \; C^6H^7N \; + \; 2H^2O \; + \; 3S$$

Nitro-   Sulphuretted   Aniline.   Water.   Sulphur
benzol.   Hydrogen.

Dr. Hofmann remarks that sulphuretted hydrogen is not by any means the most convenient reducing agent to effect this conversion, and he has shown that when nitrobenzol is placed in contact with metallic zinc and hydrochloric acid, it is rapidly converted into aniline. Béchamp submitted nitrobenzol to the action of metallic iron and acetic acid, and thus transformed it into aniline. This process is now almost universally adopted. Equal weights of nitrobenzol, acetic acid, and cast-iron turnings are very gradually mixed in cast-iron vessels, so that the heat produced by the reaction does not raise the temperature of the mixture too high. The semi-solid mass which is produced consists of acetate of iron and acetate of aniline. This is distilled sometimes alone, or by some manufacturers with the addition of lime; the distillate consisting generally of acetone, aniline, unaltered nitrobenzol, and several other products arising from the impurity of the nitrobenzol. The crude aniline mixture is redistilled, and the aniline obtained sufficiently pure by collecting the products distilling between 175° C. and 190° C. Thus produced, aniline is a slightly brownish liquid, a little heavier than water.

ANILINE-BLACK. This colour can scarcely be said to have been satisfactorily produced. The green tints (see ANILINE-GREEN) are turned black, according to a process devised by Messrs. Wood and Wright, by mixing chlorate of potash with a metallic salt and a salt of aniline; for the metallic salt they prefer ferric salts. Aniline-black may also be produced by treating the colour on the fabric by solutions of bichromate of potash, or of weak bleaching-powder. Nitrate of copper may be mixed with hydrochlorate of aniline, without the addition of chlorate of potash, and the mixture printed on the fabric, when gradually a black tint is produced.

According to Brandt aniline-blacks are very variable in their composition and properties. Some of them resist the action of light and of reagents much better than others. Some turn of an unpleasant greenish hue if exposed to air charged with acid or sulphurous vapours. The more intense an aniline-black the better it resists reagents. It is true that this intensity depends partly on the degree of concentration of the colour, but other circumstances influence its solidity. A black developed in presence of an excess of aniline is always faster than one of the same degree of concentration which is developed in presence of an excess of acid. In the latter case, beside weakening the tissue, blacks are obtained which turn green, and cannot stand the application of bleaching-powder. In this case, if the gas used for lighting the premises contains a little sulphur, the fumes cause the folds of every piece in the warehouse to turn green.

With excess of base a black is produced which shows less disposition to turn green, and bears chlorine better. Such a black must be developed rapidly enough to avoid the volatilisation of the aniline. For this end chlorate of aniline is used instead of chlorate of potash, diminishing the amount of the aniline salt by a corresponding amount. Chlorate of potash, in presence of an excess of aniline, does not decompose very rapidly.

Aniline-blacks result from two distinct reactions. There is, firstly, decomposition of the chlorate of aniline; and secondly, oxidation of the other salt of aniline mixed with the chlorate. The decomposition of the former gives rise to chlorinised products derived from aniline. There are probably various stages of substitution—a fact which explains the diversity of the results. Besides these, there is formed another product, the result of the oxidation of the salt of aniline.

Aniline-black consists, therefore, of two distinct blacks: the one, formed of the chlorine substitution of aniline, is exceedingly fast, and resists almost all chemicals, but it is not so fine as that produced by a judicious mixture of the two blacks, as it does not acquire its lustre and effect without the aid of the second. This latter is an intense violet-blue, which appears black when concentrated. It is less solid than the former, and turns greenish with the smallest amount of acid. It resists the action of soap very well. The brown-black and blue-black mixed together form a fine aniline-black. The object of the maker is to combine the maximum of beauty with the maximum of solidity. This depends on the due proportion of the chlorate.

Comparative trials have been made with pure aniline on the one hand, and, on the other, with anilines containing toluidine and pseudo-toluidine. The results were similar in each case.

ANILINE-BLUE. MM. Girard and De Laire, in M. Pelouze's laboratory, discovered the reactions which give rise to the aniline-blues. This reaction consists in heating a salt of rosaniline, or a mixture of substances capable of giving rise to its formation, for several hours with an excess of aniline. The blue colouring-matters thus obtained are the *Bleu de Paris* and the *Bleu de Lyons*. The operation on a large scale is carried out by allowing the mixture of a salt of rosaniline, with an excess of aniline, to digest at a temperature of 150° or 160° for a considerable time. If a mixture of 2 kilogrammes of dry hydrochlorate of rosaniline and 4 kilogrammes of aniline be employed, the operation is completed in four hours. The crude blue is purified, by treating it successively with boiling water, acidulated with hydrochloric acid, and with pure water, until it presents the purest possible hue. Mr. Nicholson has devised and patented a process of purifying the blue colouring-matter, which he dissolves for this purpose in concentrated sulphuric acid, afterwards digesting the solution for half an hour at a temperature of 150° C. On adding water to this solution, the blue colouring-matter is precipitated in a modified condition, having, in fact, become soluble in pure water.

Dr. Hofmann has determined the nature of aniline-blue, which he thus describes:—
'The blue colouring-matters, as might have been expected, are saline compounds of a colourless base, which may be obtained in a state of perfect purity by dissolving one of the salts (the hydrochlorate, for instance) in alcohol, and filtering the solution into alcoholic ammonia. The deep blue immediately disappears, and the slightly reddish solution yields the free base on addition of water, in the form of a white curdy precipitate, which gradually assumes an indistinctly crystalline character. Dried *in vacuo*, this substance remains colourless, or assumes a slightly bluish tint; at 100° it cakes, and becomes brown; and is found by analysis to contain—

$$C^{38}H^{33}N^3O = C^{38}H^{31}N^3, H^2O.$$

This formula exhibits an extremely simple relation between aniline-blue and aniline-red; indeed, aniline-blue is triphenylic rosaniline:—

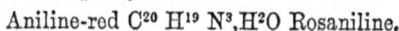

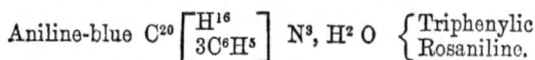

Aniline-red $C^{20} H^{19} N^3, H^2O$ Rosaniline.

Aniline-blue $C^{20} \begin{bmatrix} H^{16} \\ 3C^6H^5 \end{bmatrix} N^3, H^2 O$ {Triphenylic Rosaniline.

The salts of the triphenylic derivative correspond to the rosaniline salts. The composition of the hydrochlorate, which Mr. Nicholson prepared in a state of perfect purity, is analogous to that of the monacid hydrochlorate of rosaniline:—

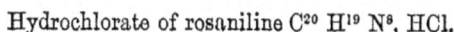

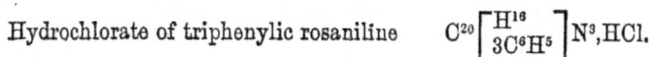

Hydrochlorate of rosaniline $C^{20} H^{19} N^3, HCl.$

Hydrochlorate of triphenylic rosaniline $C^{20} \begin{bmatrix} H^{16} \\ 3C^6H^5 \end{bmatrix} N^3, HCl.$

The genesis of aniline-blue is represented by the following equation:—

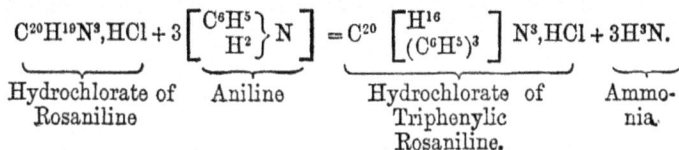

$$C^{20}H^{19}N^3,HCl + 3\begin{bmatrix} C^6H^5 \\ H^2 \end{bmatrix} N = C^{20} \begin{bmatrix} H^{16} \\ (C^6H^5)^3 \end{bmatrix} N^3,HCl + 3H^3N.$$

Hydrochlorate of Rosaniline — Aniline — Hydrochlorate of Triphenylic Rosaniline. — Ammonia.

Aniline-blue, when submitted to the action of reducing agents, such as nascent hydrogen or sulphide of ammonium, is converted into a colourless, difficultly crystallisable substance, which in composition corresponds to leucaniline. It contains $C^{38}H^{33}N^3$.'

The recognition of the nature of aniline-blue led Dr. Hofmann to some experiments which soon became of great industrial importance. Seeing that the substitution of three atoms of phenyl for three atoms of hydrogen in rosaniline induces a change from red to blue, the idea naturally suggested itself to replace the hydrogen by other radicals, such as methyl, ethyl, and amyl. Experiment furnished results of much interest. Rosaniline is readily attacked by the iodides of these radicals: a series of new substances being produced, obviously the salts of trimethyl, triethyl, and triamyl rosaniline, the blue and violet colours of which are similar to that of the phenylated compound. These new colouring-matters are now manufactured on a large scale by Messrs. Brooke, Simpson, and Spiller, of London.

Under the title of '*Improvements in preparing Colouring-Matters for Dyeing and Printing*,' Dr. Hofmann patented (sealed August 29th, 1863) the following processes:—
'I take the substance now well known as "rosaniline," being the base obtained from the various salts of rosaniline found in commerce under the names of "roseine," "magenta," and also by other names, and which is usually prepared from aniline and the homologues thereof, and I mix it with the iodides, bromides, or other salts of the "alcohol radicals," such as iodide of ethyl, methyl, or amyl, or bromides of the same. I employ the substances, by preference, in the proportion of one equivalent of rosaniline to three equivalents of the salt of the alcohol radical; I then heat the mixture, either alone or together with methylated spirit, to a temperature between 212° and 300° F.

in a close vessel under pressure; it is convenient to use an iron boiler provided with a safety-valve. I continue the heat until the desired result is obtained. During the heating the mixture passes through several phases of colouration, being eventually converted into a blue substance. If the process is stopped before the whole is converted into the blue, the mixture is then of a violet or purple colour. For the purpose of dyeing and printing the mixture may be used in the same manner as that in which the aniline colours are employed.'

Nicholson's method of making aniline-blue soluble in water was discovered in 1862, but other soluble aniline-blues are now in the market. Sulphuric acid acting upon aniline-blue can give a series of products varying according to the intensity of the reaction. All are sulphacids of triphenylrosaniline. Bulk has proved the existence of four of these bodies. Sulphuric acid gives, according to circumstances, sulphate of triphenylrosaniline, or its mono- bi- tri- or tetra-sulphuric acid. When we treat hydrochlorate of triphenylrosaniline with strong sulphuric acid and cool the mixture, we obtain a deep red liquor, and hydrochloric acid is liberated. On putting this mixture into water, sulphate of triphenylrosaniline is precipitated unaltered in the form of a fine blue powder. If, instead of cooling the mixture, it is heated and kept for five or six hours at a temperature of 30° C., it yields equally, when poured into water, a blue precipitate, insoluble in that liquid, but which differs from the last-mentioned blue precipitate in being soluble in a solution of soda, in which it gives a red solution. This latter precipitate is the monosulphuric compound of aniline-blue. When recently prepared, it forms deep blue masses, which, when dried in the water-bath, take a fine metallic lustre. It is a monobasic acid, forming with the alkalies salts soluble in water; those of the earths are sparingly soluble. To obtain these salts it is needful to treat the freshly-prepared acids with caustic alkalies. They are scarcely soluble in cold water, and dissolve in hot water with a feeble colouration. The soda salt of this acid is known in commerce as Nicholson's or alkali-blue. It is prepared by digesting the monosulphuric acid of triphenylrosaniline with a solution of caustic soda, not enough to saturate the acid. It is then filtered and evaporated down to dryness at 100° C. It is an amorphous black-grey mass. It dissolves in hot water with a blue colour. The colour of the aqueous solutions of the salts in question is very feeble, but becomes strong if the acid is set free. If acetic acid is used the colour is unalterable by air in the cold. It is decomposed by hot acetic acid and by cold mineral acids. Wool extracts these salts from their solutions in a colourless state if borax or silicate of soda is added. The salt thus fixed on the wool adheres very firmly, and cannot be removed by washing. When the wool is plunged into an acid bath, the colour appears in its full beauty and intensity. The bisulphuric compound is formed by dissolving the aniline-blue in six times its volume of sulphuric acid, and keeping it for five hours at 60° C. It is then poured into water. The greater part is precipitated, but a little remains dissolved, forming a blue liquid. The blue precipitate is bisulphuric acid, and the liquid is the trisulphuric. The bisulphuric compound is scarcely soluble in water, but dissolves in alkalis forming salts soluble in cold water. The soda-salt is known in commerce as ' soluble blue.' It is more soluble than the soda-salt of the former acid. The salts of the heavy metals are mostly insoluble. The trisulphuric acid is prepared by decomposing the blue liquid formed along with the bisulphuric, by means of hydrochloric acid. The precipitate is soluble in water and in alcohol. The highest compound, the tetrasulphuric, is formed by digesting aniline-blue in fuming sulphuric acid at 140° C. The liquid, when poured into water, forms a blue solution, from which the free sulphuric acid may be withdrawn by means of carbonate of lead. On filtering and evaporating we obtain a salt of lead saturated with the tetra-acid. It is soluble in water, and precipitable by alcohol. Its alkaline salts are soluble in water and in excess of alcohol. Those of the heavy metals are soluble in water, but not in alcohol. Silk scarcely withdraws the colour from alkaline and neutral solutions of this acid, but is readily dyed in an acidulated bath. The sulphuric compounds of aniline-violet are analogous, but as their colours are not fine, they are less interesting.

ANILINE-GREEN. Aniline assumes a beautiful indigo-blue colour by the action of chlorate of potash, to which a quantity of hydrochloric acid has been added, and also under the influence of a solution of chlorous acid. Dr. Crace Calvert and Messrs. Lowe and Clift have produced similar blues, and described them under the name of *Azurine*. Most of these blues possess the property of acquiring, under the influence of acids, a green tint called *Emeraldine*. Dr. Calvert obtains this colour directly upon cloth by printing with a mixture of an aniline salt and chlorate of potash, and allowing it to dry. In about twelve hours the green colour is developed. This colour may be converted into blue by being passed through a hot dilute alkaline solution, or through a bath of boiling soap. See VERDINE.

In the process of forming the bluer shades of ethylated violet by Hofmann's patent, described above, there is always produced simultaneously a certain quantity of a green colouring-matter, which may be purified by taking advantage of the circumstance that it is freely soluble in alkaline solutions. When crystallised or precipitated by suitable reagents, it is commonly known by the name of 'iodine-green,' and may be regarded chemically as a double compound, resulting from the union of iodide of ethyl with the already ethylated rosaniline. The colour has an affinity for silk and wool, it is remarkably brilliant, and is much used on that account for dyeing bright green, the shades being modified at pleasure by developing with picric acid. This body undergoes a remarkable alteration by heat, which resolves it again into its constituents, the colour changing from green to violet.

The following method of applying the aniline-green dye on straw will be useful. The straw is laid for some time in boiling water and then washed in cold water. It is next bleached in a bath containing 20 grammes of chloride of lime, and 7 to 9 grammes of sulphuric acid. No more water is used than is needful to give sufficient room for the straw to be well covered and turned about. It is then well washed in cold water. A mordant is then made up of sumach, alum, and tartar. In this it is well worked, and allowed to steep for 15 minutes. Half the mordant is then run off, and the vessel is filled up with pure water. The straw having been taken out, aniline-green, and, if necessary, picric acid, are added, and the straw is worked in this till the right shade is obtained.

ANILINE-RED. The discovery of this colour is clearly due to Dr. Hofmann. In 1858 this chemist wrote, in the 'Proceedings of the Royal Society' (vol. ix. p. 284) as follows:—'The aqueous solution yields, on addition of potassa, an oily precipitate containing a considerable portion of unchanged aniline; on boiling this precipitate with dilute potassa in a retort, the aniline distils over, whilst a viscid oil remains behind, which generally solidifies with a crystalline structure. Washing with cold alcohol, and two or three crystallisations from boiling alcohol, render this body perfectly white and pure, *a very soluble substance of a magnificent crimson colour* remaining in solution. The portion of the black mass, which is insoluble in water, dissolves almost entirely in dilute hydrochloric acid, from which it is re-precipitated by the alkalies in the form of an amorphous pink or dingy precipitate soluble in alcohol, with a *rich crimson colour*. The greater portion of this body consists of the same colouring principle, which accompanies the white crystalline substance.'

This red colouration was indeed noticed in 1843 by Dr. Hofmann, while studying the action of fuming nitric acid upon aniline. In 1856 Natanson observed it when examining the action of Dutch liquid upon aniline. The industrial discovery of aniline-red was made in 1859 by Messrs. Verguin and Renard Brothers, of Lyons. Their process for obtaining it was as follows:—A mixture of ten parts of aniline, and from six to seven parts of tetrachloride of tin, either anhydrous or hydrated, is heated to ebullition for fifteen or twenty minutes. The liquid first becomes yellow, and then gradually more and more red, until at last the colour is so intense that the mass appears black. The mixture is allowed to cool, and then treated with a large quantity of boiling water, which acquires a magnificent red colour, and, without any other preparation, forms a splendid dye both for silk and wool. It is found advisable to previously purify the red colouring-matter, for which purpose its insolubility in saline solutions is made available. If the concentrated red liquid be partially saturated with carbonate of soda, and a quantity of common salt added, the aniline-red is precipitated in a solid state, and constitutes the *fuchsine* of the chemist. This has only to be dissolved in water, alcohol, or acetic acid to prepare the dye-bath.

Renard and Franc stated, at the same time, that anhydrous mercuric, ferric, and cupric chlorides might be used in the place of the chloride of tin.

Several other processes for obtaining aniline-red were suggested, and some of them used. Gerber-Keller treated aniline with the nitrates of mercury. Lauth and Depouilly used nitric acid; and six months before the discovery by these French dyers, two English chemists—Medlock and Nicholson—had separately patented, within a few days of each other, as the result of their experiments, a similar process.

Medlock and Nicholson, and Girard and De Laire, all, in 1860, patented the use of arsenic acid. This process, being now almost exclusively employed, must be described. Arsenic acid is combined with a slight excess of aniline; the crystalline mass is heated by means of a slow fire to about 120° to 140° C., care being taken not to exceed 160° C. The operation, according to the scale on which it is carried on, requires from four to nine hours for completion. A perfectly homogeneous mass, fluid above 100° C., is thus obtained, which on cooling solidifies to a hard substance, with metallic bronze-coloured lustre. When dissolved in boiling water it produces a solution of great richness and purity of colour. If, in the treatment of aniline with arsenic acid, the latter be considerably beyond the proportion of aniline employed, *violet* and *blue dyes* may be formed. The production of such has been patented by Girard and De Laire.

Laurent and Casthélaz have obtained aniline-red direct from benzol, without the preliminary isolation of aniline. Nitrobenzol is treated with a mixture of iron and hydrochloric acid, or with ferric chloride. On heating the mixture, the ferric chloride reacts on the aniline contained in the mixture, transforming it into aniline-red. It is doubtful if the colouring-matter obtained by this process is equal in beauty to that procured from the aniline, and the process is no longer employed. The name of *erythrobenzol* was given by the discoverers to the colouring-matter thus obtained, but it probably consists principally of rosaniline.

The processes described are amongst the best yet devised for the preparation of crude aniline-red. Numerous other methods have been patented, amongst others the following :—

Messrs. Renard Brothers include in their patent the ebullition of aniline with stannous, stannic, mercurous, and mercuric sulphates, with ferric and uranic nitrates and nitrate of silver, and with stannic and mercuric bromides.

Messrs. John Dale and Caro patent the action of nitrate of lead upon aniline, or hydrochlorate of aniline.

Mr. Smith claims the ebullition of aniline with perchloride of antimony, or the action of antimonic acid, peroxide of bismuth, stannic, ferric, mercuric, and cupric oxides upon hydrochlorate or sulphate of aniline at the temperature of 180°.

M. Gerber-Keller (Heilmann in England) claims the production of aniline red from all the metallic salts of the oxacids of nitrogen, sulphur, chlorine, bromine, iodine, phosphorus, arsenic, and, in fact, almost every compound within the range of chemistry. It may well be said of such patents, that 'scientific men cannot speak otherwise than in terms of reprehension. Their claims are founded on random guesswork, not on the results of patient investigation. They are attempts to pre-occupy the whole field, and forestall all the rewards which should be left open to real inventive genius to cultivate and win.'

These processes have reference to the preparation of crude aniline-red. The crude colours contain some undecomposed aniline, mostly in the form of salts. They contain also tarry matters, some insoluble in water and dilute acids; others soluble in bisulphide of carbon, naphtha, or in caustic or carbonated alkalis. If, therefore, the crude red be boiled with an excess of alkali, the undecomposed aniline is expelled, the acid which exists in the product being fixed. On treating the residue with acidulated boiling water, the red is dissolved, while certain tarry matters remain insoluble. If now the boiling solution be filtered, and then saturated with an alkali, the colouring-matter is precipitated in a tolerable state of purity. By re-dissolving the precipitated red in an acid, not employed in excess, a solution is obtained which frequently crystallises, or from which a pure red may be thrown down by a new addition of chloride of sodium, or other alkaline salt. The hydrochlorate of aniline-red is employed in dyeing in France, while the acetate is used in England.

To Dr. Hofmann we are principally indebted for the investigation into the nature of aniline-red. In his paper on the 'Formation of Aniline-Red,' he says, he is 'painfully aware of the imperfections of his researches upon this subject : as yet only a corner of the veil which conceals the truth is raised. The genesis and constitution of aniline-red still remain to be investigated, though the chemical nature and composition of the substance itself are no longer doubtful.'

Aniline-reds are salts of a very remarkable compound, which plays the part of a well-defined base, and to which Dr. Hofmann gave the name of *rosaniline*. This compound, in its anhydrous state, is represented by the formula of $C^{19} H^1 {}^9N^3$. (See ROSANILINE.)

The formation of aniline-red will be best given in Dr. Hofmann's own words :—

'It had been observed by many manufacturers that some varieties of commercial aniline yield much more rosaniline than others. Samples of aniline, boiling at temperatures much higher than the boiling point of the pure compound, are found to be particularly adapted for the production of the red. This observation led Dr. Hofmann to examine carefully the deportment of *pure* aniline under the influence of the several agents by which *commercial* aniline is converted into aniline-red. To this examination he subjected a sample of pure aniline derived from indigo, and other samples made from pure benzol ; this being derived in some cases from benzoic acid, in other cases from coal-tar. These experiments elicited the remarkable fact, *that pure aniline, from whatever source obtained, is incapable of furnishing the red dye*—a result fully confirmed by Mr. E. C. Nicholson, who indeed had been long acquainted with this circumstance. It thus became obvious that commercial aniline must contain another base, the presence of which determines the formation of the colouring-matter. The idea very naturally suggested itself that *toluidine*—which, owing to the difficulty of separating toluol from benzol, is always present in commercial aniline—might be the true source of the colouring-matter. Experiments made with *pure* toluidine showed, however, that this base is not more capable of yielding the red than pure aniline itself. But *the red colouring-matter is instantaneously produced when a mixture of pure aniline and pure toluidine is treated with the chlorides of mercury or tin, or with arsenic acid*, plainly showing that the two bases must co-operate in the formation of the red.'

This result, Dr. Hofmann believes, contains the clue by which may be explained not only the genesis of aniline-red, but also that of the tinctorial ammonias generally. It points, moreover, to the necessity of ascertaining how far the formation of the violet and other colouring-matters, hitherto believed to be exclusively derived from aniline, require the co-operation of toluidine.

Returning to the red derivatives of aniline obtained by the different processes above described, we may state broadly that all these products are composed essentially of rosaniline salts. The red, prepared by the process of Messrs. Renard and Franc, or fuchsine, consists chiefly of hydrochlorate of rosaniline. The azaléine, or aniline-red prepared by nitric acid, is principally nitrate of rosaniline.

In the crude red, produced by the action of arsenic acid, we should find the arseniate of rosaniline, which, by the subsequent treatment, for the sake of purification, is converted into hydrochlorate or acetate of rosaniline.

This is the place to record the fact that for some time past a colourless (or at least slightly rose-coloured) paste, with an alkaline reaction, has been delivered into commerce from Mulhouse, in France; which paste has only to be treated with acetic acid, in which it dissolves with the greatest facility, in order to obtain an extremely rich and beautiful carmine solution, capable of being at once employed for printing stuffs. Now that the characters of rosaniline are known, there cannot be the least doubt that this colourless paste, and certain pink powders of similar properties, consist almost entirely of rosaniline more or less pure, and that they have been prepared by precipitating a solution of a rosaniline salt by an excess of a powerful base, such as soda or lime.

Remarks on the Phenomena observed in the Applications of Aniline-Red.—We are now, moreover, enabled to explain perfectly what takes place when a stuff which has been dyed with aniline-red is acted upon by a powerful acid or alkali. On printing with a powerful acid, the stuff is decolorised with the formation of a yellowish stain, because a rosaniline salt with three equivalents of acid is formed; the triacid salts of this substance being in fact all yellowish, and possessing but little colour. When the material is washed with water, the excess of acid is removed, and the monacid salt reproduced, the red colour being restored.

On printing with a powerful base, for example, with caustic soda, the red disappears as the red rosaniline salt is decomposed, and rosaniline liberated in a colourless condition. But on washing out the soda with water, the red colour reappears, the rosaniline becoming probably carbonated.

If a powerful volatile base be employed, as ammonia, the red also disappears, on account of the liberation of the colourless rosaniline; but in proportion as the ammonia evaporates the red colouration returns, particularly on slightly warming—as the rosaniline, which is a fixed base, expels the ammonia, and re-forms the primitive salt of rosaniline with its peculiar colour. If the rosaniline-dyed fabric be left for a considerable length of time (from twelve to twenty hours) in contact with weak ammonia, the colour, as has been pointed out by Mr. W. Crum, scarcely returns on rinsing with water. This is obviously due to the increased solubility of rosaniline in water containing ammonia, which separates the colouring-matter even from the mordant.

The salts of rosaniline, which are chiefly employed for dyeing silk and wool, are the acetate and the hydrochlorate, and their application is simple in the extreme. The silk is dyed by passing it through a warm aqueous solution of the salt: for the dyeing of wool the solution is heated to a temperature varying between 50° and 60° C.

The force and rapidity with which rosaniline is fixed by silk and wool is the only difficulty to be encountered in this branch of dyeing. In fact, this magnificent colour is precipitated and fixed with such avidity and promptitude by silk and wool, that it is necessary to take particular precautions, and to operate with solutions that are at first comparatively weak, and are only gradually strengthened, to prevent the dyeing being unequal, and the portions first immersed in the bath being more strongly coloured than those afterwards introduced. Cotton is also difficult to dye with rosaniline salts, but for the exactly opposite reason—that it does not present any attraction for this colouring-matter. The fixation of the colour on cotton can therefore only be effected by first treating the cotton with some animal mordant, or with tannic acid.

There are two modes of proceeding for this purpose :—

1. The fabric is printed with the thickened organic mordant ; for goods intended to be dyed throughout the mordant is uniformly spread on the whole surface of the stuff, and fixed either by drying or steaming before the fabrics are introduced into the dye-bath. The colour is only fixed on the mordanted portions, and the shades themselves may be varied according to the nature and composition of the mordant.

Among the substances employed as organic mordants for rosaniline are :—Albumen, whether made from white of egg or from blood ; prepared gluten, prepared casein, gelatine, and tannin—this latter being used either in its combinations with the metallic oxides (as antimonic, stannic, or plumbic), or as tannate of gelatine. For some time oily preparations were employed, as, for example, the sulphomargaric and sulpholeic acids.

2. The mordant is thickened, and at the same time some aniline-red is dissolved in it ; the stuff is printed therewith, dried, and steamed ; the whole is then fixed on the fabric, which then has only to be washed and dried.

This method is principally employed when using albumen, in which acetate of rosaniline is dissolved. Latterly tannin has been employed in preference for fixing aniline-red, particularly in dyeing ordinary articles ; for the mordanting of which albumen, although giving the most satisfactory results, is too costly an article.

It is to Mr. Perkin that we are indebted for the first application of tannin for fixing aniline colours upon cotton.

MM. Kuhlmann and Lightfoot have called attention to the advantages presented by the use of tannate of gelatine ; and Mr. Walter Crum has minutely indicated the treatment by which gluten, the cheapest substitute for albumen, may be rendered available in printing and dyeing with aniline colours.

ANILINE-VIOLET. To this colour in its varieties the names of *Mauve, Anileine, Indisine, Phenameine, Violine, Rosolane, Tyroline,* &c. have been given. Mr. Perkin's patent dates from 26th August, 1856, and this was the original of all the numerous colorific compounds commercially produced. Aniline-violet was first obtained in the crystalline condition in 1860 by M. Scheurer-Kestner, who used mono-hydrated acetic acid as a solvent. Dr. Hofmann informs us that in 1862 Kestner obtained 'splendid well-developed prisms of perfectly pure aniline-violet, which that chemist produced by operating on a very large scale.' The chemical composition of this colour has not yet been definitely established, but the aniline-purple prepared by Perkin's process is the sulphate of a base called Mauveine, having the composition $C^{27}H^{21}N^4$. The process of manufacture is as follows :—A cold and dilute solution of sulphate or any other salt of commercial aniline is mixed with a solution, also cold and dilute, of bichromate of potash. The mixture is well stirred, and allowed to stand for ten or twelve hours. A black precipitate is produced, which is collected upon a filter, washed with cold water, and dried. The black matter is digested with light coal-tar oil, when a brownish-black tarry substance is dissolved from the colouring-matter obtained in the precipitate. The insoluble residue is then dried and digested with wood-spirit or alcohol, or indeed with any liquid capable of dissolving the colouring-matter. The clear solution is separated by filtration or decantation, and distilled in order to recover the alcohol or wood-spirit ; the residue left in the retort is Mr. Perkin's aniline-violet.

The black precipitate, after having been washed with cold water, is extracted by a prolonged ebullition with large quantities of water (sometimes acidulated with from one to two per cent. of acetic acid), an operation which effects the solution of the colouring-matter. The filtered solutions are concentrated as much as possible, and while boiling are precipitated by the addition of caustic soda. The precipitate is filtered off and washed for some time with an alkaline solution, which facilitates the extraction of the excess of bichromate of potash, and removes a reddish colouring-matter affecting the purity of the aniline-violet. It is then treated with cold water until the alkali is removed, and the washings become coloured. The violet is thus obtained in the form of a paste.

The following processes have also been proposed for the production of aniline-violet:—

1. Oxidation of an aniline salt by a solution of permanganate of potassium.—*Williams.*

2. Oxidation of an aniline salt by a solution of ferricyanide of potassium.—*Smith.*

3. Oxidation of a cold and dilute solution of hydrochlorate of aniline by a dilute solution of chloride of lime.—*Bolley, Beale, and Kirkman.*

4. Oxidation of a salt of aniline in an aqueous solution by peroxide of manganese.—*Kay.*

5. Oxidation of a salt of aniline by the peroxide of lead under the influence of an acid.—*Price.*

6. Oxidation of a salt of aniline by free chlorine or free hypochlorous acid.—*Smith.*

7. Oxidation of a salt of aniline by the double chloride of copper and sodium.—*Dale and Caro.*

The only processes which are employed industrially are those in which bichromate of potash, chloride of lime, and chloride of copper are used. The dyeing of silk or wool by means of aniline-violet is a process of the easiest description.

Dyeing Silk.—An alcoholic solution of the violet purple is diluted with eight times its volume of hot water previously acidulated with tartaric acid. This liquid is poured into the dyeing-bath of cold water slightly acidulated. Through this the silk is passed until the required shade is attained. The tint is rendered bluish by means of indigo-carmine. Sulphuric acid added to the dye-bath causes the violet to assume a greyish shade. This may be increased until a very beautiful grey (*gris perle*) is obtained. This colour is much used by the silk-dyers of Lyons.

Dyeing Wool.—This is conducted at a temperature of 50° or 60° C., the dye-bath consisting simply of a dilute aqueous solution of colouring-matter, without any acid.

Printing upon Silk and Wool.—The paste of aniline-violet is dissolved in about five times its weight of acetic acid (specific gravity, 1·060), and mixed with enough gum-water to form a printing material. The fabrics when printed are submitted to the action of steam, and then washed.

Dyeing Cotton—Since cotton does not, like silk or wool, present much attraction for the aniline colours, the dyer employs albumen, soluble gluten, or tannin. In some cases the oxides of tin, of aluminium, of lead, or of antimony are used. Sulphuric acid has also the property of fixing the aniline-violet on cotton. The animal or tannin mordants are printed on the cotton, which is steamed so as to fix it, and it is then dyed in an acidulated solution of the colour.

Violet Impérial.—This violet, which is essentially different from the mauve, is formed by modifications of the aniline reds and blues. It is produced thus :—Equal quantities of aniline and dry hydrochlorate of rosaniline are heated to a temperature of 180° C. for about four hours. MM. Girard and De Laire first patented this colour, and on account of its great beauty it is much used, although not quite so permanent as the mauve. Mr. ·E. C. Nicholson forms another violet by heating aniline-red in a suitable apparatus to a temperature between 200° and 215° C. This mass is exhausted with acetic acid, and the deep-violet solution diluted with enough alcohol to give to the dye a convenient strength.

Aniline-violet resists the action of light to a very considerable extent, although Chevreul has shown that it is inferior in this respect to either madder, cochineal, or indigo.

ANILINE-YELLOW. In the preparation of aniline-red there arises a great number of secondary products. Amongst others, a yellow colouring-matter has been separated by Mr. Nicholson and examined by Dr. Hofmann. The name of *Chrysaniline* has been given to this very beautiful yellow colour, which has been proved to be a well-defined base. The preparation of chrysaniline is simple. The residue from which the rosaniline has been extracted is submitted for some time to a current of steam, when a quantity of the base passes into solution. Addition of nitric acid to this solution precipitates the chrysaniline in the form of a difficultly soluble nitrate.

Hofmann has shown that chrysaniline is intimately related to rosaniline and leucaniline, only differing from the first by two equivalents, and from the second by four equivalents of hydrogen :—

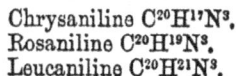

Chrysaniline $C^{20}H^{17}N^3$.
Rosaniline $C^{20}H^{19}N^3$.
Leucaniline $C^{20}H^{21}N^3$.

Chrysaniline forms two series of salts, the greater number of which are well crystallised. The most remarkable salt of chrysaniline is the nitrate, which is so insoluble in water that nitric acid may be precipitated, even from a dilute aqueous solution, by means of the more soluble hydrochlorate or acetate of chrysaniline. These, when poured into a nitric solution, rapidly give rise to the formation of an orange-red chrysaniline precipitate of nitrate of chrysaniline. This chrysaniline and its salts dye silks and wools a splendid golden-yellow colour. Such is the general character of the aniline colours. They have been used as printing-inks, which are very permanent. See 'Watts's Dictionary of Chemistry.'

E. Waller, E.M., in the 'American Chemist,' gives the following list of the names of the various coal-tar colours, both commercial and chemical, together with their chemical formulæ, when those could be found. (It should be observed that the old notation has been employed throughout). 'Many of the compounds here mentioned are not now in use as dyes, either because they are too expensive, or because their use is inconvenient, requiring too complicated a treatment or rare chemicals to fix them upon the goods, or because they have been superseded by dyes of better quality. Several colours, black especially, are usually produced on the fibre of the goods by printing them with various salts of aniline and rosaniline, and then with salts of copper, chlorates, &c. Most of the dyes called aniline-blacks give, when dissolved, deep green solutions. Of those to which the formulæ are not given, the chemical formulæ are not as yet known, or they have not been given by those works to which I have resorted on the subject. The derivatives of aniline and toluidine are given together, as the two are with difficulty separated from each other, and in course of manufacture the separation is never attempted.'

COLOURS DERIVED FROM ANILINE OR PHENYLAMINE ($C^{12}H^7N$) AND TOLUIDINE OR TOLUYLAMINE ($C^{14}H^9N$).

Reds.

Hydrochlorate of rosaniline—
$C^{40}H^{19}N^3$, HCl.
Called also aniline red, new red, magenta, solferino, fuchsine, anileine rougé, roseine, and azaline.

Acetate of rosaniline—
$C^{40}H^{19}N^3$, HO, $C^4H^3O^3$.
Known also by the same names as the above.

Nitrate of rosaniline—
$C^{40}H^{19}N^3$, HO, NO^5.
Known by the same names as the hydrochlorate; also as rubine and rubine imperial.

Dicodhydrate of trimethylchrysaniline—
$C^{40}H^{14}(C^2H^3)^3N^3$, $2(HOI)$.
Called also chrysaniline red.

Nitrosophenyline, $C^6H^6N^2O$.

Chemical formula unknown—
Xylidine, tar red, soluble ruby.

Blues and Violets.

These shade into one another so gradually that they cannot well be separated.

Hydrochlorate of monophenylrosaniline,
$C^{40}H^{18}(C^{12}H^5)$ N^3,HCl.
Called also rosaniline violet, red monophenylrosaniline, and Hofmann's violet.

Hydrochlorate of diphenylrosaniline—
$C^{40}H^{19}(C^{12}H^5)^2N^3$,HCl.
Also known as rosaniline violet and Hofmann's violet.

Triphenylrosaniline, or triphenyl rosaniline, $C^{40}H^{16}(C^{12}H^5)^3$,$N^3$.
Called also aniline blue, rosaniline blue, Hofmann's blue; bleu de Paris, bleu de Lyons, bleu de Mulhouse, bleu de Mexique, bleu de nuit, bleu lumière, bleuine, azurine, and night blue.

Hydrochlorate of triphenylrosaniline—
$C^{40}H^{16}(C^{12}H^5)^3N^3$,HCl.
Known also by the same names as the above.

Acetate of triphenylrosaniline—
$C^{40}H^{16}(C^{12}H^5)^3N^3$,HO,$C^4H^3O^3$.
Known also by the same names as the above.

Bisulphotriphenylrosaniline acid—
$C^{40}H^{16}(C^{12}H^5)^3N^3$,$4SO^3$.
Called also Nicholson's blue and soluble blue.

Hydrochlorate of monethylrosaniline—
$C^{40}H^{18}(C^{12}H^3)N^3$,HCl.
Called also Hofmann's red violet.

Hydriodate of ethylrosaniline—
$C^{40}H^{18}(C^4H^5)N^3$,HI.
Called also Hofmann's red violet.

Ethyliodate of ethylrosaniline—
$C^{40}H^{18}(C^4H^5)N^3C^4H^5I$.
Called also fuchsine with a blue tint, and Hofmann's violet red.

Hydrochlorate of diethylrosaniline—
$C^{40}H^{17}(C^4H^5)^2N^3$,HCl.
Called also Hofmann's blue.

Ethyliodate of diethylrosaniline—
$C^{40}H^{17}(C^4H^5)^2N^3$,$C^4H^5I$.
Called also Hofmann's red violet and ethylic rosaniline violet.

Hydrochlorate of triethylrosaniline—
$C^{40}H^{16}(C^4H^5)^3N^3$,HCl.
Called also Hofmann's blue.

Ethyliodate of triethylrosaniline—
$C^{40}H^{16}(C^4H^5)^3N^3$,$C^4H^5I$.
Called also Hofmann's blue and ethylic rosaniline violet.

Ethylbromate of triethylrosaniline—
$C^{40}H^{16}(C^4H^5)^3N^3$,$C^4H^5Br$.
Called also brimula.

Hydrochlorate of methylrosaniline—
$C^{40}H^{18}(C^2H^3)N^3$,HCl.

Hydriodate of methylrosaniline—
$C^{40}H^{16}(C^2H^3)N^3$,HI.

Hydrochlorate of dimethylrosaniline—
$C^{40}H^{17}(C^2H^3)^2N^3$,HCl.

Hydrochlorate of trimethylrosaniline—
$C^{40}H^{16}(C^2H^3)^3N^3$,HCl.

Methylaniline, $C^{12}H^6(C^2H^3)N$.
Called also methylic rosaniline violet and violet de Paris.

Mauvaniline, $C^{38}H^{17}N^3$.

Voilanile, $C^{36}H^{15}N^3$.

Mauveine, $C^{54}H^{24}N^4$.
Called also mauve, aniline purple, Perkin's violet, indisine, analeine harmaline, violine, and mauve rosolane.

Hydrochlorate of mauveine—
$C^{54}H^{24}N^4$,HCl.
Known also by the same names as mauveine.

Hydrochlorate of ethylmauveine—
$C^{54}H^{23}(C^4H^5)N^4$,HCl.
Called also dahlia.

Ditolylrosaniline. $C^{40}H^{17}(C^{14}H^7)^2N^3$.

Called also toluidine blue.

Tritolylrosaniline, $C^{40}H^{16}(C^{14}H^7)^3N^3$.

Chemical formulæ unknown—

Regina blue, opal blue, regina purple, bleu de Fayolle, violet de Mulhouse, Britannia violet, geranosine, violet imperial.

Greens.

$C^{40}H^{13}(C^4H^5)N^3,2HO$.

Known as Aldehyde green, aniline green, viridine, and emeraldine.

$C^{40}H^{13}(C^2H^3)^6N^3,2HO$.

Known as iodine green and iodide of methyl green.

Chemical formulæ unknown—

Iodide of ethyl green, Perkin's green.

Yellows.

Chrysaniline, $C^{40}H^{17}N^3$.

Called also Phosphine, aniline yellow, and yellow fuchsine,

Nitrophenyldiamine. $C^{20}H^6O^6,HCl$.

Chrysotoluidine, $C^{42}H^{20}N^3$.

Zinaline, $C^{40}H^{19}N^2O,^2(?)$.

Chemical formulæ unknown—

Dinitroaniline, Field's orange (?).

Browns.

Chemical formulæ unknown.

Havanna brown, Bismarck brown, aniline brown, aniline maroon, Napoleon brown.

Greys.

Chemical formulæ unknown—

Aniline grey, argentine.

Black.

Chemical formulæ unknown—

Aniline black.

COLOURS DERIVED FROM NAPHTHALINE OR NAPHTHYLHYDRATE—($C^{20}H^8$).

Reds.

Chloroxynaphthylic acid, $C^{20}H^5ClO^6$.

Called also pseudoalizarine, naphthylic red, and chloronaphthaline acid.

Chemical formulæ unknown—

Roseonaphthaline, carminaphtha.

Yellows.

Binitronaphthaline, $C^{20}H^6(NO^4)^2$.

Called also binitronaphthal, naphthalamine yellow, naphthylic yellow, golden yellow, and Manchester yellow.

Binitronaphthylic acid—

$C^{20}H^5(NO^4)^2O,HO$.

Known also by the same names as the above.

Trinitronaphthylic acid—

$C^{20}H^4(NO^4)^3O,HO$.

COLOURS DERIVED FROM CARBOLIC ACID AND PHENIC ACID, PHENYLHYDRATE OR PHENOL—($C^{12}H^6O^2$).

Reds.

Picramic acid, $C^{12}H^3(NO^4)^2NO^2$.

Called also picramine acid.

Coralline, $C^{20}H^8O^4$.

Called also peonine.

Coralline amide, $C^{20}H^9NO^2$.

Called also red coralline.

Blue.

Isopurpuric acid, $C^{12}H^3(NO^4)^2NO^3,2Cl$.

Called also bicyanide of picramyl and Grénat.

Green.

Chemical formulæ unknown—

Chloropicrine.

Yellows.

Picric acid, $C^{12}H^2(NO^4)^3O,HO$.

Called also trinitrophenic acid and carbazotic acid.

Aurine, $C^{24}H^{12}O^6$.

Called also rosolic acid.

Browns.

Picrate of ammonia—

$NH^4O,C^{,2}H^2(NO^4)^2O$.

Isopurpurate of potash.

Chemical formulæ unknown.

Phenyl brown, or rotheine, or phénicienne.

Azuline (blue), $C^{24}H^{11}NO^4$, and another viridine (formula unknown), are both an aniline and a carbolic acid colour, being produced by the action of carbolic acid on a derivative of aniline.

Cyanine (blue), $C^{60}H^{35}N^2I$, is described in some works among the coal-tar colours, but is derived from chinchonine.

Among the blues and violets, the names Hofmann's blue or Hofmann's violet are seen frequently to occur. These are distinguished in commerce by suffixing the letters B or R the number of times that either is repeated, showing the relative blueness or redness of the dye. They range from BBBB to RRRR. The reddish shades are those in which the least substitution has taken place, as in the monethyl- or monophenyl-rosaniline, &c., while the bluest of these are those which are triethyl- triphenylrosanilines, &c. The series of names given for triphenylrosaniline and the hydrochlorate of the same base are frequently interchanged. On the ethyliodates and ethylbromates. authorities appear to differ as to whether they really are ethyliodates, &c., or not. The colours are prepared by the action of iodide of ethyl, &c. upon rosaniline or some of its salts, and iodine is given off in the operation; but whether one equivalent of the iodide of ethyl remains behind or not in a state of chemical combination, does not appear to be fully established. Were the latter supposition the case, the C⁴H⁵I of those formulæ would be replaced by 2HO, and the chemical name would necessarily be changed to correspond. The same question might be raised regarding some of the Hofmann violets with their equivalent of HCl or HO, C⁴ H³O³, but as one of these acids is used in the solution when purifying the colour, the probabilities are that the base unites with it, and the colour goes to market as a salt and not as an isolated base. The terms, direct blues and purified blues, are simply commercial terms indicating the amount of purification which the dyes have received, the first-named being the most impure. Among the greens the terms aniline-green and emeraldine are synonymous terms applied to a colour formed in the fibre of the goods. Viridine is a name applied to a true green, but the term has also been used for a mixture of indigo and picric acid, which cannot properly be called an aniline colour.

ANIMAL BLACK. Refuse animal matters are placed in a retort, and submitted to destructive distillation. The gases, evolved on decomposition, are usually burnt, while water, oily matter, and ammoniacal compounds distil over, and are condensed. There remains in the retort a carbonaceous mass, which, when levigated and ground in a mill, forms 'animal black.' It is in a more finely-divided state than bone-black, and is used in the preparation of blacking and of printing-ink.

ANIMAL CHARCOAL. See BONE-BLACK.

ANIMÉ. A resin of a pale brown yellow colour, transparent and brittle. It exudes from a large American tree, called by Piso, *jetaiba;* and by the Indians *courbaril.* It appears to be a species of *Hymenæa.* It occurs in pieces of various sizes, and it often contains so many insects belonging to living species, as to have merited its name, as being animated. It contains about a fifth of 1 per cent. of a volatile oil, which gives it an agreeable odour. Alcohol does not dissolve the genuine animé, as I have ascertained by careful experiments, nor does caoutchoucine; but a mixture of the two, in equal parts, softens it into a tremulous jelly, though it will not produce a liquid solution. When reduced to this state, the insects can be easily picked out, without injury to their most delicate parts. On the contrary, Dr. R. D. Thomson says, animé resin is distinguished from copal by its ready solubility in alcohol; and that when digested in cold alcohol a portion remains undissolved, which may be dissolved in hot alcohol, from which it crystallises on cooling. Sir R. Kane gives C⁴⁰H³³O (**C⁴⁰H⁶⁶O**), as the composition of this gum-resin.—See 'Watts's Dictionary of Chemistry.'

The specific gravity of the different specimens of animé varies from 1·054 to 1·057. When exposed to heat, in a glass retort over a spirit-flame, it softens, and, by careful management, it may be brought into liquid fusion without discolouration. It then exhales a white vapour of an ambrosial odour, which being condensed in water, and the liquid being tested, is found to be succinic acid.

It is extensively used by the varnish-makers, who fuse it at a pretty high heat, and in this state combine it with their oils or other varnishes. It is also employed, on account of its agreeable smell when burning, in the manufacture of pastilles.

Gum-animé is sometimes mistaken for amber, but the fossil resin can generally be distinguished by its greater hardness. The gum-animé of Zanzibar is a semi-fossil resin, believed to be the produce of a species of *Trachylobium.*

ANISEED. (*Anis,* Fr.; *Anis,* Ger.) The fruit or seed of the *Pimpinella anisum,* largely cultivated in Malta, Spain, and Germany; used in the preparation of the oil of anise (*oleum anisi*), the spirit of anise (*spiritus anisi*), and anise-water (*aqua anisi*). It is also used in cordials. In 1855, 963 cwts. were imported. The *oleum badiani,* or the *oil of star anise* (*illicium anisatum*), has the colour and taste of the oil of anise; but it preserves its fluidity at 35·6° F. It is sometimes fraudulently substituted for *oleum anisi.*—*Pereira.*

ANKER. A liquid measure of Amsterdam, which contains 32 gallons English. During the war, when communication with Holland was constant, and sailors and soldiers were constantly passing from one country to the other, the anker was as commonly used as a measure in our seaports as in those of Holland. The anker of brandy was frequently smuggled into this country.

ANNEALING or **NEALING.** (*Le recuit,* Fr.; *das Anlassen,* Ger.) A process by which glass is rendered less frangible; and metals which have become brittle, either in consequence of fusion or long-continued hammering, are again rendered malleable. When a glass vessel is allowed to cool immediately after being made, it will, if a small splinter of flint, or an angular fragment of quartz, is dropped gently into it, fly to pieces with great violence, sometimes immediately, sometimes after a few minutes. This extreme fragility is prevented by annealing, or placing the vessels in a hot oven, where they take several hours, or even some days, to cool.

Similar phenomena are exhibited in a higher degree by glass-tears, or Prince Rupert's drops, produced by letting drops of melted glass fall into cold water. Their form resembles that of a pear, rounded at one extremity, and tapering to a very slender tail at the other. If a part of the tail be broken off, the whole drop flies to pieces with a loud explosion; and yet the tail of a drop may be cut away by a glass-cutter's wheel, or the thick end may be struck smartly with a hammer, without the fear of sustaining any injury. When heated to redness, and permitted to cool gradually in the open air, they lose these peculiarities, and do not differ sensibly from common glass.

The peculiar brittleness of unannealed glass is, by many manufacturers, referred to the following conditions. The exterior surface of the glass cooling quicker than the layers of glass beneath, the two portions of glass are supposed to be in different degrees of tension; as they technically express it, *a stretched skin of glass* is formed; and as the arrangement of the particles is different in this film from their disposition in those parts which have cooled more slowly, there is a constant tendency to fracture, the slightest scratch upon this 'skin' disturbing the entire molecular arrangement.

If any mass of glass or of metal cools rapidly, there will be, according to the thickness of the mass, a greater or less difference between the arrangement of the constituent particles on the outer and inner sections. The process of annealing secures an equal arrangement throughout the mass.

When metals have been extended to a certain degree under the hammer, they become brittle, and incapable of being further extended without cracking. In this case the workman restores their malleability, sometimes by annealing, or, in other cases, by heating them red-hot and allowing them to cool slowly. The rationale of this process seems to be, that the hammering and extension of the metal destroys the kind of arrangement which the particles of the metal had previous to the hammering; and that the annealing, by softening the metal, enables it to recover its original structure.

Of late years a mode has been discovered of rendering cast-iron malleable, without subjecting it to the action of puddling. The process is somewhat similar to that employed in annealing glass. The metal is kept imbedded in ground charcoal, or in powdered hæmatite, for several hours at a high temperature, and then allowed to cool slowly. In this manner vessels are made of cast-iron which can sustain considerable violence without being broken. See IRON, MALLEABLE.

ANNOTTO or ANATTO. See ARNATTO.

ANORTHITE. A lime felspar. See FELSPAR.

ANTELOPE HORN is used occasionally for ornamental knife-handles. See HORN.

ANTHRACENE. $C^{28}H^{10}$ ($C^{14}H^{10}$). A hydrocarbon, known also as paranaphthaline, discovered by J. Dumas in 1831. It has become of considerable commercial importance since Messrs. Graebe and Liebermann discovered, in 1869, that anthracene could be converted into a valuable colouring-matter identical with the natural alizarine of the madder-root.

Anthracene is produced in the dry distillation of coal, bituminous shale, or wood; and is found in the heavy semi-fluid portion of the tar which comes over towards the close of the distillation. The substance known as 'green grease,' obtained by distilling coal-tar, and used as a common lubricating agent for machinery, contains about 20 per cent. of anthracene associated with naphthaline and other hydrocarbons. From this product, crude anthracene may be obtained by the use of the hydro-extractor, and by submitting the raw product to strong pressure. The crude anthracene is purified by solution in hot coal-tar naphtha and repeated recrystallisation. A yellow tint, due to the presence of chrysogen, may be expelled by exposure to sunlight, and the anthracene is finally purified from any other hydrocarbons by boiling with alcoholic picric acid.

Thus obtained, the pure anthracene appears in small, well-defined, lustrous crystalline laminæ of a clear white colour, and exhibiting, when pure, a beautiful violet fluorescence. The specific gravity of anthracene is 1·149. It melts at about 415° F., and sublimes at higher temperatures. Anthracene is insoluble in water, but readily soluble in boiling alcohol, in ether, benzole, volatile oils, and bisulphide of carbon. By prolonged exposure to light it passes into an isomeric modification known as *paranthracene*. Under the influence of oxidising agents it is converted into *anthraquinone*, from which artificial alizarine may be prepared. See ALIZARINE.

ANTHRACENE-RED. A name for artificial alizarine. See ALIZARINE.

ANTHRACITE. (ἄνθραξ, *coal.*) A variety of coal containing a larger proportion of carbon and less bituminous matter than common coal.—*De la Beche.*

'We see the same series of coal-beds becoming so altered in their horizontal range, that a set of beds *bituminous* in one locality is observed gradually to change into *anthracitic* in another. Taking the coal-measures of South Wales and Monmouthshire, we have a series of accumulations in which the coal-beds become not only more anthracitic towards the west, but also exhibit this change in a plane which may be considered as dipping SSE. at a moderate angle, the amount of which is not yet clearly ascertained, so that in the natural sections afforded we have bituminous coals in the high grounds and anthracitic coals beneath. This fact is readily observed either in the Neath or Swansea valleys, where we have bituminous coals on the south and anthracite on the north; and more bituminous coal-beds on the heights than beneath, some distance up these valleys—those of the Nedd and Tawe. Though the terms bituminous coal and anthracite have been applied to marked differences, the changes are so gradual that there is no sudden modification to be seen. To some of the intermediate kinds the term 'free-burning' has been given, and thus three chief differences have been recognised.'—*Memoirs of the Geological Survey.*

The term *Culm* is applied both to an inferior kind of anthracite only worked for making lime, or for mixing with clay, and to the small pieces of good anthracite obtained in working the true anthracite beds. It is also called *Blind Coal, Glance Coal,* and *Kilkenny Coal.*

The term *Culm* is applied generally to anthracite in our parliamentary returns.

There are three very distinct 'trades' in anthracite. There is, first, that where the coal is sold exactly as it is worked, 'through and through,' as it is termed, or *Through Culm,* which is used entirely for lime-burning. This coal is not of so pure a kind as that from which the large coal is picked out, and is sometimes called *Bastard Stone Coal.* The trade in the Neath district is entirely of this kind. In Swansea and Llanelly it is partly of this kind, and partly of the kind where the large coal is picked out, and sold as *Stone Coal* for the various purposes to which that coal is applied, leaving the small to be shipped, also for lime-burning purposes, under the name of *Stone Coal Culm.* In Pembrokeshire no 'through culm' is shipped. There is one curious lot of 4,000 tons annually shipped in Swansea under the name of *Lambskin,* which is almost dust; it is sent to one market—Cardiganshire, where it is used entirely for mixing with clay; the mixture, under the name of *Fireballs,* being used for household purposes. This mixture, made of the ordinary *Stone Coal Culm,* is also very commonly used in parts of Pembrokeshire and Caermarthenshire.

Anthracite coal is obtained in the western divisions of the South Wales coal-field, at Bideford in Devonshire, at Walsall in Staffordshire, in Ireland, and in Scotland, in Switzerland, Savoy and Italy. Commencing at the top of the Neath valley, and following the north crop of the South Wales coal-field downwards to Kidwelly, from east to west, there are 48 anthracite collieries—and in Pembrokeshire there are 16 of these collieries. It is found abundantly in America. Professor H. D. Roger's 'Transactions of American Geologists' states that in the great Apalachian coal-field, extending 720 miles, with a chief breadth of 180 miles, the coal is bituminous towards the western limit, where it is level and unbroken, becoming anthracitic towards the south-west, where it is disturbed. Anthracitic coal is also found in the coal-fields of France, especially in the departments of Isère, the High Alps, Gard, Mayenne, and of Sarth; about 42,271,000 kilogrammes (of 2·2046 avoirdupois pounds each) are produced annually. Anthracite is also raised in Belgium.

The following analyses of bituminous and anthracite coals will sufficiently show the differences:—

Locality	Name of Coal	Carbon	Volatile Matter	Ashes
	BITUMINOUS			
Birtley Works, Newcastle-on-Tyne .	. . . .	60·50	35·50	4·00
Alfreton, Derbyshire	. . . .	52·46	42·50	2·04
	ANTHRACITE			
Neath Abbey . .	Pwlferon Vein, 5th bed . .	91·08	8·00	0·92
Swansea . . .	Peacock Coal . . .	89·00	7·50	3·50
Ystalyfera . .	Brass Vein . . .	92·46	6·04	1·50
Cwm Neath . .	Nine-feet Vein . . .	93·12	5·22	1·50
France . . .	Anthracite, common . .	79·15	7·37	13·25
„ . . .	Côte-d'Or . . .	82·60	8·60	8·80
„ . . .	Mais Saize . . .	83·80	7·50	9·50
Pennsylvania . .	Beaver Meadow . . .	92·30	6·42	1·28
„ . .	Shenoweth Vein . . .	94·10	1·40	4·50
„ . .	Black Spring Gap . .	80·57	7·15	3·28
„ . .	Nealey's Tunnel . . .	89·20	5·40	5·40
Massachusetts . .	Mansfield Mine . . .	97·00	...	3·00
Rhode Island . .	Portsmouth Mine . . .	85·84	10·50	3·66
Westphalia . .	Schafberg, Alexander Seam .	82·02	8·69	9·29

Anthracite is not an original variety of coal, but a modification of the same beds which remain bituminous in other parts of the region. Anthracite beds, therefore, are not separate deposits in another sea, nor coal-measures in another area, nor interpolations among bituminous coals; but the bituminous beds themselves, altered into a natural coke, from which the volatile bituminous oils and gases have been driven off.—*J. P. Lesley, on Coal.*

Anthracite—now exclusively used for iron-making, steam-engines, and for domestic purposes in the United States—was some 50 years since regarded as incombustible refuse, and thrown away.

Principal Localities of Anthracite and Anthracitic Coal, &c.

	Specific Gravity.	Weight of a Cubic Yard in lbs.
EUROPE.		
South Wales:—Swansea	1·263	2131
Cyfarthfa	1·337	2256
Yniscedwin	1·354	2284
Average	1·445	2278
Ireland, mean	1·445	2376
France, Allier	1·380	2207
Tantal	1·390	2283
Brassac	1·430	2413
Belgium:—Mons	1·307	2105
Westphalia	1·305	2278
Prussian Saxony	1·466	2474
Saxony	1·300	2193
Average of Europe		2281
AMERICA.		
Pennsylvania:—Lykens Valley	1·327	2240
Lebanon co., grey vein	1·379	2327
Schuylkill co., Lorberry Creek	1·472	2484
Pottsville, Sharp Mountain	1·412	2382
„ Peach	1·446	2440
„ Salem Vein	1·574	2649
Tamaqua, north vein	1·600	2700
Manch Chunk	1·550	2615
Nesquehoning	1·558	2646
Wilkesbarre, best	1·472	2884
West Mahoney	1·371	2313
Beaver Meadow	1·600	2700
Girardville	1·600	2700
Hazelton	1·550	2615
Broad Mountain	1·700	2869
Lackawanna	1·609	2715
Massachusetts:—Mansfield	1·710	2882
Rhode Island:—Portsmouth	1·810	3054
Average in United States		2601

The calorific value of anthracite coal is well shown by the following results from Dr. Fyfe's experiments to compare Scotch and English bituminous coals with anthracite, in regard to their evaporative power, in a high-pressure boiler of a 4-horse engine having a grate with 8·15 square feet of surface; also in a waggon-shaped copper boiler, open to the air, surface 18 feet, grate 1·55.

Kind of Fuel employed	Pounds burnt per Hour on the Grate	Duration of the Trial in Hours	Temperature of the Water	Pounds of Water evaporated from the initial Temperature by 1 lb. of Coal	Pounds of Water at 212° from 1 lb. of Coal	Coal per Hour on 1 Square Foot of Grate	Time in Seconds of consuming 1 lb. of Coal	Pounds evaporated per Hour from each Square Foot of Surface	Remarks
Middlerig Scotch coal.	81·33	9	45°	6·66	7·74	10·00	44·27	..	Pressure 17 lbs. per sq. inch.
Scotch coal, different variety from preceding	108	5	170	6·62	6·89	13·25	33·33	..	Ditto.
ANTHRACITE	47·94	8½	45	8·73	10·10	5·88	75·09	..	Ditto.
Scotch coal, from near Edinburgh	8·24	8½	50	5·38	6·90	5·31	436·89	3·15	Low pressure, open copper boiler.
English bituminous coal.	6·07	8·4	50	7·84	9·07	3·91	503·08	3·06	Ditto.

Space will not admit of our entering fully into the question of the evaporative power of anthracite ; but its advantages under certain conditions are fully established.

In this country anthracite coal is used in the manufacture of iron in the following furnaces :—

Ystalyfera in Glamorganshire   .   .   . 11 furnaces in blast in 1871
Yniscedwyn in Brecknockshire   .   .   . 2   ,,   ,,

The quantity of anthracite-iron made in 1871 being 34,761 tons.

The following table shows the progress of production in America of anthracite from 1862 to 1871 inclusive, from Schuylkill, Lehigh, and Wyoming :—

Years	Tons	Years	Tons
1862	7,387,422	1867	11,725,588
1863	9,187,588	1868	12,912,751
1864	9,657,723	1869	12,746,938
1865	8,814,995	1870	14,266,190
1866	10,498,970	1871	13,855,307

Mr. P. W. Sheafer, in an address recently delivered to the students of the Pardee Scientific Department in Lafayette College, says :—

'In our estimates of the areas of the anthracite coal-fields of Pennsylvania, we place that of the

Southern coal-field at   .   .   .   .   .   . 146 square miles
Of the Shamokin district 50   ,,
Of the Mahanog district 41   ,,
Of the Upper Lehigh field   35   ,,
Of the Wyoming and Lackawanna field   .   .   . 198   ,,

Total,   470 square miles,
or 300,800 acres.

'Averaging the total coal thickness of the southern coal-field at 75 feet, and that of the middle and northern fields at 45 feet, we have a total content (one cubic yard equalling one ton) of say   .   .   .   .   .   . 26,361,076,000 tons
Deduct one-half for waste in mining, preparing,
and faults   .   .   .   . 13,180,538,000 tons

and we have a net result of.   .   .   .   . 13,180,538,000 tons

'The amount mined from 1820 to 1870, the first fifty years of the anthracite coal-trade, was 206,666,325 tons; so that we have yet in store 12,973,878,675 tons. The progress of our coal-trade is thus shown :—

In 1820 the production was .   .   .   .   .   . 365 tons
from 1820 to 1830   .   .   .   . 533,194 ,,
,, 1830 to 1840   .   .   .   . 5,406,711 ,,
,, 1840 to 1850   .   .   .   . 15,952,893 ,,
,, 1850 to 1860   .   .   .   . 42,088,644 ,,
,, 1860 to 1870   .   .   .   . 50,337,354 ,,

'The production of anthracite coal in Pennsylvania in the year 1872 was unprecedently large, as will be seen by the following Table, illustrating the progress of the extraction year by year during the last thirty years :

Year	Tons	Year	Tons
1843	1,263,598	1858	6,839,369
1844	1,630,850	1859	7,808,255
1845	2,013,013	1860	8,513,123
1846	2,344,005	1861	7,954,264
1847	2,882,309	1862	7,869,407
1848	3,089,238	1863	9,566,006
1849	3,242,966	1864	10,177,475
1850	3,358,899	1865	9,652,391
1851	4,448,916	1866	12,703,882
1852	4,993,471	1867	12,988,725
1853	5,195,151	1868	13,834,132
1854	6,002,334	1869	13,723,030
1855	6,608,567	1870	15,849,899
1856	6,927,580	1871	15,113,407
1857	6,644,941	1872	18,400,000

ANTHRAPURPURIN. A colouring-matter recently obtained by Mr. W. H. Perkin from commercial artificial alizarine. The crude alizarine is dissolved in dilute solution of carbonate of soda, and the product well agitated with freshly-precipitated alumina, which combines with the alizarine, leaving the anthrapurpurin in solution. This solution, having been filtered and heated to the boiling point, is acidified with hydrochloric acid, whereby the colouring-matter is precipitated; this may be purified by repeated boiling in alcohol.

As a dyeing agent anthrapurpurin greatly resembles alizarine, giving red colours with alumina, and purple and black with iron mordants. The shades of colour, however, are different with the two materials; the anthrapurpurin reds being much purer and less blue, whilst the purples are bluer and the blacks more intense than those with alizarine. (See 'Journ. Chem. Soc.' May, 1873.)

ANTI-ATTRITION, or, ANTI-FRICTION COMPOSITION. Various preparations have been, from time to time, introduced for the purpose of removing, as much as possible, the friction of machinery. Black lead, or plumbago, mixed with a tenacious grease, has been much employed. Peroxide of iron, finely divided hæmatite, &c., have also been used.

ANTICHLORE. A term employed by bleachers to the means of obviating the pernicious after-effects of chlorine upon the pulp of paper, or stuffs, which have been bleached therewith. Manufacturers have been in the habit of using sulphite of soda, whose action upon the adhering bleaching salt, which cannot be removed by washing, gives rise to the formation of sulphate and hydrosulphate of soda and chloride of sodium. Chloride of tin has been recommended by some chemists for this purpose.

Hyposulphite of soda is now extensively used as an antichlore, as also are certain salts of lime, as sulphide of calcium.

ANTI-FRICTION METAL. Tin and pewter are often employed as anti-friction metals for the bearings of locomotive engines. One-half of each tin and copper is now used at some of the large railway works.

Babbet's metal is prepared by taking about fifty parts of tin, five of antimony, and one of copper.

Tin, or pewter, used alone, owing to its softness, spreads out and escapes under the superincumbent weight of the locomotive, or other heavy machinery. It is usual, therefore, to add antimony, for the purpose of giving these metals hardness.

Fenton's anti-friction metal, which is much employed, is a mixture of tin, copper, and spelter. Its advantages are stated to be cheapness in first cost, low specific gravity, being 20 per cent. lighter than gun-metal; and being of a more unctuous or soapy character than gun-metal, less grease or oil is required.

The softer metal is often supported by brasses cast of the required form, the tin alloy being cast upon them. The brasses, or bearings, being properly tinned, and an exact model of the axle having been turned, the parts are heated, put together in their relative positions, luted with plastic clay, and the fluid anti-friction metal poured in, which then becomes of the required form, and effectually solders the brass.

The following compositions are recommended to railway engineers as having been employed for several years in Belgium. In those cases where the objects are much exposed to friction, 20 parts of copper, 4 of tin, 0·5 of antimony, and 0·25 of lead. For objects which are intended to resist violent shocks, 20 parts of copper, 6 of zinc, and 1 of tin. For those which are exposed to heat, 17 parts of copper, 1 of zinc, 0·5 of tin, and 0·25 of lead. The copper is added to the fused mass containing the other metals. See ALLOY and KINGSTON'S METAL; ANTIMONY.

ANTI-GUGGLER. A small syphon of metal, which is inserted into the mouths of casks, or large bottles called carboys, to admit air over the liquor contained in them, and thus to facilitate their being emptied without agitation or a guggling noise.

ANTIMONY. (*Antimoine*, Fr.; *Antimon, Spiessglanz* or *Spiessglas*, Ger.) Symbol Sb. (*Stibium*, Lat.); *Atomic Weight*, 122; *Specific Gravity*, 6·715. The sulphide or sulphuret is the only ore of this metal found in sufficient abundance to be largely smelted, and therefore forms the chief and most common source of the antimony of commerce, and of the greater number of the pharmaceutical preparations of that metal.

Antimony Glance, Antimonite, Stibnite, or Grey Antimony Ore, sometimes occurs compact, but usually in very long prismatic or acicular crystals, or in a fibrous form. It is of a lead or steel-grey colour, sometimes with an iridescent lustre, sectile and flexible when in thin laminæ. It may be distinguished from a similar ore of manganese by its perfect diagonal cleavage and easy fusibility. Grey antimony is composed of antimony 72, sulphur 28, corresponding to the formula SbS^3 (**Sb^2S^3**). It fuses readily in the flame of a candle, to which it imparts a greenish tint. On charcoal, in the flame of a blowpipe, it gives out a strong smell of sulphur, with white fumes, and

o 2

yields a white slag. When pure, it is perfectly soluble in muriatic acid. Its specific gravity is 4·5.

The most celebrated localities of this ore are Felsöbanya, Schemnitz, and Kremnitz, in Hungary, where it occurs in diverging prisms several inches long. It is also found in the Hartz, at Andreasberg; in Cornwall, at Padstow and Tintagel; at New Cumnick, in Ayrshire; in Victoria and South Australia; and abundantly in Borneo.

This ore was called by the ancients πλατύόφθαλμον—πλατὺs broad φθαλμὸs eye —from the use to which it was applied in increasing the apparent size of the eye, as is still practised among Oriental nations, by staining the upper and under edges of the eyelids. It was also used as a hair-dye and to colour the eyebrows.

It was the *Lupus Metallorum* of the alchemists. 'Crude antimony' is obtained from it by simple fusion, and from this product the pure metal is extracted.

The other principal ores of antimony are the following:—

Native Antimony is a mineral of a tin-white colour and streak, and of a metallic lustre; it sometimes contains silver, iron, and arsenic, with which last it is commonly associated. It is brittle, and possesses a specific gravity of 6·62 to 6·72. It is generally lamellar, sometimes botryoidal, or reniform. Before the blowpipe it soon melts, and continues to burn after the heat is removed; but if the heat be continued, it evaporates in white fumes, and is redeposited around the globule.

Native antimony occurs at Sahlberg in Sweden, Andreasberg in the Hartz, Allemont in Dauphiny, in Mexico, in Borneo, &c.

Allemontite, or *Arsenical Antimony.* See ARSENIC.

Dyscrasite, or *Antimonial Silver*, is a silver-white metallic mineral of somewhat variable composition, containing from 15 to 27 per cent. of antimony, and from 73 to 85 per cent. of silver. It is a rare mineral, occurring at Andreasberg in the Hartz, at Allemont in Dauphiny, in Bolivia, &c.

Breithauptite or *Antimonial Nickel* is a mineral containing 67·5 of antimony, and 32·5 of nickel, found at Andreasberg in the Hartz.

Oxides of Antimony.—Three mineral species consist wholly of native oxides of antimony—the result of the alteration of grey antimony, native antimony, and other ores of that metal. *Valentinite*, teroxide of antimony, or antimonious oxide, SbO^3 (Sb^2O^3), occurs in rectangular plates and acicular prisms belonging to the orthorhombic system. It possesses a shining pearly lustre and a snow-white colour, but is sometimes pinkish, or ash-grey, or brownish. It affords a white streak. It is composed of antimony 84·32, oxygen 15·68. Specific gravity = 5·56. It is found in tabular crystals in veins traversing the primary rocks at Przibram in Bohemia, near Freiberg in Saxony, Allemont in Dauphiny, &c. *Senarmontite.*—This also consists solely of teroxide of antimony SbO^3 (Sb^2O^3); but, unlike Valentinite, crystallises in regular octahedrons: hence the native oxide is dimorphous. The crystals are colourless or greyish, with a resinous or subadamantine lustre. The per-centage composition is, of course, the same as that of Valentinite. Senarmontite occurs in the province of Constantine in Algeria; at Pernick in Hungary; at Endellion in Cornwall; and at South Ham in Canada. *Cervantite*, or *Antimony Ochre.*—This is an oxide containing Sb O⁴ (Sb^2O^4), probably a combination of antimonious and antimonic oxides ($SbO^3 + SbO^5$). It occurs as a crust or powder, or in acicular crystals, with a greasy or earthy lustre, and of a pale yellow or nearly white colour. Specific gravity = 4·08. It is found at Cervantes, in Spain; in Hungary, and the Auvergne.

Red Antimony (*Kermesite*) is a compound of oxide of antimony 30·2, and sulphide of antimony 69·8; or antimony 74·45, oxygen 5·29, and sulphur 20·49. It occurs generally in capillary six-sided prismatic crystals of a cherry-red colour, affording a brownish-red streak. It has a specific gravity of from 4·5 to 4·6. It is feebly translucent, and possesses an adamantine lustre. It occurs at Malaczka in Hungary, Bräunsdorf in Saxony, and at Allemont in Dauphiny.

Antimony also occurs in a large number of other minerals, which are for the most part double sulphides, such as Jamesonite, Zinckenite, Bournonite, Plumosite, Boulangerite, Wolfsbergite, Panabase, Berthierite, Miargyrite, Pyrargyrite, &c.

ASSAYING OF ANTIMONY ORES.—The chief mineral or ore which has to be submitted to assay is the sulphide of antimony (SbS^3), sometimes the oxides of antimony (SbO^3, SbO^4, and SbO^5), and occasionally native antimony.

I. *Sulphide of Antimony.*

(*a.*) *Estimation of the Sulphide of Antimony when it occurs intermixed with more or less of vein-stuff.*—About 2,000 to 7,000 grains of the ore are broken into fragments from about ½ to 1 inch in diameter, so as to produce as little dust as possible. Two crucibles are selected, so that the bottom of the upper one can be inserted into the mouth of the lower one to the extent of about 1 inch; a hole is made in the bottom of the upper crucible. This hole is partially closed by placing over it a small lump of the ore or a fragment of charcoal. The ore is then introduced; portions of charcoal about the size of the ore being intermixed during the charging, the fine ore placed on top, a layer of charcoal afterwards added, and the crucible-cover fitted and well luted down. The bottom of the pot thus charged is inserted into the mouth of the lower one. Heat is now applied; the two pots thus arranged being placed so that the lower pot is under the bars of the furnace and the upper one surrounded with hot fuel. The temperature should be carefully regulated, and the operation completed in about 1 to 1½ hours. When cold, the liquated regulus or sulphide of antimony will be found in the lower crucible, and from its weight the per-centage of pure ore contained in the sample operated on can be calculated. The regulus should be well fused, bluish grey in colour, and the fracture bright and fibrous-crystalline. When pure, sulphide of antimony contains 71·76 per cent. of metallic antimony; so that, if desirable, from the weight of the regulus obtained the quantity of metal in the sample operated on can readily be calculated. The residual vein-stuff in the upper crucible should be examined, to see that it is practically free from sulphide of antimony.

(b.) *Assay of Ore rich in Sulphide of Antimony, or Regulus obtained by Liquation (a) or otherwise, by roasting, &c.*—100 to 500 grains of the finely powdered ore are placed in a crucible or roasting-dish, and roasted at a very low and carefully regulated temperature, with frequent stirring, especially at the first part of the operation, so as to prevent clogging or loss from antimony fume being given off. The roasted product, which is generally grey or greyish white in colour, is then mixed with carbonate of soda and charcoal powder, or tartar, or with black flux, and the assay made as for oxide of antimony.

(c.) *By Cyanide of Potassium.*—With 100 to 200 grains of the finely powdered ore are mixed about four times its weight of coarsely powdered cyanide of potassium, the mixture transferred to a crucible, and the whole submitted to a low red heat for about 20 to 30 minutes. The fused contents are poured out into a mould, and when cold the slag detached and the button of metallic antimony weighed. It should be bright, bluish white, brittle, and break with a largely crystalline fracture.

II. *Oxides of Antimony.*

(a.) *By Carbonate of Soda and Carbon.*—100 to 500 grains of the finely powdered ore are mixed with from 300 to 500 grains of carbonate of soda, and from 20 to 50 grains of charcoal powder, and the mixture submitted in a crucible to a temperature gradually increasing to a red heat at the end of from 20 to 30 minutes. When the fused contents are tranquil, it is poured out into a mould, and when cold the slag cautiously detached, and the button of antimony cleaned and weighed.

(b.) *By Cyanide of Potassium.*—100 to 200 grains of the ore are weighed and mixed with about four times its weight of cyanide of potassium, and from 20 to 30 grains of charcoal powder, the whole exposed in a crucible to a low red heat for about 20 to 30 minutes, and the process completed as before described for the assay of sulphide of antimony with cyanide of potassium.

Professor Henry Rose, of Berlin, in a memoir on the natural, not oxidised, combinations of antimony and arsenic, gives the following analyses:[1]—

	1	2	3	4	5	6	7	8
Sulphur	22·58	21·95	22·15	22·53	19·72	16·42	20·31	17·04
Antimony	44·39	39·14	34·40	34·9	31·04	14·68	26·28	5·09
Lead	31·84	...	40·75	36·71	46·87	...	40·84	
Silver	...	36·40	...	...	...	68·54	...	64·29
Copper	0·42	1·06	0·13	0·19	...	0·64	12·65	9·23
Iron	...	0·62	2·30	2·65	1·30	...	...	0·06
Lime	...	...	...	...	0·08			
Arsenic	...	...	...	...	...	...	...	3·74
	99·23	99·17	99·73	96·17	99·01	100·28	100·08	100·15

1. *Zinkenite*, from Wolfsberg, in the Eastern Hartz.
2. *Miargyrite*, from Bräunsdorf, in Saxony.
3, 4. *Jamesonite*, from Cornwall.
5. *Plumose Grey Antimony*, from Wolfsberg, in the Eastern Hartz.
6. *Brittle Silver Glance*, from Schemnitz, Hungary.
7. *Bournonite*, from the Pfaffenberg mine, Eastern Hartz.
8. *Polybasite*, from Mexico.

[1] Brewster's Edin. Journ. ii, 359; Pogg. Ann. xv.

METALLURGY OF ANTIMONY.—In treating certain ores to obtain the metal, the first object is to separate the gangue, which was formerly done by filling crucibles with the

71　　　　　　　　　　72

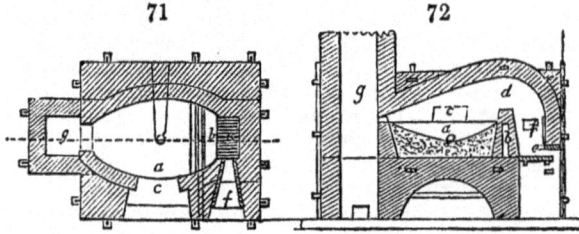

mixed materials, placing them on the hearth of an oven, and exposing them to a moderate heat. As the sulphide easily melts, it runs out through a hole in the bottom of the crucible into a pot placed beneath, and out of the reach of the fire. But the great loss from the breakage of the crucibles has caused another method to be adopted. In this, the broken ore, being sorted, is laid on the bottom of a concave reverberatory hearth, where it is reduced.

Figs. 71 and 72 represent a wind or flame furnace, for the reduction of antimony. The hearth is formed of sand and clay solidly beat together, and slopes from all sides towards the middle, where it is connected with the orifice a, which is closed with dense coal-ashes; b is the air-channel up through the bridge; c, the door for introducing the prepared ore, and running off the slags; d, the bridge; e, the grate; f, the fire or fuel-door; g, the chimney. With 2 or 3 cwts. of ore, the smelting process is completed in from 8 to 10 hours. The metal thus obtained is not pure enough, but must be fused under coal-dust, in portions of 20 or 30 pounds, in crucibles placed upon a reverberatory hearth.

At Malboac, in the department of Ardèche, in France, the separation of the sulphide

73

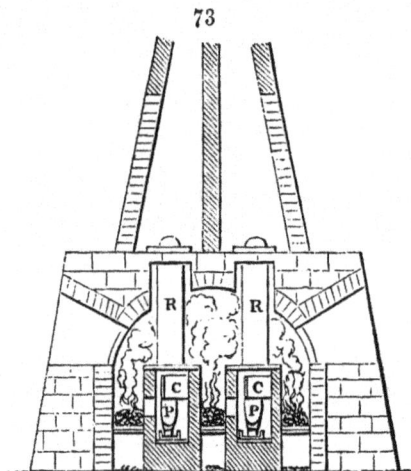

of antimony from its associated gangue is, or was, effected by means of a peculiar apparatus (*fig.* 73). The mineral is placed in large retorts, R R, of which four are set in each furnace. An aperture is left at the bottom of each of these cylinders, which corresponds with a similar opening by which they are supported. Beneath these, in the chambers, c c, are placed earthen pots, P P, in which is received the melted sulphide as it descends through the openings in the cylinders. The fuel consumed on the grate consists of fir-wood; and the sulphide obtained is converted into metallic antimony by roasting in a reverberatory furnace, and subsequent reduction by a mixture of 20 per cent of powdered charcoal which has been saturated with a strong solution of the carbonate of soda.

Metallic antimony, as obtained by the preceding process, is the antimony of commerce, but is not absolutely pure; containing frequently minute portions of iron, lead, and even arsenic, the detection and separation of which belong to the province of analytical chemistry; but considerable purity may be secured by repeatedly fusing the metal, mixed with a little of its sulphide and some carbonate of soda, in a crucible. From 100 parts of the impure metal in this way 94 of pure antimony are obtained. The addition of sulphide serves the purpose of making fluid compounds of the sulphides of iron, arsenic, and copper, with the soda. Wöhler purifies antimony completely from arsenic (not from iron and copper) by deflagrating 10 parts of the crude ore with 12 of nitre and 15 of carbonate of soda; washing away the arsenic salt, and then smelting the residuary antimoniate of potash with black flux. Lead can be separated only by the humid analysis.

To obtain antimony free from iron, it should be fused with some antimonic oxide in a crucible, whereby the iron is oxidised and separated. The presence of arsenic in antimony is detected by the garlic smell, emitted by such an alloy when heated at the blowpipe; or, better, by igniting it with nitre in a crucible; in which case insoluble antimonite and antimonate of potash will be formed along with soluble arsenate. Water digested upon the mixture, filtered, and then tested with nitrate of silver, will afford the brown-red precipitate characteristic of arsenic acid.

According to Berthier, the following materials afford, in smelting, an excellent product of antimony. From 100 parts of sulphide, 60 of protoxide of iron from the shingling or rolling mills (*Hammerschlag*), 45 to 50 of carbonate of soda, and 10 of charcoal powder, from 65 to 70 parts of metallic antimony or regulus should be obtained. Glauber salts may be used advantageously instead of soda. Another formula is, 100 parts of sulphide of antimony, 42 of metallic iron, and 10 of dry sulphate of soda. The product thence is said to be from 60 to 64 parts of metal.

In the works where antimonial ores are smelted, by means of tartar (argol, bitartrate of potash), the alkaline scoriæ which cover the metallic ingots are not rejected as useless, for they hold a certain quantity of antimonial oxide in combination—a property of the potash flux which is propitious to the purity of the metal. These scoriæ, consisting of sulphide of potassium and antimonate of potash, being treated with water, undergo a reciprocal decomposition; the elements of the water act on those of the sulphide, and the resulting alkaline hydrosulphide reacts on the antimonial solution so as to form a species of *kermes mineral*, which precipitates. This is dried, and sold at a low price as a veterinary medicine under the name of *kermes, by the dry way.*

Metallic antimony is now largely obtained from the native sulphide by the reducing action of iron. A quantity of scrap-iron or of tin-plate clippings is thrust into the molten sulphide, previously separated from the gangue, and the antimony is thus reduced, with formation of a regulus of protosulphide of iron (ferrous sulphide). The process of smelting antimony by means of iron resolves itself into three distinct operations, which may be thus described:—[1]

1. *Singling.*—A charge of about 40 lbs. of the ore, broken up into pieces each about half the size of an egg, is introduced into a red-hot crucible, with a quantity of slag obtained in the operation of *doubling* at a previous smelting. Above this ore and slag is placed a mass of refuse iron, consisting generally of tin-plate in the form of old kettles and saucepans, and beaten for convenience' sake into the shape of a cone. Assuming that the ore contains from 50 to 55 per cent. of antimony, about 20 lbs. of iron would be added to the quantity of ore and slag specified above. When the charge has melted, the iron cone is pressed into the molten mass, and the reduction thus effected by action of the metal on the fused sulphide. The crucible is then removed from the fire, and the contents poured into a large conical cast-iron mould. On the cooling of the mass, a button of crude antimony is found below the regulus, from which it is readily separated by a tap with the hammer.

2. *Doubling.*—The 'singles,' or buttons of metallic antimony from the first melting are sorted, so that those which contain an excess of sulphur may be melted with those which have an excess of iron. Seventy or eighty pounds of these sorted singles are put into a crucible with a little salt-cake (crude sulphate of soda) and melted. This re-melted antimony is then poured into a cast-iron bowl, where it solidifies, and forms the product known as 'bowl metal.'

3. *Refining* or *Frenching.*—A charge of from 60 to 70 lbs. of bowl metal is introduced into a red-hot crucible, with a pound or two of American potash and about 10 lbs. of slag from the previous refining. When melted, the mass is stirred with an iron bar, and the character of the slag adhering to the stirrer enables the workman to judge whether the refining be complete or no. The refined metal is poured into moulds, where it slowly cools and acquires the crystalline structure characteristic of this metal; to favour this crystallisation the metal, while cooling, is covered with slag, and should be left quite undisturbed.

It was shown by the late Dr. Matthiessen that the tendency of antimony to crystallise is due to the presence of a small proportion of impurity; antimony, in a pure state, cannot be readily caused to crystallise.

Antimony is a brittle metal, of a silvery white colour, with a tinge of blue, a lamellar texture, and crystalline fracture. When heated at the blowpipe, it melts with great readiness, and diffuses white vapours, possessing somewhat of a garlic smell. If thrown in this melted state on a flat sheet of paper, the globule sparkles and bursts into a multitude of small spheroids, which retain their incandescence for a long time, and run about on the paper, leaving traces of the white oxide produced during the combustion. When this oxide is fused with borax, or other vitrifying matter, it imparts a yellow colour to it. Metallic antimony, treated with hot nitric acid in a concentrated state, is converted into a powder, called antimonious acid, which is altogether insoluble in the ordinary acid menstrua—a property by which the chemist can separate that metal from iron and copper. According to Bergmann, the specific gravity of antimony is 6·86; but that of the purest is 6·715. The alchemists had conceived the most brilliant hopes of this metal; the facility with which it is alloyed with gold, since its fumes alone render this most ductile metal immediately brittle, led them to assign to it a royal lineage, and distinguished it by the title of *regulus*, or the little king.

[1] The substance of this description is taken from some 'Notes on Antimony,' in the 'Mining and Smelting Magazine,' vol. iii. p. 136.

Its chief employment is in making the alloys called type metal, stereotype metal, music plates, and Britannia metal; the first consisting of 6 of lead and 2 of antimony; the second of 6 of lead and 1 of antimony; the third of lead, tin, and antimony; and the fourth also of lead, tin, and antimony, with occasionally a little copper, bismuth, and nickel. Antimony is much used in alloys with tin, tin and lead, and in some cases copper, in various proportions, for machinery bearings, instead of gun-metal. In cases of rapid and continuous revolution, as the shafts of screw-steamers, these are found much better than gun-metal. It is also used by the Ordnance in hardening bullets and shot.—*Watts's Dictionary of Chemistry.*

Melted with tin, antimony has of late been used as an antifriction alloy for railway axles, and other bearings; in metallic rings, or collars, for machinery. As this alloy is not so much heated by friction as the harder metals, less grease is consumed. See ALLOYS; ANTIFRICTION METAL.

The shipments of Antimony Ore and Regulus from Victoria have been as follows :—

1866	. . . . .	530 tons valued at £3,582
1867	. . . . .	518 „ „ 5,106
1868	. . . . .	649 „ „ 8,810
1869	. . . . .	593 „ „ 11,258
1870	. . . . .	3,118 „ „ 32,870
1871	. . . . .	No returns given

From Borneo the shipments were :—In

1866	. . . .	316 tons valued at £3,859
1867	. . . .	336 „ „ 3,449
1868	. . . .	1,154 „ „ 15,409
1869	. . . .	1,072 „ „ 15,080
1870	. . . .	3,578 „ „ 26,888
1871	. . . .	Included in ' *Ores unenumerated.*'

ANTIMONY, CHLORIDES OF. Two chlorides are known—the *terchloride*, or *antimonious chloride* (Sb Cl³), and the *pentachloride*, or *antimonic chloride* (Sb Cl⁵). The former, known to the older chemists as *butter of antimony*, may be prepared by distilling metallic antimony with corrosive sublimate, or by acting on the tersulphide of antimony with hydrochloric acid, and distilling the product. The pentachloride is obtained by passing chlorine over metallic antimony, and separating the mixed chlorides by distillation. The old *Powder of Algaroth* was an oxychloride of antimony.

ANTIMONY, CROCUS OF. An impure sulphide of antimony and sodium, forming the scoria which is produced in smelting antimony by heating the roasted sulphide with charcoal and carbonate of soda.

ANTIMONY GLANCE. Native tersulphide of antimony, the principal ore of this metal. See ANTIMONY.

ANTIMONY, GLASS OF. This substance, according to M. Soubeiran, contained:—Teroxide of antimony, 91·5; silica, 4·5; peroxide of iron, 3·2; sulphuret of antimony, 1·9. = 101·1.

ANTIMONY VERMILION. A red pigment consisting of artificial tersulphide of antimony, formed by pouring a solution of chloride of antimony in hydrochloric acid into a dilute solution of hyposulphite of lime in excess; when the liquid is heated, a yellow precipitate falls, and this gradually assumes an orange-red colour.

ANTISEPTICS. (From ἀντὶ *against*; σηπτὸς *putrid.*) Substances which prevent the spontaneous decomposition of animal and vegetable substances. These are chiefly the mineral acids, charcoal, chloride of lime, chlorine, culinary salt, nitre, spices, sugar, creosote, and yeast—which operate partly by inducing a change in the animal or vegetable fibres, and partly by combining with and rendering the aqueous constituent unsusceptible of decomposition. See DISINFECTANTS; FOOD; PROVISIONS, CURING OF; and PRESERVED MEATS.

ANVIL. A mass of iron, having a smooth and nearly flat top-surface of steel, upon which blacksmiths, and various other artificers, forge metals with the hammer. The common anvil is usually made of seven pieces: 1, the core, or body; 2, 3, 4, 5, the four corner-pieces, which serve to enlarge its base; 6, the projecting end, which has a square hole for the reception of the tail, or shank of a chisel, on which iron bars may be cut through; and 7, the beak, or horizontal cone, round which rods or slips of metal may be turned into a circular form, as in making rings. These six pieces are welded separately to the first, or core, and then hammered into a uniform body. In manufacturing large anvils, two hearths are needed, in order to bring each of the two pieces to be welded to a proper heat· by itself; and several men are employed in working them together briskly in the welding state, by heavy swing hammers. The steel facing is applied by welding in the same manner. The anvil is then hardened, by heating it to a cherry red, and plunging it into cold water—a running stream being preferable to a pool or cistern. The facing should not be too thick a plate; for, when such, it is apt to crack in the hardening. The face of the anvil is now smoothed upon a grindstone, and finally polished with emery and crocus, for all delicate purposes of art.

The blacksmith, in general, sets his anvil loosely upon a wooden block, and in preference, on the root of an oak tree. The cutlers and file-makers fasten their anvils to a large block of stone, their peculiar work rendering it an advantage to have the anvil fixed as firmly and solidly as possible.

The *whitesmith*, or *brightsmith*, when working at the anvil, unless the piece under the hammer should be very light, is assisted by a striker, who wields a sledge-hammer. In forging round articles, such as bolts, axles, &c., the smith makes use of swages— pieces of steel formed somewhat like hammer-heads—with a groove in one corresponding with a hollow in the other. In forging small spindles, the boss, or lower piece, is permanently fixed upon the anvil. For convenience in managing heavy articles, a crane is so fixed in the workshops, that the arm traverses between the fire and the anvil.

APATITE. (ἀπατάω *to deceive*). A name proposed by Werner, in 1786, for the native crystallised phosphate of lime of Saxony, and since extended to all minerals of like chemical composition. The name is suggestive of the deceptive appearances which the mineral often presents, and which naturally enough led the early mineralogists into the error of mistaking many of its varieties for widely-different substances. As apatite, when occurring in sufficient quantity to be advantageously worked, has always a high economic value, it is desirable to describe the species somewhat in detail.

Apatite crystallises in forms belonging to the hexagonal system, frequently in short six-sided prisms, each terminated either by a pyramid of as many faces, or by a simple flat plane. The horizontal edges at the ends of the crystal are often variously modified, and the lateral faces of the prism frequently exhibit vertical striæ. Cleavage is generally not well marked. In colour the mineral varies from white to various shades of green and blue, passing sometimes into violet and brown; but the 'streak,' readily seen on scratching the mineral, is invariably white. The lustre is generally glassy, but rather inclined to resinous. Some varieties of the mineral are transparent, while others are quite opaque: it is notable that a bluish opalescence may occasionally be detected in the direction of the vertical axis of the crystal. For a salt of lime, apatite is rather hard, readily scratching glass, but being itself scratched by felspar. Its specific gravity varies from 2·92 to 3·25. In chemical composition all apatite consists mainly of phosphate of lime (calcium phosphate), but it was shown by Rose in 1827 that this phosphate is almost invariably associated to a greater or less extent with either chloride or fluoride of calcium, or with both. The general composition of apatite may be thus formulated: $3 (3CaO, PO^5) + Ca (Cl,F)$; $[3 (Ca^3P^2O^8) + Ca (Cl^2, F^2)]$. The amount of phosphoric acid (phosphoric anhydride) in apatite usually varies from 40 to 45 per cent. Heated before the blowpipe, the mineral fuses, with difficulty, on the edges. Many massive varieties emit a phosphorescent glow when heated, and are hence termed *phosphorite*.

Among the minerals commonly found in association with apatite, may be specially mentioned tin-stone, topaz, and tourmaline. It is with such associates that apatite occurs in veins in St. Michael's Mount, and in several Cornish tin-mines; and it is also found under similar conditions in the tin-deposits on both the Saxon and the Bohemian sides of the Erzgebirge, especially at Ehrenfriedersdorf, Zinnwald, and Schlaggenwald. A variety in small white crystals, with curved faces, and in crystalline masses, occurring at Huel Franco and Fowey Consols, in Cornwall, has been termed *Francolite*. Near Bovey Tracey, in Devonshire, apatite was formerly found in large white crystals, associated with fine specimens of black tourmaline. At Carrock Fells, in Cumberland, it occurs in green crystals, with smoky quartz, molybdenite and gilbertite. The dark greenish-blue crystals found in Norway and elsewhere have been termed *Moroxite*. Snarum, in Norway, yields large white crystals, apparently decomposed. A crystalline apatite, flesh-red in colour, and looking much like a felspar, is found at Krageröe in Norway, where it has been largely worked for export to England. The variety termed by Werner *Spargelstein* ('asparagus stone') occurs in beautifully formed clear yellowish-green crystals, associated with specular iron-ore, in a peculiar rock, apparently volcanic, at Jumilla, in the province of Murcia, Spain. A proposal was lately made to work the rock containing these crystals. At Logrossan, in the province of Estremadura, there are vast deposits of massive or con·

cretionary hard phosphate of lime, known as *phosphorite*. These deposits were described in 1844 by the late Dr. Daubeny, and have been worked for many years on a very extensive scale. In the neighbourhood of Staffel, near Limburg, on the Lahn, and elsewhere in Nassau, valuable deposits of phosphorite have been actively worked. At Staffel the phosphorite is sometimes incrusted with a peculiar mineral, generally in botryoidal or reniform masses, termed *Staffelite*. This may have been derived from the alteration of the phosphorite, and is said to contain, in addition to phosphate of lime, upwards of 9 per cent. of carbonate of lime, and is further peculiar in containing traces of iodine. Phosphorite is also worked at Amberg, Diez, and other localities in Bavaria. The mineral called *Osteolite* is said by Professor Church to be an altered impure form of apatite. In the United States there are a large number of localities yielding apatite. Crystals of considerable size have been found in St. Lawrence co., in Orange co., in Rossie, and elsewhere in the State of New York. At Hurdstone, in Sussex co., New Jersey, 'a shaft has been sunk, and the apatite mined ; masses brought out weigh occasionally 200 lbs., and some cleavage prisms have the planes 3 in. wide' (*Dana*). Apatite is widely disseminated through many of the crystalline limestones of the Laurentian series in Canada ; indeed, in some parts of the limestone it is so abundant as to form a large proportion of the rock. The most remarkable deposits of Laurentian apatite are in the townships of Burgess and Elmsley. 'In North Elmsley it forms an irregular bed parallel to the stratification of the limestone ; the breadth of the bed seems to be about 10 feet, of which 3 feet are nearly pure crystalline apatite, sea-green in colour, and with a small admixture of black mica. Masses of this gave an average of 88 per cent. of phosphate of lime' (*T. Sterry Hunt*).

When apatite or phosphorite occurs in sufficient quantity to be systematically worked, it becomes a mineral of great commercial value. Treated with oil of vitriol, it is converted into superphosphate of lime, and in this soluble form is highly valued by the agriculturist as a fertilising agent for the soil. Apatite has also been used, in the place of bone-ash, as a constituent of certain kinds of soft porcelain. For other mineral substances containing phosphate of lime, see SOMBRERITE, COPROLITES, and GUANO.—F.W.R.

APPLES. The fruit of the *Pyrus malus* (apple-tree). Employed in the manufacture of cider. See CIDER.

APPLE-TREE. (*Pyrus malus.*) The wood of the apple-tree is much used in the Tunbridge turnery manufacture, and the millwright employs the wood of the crab-tree for the teeth of mortice wheels.

APPLE-WINE. Cider. Winckler finds that the wine from apples is distinguished from the wine from grapes by the absence of bitartrate of potash and of œnanthic acid, by its containing a smaller amount of alcohol and more tannin, but especially by the presence of a characteristic acid, which he regards as lactic acid, notwithstanding that this opinion is not confirmed by the degree of solubility of its salts with oxide of zinc, lime, and magnesia. See CIDER.

AQUAFORTIS. Nitric acid, somewhat dilute, was so named by the alchemists on account of its strong solvent and corrosive action upon many mineral, vegetable, and animal substances. It is still employed as the commercial name of nitric acid. See NITRIC ACID.

This acid is usually obtained by distilling either common nitre or cubic nitre with sulphuric acid.

It may, however, be usefully borne in mind, that this term of *aquafortis*, or *strong water* of the old chemist, was also applied to solutions which answered their special purposes. Thus Salmon, in 1685, gives the composition of aquafortis from certain mixtures of acids, not nitric, and salts, and distinctly refers to the Pharmacopœia for the other kind. This may be of service when applying old recipes for processes in the arts. Aquafortis did not always mean nitric acid.

AQUAMARINE is the name given to those varieties of beryl which are of clear shades of sky-blue, or greenish-blue. It occurs in longitudinally-striated hexagonal crystals, sometimes a foot long, and is found in the Brazils, Hindostan, and Siberia. See BERYL.

AQUA REGIA. *Royal water.* The name given by the alchemists to that mixture of nitric and muriatic acids which was best fitted to dissolve gold ; it is now called *nitro-muriatic acid*, or *nitro-chlorohydric acid*, or *hypochloro-nitric acid*.

Aqua regia, prepared under different conditions, appears to give different results. Gay-Lussac observed that aqua regia, when heated in a water-bath, evolves a gaseous body which, dried and exposed to a frigorific mixture, separates into chlorine and a dark lemon-yellow liquid, boiling at 70° F. This yellow liquid was found to contain 60·4 per cent. of chlorine, the calculated quantity for the formula, NO^2Cl^2, being 70·2. Gay-Lussac refutes the assertion of E. Davy and Baudrimont, that the properties of aqua regia are due to its containing a compound of chlorine, nitrogen, and oxygen, and confirms the generally received view, that its action depends upon free chlorine. From the vapour evolved in the action of nitric upon hydrochloric acid, a liquid may be condensed which is nearly of the composition NO^2Cl^2 ($\mathbf{NOCl^2}$), containing, however, no *free* chlorine: this compound, in the gaseous form, is known as *chloronitric gas*.

The best proportions for forming aqua regia appear to be about one volume of strong nitric to three of hydrochloric acid. Aqua regia is used for dissolving both gold and platinum.

AQUA VITÆ. The name given to alcohol when used as an intoxicating beverage. It is derived from the alchemists, who, having obtained—in all probability from the Arabian physicians, since Avicenna uses the term—the product by distillation of saccharine fermentation, *al-kohol* (alcohol), gave, upon the same principle as guided them in calling the nitro-muriatic acid *aqua regia*, the name of *aqua vitæ* to several ardent spirits; and it has been retained especially with reference to whisky and brandy.

ARABIC, GUM. Gum Arabic exudes from several species of *Acacia*, as *A. vera*. It is also found in the roots of the mallow, comfrey, and some other plants. Gum Arabic never crystallises, is transparent, and has a vitreous fracture.

ARABIN. The principal constituent of Gum Arabic. If gum is treated with hydrochloric acid and alcohol, the lime, magnesia, and potash, in combination, are decomposed, and the arabin is separated as a gum, exhibiting the properties of an acid. In the moist state it dissolves in cold water, forming *mucilage*, from which it is precipitated by alcohol. After drying, it no longer dissolves, but swells into a gelatinous mass. Dried at 212° F. it has the composition $C^{12}H^{11}O^{11}$ ($\mathbf{C^{12}H^{22}O^{11}}$). See ACACIA, CERASINE, DEXTRINE, GUM.

ARAGONITE. So called from Aragon, in Spain, where it was first discovered. A carbonate of lime, crystallised in rhombic prisms, or in forms derived from the same. Sometimes written ARRAGONITE. See LIME.

ARBOR VITÆ. Several species of *Thuja*, found in America and China, are called *arbor vitæ*. It is a light, soft, and fine-grained wood, which is used in several kinds of carpentry.

ARCH. As this dictionary is not intended to include articles connected with engineering or with architecture, it would be out of place to describe the conditions required to ensure the stability of the arch, which is manifestly one of great importance to the practical builder. (For the theory of the equilibrium of the arch, Gwilt's treatise on the subject should be consulted, or the article Arch, 'Encyclopædia Britannica.') It simply remains to define the arch as a structure of stone or brick, supported by its own curve; or of wood or iron, supported by the mechanical arrangements of the work.

The curvature of an arch may vary very considerably. Where the arch is low, the circle it belongs to becomes very large; and the strength of arches varies greatly with their forms; they may be either segments of a circle, a parabola, an ellipse, an hyperbola, or a catenary.

The arch in architecture is the means of passing from one pillar to another; and we have the circular form, which was succeeded by the pointed arch, and all its modified forms of foliation, &c.

ARCHERY BOW. These are divided into the '*single-piece bow*' and the '*back or union bow*.'

The single-piece bow is made of one rod of hickory, lance-wood, or yew-tree, which last, if perfectly free from knots, is considered the most suitable wood.

The union bow is made of two or sometimes three pieces glued together. The *back*' piece, or that furthest from the string, is of rectangular section, and always of lance-wood or hickory; the 'belly,' which is nearly of semicircular section, is made of any hard wood that can be obtained straight and clean, as ruby-wood, rose-wood, green-heart, king-wood, snake-wood, &c. Sometimes the union bow is imitated by one solid piece of straight cocoa-wood of the West Indies (not that of the cocoa-nut palm), in which case the tough fibrous sap is used for the back. The Palmyrea is also used for bows.—*Holtzapffel*.

ARCHIL. (*Orseille*, Fr.; *Orseille*, Ger.; *Oricello*, Ital.) The name of archil is given to a colouring-matter obtained, by the simultaneous action of the air, moisture, and an ammoniacal liquor, from many of the *lichens*, the most esteemed being the *Roccella*.

It appears in commerce in three forms: 1, as a pasty matter called *archil*; 2, as a mass of a drier character, named *persis*; and 3, as a reddish powder called *cudbear*.

The lichen from which archil is prepared is known also as the canary weed or orchilla weed. It grows in great abundance on some of the islands near the African coast, particularly in the Canaries and several of the islands of the Archipelago. Its colour is sometimes a light and sometimes a dark grey.

There appears to be good evidence for supposing that archil was known to the Romans, and Beckmann is disposed to believe that the ancient Greeks were familiar with this dye. This ingenious and industrious author gives the following account of the modern introduction of the archil.

'Among the oldest and principal Florentine families is that known under the name of Oricellarii or Rucellarii, Ruscellai or Rucellai, several of whom have distinguished themselves as statesmen and men of letters. This family is descended from a German nobleman, named Ferro or Frederigo, who lived in the beginning of the 12th century. One of his descendants, in the year 1300, carried on a great trade in the Levant, by which he acquired considerable riches, and returning at length to Florence with his fortune, first made known in Europe the art of dyeing with archil. It is said that a little before his return from the Levant, happening to make water on a rock covered with this lichen, he observed that the plant, which was there called *respio* or *respo*, and in Spain *orciglia*, acquired by the urine a purple colour, or, as others say, a red colour. He, therefore, tried several experiments, and when he had brought to perfection the art of dyeing wool with this plant, he made it known at Florence, where he alone practised it for a considerable time, to the great benefit of the state. From this useful invention the family received the name of Oricellarii, from which at last was formed Rucellai.'—*History of Inventions.*

For more than a century Italy possessed the exclusive art of making archil, obtaining the lichens from the islands of the Mediterranean. Teneriffe furnished annually 500 quintals (of 110 lbs. each) of lichen; the Canary Isles, 400; Fuerta Ventura, 300; Lancerot, 300; Gomera, 300; Isle of Ferro, 800. This business, in the islands of Teneriffe and Canary, belonged to the Crown of Spain, and in 1730 brought in a revenue of 1500 piastres. The farmers paid from 15 to 20 reals for the right to gather each quintal.

Since 1402 the largest quantity of the lichens for the preparation of archil has been obtained in the Canary Islands; a smaller quantity has, however, been procured from the Cape de Verde Islands. It is stated that the archil from the lichens of the latter place dye wool of a deeper colour than the archil from the Canaries, but that the dye is not so rich. The labour of collecting these lichens is very great, and men are exposed to the greatest risks, being suspended by cords over the face of stupendous cliffs. Upon the coasts of Spain, Scotland, and Ireland, the peasantry have for a very long period used lichens for the purpose of dyeing red.

The chemical constitution of archil was first investigated by M. Cocq ('Annales de Chimie,' vol. lxxxi.); and subsequently, yet more extensively, by Robiquet ('Annales de Chimie,' vol. xlii. 2nd series).

From the *Variolaria*, Robiquet obtained *Orcine*, by digesting the lichen in alcohol, evaporating to dryness, dissolving the extract in water, concentrating the solution to the thickness of a syrup, and setting it aside to crystallise. It forms, when quite pure, colourless prisms, of a nauseous sweet taste, which fuse easily, and may be sublimed unaltered. Its formula is $C^{14}H^8O^4$ ($\mathbf{C^7H^8O^2}$); when crystallised from its aqueous solution it contains 5 Aq.

If orcine be exposed to the combined action of air and ammonia, it is converted into a crimson powder *orcëine*, which is the most important ingredient in the archil of commerce. *Orcëine* may be obtained by digesting dried archil in strong alcohol, evaporating the solution in a water-bath to dryness, and treating it with ether as long as anything is dissolved; it remains as a dark blood-red powder, being sparingly soluble in water or ether, but abundantly in alcohol. Its formula is $C^{14}H^7NO^6$ ($\mathbf{C^7H^7NO^3}$).

Orcëine dissolves in alkaline liquors with a magnificent purple colour; with metallic oxides it forms lakes, also of rich purple of various shades. In contact with deoxidising agents, it combines with hydrogen as indigo does, and forms leuc-orcëine. When bleached by chlorine, a yellow substance is formed, *chlor-*orcëine.

Dr. Schunck, by an examination of several species of *Lecanora*, has proved that, although under the influence of ammonia and of air, they ultimately produce orcëine, these lichens do not contain orcine ready formed, but another body, *Lecanorine*, which, under the influence of bases, acts as an acid, and is decomposed into orcine and carbonic acid. If lecanoric acid be dissolved in boiling alcohol, it unites with ether, forming lecanoric ether, which crystallises beautifully in pearly scales. In the *Roccella tinctoria* and the *Evernia prunastri* erythric acid is found By the oxidation of this acid *amarythrine* or *erythrine bitter* is formed. These substances have been carefully examined by Schunck, Stenhouse, and Kane. The chemical history of these and some other compounds is of great interest; but as they do not bear directly upon the manufacture of archil, or its use in dyeing, further space cannot be devoted to their consideration.

Kane found archil and litmus of commerce to contain two classes of colouring-matters, as already stated, *orcine* and *orcëine*, derived from it. Beyond these there were two bodies, one containing nitrogen, *azocrythrine*, and the other destitute of nitrogen, *erythroleic* acid. This latter acid is separated from the other bodies present in archil by means of ether, in which it dissolves abundantly, forming a rich crimson solution. It gives with alkalis purple liquors, and with earthy and metallic salts coloured lakes.

Beyond those already named there are several other species of lichen which might be employed in producing an analogous dye, were they prepared, like the preceding, into the substance called *archil*. Hellot gives the following method for discovering if they possess this property. A little of the plant is to be put into a glass vessel; it is to be moistened with ammonia and lime-water in equal parts; a little muriate of ammonia (sal-ammoniac) is added, and the small vessel is corked. If the plant be of a nature to afford a red dye, after three or four days the small portion of liquid which will run off on inclining the vessel, now opened, will be tinged of a crimson red, and the plant itself will have assumed this colour. If the liquor or the plant does not take this colour, nothing need be hoped for; and it is useless to attempt its preparation on the great scale. Lewis says, however, that he has tested in this way a great many mosses, and that most of them afforded him a yellow or reddish-brown colour; but that he obtained from only a small number a liquor of a deep red, which communicated to cloth merely a yellowish-red colour.

Prepared archil gives out its colour very readily to water, ammonia, and alcohol. Its solution in alcohol is used for filling spirit-of-wine thermometers; and when these thermometers are well freed from air, the liquor loses its colour in some years, as Abbé Nollet observed; but the contact of air restores the colour, which is destroyed anew, *in vacuo*, in process of time; but the watery infusion loses its colour, by the privation of air, in a few days; a singular phenomenon, which merits new researches.

The infusion of archil is of a crimson bordering on violet. As it contains ammonia, which has already modified its natural colour, the fixed alkalis can produce little change on it, only deepening the colour a little, and making it more violet. Alum forms in it a precipitate of a brown red; and the supernatant liquid retains a yellowish-red colour. The solution of tin affords a reddish precipitate, which falls down slowly; the supernatant liquid retains a feeble red colour.

The researches on the lichens, as objects of manufacture, by Westring, of Stockholm, are worthy of attention. He examined 150 species, among which he found several which might be rendered useful. He recommends that the colouring-matter should be extracted in the places where they grow, which would save a vast expense in curing, package, carriage, and waste. He styles the colouring substance itself cudbear, persio, or turnsole; and distributes the lichens as follows:—1st. Those which, left to themselves, exposed to moderate heat and moisture, may be fixed without a mordant upon wool or silk; such are the *Lichenes cinereus, æmatonta, ventosus, corallinus, Westringii, saxatilis, conspassus, barbatus, plicatus, vulpinus*, &c.

2. Those which develop a colouring-matter fixable likewise without mordant, but which require boiling and a complicated preparation; such are the *Lichenes subcarneus, dillenii, farinaceus, jubatus, furfuraceus, pulmonareus, cornigatus, cocciferus, digitatus, ancialis, aduncus*, &c. Saltpetre or sea-salt is requisite to improve the lustre and fastness of the dye given by this group to silk.

3. Those which require a peculiar process to develop their colour, such as those which become purple through the agency of stale urine or ammonia. Westring employed the following mode of testing:—He put 3 or 4 drachms of the dried and powdered lichen into a flask, moistened it with 3 or 4 measures of cold spring water, put the stuff to be dyed into the mixture, and left the flask in a cool place. Sometimes he added a little salt, saltpetre, quicklime, or sulphate of copper. If no colour appeared, he then moistened the lichen with water containing $\frac{1}{20}$th of sal-ammoniac and $\frac{1}{10}$th of quicklime, and set the mixture aside in a cool place from 8 to 14 days. There appeared in most cases a reddish or violet coloured tint. Thus the *Lichene cinereus* dyed silk a deep carmelite and wool a light carmelite; the *L. physodes* gave a yellowish-grey; the *pustulatus*, a rose red; *sanguinarius*, grey; *tartareus*, found on the rocks of Norway, Scotland, and England, dyes a crimson-red. Cudbear is made from it in Jutland by grinding the dry lichen, sifting it, then setting it to ferment in a close vessel with ammonia. The lichen must be of the third year's growth to yield an abundant dye; and that which grows near the sea is the best. It loses half its weight by drying. A single person may gather from 20 to 30 pounds a day in situations where it abounds. No less than 2,239,685 pounds were manufactured at Christiansund, Flekkefiord, and Fakrsund, in Norway, in the course of the six years prior to 1812. Since more solid dyes of the same shade have been invented, the archil has gone much into disuse.

To prepare archil, the lichens employed are ground up with water to a uniform pulp, and this is then mixed with as much water as will make the whole fluid; ammoniacal liquors from gas or from ivory-black works, or stale urine, are from time to time added, and the mass frequently stirred so as to promote the action of the air. The orcine or erythrine which exists in the lichen absorbs oxygen and nitrogen, and forms orcëine. The roccelline absorbs oxygen and forms *erythroleic acid ;* these being kept in solution by the ammonia, the whole liquid becomes of an intense purple, and constitutes ordinary archil.—*Kane.*

Archil alone is not used for dyeing silk, unless for lilacs; but silk is frequently passed through a bath of archil, either before dyeing it in other baths or after it has been dyed, in order to modify different colours or to give them lustre. It is sufficient here to point out how white silks are passed through the archil bath. The same process is performed with a bath more or less charged with this colour, for silks already dyed.

Archil, in a quantity proportioned to the colour desired, is to be boiled in a copper. The clear liquid is to be run off quite hot from the archil bath, leaving the sediment at the bottom, into a tub of proper size, in which the silks, newly scoured with soap, are to be turned round on the skein-sticks with much exactness, till they have attained the wished-for shade. After this they must receive one beetling at the river.

Archil is, in general, a very useful ingredient in dyeing; but as it is rich in colour, and communicates an alluring bloom, dyers are often tempted to abuse it, and to exceed the proportions that can add to the beauty without at the same time injuring, in a dangerous manner, the permanence of the colours. Nevertheless, the colour obtained when solution of tin is employed, is less fugitive than without this addition : it is red, approaching to scarlet. Tin appears to be the only ingredient which can increase its durability. The solution of tin may be employed, not only in the dyeing bath, but for the preparation of the silk. In this case, by mixing the archil with other colouring substances, dyes may be obtained which have lustre with sufficient durability.

To dye wool with archil, the quantity of this substance deemed necessary according to the quantity of wool or stuff to be dyed, and according to the shade to which they are to be brought, is to be diffused in a bath of water as soon as it begins to grow warm. The bath is then heated till it be ready to boil, and the wool or stuff is passed through it without any other preparation except keeping that longest in which is to have the deepest shade. A fine gridelin, bordering upon violet, is thereby obtained; but this colour has no permanence. Hence archil is rarely employed with any other view than to modify, heighten, and give lustre to the other colours. Hellot says, that having employed archil on wool boiled with tartar and alum, the colour resisted the air no more than what had received no preparation. But he obtained from herb archil (*l'orseille d'herbe*) a much more durable colour, by putting in the bath some solution of tin. The archil thereby loses its natural colour, and assumes one approaching more or less to scarlet, according to the quantity of solution of tin employed. This process must be executed in nearly the same manner as that of scarlet, except that the dyeing may be performed in a single bath.

Archil is frequently had recourse to for varying the different shades and giving them lustre ; hence it is used for violets, lilacs, mallows, and rosemary-flowers. To obtain a deeper tone, as for the deep *soupes au vin,* sometimes a little alkali or milk of lime is mixed with it. The suites of this browning may also afford agates, rosemary-flowers, and other delicate colours, which cannot be obtained so beautiful by other processes.

The herb archil, just named, called especially *orcëille de terre,* is found upon the volcanic rocks of the Auvergne, on the Alps, and the Pyrenees.

These lichens are gathered by men whose whole time is thus occupied; they scrape them from the rocks with a peculiarly shaped knife. They prefer collecting the orcëille in rainy weather, when they are more easily detached from the rocks. They gather about 2 kilogrammes a day, or about 4½ pounds. When they take their lichens to the makers of archil or litmus for the purpose of selling them, they submit a sample to a test, for the purpose of estimating their quality. To this end they put a little in a glass containing some urine, with a small quantity of lime. As the lichens very rapidly pass into fermentation if kept in a damp state, and thus lose much of their tinctorial power, great care is taken in drying them; when dry they may be preserved without injury for some time.

Archil is perhaps too much used in some cloth factories of England, to the discredit of our dyes. It is said, that by its aid ⅓rd of the indigo may be saved in the blue vat; but the colour is so much the more perishable. The fine soft tint induced upon much of the black cloth by means of archil is also deceptive. One half pound of cudbear will dye one pound of woollen cloth. A crimson red is obtained by adding to the decoction of archil a little salt of tin (muriate), and passing the cloth through the bath after it has been prepared by a mordant of tin and tartar. It must be afterwards passed through hot water.

Dyeing with archil with the aid of oil has been patented by Mr. Lightfoot, on the same principle as has been so long used in the Turkey-red cotton dye, who also has recourse to metallic and earthy bases. See CUDBEAR and LITMUS.

Under the names of *archil carmine* and *archil purple*, or *French Purple*, two brilliant dyes were introduced about a dozen years ago; these contained the colouring principles of the lichens in a very pure form. But since the introduction of the brilliant and stable colours derived from coal-tar, archil and the other dye-stuffs yielded by lichens have greatly fallen into disuse.

ARCHITECTURE. The art of constructing buildings, which involves the consideration of very dissimilar points.

    1. UTILITY,—as it regards any specified object, as—
        a. Domestic accommodation in a dwelling-house.
        b. Acoustic arrangements in all buildings intended for public purposes. This consideration is entirely lost sight of by many modern architects.
        c. Ventilation, which is a matter upon which a very large amount of empiricism has been expended with exceedingly small results.

    2. DURABILITY.—If we examine the walls of our ruined abbeys and castles, we shall find that the stones employed still retain the marks of the workman's tool; and that in numerous cases the ornamental work is as sharp as if it had been executed but yesterday. This should prove to us that the selection of stone was of great importance.

ARDENT SPIRITS—called formerly *Aqua ardens*—are the spirituous products of a considerable variety of fermentable substances. The term is more strictly applicable to those spirits which, by careful distillation, have been deprived of a large quantity of the water in combination. Rectified spirit is alcohol with 16 per cent. of water. Proof spirit is 5 pints of rectified spirit with 3 pints of distilled water.

ARECA. A genus of palms, containing two species—1. The *Areca catechu*, producing the betel nut, which is so universally chewed in the East Indies. 2. The *Areca oleracea*, or cabbage-palm; the cabbage is eaten in the West Indies, both raw and boiled; and the trunk, which is often 100 feet long, is used in Jamaica for water-pipes, which are said to become, when buried, almost as hard as iron.

A. catechu is one of the most beautiful palm-trees growing in India. It is chiefly cultivated in Malabar, Ceylon, and Sumatra. One tree will produce, according to situation, age, and culture, from 200 to 800 nuts. See ACACIA CATECHU.

AREOMETER. An instrument to measure the densities of liquids. (See ALCOHOLOMETRY.) The principle will be well understood by remembering that any solid body will sink further in a light liquid than in a heavy one. The areometer is usually a glass tube, having a small glass bulb loaded with either shot or quicksilver, so as to set the tube upright in any fluid in which it will swim. Within the tube is placed a graduated scale: we will suppose the tube placed in distilled water, and the line cut by the surface of the fluid to be marked; that it is then removed and placed in strong alcohol—the tube will sink much lower in this, and consequently we shall have two extremities of an arbitrary scale, on which we can mark any intermediate degrees.

The areometer of Baumé is used in France, and the following scale is adopted by the French chemists :—

Specific Gravity Numbers corresponding with Baumé's Areometric Degrees.

Liquids denser than Water						Less dense than Water			
Degrees	Specific Gravity	Degrees	Specific Gravity	Degrees	Specific Gravity	Degrees	Specific Gravity	Degrees	Specific Gravity
0	1·0000	26	1·2063	52	1·5200	10	1·0000	36	0·8488
1	1·0066	27	1·2160	53	1·5353	11	0·9932	37	0·8439
2	1·0133	28	1·2258	54	1·5510	12	0·9865	38	0·8391
3	1·0201	29	1·2358	55	1·5671	13	0·9799	39	0·8343
4	1·0270	30	1·2459	56	1·5833	14	0·9733	40	0·8295
5	1·0340	31	1·2562	57	1·6000	15	0·9669	41	0·8249
6	1·0411	32	1·2667	58	1·6170	16	0·9605	42	0·8202
7	1·0483	33	1·2773	59	1·6344	17	0·9542	43	0·8156
8	1·0556	34	1·2881	60	1·6522	18	0·9480	44	0·8111
9	1·0630	35	1·2992	61	1·6705	19	0·9420	45	0·8066
10	1·0704	36	1·3103	62	1·6889	20	0·9359	46	0·8022

Liquids denser than Water						Less dense than Water			
De-grees	Specific Gravity	De-grees	Specific Gravity	De-grees	Specific Gravity	De-grees	Specific Gravity	De-grees	Specific Gravity
11	1·0780	37	1·3217	63	1·7079	21	0·9300	47	0·7978
12	1·0857	38	1·3333	64	1·7273	22	0·9241	48	0·7935
13	1·0935	39	1·3451	65	1·7471	23	0·9183	49	0·7892
14	1·1014	40	1·3571	66	1·7674	24	0·9125	50	0·7849
15	1·1095	41	1·3694	67	1·7882	25	0·9068	51	0·7807
16	1·1176	42	1·3818	68	1·8095	26	0·9012	52	0·7766
17	1·1259	43	1·3945	69	1·8313	27	0·8957	53	0·7725
18	1·1343	44	1·4074	70	1·8537	28	0·8902	54	0·7684
19	1·1428	45	1·4206	71	1·8765	29	0·8848	55	0·7643
20	1·1515	46	1·4339	72	1·9000	30	0·8795	56	0·7604
21	1·1603	47	1·4476	73	1·9241	31	0·8742	57	0·7656
22	1·1692	48	1·4615	74	1·9487	32	0·8690	58	0·7526
23	1·1783	49	1·4758	75	1·9740	33	0·8639	59	0·7487
24	1·1875	50	1·4902	76	2·0000	34	0·8588	60	0·7449
25	1·1968	51	1·4951			35	0·8538	61	0·7411

ARENACEOUS. (*Arena*, sand.) Sandy. Rocks composed of particles of sand, or containing much sand, as the grits and sandstones, are said to be *arenaceous*. If they contain lime they are called *arenaceo-calcareous*.

ARGAN OIL. An oil expressed from the kernels of the *Argania Sideroxylon*, a shrub growing in Morocco.

ARGILLACEOUS. Composed of clay, or clayey. This name is applied to all rocks composed of clay. If containing also sand or lime, they are distinguished as *argillo-arenaceous* or *argillo-calcareous*. Argillaceous rocks, when breathed on, have a peculiar earthy odour, by which they may be distinguished.

ARGILLACEOUS EARTH. (*Argilla*, clay, Lat.) The earth of clay, called in chemistry, alumina, because it is obtained in greatest purity from alum. See ALUMINA, CHINA CLAY, CLAY, KAOLIN.

ARGOL, or **ARGAL.** (*Tartre*, Fr.; *Weinstein*, Ger.) The tartrate of potash is known in commerce as the white and red argol; the white being the crust let fall by white wines, which is of a pale pinkish colour, and the red the crust deposited from red wines, and of a dark red colour. See TARTAR, CREAM OF TARTAR, &c.

ARICINE. An alkaloid discovered by Pelletier and Corriol in a cinchona bark from Arica in Peru. It is separated by the same process as quinine.

ARMENIAN BOLE. See BOLE.

ARMENIAN STONE. ARMENITE. A name formerly given to an earthy copper ore mixed with limestone, of an azure colour, or to quartz coloured with carbonate of copper. See LAPIS LAZULI.

ARMOUR-PLATES. Massive wrought-iron plates used for coating ships of war. The iron for these plates should be as tough and soft as possible; and steel, though possessing high tensile strength, should not be used. It is an object of the manufacturer to produce a plate of considerable thickness, as it is known that the resistance of a single solid plate is greatly superior to that of a number of superimposed plates of the same aggregate thickness, however carefully the several plates may have been fastened together. It is difficult, however, in manufacturing thick plates, to completely squeeze out the liquid cinder interposed between the several layers of iron which are welded together; and hence armour-plates, when exposed to the impact of heavy shot, often exhibit a tendency to lamination. The large plates are manufactured either by rolling in a mill or by forging under the steam-hammer: it is said that the structure of a hammered plate is more likely to be uniform than that of a rolled plate. 'The desideratum in all armour-plates is that they shall bulge with the least possible amount of cracking. Large radiating fractures at the back indicate brittleness, and should immediately condemn a plate.'—(*Percy.*)

ARNATTO, ARNOTTO, or **ANNOTTO.** (*Rocou* or *roucou*, Fr.; *Orleans*, Ger.) A somewhat dry and hard paste, brown without and red within. It is usually imported in cakes of two or three pounds weight, wrapped up in leaves of large reeds, packed in casks, from America, where it is prepared from the seeds of a certain tree, called the *arnatto tree*; it is the *Bixa orellana* of Linnæus.

The shrub producing the arnatto is originally a native of South America; it is now cultivated in Guiana, St. Domingo, and in the East Indies. In the 'Annales de Chimie' we have the following description of the arnatto tree :—' The tree produces oblong bristled pods, somewhat resembling those of a chestnut. These are at first of a beautiful rose-colour, but, as they ripen, change to a dark brown ; and bursting open, display a splendid crimson farina or pulp, in which are contained from thirty to forty seeds, somewhat resembling raisin-stones. As soon as they arrive at maturity, these pods are gathered, divested of their husks, and bruised. Their pulpy substance, which seems to be the only part which constitutes the dye, is then put into a cistern, with just enough water to cover it, and in this situation it remains for seven or eight days, or until the liquor begins to ferment, which, however, may require as many weeks, according to circumstances. It is then strongly agitated with wooden paddles or beaters, to promote the separation of the pulp from the seeds. This operation is continued until these have no longer any of the colouring-matter adhering to them ; it is then passed through a sieve, and afterwards boiled, the colouring-matter being thrown to the surface in the form of scum, or, otherwise allowed to subside : in either case, it is boiled in coppers till reduced to a paste, when it is made into cakes and dried.'

Instead of this long and painful labour, which occasions diseases by the putrefaction induced, and which affords a spoiled product, Leblond proposed simply to wash the seeds of the bixa till they are entirely deprived of their colour, which lies wholly on their surface ; to precipitate the colour by means of vinegar or lemon-juice, and to boil it up in the ordinary manner, or to drain it in bags, as is practised with indigo.

The experiments which Vauquelin made on the seeds of the bixa, imported by Leblond, confirmed the efficacy of the process which he proposed ; and the dyers ascertained that the arnatto obtained in this manner was worth at least four times more than that of commerce ; that, moreover, it was more easily employed ; that it required less solvent ; that it gave less trouble in the copper, and furnished a purer colour.

Arnatto dissolves better and more readily in alcohol than in water, when it is introduced into the yellow varnishes for communicating an orange tint.

The decoction of arnatto in water has a strong peculiar odour, and a disagreeable taste. Its colour is yellowish-red, and it remains a little turbid. An alkaline solution renders its orange-yellow clearer and more agreeable, while a small quantity of a whitish substance is separated from it, which remains suspended in the liquid. If arnatto be boiled in water along with an alkali, it dissolves much better than when alone, and the liquid has an orange hue.

The acids form with this liquor an orange-coloured precipitate, soluble in alkalis, which communicate to it a deep orange colour. The supernatant liquor retains only a pale yellow hue.

When arnatto is used as a dye, it is always mixed with alkali, which facilitates its solution, and gives it a colour inclining less to red. The arnatto is cut in pieces, and boiled for some instants in a copper with its own weight of crude pearl-ashes, provided the shade wanted do not require less alkali. The cloths may be afterwards dyed in this bath, either by these ingredients alone, or by adding others to modify the colour ; but arnatto is seldom used for woollen, because the colours which it gives are too fugitive, and may be obtained by more permanent dyes. Hellot employed it to dye a stuff prepared with alum and tartar ; but the colour acquired had little permanence. It is almost solely used for silks.

For silks intended to become aurora and orange, it is sufficient to scour them at the rate of 20 per cent. of soap. When they have been well cleansed, they are immersed in a bath prepared with water, to which is added a quantity of alkaline solution of arnatto more or less considerable, according to the shade that may be wanted. This bath should have a mean temperature between that of tepid and boiling water.

When the silk has become uniform, one of the hanks is taken out, washed, and wrung, to see if the colour be sufficiently full ; if it be not so, more solution of arnatto is added, and the silk is turned again round the sticks : the solution keeps without alteration.

When the desired shade is obtained, nothing remains but to wash the silk, and give it two beetlings at the river, in order to free it from the redundant arnatto, which would injure the lustre of the colour.

When raw silks are to be dyed, those naturally white are chosen, and dyed in the arnatto bath, which should not be more than tepid, or even cold, in order that the alkali may not attack the gum of the silk, and deprive it of the elasticity which it is desirable for it to preserve.

What has now been said regards the silks to which the aurora shades are to be given : but to make an orange hue, which contains more red than the aurora, it is requisite, after dyeing with arnatto, to redden the silks with vinegar, alum, or lemon-juice. The acid, by saturating the alkali employed for dissolving the arnatto, destroys the shade of yellow that the alkali had given, and restores it to its natural colour, which inclines a good deal to red.

For the deep shades, the practice at Paris, as Macquer informs us, is to pass the silks through alum; and if the colour be not red enough, they are passed through a faint bath of Brazil wood. At Lyons, the dyers who use carthamus sometimes employ old baths of arnatto for dipping the deep oranges.

When the orange hues have been reddened by alum, they must be washed at the river; but it is not necessary to beetle them, unless the colour turns out too red.

Shades may be obtained also by a single operation, which retain a reddish tint, employing for the arnatto bath a less proportion of alkali than has been pointed out.

Guhliche recommends to avoid heat in the preparation of arnatto. He directs it to be placed in a glass vessel, or in a glazed earthen one; to cover it with a solution of pure alkali; to leave the mixture at rest for 24 hours; to decant the liquor, filter it, and add water repeatedly to the residuum, leaving the mixture each time at rest for two or three days, till the water is no longer coloured; to mix all these liquors, and preserve the whole for use in a well-stopped vessel.

He macerates the silk for 12 hours in a solution of alum, at the rate of an eighth of this salt for one part of silk, or in a water rendered acidulous by the aceto-citric acid above described, and he wrings it well on its coming out of this bath.

Silk thus prepared is put into the arnatto bath quite cold. It is kept in agitation there till it has taken the shade sought for; or the liquor may be maintained at a heat far below ebullition. On being taken out of the bath, the silk is to be washed and dried in the shade.

For lighter hues, a liquor less charged with colour is taken; and a little of the acid liquor which has served for the mordant may be added, or the dyed silk may be passed through the acidulous water.

We have seen the following preparation employed for cotton velvet:—1 part of quicklime, 1 of potash, 2 of soda.

Of these a ley is formed, in which one part of arnatto is dissolved; and the mixture is boiled for an hour and a half. This bath affords the liveliest and most brilliant auroras. The buff (chamois) fugitive dye is also obtained with this solution. For this purpose only a little is wanted; but we must never forget that the colours arising from arnatto are all fugitive.

Dr. John found in the pulp surrounding the unfermented fresh seeds, which are about the size of little peas, 28 parts of colouring resinous matter, 26·5 of vegetable gluten, 20 of ligneous fibre, 20 of colouring extractive matter; 4 formed of matters analogous to vegetable gluten and extractive, and a trace of spicy and acid matters.

The Gloucestershire cheese is coloured with arnatto, in the proportion of 1 cwt. to an ounce of the dye: butter is sometimes coloured with it.

When used in calico-printing, it is usually mixed with potash or ammonia and starch.

Arnatto was considered to contain two distinct colouring-matters, a yellow and red, till it was shown by M. Preisser that one is the oxide of the other, and that they may be obtained by adding a salt of lead to a solution of arnatto, which precipitates the colouring-matter. The lead is separated by sulphuretted hydrogen; and the substance being filtered and evaporated, the colouring-matter is deposited in small crystals of a yellow-white colour. These crystals consist of *bixine*; they become yellow by exposure to the air, but if they are dissolved in water they undergo no change. When ammonia is added to *bixine*, with free contact of air, there is formed a fine deep red colour, like arnatto, and a new substance, called *bixeine*, is produced, which does not crystallise, but may be obtained as a red powder; this is coloured blue, by sulphuric acid, and combines with alkalis; it is *bixine* with addition of oxygen. When arnatto, in the form of paste, is mixed from time to time with stale urine, it appears probable that the improvement consists in the formation of *bixeine* from the *bixine* by the ammonia of the urine. It has hence been suggested that, to improve the colour of arnatto, it might be mixed with a little ammonia, and subsequently exposed to the air, previously to its being used for dyeing.

A solution of arnatto and potash in water is sold under the name of *Scott's Nankeen Dye*.

Flag arnatto paid a duty of 18s. 8d. per cwt., and the other sorts 5l. 12s., previously to 1832. The duty was subsequently reduced to 1s. per cwt. on the former and 4s. on the latter. It was repealed in 1845.

ARNICA. A genus of plants belonging to the Natural order *Compositæ*, and Suborder *Corymbifera*. The *Arnica montana*, called Leopard's Bane, or Mountain Tobacco, is a native of the North of Europe, and of the Alps. The plant contains a volatile oil, *oil of Arnica;* and an alkaline bitter principle, *Arnicine.* It is used occasionally in medicine.

AROMATIC VINEGAR. (*Acetum aromaticum.*) This is a compound of strong acetic acid with certain powerful essential oils or aromatic herbs. The 'Edinburgh Pharmacopœia' orders it to be made with concentrated acetic acid, 1½ pints; rosemary and thyme dried, of each 1 oz.; lavender, also dried, ½ oz.; cloves, bruised, ½ drachm. Macerate for seven days, strain, and express strongly, and filter the liquor. *Henry's aromatic vinegar* is prepared by dissolving oils of cloves, lavender, rosemary, and the like, in concentrated acetic acid. Camphorated acetic acid is sometimes substituted for the *acetum aromaticum.* These preparations have been in great repute as prophylactics in contagious fevers. The name of '*Le vinaigre des quatre voleurs*' has been given to aromatic vinegar in France—it is said from the confessions of four thieves who, during the plague at Marseilles, plundered the dead bodies with perfect impunity after protecting themselves with aromatic vinegar.

ARQUERITE. A silver amalgam from the mines of Arqueros, near Coquimbo. It occurs crystalline. Domeyko finds it to consist of silver 86·49, mercury 13·51.

ARRACK. A spirituous liquor from the East Indies. This term, or its corruption, *rack*, is applied to any spirituous liquor in the East. The true arrack is said to be distilled from *toddy*—the fermented juice of the cocoa-nut tree. It is, however, frequently distilled from rice and sugar, fermented with the cocoa-nut juice.

ARROBA. A measure of capacity and weight in general use throughout all those parts of South America which ever belonged to Spain. It is also used in Manilla and the East. According to Spanish standard weight it should be 25·36 lbs. English. As a wine measure it is equal to 3·54 imperial gallons; as an oil measure it is but 2·78 imperial gallons.

ARROPE. Sherry boiled to a syrup; used for colouring other wines.

ARROWROOT. (*Racine fléchière*, Fr.; *Pfeilwurz*, Ger.) The rhizome of the *Maranta arundinacea*, a plant which grows in the West Indies, and furnishes, by pounding in mortars, and elutriation through sieves, a peculiar species of starch, commonly, but improperly, called arrowroot. It is reckoned more nourishing than the starch of wheat or potatoes, and is generally also freer from peculiar taste or flavour. The fresh root consists, according to Benzon, of 0·07 of volatile oil; 26 of starch (23 of which are obtained in the form of powder, while the other 3 must be extracted from the parenchyma in a paste by boiling water); 1·58 of vegetable albumen; 0·6 of a gummy extract; 0·25 of chloride of calcium; 6 of insoluble fibrine; and 65·5 of water. This plant was brought from the Island of Dominica, by Colonel James Walker to Barbadoes, and there planted. From thence it was sent to Jamaica. The root appears to have been used by the Indians to yield a poison with which to smear their arrows, and hence its name.

This plant has been lately cultivated with great success, and its root manufactured in a superior manner, upon the Hopewell estate, in the Island of St. Vincent. It grows there to the height of about 3 feet, and it sends down its tap roots from 12 to 18 inches into the ground. Its maturity is known by the flagging and falling down of the leaves, which takes place when the plant is from 10 to 12 months old. The roots being dug up with the hoe, are transported to the washing-house, where they are thoroughly freed from all adhering earth, and next taken individually in the hand, and deprived by a knife of every portion of their skins, while every unsound part is cut away. This process must be performed with great nicety, for the cuticle contains a resinous matter which imparts colour and a disagreeable flavour to the fecula which no subsequent treatment can remove. The skinned roots are thrown into a large cistern, with a perforated bottom, and there exposed to the action of a copious cascade of pure water till this runs off quite unaltered. The cleansed roots are next put into the hopper of the mill, and are subjected to the powerful pressure of two pairs of polished rollers of hard brass, the lower pair of rollers being set much closer together than the upper. (See *fig.* 74.) The starchy matter is thus ground into a pulp, which falls into the receiver placed beneath, and is thence transferred to large fixed copper cylinders, tinned inside, and perforated at the bottom with numerous minute orifices, like a kitchen drainer. Within these cylinders, wooden paddles are made to revolve with great velocity, by the power of a water-wheel, at the same time that a stream of pure water is admitted from above. The paddle-arms beat out the fecula from the fibres and parenchyma of the pulp, and discharge it in the form of a milk through the perforated bottom of a cylinder. This starchy water runs along pipes, and then through strainers of fine muslin, into large reservoirs, where, after the fecula has subsided, the supernatant liquid is drawn off, and fresh water being let on, the whole is agitated and left again to repose. When the water ceases to remove anything from the arrowroot, all the deposits of fecula are collected into one cistern, covered, and agitated with a fresh charge of water, and left until the following morning. The water being allowed to run off, the surface of the deposit is carefully scraped with German-silver palette-knives, to remove any impure or coloured parts, and the lower portions only are dried and prepared for the market. The greatest care is taken in drying; and when dry, the fecula is packed in tin-cases for exportation.

Fig. 74, plan of arrowroot grinding mill, and two sets of copper cylinder

74

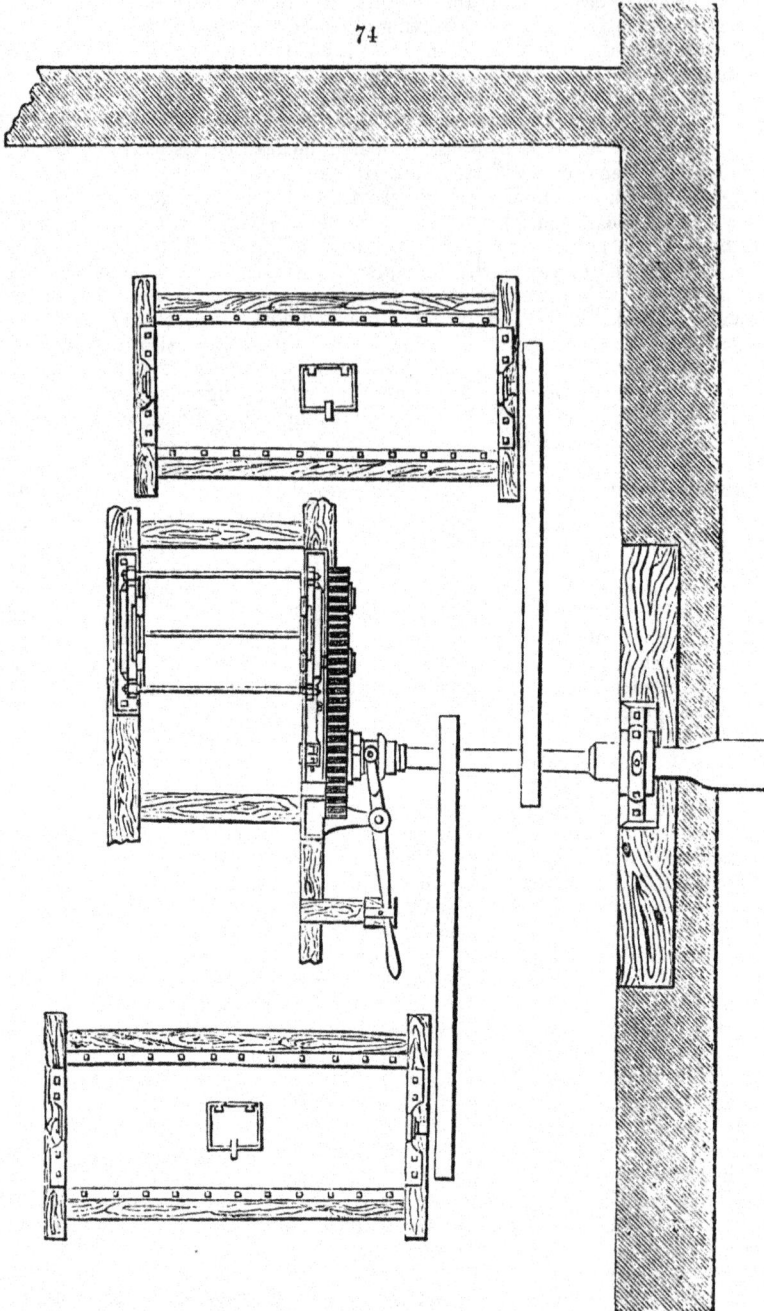

washing-machines, with the connecting machinery for driving them, the washing-agitator being driven from the connecting shaft with leathern belts. *Fig.* 75, end-elevation of copper washing-cylinder, with press framing, &c. The washing-cylinders are 6½ feet long and 3½ in diameter. The mill rollers are 3 feet long and 1 foot in diameter. *Fig.* 76, end-elevation of arrowroot mill, with wheels and pinions, dis-engaging lever, &c.

Arrowroot is brought into the market from Bermuda, St. Vincent, Jamaica, Brazil, the East Indies, Natal, and Sierra Leone. It is subject to a duty of 4s. per cwt. The Bermuda arrowroot was in 1865 sold wholesale at 1s. 2d. the pound, the other sorts varying from 2½d. to 6d.

75

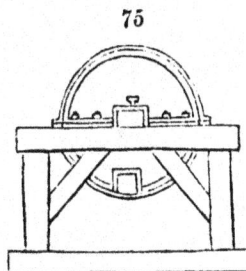

The uses of arrowroot are too well known and acknowledged to require recounting here. It is the most elegant and the richest of all the feculas. Liebig places the powers of arrowroot, as a nutriment to man, in a very remarkable point of view, when he states that 15 pounds of flesh contain no more carbon for supplying animal heat by its combustion into carbonic acid in the system than 4 pounds of starch; and that if a savage, with one animal and an equal weight of starch, could maintain life and health for a certain number of days, he would be compelled, if confined to flesh alone, in order to procure the carbon necessary for respiration during the same time, to consume five such animals. All

76

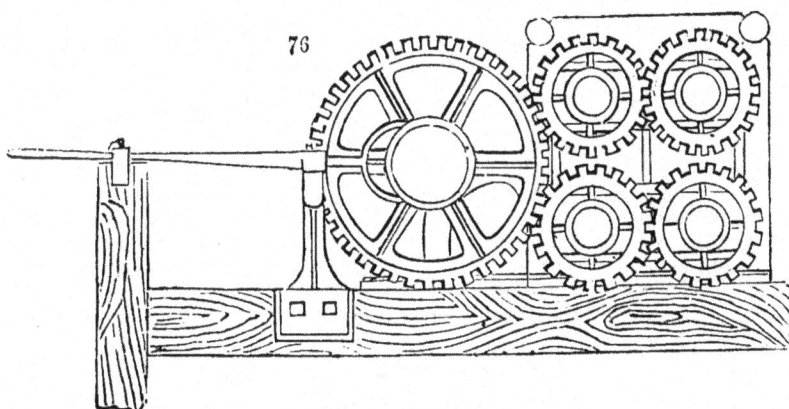

the starches are readily converted into sugar and fat, but they are low in their flesh-producing power.

In commerce, the term *arrowroot* is frequently used generically to indicate a starch or fecula, as:—*East India arrowroot*, prepared from the *Curcuma angustifolia*. *Brazilian arrowroot* or *Cassava*, the fecula of *Jatropha manihot*. *English arrowroot*, the starch of the potato (*Solanum tuberosum*). *Portland arrowroot*, a white amylaceous powder, formerly prepared in the Isle of Portland, from the *Arum maculatum*, the *common Cuckoo-pint*, called also *Wake-robin* and *Lords and Ladies*. *Tahiti arrowroot*, the fecula of *Tacca oceanica*, which has been imported into London and sold as 'arrowroot prepared by the native converts at the missionary stations in the South Sea Islands.'

The presence of potato-starch in arrowroot, with which it is often adulterated, may be discovered by the microscope. Arrowroot consists of regular ovoid particles of nearly equal size, whereas potato-starch consists of particles of an irregular ovoid or truncated form, exceedingly irregular in their dimensions, some being so large as $\frac{1}{300}$th of an inch, and others only $\frac{1}{2000}$th. Their surfaces in the arrowroot are smooth and free from the streaks and furrows to be seen in the potato-particles by a good microscope. The arrowroot, moreover, is destitute of that fetid unwholesome oil extractable by alcohol from potato-starch. But the most convenient test is dilute nitric acid of 1·10 (about the strength of single aquafortis), which, when triturated in a mortar with the starch, forms immediately a transparent, very viscid paste or jelly. Flour-starch exhibits a like appearance. Arrowroot, however, forms an opaque paste, and takes a much longer time to become viscid.

ARSENATES. Compounds of arsenic acid with alkaline and metallic bases.

ARSENIC, derived from the Greek ἀρσενικὸν, *masculine*, a name applied to orpiment on account of its potent powers. Arsenic occurs native, in veins, in crystalline rocks, and the older schists; it is found in the state of oxide, and also combined with sulphur, when it is known under the names of *yellow* and *red arsenic* (*orpiment* and *realgar*). Arsenic is associated with a great many metallic ores; in this country chiefly with those of tin, but on the Continent arsenical cobalt is the chief source of the compounds of arsenic.

The following are the principal ores of arsenic :—

Native Arsenic.—The most common form of native arsenic is that of reniform and stalactitic masses, often mammillated, and splitting off in thin successive layers like those of a shell. It possesses a somewhat metallic lustre, and a tin-white colour and streak, which soon tarnishes to a dark grey. Its specific gravity is 5·93. Before the blowpipe it gives out an alliaceous odour, and volatilises in white fumes. It is found in the silver mines of Freiberg, Annaberg, Marienberg, and Schneeberg in Saxony ; also at Joachimstahl in Bohemia, Andreasberg in the Hartz, Kapnik in Transylvania, Orawitza, in the Bannat, Kongsberg in Norway, Zimeoff in Siberia, in Alsace, in Borneo, and, according to Dana, at Haverhill, and at Jackson, N. H. in the United States.

Arsenical Antimony.—This mineral occurs at Allemont ; also at Przibram in Bohemia, where it occurs in metallic veins associated with blende, antimony, and spathic iron ; at Schladming in Styria ; and Andreasberg in the Hartz. Its composition is :—Arsenic, 63·62 ; antimony, 36·38. When exposed to the action of the blowpipe, this mineral emits fumes of arsenic and antimony ; and fuses to a metallic globule, which takes fire and burns away, leaving oxide of antimony on the charcoal.

White Arsenic or Arsenious Acid (Arsenolite) is often formed by the decomposition of other arsenical ores, and is composed of arsenic 75·76, and oxygen 24·24. It occurs either in minute radiating capillary crystals and crusts investing other substances, or in a stalactitic or botryoidal form. Before the blowpipe it volatilises in white fumes : in the inner flame it blackens and gives out an alliaceous odour ; its specific gravity is 3·69. It is white, sometimes with a yellowish or reddish tinge, and has a silky or vitreous lustre. It possesses an astringent, sweetish taste.—H. W. B.

Realgar (anciently called *Sandaraca*), red orpiment, or ruby sulphur, is a *sulphide of arsenic,* having a composition, sulphur 29·91, arsenic 70·09 = AsS² (**As²S²**). It occurs in Hungary, Saxony, Switzerland, and China.

Orpiment (a corruption of its Latin name, *auripigmentum*—golden paint), yellow sulphide of arsenic : its composition is, sulphur 39, arsenic 61 = AsS³ (**As²S³**.) Burns with a blue flame on charcoal, and emits fumes of sulphur and arsenic. Dissolves in nitro-muriatic acid and ammonia. It is found in Hungary, the Hartz, &c.

Both realgar and orpiment are artificially prepared and used as pigments. See ORPIMENT, REALGAR.

ARSENIC is a brittle metal, of an iron-grey colour, with a good deal of brilliancy. It may be prepared by triturating arsenious acid, or the white arsenic of commerce, with black flux (charcoal and carbonate of potash), and subliming in a tube. If arsenical pyrites be ignited in close tubes, metallic arsenic sublimes, and sulphuret of iron remains. This metal, when exposed in the air, gradually absorbs oxygen, and falls into a grey powder (suboxide). This is sold on the Continent as *fly-powder.*

To prepare arsenic on a larger scale, *mispickel,* or the other ores employed, are pounded ; some pieces of old iron are mixed with the ore, to retain the combined sulphur, and the mixture placed in retorts between four and five feet in length, to which receivers are adapted. The retorts are moderately heated by a fire placed beneath them ; the ores are decomposed, and metallic arsenic is sublimed and condensed in the receivers. The arsenic obtained in this way is purified by a second distillation with a little charcoal. The atomic weight of arsenic is 75 ; its symbol As.

Arsenic is used in small quantities in the preparation of several alloys ; whilst arsenious acid is employed in the manufacture of opal glass ; and is much used in the manufacture of shot, to which the reduced arsenic imparts a certain degree of hardness ; and, by preventing the distortion of the falling drops of metal, and thus securing regular globules, the manufacture is greatly facilitated. It is also used in pyrotechny.

ARSENIC ACID. AsO⁵. 3HO (**H³AsO⁴**). This acid was first produced on a large scale by M. G. Kopp. He employs nitric acid to convert arsenious acid by oxidation into arsenic acid, and by passing the nitrous acid fumes evolved, together with air, over coke moistened with water, he recovers two-thirds or three-fourths of the nitric acid employed. The proportions he adopts are 303 kilogrammes (*nearly* 2¼ lbs. *avoirdupois each*) of nitric acid of 1·35 sp. gr. to 400 kilogrammes of arsenious acid, and by adding the nitric acid gradually, the oxidising action may be accomplished without the application of heat.

Arsenic acid is now almost universally employed in the manufacture of *Rosaniline,* and is therefore an article of great consumption. It is also largely used for the white discharge of Turkey red.

M. Kopp has noticed, that without any injury to the general health, a natural tendency to stoutness was produced whilst working with arsenic acid. In the course of ten weeks, while engaged on experiments with arsenic acid, M. Kopp himself increased in weight considerably more than twenty pounds, which he lost again when the experiments were concluded. The workpeople engaged in the manufacture of Rosaniline are similarly affected.

Arsenate of Potash is prepared, in the small way, by exposing to a moderate heat, in a crucible, a mixture of equal parts of white arsenic and nitre in powder. After fusion the crucible is to be cooled; the contents being dissolved in hot water, and the solution filtered, will afford regular crystals on cooling. It is an acid salt, usually called the binarsenate of potash. This article is prepared upon a great scale, in Saxony, by melting nitre and arsenious acid together in a cylinder of cast-iron. A neutral arsenate also is readily formed by saturating the excess of acid in the above salt with potash; it does not crystallise. The acid arsenate is occasionally used in calico-printing, for preventing certain points of the cotton cloth from taking on the mordant; with which view it is mixed up with gum-water and pipe-clay into a paste, which is applied to such places with a block.

Arsenate of Soda.—An acid arsenate of soda, prepared by heating white arsenic and nitrate of soda, is now used in calico-printing.

ARSENIC, SULPHIDES OF. See ORPIMENT; REALGAR.

ARSENILLO. Ground atacamite, or native oxychloride of copper, sometimes used in Chili as sand for letters.

ARSENIOUS ACID. *White Arsenic, Flowers of Arsenic.* AsO^3 (As^2O^3).— This is the white arsenic of commerce, usually called Arsenic. It is obtained in this country from the arsenical ores of iron, tin, &c., and on the Continent from those of cobalt and nickel. It is prepared by heating the ores containing arsenic on the sole of a reverberatory furnace, through which a current of air, after passing through the grate, is allowed to play. The following ores are the more remarkable of this class —the quantity of arsenic in 100 parts is given in each case.

Mispickel, or arsenical iron	42·88
Lölingite, arsenical pyrites	65·88
Kupfernickel, arsenical nickel	54·73
Rammelsbergite, white arsenical nickel	72·64
Smaltine, tin-white cobalt	74·22
Safflorite, arsenical cobalt	70·37

In the roasting of tin ores, a considerable quantity of arsenious acid is collected in the flues leading from the furnaces in which this process is effected.

The extraction of white arsenic from the cobalt ores is performed at Altenberg and at Reichenstein, in Silesia, with an apparatus excellently contrived to protect the health of the smelters from the vapours of this poisonous sublimate.

Figs. 77 to 80 represent the arsenical furnaces at Altenberg. *Fig.* 77 is a vertical section of the poison tower; *fig.* 78, a longitudinal section of the subliming furnace A, with the adjoining vault B, and the poison tower in part at *n;* *fig.* 79, the transverse section of the furnace A, of *fig.* 78; *fig.* 80 ground-plan of the furnace A, where the left half shows the part above, and the right the part below the muffle or oblong retorts; B′ is the upper view, B″ the ground plan of the vault B, of *fig.* 78; *m, n,* the base of the poison tower. In the several figures the same letters denote the same objects; *a* is the muffle; *b* is its mouth for turning over the arsenical schlich, or ground ore; *c, c, c,* fire-draughts or flues; *d,* an aperture for charging the muffle with fresh schlich; *e,* the smoke chimney; *f,* two channels or flues for the ascent of the arsenious fumes, which proceed to other two flues *g,* and then terminate both in *h,* which conducts the fumes into the vault B. They issue, by the door *i,* into the conduit *k,* thence by *l* into the spaces *m, n, o, p, q, r,* of the tower. The incondensable gases escape by the chimney *s.* The cover *t* is removed after completion of the process, in order to push down the precipitate into the lower compartments.

The arsenious schlichs, to the amount of 9 or 10 cwt. for one operation (1 *roast-post,* or roasting round), are spread 2 or 3 inches thick upon the bottom of the muffle, and heated with a brisk fire to redness, then with a gentler heat, in order to oxidise completely, before subliming, the arsenical ore. With this view the air must have free entrance, and the front aperture of the muffle must be left quite open. After 11 or 12 hours, the calcined materials are raked out by the mouth of the muffle, and fresh ones are introduced by the openings indicated above, which are closed during the sublimation.

The arsenious acid found in these passages is not marketable till it be resublimed in large iron pots, surmounted with a series of sheet-iron drums or cast-iron cylinders, upon the sides of which the arsenic is condensed in its compact glassy form. The top cylinder is furnished with a pipe which terminates in a condensing chamber.

Figs. 81, 82, represent the arsenic-refining furnaces at Reichenstein. *Fig.* 81 shows at A, a vertical section of the furnace, the kettle, and the surmounting drums or cylinders; over B it is seen in elevation; *fig.* 82 is a ground-plan of the four fireplaces. a is the grate; b, the ash-pit; c, the openings for firing; d, the fire-place; e, iron pots or kettles which are charged with the arsenious powder; f, the fire-flues

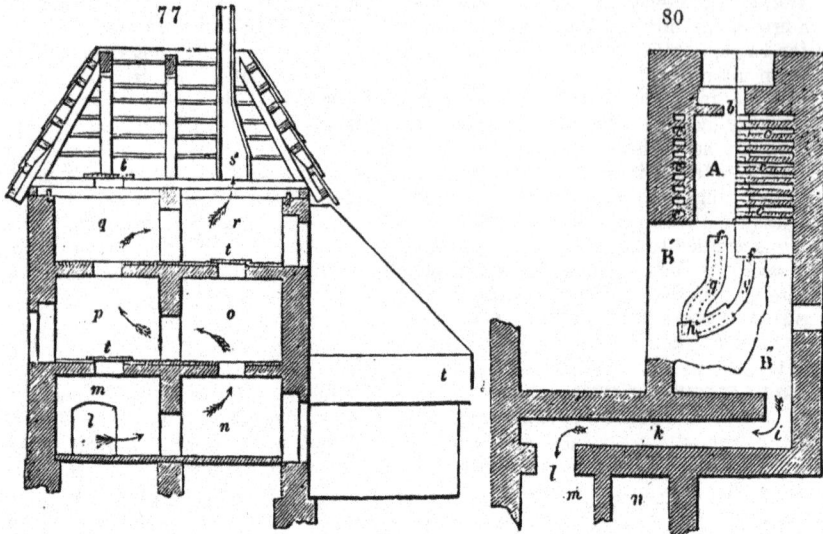

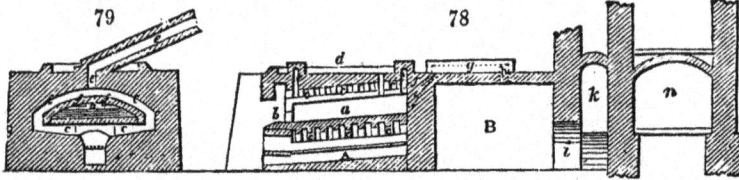

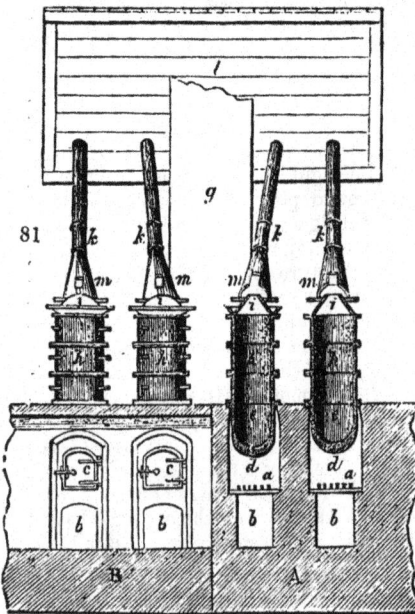

77

80

79

78

proceeding to the common chimney g; h iron cylinders; i, caps; k, pipes leading to the poison-vent l; m, openings in the pipes for introducing the probing-wires.

The conduct of the process is as follows: The pot is filled nearly to its brim with $3\frac{1}{2}$ cwt. of the arsenic meal; the cylinders are fitted on by means of their handles, and luted together with a mixture of loam, blood, and hair; then is applied first a gentle, and after half an hour, a strong fire, whereby the arsenic is raised partly in the form of a white dust, and partly in crystals; which, by the continuance of the heat, fuse together into a homogeneous mass. If the fire be too feeble, only a sublimate

81

82

is obtained; but if too violent, much of the arsenic is volatilised into the pipes. The workmen judge by the heat of the cylinders whether the operation be going on well or not. After 12 hours the furnace is allowed to cool, provided the probe-wires show that the sublimation is over. The cylinders are then lifted off, and the arsenious glass is detached from their inner surface. According to the quality of the poison-flour, it yields from $\frac{3}{4}$ths to $\frac{7}{8}$ths of its weight of the glass or enamel. Should any dark particles of metallic arsenic be intermixed with the glass, a fresh sublimation must be had recourse to.

In these operations, if any sulphur is present it is converted into sulphurous acid, which escapes through the chimney, while the arsenious acid is condensed in proper chambers, placed in the flues to receive it. Freshly prepared arsenious acid is a perfectly transparent solid mass; but by exposure it becomes transformed into an opaque body resembling porcelain.

White arsenic is extensively used in the preparation of various pigments, as the *bisulphide*, or realgar, the *tersulphide*, or orpiment, and also in the mineral greens used by paper-stainers. It has been stated that paper stained with the arsenical greens is injurious to health. Very much has been said on this subject; but the following remarks by Mr. Alfred Fletcher appear to settle the question :—'Now, it is stated that in a medical work an instance is noted in which injury has been received by those living in rooms decorated with these colours : surely, were the proximity of such materials injurious, it would not be necessary to search in recondite books for the registry of isolated cases. The fact of the large extent to which such materials have always been employed is a sufficient proof that there is no danger attending their use; moreover, workmen who have been daily employed for many years in manu-facturing large quantities of these colours, under the necessity of constantly handling them, are in the regular enjoyment of perfect health, though exposed also to the general influences of a chemical factory. Let blame be laid at the right door, and let the public be assured that it is not the looking at cheerful walls, the fingering of brightly ornamented books, nor the wearing of tastefully coloured clothing, that will hurt them, but the dwelling in ill-ventilated rooms.'

Arsenite of Copper.—Scheele's green is a combination of arsenious acid with oxide of copper, or an arsenite of copper. See SCHEELE'S GREEN.

ARSENIC, POISONING BY.—This poison is so commonly the cause of death, by accident and by design, that it is important to name an antidote which has been em-ployed with very great success.

This is the *hydrated peroxide of iron.* This preparation has no action on the system, and it may therefore be administered as largely and as quickly as possible. The following statement will render the action of this hydrated salt intelligible. When hydrated peroxide of iron is mixed in a thin paste with the solution of arse-nious acid, this disappears, being changed into arsenic acid (a far less active oxide), and the iron into protoxide, $2Fe^2O^3$ and AsO^3, producing $4FeO + AsO^5$. The hydrated peroxide of iron may be made in a few minutes by adding carbonate of soda to any salt of the red oxide of iron (perchloride, acetate, &c.). It need not be washed, as the liquor contains only a salt of soda, which would be, if not beneficial, certainly not injurious.—*Kane.*

Detection of Arsenic in Cases of Poisoning.

Arsenious acid, which is almost always the form in which the arsenic has entered the system, possesses the power of preventing the putrefaction of animal substances; and hence the bodies of persons that have been poisoned by it do not readily putrefy. The arsenious acid combines with the fatty and albuminous tissues to form solid compounds, which are not susceptible of alteration under ordinary circumstances. It hence has frequently occurred that the bodies of persons poisoned by arsenic have been found, long after death, scarcely at all decomposed; and even where the general mass of the body had completely disappeared, the stomach and intestines had remained preserved by the arsenious acid which had combined with them, and by its detection the crimes committed many years before have been brought to light and punished.—*Kane.*

The presence of arsenic may be determined by one of the following methods :—

1. Portions of the contents of the stomach or bowels being gently heated in a glass tube, open at both ends, the arsenic, if in any quantity, will be sublimed, and collected as minute brilliant octahedrons of arsenious acid.

2. Or if the ignition is effected in a tube closed at one end, metallic arsenic sub-limes, forming a steel-grey coat, and emitting a strong smell of garlic.

3. *Ammoniacal Nitrate of Silver* produces a canary-yellow precipitate of arsenite of silver in a solution of arsenious acid. The tribasic phosphate of soda produces a

yellow precipitate of tribasic phosphate of silver, which exactly resembles the arsenite. The phosphate is, however, the more soluble in ammonia, and when heated gives no volatile product; while the arsenite is decomposed into white arsenic and oxygen, leaving metallic silver behind.

4. *Ammoniacal Sulphate of Copper* produces a fine apple-green precipitate of arsenite of copper, which is dissolved in an excess of either acid or ammonia. It is, however, uncertain, unless the precipitate be dried and reduced.

5. *The Reduction Test.*—Any portion of the suspected matter, being dried, is mixed with equal parts of cyanide of potassium and carbonate of potash, both dry. This mixture is to be introduced into a tube terminating in a bulb, to which heat is applied, when metallic arsenic sublimes.

6. *Marsh's Test.*—This is one of the most delicate and useful of tests for this poison, and when performed with due care there is little liability to error. The liquid contents of the stomach, or any solution obtained by boiling the contents, is freed as much as possible from animal matter by any of the well-known methods for doing so. This fluid is then rendered moderately acid by sulphuric acid, and introduced into a bottle properly arranged.

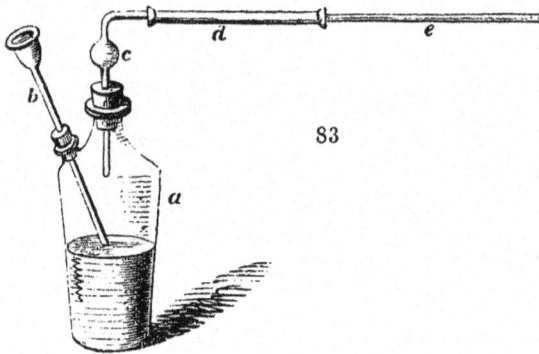

83

Fig. 83 is the best form for Marsh's apparatus:—*a* is a bottle capable of holding half, or, at most, a pint. Both necks are fitted with new perforated corks, which must be perfectly tight. Through one of these the funnel-tube *b* is passed air-tight, and through the other the bent tube *c*, which is expanded at *e* into a bulb about an inch in diameter. This bulb serves to collect the particles of liquid which are thrown up from the contents of the bottle, and which drop again into the latter from the end of the tube. The other end of the tube is connected, by means of a cork, with the tube *d*, about six inches long, which is filled with fused chloride of calcium, free from powder, destined to retain the moisture. In the opposite end of the tube *d* is fixed, air-tight, another tube, *e*, made of glass free from lead, 12 inches long, and, at most, $\frac{1}{12}$th of an inch in internal diameter. It must be observed that the funnel-tube *d* is indispensably necessary to introduce the fluid to the pieces of perfectly pure metallic zinc already placed in the bottle. Hydrogen gas is at once formed, and if arsenic be present, in even the smallest quantity, it combines with the hydrogen, and escapes as arseniuretted hydrogen. If the gas as it issues from the jet is set on fire, no product but water is generated if the hydrogen be pure; and by holding against the flame a cold white porcelain basin, or piece of glass, or of mica, no steam is produced, and a dew is formed upon the cold surface. If arsenic be present, a deposit is obtained, which, according to the part of the flame in which the substance to receive it is placed, will be either a brown stain of metallic arsenic, or a white one of arsenious acid. If the quantity of arsenic is too small to be detected in this way, it will be well to ignite the horizontal part of the tube. All the arseniuretted hydrogen will, in passing that point, become decomposed, and deposit its arsenic. The heat will drive this forward, and a little beyond the heated portion metallic arsenic will be condensed. Several precautions are necessary to be observed; but for the details of those we must refer to works especially directed to the consideration of this subject. One source of error must, however, be alluded to. A compound of antimony and hydrogen is formed under similar circumstances; and this gas in many respects resembles the compound of arsenic and hydrogen. If the stain formed by the flame is arsenic, it will dissolve, when heated, in a drop or two of sulpho-hydride of ammonia, and a lemon-yellow spot is left; if antimony is present, it leaves a yellow stain.—*Wöhler.*

If a drop of bromine is placed on a saucer, and a capsule containing arsenical spots inverted over it, the spots take a very bright lemon-yellow tinge in a short time. Antimonial spots, under the same circumstances, are acted on much more rapidly (in about five seconds at a temperature of 52° F.), and assume an orange shade. Both become colourless if exposed to the air, and are again restored if treated with a strong solution of sulphuretted hydrogen. The secondary yellow of the arsenical spots, as observed by Lassaigne, disappears on the addition of ammonia, whilst that of the antimonial spots remains untouched. A concentrated solution of iodate of potash turns arsenical spots of a cinnamon-red and dissolves them almost immediately. On anti-monial spots it has no visible action within three or four hours. Solutions of the hypochlorites (chlorides) of soda and lime and chlorine-water dissolve arsenical spots instantaneously, leaving those of antimony. A concentrated solution of the chlorate of potash gradually acts upon arsenical spots, but not upon those of antimony. The nitroprusside of potassium, on the other hand, slowly dissolves antimony, producing no perceptible effect upon arsenic. The statement of Bischoff, that arsenical spots were soluble, antimonial insoluble, in a solution of the chloride of sodium, could not be verified, as, after repeated trials, it was found to leave both not perceptibly affected. The chloride of barium, the hypochlorate and the sulphite of ammonia, afforded like-wise no distinguishing action. The nitrate of ammonia dissolves arsenical more rapidly than antimonial stains. Of these reactions the most decisive are those of iodate of potash, hypochlorites of soda and lime, and fresh chlorine-water.

It is well known that fluids mixed with glutinous matter are very liable to froth up when hydrogen is disengaged in them, from the mutual action of zinc and a dilute acid ; and that the froth obstructs the due performance of the experiment of Marsh. A committee appointed by the Prussian Government contrived an ingenious modi-fication of Marsh's apparatus, the annexed form (*fig.* 84) representing a convenient simplification of it by Dr. Ure :—A, is a narrow glass cylinder, open at top, about 10 inches high, and 1¼ or 1½ inch diameter inside; B is a glass tube, about 1 inch dia-meter outside, drawn to a point at bottom, and shut with a cork at top. Through the centre of this cork the small tube c passes down air-tight, and is furnished at top with a stopcock, into which the bent small tube of glass (without lead) E is cemented. The bent tube F is joined to the end of E with a collar of caoutchouc, or a perforated cork, which will be found more convenient.

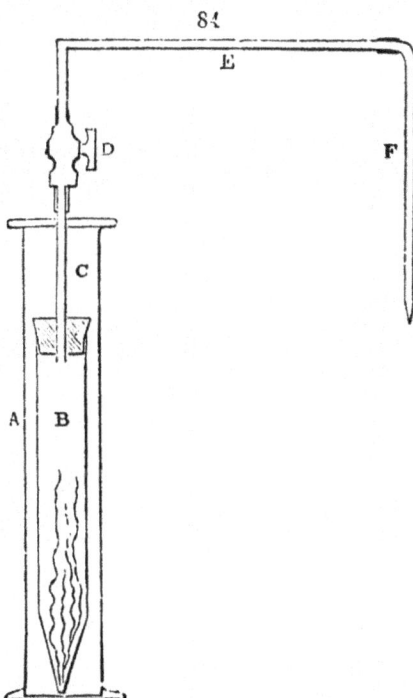

The manner of using this apparatus is as follows:—Introduce a few oblong slips of zinc, free from arsenic, into B, and then insert its air-tight cork with the attached tubes. Having opened the stopcock, pour into A as much of the suspected liquid, acidulated with dilute hydrochloric or sul-phuric acid (each pure) as will rise to the top of the cork, after B is full, and imme-diately shut the stopcock. The generated hydrogen will force down the liquid out of the lower orifice of B into A, and raise the level of it above the cork. The extremity of the tube F being dipped beneath the surface of a weak solution of nitrate of silver, and a spirit-flame being placed a little to the left of the letter E, the stopcock is then to be slightly opened, so that the gas which now fills the tube B may escape so slowly as to pass off in separate small bubbles through the silver-solution. By this means the whole of the arsenic contained in the arseniuretted hydrogen will be deposited either in the metallic state upon the inside of the tube E, or with the silver in the characteristic black powder. The first charge of gas in B being expended, the stopcock is to be shut till the liquid be again ex-pelled from it by a fresh disengagement of hydrogen. The ring of metallic arsenic deposited beyond E may be chased onwards by placing a second flame under it, and thereby formed into an oblong brilliant steel-like mirror. It is evident that by the patient use of this apparatus the whole arsenic in any poisonous liquid may be collected, weighed, and subjected to every kind of chemical verification. If F be joined to E by means of a perforated cork, it may readily be turned about, and its taper point raised into a position such as when the hydrogen issuing from it is kindled, the flame may be made to play upon a surface of glass or porcelain, in order to produce the arsenical mirror,

7. *Reinsch's Test.*—Professor Reinsch proposed an entirely different method of detecting arsenic, which consists in acidulating any suspected fluid with hydrochloric acid, heating in it a thin plate of bright copper, upon which the arsenic is deposited in the form of a thin metallic crust, and then separating the arsenic from the copper in the state of oxide by subjecting the copper to a low red heat in a glass tube. Organic

fluids and solids suspected to contain arsenic, may be prepared for this purpose by boiling them for half an hour with a little hydrochloric acid; solid matters being cut into small shreds, water being added in sufficient quantity to let the ebullition go on quietly, and care being taken to continue the boiling until the solids are either dissolved, as generally happens, or are reduced to a state of minute division.

The method of Reinsch is exceedingly delicate, for it is adequate to detect a 250,000th part of arsenic in a fluid. It is also perfect in another respect: it does not leave any arsenic in the subject of analysis; none, at least, which can be detected by any other means, even by the most delicate process yet proposed, that of Mr. Marsh.

Cut the copper on which the arsenic is deposited into small chips, so that they may be easily packed in the bottom of a small glass tube, and apply a low red heat. A white crystalline powder sublimes; and if this be examined in the sunshine, or with a candle near it, a magnifier of four or five powers will enable the observer to distinguish the equilateral triangles composing the facets of the octahedral crystals, which are formed by arsenious acid when it sublimes. Sometimes the three equal angles, composing a corner of the octahedron, may be seen by turning the glass in various directions. If triangular facets cannot be distinguished, owing to the minuteness of the crystals, then shake out the copper chips, close the open end of the tube with the finger, and heat the sublimed powder over a very minute spirit-lamp flame, chasing it up and down the tube till crystals of adequate size are formed. Next boil a little distilled water in the tube over the part where the crystalline powder is collected; and when the solution is cold, divide it into three parts, to be tested with ammoniacal nitrate of silver, ammoniacal sulphate of copper, and sulphuretted hydrogen, either in the state of gas or dissolved in water.

8. *Fleitmann's Test.*—If a solution containing arsenic be mixed with a large excess of concentrated solution of potassa, and boiled with fragments of granulated zinc, arseniuretted hydrogen is evolved, and may be easily recognised by allowing it to pass on to a piece of filter paper spotted over with solution of nitrate of silver. These spots assume a purplish-black colour, even when a small quantity of arsenic is present. This experiment may be performed in a small flask, furnished with a perforated cork carrying a piece of glass tube of about $\frac{1}{4}$ inch diameter. It will be observed that this test serves to distinguish arsenic from antimony.

The following remarks on the *Toxicological Discovery of Arsenic* deserve attention:—

'This active and easily administered poison is fortunately one of those most easily and certainly discovered; but the processes require great precaution to prevent mistaken inferences: if due care is taken, arsenic can be found after any lapse of time, as well as after the most complete putrefaction of the animal-remains. The longest time after which it has been discovered by myself is eight years, which was the case of an infant; nothing but the bones of the skeleton remained, the coffin was full of earth, and large roots of a tree had grown through it. The metal was obtained from the bones, and in the earth immediately below where the stomach had existed. Many cases have occurred in my experience, where one, two, three, four, and five years have elapsed; in one case, after fourteen months, where the body of a boy had been floating in a coffin full of water. The poison is given in one of three states, white arsenious acid, yellow sulphuret ("orpiment"), or "realgar," red sulphuret of arsenic; and it is worthy of notice that putrefaction will turn either white or red into yellow, but will never turn yellow into either white or red; this is owing to the hydrosulphuret of ammonia disengaged during decomposition.

'Modern toxicologists have abandoned all the old processes for the detection of this poison, and have adopted one of two, which have been found more expeditious, as well as more certain. The first was proposed by Marsh, of Woolwich: it is founded upon the principle that nascent hydrogen will absorb and carry off any arsenic which may be present, as arseniuretted hydrogen; but as I prefer the principle first proposed by Reinsch, and have always acted upon it, I shall confine my description to the processes founded upon it. The principle is this: arsenic mixed or combined with any organic matter will, if boiled with pure hydrochloric acid and metallic copper, be deposited upon the copper; but as this depositing property is also possessed by mercury, antimony, bismuth, lead, and tellurium, subsequent operations are required to discriminate between the deposits. I take pieces of copper wire, about No. 13 size, and $2\frac{1}{2}$ inches long; these I hammer upon a polished plane with a polished hammer, for half their length (*fig.* 85), and having brought the suspected matters to a state of dryness, and boiled the copper blade in the pure hydrochloric acid, to prove that it contains no metal capable of depositing, I introduce a portion of the suspected matter

85

and continue the boiling; if the copper becomes now either steel-grey, blue, or black, I remove it, and wash it free of grease in another vessel in which there is hot diluted hydrochloric acid; I now dry it, and, with a scraper with a fine edge, take off the deposit with some of the adhering copper, and repeat the boiling, washing and scraping, so as to have four or five specimens on copper; one of these is sealed up hermetically in a tube for future production. I now take a piece of glass tube, and having heated it in the middle, draw it out, as in *fig.* 86, dividing it at A, each section being about 2 inches long, the wide orifices being about $\frac{3}{10}$ths of an inch in diameter, and $\frac{1}{2}$ an inch long, the capillary part $\frac{1}{8}$th of an inch in diameter and $1\frac{1}{2}$ inch long; now, by putting one portion of the scrapings into one of the tubes at B, and holding it upwards over a very small flame, so that the volatile products may slowly ascend into the narrow portion of the tube, we prove the nature of the deposit: if mercury, it condenses in minute white shining globules; if lead or bismuth, it does not rise, but melts into a yellowish glass, which adheres to the copper; if tellurium, it would fall as a white amorphous powder; if antimony, it would not rise at that low temperature; but arsenious acid condenses as minute octahedral crystals, looking with the microscope like very transparent grains of sand. I make three such sublimates, one of which is sealed up like the arsenic for future production. I now cut the capillary part of another of the tubes in pieces, and boil it in a few drops (say 10) of distilled water, and when cold drop three or four drops on a plate of white porcelain, and with a glass rod drop one drop of ammoniacal sulphate of copper in it: and now to make the colours from this and the next test more conspicuous, I keep a chalk-stone, planed and cleaned, in readiness, and placing on it a bit of clean white filtering paper, I conduct the drops of copper-test upon the paper, which permits the excess of copper-solution to pass through into the chalk, but retains the smallest proportion of Scheele's green; the other few drops of the solution are treated the same way with the ammoniacal nitrate of silver. When I get the yellow precipitate of arsenite of silver, the papers, with these two spots, are now dried and sealed up in a tube as before, and that with the silver must be kept in the dark, or it will become black. I have still one of the tubes with the arsenical sublimate remaining; through this I direct a stream of hydrosulphuric acid gas for a few seconds, which converts the sublimate into yellow orpiment. I have now all **five** tests: the metal, the acid, arsenite of copper, arsenite of silver, and yellow sulphuret; and the $\frac{1}{100000}$th of a grain of arsenic is sufficient in adroit hands to produce the whole; but all five must be present, or there is no positive proof, for many matters will cause a darkness of the copper in the absence of arsenic,—sulphurets even from putrefaction;—but there is no sublimate in the second operation, because the sulphur burns into sulphurous acid and passes off upwards. Corn, grasses, and earth slightly darken it from some unknown cause, but produce no sublimate; so, if the solution of suspected arsenious acid is tested with the copper-test while hot, it will produce a greenish deposit of oxide of copper, through the heat dissipating a little ammonia, or if the copper blade has not been deprived of grease by the diluted hydrochloric acid, the sublimed acid from the grease will precipitate copper from that test; but as much of the sulphuric acid of commerce, and nearly all such hydrochloric acid and some commercial zinc contains arsenic, nothing can excuse a toxicologist who attempts to try for arsenic if he has not previously experimented with all his reagents before he introduces the suspected matters. I should also mention that this metal is to be found in all parts of the body, but longest, and in greatest quantity, in the liver, where it is frequently found many days after it has disappeared from the intestines.'—*W. Herapath.*

Arsenious acid of commerce is frequently adulterated with chalk or plaster of Paris. These impurities are very easily detected, and their proportions estimated. Arsenious acid is entirely volatilised by heat, consequently it is sufficient to expose a weighed quantity of the substance to a temperature of about 400° F. in a capsule or crucible. The whole of the arsenic will pass off in fumes, while the impurities will be left behind as a fixed residuum, which can, upon cooling, be weighed.

The mines of Cornwall and Devonshire produced in 1871. 4,147 tons, 15 cwt. of arsenic, the value of which was 15,519*l.* 18*s.*; a considerable quantity is also produced at Swansea, from the roasting of arsenical copper ores.

ARSINE. A name used by some modern chemists for arseniuretted hydrogen.

ARTESIAN WELL. This is a description of well or borehole in which water is obtained by means of a perforation bored vertically down through impermeable strata to an underlying stratum of a more or less permeable character, such stratum to be charged with water and to exist either in the shape of a basin-shaped depression, or to be so inclined as to reach, at some distance from the point at which the borehole may be made, the surface of the earth. The name is derived from the

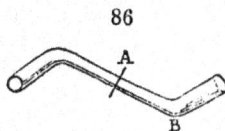

fact that wells of this description were first known in North-Western Europe, in the province of Artois in France, where this method of obtaining water has been practised from a very early period. Properly speaking, an Artesian well is one in which the water from the lower stratum rises *above* the surface of the superincumbent impermeable stratum; but by extension the phrase has been applied of late years to any well in which the waters of a lower stratum are enabled to rise sufficiently near to the surface to allow of their being economically used. It will be seen hereafter that in many instances, borings, which were originally strictly Artesian, have at a later period lost the characteristic property of yielding waters flowing *over* the surface.

When the water falls upon the exposed surface of the outcrop of the permeable stratum from which the supply for any Artesian well is derived, it passes under the edge of the overlapping impermeable stratum, and over such inferior retentive stratum as it may meet with. Then if it cannot find, or make to itself an outlet, it will follow the surface of the impermeable upholding stratum, in strict accordance with the laws which regulate the flow of water above ground. If, under these circumstances, an opening should be made through the overlying impermeable stratum, the water will rise to a height corresponding to the level at which it passed under such stratum, excepting in so far as it may be affected by friction, or by the existence of any natural overflows, created by interruptions of the containing basin, or by any disturbance of the lower retentive strata of a nature to place the water-bearing stratum in contact with still lower strata having no communication with the surface.

M. Lefebvre ('Comptes Rendus de l'Acad. des Sciences, 1838,') describes several very ancient Artesian wells, which were discovered by M. Ayme in the Oasis of Thebes. These appear to have been sunk through 80 feet of clay and marls, and then through 300 feet of limestone. M. Ayme states that in the Libyan desert, where there are no rivers or springs, and upon which rain never falls, formerly a large population was supplied with water by Artesian wells, several of which have been cleared out and restored by this French engineer with perfect success. The 'Wells of Solomon,' in the plains of Tyre, are supposed to be of this description.

The first Artesian well in London was put down in the year 1794. This description of well has been used for a long period in the East and in Italy.

The term Artesian may really be applied to all wells or borings which may be put down, having for their special purpose the obtaining of water; and the advisability of endeavouring to find water by means of such wells will depend upon several considerations, namely:—on the quantity and quality of water required; on the physical position of the strata existing in the district where the water-supply is required, and of the surface of the ground where the water-bearing rocks are known to come to the surface, and on the outcrop of such rocks being denuded or covered with any description of drift; on the mechanical formation of the rocks to be perforated, with special reference to their compactness or porosity as the case may be, and on the lithological character and thickness of the water-bearing deposit; lastly, on the application of the processes by means of which the impermeable strata can be passed through, and the water-bearing strata reached.

The first three of these considerations will now be dealt with; the fourth point, which comprises the engineering of the work, will be brought into notice under the head of BORING. Overflowing wells owe their origin, as a rule, to the infiltration of the waters falling upon the surface of the globe, which, percolating through the various pores and fissures of the strata, are passed into, and held by such strata of sand or gravel as will contain water in very large quantities. If the water be carried in this manner from some high point on the surface of the globe to some subterranean point where the surface of the ground is at a lower level than the point at which the source of the water is formed, the hydrostatic pressure is sufficient in case a connection with the surface is formed, either by faults or fissures in the strata, or by a borehole put down from the surface, to cause the water to rise and overflow in a stream more or less constant.

In the case of all borings used for the purpose of obtaining water, the chief considerations are naturally as follows:—

1st. To obtain a certain quantity of water.
2nd. To have such water pure.
3rd. To have the position of the borehole so fixed as to make a constant supply over a certain period of time to be depended upon.

The site of a boring for water may of necessity have to be fixed upon within a certain limited space. The strata to be passed through, and the physical character of the surface of the ground adjacent to the site of the boring, will probably partake of one of the following conditions:—

1st. The ground to be passed through may have a steep inclination extending to the bottom of the water-bearing beds. In this case the quantity of water which can be obtained by the borehole is necessarily limited. A large quantity of water may, however, be obtained under these conditions (which are illustrated by *fig.* 87) should the water-bearing strata be very porous, and have a considerable lateral extension.

87

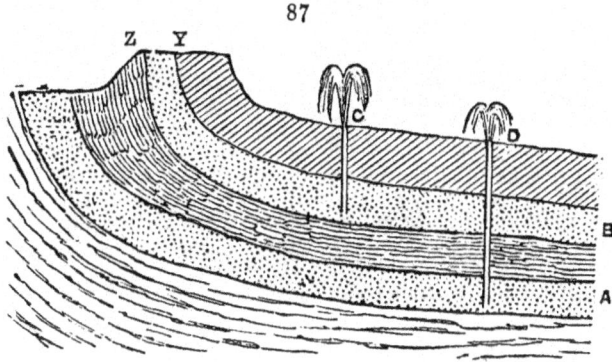

2nd. On the other hand the inclination of the strata may be very gradual, as shown in *fig.* 88, and in this case the area of surface receiving the rainfall is much greater. This is due not only to the surface of the water-bearing rocks having a larger superficial area, but also to the fact that near to the surface the overlying rocks are generally found to be more open than they are at a considerable depth from the surface. Hence, whilst in *fig.* 87 the rainfall from z to y is the

88

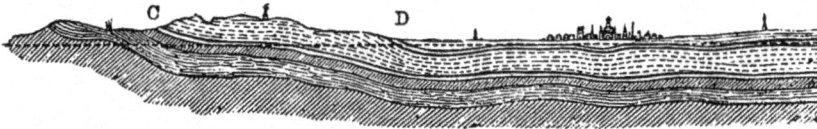

most that can be expected to reach the borehole, in *fig.* 88 it is probable that most of the rainfall on the area from c to D will percolate through to the water-bearing strata. This is the condition under which the largest quantity of water may be expected to be obtained in the prosecution of Artesian wells.

3rd. Another condition is where a boring has to be made to water-bearing strata through other rocks, which, though compact in their nature, are not impermeable. This condition naturally affects the quantity of water obtainable, and in such a case it is important to obtain increased hydrostatic pressure.

4th. In some cases several qualities of water may be met with in one boring, some of which may be found chemically objectionable. When satisfactory water has been found, the impure water can only be kept back by the insertion of tubes in the borehole. With the third condition mentioned above, the application of tubes will also sometimes be found advantageous. They are always necessary where running sand or very loose strata are met with.

5th. Another case occurs when the water met with by a boring has so little hydrostatic pressure that it will not rise in the borehole to the surface. In this case the water has to be raised, when its level is within 30 feet of the surface, by some description of pump. When the level of the water is at a greater distance than this from the top, a plunger-pump has to be used.

In cases 1 and 2 a bed of impermeable rock is assumed to intervene between the surface and the water-bearing strata. It need hardly be mentioned that the quantity of water found in any class of strata does not depend only on the surface of such strata exposed to the rainfall, but is much influenced by the degree of porosity of the strata, which is the test of its saturative capability.

An illustration of this is afforded by the results of the sinkings of many of the deepest coal-mines in Great Britain, where such sinkings have passed through the Permian beds before reaching the coal-measures. Between the magnesian limestone and coal-measures is found in nearly every instance a bed of red sand, varying in thickness from a few inches to 12 feet. Whilst feeders of water of a few hundred gallons per minute only have been encountered whilst passing through the limestone, the feeders met with on reaching the more porous sand-bed referred to, have frequently been enormous, in several instances amounting to over 4,000 gallons per minute. In such cases the quantity of water can doubtless be traced to the principles indicated on *fig.* 88.

Under the conditions referred to in the fifth head, may be mentioned cases where water may be obtained by short holes, bored a few yards into the ground, the object being to collect the surface-drainage, and the water being obtained by small pumps.

Where gravel only is found, water cannot generally be procured by short holes, but where gravel rests on an impervious clay, success is almost certain.

In cases where there is apparently a considerable hydrostatic pressure, there is a condition which will prevent any large quantity of water falling upon porous strata, passing to subterranean depths. Should any river emanate from, or pass through, such strata, the river will probably carry away a large proportion of the water which otherwise would have saturated the permeable rocks.

It will be understood that the geological formations in which Artesian explorations can be made with most prospects of success are those which combine compact and impermeable strata with porous and open rocks. The particular systems of rocks which appear to present as a rule these conditions are those contained by and lying adjacent to the chalk series, embracing the London clay, the chalk, upper greensand, the gault, and the lower greensand. These rocks present the necessary conditions, and in the sites where they are chiefly found, the north of France and south-east of England, a large number of wells have been put down, many of which are producing large volumes of water.

In older formations it is much more difficult to discover rocks of sufficient openness to carry large quantities of water, and further than this, as the older rocks lie very irregularly, and frequently at a heavy inclination, they are not so suitable for the purpose of obtaining water by means of boring. Hence it is usual in districts where such rocks prevail to obtain the water-supply, where river-water either is not used or is not obtainable, from reservoirs situated at some high level where they can be arranged to catch the surface-drainage.

The hot springs which burst out of the ground in districts where the so-called primary formations are found, came undoubtedly from a great depth beneath the surface, and derive their heat from an exalted subterranean temperature; but it would not be practicable to bore to such extreme depths as would be necessary in these rocks. A miniature representation of such springs is exhibited in the intermitting fountains of fresh water on the shoulder of Vesuvius.

It will be interesting to record the results of some of the chief artesian borings which have been made in this and other countries. The most famous example is that of the boring commenced in 1833 at Grenelle, a suburb of the SW. of Paris where there was a great scarcity of water. Here the chalk was overlaid by gravels, marls, and clays, which were known to be capable of intercepting the passage of water. Hence, as it was known that below the chalk water-bearing sand would be met with, M. Mulot, the engineer of the well, supported by the authority of MM. Arago and Walferdin, resolved to seek a supply of water by boring through the chalk into the sub-cretaceous strata. At Elbœuf the chalk had been traversed in this manner, and the water had risen to a height of 82 feet above the level of the ground, or 109 feet above the level of the sea, and it was considered that as the surface of the ground at Grenelle was about 104 feet above the level of the sea, and as the outcrop of the water-bearing strata was nearer to the proposed borehole than at Elbœuf, the water at Grenelle might be expected to flow over the surface. This reasoning was found to be correct, and in February, 1841, after eight years' labour, the rods suddenly descended several yards, having pierced into the vault of the subterranean waters so long sought after by the indefatigable engineer. A few hours afterwards he was rewarded for all his anxious toils; for the water, rising to the surface, discharged itself at the rate of 881,884 gallons in every twenty-four hours; the temperature of the water being nearly 82° F. At first it brought up so great a quantity of sand that the tube was several times choked up by it, and even now it is not free from occasional though rare interruptions, but the force of the column of water has always proved sufficient to clear its way after a short interval. The water flows in a clear, continuous stream, and is carried by pipes to a reservoir near the Pantheon, whence it is distributed over the adjacent parts of the city, as well as along the line of the Boulevards from the *abattoir* to the Observatory. By means of small pipes, the École Militaire, the Invalides, and two or three other public establishments, are also supplied with this water. The surface of the ground at the well is 102 feet above the level of the sea, and the water is capable of being carried above this to a height of 120 feet. The exposed surface of the water-bearing beds which supply the well of Grenelle is about 117 square miles; the subterranean area in connection with these lines of outcrop may possibly be about 20,000 square miles, and the average thickness of the sand of the *grès verts*, serving in their underground range as a reservoir for the water, does not probably exceed thirty or forty feet.—*Prestwich on the Water-bearing Strata of London.*

After the completion of the Grenelle well others were quickly undertaken. Amongst the most important of these were the borings undertaken in the Rhenish provinces for bringing to the surface the waters of the brine-springs of that district, some of which even exceeded the depth of 2,400 feet from the surface. M. Degoussée mentions in his ' Guide de Sondeur ' (1847), that he himself had executed no less than sixteen deep borings in the Département de l'Indre et Loire, of which ten are in the town of Tours and six in its neighbourhood, presenting an average depth of about 500 feet. Two of these borings were, however, unsuccessful, and it appears that the conditions under which they occurred with respect to the great watercourses of the district, led to the supposition that the underground course of the waters was interrupted by means of a fault or upheaval.

At Calais the results obtained by the great artesian well there sunk were even more striking than those obtained near Tours ; for after having in this place passed through the drift above the chalk, the chalk itself and the whole of the sub-cretaceous strata, the boring was continued *in the transition rocks* until it had attained a total depth from the surface of about 1,150 feet. It will be necessary hereafter to refer to this well, and to the abnormal state of the geological formations under this district.

An important Artesian well was also put down at Chichester, being carried through the great Hampshire tertiary basin to the upper greensand, where it was stopped at a depth of 1,054 feet from surface. Very little water was obtained.

At Southampton the upper and lower chalk and chalk-marl were passed through, but at a depth of 1,317 feet no valuable supply of water was obtained. A great number of Artesian wells had in the meantime been sunk in the tertiary basins of both London and Hampshire, and the drain thus established upon the subterranean water-courses of those formations was so great that the waters which originally had flowed over the surface of the ground, were no longer able to reach that height; and it became evident that the demand upon these water-bearing strata was rapidly exceeding the supply. Under these circumstances the Hampstead and Highgate Waterworks Company resolved to renew under London the attempt which had been abandoned at Southampton ; and their advisers argued that, inasmuch as the outcrop of the sub-cretaceous formations was continuous around the margin of the cretaceous basin surrounding and underlying the London tertiaries, excepting on the eastern border, those sub-cretaceous strata would be found under London just as they had been actually found at Paris.

This reasoning proved to be correct so far as the chalk-marl, the upper greensand, and the gault were concerned ; but when those formations had been traversed (to a depth of $1,113\frac{1}{2}$ feet), the boring tools, instead of entering upon the lower greensand, which theoretically had been expected, entered upon and traversed, to a total depth of 1,302 feet, a series of marls, clays, and sandstones, which appear in all probability to belong to the *new red-sandstone* series : all the intermediate strata being absent.

A boring at Harwich also proved the existence of transition rocks of an early period at a depth of 1,200 feet from the surface ; various rocks from the tertiaries to the upper greensand and gault having been passed through.

From the above data the interesting fact will be observed that no borehole in the London basin has as yet succeeded in proving and obtaining water from the lower greensand rocks; the Southampton, Calais, Highgate, and Harwich wells having all proved failures in this respect. It is a question to be proved by experiment whether to the north-west of London the tertiary rocks would not be less likely to give place to rocks of older formations, as they appear to do in the boreholes referred to. It will be understood from the particulars given of the few boreholes, how much uncertainty attends the art of boring, at least, as regards the obtaining of water by this means.

Some particulars may now be given of a number of the chief Artesian boreholes put down in France and England. The following Table shows the depth and cost of several of the French Artesian wells :—

Grenelle,	Dept.	Seine .	.	.	1,798 feet	.	.	.	£14,500
Calais	,,	Pas de Calais	.	1,138	,,	.	.	.	3,560
Douchery	,,	Ardennes	.	.	1,215	,,	.	.	.	3,045
St. Fargeau	,,	Yonne	.	.	666	,,	.	.	.	1,216
Lille	,,	Nord .	.	.	592	,,	.	.	.	320
Crosne	,,	Seine et Oise	.	333	,,	.	.	.	190
Brou	,,	Marne	.	.	246	,,	.	.	.	200
Ardres	,,	Nord	.	.	155	,,	.	.	.	64
Claye	,,	Seine et Marne	.	108	,,	.	.	.	78
Chaville	,,	Oise .	.	.	65	,,	.	.	.	15

The deep wells of London are all in the chalk. The depths of some of the most important are given in the following Table, which has been compiled from data given by Mr. W. Whitaker, ' Memoirs of the Geological Survey,' vol. iv. (1872) :—

Sections of some of the Deep Wells in London and the adjoining Country.

MIDDLESEX	Soil, made Ground, Brick Earth and Gravel	London Clay	Woolwich and Reading Beds	Thanet Sand	Depth to the Chalk	In Chalk
	ft.	ft.	ft.	ft.	ft.	ft.
Apothecaries' Hall, Blackfriars	12	114	48	44	218	76
Bank of England	26	111	58½	39	234½	100
Blackwall, Trinity Wharf	63	68	34	72	237	10
Bow	19	48	56	51	174	150
Broad Street, Golden Square	10½	98	58	25	191½	25
Camden Station	18	144	64	8	234	166
Castleboar Hill, near Ealing	...	300	60	...	360	...
Chiswick, Griffin Brewery	40	140	90	29	299	46
Colney Hatch Lunatic Asylum	...	137	27	25	189	141
Fulham	25	135	90	...	250	66
Hackney Road	14	48½	48	42	152½	259
Haggerstone	16	56½	44½	47½	164½	256
Hampstead, Lower Heath	...	289	89		378	72
Hampstead Road	23	59	39½	24½	146	37
Hanwell Lunatic Asylum	21	194	75	...	290	30
Harrow Waterworks	...	111	48	...	159	254
Haverstock Hill	...	223	61	28	312	78
Hayes	14	134	88½	...	231	88
Highbury	...	106	57½	16½	180	134
Holloway City Prison	...	135	69	13	217	102
Hoxton	18	69	34	30	151	...
Hyde, The, Edgeware Road	...	66	34½	...	100½	37
Hyde Park Corner	5	229	64	21	319	18
Isle of Dogs	39	...	43	42½	124½	239½
Islington Green	12	48	100 ?	16	176	144
Kensington, Horticultural Society	40	198	54	25	317	84
Kensington Gardens, N.	2	172	56	33	263	58
Kentish Town Waterworks	...	236	61½	27	324½	645[1]
Leicester Square	5½	148½	60	28	244	101
Limehouse	29	19	47	44½	139½	...
Long Acre	20	120½	58½	24	222	258[2]
Mile End	13	86	63	40½	202½	2[2]
Mile End Road (City of London Union)	35	60½	41	38½	175	10
Pentonville Model Prison	17	113	54½	35	219½	151
Pimlico, Simpson's Factory, Grosvenor Road	26	112	67½	25½	231	100
Pinner	3½	29	27½	...	60	80
Ponder's End	13	15	49½	35 ?	112½	290½
Ratcliffe	14	56	26	54	150	102
Shoreditch, Truman's Brewery	22½	80½	53	43	199	331
Shoreditch Workhouse	18	60	40	39	157	100
Staines	33	267	79	...	369	154
Sudbury	2	68	60	...	120	80
Tottenham	20	52	61	15	148	250[2]
Tottenham Court Road (Meux's)	22	64	51½	21	158	207[3]
Tower Hill (Royal Mint)	24	94	57	20½	195½	202
Trafalgar Square	23	142	41	42	248	147
Twyford, near Ealing	...	211	41	...	...	...
Uxbridge Union	12	94	75	...	175	38
Westbourne Estate Waterworks	...	217	62	18	297	15
West Drayton	32	88	66	...	186	100
Westminster, Elliot's Brewery	32	140	67½	31½	271	127
,, Thorne's Brewery	27½	100	66½	36	230	70
Winchmore Hill	...	186	44	...	230	...

[1] This boring was carried down 332 feet below the bottom of the chalk.
[2] Or more. [3] More since.

SURREY, HERTFORDSHIRE, ESSEX	Soil, made Ground, Brick Earth and Gravel	London Clay	Woolwich and Reading Beds	Thanet Sand	Depth to the Chalk	In Chalk
	ft.	ft.	ft.	ft.	ft.	ft.
Balham Hill, near Clapham Common	15	239	53	40	...	...
Battersea	32	127	55	35	249	...
Bermondsey	23	...	30	38½	91½	140½
Claremont	50	450	60 ?	... ?	560	...
Horselydown	32	51	75		158	104
Kingston on Thames	13	245	88	25	371	99
Lambeth (Bedlam)	28	80½	35½	47	191	...
Mitcham	4	101	46	38	189	72
Mortlake Brewery	10	199	58	...	267	3
New Barnet Railway Station	...	115	44	...	159	280
New Cross (Naval School)	...	23	51	48	125	25
Penge (Crystal Palace)	...	259	47½	54½	361	149
Richmond	...	191	85		276	103
Rotherhithe	29	...	35	43	107	145
Southwark, Barclay's Brewery	27½	77½	62	36	203	{ over 100
Wandsworth, County Lunatic Asylum	...	231	60 {	over 40	over 330	...
West Ham	33	...	42	57	132	306

The Artesian wells in Essex which overflow, are of the following depths, according to Dr. Mitchell :—Foulness Island, 450 feet; Mersey, and adjoining islands, 300 feet; Wallis Island, 400 feet; Little Wigborough, 250 feet; Woodham, 350 feet; North Ockenden, 80; Fobbing, 100 feet; Bulpham Fen, 70–80.

The difficulty of making any calculation, even in a well-known district, as to the quantity of water which can be expected to drain to any one borehole, is considerable, since, though it may be possible to judge of the breadth of surface over which the rainfall may be expected to sink into the water-bearing strata, it is impossible to tell with any degree of exactness the lateral extension of the drainage, except the conditions happen to be those in which the borehole is put down in the centre, or some part of a basin. Naturally the more porous and saturable the water-bearing strata are, the greater the proportion of the drainage which may be expected to be conveyed to any one point.

Some years ago Mr. Prestwich computed the quantity of rain falling over the district surrounding London with a view to estimate the supply of water which a boring through the chalk to the lower greensand formation would furnish. The following Table exhibits the results of his investigation :—

	Probable extent of effective Area	Quantity of Rainwater received		Probable Quantity absorbed	
	Sq. miles	Inches annually	Gallons in 24 hours	Inches annually	Gallons in 24 hours
Lower Tertiaries	24	25 =	23,749,656	12 =	11,411,352
Upper Greensand	70	28 =	77,660,660	10 =	27,735,960
Lower Greensand	230	26½ =	241,500,920	16 =	145,811,720

'These calculations, although offered as only very general approximations, give results sufficiently marked and decided, that even admitting the necessity of not inconsiderable corrections, I think they establish strong *primâ facie* evidence in favour of the upper and lower greensands beneath London containing unusually large quantities of water, which may be rendered available for the supply of the metropolis by means of Artesian wells. What their yield might be could only be determined exactly by actual experiment; but, judging from analogy, if the lower tertiary sands, with dimensions comparatively so limited, can nevertheless furnish not less than 3,000,000 to 4,000,000 gallons daily (and if, as is probable, they supply much of the water found in the upper beds of the chalk beneath London, their yield may amount to 8,000,000 or 10,000,000), then, I submit, that there is a reasonable probability, after allowing for the present over-drainage, of the tertiaries of the upper greensand, with an effective area and a thickness 3 times greater than those of the lower tertiaries, yielding daily, and without diminution, from 6,000,000 to 10,000,000, and of the lower greensands, which exceeds by 10 times the lower tertiaries in both respects, of their yielding daily and without diminution from 30,000,000 to 40,000,000 gallons of water in the twenty-four hours, taken at about surface level.

'Since the beds of the lower greensand are 200 feet thick, and they occupy an area above and below ground of 4,600 square miles, and since a mass of one mile square and one foot thick will hold more than 60,000,000 of gallons of water, it is evident that a year's consumption of water by the population of London would not occasion a fall of one foot in the water-level over the entire area; that is, supposing no rain had fallen during the year. Such wells, too, would have the advantage of adding to the adornment of the metropolis, as if the water of the lower greensand was liberated by means of Artesian wells, fountains would be at once formed, projecting their water from 100 to 150 feet above the level of Trinity high-water mark.'[1]—E. B.

ARTESIAN WELLS, *Negative.* Borings into the earth which are intended to carry off the waters from the surface. They have been proposed for the purpose of draining large tracts of swampy country. Especial information on this subject will be found in the 'Society of Arts' Journal' for 1856, and Ansted's 'Geology.'

ARTICHOKE. (*Cynara Scolymus*). A thistle-like plant, a native of the South of Europe, cultivated for the sake of the fleshy sweet receptacle of its flowers. JERUSALEM ARTICHOKES are the tubers of the *Helianthus Tuberosus*, and derive their name by a corruption, from the Italian *girasole*, sunflower.

ARTICULITE. A name proposed by Dr. Wetherill for flexible sandstone, in allusion to the articulated structure of the stone, seen on microscopic examination.

ARTIFICIAL STONE. See STONE, ARTIFICIAL.

ARTILLERY. The earliest European artillery of large size consisted of 'serpentines' and 'bombards,' both being formed of longitudinal bars of wrought-iron, arranged like the staves of a cask, and hooped all over, or nearly so, with wrought-iron rings, shrunk-on hot upon the bars. The serpentine was of small calibre, but of enormous length. A gun of this character, taken by the Swiss from Charles le Téméraire, at the battle of Granson, in 1476, is described and figured in the Emperor Napoleon's work, 'Passé et l'Avenir d'Artillerie.' This example is preserved in the collection of the Arsenal of Neuville, Canton of Berne; it is only about two inches calibre, but about ten feet in length of chase, formed with wrought-iron, with rings shrunk-on at some inches apart. It is embedded to its horizontal diameter, and for its whole length, in a timber bed.

The bombard was usually a much shorter piece, often of immense calibre. The great gun of Ghent, known as *Dulle Griette*, or the Raging Meg, is of this character. Voisin thus describes it:—'This enormous cannon, or ancient bombard, is one of the most curious pieces of artillery known, both in dimensions and construction, which is a *chef-d'œuvre* of the art of forging. It is 18 feet in length, by 10 feet 6 inches in circumference; the mouth is 2¾ feet in circumference; it is forged from bars of iron, and weighs 33,606 lbs., and throws a stone ball of 600 lbs. weight. Its construction appears to date from the early years of the invention of artillery; in all probability it was forged while Philip Van Artevelde, Riswaert of Flanders, was besieging Oudenarde, in 1382. It is certain that the people of Ghent, at war with their Duke, Philippe, used it in 1411, and at the attack of Oudenarde, in 1452.'

In the arsenal of St. Petersburg is a bombard which is 21 feet long; but it only weighs 17,435 lbs., and its calibre is only 68 lbs.

The Mons Meg of Scotland, which now quietly reposes on the King's Bastion, Edinburgh, is formed of longitudinal stave bars, in one ply only, and of superimposed rings, driven and shrunk-on upon the taper. This will be understood from the accompanying figures (89, 90). This gun was made by one M'Kin, to whom the people of Kirkcudbright contributed the bars of iron. Mons Meg was used at the siege of Dumbarton, in 1489; at Norham, in 1497; it was used to fire a salute in 1548; and in 1682, when firing a salute in honour of the Duke of York, the iron rings, which are now partly wanting near the breech, were blown away without much disturbing the longitudinal bars. The gun actually discharged balls of Galloway granite against

---

[1] Consult Prestwich, 'Water-bearing Strata of the Country round London;' 'Mylne's Sections of the London Strata;' M. Garnier's 'Traité sur les Puits Artésiens;' Swindell, 'Rudimentary Treatise on Well Digging and Boring;' Buckland's 'Bridgewater Treatise on Geology and Mineralogy;' De la Beche's 'Geological Observer;' Héricart de Thury's 'Considérations sur la Cause du Jaillissement des Eaux des Puits Forcés;' Dégousse and Laurent, 'Guide du Sondeur;' Whitaker, 'Geological Survey Memoirs,' vol. iv., 1872, etc. etc.

Threave Castle. The weight of a granite ball of 19½ inches diameter is about 330 lbs.

Colonel Symes, in his 'Embassy to Ava, in 1795,' informs us that he found that cannon formed of prismatic bars of wrought hoop-iron hooped together were known

89

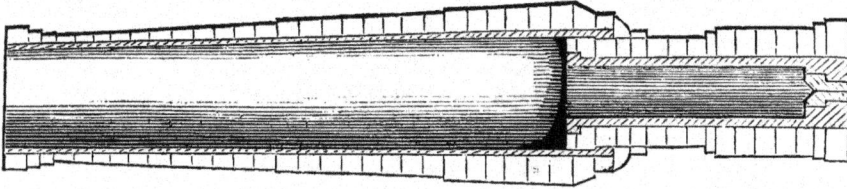

90

in India from a remote antiquity. In Meyer's 'Historical Manual' will be found a curious history of the progress of wrought-iron cannon, from 1494—when Charles VIII. suppressed wrought-iron bombards, and had no other artillery than that of bronze—to the present day. In 1856, Daniel Treadwell published a memoir 'on the Practicability of constructing Cannon of Great Calibre, capable of enduring long-continued Use under full Charges.' In this he proposes a very large wrought-iron gun, which should be capable of projecting a shot or shell of a ton weight through the space of six miles. He says, in a note to this paper, 'Between the years 1841 and 1845, I made upwards of twenty cannon of this material (wrought-iron). They were all made up of rings, or short hollow cylinders, welded together endwise. Each ring was made of bars wound upon an arbour spirally, like winding a ribbon upon a block, and, being welded and shaped in dies, were joined endwise when in the furnace and at a welding heat, and afterwards pressed together in a mould by a hydrostatic press of 1,000 tons force.' Finding in the early stage of the manufacture that the softness of the wrought-iron was a serious defect, he formed those made afterwards with a lining of steel, the wrought-iron bars being wound upon a previously formed steel ring.

Mr. Nasmyth undertook, in 1854, an enormous wrought-iron gun, of 13 inches calibre; but there was some failure in the forging.

In 1856, Messrs. Horsfall, of Liverpool, completed, and proved with a solid shot of 300 lbs. and 45 lbs. of powder, a wrought-iron gun, 13 inches calibre, and 13½ feet length of chase, perhaps the largest and most remarkable forging ever made. Two wrought-iron mortars, of 36 inches calibre, built up of separate pieces, were constructed about the same time for the Government, from the designs of Mr. Mallet. A detailed account of this monster mortar is given at page 235.

Cast-Iron Guns.—The date of the introduction of cast-iron guns is very uncertain. Blast furnaces for smelting replaced the old Catalan methods about the commencement of the fifteenth century, were known in the Hartz, in Westphalia, in Flanders, and seem to have come to us thence, and were not uncommon about the middle of the century. There is in the repository at Woolwich an 18-inch *Pierrière*, captured at Corfu, with the date 1684 upon it, an early example of cast-iron.

In the sixteenth and seventeenth centuries, the average sizes of guns in England were as follow :—

	Length feet	Calibre lbs.	Weight lbs.
The cannon royal, or piece of eight	12	48	8,000
The demi-cannon	12	36	6,000
The culverin	12	20	4,800
The demi-culverin	11	10	2,700
The saker	10	6	1,500

The smaller sizes were called minion, falcon, falconet, rabinet, and base, the last of which only carried a 5-ounce ball of lead.

Cannon of Bronze.—The earliest bronze guns appear to have been cast in Europe about 1370. Between that and 1400, bombards were cast (after the more ancient models of iron) in bronze with separate and with attached chambers (*canons à boîte*), the ancestors of all modern breech-loading guns; and culverins, which replaced the iron serpentines, and were of enormous length, 35 to 60 calibres, and great strength towards the breech, but of small calibre. Many examples remain of a later date: one at Dover Castle, another in the Dial Square, Woolwich Arsenal, and the celebrated one of Nancy (1598), above 21 feet in length, carrying about an 18-pound iron ball. In England the earliest bronze guns are said to have been cast by one John Owen, in 1535.

Few examples are met with of guns formed of metal in strictly atomic proportions; but alloys are found therein presenting every formula, from 7Cu + Sn up to 83Cu + 4Sn. The proportions most approved of in the arsenals of Europe appear to vibrate between 100 by weight of copper to 9 of tin, up to 100 of copper and 12 of tin. In France, 100 copper + 11 tin by weight is the proportion fixed by law, and invariably aimed at. In the United States, 100 copper + 12·5 tin is adopted for certain species of guns.

The proportions of tin and copper used in making bronze guns in the United States:—

	Density	Tenacity
Tin, 1 part	7·297	2,122
Copper, 8 parts . . .	8·672	24,252
Mean proportional . . .	8·519	21,793
Mean of 83 guns , .	8·751	
Mean of 83 gun-heads . .	8·523	29,655

Bronze guns are liable to drop at the muzzle; this is due to the unequal temperature of the inside and of the outside of the gun.

Brass ordnance are made of what is called GUN-METAL, composed of about 10 parts of copper and 1 of tin.

One of the first inquiries of importance in connection with the construction of pieces of artillery is that of the liability to fracture in the metal. Upon this point the researches of Mr. Mallet furnish much important matter. He tells us, as the result of his investigation, that *it is a law of the molecular aggregation of crystalline solids, that when their particles consolidate under the influence of heat in motion, their crystals arrange and group themselves with their principal axes in lines perpendicular to the cooling or heating surfaces of the solid: that is, in the lines of the direction of the heat-wave in motion, which is the direction of least pressure within the mass.* And this is true, whether in the case of heat *passing from* a previously fused solid in the act of cooling and crystallising in consolidation, or of a solid not having a crystalline structure, but capable of assuming one upon its temperature being sufficiently raised, by heat applied to its external surfaces, and so *passing into* it.

Cast-iron is one of those crystallising bodies which, in consolidating, obeys, more or less perfectly according to conditions, the above law. *In castings of iron the planes of crystallisation group themselves perpendicularly to the surfaces of external contour.* Mr. Mallet, after examining the experiments of Mr. Fairbairn—who states ('Trans. Brit. Ass.' 1853) that the grain of the metal and the physical qualities of the casting improve by some function of the number of meltings; and he fixes on the thirteenth melting as that of greatest strength—shows that the size of crystals, or coarseness of grain in castings of iron, depends, for any given 'make' of iron and given mass of casting, upon *the high temperature of the fluid iron above that just necessary to its fusion, which influences the time that the molten mass takes to cool down and assume again the solid state.*

The very lowest temperature at which iron remains liquid enough fully to fill every cavity of the mould without risk of defect, is that at which a large casting, such as a heavy gun, ought to be ' poured.' Since the cooling of any mass depends upon the thickness of the casting, it is important that sudden changes of form or of dimensions in the parts of cast-iron guns should be avoided. In the sea and land service 13-inch mortars, where, at the chamber, the thickness of metal suddenly approaches twice that of the chase, there is evidently a malconstruction.

The following statements of experiments made to determine the effect produced on the quality of the iron in guns, by slow or rapid cooling of the casting, are from the report of Major W. Wade, of the South Boston Foundry, to Colonel George Bomford, of the Ordnance Department of the United States. Three six-pounder cannon were cast at the same time from the same melting of iron. The moulds were similar and prepared in the usual manner. That in which No. 1 was cast was heated before casting, and kept heated afterwards by a fire which surrounded it, so that the flask and mould were nearly red hot at the time of casting; and it was kept up for three days. Nos. 2 and 3 were cast and cooled in the usual way.

At the end of the fourth day the gun No. 1 and flask were withdrawn from the heating cylinder while all parts were yet hot. Nos. 1 and 2 were bored for 6-pounders in the usual way; No. 3 for a 12-pounder howitzer, with a 6-pounder chamber. The firing of the guns was in every respect the same. Nos. 1 and 2 were fired the same number of times with similar charges. No. 1 burst at the 27th fire, and No. 2 at the 25th. It appears from these results, that no material effect is produced on the quality of the iron by these different modes of cooling the castings.

A very extensive series of experiments was made, by the order of the United States' Government, on the strength of guns cast solid or hollow. In these it was confirmed that the guns cast hollow endured a much more severe strain than those cast solid. Considerable differences were also observed, whether the casting was cooled from within or without; and Lieutenant Rodman's method of cooling from the interior is regarded as tending to prevent injurious strains in cooling.

Major Wade informs us that time and repose have a surprising effect in removing strains caused by the unequal coolings of iron castings.

Great advances have been made in improving the quality of iron guns. Guns cast prior to 1841 had a density of 7·148, with a tenacity of 23,638. Guns cast in 1851 had a density of 7·289, with a tenacity of 37,774.

The following Table gives the results of all the trials made for the United States Government, showing the various qualities of different metals :—

Metals	Density	Tenacity	Transverse Strength	Torsion		Compressive Strength	Hardness
				At Half Degree	Ultimate		
Cast-iron :—							
Least . .	6·900	9,000	5,000	3,861	5,605	84,592	4·57
Greatest . .	7·400	45,970	11,500	7,812	10,467	174,120	33·51
Wrought-iron :—							
Least . .	7·704	38,027	6,500	3,197	...	40,000	10·45
Greatest . .	7·858	74,592	...	4,298	7,700	127,720	12·14
Bronze :—							
Least . .	7·978	17,698	...	2,021	5,511	...	4·57
Greatest . .	8·953	56,786	...	...	...	...	5·94
Cast-steel :—							
Least . .	7·729	...	...	...	...	198,944	
Greatest . .	7·862	128,000	23,000	...	...	391,985	

The following analyses of the metal of iron guns of three qualities are important :—

Influence of Single Ingredients.

Classes	Mechanical Tests		Chemical Constituents						
	Specific Gravity	Tensile Strength	Combined Carbon	Graphite	Silicium	Slag	Phosphorus	Sulphur	Earthy Metals
1	7·204	28,865	·0977	·0507	·0417	·0215	·0239	·0017	·0117
2	7·140	24,767	·0819	·0576	·0538	·0200	·0300	·0021	·0094
3	7·088	20,176	·0726	·0560	·0531	·0219	·0321	·0021	·0144

Influence of Two or more Ingredients.

Classes	Mechanical Tests		Chemical Constituents					
	Specific Gravity	Tensile Strength	Silicium and Carbon	Silicium and Slag	Graphite and Slag	Graphite, Silicium, and Slag	Graphite, Slag, Silicium, and Phosphorus	Total Carbon
1	7·204	28,865	·1394	·0632	·0722	·1139	·1378	·1484
2	7·140	24,767	·1357	·0738	·0776	·1314	·1614	·1395
3	7·088	20,176	·1257	·0750	80 ·'	·1311	·1632	·1286

An inspection of the first of the foregoing Tables, representing the average amount of each foreign ingredient in gun-metal deduced from all the analyses, shows a considerable difference in the proportions of those ingredients in each of the three classes into which guns are divided. It will be observed, that while the proportion of combined carbon diminishes from the 1st to the 3rd class, that of silicium similarly increases, so that their united amounts are nearly the same. In other words, it appears that silicium can replace the carbon to a certain extent; but that the quality of the metal is injured where the amount of the silicium approaches that of the carbon. Karsten made a similar observation in determining the limits between cast-iron and steel, but did not notice the influence of that substitution.

But the differences become more striking by combining the ingredients variously together, as in the second of those Tables; and especially by comparing the extremes, which are each derived from a larger number of observations than the mean.

After showing the total amount of carbon (both combined and uncombined), silicium and combined carbon are thrown together, which indicates the replacement by silicium of that portion of carbon set free in the form of graphite. The column 'silicium and slag' shows the general depreciation of the metal as the silicious metal increases.—*From the Report of Campbell Morfit and James C. Booth to the Ordnance Office, United States' Army.*

The following analyses (rejecting those substances of which only a mere trace has been discovered), from the same chemists, are selected as showing striking peculiarities :—

Class	Iron	Graphitic Carbon	Combined Carbon	Silicium	Slag	Phosphorus	Manganese	Magnesium	Calcium	Aluminium	Sodium and Potassium
1. 32-pounder, which endured the extreme proof	·93520	·02000	·02200	·00776	·00250	·00036	·02100	..	·00028	·00106	
2. 32-pounder, which endured the extreme proof. Hot blast iron	·88480	·02800	·00200	·02000	·00400	·00666	·05212	·00072	·00043	..	·00034
24-pounder, which endured the extreme proof. Hot blast iron	·92400	·03000	·01200	·01790	·00200	·00626	·02244	·00080	·00028	·00234	
3. 42-pounder	·92155	·03200	·00700	·01130	·00100	·00800	·01448	·00074	·00086	·00316	·00220
32-pounder	·92540	·02800	·00150	·00730	·00200	·00738	·02317	·00061	·00057	·00170	
32-pounder	·93450	·02900	·00900	·00900	·00200	·01290	·01810	..	?	·00158	·00026

Comparison of Weight, Strength, Extensibility, and Stiffness; Cast-Iron being unity within practical limits to static forces only.

Material	Weight for = Volume	Strength	Extensibility	Stiffness	Torsion
Cast-iron	1·00	1·00	1·00	1·00	1·00
Gun-metal	1·18	0·65	1·27	0·53	0·55
Wrought-iron	1·07	3·00	0·45	2·20	1·11
Steel	1·07	4·75	0·32	3·15	2·11

We find that wrought-iron guns are more than fivefold as durable as those of gun-metal, and twenty-two times as durable as those of cast-iron. And taking first cost and durability together, gun-metal cannon are about seventy-seven times, and cast-iron guns about thirty times, as dear as wrought-iron artillery. Again: the cost of horse-labour, or other means of transport for equal strength (and, of course, therefore, for equal effective artillery power), is about five times as great for gun-metal, and nearly three times as great for cast-iron as for wrought-iron guns. In every respect in which we have submitted them to a comparison, searching and rigid, and that seems to have omitted no important point of inquiry, wrought-iron stands pre-eminently superior to every other material for the fabrication of ordnance.—*United States' Report.*

The advantages possessed by rolled bars for the construction of artillery are thus summed up by Mr. Mallet, in his 'Memoir on Artillery:'—

1. The iron constituting the integrant parts is all in moderate-sized, straight, prismatic pieces, formed of rolled bars only; hence, with its fibres all longitudinal, perfectly uniform, and its extensibility the greatest possible, and in the same direction in which it is to be strained; it is, therefore, a better material than any forged iron can, by possibility, be made.

2. The limitation of manufacture of the iron, thus, to rolling, and the dispensing with all massive forgings, insures absolute soundness and uniformity of properties in the material.

3. The limited size of each integrant part, and the mode of preparation and combination, afford unavoidable tests of soundness and of perfect workmanship, step by step, for every portion of the whole: unknown or wilfully concealed defects are impossible.

4. Facility of execution by ordinary tools, and under easily obtained conditions, and without the necessity either for peculiarly skilled labour on the part of 'heavy forgemen,' or for steam or other hammers, &c., of unusual power, and very doubtful utility; and hence very considerable reduction in cost as compared with wrought-iron artillery forged in mass.

5. Facility of transport by reduction of weight, as compared with solid guns of the same or of any other known material.

6. A better material than massive forged iron, rolled bars are much more scientifically and advantageously applied; the same section of iron doing much more resisting work, as applied in the gun built-up in compressed and extended plies, than in any solid gun.

7. The introduction thus into cannon of a principle of elasticity, or rather of elastic range (as in a carriage-spring divided into a number of superimposed leaves), greater than that due to the modulus of elasticity of the material itself; and so acting, by distribution of the maximum effort of the explosion, upon the rings successively recipient of the strain during the time of the ball's trajet through the chase, as materially to relieve its effects upon the gun.

Considerable attention has been given, of late years, to the construction of very powerful pieces of ordnance. Cast-iron cannon are usually employed, but these very soon become useless when exposed to the sudden shocks of rapid firing. Cast-iron is, comparatively speaking, a weak substance for resisting extension, or for withstanding the explosive energy of gunpowder, compared with that of wrought-iron, the proportion being as 1 is to 5; consequently, many attempts have been made to substitute wrought-iron cannon for cast.

A gun, exhibited in 1851 by the Belgian Government, made of cast-iron '*prepared with coke and wood*,' was said to have stood 2,116 rounds, and another, 3,647 rounds, without much injury to the touch-hole or vent. Another is said to have been twice 'rebouched,' and has stood 6,002 rounds without injury. As few guns of cast-iron will stand more than 800 rounds without becoming unserviceable, this mode of preparing the iron appears to be a great improvement. At St. Sebastian 2,700 rounds were fired from the English batteries, but, as was observed by an eye-witness, 'you could put your fist into the touch-holes.'—*Colonel James*, R.E.

In Prussia they have for some time made cannon of 'forged cast-steel.' To get over the difficulty of forging the gun with the trunnions on, the gun has been made without them, and a hollow casting with trunnions afterwards slipped over the breech, and secured in its proper position by screening in the cascable. The tenacity of this metal must be very great.

CASTING OF GUNS.—Guns have long been cast in a vertical position, and with a certain amount of 'head of metal' above the topmost part of the gun itself. One object gained by this (of great value) is to afford a gathering-place for all scoria, or other foreign matter; an end that might be much more effectually accomplished were the metal always run into the cavity of the mould by 'gaits' leading to the bottom, or lowest point, in place of the metal being thrown in at the top, with a fall, at first, of several feet, as is now the common practice, by which much air and scoria are carried down and mixed with the metal, some of which never rises up again, or escapes as 'air-bubbles.'

The value of the 'head of metal' in casting of guns is shown by the following Table, constructed by Mr. Robert Mallet, after a series of carefully conducted experiments, which he published in a paper entitled ' *On the Physical Conditions involved in the Construction of Artillery* ':—

General Classification of the Principal Makes of British Cast-Irons as applicable to Artillery. (All deduced from equal Pieces, cast One Inch thick and Five Inches square.)

S.N.	Class of Iron	Hot or Cold	Commercial No.	Fracture	Character in Working	Sp. Gr.	How Cast	Physical Maxima and Minima
1	Apedale	Cold	No. 2	Silvery	Least fusible; thickening rapidly when fluid by a spontaneous 'puddling,' vesicular, often crystalline, incapable of being cut by chisel or file; ultimate cohesion a maximum, and elastic range generally a minimum.	7·603	Chilled	
2	Hardest Procurable.		Scrap	,,		7·624	Sand	Maximum density.
3	Oldberry	Hot	No. 3	,,		7·501	Sand	
4	Ponkey	Cold	No. 3	,,		7·233	Sand	Maximum ultimate strength.
5	Pentwyn	Hot	No. 2	,,		7·629	Chilled	
6	Calder	Hot	No. 4	,,		7·527	Sand	
7	Shotts	Hot	No. 4	,,		7·158	Sand	
8	Dowlais (Finery Pig).	Hot	No. 4	,,		6·378	Sand	Full of microscopic vesicles.
9	Arigna	Cold	No. 1	Micaceous	Very soft; feels greasy; peculiar micaceous appearance, generally owing to excess of manganese; soils the fingers strongly, crystals large; runs very fluid; contraction large.	7·015	Sand	
10	Burchill's	Cold	No. 1	,,		6·928	Sand	
11	Muirkirk	Hot	No. 2	,,		6·980	Sand	
12	Pentwyn (peculiar)	Hot	No. 1	,,		7·000	Sand	
13	Arigna	Cold	No. 3	Mottled	Tough and hard, can be with difficulty filed or cut; crystals large and small mixed; sometimes runs thick; contraction on cooling a maximum.	7·308	Chilled	
14	Apedale (Cylinder Iron).	Hot	No. 2	,,		7·116	Sand	
15	Pentwyn	Hot	No. 2	,,		7·017	Sand	
16	Calder No. 1, + Pentwyn.	..	..	,,		7·168	Sand	
17	Do. No. 2, + p Grey Cast-iron (Blaenavon No. 2 Scrap).	..	..	,,		7·138	Sand	Maximum contraction in cooling.
18	Monkland	Hot	No. 4	,,		7·294	Sand	
19	Clyde	Cold	No. 1	,,		7·140	Sand	
20	Parkfield	Cold	No. 1	,,		7·248	Sand	
21	Apedale	Hot	No. 1	,,		7·268	Sand	
22	Devon	Cold	No. 3	,,		7·280	Sand	Maximum.
23	Calder	Hot	No. 1	,,		7·079	Chilled	
24	Arigna ½, Scrap ½.	..	..	,,		7·134	Chilled	
25	Calder ½, Scrap ½.	..	..	Bright Grey	Toughness and hardness most suitable for working; ultimate cohesion and elastic range generally are balanced most advantageously; crystals uniform, very minute.	6·329	Chilled	Minimum density forms as No. 8.
26	Gartsherrie	Hot	No. 2	,,		7·115	Sand	
27	Low Moor	Cold	No. 2	,,		7·150	Sand	
28	Shotts	Hot	No. 2	,,		7·152	Sand	
29	Blaina	Cold	No. 3	,,		7·159	Sand	
30	Arigna	Cold	No. 3	,,		7·141	Sand	
31	Gartsherrie	Hot	No. 1	,,		7·001	Sand	
32	Shotts	Hot	No. 3	,,		7·183	Sand	
33	Varteg Hill	Hot	No. 2	,,		7·074	Sand	
34	Calder	Hot	No. 3	,,		7·064	Sand	
35	Summerlie	Hot	No. 2	,,		7·156	Sand	
36	Madeley Wood	Cold	No. 1	,,		7·115	Sand	
37	Elsecar	Cold	No. 1	,,		7·097	Sand	
38	Cinderford	Cold	No. 1	,,		7·049	Sand	
39	Carron	Hot	No. 2	,,		7·081	Sand	
40	Gartsherrie	Hot	No. 3	,,		7·047	Sand	
41	Muirkirk	Hot	No. 3	Dull Grey	Less tough and hard than the preceding, other characters alike; contraction on cooling generally a minimum.	6·838	Sand	
42	Monklands	Hot	No. 3	,,		7·124	Sand	
43	Dowlais	Hot	No. 1	,,		7·164	Sand	Minimum density, solid.
44	Arigna	Cold	No. 2	,,		6·809	Sand	
45	Shotts	Hot	No. 1	,,		7·109	Sand	
46	Lilleshall	Cold	No. 1	,,		7·205	Sand	
47	Shotts	Hot	No. 2	,,		7·152	Sand	
48	Coed Talon	Hot	No. 2	,,		7·030	Sand	
49	Butterly	Hot	No. 1	,,		7·063	Sand	
50	Coed Talon	Cold	No. 2	,,		7·020	Sand	

No.	Class of Iron	Hot or Cold	Com-mercial No.	Fracture	Character in Working	Sp. Gr.	How Cast	Physical Maxima and Minima
51	Carron .	Cold	No. 2	Dark Grey		7·107	Sand	
52	Dowlais .	Cold	No. 3	,,		7·159	Sand	
53	Dowlais .	Cold	No. 1	,,	Most fusible ; remains long fluid, exudes graphite in cooling ; soils the fingers; crystals large and lamellar ; ultimate cohesion a minimum, and elastic range generally a maximum.	7·192	Sand	
54	Blaenavon .	Cold	No. 1	,,		7·143	Sand	
55	Muirkirk .	Cold	No. 2	,,		7·076	Sand	Minimum ultimate strength.
56	Milton .	Hot	No. 1	,,		7·073	Sand	
57	Calder .	Hot	..	,,		7·027	Sand	
58	Calder ½, Pentwyn ½.	..	..	,,		6·978	Sand	
59	Arigna ½, Pentwyn ½	..	..	,,		7·050	Sand	

Table showing the Increase of Density in Castings of large Size, due to their Solidification under a Head of Metal, varying from two to fourteen Feet :—

No. of Experiment	Calder Cast-iron, No. 1, Hot Blast			Blaenavon, No. 1, Cold Blast			Apedale, No. 2, Hot Blast			Quam prox. Pressure when fluid in lls. per square inch
	Depth of Casting in Inches	Specific Gravity	First Difference	Depth of Casting in Inches	Specific Gravity	First Difference	Depth of Casting in Inches	Specific Gravity	First Difference	
1	0	6·9551		0	7·0479		0	7·0328		·0
2	24	6·9633	·0082	24	7·0576	·0097	24	7·0417	·0089	6·4
3	48	7·0145	·0512	48	7·0777	·0201	48	7·0558	·0141	12·8
4	72	7·0506	·0361	72	7·0890	·0113	72	7·0669	·0111	19·2
5	96	7·0642	·0136	96	7·1012	·0122	96	7·0789	·0120	25·6
6	120	7·0776	·0134	120	7·1148	·0136	120	7·0915	·0126	32·0
7	144	7·0907	·0131	144	7·1288	·0140	144	7·1046	·0131	38·4
8	168	7·1035	·0128	168	7·1430	·0142	168	7·1183	·0137	44·8

The experiments were made upon cylindrical shafts of cast-iron, cast vertically in dry sand-mould, under heads gradually increasing up to fourteen feet in depth, and all poured from 'gaits' at the bottom.

These experiments show an increase of density due to fourteen feet head, about equal to a pressure of 44·8 lbs. per square inch on the casting; from 6·9551 to 7·1035 for Scotch cast-iron.

About the latter end of 1854, the attention of Mr. Robert Mallet, C.E., was directed to the mathematical consideration of the relative powers of shells in proportion to their increase of size or of diameter. His inquiries resulted in a memoir presented by him to Government, in which he investigated the increase of power in shells with increase of diameter, under the heads of:—1. Their penetrative power. 2. Their increased range and greater accuracy of fire. 3. Their explosive power. 4. Their power of demolition, or of levelling earthworks, buildings, &c. 5. Their fragmentary missile power. 6. and lastly, their moral effect,—in every case viewing the shell, not as a weapon against troops, but as an instrument of destruction to an enemy's works. The result so convinced Mr. Mallet of the rapid rate at which the destructive powers of a shell increase with increase of size, that he was induced to propose to Government the employment of shells of a magnitude never before imagined by any one, namely, of a yard in diameter, and weighing, when in flight, about a ton and a quarter each : and to prepare designs, in several respects novel and peculiar, for the construction of mortars capable of projecting these enormous globes. Such a mortar was made, and on the 19th of October, 1857, the first of those colossal mortars, constructed from Mr. Mallet's design (*fig.* 91), was fired on Woolwich Marshes, with charges (of projection) gradually increasing up to 70 lbs. ; and with the latter charge a shell weighing 2,550 lbs. was thrown a horizontal range of upwards of a mile and a half, to a height of probably three-quarters of a mile, and falling, penetrated the compact and then hard dry earth of the Woolwich Range to a depth of more than 18 feet, throwing about cartloads of earth and stones by the mere *splash* of the fall of the empty shell.

The drawing of this remarkable piece of artillery is presented—although, except experimentally, the mortar has never been used. It certainly is a remarkable example

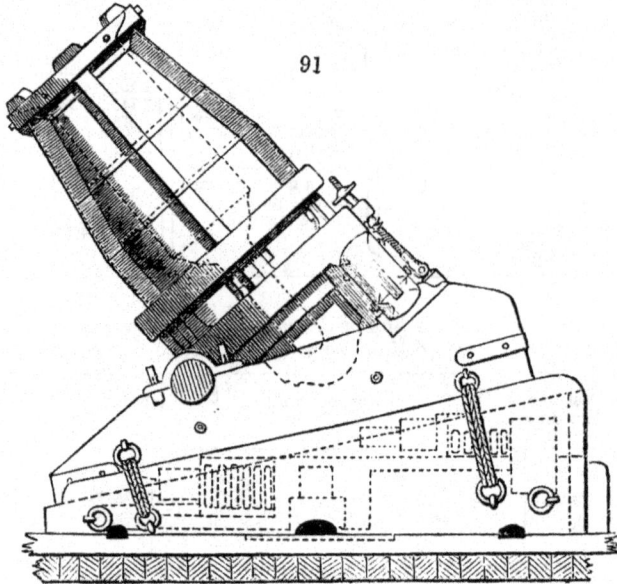

91

of engineering skill. Mallet's mortar is formed wholly of wrought-iron in concentric rings, and each mortar is separable at pleasure with 13 pieces, the heaviest weighing about 11 tons, the entire mass being 52 tons.

The position attained by Rifled Ordnance manufactured on the principles advocated by Sir William Armstrong is such, that it appears desirable to describe the mode of constructing those guns. Sir William Armstrong himself describes the principles by which he has been guided in the construction of his guns, in his paper communicated to the 'British Association,' and reprinted in 'The Industrial Resources of the Tyne, Wear, and Tees.' With some slight alteration this has been retained as the best possible source of information.

'In the month of December, 1854, my friend Mr. Rendell, the well-known engineer, submitted to Sir James Graham a communication he had received from me suggesting the expediency of enlarging the ordinary rifle to the standard of a field-gun, and using elongated projectiles of lead instead of balls of cast-iron. This communication was handed by Sir James Graham to the Duke of Newcastle, then Minister of War, with whom I had an interview on the subject in company with Mr. Rendell.

'At this interview I was authorised by his Grace to carry my views into effect, by constructing, upon the plan I had suggested, one or more guns, not exceeding six in number, and to make the necessary experiments in connection with the subject.

'In acting upon the authority thus received, I deemed it expedient to confine myself, in the first instance, to the production of a single gun, but to make that one gun the test, not only of the principles I had recommended, but also of the feasibility of loading field-pieces at the breech, and applying certain mechanical arrangements to counteract recoil, and facilitate the pointing of the gun.

'The substitution of elongated solid projectiles for spherical bullets is an essential step to the attainment of very extended range in artillery-practice; but the lengthening of a solid projectile involves the necessity of strengthening the gun to enable it to resist the greater intensity of force which becomes necessary to give the required velocity; and this object can only be effected, consistently with lightness, by constructing the gun of steel or wrought-iron instead of cast-iron or bronze. The tensile strength of these several materials is exhibited in the following Table:—

	Breaking strain per square inch of section.
Cast-steel, about	60 tons.
Sheer-steel	42 ,,
Wrought-iron	26 ,,
Bronze or gun-metal, about	16 ,,
Cast-iron	8 ,,

'The first and strongest of these substances, viz. cast-steel, may be set out of the question, as it appears impracticable, in the present state of manufacture, to produce it in masses sufficiently large without the occurrence of flaws, which, in the great majority of cases, would destroy its efficiency. Sheer-steel may be forged, like wrought-iron, into large pieces : but in a gun made from a solid mass of either of these substances, the full strength of the material can never be realised, because the tenacity of wrought-iron or steel is always less in the lateral than in the longitudinal direction : and it is the lateral strength which, in a gun so manufactured, would be chiefly brought into action. There is also much uncertainty in the lateral strength of wrought-iron or steel, because the flaws or imperfections of welding which exist in all thick masses of those materials almost invariably run in the direction of the length, and in general, therefore, only detract from the strength in the transverse direction. It is for these reasons that the barrels of muskets and sporting guns are formed by twisting long slips of iron into spiral tubes, and then welding together the edges, by which means the longitudinal strength of the slip becomes opposed to the explosive force of the powder, and the weldings being transverse with the bore, have no important influence in lessening the strength of the barrel. It is also to be observed, in reference to the strength of steel or wrought-iron cannon, that the resistance of a cylinder to internal pressure does not increase in the ratio of its thickness. If the cylinder be regarded as made up of a number of concentric layers, each capable of sustaining without injury a degree of extension proportionate to its length, it is obvious, that the greater the circumference of each layer, the less will it be stretched by a given distention of the bore, and, consequently, the less will it contribute to the general strength of the cylinder. The ratio of this decrease is very rapid, being as the square of the circumference, or distance from the centre inversely ; and, consequently, when the cylinder is thick, the deficiency of strength from this cause becomes very great.

'Now this defect can only be remedied by giving to the external portion of the cylinder a certain initial tension, gradually decreasing and finally passing into compression towards the centre ; and although this condition cannot be effected by any known process of forging or casting, yet where wrought-iron or steel is the material used, it may in a great measure be attained by shrinking an outer cylinder upon an inner one, and in like manner superadding others until the requisite thickness has been acquired.

'The method, however, of forming steel or wrought-iron guns, by simply forging the material into the required form, and boring it in the usual manner, was so much recommended by its facility, that I was induced to make some experiments to test its sufficiency.

'With this view a number of cylinders were forged, each twelve inches long and five inches in the outward diameter. These were bored to an internal diameter of one and three-quarter inches, and tested in the following manner :—Each cylinder was entirely filled with gunpowder, and the open end was pressed by screws against a very thick iron tube bored to the same diameter, and containing a cylindrical shot of lead equal in weight to about three spherical shot of the same diameter and material. Several of the cylinders burst on the first discharge, and those which remained uninjured were afterwards reduced in thickness, and tested a second time. If they still resisted the explosion, the thickness was further diminished ; and this mode of proceeding was continued until fracture took place in all of them.

'The results obtained in this manner showed, as had been apprehended, great uncertainty in the strength of the material, and rendered it impossible to define the thickness necessary to resist a given charge of powder. I felt compelled, therefore, to dismiss this mode of construction, and to adopt another more correct in principle, but more difficult of execution.

'In the above experiment it was found that steel was more subject to defects of welding than iron ; but being a harder substance, and therefore more fitted to form the surface of a bore, I determined to apply it as an internal lining, and to obtain the necessary strength by encircling it with twisted cylinders of wrought-iron, tightly contracted upon the steel core by the usual process of cooling after previous expansion by heat. Considerable difficulties were encountered in carrying this plan into practice ; but I ultimately succeeded in completing a gun, of which the following is a description.

'The gun, when fired, recoils upon an ascending slide without displacing the carriage, and then returns to its place by gravity. The slide-frame turns upon a pivot, which permits the gun to be pointed to either side without moving the carriage. The gun is elevated and depressed by means of a screw, which is fixed to and moves with the slide, and a similar screw is applied for the traversing or horizontal movement. The arrangement for loading at the breech may be described as follows :—At the back end of the gun a powerful screw is applied, having a hole through the centre, forming a prolongation of the bore, and through which hole the bullet and charge are delivered into the gun. A 'breech-piece' with a mitred face, fitting a similar face at the end of the bore, is then dropped into a recess, and by the action of the screw pressed tightly into its seat, so as effectually to close the bore.

'In order to facilitate the loading, the bullet and cartridge are placed in a tube, from which they are thrust into the gun by means of a rammer.

'The breech-piece contains a vent, with a cavity for receiving a small quantity of powder to ignite the charge; and as the breech-piece is prepared for firing while the gun is being loaded, no time is lost in subsequent priming.

'Several of these breech-pieces accompany the gun, some being arranged to fire by percussion-caps, and others by friction-tubes or port-fires.

'The bore of the gun is one and three-quarter inches in diameter, and contains eight spiral grooves, having an inclination equal to one turn in twelve feet. These grooves terminate at a distance of fourteen inches from the breech, and the bore then gradually expands in a length of three inches, from one and three-quarters inches to one and seven-eighths inches in diameter. The bullet, in the operation of loading, passes freely through this widened space; but its diameter being a little in excess of the bore, it lodges in the tapered contraction at the commencement of the grooves.

'The mode in which the gun is made up of separate parts consists in surrounding the steel centre with twisted cylinders of wrought-iron, made in a similar manner to gun-barrels, and being shrunk upon the steel, they are in that state of initial tension which is necessary to bring their entire strength into operation.

'The weight of the gun by itself is about 5 cwts.; but, including the carriage, its weight is nearly identical with that of a light 6-pounder with its carriage complete. It is probably heavier than necessary, but recoil might be inconveniently increased if the weight were much reduced.

'Having now described the gun and its carriage, I shall proceed to speak of the projectile.

'The resistance which a projectile encounters in passing through the air is mainly dependent upon the area of its cross-section, and the advantage of lengthening a bullet consists in augmenting the weight without increasing this sectional area; but in order to realise this advantage it is essential that the bullet be guided endways in its course, and this can only be effected by causing it to rotate rapidly upon its longer axis, which is accomplished by firing it from a rifled bore.

'This peculiar influence of rotation, in giving persistency of direction to the axis of a projectile, is entirely distinct from that which it also possesses of correcting the tendency to aberration arising from irregular form or density; and in order to investigate experimentally the nature of this action, I constructed an apparatus by which a cylindrical bullet could be put into extremely rapid rotation, and be then suspended in a manner which left it free to turn in any direction.

'When thus suspended, the rotating bullet exhibited the same remarkable properties as are possessed by the revolving disc in the recently invented instrument called the 'Gyroscope.' When pressure was applied to either end of the axis, the movement which took place was not in the direction of the pressure, but at right angles to it. Thus a vertical pressure deflected the axis horizontally, while lateral pressure deflected it vertically. But the important point elicited was this, that the time required to produce these indirect movements became greater as the velocity was increased, and, consequently, that the amount of deflection produced in a given time by a given pressure, diminished as the rotation was accelerated. Now, all disturbing forces which operate upon a projectile during its flight must necessarily be of very short continuance, and can therefore have but little influence in diverting the axis when thus stiffened by rapid rotation.

'I also found that a cylindrical bullet with tapered extremities was more easily deflected than one of equal weight with flat or merely rounded ends, because the mean diameter of the bullet, and consequently the mean velocity of rotation, were thereby diminished. So far, therefore, as accuracy of flight depends upon the rigidity of the axis, it would appear that the nearest practicable approach to a plain cylinder is the most desirable form for a projectile, but there are other considerations which modify this conclusion.

'It is also to be observed, that since the rigidity of the axis (relatively to the magnitude of the projectile) depends upon the mean velocity of rotation, the inclination of the spiral grooves in a rifled gun should vary inversely with the diameter of the bore. Thus, if one turn in eight feet be assumed as sufficient for a rifled bore of one inch in diameter, one turn in forty-eight feet should be sufficient for a bore of six inches, provided the same form of projectile be used.

'The forms of bullet which I actually tried with the gun were exceedingly numerous, and the materials used for these bullets was in all cases lead hardened by an intermixture of antimony and tin; and the weight varied from two to three and a half pounds.

'In trying these various bullets, a number of each kind was fired against a vertical bank at a distance of 435 yards. The gun was constantly pointed at the same object ,and the closeness of the bullet-holes to each other was taken as the criterion of accuracy, while the drop below the level of the aim furnished an indication of comparative range.

'The conclusions arrived at from these and other experiments may be concisely stated as follows :—

'1st.—A pointed form at the front end of the bullet is unfavourable to accuracy of flight, unless the cylindrical part of the bullet be of considerable length ; but, on the other hand, a pointed or conoidal form behind, has the effect of increasing the accuracy attained. This may be explained upon the very probable supposition that the blast from the mouth of the gun, impinging upon the rear of the bullet, will operate more unfavourably upon a flat or hollow end than upon a rounded or conical one.

'2nd.—Increase of length in the cylindrical part of a bullet always increases precision ; but, when carried beyond a certain limit, lessens the initial velocity, even where the charge is proportionately augmented.

'3rd.—Both range and accuracy were affected in an important degree by the manner in which the bullet fitted the contraction in the gun. When the fitting part was in front of the bullet, the pressure of the gas operating upon its sides compressed it, and the same effect was produced, though in a less degree, when the conical, or rounded end at the back, projected too far into the powder-chamber.

'These effects were rendered apparent by inspection of bullets recovered after firing, many of which were found in nearly the precise condition in which they quitted the gun.

'The bullet ultimately selected is a little longer and heavier than those experimented with, and differs from the pointed bullet, in being longer in the cylindrical part and having a coned, instead of a rounded, end behind ; and although its drop in a range of 435 yards is considerably more than that of several of the shorter bullets, yet there is little doubt it will excel them in range at higher elevations of the gun ; because I have found that a pointed front only operates in sustaining the flight of the bullet when the range is long ; and a high initial velocity, which materially lessens the drop in short distances, does not produce the same effect, in a corresponding degree, when the distance is increased.

'Great improvements were effected in the accuracy of the firing, by modifying the shape of the projectile ; but although the experiments were very protracted, I feel that they require to be further prolonged in order to arrive at the greatest attainable perfection in the form of the bullet.

'The ranges at different elevations were not ascertained with the form of bullet ultimately adopted ; but with a three-pound pointed bullet and charges of twelve ounces of powder, they were as follows :—

Ranges with the rifled gun and three-pound bullets.

Elevation.	Range in Yards.	
$\frac{1}{4}$°	408	
1°	770	
2°	1,112	Measured to first graze
3°	1,500	upon a plane about five
4°	1,840	feet below the centre of
5°	2,056	the gun.
6°	2,300	
7°	2,600	

'The powder used was a mixture of blasting and 'double-seal' powder in equal proportions. The distances given are in most cases averages of several shots ; but in some instances they were only approximately determined. When the gun had more elevation than 7° the bullets could only be fired out to sea, and the range could not be ascertained.

'By way of comparison with these results, an extract is here given from the last edition of Sir H. Douglas's 'Naval Gunnery,' specifying the ranges obtained with a 68-pounder throwing shot with full charges, which ranges, it will be seen, are, upon the whole, no greater than those of the three-pound bullet fired from the rifled gun :—

Ranges with a 68-pounder.

Elevation.	Range in Yards.
$\frac{1}{4}$°	340
1°	833
2°	1,247
3°	1,558
4°	1,737
5°	2,035
6°	2,337
7°	2,440

'In trying the initial velocity of the shot by means of a ballistic pendulum, I was enabled to observe its penetrating power. When fired with charges of 13 oz. of powder, a 3-lb. bullet passed through 2 feet 2 inches of hard elm timber, and flattened against a cast-iron block forming the back of the pendulum. The initial velocity was similar to that generally obtained with round shot fired with proportionate charges, viz. about 1,550 feet per second.

'In the course of the experiments made with the gun, upwards of 500 rounds were fired; and ample opportunity was thus afforded of judging as to the durability of the parts affected by the loading at the breech. At first the fitting surfaces which closed the bore were of unhardened steel; but these soon failed, being cut away in numerous small channels by the ignited gases. The steel was then hardened; but instead of being rendered more durable, it yielded to the action of the powder more rapidly than before. Conceiving, therefore, that the erosion was not a mechanical action, but a chemical effect of combustion, and that a metal which was a better conductor of heat than steel or iron would be less liable to burn on the surface, I was led to substitute copper as the material of the parts affected, and no further difficulty was experienced. The copper fittings applied for this purpose consist of two annular pieces, one of which is screwed into the breech end of the gun, and the other fixed upon the breech-piece. These fittings can very easily and quickly be repaired, when necessary, by means of a tool provided for that purpose, and can also be removed and replaced by others kept in readiness for use; and there is nothing to prevent these operations being performed by the gunners when on service, if they be previously instructed.

'The advantages of loading at the breech may be stated as follows:—

'1st.—It permits of a bullet being used of a larger diameter than the bore, by which means accuracy of fit is secured, and the material of the bullet is forced into the grooves of the bore.

'2nd.—Any ignited matter remaining in the gun after firing may with ease and certainty be removed, or, if left in the gun, it will be thrust forward from the part where its presence would be dangerous, by the insertion of the succeeding bullet.

'3rd.—In the arrangement which I have adopted, the perishable part of the gun, viz. the vent and its vicinity, is comprised in the moveable breech-piece, which may be easily replaced when worn or otherwise injured.

'4th.—A rifled gun loaded at the breech may be more rapidly fired than a rifled gun loaded at the muzzle, because the fouling of the bore presents no impediment to the insertion of the bullet when introduced from behind; but as compared with smooth bored ordnance of the ordinary description, there is probably nothing to gain in point of quickness of firing.

'The gun was remarkably free from tendency to become heated by firing, a fact which can only be explained upon the supposition that the heating of a cannon is occasioned, not by the contact of the flame, but by some molecular action of the metal, produced by the explosion, and more effectually resisted by wrought-iron than by cast-iron or bronze; but possibly the compound structure of this gun may also operate to deaden vibration, and prevent the evil in question.

'It may, perhaps, be objected to this gun, that from the smallness of the bore, it cannot be applied for throwing shells as well as solid projectiles; but the fact is, these two purposes are incompatible with each other, unless both be imperfectly attained, for while the one necessarily requires a large bore, the other demands a small one; and it therefore seems preferable to have separate guns specially adapted for each application. As a civilian, I speak with diffidence upon the advantages which I believe the long range of this description of field-gun will afford in its military application; but I may be permitted to observe, that the incident which chiefly contributed to direct my attention to this subject still appears to furnish a forcible illustration of its importance. I allude to the memorable service rendered at Inkermann, by means of two 18-pounders, laboriously dragged from the batteries, and ultimately directed with great gallantry and success against the Russian artillery, at a distance from which the numerous but lighter guns of the enemy could not effectually reply. Now, these two battery-guns were but a clumsy substitute for light, long-range guns, which would have rendered the same important service with more promptitude and ease, and could have operated at a greater distance from the enemy's fire. It is, perhaps, chiefly as 'guns of position,' commanding important points at great but ascertained distances, that these rifled guns would be valuable, because long range can only be made available where distance can be determined, which it cannot easily be in the rapid operations for which 'field-pieces' are employed. It is, therefore, as adjuncts to, and not as substitutes for, the present description of field ordnance that I propose the adoption of these guns; and when fully brought to perfection, I believe they will furnish a most important addition to the artillery of an army.

'With respect to the construction of heavy ordnance by the process of twisting wrought-iron bars into cylinders and combining them in the manner described, there appears to be no great difficulty in so doing, if proper apparatus be provided for the purpose. It would not, however, be advisable (except in peculiar cases) to apply the principle of loading at the breech except to guns of small dimensions, because in heavy ordnance the moveable parts would become too cumbrous to be conveniently handled.'

The essential features of the Armstrong method of construction are:—

1st. The disposal of the fibre of the metal round the bore by coiling, so as to resist the tangential strain, the welds running in the direction of the least strain as regards their separation.

2nd. The employment of a breech-piece, to support the bottom of the bore, with the fibre running lengthwise so as to resist longitudinal strain.

3rd. The shrinking-on the different portions, so that the exterior of the gun takes a due share of the strain. Mr. Whitworth's method of building-up is as follows:— 'The tube of the gun is made taper, being in the $5\frac{1}{2}$-inch-bore gun 1 inch larger in diameter at the breech end than at the muzzle end; then a series of hoops are made, which are screwed together so as to form another tube, that is put on by hydraulic pressure; each layer is put on a little tighter than the succeeding one.'—*Evidence Report on Ordnance.*

The method of closing the bore of a built-up gun is an important question. The inner tubes of some of the large M. L. ordnance lately constructed in the Royal Gun Factories, as well as those of some of Blakely's guns, have what are termed closed ends, that is, the tube is not bored through to the bottom; the solid end of the tube in service-guns is supported by a cascable screwed into the breech-piece, and in some of them also by a shoulder in the breech-piece. Sir W. Armstrong, Mr. Whitworth, and Major Palliser use open tubes and close them by a plug of wrought-iron or copper. The cascable in the Whitworth guns is not, like Armstrong's, cylindrical in form, but is shaped into two or more (screwed) cylinders, their respective diameters increasing from bore to breech.

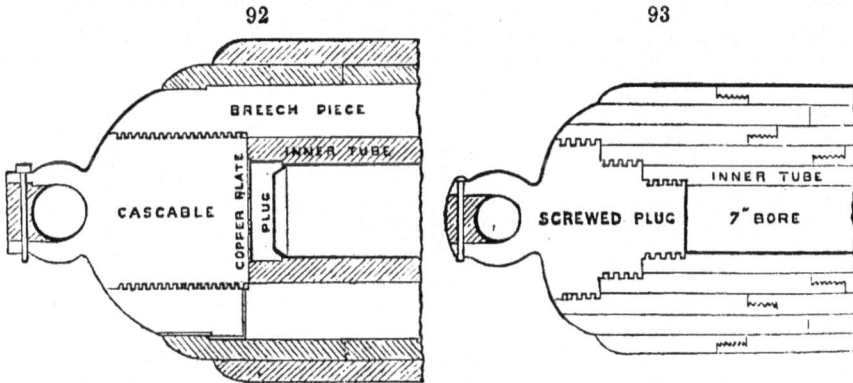

Breech of Armstrong's 10·5-inch gun.

Breech of Whitworth's 7-inch gun.

In closing the bore of a M. L. or B. L. gun, one important principle should not be neglected, viz. that as the gas exerts an equal force in every direction, the thickness of the metal should be as great, or nearly so, behind as over the charge. Inattention to this principle, or its sacrifice to other considerations, is a source of weakness in many B. L. guns. One advantage of an open end is, that the metal of the inner tube is relieved to some extent from longitudinal strain.

The relative cost of large ordnance made in different ways was, when the last edition was published, as follows:—

		£
Cast-iron guns	. . . . .	21 per ton.
Armstrong built-up ditto	. . . .	100 „ (lately 87*l*.)
Krupp's steel ditto	. . . .	170 „
Gun-metal ditto	. . . . .	187 „

and, excepting the variation due to the price of the metal, it continues relatively about the same.

Bronze guns are valuable for recasting. Mr. Frazer has introduced modifications, by which it is said the cost of built-up ordnance will be much reduced, viz. to 40*l*. a ton with a coiled inner tube, and to 55*l*. a ton with a steel tube. Mr. Whitworth told the Committee on Ordnance that his $5\frac{1}{2}$-inch gun weighing 4 tons, and made of homogeneous metal (soft steel) cost 700*l*., which is about 175*l*. per ton. The question of the relative advantages of breech- and muzzle-loading ordnance has been frequently discussed. The subject appears very fairly put by Major C. H. Owen, Professor of Artillery, at Woolwich. He says:—'Various opinions are held as to the relative advantages of breech- and muzzle-loading ordnance, but the latter would appear to be the best adapted to general service, as they are stronger for equal weights of metal and simpler in construction. The advantages of loading cannon at the breech are, that a projectile of larger diameter than the bore can be used, and its axis will consequently be stable; that the gun can be loaded when run-up, the gunners being therefore less exposed; that the gun can be worked in a smaller space (than a M. L. piece); the clearing of the bore can be more readily effected, and any ignited substance left in the bore can be seen and removed; also there is no danger of the shot not being *home*. This plan, however, is attended with the following disadvantages, viz. that the construction is more complicated than that of a muzzle-loading piece; that if the gun be of large calibre, the breech-loading apparatus, when sufficiently strong and heavy, will be unwieldy; and that with the same weight of metal, the breech-loading is a weaker and less enduring construction than the muzzle-loading. On the other hand, a muzzle-loading gun has a simpler and stronger construction, but the gun detachments are more exposed than with a breech-loading gun, and if loaded carelessly, the shot may not be rammed *home*, in which case the metal of the gun may be fractured by the suddenly condensed gas.'

On the Systems of Rifling, Major Owen, R. A., one of our best authorities, writes:—'In what does a system of rifling consist? Essentially in the method of giving the rotatory motion to the projectile. This definition will not satisfy some inventors, who wish to claim a particular *twist* as a part of their *system of rifling*. It would, however, be quite as reasonable to claim a particular charge. The rotatory motion, as you all know, is given to prevent the projectile from turning over in flight; and the velocity of rotation required depends upon the form, length, and weight of the projectile, no matter what the system of rifling may be; in fact, the number of revolutions made by a shot $=\frac{\text{initial velocity}}{\text{length of twist}}$, and therefore, with the same charge, the same twist must be obviously necessary.'[1]

'A twist, like a charge, may suit a particular rifled gun, but this is quite another thing. A *gaining twist* is advantageous, for, by employing it, the initial strain upon the gun is reduced, the rotatory motion not being given when the shot is set in motion, but gradually acquired as it moves down the bore. It is better to give rather more twist than is required under ordinary circumstances at the expense of a little extra strain; for should the twist be merely sufficient to impart the necessary rotatory motion with the service-charge, the velocity of rotation will probably be too low with a reduced charge to keep the projectile steady in flight.'[2]

The diameter of the bore has also been often mixed up with the system of rifling, with which it can have nothing whatever to do. As the diameter is decreased, so will the elongated projectile oppose a less surface (in proportion to its weight) to the resistance of the air, or that of the substance fired at; but, on the other hand, it will expose a less area to the force of the gas, and will therefore have a lower initial velocity; it will have less capacity as a shell; its cartridge must be elongated, thereby throwing the strain forward; the amount of powder that can be usefully employed will be less; and if the length of the bore be not increased, the expansion of the gas will be more limited. This question has been discussed, and should be thoroughly understood. In the Table below the loss of initial velocity by decrease in the size of the bore is clearly shown:—

| Ordnance | Charge | Projectile | | Initial Velocity |
		Weight	Diameter	
	lbs.	lbs.	inches	
Britten's (32-pounder rifled) . . .	5	50·36	6·24	1,209
Armstrong's 40-pounder . . .	...	41·25	4·75	1,197
„ 3-grooved shunt . . .	9	68·40	6·4	1,283
Whitworth's 70-pounder . . .	...	68·56	$\left\{\begin{array}{c}5·5\\5·\end{array}\right\}$	1,132
Armstrong's 70-pounder . . .	10	74·60	6·4	1,271
Whitworth's 70-pounder . . .	...	68·56	$\left\{\begin{array}{c}·5\\5·\end{array}\right\}$	1,199

[1] The Initial Velocity is very little affected by the system of rifling.
[2] This was particularly shown by the inaccurate practice of the 600-pounder, when fired with a small charge.

Mr. Whitworth and his admirers have constantly asserted that his small-bore gives a flatter trajectory than the larger bores chosen by Armstrong, Britten, and others. This is, however, not the case under all circumstances, and arose partly from the fact of the Whitworth guns first tried being fired with charges of $\frac{1}{6}$th of the weight of the projectile, whereas the greater number of other rifled guns used charges of only $\frac{1}{8}$th or $\frac{1}{10}$th. Mr. Whitworth is quite right to use as large a charge as he can, but it must be taken into account in drawing comparisons. In practice from two rifled guns of different calibres, but firing projectiles of the same weight with equal charges, the large bore will give a lower trajectory; but as the projectile with the smaller diameter is less retarded, its trajectory will gradually become lower, as compared with the other, until beyond a certain range the small bore will give the lower trajectory. Small bores have found little favour on the Continent, and it is for the authorities to demand either a large or a small bore as circumstances may require.

The following conditions are requisite in any rifled gun to ensure accuracy of fire:—a rotatory motion must be given to the projectile round an axis parallel to, or coincident with, that of the bore; and the velocity of rotation imparted to the projectile must be sufficient to counteract the pressure of air tending to turn the shot over or render it unsteady in flight.

Great numbers of rifled guns with projectiles to correspond have been proposed, but most of the systems of rifling that have been adopted by any service, or tried on the practice-ground, may be divided into the following classes:—

(1.) Muzzle- or breech-loading guns, having projectiles of iron fitting the peculiar form of the bore mechanically.

(2.) Muzzle-loading guns, with projectiles having soft-metal studs or ribs to fit the grooves.

(3.) Muzzle-loading guns, with projectiles having a soft-metal envelope, coating, or cup, which is expanded by the gas in the bore.

(4.) Breech-loading guns, with projectiles having a soft-metal coating larger in diameter than the bore, but which is compressed by the gas to the form of the bore.

The effects of those guns, and consequently their relative values, will be best shown by extracting from the 'Proceedings of the Royal Artillery Institution' some of the results as officially stated by the officers in charge of the experiments. The more important of the targets have been selected, as representing the actual conditions of our ships at the time (1866), and of the power which can be brought to bear upon the armour-clad ships of an enemy.

'Warrior' Target.

This target was 10 feet by 12 feet, consisted of three plates, made at the Park Head forge, all $4\frac{1}{2}$ inches thick, and varying from 12 feet by 3 feet to 12 feet by 3 feet 4 inches.

The Horsfall gun used weighed 24 tons 3 qrs. 2 lbs., diameter of bore 13·014 inches, diameter of shot 12·8 inches. It was first fired at 200 yards' range, with a solid cast-iron shot, weighing 279 lbs. and a charge of powder 74·40 lbs., which gave an initial velocity of 1,630 feet, reduced at 40 yards to about 1,610 feet per second.

The shot completely pierced the target through and through, making an irregular hole in the armour 2 feet square, and cracking but not buckling it.

From this and other similar experiments it appeared that the 'Warrior' ship at 200 yards would be completely pierced by the Horsfall shot. A solid shot of annealed cast-iron weighing 285 lbs. was fired at the same target with the same charge as before, from a range of 800 yards. This grazed the ground 17 yards short, and struck the target in the junction of two plates, breaking a large hole about 2 feet square through the armour, and burying itself in the timber backing. This proves that at 800 yards the real 'Warrior' would be severely injured, but the skin would not be penetrated by an individual shot.

Mr. Whitworth made a series of experiments to prove the penetration of his projectiles. The shot and shell were fired from a 12-pounder breech-loader, a 70-pounder muzzle-loader, and a 120-pounder muzzle-loader. Most of the shot and shell pierced the target; the following were the more remarkable results. A target was made in the form of a box, with the object of putting to the test Mr. Whitworth's boast that he could drive a shell through the side of an armour-clad ship, and make it burst between decks. The shell fired on this occasion, with an initial velocity of 1,275 feet, passed completely through the 4-inch armour-plate and its oak backing, and exploded on the rear side of the box, the plate of which was indented $2\frac{1}{2}$ inches, bursting the box and blowing all six sides outwards.

A shell of homogeneous metal, weighing 127 lbs., with a bursting charge of 3 lbs. 8 oz. and without a fuse, was fired at the same range with a charge of 25 lbs. of powder, giving a terminal velocity of about 1,263 feet. This shell went completely through everything, much to the astonishment of every one present.

Some experiments were made on the 'Warrior' target to prove the effect of steel shell fired from a 13·3″ Armstrong M. L. wrought-iron shunt rifled gun at 2,000 yards' range. The initial velocity of the shell, with 51½ lbs. charge, is about 990 feet, and the striking velocity 940′.

Mean weight of shell empty	585 lbs.
Burster	24 „
Diameter of shell	13″24 „
Length { over all	23″
{ of shell	19·75
Mean recoil	6 feet 1 inch

The third round struck about 10 yards short, and ricochetted on to centre of target, striking centre plate 4′ 2″ from left side; hole in plate 16″ × 13½″, centre plate started forward 6½″ at top and 4¼″ at bottom on right side, and 3″ at top, and 0·5″ at bottom on left side; 11 armour-plate bolts started in centre plate and one in bottom plate. Upper plate blown off and lying at foot of target in front; all the bolts (except three) of this plate broken at nut—the three being drawn bodily out of the plate; bottom of upper plate, where shell entered, indented 1½″ in length of 1 foot. At the back ragged hole 4′ × 2′ 3″ between third and fourth ribs from right side; two ribs broken and forced out, second rib from right bulged, angle-iron cracked; skin cracked and opened for length of 3′ below hole. Seventeen armour-plate holes, twenty-one rivets, and thirteen backing bolts broken. A great many splinters of iron, timber, bolt-heads, &c., on raft. Shell on platform in rear of target broken up into four pieces.

The 'Bellerophon' Target.

The part of the ship which was tested by the target is that situated between the main and lower decks, and not in the line of ports, the object being to test the strength of the general side of the ship. Special arrangements are made to strengthen the side in the vicinity of the ports, which will be few in number, as the 'Bellerophon' carries a small number of very large guns. These few ports are strengthened by the introduction of additional iron to an extent which would not be practicable if the number of ports were large.

Each frame of the target was made of angle-iron 10″ × 3½″ × ½″, and two angle-irons 3½″ × 3½″ × ⅝″ riveted together; to the double angle-irons of this frame the skin, which is composed of two thicknesses of ¾″ plating, making together 1½″, with a layer of painted canvas between, is riveted. On the outside of the skin-plating, four horizontal angle-iron stringers are attached, two under the upper armour-plate 9½″ × 3½″ × ½″, the broad flange being square to the skin, and not reaching out to the armour by half an inch; the other two are placed behind the lower plate 10″ × 3½″ × ½″. The breadth of the broader flange being the same as the thickness of the backing, it reaches out to, and comes in contact with, the armour. Wood backing 10″ thick, is worked longitudinally on the skin-plating and between the angle-stringers, bolted with nut and screw bolts through the skin-plating. The armour consists of two rolled plates, 6″ thick, manufactured at the Millwall works, weighing upwards of 9 tons each. The upper armour-plate is bolted with bolts 2½″ diameter, and the lower plate with bolts 2¾″ diameter. In one half of the target, divided vertically, the armour-bolts have elastic washers, and are clenched on single nuts. In the other half the bolts have common washers with double nuts, and bolts not clenched. In erecting the target, care was taken to support it behind with beam-ends, &c., so that the actual condition of the proposed ship's side might be approximated to as closely as possible. All the portions of the target were carefully weighed, and the weight, as reported by the Admiralty overseer, was 389 lbs. per square foot.

The range was 200 yards, and the shot named below struck the target. The most decided effects were, however, produced by the guns named in the Table on the next page:—

	lbs. weight
From 10·5″ Armstrong rifled gun:—	
Spherical cast-iron solid shot, one	150
„ steel solid shot, one	165
Cylindrical cast-iron solid shot, one	308
From 7·1″ Ordnance Select Committee gun:—	
Steel shell, one	119
From 7″ Whitworth rifled gun:—	
Steel shell, one	149

From 5½" Whitworth rifled gun :—   lbs. weight
    Steel shell, *one* 69
From 110-pounder Armstrong breech-loading rifled gun :—
    Solid cast-iron shot, *four* . . . . . . 66¼ each.
From 68-pounder smooth-bore gun :—
    Solid cast-iron shot, *three* . . . . . . 66½ „

Nature of Ordnance	Weight in lbs. of Projectile	Forms of Projectile	Charge in lbs.	Remarks
5½" Whitworth gun.	69 Steel shell	*Cylindrical.* Bursting charge 2 lbs. 6 oz.	12	Struck the lower plate 8" from top and 5" from right side, on a bolt; narrow crack on face of indent; armour-plate bolt driven in ½-inch; nut on bolt loose; one balk of timber in backing split through.
10·5" Armstrong gun.	150 Solid cast-iron shot.	*Spherical.* 10·36 diam.	35	Struck the upper plate 6" from the lower edge on a bolt; plate cracked from bolt to bottom; crack 9" long on face of indent; crack 10" long and 1" wide at 5" from circumference of indent on right side; also two small cracks from bottom of plate at 5" and 10" respectively from left side of circumference; plate driven in 3½ at lower edge in length of 3'; plate started out 0·3" at top on left side, and 0·2" from lower plate. At the back a through armour-plate bolt driven out 2"; the heads of two backing-bolts and one rivet broken off; one backing bolt driven out 1¼"; skin bulged slightly over area 1¼ square.
10·5" Armstrong gun.	308 Solid cast-iron shot.	*Cylindrical.*	35	Struck the armour-plate on the third bolt from the right side, lower row; plate driven in 2·1" at bottom in a length of 5'; a crack 18" long through a bolt hole at 2' from impact plate, started at 0·4" from the backing on the right side for a length of 2' at top. At the back one through armour-plate bolt driven out 2", the heads of four rivets and one backing-bolt broken off; vertical frame-piece cracked through and bent out slightly; beam-knee crushed; skin slightly bulged.
7" Whitworth rifled-gun.	149·5 *Steel Shell*	*Cylindrical.* Bursting charge 5 lbs. 8 oz. in flannel bag.	27	Struck lower plate; head of shell remained in hole; depth to nearest point of shell 9½ inches. At the back of the skin bulged at junction of skin plates, bottom plate 2"; upper plate 1"; rib bulged out 2" at 2' from ground; two deck-knees separated from angle-iron 0·3; one armour-plate bolt and three backing-bolts broken; burst in backing.

'Minotaur' Target.

The armour is 5½ inches thick, the thickness of the teak backing is reduced from 18 inches, as in the 'Warrior,' to 9 inches, which is considered as equivalent to 1 inch of wrought-iron. The target used July 7, 1862, constructed on those principles, presented a front of three armour-plates, one made by Messrs. Brown, of Sheffield, another by the Thames Iron Works, and the third by Messrs. Beale.

The guns used against this target were the 12-ton Armstrong muzzle-loading gun, throwing spherical 150-lb. cast-iron, and 162-lb. wrought-iron shot, with 50-lb. charges of powder, the former having an initial velocity of 1,750 feet, and the latter of about 1,700 feet per second; and a service 68-pounder throwing 67-lb. cast-, and 71-lb. wrought-iron shot, with 16 lbs. of powder; the cast shot having an initial velocity of 1,580 feet, the wrought-iron about 1,530 feet per second; all at 200 yards' range. The first 150-lb. cast shot struck the Thames Iron Company's plate, and made a hole about a foot square through the armour, and bedded itself deep in the teak. The plate was buckled considerably, several bolts were started, two ribs cracked, the skin much bulged in, four bolts were broken, and a number of rivets.

The second 150-lb. shot struck the Sheffield plate, made a hole 13 inches by 12 inches in the armour, and sent pieces of the armour-plate, shot, and teak, through a large irregular hole in the skin, the armour-plate was buckled, three bolts broken, and other damage done. The third 150-lb. shot struck Messrs. Beale's plate, and did similar injury. These were the more important of the trials made upon this armour, proving that the powers of resistance in the 'Minotaur' were inferior to those of the 'Warrior.'

The 'Lord Warden' Target.

The target, 20 feet by 9 inches, represented the ordinary construction of a wooden ship, armour-plated, with the addition of a thick iron skin worked outside of the frame-timbers of the ship. The following were the scantlings; frame-timbers moulded $12\frac{1}{2}$ inches; iron diagonal riders connecting the frame-timbers, 6 inches by $1\frac{1}{4}$ inches: inner planking 8 inches thick; iron skin, $1\frac{1}{2}$ inches thick; outside planking $8\frac{1}{2}$ inches thick; rolled armour plates 20 feet × 4 feet 6 inches × 4·5 inches manufactured by the Millwall Company. The guns used were as follows (see Table, p. 247):

	Weight		
	Tons	cwt.	qrs.	lbs.
One 68-pounder smooth-bore muzzle-loading gun . .	0	95	0	0
One 9·22 inches' muzzle-loading rifle gun 11 feet long, 6 grooves	6	11	2	11
One 9·22-inch muzzle-loading rifled gun 13 feet 3 inches long, 6 grooves	12	2	2	0
One 10·5-inch muzzle-loading rifle gun 11 feet 7 inches long, 10 grooves	11	15	2	0
One 7-inch muzzle-loading rifled gun, 10 feet 9 inches long, 6 grooves	6	13	3	0

Some experiments were made to test the resistance of some rolled armour-plates made by Messrs. John Brown and Co., Sheffield.

The plates were of the following dimensions :—

One 13 feet $4\frac{1}{2}$ inches, by 3 feet 7 inches, and $5\frac{1}{2}$ inches thick.
One 12 „ $2\frac{3}{4}$ „ „ 3 „ $7\frac{1}{2}$ „ „ $6\frac{1}{2}$ „ „
One 11 „ 9 „ „ 3 „ $8\frac{1}{2}$ „ „ $7\frac{1}{2}$ „ „

They were secured by $2\frac{1}{2}$-in. screw-bolts to the skin and frame of Mr. Samuda's old target; one-half of each plate had a backing of from 7 inches to 9 inches of teak, and at the back of the other half, it was left hollow for an equal interval between the plates and the skin. India-rubber washers were used under the nuts.

The guns in position for trial were :—

One 300-pounder Armstrong muzzle-loading shunt gun.
One 9-inch Lynall Thomas gun.
One 7-inch Whitworth rifle gun.
One 110-pounder Armstrong breech-loader.
One 68-pounder service 95-cwt. gun.

All were fired at a range of 200 yards.

The first three shots (all cast-iron) were fired from the 68-pounder; one shot struck each plate and made indents $1\frac{3}{4}$ inches deep in the $6\frac{1}{2}$-inch and $7\frac{1}{2}$-inch plates, and 2 inches deep in the $5\frac{1}{2}$-inch plate.

These were followed by three shots from the 110-pounder, also of cast-iron; the indent upon the $5\frac{1}{2}$-inch plate was 1·9 inch deep, that upon the $6\frac{1}{2}$-in. was 2·05 inches deep, that upon the $7\frac{1}{2}$-inch was 1·65 inches deep. There was scarcely any other effect visible.

The most remarkable effects were as follows :—

Nature of Ordnance	Projectiles			Charge in lbs.	Remarks
	Nature	Weight in lbs.	Form and Diameter		
10 ft. 5 in. Armstrong rifled gun.	Steel solid shot.	168·25	*Spherical.* 10·43	50	Struck upper plate 10 ft. from bottom, and 9′ 6″ from left side on a bolt, penetrated the armour-plate, making a hole in plate 11·5″ × 11, depth to surface of shot 12″, plate driven in 1′ 8″ at bottom ; much damage was done at the back ; two inner timbers were rent and splintered and thrust out, fragments projecting about 1′. Shot remained in hole apparently whole.
10 ft. 5 in. rifled gun.	Steel solid shot.	301	*Cylindrical.* 10·46	45	Struck at junction of plates 5′10″ from left of target ; bolts at 15″, 13″ and 14″ from hole started 0·8″, 0·7″ and 0·4″ respectively ; both plates laminated round the circumference of the hole, and two small cracks on front of lower plate from edge of hole. At the back, iron knee broken right off, and lower limb (4′ long with three bolts in it), driven 50′ to the rear. Area of damage 8′ × 4′, five or six plank bolts started and heads off ; inner timbers rent in fragments and thrust out 1′ 6″ ; large splinters of wood scattered all around. Shot struck a large block of granite in rear, and broke itself into four pieces.

The next shot was from the Armstrong 300-pounder, with a cylindrical steel shot weighing 301 lbs., and fired with a 45-lb. charge of powder. This shot had a velocity of 1,295 feet per second at 30 yards in front of the target, and struck the 7½-inch plate where it had the teak backing. The indent made was 6·2 inches deep, and its diameter about 12 inches, or rather a circular piece of this diameter was driven in to a depth of 6·2 inches, and nearly, if not quite, separated from the plate, which was of very good quality. There is, therefore, here, a well-defined measure of the full force of this shot. Besides this local effect, the target had evidently received a serious shake ; one rib was cracked through and bent out ; a number of small rivets were broken ; the plate struck was buckled about 1¼ inch and slightly cracked. The shot, which rebounded from the target, was set up about 2½ inches, and was of excellent material.

A cylindrical steel shell, with a cast-iron head, made on a principle designed by Sir William Armstrong for the purpose of penetrating iron plates by directing the force of the explosion of the bursting charge *forward*, was next fired from the same gun. It weighed 288 lbs., had a bursting charge of 11 lbs., and was fired with a charge of 45 lbs. of powder, which gave at 25 yards in from the target, a velocity of 1,320 feet per second. It struck the 5½-inch plate on the part supported by the teak backing. It completely penetrated the armour-plate, leaving a hole about 14 inches in diameter, burst in the teak backing, tearing away the inner skin, and breaking a rib, and carried a shower of fragments and splinters in board. The teak was set on fire by the explosion, but easily extinguished; one bolt was broken, and other injuries done.

Altogether, for completeness of penetration and for the destructive effects which would have been produced both upon the ship and crew, this experiment carries with it great significance.

After this a cylindrical flat-headed homogeneous metal shell, weighing 148 lbs., with a bursting charge of 5 lbs. 12 oz., was fired from the Whitworth 7-inch gun, with a charge of 25 lbs. of powder, which gave velocity at 30 yards in front of the target of 1,265 feet per second. This shell struck the $5\frac{1}{2}$-inch plate near the hole made by the last Armstrong shell, punched out a clean-cut hole about 9 inches in diameter, and burst in the teak backing; beyond blowing out some of the timber, it added very little indeed to the injury done by the Armstrong shell.

Lynall Thomas's 9-inch gun next missed the target with a round-headed solid steel shot weighing 327 lbs., fired with a charge of 50 lbs. of powder, which at 546 feet from the gun, gave a velocity of 1,220 feet per second.

The same gun next fired a wrought-iron solid flat-headed shot, weighing 302 lbs., with a charge of 50 lbs. of powder. The velocity of this shot was not obtained with certainty, it struck partly on the $6\frac{1}{2}$-inch and partly on the $7\frac{1}{2}$-inch armour; the greatest depth of impression on the latter plate was 6 inches, and on the former 4 inches. The $7\frac{1}{2}$-inch plate was cracked through a bolt-hole and round the indent, as was also the $6\frac{1}{2}$-inch plate, but altogether the injury done was less than had been expected.

A hardened steel shot was next fired from the same gun; it weighed 330 lbs., was round-headed, was fired with a charge of 50 lbs. of powder, which gave a velocity of 1,220 feet per second at 25 yards in front of the target. It struck close to the lower edge of the $7\frac{1}{2}$-inch plate, and made an irregular indentation, measuring about 1 foot by 1 foot 8 inches, and 7 inches deep; two bolts were broken, one rib broken through, two others much bent, and the skin bulged in. The shot itself broke in half lengthways.

After this the 300-pounder Armstrong shunt gun fired a spherical wrought-iron solid shot, weighing 163 lbs. with a charge of 45 lbs., which at 30 yards in front of the target, gave a velocity of 1,630 feet per second. It struck the $7\frac{1}{2}$-inch plate where it had no teak backing, and made an indent $3\frac{3}{4}$ inches deep and 13 inches in diameter, with a crack on the face of the indent; the plate was considerably bulged in; and at the back it showed a large starred crack. The shot was flattened out to a diameter of 13 inches.

The material of which these armour-plates was made proved itself to be of uniform and excellent quality.

The practical lessons to be learnt from such experiments seem to be these:—

1st. That guns are already in existence which can completely penetrate with shot the best $7\frac{1}{2}$-inch armour that can be made, and which can, with shell, pierce the side of a ship built, as to frame, much more strongly than our best ship, and protected with our best $5\frac{1}{2}$-inch armour.

2nd. That iron plates can now, with the improved manufacture of the country and the energy brought out by the occasion, be made of dimensions hitherto quite unattainable, and yet without losing anything in quality.

With the exception of America, other nations have done little or nothing in the manufacture of guns throwing projectiles over 100 lbs. in weight. The United States also boast the possession of two large rifled guns.

<blockquote>
1st, an 8-inch gun . . . 175 lb. projectile, 16 lbs. charge.
2nd, a 10 ,, ,, . . . 250 lb. ,, 25 lbs. ,,
</blockquote>

The Table (p. 249) gives the comparative values of the British muzzle-loading built-up ordnance and the American smooth-bore ordnance.

All cast hollow except the 10-inch of 5·35 tons.

All shell-guns except 10-inch 125-pounder.

20-inch gun only, at present experimental.

Solid shot are only to be fired from the 15-inch N. S. gun at iron-clad vessels, and then with 50 lbs.; 20 rounds may, however, be fired with 60 lbs.

The S. B. guns are formidable weapons, although they are merely cast-iron shell-guns. Our guns being made of wrought-iron will not, on failure, break up like cast-iron or steel ordnance; and from their accuracy of fire, the capacity of their shells, and the power these latter have of maintaining a comparatively high velocity (in consequence of their elongated form) the British are in all probability greatly superior as weapons to the American guns.

Professor Major Owen, R.A., has ably dealt with the following important question:

'One of the most important questions at the present time is this: are monster guns

British Muzzle-Loading Built-up Ordnance.

Gun			Projectile	
Nature	Weight	Charge	Weight	Burster
	Tons	lbs.	lbs.	lbs.
RIFLED :—				
13·3″ (600-pounder)	23	7	Steel shot . . . 603 „ shell . . 585 Cast-iron shell . . 554	24 42½
10·5″ (300-pounder)	12	35	Steel shot . . . 301 „ shell . . 297	15
9·2″ . . .	12	44	Steel shot . . . 221 „ shell . . 206 Cast-iron shell . . 202	11 15½
7″ L. S. . . .	7	25	Steel shot . . . 100 Cast-iron shot . . 100 „ „ shell . . 93	7½
7″ N. S. . . .	6½	25	Ditto.	
64-pounder . .	3¼	8	Cast-iron shot . . 63½ „ „ shell . . 60	4½
SMOOTH-BORE :—				
150-pounder . .	12	40 35 20	Steel shot . . . 168 Cast-iron shot . . 150 „ „ shell . . 104	6½
100-pounder . .	6	25 20 12	Steel shot. Cast-iron shot . . 94 „ „ shell . . 66	

Smooth-Bore Cast-Iron American Ordnance.

Gun	Weight of Gun	Charge		Weight of Shot	Weight of Shell	Bursting Charge of Shell
		Service	Minimum			
	Tons	lbs.	lbs.	lbs.	lbs.	lbs.
20-in. L.S. . .	51·42	100	...	1,000		
„ N.S. . .	44·64	100	...	1,000		
15-in. L.S. . .	21·91	50	...	440	330	17
„ N.S. . .	18·75	35	60	400		
13-in. L.S. . .	14·61	30	...	300	224	7
„ N.S. . .	16·07	40	...	280	224	
11-in. N.S. . .	7·14	15	20	170	130	
10-in. L.S. . .	6·72	15 shell 18 shot	...	172½	100	3
„ N.S. . .	5·35	12½	16	125	100	
„ N.S. . . (or 125-pounder)	7·36	40	...	125	100	

required ? Opinions are divided; but let us turn to facts, and see what has been done. I have endeavoured in the following Table (p. 250) to arrange some of the leading facts in order, so as to give an idea (necessarily a rough one) of the projectiles and charges necessary to actually penetrate certain structures at different ranges. I have not chosen the targets in preference to any others, but simply believing that they represent the average resistance offered by sea-going vessels, and also for convenience of comparison.

'It appears then, from what has been already accomplished, that there is at present no occasion to employ monster ordnance for the destruction of ordinary plated vessels.

'The guns we are now making, which will throw projectiles of 200 or 300 lbs. weight with charges of 45 lbs. are, if properly used, which no doubt they will be, quite sufficient for the purpose. Further than this, however, it is probable that few iron-

Target Penetrated by Steel Elongated Projectiles.

Range	Weight of gun	Projectiles		Charge	Target
		Nature	Diameter		
Yards	cwts.	lbs.	in.	lbs.	
200 . . .	8	12 shot	3	1¾	2½″ iron plate.
,, . . .	,,	12 shell	,,	,,	2½″ iron plate and 12″ wood backing.
,, . . .	81	110 shot	7	12	5½ iron plate.
,, . . .	134	104 ,,	,,	25	Warrior.
600 . . .	148	130 ,,	6·4	25	,,
	tons				
800 . . .		130 ,,	,,	27	,,
1,500 [1] . . .	12	221 ,,	9·2	44	Small plate.[2]
,, [3] . . .	,,	301 ,,	10·5	45	,, ,,
2,000 . . .	22	610 shell	13	70	Warrior.

plated sea-going vessels (now afloat) could withstand the fire of our rifled 7″ guns of 130 cwt., fired with 25-lbs. charges, at 800 or even 1,000 yards' range; [4] for we must remember that in actual warfare, vessels are constantly subjected to a continual fire, and not merely a few blows delivered at certain intervals of time; and that a structure may thus be kept in a constant state of vibration by the repeated impacts of shots, and will offer less resistance than when time is allowed between the rounds, for the metal of the armour to resume its former condition of repose. We should also remember that the few plates upon which experiments are usually made, are in all probability of sounder construction than those produced in quantities for the plating of several vessels; also that when a ship has been for some time at sea, and may in addition have been in action, the armour (bolt-plates and fastenings) will have been subjected to many shocks and strains, and will, therefore, have been considerably weakened.'

One of the most extraordinary of these large guns is the so-called 'WOOLWICH IN-FANT,' which has been recently (1873) severely injured by the heavy charges which have been fired from it. The report of the Inspector of Ordnance upon the state of the interior of the first 35-ton muzzle-loading rifled gun built for the 'Devastation,' after 38 horizontal discharges from its 12-inch bore, is illustrated by the accompanying

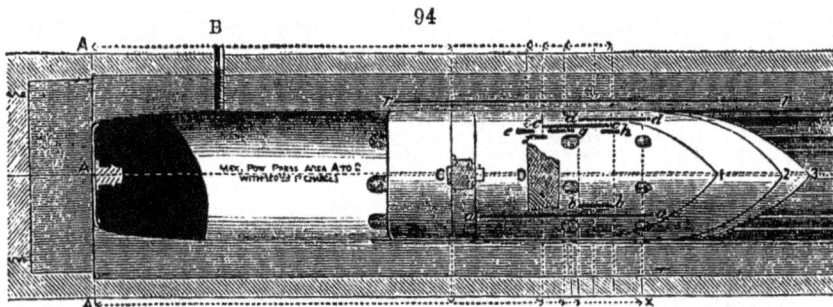

diagram, in which a section of the inner portion is shown to scale. A is the inner end of the bore, where the maximum pressure, varying from 20 to 66 tons per square inch from identical powder-charges, was registered by crushing gauge. B is the vent, where the lowest pressures in the chamber were generally registered. C shows the base of the shot six inches in advance of its seat, where it experienced the greatest pressure, varying from 18 to 53 tons per square inch from similar powder-charges. The positions of the 700-lbs. shot are shown with 120-lbs. powder-charge, 1st, in its seat; 2nd, registering the greatest pressure; and, 3rd, with the rear-studs coming into

[1] Ascertained for this range by using a 30-lbs. charge at 200 yards.
[2] 5½ inches of iron and 27 inches of wood; the wood and iron not disposed in such an advantageous manner for resistance as in the 'Warrior' target.
[3] Ascertained for this range by using a 35-lbs. charge at 200 yards.
[4] The result of a recent experiment shows 'that a structure such as the "Warrior" can be penetrated at 200 yards' range with elongated shot, and shot cast in chill when the form of the latter is elliptical, fired from a 7-inch rifled gun with ½ charges;' and the report adds, 'but it is probable that had the 7-inch steel shot been elliptical-headed, instead of hemispherical-headed, penetration would also be effected at the longer range (1,200 yards.)'

'driving' bearing eight inches in advance of their seat. This latter point corresponds nearly with that at which the front-studs hammer at starting. With shorter powder-charges these several positions of the shot would be nearer the chamber.

The longitudinal positions of the four cracks, four fissures, and the deep roughness or erosion caused by the escaping gases, are shown by dark lines; that of the greatest enlargement of the bore by dark shading, at D; those of the burrs on the edges of the grooves are not stated in the official report. The nature of these injuries would be hardly visible on so small a scale, and the vertical positions could not be shown in a section. Two of the cracks were on the lower side of the bore, all the other injuries on the upper side, and their centres were $3\frac{1}{2}$ to 4 feet from A, where the greatest powder-pressure occurred, but coincided with the point where the front-studs hammer and the rear-studs come into 'driving' bearing. The gun is being rebuilt, at a cost of about 700l. or 800l.

In detail, the drawing shows the following effects :—Four cracks, aa, $15\frac{1}{2}$ inches long, centre $44\frac{1}{4}$ inches from the rear end of the bore at A; bb, 3 inches long, centre 47 inches from A; cc, $5\frac{1}{2}$ inches long, centre 45 inches from A; dd, $6\frac{1}{2}$ inches long, centre $48\frac{5}{8}$ inches from A; four fissures, e, $1\frac{3}{4}$ inches long, centre $40\frac{7}{8}$ inches from A; f, $1\frac{1}{4}$ inches long, centre $42\frac{3}{8}$ inches from A; g, $2\frac{3}{4}$ inches long, centre $44\frac{1}{4}$ inches from A; h, 2 inches long, centre $48\frac{1}{2}$ inches from A; rr, a roughness extending from 1 inch in front of the seat of the shot ($28\frac{1}{2}$ inches from A), to 65 inches from A; x, burrs, of which the position is not specified, but approximately about 50 to 52 inches from A. The powder-pressure is relieved at c, $33\frac{1}{2}$ inches from A (6 inches in front of seat of shot); the greatest enlargement of the bore is at D, 42 inches from A ($14\frac{1}{2}$ inches in front of seat of shot); the hammering of front-stud is located $15\frac{1}{4}$ inches away from seat of shot, at $43\frac{1}{4}$ inches from A; and the rear-studs come into driving contact $\frac{3}{4}$ of an inch further on.

In the 'Philosophical Magazine,' Captain Noble, of the Elswick Works, published an elaborate paper on the influence of the spiral in rifled ordnance. The following abstract of that paper, freed from its mathematical formulæ, with the critical remarks, is from an experienced hand.

'Every one is aware that elongated rifled projectiles are the subjects of two principal motions during their exit from the bore, viz., a motion of translation and a motion of rotation. If the rotation be efficiently accomplished, no other considerable motion ought to take place. But if unmechanical devices be resorted to for the purpose of effecting the revolution of the elongated projectile, other undesirable movements are set up within the gun. However, under any sound mechanical arrangement for supporting and rotating heavy elongated projectiles, it is an ascertained experimental fact, that the force necessary to impart rotation is only a small fraction of that required to give a high velocity of translation. Hence it follows, both in theory, and as an ascertained experimental fact, that the increment of gaseous pressure due to rifling is quite insignificant. It is with this small fraction of expulsive force, and this insignificant increment of gaseous pressure, that Captain Noble deals in his very neat mathematical investigation. He takes two utterly unmechanical systems of rotating heavy projectiles—one with an uniform angle of spiral, and the other with an ever-changing angle—both employing studs, and he yields the unmechanical precedence to the stud acting in an uniform spiral. Whether this be so or not, is a philosophical question which appears to us to have been decided by Captain Noble on erroneous data. Still, the formulas adduced will strike mathematicians as particularly neat; and, if they leave out of sight the whole of the practical objections to the increasing spiral, these formulas cannot fail to form most instructive beacons to all mathematical artillerists.

'Captain Noble assumes that the action of studs within their grooves is uniform in all the grooves. Now this cannot be, unless the major axis of the projectile coincides with that of the gun throughout the whole of its transit. He also assumes that, previous to starting, the studs are all in "driving" bearing, and at equal depths in their several grooves; whereas the lower studs, on which the shot rests, and which are the only points in contact with the bore, are then touching the "loading" side of their groove, and all the other studs are more or less on the same, or "off" side of their grooves. Before they can come into "driving" bearing, the shot must move forward, slightly in the case of the uniform spiral, and about six or eight inches in the parabolic groove. In the former case, the so-called "pressure" is a succession of light blows all round the bore; and in the latter, the shot having attained about one-third of its velocity, it is a succession of very heavy blows. Now these successive blows are concentrated on one-inch points of each groove, and, constantly recurring upon the same spot, produce slight enlargements and roughnesses, which prevent the smooth stud slipping away easily. The tendency of the shot's momentum, acting on a circle of points near the centre of gravity and of figure, is to exert an effort of rotation round those points, or, in other words, round the minor axis. Thus several oscillating motions are set up, the force of which varies with the amount of the obstacle and the suddenness of the force applied; *i.e.*, with the amount and nature of the powder-charge. Moreover, in the case of the increasing spiral, further mechanical forces are brought into operation at the muzzle, which have escaped Captain Noble's investigation. An ever-changing angle of groove cannot be conformed to by a constant angle of shot, any more than a male screw of one pitch can work into a female screw of a different pitch. To meet this obvious mechanical difficulty, only one stud, one inch long, bears in each groove all along the bore; but when within twelve inches of the muzzle, an angle of twist is reached which coincides with the angle formed by the front and rear studs on the shot. Now as this is the spot where most of the "increasing spiral" guns give way, a mathematical examination of the forces brought into play near the muzzle would be fraught with much interest. But these and other mechanical inquiries find no place in Captain Noble's formula. He assumes that the original action on the stud is a pressure, not a blow, and that this pressure follows a uniform law throughout the gun. Granting this singular hypothesis, the conclusions are rather of a philosophical than practical character, dealing, as we have said, with but a small fraction of the force of translation, and a quite insignificant increment of gaseous pressure. Subject to those deductions, his conclusions are worthy of note.

'Captain Noble educes from his formulas what is, we doubt not, the fact, that in a uniform twist the pressure on the studs is a constant fraction of the pressure of the base of the shot, the value of the fraction depending on the angles of the rifling. The tension of the powder-gases at the muzzle being very small when compared with their tension at the seat of the shot, the studs have, on the uniform system, scarcely any work to do at the muzzle, while they may be severely strained at the commencement of motion. He estimates the pressure on the studs due to rifling as, in this case, about $2\frac{1}{2}$ per cent. of that required to impart translation to a 400-lb. shot in the 10-inch 18-ton gun, or about $68\frac{1}{2}$ tons' pressure when it has moved four inches, and 9 tons at the muzzle; whereas the substitution of the parabolic curves for the uniform angle of spiral, according to Captain Noble's formulas, reduces this pressure one-half, so that when the stud has moved four inches (*i.e.*, *before it touches at all on the "driving" side*), it sustains 31·2 tons' pressure, gradually rising to 36 tons at the muzzle!

'As Sir William Armstrong certifies that "the maximum pressure" (in the powder-chamber) "causes the failure of the stud," the difference of powder-pressure arising from a change of spiral is noteworthy. Captain Noble tells us that, small as the increment in gaseous pressure due to rifling is, it is still less in the parabolic than in the uniform spiral. Whereas the maximum bursting pressure is reduced from 19·7 tons per square inch to 19·5 tons per square inch, by suppressing the rifling altogether in the case of uniform spirals, the decrement of pressure due to the suppression of the parabolic rifling is a reduction from 19·7 tons to 19·62 tons per square inch. The gain then, to the powder-chamber, from the employment of the increasing spiral, is ·12 of a ton per square inch. We commend this philosophical fraction to our artillery philosophers, and would make them a present of this mathematical advantage. When, however, we turn to the Tables of Pressures registered by the Committee on Explosives in the 10-inch 15-ton, which is the subject of Captain Noble's learned investigation, we are rather puzzled to which of the pressures we are to apply the ·12 of a ton. We find similar powder-charges fired under identical conditions producing most unlike results. We find these anomalous pressures with every description of powder; and we observe that the gun has this parabolic system of rifling, with its consequent stud agency. Yet, with these great philosophical advantages, the powder-pressures registered in the 10-inch gun, with $87\frac{1}{2}$ lbs. P. charges and 400-lbs. shot, varied from 25 tons on the square inch to 63·4 tons, the latter expulsive force resulting in the least velocity and striking force in the projectile. Again 60 lbs. R.L.G. charges registered powder-pressures varying from 36·5 tons to 57·8 tons on the square inch, under identical conditions, the highest expulsive force imparting the lowest velocity to the projectile. Yet it is on the register of pressures within this gun that Captain Noble's calculations are based; true, he does not select any of the above figures for his formulas, but on the pressures registered with 85 lbs. P. charge, which happened to be 19·7 tons on the square inch. But, if a selection must be made between pressures varying from 19·7 tons to 63·4 tons on the square inch, it might be quite as well to close the Report of the Committee on Explosives, and assume any number of tons at haphazard.

'Captain Noble has shown a mathematical gain of ·12 of a ton pressure on the square inch by the adoption of the parabolic or increasing spiral. What if the greater part of this astounding variation of pressure from 19·7 to 63·4 tons on the square inch was attributable to the parabolic curve, or, to speak more accurately, to the stud system which that curve necessitates? That gunpowder varies in explosive power in this way in mines, shells, or torpedoes, or anywhere, except in a stud-rifled gun, is stoutly denied. If the variation of powder-pressures be not due to the gunpowder it must be due to the shot; and if to the shot, then to the oscillations of the axis round the points of contact with the bore, which are exclusively the studs; but the studs are a necessity of the increasing spiral or parabolic groove. Hence it appears, that, while saving ·12 of a ton pressure on the square inch, by employing this most unmechanical contrivance, we are adding at least 4 tons, and, probably, more, pressure occasionally to the gun. These are the deductions which we draw from Captain Noble's formulas, and from the Report of the Committee on Explosives.'—*Iron.*

After the siege of Paris inquiries and experiments were made in all directions into the relative qualities of bronze and steel for cannon; amongst the metals tried was phosphorised bronze, of which MM. Montefiore, Lévy and Kunzel claimed to be the inventors. This claim is now refuted, and it appears that sixteen years ago the very same alloy was introduced to the French artillery by two officers, MM. de Roulz and A. de Fontenay. In the years 1870 and 1871 a series of experiments were made at Liège, in presence of a commission of artillery officers of all nations, and the results were described in a pamphlet by M. Lévy, as highly favourable to the alloy in question. It is stated in that work, that an ordinary bronze gun founded at Liège, having been fired forty-nine times with a charge of one kilogramme of powder and a shot, was so seriously injured that it was impossible to continue the experiments with it, while another gun of the same calibre (4) made of the new phosphorised bronze, and fired with the same charge, and the same number of times, exhibited no sensible injury whatever. Further comparative trials with bursting charges gave results equally favourable to the new metal. In this case, guns of each kind were fired under the same conditions, five times each, commencing with one kilogramme of powder and a single shot, and carried as high as $1\frac{3}{4}$ kilogrammes, with a cylinder of the weight of 3 shot, with one charge of $1\frac{1}{4}$ kilogrammes of powder, and 2 shot, and still more so with the same amount of powder, and a cylinder equal to 3 shot. The interior of the chamber of both guns was visibly enlarged, but rather more so in the case of the old than of the new metal gun. Finally, the phosphorised bronze gun burst with a charge of $1\frac{1}{2}$ kilogrammes of powder, and a cylinder of equal weight. These experiments seemed conclusive, but the French Government ordered further trials to be made at Bourges and other places by a commission of artillery officers, with bronze guns of various alloys, and of foreign as well as French make. The results as between ordinary and phosphorised bronze are very different from those obtained at Liège.

The projectiles used at Bourges were long solid shot, weighing from 10 kilogrammes to 20 kilogrammes for guns of 4, with charges of powder ranging from the ordinary quantity to 1,700 grammes, the bursting charge. With a charge of 1,150 grammes, and a 10-kilogramme shot, the phosphorised bronze gun began to show cracks, while the ordinary gun exhibited no serious injury whatever. The experiments were afterwards continued with full charges of powder and 20-kilogrammes projectiles: at the seventeenth or eighteenth firing the phosphorised bronze gun burst, and produced a number of small fragments, without any appearance of enlargement of the circumference. At the nineteenth round, the ordinary bronze-metal gun also burst, nearly half the piece being blown off in one mass, which, as well as the rest of the gun, exhibited expansion of the metal with longitudinal fissures. The conclusion the Commission arrived at, after these absolutely conflicting results, was, that the ordinary bronze used for guns exhibits at least as much resisting power as phosphorised bronze, and is incomparably more malleable and less brittle.

SHELLS.—The hollow explosive projectiles that we call shells, or bombs, are a very old invention. Under the name of 'coininges,' they consisted of rudely formed globes of plate-iron soldered together, filled with gunpowder and all sorts of miscellaneous 'mitraille.' These were thrown to short distances both from 'pierriers' (a sort of mortar) and from catapultæ, as early as 1495 at Naples, 1510 at Padua, 1520 at Heilsberg, 1522 at Rhodes, and 1542 at Boulogne, Liège. About the middle of the 15th century bombs of cast-iron seem to have come into use; an Englishman, named Malthus, learned the art of throwing them from the Dutch, and perfected the system for the French armies—being the first to throw shells in France, at the siege of La Mothe, in 1643. The diameter of the bomb seems at that time to have become fixed at 13 inches—the old Paris foot; and at this it remains (with very few exceptional cases) down to the present day.

A few attempts to increase the size and power of these projectiles have been made at different periods, but never with the practical skill necessary to success; for example, 18-inch shells were thrown by the French at the siege of Tournay, in 1745; whereas, just a century before, the Swedes threw shells of 462 lbs. weight, and holding 40 lbs. of powder. The French, when they occupied Algiers in 1830, found numbers of old shells of nearly 900 lbs. in weight; and in almost every arsenal and fortress in Europe one or two old 16-inch and 18-inch shells are to be found. No attempt was made in modern days to realise the vast accession of power that such large shells confer, until the year 1832, when the 'monster mortar,' as it was then called, of 24 inches calibre, designed by Colonel Paixhans (the author of the Paixhans gun), was constructed by order of Baron Evain, the Belgian Minister of War, and attempted to be used by the French at the siege of the citadel at Antwerp, but with the worst possible success. The mortar, a crude cylindrical mass of cast-iron, sunk in a bed of timber weighing about 8 tons, and provided neither with adequate means for 'laying' it, nor for charging it—the heavy shells weighing, when filled with 99 lbs. of powder, 1,015 lbs. each—could with difficulty be fired three rounds in two hours, while the shells themselves were very badly proportioned.

One of these shells fell nearly close to the powder-magazine, but did not explode; had it fallen upon the presumed bomb-proof arch of the magazine, containing 300,000 lbs. of powder, it would have pierced it, according to the opinion of all the military engineers present at the siege, and so closed the enterprise at a blow. The ill-success of this mortar prevented for several years any attempt to develop bombs into their legitimate office—as the means of suddenly transferring mines into the body of fortified places—of a power adequate to act with decisive effect upon their works; although some years afterwards a 20-inch mortar was made in England for the Pacha of Egypt, and proved at Woolwich.

But another circumstance still more tended to the neglect of large shells thrown by vertical fire. After repeated trials and many failures, it was found practicable to throw 10-inch (and since that even 13-inch) shells from cannon, or 'shell-guns,' by projecting them nearly horizontally, or at such low angles that they should 'ricochet' and roll along the ground before they burst; and, thus fired, it was soon seen that their destructive power *as against troops* was greater than if fired at angles approaching 45° of elevation from mortars. Paixhans and his school had pushed a good and useful invention beyond its proper limits, and had lost sight wholly of the all-important fact that horizontal shell-fire, powerful as it is against troops or shipping, is all but useless as an instrument of destruction to the works (the earthwork and masonry, &c.) of fortified places; for this end, weight and the penetrative power due to the velocity of descent in falling from a great height are indispensable.

A 13-inch shell, weighing about 180 lbs., is thrown, by a charge of 30 lbs. of powder, barely 4,700 yards. While, with not much more than double this amount of powder, the 36-inch shell, of more than 14 times its weight, can be thrown 2,650 yards, or much more than half the distance.

The explosive power, it is obvious, is approximately proportionate to the weight of powder; but, by calculations, of which the result only can here be given, Mr. Mallet has shown that the total power of demolition—that is to say, the absolute amount of damage done in throwing down buildings, walls, &c. &c.—by one 39-inch shell, is 1,600 times that possible to be done by one 13-inch shell; and that an object which a 13-inch shell could just overturn at one yard from its centre, will be overthrown by the 36-inch shell at 40 yards' distance.

A 13-inch shell penetrates, on falling upon compact earth, about 2½ feet. The Antwerp shell penetrated 7 feet. The 36-inch shell penetrated 16 to 18 feet. The funnel-shaped cavity, or 'crater,' of earth blown out by the explosion of a buried shell, is always a similar figure, called a 'paraboloid;' its diameter at the surface, produced by the 13-inch shell, is about 7 feet, and by the 36-inch shell about 40 feet.

No bomb-proof arch (so called) now exists in Europe capable of resisting the tremendous fall of such masses, and the terrible powers of their explosion when 480 lbs. of powder, fired to the very best advantage, puts in motion the fragments of more than a ton of iron. No precautions are possible in a fortress, no splinter-proof, no ordinary vaulting, perhaps no casement, exists capable of resisting their fall and explosion. Such a shell would sink the largest ship or floating battery.

A single 36-inch shell in flight costs 25l., and a single 13-inch 2l. 2s., yet the former is the *cheaper* projectile; for, according to Mr. Mallet's calculations, to transfer to the point of effect the same weight of bursting powder, we must give—

55 shells of 13 inches, at 2l. 2s.	.	.	.	115 10 0
Against 1 shell of 36 inches	.	.	.	25 0 0
Showing a saving in favour of the large shell of		.		90 10 0

In 1871 we have the following return of Cannon and Mortars exported:—

	Cwts.	Value.
To France.	4,276	£19,236
„ Italy	24,060	63,000
„ Austrian Territories	1,200	7,500
„ Egypt	664	6,635
„ Other Countries	3,224	11,494
	33,424	107,865

ARUM VULGARE. *A. maculatum ; The Wake-robin ; Lords and Ladies.* In the island of Portland a kind of arrowroot was prepared from this plant. See ARROW-ROOT.

ASBESTOS, from ἄσβεστος, *unconsumable.* (*Asbeste,* Fr.: *Asbest,* Ger.) When the fibres of the fibrous varieties of amphibole are so slender as to be flexible, it is called asbestos, or amianthus. It is found in Piedmont, Savoy, Salzburg, the Tyrol, Dauphiné, Hungary, Silesia; also in Corsica so abundantly as to have been made use of by Dolomieu for packing minerals; in the United States, St. Kevern in Cornwall, in Aberdeenshire, in some of the islands north of Scotland, and Greenland. Asbestos was manufactured into cloth by the ancients, who were well acquainted with its incombustibility. This cloth was used for napkins, which could be cleansed by throwing them into the fire; it was also used as the wick for lamps in the ancient temples; and it is now used for the same purpose by the natives of Greenland. It has been proposed to make paper of this fibrous substance, for the preservation of important matters. An Italian, Chevalier Aldini, constructed pieces of dress which are incombustible. Those for the body, arms, and legs were formed out of strong cloth steeped in a solution of alum; while those for the head, hands, and feet were made of cloth of asbestos. A piece of ancient asbestos cloth, preserved in the Vatican, appears to have been formed by mixing asbestos with other fibrous substances; but M. Aldini has executed a piece of nearly the same size, which is superior to it, as it contains no foreign substance. The fibres were prevented from breaking by the action of steam. The cloth is made loose in its fabric, and the threads are about the fiftieth of an inch in diameter. The Society of Encouragement, of Paris, proposed a prize for the improvement of asbestos cloth. The use of it was publicly exhibited in London in 1858.

Common Asbestos is found in fibres of a dull greenish colour, and of a somewhat pearly lustre. In the Serpentine formations at the Lizard Point, in Cornwall, it is common. Dr. M'Culloch found it in the limestone of Glentilt in a pasty state, but it hardened upon exposure.

Mountain Leather, or *Mountain Paper,* is not in parallel fibres like the preceding, but the fibres are interwoven. The thinner pieces bear the latter name. Wanlock Head is the best known locality in this country.

Elastic Asbestos, or *Mountain Cork,* floats on water. It has, like the preceding, an interlaced fibrous texture. It varies in colour, being white, grey, yellow, or brown. In appearance and feel it is not unlike common cork, and it has a certain degree of elasticity, hence its name.

Mountain Wood, or *Ligniform Asbestos.* This variety is usually massive, and of a brown colour, having much the appearance of wood. It is found in several localities in Scotland.

ASH. (*Fraxinus excelsa.*) Ash is superior to any other British wood for its toughness and elasticity. It is therefore used for the frames of machines, for agricultural implements, and the felloes of wheels. This wood is split into pieces for the springs of bleachers' rubbing-boards. Handspikes, hammer-handles, rails for chairs, &c., are made from the ash. All these and similar works are much stronger when they follow the natural fibre of the wood. Hoops are also frequently made of the young branches of the ash. Rankine gives its tenacity as 17,000, and its modulus of elasticity, or resistance to stretching, as 1,600,000.

Certain species of *Fraxinus* in the South of Europe yield a sweet exudation known as *Manna.*

ASHES. In commerce, the word ashes is applied to the ashes of vegetable substances from which the alkalis are obtained. See KELP, BARILLA, &c.

It is the popular name of the vegetable alkali, potash, in an impure state, as procured from the ashes of plants by lixiviation and evaporation. The plants which yield the greatest quantity of potash are wormwood and fumitory. See POTASH, PEARLASH, and, for the mode of determining the value of ashes, ALKALIMETRY.

Commercially ashes are divided into soap-ashes, wood-ashes, and weed-ashes.

ASHES OF PLANTS. The ashes of all species of woods and weeds are found to contain some alkali; hence it is that the residuary matter, after the combustion of any vegetable matter, acts as a stimulant to vegetable growth.

The following analyses of plants have been selected from the Tables which have been published by Messrs. Thomas Way and G. Ogston, in the 'Journal of the Agricultural Society:'—

	Peas	Beans	Red Clover	Sainfoin	Wheat Grain	Straw	Barley	Oats	Turnip Root	Turnip Leaves	Beet-Root	Carrot Root
Potassa	42·43	36·72	18·44	31·90	29·76	10·51	20·97	17·70	23·70	11·56	21·68	37·55
Soda	3·27	0·14	2·79	..	5·26	1·03	4·56	3·84	14·75	12·43	2·13	12·63
Lime	5·73	12·06	35·02	24·30	2·88	5·91	1·48	2·54	11·82	28·49	1·90	9·76
Magnesia	5·92	6·00	11·91	5·03	11·06	1·25	7·45	7·33	3·28	2·62	1·79	3·78
Sesquioxide of iron	0·44	0·65	0·98	0·61	0·23	0·07	0·51	0·49	0·47	3·02	0·52	6·74
Sulphuric acid	6·23	4·28	3·91	3·28	0·11	2·14	0·79	1·10	16·13	10·36	3·14	6·34
Silica	1·74	1·52	4·03	3·22	2·23	73·57	32·73	38·48	2·69	8·04	1·40	0·76
Carbonic acid	4·38	1·63	12·92	15·20	0·22	..	..	..	10·47	6·18	15·23	15·15
Phosphoric acid	29·92	33·74	5·82	9·35	48·21	5·51	31·69	26·46	9·31	4·85	1·65	8·37
Chloride of potassium	..	..	..	6·24	..	..	..	0·92				
Chloride of sodium	..	3·26	4·13	0·78	..	..	..	..	7·05	12·41	49·51	4·91
Total amount	99·96	100·00	99·95	99·96	99·96	99·99	99·98	99·96	99·93	99·96	99·96	99·99
Per-centage of ash in the dry substance	2·60	2·90	7·87	6·37	2·05	..	2·50	2·50	6·00	16·40	11·32	5·12
Per-centage of ash in the fresh substance	2·24	2·54	6·77	5·65	1·81	..	2·25	2·27	0·75	1·97	1·02	0·77

A few additional analyses, by Prof. Way and other chemists, are given for the purpose of showing the variations which exist in the constituents of plants as determined by the analysis of their ashes :—

	Potatoes[1]	Lettuce Leaves and Stalk[2]	Olive-tree Wood[3]	Hops[4]	Hay[5]	Sprouts: Clupea Sprotus[6]
Potassa	25·41	22·37	20·60	24·88	11·93	17·23
Soda	...	18·50	...	...	1·07	1·19
Lime	2·34	10·43	63·02	21·59	14·76	23·57
Magnesia	4·17	5·68	2·31	4·69	5·30	3·01
Sesquioxide of iron	0·50	2·82	...	1·75	2·75	0·28
Sulphuric acid	4·71	3·85	3·09	7·27	0·20	
Silica	3·64	11·86	3·82	19·71	53·43	
Carbonic acid	...	...	...	2·17		
Phosphoric acid	10·38	9·38	4·77	14·47	6·34	43·52
Chloride of potassium	12·40	...	1·09			
Chloride of sodium	trace	15·09	...	3·42	2·27	11·19
Total amount	100·00	99·99	100·00	99·95	100·00	100·00
Per-centage of ash in the dry substance	4·86	...	0·58	5·95	6·97	
Per-centage of ash in the fresh substance	...	...	...	...	6·15	

The large amount of silica found in the grasses, constituting, as it does, much of their outer coating, cannot fail to be noticed. The variations in the quantities of phosphoric acid are instructive.

A vast number of analyses of the ashes of plants have been collected and systematically arranged by Dr. Emil Wolff in his 'Aschen-Analysen von landwirthschaftlichen Producten, Fabrik-Abfällen und wildwachsenden Pflanzen.' 4to., Berlin, 1871.

---

[1] Griepenkerl.   [2] Griepenkerl.   [3] A. Müller.   [4] Way.   [5] Hubert.   [6] Way.

ASHLAR or **ASHLER.** When stones are worked in regular beds and joints, and are dressed for facing work, they are called ashlar. The stone used as ashlar is called *ashlaring*, when in thin slabs, and made to serve merely as a case to the regular body of the wall.

ASHLERING, in carpentry, are the short upright pieces of timbering or quartering fixed, in garrets, to the floor and rafters, to cut off the acute angle which they form.

ASPARAGINE. *Syn.* Asparamide, altheine. $C^8H^8N^2O^6 + 2Aq.$ ($C^4H^8N^2O^3 + H^2O$.) A beautifully crystallised substance, first found in asparagus juice, by Vauquelin and Robiquet, in 1805. It not only exists in a great number of vegetables, but some which do not contain it naturally may be made to afford it by being grown in dark damp cellars. Many plants normally containing only small quantities of it may be made to yield more by being allowed to germinate in that manner. Among the vegetables from which it can be directly obtained may be mentioned the following:— *Althæa officinalis, Asparagus acutifolius, A. off., Atropa belladonna, Convallaria majalis, C. multiflora, Cynodon dactylon, Glycyrrhiza glabra, Lactuca sativa, Ornithogalum caudatum, Paris quadrifolia, Robinia pseudacacia, Solanum tuberosum,* and *Symphytum off.* The following list contains the names of some plants normally containing no asparagine, but yielding it when allowed to germinate in darkness in damp cellars:— *Colutea arborescens, Cytisus laburnum, Ervum lens, Genista juncea, Hedysarum onobrychis, Lathyrus odoratus, L. latifolius, Phaseolus vulgaris, Pisum sativum, Trifolium pratense, Vicia Faba,* and *V. sativa.*

Preparation.—Perhaps the most convenient and economical mode of procuring asparagine is from the etiolated (blanched) shoots of vetches. When they have acquired a length of two inches—which, under favourable circumstances, will be in about three weeks—they are to be crushed, and the juice pressed out. The quantity yielded will be rather less than three-fourths of the weight of the plant. It is then to be boiled for a short time, to coagulate the vegetable albumen, and strained. This clarified fluid is to be evaporated until almost syrupy, and put aside to crystallise. The product is at first brown, but by washing with cold water, afterwards dissolving in boiling water, and subsequent crystallisation, it may be obtained pure. If, previous to putting the hot fluid aside to crystallise, a little pure animal-charcoal be added, and the whole be digested a short time, and then filtered, the crystals will be obtained brilliantly white at one operation. Some chemists advise the germination to be allowed to go much further than was mentioned above, so that the shoots may be as long as 15 inches. The crystals obtained by the process given have the formula $C^8 H^8 N^2 O^6 + 2$ Aq., but the water is expelled at 212°. Asparagine possesses the peculiarity of behaving like a base towards strong oxides and like an acid towards bases. The crystals obtained by the method given contain, in the 100 parts, carbon 32·00, hydrogen 6·67, nitrogen 18·67, oxygen 42·66. Dried at 212°, it has the following composition: carbon 36·36, hydrogen 6·06, nitrogen 21·21, oxygen 36·37.— C. G. W.

ASPARAGOLITE. A name given to a variety of apatite of the colour of asparagus.

ASPARAGUS OFFICINALIS. An esculent vegetable belonging to the natural order *Liliaceæ.* The young shoots sent up from the underground stem are the parts used.

ASPEN. The *Populus tremula.* A tree native of almost all parts of Europe as far north as Siberia. The wood is white, and is applied to many useful purposes. The charcoal prepared from the aspen is said to be well adapted for gunpowder. See POPLAR TREE.

ASPHALT, ASPHALTUM, or **MINERAL PITCH.** (*Asphalte,* Fr.; *Asphalt, Bergpech,* Ger.) A name applied to the solid varieties of bitumen. In its purest form asphalt presents the appearance of a black or brownish-black solid substance, possessing a bright conchoidal fracture. It fuses at 212° F., burning with a brilliant flame and emitting a bituminous odour. Specific gravity = 1 to 1·2. Asphalt is insoluble in alcohol, but soluble in about five times its weight of naphtha.

The mineral substances included under the rather wide term of asphalt appear to differ considerably in chemical composition. They may generally be resolved proximately into certain oils, resins, and pitch-like solids; whilst ultimately they yield carbon, hydrogen, and oxygen, associated with a small proportion of nitrogen and mineral matter. The asphalts appear to have been formed by the evaporation, solidification, and consequent partial oxidation of certain liquid hydrocarbons, such as petroleum. Their ultimate origin may no doubt be traced to organic sources.

Asphalt is found in small quantity in the carboniferous limestone of Derbyshire,

Staffordshire, and elsewhere. It is generally said that masses of asphalt float on the surface of the Dead Sea, or Lake Asphaltites—whence the name—but according to modern observers, the quantity found at present is but small. The vast deposit of asphalt in the Great Pitch Lake of Trinidad is described under the head of BITUMEN. A substance known as *chapapote*, or Mexican asphalt, is imported from Cuba.

Large masses of rock impregnated with asphalt are found in certain localities on the Continent, and are important as furnishing most of the asphalt used commercially. Perhaps the best known of these deposits is the great mass of Jurassic limestone in the Val de Travers, at Seyssel, on the Rhone. Similar rocks occur at Limmer, near Hanover; in the Isle of Brazza in Dalmatia; at Hölle, near Heide, in Holstein; in the Tyrol, and in Alsace.

Under the head of BITUMEN will be found some historical notices of the ancient use of asphalt and kindred substances for building purposes. In modern times attention has frequently been directed to the utilisation of the asphaltic rocks of Switzerland, especially as a source of asphalt for paving. Without following the vicissitudes of the Swiss workings since they were originally commenced by Erinus, in 1712, it may suffice to say that within the last few years considerable attention has been directed to their development, and that they are now actively worked. Originally the asphalt obtained from the rocks of these quarries was employed in the form of a liquid, melted out from the limestone, and spread over the pavement—durability being imparted to the material by admixture of coarse sand and by sprinkling sand or gravel over the surface. The following is the modern method of laying down asphaltic foot-paths, as practised in Paris:—A foundation is first formed by a layer of concrete, the surface of which is carefully flattened. On this even surface, when dry, the melted asphalt is spread. This asphalt is melted in a cauldron, and a proper proportion of sand added—the mixture being kept stirred to prevent subsidence of the sand. The asphalt is spread with a wooden trowel over the concrete, and the surface is finally smoothed over.

Of late, a very great improvement in the construction of asphalt roads has been introduced, the merit of the new method being due to M. A. Merian, of Basle. The asphalt is laid down in the form of a hot powder, and the powder is then beaten into a compact mass. The process has been thus described by M. Léon Malo:—'The asphalt stone is brought direct from the quarries, and broken up into small pieces about the size of those used for macadamized roads; it is then heated over a stove, in a drum-shaped iron vessel with feet, till it crumbles into powder; and in order that the powder may not lose its heat, the whole apparatus is conveyed on to the street where it is to be applied. Then a foundation of *béton* (concrete) is laid, about 4 inches deep, which may, however, be thicker or thinner according to the nature of the soil.' The concrete having hardened, its surface is brought to the required curve, and a layer of powdered asphalt, 16 to 20 inches thick, laid down and compressed by stamping, the surface being finally smoothed by a heavy roller.

The Val de Travers asphalt quarries are now largely worked, and several experimental patches of paving with this asphalt have been laid down in some of the main thoroughfares of London, and have in general proved highly successful.

In addition to the use of asphalt for pavements and roadways, the material is of value as a waterproof lining for cisterns, and as a cement. It also finds application in the arts as a component of certain varnishes. See BITUMEN and PAVEMENT, ASPHALT.

ASPHALTENE. A product obtained from asphaltum by volatilising the oily and volatile product *petrolene*.

ASPHALTIC MASTIC, used in Paris for large works, is brought down the Rhone from Pyrimont, near Seyssel. It is composed of nearly pure carbonate of lime, and about 9 or ten per cent. of bitumen.

When in a state of powder it is mixed with about 7 per cent. of bitumen or mineral pitch, found near the same spot. The powdered asphalt is mixed with the bitumen in a melted state along with clean gravel, and consistency is given to pour it into moulds. Sulphur added to about 1 per cent. makes it very brittle. The asphalt is ductile, and has elasticity to enable it, with the small stones sifted upon it, to resist ordinary wear. Walls having cracked, and parts having fallen, the asphalt has been seen to stretch and not crack. It has been regarded as a sort of mineral leather. The sun and rain do not appear to affect it; and it answers for *abattoirs* and barracks, keeps vermin down, and is uninjured by the kicking of horses.

ASPHALT OIL. An oil obtained from asphaltum by dry distillation.

ASPHALTUM. See ASPHALT.

ASPHALTUM, GAS-TAR, or ARTIFICIAL. When, with the thick pitchy residue, obtained by evaporating off the more volatile portions of gas-tar, sand, chalk or lime are mixed, it is called artificial asphaltum. The mineral substances are strongly heated to expel all moisture, and then added to the pitch while in the melted state. This is used for pavements, for lining tanks, &c.

ASPIRATOR. An apparatus used for drawing a stream of air through a tube or other vessel. There are several varieties used by chemists in the analyses of air. One or two only need be mentioned here.

Brumier's consists of two equal cylindrical vessels placed one above another and communicating by tubes, which can be opened or closed, so that when the water has run from the upper to the lower vessel, the apparatus, turning for the purpose on a horizontal axis, may be inverted, so as to repeat the process.

An aspirator devised some years ago by Mr. M. W. Johnson is of considerable interest, as the principle of its action has of late received extensive application in the construction of certain forms of exhausting apparatus. The arrangement of Johnson's aspirator will be readily understood from the accompanying figure (*fig.* 95). A tap in connection with a supply of water is fitted by means of a piece of india-rubber tubing to a small cylinder, A, opening below into a long straight glass tube, B, and communicating by means of a lateral branch, c, with the vessel through which the stream of air is to be drawn. On opening the tap, the water runs down the tubes A B, carrying with it air, which it sucks in through the branch-tube, c ; in this way a stream of air continues to flow in at c as long as water is allowed to run through A B. An aspirator of this form was fitted up by Mr. Johnson at the Royal College of Chemistry, and was described before the Chemical Society in 1852. ('Journ. Chem. Soc.' vol. iv. p. 186.)

Johnson's aspirator is similar in principle to the water-blowing machine known as the *trompe*, used with the old Catalan iron-furnaces, still working in the Pyrenees and other parts of Southern Europe. In the trompe, a cistern of water is connected with wooden pipes having small openings called *aspirateurs*, communicating with the external atmosphere. As the stream of water descends from the cistern

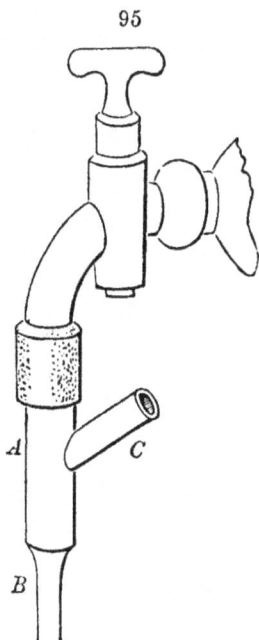

95

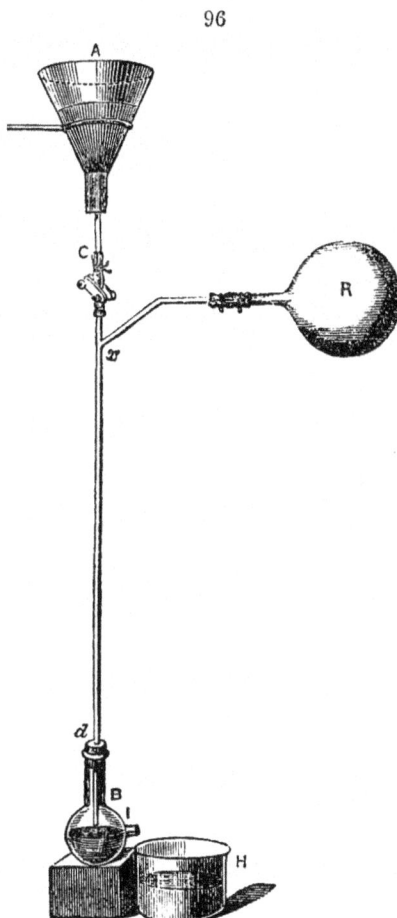

96

through the pipes, it draws down with it a current of air entering through these *aspirateurs*, and the mixed air and water passes into a vessel below, whence the water flows out through a special aperture, whilst the air passes to the tuyère.

On referring to the previous figure of Johnson's aspirator, it is clear that if the lateral tube, c, instead of being connected with an open tube through which air can be drawn, be connected with a closed receiver, the air will be gradually sucked out of this vessel by the descending current of water, and a vacuum, more or less perfect, may be thus obtained. This is, indeed. the principle of the admirable, though simple, exhausting apparatus introduced by Dr. Sprengel, in which a vacuum is obtained by the descent of a column of mercury. The mercury is placed in a large funnel, A (*fig.* 96), which communicates with a glass tube, c, d, longer than the tube of the mercurial barometer, and open at both ends. The receiver, R, to be exhausted, is connected with a lateral tube, opening into the main tube at x. On pressing a spring-clamp attached to the india-rubber connection below c, the mercury flows down the tube, c, d. As the lower end of this tube opens a little below the lateral spout of the bulb, B, the first portions of mercury hermetically seal this open end, and prevent any ingress of air. The descending column of mercury is broken up into detached cylinders separated by columns of air sucked in from the vessel R. The mercury and air pass out at the lateral aperture of the bulb B ; and to economize the mercury, it is from time to time poured back from the vessel H to the funnel A. As rarefaction proceeds, the quantity of air enclosed with the mercury becomes less and less, and as the exhaustion approaches completion the mercurial column is almost uninterrupted by any air. At this stage of the operation, the falling mercury makes the characteristic sound of a liquid moving in a vacuum, familiar in the common water-hammer. When the exhaustion is complete, about 30 inches of mercury will be supported in the tube, c, d, and the remaining part of the tube, together with the lateral branch x and receiver R, is in the condition of the Torricellian vacuum—that is to say, it is a space containing nothing but vapour of mercury at very low tension. By means of this mercurial pump a higher degree of rarefaction can be attained than with the ordinary air-pump. Dr. Sprengel found no difficulty, even with common cold mercury, in rarefying the air to one-millionth of its original density. The inventor recommends the use of an exhausting-syringe to remove the bulk of the air, employing the mercurial pump only as an auxiliary in completing the exhaustion. In practice, the Sprengel pump is not so simple in construction as that previously figured, but is furnished with certain accessory parts, which do not, however, affect the general principles of its action. Some improvements in the pump have been introduced by Prof. McLeod. (For Sprengel's original researches, see 'Journ. Chemical Soc.' 1865, p. 9 : for McLeod's improvements, see same journal, 1867, p. 307).

Dr. Sprengel, in explaining the action of his mercurial pump, says : 'My instrument is merely the reverse of the trompe, with this addition, that the supply of air is limited, while that of the trompe is unlimited.'

An important application of the principle of the Sprengel pump has been recently made by Professor Bunsen, in his new method of filtering. The operation of filtering is usually very tedious, and in many branches of manufacture a rapid method of filtration is highly desirable. Bunsen's great improvement consists in accelerating the operation by filtering into a flask from which the air has been partially withdrawn : the pressure of the atmosphere on the surface of the liquid in the filter forces the liquid through the pores of the paper, and the partial vacuum on the other side offers but little resistance to its passage. To effect the exhaustion, the vessel which receives the filtered solution is placed in connection with a water air-pump, that is, an apparatus on Sprengel's principle, but working with water instead of mercury. This water air-pump is recommended by Bunsen, not only for washing precipitates, but for crystallising substances from syrupy mother-liquors. Both the mercurial and water air-pumps may become of great use in the arts, where a ready and perfect means of exhaustion may be needed.

(For translation of Bunsen's paper on filtration with the filter-pump, see 'Philosophical Magazine,' Jan. 1869, p. 1.)

The following form of spirator, devised by Professor Guthrie, will be found useful in establishing a current of air for an indefinite length of time, by means of a continuous current of water. It may be employed either as aspirator in drawing, or as expirator in forcing air through an apparatus. Its action will be readily understood by referring to the accompanying diagram (*fig.* 97.).

A is a wide-mouthed 12-ounce bottle, whose bottom is covered with a few millimetres of mercury, m. Through its well-fitting cork, c, four holes are bored. Into the first of these, the wide tube open at both ends, g, is fitted, so that its lower end is a little above the mercury, m. The upper end of g is provided with a cork, through which the syphon-tube f passes. In the second hole of c the bent tube h is fixed, in such a manner that its lower end dips beneath the surface of the mercury, m. Through the third hole of the cork c, a straight tube, c, is passed, whose office is to convey water into the bottle, A ; the lower end of c is a little above the mercury, m. Through the fourth hole in c a narrow tube, e, is fastened, whose longer exterior limb dips under the surface of the mercury, *n*, in the tube B. B is a small test-tube, widened at the bottom in three directions, and containing a few millimetres in depth of mercury, *n*. It is fastened with sealing-wax to A, and is provided with a cork, the one orifice of which admits the tube *e*; through the other passes the bent tube *d*.

The lower extremity of the tube *f* being placed far down a sink, and a gradual stream of water being allowed to enter by *c*, as indicated by (1), the water in A rises (2), the air is driven out of A (3), bubbles through the mercury, *n*, and passes by *d* (4), through the apparatus employed. During this filling of A with water, the mercury, *m*, prevents the retrograde flux of water through *h*. After A is filled, the water

97

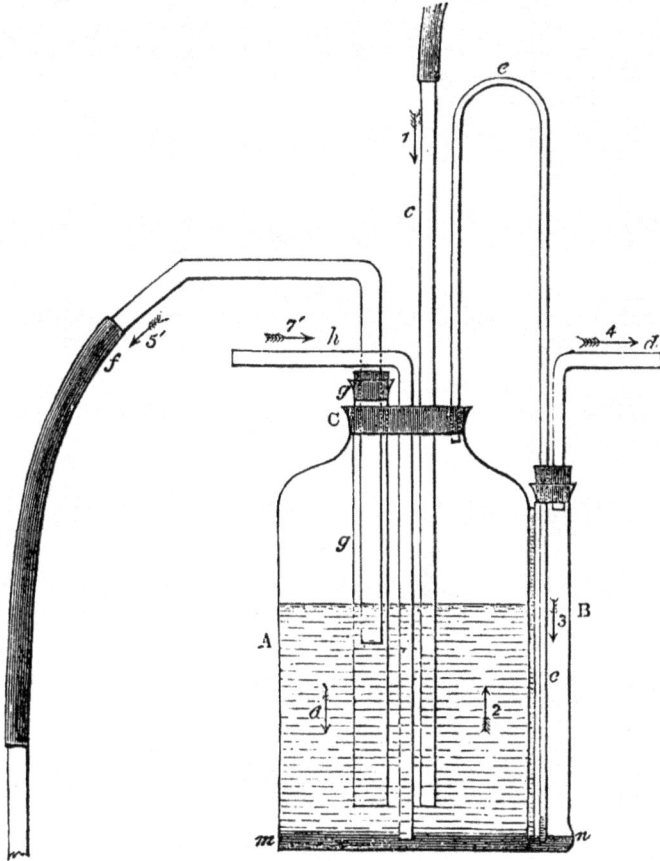

rises in the tubes *f* and *e* until it reaches the top of *f*, when this tube acts as a syphon (5'), and being wider than the ingress tube *c*, gradually empties the bottle A (6). To supply the place of this water, the air must enter by *h* (7'), and may thus be drawn through the apparatus in use, while the mercury *n*, in B, prevents the regression of the air through *e*.

The instrument has of course a simpler form when required to act only as an aspirator, for then the tube B and its appendages may be dispensed with.

When an increased resistance has to be overcome (the instrument being used either as aspirator or as expirator), the tube *f* is drawn further out of the tube *g*.

This form of spirator has been found to be certain in its action; for with a continuous stream of water, the volume of air which passes through is in definite proportion to the volume of water employed; and, indeed, the slower stream of water the more nearly equal are these volumes, for in this case the amount of water passing through *c* during the action of the syphon *f*, is inconsiderable.

ASSAFŒTIDA. (*Assus*, dried; *fœtidus*, fetid.) A fetid gum-resin obtained from the root of the *Narthex Assafœtida*, and probably from some other species belonging to the *Umbelliferæ*.

ASSAMAR. (*Assare*, to roast; *Amarus*, bitter.) A name given to the bitter substance produced when gum, sugar, starch, or bread are roasted until they turn brown. See CARAMEL.

ASSAY. (*Essai*, Fr., *Probe*, Ger.) **ASSAYING.** (*Docimasie*, Fr., *Probirkunst*, Ger.) Assaying is the art of estimating the proportion of metals in minerals, ores, metallurgical products, and various alloys used for monetary and other purposes. It is generally regarded as a branch of metallurgy, and should occupy an important place in metallurgical instruction. A knowledge of chemistry is essential to a correct understanding of the nature of the operations, and of the reactions which occur in the various assay-processes. To the practical metallurgist it is essential that the ores under treatment at smelting works should be submitted to assay, to afford a clear indication of the quantity of metal obtainable, and that the products of furnaces, &c., obtained at various stages of the operations should also be tested, so as to exercise a salutary control over the working of the various processes. To the miner, also, it is indispensable to have the various parcels of ore submitted to assay, to ascertain their economical value. Assaying may likewise be advantageously employed to test the working capabilities of dressing machinery, or to control the dressing processes. It is also of the utmost importance that the alloys employed for monetary and other purposes should be submitted to careful and exact assay, to ascertain that they are of the correct standard, and to prevent fraud. To the colonist and explorer, a knowledge of assaying would often prove of great service, in enabling them to ascertain the nature and economical value of metalliferous minerals, or ores which they may discover. Assaying has been practised for many generations; formerly the assays were made by the agency of fire, and were, more or less, but miniature smelting processes. Since the study of chemistry has advanced, and within comparatively recent times, other methods by the use of liquid reagents have been introduced. The various methods of assaying, exclusive of those made by the blowpipe, are, therefore, conveniently divided into (1) assays by the dry way, (2) assays by the wet way.

1. *Assays by the Dry Way.*—These assays are made by the agency of fire, by fusion of the ores or other substances, with or without the addition of appropriate fluxes and reagents in crucibles or other suitable vessels of iron, clay, or black-lead; the requisite temperature being obtained in an *air-furnace, muffle-furnace,* or small *blast-furnace.*

2. *Assays by the Wet Way.*—These assays are made by the agency of water, or liquid reagents.

1. By volumetric methods.
2. By analysis.
3. By mechanical means.

1. *The Volumetric Methods* of assay are of comparatively recent introduction. These assays are made by the use of *standard solutions* of known strength, supplied from graduated vessels, as *burettes, alkalimeters,* or *pipettes;* unfortunately only a few of the numerous volumetric methods which are known can be applied practically for the purposes of assaying, as they are not sufficiently reliable, consume too much time, or do not work with the requisite degree of accuracy.

2. *Analysis.*—The methods of assay by analysis are only used when other methods are not available, or in special cases.

3. *Mechanical Methods.*—These assays consist in the separation, by the agency of water, of the substances associated or occurring with metalliferous minerals and ores, and are performed by *hand-washing* on a *vanning-shovel,* or in a *washing-bowl* of wood or metal. A known quantity of the pulverised ore is put on a shovel, or in a bowl with water, and by certain rotary and other movements, to be acquired only by practice, the lighter substances are separated from those of greater specific gravity. The vanning-shovel is usually employed for tin ores, and the washing-bowl, or *tin dish,* for gold ores. Washing may also be practised to ascertain the nature and proportion of certain minerals, as galena, iron pyrites, &c. present in samples of ores. It may likewise be had recourse to for ascertaining the proportion of metallic grains present in slags or other furnace-products, and which may be afterwards extracted from them by stamping and washing on the large scale.

EXPLANATION OF TERMS USED IN ASSAYING (BY THE DRY METHOD).

Fusion.—Rendering fluid by the aid of heat. The term *fritting,* or semi-fusion, is applied to materials which have softened sufficiently by heat to become cemented together.

Reduction.—When a metal is separated from its compounds by another agent, it is said to be *reduced,* and the operation is called *reduction.* Thus the reduction of

ASSAY

263

galena occurs when it is heated with iron, the products being metallic lead and sulphide of iron; the iron in this instance is called the *reducing agent*. When a metallic oxide passes from a higher to a lower state of oxidation, it is also said to be reduced.

Calcination, Roasting.—When a powdered substance is exposed to the oxidising action of heat and air, in order to expel the sulphur, arsenic, carbonic acid, and other matters, the process is called roasting, or calcination. If it is continued until practically complete, it is said to be roasted *sweet* or *dead*. Accidental softening of the particles, so that they cohere, is called *clotting*.

Scorification.—A roasting-fusion process, employed in assaying silver ores.

Cupellation.—An oxidising-fusion process conducted on a porous vessel called a cupel, used in silver assaying.

Distillation.—When a metal is volatilised by heat, and afterwards condensed in the liquid form, the process is called *distillation*. The term *sublimation* is applied when condensation occurs in the solid state.

Liquation.—When an ore or other substance, part of which is fusible and the other infusible, or fusible at a higher temperature, is exposed to a temperature sufficient to melt one portion and not the other, the fused product is said to be *liquated*, and the operation is named *liquation*. For example, when sulphide of antimony is liquated out from associated vein-stuff.

Flux.—The substance which is added to another to render it fusible by the application of heat, is called a flux. Thus protoxide of lead or litharge is a flux for silica, the melted product being silicate of protoxide of lead.

Slag.—The product resulting from the fusion of an ore or other substance, which floats on the top of the metal, regulus, or speiss. Those obtained in assay processes are very variable in composition, such as silicates, boro-silicates, metallic alkaline sulphides, metallic oxides, fluo-silicates, &c.

Regulus.—A compound of one or more metals with sulphur.

Speiss.—A compound of one or more metals with arsenic.

Button of Metal.—The metal, or alloy, the result of assay, which is found at the bottom of the crucible or ingot mould, after cooling. The small more or less rounded metallic particles are called *shots*, or *globules*, or *pills*.

For an explanation of the terms used in the wet way, such as *filtration, precipitation*, &c., the reader is referred to works on chemical analysis.

Furnaces, Implements, Apparatus, &c. used in Assaying.

Furnaces.—They are of three kinds. For a description of an *air-furnace*, see Copper; of a *cupellation furnace*, see Silver; of a *small blast-furnace*, see Iron.

Crucibles.—Open-mouthed vessels of clay, iron, or black-lead. Clay crucibles should be well dried before use. When a crucible is charged with the assay mixture, it should not be more than from ½ to ⅔rds full. The following may be noticed:—

Cornish Crucibles.—These crucibles are the best for general assay purposes, as they withstand great and sudden alternations of temperature without cracking. They also resist fairly the corrosive action of fluxes, and although they soften when exposed to extreme temperatures, yet iron assays can be made in them, provided the precaution be taken of lowering the temperature somewhat, so that they become firm before removal from the furnace. They are greyish-white, coarse in grain, and composed chiefly of silica. They are generally sold in nests of two, and sometimes three, each as used by copper assayers. The larger size are 3 inches diameter at top, and 3½ inches high, outside measure. They may now be obtained of various shapes and sizes.

Hessian Crucibles.—These crucibles, when genuine, have nearly the same qualities as Cornish pots, to which they approximate in composition. They are reddish-brown in colour, generally triangular at the top, and are sold in nests of six crucibles, which fit successively into each other.

London Crucibles.—These pots vary somewhat in shape and quality. They are light reddish-brown in colour, close in grain, and have a smooth surface. They resist the corrosive action of litharge and fluxes very well, but require care in using to prevent cracking. They resist high temperatures well enough to be employed in assaying iron ores. Crucibles known as 'skittle pots,' and made of the same materials as London crucibles, are still used by some assayers. They are deep, drawn in towards the top, to allow of plenty of room for effervescence during fusion, especially when undried materials are used.

French Crucibles.—These crucibles have a greyish-white or cream colour, are thin, firm, very perfect in form, and smooth externally. They withstand the highest temperature of ordinary furnaces, and resist well the action of fluxes. They are more expensive than other varieties of clay crucibles. The so-called *white fluxing pots* made in London of French fire-clay have the same shape, but are rather thicker than the true French crucibles. They also answer very well for assay purposes.

Black-lead, or Plumbago Crucibles.—These pots are made of a mixture of plumbago and fire-clay. The best varieties withstand sudden alternations of temperatures; resist the highest temperatures without softening or cracking, but they slowly burn away externally by repeated use. They are employed in iron and tin assaying.

Iron Crucibles.—Wrought-iron pots of various sizes and shapes are used in lead assaying. Those made out of one piece of iron, without a weld, are preferable; but they cost more than those made from boiler-plate, or iron-tubing by hammering and welding.

Porcelain Crucibles.—These crucibles are made of various sizes and shapes. They are chiefly used in assays by analysis.

Roasting Dishes.—Flat, shallow, thin circular vessels of fire-clay of various sizes, used for the calcination of ores, &c., in muffles. The most useful sizes vary from 2 to 3 inches in diameter, and from $\frac{3}{4}$ to $\frac{7}{8}$ of an inch in depth, inside measure.

Scorifiers.—Cup-shaped vessels of fire-clay used in assaying silver ores; they should withstand sudden alternations of temperature, and resist the corrosive action of litharge and metallic oxides. Those commonly used are from $1\frac{3}{4}$ to $2\frac{1}{4}$ inches diameter at top, and from $\frac{6}{8}$ to $\frac{7}{8}$ of an inch in depth, inside measure.

Cupels.—Small circular vessels, having a shallow hemispherical cavity. They are generally made of bone-ash, or other material which is porous, and resists the corrosive action of litharge at the required temperature. They vary from $\frac{1}{2}$ inch to 2 inches in diameter, according to circumstances.

Tongs, Scoops, Stirring Rods, Ingot Moulds, &c.—For a description of these implements, see the assays of the various metals.

Balances.—For general assay purposes, three kinds of balances will suffice. (1.) To carry 500 grains, and turn with $\frac{1}{1000}$th of a grain: this may be used for gold and silver assays, and for all purposes of exact weighing. (2.) To carry 1000 grains, and turn with from $\frac{1}{10}$th to $\frac{1}{20}$th of a grain. This will be found suitable for the dry assay of copper, tin, lead, &c. (3.) To carry 10,000 grains, and turn with $\frac{1}{10}$th to $\frac{5}{10}$th of a grain. Used for weighing out fluxes and other substances. In special branches of assaying, where a large number of assays of the same kind have to be made, it is desirable to have balances constructed suitable for that specific work.

Weights.—For general assay purposes the grain weights divided on the decimal system are most convenient. Special weights are used by tin assayers, copper assayers, bullion assayers, and others, to facilitate calculation. These will be noticed under the respective metals when necessary.

Burettes, pipettes, and any special apparatus employed in wet assays, or otherwise, will be described under the assays of the several metals, when necessary.

FLUXES, REAGENTS, AND OTHER SUBSTANCES USED IN ASSAYING.

They should be kept in covered earthenware jars, or in a covered long rectangular wooden box divided into compartments; all fluxes, when practicable, should be used in the dry state. Those employed in the dry way may be classified as follows:—

FLUXES. *Carbonate of Soda, dried.*—Crystallised carbonate of soda contains about 63 per cent. of water, which it loses on heating. Bicarbonate of soda is a convenient substitute. Carbonate of potash may also be used instead. The alkaline carbonates form fusible compounds with silica, &c.

Borax or *Biborate of Soda, dried or calcined.*—Crystallised borax contains about 47 per cent. of water; when heated it loses this water, and swells up to a very light bulky mass, which is dried or *calcined* borax. If the temperature is increased, it melts into a clear, colourless liquid, which on cooling constitutes *glass of borax*. It forms fusible compounds with earthy and metallic oxides, as lime, oxide of iron, &c.

Glass.—White glass, free from oxide of lead, such as plate-glass or window-glass, is suitable for some purposes. Green bottle-glass may also be used where the presence of oxide of iron is not objectionable. It serves to increase the fusibility of earthy silicates, &c., and in some cases as a substitute for borax.

Silica.—White sand, or powdered quartz; it serves as a flux for oxides of iron, lime, &c.

Fluor Spar, Fluor, or *Fluoride of Calcium.*—It should be selected free from galena, copper pyrites, and other minerals. It forms very fusible compounds with sulphate of baryta, sulphate of lime, phosphate of lime, silica, &c.

China Clay, Kaolin, or *Hydrated Silicate of Alumina.*—When pure it contains about 12 per cent. of water. It can be deprived of this water by heating the powdered clay to a strong red heat. Fire-clays and shale are sometimes used as substitutes for china clay.

Lime.—Unslaked lime is preferable. It forms fusible compounds with silica, silicates of alumina, &c.

Litharge, or *Protoxide of Lead.*—It forms fusible compounds with silica, and earthy and metallic oxides, &c. Red lead, or white lead, or carbonate of lead may also be employed.

Oxides of Iron.—Hæmatite, or iron-scale, may be used as a flux, for silica, and difficultly fusible silicates, &c.

Black Flux may be practically regarded as a mixture of carbonate of potash and charcoal. It is prepared as follows : 1 part of nitre, and from 2 to 3 parts of tartar, by weight, are mixed, and deflagrated by stirring with a hot iron rod until action ceases, or by projecting portions of the mixture from time to time into a hot crucible. The product is reduced to powder and kept in a closely covered jar, as it is liable to absorb moisture rapidly. The quantity of carbon in the product varies with the proportion and purity of the tartar, or argol, employed. Very convenient substitutes are now used by mixing carbonate of soda with from 5 to 10 per cent. of charcoal powder, or with larger proportions of tartar, starch, or flour.

White Flux is essentially carbonate of potash. It is prepared in the same way as black flux, by deflagrating a mixture of equal parts by weight of nitre and tartar. The nitric acid of the nitre converts the carbon of the tartaric acid in the so-called bi-tartrate of potash into carbonic acid, which combines with the alkali, and carbonate of potash is formed.

Refining Flux is a variety of white flux, generally made in a similar manner, with salt intermixed. It is used by copper-assayers for refining impure copper.

REDUCING AGENTS. *Charcoal Powder.*—Coke dust, and culm or anthracite powder, are also used for some purposes, as they burn away less rapidly than charcoal powder.

Tartar.—Cream of tartar, known in the crude state as *red argol* and *white argol,* and when purified, as bitartrate of potash. Starch and flour form convenient substitutes.

Cyanide of Potassium.—Two varieties are used, one known as *gold cyanide,* and the other *common,* which contains a large amount of carbonate of potash. As cyanide of potassium has little fluxing power, for some purposes the latter variety is preferable, as the carbonate of potash forms fusible compounds with silica, &c.

Iron.—Wrought-iron in the form of iron nails, iron rod, or hoop-iron.

OXIDISING AGENTS. *Atmospheric Air.*—This is the chief agent which acts in roasting processes, in removing sulphur, as sulphurous acid, &c.

Nitre, or *Nitrate of Potash.*—It is an anhydrous salt, and acts as a powerful oxidising agent, on account of the large proportion of oxygen which it contains. Nitrate of soda may also be used.

Litharge. Red Lead.—These are also used for oxidising sulphur, &c.

Salt, or *Chloride of Sodium.*—It acts as an oxidising agent upon metallic copper. By some assayers it is used in nearly every dry assay process, to top-up with, or cover the other ingredients. On account of its easy fusibility and comparatively low specific gravity, it floats on the top of the products of fusion, and allays effervescence or ebullition when fused. It also acts as a lubricator to the interior of the crucibles, and enables the particles of matter to run down more freely. However, it can readily be dispensed with, and as in most cases its use injuriously affects the result of the assay methods, it is not advisable to employ it.

SULPHURISING AGENTS, used for forming metallic sulphides, or regulus. *Sulphur.*—Flowers of sulphur or powdered brimstone may be used.

Iron Pyrites.—For some purposes it should be selected free from copper.

Sulphide of Iron.—Made by heating iron and sulphur together, or by fusing iron pyrites with hoop-iron.

DESULPHURISING AGENTS, used for the removal of sulphur by forming other sulphides, or by oxidation into sulphurous acid. *Iron.*—Hoop-iron, thin bar-iron, iron rod, or nails, may be used.

Cyanide of Potassium.

Carbonate of Soda, dried, or bicarbonate of soda.

Litharge or *Red Lead.*

ARSENICISING AGENTS, used for forming metallic arsenides or speiss. *Arsenic,* metallic.

Arsenious Acid, in admixture with carbon.

DEARSENICISING AGENTS, used for the removal of arsenic as a speiss, or by oxidation. *Iron,* hoop-iron, &c.

Atmospheric Air, in roasting.

Nitre, by conversion into arsenate of potash.

COLLECTING AGENTS, used for collecting or dissolving gold and silver in an assay. *Lead*, granulated.

Litharge, or galena, which yields lead when heated with carbon or iron respectively. *Mercury.*

REAGENTS, &C., EMPLOYED IN THE WET WAY.

SOLVENTS, or agents used in dissolving various substances.—*Nitric Acid. Hydrochloric Acid. Sulphuric Acid.*

REDUCING AGENTS, or substances used to reduce a metallic compound in solution to a lower state of combination. *Zinc*, granulated.—That in the form of *bean shot*, obtained by pouring the metal into hot water, is preferable.

Sulphite of Soda. Protochloride of Tin.

METALLIC PRECIPITANTS. *Zinc*, in form of sheet. *Iron.*—Wrought-iron, in form of thin clean sheet, or round or flat bar. *Protochloride of Tin.*

SPECIAL REAGENTS, as permanganate of potash, sulphide of sodium, iodide of potassium, &c., will be noticed when necessary.

For the methods of assaying the various metals, see COPPER, LEAD, GOLD, &c.—R.S.

ASTERIA. (*Starstone*). The name first used by Pliny to denote those varieties of sapphire which display diverging rays of light.

ASTRAGAL. An ornamental moulding, generally used to conceal a junction in either wood or stone.

ASTRAGAL PLANES. Planes fitted with cutters for forming astragal mouldings. They are commonly known as moulding-planes.

98

ASTRAGAL TOOL, for turning. By using a tool shaped as in *fig.* 98, the process of forming a moulding or ring is greatly facilitated, as one member of the moulding is completed at one sweep, and we are enabled to repeat it any number of times with exact uniformity.

ASTRALITE. A glass resembling AVENTURINE, but containing crystals of a compound of copper, which by reflected light exhibit a dichroic iridescence of dark red and greenish-blue. It is said to be made with 80 parts of flint, 120 parts of oxide of lead, 72 parts of carbonate of soda, and 18 parts of anhydrous borax. To this are added 24 parts of scale oxide of copper, and 1 part of scale oxide of iron. These are melted in a Hessian crucible, at the heat of an ordinary air-furnace, and left to cool slowly without being moved.

ATACAMITE. A native oxychloride of copper, originally found in the desert of Atacama in Peru. It forms small rhombic crystals, varying in colour from leek to emerald green. Splendid examples of this mineral have been found at Wallaroo, on Yorke Peninsula, and at Burra Burra, in South Australia.

ATHERINA. See SARDINE.

ATMOMETER. (ἀτμὸς, *vapour*; μέτρον, *a measure*.) An instrument to measure the quantity of water evaporated in a given time under ordinary atmospheric conditions.

ATMOSPHERE. The gaseous envelope surrounding this globe. The term is also applied to any gaseous body enveloping any mass of matter.

The extent of the earth's atmosphere has not been determined with any great degree of accuracy. The height of the air above the surface of the earth should vary with the increase of the attractive force at the poles, and its diminution at the equator, and the variations of temperature also affect the mass, but, owing to the influence of centrifugal force, the spheroidal mass of air has a diameter shorter at the poles than at the equator. The volume which a given quantity of air occupies is directly dependent upon the pressure to which it is subjected—and upon the temperature—so that the density diminishes as the distance from the earth's surface increases.

All the influences having been carefully examined and allowed for, calculations have been made which appear to show that the atmosphere reaches, in a state of density, which can be measured, to the height of about 45 miles. It may be assumed that in a state of continually increasing tenuity, it extends to a considerably greater distance from the earth's surface.

The composition of the air has been determined under a considerable number of conditions, the mean result being to show that it is a chemical mixture of about 20 volumes of oxygen and 80 volumes of nitrogen (see Watts's 'Dictionary of Chemistry' for a full account of the chemical examinations of the air.) Carbonic acid exists in the atmosphere in variable proportions; the mean average being about 4 volumes of carbonic acid in 10,000 of air. Ammonia and all the exhalations from the earth exist as mixtures in the air, and on the presence or absence of these depends its healthfulness or otherwise.

The following remarks are from 'Travels in the Air,' by Mr. James Glaisher, F. R. S., and as giving the results of his practical experience and careful observations made during the numerous balloon ascents by that gentleman, they have considerable value :—

'Every one knows that *the pressure of the atmosphere* is measured by means of the barometer. A column of air extending to its limit, of the same area as the barometer tube, is balanced by the column of mercury in the tube; and if we weigh the mercury, we know the weight or pressure of the column of atmosphere upon that area. If the area of the barometer tube be one square inch, then this would tell us the pressure of the atmosphere on one square inch. The length of a column of mercury thus balanced by the atmosphere, near the level of the sea, is usually about 30 inches, and if this be weighed, it will be found to be nearly 15 lbs.; therefore the atmospheric pressure on every square inch of surface is about 15 lbs., just one-half as many pounds as the number of inches which expresses the height of the column of mercury.

'Now, in ascending into the air, part of the atmosphere is below, and part above: the barometer, therefore, has to balance that which is above only, and will, therefore, read less.

'At the height of three miles and three-quarters, the barometer will read about 15 inches; there is, therefore, as much atmosphere above this point as there is below, and the pressure on a square inch is 7½ lbs.

'At a height of between five and six miles from the earth, the barometer-reading will be about ten inches; one-third of the whole atmosphere is then above and two-thirds beneath, and the pressure of a square inch is reduced to 5 lbs.

'The reading of the barometer varies with the altitude at which it is observed, and indicates, by its increasing or decreasing readings, corresponding changes in the pressure of the atmosphere.

'At the height of 1 mile the barometer reading is 24·7 inches.

,,	,,	2	miles	,,	20·3 ,,
,,	,,	3	,,	,,	16·7 ,,
,,	,,	4	,,	,,	13·7 ,,
,,	,,	5	,,	,,	11·3 ,,
,,	,,	10	,,	,,	4·2 ,,
,,	,,	15	,,	,,	1·6 ,,
,,	,,	20	,,	,,	1·0 less.

'By the reading of the barometer in the balloon, the distance from the earth is known; and if the balloon be situated above clouds, or in a fog, the reading of the barometer indicates the near approach of the earth, and acts as a warning to the occupants of the car to prepare accordingly. In addition to this temporary use, the readings combined with those of temperature enable us to calculate the height of the balloon at every instant at which such readings have been taken.

'*The temperature of the dew-point* also deserves a few explanatory words.

'There is always mixed with the air a certain quantity of water, in the invisible shape of vapour, sometimes more, sometimes less, but there is a definite amount which saturates the air at every temperature, though this amount varies considerably with different temperatures.

'A cubic foot of air at the temperature of—

30° is saturated with 2 grains of vapour of water.
49°	,,	,,	4	,,	,,
70°	,,	,,	8	,,	,,
92½°	,,	,,	16	,,	,,

'The capacity of air for moisture, therefore, doubles for every increase of temperature of about 20 degrees. The temperature of the dew-point is the temperature to which air must be reduced in order to become saturated by the water then mixed with it; or it is that temperature to which any substance, such as the bright bulb of a hygrometer, must be reduced before any of the aqueous vapour present will be deposited as water, and become visible as dew. The temperature at which this first bedewing or dulling of bright surfaces takes place is the temperature of the dew-point.

For instance, I have already said that two grains of water saturate a cubic foot of air at 30°; if, therefore, the temperature of the air be 40°, and there be two grains of moisture in a cubic foot of air, then if the bulb of the hygrometer be reduced to 30°, a ring of dew will appear on it, caused by the deposition of the water in the air. The determination of the dew-point at once tells us, therefore, the amount of water present, and, combined with the temperature, enables us to determine the hygrometrical state of the atmosphere.

'If the air be saturated with moisture, the temperature of the air and that of the dew-point are alike; if it be not saturated, the temperature of the dew-point is lower than that of the atmosphere; if there be a great difference between the two temperatures, the air is dry, and if this happen when the temperature is low, there is very little water present in the air. By the careful simultaneous readings of two thermometers, one with a moistened bulb, and the other dry, or by the use of a Daniell's or Regnault's hygrometer, the amount of water present in the air in the invisible shape of vapour can be determined, as well as the temperature of the dew-point and the degree of humidity.

' *The degree of humidity of the air* expresses the ratio between the amount of water then mixed with it, and the greatest amount it could hold in solution at its then temperature, upon the supposition that the saturated air is represented by 100, and the air deprived of all moisture by 0. Thus: Suppose the water present to be one-half of the quantity that could be present, the degree of humidity in this case will be 50. If the air were at the temperature of 30°, and there were two grains of moisture in the air, it would be saturated, and the degree of humidity would be 100. If there were one grain, that is, one-half of the whole quantity that could be present, the air would be one-half saturated, and the degree of humidity would be represented by 50.

'At 49°   with   4 grains of moisture
   70°   „   8   „   „ } The air is saturated and the degree of humidity is 100.
   92½   „   16   „   „

'But at 49°   with 2 grains of moisture
  „   70°   „   4   „   „ } The air is one-half saturated, and the degree of humidity is 50.'
  „   92½°   „   8   „   „

ATOM. (ά, *not*; τέμνω, *I cut.*) An indivisible particle.

With few exceptions, the views promulgated by Dr. Dalton are received by chemists. They may be thus expressed: All elementary bodies are formed of individual atoms, the different species of which unite, generally by twos, in a small number of groups, constituting compound atoms of the first order, always mechanically indivisible, but chemically divisible, and, in their turn, constituting all the other orders of composition by a series of analogous combinations.

We are not enabled by direct experiment to determine the condition of any ultimate atom of matter; but the results furnished by chemical science clearly point to the existence of elementary units, from which all the infinite varieties of matter are formed. Sir Isaac Newton thus expresses himself :—' All things considered, it seems probable that God, in the beginning, formed matter in solid, massy, hard, impenetrable, movable particles, of such sizes, figures, and with such other properties, and in such proportions to space, as most conduced to the end for which He formed them ; and that these primitive particles, being solids, are incomparably harder than any porous bodies compounded of them ; even so hard as never to wear or break to pieces ; no ordinary power being able to divide what God Himself made one in the first creation. While the particles continue entire, they may compose bodies of one and the same nature and texture in all ages ; but should they wear away, or break in pieces, the nature of things depending on them would be changed. Water and earth composed of old worn particles would not be of the same nature and texture now with water and earth composed of entire particles at the beginning. And therefore, that nature may be lasting, the changes of corporeal things are to be placed only in various separations, and new associations, and motions of these permanent particles ; compound bodies being apt to break, not in the midst of solid particles, but where those particles are laid together and touch in a few points.'—*Horsley's Newton.*

With the metaphysical theories, which would lead us to regard all matter as mere accumulations of force, it would not be proper at present to deal.

Experimental philosophy has proved to us that the conditions of matter are determined by certain *polar-attractive* forces ; and that these are opposed or balanced by *heat, electricity,* and the force which regulates chemical combination. Consequently, every ultimate atom of matter may be regarded as the centre of such a set of physical forces surrounding it as an atmosphere.

In modern chemistry an *atom* is defined to be the smallest particle of any element which can exist in combination. The atom is thus distinguished from the *molecule*, the latter term being now applied to the smallest quantity of the substance capable of existing in a free state. The molecule and the atom may coincide, or the molecule may be made up of two or more atoms. Thus, an *atom* of chlorine, or 35·5 parts by weight, is represented by the symbol Cl, since this denotes the smallest quantity of chlorine capable of existing in any of its compounds—hydrochloric acid (HCl) for example; while the *molecule* of chlorine, or smallest quantity set free in any reaction, will be represented by two atoms, or Cl^2.

ATOMICITY, or EQUIVALENCE. Terms employed by modern chemical writers to denote the combining capacity of an element, or a radical, as determined by the number of atoms of hydrogen, or other monatomic element, with which it can combine. Thus chlorine, oxygen, boron, carbon, and phosphorus (using the atomic weights, $Cl = 35·5, O = 16, B = 11, C = 12$, and $P = 31$) may be said to be respectively monatomic, diatomic, triatomic, tetratomic, and pentatomic elements; or, to use equivalent expressions, they may be described as univalent, bivalent, tervalent, quadrivalent, and quinquivalent: in other words, the elements just cited may be termed respectively a monad, diad, triad, tetrad, and pentad. The atomicity, or equivalence, is often indicated by dashes or by Roman numerals, placed at the upper right-hand side of the symbol; thus, B''' indicates the triad boron, P^v the pentad phosphorus, and so forth. It should be remembered, however, that mineralogists were formerly in the habit of employing dashes in this way to represent so many atoms of sulphur, just as they used, and still use, dots placed above a symbol to denote so many atoms of oxygen. Hence, to a mineralogical reader, such expressions have now become ambiguous; Sb''', for instance, may either represent tersulphide of antimony, or merely indicate that the metal antimony is a triad.

Elements of *equal* atomicity are termed *artiads*; and those of *unequal* atomicity *perissads*. For a full discussion of the modern doctrine of atomicity, see Watts's 'Dictionary of Chemistry,' and the supplementary volume.

ATOMIC THEORY. The question as to whether matter be or be not infinitely divisible, has been debated from the earliest times, and is probably as far from a settlement as ever; we can, however, scarcely conceive of the existence of matter at all, if there be no limit to its divisibility. It is easy to demonstrate that a mathematical line is infinitely divisible, but a mathematical line is only an ideal thing; having only one dimension, it can have no physical existence. We have, therefore, no hesitation in admitting the existence of atoms of matter—of particles infinitely small, it is true, as regards our perceptions, far exceeding in minuteness the finest subdivision to which we can submit a body, but yet incapable of further subdivision. To such insectible molecules the term *atom* has been applied.

If we take any substance chemically complex, we may suppose the existence of atoms in this body, held together by the force of cohesion, which are themselves heterogeneous, being made up, in fact, of atoms of the elementary chemical constituents.

Dr. Dalton suggested the happy idea, which has been most fruitful in its results, of accounting for the constancy of chemical combinations by assuming that they were composed of one or more atoms of the several elements, the weight of which atoms is represented by the combining proportions; that carbonic oxide, for instance, contains single atoms of carbon and oxygen, whilst carbonic acid is composed of one atom of carbon and two of oxygen.

It must always be remembered that the combining proportions are purely the results of experiment, and, therefore, incontestable, whatever may be the fate of this theory, which, however, has now stood its ground for many years, and done excellent service to science.

This theory offers a most satisfactory explanation of the different laws of chemical combination.

The fact of bodies uniting only in certain proportions, or multiples of those proportions, is a necessary consequence of the assumption that the weight of the elementary atoms is represented by the combining proportions; for, if they united in any other ratio, it would involve the splitting up of these atoms, which are assumed to be indivisible.

And, of course, the combining proportion of a compound must be the sum of the combining proportions of the constituents, since it contains within itself one or more atoms of the several constituents.

The term atom is, therefore, very often used instead of combining proportion, a body being said to contain so many atoms of its elements.

All that is assumed in this theory is, that the atoms are of constant value *by weight ;* the same atoms may be arranged in a different way, and hence, although any particular compound contains always the same elements in the atomic ratios, yet the same atoms may, by difference in arrangement, give rise to bodies agreeing in composition by weight, but differing essentially in properties. See ISOMERISM.

The atomic theory is further confirmed by the observation, that if the specific heat of the elements be compared, it is found that in a large number of cases the specific heats of quantities of the bodies represented by their atomic weights coincide with each other in a remarkable manner.

For a full examination of this subject, consult 'An Introduction to the Atomic Theory,' by Charles Daubeny, M.D.; and 'Memoirs of John Dalton and History of the Atomic Theory,' by Robert Angus Smith, Ph. D.[1]

ATOMIC VOLUMES. Of late years it has been assumed that the elements, when in the gaseous state, unite invariably in equal volumes, or, in other words, that the atoms of bodies have always the same volume. If this doctrine be maintained, it becomes necessary to alter the atomic weights or combining numbers of certain elements. For example, water contains two volumes of hydrogen to one of oxygen; but, according to the old idea, it consists of single atoms of each element; it is clear, therefore, that if we are to assume that the atoms of hydrogen and oxygen have the same volume, we must either halve the atomic weight of hydrogen or double that of oxygen.

Berzelius suggested that all the atomic weights should remain the same, except those of hydrogen, nitrogen, phosphorus, chlorine, bromine, and iodine, which should halve their present values. Gerhardt, on the other hand, adopted the more convenient practice of allowing hydrogen and its congeners to retain their present atomic weights, doubling those of oxygen, sulphur, tellurium, and carbon. This practice has of late years been extended to many other elements. See ATOMIC WEIGHTS, and Watts's 'Dictionary of Chemistry.'

ATOMIC WEIGHTS, COMBINING WEIGHTS or PROPORTIONS. The atomic weights of the elements represent the proportions in which they severally combine with each other, referred to some standard element as unity. In accordance with Dalton's atomic theory, explained in a previous article, it is supposed that the numbers assigned to the elements as their respective combining proportions represent the relative weights of their atoms, and hence the adoption of the term *atomic weight* —a term extremely convenient to retain whatever views may be held as to the ultimate constitution of matter. By Berzelius, oxygen was selected as the standard to which all atomic weights were referred, but it is now almost universal among chemists to take hydrogen as the standard of comparison, since it is found that of all the elements hydrogen has the smallest combining number. It was believed by Prout that the atomic weights of all substances were multiples of the atomic weight of hydrogen, but it has been shown by Stas—who has made the most refined experiments on this subject—that the theory is only approximately true.

In establishing the atomic weights, or proportional numbers, of the elements, it is not only necessary to determine exactly the ratios in which they severally combine—which is merely a matter of accurate experiment—but also to interpret these ratios by the light derived from an extensive range of physical and chemical phenomena—such as isomorphism, specific heat, combining volume of vapour, and the like. Hence, as science has advanced, the necessity has been recognised by most chemists, of altering the numbers assigned to certain of the elements as their atomic weights, and, in fact, within the last few years many of these numbers have been doubled. It has, however, been considered, in the preparation of the new edition of this Dictionary, that the convenience of manufacturers and others accustomed to the use of the old atomic weights would be best served by retaining these familiar figures; and hence in all cases throughout this work, unless otherwise stated, the formulæ are

---

[1] Dr. Angus Smith, in his 'Memoirs of Dalton,' thus sums up the labours of this deep thinker :— 'This Dalton did. He gave the first idea of *atomic weights.* Under this head came Richter and Fischer's numbers. Richter, grappling with those numbers, never could obtain a rational theory from the phenomena. Dalton's plan explains these numbers with the greatest ease, and looks on such as a necessity of the fundamental law, instead of the beginning of the inquiry, as it was to them. It seems to me, then, that what happened historically happened also intellectually. Dalton had included his predecessors in his more extensive system. He had gone to the summit of the hill, and when coming down found proofs that they had been making good progress upwards. Higgins had gone at once to the top, as it appears to me, but took no heed to make the needful observations when he was up, or he found the prospect entirely obscured. We are compelled to put reciprocal proportions in a secondary position, as it seems to me it cannot be called a law, but one of the consequences of a law ; and the evidence brought to support it, otherwise than empirically, presupposes some of the principles on which the general laws depend. It was by a careful mechanical juxtaposition of parts that Dalton arrived at the idea ; it is eminently mechanical, and it is remarkable that all progressive views on the subject have been so. *He introduced proportional weights into the theory, and found it to agree with facts.* His is, therefore, the *quantitative atomic theory.*'

constructed with the old system of atomic weights. At the same time it appears desirable also to introduce the use of the modern atomic weights; and, therefore, in almost every chemical expression in this work both the old and the new formulæ are given—the latter being printed, for sake of distinction, in a thick black type.

In the following comparative Table the first column of figures gives (approximately) the old combining weights of the elements, whilst the second column gives the modern atomic weights, as employed by the most advanced chemists of the present day. A glance at this Table is therefore sufficient to show which of the elements have retained their old atomic weights, and which have had them doubled. Moreover, it is easy from these data to translate any of the formulæ on the old system into formulæ constructed with the recent values of the atomic weights. For example, in our article ALCOHOL, that compound is said to be composed of $C^4 H^6 O^2$; but reference to the Table shows the atomic weights of carbon and of oxygen have been doubled, whilst that of hydrogen remains unaltered. It is, therefore, obviously necessary to halve the number of atoms of carbon and of oxygen in the old formula, and consequently the symbolic expression for alcohol, instead of being $C^4 H^6 O^2$, becomes on the modern system $\mathbf{C^2 H^6 O}$.

Elements					Symbols	Old at. weights	New at. weights
Aluminium	.	.	.	.	Al	13·75	27·5
Antimony	.	.	.	.	Sb	122	122
Arsenic .	.	.	.	.	As	75	75
Barium .	.	.	.	.	Ba	68·5	137
Bismuth	.	.	.	.	Bi	210	210
Boron .	.	.	.	.	B	11	11
Bromine	.	.	.	.	Br	80	80
Cadmium	.	.	.	.	Cd	56	112
Cæsium .	.	.	.	.	Cs	133	133
Calcium .	.	.	.	.	Ca	20	40
Carbon .	.	.	.	.	C	6	12
Chlorine	.	.	.	.	Cl	35·5	35·5
Chromium	.	.	.	.	Cr	26·25	52·5
Cobalt .	.	.	.	.	Co	29·5	59
Copper .	.	.	.	.	Cu	31·75	63·5
Fluorine	.	.	.	.	F	19	19
Gold .	.	.	.	.	Au	98·5	197
Hydrogen	.	.	.	.	H	1	1
Indium .	.	.	.	.	In	76	76
Iodine .	.	.	.	.	I	127	127
Iridium .	.	.	.	.	Ir	98·5	197
Iron .	.	.	.	.	Fe	28	56
Lead .	.	.	.	.	Pb	103·5	207
Lithium	.	.	.	.	Li	7	7
Magnesium	.	.	.	.	Mg	12	24
Manganese	.	.	.	.	Mn	27·5	55
Mercury	.	.	.	.	Hg	100	200
Molybdenum	.	.	.	.	Mo	48	96
Nickel .	.	.	.	.	Ni	29·5	59
Nitrogen	.	.	.	.	N	14	14
Osmium	.	.	.	.	Os	99·5	199
Oxygen .	.	.	.	.	O	8	16
Palladium	.	.	.	.	Pd	53	106
Phosphorus	.	.	.	.	P	31	31
Platinum	.	.	.	.	Pt	98·5	197
Potassium	.	.	.	.	K	39	39
Rubidium	.	.	.	.	Rb	85	85
Selenium	.	.	.	.	Se	39·75	79·5
Silicon .	.	.	.	.	Si	21	28
Silver .	.	.	.	.	Ag	108	108
Sodium .	.	.	.	.	Na	23	23
Strontium	.	.	.	.	Sr	43·75	87·5
Sulphur .	.	.	.	.	S	16	32
Tellurium	.	.	.	.	Te	64·5	129
Thallium	.	.	.	.	Tl	204	204
Tin .	.	.	.	.	Sn	59	118

Elements	Symbols	Old at. weights	New at. weights
Titanium	Ti	25	50
Wolfram	W	92	184
Uranium	U	60	120
Vanadium	V	51	51
Zinc	Zn	32·5	65
Zirconium	Zr	44·5	89

The term 'atomic weight' was formerly employed as synonymous with 'chemical equivalent,' but the ideas involved in the two terms, as applied in modern chemistry, are essentially distinct.

Every chemical manufacturer should be thoroughly acquainted with the combining ratios, which are, for the same two substances, not only definite, but often multiple; two great truths, upon which are founded, not merely the *rationale* of his operations, but also the means of modifying them to useful purposes. The discussion of the doctrine of atomic weights belongs to pure chemistry; but several of its happiest applications are to be found in the processes of art, as pursued upon the largest scale.

The following propositions may be regarded as the laws regulating atomic combination :—

1. *The combining proportions of elementary bodies represent the smallest proportions in which they enter into combination with each other.*

2. *The combining proportion of a compound body is the sum of the combining proportions of its elements.*

3. *Combination takes place, whether between elements or compounds, either in the proportions of their combining weights, or in multiples of these proportions, and never in sub-multiples.*

4. *The law of definite proportion teaches that individual compounds always contain exactly the same proportions of their elements.* See EQUIVALENTS, CHEMICAL. See also Watts's 'Dictionary of Chemistry.'

ATRAMENTUM. An old name for iron-vitriol, or sulphate of iron. A product of the partial oxidation of iron pyrites, which is sometimes used in making ink.

ATROPINE, or **DATURINE.** $C^{34}H^{23}NO^6$. ($C^{17}H^{23}NO^3$). An exceedingly poisonous alkaloid, found in deadly nightshade (*Atropa Belladonna*) and in stramonium (*Datura Stramonium*), and probably in some other plants. One-sixth of a grain of atropine produces unconsciousness and delirium. To the freshly prepared extract of belladonna add a strong solution of caustic potash, and well mix in a mortar. Digest the resulting mass at a temperature of 80° with benzole; separate the latter, and distil off the hydrocarbon in a retort on the water-bath. The residue in the retort is to be treated with water acidulated with sulphuric acid; the acid solution is to be precipitated by carbonate of soda, and the resulting atropine may then be obtained pure by crystallisation from alcohol. Atropine is used in medicine, $\frac{1}{30}$th of a grain being a full dose, and it is applied externally for producing dilatation of the pupil of the eye. The smallest portion of a very dilute solution rubbed on the eyelid suffices to produce the result.

ATTALEA. *A. funifera* yields the coquilla nut much used in turnery. It was formerly supposed that this species of *Attalea* also yielded the Piassaba fibre used in Brazil for ropemaking, and in this country for the manufacture of bast-brooms, but it is now known that the Piassaba fibre is the produce of another palm—the *Leopoldina Piassaba*. See COQUILLA.

ATTAR OF ROSES, more commonly, **OTTO OF ROSES.** An essential oil, obtained in India, Turkey, and Persia, from some of the finest varieties of roses. It is procured by distilling rose-leaves with water, at as low a temperature as possible. It is said that this perfume is prepared also by exposing the rose-leaves in water to the sun; but, from the fact that under the circumstances fermentation would be speedily established, it is not probable that this is a method often resorted to. By dry distillation from salt-water baths, no doubt the finest attar is obtained. This essential oil is only used as a perfume. Attar of roses is adulterated with spermaceti and with castor-oil dissolved in strong alcohol.

This adulteration may be detected by putting a small drop of the otto of roses on a piece of clean writing-paper; by agitation in the air, the volatile oil soon evaporates, leaving no stain if pure; if any fixed oil is present, a greasy spot is left on the paper.

ATTEMPERATOR. In brewing, the name of several arrangements devised for the purpose of regulating the temperature to which the fermenting wort is exposed. It is also employed to regulate the temperature of malting-rooms. Without them it is impracticable to make malt in the summer equal to that made in winter. In all cases either air or water is the attemperating agent.

ATTENUATION. Brewers and distillers employ this term to signify the weakening of saccharine worts during fermentation, by the conversion of the sugar into alcohol and carbonic acid.

ATTLE. A miner's term for the 'deads' or refuse-matter of a mine. The 'attle-heap' is the mine-burrow or rubbish-heap.

AUGER. The auger is a tool for boring either wood or stone. The *single-lip auger* is forged as a half-round bar; it is then coiled into an open spiral, with the flat side outwards. The ordinary *screw auger* is forged; it is twisted red-hot; the end terminates in a worm, by which the auger is gradually drawn into the work as in the gimlet; and the two angles, or lips, are sharpened to cut at the extreme ends, and a little up the sides also. The *American screw auger* has a cylindrical shaft, around which is brazed a single fin or rib; the end is filed into a worm, as usual, and immediately behind the worm a small diametrical mortice is formed for the reception of a detached cutter, which exactly resembles the chisel-edge of the centre-bit. —*Holtzapffel.*

AUGITE. (αὐγή, *brilliancy.*) A sub-species of Pyroxene. The name is confined to the opaque and greenish-black varieties, common in basaltic, doleritic, and recent volcanic rocks, in which it forms an important constituent, but it is never found in granite. It has a base of magnesia, lime, protoxide of iron, and alumina. The term augite is often used by English geologists as synonymous with pyroxene. For the means of distinguishing between augite and hornblende—two minerals which often closely resemble each other—see HORNBLENDE.

AURATES. Crystalline compounds of the peroxide of gold.

AURIC ACID. (*Aurum*, gold.) A term sometimes used for the peroxide of gold.

AURIFEROUS. Containing gold, as 'auriferous quartz,' 'auriferous pyrites,' &c.

AURINE. A red colouring-matter obtained from phenol, or carbolic acid. It appears in commerce as a brittle resinous solid, having a beetle-green lustre, and yielding a red powder. See CARBOLIC ACID.

AURUM MUSIVUM or MOSAICUM. MOSAIC GOLD.—For the preparation of Mosaic gold the following process is recommended by Woolfe. An amalgam of 2 parts of tin and 1 part of mercury is prepared in a hot crucible, and triturated with 1 part of sal-ammoniac, and 1 part of flowers of sulphur; the mixture is sublimed in a glass flask upon the sand-bath. In breaking the flask after the operation, the sublimate is found to consist, superficially, of sal-ammoniac, then of a layer of cinnabar, and then of a layer of mosaic gold.

Bergmann mentions a native *aurum musivum* from Siberia, containing tin, sulphur, and a small proportion of copper. Dr. John Davy gave the composition as—tin, 100; sulphur, 56·25; and Berzelius, as tin, 100; sulphur, 52·3.

Mosaic gold is employed as a bronzing powder for plaster figures, and it is said to enter sometimes into the composition of artificial aventurine.

AUSTRALENE, or *Austraterebinthene.* A liquid hydrocarbon resembling terebinthine, obtained by neutralising English turpentine oil with an alkaline carbonate, and distilling the product.

AUTOGENOUS SOLDERING. A process of soldering by which metals are united, either by the ordinary solders or by lead, under the influence of a flame of hydrogen, or of a mixture of hydrogen and common air.

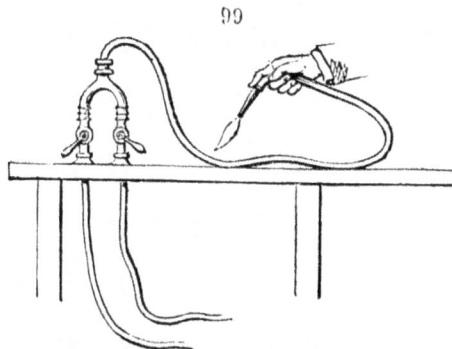

The process of using air and hydrogen was invented in France, by the Count de Richemont. Hydrogen gas is contained in a gasometer, to which a flexible tube is connected, and air is urged, from a bellows worked by the foot, through another tube, and on to the blowpipe, where the hydrogen is ignited. By means of the flexible tubes the flame can be moved up and down the line of any joint, and the connecting medium melted. *Fig.* 99.

This process has been a good deal employed for plumbers' work, especially in our naval arsenals. In Devonport dockyard, the autogenic process has been largely used.

AUTOMATIC. A term employed to designate such economic arts as are carried on by self-acting machinery. The word is employed by the physiologist to express involuntary motions.

The term *automatic* is now applied to self-acting machinery, or such as has within itself the power of regulating entirely its own movements, although the moving force is derived from without; and to what pertains to such machinery; as *automatic* operations or improvements.—*Webster*.

The word 'manufacture,' in its etymological sense, means any system or objects of industry executed by the hands; but, in the vicissitude of language, it has now come to signify every extensive product of art which is made by machinery, with little or no aid of the human hand, so that the most perfect manufacture is that which dispenses entirely with manual labour. It is in our modern cotton and flax mills that automatic operations are displayed to most advantage; for there the elemental power HEAT has been made to animate complex organs, imparting to forms of wood, iron, and brass, an agency of seeming intelligence. And as the philosophy of the fine arts, poetry, painting, and music, may be best studied in their individual master-pieces, so may the philosophy of manufactures in these its noblest creations.

The constant aim and effect of these automatic improvements in the arts are philanthropic, as they tend to relieve the workman either from niceties of adjustment, which exhaust his mind and fatigue his eyes, or from painful repetition of effort, which distort and wear out his frame. A well-arranged power-mill combines the operation of many work-people, adult and young, in tending with assiduous skill a system of productive machines continuously impelled by a central force. This great era in the useful arts is mainly due to the genius of Arkwright. Prior to the introduction of his system, manufactures were everywhere feeble and fluctuating in their development; shooting forth luxuriantly for a season, and again withering almost to the roots like annual plants. Their perennial growth then began, and attracted capital, in copious streams, to irrigate the rich domains of industry. When this new career commenced, about the year 1770, the annual consumption of cotton in British manufactures was under four millions of pounds' weight, and that of the whole of Christendom was probably not more than ten millions. In 1850 the consumption in Great Britain and Ireland had risen to five hundred and eighty-eight millions of pounds, and that of Europe and the United States together to one thousand and ninety-two millions. In our spacious factory apartments the benignant power of Steam summons around him his myriads of willing menials, and assigns to each the regulated task, substituting, for painful muscular effort upon their part, the energies of his own gigantic arm, and demanding in return only attention and dexterity to correct such little aberrations as casually occur in his workmanship. Under his auspices, and in obedience to Arkwright's policy, magnificent edifices, surpassing far in number, value, usefulness, and ingenuity of construction, the boasted monuments of Asiatic, Egyptian, and Roman despotism, have, within a short period, risen up in this kingdom, to show to what extent capital, industry and science may augment the resources of a State, while they ameliorate the condition of its citizens. Such is the automatic system, which promises, in its future growth, to become the great minister of civilisation to the terraqueous globe, enabling this country to diffuse, along with its commerce, the life-blood of knowledge to myriads of people.

AUTOMATIC ARTS. Such arts or manufactures as are carried on by self-acting machinery.

AUTOMATON. (αὐτόματος—automatos—*self-moving*.) In the etymological sense, this word (self-working) signifies every mechanical construction which, by virtue of a latent intrinsic force, not obvious to common eyes, can carry on, for some time, certain movements more or less resembling the results of animal exertion, without the aid of external impulse. But the term automaton is, in common language, appropriated to those mechanical artifices in which the purposely concealed power is made to imitate the arbitrary or voluntary motions of living beings. Human figures, of this kind, are sometimes styled *Androides*, from the Greek term, *like a man*.

Although, from what has been said, clockwork is not properly placed under the head Automaton, it cannot be doubted that the art of making clocks, in its progressive improvement and extension, has given rise to the production of automata. The most of these, in their interior structure, as well as in the mode of applying the moving power, have a distinct analogy with clocks; and these automata are frequently mounted in connection with watchwork. Towards the end of the 13th century, several tower clocks, such as those at Strasburg, Lübeck, Prague, and Olmütz, had curious mechanisms attached to them. The most careful historical inquiry proves that automata, properly speaking, are not older than *wheel*-clocks; and that the more perfect structures of this kind are subsequent to the general introduction of *spring*-clocks. Many accounts of ancient automata, such as the flying pigeon of Archytas of Tarentum, appear to have been but poor mechanical contrivances. 'The Pneumatics of Hero of Alexandria' have been rendered accessible to the English reader by the translation of Mr. Bennett Woodcroft. In this work will be found descriptions and drawings of several curious contrivances which must be included amongst automata. The following, amongst others, may be quoted:—

'An automaton which drinks at certain times only, on a liquid being presented to it.

'An automaton which may be made to drink at any time on a liquid being presented to it.

'An automaton which will drink any quantity which may be presented to it.

'An automaton, the head of which continues attached to the body after a knife has entered the head at one side, passed completely through it, and out at the other; which animal will drink immediately after the operation.'

Beckmann informs us, quoting from Plato, that Dædalus made statues which could not only walk, but which it was necessary to tie, in order that they might not move; and, on the authority of Aristotle, he speaks of a wooden Venus, and remarks, that the secret of its motion consisted in quicksilver having been poured into it.

The moving power of almost all automata is a wound-up steel spring; because, in comparison with other means of giving motion, it takes up the smallest room, is easiest concealed and set a-going. Weights are seldom employed, and only in a partial way. The employment of other moving powers is more limited; sometimes fine sand is made to fall on the circumference of a wheel, by which the rest of the mechanism is moved. For the same purpose water has been employed; and, when it is made to fall into an air-chamber, it causes sufficient wind to excite musical sounds in pipes. In particular cases quicksilver has been used, as, for example, in the Chinese tumblers, which is only a physical apparatus to illustrate the doctrine of the centre of gravity.

Fig. 100 exhibits the outlines of an automaton, representing a swan, with suitably combined movements. The mechanism may be described, for the sake of clearness of explanation, under distinct heads. The first relates to the motion of the whole figure. By means of this part it swims upon the water, in directions changed from time to time without exterior agency. Another construction gives to the figure the faculty of bending its neck on several occasions, and, to such an extent, that it can plunge the bill and a portion of the head under water. Lastly, it is made to move its head and neck slowly from side to side.

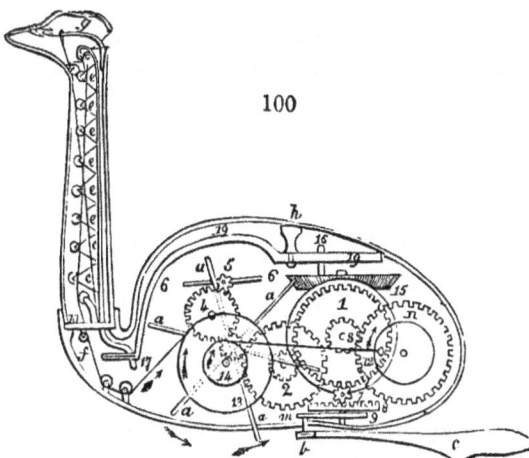

100

On the barrel of the spring exterior to the usual ratchet wheel, there is a main-wheel, marked 1, which works into the pinion of the wheel 2. The wheel 2 moves a smaller one, shown merely in dotted lines, and on the long axis of the latter, at either end, there is a rudder, or water-wheel, the paddles of which are denoted by the letter *a*. Both of these rudder-wheels extend through an oblong opening in the bottom of the figure down into the water. They turn in the direction of the arrow, and impart a straightforward movement to the swan. The chamber in which these wheels revolve is made water-tight, to prevent moisture being thrown upon the rest of the machinery. By the wheel 4, motion is conveyed to the fly-pinion 5; the fly itself, 6, serves to regulate the working of the whole apparatus, and it is provided with a stop bar, not shown in the engraving, to bring it to rest, or set it a-going at pleasure. Here, as we may imagine, the path pursued is rectilinear, when the rudder-wheels are made to work in a square direction. An oblique bar, seen only in section at *b*, movable about its middle point, carries at each end a web foot *c*, so that the direction of the bar *b*, and of both feet towards the rudder-wheels, determines the form of the path which the figure will describe. The change of direction of that oblique bar is effected without other agency. For this purpose the wheel 1 takes into the pinion 7, and this carries round the crown-wheel 8, which is fixed, with an eccentric disc 9, upon a common axis. While the crown-wheel moves in the direction of the arrow, it turns the smaller eccentric portion of the elliptic disc towards the lever *m*, which, pressed upon incessantly by its spring, assumes, by degrees, the position corresponding with the middle line of the figure, and afterwards an oblique position; then it goes back again, and reaches its first situation; consequently, through the reciprocal turning of the bar *h* and the swim-foot, is determined and varied the path which the swan must pursue. This construction is available with all automata which work by wheels; and it is obvious, that we may, by different forms of the disc 9, modify, at pleasure, the direction and the velocity of the turnings. If the disc is a circle, for instance, then the changes will take place less suddenly; if the disc is an outward and inward curvature, upon whose edge the end of the lever presses with a roller, the movement will take place in a serpentine line.

The neck is the part which requires the most careful workmanship. Its outward case must be flexible, and the neck itself should therefore be made of a tube of spiral wire, covered with leather, or with a feathered bird-skin. The double line in the interior, where we see the triangles *e e e*, denotes a steel spring made fast to the plate 10, which forms the bottom of the neck; it stands loose, and needs to be merely so strong as to keep the neck straight, or to bend it a little backwards. It should not be equally thick in all points, but it should be weaker where the first graceful bend is to be made; and, in general, its stiffness ought to correspond to the curvature of the neck of this bird. The triangles *e* are made fast at their base to the front surface of the spring; in the points of each there is a slit, in the middle of which a movable roller is set, formed of a smoothly turned steel rod. A thin catgut string *f*, runs from the upper end of the spring, where it is fixed over all these rollers, and passes, through an aperture pierced in the middle of 10, into the inside of the rump. If the catgut be drawn straight back towards *f*, the spring, and consequently the neck, must obviously be bent, and so much the more, the more tightly *f* is pulled and is shortened in the hollow of the neck. How this is accomplished by the wheel-work will presently be shown. The wheel 11 receives its motion from the pinion *s*, connected with the main wheel 1. Upon 11 there is, moreover, the disc 12, to whose circumference a slender chain is fastened. When the wheel 11 turns in the direction of the arrow, the chain will be so much pulled onwards through the corresponding advance at the point at 12, till this point has come to the place opposite to its present situation, and, consequently, 11 must have performed half a revolution. The other end of the chain is hung in the groove of a very movable roller 14; and this will be turned immediately by the unwinding of the chain upon its axis. There turns, in connection with it, however, the large roller 13, in which the catgut *f* is fastened; and as this is pulled in the direction of the arrow, the neck will be bent until the wheel 11 has made a half revolution. Then the drag ceases again to act upon the chain and the catgut; the spring in the neck comes into play: it becomes straight, erects the neck of the animal, and turns the rollers 13 and 14 back into their first position.

The roller 13 is of considerable size, in order that through the slight motion of the roller 14, a sufficient length of the catgut may be wound off, and the requisite shortening of the neck may be effected; which results from the proportion of the diameters of the rollers 11, 13, 14. This part of the mechanism is attached as near to the side of the hollow body as possible, to make room for the interior parts, but particularly for the paddle-wheels. Since the catgut *f* must pass downwards on the middle from 10, it is necessary to incline it sideways and outwards towards 13, by means of some small rollers.

The head, constituting one piece with the neck, will be depressed by the complete flexure of this; and the bill, being turned downwards in front of the breast, will touch the surface of the water. The head will not be motionless; but it is joined on both sides, by a very movable hinge, with the light ring which forms the upper part of the clothing of the neck. A weak spring, *g*, also fastened to the end of the neck, tends to turn the head backwards; but in the present position it cannot do so, because a chain at *g*, whose other end is attached to the plate 10, keeps it on the stretch. On the bending of the neck, this chain becomes slack; the spring *h* comes into operation, and throws the head so far back that, in its natural position, it will reach the water.

Finally, to render the turning of the head and neck practicable, the latter is not closely connected with the rump, while the plate 10 can turn in a cylindrical manner upon its axis, but cannot become loose outwardly. Moreover, there is upon the axis of the wheel 1, and behind it (shown merely as a circle in the engraving) a bevel wheel, which works into a second similar wheel, 15, so as to turn it in a horizontal direction. The pin, 16, of the last wheel works upon a two-armed lever, 19, movable round the point *h*, and this lever moves the neck by means of the pin 17. The shorter arm of the lever 19 has an oval aperture in which the pin 16 stands. As soon as this, in consequence of the movement of the bevel-wheel 15, comes into the dotted position, it pushes the oval ring outwards on its smaller diameter, and thereby turns the lever upon the point *h*, into the oblique direction shown by the dotted lines. The pin 16, having come on its way right opposite to its present position, sets the lever again straight. Then the lever, by the further progress of the pin in its circular path, is directed outwards to the opposite side; and, at last, when 15 has made an entire revolution, it is quite straight. The longer arm of the lever follows, of course, these alternating movements, so that it turns the neck upon its plate 10, by means of the pin 17: and, as 18 denotes the bill, this comes into the dotted position. It may be remarked, in conclusion, that the drawing of *fig.* 100 represents about half the size of which the automaton may be constructed, and that the body may be formed of thin sheet copper or brass.

In the former edition another example of an automaton was given, but it is thought unnecessary to retain it. In many of the machines now employed, we have examples of useful automata, superior in correctness of action to any of those which are at the best only scientific toys.

AUTOTYPE. See PHOTOGRAPHY.

AVENA. A genus of corn-bearing grasses. The *A. sativa* is the common oat.

AVENTURINE. (*Aventurine*, Fr.) A variety of quartz, which is minutely spangled throughout with yellow scales of mica, is known as *Aventurine quartz*. It is usually translucent, and of a grey, brown, or reddish-brown colour. There is also an *Aventurine felspar* (*Feldspath aventuriné*, Fr.), frequently termed *sunstone* (*Pierre de soleil*); some lapidaries, however, calling this stone by the name of *Aventurine orientale*. Aventurine quartz occurs at Capa de Gata, in Spain; and the aventurine felspar, or sunstone, at Tvedestrand, in Norway.

AVENTURINE, ARTIFICIAL, or GLASS, called also *Gold Flux*, has been manufactured on a large scale, for a long period, at the glass-works of Murano, near Venice. According to Wöhler's examination, aventurine glass owes its golden iridescence to a crystalline separation of metallic copper from the mass coloured brown by the peroxide of iron. C. Karsten analysed the artificial aventurine from the glass manufactory of Bigaglia, in Venice, and found it to contain—

Silicic acid	67·3
Lime	9·0
Protoxide of iron	3·4
Binoxide of tin	2·3
Protoxide of lead	1·0
Metallic copper	4·0
Potash	5·3
Soda	7·0

These numbers agree in a remarkable manner with the results formerly obtained by Péligot, and may therefore be regarded as truly representing the composition of the glass.

AVENTURINE GLAZE, for porcelain, exhibits a crystalline separation of green oxide of chromium from the brown ferruginous mass of the glaze producing a similar effect to the glass. This glaze is prepared as follows, according to A. Wächter:—

31 parts of fine lixiviated dry porcelain-earth from Halle,
43 „ „ dry quartz sand,
14 „ „ gypsum,
12 „ „ fragments of porcelain,

are stirred up with 300 parts of water, and by repeated straining through a linen sieve, uniformly suspended in it, and intimately mixed. To this paste are added, under constant agitation, and one after the other, aqueous solutions of

19 parts bichromate of potash,
100 „ protosulphate of iron,
47 „ acetate of lead,

and then so much solution of ammonia that the iron is completely separated. The salts of potash and ammonia are removed by frequent decantation with spring water. The baked porcelain vessels are dipped into the pasty mixture obtained as above described, in the same manner as with other glazes, and then fired in the porcelain furnace. After this they are covered with a brown glaze, which in reflected light appears to be filled with a countless number of light gold spangles.

A thin fragment of the glaze appears, under the microscope, by transmitted light, as a clear brownish glass, in which numerous transparent green six-sided prisms of oxide of chromium, and some brownish crystals, probably of oxide of chromium and peroxide of iron, are suspended. The oxide of chromium, therefore, separates on the slow cooling of the glaze in the porcelain furnace, from the substance of the glaze— a silicate of potash, lime, and alumina, saturated with the peroxide of iron—and shines through the brownish mass with a golden colour. When the aventurine glaze is mixed with an equal amount of colourless porcelain glaze, the glassy mass no longer has a brown colour after the burning, but a light greenish-grey, and the eliminated crystalline spangles likewise exhibit in reflected light their natural green colour.

AVERRUNCATOR. A pair of pruning shears, which, on being mounted on a pole some ten feet long, and actuated by a string of catgut, can be used for pruning at a considerable distance above the head.

AVOCADO-PEAR OIL. An oil obtained from the oleaginous fruit, the Avocado pear-tree (*Persea gratissima*), a native of Trinidad. A portion of this oil having been submitted to Dr. Hofmann by the Governor of Trinidad, he reported on its character: —'According to my present experience, the oil of the Avocado pear is less valuable as a lubricating material. To make it fit for the higher classes of machinery, its mucilaginous constituents must be removed by the same refining process requisite for its adaptation in illuminating purposes.

'On the other hand, the oil of the Avocado pear is very applicable for the production of good soap. I have the honour of transmitting to your Excellency specimens prepared with the oil: the smaller one, which possesses a yellow colour, is prepared with the oil in its original condition; the larger one is made with a portion of oil which had previously been bleached by chlorine. From this specimen it is obvious that the oil, although poor in stearine, nevertheless furnishes a soap which is tolerably hard and solid. I have even now no hesitation in stating that, for the purposes of the soap-maker, the oil of the Avocado pear will have, at least, the same value as palm oil.'

AXE. A tool much used by carpenters for cleaving and roughly fashioning blocks of wood. It is a thin iron wedge, with an oblong steel edge, parallel to which, in the short base, is a hole for receiving and holding fast the end of a strong wooden handle.

AXE-STONE. A sub-species of *jade*, found in Corsica, Saxony, and on the banks of the Amazon. It is a silicate of magnesia and alumina, coloured by oxide of chromium. See JADE.

AXINITE, called also *Thumite*. A silicate of magnesia, alumina, and iron, containing boracic acid. It derives its name from the axe-like bevelling of its lateral edges. This mineral is harder than felspar, and varies in colour from a violet-brown to a leek-green. It is found in many parts of the Continent, and at Botallack, St. Just, and at Trewellard, Cornwall, in fine brilliant clove-brown crystals.

AXLE-GREASE. Several kinds of unguents employed to reduce the friction of wheels circulating on their axles. See ANTI-ATTRITION.

AXLES, of carriages. See WHEEL CARRIAGES.

AXUNGE. Hog's lard. See FAT and OILS.

AYR STONE, called also Scotch stone and snake-stone, is much in request as a polishing stone for marble and for copper plates. These stones are always kept damp, or even wet, to prevent their becoming hard.

The harder varieties of Ayr stone are now employed as whetstones.

AZALE (from *Azala*, Arabic for madder). A colouring-matter obtained from 'flowers of madder,' perhaps crude alizarine. It has been proposed to introduce azale in France as a dye-stuff.

AZALEINE. A name for aniline-red.

AZIMUTH COMPASS. The azimuth compass is used chiefly to note the actual magnetic azimuth, or that arch of the horizon intercepted between the azimuth, or vertical circle passing through the centre of any heavenly body, and the magnetic meridian.

The card of the azimuth compass is subdivided into exact degrees, minutes, and seconds. To the box are fixed two 'sights,' through which the sun or a star may be viewed. The position into which the index of the sights must be turned to see it, will indicate on the card the azimuth of the star. When the observations are intended to be exact, telescopes take the place of the sights. By this instrument we note the actual magnetic azimuth: and as we know the azimuth calculated from the N. and S. line, the variation of the needle is readily found.

AZOBENZENE, AZOBENZIDE, or **AZOBENZOL.** $C^{24}H^{10}N^2$ ($C^{12}H^{10}N^2$). A peculiar substance formed by acting with an alcoholic solution of potash upon nitrobenzole, or, as it is sometimes called, artificial oil of bitter almonds. If nitrobenzole, dissolved in alcohol, with the addition of solid potash, be distilled, a complex and by no means well understood reaction occurs. The azobenzide distils over mixed with aniline. The fluid treated with hydrochloric acid, to dissolve the aniline, is passed through a wet filter; the aniline salt passes through, leaving the azobenzide as a red oil, which in a few moments solidifies into a mass of rich golden-brown crystals of considerable size, even when working on a very small quantity. The alcohol enters into the reaction, and oxalic acid is formed, which unites with the potash. Four equivalents of nitrobenzole and two equivalents of alcohol appear to yield one equivalent of azobenzide, two equivalents of aniline, four equivalents of oxalic acid, and eight equivalents of water. See NITROBENZOLE.

Azobenzene yields numerous derivatives. With fuming nitric acid it gives two nitro-compounds; viz., nitroazobenzide and binitroazobenzide. Azobenzide, treated with sulphide of ammonium, yields an alkaline called benzidine, $C^{24}H^{12}N^2$ ($C^{12}H^{12}N^2$). —C. G. W.

AZOBENZOIDE. When bitter almonds are distilled, *per descensum*, an oil is obtained; if the latter be treated with ammonia, and the substance thus formed be treated with ether, a white powder remains, which is probably impure hydrobenzamide.—C. G. W. See 'Watts's Dictionary of Chemistry.'

AZOBENZOYLE. A substance formed simultaneously with hydrobenzamide and benzydramide, when oil of bitter almonds is treated with ammonia.—C. G. W.

AZOTE. An old name for NITROGEN.

AZOTISED, said of certain vegetable substances, which, as containing azote, were supposed at one time to partake, in some measure, of the animal nature. The vegetable products, indigo, caffeine, gluten, and many others, contain abundance of azote.

AZURE. This term was applied by Pliny to the blues of the ancients. 'Cæruleum, or azure, is of three kinds: the Egyptian (artificial); the Scythian (natural), which is inferior; the Cyprian, the best.'—*Theophrastus*, also *Pliny*. Girardin, writing of the ancient colours, says, ' This *azure*, which has thus endured above 1,700 years, may be cheaply and easily made thus: 15 parts, *by weight*, of carbonate of soda, 20 parts of opaque flints, and 3 parts of copper filings, are strongly heated for two hours, and the mixture will result in a fine deep sky-blue.' The Egyptian blue, or Alexandrian frit, is a pulverised blue glass; it was once thought to contain cobalt, but all analyses prove it to contain silicate of copper.

The term Azure has been applied to smalts. See COBALT, SMALT, and ULTRAMARINE.

AZURINE. See ANILINE-BLUE and ANILINE-GREEN.

AZURITE. This term is now usually restricted to the blue carbonate of copper, otherwise known as *Chessylite*. It is a mineral of fine blue colour, crystallising in the oblique system. The old mines of Chessy, near Lyons, in France, were famous for yielding groups of magnificent crystals of this species. It is also found in the shallow workings of many other copper mines, often associated with malachite, or green carbonate of copper. Azurite contains, when pure, 55·16 per cent. of copper, and hence forms a valuable ore. It has also been used as a blue pigment, though too liable to turn green, the absorption of carbonic acid readily converting it into malachite.

It is right to remark that the term *Azurite* has also been applied to certain other blue minerals, such as the phosphate of alumina and magnesia, usually known as *Lazulite*, and even to the *lapis lazuli*.

The want of agreement between mineralogists—leading them to adopt names independent one of the other (names frequently taken from some locality in which the writer knows the mineral to be found)—produces great confusion, and retards the progress of knowledge.

B

BABBIT'S METAL. An alloy which, from its smoothness of surface, is called an anti-attrition metal. It is composed of 25 parts of tin, 2 parts of antimony, and $\frac{1}{2}$ a part of copper.

BABINGTONITE. An anhydrous silicate of iron and lime, found in small, greenish-black, doubly-oblique crystals, at Arendal, in Norway. A fibrous variety, much resembling hornblende, was discovered in a railway-cutting in Devonshire, in 1854, and was sufficiently abundant to be worked as an ore of iron. A specimen received from the late Mr. S. Blackwell was analysed by Mr. David Forbes, with the following results:—Silica, 49·12 ; alumina, 1·60 ; peroxide of iron, 9·78 ; protoxide of iron, 12·87 ; protoxide of manganese, 1·25 ; lime, 20·87 ; magnesia, 3·67 ; loss on ignition, 0·73.

BABLAH. The rind or shell of the fruit of the *Mimosa cineraria*. It is brought from the East Indies under the name of *Neb-Neb*. On account of the tannin it contains, it has been used for dyeing cotton, and for producing various shades of drab.

BABUL GUM. The gum of the Babul tree, a species of the *Acacia*, growing in Bengal. It is sometimes imported as Bengal gum.

Babul Bark is extensively used in India as a tanning material, and has occasionally been imported into this country.

BACK. In *mining*, that side of an inclined mineral lode which is nearest the surface of the ground. The back of a level is the ground between it and the level above it. In *brewing*, a brewer's utensil, a large vessel for receiving the wort. In *building*, that part of a stone opposite the face.

BACK-MILL. A fulling mill.

BACULUS. A forked branch of hazel, used by the superstitious with a view to the discovery of springs and mineral lodes. See DIVINING ROD.

BADGER. (*Blaireau*, Fr. ; *Dachs*, Ger.) A genus of carnivorous animals belonging to the family *Mustelidæ*. The common badger, *Meles Taxus*, inhabits the northern parts of Europe and Asia. The hide of the badger is employed for pistol furniture. The fine hair is used for making brushes for the use of the artist, and for the best class of shaving-brushes. The hind-quarters, salted and smoked, make excellent hams.

BADIGEON. A mixture for stopping holes in wood or stone. The badigeon for stonework is composed of plaster of Paris and freestone ground together. That for wood is usually sawdust and glue, or sometimes putty and chalk.

BAG. A measure equal to a striked Winchester bushel. Twenty-five bags of lime make a ton. A bag of plaster of Paris is fourteen pounds. Eight bags are considered to equal a bushel.

BAGASSE. The sugar-cane, in its dry crushed state, much employed for fuel in the colonial sugar-houses.

BAIN-MARIE. A vessel of water in which saucepans, &c. are placed to warm food, or to prepare it and some pharmaceutical preparations.

BAIZE. A coarse woollen stuff with a long nap, sometimes friezed on one side.

BAKERS' SALT. The sesquicarbonate of ammonia, so called because it is often used as a substitute for yeast in bread and pastry.

BAKING. (*Cuire*, Fr. ; *Backen*, Ger.) The exposure of any body to such a heat as will dry and consolidate its parts without wasting them. Thus wood, pottery, and porcelain, are baked, as well as bread and meat. See BISCUIT ; BREAD.

BAL. An ancient Cornish miner's term for a mine.

BAL-MAIDEN, BAL-BOY. A girl or boy working at a mine.

BALACHONG. An article of food much used in the Eastern Archipelago, consisting of fish and shrimps pounded together.

BALÆNA. A genus of cetacean mammals, including the Greenland, or Right Whale (*Balæna mysticetus*), and the Southern Whale (*B. australis*). The former inhabits the Arctic Seas, and its capture forms the object of the Northern whale-fishery, while the latter is found in the Antarctic, South Pacific, and Indian Oceans. These species, in the adult state, are destitute of teeth, but the mouth is furnished with numerous plates of a horny substance, called *baleen*, or *whalebone*, which hang freely from each side of the palate, and thus form a sieve for straining off the water from the small prey taken into the mouth. Large quantities of oil are obtained from the *blubber*, or thick layer of fat which immediately underlies the naked skin, and serves to protect the warm-blooded whale from the cold of the surrounding medium. The Esquimaux not only eat the flesh of the whale, but use some of the internal membranes in the preparation of certain articles of clothing, and of a curious semi-transparent substance serving instead of glass for the windows of their huts. The species of *Balæna*, or true Whalebone Whales, are to be distinguished from the Sperm Whales, which belong to a totally distinct genus, and though possessing teeth, and therefore not yielding whalebone, are nevertheless valued for the sake of their spermaceti and ambergris. See AMBERGRIS ; SPERMACETI ; WHALEBONE.

BALANCE. To conduct arts and manufactures with judgment, recourse must be had to a balance. Experience proves that all material bodies existing upon the surface of the earth are constantly solicited by a force which tends to bring them towards its centre, and that they fall to the earth when they are free to move. This force is called gravity. Though the bodies be not free, the effort of gravity is still sensible, and the resultant of all the actions which it exercises upon their material points constitutes what is called their *weight*. Weights are, therefore, forces which may be compared together, and by means of machines may be made to correspond or be counterpoised.

To discover whether two weights be equal, we must oppose them to each other in a machine where they act in a similar manner, and then see if they maintain an equilibrium; for example, we fulfil this condition if we suspend them at the two extremities of a lever supported at its centre, and whose arms are equal. Such is the general idea of a balance. The beam of a good balance ought to be a bar or double cone of metal, of such strength as to secure perfect inflexibility under any load which may be fitly applied to its extremities. Its arms should be quite equal in weight and length upon each side of its point of suspension; and this point should be placed in a vertical line over the centre of gravity; and the less distant it is from it, the more delicate will be the balance. Were it placed exactly in that centre, the beam would not spontaneously recover the horizontal position when it was once removed from it. To render its indications more readily commensurable, a slender rod or needle is fixed to it, at right angles, in the line passing through its centres of gravity and suspension. The point, or rather edge, of suspension, should be made of perfectly hard steel, and turn upon a bed of the same. For common uses the arms of a balance can be made sufficiently equal to give satisfactory results; but, for the more refined purposes of science, that equality should never be presumed nor trusted to; and, fortunately, exact weighing is quite independent of that equality. To weigh a body is to determine how many times the weight of that body contains another species of known weight, as of grains or pounds, for example. In order to find it out, let us place the substance, suppose a piece of gold, in the left hand scale of the balance; counterpoise it with sand or shot in the other, till the index needle be truly vertical, or stand in the middle of its scale, proving the beam to be horizontal. Now remove gently the piece of gold, and substitute in its place standard multiple weights of any graduation, English or French, until the needle again resumes the vertical position, or until its oscillations upon either side of the zero-point are equal. These weights will represent precisely the weight of the gold, since they are placed in the same circumstances with it, and make the same equilibrium with the weight laid in the other scale.

This method of weighing is obviously independent of the unequal length as well as the unequal weight of the arms of the beam. For its perfection two requisites only are indispensable. The first is that the points of suspension should be rigorously the same in the two operations; for the power of a given weight to turn the beam being unequal, accordingly as we place it at different distances from the centre of suspension, did that point vary in the two consecutive weighings, we should require to employ, in the second, a different weight from that of the piece of gold, in order to form an equilibrium with the sand or shot originally put in the opposite scale; and as there is nothing to indicate such inequality in the states of the beam, great errors would result from it. The best mode of securing against such inequality is to suspend the cords of the scales from sharp-edged rings, upon knife-edges, at the ends of the beam, both made of steel so hard-tempered as to be incapable of indentation. The second condition is, that the balance should be very sensible—that is, when in equilibrium and loaded, it may be disturbed, and its needle may oscillate, by the smallest weight put into either of the scales. This sensibility depends wholly upon the centre of suspension; and it will be the more perfect the less friction there is between that *knife-edge* surface and the plane which supports it. Both should therefore be as hard and highly polished as possible; and should not be suffered to press against each other, except at the time of weighing. Every delicate balance of moderate size, moreover, should be suspended within a glass case, to protect it from the agitations of the air, and the corroding influence of the weather. In some balances a ball is placed upon the index or needle (whether that index stand above or below the beam), which may be made to approach or recede from the beam by a fine-threaded screw, with the effect of varying the centre of gravity relatively to the point of suspension, and thereby increasing, at will, either the sensibility or the stability of the balance. The greater the length of the arms, the less distant the centre of gravity is beneath the centre of suspension, the better polished its central knife-edge of 30°, the lighter the whole balance, and the less it is loaded, the greater will be its sensibility. In all cases the arms must be quite inflexible. A balance made by Ramsden for the Royal Society is capable of weighing ten pounds, and turns with one hundredth of a grain, which is the seven-millionth part of the weight. See WEIGHING MACHINE.

BALANCE FOR WEIGHING COIN, introduced at the Bank of England in
the year 1841, requires an especial notice.

Mr. William Cotton, then Deputy-Governor, and during the two succeeding years
Governor of the Bank, had long regarded the mode of weighing by common hand-
balances with dissatisfaction, on account of its injurious effect upon the 'teller,' or
weigher, owing to the straining of the optic nerve by constant watching of the beam-
indicator, and the necessity of reducing the functions of the mind to the narrow office
of influencing a few constantly repeated actions. Such monotonous labour could not
be endured for hours together without moments of forgetfulness resulting in errors.
Errors more constant, although less in amount, were found to be due to the rapid
wearing of the knife-edges of the beam; currents of air also acting upon the pans
produced undesired results; and even the breath of the 'teller' sometimes turned the
scale; so that in hand-weighing the errors not unfrequently amounted to $\frac{1}{3}$rd, and
even $\frac{1}{2}$ grain. At the very best, the hand-scale working at the rate of 3,000 per six
hours could not indicate nearer than $\frac{1}{25}$th grain.

Upon taking into consideration the inconveniences and defects of the hand-weighing
system, Mr. Cotton conceived the idea that it might be superseded by a machine de-
fended from external influences, and contrived so as to weigh coins as fast as by hand,
and within the fourth of a grain. He subsequently communicated his plan to Mr.
David Napier, of York Road, Lambeth, engineer, who undertook the construction of
an experimental machine. Its capabilities were tested and reported upon by Mr.
William Miller, of the Bank. The result was most satisfactory: more 'automaton
balances' were ordered; and from time to time further additions have been made, so
that at present there are ten in daily operation at the Bank of England. But it was
not without a struggle that the time-hallowed institution of 'tellers' passed away.
There were interests opposed to the introduction of improved, more ready, and less expensive methods; and it required all Mr. Cotton's energy of character, the influence of
his intelligence in mechanics, as well as that arising from his position in the Direction,
to obtain the adoption of an invention by which a very large annual saving has been
effected.

The mechanical adaptation of the principles involved in the Automaton Balance, as
contrived by Mr. Napier, may be shortly explained:—The weighing-beam, of steel, is
forked at the ends, each extremity forming a knife-edge; and in the centre the fulcrum
knife-edge extends on each side of the plate of the beam, and rests in hollows cut in
a bowed cross-bar fixed to the under side of a rectangular brass plate, about 12 inches
square, which is supported at the corners by columns fixed to a cast-iron table raised
a convenient height on a stand of the same metal. To form a complete enclosing
case, plates of metal or glass are slid into grooves down the columns. When the beam
is resting with its centre knife-edge in the hollows of the cross-bar just referred to,
its upper part is nearly on a level with the under-side of the brass plate, in which a
long slot is made, so that the beam can be taken out when the feeding slide-box, and
its plate, which covers this slot, are removed. On the top of the covering plate of
the feeding slide a tube-hopper is placed, and a hole in the plate communicates with
the slide; another hole is pierced in the same plate exactly over one end of the beam,
upon the knife-edges of which a long rod is suspended by hollows formed in a cross-
bar close to its upper end, where the weighing platform is fitted. A rod is also suspended at the other end of the beam in a similar manner; but instead of a weighing-
plate, it has a knob at top, which, when the beam is horizontal, comes into contact
with an adjustable agate point. The lower end of this pendent rod is stirrup-shaped,
for holding the counterpoise. Two displacing slides are provided, one on each side of
the feeding-slide, and at right angles to each other; and a gripping apparatus is fixed
to the under side of the brass top-plate, arranged so as to hold the pendant on which
the scale-plate is fitted during the change of the coin. A dipping-finger is also attached to the frame of the gripping apparatus, its end passing into a small slot in the
pendent rod, and acting upon a knife-edge at the lower end of the slot. There are
four shafts crossing the machine; the one through which the power is applied is
placed low and at the centre, and carries a pinion which gears with a wheel of twice
its diameter on a shaft above; this wheel gears with two similar wheels fixed to shafts
on each side of the centre. Cams for acting upon the feeding slide, through the
medium of a rocking frame, are carried by the shaft placed at the end of the machine
where the counterpoise hangs, and the other two shafts on the same level bear cams
for working the gripping apparatus, the dipping-finger, and the displacing slides.

Having described, as clearly and as popularly as we can, the general features of the
mechanism, we will proceed to indicate its manner of action. Suppose, then, the
hopper filled, and a hollow inclined plane about two feet long, which has been added
to the hopper by the inventive genius of one of the gentlemen in the weighing-room,
also loaded its whole length with the pieces to be weighed, the machine is set in

motion, and the feeding slide pushes the lowest piece forward on to the weighing-plate, the grippers meantime holding fast by the neck of the pendant, so as to keep the plate perfectly steady; the dipping-finger is also at its lowest position, and resting upon the knife-edge at the bottom of the slot in the pendent rod, thus keeping the beam horizontal, and the knob on the counterpoise-pendant in contact with the agate point already mentioned. When the coin is fairly placed on the weighing-plate, the grippers let go their hold of the pendent rod, and the dipping-finger is raised by its cam; if then the coin is too light, the coin end of the beam will rise along with the dipping-finger, and the counterpoise end will descend; if heavy, the beam will remain without motion, the agate point preventing it. As soon as the dipping-finger attains the proper height, and thus has allowed sufficient time for the weight of the coin to be decided, the grippers close and hold the pendant, and consequently the scale or weighing-plate, at the high level, if the coin has proved light, and been raised by the excess of weight in the counterpoise; and at the low or original level, if the coin has proved heavy. One of the displacing slides now comes forward and passes under the coin, if it is light, and therefore raised to the high level; but knocks it off, if remaining on the low level, into the 'heavy box.' The other displacing slide then advances. This strikes higher than the first, and removes the light piece which the other has missed, into the receptacle for the light coin. During these operations the feeding-slide has brought forward another coin, and the process just described is repeated. The attendant is only required to replenish the inclined plane at intervals, and remove the assorted coin from the boxes. The perfection of the workmanship, and the harmony of the various actions of the machine, will be best appreciated from the fact, that 25 pieces are weighed per minute to the fineness of $\frac{1}{100}$th of a grain. This combination of great speed and accuracy would not have been possible with a beam made in the ordinary way, having the centre of gravity below the centre of action; and it was pronounced to be so by the late Mr. Clement, the constructor of Mr. Babbage's Calculating Machine. But Mr. Napier overcame the difficulty by raising the centre of gravity so as to coincide with the centre of action, which gave it much greater sensibility; and he provided the dipping-finger, to bring the beam to a horizontal position after each weighing, instead of an influencing weight in the beam itself.

The wear and tear of these machines is found to be very small indeed; those supplied in 1842 and 1843, and in daily use ever since, weigh with the same accuracy as at first, although they may be said to have cost nothing for repairs. The principal cause of this long-continued perfection is that the beam does not oscillate, unless the coin is light, and even then the space passed through does not exceed the thickness of the coin.

In 1851, when the Moneyers were no longer *masters* of the Royal Mint, and the new authorities began to regard the process of weighing the coin in detail by hand as a laborious, expensive, and inaccurate method, the firm of Napier and Son, at an interview with Sir John Herschel, the Master, and Captain Harness, the Deputy-Master, received an order for five machines, to be designed to suit the requirements of the Mint, which involved a complete change in the mechanical arrangement of the machine as used at the Bank, it being necessary to divide the 'blanks,' or pieces before they are struck, into three classes, 'too light,' 'too heavy,' and 'medium,' or those varying between certain given limits. It would occupy too much space to attempt a description of the mechanical disposition of this machine, and it could not be satisfactorily accomplished without the aid of drawings; let it suffice, then, to say that the displacing-slides are removed, and a long vibrating conducting-tube receives the blanks as they are in turn pushed off the weighing-plate by the on-coming blanks; but, according to the weight of the blank, so the lower end of the tube is found to be opposite to one of three openings leading into three boxes. The tube is sustained in its proper position, during the descent of the blank last weighed through it, by a stop-finger, the height of which is regulated by a dipping-finger, which comes down upon a knife-edge at the lower end of a slot in the pendent rod just when the grippers have laid hold of the rod after the weighing is finished; this finger thus ascertains the level which the knife-edge has attained, and as it brings down the stop-finger with it, the guide-tube, which is furnished with three rests, as steps in a stair, vibrates against the stop-finger, one of the three steps coming in contact with it, according to the level of the stop-finger; and the end of the guide-tube takes its place opposite the channel leading to the box in which the blank should be found. The counterpoise employed is less than the true standard weight, by the quantity which may be allowed as the limit in that direction; and in case a blank is too heavy, not only is the counterpoise raised, but a small weight, equal to the range allowed between the 'too light' and 'too heavy,' is raised also; this small weight comes to rest on supports provided for it when the beam is horizontal, and is only disturbed by a *too heavy* blank.

These machines have proved even more accurate and rapid than those made for the Bank; and Professor Graham, the late Master, amongst the improvements introduced by him into the system of the Mint, added to the number, and dispensed entirely with the hand-weighing. It is said that the saving accruing from this change alone amounts to nearly 2,000*l.* per annum. See HYDROSTATIC BALANCE; WEIGHING MACHINE.

BALAS, BALLUS, or **BALAIS RUBY.** The names applied to the *rose-red* and *reddish-white* varieties of spinel. See RUBY.

BALE. A package of silk, linen, or woollen, is so called.

BALLESTEROSITE. A variety of iron pyrites found in Asturia.

BALLISTIC PENDULUM. An instrument for measuring the force of cannon-balls. The ballista was an instrument used by the ancients to throw darts, &c. The ballistic pendulum derives its name from this: it consists of an iron cylinder, closed at one end, suspended as a pendulum. A ball being fired into the open end, deflects the pendulum according to the force of the blow received from the ball, thus measuring its power.

BALLOON. In France, a quantity of glass. Of *white glass*, 25 bundles of six plates each; of *coloured glass*, 12½ bundles of three plates each, are called balloons. Chemists call receivers and flasks of a spherical form balloons.

BALLOONS. See AEROSTATION.

BALL SODA, BLACK BALLS, or **BLACK ASH.** Crude carbonate of soda, obtained in the manufacture of soda-ash. See SODA.

BALM OF GILEAD. See BALSAM, MECCA.

BALSAM. (*Baume*, Fr.; *Balsam*, Ger.) A native compound of ethereal or essential oils, with resin, and frequently benzoic acid. Most balsams have the consistence of honey; but a few are solid, or become so by keeping. They flow either spontaneously, or by incisions made in trees and shrubs in tropical climates. They have peculiar and sometimes powerful smells, aromatic hot tastes, but lose their odoriferous properties by long exposure to the air. They are insoluble in water; soluble to a considerable degree, in ether; and completely in alcohol. When distilled with water, ethereal oil comes over, and resin remains in the retort.

BALSAM, CANADA. See CANADA BALSAM.

BALSAM COPAIVA, or **CAPIVI,** or **CAPAIBA.** (*Baume de Copahu*, Fr.; *Kopaiva Balsam*, Ger.) *Capaiva balsam*, balsam of copahu, or capivi, is obtained from incisions made in the trunk of the *Copaifera officinalis*, a tree which grows in Brazil and Cayenne. It is also very frequently obtained from the *C. multijuga, C. Langsdorfi*, and *C. Coriacea*. It is pale yellow, semi-liquid, clear and transparent, has a bitter, sharp, hot taste; a penetrating disagreeable smell; a specific gravity of from 0·950 to 0·996. It dissolves in absolute alcohol, and partially in spirits of wine, and forms with alkalis crystalline compounds. It consists of 45·59 ethereous oil, 52·75 of a yellow brittle resin, and 1·66 of a brown viscid resin. The oil contains no oxygen, has a composition like that of oil of turpentine; it dissolves caoutchouc (according to Durand), but becomes oxidised, in the air, into a peculiar species of resin.

This substance is extensively used in medicine. It was formerly often adulterated; some unctuous oil being mixed with it, but as this is easily discovered by its insolubility in alcohol, castor-oil has since been used. The presence of this cheaper oil may be detected,—1, by agitating the balsam with a solution of caustic soda, and setting the mixture aside to repose, when the balsam will come to float clear on the top, and leave a soapy thick magma of the oil below; 2, when the balsam is boiled with water, in a thin film for some hours, it will become a brittle resin on cooling; but it will remain viscid if mixed with castor-oil; 3, if a drop of the oil on white paper be held over a lamp, at a proper distance, its volatile oil will evaporate, and leave the brittle resin, without causing any stain around, which the presence of oil will produce; 4, when three drops of the balsam are poured into a watch-glass, alongside of one drop of sulphuric acid, it becomes yellow at the point of contact, and altogether of a saffron hue when stirred about with a glass rod; but if sophisticated with castor-oil, the mixture soon becomes nearly colourless, like white honey, though after some time the acid blackens the whole in either case; 5, if three parts in bulk of the balsam be mixed with one of good water of ammonia (of 0·970 specific gravity) in a glass tube, it will form a transparent solution if it be pure, but will form a white liniment if it contain castor-oil; 6, if the balsam be triturated with a little of the common magnesia alba, it will form a clear solution, from which acids dissolve out the magnesia, and leave the oil transparent if it be pure, but opaque if it be adulterated. When turpentine is employed to falsify the balsam, the fraud is detected by the smell on heating the compound.

This balsam is used in the manufacture of some varieties of *tracing paper;* and many lacquers and varnishes have the balsam of copaiva as one of their constituents.

It is no longer possible to ascertain the quantity of Balsam Copaiva imported ; by, as it appears to us, a very mistaken regulation of the Custom-house, it, and a great many other articles, are entered under the head of ' *Drugs unenumerated.*'

BALSAMITO and **WHITE BALSAM.** By digesting the fruit of the Balsam of Peru tree in rum, a liquid having a bitter taste, a light sherry colour, and the odour of the tonquin-bean, is produced, called Balsamito. It is taken internally, and used as an application to sloughing sores—especially those of the chigoe. By subjecting this fruit to pressure, without heat, *White Balsam* is obtained. It resembles strained Bordeaux turpentine, and is sometimes confounded with balsam of Tolu.

BALSAM, MECCA. (*Baume de la Mecque, Baume du Judée*, Fr.) *Mecca balsam*, or *opobalsam*, or *Balm of Gilead*, is obtained both by incisions in, and by boiling, the branches and leaves of the *Balsamodendron opobalsamum*, a shrub which grows in Arabia Felix and Egypt. When fresh it is turbid and whitish, but becomes by degrees transparent, yellow, thickish, and eventually solid. Its smell is peculiar, but agreeable ; it tastes bitter and spicy ; does not dissolve completely in hot spirit of wine, and contains 10 per cent. of ethereal oil of the specific gravity 0·876. It is also obtained from *B. Gileadense*.

BALSAM OF PERU. (*Baume du Pérou*, Fr. ; *Peruvianischer Balsam*, Ger.) *Balsam of Peru* is extracted from the *Myroxylon Peruiferum*, a tree which grows in Peru, Mexico, &c. ; sometimes by incision, and sometimes by evaporating the decoction of the bark and branches of the tree. The former kind is very rare, and is imported in the husk of the cocoa-nut, whence it is called balsam *en coque*. It is brown, transparent only in thin layers of the consistence of thick turpentine, of an agreeable smell, an acrid and bitter taste ; formed of two matters, the one liquid, the other granular, and somewhat crystalline. In 100 parts it contains 12 of benzoic acid, 88 of resin, with traces of a volatile oil.

The second sort, the *black* balsam of Peru, is much more common than the preceding ; translucent, of the consistence of well-boiled syrup, very deep red-brown colour, an almost intolerably acrid and bitter taste, and a stronger smell than the other balsam. Stoltze regards it as formed of 69 parts of a peculiar oil, 20·7 of a resin little soluble in alcohol, of 6·4 of benzoic acid, of 0·6 of extractive matter, and 0·9 of water.

The celebrated *Pomade Divine*, which was a few years since very celebrated, contained a considerable quantity of the balasm of Peru. One of the best recipes for its preparation was the following :—

Fine olive oil	18 ozs.
Balsam of Peru	1 oz.
Orris-root	6 drachms.
Strained Storax	1 drachm.

This, with some bruised nutmegs and cinnamon, was macerated in a water-bath for three hours, and then filtered.

A French authority states that, dissolved in four times its weight of alcohol, and spread upon sarsanet already covered with a layer of isinglass, it formed the *taffetas d'Angleterre*.

One thousand parts of good balsam should, by its benzoic acid, saturate 75 parts of crystallised carbonate of soda. It is employed as a perfume for pomatums, tinctures, lozenges, sealing-wax, and for chocolate and liqueurs, instead of vanilla, when this happens to be very dear.

M. Victor le Nouvel, who has been engaged in collecting this balsam since 1836, gives the following as the process used by the Indians to obtain it. An incision is made into the tree of about two or three inches broad, and three to four inches long. They raise the bark from the wood and apply cotton rags to it ; a fire being lighted round the tree to liquefy the balsam. Fresh incisions are made higher and higher up the tree, till the cotton rags are quite saturated. It takes from ten to twelve days to effect this. The rags are next boiled, and when the liquor is cold, the balsam collects below.—*Pereira's Materia Medica.*

Balsam of Peru has been for some years exported from the State of Salvador On the coast of Chiquimulilla (Guatemala) there are many trees of the description that yield the balsam, but hitherto it has not attracted the attention of the people to collect it.

The Balsam of Peru of Salvador is procured within the department of Sonsonate. The British Consul thus describes its production :—

In the district of Cuisnagua there are 3,574 trees, which yield altogether only 600 lbs. of the gum annually. With proper care in the extraction, each tree would yield 2 lbs. to 3 lbs., making the total quantity capable of being produced in the before-mentioned district about 10,000 lbs. When the season has been more rainy than usual the product is much lower ; but in order to meet this difficulty, the Indians heat the body of the tree by fire, by this means causing the gum to exude more freely ; but this operation invariably causes the decay of the tree.

The Indians employed in collecting the gum say that such trees as are well shaded yield a greater quantity ; but that those which have been planted by hand yield the most. This has been proved by experience, particularly in Calcutta, where a considerable quantity is yearly collected from trees which have been so planted. During the months of December and January the gum oozes away spontaneously. This class of gum is called 'calcawzate.' It is orange-coloured, weighs less than the other, and emits a strong odour ; is volatile and pungent.

BALSAM STORAX. See STORAX.

BALSAM OF TOLU. (*Baume de Tolu*, Fr. ; *Tolutanischer Balsam*, Ger.) *Balsam of Tolu* flows from the trunk of the *Myrospermum toluiferum*, a tree which grows in South America, on the mountains of Tolu, Timbaceo, &c. It is, when fresh, of the consistence of turpentine ; is brownish-red, dries into a yellowish or reddish brittle resinous mass, of a smell like benzoin ; is soluble in alcohol and ether ; affords, with water, benzoic acid. It appears probable that both the balsams of Peru and of Tolu are obtained from one tree. *Balsam of Tolu* is used to manufacture Tolu lozenges, and the Syrup of Tolu for irritating coughs. It is sometimes employed by confectioners to flavour sweetmeats, by perfumers, and in the formation of *fumigating* pastils.

BALTIMORITE. A variety of fibrous serpentine found at Baltimore.

BAMBOO. (*Bambou*, Fr. ; *Indianisches Rohr*, Ger.) A species of cane, the *Bambusa arundinacea* of botanists. A most important vegetable product in the East, where it is used in the construction of houses, boats, bridges, &c. Its grain is used for bread ; its fibre is manufactured into paper. Walking-sticks are said to be of bamboo ; they are the *ratan*, a different plant. A siliceous secretion called *tabasheer* is frequently found in the joints of the bamboo. See RATAN and TABASHEER.

BAMLITE. A silicate of alumina found at Bamle, in Norway.

BANANA. An herbaceous endogenous plant, *Musa sapientum*, growing in the West Indies, East Indies, and generally throughout the tropics. The Plantain has a fruit which is used for food to an immense extent by the inhabitants of hot climates, forming, indeed, a necessary article of diet.

BANDANNA. A style of calico-printing, in which white or brightly-coloured spots are produced upon a red or dark ground. It seems to have been practised from time immemorial in India, by binding up firmly with thread those points of the cloth which were to remain white or yellow, while the rest of the surface was freely subjected to the dyeing operations.

The European imitations have now far surpassed, in the beauty and precision of the design, the Oriental patterns, having called into action the refined resources of mechanical and chemical science. The white spots are produced by a solution of chlorine made to percolate down through the Turkey-red cotton cloth, in certain points defined and circumscribed by the pressure of hollow lead types in plates, in an hydraulic press. *Fig.* 101 is an elevation of one press ; A, the top of the entablature ; B B, the cheeks or pillars ; c, the upper block for fastening the upper lead perforated pattern to ; D, the lower block, to which the fellow pattern is affixed, and which moves up and down with the piston of the press ; E, the piston or ram ; F, the sole or base ; G, the water-trough for the discharged or spotted calico to fall into ; H, the small cistern for the aqueous chlorine or liquor-metre, with glass tubes for indicating the height of liquor inside the cistern ; e e, glass stopcocks, for admitting the liquor into that cistern from the general reservoir ; f f, stopcocks for admitting water to wash out the chlorine ; g g, the pattern lead-plates, with screws for setting the patterns parallel to each other ; m m, projecting angular pieces at each corner, perforated with a half-inch hole to receive the four guide-pins rising from the lower plate, which serve to secure accuracy of adjustment between the two faces of the lead pattern-plates ; h h, two rollers, which seize and pull through the discharged pieces, and deliver them into the water-trough. To the left of D there is a stopcock for filling the trough with water ; l is the waste tub for chlorine-liquor and water of washing. The contrivance for blowing a stream of air across the cloth through the pattern holes is not represented in the figure.

Sixteen engines, similar to the above, each possessing the power of pressing with several hundred tons, are arranged in one line, in subdivisions of four, the spaces between each subdivision serving as passages to allow the workmen to go readily from the front to the back of the presses. Each occupies 25 feet, so that the total length of the apartment is 100 feet.

To each press is attached a pair of patterns in lead (or plates as they are called), the manner of forming which will be described in the sequel. One of these plates is fixed to the upper block of the press. This block is so contrived that it rests upon a kind of universal joint, which enables this plate to be applied exactly to the under fellow-plate. The latter sits on the movable part of the press, commonly called the sill. When this is forced up, the two patterns close on each other very nicely by means of the guide-pins at the corners, which are fitted with the utmost care.

101

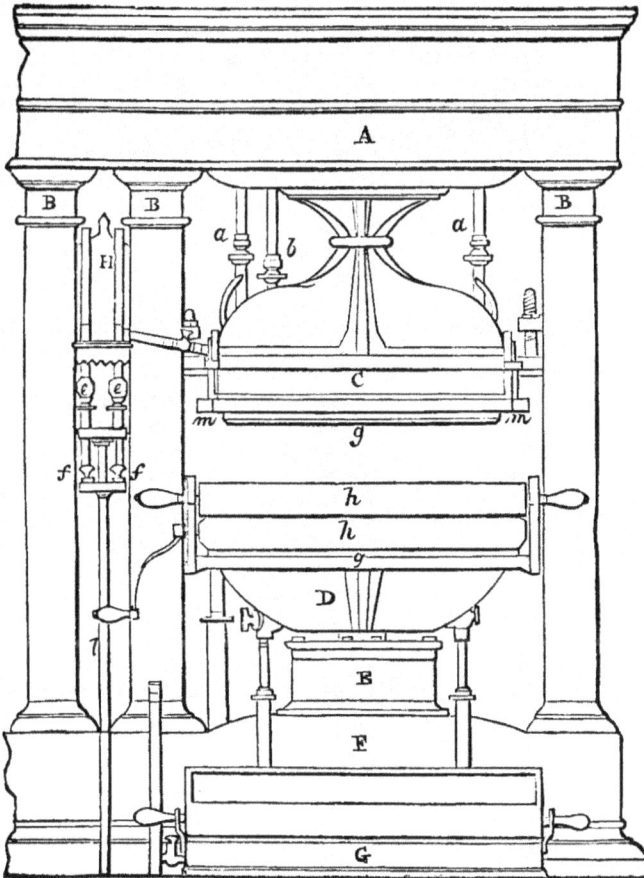

The power which impels this great hydrostatic range is placed in a separate apartment, called the machinery-room. This machinery consists of two press-cylinders of a peculiar construction, having solid rams accurately fitted to them. To each of these cylinders three little force-pumps, worked by a steam-engine, are connected.

The piston of a large cylinder is eight inches in diameter, and is loaded with a top weight of five tons. This piston can be made to rise about two feet through a leather stuffing or collar. The other cylinder has a piston of only one inch in diameter, which is also loaded with a top weight of five tons. It is capable, like the other, of being raised two feet through its collar.

Supposing the pistons to be at their lowest point, four of the six small force-pumps are put in action by the steam-engine, two of them to raise the large piston, and two the little one. In a short time so much water is injected into the cylinders that the loaded pistons have arrived at their highest points. They are now ready for working the hydrostatic discharge-presses, the water-pressure being conveyed from the one apartment to the other, under ground, through strong copper tubes of small calibre.

Two valves are attached to each press, one opening a communication between the large driving cylinder and the cylinder of the press, the other between the small driving cylinder and the press. The function of the first is simply to lift the under block of the press into contact with the upper block; that of the second is to give the requisite compression to the cloth. A third valve is attached to the press for the purpose of discharging the water from its cylinder, when the press is to be relaxed in order to remove or draw through the cloth.

From 12 to 14 pieces of cloth, previously dyed Turkey red, are stretched over each other as parallel as possible, by a particular machine. These parallel layers are then rolled round a wooden cylinder, called by the workmen a drum. This cylinder is now placed in its proper situation at the back of the press. A portion of the 14 layers of cloth, equal to the area of the plates, is next drawn through between them by hooks attached to the two corners of the webs. On opening the valve connected with the eight-inch driving cylinder, the water enters the cylinder of the press, and instantly lifts its lower block so as to apply the under plate with its cloth close to the upper one. This valve is then shut and the other is opened. The pressure of five tons in the one-inch prime cylinder is now brought to bear on the piston of the press, which is eight inches in diameter. The effective force here will therefore be $5 \text{ tons} \times 8^2 = 320 \text{ tons}$, the areas of cylinders being to each other as the squares of their respective diameters. The cloth is thus condensed between the leaden pattern-plates with a pressure of 320 tons in a couple of seconds.

The next step is to admit the bleaching or discharging liquor (aqueous chlorine, obtained by adding sulphuric acid to solution of chloride of lime) to the cloth. This liquor is contained in a large cistern in an adjoining house, from which it is run at pleasure into small lead cisterns, H, attached to the presses, which cisterns have graduated index-tubes for regulating the quantity of liquor according to the pattern of discharge. The stopcocks on the pipes and cisterns containing this liquor are all made of glass.

From the measure-cistern, H, the liquor is allowed to flow into the hollows in the upper lead plate, whence it descends on the cloth, and percolates through it, extracting in its passage the Turkey-red dye. The liquor is finally conveyed into the waste pipe from a groove in the under block. As soon as the chlorine liquor has passed through, water is admitted in a similar manner to wash away the chlorine, otherwise upon relaxing the pressure, the outline of the figure discharged would become ragged. The passage of the discharge liquor, as well as of the water through the cloth, is occasionally aided by a pneumatic apparatus, or blowing machine, consisting of a large gasometer from which the air, subjected to a moderate pressure, may be allowed to issue and act, in the direction of the liquid, upon the folds of the cloth. By an occasional twist of the air-stopcock, the workmen also can ensure the equal distribution of the discharging liquor over the whole excavations in the upper plate. When the demand for goods is very brisk, the air apparatus is much employed, as it enables the workman to double his product.

The time requisite for completing the discharging process in the first press is sufficient to enable the other three workmen to put the remaining fifteen presses in play. The discharger proceeds now from press to press, admits the liquor, the air, and the water; and is followed at a proper interval by the assistants, who relax the press, move forwards another square of the cloth, and then restore the pressure. Whenever the sixteenth press has been liquored, &c., it is time to open the first press. In this routine about ten minutes are employed, that is, 224 handkerchiefs (16 × 14) are discharged every ten minutes. The whole cloth is drawn successively forward, to be successively treated according to the above method.

When the cloth is removed from the press it is passed between the two rollers in front, from which it falls into a trough of water placed below. It is finally carried off to the washing and bleaching department, where the lustre of both the white and the red is considerably brightened.

By the above arrangement of presses, 1,600 pieces, consisting of 12 yards each = 19,200 yards, are converted into bandannas in the space of ten hours, by the labour of four workmen.

The patterns, or plates, which are put into the presses to determine the white figures on the cloth, are made of lead in the following way:—A trellis frame of cast iron, one inch thick, with turned-up edges, forming a trough rather larger than the intended lead-pattern, is used as the solid groundwork. Into this trough a lead plate, about one half-inch thick, is firmly fixed by screw-nails passing up from below. To the edges of this lead plate the borders of the piece of sheet lead are soldered, which covers the whole outer surface of the iron frame. Thus a strong trough is formed, one inch deep. The upright border gives at once great strength to the plate and serves to confine the liquor. A thin sheet of lead is now laid on the thick lead plate, in the manner of a veneer on toilette tables, and is soldered to it round the edges. Both sheets must be made very smooth beforehand, by hammering them on a smooth stone table, and then finishing with a plane; the surface of the thin sheet (now attached) is to be covered with drawing-paper, pasted on, and upon this the pattern is drawn. It is now ready for the cutter. The first thing which he does is to fix down with brass pins all the parts of the pattern which are to be left solid. He now proceeds with the little tools generally used by block-cutters, which are fitted to the different curvatures of the pattern, and he cuts perpendicularly quite through the thin sheet. The pieces thus detached are easily lifted out, and thus the channels are formed which design the white figures on the red cloth. At the bottom of the channels a sufficient number of small perforations are made through the thicker sheet lead, so that the discharging liquor may have free ingress and egress. Thus one plate is finished, from which an impression is taken in the hydrostatic press, by means of printers' ink, on paper pasted upon another plate. Each pair of plates constitutes a set which may be put into presses and removed at pleasure.

BANDOLINE, called also *clysphitique* and *fixature,* a mucilage of Carrageen moss; used for stiffening the hair and keeping it in order.

BANG or **BHANG.** When common hemp (*Cannabis sativa*) is grown in tropical countries, its fibre becomes much less valuable, but its peculiar narcotic resin is much more abundantly secreted. The leaves and capsules of such hemp furnish the substance known as *bang,* which is largely used in the East as an intoxicating drug.

BANTAM-WORK. Carved and painted work in imitation of Japan ware.

BAOBAB TREE. See ADANSONIA.

BAP or **BAT.** In Leicestershire a dark bituminous shale is so named.

BARBADOES TAR. A mineral pitch of a peculiarly odorous character. This bitumen was formerly obtained from Barbadoes ; but several kinds now pass under the name.

BARBARY GUM. Sometimes called *Morocco gum.* The product of the *Acacia gummifera.* Imported from Tripoli, Barbary, and Morocco. See ARABIC, GUM.

BARBERRY. (*Berberis,* Lat. ; *Épine-vinette,* Fr.) It is probable that this name has been given to this plant from its spines, or *barbs.* The name, *Oxycanthus,* also given to it, indicates a like origin.

The barberry is a shrubby plant, common in hedges in England; sometimes called the pipperidge bush. The berries are used in housewifery. The wood and bark of this plant contain a yellow colouring-matter which is soluble in water and alcohol, and is rendered brown by alkalis. The solution is employed in the manufacture of morocco leather. The yellow crystalline colouring-principle of the barberry is termed *Beberine.*

It is a common notion among farmers that barberry bushes cause the neighbouring wheat to become blighted. This was long regarded by botanists as nothing more than a popular prejudice, but the recent researches of Oersted and De Bary have shown that it really has foundation in fact. It is now proved that the two kinds of fungus, of which one infests the barberry and the other the wheat, though so different as to be placed in distinct genera, are really alternating forms of one and the same species. In one condition of its existence the fungus grows only on the barberry bush, but at a later period of its development it gives rise to an organism which produces the rust of wheat. Hence, a scientific relation is established between the appearance of the disease and the presence of the barberry.

BARILLA. (*Soude, Barille,* Fr. ; *Barilla,* Ger.) A crude soda, procured by the incineration of the *Salsola soda,* a plant cultivated for this purpose in Spain, Sicily, Sardinia, and the Canary Islands. In Alicante the plants are raised from seed, which is sown at the close of the year, and they are usually fit to be gathered in September following. In October the plants are usually burned. For this purpose holes are made in the earth, capable of containing a ton or a ton and a half of soda. Iron bars are laid across these cavities, and the dried plants, stratified with dry reeds, are placed upon them. The whole is set on fire. The alkali contained in the plants is fused, and it flows into the cavity beneath, a red-hot fluid. By constantly heaping-on plants, the burning is continued until the pits are full of barilla ; they are then covered up with earth and allowed to cool gradually. The spongy mass of alkali, when sufficiently cold, is broken out, and, without any further preparation, it is ready for shipment. Good barilla usually contains, according to Dr. Ure's analysis, 20 per cent. of real alkali associated with muriates and sulphates, chiefly of soda, some lime, and alumina, with very little sulphur. Caustic leys made from it were formerly used in the finishing process of the hard-soap manufacture.

The manufacture of barilla has greatly declined since the introduction of Le Blanc's process for artificially manufacturing soda from common salt.

BARILLA DE COBRE. (*Copper Barilla.*) A commercial name for the native copper of Corocoro in Bolivia. The copper is obtained in the state of powder by crushing and washing the red Permian sandstone, which contains the metal.

BARITE. A form of spelling adopted by Dana for the mineral usually called *barytes* or *heavy spar.* Professor Dana has proposed that a distinction should be established between the names of minerals and those of rocks, by terminating the former in -*ite* and the latter in -*yte.* Hence the change of spelling from *baryte* to *barite.*

BARIUM. (From βαρὺς, *heavy.*) The metallic basis of the earth baryta was obtained by Davy, in 1808, by the voltaic decomposition of the moistened carbonate of baryta in contact with mercury. It may likewise be procured by passing potassium in vapour over baryta heated to redness in an iron tube, and afterwards withdrawing the reduced barium which the residuum contains, by means of mercury. The latter metal is separated by distillation in a glass retort, care being taken not to raise the temperature to redness, for the barium then decomposes glass. Mr. Crookes has prepared metallic barium by adding a saturated solution of chloride of barium to his sodium-amalgam, and heating it to about 200° F. The sodium is thus replaced by barium, and this barium-amalgam, when purified, is heated under naphtha, and the mercury thus distilled off, leaving metallic barium.

Barium is a white metal, like silver, fusible under a red heat, and denser than oil of vitriol, in which it sinks.—*Graham.*

BARIUM, OXIDES OF. There are two oxides of barium, a protoxide BaO (baryta) and a peroxide BaO^2. The *protoxide* will be described under **BARYTA.** The peroxide may be obtained by passing oxygen over caustic baryta heated to dull redness; the oxygen thus absorbed may be expelled at a higher temperature, and the peroxide thus reduced to the state of protoxide. Availing himself of these reactions, Boussingault has proposed to prepare oxygen gas on a large scale by first forming peroxide of barium by the passage of atmospheric air over baryta at a low red heat, and then decomposing this peroxide by ignition. The oxygen would thus be really derived from the air, and the barium-oxide would merely act as a medium for its alternate absorption and evolution, and might therefore be used over and over again indefinitely. Though economy seems to recommend this process, there are practical difficulties which have hitherto interfered with its working. See **BARYTA.**

BARIUM, SALTS OF:—

BROMIDE OF BARIUM. Prepared by saturating baryta water with hydrobromic acid.

CHLORIDE OF BARIUM. Made from the native sulphate (heavy spar), by igniting it in a crucible with pounded coal, and then dissolving this sulphide in hydrochloric acid, or by fusing the native sulphate with chloride of calcium. The commercial chloride frequently contains small quantities of the chlorides of strontium and calcium. Chloride of barium is especially used for the detection and estimation of sulphuric acid.

FLUORIDE OF BARIUM. Prepared by neutralising baryta-water by hydrofluoric acid.

IODIDE OF BARIUM is formed when hydriodic acid is passed over baryta at a red heat.

BARK. The outer rind of plants. Many varieties of barks are known to commerce, but the term is especially used to express either Peruvian or Jesuits' bark, a pharmaceutical remedy, or Oak bark, which is very extensively used by tanners and dyers. The varieties known in commerce are:—

CORK BARK. (Fr. *Liège*; *Kork*, Ger.). OAK BARK. (*Tan brut*, Fr.; *Eichenrinde*, Ger.). PERUVIAN BARK. (*Quinquina*, Fr.; *Chinarinde*, Ger.). QUERCITRON BARK. WATTLE BARK. See these respectively.

BARK BREAD. A kind of bread prepared in many parts of Norway by the poorer peasants from the inner bark of the *Pinus sylvestris.* See PINUS.

BARLEY. (*Orge*, Fr.; *Gerste*, Ger.) *Hordeum*, Linn. This term is supposed to be derived from *hordus*, heavy, because the bread made from it is very heavy. Barley belongs to the class *Endogens*, or *Monocotyledons*; *Glumel Alliance*, of Lindley: natural order, *Graminaceæ.*

There are four species of barley cultivated in this country:—

1. *Hordeum hexastichon.* Six-rowed barley, or Winter barley.
2. *Hordeum vulgare.* The Scotch bere or bigg; the four-rowed barley.
3. *Hordeum zeocriton.* Putney, fan, sprat, or battledore barley.
4. *Hordeum distichon.* Two-rowed long-eared barley, or Summer barley.

Barley and oats are the cereals whose cultivation extends farthest north in Europe.

The specific gravity of English barley varies from 1·25 to 1·33; of bigg from 1·227 to 1·265; the weight of the husk of barley is $\frac{1}{6}$, that of bigg $\frac{2}{9}$. Specific gravity of barley is 1·235, by Dr. Ure's trials. 1,000 parts of barley-flour contain, according to Einhof, 720 of starch, 56 sugar, 50 mucilage, 36·6 gluten, 12·3 vegetable albumen, 100 water, 2·5 phosphate of lime, and 68 fibrous or ligneous matter.

From the examination instituted by the Royal Agricultural Society of England, and carried out under the directions of Messrs. Way and Ogston, the following results have been arrived at :—

Kind of Barley employed	Moisture in 100 Parts of Grain	Specific Gravity of Grains	Ash in 100 Parts of dried Grain
Unknown	12·00	...	2·43
Chevalier barley	10·00	1·260	2·50
Ditto	16·00	1·234	2·82
Ditto, from Moldavia	11·00	1·268	2·38
Ditto	16·00	...	2·75
Grains of Chevalier barley	15·00	...	14·23

The analyses of several varieties gave as the composition of the ashes of the grains of barley :—

	Unknown	Chevalier Barley	From Moldavia	Chevalier Barley
Potash	21·14	20·77	37·55	7·70
Soda	...	4·56	1·06	0·36
Lime	1·65	1·48	1·21	10·36
Magnesia	7·26	7·45	10·17	1·26
Sesquioxide of iron	2·13	0·51	1·02	1·46
Sulphuric acid	1·91	0·79	0·27	2·99
Silica	30·68	32·73	24·56	70·77
Phosphoric acid	28·53	31·69	28·64	1·99
Chloride of sodium	1·01	...	1·47	1·10

In the 'Synopsis of the Vegetable Products of Scotland,' by Peter Lawson and Son, will be found the best description of all the different varieties of barley; and, since the Lawsonian collection is in the museum of the Royal Botanic Gardens at Kew, the grains can be examined readily by all who take any interest in the subject. A few only of the varieties will be noticed.

The true six-rowed Barley, known also as Pomeranian and as six-rowed white winter barley.—This is a coarse barley, but hardy and prolific. It is occasionally sown in France, and also in this country, sometimes as a winter and sometimes as a spring barley, and is found to answer pretty well as either.

Naked two-rowed.—Ear long, containing twenty-eight or thirty very large grains, which separate from the paleæ, or chaff, in the manner of wheat. This variety has been introduced to the notice of agriculturalists at various times, and under different names, but its cultivation has never been carried to any great extent.

Common Bere, Bigg, or rough Barley.—This variety is chiefly cultivated in the Highlands of Scotland, and in the Lowlands on exposed inferior soils.

Victoria.—A superior variety of the old bigg, compared with which it produces longer straw, and is long-eared, often containing 70 or 100 grains in each. Instances have been known of its yielding 13 quarters per acre, and weighing as much as 96 lbs. per bushel.

Beyond these there are the winter black; the winter white; old Scottish four-rowed; naked, golden, or Italian; Suffolk or Norfolk, and Short-necked; cultivated in various districts, and with varying qualities. See BEER.

Total Acreage of Barley grown in Great Britain in each year from 1868 to 1872,

Barley	1868	1869	1870	1871	1872
England	1,780,201	1,864,088	1,963,744	1,964,210	1,896,403
Wales	151,608	157,582	163,853	169,751	168,014
Scotland	219,515	229,810	244,142	251,822	251,915
Great Britain	2,151,324	2,251,480	2,371,739	2,385,783	2,316,332

Statement of Quantities of Barley produced in Foreign Countries in the following years :—

Years		Countries					Quantity
							Bushels
1870	. .	Sweden	.	.	.	.	12,377,827
1870	. .	Norway	:	:	:	:	3,749,872
1871	. .	Prussia	:	.	.	:	113,920,223
1871	. .	Würtemberg	.	:	.		6,028,400
1863	. .	Bavaria	.	:	:	:	16,910,539
1870	. .	Holland	:	:	:	:	5,088,682
1866	. .	Belgium	:	:	:	:	3,665,643
1869	. .	France	.	.	.	.	56,495,697
1865	. .	Portugal	.	.	.	.	1,925,000
1857	. .	Spain	.	.	.	.	76,427,587
1871	. .	Austria	.	.	.	.	44,933,867
1865	. .	Italy	.	.	.	.	20,534,907
1867	. .	Greece	.	.	.	.	2,128,430
1871	. .	United States	.	.	.		26,718,500

BARLEY, SCOTCH, HULLED, POT, and **PEARL.** When barley is deprived of its husk by a mill, it forms the *Scotch, Hulled,* or *Pot Barley.* When all the integuments of the grains are removed, and the seeds are rounded and polished, they constitute *Pearl-Barley.* The flour obtained by grinding pearl-barley to powder is called *Patent Barley.*

BARLEY-SUGAR. Sugar boiled, formerly in barley-water, until it is quite transparent and crisp. It is flavoured with either orange or lemon peel.

BARM. (Derived from the Saxon *beorme ;* or from *beer-rahm,* beer-cream.) The yeasty top of fermenting beer. It is used as leaven in bread, and to establish fermentation in liquors. See BEER, FERMENTATION.

BAR-MASTER. In Derbyshire, the authority to whom all disputes in lead-mining are referred. He has charge of the standard 'dish' or measure used for measuring the ore. It is the same as *Bargh-master.*

BARMOTE or **BARGMOTE.** A court held for determining such questions as may arise in lead-mining. It is usually held in Derbyshire twice a year.

BAR OF GROUND. A course of rock dissimilar to the ordinary vein-stone—which runs across a mineral lode.

BAROMETER. This name signifies a *measurer of weight*—the column of mercury in the tube of the barometer being exactly balanced against the weight of a column of air of the same diameter, reaching from the surface of the earth to the extreme limits of the atmosphere. The length of this column of mercury is never more than thirty-one inches; below that point it may vary, according to conditions, through several inches. There have been many useful applications of the barometer, but the only one with which this Dictionary has to deal appears to be the use of the instrument in coal mines. It is now necessary, under the Coal Mines' Regulation Act, that a barometer and a thermometer should be found in every colliery. This has arisen from a prevailing idea that the explosions of fire-damp have, in numerous instances, arisen from the alteration of atmospheric pressure.

The relation between the state of the barometer and the occurrence of colliery explosions has been investigated by Messrs. R. H. Scott, F. R. S., and W. Galloway, in a paper 'On the Connection between Explosions in Collieries and Weather.'—*Proceedings of the Royal Society,* April 18th, 1872.

Mr. T. Dobson read a paper 'On the relation between Explosions in Collieries and Revolving Storms' at the meeting of the British Association at Glasgow in 1855, which is printed in the Reports for that year. Mr. Bunning has given in the 'Transactions of the North of England Institute of Mining Engineers' diagrams showing the meteorological records from the observatories of Kew and Glasgow, and the explosions in collieries reported in those years. It is not possible in this place to examine a question complicated as this one is by the numerous conditions which surround the operations of working coals, and ventilating a colliery. The results of the examinations made from time to time before Committees of the House of Commons, and other Committees, and by individuals, many of which are carefully recorded in the paper already referred to, go to show that meteorological changes are the proximate causes of a large majority of colliery explosions, and hence, therefore, the necessity of carefully watching the changes of the barometer, and of regulating the ventilation in obedience to its indications. So strongly was this felt by the Meteorological Committee who, in 1868, carefully examined the question, that they proposed to send telegraphic intelligence of storms—arising as they always do from disturbances of the atmospheric pressure—to colliery proprietors. Messrs. Scott and Galloway conclude their paper—above referred to—in the following words :— ' Whether, therefore, the barometer falls or the temperature rises, it is absolutely necessary to keep a most careful watch over the amount of air passing through the workings, in order to prevent the formation of dangerous accumulations of explosive mixtures of air and fire-damp in all mines in which the margin between danger and safety is very small. . . . The one cry—whether we look to security against explosion, or to afford to miners an atmosphere which is respirable without injury to health— is more air.' See COAL-MINING and VENTILATION OF MINES.

BARRÈGE. A woollen fabric, in both warp and woof, which takes its name from the district in which it was first manufactured—the especial locality being a little village named Arosons, in the beautiful valley of Barrèges. It was first employed as an ornament for the head, especially for sacred ceremonies, as baptism and marriage. Paris subsequently became celebrated for its barrèges, but these were generally woven with a warp of silk. Enormous quantities of cheap barrèges are now made with a warp of cotton.

BARREL. (*Baril*, Fr.) A round vessel, or cask, of greater length than breadth, made of staves, and hooped.

The English barrel—wine measure contains 31½ gallons.

,,	(old) beer ,,	,,	36	,,
,,	(old) ale ,,	,,	32	,,
,,	beer vinegar ,,	34	,,	
,,	contains 126 Paris pints.			

The ale and beer barrels were equalised to 34 gallons by a statute of William and Mary. The wine gallon, by a statute of Anne, was declared to be 231 cubic inches ; the beer gallon being usually reckoned as 282 cubic inches. The imperial gallon is 277·274 cubic inches. The old barrels now in use are as follows :—

Wine barrel	.	.	$26\frac{1}{4}$ imperial gallons.
Ale ,, (London)	.	.	$33\frac{32}{59}$,,
Beer ,,	.	.	$36\frac{38}{59}$,,
Ale and beer, for England	.	.	$34\frac{34}{59}$,,

The *baril de Florence* is equivalent to 20 bottles.

The Connecticut barrel for liquors is 31½ gallons, each gallon to contain 231 cubic inches. The statute barrel of America must be from 28 to 31 gallons. The barrel of flour, New York, must contain either 195 lbs. or 228 lbs. nett weight. The barrel of beef or pork in New York and Connecticut is 200 lbs. A barrel of Essex butter is 106 lbs. A barrel of Suffolk butter is 256 lbs. A barrel of herrings should hold 1,000 fish. A barrel of salmon should measure 42 gallons. In *machinery*, anything hollow and cylindrical.

BARROWS. In *mining*, heaps of waste stuff raised from the mine ; rubbish, called in Cornwall ' deads.'—The conical baskets into which salt is put.

BARWOOD. An African red dye-wood, the produce of the *Baphita nitida*, belonging to the *Leguminosæ* or pea-order—a tree which also yields Camwood. Although distinctions are made between sandal or saunders wood, camwood, and barwood, they appear to be very nearly allied to each other—at least, the colouring-matter is of the same composition. They come, however, from different places. See CAMWOOD and SANDAL WOOD.

MM. Girardin and Preisser thus describe barwood :—

This wood, in the state of a coarse powder, is of a bright red colour, without any odour or smell. It imparts scarcely any colour to the saliva.

Cold water, in contact with this powder, only acquires a fawn tint after five days' maceration. 100 parts of water only dissolve 2·21 of substances consisting of 0·85 colouring-matter and of 1·36 saline compounds. Boiling water becomes more strongly coloured of a reddish yellow ; but, on cooling, it deposits a part of the colouring-principle in the form of a red powder. 100 parts of water at 212° dissolve 8·86 of substances consisting of 7·24 colouring-principle, and 1·62 salts, especially sulphates and chlorides. On macerating the powder in strong alcohol, the liquid almost immediately acquires a very dark vinous red colour. To remove the whole of the colour from fifteen grains of this powder, it was necessary to treat it several times with boiling alcohol. The alcoholic liquid contained 0·23 of colouring-principle and 0·004 of salt. Barwood contains, therefore, 23 per cent. of red colouring-matter; whilst saunders wood, according to Pelletier, only contains 16·75.

The alcoholic solution behaves in the following manner towards reagents :—

Distilled water added in great quantity .	Produces a considerable yellow opalescence. The precipitate is re-dissolved by the fixed alkalis, and the liquor acquires a dark vinous colour.
Fixed alkalis	Turn it dark crimson, or dark violet.
Lime-water	Ditto.
Sulphuric acid	Darkens the colour to a cochineal red.
Sulphuretted hydrogen . . .	Acts like water.
Salt of tin	Blood-red precipitate.
Chloride of tin	Brick-red precipitate.
Acetate of lead	Dark violet gelatinous precipitate.
Salts of the protoxide of iron . .	Very abundant violet precipitates.
Copper salts	Violet-brown gelatinous precipitates.
Chloride of mercury . . .	An abundant precipitate of a brick-red colour.
Nitrate of bismuth	Gives a light and brilliant crimson red.
Sulphate of zinc	Bright red flocculent precipitate.
Tartar emetic	An abundant precipitate of a dark cherry colour.
Neutral salts of potash . . .	Act like pure water.
Water of baryta	Dark violet-brown precipitate.
Gelatine	Brownish-yellow ochreous precipitate.
Chlorine	Brings back the liquor to a light yellow, with a slight yellowish-brown precipitate, resembling hydrated peroxide of iron.

Pyroxylic spirit acts on barwood like alcohol, and the strongly coloured solution behaves similarly towards reagents. Hydrated ether almost immediately acquires an orange-red tint, rather paler than that with alcohol. It dissolves 19·47 per cent. of the colouring-principle. Ammonia, potash, and soda, in contact with powdered barwood, assume an extremely dark violet-red colour. These solutions, neutralised with hydrochloric acid, deposit the colouring-matter in the form of a dark reddish-brown powder. Acetic acid becomes of a dark-red colour, as with saunders wood.

Barwood is but slightly soluble; but the difficulty arising from its slight solubility is, according to Mr. Napier, overcome by the following very ingenious arrangement :—The colouring-matter while hot combines easily with the proto-compounds of tin, forming an insoluble rich red colour. The goods to be dyed are impregnated with proto-chloride of tin combined with sumach. The proper proportion of barwood for the colour wanted is put into a boiler with water and brought to boil. The goods thus impregnated are put into this boiling water containing the rasped wood, and the small portion of colouring-matter dissolved in the water is immediately taken up by the goods. The water, thus exhausted, dissolves a new portion of colouring-matter, which is again taken up by the goods, and so on till the tin upon the cloth has become (if we may so term it) saturated. The colour is then at its brightest and richest phase.

BARYTA. (*Baryte*, Fr.) One of the simple earths, protoxide of barium (BaO). It may be obtained most easily by dissolving the native carbonate of baryta in nitric acid, evaporating the neutral nitrate till crystals be formed, draining and then calcining these, by successive portions, in a covered platina crucible, at a bright red heat. A less pure baryta may be obtained by igniting strongly a mixture of the carbonate and charcoal, both in fine powder and moistened. It is a greyish-white earthy looking substance, fusible only at the jet of the oxy-hydrogen blowpipe, has a sharp caustic taste, corrodes the tongue and all animal matter, is poisonous even in small quantities, has a very powerful alkaline reaction; a specific gravity of 4·0; becomes hot, and slakes violently when sprinkled with water, falling into a fine white powder, called the hydrate of baryta, which contains 10½ per cent. of water, and dissolves in 10 parts of boiling water. This solution lets fall abundant columnar crystals of hydrate of baryta as it cools; but it still retains one-twentieth its weight of baryta, and is called baryta water. The above crystals contain 61 per cent. of water, of which, by drying, they lose 50 parts. This hydrate may be fused at a red heat without losing any more water. Of all the bases, baryta has the strongest affinity for sulphuric acid, and is hence employed—either in the state of the above water, or in that of one of its neutral salts, as the chloride—to detect the presence and determine the quantity of that acid present in any soluble compound,

BARYTA, CARBONATE OF. The composition of the native carbonate of baryta, called *Witherite*, after Withering, who described it ('Phil. Transactions,' 1784), may be regarded as baryta, 77·59, and carbonic acid 22·41. It is found in Shropshire, Cumberland, Westmoreland, and Northumberland. The carbonate of baryta is employed in our colour-manufactories as a base for some of the more delicate colours; it is also used in the manufacture of plate-glass, and of Wedgwood-ware; and, in France, it is much used in the preparation of beet-root sugar.

A small quantity only of carbonate of baryta is now produced in this country; in 1870 about 2,613 tons, 19 cwt., were raised in Northumberland; a few tons were sold from Alston Moor, and from Snailbeach, in Shropshire.

BARYTA, NITRATE OF. This salt is used in pyrotechny for making *green fire*. The best mixture is nitrate of baryta 77 parts, sulphur 13 parts, chlorate of potash 5 parts, metallic arsenic 2 parts, charcoal 3 parts. The nitrate is prepared by dissolving carbonate of baryta in nitric acid.

BARYTA, SULPHATE OF. This compound occurs native, forming the mineral-species known variously as *barite*, *baryte*, or *barytes*. Its comparatively high density for a non-metallic mineral (4·7) led to its recognition by the older mineralogists as *spathum ponderosum*, or *terra ponderosa*, and it is still commonly known as *heavy spar*. The mineral frequently occurs in large crystals, usually tabular in form. Massive varieties, common in many of the lead-mines worked in the mountain limestone of Derbyshire and Shropshire, are usually termed *cawk;* certain columnar varieties from Saxony are known to German mineralogists as *Stangenspath;* and a peculiar form occurring, near Bologna, in nodules which present a radiated structure, is called *Bologna stone*. This Bologna spar is notable for the phosphorescence which it exhibits when heated; the so-called '*Bologna Phosphorus*' was made by powdering this stone, and cementing the powder into the form of sticks, by means of gum.

Sulphate of baryta is composed of baryta 65·63, sulphuric acid 34·37, with sometimes a little iron, lime, or silica.

This salt of baryta is very extensively spread over various parts of the British islands. It might be obtained in very large quantities in Devonshire, Cornwall, and other places, if the demand for it sufficiently increased the price, so as to render the working of it profitable. It is worked in Derbyshire, Yorkshire, Shropshire, the Isle of Arran, and in Ireland.

Cawk, or massive sulphate of baryta, was introduced by Josiah Wedgwood as an important ingredient in his celebrated 'jasper ware,' and is still employed by the potter in producing a similar fine paste. But the mineral is chiefly used as a pigment, or rather for adulterating other pigments.

The white varieties are ground after being heated and thrown into water, and the heavy white powder is employed in adulterating white lead. On this account it is very difficult to obtain correct returns. The production of 1871 was:—

	Tons	Cwts.
Derbyshire	2,189	5
Shropshire	595	1
Northumberland	1,690	0
Isle of Arran	400	0
Cumberland	57	15

BARYTES. Heavy spar, or native sulphate of baryta.

BASALT. One of the most common varieties of trap-rock. It is a dark green or black stone, composed chiefly of augite and labradorite-felspar, very compact in texture, and of considerable hardness, often found in regular pillars of three or more sides, called basaltic columns. Remarkable examples of this kind are seen at the Giant's Causeway in Ireland, and at Fingal's Cave, in Staffa, one of the Hebrides. Messrs. Chance (brothers), of Birmingham, at one time adopted the process of melting the Rowley rag, a basaltic rock forming the plateau of the Rowley hills, near Dudley, South Staffordshire, and then casting it into moulds for architectural ornaments, tiles for pavements, &c. Not only the Rowley rag, but basalt, greenstone, whinstone, or any similar mineral, might be used. The material was melted in a reverberatory furnace, and when in a sufficiently fluid state poured into moulds of sand encased in iron boxes, these moulds having been previously raised to a red heat in ovens suitable for the purpose. The object to be attained by heating the moulds previous to their reception of the liquid material is to retard the rate of cooling; as the result of slow cooling is a hard, strong, and stony substance, closely resembling the natural stone, while the result of rapid cooling is a dark brittle glass.

BASILICON. The name given by the old apothecaries to a mixture of oil, wax, and resin, which is represented by the *Cerat resinæ* of the present day.

BASKETS. Weaving of rods into baskets is one of the most ancient of the arts amongst men; and it is practised in almost every part of the globe, whether inhabited by civilised or savage races. Basket-making requires no description here.

BASS, or **BAST.** The Russian mats used by gardeners and upholsterers, made from the bark of the Lime or Linden tree, are called Bast mats. The name is also used for the bark or tough fibres of the flax and hemp plants of which Bast brooms are made. The thick mat or hassock used by persons to kneel on at church is called a Bass.

BASSET. A miner's term for the outcrop of strata. When a seam of coal comes to the surface, it is said to ' basset.'

BASSORA GUM. A gum obtained from the *Acacia leucophlæa*, brought from Bassora. It has a specific gravity of 1·3591, and is yellowish white in colour.

BASSORINE. A constituent part of gum Bassora, as also of gum tragacanth. It is semi-transparent, difficult to pulverise, swells considerably in cold or boiling water, and forms a thick mucilage without dissolving.

BATEA. A dish made slightly conical, which is employed for washing soil or gravel, in search of gold. It is usually about 20 inches in diameter, and 2½ inches deep. Before using the *batea*, to ascertain if there be any gold, and what amount, it is necessary to be very careful in the selection of the sample to be experimented upon. The usual manner of obtaining such a sample is as follows:—The produce of gold is so very irregular that it is necessary, in the first place, to break from the rock several hundredweights to secure a good average sample; all of which should be broken in pieces about the size of a walnut, the whole well mixed together, and made into a round flat heap; this heap is cut through the middle, and an equal quantity of stuff being taken from each side of the trench formed by the cutting, may, for a rough estimation, be at once pulverised and subjected to washing in the batea or horn-spoon; but if greater accuracy be desired, it is well to take about half a hundredweight from each side of the trench, and this be again reduced to pieces of about the size of a pea, then formed in a heap, and cut as before, and about two pounds should be taken from each side the trench, and this after pulverisation, and being passed through a very fine wire sieve, is ready for a very accurate trial with the batea; or is quite fit for assay. This is, indeed, the process by which samples are taken of the poorer copper ores in Cornwall.

BATH BRICK. A brick made of calcareous and siliceous earth, used in cleaning knives and for polishing purposes. They are made very extensively at and near Bridgewater from a deposit found in the estuary there; a similar deposit is also worked at Cumwick, at the entrance of the Parrot River, and at Highbridge. At Bridgewater the average make is about 3,000,000 scouring bricks annually, which sell at about 2*l.* per thousand.

BATH METAL. An alloy in nearly equal quantities of copper and zinc. Bath metal consists of 3 oz. of zinc to 1 lb of copper. See BRASS.

BATHS. (*Bains*, Fr.; *Baden*, Ger.) The importance attached by the Greeks and Romans to bathing is sufficiently attested by the remains of magnificent structures, which still excite the admiration of the beholder, and by the beautiful specimens of fresco-painting and sculpture discovered in their baths.

It is computed that in the baths of Caracalla, as many as three thousand people could bathe at the same time, in water at various degrees of temperature, to suit their inclinations. The warm and hot baths were, however, almost exclusively in use under the Emperors.

During the Republic the baths were cold. Mæcenas was the first to erect warm and hot ones for public use; they were called Thermæ. and were placed under the direction of ædiles, who regulated the temperature, enforced cleanliness in the establishment, and order and decorum among the visitors. Agrippa, during the time he was ædile, increased the number of thermæ to 170, and in the course of two centuries, there were no less than eight hundred in imperial Rome. The inhabitants resorted to the baths at particular hours, indicated by striking a bell or gong. Adrian forbade their being open before eight in the morning, except in cases of sickness; whereas Alexander Severus not only permitted them to be open during the whole day, but also to be used through the night in the great heats of summer.

It was a common practice with the Romans to bathe towards evening, and particularly before supper: some of the more luxurious made use of the bath even after this meal. We are told of many citizens of distinction who were in the habit of bathing four, or five, and even eight times a day. Bathing constituted a part of public rejoicings, equally with the other spectacles, and like them was prohibited when the country suffered under any calamity. All classes resorted to the baths; the emperors themselves, such as Titus, Adrian, and Alexander Severus, were occasionally seen among the bathers. The price of admission was very small, amounting to no more than a farthing.—*E. Lee, on Mineral Waters and Baths.*

Warm baths have come into very general use in England, and they are now considered as indispensably necessary in all modern houses of any magnitude, as also in club-houses, hotels, and hospitals; and the mode of constructing baths, and of obtaining the necessary supplies of hot and cold water, has undergone much improvement with the extension of their employment.

The several points in regard to warm baths are,

1. The materials of which they are constructed.
2. Their situation.
3. The supply of cold water.
4. The supply of hot water.
5. Minor comforts and conveniences.

1. As to the materials of which they are constructed.—Of these the best are slabs of polished marble, properly bedded with good water-tight cement, in a seasoned wooden case, and neatly and carefully united at their respective edges. These, when originally well constructed, form a durable, pleasant, and agreeable-looking bath, but the expense is often objectionable, and, in upper chambers, the weight may prove inconvenient. If of white or veined marble, they are also apt to get yellow or discoloured by frequent use, and cannot easily be cleansed; so that large Dutch tiles, as they are called, or square pieces of white earthenware, are sometimes substituted. Welsh slate has now superseded marble to a great extent; and very superior baths are now manufactured of Stourbridge clay, at Stourbridge. Copper, tinned or galvanised iron, are also employed; the first is most expensive in the outfit, but far more durable than the latter.

2. As to the situation of the bath, or the part of the house in which it is to be placed.—In hotels and club-houses, this is a question easily determined; several baths are usually here required, and each should have annexed to it a properly warmed dressing-room. Whether they are upstairs or downstairs is a question of convenience, but the basement story, in which they are sometimes placed, should always be avoided: there is a coldness and dampness belonging to it, in almost all weathers, which is neither agreeable nor salubrious.

In hospitals, there are usually several baths on each side of the house (the men's and women's), and the supply of hot water is ready at a moment's notice.

In private houses, the fittest places for warm baths are dressing-rooms annexed to the principal bed-rooms; or, where such convenience cannot be obtained, a separate bath-room connected with the dressing-room, and always upon the bed-room floor.

3. The supply of water is a very important point, as connected with the present subject. The water should be soft, clean, and pure; and as free as possible from all substances mechanically suspended in it.

4 and 5.—In public bathing establishments, where numerous and constant baths are required, the most effective means of obtaining hot water for their supply are now employed. It is drawn directly into the baths from a large boiler, placed somewhere above their level. The hot water enters the bath by a pipe at least an inch and a half in diameter, and the cold water by one of the same dimension. The relative proportions of the hot and cold water, are of course to be adjusted by a thermometer; and every bath has a two-inch waste-pipe, opening about two inches from the top of the bath, and suffering the excess of water freely to run off; so that when a person is immersed in the bath, or when the supplies of water are accidentally left open, there may be no danger of an overflow.

A contrivance of some ingenuity consists in suffering the water for the supply of the bath to flow from a cistern above it, through a leaden pipe of about one inch diameter, which is conducted into the kitchen or other convenient place, where a large boiler for the supply of hot water is already fixed. The bath-pipe is immersed in this boiler, in which it makes many convolutions, and again, emerging, ascends to the bath. The operation is simply this:—the cold water passing through the convolutions of that part of the pipe which is immersed in the boiling water, receives there sufficient heat for the purpose required, and ascending, in obedience to the law of fluid pressure, it is delivered in that state by the ascending pipe into the bath, which is also supplied with cold water and waste-pipes as usual. The pipe may be of lead, as far as the descending and ascending parts are concerned, but the portion forming the worm or convolutions immersed in the boiler, should be copper, in order that the water within it may receive heat without impediment.

The facilities which are now afforded for the construction of baths in private houses, and for the use of them at a very cheap rate in public establishments, render it quite unnecessary to retain the remarks made by Dr. Ure.

Public baths and wash-houses have now become common amongst us, and with them an increased cleanliness is apparent, and improved health throughout the population.

The steady increase of the revenue derived from the baths and wash-houses in London, from the commencement of the undertaking in 1846, shows the practical utility of these institutions, and their effect on the physical and social condition of the industrious classes; viz. :—

	£	s.	d.
The aggregate receipts of nine establishments, during 1853, amount to	18,213	5	8
1852. Eight establishments	15,629	5	8
1851. Six establishments	12,906	12	5
1850. Four establishments	9,823	10	6
1849. Three establishments	6,379	17	2
1848. Two establishments	2,896	5	1
1847.{ 1846.} Ditto	3,222	1	5

A similar increase has continued to the present time, the receipts being now, 1865, above 25,000*l*. Those conveniences—now, indeed, become absolute necessities—are extending in every part of the country.

Baths, as curative agents, are of various kinds. TURKISH BATHS, for Rheumatism and other complaints—in which are adopted all the processes which have been so much extolled in the Oriental bath system—have been introduced with success during the last few years. Although much lauded by some, they have not been so satisfactory to others; and do not therefore appear to be extending. VAPOUR BATHS are stimulant and sudorific; they may be either to be breathed, or not to be breathed. Dr. Pereira has given the following Table as a comparative view of the heating powers of vapour and of water :—

Kind of Bath	Water	Vapour	
		Not breathed	Breathed
Tepid bath . . .	85° to 92°	96° to 106°	90° to 100°
Warm bath . . .	92 „ 98	106 „ 120	100 „ 110
Hot bath . . .	98 „ 106	120 „ 160	110 „ 130

Local vapour baths are applied in affections of the joints, and the like.

Vapour douche is a jet of aqueous vapour directed on some part of the body.

Medicated vapour baths are prepared by impregnating vapour with the odours of medicinal plants.

Sulphur, chlorine, sulphurous acid, iodine and camphor, are occasionally employed in conjunction with aqueous vapour.

Warm, tepid, and *hot baths* are sufficiently described above.

BATH STONE. A building stone raised in the vicinity of the city of Bath. See OOLITE.

BATHVILLITE. Dr. C. Greville Williams, who has been largely employed in the distillation of bituminous minerals, and amongst others of the *Torbanite* from Torbane Hill, near Bathgate, in Scotland, has discovered a brown friable substance occasionally filling the hollows of the above mineral. This is inflammable, and has been named *Bathvillite* by its discoverer.

BATT. A name given to a highly bituminous shale, which is often found interstratified with the coal. It occurs in the South Staffordshire coal-field, and has been well described by Jukes in his 'Geology of the South Staffordshire Coal-Field.' In Lancashire this shale is called *Black Bass*, and in Flintshire, where they are distilling it in considerable quantities, it is known as *Black Slag*.

Batt or *bat* is also a term applied by the potter to a plate of gelatine, used in printing on to pottery, or porcelain *over* the glaze. In *bat-printing*, the impression is transferred from an engraved copper plate to a bat of gelatine or glue, whence it is printed on the glaze, in oil or tar. Enamel powder being then dusted over the print, adheres to the oiled surface, and the porcelain is then fired at a low temperature. See POTTERY.

BATTER. In *metallurgy*, a process of flattening a piece of iron by a blow with a hammer, so as to compress it inwardly, and spread it outwardly on all sides around the place of impact. See STAMPS.

BATTERY. In *mining*, a stamping mill. In *electricity*, a combination of glass plates or jars, with both surfaces coated with tinfoil. A combination of zinc and copper, or of other dissimilar metal plates, which are placed in an acid solution, or some other exciting fluid. The galvanic battery. See ELECTRICITY.

BAULK. A piece of timber—the whole trunk of a tree. The term is applied by London timber-merchants to wood in lengths of from 20 to 25 feet and 10 inches square.

BAUXITE. A mineral which was at one time regarded as an ore of iron. It is so called from Baux, near Arles, the name of one of the localities in France where it is found. Its composition varies, but the following analysis of a specimen from Revest, near Toulon, may be taken as typical.—

Silica	2·8
Oxide of titanium	3·1
Sesquioxide of iron	25·5
Alumina	57·4
Carbonate of lime	0·4
Water	10·8

It is used as the source from which to obtain aluminium with the most facility and in the greatest purity. See ALUMINIUM.

BAY SALT. The larger crystalline salt of commerce. See SALT.

BAY, THE SWEET. (*Laurus nobilis.*) Bay-leaves have a bitter aromatic taste, and an aromatic odour, which leads to their use in cookery.

BAYLDONITE. A hydrated arsenate of lead and copper from Cornwall. It occurs in little concretions of a grass-green colour; and was described by Prof. Church in the 'Journal of the Chemical Society' for 1865.

BAYS, OIL OF. This oil is imported in barrels from Trieste. It is obtained from the fresh and ripe berries of the bay-tree by bruising them in a mortar, boiling them for three hours in water, and then pressing them. When cold, the expressed oil is found floating on the top of the decoction. Its principal use is in the preparation of veterinary embrocations.

BDELLIUM. Two gum-resins pass in commerce by this name. One is the false myrrh (the *Bdellium* of Scripture), the produce of the *Amyris commiphora*. The other is the *African Bdellium*, obtained from *Heudolatia Africana*. Pelletier gives the composition of the African bdellium as—resin, 59·0; soluble gum, 9·2; bassorine, 30·6; volatile oil and loss, 1·2.

BEADS. (*Grain*, Fr.) Perforated balls of glass, porcelain, or gems, strung and worn for ornaments. Amongst some of the uncivilised races, beads are employed instead of money.

The use of beads is of the highest antiquity. They are found in the tombs of Thebes and in the ruined temples of Assyria. They are discovered buried with the mighty dead of Greece. The Roman lady had them placed with her in her grave; and even in the burial-places of the ancient Britons we find beads, and these, too, of a similar pattern to such as we have every reason to believe are as old as Moses. Indeed, the peculiar ornamented zigzag pattern of the most ancient beads has been always, and still is manufactured at Venice, and found over the entire continent of Africa.

Glass beads have long been made in very large quantities in the glass-houses of Murano, at Venice.

Glass-tubes, previously ornamented by colour and reticulation, are drawn out in proper sizes, from 100 to 200 feet in length, and of all possible colours. Not less than 200 shades are manufactured at Venice. These tubes are cut into lengths of about 2 feet, and then, with a knife, are cut into fragments, having about the same length as their diameter. The edges of these beads are, of course, sharp; and they are subjected to a process for removing this. Sand and wood-ashes are stirred with the beads, so that the perforations may be filled by the sand; this prevents the pieces of glass from adhering in the subsequent process, which consists in putting them into a revolving cylinder and heating them. The finished beads are sifted, sorted in various sizes, and strung by women for the market.

In the Jurors' Report of the Great Exhibition of 1851, are the following remarks on this manufacture:—

'The old Venetian manufactures of glass and glass-wares fully sustain their importance; and those of paper, jewellery, wax-lights, velvets, and laces, rather exceeded their ordinary production. The one article of beads employs upwards of 5,000 people at the principal fabric on the island of Murano; and the annual value is at least 200,000l. They are exported to London, Marseilles, Hamburg, and thence to Africa and Asia, and the great Eastern Archipelago.' The *perles à la lune* are a finer, and, consequently, more expensive bead, which are prepared by twisting a small rod of glass, softened by a blow-pipe, about an iron wire. The preparation and cutting of gems into beads belong especially to the lapidary. The production of beads of PASTE, and of artificial PEARLS, will be noticed under those heads respectively. In India beads of rock-crystal are often very beautifully cut. In 1871 we imported 2·204,241 lbs. of glass beads. See PASTE ; PEARLS.

BEAM TREE. (*Pyrus Aria.*) The wood is used for axle-trees, naves of wheels, and the cogs of machinery.

BEAN. (*Faba* and *Phaseolus.*) See LEGUMINOSÆ.

BEAN ORE. (*Bohnerz*, Ger.) Brown iron ore occurring in ellipsoidal concretions.

BEARINGS. The parts of a machine upon which the movable portions are supported. Upon the correct adaptation of the rubbing surfaces to each other depends the value of a machine. If, for example, there should be much friction between the axles of a railway-carriage and its *bearings*, there would be a large amount of power lost in overcoming that friction.

It has, therefore, been the study of engineers to produce bearings which should offer great resistance to pressure, and from their smoothness produce as little friction as possible. Kingston's metal has been lately used in the large engines for our iron-clad fleet. Some of the railway companies are using an alloy of equal parts of tin and copper. Gun-metal is, however, commonly employed for the bearings of machines. See BRONZE ; COPPER ; KINGSTON'S METAL ; UNGUENTS.

BEAT-AWAY. In *mining*, the process of working away hard ground by a rough method—with wedges and sledge-hammers—in the process of excavation.

BEAUXITE. See BAUXITE.

BEAVER. (*Castor Fiber.*) This animal is captured for its skin, and for the castor (*castoreum*), which is employed medicinally. See FURS.

BEBIRINE, or **BEBEERINE.** $C^{38}H^{21}NO^6$ ($C^{19}H^{21}NO^3$). An alkaloid discovered by Dr. Rodie, of Demerara, in the bark of the bebeern tree. It was examined more minutely by Madagan and Tilley, and still more recently by Von Planta, who has determined its true formula. It is very bitter, and highly febrifuge.

BEDE. In *mining*, a name given to a peculiar kind of pickaxe.

BEECH, (*Hêtre commun*, Fr. ; *Gemeine Buche*, Ger.) The beech-tree (the *Fagus sylvatica* of Linnæus) is one of the most magnificent of our English trees, attaining, in about sixty or seventy years, in favourable situations, a height of from 70 to 100 feet, and its trunk a diameter of 5 feet. The wood, when green, is the hardest of British timbers, and its durability is increased by steeping in water ; it is chiefly used by cabinet-makers, coopers, coach-builders, and turners.

BEEF WOOD. An Australian wood, of red colour, the produce of certain species of *Casuarina*. It is used for inlaying and marqueterie work.

BEER. The fermented infusion of malted barley, flavoured by hops, constitutes the best species of beer ; known also as ale, bitter ale, porter, or brown stout, according to its varied flavour, colour, and strength. But there are many beverages of inferior quality to which the name of beer is given ; such as spruce-beer, ginger-beer, &c., all of which consist of a saccharine liquor, partially advanced into the vinous fermentation, and flavoured with peculiar substances.

The ancients were acquainted with beer, and the Romans gave it the appropriate name of Cerevisia (quasi Ceresia), as being the product of corn, the gift of Ceres. The most celebrated liquor of this kind in the old time was the Pelusian potation, so called from the town where it was prepared, at the mouth of the Nile. Aristotle speaks of the intoxication caused by beer, and Theophrastus justly denominated it the wine of barley. We may, indeed, infer, from the notices found in historians, that drinks analogous to beer were in use among the ancient Gauls, Germans, and, in fact, almost every people of our temperate zone ; and they are still the universal beverage in every land where the vine is not an object of rustic husbandry.

In the production of beer, the raw Barley, and Hops, which are the only materials necessary, have to undergo various processes which will be more fully described under the separate articles on MALTING and BREWING, but the changes which take place in those operations will now be considered.

1. THE MATERIALS.

BARLEY.—Barley, wheat, maize, and several other kinds of grain, are capable of undergoing those changes which develop the saccharine principle from which beer can be made ; but the first-named is by far the most fit, and in this country is almost exclusively used. There are two species of barley; the '*Hordeum vulgare*,' or common barley, having its corns arranged in two rows on its spikes; and the '*Hordeum hexastichon*,' in which three seeds spring from one point, so that its double row has apparently six corns. The former is the proper barley, and is much the larger sized grain. The latter is little known in England, but is much cultivated in Scotland under the name of *bere*, or *bigg*, being a hardy plant, adapted to a colder climate. Bigg is a less compact grain than barley, the weight of an imperial bushel (2218·192 ins.) of the former being only 48 lbs., while that of the latter will be from 52 to 56 lbs. Their constituents are, however, similar.

By chemical analysis, 100 parts of barley-meal appear to consist of:—

Gluten	.	.	.	. 3·76	Albumen.	.	.	.	2·23
Starch	.	.	.	. 72·00	Phosphate of lime	.	.	0·25
Sugar	.	.	.	. 5·60	Water	.	.	.	10·00
Gum	.	.	.	. 5·00	Loss	.	.	.	1·16

Another analysis gives :—

Gluten . . . . 3·52	Phosphates	.	.	.	0·24
Hordeum, or starch and gluten	Oil .	.	.	.	0·30
intimately combined . . 67·18	Vegetable fibre	.	.	7·29
Sugar . . . . 5·21	Water	.	.	.	9·37
Gum . . . . 4·62	Loss	.	.	.	1·12
Albumen. . . . 1·15					

Hermstadt gives the mean of several analyses of barley to be :—

Gluten . . . . 4·92	Oils	.	.	.	0·35
Starch . . . . 60·50	Phosphates	.	.	0·36
Sugar . . . . 4·66	Husk	.	.	.	11·56
Gum . . . . 4·51	Water	.	.	.	10·48
Albumen. . . . 0·35	Loss	.	.	.	2·31

Proust thought he had discovered in barley a peculiar principle, to which he gave the name of *Hordeine*, and which he separated from the starch by the action of both cold and boiling water. He found that, by treating barley-meal successively with water, he obtained from 89 to 90 parts of a farinaceous substance, composed of from 32 to 33 of starch, and from 57 to 58 of hordeine. His analysis also gives, gluten, 3·0 ; sugar, 5·0 ; gum, 4·0 ; and resinous extract, 1·0.

Dr. S. Thomson gives no hordeine, but the starch as 88 per cent., sugar 4.

Einhof gives the constituents of barley as 70·05 flour; 18·75 husk; and 11·20 water.

The hordeine of Proust is a yellowish powder, contains no nitrogen, and is, therefore, dissimilar to gluten. In the process of malting the proportion of hordeine is greatly diminished by its conversion into starch and sugar, so that many chemists view hordeine as only an allotropic condition of sugar; but the subject will evidently bear yet more extended and careful research.

In giving the foregoing analyses, it may be remarked that they are not intended as a basis for any estimate of the value for brewing purposes of even the various samples from which they have been drawn, as the quality of the extract is affected by every variation of the soil on which the barley was grown, the quality of the seed, the climate, the season, and the care bestowed on its proper cultivation.

The quality of barley is much influenced by the soil on which it is grown; the best being from a light calcareous soil, or that known by farmers as good turnip-land ; and crops of excellent quality are also grown on a rich land.

Much also depends on the seed, the climate, and the care of the husbandmen in the harvesting, stacking, and the threshing at the proper season.

The barley should have a thin, bright, clean, wrinkled husk, closely adhering to a plump, well-fed kernel, which, when broken, appears white and chalky, with a full uninjured germ of a pale yellow colour. If it breaks hard and flinty, it should be avoided; and, although not in a proper condition for malting until it has sweated or seasoned in the stack or mow, care must be taken that it has not heated so as to destroy the vitality of the germ. Mixed or uneven samples should also be avoided, as it is important that all should grow simultaneously or evenly on the floors.

The Saale district of Germany is generally considered to produce the finest quality of barley, although its weight per imperial bushel is less than the average of English barley, and much less than the Scotch.

The Saale	weighs from 50 to 54 per bushel
The English	,, ,, 52 ,, 58 ,,
The Scotch	,, ,, 54 ,, 59 ,,

And as barleys, when equally well malted, yield the valuable saccharine principle nearly in proportion to their weight, the heavier English or Scotch barley, in a favourable season, is of the most value to the brewer of strong mild ales, where peculiar delicacy of flavour is not so much required.

Hops.—The female flowers, or catkins, of a diœcious plant (*Humulus lupulus*) belonging to the natural order *Urticaceæ*, which grows wild in many English hedge-rows, but requires the most careful cultivation to produce the highly odoriferous and cordial properties so valued by the brewer. The plant springs up annually from the old roots in April, flowers the latter end of June, and ripens towards the end of August and September, when they are gathered, dried, and packed very tightly in pockets or bags, for preservation and use. Hops are grown to the greatest extent in Kent and Sussex; but a strong hop is also grown in the north clay-district of the county of Nottingham, and a very grateful mild hop in the Worcestershire district.

The flavour of the Goldings, or Farnham hop, a district in Surrey, is rich, and in high estimation; but the plant is one of the most tender cultivated, the flower small, but heavy with the farina, and the crop very uncertain. The Canterbury grape-hop is much cultivated in the districts of Kent and Sussex, and deservedly esteemed as a good useful hop.

The Flemish plant produces a large flower, but of light weight and of inferior flavour; it is considered a hardy kind, and very productive. Hops require a rich soil, well manured and cleaned, a sunny aspect, and to be sheltered from the east winds, which not only check the growth of the plants, but cause them to be infested with vermin, which are sometimes so numerous as to destroy nearly the entire crop. The flower, during the ripening season, is also sometimes attacked by the red or blue mould, which often consumes a considerable portion of the farina, and may be discovered by the strig of the flower being bare of leaf. The catkins or strobils of the hop consist of the scales, or large and persistent bracts, which, in the early period of their growth, are of a light green colour (afterwards changing to a pale yellow), at the bottom of which are small round seeds, that, when ripe, have a hard shell of a brown or reddish colour. They are imbedded in the farina, or yellow powder, which is the most valuable part of the hop. No hop should be gathered till the seed is matured; not for the sake of the seed itself, but the nectarium, or farina, technically known as 'the condition,' will be in larger particles, and its essential aromatic and bitter qualities more perfectly developed when ripe. Good hops, when rubbed in the hand, leave an oily, or resinous, and rather clammy feeling, with a pungent and gratifying odour; the scales should also be even in colour, and without any green specks, or any appearance of mould on the sprig, or small stem of the flower.

The drying of the hop is an important part of its management, and requires great care; it is performed in kilns, in Sussex, termed oast-houses.

The heat should be moderate and regular, in no case exceeding 120° F., as to over-dry them would injure the flavour, and if not sufficiently dry they are liable to become mouldy.

The general practice is to try the strig or stalk of the flower, which, if it snaps from brittleness, is sufficiently dried, but if it bends without breaking, more drying is necessary.

In the process of drying every means should be used to avoid separating the farina from between the scales of the hop, and the practice of passing the hops, after drying, through what is termed a mill, for the purpose of giving more evenness to the appearance of the sample, must be highly injurious, as it breaks up the hop and exposes to loss the most valuable part of the plant. The packing has also much influence in the preservation of the valuable but volatile aroma. The finer flavoured and pale hops are well rammed into sacks of canvas, called pockets, which weigh about 1½ cwt. each; the stronger and dark-coloured hops into sacks of a coarser texture, called hop-bags, and weigh from 2½ cwts. to 3 cwts. each.

If intended for export, the bags are sometimes subjected to the action of the hydraulic press; and if not required for immediate use, the simple screw-press may be used with great advantage.

Dr. Ives first directed attention to the yellow pulverulent substance that has been alluded to as the farina or pollen of the hop, which in good samples will amount to one-sixth of their weight. This powder bears some resemblance to lycopodium; and its analysis by Dr. Ives gives, tannin, 4·16; extractive, 8·33; bitter principle, 9·16; wax, 10·00: resin, 30·00; lignin, 38·33; and loss, 0·02. About 65 per cent. of the farina is soluble in alcohol, and the solution, distilled with water, leaves a resin amounting to 52·5 per cent., which has no bitter taste, and is soluble in alcohol or ether. The distillate from which the resin has thus been separated contains the bitter principle, which has been called *lupuline* (by Payen and Chevallier), mixed with a little tannin and malic acid.

To obtain this in a state of purity, the free acid must be saturated with lime, the solution evaporated to dryness, and the residuum treated with ether, which removes a little resin; after which the lupuline is dissolved out by alcohol, leaving the malate of lime. On evaporating the alcohol, the lupuline remains, weighing from 8·3 to 12·5 per cent. It is sometimes white, or slightly yellowish, and opaque, sometimes orange-yellow and transparent.

At ordinary temperatures it is inodorous, but when heated emits the peculiar smell and possesses the characteristic taste and bitterness of the hop. Water dissolves it in the proportion of about 1 part to 20, or 5 per cent., and acquires a yellow colour. It is quite soluble in alcohol and slightly so in ether.

Lupuline is neither acid nor alkaline, nor is it acted upon by solutions of the metallic salts; it contains only a small quantity of nitrogen, and an essential oil.

The analysis by Payen and Chevallier gives the following:—Volatile oil, 2·00; lupuline, 10·30; resin, 55·00; lignin, 32·00; loss, 0·70. There are also traces of fatty, astringent, and gummy matters, malic and carbonic acids, and various salts.

The volatile oil was procured by Dr. Wagner by distilling fresh hops with water. It constituted about 8 per cent. of the air-dried flowers, it possessed a clear brownish-yellow colour, had an acrid taste and a strong odour of the hop. Its specific gravity is about 0·910; it is partially soluble in water, but more so in alcohol and ether, and becomes resinified by keeping. The tannin of the hop is also important in brewing, as it serves to precipitate the nitrogenised or albuminous matter of the barley, and assist the clearing of the liquor. Ives thought the scales of the hop, when freed from the yellow powder, contained no principles analogous to it; but it is almost impossible to free them entirely from the lupulinic grains; and Payen and Chevallier found the same principles in the different parts of the hop, but in different proportions.

2. The Preparation of the Barley by the Process of Malting.

In this process (for the conduct of which we refer to the article MALTING) the raw grain is steeped in cisterns of water until it has imbibed sufficient to cause it to germinate; it is then spread on the floor of the malt-house, and frequently turned, until the germination has advanced to the stage when the plumula is about to make its appearance, and its further germination is stopped by being rapidly dried on the malt-kiln.

During germination a remarkable change has taken place in the substance of the grain. The glutinous constituent has almost entirely disappeared, and is supposed to have passed into the matter of the radicles, or roots, which during the process will have grown rapidly to nearly one and a half the length of the grain, while a portion of the starch is converted into sugar and mucilage.

The change is similar to that which starch undergoes when dissolved in water and digested in a heat of about 160° F. along with a little gluten. The thick paste becomes gradually liquid, transparent and sweet-tasted, and the solution contains now sugar and gum, with some unaltered starch. The gluten suffers a change at the same time, and becomes acescent, so that only a small quantity of starch can thus be converted by a quantity of gluten.

By the artificial growth upon the malt-floor all the gluten and albumen present in barley are not decomposed, and only about one-half of the starch is converted into sugar, as a continuance of the germination would exhaust the grain, and the valuable products would be taken up by the growth of the roots and stems of the plant. It is, therefore, the chief art of the maltster to regulate the germination and stop it at the point when the utmost conversion is attained with the least loss. This is generally considered to be done when the plumula, technically known as the *acrospire*, has advanced two-thirds the entire length of the grain, starting from the germ and proceeding under the skin toward the other end of the grain, beyond which it must never be suffered to protrude; the conversion of the hordeine into starch and sugar keeping pace with the growth of the acrospire, and being thus prepared for its nearly complete conversion in the subsequent operations of the brewer.

Malt is generally distinguished by its colour—as pale, amber, brown, or black malt —arising from the different degrees of heat and management in the process of drying. The first is produced when the highest heat to which it has been subjected is from 90° to 100° F., the amber-coloured when the heat has been raised to 120° or 125°, and the brown at a heat of from 150° to 170°. The black malt, commonly called patent malt, is prepared by roasting in cylinders, like coffee, at a heat of from 360° to 400°, and is the only legal colouring-matter that may be used in the brewing of porter.

The action of the kiln in drying is not confined to the mere expulsion of the moisture from the germinated seeds, but it serves to convert into sugar a portion of the starch which remained unchanged, not only by the action of the gluten upon the fecula at an elevated temperature, but also by the species of roasting which the starch undergoes, which renders it of a gummy nature. We have a proof of this if we dry one portion of the malt in a naturally dry atmosphere, and another portion in a moderately warm kiln; we shall find the former yield a less saccharine extract than the latter. Moreover, kiln-dried malt has a peculiar, agreeable, and faintly-burned taste, probably from a small portion of empyreumatic oil formed in the husk, which not only imparts its flavour to the beer, but also contributes to its preservation.

As the quality of the malt depends much on that of the barley, so its skilful preparation has the greatest influence both on the quantity and quality of the worts made from it. If the germination has been imperfect or irregular, a portion of the malt will be raw, and too much of its substance remain unchanged and flinty; if it has been pushed too far, a part of the extractible matter is wasted.

If not thoroughly dried, the malt will not keep, but becomes soft and liable to mildew; and if too highly kiln-dried, a portion of its sugar will be caramelised and become bitter.

Good malt possesses the following characteristics:—The grain is round and full, breaks freely between the teeth, and has a sweetish taste, an agreeable smell, and is full of a soft flour from end to end. It affords no unpleasant flavour on being chewed; is not hard, so that when drawn along an oaken board across the fibres it leaves a white streak like chalk. It swims upon water, while unmalted barley sinks in it.

The bulk of good malt exceeds that of the barley from which it is made by from 5 to 8 per cent., but at the same time it becomes lighter in weight, 100 lbs. of good barley, judiciously malted, weighing, after being dried and screened, no more than about 80 lbs., the loss being about 12 per cent. of water, 5 per cent. waste, and about 3 per cent. by the growth of the roots, which, in drying, have been rendered brittle, and are removed by passing the malt over a wire screen.

The change which the barley has undergone by malting will be readily seen in the following comparative analysis by Proust:—

	Barley	Malt
Gluten	3	1
Hordeine	55	12
Starch	32	56
Sugar	5	15
Mucilage	4	15
Resin	1	1
	100	100

We thus see the amount of the convertible starch and sugar has been nearly doubled at the expense of the hordeine, a portion of which has also passed into the condition of mucilage, or a soluble gum, while the gluten is much diminished.

The researches of Payen and Persoz show there is also a new proximate principle formed during the malting, which may be considered as a residuum of the gluten or vegetable albumen, in the germinating grain.

If we moisten the malt-flour for a few minutes with cold water, press it out strongly, filter the solution, and heat the clear liquid in a water-bath to the temperature of 158°, the greater part of the albuminous azotised substance will be coagulated, and should be separated by a fresh filtration, after which the clear liquid is to be treated with alcohol, when a flocky precipitate appears, to which has been given the name of diastase. To purify it still further, especially from the nitrogenous matter, we should dissolve it in water, and precipitate again with alcohol. When dried at a low temperature it appears as a solid white substance, which contains no nitrogen, is insoluble in alcohol, but dissolves in water and proof spirit. Its solution is neutral and tasteless; it changes with greater or less rapidity according to the temperature, and becomes sour at a temperature from 149° to 167°. It has the property of converting starch into gum, or dextrine (so called by the French chemists, from its polarising light to the right hand, whereas common gum does it to the left) and sugar; and, indeed, when sufficiently pure, the diastase operates with such energy that one part of it disposes 2,000 parts of dry starch to that change, but it operates the quicker the greater its quantity.

Whenever the solution of diastase with starch is heated to the boiling point, it loses the converting property.

One hundred parts of the starch solution from good malt appear to contain about one part of this substance, which is of the greatest importance in effecting the further changes which take place in the process of brewing.

3. The Formation of a Saccharine Liquid, or Wort,

from the malt and hops, and production of the finished beer, is the province of the brewer; and the process will be found at length under the article Brewing.

The peculiar properties contained in wort do not exist ready formed in malt, but are the result of the joint action of water and heat which is employed in the initiatory process of the brewer on that substance, and is termed the mashing.

The Mashing.—This operation requires the greatest care, as on it, almost as much as on the malt employed, depends the character of the liquor.

Payen and Persoz, already alluded to, show that the mucilage formed by the reaction of malt upon starch may be either converted into sugar or be made into a permanent gum, according to the temperature of the water in which the materials are digested. We take of pale barley-malt, ground fine, from 6 to 10 parts, and 100 parts of starch; we heat, by means of a water-bath, 400 parts of water in a copper to about 80° F.; we then stir in the malt, and increase the heat to 140° F., when we add the starch, and stir well together. We next raise the temperature to 158°, and endeavour to maintain it constantly at that point, or, at least, to keep it within the limits of 167° on the one side and 158° on the other. At the end of twenty or thirty minutes the original milky and pasty solution becomes thinner, and soon after as fluid nearly as water. This is the moment when the starch is converted into gum or dextrine. If this merely mucilaginous solution, which seems to be a solution of gum with a little liquid starch and sugar, be suitably evaporated, it may serve for various purposes in the arts to which gum is applied; but, with this view, it must be quickly raised to the boiling point, to prevent further change. If we wish, on the contrary, to produce a saccharine fluid, such as the wort for beer, we must maintain the temperature at between 158° and 167° for three or four hours, when the greatest part of the starch will have passed into sugar, and by evaporation of the liquid at the same temperature, a starch syrup may be obtained like that procured by the action of sulphuric acid upon starch.

In the operation of mashing, the finished and mellowed malt, having been well cleansed from all extraneous matters by screening, is coarsely ground, or better if only crushed between iron rollers, as is now generally practised. It is then gradually mixed with water in the mash-tun, at the proper heat, and intimately blended by stirring with the mashing-rakes, so that it may be uniformly moistened and no lumps remain. After being allowed some time to stand and settle, the liquor is drawn off, and more water at a higher temperature is added, again intimately blended with the malt—now termed the ' goods '—again allowed to rest, and drawn off; the operation being repeated until the complete exhaustion of the saccharine and amylaceous substances of the malt is effected.

We can now see, from Payen and Persoz's experiment just given, the temperature at which the liquor ought to be maintained in this operation; namely, the range between 158° and 167°; and it has been ascertained, as a principle in mashing, that the best and soundest extract of the malt is to be obtained, first, by beginning to work with water at the lowest of these heats, and to conclude with water at the highest; secondly, not to operate the extraction at once with the whole of the water that is to be employed, but with separate portions and by degrees.

The first portion has the task of penetrating equally the crushed malt, extracting the more soluble ingredients and subjecting the dissolved starch to the action of the diastase and free sugar; the second and further portions are for the purpose of converting the remaining starch and completing the extraction of all the available products. By this means also the starch is not allowed to run into a cohesive paste, or, as it is termed, ' lock up the goods,' and the extract is more easily drained from the mass, and comes off a nearly limpid wort. The thicker, moreover, or the less diluted the mash is, so much the easier is the wort fined in the boiler or copper by the coagulation of the albuminous matter. These principles indicate the true mode of conducting the mashing process, but different kinds of malt require a different treatment; pale and slightly kilned malt requires a somewhat lower heat than malt highly kilned, because the former is more ready to become pasty, and, for the same reason, needs a more leisurely infusion than the latter; and this is still more applicable to the case of a mixture of raw grain with malt, for it requires still gentler heats and more cautious treatment.

It is quite practicable to obtain from 1 part of malt and 8 parts of barley, a wort precisely similar to that procured from 9 parts of pure malt alone. But, of course, this could not be done without modifying considerably the process of mashing; and it happens, unfortunately, that the practice of the present day, amongst brewers, is to maintain, as closely as possible, one uniform system of mashing, whatever may be the nature or quality of the malt employed. Thus a difference in the malt is made to produce a difference in the wort, and all the energy and skill of the practical brewer are sometimes insufficient to compensate for the alterations which this difference induces in the subsequent working of the beer. With a regular and certain composition, as to the constituents of his wort, the operations of the brewer would assume a fixed and definite character, which, at present, they are very far indeed from possessing; and by which he not unfrequently suffers the most severe pecuniary loss and mental anxiety. With the exception of a trifling quantity of vegetable albumen, the only solid ingredients of beer-wort are dextrine and sugar; the latter of which ferments with great ease and rapidity, whilst the dextrine, though capable of fermentation, enters into the process only with difficulty, and requires, for its successful termination, not only much more yeast, but also a much higher temperature in the fermenting vat. At the same time, it is this very sluggishness in the fermentative quality of dextrine which is essential to the production of good beer; for, with sugar alone, the fermentation cannot be checked at ordinary temperatures, until the full measure of its decomposition has taken place, and it has become either a vapid admixture of alcohol and water, or, by the absorption of oxygen, is resolved into vinegar. It is indeed a notorious fact, that beer made with sugar will not keep so well as that made from malt; though, for rapid consumption, the use of sugar is, under some circumstances, to be commended, more especially on the small scale and in cold weather. The peculiarity of dextrine is, however, as we have stated, to undergo fermentation only with difficulty and by slow degrees; hence its decomposition spreads over a long space of time, and, in very cold weather, amounts to nothing; so that for months, or even years, after all the sugar of the wort has been destroyed, the evolution of carbonic acid gas from the still fermenting dextrine, keeps up a briskness and vitality in the beer; and, by excluding oxygen, all chance of acidification is shut off. A perfect beer-wort should therefore have reference to the period of its consumption: if this be speedy and pressing, the proportion of sugar ought to be large; if remote, the dextrine should greatly predominate. Under the first condition, the attenuation would proceed quickly, and, provided the temperature of the fermenting vat was not allowed to exceed 78°, the beer would soon cleanse and become ripe and bright; under the second, the attenuation in the vat would be slow and trifling, and require, perhaps, several years for its completion in the cask. Nevertheless, if the attenuation in the vat had gone on to the complete destruction of all the sugar, this kind of beer would prove in the end both the better and more healthy beverage of the two; for by the mode of its formation the presence of œnanthic ether or fusel oil is avoided. The importance therefore of placing in the hands of the brewer a means of determining the relative amounts of sugar and dextrine in his wort is sufficiently obvious. Now, this may be done in two ways: either by ascertaining, in wort of a determinate strength, the proportion of the one or the other of these substances. The dextrine is easier of calculation than the sugar, in a rough or approximate way; but the sugar can be determined with much more minute accuracy than the dextrine. Yet, in practice, the former plan is preferable, from its simplicity, as we shall proceed to show. If, to a certain volume of strong wort (say of 30 lbs. per barrel), we add an equal amount of alcohol or spirits of wine, the whole of the dextrine will precipitate as a dense coagulum; and by examining the bulk of this deposit in the tube, its weight may be inferred pretty nearly if the tube has been previously graduated, so as to indicate, from actual experiment, the weight of the different measures of the coagulated dextrine. With weaker wort, more alcohol must be used, and with a denser wort, less alcohol,—the relations of which to each other may easily be kept recorded on a small card or scale affixed to the tube. This instrument is very easy of application, and has been found extremely useful to more than one practical brewer of the present day; and the accompanying record of brewing operations has reference to this mode of analysing wort. The determination of sugar in wort is best effected by boiling 100 grains of it with about half a pint of the following solution, and collecting and weighing the red-coloured precipitate which ensues,—every three grains of which indicate one grain of grape-sugar in the wort.

Grape-Sugar Test-Solution.

Sulphate of copper in crystals	100 grains.
Bitartrate of potash	200 ,,
Carbonate of soda in crystals	800 ,,
Boiling water, one pint, or	8,750 ,,

First dissolve the sulphate of copper, then the bitartrate of potash, after which add the carbonate of soda, and filter if necessary. This solution is not affected when boiled with cane-sugar, dextrine, gum, or starch.

We have retained from Dr. Ure's original article the result of two brewings, taken from one mash at two different periods, and analysed to determine their relative contents of dextrine and sugar, according to the tube or alcohol process :—March 28th, 1851, proceeded to mash for experimental brewings ; weather clear and open ; thermometer outside at 51°,—in fermenting room 58° ; difference between wet and dry bulb, 5·750° ; barometer, 39·4 inches. Composition of the malt :—Moisture, 6·1 ; insoluble matter, 27 ; extract, 66·9. Quantity of malt employed, 70 bushels ; of water at 180° F., 700 gallons ; made the mixture with a common mashing-oar, and finished in 15 minutes. One hour afterwards, drew off 200 gallons of wort ; and three hours from commencing to mash, drew off 200 gallons more,—continuing the mash for table-beer wort. The first-drawn wort contained 7·5 parts of dextrine to 1 of sugar ; the second, 6·3 parts of dextrine, 2·2 of sugar ;—their densities were, respectively, 30 and 36·5 lbs. per barrel. They were each boiled separately, with relative amount of hop,—the first having 30 and the second 36½ lbs. added ; and the boiling in each case was kept up for three hours. At the end of this time both were cooled and diluted with water to a gravity of 27½ lbs. per barrel, and 250 gallons of each let down into separate fermenting-vats placed side by side ; after which, they both received three quarts of good yeast,—the temperature being at 68° F. Two hours afterwards, the following observations commenced :—No. 1 being the wort containing 7·5 parts of dextrine to 1 of sugar, and No. 2 the wort having 6·3 of dextrine to 2·2 of sugar.

1851.	No. 1.	Temp.
March 28, 5 P.M.	No action	67·5°
,, ,, 10 P.M.	Light thin cream	67·5
,, 29, 9 A.M.	White head	70·0
,, ,, 6 P.M.	Fine white head	71·0
,, 30, 9 A.M.	Thick tough head	74·0
,, ,, 6 P.M.	Tough brown head	75·0
,, 31, 2 P.M.	Ferment well roused up . . .	75·0
	Attenuation of No. 1.	8·5
April 2, 2 P.M.	(Skimmed off yeast)	10·0
,, 11, 2 P.M.	,, ,, ...	15·0
,, 13, 2 P.M.	,, ,, ...	15·5

	No. 2.	
March 28, 5 P.M.	No action	68·0
,, ,, 10 P.M.	Fine white head	70·0
,, 29, 9 A.M.	Thick yellow head	74·0
,, ,, 6 P.M.	Fine tough brown head . . .	77·0
,, 30, 9 A.M.	High roused-up rocky head . . .	77·0
,, ,, 6 P.M.	In rapid fermentation . . .	76·5
,, 31, 2 P.M.	Throws up much yeast (skimmed off yeast) .	76·0
	Attenuation of No. 2.	12·7
April 2, 2 P.M.	,, ,, ...	15·5
,, 11, 2 P.M.	,, ,, ...	17·5
,, 13, 2 P.M.	,, ,, ...	18·2

The temperature of both had now fallen to 69° F., though each had been roused repeatedly ; the yeast was therefore again skimmed off, and the beer run into barrels, and filled up with reserved wort three times a day as it worked over. On April the 18th the barrels were closed, having then lost, by attenuation—No. 1, 16·2 lbs., and No. 2, 19·6 lbs. Six weeks afterwards these ales were examined :—No. 1 was found muddy and unpleasant; whilst No. 2 had a fine fragrant aroma, a brisk, lively appearance, and was perfectly bright. On January 2nd, 1852, the casks were again examined;—No. 1 had now lost 17·9 lbs., and was bright, rich, and fine-flavoured; whilst No. 2, though bright and pleasant, had contracted a little acidity, and was becoming flat: it had lost, in all, 21½ lbs.

Two similar experiments, made about the same time in another quarter, gave almost exactly the same results; and, consequently, there can be little doubt that, where a quick sale and rapid consumption of beer can be ensured, the great object of the brewer should be to convert as much of the dextrine of his wort into sugar as is proportional to the rapidity of that consumption; whereas, for beer intended to keep, the opposite practice should be followed.

The conversion of any given amount of the dextrine-wort into sugar may be effected either by keeping up the temperature of the mash-tun, and prolonging the operation of mashing; or, which is better and simpler, by merely preserving the wort for a few hours at a heat of 165° F., either in the underback or any other convenient vessel. We have found from experiment that a wort which when run out from the mash-tun had only 3 parts of sugar to 16 of dextrine, became by 10 hours' exposure to a heat of 165° converted almost altogether into sugar,—the proportions then being 17·8 of sugar to 1·2 of dextrine.

A very important part of the duty of a brewer should therefore be, first, the determination of the relative amounts of dextrine and sugar required to suit the taste of his customers, or the circumstances of the market, and next, the continued careful examination of his wort, so as to ensure that these proportions are regularly maintained; for by no other plan is it possible to ensure that certainty of result and uniformity of quality which are essential to the proper conducting of an expensive business like brewing. Far too little attention has hitherto been given to the fluctuating qualities of beer-wort; in warm weather, this wort should probably contain at least twice as much dextrine as in winter; yet this is the very period when, from the increased temperature of the air and materials, the largest quantity of sugar must be formed by those who mash upon a fixed and unvarying principle. Hence the proneness of the wort to ferment violently in summer is still further increased by the presence of an extra proportion of sugar;—whereas prudence would suggest, under such circumstances, a predominance of dextrine, and seek to effect this purpose by a low temperature in the mash-tun, and by shortening the period of mashing. As a general rule, in the management of wort, more sugar is requisite where small quantities are brewed at a time, than where large operations are conducted, for the loss of heat is relatively larger in small masses than in large ones; and, from what has been stated, it must be apparent, that, as the fermentation of dextrine is more easily checked by cold than that of sugar, the beer brewed in trifling quantities could not preserve a fermentative temperature, but would become chilled and dead from the excessive radiation of heat, unless a principle existed in it capable of fermentation at the most ordinary temperatures of this country. If, therefore, beer-wort consisting chiefly of dextrine be fermented in very cold weather, or with an insufficiency of yeast, or if the temperature happen to rise too high, so as to destroy or impair the fermentative power of the yeast, then a dull languid action will ensue, accompanied by what has been called the viscous fermentation, and beer becomes permanently ropy, and is spoiled.

Although, clearly, it would be impossible to lay down any specific rule for the proper proportion of dextrine and sugar in beer-wort, yet there could be no difficulty in each brewer determining for himself, and for the conditions of quantity, time of sale, time of year, and other contingencies, the requisite ratio to be established in his own case; and, as we have shown, nothing can be simpler than the means proposed for ascertaining the composition of wort, remembering that, though a dextrine-wort may be thought to have a superior keeping property, it should be rather said that it is slower in arriving at maturity, whereas a full saccharine wort can be fermented more readily, is more under control, and the beer sooner becomes a brilliant and matured beverage.

The quantity of extract per barrel weight, which a quarter of malt yields to wort, amounts to about 84 lbs. The wort of the first extract is the strongest; the second contains, commonly, one-half the extract of the first; and the third, one-half of the second, according to circumstances.

To measure the degrees of concentration of the worts drawn off from the tun, a particular form of hydrometer, called a saccharometer, is employed, which indicates the number of pounds' weight of liquid contained in a barrel of 36 gallons imperial measure. Now, as the barrel of water weighs 360 lbs., the indication of the instrument, when placed in any wort, shows by how many pounds a barrel of that wort is heavier than a barrel of water; thus, if the instrument sinks with its poise till the mark 10 is upon a line with the surface of the liquid, it indicates that a barrel of that wort weighs ten pounds more than a barrel of water. See SACCHAROMETER.

Or, supposing the barrel of wort weighs 396 lbs., to convert that number into specific gravity, we have the following simple rule :—

$$360 : 396 :: 100 : 1\cdot100 ;$$

at which density the wort contains about 25 per cent. of solid extract.

Now the ordinary German chemical thermometer, as supplied from all laboratories is by far the more reliable and useful instrument ; some men have for years used them in the mashing, and are quite proud of the exactness and facility with which they are enabled thereby to manage the process. The hair stem is enclosed along with a paper scale (properly adjusted and accurately divided) within a glass tube annealed at the top, and the lower end on to the upper portion of the bulb; thus, with certainty, exposing the bulb alone to the influence of apparent heat. By fine copper wire twisted round the top and lower portions, this tube is attached to a long wood stick 1 inch × 1½, cheeked on either side with a lath of 3 or 4 feet long, and rising to the front nearly ¾ of an inch, to protect the thermometer from actual contact in the event of an accidental knock ; upon the lower end of the stick I attach a small tin box or cover about 4 inches long, just the width of the stick, and about an inch in depth. This covers the bulb, and is fitted at the lower end with a simple tin trapdoor valve arrangement, which opens upward on the inside, whenever the slightest pressure is applied underneath it by contact with the mash, and the instrument is complete.

When this apparatus is thrust into the goods, their upward pressure pushes open the valve, and allows them to pass over the bulb, and immediately on attempting to withdraw the instrument the valve again closes. This of course can be repeated at pleasure, and changes the goods in immediate contact with the bulb, with every fresh motion of the hand, be it ever so slight, and these are distinctly marked by the click of the valve as it closes being felt. By this simple and inexpensive arrangement, the brewer has a trusty, useful thermometer, with which he can easily obtain a sample of his mash from any part of his tub whatever. The thermometer can be read with the greatest deliberation ; its indications are almost instantaneous and quite reliable, and a slight jerk is all that is required to free it entirely from every grain the box contains, when reading the stem.

We will here give a few moments' consideration to the amount of extract to be obtained from a certain quantity of malt, and for practical purposes let us say eight bushels, or one imperial quarter.

It is ascertained from experiment that, on an average, 60 lbs. of ordinary glucose (grape-sugar) are equal to 2 bushels of malt in producing a barrel of beer. A bushel of malt usually weighs about 40 lbs. ; if it weighs less, on account of being more thoroughly malted, it is all the better. This proves that 80 lbs. of dry malt, at least 60 lbs., or 75 per cent., are taken up by the brewing liquor. It has been further ascertained by experiment that the amount of these substances just given, namely 60 lbs. of glucose, or 80 lbs. of malt, will produce a barrel of beer of 20 lbs. per barrel gravity.

From this the practical brewer may deduce that, to ascertain the amount of dry extract taken from the malt he has been brewing, he must multiply the lbs. per barrel gravity by 3, and even this will but show the proportion of dry extract taken up by the brewing liquor alone. This multiplier is somewhat more than that allowed by the Excise, theirs being 2·6 instead of 3 ; but it must be borne in mind that their Tables were framed upon the basis of cane-sugar instead of malt, and that 90 parts cane-sugar are equal in atomic equivalent to 95 parts pure glucose. On this account, therefore, also, their multiplier ought to be 2·7368 instead of 2·6. The knowledge of this is of course extremely galling to the export brewer. It will at once be seen that, in order to determine by a rough and ready estimate what a certain amount of malt should produce, simply divide the total number of lbs. of malt by 4. This will give the total gravity of extract obtainable from good malt for common beers, and if it is desired to know the lbs. per barrel that should be obtained for a particular brewing, simply divide this total extract gravity by the number of barrels brewed; thus 20 quarters of malt at 40 lbs. per bushel = 6,400 lbs. malt :—

$$\begin{array}{r} 4)\ 6400 \\ \hline 1600 \end{array} \text{ lbs. gravity of extract.}$$

When cooled down and got into the fermenting-tun, if there were 66 barrels of it, 1600 ÷ 66 = 24·2 lbs. per barrel, would be the weight of the beer. This is found practically correct, though it must not be contended that you have here an account of all that has been obtained from the malt; there is no account of all the losses that are inevitable in the process of brewing, and these of course vary according to the peculiarities of each brewing. As to the amount a quarter of malt ought to yield, there is much diversity of opinion, and of a necessity this must continue to be so according to the circumstances and class of trade of a brewer, and the kind of ale most suitable to him; but to ale adapted to the prevailing taste of the present day, the experienced brewer will find that the more he can afford to be below 80 lbs. per quarter when cooled down and got into the fermenting-tun, the quicker and more certain will be his profits, and the less annoyances will he have; indeed, for ale that is not vatted it is most advisable, and for those that are, it is prudent, especially in warm weather.

The object of boiling the wort is not merely evaporation and concentration, but extraction, coagulation, and, finally, combination with the hops; purposes which may be accomplished in a deep confined copper, by a moderate heat, or in an open shallow pan with a quick fire.

The copper, being encased above in brickwork, retains its digesting temperature much longer than the pan could do. The waste steam of the close kettle, moreover, can be economically employed in communicating heat to water or weak worts, whereas the exhalations from an open pan would prove a nuisance, and would need to be carried off by a hood.

The boiling has a fourfold effect: first, during the earlier stages of heating, it converts the starch into sugar, dextrine, and gum, by means of the diastase; secondly, it concentrates the wort; thirdly, it extracts the substance of the hops diffused through the wort; fourthly, it coagulates the albuminous matter present in the grain, or precipitates it by means of the tannin of the hops.

The degree of evaporation is regulated by the nature of the wort and the quality of the beer. Strong ale and stout, for keeping, require more boiling than ordinary porter or table-beer, brewed for immediate use. The proportion of the water carried off by evaporation is usually from a seventh to a fourth of the volume.

The hops are introduced at the commencement of the process. They serve to give the beer not only a bitter aromatic taste, but also a keeping quality, as they counteract its natural tendency to become sour—an effect partly due to the precipitation of the albumen and starch, by their resinous and tanning constituents, and partly to the antifermentable properties of the lupuline, bitter principle, ethereous oil, and resin. In these respects, there is none of the bitter plants which can be substituted for hops with advantage.

For strong beer, powerful fresh hops should be selected; for weaker beer an older and weaker article will suffice.

The stronger the hops are, the longer time they require for the extraction of their virtues; for strong hops an hour and a half, or two hours' boiling may be proper; for a weaker sort, an hour may be sufficient; but it is never advisable to push this process too far, lest a disagreeable bitterness, without aroma, be imparted to the beer. In some breweries it is the practice to boil the hops with a part of the wort, and to filter the decoction through a drainer, called the hop-back. The proportion of hops to malt is very various; but, in general, from $1\frac{1}{4}$ lbs. to $1\frac{1}{2}$ lbs. of the former are taken for 100 lbs. of the latter in making good table-beer.

For porter and strong ale, 2 lbs. of hops are used, or even more: for instance, from 2 lbs. to $2\frac{1}{2}$ lbs. of hops to a bushel of malt, if the beer be destined for consumption in India.

During the boiling of the two ingredients, much coagulated albuminous matter, in various stages of combination, makes its appearance in the liquid, constituting what is called the breaking or curdling of the wort, when numerous minute flocks are seen floating in it. The resinous, bitter, and oily ethereous principles of the hops combine with the sugar and gum or dextrine of the wort; but for this effect they require time and heat; showing that the boil is not a process of mere evaporation, but one of chemical reaction. A yellowish green pellicle of hop-oil and resin appears upon the surface of the boiling wort, in a somewhat frothy form; when this disappears the boiling is presumed to be completed, and the beer is strained off into the cooler. The residuary hops may be pressed and used for an inferior quality of beer; or they may be boiled with fresh wort, and be added to the next brewing charge.

Many prefer adding the hops when the wort has just come to the boiling point. Their effect is to repress the passage into the acetous stage, which would otherwise inevitably ensue in a few days. In this respect no other vegetable production hitherto discovered can be a substitute for the hop.

The odorant principle is not so readily volatilised as would at first be imagined; for when hop is mixed with strong beer-wort, and boiled for many hours, it can still impart a very considerable degree of its flavour to weaker beer.

By mere infusion in hot beer or water, without boiling, the hop loses very little of its soluble principles. The tannin of the hop combines, as we have said, with the vegetable albumen of the barley, and helps to clarify the liquor.

If the hops be boiled in the wort for a longer period than five or six hours, they lose a portion of their fine flavour; but if their natural flavour be rank, a little extra boiling improves it. Many brewers throw the hops in upon the surface of the boiling wort, and allow them to swim there for some time, that the steam may penetrate them, and open their pores for a complete solution of their principles when they are pushed down into the liquor.

The quantity of hop to be added to the wort varies according to the strength of the beer, the length of time it is to be kept, or the heat of the climate where it is intended to be sent.

For weak beer $4\frac{1}{2}$ lbs. of hops are required to a quarter of malt; but when it is intended to be highly aromatic and remarkably clear, and for the stronger kinds of ale and porter, the rule, in England, is to take 1 lb. of hops for every bushel of malt, or 8 lbs. to a quarter. Common beer has seldom more than $\frac{1}{4}$ lb. of hops to a bushel of malt.

The form, size, and setting, the extent of fire-bed and dimensions of the flues, as also the power of draught procurable of a wort copper, are each and all of such importance that none but men of experience should be entrusted with the work of placing it.

With respect to the first of these qualifications, the rapid evaporation required will suggest an open shallow basin, turned in at the top, so as to roll violent ebullition into the pan; the flue should not expose the lower part of the pan higher than can be covered by the first charge run off from the mash-tun, or the thin edge of its contents are liable to burn and thereby colour and perhaps flavour the brewing.

It should be set so that the whole bottom is freely exposed to the fire, and the bridge so placed as to direct the flame straight up against it, midway between the centre and edge in front. In size it should be capable of boiling away one-fourth of the brewing; a pan, say of 60 barrels contents, would turn out, after boiling, 45 barrels.

In estimating for a copper of any size, it is usual to reckon thus: suppose you desire a copper to boil for a 60-barrel brewing, the contents of the copper should be 80 barrels, and this will only just allow for expansion of bulk and the violent ebullition.

The extent of fire-bed and power of draught should be such as would enable the boiling to be finished within two hours from the time the pan was fully charged. All beers should be boiled at least two hours, or much more of the value of the hops will be thrown away than is necessary: it will not endanger either the colour or the flavour of the palest ales, and it is time sufficient to ensure much of the benefit arising from the depuration of the flocks by the coagulation consequent on boiling.

The colour desired should also partially regulate the time required for boiling; for pale ales about two hours is sufficient, but not too much: for deep amber, two and a half to three hours; for rich brown ales from three to four hours will not be found too long; but in deciding this, the colour of the malt-extract, of the hops, and the gravity of the wort must each be considered.

The following considerations are submitted for the guidance of the brewer in this operation.

In the first place, except in steam-tight boilers, you cannot raise the heat above 212°, however hard you boil; by increasing the fire, therefore, you gain rapidity of concentration, and colour is obtained not by hard, but by long boiling.

Secondly, if wort, boiled either with or without hops, be examined by any of the simple tests for the albumenoids at different times in the process of boiling, it will be found that the longest boiled will be the most free from the albuminous constituents, and that it is almost impossible to boil wort long enough to free it entirely from them; in this, again, a good boiling proves of value, for it enhances the keeping power of the beer by ejecting from it those constituents which are so troublesome to the brewer.

Again, the more concentration that can be permitted in the pan, the more of the valuable properties that most deep-spring waters contain are utilised, and these assist greatly the clarifying and soundness of the ultimate product.

Thirdly, with regard to the boiling with hops, the same, almost precisely, may be said, for the lupuline and tannin of the hop are very difficult to draw from their covert, but as this is being accomplished, it does its work of depuration, separating with its load of albuminous flocks, as tannate of albumen.

In apportioning the hops that are to be boiled with the wort, quantity must be considered quite as much as quality, for it is on the amount of tannin utilised that the clarifying, and therefore the keeping power of the beer, depends.

The hops used for this purpose may be mixed with yearlings and a small proportion of old hops, but these latter must be carefully selected, for in very old hops the tannin is apt to degenerate into the gallic form, and then it is useless as an agent to precipitate the albuminous flocks from the wort.

Refrigerators have now become so generally used, that the slow process of cooling is quite the exception in breweries, but the great benefit resulting from the quiet separation of the flocks as it rested on the cooler should not be lost sight of; but it is very much feared that the great advantages derivable from using powerful refrigerators have led many away from the slow but prudent course, for by allowing the sediment to pass into the fermenting tun, the soundness and qualities of the beers concerned are very much impaired. But by the exercise of a little ingenuity and careful management, all the best benefits expected from using the most powerful refrigerators may be obtained without any additional risk.

In the first place, let the hop-back be provided with some arrangement which shall include a guard to keep the hops, with ports to prevent a disturbance of the sediment settled under the plates, and a floating syphon provided with a flattened tin mouth-piece.

After the wort is discharged from the copper, allow it to rest in the hop-back until such time as the whole of the flocks and hops shall have settled to the bottom, open the ports, and push the mouth of the syphon below the surface; it will then draw off all the wort clean, bright, and freed from every particle of flocks at any speed desired.

Now this is a simple and not expensive arrangement.

About an hour will be found long enough for a 90 or 100 barrel brewing to stand. It should then be passed through the refrigerator within two hours after, the machine of course being of such actual power as to be capable of cooling a whole brewing, no matter what the size, in that time.

It will then be found that the brewing has passed on to the refrigerator before the wort in the hop-back has fallen even to 150 degrees, and this precludes all probability of the wort attaining acetancy from exposure on account of cooling.

Another very excellent mode of fermentation, very general in the Northern Counties and Scotland, is that known as the stone-square system, and it has certainly a claim to the most serious consideration of the practical brewer on account of its many merits. It is very cleanly and simple in process, thorough in its work, most easily and perfectly under control, will prepare the beer for consumption in less time than any other process, and is worked at heats far removed from all dangerous tendencies, and these are all qualities which must greatly commend the system in a commercial point.

It is thus conducted:—

The stone square is a cistern made of hard blue stone or slate nearly six feet deep. This is for the reception of the wort to be fermented: it should hold from 20 to 25 barrels. Upon it is placed another stone cistern of sufficient dimensions to contain the whole of the yeast head that may be made. This is called the yeast-back. It is usually capable of holding about half the contents of the wort square; it has a man-hole in the centre, surrounded on the top by a circular stone ring of a section of about six inches square. Some twelve inches in front of this man-hole is another hole, about five or six inches diameter, fitted with a valve arrangement, to the underside of which is screwed a large tin pipe called the organ-pipe, conducting the wort to within about two inches from the bottom. There is also in the corner another hole, fitted with a plug at the top, and having a pipe attached to conduct the yeast (after the fermentation is finished) to the yeast waggon in the cellar below; the yeast-back usually projects some eighteen inches around the wort cistern, and is from thirty to thirty-six inches deep.

The wort cistern is contained within another stone cistern as deep as itself, within 3 or 4 inches from the top. This is called the shell; it allows of a free space all around the outside of the wort square of about 5 or 6 inches. This is to allow of the application of a suitable bath of warm or cold water, as may be required, to control the temperature of the fermenting wort; to assist in this operation a notch is cut at the back of the shell, at the top of the side slab: from this the water is allowed to overflow as required.

All the slabs composing these cisterns should be sawn plain and parallel on both sides. The bottom slab, of course, serves for both the wort cistern and shell: it has two taps let into it to drain each respectively, and in front, about 1½ or 2 inches up from the bottom, a racking pipe with tap attached is let in horizontally through the shell and wort-back slabs. To this a hose pipe is screwed, and the wort is thus drawn from the cistern into the casks to be sent out to the consumer, bright, clean, and quite free from the sediment settled at the bottom of the square.

There are two ways of working the stone-square system : in the one, or what we may call the quiet process, as the wort is run into the square the yeast is added, and the whole remains undisturbed till the fermentation is finished (this is known by the falling of the yeast), when it is allowed to run off through the yeast-pipe in the corner, the wort remaining in the square till perfectly quiet, when it is also bright and ready for racking into the casks to be sent out to the consumer.

In the other process, after the wort and yeast are mixed in the square, it is allowed to rest and work of itself till there is an evidence of the head just beginning to fall. This will usually occur about thirty-six hours after the square has been filled, sooner with light, later with heavy ones. Hand-pumps are then placed in the man-hole, and the wort is pumped on to the back above, well mixed with the new head, and let down into the bottom of the square again by the means of the valve and organ-pipe. This is repeated every $1\frac{1}{2}$ or 2 hours, and the attenuation watched by the aid of the brewer's saccharometer. When it is desired to stop the progress of the fermentation, it is merely allowed to rest 6 hours ; when the yeast is let off the back and the wort in the square allowed to rest till it is bright and ready for racking. The time occupied by the pumping varies with the character and gravity of the beer in the square from 12 to 30 hours ; and the time for rest afterwards from 30 to 48 or 90 hours, according as it is required to be ready for the consumer, sooner or otherwise.

As to the amount of yeast to be apportioned to the setting on, the brewer must be principally guided by his experience, for in addition to the gravity of the wort and the amount of attenuation required, many other points have to be considered, as the particular kind of ale, the state of briskness in which it is most acceptable to the consumer, the character of the malt, and the extent to which exhaustion has been carried, the amount of hops and the length of time it has boiled, the age and constitution of the yeast, the season and state of the atmosphere—all these considerations make it nearly impossible to construct a table of quantities, or even give a general rule as a guide that may be relied on by the brewer.

From circumstances peculiar to every brewer's trade, it will be seen at once how much difficulty there is in framing a table for the quantities of the yeast to be added to the wort at the setting on. In order to render this article as complete and practical as possible, it may be stated for wort mashed in the latter of the processes described, and fermented by the second of the processes of the stone-square systems, the extent of extract being about 83 lbs. per quarter when cooled down and got into the squares (this, of course, being less than the real amount taken from the malt), that for a gravity of about 24 lbs. per barrel, $2\frac{1}{2}$ lbs. of yeast per barrel has been found to be the quantity answering the requirements best, the ale generally becoming bright in the square within six days, racking bright and in first-class condition for sending out within a week afterwards.

As the gravity per barrel decreases, the proportion of yeast to be added must decrease in greater ratio, owing to the constitution of the wort being of a more albuminous nature, and for porters more so still, and *vice versâ*, as the gravity is increased so must the quantity of yeast added be increased, but in a greater ratio, on account of the more saccharific quality of the wort.

The malt used in experimental trials was made from good Yorkshire barley, and weighed about $39\frac{1}{2}$ lbs. per bushel. It was dried a nice high amber, was three months old, and the time of the year was March, April, May.

For reasons very similar to those applied to yeast, it is equally difficult to make a rule as to the stopping-point in the process of fermentation, and the amount of attenuation necessary, other than this, the longer a beer has to remain on tap the further should attenuation be carried.

In porter it should be to nearly $\frac{2}{3}$ of the original gravity.
In common and mild ales at least $\frac{2}{3}$ of the original gravity.
In strong ales nearly $\frac{3}{4}$ of the original gravity.
In bitter ales quite $\frac{3}{4}$ or nearly $\frac{4}{5}$ of the original gravity.

It will be well here to consider some of the influences which act so adversely upon the reputation of the brewer from the quality of the materials he may have to use. Every brewer should make malt and malting his anxious study, quite as much as he should any other portion of his operations, for on it mainly depends the quality of his productions, and he should not forget that it costs much less in time, care, and money, to make bad malt than good, and that it is easy to make bad malt yield over-measure or overweight, just as it is desired by the local customs of the market : therefore it is necessary for the brewer to be very careful in his selection and examination of all malt that comes to his hand, for he is very soon made to feel that any evil result from using it is not the fault of the maltster, but of his mismanagement in brewing; therefore he must neglect nothing that will enable him to secure to his use a suitable and trustworthy article.

In an early paragraph of this article, under the head of MATERIALS, is the description of good malt, and we will here state the characteristic appearances of barley that has been improperly malted.

First, there is a deficiency in the growth of the acrospire; the cause of this is generally an insufficient steep in the cistern; the inducements to it are two—it will require less turning on the malting floor, and pay somewhat less duty. The results are a plumpness and weight in the malt, but with it a perceptible deficiency in the sweetness and saccharine constituent in the product, though an apparently greater gravity of extract is obtainable from the excessive proportion of the albuminous constituent present. It may be observed in brewing it, there is a large amount of sediment and flocks, and in the fermenting-tun abundance of yeast; the beer from it will be fretful and soon turn off.

In the crushing of such malt in the rolls, it will be perceived there is an abundance of hard rice-like ends, and the more of these the more harm and loss to the brewer, for he is either deprived of the use of them if not crushed well up, or disappointed by the fretfulness of his ale if he crushes them so as to gain a greater apparent gravity from his mash-tun. Another common fault is the tendency of the maltster to crowd his floors. This increases the evil begun with the inadequate steep, for the heat generated forces up the acrospire beyond what the real state of the grain would warrant, causing it to appear in an advanced state when really not so.

The maltster, taking advantage of this forward appearance, puts in on the kiln at seven or eight days old, which is utterly at variance with the interests of the brewer, to whom the development of the saccharine principle is the true value of malting.

The treatment described above involving heavy sprinkling on the floor encourages acidity and mould, and it is not possible to eradicate this tendency when once fairly set in.

Perhaps it may be practically impossible to produce malt without a trace of acetic acid, but the trace should be all that should be there, and where mould has occurred, the consequences are much worse, for much of the sugar of the malt has become lactic, and of irreparable lactic tendency; a sound wort can never be made from such malt. Malt of this description will have a close-fitting skin that good malt should not have, and many of the mouldy grains will have a dark spot where the mould has been attached before it was rubbed off by the screening. Acidity is not always to be perceived by the taste, but mould is much easier of detection and should be most rigidly rejected.

We will next consider the results arising from injudicious drying. As in the former instance, the desire to tax to its utmost the working ability of the kiln is the incentive, and the kiln is therefore overloaded, sometimes to the depth of 15, 16, or 18 inches; but it is not always the depth that is at fault—it is often the irregularity of density of different parts of the floor, an improper pack generally, unevenness in the distribution of the heat, want of draught power to penetrate the raw floor, or too much heat attained at first and insufficient at last. All these things have very baneful effects on the malt, varying according to the circumstances, and doing injury to the extent and degree of the irregularity—but the most common and serious among them are, overloading and insufficient fire at the finish. By the first of these, grain that has been in all other respects properly treated, and would have been turned off the kiln a first-rate article, will be disappointing in the mash-tun, and almost useless; the moisture that should pass quickly away is retained in the upper portion of the malt when it is permanently injured according to the extent of over-loading.

It is at all times difficult to detect this kind of malt, but it may be observed that there is a sort of biscuity crispness in breaking it with the teeth, quite unlike the soft friableness of good malt. Moreover, many of the grains will appear hard and glossy, as, from being subjected to an excess of heat at first, the outside has become hard before the moisture has been efficiently expelled from the interior.

In conclusion, let it be remembered that no art of the brewer can make a first-class quality of extract from inferior or unsound malt. Great weights of extract may be obtained from the worst quite as easily as from the best of malts, but it is certain the less got the better, for with increase of extract out of indifferent samples of malt, there will be increase of trouble, anxiety, and loss, whilst by due care in the selection and use of good sound malt and healthy well-cured hops, no brewer need fail of procuring a sound and satisfactory ale.

Beer in its perfect condition is an excellent and healthful beverage, combining, in some measure, the virtues of water, of wine, and of food, as it quenches thirst, stimulates, cheers, and strengthens. The vinous portion of it is the alcohol, proceeding from the fermentation of the malt-sugar. Its amount, in common strong ale or beer, is about 4 per cent., or four measures of spirits, specific gravity 0·825, in 100 measures of the liquor. The best brown stout porter contains 6 per cent., the strongest ale even 8 per cent., but common beer only one. The nutritive part of the beer is the undecomposed gum-sugar, and the starch-gum not changed into sugar. Its quantity is very variable, according to the original starch of the wort, the length of the fermentation, and the age of the beer.

The main feature of good beer is fine colour and transparency; the production of which is an object of great interest to the brewer. Attempts to clarify it in the cask seldom fail to do it harm. The only thing that can be used with advantage for *fining* foul or muddy beer, is isinglass. For porter, as commonly brewed, it is frequently had recourse to. A pound of good isinglass will make about 12 gallons of *finings*. It is cut into slender shreds, and put into a tub with as much vinegar or hard beer as will cover it, in order that it may swell and dissolve. In proportion as the solution proceeds, more beer must be poured upon it, but it need not be so acidulous as the first, because, when once well softened by the vinegar, it readily dissolves. The mixture should be frequently agitated with a bundle of rods, till it acquires the uniform consistence of thin treacle, when it must be equalised still more by passing through a tammy-cloth, or a sieve. It may now be made up with beer to the proper measure of dilution. The quantity generally used is from a pint to a quart per barrel, more or less, according to the foulness of the beer. But before putting it into the butt, it should be diffused through a considerable volume of the beer with a whisk, till a frothy head be raised upon it. It is in this state to be poured into the cask, and briskly stirred about; after which the cask must be bunged down for at least 24 hours, when the liquor should be limpid. Sometimes the beer will not be improved by this treatment; but this should be ascertained beforehand, by drawing off some of the beer into a cylindric jar or phial, and adding to it a little of the finings. After shaking and setting down the glass, we shall observe whether the feculencies begin to collect in flocky parcels, which slowly subside; or whether the isinglass falls to the bottom without making any impression upon the beer. This is always the case when the fermentation is incomplete, or a secondary decomposition has begun. Mr. Jackson has accounted for this clarifying effect of isinglass in the following way.

The isinglass, he thinks, is first of all rather diffused mechanically, than chemically dissolved, in the sour beer or vinegar, so that when the finings are put into the foul beer, the gelatinous fibres, being set free in the liquor, attract and unite with the floating feculencies, which before this union were of the same specific gravity with the beer, and therefore could not subside alone; but having now acquired additional weight by the coating of fish-glue, precipitate as a flocculent magma. This is Mr. Jackson's explanation; to which we might add, that if there be the slightest disengagement of carbonic acid gas, it will keep up an obscure locomotion in the particles, which will prevent the said light impurities, either alone or when coated with isinglass, from subsiding. The beer is then properly enough called *stubborn* by the coopers. The true theory probably of the action of isinglass is, that the tannin of the hops combines with the fluid gelatine, and forms a flocculent mass, which envelops the muddy particles of the beer, and carries them to the bottom as it falls, and forms a sediment. When, after the finings are poured in, no proper precipitate ensues, it may be made to appear by the addition of a little decoction of hop.

Mr. Richardson, the author of the well-known brewer's saccharometer, gives the following as the densities of different kinds of beer :—

Beer				Pounds per Barrel	Specific Gravity
Burton ale, 1st sort	.	.	.	40 to 43	1·111 to 1·120
„ 2nd „	.	.	.	35 to 40	1·097 to 1·111
„ 3rd „	.	.	.	28 to 33	1·077 to 1·092
Common ale .	.	.	.	25 to 27	1·070 to 1·073
Ditto ditto .	.	.	.	21	1·058
Porter, common sort	.	.	.	18	1·050
„ double .	.	.	.	20	1·055
„ brown stout	.	.	.	23	1·064
„ best brown stout .	.	.	26	1·072
Common small beer	.	.	.	6	1·014
Good table beer	.	.	.	12 to 14	1·033 to 1·039

It may be remarked that Mr. Richardson somewhat underrates the gravity of porter, which is now seldom under 20 lbs. per barrel. The criterion for transferring from the gyle-tun to the cleansing butts is the attenuation caused by the production of alcohol in the beer: when that has fallen to 10 lbs. or 11 lbs., which it usually does in 48 hours, the cleansing process is commenced. The heat is at this time generally 75°, if it was pitched at 65°; for the heat and the attenuation go hand in hand.

About forty years ago, it was customary for the London brewers of porter to keep immense stocks of their beer for eighteen months or two years, with the view of improving its quality. The beer was pumped from the cleansing butts into store-vats holding from twenty to twenty-five 'gyles' or brewings of several hundred barrels each. The store-vats had commonly a capacity of 5,000 or 6,000 barrels; and a few were double, and one was treble, this size. The porter, during its long repose in these vats, became fine, and by obscure fermentation its saccharine mucilage was nearly all converted into vinous liquor, and partly dissipated in carbonic acid. Its hop-bitter was also in a great degree decomposed. *Good hard beer* was the boast of the day. This was sometimes softened by the publican, by the addition of some mild new-brewed beer. Of late years, the taste of the metropolis has undergone such a complete revolution in this respect, that nothing but the mildest porter will now go down. Hence, six weeks is a long period for beer to be kept in London; and much of it is drunk when only a fortnight old. Ale is for the same reason come greatly into vogue; and the two greatest porter houses, Messrs. Barclay, Perkins, and Co., and Truman, Hanbury, and Co., have become extensive and successful brewers of mild ale, to please the changed palate of their customers.

We shall add a few observations upon the brewing of Scotch ale. This beverage is characterized by its pale amber colour and its mild balsamic flavour. The bitterness of the hop is so mellowed with the malt as not to predominate. The ale of Preston Pans is, in fact, the best substitute for wine which barley has hitherto produced. The low temperature at which the Scotch brewer pitches his fermenting tun restricts his labours to the colder months of the year. He does nothing during four of the summer months. He is extremely nice in selecting his malt and hops; the former being made from the best English barley, and the latter being the growth of Farnham or East Kent. The yeast is carefully looked after, and measured into the fermenting tun in the proportion of one gallon to 240 gallons of wort.

Only one mash is made by the Scotch ale brewer, and that pretty strong; but the malt is exhausted by eight or ten successive sprinklings of liquor (hot water) over the goods (malt), which are termed, in the vernacular tongue, *sparges*. These waterings percolate through the malt on the mash-tun bottom, and extract as much of the saccharine matter as may be sufficient for the brewing. By this simple method much higher specific gravities may be obtained than would be practicable by a second mash. With malt, the infusion or saccharine fermentation of the *diastase* is finished with the first mash; and nothing remains but to wash away from the goods the matter which that process has rendered soluble. It will be found on trial that 20 barrels of wort drawn from a certain quantity of malt, by two successive mashings, will not be so rich in fermentable matter as 20 barrels extracted by ten successive sparges of two barrels each. The grains always remain soaked with wort like that just drawn off, and the total residual quantity is three-fourths of a barrel for every quarter of malt. The gravity of this residual wort will on the first plan be equal to that of the second mash; but, on the second plan, it will be equal only to that of the tenth sparge, and will be more attenuated in a very high geometrical ratio. The only serious objection to the sparging system is the loss of time by the successive drainages. A mash-tun with a steam-jacket promises to suit the sparging system well, as it would keep up an uniform temperature in the goods, without requiring them to be sparged with very hot liquor.

The first part of the Scotch process seems of doubtful economy; for the mash liquor is heated so high as 180°. After mashing for about half an hour, or till every particle of the malt is thoroughly drenched, the tun is covered, and the mixture left to infuse about three hours; it is then drained off into the underback, or preferably into the wort-copper.

After this wort is run off, a quantity of liquor (water), at 180° of heat, is sprinkled uniformly over the surface of the malt; being first dashed on a perforated circular board, suspended horizontally over the mash-tun, wherefrom it descends like a shower upon the whole of the goods. The percolating wort is allowed to flow off by three or more small stopcocks round the circumference of the mash-tun, to insure the equal diffusion of the liquor.

The first sparge being run off in the course of twenty minutes, another similar one is affused; and thus in succession till the whole of the drainage, when mixed with the first mash-wort, constitutes the density adapted to the quality of the ale. Thus, the strong worts are prepared, and the malt is exhausted either for table beer, or for a *return*, as pointed out above. The last sparges are made 5° or 6° cooler than the first.

The quantity of hops seldom exceeds four pounds to the quarter of malt. The manner of boiling the worts is the same as that above described; but the conduct of the fermentation is peculiar. The heat is pitched at 50°, and the fermentation continues from a fortnight to three weeks. Were three brewings made in the week, seven or eight working tuns would thus be in constant action; and, as they are usually in one room, and some of them at an *elevation* of temperature of 15°, the apartment must be propitious to fermentation, however low its heat may be at the commencement. No more yeast is used than is indispensable: if a little more be needed, it is made effective by rousing up the tuns twice a day from the bottom.

When the progress of the attenuation becomes so slack as not to exceed half a pound in the day, it is prudent to cleanse, otherwise the top barm might re-enter the body of the beer, and it would become *yeast-bitten*. When the ale is cleansed, the head, which has not been disturbed for some days, is allowed to float on the surface till the whole of the *then* pure ale is drawn off into the casks. This top is regarded as a sufficient preservative against the contact of the atmosphere. The Scotch do not skim their tuns, as the London ale brewers commonly do. The Scotch ale, when so cleansed, does not require to be set upon close stillions. It throws off little or no yeast, because the fermentation was nearly finished in the tun. The strength of the best Scotch ale ranges between 32 and 44 pounds to the barrel; or it has a specific gravity of from 1·088 to 1·122, according to the price at which it is sold. In a good fermentation, seldom more than a fourth of the original gravity of the wort remains at the period of the cleansing. Between one-third and one-fourth is the usual degree of attenuation. Scotch ale soon becomes fine, and is seldom racked for the home market. The following Table will show the progress of fermentation in a brewing of good Scotch ale:—

$$20 \text{ barrels of mash-worts of } 42\tfrac{2}{3} \text{ pounds gravity} = 860\cdot6$$
$$20 \text{ ,, \qquad returns \qquad } 6\tfrac{1}{10} \text{ ,, \qquad ,, } = 122$$

$$12\,)\,982\cdot6$$

pounds weight of extract per quarter of malt = 81

Fermentation :—

March 24, pitched the tun at 51°: yeast 4 gallons.

		Temp.	Gravity.
,,	25.	52 degrees.	41 pounds
,,	28.	56 ,,	39 ,,
,,	30.	60 ,,	34 ,,
April	1.	62 ,,	32 ,,
,,	4.	65 ,,	29 added 1 lb. of yeast.
,,	5.	66 ,,	25 pounds.
,,	6.	67 ,,	23 ,,
,,	7.	67 ,,	20 ,,
,,	8.	66 ,,	18 ,,
,,	9.	66 ,,	15 ,,
,,	10.	64 ,,	14·5 cleansed.[1]

Dr. Ure was employed to make experiments on the density of worts, and the fermentative changes which they undergo, for the information of a Committee of the House of Commons, which sat in July and August, 1830: the following is a short abstract of that part of his evidence which bears upon the present subject:—

'My first object was to clear up the difficulties which, to common apprehension, hung over the matter, from the difference in the scales of the saccharometers in use among the brewers and distillers of England and Scotland. I found that one quarter of good malt would yield to the porter brewer a barrel imperial measure of wort, at the concentrated specific gravity of 1·234. Now, if the decimal part of this number be multiplied by 360, being the number of pounds weight of water in the barrel, the product will denote the excess, in pounds, of the weight of a barrel of such concentrated wort over that of a barrel of water, and that product is, in the present case, 84·24 pounds.

'Mr. Martineau, jun., of the house of Messrs. Whitbread and Company, and a

[1] 'Brewing,' Society for Diffusing Useful Knowledge, p. 156.

gentleman connected with another great London brewery, had the kindness to inform me that their average product from a quarter of malt was a barrel of 84 lbs. gravity. It is obvious, therefore, that by taking the mean operation of two such great establishments, I must have arrived very nearly at the truth.

'It ought to be remarked that such a high density of wort as 1·234 is not the result of any direct experiment in the brewery, for infusion of malt is never drawn off so strong; that density is deduced by computation from the quantity and quality of several successive infusions; thus, supposing a first infusion of the quarter of malt to yield a barrel of specific gravity 1·112, a second to yield a barrel at 1·091, and a third a barrel at 1·031, we shall have three barrels at the mean of these three numbers, or one barrel at their sum, equal to 1·234.

'I may here observe that the arithmetical mean or sum is not the true mean or sum of the two specific gravities; but this difference is either not known or disregarded by the brewers. At low densities this difference is inconsiderable, but at high densities it would lead to serious errors. At specific gravity 1·231, wort or syrup contains one-half of its weight of solid pure saccharum, and at 1·1045 it contains one-fourth of its weight; but the brewer's rule, when here applied, gives for the mean specific gravity $1·1155 = \dfrac{1·231 + 1·000}{2}$. The contents in solid saccharine matter at that density are, however, $27\frac{1}{4}$ per cent., showing the rule to be $2\frac{1}{4}$ lbs. wrong in excess on 100 lbs., or 9 lbs. per barrel.

'The specific gravity of the solid dry extract of malt-wort is 1·264; it was taken in oil of turpentine, and the result reduced to distilled water as unity. Its specific volume is 0·7911, that is, 10 lbs. of it will occupy the volume of 7·911 lbs. of water. The mean specific gravity, by computation of a solution of that extract in its own weight of water, is 1·1166; but, by experiment, the specific gravity of that solution is 1·216, showing considerable condensation of volume in the act of combination with water.

'The following Table shows the relation between the specific gravities of solutions of malt-extract and the percentage of solid extract they contain:—

Extract of Malt		Water	Malt-Extract in 100	Sugar in 100	Specific Gravity
600	+	600	50·00	47·00	1·2160
600	+	900	40·0	37·00	1·1670
600	+	1,200	33·3	31·50	1·1350
600	+	1,500	28·57	26·75	1·1130
600	+	1,800	25·00	24·00	1·1000

'The extract of malt was evaporated to dryness, at a temperature of about 250° F., without the slightest injury to its quality or any empyreumatic smell. Bate's tables have been constructed on solutions of sugar, and not with solutions of extract of malt, as they agree sufficiently well with the former, but differ materially from the latter. Allen's tables give the account of a certain form of solid saccharine matter extracted from malt, and dried at 175° F., in correspondence to the specific gravity of the solution; but I have found it impossible to make a solid extract from infusions of malt, except at much higher temperatures than 175° F. Indeed, the numbers on Allen's saccharometer-scale clearly show that his extract was by no means dry: thus, at 1·100 of gravity he assigns 29·669 per cent. of solid saccharine matter; whereas there is at that density of solid extract only 25 per cent. Again, at 1·135, Allen gives 40 parts per cent. of solid extract, whereas there are only $33\frac{1}{3}$ present.'

The Table (p. 319) shows the origin and effect of fermentation in the reduction of gravity, in a number of practical experiments.

The second column here does not represent the solid extract, but the pasty extract obtained as the basis of Mr. Allen's saccharometer, and therefore each of its numbers is somewhat too high. The last column, also, must be in some measure erroneous, on account of the quantity of alcohol dissipated during the process of fermentation. It must be likewise incorrect, because the density due to the saccharine matter will be partly counteracted by the effect of the alcohol present in the fermented liquor. In fact, the attenuation does not correspond to the strength of the wort; being greatest in the third brewing and smallest in the first. The quantity of yeast for the ale brewings given in the Table was, upon an average, one gallon for 108 gallons; but it varied with its quality, and with the state of the weather, which, when warm, permits much less to be used with propriety.

The good quality of the malt, and the right management of the mashing, may be tested by the quantity of saccharine matter contained in the successively drawn worts.

Original Gravity of the Worts	lbs. per Barrel of Saccharine Matter	Specific Gravity of the Ale	lbs. per Barrel of Saccharine Matter	Attenuation, or Saccharum decomposed
1·0950	88·75	1·0500	40·25	0·478
1·0918	85·62	1·0420	38·42	0·552
1·0829	78·125	1·0205	16·87	0·787
1·0862	80·625	1·0236	20·00	0·757
1·0780	73·75	1·0280	24·25	0·698
1·0700	65·00	1·0285	25·00	0·615
1·1002	93·75	1·0400	36·25	0·613
1·1025	95·93	1·0420	38·42	0·600
1·0978	91·56	1·0307	27·00	0·705
1·0956	89·37	1·0358	32·19	0·640
1·1130	105·82	1·0352	31·87	0·661
1·1092	102·187	1·0302	26·75	0·605
1·1171	110·00	1·0400	36·25	0·669
1·1030	96·40	1·0271	23·42	0·757
1·0660	61·25	1·0214	17·80	0·709

With this view, an aliquot portion of each of them should be evaporated by a safety-bath heat to a nearly concrete consistence, and then mixed with twice its volume of strong spirit of wine. The truly saccharine substance will be dissolved, while the starch and other matters will be separated; after which the proportions of each may be determined by filtration and evaporation. Or an equally correct, and much more expeditious, method of arriving at the same result would be, after agitating the viscid extract with the alcohol in a tall glass cylinder, to allow the insoluble fecula to subside, and then to determine the specific gravity of the supernatant liquid by a hydrometer. The additional density which the alcohol has acquired will indicate the quantity of malt-sugar which it has received. The following Table, constructed by Dr. Ure, at the request of Henry Warburton, Esq. M.P., chairman of the Molasses Committee of the House of Commons in 1830, will show the brewer the principle of this important inquiry. It exhibits the quantity in grains' weight of sugar requisite to raise the specific gravity of a gallon of spirit of different densities to the gravity of water = 1·000.

Specific Gravity of Spirit.	Grains' Weight of Sugar in the Gallon Imperial
0·995	·980
0·990	1·890
0·985	2·800
0·980	3·710
0·975	4·690
0·970	5·600
0·965	6·650
0·960	7·070
0·955	8·400
0·950	9·310

The immediate purpose of this Table was to show the effect of saccharine matter in disguising the presence or amount of alcohol in the weak feints of the distiller. But a similar Table might easily be constructed, in which, taking a uniform quantity of alcohol of 0·825, for example, the quantity of sugar in any wort-extract would be shown by the increase of specific gravity which the alcohol received from agitation with a certain weight of the wort, inspissated to a nearly solid consistence by a safety-pan made on the principle of Dr. Ure's patent sugar-pan. (See SUGAR). Thus, the normal quantities being 1,000 grains' measure of alcohol, and 100 grains by weight of inspissated mash-extract, the hydrometer would at once indicate, by help of the Table, first, the quantity per cent. of truly saccharine matter, and next, by subtraction, that of farinaceous matter present in it.

The advance of the arts is gradually assuming a character which will no longer permit any manufacturer to neglect the assistance of science ; and those who first take advantage of the power of knowledge will assuredly leave their fellow-labourers behind. From being an uncertain and hazardous operation, brewing must ere long become a fixed and definite principle based upon facts well understood, and capable of perpetual repetition and reproduction at will. To sum up briefly the general details of ale-brewing, we may state, that, for most kinds of ale, the attenuation in the first instance should be finished in from six to twenty-one days, according to the strength of the wort; that this attenuation should approach to two-thirds of the whole weight; and that after tunning and cleansing, the ale itself should weigh about one-fourth of the original gravity of the wort. Thus, if the fermenting tun be set with wort of 27 lbs., then the attenuation should bring it down to 9 or 10 lbs., and the subsequent operations produce an ale weighing from 6 to 7 lbs. When these conditions are fulfilled, without much extra trouble or attention, the ale is pretty certain to turn out well, though, in some localities, ale is never attenuated to more than one-half its original gravity: this kind of ale is, however, very apt to become sour in hot weather and ropy in cold.

Some additional remarks on the brewing of porter, which differs from that of ale both in the nature of the materials used and in the mode of finishing the fermentation, are required. Porter owes its peculiar colour and flavour to burnt saccharine or starchy matter; and this was formerly obtained by burning sugar until it exhaled the odour called by French writers *caramel*. At present, however, nothing but highly-torrefied malt is used; and of this there are several kinds, as brown malt, imperial malt, and black malt; all of which are used by some brewers, whilst others employ only the brown and black, and a few the black alone, for giving colour and flavour. The fermentative quality or saccharine is, however, the same as that of ale, and is derived from pale or amber malt. As a general rule, the ratio of the colouring and flavouring malts are to the saccharine as about 1 to 5 or 1 to 4; but where black malt only is used, the proportion does not exceed 1 to 10.

The employment of these burnt malts permits a singular act of injustice on the part of the Excise, as regards the drawback on exportation. By the Excise regulations, it is assumed that a quarter of malt will produce four barrels of ale brewed from wort of the sp. gr. 1·054, or 19·4 lbs. per barrel; but, although this is hopeless even with pale malt, yet with an admixture of brown and black malt the assumption becomes absurd in the extreme. Admitting that, by good management, on the average, four barrels of wort, weighing 20 lbs., can be obtained from one quarter of fine pale malt, yet, in the operations of cooling, fermenting, tunning, skimming, and cleansing, a loss of fully 10 per cent. occurs under the most vigilant superintendence; and, taking the great bulk of our metropolitan breweries, it would be nearer the truth to estimate this loss at 12 per cent. In plain words, 100 gallons of wort will not, by any management, produce more than about 88 gallons of saleable beer, though no allowance is made for this by the Excise; and the brewer who has paid duty upon 100 gallons gets a drawback upon but 88. This, however, is the most favourable view of the case; and we solicit attention to the force with which the argument returns in the instance of porter.

If a quarter of pale malt be assumed at 84 lbs. of saccharine strength, then such an admixture of brown and black malt as is usually employed by brewers of porter will not give more than about 24 lbs.; and as this constitutes at least one-fifth of the whole bulk used in porter-brewing, we see that a quarter of such mixed malt can never give more than 70 lbs.; that is to say, 80 parts of pale malt, mixed with 20 of brown and black, instead of giving at the rate of 84 lbs., as pale malt alone does, would give but 70 lbs., or produce a difference between the actual return and that taken for granted by the Excise authorities, of no less than 16·6 per cent.; to which, if we add the loss previously mentioned as arising from fermentation, yeast, &c., and which we have called 12 per cent., a total difference ensues of 28·6 per cent. between the duty paid by the brewer and the drawback allowed by Act of Parliament. But the grievance does not stop here; for the only return allowed by Act of Parliament is based upon the malt duty, and nothing whatever is said of the duty on hops. This, however, is at the rate of 19s. 7d. per cwt.; and since hops yield only about 35 per cent. of their weight of soluble matter, it would require 168 lbs. of hops to produce a barrel of fluid or wort weighing 19·4 lbs., or having the requisite parliamentary specific gravity of 1·054. Upon this barrel, when exported, the drawback is 5s.; but, as may easily be seen on calculation, the duty paid by the brewer has been 29s. 3d. In fact, upon every 168 lbs. of hops consumed by the export brewer, he suffers a dead loss of 24s. 3d. independently of the waste incidental to his various processes. These things may seem startling; but the whole Board and Staff of the Excise are unable to prove that they are in the least over-estimated. At the same time, the intelligent reader will gather that the profits of brewing are not by any means so large as a cursory glance at the subject might appear to warrant. No doubt the brewing business is at times very remunerative; but a continued high price of the raw materials sometimes proves ruinous to the large brewer, as it must not be forgotten that the capital required is large, and invested in very perishable materials, such as casks and other wooden utensils, the wear and tear upon which is a very large item; nor, again, as we have shown, must a speculator begin by assuming, with the Excise authorities, that a quarter of malt will produce four barrels of beer, for he will be much nearer the truth if he estimates his saleable produce at three barrels. As, however, it forms no part of our present task to enter into the financial statistics of brewing, we return to the object more immediately in view, merely throwing out, *en passant*, the above hints for the benefit of those whom they may concern.

If the analyses of malt and malt-wort are requisite to enable the brewer to perform his operations with safety and success, the analysis of beer is not less indispensable to qualify him for the harassing labour of competition with his neighbours, and for the protection of his interest against Excise confiscation. Although beer may have been brewed of the requisite gravity for justifying a drawback on exportation, yet this is very far indeed from ensuring a return of the malt-duty, even to the limited extent awarded by law. The question is, How are the Excise officials to know the real weight of the wort from which the beer was brewed? This may be ascertained by the following method, which should take the place of the present indefinite system :— Having agitated a portion of the ale or beer so as to dissipate its carbonic acid gas, measure out exactly 3,600 grains' measure of it, and pour these into a retort; then distil with great care into a receiver surrounded by ice-cold water about one-third of the whole fluid, or rather more than this if the ale or beer is known to be highly alcoholic. Next weigh the distilled fluid, and then ascertain its specific gravity, from whence, by any of the proper tables of *alcohol*, the total quantity of absolute alcohol in the distilled fluid may be known. This alcohol is to be converted by calculation into its equivalent of sugar, at the rate of 171 parts of sugar for every 92 of alcohol found; after which the sugar must be brought into pounds per barrel by the rule before given, which is 52½ lbs. of sugar for every 20 lbs. of gravity. The amount of vinegar is next to be determined by any of the known forms of acidimetry. (See ACIDIMETRY.) This vinegar, or acetic acid, must, like the alcohol, be also converted into its representative of sugar, by assigning 171 of sugar to every 102 of anhydrous acetic acid present in the beer, this sugar being, as before, converted into pounds per barrel. To the beer remaining in the retort, sufficient distilled water is then to be added, that the entire bulk of fluid may once more be equal to 3,600 grains' measure; and the temperature of the mixture having fallen to 60° F., its specific gravity must be determined in the usual way, and this reduced to pounds per barrel, by multiplying the excess above 1,000 by 360, and dividing the product by 1,000. The whole of these weights, added together, gives the original weight of the wort. Thus, for example, we will suppose that 3,600 grains of a particular beer have given 1,300 grains of a dilute alcohol, of specific gravity 0·9731, and consequently containing about 17½ per cent. by weight of alcohol; again, that the same quantity of beer, when tested by ammonia, has indicated 30 grains of acetic acid; and lastly, that the spent wash, when filled up with distilled water to its primary bulk, has, at 60°, a specific gravity of 1·016; then the total alcohol would be in 360 grains, or the representative of a barrel, 22¾ grains, and the acetic acid in the same quantity, 3 grains: hence we have the following results :—

	Grs. of sugar.		Brewers' lbs.
Alcohol, 22¾ grains, equal to . . .	42·2	or	16.
Acetic acid, 3 grains	5·	,,	1·9
Spent wash, of specific gravity 1·016 .	...	,,	5·76
Total weight . .			23·66

It might be thought that the proper kind of sugar to select in this instance as the representative of alcohol and acetic acid should be grape-sugar, whose atomic weight is 180; but it has been shown by Dr. Ure that the kind of sugar actually employed in the construction of our saccharometer tables must have been cane-sugar, the atom of which is 171; and hence the reason why it must be employed in this calculation.

ALE, Pale or Bitter; *brewed chiefly for the Indian market and for other tropical countries.*—It is a light beverage, with much aroma, and, in consequence of the regulations regarding the malt-duty, is commonly brewed from a wort of specific gravity 1·055 or upwards; for no drawback is allowed by the Excise on the exportation of beer brewed from worts of a lower gravity than 1·054. This impolitic interference with the operations of trade compels the manufacturer of bitter beer to employ wort of a much greater density than he otherwise would do; for beer made from wort of the specific gravity 1·042 is not only better calculated to resist secondary fermentation and the other effects of a hot climate, but is also more pleasant and salubrious to the consumer. Under present circumstances the law expects the brewer of bitter beer to obtain four barrels of marketable beer from every quarter of malt he uses, which is just barely possible when the best malt of a good barley year is employed. With every quarter of such malt 16 lbs. of the best hops are used ; so that, if we assume the cost of malt at 60s. per quarter, and the best hops at 2s. per lb., we shall have, for the prime cost of each barrel of bitter beer—in malt, 15s. ; in hops, 8s. ; together, 23s. ; from which, on exportation, we must deduct the drawback of 5s. per barrel allowed by the Excise, which brings the prime cost down to 18s. per barrel, exclusive of the expense of manufacture, wear and tear of apparatus, capital invested in barrels, cooperage, &c., which constitute altogether a very formidable outlay. As, however, this ale is sold as high as from 50s. to 65s. per barrel, there can be no doubt that the bitter-ale trade has long been, and still continues, an exceedingly profitable specula-tion, though somewhat hazardous, from the liability of the article to undergo decom-position ere it finds a market.

The East Indian pale ale, or bitter beer, is now brewed in large quantities for the home market at Burton-on-Trent, London, Glasgow, and Leeds, but differs slightly from that exported, as being less bitter and more spirituous. It is brewed solely from the best and palest malts and the finest and most delicate hop, and much of its success depends on the care taken in selecting the best materials for its composition. It also requires the utmost care and attention at every stage of its progress to preserve the colour, taste, and other properties of this ale in their fulness and purity.

For further description of the brewhouse and its appliances, with the various modes of operations, see the article BREWING.

The English ale-drinkers were a few years since startled by a public report, apparently well authenticated, that the French chemists were largely engaged in preparing immense quantities of that most deadly poison *strychnine* for the purpose of drugging the pale bitter ale, in such great vogue at present in Great Britain and its colonies. The follow-ing are a few amongst many reasons which might be quoted, to show the absurdity of this report:—1. Strychnine is an exceedingly costly article. 2. It has a most un-pleasant metallic bitter taste. 3. It is a notorious poison, and its use in any brewery being known would ruin the reputation of the brewer. 4. It cannot be introduced into ordinary beer brewed with hops, because it is entirely precipitated by infusions of that wholesome and fragrant herb. In fact, the quercitannic acid of hops is in-compatible with strychnia and all its kindred alkaloids. Hence hopped beer becomes in this respect a sanitary beverage, refusing to take up a particle of strychnia and other noxious drugs of like character. Were the *nux vomica* powder, from which strychnia is extracted, even stealthily thrown into the mash-tun, its dangerous prin-ciple would be all infallibly thrown down with the grounds in the subsequent boiling with the hops.

The varieties of beer depend either upon the difference of their materials, or upon a different management of the brewing processes. With regard to the materials, beers differ in the proportion of their malt, hops, and water, and in the different kinds of malt or other grain. To the class of ' table ' or ' small beers,' all those sorts may be referred whose specific gravity does not exceed 1·025, which contain about 5 per cent. of malt extract, or nearly 18 lbs. per barrel. Beers of middling strength may be reckoned those between the density of 1·025 and 1·040, which contain, at the average, 7 per cent., or 25 lbs. per barrel. The latter may be made with 400 quarters of malt to 1,500 barrels of beer : stronger beers have a specific gravity of from 1·050 to 1·080, and take from 450 to 750 quarters of malt to the same quantity of beer. The strongest beer found in the market is some of the English and Scotch ales, for which from 18 to 27 quarters of malt are taken for 1,500 gallons of beer : good porter requires from 16 to 18 quarters for that quantity. Beers are sometimes made with the addition of other farinaceous matter to the malt ; but when the latter con-stitutes the main portion of the grain, the malting of the other kinds of corn becomes unnecessary, for the diastase of the barley-malt changes the starch into sugar during the mashing operation. Even with entirely raw grain, beer is made in some parts of the Continent, the brewers trusting the conversion of the starch into sugar to the action of the gluten alone, at a low mashing temperature, on the principle of Saussure's and Kirchoff's researches.

The colour of the beer depends upon the colour of the malt and the duration of the boil in the copper. The pale ale is made, as we have stated, from steam- or sun-dried malt and the young shoots of the hop ; the deep yellow ale from a mixture of pale-yellow and brown malt ; and the dark-brown beer from well-kilned and partly car-bonised malt, mixed with a good deal of the pale to give body. The longer and more strongly heated the malt has been in the kiln, the less weight of extract, *cæteris paribus*, does it afford. In making the fine mild ales, high temperatures ought to be avoided, and the yeast ought to be skimmed off, or allowed to flow very readily from its top, by means of the cleansing-butt system, so that little ferment being left in it to decompose the rest of the sugar, the sweetness may remain unimpaired. With regard to porter, in certain breweries each of the three kinds of malt employed for it is separately mashed, after which the first and the half of the second wort is boiled along with the whole of the hops, and thence cooled, and set to ferment in the gyle-tun. The third-drawn wort, with the remaining half of the second, is then boiled with the same hops, saved by the drainer, and, after cooling, added to the former in the gyle-tun, when the two must be well roused together.

It is obvious from the preceding development of principles, that all amylaceous and saccharine materials, such as potatoes, beans, turnips, as well as cane- and starch-syrup, molasses, &c. may be used in brewing beer. When, however, a superior quality of brown beer is desired, malted barley is indispensable, and even with these substitutes a mixture of it is most advantageous. The washed roots of the common carrot, of the red and yellow beet, or of the potato, must be first boiled in water, and then mashed into a pulp. This pulp must be mixed with water in the copper along with wheaten- or oat-meal and the proper quantity of hops, then boiled during eight or nine hours. This wort is to be cooled in the usual way, and fermented with the addition of yeast. A much better process is that now practised on a considerable scale at Strasbourg, in making the ale for which that city is celebrated. The mashed potatoes are mixed with from a twentieth to a tenth of their weight of finely-ground barley-malt and some water. The mixture is exposed in a water-bath to a heat of 160° F. for four hours, whereby it passes into a saccharine state, and may then be boiled with hops, cooled, and properly fermented into good beer.

Maize, or Indian corn, has also been employed to make beer; but its malting is somewhat difficult, on account of the rapidity and vigour with which its radicles and plumula sprout forth. The proper mode of causing it to germinate is to cover it a few inches deep with common soil, in a garden or field, and to leave it there till the bed is covered with green shoots of the plant. The corn must be then lifted, washed, and exposed to the kiln.

The Board of Excise, or Inland Revenue, having, a few years ago, been permitted by the Legislature to grant leave to use sugar in the place of barley-malt in breweries, an extensive sugar-merchant in London, hoping, under this boon, to acquire a new and wealthy class of customers, employed Dr. Ure to ascertain by experiment the relative values of malt and sugar for the manufacture of beer. Ten samples of Muscovado sugar, of several qualities, were examined, and were found to vary very slightly in the proportions of alcohol they could furnish by fermentation in a brewer's tun, the average being 12 gallons of proof spirit for 112 lbs. of the sugar; whereas an equal quantity of proof spirit could be obtained from $4\frac{8}{10}$ bushels of malt. One pound of malt yields $\frac{3}{4}$ lb. of extract capable of making as much beer as that weight of sugar. On comparing the actual price of sugar and malt, we shall see how ruinous a business it would be to use sugar instead of malt in a brewery, and hence the delusiveness of the Excise generosity towards the beer trade.

Although the object of the brewer is not the formation of a mere saccharine wort, as we have already shown (and malt contains other substances necessary to the formation of a sound beer), the amount of proof spirit producible from various substances will be some index to their relative value and it has been found that, with proper management, a quarter of good malt, weighing 42 lbs. per bushel, or 336 lbs. per quarter, will yield 18 gallons of proof spirit; a quarter of barley, weighing 55 lbs. per bushel, or 440 lbs. per quarter, will yield from 18 to 20 gallons. An equal quantity of spirit, say 18 gallons at proof, can be obtained from 175 lbs. of best West India sugar; from 234 lbs. of inferior Jamaica raw sugar; from 275 lbs. of West India molasses; or from 295 lbs. of refined or sugar-house molasses. Bauerstock gave the average of sugar 200 lbs., and of honey 226 lbs., as equivalent to a quarter of malt.

Ropiness is a morbid state of beer, which is best remedied, according to Mr. Black, by putting the beer into a vat with a false bottom, and adding, per barrel, 4 or 5 pounds of hops, taken away after the first boilings of the worts; and to them may be added about half a pound per barrel of mustard-seed. Rouse the beer as the hops are gradually introduced, and, in some months, the ropiness will be perfectly cured. The beer should be drawn off from below the false bottom.

For theoretical views, see FERMENTATION; and for wort-cooling apparatus, see REFRIGERATOR.

BEER, BAVARIAN. (*Baierisches Bier*, Ger.) The Germans from time immemorial have been habitually beer-drinkers, and have exercised much of their technical and scientific skill in the production of beer of many different kinds, some of which are little known to our nation, while one at least, called Bavarian, possesses excellent qualities, entitling it to the attention of all brewers and consumers of this beverage. The peculiarities in the manufacture of Bavarian beer some time ago attracted the attention of the most eminent chemists in Germany, especially of the late Professor

Liebig, and much new light was thereby thrown upon this curious portion of vegetable chemistry.

The following is a list of the principal beers brewed in Germany:—

1. Brown beer of Merseburg; of pure barley malt.
2.   „   „   „   and beet-root sugar.
3.   „   barley malt, potatoes, and beet-root syrup.
4.   „   refined beet-root syrup alone.
5. Covent or thin beer.
6. Berlin white beer, or the champagne of the north.
7. Broyhan, a famous Hanoverian beer.
8. Double beer of Grünthal.
9. Bavarian beer: 1. Summer beer; 2. Winter beer.
10.   „   Bock beer.
11. Wheat *Lager*-beer (slowly fermented).
12. White bitter beer of Erlangen.

Considerable interest among men of science, in favour of the Bavarian beer process, has been excited ever since the appearance of ' Liebig's Organic Chemistry.' In the introduction to this admirable work, he says, ' The beers of England and France, and for the most part those of Germany, become gradually sour by contact of air. This defect does not belong to the beers of Bavaria, which may be preserved at pleasure in half-full casks, as well as full ones, without alteration in the air. This precious quality must be ascribed to a peculiar process employed for fermenting the wort, called in German *Untergährung*, or fermentation from below; which has solved one of the finest theoretical problems.

' Wort is proportionally richer in soluble gluten than in sugar. When it is set to ferment by the ordinary process, it evolves a large quantity of yeast, in the state of a thick froth, with bubbles of carbonic acid gas attached to it, whereby it is floated to the surface of the liquid. The phenomenon is easily explained. In the body of the wort, alongside of particles of sugar decomposing, there are particles of gluten being oxidised at the same time, and enveloping, as it were, the former particles, whence the carbonic acid of the sugar and the insoluble ferment from the gluten being simultaneously produced, should mutually adhere. When the metamorphosis of the sugar is completed, there remains still a large quantity of gluten dissolved in the fermented liquor, which gluten, in virtue of its tendency to appropriate oxygen, and to get decomposed, induces also the transformation of the alcohol into acetic acid (vinegar). But were all the matters susceptible of oxidisement as well as this vinegar ferment removed, the beer would thereby lose its faculty of becoming sour. These conditions are duly fulfilled in the process followed in Bavaria.

' In that country the malt-wort is set to ferment in open backs, with an extensive surface, and placed in cool cellars, having an atmospheric temperature not exceeding 8° or 10° C. (46½° or 50° F.) The operation lasts from three to four weeks; the carbonic acid is disengaged; not in large bubbles that burst on the surface of the liquid, but in very small vesicles, like those of a mineral water, or of a liquor saturated with carbonic acid, when the pressure is removed. The surface of the fermenting wort is always in contact with the oxygen of the atmosphere, as it is hardly covered with froth, and as all the yeast is deposited at the bottom of the back, under the form of a very viscid sediment, called in German *Unterhefe*.

' In order to form an exact idea of the difference between the processes of fermentation, it must be borne in mind that the metamorphosis of gluten, and of azotised bodies in general, is accomplished successively in two principal periods, and that it is in the *first* that the gluten is transformed in the interior of the liquid into an insoluble ferment, and that it separates alongside of the carbonic acid proceeding from the sugar. This separation is the consequence of an absorption of oxygen. It is, however, hardly possible to decide if this oxygen comes from the sugar, from the water, or even from an intestine change of the gluten itself; or, in other words, whether the oxygen combines directly with the gluten, to give it a higher degree of oxidation, or whether it lays hold of its hydrogen to form water.

' This oxidation of the gluten, from whichever cause, and the transformation of the sugar into carbonic acid and alcohol, are two actions so correlated, that by an exclusion of the one, the other is immediately stopped,'

The *superficial* ferment (*Oberhefe* in German) which covers the surface of the fermenting works, is gluten oxidised in a state of putrefaction; and the ferment of *deposit* is the gluten oxidised in a state of *eremacausis*, or slow combustion.

The surface yeast, or barm, excites in liquids containing sugar and gluten the same alteration which itself is undergoing, whereby the sugar and the gluten suffer a rapid and tumultuous metamorphosis. We may form an exact idea of the different states of these two kinds of yeast by comparing the *superficial* to vegetable matters putrefying at the bottom of a marsh, and the *bottom* yeast to the rotting of wood in a state of *eremacausis*. The peculiar condition of the elements of the *sediment* ferment causes them to act upon the elements of the sugar in an extremely slow manner, and excites the change into alcohol and carbonic acid, without affecting the dissolved gluten.

If to wort at a temperature of from 46½° to 50° F. the top yeast be added, a quiet slow fermentation is produced, but one accompanied with a rising-up of the mass, while yeast collects both at the surface and bottom of the backs. If this deposit be removed to make use of it in other operations, it acquires by little and little the characters of the *Unterhefe*, and becomes incapable of exciting the phenomena of the first fermenting period, causing only, at 59° F., those of the second, namely, sedimentary fermentation. It must be carefully observed that the right *Unterhefe* is not the precipitate which falls to the bottom of backs in the ordinary fermentation of beer, but is a matter entirely different. Peculiar pains must be taken to get it genuine, and in a proper condition at the commencement. Hence the brewers of Hesse and Prussia, who wished to make Bavarian beer, found it more to their interest to send for the article to Würzburg, or Bamberg, in Bavaria, than to prepare it themselves. When once the due primary fermentation has been established and well regulated in a brewery, abundance of the true *Unterhefe* may be obtained for all future operations.

In a wort made to ferment at a low temperature with deposit only, the presence of the *Unterhefe* is the first condition essential to the metamorphosis of the *saccharum*, but it is not competent to bring about the oxidation of the gluten dissolved in the wort, and its transformation into an insoluble state. This change must be accomplished at the cost of the atmospherical oxygen.

In the tendency of soluble gluten to absorb oxygen, and in the free access of the air, all the conditions necessary for its *eremacausis* are to be found. It is known that the presence of oxygen and soluble gluten are also the conditions of acetification (vinegar-making), but they are not the only ones; for this process requires a temperature of a certain elevation for the alcohol to experience this slow combustion. Hence by excluding that temperature, the combustion (oxidation) of alcohol is obstructed, while the gluten alone combines with the oxygen of the air. This property does not belong to alcohol at a low temperature, so that during the oxidation in this case of the gluten, the alcohol exists alongside of it, in the same condition as the gluten alongside of sulphurous acid in the *muted* wines. In wines not impregnated with the fumes of burning sulphur, the oxygen which would have combined at the same time with the gluten and the alcohol does not seize either of them in wines which have been subjected to *mutism*, but it unites itself to the sulphurous acid to convert it into the sulphuric. The action called *sedimentary* fermentation is therefore merely a simultaneous metamorphosis of putrefaction and slow combustion; the sugar and the *Unterhefe* putrefy, and the soluble gluten gets oxidised, not at the expense of the oxygen of the water and the sugar, but of the oxygen of the air, and the gluten then falls in the insoluble state. The process of Appert for the preservation of provisions is founded upon the same principle as the Bavarian process of fermentation, in which all the putrescible matters are separated by the intervention of the air at a temperature too low for the alcohol to become oxidised. By removing them in this way, the tendency of the beer to grow sour, or to suffer a further change, is prevented. Appert's method consists in placing, in presence of vegetables or meat which we wish to preserve, the oxygen at a high temperature, so as to produce slow combustion, but without putrefaction or even fermentation. By removing the residuary oxygen after the combustion is finished, all the causes of an ulterior change are removed. In the sedimentary fermentation of beer, we remove the matter which *experiences* the combustion; whereas, on the contrary, in the method of Appert, we remove that which *produces* it.

The temperature at which fermentation is carried on has a very marked influence upon the quantity of alcohol produced. It is known that the juice of beets set to ferment between 86° and 95° F., does not yield alcohol, and its sugar is replaced by a less oxygenated substance, *mannite*, and lactic acid, resulting from the mucilage. In proportion as the temperature is lowered the mannite fermentation diminishes. As to azotised juices, however, it is hardly possible to define the conditions under which the transformation of the sugar will take place, without being accompanied with another decomposition which modifies its products. The fermentation of beer by *deposit* demonstrates that by the simultaneous action of the oxygen of the air and a low temperature, the metamorphosis of sugar is effected in a complete manner; for the vessels in which the operation is carried on are so disposed that the oxygen of the air may act upon a surface great enough to transform all the gluten into insoluble yeast, and thus to present to the sugar a matter constantly undergoing decomposition. The oxidisement of the dissolved gluten goes on, but that of the alcohol requires a higher temperature, whence it cannot suffer acetification, or conversion into vinegar.

In several States of Germany the favourable influence of a rational process of fermentation upon the quality of the beers has been fully recognised. In the Grand Duchy of Hesse considerable premiums were proposed for the brewing of beer according to the process pursued in Bavaria, which were decreed to those brewers who were able to prove that their product (neither strong nor highly hopped) had kept six months in the casks without becoming at all sour. When the first trials were being made, several thousand barrels were being spoiled, till eventually experience led to the discovery of the true practical conditions which theory had foreseen and prescribed.

Neither the richness in alcohol, nor in hops, nor both combined, can hinder ordinary beer from getting tart. In England, says Liebig, an immense capital is sacrificed to preserve the better sorts of ale and porter from souring, by leaving them for several years in enormous tuns quite full, and very well closed, while their tops are covered with sand. This treatment is identical with that applied to wines to make them deposit the wine-stone. A slight transpiration of air goes on in this case through the pores of the wood; but the quantity of azotised matter contained in the beer is so great, relatively to the proportion of oxygen admitted, that this element cannot act upon the alcohol. And yet the beer thus managed will not keep sweet more than two months in smaller casks, to which air has access. The grand secret of the Munich brewers is to conduct the fermentation of the wort at too low a temperature to permit of the acetification of the alcohol, and to cause all the azotised matters to be completely separated by the intervention of the oxygen of the air, and not by the sacrifice of the sugar. It is only in March and October that the good store beer is begun to be made in Bavaria.

The following Table exhibits the results of the chemical examination of the undermentioned kinds of Beer:—

Name of the Beer	Quantity in 100 parts by weight				Analyst
	Water	Malt extr.	Alcohol	Carb. acid	
Augustine double beer—Munich	88·36	8·0	3·6	0·14	Kaiser.
Salvator beer—do. . .	87·62	8·0	4·2	0·18	Do.
Bock beer from the Royal Brewery—do. . . .	88·64	7·2	4·0	0·16	Do.
Schenk (pot) beer, from a Bavarian country brewery; a kind of small beer . .	92·94	4·0	2·9	0·16	Do.
Bock beer, of Brunswick, of the Bavarian kind . .	88·50	6·50	5·0	...	Balhorn.
Lager (store) beer, of Brunswick, of the Bavarian kind.	91·0	5·4	3·50	...	Otto.
Brunswick sweet small beer .	84·70	14·0	1·30	...	Do.
Brunswick mum . . .	59·2	39·0	1·80	0·1	Kaiser.

Malting in Munich.—The barley is steeped till the acrospire, embryo, or seed-germ seems to be quickened, a circumstance denoted by a swelling at that end of the grain which was attached to the foot-stalk, as also when, on pressing a pile between two fingers against the thumb-nail, a slight projection of the embryo is perceptible. As long, however, as the seed-germ sticks too firm to the husk, it has not been steeped enough for exposure on the under-ground malt-floor. Nor can deficient steeping be safely made up for afterwards by sprinkling the malt-couch with a watering-can, which is apt to render the malting irregular. The steep-water should be changed repeatedly, according to the degree of foulness and hardness of the barley: first, six hours after immersion, having previously stirred the whole mass several times: afterwards, in winter every 24 hours, but in summer every 12 hours. It loses none of its substance in this way, whatever vulgar prejudice may think to the contrary. After letting off the last water from the stone cistern, the Bavarians leave the barley to drain in it during 4 or 6 hours. It is now taken out, and laid on the couch floor in a square heap, 8 or 10 inches high, and it is turned over, morning and evening, with dexterity, so as to throw the middle portion upon the top and bottom of the new-made couch. When the acrospire has become as long as the grain itself, the malt is carried to the *withering* (*Welkboden*) or drying floor, in the open air, where it is exposed (in dry weather) during from 8 to 14 days, being daily turned over three times with a winnowing shovel. It is next dried in a well-constructed cylinder or flue-heated malt-kiln, at a gentle clear heat, without being browned in the slightest degree, while it turns into a fine friable white meal. Smoked malt is entirely rejected by the best Bavarian brewers. Their malt is dried on a series of wove wire horizontal shelves, placed over each other, up through whose interstices, or perforations, streams of air, heated to only 122° F., rise, from the surfaces of rows of hot sheet-iron pipe-flues, arranged a little way below the shelves. Into these pipes the smoke and burned air of a little furnace on the ground are admitted. The whole is enclosed in a vaulted chamber, from whose top a large wooden pipe issues for conveying away the steam from the drying malt. Each charge of malt may be completely dried on this kiln in the space of from 18 to 24 hours, by a gentle uniform heat, which does not injure the diastase or discolour the farina.

The malt for store beer should be kept three months at least before using it, and be freed by rubbing and sifting from the acrospires before being sent to the mill, where it should be crushed pretty fine. The barley employed is the best *distichon* or common kind, styled *Hordeum vulgare*.

The hops are of the best and freshest growth of Bavaria, called the fine *spalter*, or *saatser Bohemian townhops*, and are twice as dear as the best ordinary hops of the rest of Germany. They are in such esteem as to be exported even into France.

In Munich the malt is moistened slightly 12 or 16 hours before crushing it, with from two to three *Maas*[1] of water for every bushel, the malt being well dried, and several months old. The mash-tun into which the malt is immediately conveyed is, in middle-sized breweries, a round oaken tub, about 4½ feet deep, 10 feet in diameter at bottom and 9 at top, outside measure, containing about 6,000 Berlin quarts. Into this tun cold water is admitted late in the evening, to the amount of 25 quarts for each *scheffel*, or 600 quarts for the 26 *scheffels* of the ground malt, which are then shot in and stirred about, and worked well about with the oars and rakes, till a uniform paste is formed without lumps. It is left thus for three or four hours; 3,000 quarts of water being put into the copper and made to boil; and 1,800 quarts are gradually run down into the mash-tun and worked about in it, producing a mean temperature of 142·5° F. After an hour's interval, during which the copper has been kept full, 1,800 additional quarts of water are run into the tun, with suitable mashing. The copper being now emptied of water, the mash-mixture from the tun is transferred to it, and brought quickly to the boiling point, with careful stirring to prevent its settling on the bottom and getting burned, and it is kept at that temperature for half an hour. When the mash rises by the ebullition, it needs no more stirring. This process is called, in Bavaria, boiling the thick mash, *dickmeisch Kochen*. The mash is next returned to the tun, and well worked about in it. A few barrels of a thin mash-wort are kept ready to be put into the copper the moment it is emptied of the thick mash. After a quarter of an hour's repose the portion of liquid filtered through the sieve part of the bottom of the tun into the wort-cistern is put into the copper, thrown back boiling hot into the mash in the tun, which is once more worked thoroughly.

The copper is next cleared out, filled up with water, which is made to boil for the after, or small-beer, brewing. After two hours' settling in the open tun, the worts are drawn off clear.

Into the copper, filled up one foot high with the wort, the hops are introduced, and the mixture is made to boil during a quarter of an hour. This is called *roasting the hops*. The rest of the wort is now put into the copper, and boiled along with the hops during at least an hour or an hour and a half. The mixture is then laded out through the hop-filter into the cooling cistern, where it stands three or four inches deep, and is exposed upon an extensive surface to natural or artificial currents of cold air, so as to be quickly cooled. For every 20 barrels of *Lagerbier* there are allowed 10 of small beer; so that 30 barrels of wort are made in all.

For the winter or pot-beer the worts are brought down to about 59° F. in the cooler, and the beer is to be transferred to the fermenting tuns at from 54·5° to 59° F.; for the summer or *Lagerbier*, the worts must be brought down in the cooler to from 43° to 45½°, and put into the fermenting tuns at from 41° to 43° F.

A few hours beforehand, while the wort is still at the temperature of 63½° F., a quantity of *lobb* must be made, called *Vorstellen* (*fore-setting*) in German, by mixing the proportion of *Unterhefe* (yeast) intended for the whole brewing with a barrel or a barrel and a half of the worts, in a small tub called the *Gähr-tiene*, stirring them well together, so that they may immediately run into fermentation. This *lobb* is in this stage to be added to the worts. The *lobb* is known to be ready when it is covered

---

[1] A Bavarian *maas* = 1¼ quarts English measure.

with a white froth from one quarter to one half an inch thick, during which it must be well covered up. The large fermenting tun must in like manner be kept covered even in the vault. The colder the worts, the more yeast must be used. For the above quantity, at

From 57° to 59° F.	.	.	.	.	6	*Maas of Unterhefe.*
„ 53° to 55°	.	.	.	.	8	„ „
„ 48° to 50°	.	.	.	.	10	„ „
„ 41° to 43°	.	.	.	.	12	„ „

Some recommend that wort for this kind of fermentation (the *Untergährung*) should be set with the yeast at from 48° to 57°; but the general practice at Munich is to set the summer or *Lagerbier* at from 41° to 43° F.

By following the preceding directions, the wort in the tun should, in the course of from 12 to 24 hours, exhibit a white froth round the rim, and even a slight whiteness in the middle. After another 12 to 24 hours, the froth should appear in curls; and, in a third like period, these curls should be changed into a still higher frothy brownish mass. In from 24 to 48 hours more, the barm should have fallen down in portions through the beer, so as to allow it to be seen in certain points. In this case it may be turned over into the smaller ripening tuns in the course of other five or six days. But when the worts have been set to ferment at from 41° to 43° F., they require from eight to nine days. The beer is transferred, after being freed from the top yeast by a skimmer, by means of the stopcock near the bottom of the large tun. It is either first run into an intermediate vessel, in order that the top and bottom portions may be well mixed, or into each of the *Lager* casks, in a numbered series, like quantities of the top and bottom portions are introduced. In the ripening cellars the temperature cannot be too low. The best keeping beer can never be brewed unless the temperature of the worts at setting, and of course the fermenting vault, be as low as 50° F. In Bavaria, where this manufacture is carried on under Government inspectors, a brewing period is prescribed by law, which is, for the under-fermenting *Lagerbier*, from Michaelmas (29th September) to St. George (23rd April). From the latter to the former period the ordinary top-barm beer alone is to be made. The ripening casks must not be quite full, and they are to be closed merely with a loose bung, in order to allow of the working over of the ferment. But should the fermentation appear too languid, after six or eight days, a little briskly fermenting *Lagerbier* may be introduced. The *store Lagerbier* tuns are not to be quite filled, so as to prevent all the yeasty particles from being discharged in the ripening fermentation; but the *pot Lagerbier* tuns must be made quite full, as this beverage is intended for speedy sale within a few weeks of its being made.

As soon as the summer-beer vaults are charged with their ripening casks and with ice-cold air, they are closed air-tight with triple doors, having small intervals between, so that one may be entered and shut again before the next is opened. These vaults are sometimes made in ranges radiating from a centre, and at others in rooms set off at right angles to a main gallery, so that in either case, when the external opening is well secured with triple air-tight doors, it may be entered at any time, in order to inspect the interior without the admission of warm air to the beer-barrels. The wooden bungs for loosely stopping them must be coated with the proper pitch, to prevent the possibility of their imparting any acetous ferment.

The Government has taken great pains to improve this national beverage, by encouraging the growth of the best qualities of hops and barley. The vaults in which the beer is fermented, ripened, and kept, are all under ground, and mostly in stony excavations called *Felsenkeller*, or rock-cellars. The beer is divided into two sorts, called *summer* and *winter*. The latter is light, and, being intended for immediate retail in tankards, is termed *Schenkbier*. The other, or the *Lagerbier*, very sensibly increases in vinous strength in proportion as it decreases in sweetness, by the judicious management of the *Nachgährung*, or fermentation in the casks. In several parts of Germany a keeping quality is communicated to beers by burning sulphur in the casks before filling them, or by the introduction of sulphite of lime; but the flavour thus imparted is disliked in Munich, Bayreuth, Regensburg, Nürnberg, Hof, and the other chief towns of Bavaria, instead of which a preservative virtue is sought for in an aromatic mineral, or Tyrol *pitch*, with which the inside of the casks are carefully coated, and in which the ripe beer is kept and exported. In December and January, after the casks are charged with the summer or store beer, the double doors of the cellars are closed, and lumps of ice are piled up against them, to prevent all access of warm air. The cellar is not opened till next August, in order to take out the beer for consumption. In these circumstances the beer becomes transparent like champagne wine; and, since but little carbonic acid gas has been disengaged, little or none of the additionally generated alcohol is lost by evaporation.

The winter or schenk (pot) beer is brewed in the months of October, November, March, and April; but the summer or store beer, in December, January, and February, or the period of the coldest weather. For the former beer, the hopped worts are cooled down only to from 51° to 55°, but for the latter to from 41° to 42½° F. The winter beer is also a little weaker than the summer beer, being intended to be sooner consumed; since four bushels [1] (Berlin measure) of fine, dry, sifted malt, of large heavy *Hordeum vulgare distichon*, affords seven *Eimers* of winter beer, but not more than from five and a half to six of summer beer. [2] At the second infusion of the worts small beer is obtained to the amount of 20 quarts for the above quantity of malt. For the above quantity of winter beer, 6 lbs. of middling hops are reckoned sufficient; but for the summer beer, from 7 to 8 lbs. of the finest hops. The winter beer may be sent out to the publicans in barrels five days after the fermentation has been completed in the tuns, and, though not quite clear, it will become so in the course of six days; yet they generally do not serve it out in pots for two or three weeks; but the summer beer must be perfectly bright and still before it is racked off into casks for sale.

Bock Beer of Bavaria.—This is a favourite double-strong beverage of the best *lager* description, which is so named from causing its consumers to prance and tumble about like a buck or a goat;—for the German word *Bock* has both these meanings. It is merely a beer having a specific gravity one-third greater, and is therefore made with a third greater proportion of malt, but with the same proportion of hops, and flavoured with a few coriander seeds. It has a somewhat darker colour than the general *Lagerbier*, occasionally brownish, tastes less bitter on account of the predominating malt, and is somewhat aromatic. It is an eminently intoxicating beverage. It is brewed in December and January, and takes a long time to ferment and ripen; but still it contains too large a quantity of unchanged saccharine matter and *dextrine* for its hops, so that it tastes too luscious for habitual topers, and is drunk only from the beginning of May till the end of July, when the fashion and appetite for it are over for the year.

On the Clarifying or Clearing of Beers.—Clarifiers act either chemically,—by being soluble in the beer, and by forming an insoluble compound with a vegetable gluten, and other viscid vegetable extracts; gelatine and albumen, under one shape or other, have been most used: the former for beer. the latter, as white of egg, for wine,—or mechanically, by being diffused in fine particles through the turbid liquor, and, in their precipitation, carrying down with them the floating vegetable matters. To this class belong sand, bone-black (in some measure, but not entirely), and other such articles. The latter means are very imperfect, and can take down only such matters as exist already in an insoluble state; of the former class, milk, blood, glue, calves'-feet jelly, hartshorn shavings, and isinglass, have been chiefly recommended. Calves'-feet jelly is much used in many parts of Germany, where veal forms so common a kind of butcher-meat; but in summer it is apt to acquire a putrid taint, and to impart the same to the beer. In these islands, isinglass, swollen and partly dissolved in vinegar, or sour beer, is almost the sole clarifier, called finings, employed. It is costly, when the best article is used; but an inferior kind of isinglass is imported for the brewers.

The solvent or medium through or with which it is administered is eminently injudicious, as it never fails to infect the beer with an acetous ferment. In Germany their tart wine has been used hitherto for dissolving the isinglass; and this has also the same bad property. Mr. Zimmermann professes to have discovered an unexceptionable solvent in tartaric acid, one pound of which dissolved in 24 quarts of water is capable of dissolving two pounds of ordinary isinglass; forming finings which may be afterwards diluted with pure water at pleasure. Such isinglass imported from Petersburg into Berlin costs there only 3s. per lb. These finings are best added, as already mentioned, to the worts prior to fermentation, as soon as they are let into the setting-back, or tun, immediately after adding the yeast to it. They are best administered by mixing them in a small tub with thrice their volume of wort, raising the mixture into a froth with a whisk (*twig-besom* in German), and then stirring it into the worts. The clarification becomes manifest in the course of a few hours, and when the fermentation is completed, the beer will be as brilliant as can be wished; the test of which with the German topers is when they can read a newspaper while a tall glass beaker of beer is placed between the paper and the candle. One quart of finings of the above strength will be generally found adequate to the clearing of 100 gallons of well-brewed lager-beer, though it will be surer to use double that proportion of finings. The Carrageen moss, as finings, is to be cut in fine shreds, thrown into the boiling

---

[1] An English quarter of grain is equal to 5 bushels (*scheffel*) and nearly one-third Prussian measure.
[2] 1 Eimer Prussian=15¼ English imperial gallons; 1 Munich *scheffel* is equal to 4 Berlin *scheffels*; 1 Lib. Munich=1·235 English pounds avoird.; 1 Lib. Berlin=1·031 pounds avoird.

thin wort, when the flocks begin to separate, and before adding the hops; after which the boiling is continued for an hour and a half or two hours, as need be. The clarifying with this kind of finings takes place in the cooler, so that a limpid wort may be drawn off into the fermenting back.

Zimmermann assumes the merit of having introduced Carrageen moss as a clarifier into the beer manufacture. He says that 1 ounce of it is sufficient for 25 gallons of beer; and that it operates, not only in the act of boiling with the hops, but in that of cooling, as also in the squares and backs before the fermentation has begun. Whenever this change, however, takes place, the commixture throws up the gluten and moss to the surface of the liquid in a black scum, which is to be skimmed off, so that the proper yeast may not be soiled with it. It occasions the separation of much of the vegetable slime, or mucilage, called by the German brewers *Pech* (pitch).

Berlin White or Pale Beer (*Weiss-bier*).—This is the truly national beverage of Prussia Proper. It is brewed from 1 part of barley malt and 5 parts of wheat malt, mingled, moistened, and coarsely crushed between rollers. This mixture is worked up first with water at 95° F., in the proportion of 30 quarts per *scheffel* of the malt, to which pasty mixture 70 quarts of boiling water are forthwith added, and the whole is mashed in the tun. After it has been left here a little to settle, a portion of the thin liquor is drawn off by the tap, transferred to the copper, and then for each bushel of malt there is added to it a decoction of half a pound of *Altmark* hops separately prepared. This hopped wort, after half an hour's boiling, is turned back with the hops into the mash-tun, of which the temperature should now be 162½° F., but not more. In half an hour the wort is to be drawn off from the grains, and pumped into the cooler. The grains are afterwards mashed with from 40 to 50 quarts of boiling water per *scheffel* of malt, and this infusion is drawn off and added to the former worts. The whole mixture is set at 66° F. with a due proportion of top yeast or ordinary barm, and very moderately fermented.

Potato Beer.—The potatoes being well washed are to be rubbed down to a pulp by such a grating cylinder machine as is represented in *fig.* 102, where *a* is the

102

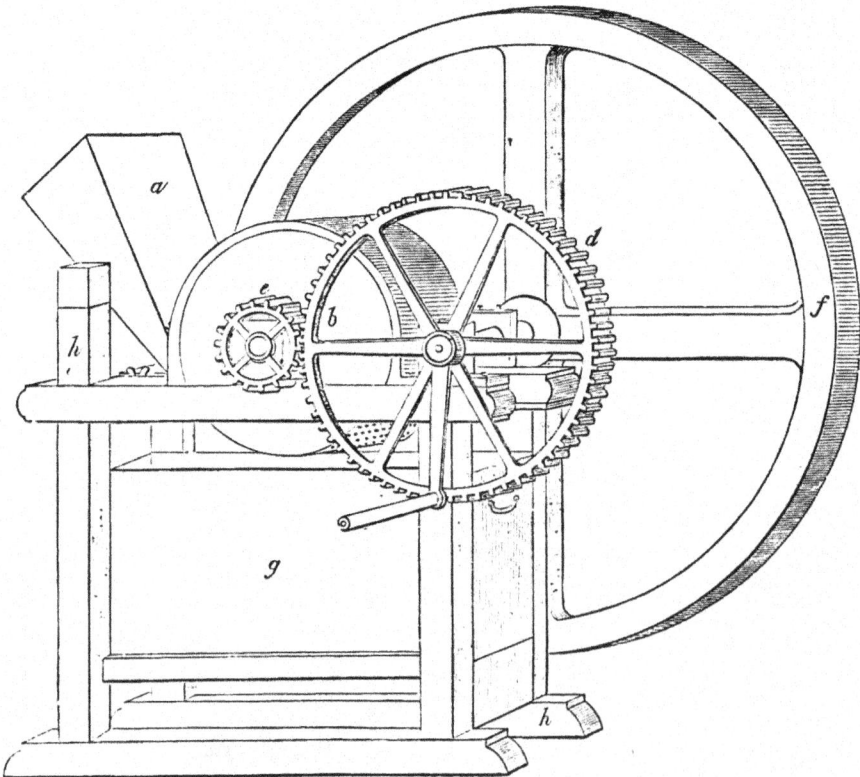

hopper for receiving the roots (whether potato or beet, as in the French sugar factories); *b* is the crushing and grinding drum; *c*, the handle for turning the spur-wheel *d*, which drives the pinion *e*, and the fly-wheel *f*; *g*, *h*, is the frame. The dotted lines above *c* are the colander through which the pulp passes. For every *scheffel* of potatoes 80 quarts of water are to be put with them into the copper, and made to boil.

Crushed malt, to the amount of 12 *scheffels*, is to be well worked about in the mash-tun with 360 quarts, or 90 gallons (English), of cold water, to a thick pap, and then 840 additional quarts, or about 6 barrels (English), of cold water are to be successively introduced, with constant stirring, and left to stand an hour at rest.

The potatoes having been meanwhile boiled to a fine starch paste, the whole malt-mash, thin and thick, is to be speedily laded into the copper, and the mixture in it is to be well stirred for an hour, taking care to keep the temperature at from 144° to 156° F. all the time, in order that the *diastase* of the malt may convert the starch present in the two substances into sugar and dextrine. This transformation is made manifest by the white pasty liquid becoming transparent and thin. Whenever this happens the fire is to be raised, to make the mash boil, and to keep it at this heat for 10 minutes. The fire is then withdrawn, the contents of the copper are to be transferred into the mash, worked well there, and left to settle for half an hour; during which time the copper is to be washed out, and quickly charged once more with boiling water.

The clear wort is to be drawn off from the tun, as usual, and boiled as soon as possible with the due proportion of hops; and the boiling water may be added in any desired quantity to the drained mash, for the second mashing. Wort made in this way is said to have no flavour whatever of the potato, and to clarify more easily than malt-wort, from its containing a smaller proportion of gluten relatively to that of saccharum.

A *scheffel* of good mealy potatoes affords from 26 to 27½ lbs. of thick well-boiled syrup, of the density of 36° Baumé (see AREOMETER); and 26 lbs. of such syrup are equivalent to a *scheffel* of malt in saccharine strength. Zimmermann thinks beer so brewed from potatoes quite equal, at least, if not superior, to pure malt beer, both in appearance and quality.

Fig. 103 is the stopcock used in Bavaria for bottling beer.

103

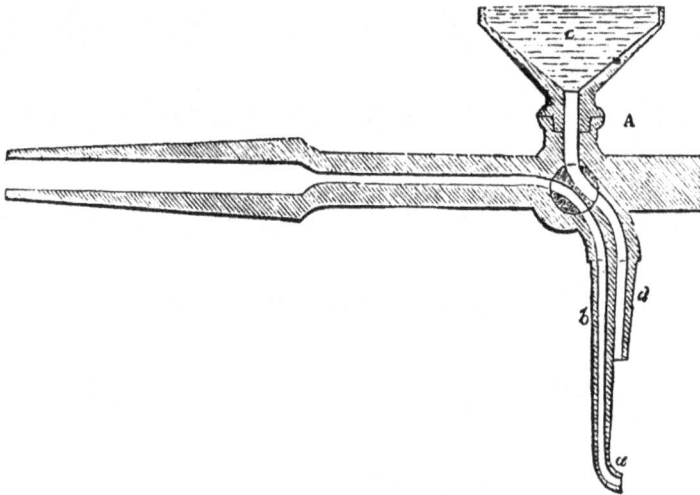

The following analyses of German beers are by Leo:—

	Lichtenhain	Upper Weimar	Ilmenau	Jena	Double Jena
Alcohol . . .	3·168	2·567	3·096	3·018	2·080
Albumen . . .	0·048	0·020	0·079	0·045	0·028
Extract . . .	4·485	7·316	7·072	6·144	7·153
Water . . .	92·299	90·097	89·753	90·793	90·739
	100·000	100·000	100·000	100·000	100·000

Under the term 'extract,' in these analyses, is meant a mixture of starch, sugar, dextrine, lactic acid, various salts, certain extractive and aromatic parts of the hop, gluten, and fatty matter.

Hoffstedt's process for the detection of spurious bitters in beer is applicable to the detection of picrotoxin, absinthin, menyanthin, quassin, and colocynthin. The bitter principles likely to occur in beer may be divided into two classes :—

I. Precipitable by Acetate of Lead.

Lupulin.—It is not precipitable by tannin. It is soluble in alcohol and ether, but not in water.

II.—Not precipitated by Acetate of Lead.

With tannin, after removal of lead by means of sulphuretted hydrogen.

   a. Not precipitated by tannin:
      Picrotoxin.—Soluble in water, alcohol, and ether.
      Absinthin.—Soluble in alcohol and ether, not in water.
   b. Precipitated by tannin:
      Menyanthin.—Sparingly soluble in ether and cold water; easily in hot water. Turns brown and then violet with strong sulphuric acid.
      Quassin.—Sparingly soluble in ether; soluble in 222 parts of cold water; not coloured by sulphuric acid.
      Colocynthin.—Insoluble in ether; soluble in cold water. Turns first red and then brown with strong sulphuric acid.

The quantities needful for examination are six litres of Bavarian or bitter beer, or four of porter. This may seem excessive, but it must be remembered that a very small quantity of the above-mentioned drugs will impart a strong bitter taste to a large volume of liquid; and, again, that the hop is never entirely omitted, since its peculiar efficacy in preventing spurious or secondary fermentation appears to be possessed by no other bitter. The beer in question is to be evaporated down, first over the naked fire, and afterwards on the water-bath. Great care must be taken that it does not dry or burn on the sides of the vessel, or bitter principles may be generated which mask the reactions to be sought for. The thick mass is well treated with alcohol in a tall beaker. At the bottom will be found a thick gummy mass, and a somewhat turbid stratum of liquor over it: this is set aside to become clear; it is then poured off and the alcohol distilled off; the residue is concentrated to a syrup and dissolved in alcohol. The solution is mixed with ten times its bulk of ether, which precipitates sugar; when clear, the liquid is decanted from the sediment and distilled. The residue is dissolved in warm water and a portion of it tested with tannin. A pure, well-hopped beer never gives a clear aqueous solution; a beer containing little of the hop may; if the solution does not clear up add a trace of alcohol. Besides lupulin, absinthin is insoluble in water. Filter off the resinous matter which may have been deposited, then precipitate the warm filtrate with acetate of lead, which must not be too acid; lupulin is then thrown down. Excess of lead must be carefully avoided, or menyanthin may fall down also: allow it to settle, filter, and wash the precipitate with hot water.

Filtrate.—Treat with sulphuretted hydrogen till all the lead is precipitated; filter and wash, first with warm water and then with alcohol; remove sulphuretted hydrogen and free acetic acid by evaporation almost to dryness. If the residue is free from bitterness no adulteration is present; absinthin never gives a clear aqueous solution, and menyanthin never a clear cold one. A turbid solution may contain all the spurious bitters; add a little alcohol till the solution becomes clear, and then tannin.

1. The precipitate formed is dried up along with hydrated oxide of lead suspended in water, and extracted with boiling spirit. In the residue of this extract colocynthin, menyanthin, and quassin are separated by means of their behaviour with ether and water.

2. The precipitate is freed from tannin by means of acetate of lead, the precipitate filtered off, the lead removed by means of sulphuretted hydrogen and evaporated. Picrotoxin separates out in crystals; absinthin remains as a yellow mass.

Levin Ender recommends the following procedure :—

1. Precipitate with acetate of lead.
   Lupulin.—It gives no mirror with ammoniacal solution of silver.
2. Not precipitated by acetate of lead, but by tannin.
   A. Soluble in ether: *Absinthin.* Gives a mirror with the silver solution.
   B. Sparingly soluble in ether. *Menyanthin; Quassin.* The former gives a mirror; the latter not.

Picrotoxin, absinthin, menyanthin, edocynthin, reduce solution of silver; lupulin and quassia do not.

Beer and Ale.—Exports.

Countries to which exported	1871		1872	
	Barrels	£	Barrels	£
To Russia	4,253	16,131		
„ Germany	5,168	18,613		
„ Belgium	3,714	13,432		
„ France	10,152	34,149		
„ China	4,209	21,472		
„ Japan	2,421	12,454		
„ United States:—				
Atlantic	29,446	147,010	} 44,360	223,579
Pacific	6,956	34,185		
„ Foreign West Indies	16,080	82,503		
„ Peru	11,965	63,998		
„ Chili	7,107	35,223		
„ Brazil	13,267	71,903		
„ Uruguay	2,388	12,447		
„ Argentine Confederation	5,342	26,846		
„ Channel Islands	8,531	25,327		
„ Gibraltar	11.432	38,198		
„ Malta	6,742	22,152		
„ British Possessions in South Africa	15,669	64,777		
„ British India:—				
Bombay and Scinde	59,264	165,929	} 167,597	522,593
Madras	24,354	69,050		
Bengal	66,365	214,574		
„ Straits'-Settlements	3,287	13,133		
„ Ceylon	8,589	30,199		
„ Hong Kong	7,417	28,717		
„ Australia	80,511	324,021	88,184	359,701
„ British North America	11,941	50,542		
„ British West India Islands and British Guiana	28,013	106,243	27,199	102,491
„ Other Countries	28,537	110,505	194,616	876,219
Total	483,120	1,853,733	521,956	2,084,583

Beer and Ale.—Imports in 1872.

Countries whence imported	Quantities	Value	Entered for Home Consumption	Gross Amount received
	Barrels	£	Barrels	£
Mum—From all Countries	2	6	2	2
Spruce—From Germany	1,813	14,688		
„ Other Countries	7	30		
Total	1,820	14,718	1,720	2,062
Other sorts—From Germany	326	1,349		
„ Belgium	841	2,853		
„ Other Countries	1,277	3,303		
Total	2,444	7,505	2,435	1,088

BEER-STONE. A peculiar stone, composed chiefly of carbonate of lime, which is quarried extensively at Beer, in Devonshire.

BEES'-WAX. The solid matter forming the cells of the honeycomb, secreted, according to Hüber, by an organ situated in the abdomen of the bee. See WAX.

BEETLE. A name usually given to the insects of the Coleopterous order, especially to those of a dark colour. The species of Coleopterous insects known amount to nearly 40,000. The cantharides, or blistering-flies, are used medicinally. The larva of *Cerambyx heros* was regarded by the Romans as a delicacy. The American Indians eat the larva of *Calandra palmarum*. The name is applied to the annoying insects which infest the kitchens of houses in large towns; they are the *blatta* or cockroach, and belong to the *Orthopterous order*.

BEETLE's WINGS. The elytra or wing cases of the more brilliantly coloured beetles (*Coleoptera*), are used in making head-dresses for ladies, and for decorating muslins, scarfs, and ball dresses. In Brazil especially, those wings are used for ornaments, and much art is bestowed in their production. Since the Exhibition of 1862, when Brazil exhibited a collection of the beetle's wing ornaments, they have been regularly imported.

BEETLE, or *Maul*. A large mallet, with a handle about three feet in length, used for knocking the corners of framed work, and setting it in its proper position. Also a mallet used for driving piles, raised by ropes and pullies—sometimes called Boytle.

BEETLE STONES. A name given in South Wales to septarian nodules of the clay ironstone from the coal-measures.

BEETLING MACHINE. A machine used for producing ornamental figured fabrics by pressure from corrugated or indented surface rollers.

BEET-ROOT. (*Betterave*, Fr.; *rothe Rübe*, Ger.) The large fleshy root of the *beet*, a plant of the genus *Beta*. There are two distinct species cultivated, each containing several varieties. One called *Hortensis*, producing succulent leaves only; the other, the *Vulgaris*, distinguished by its long fleshy root. The variety of the *Vulgaris*, known as the *red beet*, is much cultivated in our gardens, and used as a vegetable. The *white beet* is in much repute in Belgium and France for the manufacture of sugar. See SUGAR.

The common *field beet*, for cattle, which has been long known in Germany, was introduced into England at the latter end of the last century; and its introduction is generally attributed to the late Dr. Lettsom, a physician of great repute, and one of the Society of Friends. The German name is *mangold wurzel*, or mangold root, but is commonly pronounced *mangel wurzel*, which means scarcity root; and, by a strange translation, it is called in French *racine d'abondance*, or root of plenty, as well as *racine de disette*, or root of scarcity. The name *field beet* is much more appropriate.— *Penny Cyclopædia*.

The Analyses of Way and Ogston give the following Composition for two Varieties of the Beet-root, and the Analysis of Griepenkerl for another.

Substances contained	Yellow Globe Mangold Wurzel		Long Red Mangold Wurzel		Red Beet
	Root	Leaves	Root	Leaves	Root
Potassa	25·54	8·34	21·68	27·90	51·10
Soda	19·08	12·21	3·13	3·01	
Lime	1·78	8·72	1·90	8·17	2·45
Magnesia	1·75	9·84	1·79	7·03	2·94
Sesquioxide of iron	0·74	1·46	0·52	0·96	0·35
Sulphuric acid	3·68	6·54	3·14	4·60	3·31
Silica	2·22	2·35	1·40	2·26	0·19
Carbonic acid	18·14	6·92	15·23	6·45	
Phosphoric acid	4·49	5·89	1·65	5·19	10·77
Chloride of sodium	24·54	37·66	49·51	34·39	17·04
Total amount	99·96	99·95	99·95	99·96	99·99
Per-centage of ash in the dry substance	11·32	14·00	7·10	17·90	7· 8
Per-centage of ash in the fresh substance	1·02	1·40	0·64	1·79	

The quantity of beet-root used in the Zollverein States of Germany in the manufacture of sugar was as follows :—

	Centners of 110 lbs. Eng.
For the year 1849–50	11,525,678
„ 1850–51	16,000,000
„ 1851–52	20,000,000
„ 1870–71	25,750,000
„ 1871–72	26,550,000

The centner varies, in different localities, from 100 to 112 avoirdupois pounds.

The cultivation of the sugar-beet has been introduced into the northern United States and California.

BELLADONNA. (*Belledame*, Fr.) The *Atropa Belladonna*, or deadly night-shade, a poisonous plant belonging to the *Solanaceæ* or potato-order. It is employed in medicine as an anodyne, and also for dilating the pupil of the eye in operation for cataract. It has been used in the preparation of an Italian cosmetic, whence the specific name—*Belladonna* ('fine lady'). The active principle of this plant is an alkaloid called *atropine* or *atropia*.

BELL-METAL. An alloy of copper and tin. The proportions of these con-stituents vary within certain limits. The older bell-founders appear to have aimed at producing an alloy of 3 parts of copper to 1 of tin; these proportions yield a metal of high density—a good casting having a specific gravity of 8·9, or equal to that of the unalloyed copper—but rather too brittle to be used for large bells. An alloy of 3½ of copper to 1 of tin has been largely employed, and being easy to tune is a favourite metal with bell-founders. When 4 of copper to 1 of tin is used, a soft alloy is obtained, such as is ordinarily used for small house-bells. The large bells in the New Houses of Parliament at Westminster were cast in an alloy of 22 of copper to 7 of tin; but Mr. Denison, who superintended the construction of these bells, has since suggested that the ratio of 13 to 4, or 3¼ parts of copper to 1 of tin, would probably form a better alloy, since these proportions exactly represent 6 equivalents of copper to 1 of tin. Such an alloy, being a definite compound, with its constituents in atomic propor-tions, would be more likely to remain homogeneous throughout—the component metals having less tendency to separate from each other during the cooling of the molten mass. 'I should now,' says Mr. Denison, speaking after his experience of the West-minster bells, 'require large bells to be of this 76·5 copper to 23·5 tin, or Cu^6Sn; and they should then be rejected as unhomogeneous if any part of the bell is proved to be beyond the limits of either 77 per cent. of copper or 23 of tin.'

In addition to the two chief constituents of bell-metal, small quantities of other metals have occasionally been introduced into the alloy, but apparently without any decided advantage. Thus some celebrated old bells contain a small proportion of antimony—Old Tom of Lincoln containing about ·03 per cent. The use of silver has also been recommended, but seems unwarranted.

An alloy of cast-iron and tin, called 'Stirling's Union Metal,' has been employed for bells; but, though emitting a fair sound, is far inferior to ordinary bell-metal. The same remark applies to cast-steel bells. See BRONZE and COPPER.

BELL-METAL ORE, or *Stannine*; a sulphide of tin, copper, and iron. (*Etain sulphuré*, Haüy; *Zinnkies*, Hausmann.) The composition of the ordinary variety of this ore is—

Copper	30·0
Iron	12·0
Tin	26·5
Sulphur	30·5
	99·0

It was found in many of the Cornish mines, and especially at Carn Brea, but is now rare.

BELLOWS. See METALLURGY.

BELLS. Church bells are said to have been originated in Italy; but bells were cer-tainly cast at a very early period in the East. They were evidently used by the ancient Egyptians, and at a very early date amongst the Chinese. All the more celebrated bells are manufactured of bronze, or bell-metal (these alloys are described under their respective heads).

The following are the weights of a few of the largest bells :—

	lbs.
The great bell of Moscow	443,772
The bell of St. Ivan	127,836
Another bell in the same city	39,827
Ditto ditto, cast in 1819	112,000

					lbs.
The bell in the cathedral, Paris	.	.	.	.	38,800
Ditto　　　　ditto　　Vienna	.	.	.	.	39,648
The bell in the church at Erfürt	.	.	.	.	30,800
Great Tom of Oxford	.	.	.	.	17,000
Ditto　　　　Lincoln	.	.	.	.	9,894
The bell of St. Paul's, London	.	.	.	.	8,400
Big Ben of Westminster, London	.	.	.	.	30,352

The Big Ben of the New Houses of Parliament was designed by Mr. Denison, Q.C., who undertook all the responsibility of its construction, *except the casting*. The metal, as already stated, was an alloy of 22 parts of copper to 7 of tin. The original bell was cast on August 6, 1856, by Messrs. Warner, at Norton, near Stockton-on-Tees. It was thicker than the prescribed pattern, and exceeded the intended weight by 2 cwt. Moreover, the casting was defective, and when the bell was subsequently broken up, a natural crack, 18 inches long, was found in the sound-bow. In order to bring out the full sound, a clapper of 13 cwt. was required, and the bell was consequently cracked within a year after it had been cast.

On April 10, 1858, Big Ben was recast, with certain alterations of shape, by Mr. Mears. Soon after it had been placed in the clock-tower it was found that this second casting was much more defective than the first—the metal exhibiting a number of superficial cavities and still more internal blisters. Dr. Percy and Prof. Tyndall were instructed to report officially on the bell. It was found that instead of containing 22 of copper to 7 of tin, as required by contract, two fragments from the sound-bow contained respectively 19·4 of copper to 7 of tin, and 19·9 copper to 7 tin; whilst a sample taken from the top yielded 22·3 of copper to 7 of tin. Thus, in addition to the porous structure of the casting, the alloy was far from being uniform throughout, and the lower part—which is, of course, the most important part of a bell—was harder and more brittle than the specified alloy. Both castings, therefore, were decided failures.

With regard to the general form of bells, Mr. Denison made the following remarks in a lecture at the Royal Institution :—

' Now, from these and other experiments, I have come to the conclusion that bells of the common and well-known shape, with a thick lip or sound-bow, are the most effective known instruments for producing a loud and musical sound, such as you want when you erect a large public clock, or put up a peal of church bells. And I confess, also, that after trying, at Messrs. Warners', a number of experiments with bells of the usual *general* form, but with various deviation in the details, I am equally satisfied that there is nothing to be gained by deviating materially from the established proportions of the best old bells. And I think it is some confirmation of my views to tell you that Professor Wheatstone, having been commissioned by the Board of Works with Sir C. Barry, on his own suggestion, to collect information at the late Paris Exhibition respecting the most esteemed chimes in France and Belgium, and whether there are in those countries makers acquainted with the traditions of the art, or who have applied the discoveries of science to the improvement of bells, *or to efficient substitutes for them*, has come back with the conclusion that no such efficient substitutes have been discovered ; nor is there any known improvement on the established mode and materials for casting them. Sir C. Barry and he, indeed, seem to have been rather impressed with the merits of the cast-steel bells, which you have seen noticed in the newspapers. I have not heard them myself, but I have heard such condemnation of their harshness of sound from other persons, of probably more experience in such matters, that I do not the least believe in their being received generally as an efficient (though they may be a cheap) substitute for the more expensive compound of copper and tin; and, on the whole, that seems to be Professor Wheatstone's opinion also.'

BENGAL STRIPES. Ginghams ; a kind of cotton cloth woven with coloured stripes, so called from the cottons which we formerly imported from Bengal.

BEN NUTS. (*Noix de ben*, Fr. ; *Salbnüsse*, Ger.) The tree which furnishes these nuts is the *Guilandina moringa* of Linnæus, a native of India, Ceylon, Arabia, and Egypt.

BEN OIL. The oil of ben, which may be obtained from the decorticated nuts, is said to be far less liable than other oils to become rancid, and hence it is much used by watchmakers. At a low temperature, the oil of ben separates into two parts—one solid and one fluid ; the latter only is used for watch-work. At one time oil of ben was employed as a base for the enfleurage process of making perfumed oils from flowers in the south of France, brought thence from the Levant, but from some unknown reason it has long since ceased to be imported, and oil of ben is now a very rare article of commerce. An attempt has been made in Jamaica, by Mr. Kemble, to raise the moringa for the sake of this oil, but the samples there produced remained a perfectly solid fat in England throughout the whole year.—S.P.

BENZIDINE. An alkali, discovered by Zinin, in acting with reducing agents on arzobenzide and azoxibenzide.—C.G.W.

BENZINE. See BENZOLE.

BENZOIC ACID. $C^{14}H^6O^4$ ($C^7H^6O^2$). This acid may be obtained by placing benzoin powdered, with sand, in an evaporating basin, and above it a paper cap; on applying heat carefully to the sand, acid vapours arise from the resin, and they are deposited in the form of fine light crystals within the paper cap. Stolze recommends the following process for extracting the acid :—The resin is to be dissolved in three parts of alcohol, the solution is to be introduced into a retort, and a solution of carbonate of soda dissolved in dilute alcohol is to be gradually added to it, till the free acid be neutralised; and then a bulk of water equal to double the weight of the benzoin is to be poured in. The alcohol being drawn off by distillation, the remaining liquor contains the acid, and the resin floating upon it may be skimmed off and washed, when its weight will be found to amount to about 80 per cent. of the raw material.

Benzoic acid is also obtained by boiling hippuric acid, or the urine of cows or horses which contains this acid, with hydrochloric acid.

BENZOIN, or **BENJAMIN.** (*Benjoin*, Fr.; *Benzöe*, Ger.) A species of resin, used chiefly in perfumery; improperly called a gum, since it is quite insoluble in water. It is extracted by incision from the trunk and branches of the *Styrax benzoin*, or *Lithocarpus benzoin*, which grows in Java, Sumatra, Santa Fé, and in the kingdom of Siam. The plant belongs to the natural family of the *Styracaceæ*. The benzoin flows in small quantities spontaneously from the trees; but it is collected by making incisions in the stem, just below where the branches are given off, as soon as the tree has attained an age of five or six years. These incisions are repeated each year for about twelve years, when the tree becomes exhausted. The resin flows out as a white fluid. It hardens readily in the air, and comes to us in brittle masses, whose fracture presents a mixture of red, brown, and white grains of various sizes, which, when white, and of a certain shape, have been called *amygdaloid*, from their resemblance to almonds. The *benzoe in sortis* is very impure, containing portions of wood and bark.

The fracture of benzoin is conchoidal, and its lustre greasy; its specific gravity varies from 1·063 to 1·092. It has an agreeable smell, somewhat like vanilla, which is most manifest when it is ground. It enters into fusion at a gentle heat, and then exhales a white smoke, which may be condensed into the acicular crystals of benzoic acid, of which it contains 18 parts in the hundred. Ether does not dissolve benzoin completely. The fat and volatile oils dissolve very little of it.

Unverdorben has found in benzoin, besides benzoic acid and a little volatile oil, no less than three different kinds of resin, none of which has, however, been turned, as yet, to any use in the arts.

Benzoin is principally used in perfumery; it enters into a number of preparations, among which may be mentioned fumigating pastilles, fumigating cloves (called also nails), *poudre à la maréchale*, &c. The alcoholic tincture, mixed with 20 parts of rose-water, forms the cosmetic *virginal milk*. Benzoin enters also into the composition of certain varnishes employed for snuff-boxes and walking-sticks, in order to give these objects an agreeable smell when they become heated in the hand. It is added to the spirituous solution of isinglass, with which court-plaster is made.

BENZOLE. *Syn.* Benzine, benzene, benzol, hydruret of phenyl, $C^{12}H^6$ (C^6H^6). A compound of carbon and hydrogen discovered by Faraday in the products of the destructive distillation of whale-oil. The more volatile portion of coal-naphtha has been shown by Mansfield to consist chiefly of this substance. It is produced in a great number of reactions in which organic bodies are exposed to high temperatures. It may at once be obtained in a state of purity by distilling benzoic acid with excess of quicklime. The lime acts by removing two atoms of carbonic acid from the benzoic acid. The method of obtaining benzole from coal-naphtha will be found fully described under the head of NAPHTHA, COAL. Benzole is also contained in considerable quantity in bone-oil; but it is accompanied by peculiar nitrogenised volatile fluids, which are difficult of removal. The latter, owing to their powerful and fetid odour, greatly injure the quality of the bone-oil benzole. Benzole is an exceedingly volatile fluid, boiling at ordinary pressures at 187° F. Its density is 0·850. Owing to the levity of benzole being regarded by manufacturers as a proof of its purity, it is not uncommon to find it adulterated with the naphtha from the Torbanehill mineral, or Boghead coal, which has a density as low as 0·750. Any benzole having a lower density than 0·850 is impure. Benzole is excessively inflammable, and its vapour mixed with air is explosive. Numerous lives have been lost owing to these properties, among them that of Mr. Mansfield, to whom we are indebted for an excellent investigation on coal-naphtha. Benzole is greatly used in commerce, owing to its valuable solvent properties. It dissolves caoutchouc and gutta-percha readily, and, on evaporation, leaves them in a state well adapted for waterproofing and many other purposes. Its power of dissolving fatty, oily, and other greasy matters, has caused it to become an article of commerce under the name of *benzoline*. It readily extracts grease even from the most delicate fabrics, and, as it soon, on exposure to the air, evaporates totally away, no odour remains to betray the fact of its having been used. It dissolves readily in very strong nitric acid, and, on the addition of water, it is precipitated as a heavy oil, having the composition $C^{12}H^5NO^4$ ($\mathbf{C^6H^5NO^2}$). The latter compound is *nitrobenzole*; it is regarded as benzole in which one atom of hydrogen is replaced by hyponitric acid. Nitrobenzole, in a state of tolerable purity, is a pale-yellow oil, having a sweetish taste, and an odour greatly resembling bitter almonds. Owing to its comparative cheapness, it is employed in perfumery. Nitrobenzole can be prepared with nitric acid of moderate strength, such as is ordinarily obtained in commerce; but it then becomes necessary to distil the acid and the hydrocarbon together several times. The product so obtained is darker in colour, and in other respects inferior to that obtained with highly concentrated acid. By treatment with acetate of protoxide of iron, nitrobenzole becomes transformed into aniline. This change may be effected, but far less conveniently, by means of sulphide of ammonium. Benzole is extremely valuable in many operations of manufacturing chemistry. It dissolves several alkaloids, and, on evaporation, leaves them in a state of purity. It dissolves quinine, but not cinchonine, and may therefore be employed as a means of separation. Morphia and strychnine are also dissolved by it, but not in great quantity. To obtain many natural alkaloids existing in plants, it is merely necessary to digest the dry extract with caustic potash and then with benzole. The latter is to be decanted, and then distilled off on a water-bath. The alkaloid will be left behind in a state well adapted for crystallisation or other means of purification. Benzole is becoming much used as a solvent in researches in organic chemistry. Many substances, such as chrysene and bichloride of naphthaline, crystallise better from benzole than from any other solvent.

Benzole may be employed in many ways for illuminating purposes. It is so easily inflamed that great care is necessary in using it. It does not require a wick to enable it to burn. If poured, even on an uninflammable surface and a light be applied, it takes fire like a train of gunpowder, and burns with a brilliant flame, emitting dense clouds of smoke, which, soon condensing into soot, presently fall in a shower of blacks. Even on the surface of water it burns as freely as anywhere else. If a drachm or two be poured on water contained in a pan, and a pellet of potassium be thrown in, the benzole inflames, and rises in a column of flame of considerable height. A method of destroying enemies' shipping has been founded on this principle. In consequence of the smoky nature of the flame of benzole (caused by the comparatively larger percentage of carbon), it is often convenient to burn a mixture of one volume of benzole and two volumes of alcohol. A stream of air driven through benzole becomes so inflammable as to serve for the purposes of illumination. For this mode of using the hydrocarbon, it should be kept slightly warm to assist its vaporisation. A machine on this principle, of American invention, has been employed to illuminate houses. The air is driven through the benzole by a very simple contrivance, the motive power being a descending weight. See Gas, Air.

When quite pure, benzole freezes at 32° to a beautiful snow-white substance, resembling camphor. The mass retains the solid form until a temperature of 40° or 41° is reached. This property of solidifying under the influence of cold may be made use of to produce pure benzole from the more volatile portion of coal-naphtha. To obtain it perfectly pure, it should be frozen at least three times, the portion not solidifying being removed by filtration through calico. The unfrozen portion contains hydrocarbons, homologous with olefiant gas.

Benzole dissolves free iodine and bromine, and has even been used in analysis to separate them from kelp and other substances containing them. They must of course be set free before acting with the hydrocarbon. The presence of benzole in mixtures may easily be demonstrated, even when present in very small quantity, by converting it into aniline, and obtaining the characteristic reaction with chloride of lime. For this purpose the mixture is to be dissolved in concentrated nitric acid and the nitrobenzole precipitated by water. The fluid is then agitated with ether, which dissolves the nitro-compound. The ethereal solution is mixed with an equal bulk of alcohol and hydrochloric acid: a little granulated zinc being added, hydrogen is evolved, and, by acting in a nascent state on the nitro-compound, reduces it to the state of aniline. The base is then to be separated by an excess of potash, and the alkaline fluid is shaken with ether to dissolve the base. The ethereal fluid being evaporated, leaves the aniline.

On adding water and then a few drops of solution of chloride of lime, the purple colour indicative of aniline is immediately produced.—*Hofmann.* The writer of this article has by this process detected minute traces of benzole in mixtures consisting almost entirely of homologues of olefiant gas.—C. G. W.

BENZOLINE. See BENZOLE.

BERGAMOT. (*Bergamotte*, Fr.) The *Citrus bergamia*, a citron cultivated in the centre and south of Europe. By distillation from the rind of the fruit is obtained the well-known essence of bergamot. See OILS, ESSENTIAL.

The ottoes, or essential oils, from fruits such as the bergamot, the lemon, and the orange, may all be procured by distillation, but these products thus procured are not valued by the manufacturing perfumer so much as when they are obtained by rasping the peel of the fruit and collecting the essence thus disengaged, and finally filtering. The rasps employed for this purpose are hollow cones filled with spikes, in which the fruit is dexterously revolved by hand. All essences that are distilled are modified in their composition by the presence of the watery vapour and high temperature. —S. P.

BERGAMOT. A coarse tapestry, said to have been invented at Bergamo, in Italy, made of ox and goats' hair, with cotton or hemp.

BERLIN BLACK. A black varnish, drying with almost a dead surface, used for coating the better kinds of iron-ware.

BERLIN BLUE. A fine variety of the Prussian Blue.

BERLIN CASTINGS. Delicate ornamental objects cast in a very fluid iron, smelted from bog-ores, and containing much phosphorus. These castings were formerly imported from Prussia, and used for personal decoration.

BERRY. The term is commonly applied, not only to small fruit, but in some cases to seeds. The following is Professor Lindley's definition of a berry:—' A succulent or pulpy fruit containing naked seeds, or, in more technical language, a succulent or pulpy pericarp, or seed-vessel without valves, containing several seeds, which are naked, that is, which have no covering but the pulp and rind. It is commonly round or oval. But in popular language, *berry* extends only to smaller fruits, as strawberry, gooseberry, &c., containing seeds or granules. An indehiscent pulpy pericarp, many-celled and many-seeded; the attachment of the seeds lost at maturity, and the seeds remaining scattered in the pulp.'

Berries are used in some of the processes of manufacture, but they are not of much importance.

Bay Berries.—The fruit of the *Laurus nobilis*, or the sweet bay. Both the leaves and the fruit are employed as flavourings. A volatile oil, the *oil of sweet bay*, is obtained by distillation with water; and a fixed oil, by bruising the berries, and boiling them for some hours in water; this oil, called also *Laurel fat*, is imported from Italy. See BAYS, OIL OF.

Turkey Yellow Berries.—The unripe fruit of the *Rhamnus infectorious.* They are used in calico-printing, producing a lively but fugitive yellow colour.

Persian Yellow Berries.—These are said to be produced by the same species of plant; but the colour is considered more permanent, and they fetch higher prices.

Berries of Avignon.—Another name given to the Turkey and Persian berries.

Juniper Berries.—The fruit of the *Juniperus communis.* They are chiefly used for flavouring gin and some spirituous cordials, and in the preparation of some pharmaceutical articles, as the oil of juniper and the compound spirits of juniper.

Bear Berry.—The fruit of the *Uva ursi.* The leaves only are used medicinally.

Myrobolans.—The fruit of a tree which grows in India. It has a pale-yellow colour when new, but becomes darker by age, and then resembles dried plums. It contains tannin, and has hence been used in dyeing. See JUNIPER BERRIES, &c.

In 1871 we *imported* of Myrobolans 145,450 cwt., of the value of 100,695*l.*

BERTHOLLETIA. A plant of the natural order *Lecythideæ.* The *Bertholletia excelsa* is a tree of large dimensions, forming extensive forests on the banks of the Orinoco. The Portuguese of Para have for a long time driven a great trade with the nuts of this tree, which the natives call *Iuvia*, and the Spaniards *Almendron.* They send cargoes to French Guiana, whence they are shipped for England and Lisbon. These are the common BRAZIL NUTS. The kernels yield a large quantity of oil well suited for lamps.—*Humboldt and Bonpland.*

BERYL. (*Béril*, Fr.; *Beryll*, Ger.; *Berillo*, Ital.) A beautiful mineral or gem, usually of a green colour of various shades, passing into honey-yellow and sky-blue.

Beryl and emerald are varieties of the same species, the latter including the rich green transparent specimens which probably owe their colour to oxide of chrome; the former those of other colours produced by oxide of iron. Gmelin gives the composition of a Swedish beryl as:—

Silica	.	.	.	.	.	.	.	.	69·70
Alumina	.	.	.	.	.	.	.	.	16·83
Glucina	.	.	.	.	.	.	.	.	13·39
Peroxide of iron	.	.	.	.	.	.	.	.	0·24

'Beryls of gigantic size have been found in the United States, at Acworth and Grafton, New Hampshire, and Royalston, Mass. One beryl from Grafton weighs 2,900 lbs; it is 32 inches through in one direction, and 22 in another transverse, and is 4 feet 3 inches long. Another crystal from this locality, according to Professor Hubbard, measures 45 inches by 24 in its diameters, and a single foot in length; by calculation, weighs 1,076 lbs., making it, in all, nearly 2½ tons. At Royalston, one crystal exceeded a foot in length.'—*Dana.* See EMERALD.

Some of the natural crystals of phosphate of lime, or apatite, were formerly taken for beryls, and called the *Saxony beryl.*

BESSEMER PROCESS. A process for making steel, invented by Mr. Henry Bessemer. See STEEL.

BETEL. A compound, in universal use in the East, consisting of the leaf of the betel-pepper, with the betel-nut, a little catechu, and some chunam (lime obtained by calcining shells). This is almost universally used throughout central and tropical Asia; the people are unceasingly masticating the betel. The leaf of the pepper vine (*Chavica betel*) is extensively cultivated throughout tropical Asia, and forms a large article of Eastern traffic. See PEPPER; BETEL.

BETEL-NUT, or *Areca.* The fruit of the *Areca catechu,* which is eaten both in its ripe and its unripe state. A tooth-powder used in this country is prepared by charring the areca nut, and is sold as 'areca-nut charcoal.'

BÉTON. The French name for concrete. Self-slaked hydraulic lime is mixed with sand, and when the mixture is complete it is beaten up with the ballast. See CONCRETE.

BEUHEYL. A mining term, signifying *a living stream.* It is applied by the tin-miners to any portion of a lode or of the rock which is impregnated with tin.

BEZOAR. (The most probable etymology of the word is from the Persian *Pad-zahr,* i. e. expelling poison.—*Penny Cyclopædia.*) A concretion found in the stomach of animals of the goat kind; it is said to be especially produced by the *Capra gazella.* The finest bezoar is brought to India from Borneo and the shores of the Persian Gulf; the *Capra Ægagrus,* or wild-goat of Persia, producing this concretion, which by way of eminence was called the *Lapis bezoar orientalis.* The bezoars, which were supposed to cure all diseases, have been found by the analyses of Fourcroy and Vauquelin, and of Proust, to be nothing more than some portions of the food of the animal agglutinated into a ball with phosphate of lime.

Fossil bezoars are found in Sicily, in sand and clay pits. They are concretions of a purple colour around some, usually organic, body, and of the size of a walnut. Fossil bezoar is sometimes called *Sicilian earth.*

Bezoar Mineral.—An old preparation of the oxide of antimony.

BHANG. See BANG.

BIANCO-SECCO. A carefully slaked lime, mixed with powdered marble, employed in fresco-painting.

BIBIRU and **BIBIRINE.** See GREENHEART TREE.

BICARBONATES. The ordinary carbonates of potash and soda have a strong alkaline reaction and caustic taste, making them unfit for many purposes where a soluble carbonate is required. Moreover, there are many uses to which they are applied, rendering it desirable that as large an amount of gas as possible should be given off on the addition of a stronger acid.

Bicarbonate of Potash.—There are several modes of converting the carbonate into bicarbonate. The most economical is by exposing the salt to a current of carbonic acid. For this purpose some manufacturers place it, slightly moistened, on stoneware trays, and allow the vapours of burning coke to travel slowly over it. The sources of the gas used in this manufacture will vary according to the locality in which it is undertaken. It is not unusual to produce it by the action of sulphuric acid on limestone. The gas generated in fermentation has been employed, and even that which in some places issues from the earth. The bicarbonate of potash is far less soluble than the carbonate, as it requires four parts of cold water for solution, whereas the carbonate dissolves in 0·9 of its weight of water at 54° F. Consequently, if a strong solution is saturated with carbonic acid, the bicarbonate crystallises out. When common pearl-ashes are dissolved in water, and the gas is passed in, a large quantity of a white precipitate is often thrown down; it consists chiefly of silica, but often contains alumina and other matters. Considerable heat is developed when moistened carbonate of potash is exposed to a current of carbonic acid gas. When carbonate of potash is dissolved in water, and gradually treated with acetic acid, so as to form acetate of potash, by no means the whole of the carbonic acid is expelled, and a point is arrived at when a considerable quantity of crystals is deposited; they consist of very pure bicarbonate of potash. In making acetate of potash on the large scale, the quantity of crystalline precipitate obtained in this manner is sometimes very large. Bicarbonate of potash is usually tolerably pure. If well crystallised, all the impurities remain in the mother-liquor, and on heating to redness almost exactly the theoretical amount of residue is left, viz. 69·05 per cent. Crystallised bicarbonate of potash always contains one atom of water, its formula being KO, $2CO^2 + HO$ (**KHCO³**).

Bicarbonate of Soda.—This salt is obtained by the same methods as the salt of potash. The crystals have a corresponding formula to the potash salt; namely, NaO, $2CO^2 + HO$ (**NaHCO³**). It requires about 13 parts of water at 60° to dissolve it. When pure, 100 parts leave 63·18 of NaO,CO^2 (**Na²CO³**), on ignition.

The bicarbonates of potash and soda lose carbonic acid by the boiling of an aqueous solution.

Many chemists regard carbonic acid as being bibasic, the true formula being C^2O^4, instead of CO^2. This view is probably the correct one, and it explains why the bicarbonates are neutral instead of acid salts. Moreover, C^2O^4 corresponds to 4 volumes, like organic substances generally; whereas, if we assume CO^2 as one atom of the gas, we are compelled to admit a 2-volume formula. This view has, however, been considerably modified by our modern theoretical chemists.

BICE. A light blue colour prepared from smalt. There is a green bice prepared by mixing some yellow orpiment with smalt.

BIDERY. An Indian alloy of considerable interest, named Bidery, from Bider, a city N.E. of Hyderabad. Many articles are made, remarkable for elegance of form and for gracefully-engraved patterns. Although the groundwork of this composition appears of a blackish colour, its natural tint is that of pewter or zinc. Dr. Heyne says it is composed of, copper, 16; lead, 4; tin, 2; and to every 3 ounces of alloy 16 ounces of spelter (that is, of zinc) are added, when the alloy is melted for use. To give the esteemed black colour and to bring out the pattern, it is dipped in a solution of sal-ammoniac, saltpetre, common salt, and blue vitriol. Dr. Hamilton saw, zinc, 12,360 grains, copper 400, and lead 414, melted together under a mixture of resin and bees'-wax, introduced into the crucible to prevent calcination; it was then poured into moulds of baked clay, and the articles handed over to be turned in a lathe. Though called bidery and sometimes vidry, it is manufactured in other places. In some parts of the Nizam's dominions, specimens were obtained, for the Exhibition of 1851, of great beauty. Bidery does not rust, yields little to the hammer, and breaks only when violently beaten. According to Dr. Hamilton, bidery is not nearly so fusible as zinc or tin, but melts more easily than copper.—*Dr. Royle, Lecture on the Great Exhibition of* 1851.

BIJOUTRY. (*Bijouterie,* Fr.) Jewellery;—the manufacture of and dealing in jewellery. This work is not the place in which to describe the almost endless variety of articles which come under this denomination. The principal place for the manufacture, in England, is Birmingham, but formerly the trade was largely carried on in Derby, Edinburgh, and London. During the last twenty-five years the jewellery trade of Birmingham has made rapid progress. It has been estimated that the value of the gold annually consumed in the jewellery and gilt-toy trade of that town amounts to between 600,000*l.* and 700,000*l.*, and of the silver to from 100,000*l.* to 150,000*l.*, whilst the precious stones and their imitations have been valued at a quarter of a million sterling. (See papers by Mr. J. S. Wright in 'The Resources, Products, and Industrial History of Birmingham,' 1866; and by Mr. W. G. Larkins in 'Journal of the Society of Arts,' March 1, 1872.)

The trade in jewellery forms one of the most important branches of French commerce; on which a French writer says: 'La bijouterie est une des branches les plus importantes du commerce Français, et c'est elle que constate, de la manière la plus évidente, notre supériorité dans les arts du dessin et les progrès toujours croissans de l'industrie Parisienne. Dans cette partie essentielle, elle n'a pas de rivaux, et elle rend tributaire de notre pays presque toute l'Europe et une grande partie de l'Asie et de l'Amérique.' Of late years, however, the Parisian trade has been declining; but French jewellery has still so high a reputation that English manufacturers often find it to their interest to affix French labels to their goods. A quantity of cheap jewellery is also imported from Germany. See AGATE.

The ordinary practice has been to divide articles of this character into two principal kinds—fine jewellery and false jewellery (*bijoutier en fin* and *bijoutier en faux*). Another division, among the French jewellers especially, has been to adopt four classes: 1, fine jewellery, which is all gold; 2, silver jewellery;. 3, false jewellery; and, 4, jewellery of steel or iron,

In the article ALLOYS will be found the quantity of the baser metal which is permitted to be combined with gold ; and also the proportions of the alloys forming the brasses which are employed in the false jewellery.

Under their respective heads the true gems will be described (see DIAMOND, EMERALD, &c.) ; and under GEMS, ARTIFICIAL, the imitations of them ; many of the false so nicely representing the peculiarities of the true gems as to deceive even the practised eye. The hardness is, however, an unfailing test ; if, therefore, any gem is found to be scratched with a steel file, we may depend on its being artificial. See also PEARLS, ARTIFICIAL ; LAPIDARY WORK ; GLASS, &c.

BIKH, BISH, or NABEE. An Indian poison prepared from the root of the *Aconitum ferox,* a native of Nepaul, and from other species of aconite. It is said to possess the concentrated power of all the European aconites. This is doubtful ; the poisonous properties of some of the monkshoods are little known. Recently (1873), some children from the Falmouth Workhouse, playing on the beach at Mainforth, found some roots washed on shore, and four of them ate small portions—within two or three hours three of the boys died, and the life of the other was only saved by the greatest attention. See ACONITUM.

BILE. (*Bile,* Fr. ; *Galle,* Ger.) The secreted liquor of the liver in animals.

Bile (ox's) is composed, according to Berzelius, of—biline, fellinic acid, and fat of gall, 8·00 ; mucus, 0·30 ; alkali combined with biline, &c., 0·41 ; muriate of soda, extractive matter, 0·74 ; phosphate of soda, do. of lime, &c., 0·11 ; water, 90·44 = 100·00.

Thenard's analysis gives—resin of bile and picromel (acid gallenate of soda), 10·54 ; colouring-matter, 0·50 ; soda, 0·50 ; phosphate of soda, 0·25 ; muriate of soda, 0·40 ; sulphate of soda, 0·10 ; sulphate of lime, 0·15 ; traces of oxide of iron, water, 87·56 ; = 100·00.

The analyses of Benach ('Ann. Ch. Phar.') give the following as the composition of the gall of several animals :—

	Carbon	Hydrogen	Nitrogen	Sulphur	Ash
Calves	55·4	7·7	3·3	4·9	13·15
Sheep	57·3	7·8	3·9	5·7	11·86
Goats	57·3	8·2	...	5·2	13·21
Bears	57·7	8·3	...	5·8	8·42
Fowls	57·5	8·3	3·5	5·0	10·99
Fish	56·0	8·1	2·5	5·6	14·11

Strecker and Mulder have published two treatises on ox-gall. The views advocated by these chemists will be found in the 'Annual Report of the Progress of Chemistry of Liebig and Kopp,' translated by Hofmann and De la Rue.

It has been shewn by Stricker's researches that bile is largely composed of the soda-salts of two peculiar acids called glycocholic and taurocholic acids. *Glycocholic acid* may be prepared by extracting ox-bile with cold absolute alcohol, and treating the filtered extract with ether, when crystals of alkaline glycocholates are obtained ; these were formerly termed *crystallised bile.* When the salts are decomposed by sulphuric acid, glycocholic acid is set free. This acid contains $C^{32}H^{43}NO^{12}$ ($C^{26}H^{43}NO^{6}$). Boiled with a solution of potash, it is resolved into *cholic acid* and *glycocine.* The second acid of the bile—*taurocholic acid,* formerly called *bilin*—has not hitherto been isolated in a state of purity. When boiled with alkalies the impure product is resolved into cholic acid, and a substance called *taurin,* which contains $C^4H^7NS^2O^6$ ($C^2H^7NSO^3$). A fatty matter, known as *cholesterin* is also present, to a small extent, in the bile, and forms the chief ingredient in biliary calculi.

It is notable that the liver is capable of developing, in the blood which circulates through it, an amyloid substance called *glycogen,* which is readily changed into liver-sugar, or glucose.

Heintz remarks (Poggendorff's 'Annalen'), that the change of colour sometimes produced—for it does not appear always—by nitric acid in liquids containing bile (first green, then blue, violet, red, and lastly, yellow), is occasioned only by the colouring-matter, which Berzelius has named *cholepyrrhin,* and not by the essential constituents of the bile, and can therefore be regarded only as a test for the presence of this substance.

Pettenkofer's test for bile consists in adding a drop of sulphuric acid and a solution of sugar, when a purple-violet colour is produced if bile be present.

For the further chemical examination of bile, see 'Watts's Dictionary of Chemistry ;' for its uses in the arts, see GALL.

BILE-PIGMENTS. A series of colouring matters produced from bile by Dr. Thudichum. See 'Watts's Dictionary of Chemistry.'

BIND. The name by which many of the coal-measure shales are locally known in some districts. They are generally more or less bituminous and calcareous. Since so much attention has been directed to the production of petroleum, many of those 'binds' have been subject to distillation, with variable results. See PETROLEUM.

BINDING COAL. See COAL.

BIRDLIME. (*Glu*, Fr.; *Vogelleim*, Ger.) The best birdlime may be made from the middle bark of the holly boiled seven or eight hours in water, till it is soft and tender, then laid by heaps in pits under ground, and covered with stones after the water is drained from it. There it must be left during two or three weeks, to ferment, in the summer season, and watered, if necessary, till it passes into a mucilaginous state. It is then to be pounded in a mortar to a paste, washed in running water, and kneaded till it be free from extraneous matters. It is next left for four or five days in earthen vessels to ferment and purify itself, when it is fit for use. Birdlime may be made by the same process from the mistletoe (*Viscum album*), young shoots of elder, and the barks of other vegetables, as well as from most parasitical plants.

Good birdlime is of a greenish colour and sour flavour, somewhat resembling that of linseed oil—gluey, stringy, and tenacious. By drying in the air it becomes brittle, and may be powdered; but its viscosity may be restored by moistening it. It contains resin, mucilage, a little free acid, colouring and extractive matter. The resin has been called *viscine*.

Macaire has examined a substance which exudes from the receptacle and involucre of the *Atractylis gummifera*, and describes it as the pure matter of birdlime, which he calls viscine. Common birdlime may be regarded as a mixture of *viscine*, vegetable mucilage, and vinegar.

The mistletoe yields a peculiar viscid gluey substance, consisting of a green wax and birdlime.

BISCUITS. Biscuit-baking constitutes two separate branches of manufacture, —namely, that of ordinary biscuit, or, so to speak, biscuit 'proper,' for maritime purposes, and that of fancy biscuits. Ordinary, or sailors' biscuit consists of only flour and water kneaded into a paste, cut in the proper shape, docked, and baked in an oven; fancy biscuits consist also of flour and water, but with an addition of butter, sugar, eggs, spices, or 'flavourings,' all or either of them according to the kind.

Ships' biscuits are now made by machinery, and one of the reasons for this has been that the manual preparation of them was too slow and too costly. A landsman knows very little of the true value of a biscuit: with a seaman, biscuit is the only bread that he eats for months together. There are many reasons why common loaves of bread could not be used during a long voyage: because, containing a fermenting principle, they would soon become musty and unfit for food if made previous to the voyage, while the preparation of them on board ship is subject to insuperable objections. Biscuits contain no leaven, and, when well baked throughout, they suffer little change during a long voyage.

The allowance of biscuit to each seaman on board a Queen's ship is a pound per day (averaging six biscuits to the pound). The supply of a man-of-war for several months is, consequently, very large; and it often happened during the long war that the difficulty of making biscuits fast enough was so great, that at Portsmouth waggon-loads, brought from a distance, were unpacked in the streets and conveyed to the ships.

We shall now describe the mode of making biscuits by hand, and afterwards speak of the improved method. The bakehouse at Gosport contained nine ovens, and to each was attached a gang of five men,—the 'turner,' the 'mate,' the 'driver,' the 'breakman,' and the 'idleman.' The requisite proportions of flour and water were put into a large trough, and the 'driver,' with his naked arms, mixed the whole up together into the form of dough—a very laborious operation. The dough was then taken from the trough, and put on a wooden platform called the break: on this platform worked a lever called the break-staff, five or six inches in diameter, and seven feet long; one end of this was loosely attached by a kind of staple to the wall, and the breakman, riding or sitting on the other end, worked this lever to and fro over the dough by an uncouth jumping or shuffling movement. When the dough had become kneaded by this barbarous method into a thin sheet, it was removed to the moulding board and cut into slips by means of an enormous knife; these slips were then broken into pieces, each large enough for one biscuit, and then worked into a circular form by the hand. As each biscuit was shaped it was handed to a second workman, who stamped the King's mark, the number of the oven, &c., on the biscuit. The biscuit was then docked, that is, pierced with holes by an instrument adapted to the purpose. The finishing part of the process was one in which remarkable dexterity was displayed. A man stood before the open door of the oven, having in his hand the handle of a long shovel called a peel, the other end of which was lying flat in the oven. Another man took the biscuits as fast as they were formed and stamped, and jerked or threw them into the oven with such undeviating accuracy that they should always fall on the peel. The man with the peel then arranged the biscuits side by side over the whole floor of the oven. Nothing could exceed (in manual labour alone) the regularity with which this was all done. Seventy biscuits were thrown into the oven and regularly arranged in one minute, the attention of each man being vigorously directed to his own department; for a delay of a single second on the part of any one man would have disturbed the whole gang. The biscuits do not require many minutes' baking; and as the oven is kept open during the time that it is being filled, the biscuits first thrown in would be overbaked were not some precaution taken to prevent it. The moulder therefore made those which were to be first thrown into the oven larger than the subsequent ones, and diminished the size by a nice gradation.

The mode in which, since about the year 1831, ships' biscuits have been made by machinery invented by T. T. Grant, Esq., of the Royal Clarence Yard, is this:—The meal or flour is conveyed into a hollow cylinder four or five feet long and about three feet in diameter, and the water, the quantity of which is regulated by a gauge, admitted to it; a shaft, armed with long knives, works rapidly round in the cylinder, with such astonishing effect, that in the short space of six minutes, 450 lbs. of dough are produced, infinitely better made than that mixed by the naked arms of a man. The dough is removed from the cylinder and placed under the breaking rollers; these latter, which perform the office of kneading, are two in number, and weigh 15 cwts. each; they are rolled to and fro over the surface of the dough by means of machinery, and in five minutes the dough is perfectly kneaded. The sheet of dough, which is about two inches thick, is then cut into pieces half a yard square, which pass under a second set of rollers, by which each piece is extended to the size of six feet by three, and reduced to the proper thickness for biscuits. The sheet of dough is now to be cut up into biscuits; and no part of the operation is more beautiful than the mode by which this is accomplished. The dough is brought under a stamping or cutting-out press, similar in effect, but not in detail, to that by which circular pieces for coins are cut out of a sheet of metal. A series of sharp knives are so arranged that, by one movement, they cut out of a piece of dough a yard square about sixty hexagonal biscuits. The reason for an hexagonal (six-sided) shape is, that not a particle of waste is thereby occasioned, as the sides of the hexagonals accurately fit into those of the adjoining biscuits, whereas circular pieces cut out of a large surface always leave vacant spaces between. That a flat sheet can be divided into hexagonal pieces without any waste of material is obvious.

Each biscuit is stamped with the Queen's mark, as well as punctured with holes, by the same movement which cuts it out of the piece of dough. The hexagonal cutters do not sever the biscuits completely asunder, so that a whole sheet of them can be put into the oven at once on a large peel, or shovel, adapted for the purpose. About 15 minutes are sufficient to bake them; they are then withdrawn and broken asunder by the hand.

The corn for the biscuits is purchased at the markets, and cleaned, ground, and dressed at the Government mills; in quality it is a mixture of fine flour and middlings, the bran and pollard being removed. The ovens for baking are formed of fire-brick and tile, with an area of about 160 feet. About 112 lbs. weight of biscuits are put into the ovens at once. This is called a suit, and is reduced to about 110 lbs. by the baking. From 12 to 16 suits can be baked in each oven every day, or after the rate of 224 lbs. per hour. The men engaged are dressed in clean check shirts and white linen trousers, apron, and cap, and every endeavour is made to observe the most scrupulous cleanliness.

We may now make a few remarks on the comparative merits of the hand and the machine processes. If the meal and the water with which the biscuits are made be not thoroughly mixed up, there will be some parts moister than others. Now, it was formerly found that the dough was not well mixed by the arms of the workman; the consequence of which was, that the dry parts became burnt up, or else that the moist parts acquired a peculiar kind of hardness which the sailors called ' flint:' these defects are now removed by the thorough mixing and kneading which the ingredients receive by the machine.

We have seen that 450 lbs. of dough may be mixed by the machine in three minutes and kneaded in six minutes; we need hardly say how much quicker this is than men's hands could effect it. The biscuits are cut out and stamped 60 at a time, instead of singly: besides the time thus saved, the biscuits become more equally baked, by the oven being more speedily filled. The nine ovens at Gosport used to employ 45 men to produce about 1,500 lbs. of biscuit per hour; 16 men and boys will now produce, by the same number of ovens, 2,240 lbs. of biscuits (one ton) per hour.

The comparative expense is thus stated:—Under the old system, wages and wear and tear of utensils cost about 1s. 6d. per cwt. of biscuit; under the new system, the cost is 5d.

The bakehouses at Deptford, Gosport, and Plymouth could produce 7,000 or 8,000 tons of biscuits annually, at a saving of 12,000l. per annum from the cost under the old system. The advantages of machine-made over hand-made biscuits, therefore, are many—quality, cleanliness, expedition, cheapness, and independence of Government contractors.

Fig. 104 represents the biscuit-machinery as executed beautifully by Messrs. Rennie, engineers. *a* is the breaker roller, table, and toller; *b*, the finishing roller,

104

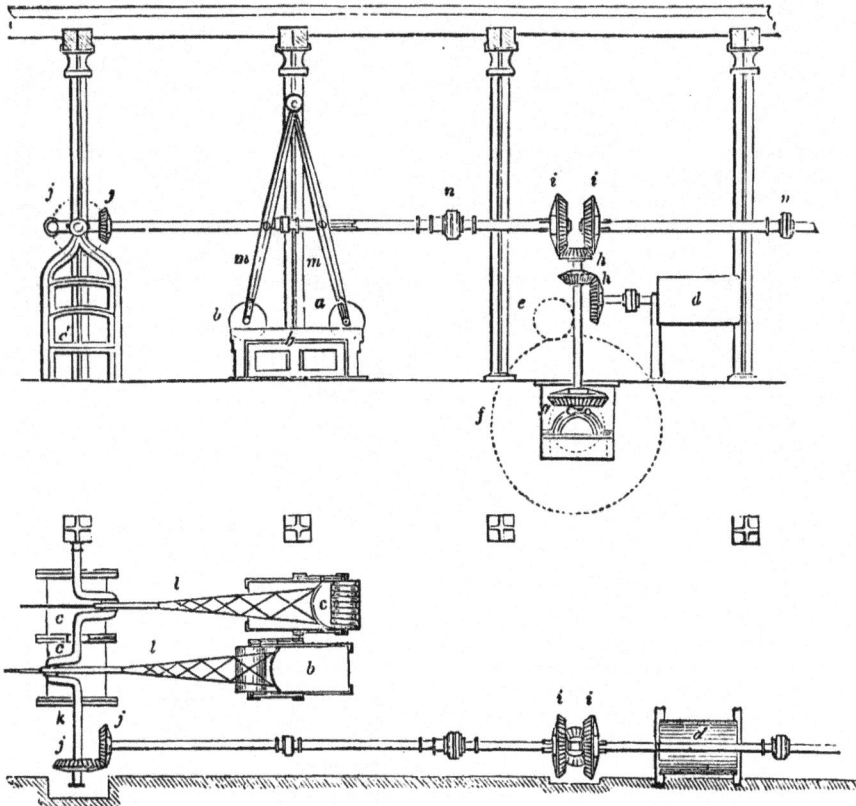

table, and toller; *c c*, docking machines, for stamping out the biscuits; *d*, mixing machine for making the dough; *e*, spur-pinion to engine-shaft; *f*, spur-wheel; *g g*, bevel mitre wheels, to give the upright motion; *h h*, bevel wheels for working the mixing machine; *i i i*, ditto, for communicating motion to the rolling machines, *j j*; *k*, the crank shaft; *l l*, connecting rods; *m m*, pendulums for giving motion to rollers; *n n*, clutches for connecting either half of the machinery to the other.

The manufacture of fancy biscuits, which in former times was confined to the pastrycook and confectioner, has of late years assumed considerable importance, and several firms are now exclusively engaged in this branch of industry, the products of which are sold under an extraordinary variety of names. Some of these, namely, the 'plain biscuit, arrowroot, captain, brown meal, cinnamon, caraway, vanilla biscuits,' &c., are intelligible enough; but, if we except 'Abernethy biscuit, macaroons, and cracknels,' with the names of which the public, from long usage, are familiar, the rest of the products of the modern biscuit-baker, 'Africans, Jamaica, Queen's routs, ratafias, Bath and other sorts of olivers, exhibition, rings and fingers, picnics, cuddy,' &c., &c. form a list of upwards of eighty fanciful names, all expressive of articles of different form, appearance, and taste, made of nearly the same materials, with but little variation in the proportion in which they are used,—the principal ingredients in all being flour and water, butter, milk, eggs, and caraway, nutmeg, cinnamon, mace, ginger, essence of lemon, neroli, or orange-flower water, called in technical language, 'flavourings.' The kneading of these materials is always performed by a kneading or mixing machine. The dough or paste produced is passed several times between two revolving cylinders adjusted at a proper distance, so as to obtain a flat, perfectly homogeneous mass, slab, or sheet. This is transferred to a stamping or cutting machine, consisting of two cylinders, through which the sheet of homogeneous paste has to pass, and by which it is laminated to the proper thickness, and at the same time pushed under a stamping and docking frame, which cuts it into discs, or into oval or otherwise shaped pieces, as occasion may require. The stamps or cutters in the frame being internally provided with prongs, push the cut pieces of dough, or raw cakes, out of the cutting frame, and at the same time dock the cakes, or cut pieces, with a series of holes, for the subsequent escape of the moisture, which, but for these vents, would distort and spoil the cake or biscuit when put in the oven. The temperature of the oven should be so regulated as to be perfectly uniform, neither too high nor too low, but just at such a heat as is sufficient to give the biscuits a light brown colour. For such a purpose the hot-water oven of Mr. Perkins, or that of Mr. Roland, is the best that can possibly be used. (See BREAD.) Roland's oven offers the peculiar advantage that, by turning the screw, the sole of the oven can be brought nearer to the top, and a temperature is thus obtained suitable for baking thoroughly, without burning, the thinnest cakes.

One of the most curious branches of the baker's craft is the manufacture of gingerbread, which contains such a proportion of molasses that it cannot be fermented by means of yeast. Its ingredients are flour, molasses or treacle, butter, common potashes, and alum. After the butter is melted, and the potashes and alum are dissolved in a little hot water, these three ingredients, along with the treacle, are poured among the flour which is to form the body of the bread. The whole is then incorporated by mixture and kneading into a stiff dough. Of these five constituents the alum is the least essential, although it makes the bread lighter and crisper, and renders the process more rapid; for gingerbread, dough requires to stand over for several days, some 8 or 10, before it acquires the state of porosity which qualifies it for the oven; the action of the treacle and alum on the potashes, in evolving carbonic acid, seems to be the gasifying principle of gingerbread; for if carbonate of potash is withheld from the mixture, the bread, when baked, resembles in hardness a piece of wood.

Treacle is always acidulous. Carbonate of magnesia and soda may be used as substitutes for the potashes. Dr. Colquhoun has found that carbonate of magnesia and tartaric acid may replace the potashes and the alum with great advantage, affording a gingerbread fully as agreeable to the taste, and much more wholesome than the common kind, which contains a notable quantity of potash. His proportions are 1 lb. of flour, $\frac{1}{4}$ of an ounce of carbonate of magnesia, and $\frac{1}{8}$ of an ounce of tartaric acid, in addition to the treacle, butter, and aromatics, as at present used. The acid and alkaline earth must be well diffused through the whole dough; the magnesia should, in fact, be first of all mixed with the flour. The melted butter, the treacle, and the acid dissolved in a little water, are poured all at once amongst the flour, and kneaded into a consistent dough, which being set aside for half an hour or an hour, will be ready for the oven, and should never be kept unbaked for more than 2 or 3 hours. The following more complete recipe is given by Dr. Colquhoun for making thin gingerbread cakes:—Flour 1 lb., treacle $\frac{1}{2}$ lb., raw sugar $\frac{1}{4}$ lb., butter 2 ounces, carbonate of magnesia $\frac{1}{4}$ ounce, tartaric acid $\frac{1}{8}$ ounce, ginger $\frac{1}{8}$ ounce, cinnamon $\frac{1}{8}$ ounce, nutmeg 1 ounce. This compound has rather more butter than common thin gingerbread. In addition to these, yellow ochre is frequently added by cheap gingerbread makers, and altogether this preparation, more generally consumed by children, is very objectionable.

Within the last few years there has been a very remarkable development of the trade in biscuits. Biscuits of all sorts, and really many curious and agreeable varieties, are now manufactured on a large scale, and machinery has been created to facilitate the process.

BISMUTH. (*Bismuth*, Fr.; *Wismuth*, Ger.) *Symbol*, Bi.; *Atomic weight*, 210. The metal bismuth occurs chiefly in a native state, but is also found in certain combinations, forming the ores noticed in the following list of bismuth-bearing minerals:—

Native Bismuth is whitish, with a faint reddish tinge, and a metallic lustre which is liable to tarnish. Streak, silver-white. Hardness, 2 to 2·5; specific gravity, 9·727. It is brittle when cold, but slightly malleable when heated. It generally occurs crystallised or in a dendritic form. It fuses readily at 476° F. Beautiful crystals can be formed artificially by fusion and subsequent slow cooling. The native metal frequently contains silver, arsenic, or tellurium. It is the source of all the metal used in the arts.

Native bismuth has been found, associated with other minerals, in Cornwall, at Dolcoath near Camborne; at Huel Sparnon, near Redruth, when that mine was worked; at Trugoo Mine, near St. Colomb (Greg), and at the Consolidated Mines, St. Ives; Caldbeck Fells, in Cumberland, with ores of cobalt. But the most abundant sources of native bismuth are the silver and cobalt mines of Saxony and Bohemia, especially those of Schneeberg, Annaberg, Marienberg, Altenberg, Joachimsthal and Johanngeorgenstadt. It is also found at Sorato, in Bolivia.

Bismuthine, Bismuth glance, or sulphide of bismuth, occurs either in acicular crystals, or with a foliated, fibrous structure. It is isomorphous with stibnite, or sulphide of antimony. Hardness, 2 to 2·5: specific gravity, 6·4 to 6·9. It is composed of bismuth, 81·25; sulphur, 18·75. It fuses in the flame of a candle.

Bismuthine occurs in Cornwall, at Botallack, and associated with tin at St. Just, and with copper at the mines near Redruth and Camborne. Large quantities are now worked and smelted in South Australia.

Acicular Bismuth, or *Aikinite,* called also *Needle Ore,* is a plumbo-cupriferous sulphide of bismuth, composed of sulphur, 16; bismuth, 34·62; lead, 35·69; copper, 11·79.

Emplectite, or *Tannenite,* is a rare mineral, containing sulphur, 18·83; bismuth, 62·16; copper, 18·72.

Telluric Bismuth, or *Tetradymite,* occurs in Cumberland, at Brandy Gill, Carrock Fells (Greg), and at Dolgelly in Merionethshire.

The purest varieties contain only bismuth and tellurium, in proportions represented by the formula, $Bi^2 Te^3$, corresponding to tellurium, 48·1, and bismuth, 51·9 per cent. Other varieties contain sulphur and selenium. It is notable that tetradymite is often found associated with gold.

Bismuth Ochre.—A dull earthy mineral, found in the Royal Restormel Iron Mine, and in small quantities in the parish of Roach, in Cornwall. Its composition is stated by Lampadius to be :—Oxide of bismuth, 86·4; oxide of iron, 5·1; carbonic acid, 4·1; and water, 3·1.

Carbonate of Bismuth, or *Bismutite.* This ore is composed of a mechanical mixture of the carbonates of bismuth, of iron, and of copper.

Eulytine or *bismuth-blende* is a silicate of bismuth, occurring in small crystals in the mines of Schneeberg, in Saxony.

Bismuth, which was formerly known as *Marcasite* and as tin-glance, was shown to be a metal 'somewhat different from lead' by G. Agricola, in 1546. It was studied by Stahl and Dufay, and still more minutely by Pott and Geoffroy, about the middle of the last century.

This metal, the demand for which is limited, is chiefly procured in Saxony, from the mines of Schneeberg; where it occurs mixed with cobalt speiss, in the proportion

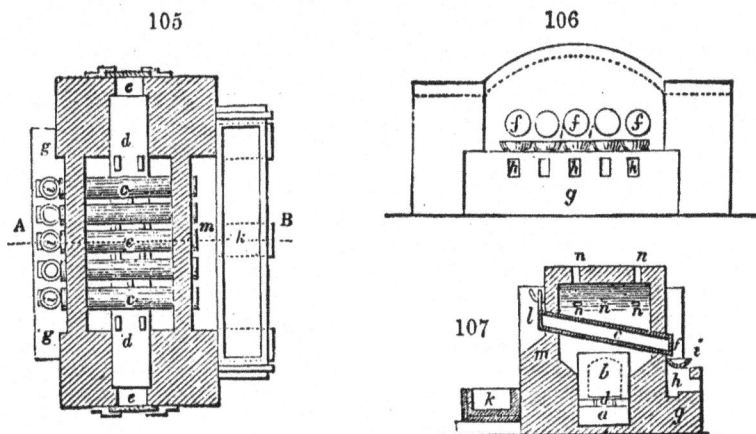

of about 7 per cent. In the metallurgical works at Schneeberg the metal is obtained by means of a peculiar furnace of liquation. This furnace is represented in *figs.* 105 and 106, of which the first is a view from above, the second a view in front; and *fig.* 107 is a transverse section on the dotted line A, B, of *fig.* 106. *a* is the ash-pit; *b,* the fire-place; *c,* the eliquation pipes; *d,* the grate, of masonry or brickwork, upon which the fuel is thrown through the fire-door, *e e.* The anterior deeper-lying orifice of the eliquation pipes is closed with the clay-plate, *f,* which has beneath a small circular groove, through which the liquefied metal flows off; *g* is a wall extending from the hearth-sole nearly to the anterior orifices of the liquation-pipes, in which wall there are as many fire-holes, h, as there are pipes in the furnace; i are iron pans which receive the fluid metal; k, a wooden water-trough, in which the bismuth is granulated and cooled; l, the posterior and higher-lying apertures of the eliquation pipes, shut merely with a sheet-iron cover. The granulations of bismuth drained from the posterior openings fall upon the flat surfaces m, and then into the water-trough. $n\,n$ are draught-holes in the vault between the two pipes, which serve for increasing or diminishing the heat at pleasure.

The ores to be eliquated (sweated) are sorted by hand from the gangue, broken into pieces about the size of a hazel nut, and introduced into the ignited pipes; one charge consisting of about $\frac{1}{2}$ cwt.; so that the pipes are filled to half their diameter, and three-fourths of their length. The sheet-iron door is shut, and the fire strongly urged, whereby the bismuth begins to flow in ten minutes, and falls through the holes in the clay-plates into hot pans containing some coal-dust. Whenever it runs slowly, the ore is stirred round in the pipes, at intervals during half an hour, in which time the liquation is usually finished. The residuum, called bismuth barley ($Graupen$), is scooped out with iron rakes into a water-trough; and the pipes are charged afresh; the pans, when full, have their contents cast into moulds, forming bars of from 25 to 50 lbs. weight. About 20 cwt. of ore are smelted in 8 hours, with a consumption of 63 Leipsic cubic feet of wood. The bismuth thus procured by liquation upon the great scale contains no small admixture of arsenic, iron, and some other metals, from which it may be freed by solution in nitric acid, precipitation by water, and reduction of the sub-nitrate by black flux. By exposing the crude bismuth for some time to a dull red heat, under charcoal, arsenic is expelled.

Bismuth is also obtained as a by-product in treating certain ores of cobalt and silver. A solution of the nitrate or chloride of bismuth is precipitated by addition of water, and the basic salt thus obtained is dried and reduced with carbonate of soda and charcoal.

Bismuth is white, and resembles antimony, but has a reddish tint; whereas the latter metal has a bluish cast. It is brilliant, and crystallises readily in small cube-like forms, often hollow, which are really rhombohedra, though long mistaken for true cubes. The beautiful iridescence often seen on specimens of crystallised bismuth is produced artificially. The metal is very brittle, and may be easily reduced to powder. Its specific gravity is 9·83; and it is said that by hammering it with care, the density may be increased to 9·8827. It melts at 515° F. (268·3° C., Riemsdijk), and may be cooled 6° or 7° below this point without fixing; but the moment it begins to solidify, the temperature rises to 480°, and continues stationary till the whole mass is congealed. Bismuth, like cast-iron, expands during solidification.

When heated from 32° to 212°, it expands $\frac{1}{710}$ in length. When pure it affords a very valuable means of adjusting the scale of high-ranged thermometers. At strong heats bismuth volatilises, may be distilled in close vessels, and is thus obtained in crystalline laminæ.

Bismuth is readily soluble in nitric acid, but is almost unacted on by hydrochloric or by sulphuric acid.

Several alloys of bismuth are used in the arts. The alloy of bismuth and lead in equal parts has a density of 10·709, being greater than the mean of the constituents; it has a foliated texture, is brittle, and of the same colour as bismuth. Bismuth, with tin, forms a compound more elastic and sonorous than the tin itself, and is, therefore, frequently added to it by the pewterers. With 1 of bismuth and 24 of tin, the alloy is somewhat malleable: with more bismuth it is brittle. When much bismuth is present, it may be easily parted by strong muriatic acid, which dissolves the tin, and leaves the bismuth in a black powder. It has been said that an alloy of tin, bismuth, nickel, and silver hinders iron from rusting.

The alloy of bismuth with tin and lead was first examined by Sir I. Newton, and has been called ever since $fusible\ metal$. The French give to this alloy the name of $métal\ fusible\ de\ D'Arcet$, and thus claim for him the merit of the discovery of it. 8 parts of bismuth, 5 of lead, and 3 of tin, melt at the moderate temperature of 202° F.; but 2 of bismuth, 1 of lead, and 1 of tin, melt at 200·75° F., according to Rose. A small addition of mercury, or of cadmium, aids the fusibility. Such alloys serve to take casts of anatomical preparations. The value of these bismuth-alloys for taking casts is due in great measure to their expansion in cooling—a sharp impression being thus secured. Indeed, the behaviour of fusible metal on exposure to heat is quite anomalous. It is said to dilate regularly from 32° to 95° F., then to contract to 131°, when it expands rapidly till it reaches 176°, and from that point again expands uniformly until it fuses.

An alloy of 1 bismuth, 2 tin, and 1 lead, is employed as a soft solder by the pewterers; and the same has been proposed as a bath for tempering steel instruments. Cake-moulds for the manufacture of toilet soaps are made of the same metal; as also excellent *clichés* for stereotype, of 3 lead, 2 tin, and 5 bismuth—an alloy which melts at 199° F. This compound should be allowed to cool upon a piece of pasteboard till it becomes of a doughy consistence, before it is applied to the mould to receive the impress of the stamp. This alloy is also used for the metallic pencils for writing on the prepared paper of pocket-books.

The employment of plates of fusible metal as safety *rondelles* to apertures in the tops of steam boilers was proposed in France, on the assumption that they would melt and give way at elevations of temperature under those which would endanger the bursting of the vessel, the fusibility of the alloy being proportioned to the quality of steam required for the engine. It has been found, however, that boilers, apparently secured in this way, burst, while the safety discs remained entire; the expansive force of the steam causing explosion so suddenly, that the fusible alloy had not time to melt or give way.

Bismuth is interesting as being a highly *diamagnetic* metal. The distinction between magnetic and diamagnetic bodies was established by the late Dr. Faraday. This may be familiarly explained, by stating that one class of bodies is influenced by magnets, as iron is, being *magnetic*. That is, if a bar of iron was hung up between the poles of a horse-shoe magnet, it would arrange itself along the line which unites the two poles; which line has been called the *axial line*. But if another class of bodies be selected, bismuth being at the head of this class, and suspended in the same way between the poles of the magnet, they arrange themselves across the axial line, or, as Faraday has termed it, *equatorially*, these bodies being called in distinction *diamagnetic* bodies. See MAGNETISM, for a further account of these phenomena.

The mines of Schneeberg produce annually about 4,000 kilogrammes of metallic bismuth; those of Johanngeorgenstadt and the cobalt mines of Saxony, about 600 kilogrammes—equal to about 10,500 avoirdupois pounds.

In 1844 bismuth was sold at from 10*d*. to 2*s*. the pound; in 1872 it had reached the high price of 30*s*. the pound; for some time this price was maintained. Up to 1844 a large quantity of bismuth was produced in this country from cobalt ores in the old way of refining, but a new method was then introduced which necessitated the loss of nearly all the bismuth. In 1845 there was a large demand for a composition to make rollers for calico-printers, which advanced the price. In 1858 the supply began to fall off, and in 1861-2 there was an increased demand for this metal for medicinal purposes, but there has been recently a considerable reduction. A company was formed in London, under the guidance of a German, who professed to have the secret of transmuting the baser metals into gold. This company had works in the Belvedere Road, Lambeth, and as bismuth was considered essential in the process, they bought all they could lay hands on. This, it is believed, more than anything led to the rapid increase in the price of the metal. The supply of bismuth is in but very few hands, and great care is taken to prevent any excess over the demand from coming into the market; by this means the price is kept up.

Solid compounds of bismuth, when heated before the blowpipe with carbonate of soda and charcoal, yield a bead of metallic bismuth, surrounded by an incrustation of yellow oxide. Salts of bismuth in solution are recognised by becoming milky white when diluted with water, owing to the formation of sparingly soluble basic salts. These basic precipitates may be distinguished from similar sub-salts of antimony by being *insoluble* in tartaric acid, and by becoming *black* when acted on by sulphuretted hydrogen.

In 'Watts's Dictionary of Chemistry' will be found various methods for the determination of bismuth. The following processes, however, appear so useful as to warrant their insertion in this place :—To detect small quantities of lead in bismuth, or in bismuth compounds, Chapman brings the somewhat flattened bead, reduced before the blowpipe, in contact with some moist basic nitrate of teroxide of bismuth, when, in a short time, in consequence of the reduction of the bismuth by the lead, arborescent sprigs of bismuth are formed around the test specimen. Since zinc and iron interfere with this reaction, they must be previously removed, the former by fusion with soda, the latter with soda and borax, in the reducing flame.

Lead and bismuth can easily be quantitatively separated from each other by the following method, proposed by Ullgren:—The solution of the two metals is precipitated by carbonate of ammonia, and the carbonates are then dissolved by acetic acid, and a blade of pure lead, the weight of which is ascertained beforehand, is plunged in the solution. This blade must be completely immersed in the liquor. The vessel is then corked up, and the experiment is left for several hours at rest. The lead precipitates the bismuth in the metallic form. When the whole of it is precipitated, the blade of lead is withdrawn, washed, dried, and weighed. The bismuth is collected on a filter, washed with distilled water which has been previously boiled, and cooled out of contact of the air; this metal is then treated with carbonate of ammonia, and the precipitate which is left, after washing and ignition, is then weighed. The total loss of the metallic lead employed indicates how much oxide of lead must be subtracted from the total weight of the protoxide of lead obtained.

BISMUTH, OXIDES OF.—There are two well-defined oxides of bismuth—the teroxide and the pentoxide, with an unimportant intermediate oxide. Of these compounds it is only necessary to notice the *teroxide* or *bismuthous oxide* BiO^3 (**Bi²O³**). This is found native as bismuth-ochre, and may be readily formed by exposing the metal to a red-white heat in a muffle, when it takes fire, burns with a faint blue flame, and emits fumes which condense into a yellow pulverulent oxide. But an easier process is to ignite the nitrate or carbonate. The oxide thus obtained has a straw-yellow colour, and fuses at a high heat into an opaque glass of a dark-brown or black colour; but which becomes less opaque and yellow after it has cooled. Its specific gravity is as high as 8·211. It consists of 89·87 of metal and 10·13 of oxygen in 100 parts. The only salt of this oxide used in the arts is the *nitrate*, which is obtained by dissolving metallic bismuth in warm nitric acid. On largely diluting a solution of the nitrate with water, a sub-nitrate or basic-nitrate is precipitated. This precipitate was termed by the older chemists, ' magestery of bismuth,' and is now sometimes called *pearl-white*, and is employed as a flux for certain enamels, as it augments their fusibility, without imparting any colour to them. Hence it is used sometimes as a vehicle of the colours of other metallic oxides. When well washed, it is employed in gilding porcelain; being added in the proportion of one-fifteenth to the gold. But pearl-white is most used by ladies, as a cosmetic for giving a delicate whiteness to a faded complexion. It is called *blanc de fard* by the French. If it contains, as bismuth often does, a little silver, it becomes grey or dingy-coloured on exposure to light. Another sort of pearl-powder is prepared by adding a very dilute solution of common salt to the above nitric solution of bismuth, whereby a pulverulent sub-chloride of the metal is obtained in a light flocculent form. A similar powder of a mother-of-pearl aspect may be formed by dropping dilute muriatic acid into the solution of nitrate of bismuth. The arsenic always present in the bismuth of commerce is converted by nitric acid into arsenic acid, which, forming an insoluble arsenate of bismuth, separates from the solution unless there be such an excess of nitric acid as to re-dissolve it. Hence the medicinal oxide, prepared from a rightly-made nitrate, can contain no arsenic. If we write with a pen dipped in that solution, the dry invisible traces will become legible on plunging the paper in water.

The nitrate of bismuth, mixed with a solution of tin and tartar, has been employed as a mordant for dyeing lilac and violet in calico-printing.

When the oxide is prepared, by dropping the nitric solution into an alkaline lye in excess, if this precipitate is well washed and dried, it forms an excellent medicine; and is given, mixed with gum tragacanth, for the relief of cardialgia, or burning and spasmodic pains of the stomach.

This sub-nitrate of bismuth is now commonly employed as a remedial agent, under circumstances which are especially liable to attack the emigrant; it is, therefore, thought advisable to give some account of its action. The following is extracted from Pereira's 'Elements of Materia Medica,' by Bentley and Redwood:—

' *Physiological Effects.*—In *small doses* it acts locally as an astringent, diminishing secretion. On account of the frequent relief given by it in painful affections of the stomach, it is supposed to act on the nerves of this viscus as a sedative. It has also been denominated tonic and antispasmodic. Vogt says, that when used as a cosmetic, it has produced a spasmodic trembling of the face, ending in paralysis.

' *Large medicinal doses* disorder the digestive organs, occasioning pain, vomiting, purging, &c.; and sometimes affecting the nervous system, and producing giddiness, insensibility, with cramps of the extremities. On the other hand, M. Momeret states, after several years' trial of this medicine, that it may be given in much larger doses than are usually administered, and that it is then of the greatest value in gastro-intestinal affections, especially those attended with fluxes.

' *Therapeutics.*—It has been principally employed in those chronic affections of the stomach which are unaccompanied by any organic disease, but which apparently depend on some disordered condition of the nerves of this viscus; and hence, the efficacy of the remedy is referred to its supposed action on these parts. It has been particularly used and recommended to relieve gastrodynia and cramp of the stomach, to allay sickness and vomiting, and as a remedy for pyrosis or water-brash. In the latter disease I give it in the form of a powder, in doses of twenty grains thrice daily, in conjunction with hydrocyanic acid mixture, and the patient rarely fails to obtain marked benefit from its use. It is also used in ulcer of the stomach. Dr. Theophilus Thompson recommends it in doses of five grains, combined with gum arabic and magnesia, in the diarrhœa accompanying phthisis, and he thinks that both in efficacy and safety, it surpasses our most approved remedies for that complaint. I have used it with advantage, in the form of ointment, applied to the septum nasi, in ulceration of this part, and as a local remedy in chronic skin diseases.'

Much of the sub-nitrate of bismuth of the shops has been found to contain nitrate of silver.

BISTRE. (*Bistre*, Fr.; *Bister*, Ger.) A brown colour which is used in water-colours, in the same way as China ink. It is prepared from wood-soot, that of beech being preferred. The most compact and best-burned parcels of soot are collected from the chimney, pulverised, and passed through a silk sieve. ' This powder is infused in pure water, and stirred frequently with a glass rod, then allowed to settle, and the water decanted. If the salts are not all washed away, the process may be repeated with warm water. The paste is now to be poured into a long narrow vessel filled with water, stirred well, and left to settle for a few minutes, in order to let the grosser parts subside. The supernatant part is then to be poured off into a similar vessel. This process may be repeated twice or thrice, to obtain a very good bistre. At last the settled deposit is sufficiently fine, and, when free from its super-natant water, it is mixed with gum-water, moulded into proper cakes and dried. It is not used in oil-painting, but has the same effect in water-colours as brown pink has in oil.

Dr. MacCulloch objects to soot as a source of bistre, both from the carelessness used in collecting it, and the uncertainty of tone and colour. If the liquids resem-bling tar, obtained from the distillation of wood, be again carefully distilled, water, acetic acid, and hydrocarbonaceous substances, as naphtha, pass over, and leave a resi-duum—brown or black, pitch-like, or brittle—according to the time and temperature employed; by prolonging the heat with care, the brittle substance becomes a powder. Dr. MacCulloch states that, by care, bistre from wood-tar may be obtained, having the fine properties of sepia with great depth of colour.

The remarkable bronze-like varnish, with almost a metallic lustre, seen upon the interior of Highland cottages, are bistre-deposits from the smoke of peat.

BITTER-ALMOND OIL. See ALMOND OIL.

BITTER-ALMOND WATER. Water containing the oil of bitter almonds in solution. It should be prepared by distillation from the bitter almonds. It is how-ever frequently made by first rubbing the essential oil of bitter almonds with mag-nesia and mixing this with water; or a solution of the oil in spirits of wine is simply added to the water and they are shaken together.

BITTER CUPS. Wooden cups in which water or other liquid is allowed to stand until it acquires a bitter taste, and thus serves medicinally as a tonic. These cups are turned in 'bitter wood,' or wood from a West Indian tree—the *Picræna excelsa*, Ldl.,—and from other plants belonging to the quassia order.

BITTERN. The mother-liquor of sea-water left after the crystallisation of the less soluble salts. The bittern is used as a source of bromine.

BITTER PRINCIPLE. (*Amer*, Fr.; *Bitterstoff*, Ger.) The 'bitter principles' consist of bodies which may be extracted from vegetable productions by the agency of water, alcohol, or ether. These are not of much importance in the arts, with a few exceptions. *Lupulin*, the bitter principle of the hop, for example, is used for pre-serving beer.

Quassin is the bitter principle of quassia; *Absinthin*, that of wormwood; and *Gentianin*, that of Gentian. These are sometimes substituted for the hop.

For particulars of these, and numerous other bitter principles, see 'Watts's Dic-tionary of Chemistry.'

The following list gives the more important of the bitter substances which have been used in the arts and in medicine. (See the articles respectively)—

Name	Part employed	Country	Observations
Quassia . . .	Wood . .	Surinam, E. Indies	Powerfully bitter
Wormwood . .	Herb . .	Great Britain .	Ditto
Aloe . . .	Inspissated juice	South Africa .	Ditto
Angustura . .	Bark . .	South America .	Ditto
Orange . . .	...	South of Europe .	Aromatic bitter
Acorus . . .	Root . .	Ditto . . .	Ditto
Carduus benedictus .	Herb . .	Greek Archipelago	
Cascarilla . .	Bark . .	Jamaica . .	Ditto
Centaury . .	Herb . .	Great Britain	
Camomile . .	Flowers . .	Ditto . . .	Ditto
Colocynth . .	Fruit . .	Levant. . .	Intolerably bitter

Name	Part employed	Country	Observations
Colombo . . .	Root . .	East Africa . .	Very bitter
Fumitory . . .	Herb . .	Great Britain .	Ditto
Gentiana lutea . .	Root . .	Switzerland . .	Ditto
Ground Ivy . .	Herb . .	Great Britain .	Ditto
Walnut . . .	Peel . .	Ditto . . .	Ditto with tannin
Iceland moss . .	Plant . .	Ditto . . .	Ditto with starch
Hops . . .	Scales of the female flowers	Ditto . . .	Aromatic bitter
Milfoil . . .	Herb, flowers .	Ditto	
Satyrion, large-leaved	Herb . .	Ditto	
Rhubarb . . .	Root . .	China, Turkey .	Disagreeable odr.
Rue . . .	Herb . .	Great Britain .	Bitter and sharp
Tansy . . .	Herb, flowers .	Ditto . . .	Bitter & offensive
Trefoil, bitter . .	Herb . .	Ditto . . .	
Simarouba . .	Bark . .	Guiana . . .	
Bryony . . .	Root . .	Great Britain .	Sharp, bitter, nauseous
Coffee . . .	Seeds . .	Arabia . . .	Agreeable

BITTER SPAR. A carbonate of lime and carbonate of magnesia. See DOLOMITE.

BITUMEN. (*Bitume*, Fr.; *Erdpech*, Ger.)—This term, as commonly applied, comprises a number of solid viscid and liquid substances, resembling pitch, tar, naphtha and the like, and consisting mainly of native hydrocarbons, more or less oxygenated. Most of these appear to be too variable in composition to take rank as distinct mineralogical species, and our knowledge of the chemical constitution of many of them is still very imperfect. Professor Dana, in the last edition of his 'System of Mineralogy' (1868), has proposed a valuable scientific classification of the numerous hydrocarbons occurring in nature. It seems convenient, however, for practical purposes to adhere to the older and more popular, if less philosophical arrangement.

Bitumen comprises several distinct varieties, of which the two most important are asphaltum and naphtha.

Asphaltum or *mineral pitch* is solid, and of a black, or brownish-black, colour, with a conchoidal brilliant fracture. It is sometimes called *Bitumen of Judea*, from its occurrence on the Dead Sea, or Lake Asphaltites. See ASPHALT.

Naphtha.—Liquid and colourless when pure, with a bituminous odour. See NAPHTHA. The darker-coloured varieties are fully described under PETROLEUM.

Springs, of which the waters contain a mixture of petroleum, and the various minerals allied to it—as bitumen, asphaltum, and pitch—are very numerous, and are, in many cases, undoubtedly connected with subterranean heat, by the agency of which organic remains undergo some of those remarkable changes which ultimately result in the formation of coal. Within a few years many discoveries have been made of sources of fluid bitumen and petroleum in both the Old and New Worlds. The importance of these natural products renders it advisable to comprehend a description of them under one general head. In one locality there are said to be 520 wells, which yield annually 400,000 hogsheads of petroleum. See PETROLEUM.

Fluid bitumen is seen to ooze from the bottom of the sea on both sides of the island of Trinidad, and to rise up to the surface of the water. It is stated that, about seventy years ago, a spot of land on the western side of Trinidad, nearly half-way between the capital and an Indian village, sank suddenly, and was immediately replaced by a small lake of pitch. In this way, probably, was formed the celebrated Great Pitch Lake. Sir Charles Lyell remarks:—'The Orinoco has for ages been rolling down great quantities of woody and vegetable bodies into the surrounding sea, where, by the influence of currents and eddies, they may be arrested and accumulated in particular places. The frequent occurrence of earthquakes, and other indications of volcanic action in those parts, lend countenance to the opinion that these vegetable substances may have undergone, by the agency of subterranean fire, those transformations or chemical changes which produce petroleum; and this may, by the same causes, be forced up to the surface, where, by exposure to the air, it becomes inspissated, and forms the different varieties of pure and earthy pitch, or asphaltum, so abundant in the island.'

The Pitch Lake is one and a half miles in circumference; the bitumen is solid and cold near the shores, but gradually increases in temperature and softness towards the centre, where it is boiling. The solidified bitumen appears as if it had cooled, as the surface boiled, in large bubbles. The ascent to the lake from the sea, a distance of three-quarters of a mile, is covered with a hardened pitch, on which trees and vegetables flourish; and about Point la Braye, the masses of pitch look like black rocks among the foliage: the lake is underlaid by a bed of mineral coal.—(*Manross*, quoted by Dana.)

The Earl of Dundonald remarks, that vegetation contiguous to the lake of Trinidad is most luxuriant. The best pine-apples in the West Indies (called black pines) grow wild amid the pitch.

Asphaltum, or solid bitumen, is abundant on the shores of the Dead Sea. It occurs in the mountain-limestone of Derbyshire and Shropshire, and has been found in granite, with quartz and fluor spar, at Poldice, in Cornwall. There is a remarkable bituminous lime and sandstone of the region of Bechelbronn and Lobsann, in Alsace. From the observations of Daubrée, we learn that probably this bitumen has had its origin as an emanation from the interior of the earth; and indeed, in Alsace, with the great elevated fissure of the sandstone of the Vosges, a fissure which was certainly open before the deposit of the Trias, but was not yet closed during the tertiary epoch, affording during this latter, moreover, an opportunity for the deposition of spathic iron ore, iron pyrites, and heavy spar.—*Annales des Mines*.

Bituminous limestones are also found abundantly at Pyrimont, near Seyssel, in the Dép. de l'Ain, France, and in the Val de Travers, Neufchâtel, in Switzerland. Both these rocks have been worked for the sake of their bitumen.

In addition to the bituminous substances already mentioned—asphalt, naphtha, and petroleum—there are a number of closely related minerals, such as *pittasphalt* and *maltha*, or *mineral tar*; *elaterite* or *elastic bitumen*; *hatchettine*, or *mineral tallow*, *ozocerite*, &c. The more important of these are described under their respective names.

Of ordinary bitumen, we give ultimate analyses of two specimens: one by Ebelmen, who obtained his sample from the Auvergne; and the other by Boussingault, of a Peruvian specimen:—

	Auvergne.	Peruvian.
Carbon	76·13	88·63
Hydrogen	9·41	9·69
Oxygen	10·34 ⎱	1·68
Nitrogen	2·32 ⎰	
Ash	1·80	
	100·00	100·00

Bitumen in many of its varieties was known to the ancients. It was used by them combined with lime, in their buildings. Not only do we find the ruined walls of temples and palaces in the East, with the stones cemented with this material, but some of the old Roman castles in this country are found to hold bitumen in the cement by which their stones are secured. At Agrigentum it was burnt in lamps, and called 'Sicilian oil.' The Egyptians used it for embalming.—*Dana*.

On the employment of bitumen for pavements, Dr. Ure has the following remarks:—It is a very remarkable fact, in the history of the useful arts, that asphalt, which was so generally employed as a solid and durable cement in the earliest constructions upon record, as in the walls of Babylon, should for so many thousand years have fallen well nigh into disuse among civilised nations. For there is certainly no class of mineral substances so well fitted as the bituminous, by their plasticity, fusibility, tenacity, adhesiveness to surfaces, impenetrability by water, and unchangeableness in the atmosphere, to enter into the composition of terraces, foot-pavements, roofs, and every kind of hydraulic work. Bitumen, combined with calcareous earth, forms a compact semi-elastic solid which is not liable to suffer injury by the greatest alternations of frost and thaw, which often disintegrate in a few years the hardest stone, nor can it be ground to dust and worn away by the attrition of the feet of men and animals, as sandstone, flags, and even blocks of granite are. An asphalt pavement, rightly tempered in tenacity, solidity, and elasticity, seems to be incapable of suffering abrasion in the most crowded thoroughfares; a fact exemplified of late in a few places in London, but much more extensively, and for a much longer time, in Paris.

The great Place de la Concorde (formerly Place Louis Quinze) is covered with a beautiful mosaic pavement of asphalt; many of the promenades on the Boulevards, formerly so filthy in wet weather, are now covered with a thin bed of bituminous mastic, free alike from dust and mud; the foot-paths of the Pont Royal and Pont Carousel, and the areas of the great public slaughter-houses, have been for several years paved in a similar manner with perfect success. It is much to be regretted that the asphalt companies of London made the ill-judged, and nearly abortive, attempt to pave the carriage-way near the east end of Oxford Street, and especially at a moist season, most unpropitious to the laying of bituminous mastic. Being formed of blocks not more than three or four inches thick, many of which contained much siliceous sand, such a pavement could not possibly resist the crash and vibration of many thousand heavy drays, waggons, and omnibuses daily rolling over it. This failure can afford, however, no argument against rightly-constructed foot-pavements and terraces of asphalt. Numerous experiments and observations have led me to conclude that fossil bitumen possesses far more valuable properties for making a durable mastic than the solid pitch obtained by boiling wood or coal tar. The latter, when inspissated to a proper degree of hardness, becomes brittle, and may be readily crushed into powder; while the former, in like circumstances, retains sufficient tenacity to resist abrasion. Factitious tar and pitch being generated by the force of fire, seem to have a propensity to decompose by the joint agency of water and air, whereas mineral pitch has been known to remain for ages without alteration.

Bitumen alone is not so well adapted for making a substantial mastic as the native compound of bitumen and calcareous earth, which has been properly called asphaltic rock, of which the richest and most extensive mine is unquestionably that of the Val de Travers, in the canton of Neufchâtel. This interesting mineral deposit occurs in the Jurassic limestone formation, the equivalent of the English oolite. The mine is very accessible, and may be readily excavated by blasting with gunpowder. The stone is massive, of irregular fracture, of a liver-brown colour, and is interspersed with a few minute spangles of calcareous spar. Though it may be scratched with the nail, it is difficult to break by the hammer. When exposed to a very moderate heat, it exhales a fragrant ambrosial smell, a property which at once distinguishes it from all compounds of factitious bitumen. Its specific gravity is 2·114,—water being 1·000,— being nearly the density of bricks. It may be most conveniently analysed by digesting it in successive portions of hot oil of turpentine, whereby it affords 80 parts of a white pulverulent carbonate of lime, and 20 parts of bitumen in 100. The asphalt rock of Val de Travers seems therefore to be far richer than that of Pyrimont, which, according to the statement in the specification of Claridge's patent of November, 1837, contains 'carbonate of lime and bitumen in about the proportion of 90 parts of carbonate of lime to about 10 parts of bitumen.'

The calcareous matter is so intimately combined and penetrated with the bitumen as to resist the action not only of air and water for any length of time, but even of muriatic acid; a circumstance partly due to the total absence of moisture in the mineral, but chiefly to the vast incumbent pressure under which the two materials have been incorporated in the bowels of the earth. It would indeed be a difficult matter to combine, by artificial methods, calcareous earth thus intimately with bitumen, and for this reason the mastics made in this way are found to be much more perishable. Many of the factitious asphalt cements contain a considerable quantity of siliceous sand, from which they derive the property of cracking and crumbling down when trodden upon. In fact, there seems to be so little attraction between siliceous matter and bitumen, that their parts separate from each other by a very small disruptive force.

Since the asphalt-rock of Val de Travers is naturally rich enough in concrete bitumen, it may be converted into a plastic workable mastic of excellent quality for foot-pavements and hydraulic works at very little expense, merely by the addition of a very small quantity of mineral or coal tar, amounting to not more than 6 or 8 per cent. The union between these materials may be effected in an iron cauldron, by the application of a very moderate heat, as the asphalt-bitumen readily coalesces with the tar into a tenacious solid.

The mode adopted for making the asphalt pavement at the Place de la Concorde in Paris was as follows :—The ground was made uniformly smooth, either in a horizontal plane or with a gentle slope to carry off the water ; the curb-stones were then laid round the margin by the mason, more than 4 inches above the level of the ground. This hollow space was filled to a depth of 3 inches with concrete, containing about a sixth part of hydraulic lime, well pressed upon its bed. The surface was next smoothed with a thin coat of mortar. When the whole mass had become perfectly dry, the mosaic pattern was set out on the surface, the moulds being formed of flat iron bars, rings, &c., about half an inch thick, into which the fluid mastic was poured by ladles from a cauldron, and spread evenly over.

The mastic was made in the following way :—The asphalt rock was first of all roasted in an oven, about 10 feet long and 3 broad, in order to render it friable. The bottom of the oven was sheet-iron, heated below by a brisk fire. A volatile matter exhaled, probably of the nature of naphtha, to the amount of one-fortieth the weight of asphalt ; after roasting, the asphalt became so friable as to be easily reduced to powder, and passed through a sieve having meshes of about one-fourth of an inch square.

The bitumen destined to render the asphalt fusible and plastic was melted, in small quantities at a time, in an iron cauldron, and then the asphalt in powder was gradually stirred in to the amount of 12 or 13 times the weight of bitumen. When the mixture became fluid, nearly a bucketful of very small, clean gravel, previously heated apart, was stirred into it; and, as soon as the whole began to simmer with a treacly consistence, it was fit for use. It was transported in buckets, and poured into the moulds.

For the reasons above assigned, I consider this addition of rounded, polished, siliceous stones to be very injudicious. If anything of the kind be wanted to give solidity to the pavement, it should be a granitic or hard calcareous sand, whose angular form will secure the cohesion of the mass. I conceive also, that liquid bitumen in moderate quantity should be used to give toughness to the asphaltic combination, and prevent its being pulverised and abraded by friction.

In the able report of the Bastenne and Gaujac Bitumen Company, drawn up by Messrs. Goldsmid and Russel, these gentlemen have made an interesting comparison between the properties of mineral tar and vegetable tar : the bitumen composed of the latter substance, including various modifications extracted from coal and gas, has, so far as they were able to ascertain, entirely failed. This bitumen, owing to the qualities and effects of vegetable tar, becomes soft at 115° of Fahrenheit's scale, and is brittle at the freezing point; while the bitumen into which mineral tar enters will sustain 170° of heat without injury. In the course of the winter, 1837–38, when the cold was at $14\frac{1}{2}$° below zero C., the bitumen of Bastenne and Gaujac, with which one side of the Pont Neuf at Paris is paved, was not at all impaired, and would, apparently, have resisted any degree of cold; while that in some part of the Boulevard, which was composed of vegetable tar, cracked and opened in white fissures. The French Government, instructed by these experiments, has required, when any of the vegetable bitumens are laid, that the pavement should be an inch and a quarter thick; whereas, where the bitumen composed of mineral tar is used, a thickness of three-quarters of an inch is deemed sufficient. The pavement of the bonding warehouses at Bordeaux has been laid upwards of 15 years by the Bastenne Company, and is now in a condition as perfect as when first formed. The reservoirs constructed to contain the waters of the Seine, at Batignolles, near Paris, have been mounted six years, and notwithstanding the intense cold of the winter of 1837, which froze the whole of their contents into one solid mass, and the perpetual water-pressure to which they are exposed, they have not betrayed the slightest imperfection in any point. The repairs done to the ancient fortifications at Bayonne have answered so well, that the Government many years ago entered into a very large contract with the company for additional works, while the whole of the arches of St. Germain and St. Cloud railways, and the pavements and floorings necessary for these works, have been laid with Bastenne bitumen.

The mineral tar in the mines of Bastenne and Gaujac is easily separated from the earthy matter with which it is naturally mixed, by the process of boiling, and is then transported in barrels to Paris or London, being laid down in the latter place to the company at 17l. per ton, in virtue of a monopoly of the article purchased by the Company at a sum, it is said, of 8,000l.

Mr. Harvey, the superintendent of the Bastenne Company, was good enough to supply me with various samples of mineral tar, bitumen, and asphaltic rock for analysis. The tar of Bastenne is an exceedingly viscid mass, without any earthy impurity. It has the consistence of baker's dough at 60° of Fahrenheit; at 80° it yields to the slightest pressure of the finger; at 150° it resembles a soft extract; and at 212° it has the fluidity of molasses. It is admirably adapted to give plasticity to the calcareous asphalts.

A specimen of Egyptian asphalt which he brought me gave, by analysis, the very same composition as the Val de Travers, namely 80 per cent. of pure carbonate of lime, and 20 of bitumen. A specimen of mastic prepared in France was found to consist, in 100 parts, of 29 of bitumen, 52 of carbonate of lime, and 19 of siliceous sand. A portion of stone called the natural Bastenne rock afforded me 80 parts of gritty siliceous matter and 20 of thick tar. The Trinidad bitumen contains a considerable portion of foreign earthy matter: one specimen yielded me 25 per cent. of siliceous sand; a second, 28; a third, 20; and a fourth, 30; the remainder was pure pitch. One specimen of Egyptian bitumen, specific gravity 1·2, was found to be perfectly pure, for it dissolved in oil of turpentine without leaving any appreciable residuum.

As the specific gravity of properly made mastic is nearly double that of water, a cubic foot of it will weigh from 125 to 130 lbs.; and a square foot, three quarters of an inch thick, will weigh very nearly 8 pounds.

It has been thought advisable to preserve these remarks on bitumen, although written several years ago, especially as the recent attempts to introduce bituminous substances for paving seem likely to be successful. During the last few years, several experimental patches of asphalt-paving have been laid down in some of the most active thoroughfares of the metropolis. Such paving recommends itself by being much cleaner and quieter under heavy traffic than an ordinary granite pavement, but has the disadvantage of becoming extremely slippery when the surface is slightly moistened by rain. It is said, however, that this slipperiness only lasts while the pavement is moderately damp, and that but few horses fall on the asphalt during either dry or thoroughly wet weather. The liquid Val de Travers asphalt, the Limner asphalt, and Barnett's liquid asphalt are all mixed with grit or sand, and thus present rougher surfaces than those pavings which consist of asphalt alone—such as the ordinary compressed asphalt of the Val de Travers Company. See PAVEMENT, ASPHALT and MASTIC.

BITUMINOUS COAL. Coal rich in bituminous matter. Pitch or caking coal, cherry coal, splint coal, cannel coal, coking coal, and some others, are varieties of bituminous coal. See COAL.

BIXINE and **BIXEINE.** Two conditions of the colouring-matter of Arnatto, according to Preisser. See ARNATTO.

BLACK AMBER. Pitch coal is so called by the amber-diggers of Prussia, and it is manufactured by them into jet-like ornaments.

BLACK BAND. A variety of the carbonate of iron, to which attention was first called by Mr. Mushet at the commencement of the present century. The iron manufacture of Scotland owes its present important position to the discovery of the value of the black-band ironstone. This ore of iron is also found in several parts of the coal-basin of South Wales, and in the north of Ireland. The chemical composition of the black-band iron ores will be given in connection with that of other minerals of the same class. See IRON ORES.

BLACK CHALK. A kind of clay containing a large amount of carbon. It is found in Carnarvonshire and in the Island of Islay.

BLACK COAL. Slate coal, cannel coal, and foliated coal, were so called by Jameson and other mineralogists of his day.

BLACK-COBALT OCHRE. See COBALT, EARTHY.

BLACK COPPER. An impure black oxide of copper. See COPPER.

BLACK DYE. (*Teinte noire*, Fr.; *Schwarze Farbe*, Ger.) Textile fabrics are dyed by various processes, according to the quality of the black required, and the kind of stuff on which the dye is to be produced. Under ANILINE-BLACK the process by which that black dye is prepared is already described; but the following process for using an aniline-black *as a dye for cotton goods* by M. J. Persol properly finds its place here:—

'Chemists have long tried to make use of the beautiful black precipitate produced by the action of bichromate of potassa for the solution of certain aniline salts as a dye for calicoes, but without success; if the solution was concentrated, the black was soon precipitated to the bottom of the bath; if, on the other hand, it was dilute, the black, owing to the absence of a sufficiently powerful oxidation, was not formed at all, or in insufficient quantity.

'This trouble it was attempted to remove by cooling down the solutions nearly to zero. But this produced another difficulty, the chromate of aniline crystallising out at that temperature when the solutions were sufficiently concentrated to produce the desired dye. Wherever these spots existed in the cloth on subsequent drying, a mutual reaction took place between the constituents of the chromate of aniline, causing such a rise of temperature as not unfrequently to set fire to the cloth.

'To overcome these various difficulties the following expedients were adopted:— By means of a horizontal brush, to which a reciprocating motion was given in a vertical direction, the solutions, either together or one after the other, were cast upon the cloth, while tightly stretched, in the form of a fine spray. By this means, however rapidly the reaction took place, it could not possibly do so until the solutions were intimately mixed together upon the cloth, the latter being at the same time thoroughly wetted with it.

'The salts found to be most suitable for this reaction are the sulphate, hydrochloride, and the nitrate. No black is obtainable with the acetate; and the tartrate, oxalate, and citrate are more or less unfitted for the production of a good colour.

'If a too nearly neutral solution is used there is great difficulty in producing the colour; if the solutions are too acid the black is formed so rapidly that the solutions have not time to mix sufficiently and to penetrate the cloth.

'As the result of numerous experiments with hydrochloric, sulphuric, and nitric acid salts, the author came to the conclusion that:—1. The employment of neutral aniline salts was ineffective. 2. The bi-acid aniline salts, especially the bi-sulphate, give good results. Of the tri-acid salts the hydrochloride is the best. 3. The sulphates give a reddish black; the hydrochloric and nitric acid salts yield a black with a blue lustre. 4. Equal volumes of bi-sulphate and bi-hydrochloride of aniline give excellent results. 5. The bi-chromate of potash solution must be concentrated, containing not less than 80 grammes of salt to the litre.

'A dark green is first produced on passing the cloth into a hot-soap bath. After washing it thoroughly this passes into pure black.

'By printing the cloth with fatty matters or resins, previous to the application of the dyeing solutions, white patterns on a black ground can be obtained.'

The following processes for dyeing woollen stuff will be found to produce excellent results. For 1 cwt. of cloth previously dyed blue:—There is put into a boiler of middle size, 18 lbs. of logwood, with the same quantity of Aleppo galls, the whole being enclosed in a bag; this is boiled in a sufficient quantity of water for 12 hours: one-third of this decoction is transferred into another boiler with 2 pounds of verdigris; and the stuff is passed through this solution, stirring it continually during two hours, taking care to keep the bath very hot without boiling. The stuff is then lifted out, another third of the bath is added to the boiler, along with 8 pounds of sulphate of iron or green vitriol. The fire is to be lowered while the sulphate dissolves, and the bath is allowed to cool for half an hour, after which the stuff is introduced, and well moved about for an hour, and then it is taken out to air. Lastly, the remaining third of the bath is added to the other two, taking care to squeeze the bag well. 18 or 22 lbs. of sumach are thrown in; the whole is just brought to a boil, and then refreshed with a little cold water; 2 pounds more of sulphate of iron are added, after which the stuff is turned through for an hour. It is next washed, aired, and put again into the bath, stirring it continually for an hour. After this, it is carried to the river, washed well, and then fulled. Whenever the water runs off clear, a bath is prepared with weld, which is made to boil for an instant; and after refreshing the bath, the stuff is turned in to soften, and to render the black more fast. In this manner a very beautiful black is obtained, without rendering the cloth too harsh.

Commonly, more simple processes are employed. Thus the blue cloth is simply turned through a bath of gall-nuts, where it is boiled for two hours. It is next passed through a bath of logwood and sulphate of iron for two hours, without boiling, after which it is washed and fulled. But in all cases the cloth, after passing through the blue vat, should be thoroughly washed, because the least remains of its alkalinity would injure the tone to be given in the black copper.

Hellot found that the dyeing might be performed in the following manner:—For 20 yards of dark blue cloth a bath is made of 2 lbs. of fustic (*Maclura tinctoria*), 4¼ lbs. of logwood, and 11 lbs. sumach. After boiling the cloth in it for three hours it is lifted out, 11 lbs. of sulphate of iron are thrown into the boiler, and the cloth is then passed through it during two hours. It is now aired, and put again in the bath for an hour. It is, lastly, washed and scoured. The black is less velvety than that by the preceding process. Experience convinced him that the maddering prescribed in the ancient regulations only gives a reddish cast to the black, which is obtained finer and more velvety without madder.

According to Lewis, the proportions which the English dyers most generally adopt are, for 112 lbs. of woollen cloth, previously dyed of a dark blue, about 5 lbs. of sulphate of iron, as much gall-nuts, and 30 lbs. of logwood. They begin by galling the cloth; they then pass it through the decoction of logwood to which the sulphate of iron has been added.

When the cloth is completely dyed, it is washed in the river, and passed through the fulling-mill till the water runs off clear and colourless. Some persons recommend, for fine cloths, to full them with soap-water. This operation requires an expert workman, who can free the cloth thoroughly from the soap. Several recommend, at its coming from the fulling, to pass the cloth through a bath of weld, with the view of giving softness and solidity to the black. Lewis says, that passing the cloth through weld, after it has been treated with soap, is absolutely useless, although it may be beneficial when this operation has been neglected.

The following German process is cheap and good. 100 lbs. of cloth or wool are put into the copper with sufficient water and 15 lbs. of Salzburg vitriol (potash-sulphate of iron) and 5 lbs. of argol, heating the bath gradually to boiling, while the goods are well worked about for two hours, taking them out, and laying them in a cool place for twenty-four hours. They are then to be put in a lukewarm bath of from 25 to 30 lbs. of logwood, and 10 lbs. of fustic, and to be worked therein while it is made to boil during two hours. The goods are now removed, and there is put into the copper 1¼ lbs. of verdigris dissolved in vinegar; the goods are restored into the improved bath, and turned in it for half an hour, after which they are rinsed and dried.

The process for dyeing merinos black is, for 100 lbs. of them to put 10 lbs. of copperas into the bath of pure water, and to work therein for a quarter of an hour, as soon as it is tepid, one-third of the goods; then to replace that portion by the second, and after another quarter of an hour, to put in the last third. Each portion is to be laid aside to air in the cold. The bath being next heated to 140° F., the merinos are to be treated as above piecemeal; but the third time it is to be passed through the bath at a boiling heat. Being now well mordanted, the goods are laid aside to air till the following day. The copper being charged with water, 50 lbs. of ground logwood, and 2 lbs. of argol, and heated, the goods are to be passed through, while boiling, for half an hour. They are then rinsed.

Different operations may be distinguished in dyeing *silk* black: the boiling of the silk,—its galling,—the preparation of the bath,—the operation of dyeing,—the softening of the black.

Silk naturally contains a gummy substance, which gives it the stiffness and elasticity peculiar to it in its native state; but this adds nothing to the strength of the silk, which is then styled raw; it rather renders it, indeed, more apt to wear out by the stiffness which it communicates; and although raw silk more readily takes a black colour, yet the black is not so perfect in intensity, nor does it so well resist the reagents capable of dissolving the colouring particles, as silk which is scoured or deprived of its gum.

To cleanse silk intended for black, it is usually boiled four or five hours with one-fifth of its weight of white soap, after which it is carefully beetled and washed.

For the galling, nut-galls equal nearly to three-fourths of the weight of the silk are boiled during three or four hours; but on account of the price of Aleppo galls, more or less of the white gall-nuts, or of even an inferior kind called galon, berry or apple galls, are used. The proportion commonly employed at Paris is two parts of Aleppo galls to from eight to ten parts of galon. After the boiling, the galls are allowed to settle for about two hours. The silk is then plunged into the bath, and left in it from twelve to thirty-six hours, after which it is taken out and washed in the river.

Silk is capable of combining with quantities, more or less considerable, of the astringent principle; whence results a considerable increase of weight, not only from the weight of the astringent principle, but also from that of the colouring particles, which subsequently fix themselves in proportion to the quantity of the astringent principle which had entered into combination. Consequently, the processes are varied according to the degree of weight which it is wished to communicate to the silk; a circumstance requiring some illustration.

The commerce of silk goods is carried on in two ways: they are sold either by the weight, or by the surface, that is, by measure. Thus the trade of Tours was formerly distinguished from that of Lyons; the silks of the former being sold by weight, those of the latter by measure. It was therefore their interest to surcharge the weight at Tours, and, on the contrary, to be sparing of the dyeing ingredients at Lyons; whence came the distinction of light black and heavy black. At present, both methods of dyeing are practised at Lyons, the two modes of sale having been adopted there.

Silk loses nearly a fourth of its weight by a thorough boiling, and it resumes, in the light black dye, one-half of this loss; but in the heavy black dye, it takes sometimes upwards of a fifth more than its primitive weight—a surcharge injurious to the beauty of the black and the durability of the stuff. The surcharged kind is denominated English black, because it is pretended that it was practised in England. Since silk dyed with a great surcharge has not a beautiful black, it is usually destined for weft, and is blended with a warp dyed of a fine black.

The peculiarity of the process for obtaining the heavy black consists in leaving the silk longer in the gall-liquor, in repeating the galling, in passing the silk a greater number of times through the dye, and even letting it lie in it for some time. The first galling is usually made with galls which have served for a preceding operation, and fresh gall-nuts are employed for the second. But these methods would not be sufficient for giving a great surcharge, such as is found in what is called the English black. To give it this weight, the silk is galled without being ungummed; and, on coming out of the galls, it is rendered supple by being worked on the jack and pin.

The silk dyers keep a black vat, and its very complex composition varies in different dye-houses. These vats are commonly established for many years; and when their black dye is exhausted it is renovated by what is called in France a *brevet*. When the deposit which has accumulated in it is too great, it is taken out, so that at the end of a certain time nothing remains of the several ingredients which composed the primitive bath, but which are not employed in the brevet.

For the dyeing of raw silk black, it is 'galled' cold, with the bath of galls which has already served for the black of boiled silk. For this purpose, silk, in its native yellow colour, is made choice of. It should be remarked, that when it is desired to preserve a portion of the gum of the silk, which is afterwards made flexible, the galling is given with the *hot* bath of gall-nuts in the ordinary manner. But here, where the whole gum of the silk, and its concomitant elasticity, are to be preserved, the galling is made *cold*. If the infusion of galls be weak, the silk is left in it for several days.

Silk thus prepared and washed takes very easily the black dye, and the rinsing in a little water, to which sulphate of iron may be added, is sufficient. The dye is made cold; but, according to the greater or less strength of the rinsings, it requires more or less time. Occasionally three or four days are necessary; after which it is washed, it is beetled once or twice, and it is then dried without wringing, to avoid softening.

Any of these processes will produce a black without the goods being previously dyed blue, but generally when such common blacks, as they are technically termed, are dyed, more of the dye drugs are required, and also a little modification in the operations. Sometimes they are 'bottomed' or 'rooted,' by first working them in a decoction of walnut-husks, and then dyed as above;—or, a good black may be dyed without any previous rooting, by working 1 cwt. of the stuff, for an hour, at a heat of 190°, in 6 lbs. of camwood: 6 lbs. of copperas are then added, and the stuff worked for another hour; the fire is then withdrawn from the boiler, and the stuff allowed to remain in the liquor for 10 or 12 hours. It is washed from this, and worked in a second bath with 60 lbs. of logwood for an hour and a half, then add 3 lbs. of copperas, and after another hour's working, it is washed.

Bichromate of potash is also used for dyeing blacks upon wool. A very good colour may be dyed direct by working, for 2 hours, 1 cwt. of the stuff in a solution of 5 lbs. of bichromate, 4 lbs. of alum, and 3 lbs. of fustic, then exposing it for an hour and washing well. It is again wrought for 2 hours, in a second bath, made up with 45 lbs. of logwood, 3 lbs. of barwood or camwood, and 3 lbs. of fustic; then adding 3 lbs. of copperas, and after half an hour's longer working, the dye is finished. A much cheaper blue black than that produced by previously dyeing the stuff in the indigo vat, is obtained by using a Prussian blue, and then proceeding as directed above.

Raw silk may be more quickly dyed by shaking it round the rods in the cold bath after the galling, airing it, and repeating these manipulations several times, after which it is washed and dried.

Macquer describes a more simple process for the black by which velvet is dyed at Genoa: and he says that this process, rendered still simpler, has had complete success at Tours. The following is his description.

For 1 cwt. (50 kilogrammes) silk, 22 lbs. (11 kilogrammes) of Aleppo galls, in powder, are boiled for an hour in a sufficient quantity of water. The bath is allowed to settle till the galls have fallen to the bottom of the boiler, from which they are withdrawn; after which 32 lbs. of copperas are introduced, and 22 lbs. of country gum, put into a kind of two-handled colander, pierced everywhere with holes. This kettle is suspended by two rods in the boiler, so as not to reach the bottom. The gum is left to dissolve for about an hour, stirring it from time to time. If, after this time, some gum remains in the kettle, it is a proof that the bath, which contains two hogsheads, has taken as much of it as is necessary. If, on the contrary, the whole gum is dissolved, from 1 to 4 lbs. more may be added. This colander is left constantly suspended in the boiler, from which it is removed only when the dyeing is going on; and afterwards it is replaced. During all these operations the boiler must be kept hot, but without boiling. The galling of the silk is performed with one-third of Aleppo galls. The silk is left in it for six hours the first time, then for twelve hours. The rest, *secundum artem*.

Lewis states that he has repeated this process in the small way; and that, by adding sulphate of iron progressively, and repeating the immersion of the silk a great number of times, he eventually obtained a fine black.

Astringents differ from one another as to the quantity of the principle which enters into combination with the oxide of iron. Hence, the proportion of the sulphate, or of any other salt of iron, and that of the astringents, should vary according to the astringents made use of, and according to their respective quantities. Gall-nut is the substance which contains most of the astringent principle; sumach, which seems second to it in this respect, throws down (decomposes), however, only half as much sulphate of iron.

The most suitable proportion of sulphate of iron appears to be that which corresponds to the quantity of the astringent matter, so that the whole iron precipitable by the astringent may be thrown down, and the whole astringent principle may be taken up in combination with the iron. As it is not possible, however, to arrive at such precision, it is better that the sulphate of iron should predominate, because the astringent, when in excess, counteracts the precipitation of the black colouring particles, and has the property of even dissolving them.

This action of the astringent is such that, if a pattern of black cloth be boiled with gall-nuts, it is reducible to grey. An observation of Lewis may thence be explained. If cloth be turned several times through the colouring bath, after it has taken a good black colour, instead of obtaining more body, it is weakened, and becomes brownish. Too considerable a quantity of the ingredients produces the same effect; to which the sulphuric acid, set at liberty by the precipitation of the oxide of iron, contributes.

It is merely the highly oxidised sulphate which is decomposed by the astringent; whence it appears that the sulphate will produce a different effect according to its state of oxidation, and call for other proportions. Some advise, therefore, to follow the method of Proust, employing it in the oxidised state; but in this case it is only partially decomposed, and another part is brought, by the action of the astringent, into the lower degree of oxidation.

The particles precipitated by the mixture of an astringent and sulphate of iron have not at first a deep colour; but they pass to a black by contact of air while they are moist.

Black dye is only a very condensed colour, and it assumes more intensity from the mixture of different colours likewise deep. It is for this reason advantageous to unite several astringents, each combination of which produces a different shade. But blue appears the colour most conducive to this effect, and it corrects the tendency to dun, which is remarked in the black produced on stuffs by the other astringents.

On this property is founded the practice of giving a blue ground to black cloths, which acquire more beauty and solidity the deeper the blue. Another advantage of this practice is to diminish the quantity of sulphuric acid which is necessarily disengaged by the precipitation of the black particles, and which would not only counteract their fixation, but would further weaken the stuff, and give it harshness. For common stuffs, a portion of the effect of the blue ground is produced by the rooting.

The mixture of logwood with astringents contributes to the beauty of the black in a twofold way. It produces molecules of a hue different from what the astringents do, and particularly blue molecules, with the acetate of copper, commonly employed in the black dyes; which appears to be more useful the more acetate the verdigris made use of contains.

The boil of weld by which the dye of black cloth is frequently finished, may also contribute to its beauty, by the shade peculiar to its combination. It has, moreover, the advantage of giving softness to the stuffs.

The processes that are employed for wool yield, according to the observation of Lewis, only a rusty black to silk; and cotton is hardly dyed by the processes proper for wool and silk. Let us endeavour to ascertain the conditions which these three varieties of dyeing demand.

Wool has a great tendency to combine with colouring substances; but its physical nature requires its combinations to be made in general at a high temperature. The combination of the black molecules may therefore be directly effected in a bath, in proportion as they form; and, if the operation be prolonged by subdividing it, it is only with the view of changing the necessary oxidation of the sulphate and augmenting that of the colouring particles themselves.

Silk has not the same disposition to unite with the black particles. It seems to be assisted by the agency of the tannin, with which it is previously impregnated, especially after it has been scoured. A very deep black may be obtained upon 100 lbs. of silk, by working it for two hours in a solution of 20 lbs. of copperas and 3 pints of nitrate of iron. Wash from this thoroughly, and then wash for two hours more in a decoction of 100 lbs. of logwood and 20 lbs. of fustic. Lift up, and add to the bath a solution of 3 lbs. of copperas, and work half an hour longer, and wash. A beautiful rich blue-black is produced by dyeing the silk a deep royal blue, then working for an hour in a solution of copperas (2 ounces to the pound of silk), washing from this, and working in a bath of logwood, using half a pound to each pound of silk, and adding, after an hour's working, a few ounces of copperas; working half an hour longer, and finishing.

Cotton has no affinity for the black dye, and has always to be impregnated or combined with astringent substances, in order to produce the dye. A good deep black will be imparted to 100 lbs. of cotton by steeping it in a decoction of 30 lbs. of sumach, at a boiling heat, and allowing it to stand till perfectly cool; then passing it through lime-water, and, immediately after this, working for an hour in a solution of 20 lbs. of copperas. After this, expose for an hour to the air; then pass through lime-water again, and wash and work for an hour in a bath of 30 lbs. of logwood and 10 lbs. of fustic; lift, and add 2 lbs. of copperas, and work 30 minutes longer, and finish.

BLACK FLUX. See ASSAYING.

BLACK HÆMATITE. An ore of MANGANESE.

BLACKING FOR SHOES. (*Cirage des bottes*, Fr.; *Schuhschwärze*, Ger.) Blacking consists of a black colouring-matter, generally bone-black, and substances that acquire a gloss by friction, such as sugar and oil. The usual method is to mix the bone-black with sperm-oil; sugar, or molasses, with a little vinegar, is then well stirred in, and strong sulphuric acid is added gradually. The acid produces sulphate of lime and acid phosphate of lime, which is soluble: a tenacious paste is formed by these ingredients, which can be smoothly spread; the oil serving to render the leather pliable. This forms a liquid blacking. Paste blacking contains less vinegar. In Germany, according to Liebig, blacking is made by mixing bone-black with half its weight of molasses, and one-eighth of its weight of hydrochloric acid, and one-fourth of its weight of strong sulphuric acid, mixing with water, to form an unctuous paste. The following method for making liquid and paste blacking is given by William Bryant and Edward James: 18 ounces of caoutchouc are to be dissolved in about 9 lbs. of hot rape-oil. To this solution 60 lbs. of fine ivory-black and 45 lbs. of molasses are to be added, along with 1 lb. of finely ground gum arabic, previously dissolved in 20 gallons of vinegar of strength No. 24. These mixed ingredients are to be finely triturated in a paint-mill till the mixture becomes perfectly smooth. To this varnish 12 lbs. of sulphuric acid are to be now added in small successive quantities, with powerful stirring for half an hour. The blacking thus compounded is allowed to stand for 14 days, it being stirred half an hour daily; at the end of which time 3 lbs. of finely ground gum arabic are added; after which the stirring is repeated half an hour every day for 14 days longer, when the liquid blacking is ready for use. In making the paste blacking, the patentees prescribe the above quantity of india-rubber oil, ivory-black, molasses, and gum arabic, the latter being dissolved in only 12 lbs. of vinegar. These ingredients are to be well mixed and then ground together in a mill till they form a perfectly smooth paste. To this paste 12 lbs. of sulphuric acid are to be added in small quantities at a time, with powerful stirring, which is to be continued for half an hour after the last portion of the acid has been introduced. This paste will be found fit for use in about seven days.

BLACK-JACK. The miner's name for blende, or sulphide of zinc. See ZINC.

BLACK LEAD. The common name of PLUMBAGO or GRAPHITE.

BLACK-LEAD PENCILS. See PENCIL MANUFACTURE.

BLACK TIN. The miner's name for tin ore ready for the smelter. See TIN.

BLACK WADD. One of the ores of manganese. See MANGANESE.

BLADDER. (*Vessie*, Fr.; *Blase*, Ger.) A bag or sack, in animals, which serves as the receptacle of some secreted fluid. Bladders are chiefly employed for securing jars, bottles, &c.

BLANKET. (*Blanchet.* Fr.) A cover for a bed made of coarse wool loosely woven. Among printers the woollen cloth which is placed between the tympans is called a *blanket*.

Blankets are largely used in Californian gold-quartz mining, for catching the particles of metal as they escape from the stamping mill. These blankets are generally of a coarse grey wool, and are woven expressly for the miner, at the woollen mills on the coast. They are made about 30 inches wide, and are spread over blanket-boards, or shallow wooden troughs, each about 16 inches wide, 3 inches deep, and from 9 to 12 feet long, and inclined in the direction of their length at an angle of from 3° or 4° to 15° to the horizon. The finely pulverised ore, suspended in water, is carried in a current, from the battery-box, over the surface of a series of these blankets. In this way a larger proportion of the gold and auriferous pyrites, or of the gold-amalgam if mercury has been used in the battery, becomes entangled in the fibres of the fabric. Any particles that may escape are finally retained by a system of amalgamated copper riffles over which the current of water is generally caused to flow after leaving the blankets. The blankets, charged with finely-divided metal, are frequently washed (the upper ones, on which the heaviest sand is deposited, being in some cases washed every quarter of an hour), and the residue from the washings is then amalgamated. It has been attempted, but without success, to substitute ox-hides or sheepskins for the blankets. See WOOLLEN MANUFACTURES.

BLAST. The current of air driven into a furnace; it may be either cold or hot air. See HOT BLAST.

BLAST-FURNACE. A furnace into which air is forcibly blown. See IRON, METALLURGY.

BLAST-HOLES. *A mining term.* The holes through which the water enters the bottom of a pump in the mines.

BLASTING. The process of rending rocks by the use of some explosive compound, as gunpowder. See MINING.

BLEACHING (*Blanchement*, Fr.; *Bleichen*, Ger.) is the process by which the textile filaments, cotton, flax, hemp, wool, silk, and the cloths made of them, as well as various vegetable and animal substances, are deprived of their natural colour, and rendered nearly or altogether white. The term bleaching comes from the French verb *blanchir*, to whiten.

The principal bleaching agents, besides alkalis, are chlorine, sulphurous acid, and the combined action of air and light. These are destroyers of colour. The chief agents for removing colours which do not require to be previously decomposed, are alkalis. The principal amount of the colouring-materials are removed from the cloth by washing with alkalis: the last tint of whiteness is not removable by this means, and it is to this last tint that the word bleaching has been more definitely applied.

In ancient times bleaching, washing, and fulling were not distinctly separated; they were all practised. We read in the Scriptures of 'fine linen, white and clean,' and in Greek authors, of 'raw linen,' of which towels were made, as well as of 'shining fine linen,' for the same purpose, thus at once making the distinction.[1] The pure white was apparently not so common as with us. A pure surface was, however, needful, in order to produce good colours, for which we are bound to give the ancients credit, as we know they were acquainted with them as pigments, and are not, therefore, to be suspected of being unable to distinguish good from bad, when transferred to textile fabrics. As their words for white and for colour are plain enough in general, we must conclude that they had the power of obtaining both fine whites and finely-dyed cloth; handkerchiefs were tied about the head in various ways, as now in Lancashire, white and coloured. The Babylonians wore white cloaks.[2] By their method of washing, the discovery of bleaching was inevitable, the cloth being washed and dried several times in the sun. But it was not left in the state of an accident only; the word *insolation* shows that the effects of the sun had been observed and classified, and this is stated to have been the chief method, as it is now, of bleaching wax. Egypt and the East seem to have been the teachers in bleaching. From Egypt were obtained alkalis, and soda mixed with lime. Both lime and alkalis were used in the process. Potashes, or the ashes of plants, were also used, and soap-plants, in all probability of various kinds, as it is not easy to decide on one. The *Saponaria officinalis*, soap-wort, is still used, and the wake-robin or cuckowpint, *Arum maculatum*; the *Gypsophila Struthium* was considered by Linnæus to be the ancient one, and is still called *Lanaria* in Italy. Nor do we require to suppose that this plant was first incinerated, as has been supposed, in the case of Borith, the fuller's soap of the Bible. Vegetable decoctions are still used in China to bleach silk, and in France also; some have been patented even in England, although but little used. The Latin method of obtaining white cloth is very well preserved, and as they got their caustic soda from Egypt, it is probable that they got also their process thence; nor is it at all likely that Nicias of Megara invented fulling, as it was evidently well known before the existence of any well-founded Greek tradition. Pictures exist in Pompeii of men dancing the fuller's dance, or stamping cloth with their feet, as women now practise in Scotland. Moderate-sized tubs were used: the clothes seem occasionally to have been taken up by the hand, in order that they might be well turned. They were then treated with ammoniacal liquors and soda. Urine was highly esteemed for the purpose. The fullers obtained it by placing vessels at the corners of the streets, which were removed when filled; this practice acting at the same time as a sanitary precaution. The same method of carefully collecting this fluid, or 'old lant,' as it is called, exists in the woollen districts of Lancashire and Yorkshire. A tax was laid on it by Vespasian, so that the fullers might not receive it without payment. The cloth was then sulphured, if it was intended to be white: this process was performed under a conical frame like a small tent, the cloth being spread round the frame, and a vessel of sulphur burned under it.[3] Potter's earth was then used according to circumstances. The fuller seems to have been a bleacher as well as domestic laundryman. He had, therefore, white as well as coloured dresses to deal with. For the first he used Sardinian potter's earth, which could not be employed for prints or such colours as easily changed (*versicolores*). For coloured cloth, sulphur was not used by the potters, but fine Cimolian earth. The potter's earth seems to have been used both before and after sulphuring, according to circumstances. This second process is allied partly to our mode of chalking white dresses, still somewhat in use: but more strongly allied to what is called dressing, stiffening, and finishing. Pliny says that the Umbrian earth was only used for polishing vestments, also that it softened fine colours and gave lustre to those that were faded in sulphuring. This shows that

[1] Philoxenus in Athenæus, ix. 77. [2] Herod. i. 195.
[3] Pompeii drawings; see Smith's Dictionary, Lardner's Cyclopædia.

they used sulphur in washing, and not merely in preparing for the bleaching process.[1] They then gave a finish of very fine clay, gypsum being used instead of clay in Greece, as amongst ourselves. If a nap was wanted, it was raised after sulphuring, by brushing, by carding, by the skin of a hedgehog, or by thistles and teasels. They seem to have got a fine nap on their woollen cloth, as garments of this kind once washed were considered less valuable, as would be the case with our broadcloth for outer dresses. Wool for under dresses could not have been injured by one washing, especially as the *fullones* seem in old Italy to have been more attentive than our washerwomen, and to have formed a college, or at least a guild. The washing was seldom done at home, except in large establishments, especially in the country. Whiteness was very much esteemed, and great pains taken to obtain it. Coloured cloth seems a later invention. This love of whiteness was so great, that those who were too poor to have their cloths fulled, rubbed them with a white fuller's earth, so as on holidays to appear clean and bright.

Clothes in ancient times required a good deal of washing, so much oil being used; alkalis alone could remove this, and people that used soft feather-beds, and pillows that sank under the weight of the head, would not be behind in having them also whitened. In India the mode was different from that used in the western world. The preparation for printing was a series of washings, beatings, and exposure to the sun, as well as wearing next the skin, and steeping in goats' and sheeps' dung. Wearing next the skin was probably instead of the oiling process in Turkey red. Bleaching with boiled rice-water was practised in India. In Jamaica the aloe was used, and in China a bean is employed: this is smaller than the Turkey bean; five parts are used to five of salt, six of flour, and twenty-five of water: this is for raw silk. The exact action of the vegetable method on the colouring-matter is not well known; but it must not be ignored. The decompositions of fermentation and putrefaction have a great power of propagating themselves; we can, in fact, readily conceive the decomposition of gums by such means, provided they are not resinous matters, consisting chiefly of carbon and hydrogen. Mucilaginous plants are even now in some places used, and have been recommended also in the most modern times.[2] It is, therefore, not easy to see why so much difficulty has been raised amongst chemical historians as to the use of plants in washing and bleaching. Vegetable products, such as oatmeal, &c., have powerful detergent qualities, and leave the skin exceedingly soft. In general we may conclude that these vegetable infusions and alkalis were the means of bleaching in ancient times, the influence of the sun being also employed. At present, alkalis are more generally used. Washing with alkalis is really the most important part of the process. The soaps of the ancients were also vegetable, or alkaline, or both; they were a σμῆγμα, but not a true soap, in general at least.—*Paulus Ægineta*, Notes by Adams.

Until modern times no improvements of great importance took place affecting the principles of bleaching; and even now the only modern changes consist in the introduction of chlorine and machinery, to which may be added the greater abundance of soap. In the last century, Holland obtained the best name for bleaching. The process passed then to Ireland and Scotland, and thence into England. It was even customary to send goods from this country to be bleached in Holland. The first attempt to vie with Holland was made in Scotland in 1749.

We find in the patent lists many crude efforts made to improve the art. Alkalis and acids are recommended in various forms, and such a variety of substances as tartar, saltpetre, sal-ammoniac, marl, loam, clay, mud, chalk, fuller's earth, oyster-shells, soot, turf, and ashes, with a great variety of washing machines.

The value of the plan in Holland was ascribed to the ashes of Muscovy (Russian potash) and the sea-water; but it is evident from the description, that it was not sea-, but very pure fresh water which was used. The Dutch process is thus described:—
' When a piece of linen is to be bleached, it is in the first place steeped in a lixivium, or lye, where other cloth has been trod; afterwards it is trod in a new lye of ashes poured upon it boiling hot. This is boiled in large copper cauldrons, and is never poured upon the cloth till it is as clear as wine. The linen is left eight days in this lye, after which it is washed and pressed in this manner:—They empty some buckets of butter-milk into wooden vessels fixed in the ground; then they throw in a piece of linen, which three men tread with their feet as much as possible. Afterwards they pour in more butter-milk, and then another piece of cloth, proceeding thus alternately till the vessels are nearly filled, when they lay planks over the linen, upon which they raise a large round piece of wood, or great stake, touching the lower side of a beam, between which and the stake they drive wedges to press the cloth. Six or seven days after they take the cloth out of these vessels, and if it be not white enough, they steep it as we have described above. Afterwards it is washed and spread

[1] Nat. Hist. xxxv. 57, &c.   [2] See Giobert's process.

out upon the ground to bleach. It must be remarked that after every dipping the cloth is washed first with black soap, then with clear water, and after each of the operations it is wrung by means of a machine that turns by means of a wheel. .... The whitening grounds are cut with canals in some places, that there may be no trouble of fetching water from a distance. The cloth is watered with long narrow shovels made in shape of a scythe. The water of these canals comes from the dams, and it is that which contributes most to the lustre of the Dutch cloth. To prevent the water from becoming thick and muddy, they are extremely careful in cleaning these canals. The washing tubs are built with bricks, with two trap-doors or sluices for admitting or excluding the water according as it is necessary.'—*Select Essays*, quoted by Parke.

The chief advantage here consists in the facility of obtaining soap, which in ancient times was either scarce or badly made. This improvement began to be more and more used from the time of its earliest introduction. Modern times have begun to exclude it to a great extent again, finding it so much cheaper to work with the alkali alone without combining it with fatty matter.

The process of bleaching then became a series of operations, consisting of, 1st, steeping in water for about three or four days, or in weak alkali for forty-eight hours. 2nd, boiling in an alkaline lye, or, in other words, *bucking* or bowking: in this operation the hot lye was poured on the cloth ; it then ran through it, was drawn off by a tap below, and then pumped up again. 3rd, crofting, or exposure to sun and air on the grass. 4th, souring : this was done by the butter-milk ; it lasted several weeks. These operations were repeated four or five times, or until the goods were pure. The whole lasted from March to September. The best months for crofting were found to be March, April, and May. It was not known that it was the acid of the butter-milk which acted ; but when sulphuric acid became cheaper, Dr. Home applied it instead of butter-milk, and caused a great revolution in bleaching, as the souring could now be done in a day which before had occupied weeks, exposing the cloth to much danger of decay by decomposition or putrefaction. Great fear was expressed in the country lest the vitriol should burn the cloth, when Dr. Home stated that he had kept linen in acid of the required dilution for some months without having it injured. Berthollet also said that the acid made a better white.

In 1784 Berthollet made known some investigations on chlorine, and in 1787 communicated them to the French Academy. By these investigations it was found that chlorine had the power of destroying colouring-matters. The use of chlorine was brought to this country by the Duke of Gordon and Professor Copeland of Aberdeen, who then gave the process to be carried out by Messrs. Milnes, of the firm of Gordon, Barron, and Co., of that place. In this discovery the theoretical portion is due, first, to Scheele, who discovered the chlorine ; and, secondly, to Berthollet, who discovered the peculiar property. The practical mode of effecting the object is the part which we claim ; but it consists of such a long series of expensive trials and ingenious contrivances, that it will take a much longer time to describe them than to give the first idea only. As the invention was at first applied only to cotton, which at that period was rising into importance, we shall begin the description of modern bleaching with the mode adopted for that material.

James Watt at the date given was in intimate communication with Berthollet, and did not rest until he had made the process successful at the bleach-field of Macgregor, near Glasgow, requesting the results to be communicated to a meeting of manufacturers to be called together at Manchester ;—so quick was Watt to see what would be for the permanent interest of a country, and so ready to act on it ! Dr. Henry did much to make it known to the manufacturers about Manchester. This is one of the early instances of scientific men being directly applied to by manufacturers for assistance—an application seldom made unless under great difficulties.

In 1798, Charles Tennant, of Glasgow, introduced chloride of lime, which is preferred above all other compounds as a means of applying chlorine.

The true theory of bleaching has not been entirely agreed upon, but there can be little doubt of the principal operations. It is known that oxygen deprives substances of colour ; this may be performed by many high oxides ; by nitric acid, manganic and chromic acids, chlorous acid, and even lower oxides which hold their oxygen lightly, as hypochlorous acid. The same effect may be produced by chlorine, bromine, and iodine. It has been said that chlorine unites with the hydrogen of the water which is present, gives off oxygen, and so acts just as oxygen would. Davy found that it would not act in dry air, so that water was needful : but Dr. Wilson found that it would act, although slowly, in dry air, if exposed to the rays of the sun. This might show that water is not necessary in order to supply oxygen, but only to allow the chlorine to be brought into thorough contact with the colouring-matter. It has also been supposed that the chlorine removes the hydrogen, or, rather, simply takes its place by an act of substitution. Now, whether the chlorine or the liberated oxygen removes the hydrogen, the result will be the same—the destruction of the compound. Chlorine so readily performs these changes, that we should at once decide on calling it the active agent, were it not for the fact that oxygen acts so readily, even when chlorine is not present: for example, peroxide of hydrogen, as well as the oxides just mentioned, and ozone also, which has no chlorine to help it. It is, then, certain that oxidation bleaches; and it is certain that dehydration bleaches, if performed by chlorine, and that the sun aids it by its active rays. We know also that water aids it: water aids bleaching or oxidation by air, partly because it contains air in solution. It aids also the bleaching performed by solutions in contact with porous bodies, because these bodies have a power of condensing gases in their pores and of compelling combinations. The next question is, Does it aid the bleaching by chlorine in the same way, by assisting the union mechanically, or by decomposing water? Chlorine acts slowly, unless water be present. The theory, therefore, does not demand the decomposition of water, and the known powerful affinities of chlorine do not require to be supplemented by oxygen. But, in order to see exactly the state of the case, let us look at the action of chlorine in hypochlorites or in chloride of lime, and we find that it is a direct oxidation. We obtain by it peroxides of metals, and not chlorides. Here we seem to be taught directly by experiment, that bleaching by hypochlorites is an oxidation of the colouring-matter. Bleaching by moist chlorine may therefore be looked on as the same; indeed, we oxidise by it; but in such cases we may obtain the base at the same time united to chlorine, giving another turn to the question, as Kane showed. The oxidation theory, therefore, seems to be sufficient when water is present. We are, however, finally to deal with dry chlorine in the sun; and in that case it is fair to conclude that it acts by direct combination with hydrogen or the colouring-matter or both. We have, then, two modes of bleaching; but the usual mode in the air becomes by that explanation an oxidation, and the direct action of chlorine obtainable only with difficulty. When sulphurous acid is used, another phenomenon may be looked for, as we find a substance whose chief quality is that of deoxidising. The removal of oxygen also decomposes bodies, and sulphuretted hydrogen can scarcely be supposed to act in any other way. Sulphurous acid, when it decomposes sulphuretted hydrogen, really acts as an oxidising agent, and we can therefore imagine it as such in the bleaching process. Investigation has not told us if it enters into combination as SO^2, and, like oxygen, destroys colour, altering the compound by inserting itself.

We may fairly conclude that the processes by chlorine and sulphurous acid are performed in a manner as different as the mode in which a salt of ammonia acts on chlorine or an oxacid, or, in Dr. Wilson's general terms, 'specific differences may be expected to occur with all the gases named, as to their action on any one colouring-matter, and with different colouring-matters, as to their deportment with any one of the gases.'—*Trans. R. S. E.*, 1848.

It has been attempted to introduce manganates, chromates, chlorates, chlorochromic acid, and sulphites, but without success, as bleaching agents.

BLEACHING OF COTTON.

Substances dealt with in Bleaching.—The object of bleaching is to separate from the textile fibre all the substances which may mask its intrinsic whiteness, or, which, in the course of dyeing or printing, may produce injurious effects on the colours. The substances present in cotton goods, and to be treated in bleaching, are as follows :—

a. The resinous matter natural to the filaments.
b. The colouring-matter of the plant.
c. The paste of the weaver.
d. A fatty matter.
e. A cupreous soap.
f. A calcareous soap.
g. The filth of the hands.
h. Iron rust, earthy matters, and dust.
i. The cotton fibre itself.
j. The carbonaceous matter caused by singeing.
k. The seed-vessels.

a. Cotton is covered with a resinous matter, which obstructs its absorption of moisture. This alone would prevent it receiving colour, and it is known that if this could be removed, some of the darker colours could be dyed without any bleaching, providing also the impurities arising from manipulation were absent, although the finest colours could not be produced in this manner on cotton in general. M. Bolly, however, has proposed the use of acetic acid, or of a sour bran liquor, as substances which are absorbed by the cotton and render it capable of absorbing colour or solutions. The matter which prevents the moistening has not been thoroughly examined. It is found to be soluble in alcohol or ether, and some of it in turpentine : it is therefore called a resinous, waxy, or fatty body. It is dissolved by alkalis, and thrown down by acids in strong solutions. The alcohol solution leaves thin yellowish scales, which may be dissolved in acid, or even in much water. But information concerning it is indistinct. For a long time the process commenced by removing this resin by means of alkali. It is called scouring.

b. The whole colouring-matter is not soluble in alkalis, but it becomes so after being altered by the action of chlorine, or by insolation or croft-bleaching. It is not even capable of being bleached, or at least but slowly, unless it be previously acted on by alkalis. The amount of colour is much less with cotton than linen. The former is so white naturally, that washing and bleaching might be dispensed with, were it not for the substances which, during its manufacture, come in contact with it, if the gum were removed which prevents the moistening. The alkaline solution from the raw linen, when precipitated by acids, throws down a nearly black resinous mass, and the total loss of weight is very great.

c. The weaver's dressing is composed chiefly of farinaceous, glutinous, or gelatinous substances, starch, flour, or size. They are usually allowed to become sour before using. They are all dissolved by water or alkaline solutions, including lime. When the dressing gets dry, the hand-weaver occasionally renders his warp-threads more pliant by rubbing some cheap kind of grease upon them. Hence it happens that the cloth which has not been completely freed from this fatty matter will not readily imbibe water in the different bleaching operations; and hence, in the subsequent processes, these greasy spots, under peculiar circumstances—somewhat like lithographic stones—strongly attract the aluminous and iron mordants, as well as the dyestuffs, and occasion stains which it is almost impossible to discharge. The acids act differently upon the fatty matters, and thence remarkable anomalies in bleaching take place. When oil is treated with the acetic or muriatic acid, or with aqueous chlorine, it evolves no gas, as it does with the sulphuric and nitric acids; but it puts these substances into a condition in which they cannot be dissolved by a strong boiling lye of caustic soda. Carbonic acid is said to have a similar action with oil.

d. Both cotton and linen contain a little fatty matter, which is removed in the same manner as the resinous. Some of it comes from the mode of treating the warp, which is occasionally greased for weaving. This prevents, like resinous matter, the thorough saturation by solutions which are not alkaline, and soap, soda, or potash may be used to remove it by solution. Lime makes an insoluble soap, and is therefore not suited to the operation. If, however, lime has been used, the insoluble soap may be removed by treating with carbonate of soda, which forms a carbonate of lime, and leaves the fat in combination with the alkali. The carbonate of lime is then removed by an acid. This is, however, an indirect method ; and the mode universally used is to decompose the lime-soap by an acid, and remove the lime, leaving the fat in the cloth; then to wash out the fat by an alkali, or by soap and alkali mixed, as is the custom almost everywhere. The soap used is in great measure a resinous one, for cheapness, and it is mixed with carbonate of soda.

e. When the hand-weavers' grease continues in contact for a night with the copper dents of his reed, a kind of cupreous soap is formed, which is sometimes very difficult to remove from the web. Lime-water does not dissolve it; but dilute sulphuric acid carries off the metallic oxide, and liberates the margaric acid, in a state ready to be acted on by alkalis.

f. When cloth is boiled with milk of lime, the grease which is uncombined unites with that alkaline earth, and forms a calcareous soap, pretty soluble in a great excess of lime-water, and still more so in caustic soda. But all fats and oils, as well as the soaps of copper and lime, cease to be soluble in alkaline lyes when they have remained a considerable time upon the goods, and have been in contact with acetic, carbonic, or muriatic acids, or chlorine. These results have been verified by experiment.

g. Cotton goods are sometimes much soiled, from being sewed or tamboured with dirty hands ; but they may easily be cleansed from this filth by hot water.

h. Any ferruginous or earthy matters which get attached to the goods in the course of bleaching are readily removable, if not allowed thoroughly to penetrate the cloth ; but the fine ferruginous clay found in suspension in water is very difficult to wash off, and it probably cannot, by any means, be removed from printed goods without spoiling the colours.

i. In all these operations it is needful to consider the most important substance of all—the fibre. Each of the operations may weaken or destroy it, if managed unwisely. Caustic lime may be allowed to act for a long time on cloth without any injury, but if allowed to act on it with free access of air, it destroys it in a few hours. Neither can cloth stand the action of alkalis of any kind very long: if very strong, they rapidly destroy it. The same thing may, in a still stronger sense, be said of acids; and chloride of lime or bleaching-powder acts in the same direction. Linen, although mechanically much stronger than cotton, has not an equal chemical resistance to decomposition. It has not, therefore, been possible to use chloride of lime so as entirely to complete the process of bleaching linen, but only to hasten it, the completion being still nearly in all cases made by crofting. The bleacher has found out these things by expensive experience, and every day shows the importance of guarding against the excessive action of any one of the bleaching agents. Goods are continually suffering from the desire of speed on the part of the trade, and especially of the buyer; nor is it easy to find them absolutely uninjured by the process of bleaching, although it seems possible to conduct the process so that no weakening will ensue. The precautions taken are such as cause the processes to appear very long and tedious. The boiling with lime is continued as long as it is safe; the cloth is then at once washed and scoured, so as to remove all the caustic earth from the fibre. The acid is not allowed to remain long, but is, within from two to four hours, washed out by machines which cause the cloth to be frequently and rapidly saturated with water; and when one of these processes is not enough, it is found better to return to it again than completely to finish it at once, to the danger of the fibre; in the same way as workmen, if they find it needful to put their hands into hot water, do it rapidly and for a short time, but bring them out to cool before they return to the charge. To dry the goods with even a very small amount of acid would infallibly render them rotten. When the chlorine has oxidised or otherwise acted on the colouring-matter, so as to render it soluble, it is washed out with alkalis, but the whole may not be acted on by the first process, and a second may be needful. Again, as to crofting: one exposure may not be found enough; another washing and another crofting are then needed, and a third, and so on, according to the method employed and the nature of the material used.

The souring by vegetable substances or by fermentation may also injure the cloth, not by the amount of acid existing in the solution, but the decomposition which becomes communicated from the vegetable matter to the cloth, and so renders it weak and rotten. The same is peculiarly the case when putrefactive action is allowed to commence. This was often the case when the gluten of the paste was removed by fermentation. It has been said that the action of carbonic and acetic acid on the fats is a great objection to the fermentation process, as they are thought to render the fat insoluble, and produce an indelible mark.

Experiments undertaken for the purpose have shown that the strength of the fibre is not impaired by being boiled in milk of lime for two hours, at the ordinary pressure, provided it is not exposed at the same time to air; but bleachers consider that, practically, the goods are not injured by boiling with lime for sixteen hours at the strength of 40 lbs. to 100 gallons. It has also been proved that caustic soda of the specific gravity of 1030· does not hurt them, even boiled under the pressure of 140 lbs. to the square inch, or immersion for eight hours in chloride of lime solution containing 3 lbs. to 100 gallons, and afterwards in sulphuric acid of the specific gravity of 1067·, or eighteen hours at the specific gravity of 1035·.

j. The carbon left by the singeing is entirely removed, but it is not clear what becomes of it. It disappears in the alkaline solution, as no traces seem to exist after this action. Probably the blackness or darkness is not caused by any pure carbon, but by compounds soluble in alkalis. If any elementary carbon exist, it is carried away almost entirely, no doubt, by mechanical means.

k. The same method gets rid of the particles of pod which remain in the cotton, and after the first washing they seem to stand out very prominently, swelling up into large dark spots. The alkali probably renders them soft, and allows them to mix readily with liquids, if not altogether actually dissolved.

General Process of Bleaching.—The process of bleaching, from what we have seen, resolves itself into treatment with alkalis, and the action of chlorine or of light. In describing the operations they seem to be very numerous; but, as explained, some require to be repeated gently, instead of being finished by one decisive operation, so as not to injure the fibre; and some are intermediate operations, such as the frequent washings needed in passing from one process to the other. The alkaline solution in which the goods are boiled does not contain above 250 lbs. of carbonate of soda to 600 gallons, but nearly always less. Lime is, however, used much more frequently than soda, which it will be seen is only employed in the second process, and the third if there be one. It is less hurtful to the cloth, and is much cheaper than the alkalis.

The chloride of lime is used at ⅓ Twaddle, or 1002·5. It is not considered so important now as formerly, and where 300 lbs. were formerly employed, 30 to 40 are now used. The goods are made nearly white by the alkalis. The chlorine gives only the last finish, and is sometimes used to whiten the ground on coloured goods. The whole process may be expressed thus :—Wash out the soluble matter; boil with lime to dissolve still more, and to make a fatty compound with the oily matter ; wash out the lime by acids ; wash out the fat with a soda-soap; clear the white by chloride of lime.

The impurities in the cloth have a certain power of retaining colour upon them. Mud and dirt, as well as grease, gluten, and albuminous matters, have this property, and fatty soaps, such as lime-compounds of fatty acids. The pure fibre, however, has no power of taking up solutions of such colouring-matter as madder. When, therefore, it is desired to try the extent to which cloth has been bleached, it is dyed or boiled up with madder exactly as in the process of dyeing. It is then treated with soap, as the madder-dyed goods are treated, and if it comes out without a stain, or nearly pure white, the goods are ready. Dyers or calico-printers who dye printed goods are exceedingly particular as to the bleaching, the dyeing and printing having now approached to such exactness, that shades invisible to any eye not very much experienced are sufficient to diminish in a material degree the value of the cloth. Any inequality from irregularity of bleaching, which causes a similar irregularity of dyeing, is destructive to the character of the goods. Many patterns, too, have white grounds; these grounds it is the pride of a printer to have as white as snow. If delicate colours are to be printed, they will be deteriorated if the ground on which they are to be printed is not perfectly white.

The stains which come out upon maddered goods in consequence of defective bleaching are sometimes called *spangs*. Their origin is such as I have described above, as the following statements of facts will show. The weaver of calicoes receives frequently a fine warp so tender, from bad spinning, or bad staple in the cotton, that it will not bear the ordinary strain of the heddles, or friction of the shuttle and reed, and he is obliged to throw in as much weft as will compensate for the weakness and thinness of the warp, and make a good marketable cloth. He of course tries to gain his end at the least expense of time and labour. Hence, when his paste dressing becomes dry and stiff, he has recourse to such greasy lubricants as he can most cheaply procure, which are commonly either tallow, or butter in a rancid state, but the former, being the lowest priced, is preferred. Accordingly, the weaver having heated a lump of iron, applies it to a piece of tallow held over the warp in the loom, and causes the melted fat to drop in patches upon the yarns, which he afterwards spreads more evenly by his brush. It is obvious, however, that the grease must be very irregularly applied in this way, and be particularly thick on certain spots. This irregularity seldom fails to appear when the goods are bleached or dyed by the common routine of work. Printed calicoes, examined by a skilful eye, will be often seen to be stained with large blotches, evidently occasioned by this vile practice of the weaver. The ordinary workmen call these *copper* stains, believing them to be communicated in the dyeing-copper. Such stains on the cloth are extremely injurious in dyeing with the indigo-vat.

Old Methods still in use.—As a specimen of the older processes, we shall give the following, adding, afterwards, a minute account of some of the plans adopted by the most successful bleachers. When grease stains do not exist, as happens with the better kind of muslins, or when goods were not required to be finely finished, the following has been adopted :—After singeing, 1. Boiling in water. 2. Scouring by the stocks or dash-wheel. 3. Bucking with lime. 4. The bleaching properly so called, viz., passing through chlorine or crofting. 5. Bucking or bowking with milk of lime. These two latter processes employed alternately several times, till the whole of the colouring-matter is removed. 6. Souring. 7. Washing.

Another routine has been, 1. Cleansing out the weavers' dressing, by steeping the cloth for twelve hours in cold water, and then washing it at the stocks or dash-wheel. 2. Boiling in milk of lime, of a strength suited to the quality of the goods, but for a shorter time than with the soda lye; two short operations with the lime, with intermediate washing, being preferable to one of greater duration. 3 and 4. Two consecutive lyes of ten or twelve hours' boiling, with about 2 lbs. of soda crystals for 1 cwt. of cloth. 5. Exposure to the air for six or eight days, or the application of chloride of lime and then sulphuric acid. 6. A lye of caustic soda. 7. Exposure to the air for six or eight days, or chlorine and acid as above. 8. Caustic soda lye as before. 9. Chlorine and the sour. 10. Rinsing in hot water, or scouring by the dash-wheel.

The Processes used in Bleaching. Singeing.—The singeing is performed by passing the cloth over a red-hot plate of iron or copper. The figure 108 shows this apparatus as improved by Mr. Thom. At *a* there is a cylinder, with the cloth wound round it to be singed; it passes over the red-hot plate at *b*, becomes singed, passes over a small roller at *c*, which is partly immersed in water, and by this means has all the sparks extinguished; then is wound on to the roller *d*, when the process is finished. As the products of combustion from the singeing are sometimes very unpleasant, they are carried by this apparatus into the fire-place, where they are consumed. The arrows show the passage of these vapours from the surface of the cloth downwards into the hearth, and thence into the fire.

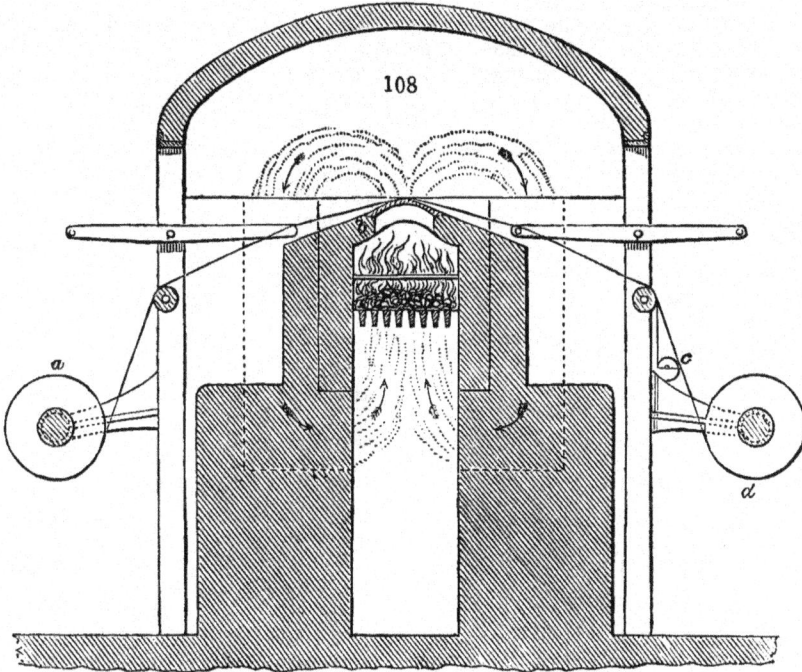

108

For goods to be finely printed both sides are singed; for market bleaching, one side. Sometimes, however, singeing is not at all desired.

The use of a line of gas jets instead of a red-hot plate was introduced by Mr. Samuel Hall. It has not, however, found its way generally into bleach-works: the plate is preferred. Gas jets are used necessarily in singeing threads. See SINGEING.

Shearing.—For fine printing, it is by some considered needful to shear the nap of the cloth instead of singeing it. The method is more expensive than singeing. Messrs. Mather and Platt have made a machine which will shear 60 to 80 yards per minute.

Bucking or *Bowking.*—This is the process of boiling goods. It is performed in alkaline liquids, generally lime, or soda, or both. The kier for bowking is a cylindrical iron vessel, the chief peculiarity of which is a method of preventing the cloth from being burnt on the bottom of the vessel, or allowed to dry on the vessel, or so to be pressed on the bottom as to prevent the boiling of the liquid in a uniform manner. This is done by simply having a false bottom to the kier, or a wooden perforated bottom, about eight or ten inches above the actual bottom.

The boiler, such as A, *fig.* 109, has a stopcock, H G, at bottom, for running off the waste lye. Kiers are commonly made of cast-iron, and are capable of containing from 300 to 600 gallons of water, according to the extent of the business done. In order that the capacity of the boilers may be enlarged, they are formed so as to admit of a crib of wood, strongly hooped, or, what is preferable, of cast-iron, to be fixed to the upper rim or edge of it. To keep the goods from the

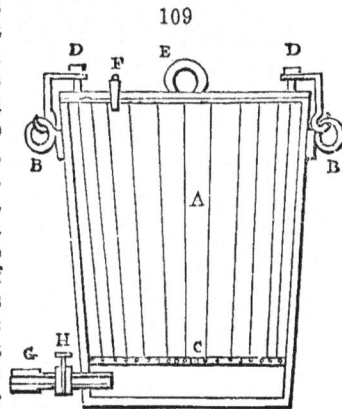

109

bottom, where the heat acts most forcibly, a strong iron ring, covered with netting made of stout rope, C, is allowed to rest six or eight inches above the bottom of the boiler. Four double ropes are attached to the ring E, for withdrawing the goods when sufficiently boiled, which have each an eye for admitting hooks from the running tackle of a crane. Where more boilers than one are employed, the crane is so placed that, in the range of its sweep it may withdraw the goods from any of them.   For this purpose, the crane turns on pivots at top and bottom; and the goods are raised or lowered at pleasure, with double pulleys and sheaves, by means of a cylinder moved by cast-iron wheels.   The lid is secured by the screw bolts D D, and rings B B.   F is a safety-valve.

To avoid the excessive heating needful to drive the liquid through the goods, Mr. John Laurie invented the kier shown at *fig.* 110.

In this figure, A B C D is the wooden kieve, or kier, containing the cloth; C E F D represent the cast-iron boiler; G G, the pump; g, K, the pipe of communication between the kier and the boiler.   This pipe has a valve on each of its extremities: that on the upper extremity, when shut, prevents the lye from running into the boiler, and is regulated by the attendant by means of the rod and handle g B.   The valve at K admits the lye: but, opening inwards, it prevents the steam from escaping through the pipe g K.   The boiler has a steam-tight iron cover, g L; and at C D in the kier is a wooden grating, a small distance above the cover of the boiler.

At M O is a broad plate of metal, in order to spread the lye over the cloth.   It is hardly necessary to say that the boiler has a furnace, as usual, for similar purposes.

While the lye is at a low temperature, the pump is worked by the mill or steam-engine.   When it is sufficiently heated, the elasticity of the steam forces it up through the valves of the pump, in which case it is disjoined from the moving power.

N P is a copper spout, which is removed at the time of taking the cloth out of the kier.

In order still further to avoid labour, the pumping has been entirely done away with.

A simple modification of the bowking apparatus is shown in *figs.* 111, 112, 113; the first being a vertical section, the second a horizontal section in the line *x*

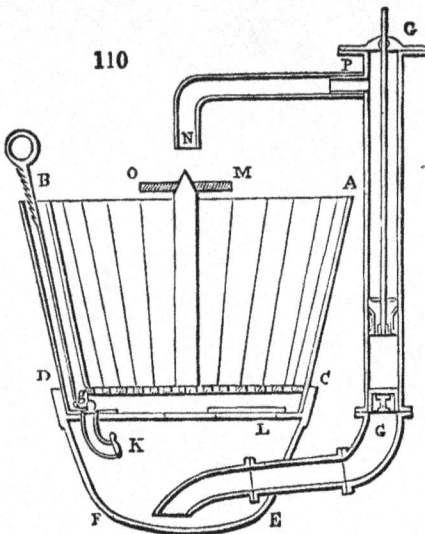

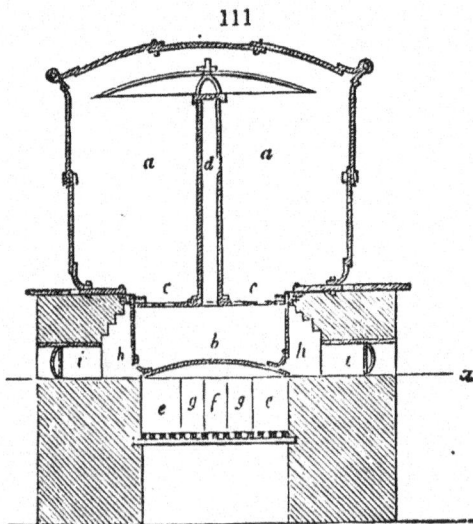

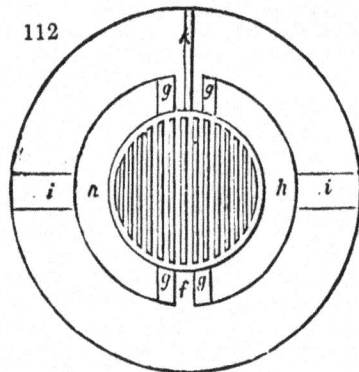

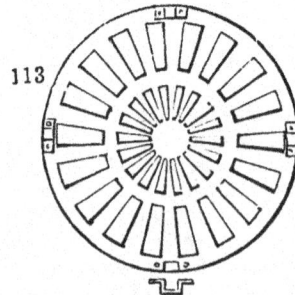

of the first.   It consists of two parts: the upper wide part, *a a*, serves for the reception of the goods, and the lower or pot, *b*, for holding the lye; *c c* is an iron grating, shown apart in *fig.* 113.   The grating has numerous square apertures in the middle of the disc, to which the rising pipe *d* is screwed fast.   The upper cylinder is formed of cast-iron, or of sheet-iron well riveted at the edges; or sometimes of wood, this being secured at its under edge into a groove in the top edge of the lye-pot. The mouth of the cylinder is constructed usually of sheet-iron. $e\ e$ is the fire-grate, whose upper surface is shown in *fig.* 111: it is made of cast-iron in three pieces. The flame is parted at f, and passes through the two apertures $g\ g$, into the flues $h\ h$, so as to play round the pot, as is visible in *fig.* 112, and escapes by two outlets into the chimney. The apertures $i\ i$ serve for occasionally cleaning out the flues $h\ h$, and are, at other times, shut with an iron plate. In the partition f, which separates the two openings $g\ g$, and the flues $h\ h$, running round the pot, there is a circular space at the point marked with k, *fig.* 112, in which the large pipe for discharging the waste lye is lodged. The upper large cylinder should be encased in wood, with an intermediate space filled with sawdust, to confine the heat. The action of this apparatus is exactly the same as that already explained.

Besides the boiling, bucking, and other apparatus above described, the machinery and utensils used in bleaching are various, according to the business done by the bleacher.

The kier of Messrs. Mather and Platt is very complete. The first figure (114) is the kier when shut or screwed down. The second (115, p. 372) is the section

114

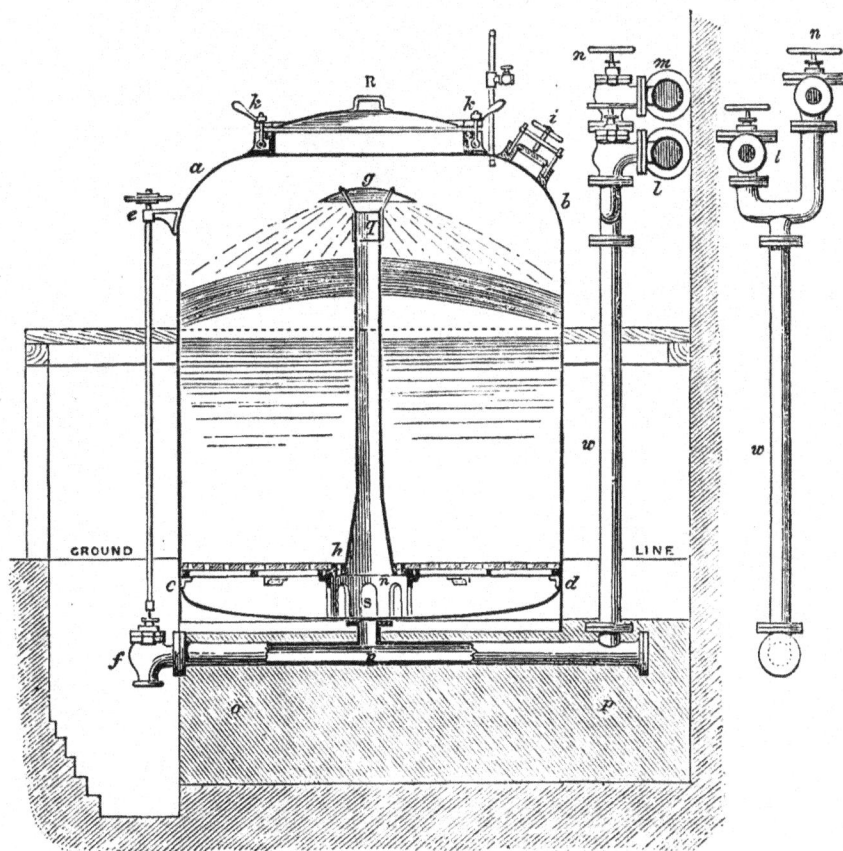

of the kier, which is very like that before given; but in this case it is steam-tight, and heated by steam which issues from a steam-pipe communicating beneath the false bottom. The dangers attending the kier before mentioned are by this means entirely averted, and all the inventions which give the washing liquid a separate and distinct place for heating are at once done away with.

An exact description of these kiers is required. a, b, c, d, represent the body of the kier, which is a cylindrical vessel, generally made of cast-iron, but sometimes of wood, or wrought iron. h represents the false bottom; a cast-iron grating, sometimes covered with boulder stones, and sometimes with wood; g, a cylindrical disc, of wrought-iron, placed on the top of 'puffer-pipe' q, to spread the liquor over the cloth. q, 'puffer-pipe,' standing on false bottom, h. s, cylindrical casting for supporting false bottom and 'puffer-pipe,' whose periphery is 'slotted,' to admit of the liquor passing through. n, cover for kier; the flanch on which this cover rests is grooved a little to admit of 'gasking' being inserted, so as to form a 'joint.' k, k, swivel-bolts, holding down the cover. i, a small aperture, covered with a lid capable of being removed easily, to enable the attendant to see that the cloth does not rise too high in the kier to endanger its working; if such happens, he checks the steam until

115

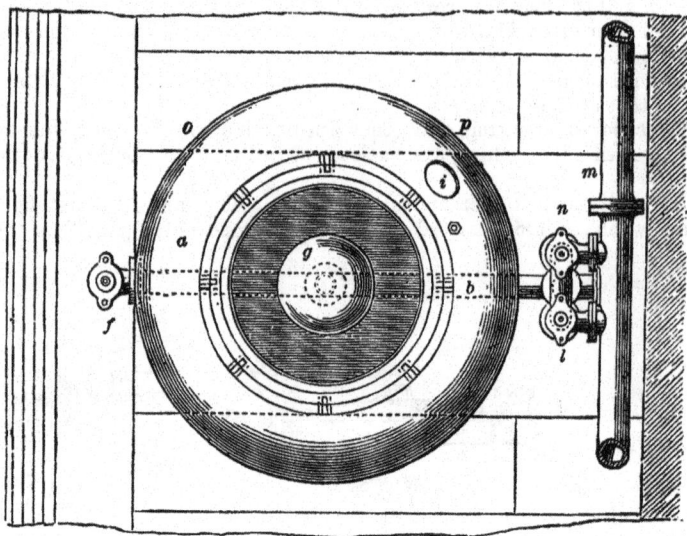

the cloth settles, after which it does not again attempt to rise. n, steam-valve; l, water-valve; both communicate with pipe w, leading to kier. p, pipe communicating with kier for supplying steam and water—also serves as escape-pipe; f, escape-valve for letting off kier; e, wheel for opening ditto; m, steam-pipe from boiler. o, p, foundation for kier.

The process of cleansing is very various. Some use lime for the first process; some use soda alone; some use them mixed. Of course when carbonate of soda and lime are used, caustic soda is at once formed, and the carbonate of lime is left idle. The practices and fancies of bleachers are numerous; and we have only to say that the principle consists in the use of alkaline lyes. Some use lime to the amount of 3 per cent.; others go as high as 10. The lime is slaked first and a portion thrown in; a portion of cloth is laid upon it, and a portion of lime again covers that: but on no account must the goods be allowed to lie in contact with the atmosphere and the lime.

When removed from the kiers the goods must be washed. Now if they are to be washed in dash-wheels, it is needful that they be in separate pieces, and in this state they are sometimes boiled in the kiers; but if they are to be washed in the washing-machines, they are lifted out of the kier in the same manner as a piece of string is drawn out of the canister in which the coil is kept.

M. Metz, of Heidelberg, has attempted to perform the work of boiling by merely extracting the air from the cloth. For this purpose the cloth is simply put into a strong upright cylinder, the top screwed down, and the air taken out by an air-pump. We have no knowledge as to the advantages gained by this process, or whether it has been found actually capable of putting cloth in a condition to be bleached for a very fastidious market.

High-Pressure Steam-Kiers.—These kiers greatly hasten the process of bleaching, and at the same time improve it. *Fig.* 116 (p. 373) is an elevation showing the original arrangement of these (which are recommended to be made of strong boiler-plate iron). One of these is shown in section. a and b are the kiers; c is a perforated platform, on which the goods to be bowked are laid; k k is the pipe connecting the bottom of the kier b with the top of the adjoining kier a; and l l, the corresponding pipe connecting the opposite ends of the kiers a and b; m m are draw-off cocks, connected with the pipes k and l, by which the kiers can be emptied of spent liquor, water, &c.; n and o are ordinary two-way taps, by which the steam is admitted into the respective kiers from the main pipe, p, and the reversing of which shuts off the steam communication, and admits the bowking liquor as it becomes expelled from the adjoining kier; *q* is a blowing-off valve or tap; *r*, the pipe through which the bowking liquor enters into the kier; *s*, manhole (closed by two cross-bars, secured by bolts and nuts) through which the goods are introduced and removed; *t t* are gauges

116

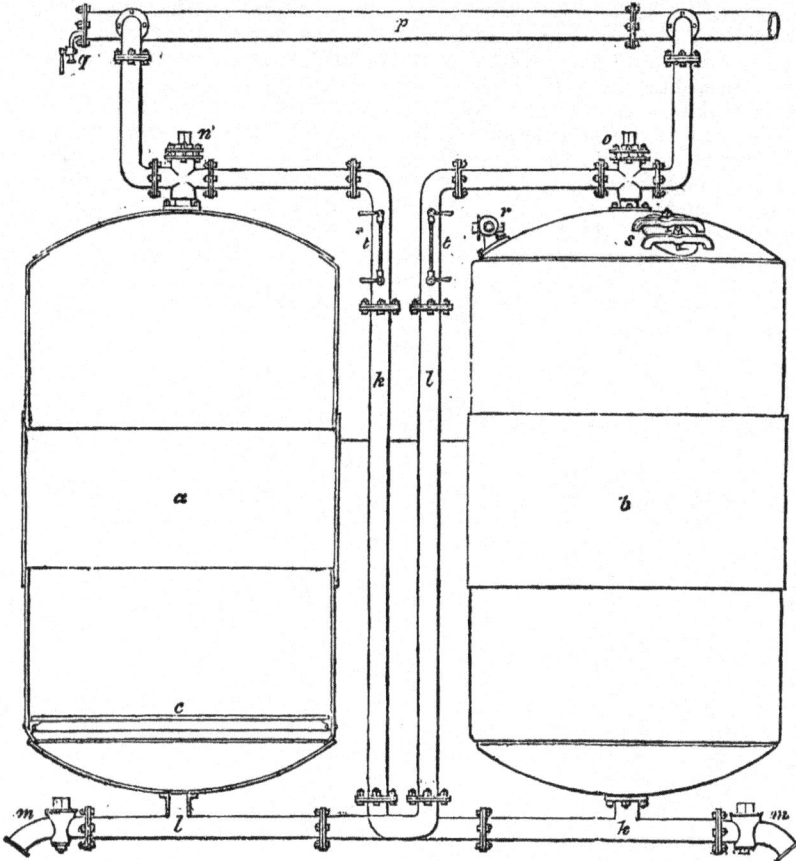

by which it is ascertained when the liquor has passed from one kier and has entered the other.

The process adopted for bleaching is as follows:

1. The box or water-trough of the washing-machine is then half filled with milk of lime of considerable consistence, and the goods are run through it, being carried forward by the winches and deposited in the kiers. The whole of the cloth in a kier is in one length, and a boy enters the vessel to lay it in regular folds until the kier is filled. All the cloth before entering the kier must pass through the lime.

2. When the kiers are filled, a grid of movable bars is laid on the top of the cloth, and the manhole of the kiers is closed. High-pressure steam is then admitted at the top; this presses down the goods and removes the lime-water, which is drawn off at the bottom. At the same time the air is also removed from the goods and replaced by steam. When this is driven off, and nothing but steam issues from the tap at the bottom, 40 lbs. of lime, which have been previously mixed with 600 gallons of water, are introduced into the first kier in a boiling state. High-pressure steam is again admitted, which forces the lime-liquor through the goods to the bottom of the vessel, then up the tube *l*, and on to the goods in the second kier. The tap is then closed which admits steam into the first kier, and the steam is now sent into the second. The same process occurs, only in this case the liquid is sent again on to the top of the goods in the first kier. This process is continued about eight hours.

High-pressure and Distributing Kiers.—Mr Barlow has effected an important improvement in his original high-pressure kiers by the addition of distributors.

Fig. 117 (p. 374) is an elevation showing a pair of kiers, fitted with distributors, &c. A and B are the kiers (which it is preferable to make of strong boiler-plate iron), the kier A being shown in section, and exhibiting the distributors, &c.

At the bottom of the kier is a plate of an umbrella shape, *c*. This plate spreads over about three-fourths of the bottom of the kier; it is perforated with holes all around its outer ridge, at $d\ d$, which rests upon the bottom of the kier; all the rest of the plate being solid. This plate is fastened in the centre to an iron block, e, which stands upon the bottom of the kier in the centre, over the outlet hole. The block e is pigeonholed at the bottom, so as to allow the liquor to pass from the kier. A socket is left in the upper part of the block e, to admit the insertion of the distributor f. This distributor is made of dimensions corresponding to the size of the kier; it is solid for some distance from the bottom, and above that is hollow and perforated as full as possible with holes until within a few inches of the top of the kier, where it is connected with the tap g (an ordinary two-way tap, which admits either steam or liquor, or shuts off both) by an inlet pipe, which dips for some distance inside the distributor. $o\ o$ is the pipe connecting the top of the kier A with the bottom of kier B, and $p\ p$ is the pipe which connects the top of kier B with the bottom of kier A; $q\ q$ are steam-pipes from the main pipe r; m is the manway, through which the goods are introduced and removed; n the pipe and tap, through which the working liquor enters the kier; $s\ s$ are gauges, by which it is seen when the liquor has passed from one kier and has entered the other; $k\ k$ are draw-off taps connected with the pipes o and p, by which the kiers can be emptied of spent liquor, water, &c.

117   118

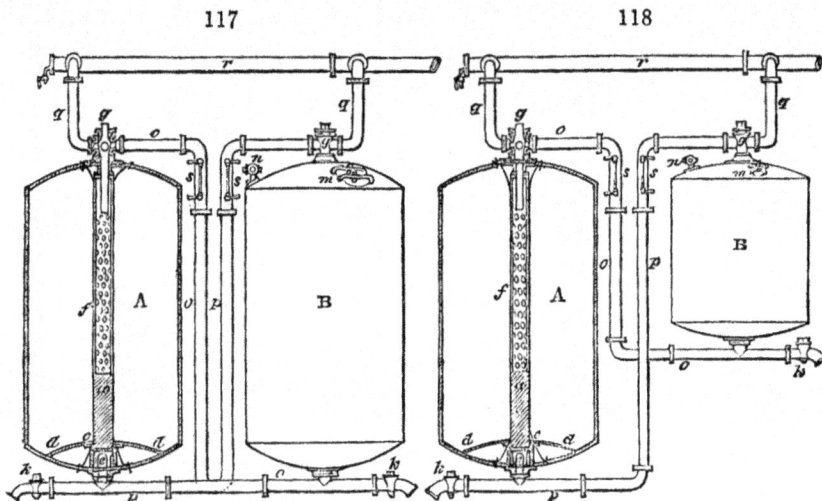

Fig. 118 is a modification of *fig.* 117. The various parts of the kiers correspond with the description of *fig.* 117; the principle and mode of working are precisely the same the only difference is, that kier B is reduced in size to about one-third that of kier A; it is not charged with goods and is only intended to receive the liquor when forced through the goods in kier A. The liquor is boiled in kier B by a modified distributor; and this is repeated until the goods in kier A are sufficiently worked.

This modification is only recommended where small quantities are done, and the kiers required would be too small for working in conveniently.

The distributors give a circulation of liquor and steam from the centre of the kiers to the goods all around, while by the action of the umbrella-plate the liquor is prevented escaping until all the goods are thoroughly saturated with it every time the liquor is forced through them; they also greatly accelerate the circulation of the liquor through the goods, and there is no necessity for anything being laid upon the goods to keep them in their place. The kiers may be crammed full of goods, and either high or low pressure steam may be used in working them.

The process adopted for bleaching is as follows: it is the shortest and simplest in use.

1. After singeing, the water-box or trough of the washing-machine is half filled with milk of lime of considerable consistence, and the goods are run through it, being carried forward by the winders and deposited in the kiers, a boy being in each kier, who lays the goods in regular folds until the kier is filled.

2. When the kiers are filled, the manholes are closed. High-pressure steam is then admitted at the top; this presses down the goods and removes the lime-water, which is drawn off at the bottom; at the same time the air is also removed from the goods and replaced by steam. When this is driven off and nothing but steam issues from the tap at the bottom, 40 lbs. lime, which have been previously mixed with 600 gallons of boiling water, are introduced into the first kier in a boiling state. High-

pressure steam is again admitted, which forces the lime-liquor through the goods to the bottom of the vessel, then up the pipe *o*, and on to the goods in the second kier. The tap is then closed, which admits steam into the first kier, and the steam is now sent into the second. The same process occurs, only in this case the liquid is sent again on to the top of the goods in the first kier. This process is continued about five hours.

In this method each 7,000 lbs. of cloth take into the kiers 2 cwts. of lime, which is equally distributed. The clear lime-water which is blown out of the steam at the commencement contains only 3 to 4 lbs. of lime in solution. At the close of the operation the liquor has a specific gravity of $3\frac{1}{2}$ to $4°$ Twaddle (1017·5 to 1020), instead of half that amount, or $1\frac{1}{2}$ to $2°$ Twaddle (1007·5 to 1010), as is usual.

3. When the liming is completed the steam-pressure in the kiers is removed, the manway opened, and the cloth in the kier attached to the washing-machine, which draws the goods out of the kiers and washes them.

4. The pieces are then passed by the winches through the souring machine, or soured by having muriatic acid of $2°$ Twaddle (1010) pumped upon them. They must remain with the acid two to three hours, either steeped in it, or after having passed through it.

5. Again attach the cloth to the washing-machine, and wash it well, passing it on by winches, as before, into the kier.

6. Introduce steam and drive off the air and the cold water; these are let out by the tap at the bottom: add then 210 lbs. of soda-ash and 70 lbs. of resin, boiled in 600 gallons of water, for 7,000 lbs. of cloth. Work the kiers by driving the liquid from one to the other as before; about five hours is a sufficient time. These proportions of soda may be varied. If the cloth is very strong a little more may be used (or if the cloth has been printed upon in the grey state, from having been used to cover the blanket of the calico-printing machine).

7. After this the cloth is passed through the washing-machine, and then submitted to chloride of lime. This may be done either by the machine or by pumping. In either case it is an advantage to warm the bleaching-liquid up to $80°$ or $90°$ F. The strength of the solution when the machine is used may be about $\frac{1}{2}°$ Twaddle, or 1002·5 specific gravity; but if the pump is used it must be much weaker. When the bleaching is for finishing white, milk of lime is added to the chloride, in order to retard the operation; the goods are also washed from the bleaching-liquor before souring them. This causes a smaller escape of chlorine, and is a more careful method: it tends to preserve the headings, or the coloured threads, which are often put into the ends of pieces of cloth in order to see if the bleaching has been performed roughly or not. The original use of this has almost been forgotten, but these headings are still carefully preserved. This method preserves also the cloth, which is also less apt to be attacked by the chlorine.

If the cloth has been well managed, it will be almost white when it leaves the second kier containing the resinate of soda; it will therefore require very little decolourising. If the goods have been printed on, more chloride will be needed. The cloth should lie from two to eight hours in the liquor, or after saturation with it. The action is quickened if warmth is used. They are soured then, as before, in muriatic and sulphuric acid, at $2°$ Twaddle, for three or four hours; then wash for drying.

The patentee claims for these kiers considerable advantages over the old, amongst others—that they are not more costly—occupy less room, and whilst the goods are more thoroughly 'bottomed' or cleansed, considerable saving is effected in fuel, water, labour, chemicals, and time. 'As regards boiling of goods in bleaching, there is, as compared with the ordinary kier, a saving of three-fourths of the coal by using these kiers.' They are perfectly safe in their action and the fibre is not 'tendered.'

From what has been said, it will be seen that the operations of the bleacher are not so numerous as at first sight appears, when we call every washing a separate process; and although it really is so, it is managed so rapidly that it can scarcely be said to occupy time, and as it is carried on at the same time as the other processes, it scarcely can be said to give trouble. The work may be divided into—

1. Singeing. 2. Bowking with lime. 3. Washing, souring, and washing. 4. Bowking with resinate of soda. 5. Washing and chlorinating. 6. Souring, washing, and drying.

Steeping.—Instead of boiling in the kier at first, the goods are sometimes, though now rarely, steeped from one to two days in water, from $100°$ to $150°$ F., for the purpose of loosening the gummy, glutinous, and pasty materials attached to the cloth. Fermentation ensues, and this process is dangerous, as the action of the ferment sometimes extends to the goods, especially if they are piled up in a great heap without being previously washed. The spots of grease on the insoluble soaps become thereby capable of resisting the caustic alkalis, and are rendered in some measure indelible; an effect due, it is believed, to the acetic and carbonic acids generated during fermentation. Some persons throw spent lyes into the fermenting vats to counteract the acids. The spots of grease are chiefly to be found in hand-loom goods, and the difficulty concerning the fats is not therefore commonly felt where power-loom goods are chiefly used, as in Lancashire.

Washing.—If the cloth is to be washed without having the pieces strung together, the following methods may be adopted. The stocks are still used, but not in any large establishments in Lancashire.

Figs. 119, 120, represent a pair of wash-stocks. A A are called the stocks or feet. They are suspended on iron pivots at B, and receive their motion from wipers

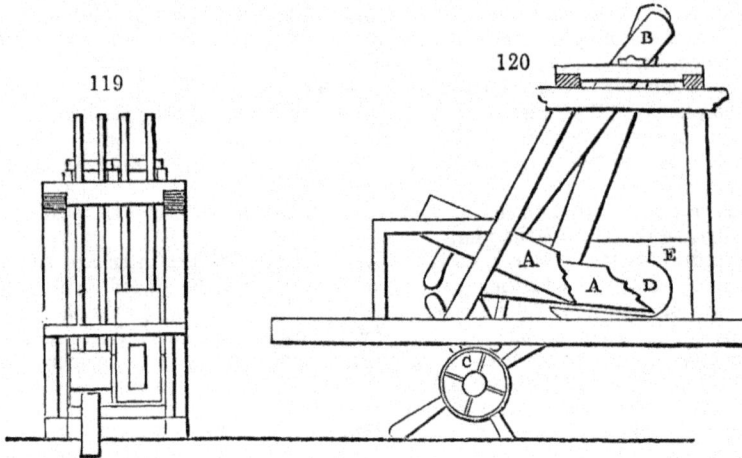

on the revolving-shaft C. The cloth is laid in at D, and, by the alternate strokes of the feet, and the curved form of the turnhead E, the cloth is washed and gradually turned. At the same time an abundant stream of water rushes on the cloth throughout holes in the upper part of the turnhead. Wash-stocks are much used in Scotland and in Ireland. In the latter country they are often made with double feet, suspended above and below two turnheads, and wrought with cranks instead of wipers. Wash-stocks, properly constructed, make from 24 to 30 strokes per minute.

This mode of washing is now entirely given up in Lancashire, where a preference is given to dash-wheels and washing-machines with squeezers. The dash are small water-wheels, the inside of which is divided into four compartments, and closed up, leaving only a hole in each compartment for putting in the cloth. There are, besides, small openings for the free admission and egress of the water employed in cleansing. The cloth, by the motion of the wheel, is raised up in one part of the revolution of the wheel; while, by its own weight, it falls in another. This kind of motion is very effectual in washing the cloth, while, at the same time, it does not injure its strength. The plan, however, where economy of water is of any importance, is very objectionable; because the wheel must move at by far too great a velocity to act to advantage as a water-wheel.

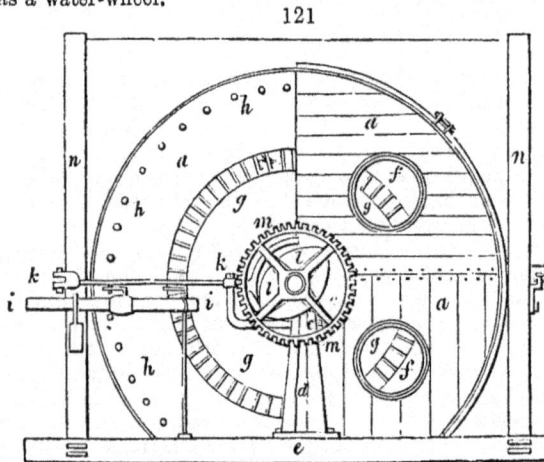

The wash or dash-wheel, now driven by steam-power in all good bleach- and print-works, is represented in *fig.* 121, upon the left side in a back view, and upon the right side in a front view (the sketch being halved). *Fig.* 122 is a ground plan.

a a is the washing-wheel; *b b* its shaft-ends; *c c* their brass bearings or plummer-blocks, supported upon the iron pillars *d d*. The frame is made of strong beams of wood, *e e*, bound together by cross-bars with mortices. *f f*, two of the circular apertures, each leading to a quadrantal compartment within the dash-wheel. **In** the back view (the left-hand half of the figure) the brass grating, $g\,g$, of a cur-vilinear form is seen, through which the jets of water are admitted into the cavity of the wheel; $h\,h$ are the round orifices, through which the foul water runs off, as each quadrant passes the lower part of its re-volution; i, a water-pipe, with a stopcock for regu-lating the washing-jets; $k\,k$, the lever for throwing the driving-crab l, or coupling-box, into or out of gear with the shaft of the wheel. This machine is so constructed, that the water-cock is opened or shut by the same lever-age which throws the wheel into or out of gear. m, a wheel, fixed upon the round extremity of

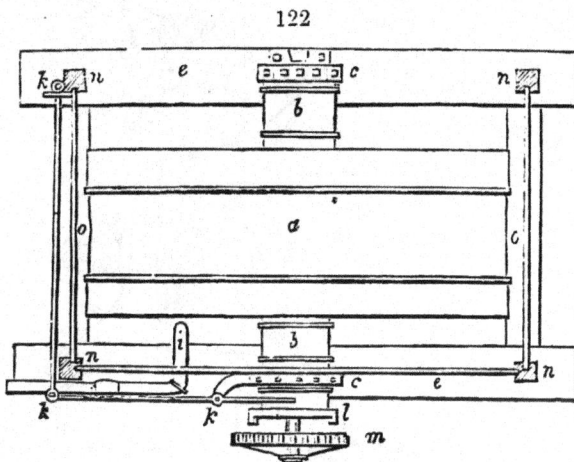

the shaft of the dash-wheel which works into the toothed pinion connected with the prime mover. When the end of the lever k, whose fork embraces the coupling-box upon the square part of the shaft, is pushed forwards or backwards, it shifts the clutch into or out of gear with the toothed wheel m. In the latter case, this wheel turns with its pinion without affecting the dash-wheel. $n\,n$, holdfasts fixed upon the wooden frame, to which the boards $o\,o$ are attached, for preventing the water from being thrown about by the centrifugal force.

The dash-wheel is generally from 6 to 7 feet in diameter, about 30 inches wide, and requires the power of about two horses to drive it.

A dash-wheel has one piece of cloth in each of the four compartments; these are washed in eight minutes, being 30 pieces an hour, or 300 pieces a day; sometimes two pieces are put in, when double the time is given. It generally requires 60 gallons of water per minute to feed it, 36,000 gallons a day, or 120 to a piece. Always after washing, the squeezers are applied, as they remove at once the super-fluous water.

The machine made by Mr. Mather (*figs.* 123 and 124) washes 800 pieces per hour, or 8,000 pieces per day of ten hours, using 400 gallons per minute, or 120,000 gallons per day, or 20 gallons to a piece. This class of machine is now in its turn superseding the dash-wheel.

This washing-machine will be understood by the general plan (*fig.* 124, and corre-sponding section, *fig.* 123). a and b represent the squeezing-bowls. a, is 18 inches diameter and 8 feet 3 inches long; it is made of deal timber. (The lapping of strong canvas at a'' is for the purpose of giving the 'out-coming' pieces an extra squeeze, in order to prepare them for the kiers.) b is 24 inches diameter and of the same length as a, making 100 revolutions per minute; it is generally made of deal, sycamore, however, being better. c, d, a strong wooden rail, in which pegs are placed in order to guide the cloth in its spiral form from the edge to the centre of the machine. h, h, the water-trough, through which the piece passes round the roller R. p (*fig.* 123), water-pipe. t, water-tap. m, m, pot-eyes, which may be adjusted to any angle, to guide and regulate the tension of the piece on entering the machine. l, side frame, for carrying bowls, &c. g, engine (with cylinder, 8 inches diameter) and gearing for driving machine. w, weight and lever for regulating pressure on the bowl.

This machine washes 800 pieces per hour, and requires 400 gallons of water per minute. It will serve also to represent the *chemick* and *souring* machine, the only difference being that the bowls are 3 feet 6 inches, instead of 8 feet 3 inches, in length.

The *chemick* and *sour* are brought by turns into the trough, or into similar separate troughs, by a leaden pipe from the mixing cisterns, and are run in to 6 or 8 inches deep.

The washing-machine of Mr. Bridson (*fig.* 125, p. 379) is worth attention. In its action the course of the cloth in the water is easily seen; it is chiefly horizontal. This motion had been given by Hellewell and Fearn in 1856; but they had a very com-plicated machine, and they did not attain the flapping motion which is given to the cloth when it becomes suddenly loose, and is driven violently against the board $a\,a$

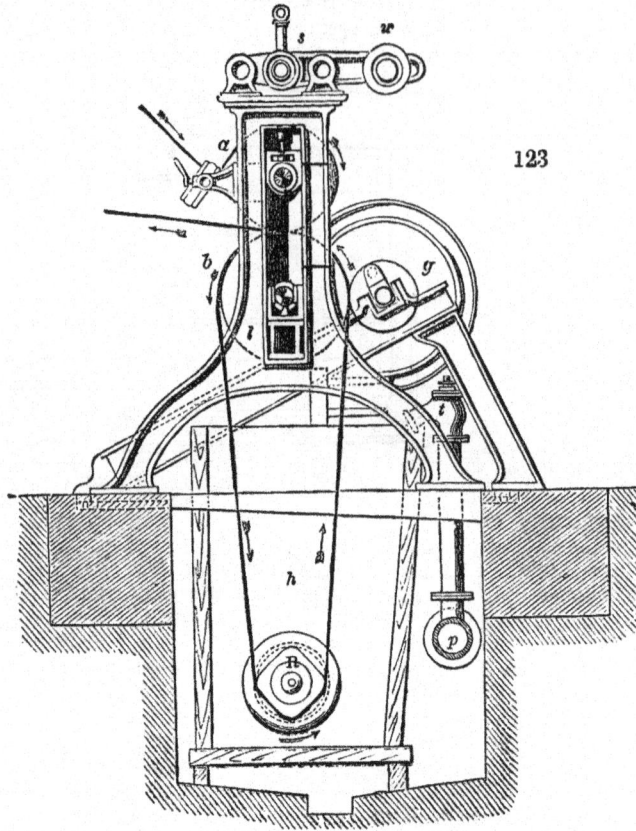

123

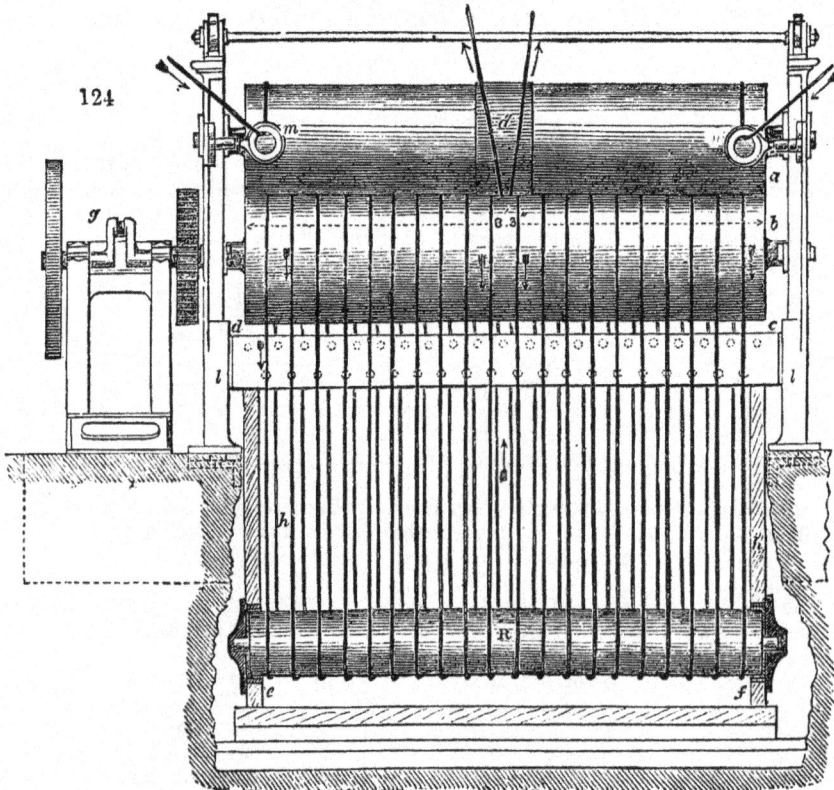

124

as often as *b c* and *e d* are in one line. It is not shown by the drawing that the cloth passes eight times round these wheels. There is a constant stream of water from the pipe *f*, which is flattened at the mouth about one and a half inch in one diameter,

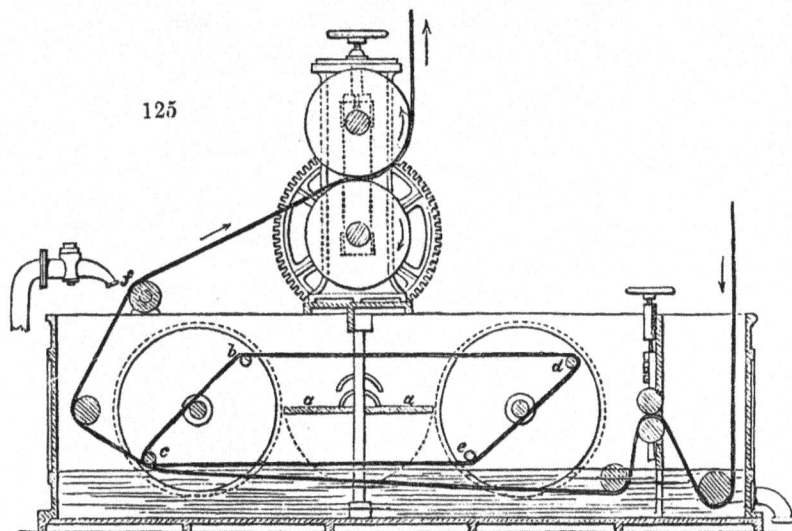

and about 10 inches in the other. This machine can wash 900 pieces in an hour. It requires about twice as much water as a dash-wheel, but washes seven and a half times more pieces. Its length is 9 feet.

Souring.—After boiling in the first kier and washing, the goods are soured in muriatic acid of 1010· specific gravity, or 6½ gallons of the usual acid, which contains 33 per cent. of real acid, mixed with 100 gallons of water. This is equal to 2° Twaddle. Muriatic acid may be replaced by sulphuric acid of 1024· specific gravity, *i.e.* 3½ gallons liquid acid to 100 of water;—or the amount of the acid may be doubled in either case, and a shorter time allowed for the souring. The souring is performed in wooden or stone cisterns, where the cloth is laid regularly as it falls over one of the rollers of the calender;—or it is passed through the acid solution by the movement of the calender in the same manner as described in the process of washing. If this method is used, it is allowed to lie on the stillages from two to three hours to allow the acid to act. The acid decomposes any lime-soap formed, and washes out the lime. Hydrochloric or muriatic acid has been preferred in the process described, as the chloride of calcium is so much more soluble than the sulphate. After souring, of course the goods must be thoroughly washed as before.

The sixth operation with soda removes the remaining fatty materials. If lime be used, it may be allowed to settle; and it is better to allow it to do so, and thus to use pure caustic soda, which will with the resin remove the impurities in a more soluble form. If, instead of adding 170 lbs. of soda crystals to 600 gallons of water, 4·6 lbs. of liquid caustic soda of specific gravity 1320· were added, the effect would be the same.

The solution of resin and carbonate of soda is a half-formed soap, which is considered to act beneficially in removing the soluble matter. It would not appear, from theory, to be capable of doing so well as the soda which has its carbonic acid removed; but tender goods will not allow the action of caustic soda, and the carbonate is therefore safer.

Powder-bleaching.—Chloride of lime is added in stone vessels where the goods are allowed to lie. It is universally called *chemick* in the manufactories. The strength used at Brickacre is half a degree Twaddle, or 1002·5. This is sometimes very much increased, so as to be even 5° in some establishments, according to the goods bleached; but it is not safe to allow the cloth to lie long in such strong solutions. In such cases it is needful to pass them rapidly through with the calender, so as to soak them thoroughly, and then to pass them on to the acid, and forward to be washed. It may be remarked that the use of the calender for these operations renders it possible to use strong solutions, even for tender goods, as there is no time given for injurious action on the fibre.

Great care is to be taken to make the solution of the chloride of lime perfectly clear. The powder does not readily wet with water, and it must therefore be pressed or agitated. This may be done by putting it in a revolving barrel with water, until complete saturation of the powder with moisture ; the amount required is then thrown into the cistern, and the insoluble matter allowed to sink. This insoluble matter must not be allowed to come into contact with the cloth, as it will be equal of course to a concentrated solution of the liquor, and will produce rottenness, or *burn the cloth*, so as to leave holes. When removing from the trough, the cloth is drawn through squeezing rollers, which press out any excess of chloride of lime.

Squeezing.—The squeezing rollers or squeezers, for discharging the greater part of the water or any liquid from the yarns and goods in the process of bleaching, are represented in *figs.* 126, 127, the former being a side view, to show how the roller

126   127

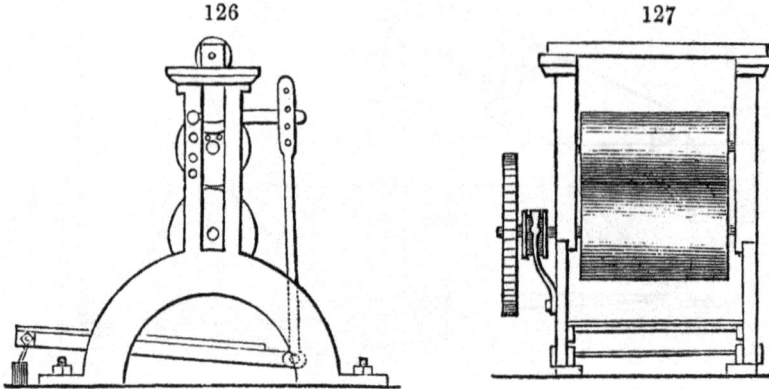

gudgeons lie in the slots of the frame, and how the shaft of the upper roller is pressed downward by a weighted lever, through a vertical junction rod, joined at the bottom to a nearly horizontal bar, on whose end the proper weight is hung. In *fig.* 128, these rollers, of birch-wood, are shown in face ; the under one receiving motion through

128

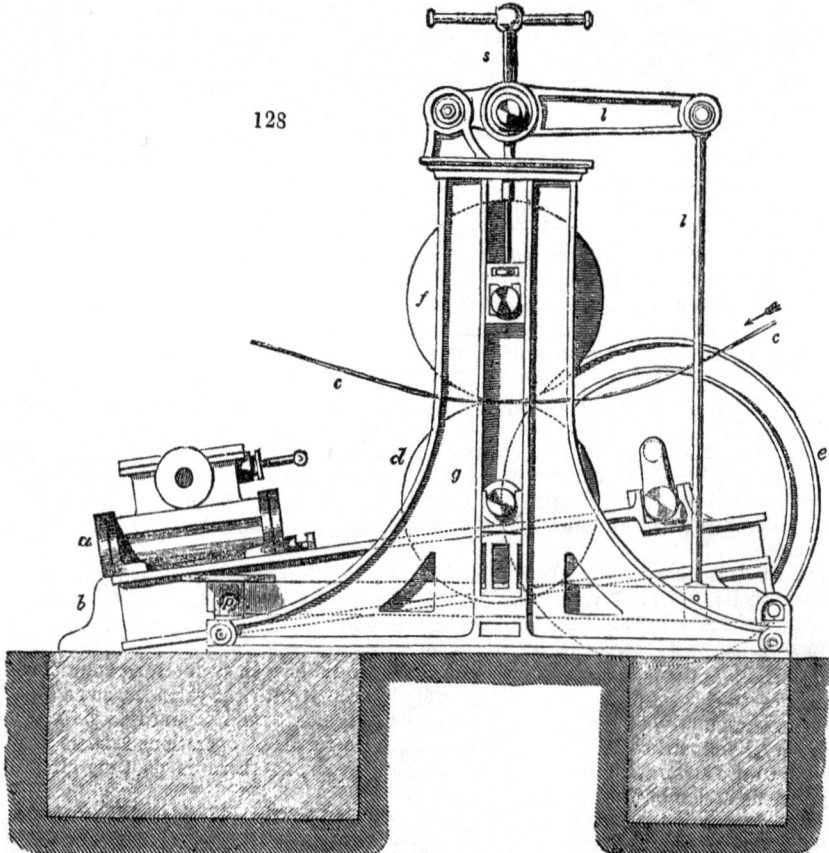

the toothed wheel on its shaft from any suitable power of water or steam. Upon the shaft of the latter, between the toothed wheel and the roller, the lever and pulley for putting the machine into and out of gear is visible. The under roller makes about 25 revolutions in the minute, by which time three pieces of goods, stitched endwise, measuring 28 yards each, may be run through the machine, from a water-trough on one side to a wooden grating upon the other.

A squeezing machine, with a small engine attached, is shown in *fig.* 128, for the drawing of which we are again indebted to the makers, Messrs. Mather and Platt.

d, f, represent the squeezing-bowls. They are as large in diameter as possible, and are generally made of sycamore; but the bottom one is better made of highly compressed cotton. *a, b,* are the engine and frame for driving; *g,* frame for carrying bowls; *l, l,* compound levers for regulating the pressure; *s* is a screw for the same purpose, and *c* is the cloth passing through the bowls.

The white-squeezers, or those used before drying, should have a box, supplied with hot water, fixed so that the piece may pass through it before going to the nip of the bowl.

When the goods are run through, they are carried off upon a grated. wheelbarrow in a nearly dry state, and transferred to the spreading machine, called at Manchester a *candroy.* In many bleach-works, however, the creased pieces are pulled straight by the hands of women, and are then strongly beat against a wooden stock to smooth out the edges. This being done, a number of pieces are stitched endwise together, preparatory to being mangled.

This squeezing machine is small, but, as will be seen, the rollers are introduced so as to act as long and as rapidly as cloth of whatever length is drawn through them.

The following figure (129) represents a pair of squeezers, for squeezing the cloth after several of the processes named, and are shown as being driven by a small

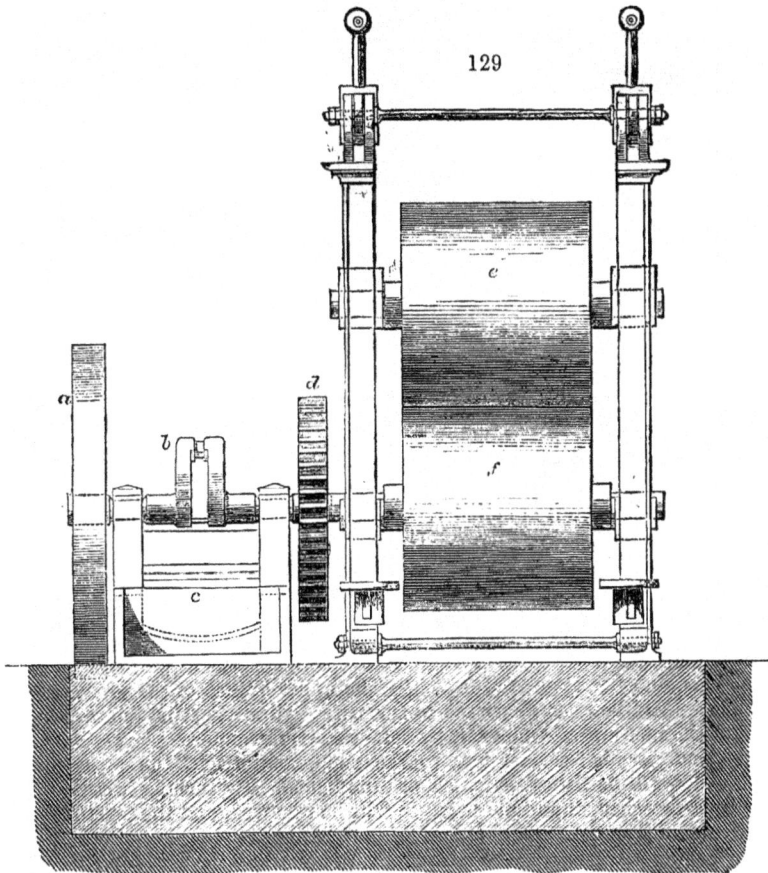

high-pressure engine. *a* is the fly-wheel of engine; *b,* crank of ditto; *c,* frame of engine; *d,* spur-wheels connecting the engine and squeezers; *e* and *f,* sycamore squeezing bowls.

The cloth when passed over the steamed rollers is not dry; but it is not smooth and ready for the market. If the cloth is wanted for printing, no further operation is needed; but if to be sold as white calico, it is finished by being starched and calendered.

The starch at large works is prepared by the bleachers themselves. At Messrs. Bridson's it is made with the very greatest care from flour. Of course it would be more expensive for them to buy it, as the manufacturer would dry it, and they would require to dissolve it. They are able also, in this manner, to obtain the purest starch. This is mixed with blue, according to the finish of the goods. A roller, which dips into the starch, lays it regularly and evenly on the cloth in the same manner as mordants are communicated in calico-printing, whilst other rollers expel the excess of the starch. The cloth is then dried over warm cylinders, or by passing into a heated apartment. It receives the final finish generally by the calender; but muslins receive a peculiar treatment.

Calender.—*Fig.* 131 is a cross-section of this machine, and *figs.* 130, 132, are front views broken off. The goods are first rolled upon the wooden cylinder *a*, near the

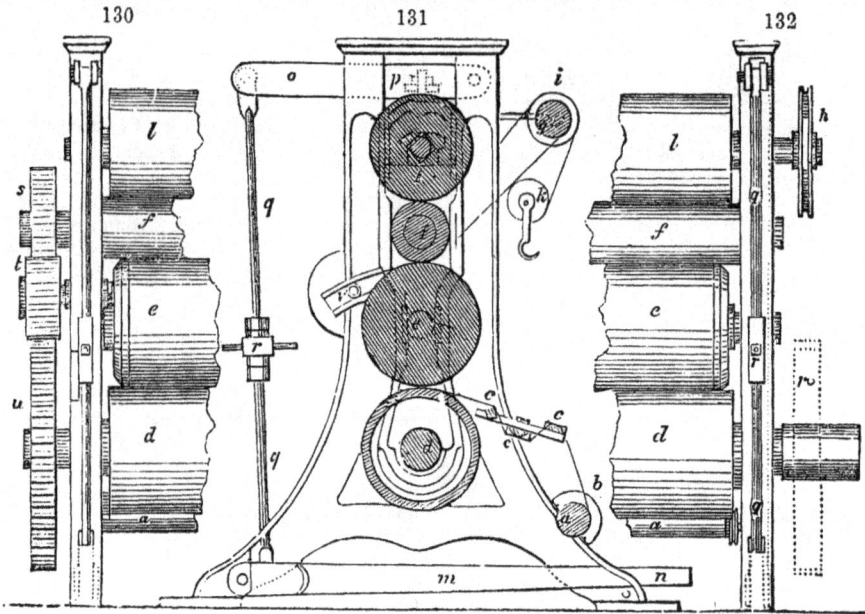

ground; by the tension-roller, *b*, upon the same cylinder, the goods receive a proper degree of stretching in the winding-off. They then pass over the spreading-bars, *c c c*, by which they are still more distended; next round the hollow iron cylinder, *d*, 16 inches diameter, and the paper cylinder, *e*, of like dimensions; thence they proceed under the second massive iron cylinder, *f*, of 8 inches diameter, to be finally wound about the projecting wooden roller, *g*. This is set in motion by the pulleys *h* (*fig.* 132), and *i* (*fig.* 131), and receives its proper tension from the hanging roller *k*; *l* is a pressing cylinder of 14 inches' diameter, made of plane-tree wood. By its means we can at all times secure an equal degree of pressure, which would be hardly possible did the weighted lever press immediately upon two points of the calender-rollers. The compression exercised by the cylinders may be increased at pleasure by the bent lever, *m*, weights being applied to it at *n*. The upper branch of the lever, *o*, is made fast, by screws and bolts at *p*, to the upper press-cylinder. The junction-leg, *q*, is attached to the intermediate piece, *r*, by left- and right-handed screws, so that according as that piece is turned round to the right or the left, the pressure of the weighted roller will be either increased or diminished. By turning it still more, the piece will get detached, the whole pressure will be removed, and the press-roller may be taken off, which is the main object of this mechanism.

The unequable movement of the cylinders is produced by the wheels *s, t, u*, of which the undermost has 69, the uppermost 20, and the carrier-wheel, *t*, either 33, 32, or 20 teeth, according to the difference of speed required. The carrier-wheel is bolted on at *v*, and adjusted in its proper place by means of a slot. To the undermost iron cylinder, the first motion is communicated by any power, for which purpose either a rigger (driving pulley) is applied to its shaft at *u*, or a crank motion. If it be desired to operate with a heated calender, the undermost hollow cylinder may be filled with hot steam, admitted through a stuffing-box at one end, and discharged through a stuffing-box at the other, or by a red-hot iron roller.

Before passing through the press they are slightly damped; this is done by a roller of brushes, which dips into the water, and throws it regularly on the cloth. They are then subjected to the powerful pressure of the calender rollers. The calendered pieces, by the powerful pressure of the rollers, are smooth and somewhat shining. There can be no doubt that cloth in this state looks to the best advantage. The pieces must, however, be put into a compact form. This is done by folding them into parcels, which are pressed by hydraulic power into firm and solid masses. Each parcel has the mark of the manufacturer, or any device that he may choose to have, stamped upon it, or bound round it.

Finishing.—Pure starch is not always used for the purpose of finishing. Fine clay, gypsum, or Spanish white is mixed with the cloth; and if weight is desired to be given, sulphate of baryta is employed. Silicate of soda was patented for this purpose, but its use has not been attended with success. Freedom from colour is of course a requisite property in whatever be added, or the excellency of the bleach is impaired. There can, however, be no doubt, that too much attention is given to this finish for home goods, or for all purposes which require the goods to be washed: they assume a solidity of appearance which they do not possess when the finishing material is removed from the pores, and the cloth appears without disguise. In some instances, however, this finish is a peculiarity of the goods, and is almost as important as the cloth itself. For example: in the case of muslins, when they are dried at perfect rest, they have a rigid inelastic feeling, somewhat allied to that of thin laths of wood, and feel very rough to the touch. They are therefore dried by stretching the cloth, and moving the lines of selvage backward and forward, so as to cause the threads of weft to rub against each other and so as to prevent them becoming united as one piece. Goods dried in this manner have a peculiar spring, and such thick muslins are for a time possessed of great elasticity. Several pieces folded up in a parcel spring up from pressure like caoutchouc.

Mr. Ridgeway Bridson invented an apparatus for giving this peculiar finish to muslins. Formerly it was done entirely by the hand, and in Scotland only. Since the invention of this machine, this trade has become a very important one in the Manchester district.

Sometimes goods are finished by the beetle, which acts by repeated hammering. This peculiar action has been transferred to a roller by T. R. Bridson, and called the 'Rotatory Beetle.' It consists of a cylinder having alternately raised and depressed surfaces, and two other cylinders which press upon it, and alternately press the cloth and give a freedom as it passes between the rollers. This is similar to the rise and fall of the hammers or mallets in the beetling process.

Sometimes a stiff finish is wanted; then muslins are dried in the usual way.

Drying.—*Figs.* 133 and 134 represent a drying machine, with eleven cylinders, each 22 inches in diameter, capable of drying 1,000 pieces of bleached calico in a day. *a*, represents cylinders heated with steam; *v*, vacuum-valves in ditto; *f*, frame for carrying cylinders; *c*, folding apparatus; *s*, steam-pipe; *g*, gearing.

133

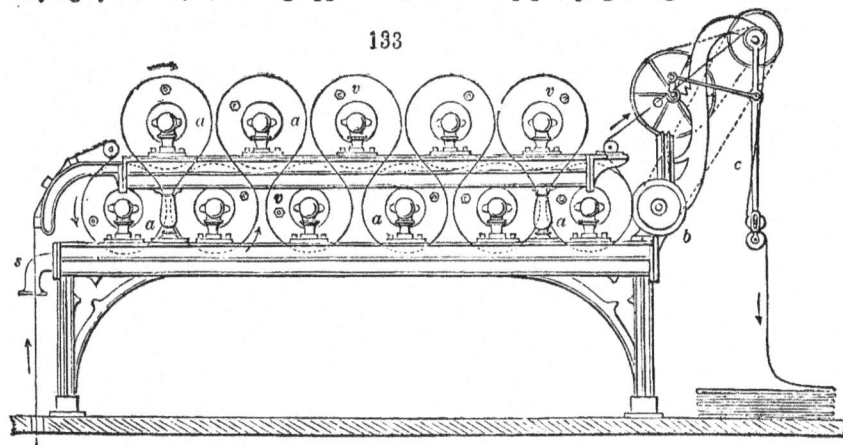

When goods are dried having a raised pattern, such as brocades, or any other, such as striped white shirting, only one side of the cloth is to be exposed; the pattern rises up from the heated surface on which the cloth is dried. For this reason, cylinders such as those just described cannot be used. Large wheels of cast-iron are employed, consisting of two concentric cylinders, between which is a closed space heated by steam. The cloth is by this means heated on one side only, not passing from cylinder to cylinder, in which case the side next to the heating surface would be changed every time. The larger the cylinder or wheel, the more rapid is the drying,

134

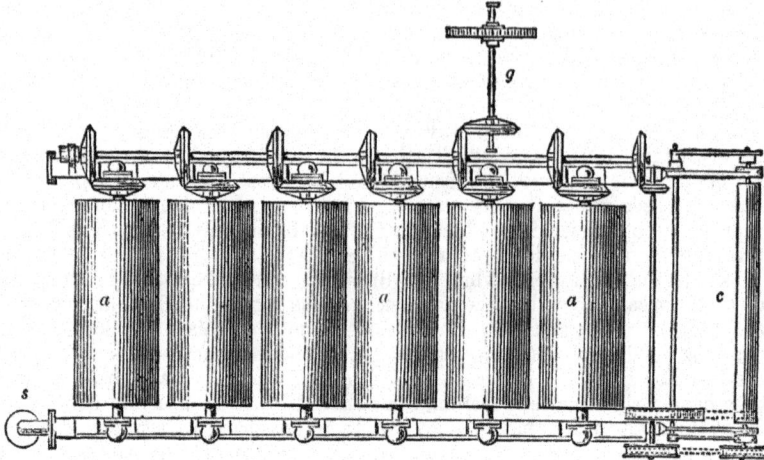

as there is more surface of cloth exposed to it at a time; it can, for the same reason, be turned more rapidly round. Well-finished goods will not rise when heated, except on the pattern. Messrs. Bridson have a large business in jacconets for artificial flowers on account of this peculiar finish. They are formed of a plain cotton cloth, but stand the pressure of hot irons without curling.

No essential difference is made in bleaching muslins, except that sometimes weaker solutions are employed for very tender goods. Mr. Barlow makes no difference as a rule in the strength given in describing his process; with very strong goods, he sometimes uses the liquids stronger.

It is desired occasionally to bleach goods which have coloured threads woven into them, or colours printed on them. In these cases great caution must be used. It is needful to use weak solutions, but more especially not to allow any one process to be continued very long, but rather to repeat it often than to lengthen it. This may be stated as a general rule in the bleaching of goods. It would indeed be possible to do the whole bleaching in one operation, but the cloth would be rotten. This arises from the fact that, at a certain strength, bleaching-liquor or soda is able to destroy the fibre; but another and less strength does not act on the fibre, but only on such substances as colouring-matters. This care is needed when printed goods which have a white ground are treated. The white ground takes up colour enough to destroy its brilliancy, and soaping does not always remove it. The bleaching then is effected by using bleaching-liquor at ½ Twaddle. Some persons put a Turkey-red thread into the ends of the pieces. The original use of this seems to be scarcely known among the manufacturers. It was used as a test of the mode of bleaching employed. If strong solutions be used, which are apt to spoil the cloth, the colour of the dyed threads will be discharged. When the separate system is employed, this is evaded easily; it is the practice to keep the ends containing the red threads out of the liquid, allowing them to rest on the side of the vessel.

Sometimes chlorate of potash is used for the same purpose, souring as with the bleaching-powder. The colours may, in this manner, be made much more brilliant than before, although a little excess will discharge them. A good deal of the effect may be owing to the better white given to the ground. Besides these processes for bleaching, another was at one time introduced, which consisted of immersing the cloth in a solution of caustic alkali, and afterwards steaming in a close vessel. It is not now in use. Alkali of 1020· specific gravity was used.

The new or continuous Process. — This method owes its introduction to David Bentley, of Pendleton, who patented it in 1828. It consists in drawing the goods in one continuous line through every solution with which it is desired to saturate them. This is done by connecting the ends of all the pieces. The motion of rollers draws the chain of cloth thus formed in any desired direction, and through any number of solutions any given number of times. We shall allow him to use his own words.

Fig. 135 is an end view of two such calenders, each having two larger rollers, B and B 1, a smaller driving-roller C, two racks D and D 1, placed upon two cisterns G

135

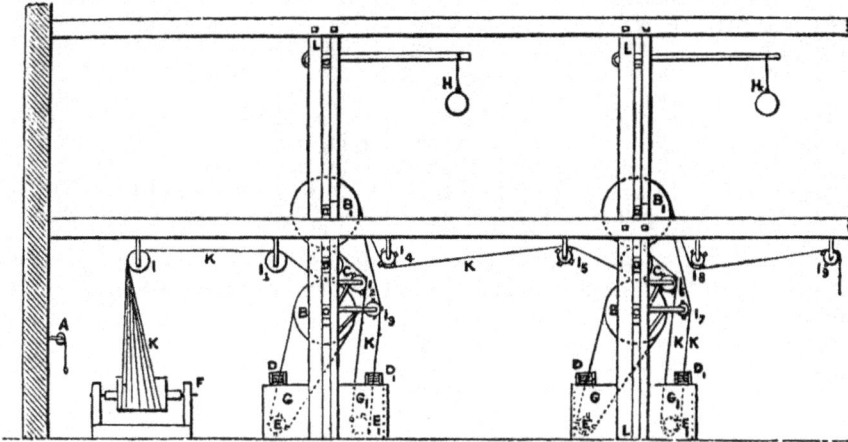

and G 1, inside of which cisterns are two rollers E and E 1, which rollers have four square ribs upon each, to shake the goods as they pass through the cisterns. At F is a frame, upon which the batches of goods are placed upon rollers shown in *fig.* 136, where they are marked K, K, K, K. The calender-cheeks are made fast at the feet, at the middle, and to the top of the building, having levers and weights H to give pressure to the calender-bowls.

Near the end-walls of the building are two rollers, one of which is shown at A; upon each of these is a soft cord used as a guide for conducting the goods through the machinery and cisterns. The operation is commenced by passing one end of the cord through the rollers B and C, down to cistern G, under roller E, through the furthermost division of rack D, and again through calender-rollers at B and C, repeating the same, but observing to keep the cord tight, and to approach one division nearer in rack D each revolution until each division is occupied, when the end must pass over C, under and round B 1, down to and over the guide-roller I 3, through the nearest division of rack D 1 into cistern G 1, under roller E 1, over guide-roller I 2, and again over roller C, under and round B 1. This course must be repeated, observing as before to keep the cord tight, and to receive one division of rack D 1 every revolution, until each division of rack D 1 is occupied, when the end must pass over from B 1 under I 4. The cord now forms a sort of spiral worm round and through the machinery and cisterns, beginning at B, C, and ending at the top of B 1 to I 4, the number of revolutions being governed by the number of divisions in the racks D and D 1, so that if there were fifteen divisions in each rack there would be fifteen revolutions under C, round B through G, under E through D, and fifteen revolutions over C round B 1, over I 3 through D 1 and G 1, under E 1 over I 2, and again over C, passing from the top of B 1 to I 4; and by this means, if one end of the back of goods marked K, and placed upon the frame F (*fig.* 136), is fastened to the end of the guide-cord, the goods will, when the calender is put in motion, be conducted and washed thirty times through the water in the cisterns, and squeezed thirty times through the calenders. As the operation proceeds and the guide-cord passes through the calender, it is wound by hand upon roller A to prevent it from becoming entangled, and to keep it in readiness for the next operation. As soon as the first end of the goods has passed through *fig.* 136, and arrives at the guide-roller I 4, it is detached from the end of the guide-cord and attached to the guide-cord at the other end, or with the opposite set of calenders. After this, by putting these in motion, the goods are washed and squeezed through its cisterns, which cisterns are supplied with hot and strong lime-lye, and the goods passing over guide-roller I 9, they are conveyed over other guide-rollers to be placed for the purpose, and taken down

136

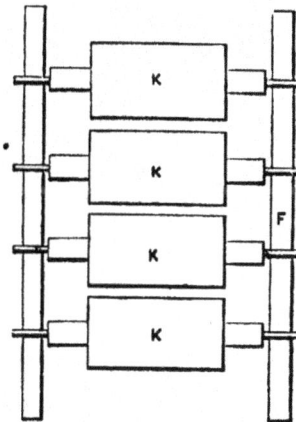

by some person or some proper machinery into one of the boiling vessels, where, steam or fire heat being added, they are suffered to remain while the lime-boiling takes effect.

We need not follow the inventor into all the particulars. When the goods were sufficiently acted on by one solution, another solution was used, so that this mode of calendering not only was a method of moving the goods from place to place by means of rollers, but it was a method also of saturating goods thoroughly with a solution and of washing them.

It was by a similar method that Mr. Bentley bleached skeins of yarn, of linen, or of cotton. The skeins are looped together by tying any soft material round the middle of the first skein, which will leave the loops from one end of the next skein to pass half way through, and which will always leave other two loops, and by repeating which any quantity of skeins may be looped together, tying the last loop with another soft material.

The mode of saturating the goods with solutions is effected by the arrangement shown in *fig.* 137. Rapid motion and frequent pressure are introduced instead of a still soaking process.

137

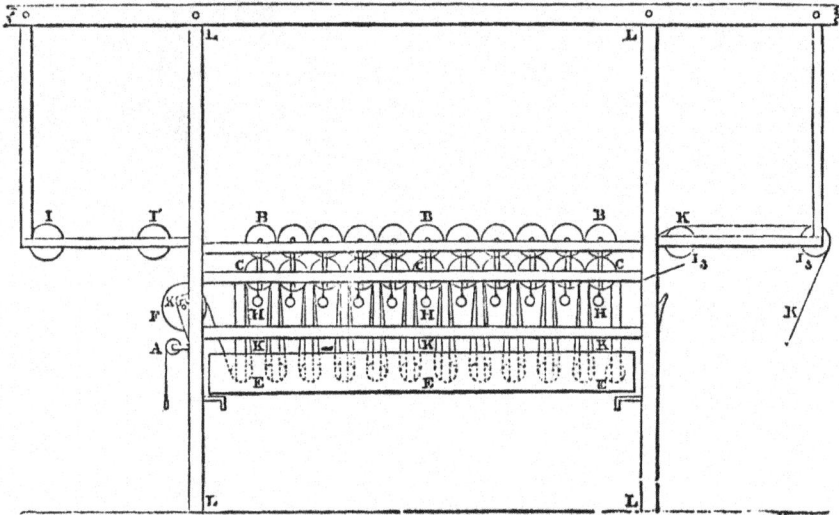

A is a roller for the guide-cords; B, B, B are eleven washing-rollers; C, C, C are speed-rollers; E, E, E are twelve rollers immersed in twelve divisions of the cistern G. The eleven staple-formed irons which pass through the frame rails on each side of the centres of the eleven rollers B, B, B, and the eleven rollers C, C, C, serve to stay these rollers in their places, at the same time allowing the eleven washing-rollers B, B, B, to rise and fall according to the pressure by which they are held down by the eleven weights attached to these irons at H, and upon the bottom rail may be placed such staves, brushes, or rollers, as may be found necessary for holding and brushing the goods in the best manner to keep them straight during the different washings in water and bleaching-liquors. The goods are prepared by steeping, as before described, and placed in batches at F, and passing under the immersing rollers E and the twelve divisions of cistern G, between the eleven speed-rollers C and the eleven washing-rollers B, as seen at K, are taken down straight and open into one of the vessels, and are then boiled by steam, which is succeeded by repeated washings alternately in water and bleaching-liquors, until they are sufficiently bleached, as before described.

The elevation and ground-plan of a bleach-house and machinery capable of bleaching 800 pieces of 4 lbs. cloth per day (for best madder work), with the labour of one man and three boys, working from 6 until 4 o'clock, exclusive of singeing and drying, are represented in *figs.* 138 and 139 (p. 387). The letter *d* represents two lengths of cloth of 400 pieces each (end of pieces being stitched together by patent sewing-machine made by Mather and Platt), making together 800 pieces, passing through washing-machine *g*, and from thence delivered over winch *w*, into kier *c*,—this operation occupies one hour,—where they are boiled for twelve hours in lime. They are then withdrawn by the same washing-machine *g*, washed, and passed into second kier *b* (operation occupying one hour), where they are boiled

138

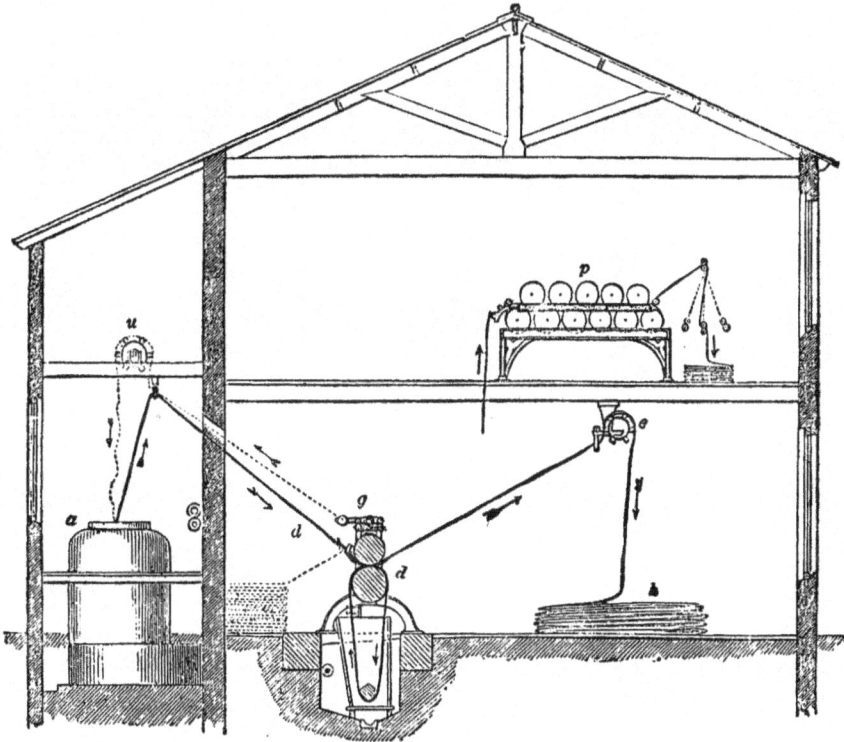

139

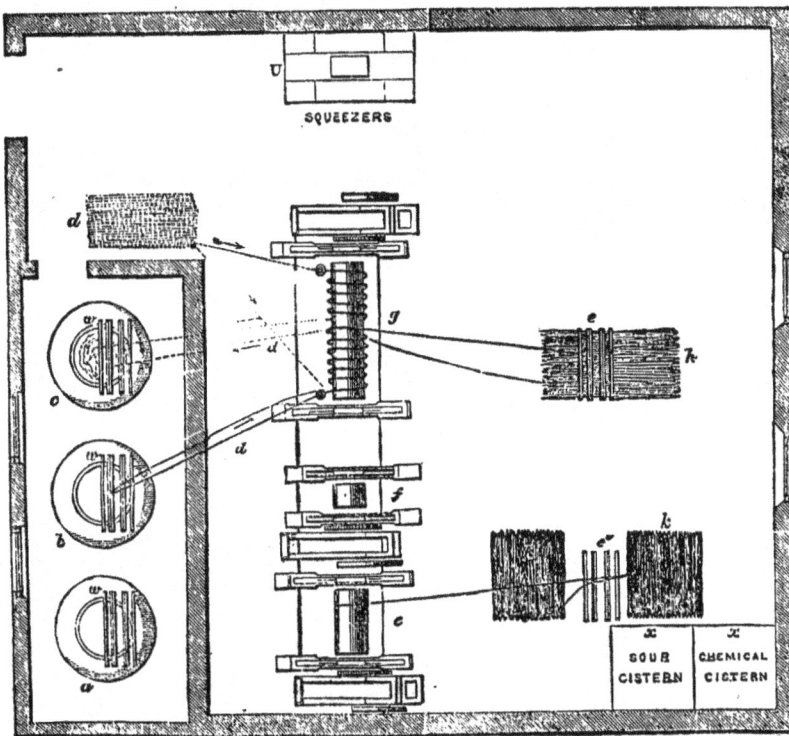

SQUEEZERS

SOUR CISTERN

CHEMICAL CISTERN

for twelve hours in ashes and resin; again withdrawn by the same machine *g*, washed, squeezed (see plan at *v*), and passed over winch *e*, and piled at *h* (this operation occupies one hour). They are then taken from pile *h*, and threaded through sour-machine *e*, soured, passed over winch *e''*, and piled at *k* (operation, one hour), where it remains in the pile for three hours. It is then squeezed at *v*, and washed through machine *g* (an hour's operation), delivered into third kier *a*, boiled for six hours, washed at *g*, squeezed at *v* (an hour's operation), and passed through *chemick-machine* (an hour's operation), and piled for one hour; after which it is soured again (an hour's operation), squeezed, and washed at *g* (an hour's operation), squeezed again at *f* (an hour's operation), and dried by machine at *p* (*fig.* 138).

There are several advantages in using the squeezing process so often in the above arrangement :—Firstly, the bowels of the washing-machine are not so much damaged by the heavy pressure which is required to be applied, if no squeezers are used, in order to prepare the pieces for the sour and chemick machines. Secondly, a drier state of the cloth than can possibly be produced by the washing-machine *alone*, thus fitting it to become better saturated with the chemick or sour. Thirdly, the piece passing from the souring to the washing-machine, in this arrangement, carries with it *less* of the acid, and thus ensures a better washing, with less water.

It may be observed, that the velocity of the above-mentioned machines is much higher than usual, experience having shown that the various operations are thus better performed than when running slower. The reason of this appears to be, firstly, that the piece, running at such velocity, carries with it, by reason of capillary attraction, a greater quantity of liquid to the nip of the bowels; secondly, the great velocity of the bowels, together with the greater quantity of water carried up, produces a more powerful current at the *nip* and down the ascending piece, thus penetrating to every fibre of it.

It may also be remarked, that the above-mentioned machines are not adapted to the bleaching of linen; for the latter cloth, not having the same elasticity as cotton, if it should become tight, would either be pulled *narrow* or torn.

In illustration of the continuous process as at present used, the plan of proceeding at Messrs. McNaughten, Barton, and Thom's, at Chorley, may be described.

1. In order that there may be no interruption in the process, the pieces are united in one continuous piece—each piece being about 30 yards, the whole varying with the weight of cloth—about 300 yards long. Each piece is marked with the name of the printer. This is sometimes done in marking-ink of silver, and sometimes in coal-tar, at the extremity of the piece. The pieces are rapidly tacked together by girls, who use in some establishments a very simple sewing-machine. (See Sewing-Machine.) The whole amount to be bleached at a time is united in one piece, and is drawn from place to place like a rope. To give them this rope-form, the goods are drawn through an aperture whose surface is exceedingly smooth, being generally of glass or earthenware. Of these many are used in transferring the cloth from place to place. They serve instead of pulleys. The cloth when laid in a vessel is not thrown in at random, but laid down in a carefully made coil. The rope-form enables the water to penetrate it more easily.

2. The pieces are singed.

3. They are boiled in the first kier. In this, 3,500 lbs. of cloth have added to them 250 lbs. of caustic lime, 1 lb. of lime to 14 of cloth. The kier is cylindrical, 7 feet deep and 8 feet in diameter; as much water is added as will cover the cloth, about 500 gallons. This boiling lasts thirteen hours.

4. They are washed in the washing-machine. Robinson and Young's machine is used.

5. They are soured in a similar machine with hydrochloric acid of specific gravity 1010·, or 2° of Twaddle.

6. The same amount of cloth being supposed to be used, it is bucked in a solution of soda-ash and resin, 170 lbs. of soda-ash to 30 lbs. of resin. The boiling lasts sixteen hours, the same amount of water being used.

7. Washed as before.

8. Passed through chloride of lime, or chemicked. The cloth is laid in a stone or wooden cistern, and a solution of bleaching-powder is passed through it, by being poured over it and allowed to run into a vessel below; this is managed by continued pumping. This solution is about half a degree Twaddle, or specific gravity 1002·5. The cloth lies in it from one to two hours.

9. Washed.

10. Boiled again in a kier for five hours with 100 lbs. of carbonate of soda crystals.

11. Washed.

12. Put in chloride of lime as before.

13. Soured, in hydrochloric acid of 1012·5 specific gravity, or $2\frac{1}{2}°$ Twaddle.

14. Lies six hours on stillages.—A stillage is a kind of low stool used to protect the cloth from the floor.

15. Washed till clean.

16. Squeezed in rollers.

17. Dried over tin cylinders heated by steam.

This is the process for calico generally; some light goods must be more carefully handled. The usual time occupied by all these processes is five days. They are sometimes dried in a hydro-extractor; after singeing, laid twenty-four hours to steep, then washed before being put into the lime-kier.

BLEACHING OF LINEN.

Linen contains much more colouring-matter than cotton. The former loses nearly a third of its weight, while the latter loses not more than a twentieth. The fibres of flax possess, in the natural condition, a light grey, yellow, or blond colour. By the operation of rotting, or, as it is commonly called, water-retting, which is employed to enable the textile filaments to be separated from the boon, or woody matter, the colour becomes darker, and, in consequence probably of the putrefaction of the green matter of the bark, the colouring-substance appears. Hence, flax prepared without rotting is much paler, and its colouring-matter may be in a great measure removed by washing with soap, leaving the filaments nearly white. Mr. James Lee obtained a patent in 1812, as having discovered that the process of steeping and dew-retting is unnecessary, and that flax and hemp will not only dress, but will produce an equal if not greater quantity of more durable fibre, when cleaned in the dry way. Mr. Lee stated that, when hemp or flax-plants are ripe, the farmer has nothing more to do than to pull, spread, and dry them in the sun, and then to break them by proper machinery. This promising improvement has apparently come to nought, having been many years abandoned by the patentee himself, though he was favoured with a special Act of Parliament, which permitted the specification of his patent to remain sealed up for seven years, contrary to the general practice in such cases.

The substance which gives steeped flax its peculiar tint is insoluble in boiling water, in acids, and in alkalis; but it possesses the property of dissolving in caustic or carbonated alkaline lyes, when it has by previous exposure been acted on only by chlorine. This process is effected in great measure by the influence of air in combination with light and moisture acting on the linen cloth laid upon the grass: but chlorine hastens the operation. In no case, however, is it possible to dissolve the colour completely at once, but there must be many alternate exposures to oxygen or chlorine, and alkali, before the flax becomes white. It is this circumstance alone which renders the bleaching of linen an apparently complicated business.

Old Method.—A parcel of goods consists of 360 pieces of those linens which are called Britannias. Each piece is 35 yards long, and weighs, on an average, 10 lbs.; the weight of the parcel is, in consequence, about 3,600 lbs. avoirdupois weight. The linens are first washed, and then steeped in waste alkaline lye, as formerly described under these processes; they then undergo the following operations:—

1. Bucked with 60 lbs. pearl-ashes, washed, exposed on the field.

2. Ditto   80   ditto   ditto   ditto   ditto.

3. Ditto   90   potashes   ditto   ditto   ditto.

4. Ditto   80   ditto   ditto   ditto   ditto.

5. Ditto   80   ditto   ditto   ditto   ditto.

6. Ditto   50   ditto   ditto   ditto   ditto.

7. Ditto   70   ditto   ditto   ditto   ditto.

8. Ditto   70   ditto   ditto   ditto   ditto.

9. Soured one night in dilute sulphuric acid; washed.

10. Bucked with 50 lbs. pearl-ashes, washed, exposed on the field.

11. Immersed in the chloride of potash or lime 12 hours.

12. Boiled with 30 lbs. pearl-ashes, washed, exposed on the field.

13. Ditto   30   ditto   ditto   ditto   ditto.

14. Soured, washed.

The linens are then taken to the rubbing-board, and well rubbed with a strong lather of black soap, after which they are well washed in pure spring-water. At this period they are carefully examined, and those which are fully bleached are laid aside to be blued, and made up for the market; while those which are not fully white are returned to be boiled, and steeped in the chloride of lime or potash; then soured, until they are fully white.

By the above process, 690 lbs. weight of alkali is taken to bleach 360 pieces of linen, each piece consisting of 35 yards in length; so that the expenditure of alkali would be somewhat less than 2 lbs. for each piece, were it not that some parts of the linens are not fully whitened, as above noted. Two pounds of alkali may therefore be stated as the average quantity employed for bleaching each piece of goods.

What is called the old method, or that used from about the introduction of bleaching-powder, at the beginning of the century, till within ten or fifteen years, required bleaching on the grass; and the mode in which it was managed in Ireland and Scotland, where it held its ground longest, is as follows:

1. They were rot-steeped in a weak solution of potash, at about 130° F., for two days, until the dressing used in manufacturing the cloth was removed.

2. Washed.

3. Boiled or bowked in potash-lye at $\frac{1}{2}$° Twaddle, for ten hours.

4. Washed, and the ends turned so that the whole might be equally exposed to the lye.

5. Boiled or bowked in a similar lye to the above for twelve hours.

6. Washed well.

7. Exposed on the grass for three days, and watered.

8. Taken up and soured with sulphuric acid, at 2° Twaddle, for four hours.

9. Taken up and washed well.

10. Boiled again for eight hours in potash-lye, at 1° Twaddle, to which had been added black or soft soap, about 20 lbs. to a kier of about 300 gallons.

11. Washed.

12. Crofted, or exposed on the grass, as before.

13. Treated with chloride of lime at $1\frac{1}{2}$° Twaddle, for four hours.

14. Washed.

15. Soured in sulphuric acid, at 2° Twaddle, for four hours.

16. Washed.

17. Boiled for six or seven hours with soap and lye, using in this case more soap and one-third less lye than in the former bowkings.

18. Drawn out and put through rub-boards. This is a kind of washing-machine, made of blocks of wood, with hard-wood teeth. The goods are washed by it in a soapy liquid. The teeth moving rapidly, drive the soap into the cloth.

19. Boiled in the lye alone for six hours.

20. Washed.

21. Crofted, keeping them very clean, as this is the last exposure.

22. Treated with chloride of lime.

23. They are then starched, blued, and beetled, to finish them for the market. These operations last six weeks.

New System, as practised in Scotland and Ireland.—*Directions given by an extensive Bleacher.*

1. Wash.

2. Boil in lime-water ten or twelve hours.

3 Sour in muriatic acid, of 2° Twaddle, for three, four, or five hours.

4. Wash well.

5. Boil with resin and soda-ash twelve hours.

6. Turn the goods, so that those at the top shall be at the bottom, and boil again as at No. 5.

7. Wash well.

8. Chemick, at $\frac{1}{2}$° Twaddle, or 1002·5, four hours.

9. Sour, at 2° Twaddle, or 1010· specific gravity.

10. Wash.

11. Boil in soda-ash ten hours.

12. Chemick again.

13. Wash and dry.

This is the system chiefly adopted when the goods are to be printed.

The following is the system practised in the neighbourhood of Perth, where the chief trade is in plain sheetings :—

1. Before putting them into operation, they are put up into parcels of about 35 cwts.

2. They are then steeped in lye for twenty-four hours.

3. Then washed and spread on the grass for about two days.

4. Boiled in lime-water.

5. Turned, and boiled again in lime-water, those at the top being put at the bottom. 60 lbs. of lime are used at a time, and about 600 gallons of water.

6. Washed, then soured in sulphuric acid of 2° Twaddle, or 1010· sp. gr., for four hours, then washed again.

7. Boiled with soda-ash for ten hours; 110 lbs. used.

8. Washed and spread out on the green, or crofted.

9. Boiled again in soda as before.

10. Crofted for three days.

11. They are then examined: the white ones are taken out; those that are not finished are boiled and crofted again.

12. Next, they are scalded in water containing 80 lbs. of soda-ash, and washed.

13. The chloride of lime is then used at $\frac{1}{2}°$ Twaddle, or 1002·5 specific gravity.

14. Washed and scalded.

15. Washed and treated with chloride of lime.

16. Soured, for four hours, with sulphuric acid, at 2° Twaddle, or 1010· specific gravity.

17. Washed.

If cloths lighter than sheetings are used, the washing liquids are used weaker. The great point is to observe them carefully during the process, in order to see what treatment will suit them best.

It will be seen that the process of bleaching linen is still very tedious; and although it may be managed in a fortnight, it is seldom that this occurs regularly for a great length of time. The action of the light introduces at once an uncertain element, as this varies so much in our climate. If, again, linen be long exposed to the air in a moist condition, it is apt to become injured in strength. To shorten the process, therefore, is important; and if no injurious agents are introduced, a shortening promises also to give increased strength to the fibre. It has not been found possible to introduce chlorine into linen-bleaching at an early stage, as in the case of cotton; and the processes for purifying it without any chlorine, render it so white that unskilled persons would call it as white as snow. The chlorine is introduced nearly at the end of the operation, after a series of boilings with alkalis, sourings, and exposures on the grass. If introduced at an earlier stage, the colour of the raw cloth becomes fixed, and cannot be removed. The technical term for this condition is ' set.' Mr. F. M. Jennings, of Cork, has patented a method which promises to obviate the difficulty. The peculiarity consists in using the alkali and the chloride of alkali at the same moment, thus giving the alkali opportunity to seize on the colouring-matter as soon as the chloride has acted, and thereby preventing the formation of an insoluble compound. He prefers the chlorides of potash or soda. His plan is as follows :—

1. He soaks the linen in water for about twelve hours, or boils it in lime or alkali, or alkali with lime, and then soaks it in acid, as he uses soaps of resin in other mixtures—the alkalis being from 3° to 5° Twaddle, 1015·–1025· specific gravity.

2. Boils in a similar alkaline solution.

3. Washes.

4. Puts it into a solution of soda, of 5° Twaddle, 1025· specific gravity, adding chloride of soda until it rises up to from 6°–7° Twaddle. It is allowed to remain in this solution for some hours, and it is better if subjected to heating or squeezing between rollers, as in the washing-machine.

5. He then soaks, sours, and washes.

6. He then puts it a second time into the solution of alkali and chloride.

7. Then washes, and boils again with soda. These operations, 6 and 7, may be repeated until the cloth becomes almost white.

The amount of exposure on the grass by this process is said to be not more than from one-half to one-fourth that required by the usual method, or it may be managed so as entirely to supersede crofting.

Chevalier Claussen has opened up the filaments of flax by the evolution of gas from a carbonate in which the plant is steeped, and at the same time bleached by chloride of magnesia, but this has not been successful.

BLEACHING OF SILK.

Silk in its raw state, as spun by the worm, is either white or yellow of various shades, and is covered with a varnish which gives it stiffness and a degree of elasticity. For the greater number of purposes to which silk is applied, it must be deprived of this native covering, which was long considered to be a sort of gum. The operation by which this colouring-matter is removed is called scouring, cleansing, or boiling. A great many different processes have been proposed for freeing the silk fibres from all foreign impurities, and for giving it the utmost whiteness, lustre, and pliancy; but none of the new plans has superseded, with any advantage, the one practised of old, which consists essentially in steeping the silk in a warm solution of soap; a circumstance placed beyond all doubt by the interesting experiments of

M. Roard. The alkalis, or alkaline salts, act in a marked manner upon the varnish of silk, and effect its complete solution; the prolonged agency even of boiling water or soap and water destroys the brilliancy of silk. It would appear, however, that the Chinese do not employ this method, but something that is preferable. Probably the superior beauty of their white silk may be owing to the superiority of their raw material.

The most ancient method of scouring silk consists of three operations. For the first, or the *ungumming*, thirty per cent. of soap is dissolved in clean water at a boiling heat; then the temperature is lowered by the addition of a little cold water, by withdrawing the fire, or at least by damping it. The hanks of silk suspended upon horizontal poles over the boiler are now plunged into the soapy solution, kept at a heat somewhat under ebullition, which is an essential point; for, if hotter, the soap would attack the substance of the silk, and not only dissolve a portion of it, but deprive the whole of its lustre. The portions of the hanks plunged in the bath get scoured by degrees: the varnish and the colouring-matter are removed, and the silk assumes its proper whiteness and pliancy. Whenever this point is attained, the hanks are turned round upon the poles, so that the portion formerly in the air may be also subjected to the bath. As soon as the whole is completely ungummed, they are taken out, wrung by the peg, and shaken out; after which the next step, called the *boil*, is commenced. About 25 lbs. or 35 lbs. of ungummed silk are enclosed in bags of coarse canvas, called *pockets*, and put into a similar bath with the preceding, but with a smaller proportion of soap, which may therefore be raised to the boiling-point without any danger of destroying the silk. The ebullition is to be kept up for an hour and a half, during which time the bags must be frequently stirred, lest those near the bottom should suffer an undue degree of heat. The silk experiences in these two operations a loss of about 25 per cent. of its weight.

The third and last scouring operation is intended to give the silk a slight tinge, which renders the white more agreeable, and better adapted to its various uses in trade. In this way we distinguish the China white, which has a faint cast of red, the silver white, the azure white, and the thread white. To produce these different shades, we begin by preparing a soap-water so strong as to lather by agitation; we then add to it for the China white a little arnotto, mixing it carefully in; and then, passing the silk properly through it, till it has acquired the wished-for tint. As to the other shades, we need only azure them more or less with a fine indigo, which has been previously washed several times in hot water, and reduced to powder in a mortar. It is then diffused through boiling water, allowed to settle for a few minutes, and the supernatant liquid, which contains only the finer particles, is added to the soap bath, in such proportion as may be requisite. The silk, on being taken out of this bath, must be wrung well, and stretched upon perches to dry; after which it is introduced into the sulphuring chamber, if it is to be made use of in the white state. At Lyons, however, no soap is employed at the third operation; after the boil, the silk is washed, sulphured, and azured, by passing through very clear river-water properly blued.

The present practice in the silk-works in Lancashire is as follows:—

The Italian silk arrives in this country with a little soap in it, put in by the throwsters there, amounting to one drachm to a pound of silk. It is received here in hanks, and bleached in that state. The hanks are hung on sticks or small poles, about three pounds of silk being on each stick. The sticks being laid across a vessel, the silk hangs down, and in this way may be immersed in any liquid. The treatment of silk is then much more tender than that of cotton.

1. The hot lather is made with 3 lbs. of soap in 50 gallons of water; to this is added 1 lb. of soda crystals. The silk is kept in this lather at a temperature of from 175° to 190° F. for three-quarters of an hour. It is then wrung or dried in the hydro-extractor (called hydro or whizzer in Lancashire works). 2. It is then, for the purpose of straightening it, rolled on a cocoa-nut roll-pin 4 in. in diameter, a little turn being given it occasionally, by the finger and thumb, to prevent entangling. 3. It is then put into bags of one yard square. The hanks are laid flat, and the bags stitched down. In this state they are boiled for 3½ hours, using for the same amount of water as before, 3 lbs. of soap to 20 lbs. of silk. 4. The silk is then washed or moved about by the hand in a cistern one yard wide and one deep, retaining as much soap as will make a pretty permanent lather. To this there is generally added a small quantity of archil, about ¼ oz. to 4 lbs. of silk. 5. It is then dried in the hydro-extractor. 6. It is then straightened and sulphured. The sulphuring is done in a small apartment, which should be very high. The size is frequently 10 feet square by 20 in height. The silk is hung up in it, and 4 lbs. of sulphur for each 40 lbs. of silk are put on the floor and set fire to. The room is closed as well as possible, and the silk is allowed to remain 4 hours. This is the bleaching, and it requires now only to be

washed by rinsing three to four times in cold water. A little indigo blue is used to give it a pearly appearance. The use of archil, which has been mentioned, depends upon the shade of white, so to speak, which is wanted. 7. The silk is now dried by the hydro-extractor first, and then by exposing to a temperature of 85°–90°. If heavily laden with gums, silk must be dried at a still cooler temperature. In this operation of bleaching, 1 lb. of good silk loses 4 oz.; but as it seldom arrives very pure, the usual loss to the pound of silk is 5 oz.

The first, or simmering operation, mentioned here, is not necessary for the white silk of China.

The silks intended for the manufacture of blondes and gauzes are not subjected to the ordinary scouring process, because it is essential in these cases for them to preserve their natural stiffness. We must therefore select the raw silk of China, or the whitest raw silks of other countries; steep them, rinse them in a bath of pure water, or in one containing a little soap; wring them, expose them to the vapour of sulphur, and then pass them through the azure water. Sometimes this process is repeated.

Before the memoir of M. Roard appeared, extremely vague ideas were entertained about the composition of the native varnish of silk. He has shown that this substance, so far from being of a gummy nature, as had been believed, may be rather compared to bees'-wax, with a species of oil and a colouring-matter which exist only in raw silks. It is contained in them to the amount of from 23 to 24 per cent., and forms the portion of weight which is lost in the *ungumming*. It possesses, however, some of the properties of vegetable gums, though it differs essentially as to others. In a dry mass, it is friable and has a vitreous fracture; it is soluble in water, and affords a solution which lathers like soap; but when thrown upon burning coals, it does not soften like gum, but burns with the exhalation of a fetid odour. Its solution, when left exposed to the open air, is at first of a golden yellow, becomes soon greenish, and ere long putrefies, as a solution of animal matter would do in similar circumstances. M. Roard assures us that the city of Lyons alone could furnish several thousand quintals of this substance *per annum*, were it applicable to any useful purpose.

The yellow varnish is of a resinous nature, altogether insoluble in water, very soluble in alcohol, and contains a little volatile oil, which gives it a rank smell. The colour of this resin is easily dissipated, either by exposure to the sun or by the action of chlorine: it forms about one fifty-fifth of its weight.

Bees'-wax exists also in all the sorts of silk, even in that of China; but the whiter the filaments, the less wax do they contain.

M. Roard has observed that, if the silk be exposed to the soap-baths for some time after it has been stripped of its foreign matters, it begins to lose body, and has its valuable qualities impaired. It becomes dull, stiff, and coloured in consequence of the solution, more or less considerable, of its substance; a solution which takes place in all liquids, and even in boiling water. It is for this reason that silks cannot be alumed with heat; and that they lose some of their lustre in being dyed brown, a colour which requires a boiling hot bath. The best mode, therefore, of avoiding these inconveniences, is to boil the silks in the soap-bath no longer than is absolutely necessary for the scouring process, and to expose them in the various dyeing operations to a temperature as moderate as may be sufficient to communicate the colour. When silks are to be dyed, much less soap should be used in the cleansing, and very little for the dark colours. According to M. Roard, raw silks, white or yellow, may be completely scoured in one hour, with 15 lbs. of water for one of silk, and a suitable proportion of soap. The soap and the silk should be put into the bath half an hour before its ebullition, and the silks should be turned about frequently. The dull silks, in which the varnish has already undergone some alteration, never acquire a fine white until they are exposed to sulphurous acid gas. Exposure to light has also a very good effect in whitening silks, and is had recourse to, it is said, with advantage, by the Chinese.

Baumé contrived a process which does not appear to have received the sanction of experience, but which may be a guide in the right way. He macerates the yellow raw silk in a mixture of alcohol at 36° (sp. gr. ·0837) and one thirty-second part of pure muriatic acid. At the end of forty-eight hours, it is as white as possible, and the more so, the better the quality of silk. The loss which it suffers in the menstruum, is only one-fortieth; showing that nothing but the colouring-matter is abstracted. The expense of this menstruum is the great obstacle to Baumé's process. The alcohol, however, might be in a very great measure recovered, by saturating the acid with chalk, and redistilling.

Wool, like the preceding fibrous matter, is covered with a peculiar varnish, which impairs its qualities, and prevents it from being employed in the raw state for the purposes to which it is well adapted when it is scoured. The English give the name *yolk*, and the French *suint*, to that native coat: it is a fatty unctuous matter, of a strong smell, which apparently has its chief origin in the cutaneous perspiration of the sheep; but which, by the agency of external bodies, may have undergone some changes which modify its constitution. It results from the experiments of M. Vauquelin, that the *yolk* is composed of several substances; namely, 1, a soap with basis of potash, which constitutes the greater part of it; 2, of a notable quantity of acetate of potash; 3, of a small quantity of carbonate, and a trace of chloride of potassium; 4, of a little lime in an unknown state of combination; 5, of a species of sebaceous matter, and an animal substance to which the odour is due. There are several other accidental matters present on sheep's wool.

The proportion of yolk is variable in different kinds of wool, but in general it is more abundant the finer the staple; the loss by scouring being 45 per cent. for the finest wools, and 35 per cent. for the coarse.

The yolk, on account of its soapy nature, dissolves readily in water, with the exception of a little free fatty matter, which easily separates from the filaments, and remains floating in the liquor. It would then appear sufficient to expose the wools to simple washing in a stream of water; yet experience shows that this method never answers so well as that usually adopted, which consists in steeping the wool for some time in simple warm water, or in warm water mixed with a fourth of stale urine. From 15 to 20 minutes of contact are sufficient in this case, if we heat the bath as warm as the hand can bear it, and stir it well with a rod. At the end of this time the wool may be taken out, set to drain, then placed in large baskets, in order to be completely rinsed in a stream of water.

It is generally supposed that putrid urine acts on the wool by the ammonia which it contains, and that this serves to saponify the remainder of the fatty matter not combined with the potash, although M. Vauquelin gave another opinion. Fresh urine contains a free acid, which, by decomposing the potash-soap of the yolk, counteracts the scouring operation.

If wools are better scoured in a small quantity of water than in a great stream, we can conceive that this circumstance must depend upon the nature of the yolk, which, in a concentrated solution, acts like a saponaceous compound, and thus contributes to remove the free fatty particles which adhere to the filaments. It should also be observed that too long a continuance of the wool in the yolk water, hurts its quality very much, by weakening its cohesion, causing the filaments to swell, and even to split. It is said then to have lost its *nerve*. Another circumstance in the scouring of wool, that should always be attended to, is never to work the filaments together to such a degree as to occasion their felting; but in agitating we must merely push them slowly round in the vessel, or press them gently under the feet. Were it at all felted, it would neither card nor spin well.

As the heat of boiling water is apt to decompose woollen fibres, we should be careful never to raise the temperature of the scouring bath to near this point, nor, in fact, to exceed 140° F. Some authors recommend the use of alkaline or soapy baths for scouring wool, but practical people do not deviate from the method above described.

When the washing is completed, all the wool which is to be sent white into the market, must be exposed to the action of sulphurous acid, either in a liquid or a gaseous state. In the latter case, sulphur is burned in a close chamber, in which the wools are hung up or spread out; in the former, the wools are plunged into water moderately impregnated with the acid. (See SULPHURING.) Exposure on the grass may also contribute to the bleaching of wool. Some fraudulent dealers are accused of dipping wools in buttermilk, or chalk-and-water, in order to whiten them and increase their weight.

Wool is sometimes whitened in the fleece, and sometimes in the state of yarn; the latter affording the best means of operating. It has been observed that the wool cut from certain parts of the sheep, especially from the groin, never bleaches well.

After sulphuring, the wool has a harsh crispy feel, which may be removed by a weak soap-bath. To this also the wool-comber has recourse when he wishes to cleanse and whiten his wools to the utmost. He generally uses a soft or potash soap, and after the wool is well soaked in the warm soap-bath, with gentle pressure he wrings it well with the help of a hook, fixed at the end of his washing-tub, and hangs it up to dry.

The actual operations of purifying wool are so blended with the methods of weaving and working it, that, to show it fully, I shall give here the process of preparing flannels, out of which the parts relating to cleansing may be taken.

1. The wool is weighed out into parcels of 120 lbs. Add, on an average, 20 to 21 lbs. or 10 quarts of oil—rape-oil or olive, or mixed, or, as is very common now, oleic acid, which may be so used as not to be hurtful to the machinery in this condition. This was introduced by Mr. M'Dougall.

2. It is then devilled or willowed, carded, slubbed, and spun.

The warp portion is made at this stage if wanted.

3. Scoured in the warp with urine and hot water, occasionally using a little ammonia.

4. Sized with a mineral sizing, and put into the looms.

5. If spun for weft, it is soaked, when on the bobbin, with cold water in a cistern, an air-pump being used to extract the air from the threads and to compel the water to enter.

6. The water is then removed by a revolving water-extractor. This process leaves the weft full and soft.

Skin-wool, so called, is taken from the skin by means of lime, which makes the oil stiff, forming a compound.

7. The piece being now woven is grey. It is sent to the finishing or fulling mill, sprinkled over with urine and pigs' dung, and put under the fulling hammers until equally wet.

8. It is then washed out or scoured with cold water, raised with teasels, dried out of doors or in a stove.

Treated a little differently, accordingly as Welsh or Lancashire is wanted.

9. It is then sprinkled again with soap-and-water, and milled one to two hours in the fulling-stock.

Three-quarters to 1 lb. of soap is given for each piece.

10. Cleared with cold water.

11. Hung up wet in a sulphur-stove; several pots of sulphur lighted. The door is shut till morning. Washed four to six hours in cold water, treated with finely-ground indigo, dried, and a little further raised, pressed, and rolled up for sale.

If the flannel is Welsh, it is dried and sprinkled with fullers' earth (instead of the soap-and-water used for the Lancashire), well milled for some time, and then cleared in cold water. It is then put into a cistern filled with water, having some soap thrown in as well as a few cakes of Prussian blue. This dipping is repeated three or four times, and between each the flannel is milled in the fulling-stock. This levels the colour. When blue enough, the pieces are dried and made up for sale.

It appears that Welsh flannel is not sulphured; the cleaning is done entirely by ammonia.

Sulphuring.—In the usual mode of sulphuring the cloth is hung on pegs or rails in rooms which are called the sulphur chambers or stoves. An iron pot containing sulphur is placed in each corner of the room, and the sulphur inflamed. The door is then shut and clayed. By the morning the process is finished, and the door is opened. This mode is objected to, because the sulphur, not being properly burnt, lodges in the cloth, and acts injuriously on it in the processes of dyeing or printing. Sparks also are apt to rise up and injure the pieces, the sulphur not being pure, and burning irregularly. Drops also of water impregnated strongly with sulphurous acid are apt to fall from the roof, doing injury to the cloth.

To avoid these inconveniences Mr. Thom has invented a method by which the cloth is rapidly carried through the sulphuring chamber, and subjected to the influence of the vapour on the principle of the washing-machine. A great deal of time and space is of course saved; it is on the same principle as the washing apparatus, vapour being used instead of water. This has not yet been applied to thick woollen. See CALICO-PRINTING.

BLEACHING OF MATERIALS FOR PAPER.

The bleaching of paper is conducted on the same principle as the bleaching of cotton. Paper is made principally of two materials, cotton and flax, generally mixed. The cotton-waste of the mills, which is that inferior portion which has become too impure for spinning, or otherwise deteriorated, and cotton rags, are the principal, if not the only, sources of the cotton used by paper-makers. The waste is sorted by hand, the hard and soft being separated, and all accidental mixtures which occur in it are removed. This is done at first roughly on a large lattice, which is a frame of wire cloth, having squares of about three-quarters of an inch, through which impurities may fall. It is then put into a duster, which is a long rectangular box,—it may be ten feet long,—lying horizontally, the inside diameter about two feet, and covered with wire gratings running horizontally, leaving openings of half an inch in width. As this revolves, the waste is thrown from one angle to the other, and throws out whatever dust or other material falls into the holes or spaces. The fibrous matter has little tendency to separate from the mass, which is somewhat agglutinated by being damp, chiefly from the oil obtained during the processes in the cotton-mill. A second duster, however, is used to retain whatever may be of value; it is a kind of riddle. It is then transferred to the lattices, which are a series of boxes covered with wire gauze, the meshes of which are about half an inch square, and so arranged as to form a series of sorting tables. The sorting generally is done by young women. Each table has a large box or basket beside it, into which the sorted material is thrown; this is removed when filled, by being pushed along a railroad or tramway. Pieces of stone, clay, leather, wood, nails, and other articles, are taken out. The cotton is then put into a devil similar to that which is used in cotton machinery, but having larger, stronger teeth, which tear it up into small fragments.

The rags are sorted according to quality, woollen carefully removed, and all the unavailable material sent back to the buyer. They are then chopped up by a knife, on the circumference of a heavy wheel, into pieces of an inch wide, devilled, and dusted.

The rags and the cotton waste are bleached in a similar manner. The cotton is put into kiers of about ten feet in diameter, of a kind similar to those described, and boiled with lime. The amount of lime used is about 6 lbs. to a cwt. of cotton or rags, but this varies according to the impurity. The lime removes a great amount of impure organic matter, and, as in bleaching cotton cloth, lays hold of the fatty matter, of which there is a great deal in the waste. When taken out, it is allowed to lie from two to three hours. The appearance is not much altered; it appears as impure as ever.

It is then put into the rag-engine and washed clean. This is a combined washing-machine and filter, the invention of Mr. Wrigley, near Bury. The washing may last an hour and a half, or more. See PAPER.

The cotton has now a bright grey colour, and looks moderately clean. It is full of water, which is removed by an hydraulic press, the cotton being put into an iron cylindrical box with perforated sides. It is then boiled in kiers or puffing boilers, where soda-ash is used, at the rate of 4 to 5 lbs. a cwt. Only as much water is used as will moisten the goods thoroughly. Much water would weaken the solution and render more soda necessary. It is then washed again in the rag-engine; afterwards put into chloride of lime, acidified as in cotton-bleaching, and washed again in the rag-engine.

The cotton rags are treated in a similar manner. The coloured rags are treated separately, requiring a different treatment according to the amount of colour; this consists chiefly in a greater use of chloride of lime.

Some points relating to bleaching are necessarily treated of under CALICO-PRINTING.

The following were the countries to which our bleaching materials were exported in 1871, and the quantities exported to each:—

	Cwts.
To Russia	49,092
„ Sweden	4,158
„ Denmark	11,059
„ Germany	61,207
„ Holland	12,698
„ Belgium	16,046
„ France	4,258
„ United States, Atlantic	294,224
„ British North America	9,085
„ Other Countries	14,293
Total	476,120

BLEACHING-LIQUIDS. These liquids, manufactured for the bleacher, contain metallic chlorides and hypochlorites. The most important are the liquid 'chlorides' of lime, magnesia, soda, and potash. See CHLORIDES.

BLEACHING-POWDER. See CHLORIDE OF LIME.

BLEAK. (*Cyprinus alburnus.*) The scales of this fish are used for making the 'essence of pearl,' or *essence d'orient*, with which artificial pearls are manufactured. In the scales of the fish the optical effect is produced in the same manner as in the real pearl, the grooves of the latter being represented by the inequalities formed by the margins of the concentric laminæ of which the scales are composed. These fish are caught in the Seine, the Loire, the Saone, the Rhine, and several other rivers. They are about four inches in length, and are sold very cheap after the scales are washed off. It is said that 4,000 fish are necessary for the production of a pound of scales, for which the fishermen of the Chalonnois get from 18 to 25 livres.

The pearl essence is obtained merely by well washing the scales which have been scraped from the fish in water, so as to free them from the blood and mucilaginous matter of the fish. See PEARLS, ARTIFICIAL.

BLENDE, from *Blenden*, Ger., to dazzle. Sulphide or sulphuret of zinc is a common ore of zinc, composed of zinc 67, sulphur 33 ; but it usually contains a certain proportion of the sulphide of iron, which imparts to it a dark colour, whence the name of 'Black Jack,' applied to it by the Cornish miner. The ore of this country generally consists of zinc 61·5, iron 4·0, sulphur 33·0. Blende occurs either in a botryoidal form or in crystals (often of very complex forms), belonging to the tetrahedal division of the cubic or monometric system. $H = 3·5$ to 4. Specific gravity $= 3·9$ to 4. See ZINC.—H.W.B.

In some districts the presence of the sulphide of zinc is regarded by the miners as a favourable indication, hence we have the phrase, '*Black Jack rides a good horse.*' In other localities it is thought to be equally unfavourable, and the miners say, '*Black Jack cuts out the ore.*' For many years the English zinc ores were of little value, the immense quantity of zinc manufactured by the Vieille Montagne Company, and sent into this country, being quite sufficient to meet the demand. Beyond this, there was some difficulty in obtaining zinc which would roll into sheets, from English sulphides.

Much of the zinc obtained from blende is used in the manufacture of brass.

Pure blende is a mineralogical rarity ; the white and colourless variety (*Cleiophane*) of New Jersey, United States, was analysed by the late T. H. Henry, and found to be absolutely pure, with the exception of a trace of cadmium. Blende nearly always contains sulphide of iron. The following analyses of varieties of blende illustrate this :—

	Sulphide of Zinc	Sulphide of Iron
Charente	82·76	13·71
English	91·8	6·4

Production of Zinc Ore in the United Kingdom in the years 1870 *and* 1871, *showing the produce of each district.*

No. of Mines	Places	1870		No. of Mines	1871	
		Zinc Ore	Value		Zinc Ore	Value
		Tons cwt. qr.	£ s. d.		Tons cwt. qr.	£ s. d.
	ENGLAND :					
10	Cornwall	926 16 3	2,523 10 0	8	952 7 2	2,325 10 6
2	Cumberland	581 18 2	1,739 10 0	2	798 8 2	2,394 10 0
1	Devonshire	346 3 1	970 6 0	1	570 11 3	1,562 10 10
	Derbyshire	57 0 0	196 13 0		57 0 0	228 0 0
3	Shropshire	399 11 0	1,274 13 0	3	380 12 0	969 6 0
1	Staffordshire	76 0 0	262 4 0	1	45 0 0	168 15 0
	WALES :					
1	Brecknockshire	48 0 0	165 12 0	1	15 0 0	60 0 0
1	Carmarthenshire	57 0 0	201 13 0	1	60 0 0	210 0 0
5	Cardiganshire	212 16 0	530 16 0	12	629 11 1	2,119 3 3
1	Carnarvonshire	61 17 2	213 10 0			
2	Denbighshire	2,919 0 0	9,069 0 0	3	3,516 0 0	14,430 4 6
3	Flintshire	2,711 0 0	7,732 5 0	5	3,187 4 0	8,139 10 0
7	Montgomeryshire	700 0 0	2,378 0 0	5	1,405 0 0	3,630 15 0
2	ISLE OF MAN	4,176 19 1	13,834 0 3	2	5,768 5 0	19,014 19 9
1	IRELAND	312 8 0	937 1 0	2	321 10 0	964 10 0
	SCOTLAND	..	..	1	30 0 0	112 10 0
40		13,586 10 0	41,058 13 3	47	17,736 10 0	56,330 4 10

Metallic zinc produced, 1870, 3,936 tons ; 1871, 4,966 tons.

IMPORTS.

Year		Tons		Tons		Tons
1870	Zinc or Spelter	28,775	Zinc Ore	44,553	Oxide of Zinc	2,328
1871	Crude Zinc	20,929	Ditto	29,418	Manufactured	8,765

EXPORTS.

1870	Zinc, British & Foreign	10,331	...		Oxide of Zinc	1,385
1871	Ditto ditto	6,452	Zinc ore	184	—	—

In 13 out of 16 analyses of blende from different localities recorded by Rammelsberg, iron is present in proportions varying from 1·18 to 18·1 per cent. Copper occasionally occurs in blende, but rarely above 1 per cent. Cadmium is a frequent, if not

a general constituent of blende.   The cadmiferous varieties are termed *Przibramite.*
The blende from the King William mine at Clausthal contains, according to Kuhle-
mann, 0·63 per cent. of antimony, 0·79 of cadmium, and 0·13 of copper, besides 1·18
of iron.   Blende is met with in association with galena, iron-pyrites and copper-pyrites, from which it should be dressed as clean as possible, although in this there is
some difficulty, owing to the very close approximation of the specific gravities of these
ores.   Blende is occasionally argentiferous, and sometimes sufficiently so to allow of
the profitable extraction of the silver.   In one of the mines in the Chiverton district,
near Truro, Cornwall, some very fine examples of this argentiferous blende have been
discovered.   In one of the zinc ores of Silesia, the new metal INDIUM has been discovered by the aid of spectrum analysis.   Plattner states that blende occasionally
contains traces of tin and manganese.—(*Percy's Metallurgy.*)   The red varieties of
blende often contain from 2 to 3 per cent. of sulphide of cadmium, especially that
which is found at Marmato, near Popayan. Dana has quoted the following analyses of
varieties of blende :—

	Sulphur	Zinc	Iron	Cadmium
Carinthia . . .	32·10	64·22	1·32	trace
New Hampshire . .	32· 6	52·00	10·0	3·2
New Jersey . .	32·22	67·46	...	trace
Tuscany . . .	32·12	48·11	11·44	1·23

See INDIUM ; MARMATITE.
BLEU DE LYONS. See ANILINE-BLUE.
BLEU DE PARIS. See ANILINE-BLUE.
BLIGHT.   A disease in plants frequently produced by atmospheric, or by physical
agencies.   A peculiar blight has been referred to the action of the extra-spectral heat
rays. Blight is sometimes of insect origin, but more frequently it arises from parasitic
fungi. See PARATHERMIC RAYS and FUNGI.
BLIND COAL, a name given to anthracite in some parts of Scotland.   See AN-
THRACITE.
BLISTER COPPER-ORE.   A botryoidal variety of copper-pyrites, which
has been found at the copper mines in the neighbourhood of Camborne, in remarkably fine masses.   Of late years it has been but rarely found in those mines. See
COPPER.
BLISTER-STEEL.   Bars of steel which exhibit blister-like protuberances.
See STEEL.
BLOCK MANUFACTURE.   Though the making of ships' blocks belongs
rather to a dictionary of engineering than of manufactures, it may be expected that
some account should be given of the automatic machinery for making blocks, so admirably devised and mounted by Sir M. I. Brunel, for the British Navy, in the dockyard of Portsmouth.
The series of machines and operations are as follows :—
1. *The straight cross-cutting saw.*—The log is placed horizontally on a very low
bench, which is continued through the window of the mill into the yard.   The saw
is exactly over the place where the log is to be divided.   It is let down, and suffered
to rest with its teeth upon the log, the back still being in the cleft of the guide.   The
crank being set in motion, the saw reciprocates backwards and forwards with exactly
the same motion as if worked by a carpenter, and quickly cuts through the tree.
When it first begins to cut, its back is in the cleft in the guide, and this causes it to
move in a straight line ; but before it gets out of the guide, it is so deep in the wood
as to guide itself ; for, in cutting across the grain of the wood, it has no tendency to be
diverted from its true line by the irregular grain.   When the saw has descended
through the tree, its handle is caught in a fixed stop, to prevent its cutting the bench.
The machine is thrown out of gear, the attendant lifts up the saw by a rope, removes
the block cut off, and advances the tree to receive a fresh cut.
2. *The circular cross-cutting saw.*—This saw possesses universal motion ; but the
axis is always parallel to itself, and the saw in the same plane.   It can be readily
raised or lowered, by inclining the upper frame on its axis ; and to move it sidewise,
the saw-frame must swing sidewise on its joints which connect it with the upper frame.
These movements are effected by two winches, each furnished with a pair of equal
pinions, working a pair of racks fixed upon two long poles.   The spindles of these
winches are fixed in two vertical posts, which support the axis of the upper frame.
One of these pairs of poles is jointed to the extreme end of the upper frame ; therefore, by turning the handle belonging to them, the frame and saw are elevated or de-

pressed; in like manner, the other pair is attached to the lower part of the saw-frame, so that the saw can be moved sidewise by means of their handles, which then swing the saw from its vertical position.

These two handles give the attendant a complete command of the saw, which we suppose to be in rapid motion, the tree being brought forward and properly fixed. By one handle, he draws the saw against one side of the tree, which is thus cut into (perhaps half through); now, by the other handle, he raises the saw up, and by the first-mentioned handle he draws it across the top of the tree, and cuts it half through from the upper side; he then depresses the saw and cuts half through the next side; and lastly a trifling cut of the saw, at the lower side, completely divides the tree, which is then advanced to take another cut.

The great reciprocating saw is on the same principle as the saw-mill in common use in America.

3. *The circular ripping saw* is a thin circular plate of steel, with teeth similar to those of a pit saw, formed in its periphery. It is fixed to a spindle placed horizontally, at a small distance beneath the surface of a bench or table, so that the saw projects a few inches above the bench through a crevice. The spindle being supported in proper collars has a rapid rotatory motion communicated to it by a pulley on the opposite end, round which an endless strap is passed from a drum placed overhead in the mill. The block cut by the preceding machine from the end of the tree is placed with one of the sides flat upon the bench, and thus slides forward against the revolving saw, which cuts the wood with a rapidity incredible to any one who has not seen these or similar machines.

4. *Boring-machine.*—The blocks prepared by the foregoing saws are placed in the machine represented in *fig.* 140. This machine has an iron frame, A A, with three legs, beneath which the block is introduced, and the screw near B being forced down upon it, confines it precisely in the proper spot to receive the borers D and E. This spot is determined by a piece of metal fixed perpendicularly just beneath the point of the borer E, shown separately on the ground at x; this piece of metal adjusts the position for the borer D, and its height is regulated by resting on the head of the screw x, which fastens the piece x down to the frame. The sides of the block are

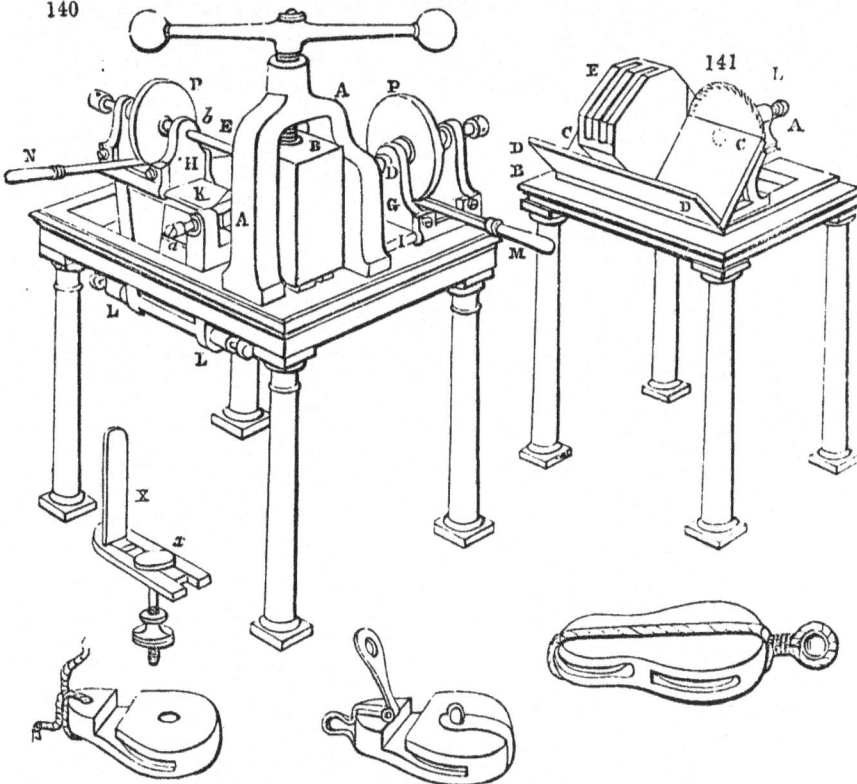

kept in a parallel position, by being applied against the heads of three screws tapped into the double leg of the frame A. The borer D is adapted to bore the hole for the centre-pin in a direction exactly perpendicular to the surface resting against the three screws; the other, at E, perforates the holes for the commencement of the sheave holes. Both borers are constructed in nearly the same manner; they are screwed upon the ends of small mandrels, mounted in frames similar to a lathe. These frames, G and H, are fitted with sliders upon the angular edges of the flat broad bars, I and K. The former of these is screwed fast to the frame; the latter is fixed upon a frame of its own, moving on the centre-screws at L L, beneath the principal frame of the machine. By this means the borer E can be moved within certain limits, so as to bore holes in different positions. These limits are determined by two screws, one of which is seen at a; the other being on the opposite side, is invisible. They are tapped through fixed pieces projecting up from the frame. A projecting piece of metal from the underside of the slider K of the borer E, stops against the ends of these screws, to limit the excursion of the borer. The frames for both borers are brought up towards the block by means of levers M and N. These are centred on a pin, at the opposite sides of the frame of the machine, and have oblong grooves through them, which receive screw-pins, fixed into the frames G and H, beneath the pulleys P P, which give motion to the spindles.

5. *The mortising-machine* is a beautiful piece of mechanism, but too complicated for description within the limits prescribed to this article.

6. *The corner saw, fig.* 141, consists of a mandrel mounted in a frame A, and carrying a circular saw, L, upon the extreme end of it. This mandrel and its frame being exactly similar to those at G and H, *fig.* 140, do not require a separate view, although they are hidden behind the saw, except the end of the screw, marked A. This frame is screwed down upon the frame B B of the machine, which is supported upon four columns. C C, D D, is an inclined bench, or a kind of trough, in which a block is laid, as at E, being supported on its edge by the plane C C of this bench, and its end kept up to its position by the other part of the bench D D.

By sliding the block along this bench, it is applied to the saw, which cuts off its angles, as is evident from the figure, and prepares it for the shaping engine. All the four angles are cut off in succession, by applying its different sides to the trough or bench. In the figure, two of them are drawn as being cut, and the third is just marked by the saw. This machine is readily adapted to different sizes of blocks, by the simple expedient of laying pieces of wood of different thickness against the plane D D, so as to fill it up, and keep the block nearer to or farther from the saw; for all the blocks are required to be cut at the same angle, though, of course, a larger piece is to be cut from large than from small blocks. The block reduced to the state of E is now taken to

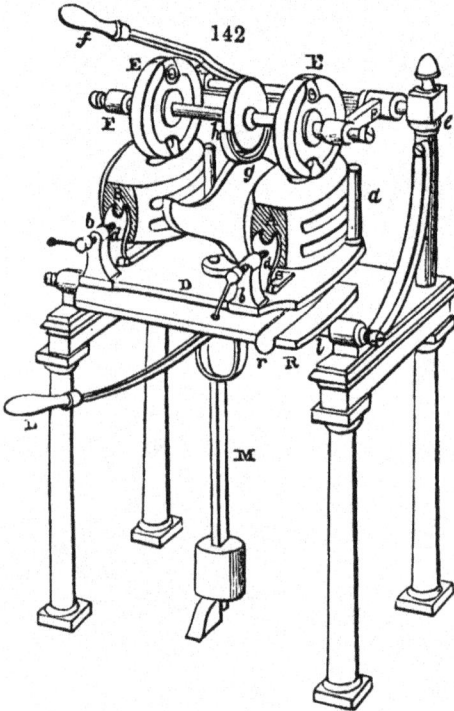

142

7. *The shaping-machine.*—A great deal of the apparent complication of this figure arises from the iron cage which is provided to defend the workmen, lest the blocks, which are revolving in the circles or chuck with an immense velocity, should be loosened by the action of the tool, and fly out by their centrifugal force. Without this provision, the consequences of such an accident would be dreadful, as the blocks would be projected in all directions, with an inconceivable force.

8. *The scoring-engine* receives two blocks as they come from the shaping-engine, and forms the groove round the longest diameters for the reception of their ropes or straps, as represented in the two snatch blocks and double block, under *figs.* 140, 141.

A, B, *fig.* 142, represent the above two blocks, each held between two small pillars a (the other pillar is hid behind the block), fixed in a strong plate D, and pressed against the pillars by a screw b, which acts on a clamp d. Over the blocks a pair of circular planes or cutters, E E, are situated, both being fixed on the same spindle, which is turned by a pulley in the middle of it. The spindle is fitted in a frame F F, moving in centres at *e e*, so as to rise and fall when moved by a handle *f*. This brings the cutters down upon the blocks; and the depth to which they can cut is regulated by a curved shape *g*, fixed by screws upon the plate D, between the blocks. Upon this rests a curved piece of metal *h*, fixed to the frame F, and inclosing, but not touching, the pulley. To admit the cutters to traverse the whole length of the blocks, the plate D (or rather a frame beneath it) is sustained between the points of two centres. Screws are seen at *l*, on these centres. The frame inclines when the handle L is depressed. At M is a lever with a weight at the end of it, counterbalancing the weight of the blocks, and plate D, all which are above the centre on which they move. The frame F is also provided with a counterpoise to balance the cutters, &c. The cutters E E are circular wheels of brass, with round edges. Each has two notches in its circumference, at opposite sides; and in these notches chisels are fixed by screws, to project beyond the rim of the wheel, in the manner of a plane-iron before its face.

This machine is used as follows:—In order to fix the block, it is pressed between the two pins (only one of which, at *a*, can be seen in this view), and the clamp *d*, screwed up against it, so as just to hold the block, but no more. The clamp has two claws, as is seen in the figure, each furnished with a ring entering the double prints previously made in the end of the block. These rings are partly cut away, leaving only such a segment of each as will just retain the block, and the metal between them is taken out to admit the cutter to operate between them, or nearly so. In putting the blocks into this machine, the workman applies the double prints to the ends of the claws of the clamps, but takes care that the blocks are higher between the pins *a* than they should be; he then takes the handle *f*, and by it presses the cutters E E (which we suppose are standing still) down upon the blocks, depressing them between their pins at the same time, till the descent of the cutters is stopped by the piece *h* resting on the shape *g*. He now turns the screws *b b*, to fix the blocks tight. The cutters being put in motion cut the scores, which will be plainly seen by the mode of adjustment just described, to be of no depth at the pin-hole; but by depressing the handle L, so as to incline the blocks, and keeping the cutters down upon their shape *g*, by the handle *f*, they will cut any depth towards the ends of the blocks, which the shape *g* admits.

By this means one quarter of the score is formed; the other is done by turning both blocks together half round in this manner. The centres *l* are not fitted into the plate D itself, but into a frame seen at R beneath the plate, which is connected with it by a centre-pin, exactly midway between the two blocks A B. A spring-catch, the end of which is seen at *r*, confines them together; when this catch is pressed back, the plate D can be turned about upon its centre-pin, so as to change the blocks, end for end, and bring the unscored quarters (*i. e.* over the clamps) beneath the cutters; the workman taking the handles *f* and L, one in each hand, and, pressing them down, cuts out the second quarter. This might have been effected by simply lifting up the handle L; but in that case the cutter would have struck against the grain of the wood so as to cut rather roughly; but by this ingenious device of reversing the blocks, it always cuts clean and smooth, in the direction of the grain. The third and fourth quarters of the score are cut by turning the other sides of the blocks upwards, and repeating the above operation. The shape *g* can be removed, and another put in its place, for different sizes and curves of blocks; but the pins *a* and holding-clamps *d* will suit many different sizes.

By these machines the shells of the blocks are completely formed, and they are next polished and finished by hand labour; but as this is performed by tools and methods which are well known, it is needless to enter into any explanation: the finishing required being only a smoothing of the surfaces. The machines cut so perfectly true as to require no wood to be removed in the finishing; but as they cut without regard to the irregularity of the grain, knots, &c., it happens that many parts are not so smooth as might be wished, and for this purpose manual labour alone can be employed.

The lignum vitæ for the sheaves of the blocks is cut across the grain of the wood by two cross-cutting saws, a circular and straight saw, as before mentioned. These machines do not essentially differ in their principle from the great cross-cutting saws we have described, except that the wood revolves while cutting, so that a small saw will reach the centre of a large tree, and at the same time cut it truly flat. These machines cut off their plates from the end of a tree which are exactly the thickness for the intended sheave. These pieces are of an irregular figure, and must be rounded and centred in the crown saw,

9. *The crown saw* is represented in *fig.* 143 (p. 402), where A is a pulley revolving by means of an endless strap. It has the crown or trepan saw *a* fixed to it, by a

screw cut within the piece, upon which the saw is fixed, and which gives the ring or hook of the saw sufficient stability to perform its office. Both the pulleys and saw revolve together upon a truly cylindrical tube *b*, which is stationary, being attached by a flanch *c* to a fixed puppet B, and on this tube as an axis the saw and pulley turn, and may be slid endwise by a collar fitted round the centre-piece of the pulley, and having two iron rods (only one of which can be seen at *d* in the figure), passing through holes made through the flanch and puppet B. When the saw is drawn back upon its central tube, the end of the latter projects beyond the teeth of the saw. It is by means of this fixed ring or tube within the saw, that the piece of wood *c* is supported together during the operation of sawing, being pressed forcibly against it by a screw D, acting through a puppet fixed to the frame of the machine. At the end of this screw is a cup or basin which applies itself to the piece of wood, so as to form a kind of vice, one side being the end of the fixed tube, the other the cup at the end of the screw D. Within the tube *b* is a collar for supporting a central axis, which is perfectly cylindrical. The other end of this axis (seen at *f*) turns in a collar of the fixed puppet E. The central axis has a pulley F, fixed on it, and giving it motion by a strap similar to the other. Close to the latter pulley, a collar *g* is fitted on the centre-piece of the pulley, so as to slip round freely, but at the same time confined to move endwise with the pulley and its collar. This collar receives the ends of the two iron rods *d*. The opposite ends of these rods are, as above mentioned, connected by a similar collar with the pulley A of the saw *a*. By this connection, both the centre-bit, which is screwed into the end of the central axis *f*, and the saw sliding upon the fixed tube *b*, are brought forward to the wood at the same time, both being in rapid motion, by their respective pulleys.

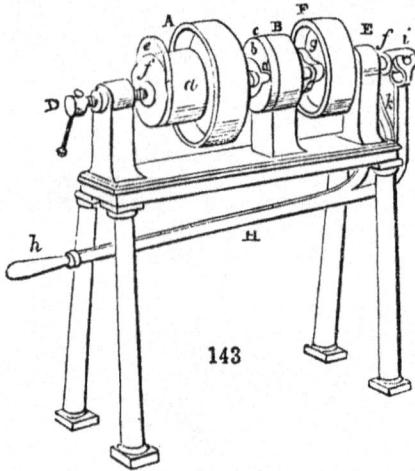

10. *The coaking-engine.*—This ingenious piece of machinery is used to cut the three semicircular holes which surround the hole bored by the crown saw, so as to produce a cavity in the centre of the disc.

11. *Face-turning lathe.*—The sheave is fixed against a flat chuck, similar to that in the coaking-engine, except that the centre-pin, instead of having a nut, is tapped into the flat chuck, and turned by a screw-driver.

A complete set of this block machinery has since been made, by Messrs. Maudslay and Field, for the Spanish Government, from the original drawings and models.

Iron blocks and sheaves have been introduced with great advantage by Messrs. Brown and Lenox, and are used extensively in the naval and merchant services. See IRON.

BLOCK TIN. Metallic tin cast into a block, the weight of which is now about 3½ cwts. Formerly, when it was the custom to carry the blocks of tin on the backs of mules, the block was regulated by what was then considered to be a load for the mule, at 2½ cwts. Subsequently, the block of tin was increased in size, and made as much as two men could lift, or 3 cwts. It was the custom to order so many blocks of tin, and the smelter, being desirous of selling as much tin as possible, continued to increase the size of the block, so that, although 3½ cwts. is the usual weight, many blocks are sold weighing 3¾ cwts. The term is also applied to articles made of tinned iron. See TIN.

BLOND METAL. A Clayband ironstone found near Wednesbury. It is used, when smelted, for making tools.

BLOOD. (*Sang*, Fr.; *Blut*, Ger.) The liquid which circulates in the arteries and veins of animals; bright red in the former and purple in the latter, among all the groups whose temperature is considerably higher than that of the atmosphere. Its specific gravity varies with the nature and health of the animal, being from 1·0527 to 1·0570 at 60° F. It has a saline sub-nauseous taste, and a smell peculiar to each animal. It consists of a transparent, nearly colourless liquid, called the *liquor sanguinis*, or *plasma*, in which vast numbers of microscopic corpuscles are suspended. These corpuscles are of two kinds, some being *white* or *colourless* transparent cells, whilst others, far more numerous, are of a *red* tint, and impart the characteristic colour to the blood. The red corpuscles are present only in the blood of vertebrated animals, and vary considerably in size and shape in different groups of the vertebrata. They are always, however, flattened disc-like bodies, oval or circular in outline, and with or without a nucleus. These corpuscles consist apparently of an albuminoid substance, enclosing a red fluid. This fluid is now recognised as a definite crystallisable compound, containing iron, and termed *hæmoglobin, hæmoglobulin* or *hæmatoglobulin*. Hæmoglobin may be resolved into two substances called *globulin* and *hæmatin*. The so-called blood-crystals vary in shape, and are in many cases characteristic of the animal from which the blood was taken. The hæmoglobin of the dog has been found to contain—

Carbon	53·85
Oxygen	21·84
Hydrogen	7·82
Nitrogen	16·17
Sulphur	0·39
Iron	0·43
	100·00

The *liquor sanguinis*, or colourless liquid in which the corpuscles freely float, contains fibrin (or rather two albuminous substances which readily form fibrin, and are called *paraglobulin* and *fibrinogen*), albumen, fatty matter, and certain saline substances. On the coagulation of blood, the fibrin separates in a gelatinous form, carrying with it the red corpuscles; this mixture of fibrin and corpuscles forms the *clot*, or *crassamentum*, whilst the remainder of the blood constitutes the liquid known as *serum*. If the warm blood be switched with a bundle of twigs as it flows from the veins, the fibrin concretes and forms long fibres and knots, while it retains its usual appearance in other respects. The clot contains fibrin and colouring-matter in various proportions. Berzelius found, in 100 parts of the dried clot of blood, 35 parts of fibrin, 58 of colouring-matter, 1·3 of carbonate of soda, 4 of an animal matter soluble in water, along with some salts and fat. The specific gravity of the serum varies from 1·027 to 1·029. It forms about three-fourths of the weight of the blood, has an alkaline reaction, coagulates at 157° F. into a gelatinous mass, and has for its leading constituent *albumen* to the amount of 8 per cent., besides fat, potash, soda, and salts of these bases. Blood does not seem to contain any gelatine. Fat and sugar are found in blood, the quantities varying with the health of the animal. For a very full account of the researches made by chemists on blood, see 'Watts's Dictionary of Chemistry.'

The red colouring-matter called *hematosine* may be obtained from the cruor, or hæmoglobin, by washing with cold water and filtering. Professor Stokes, in a paper ' On the Reduction and Oxidation of the Colouring-Matter of the Blood,' has published some very curious results. By spectrum-analysis he has been led to infer that the colouring-matter of blood, like indigo, is capable of existing in two states of oxidation, distinguishable by a difference of colour and a fundamental difference in the action on the spectrum. It may be made to pass from the more to the less oxidised state, by the action of suitable reducing agents, and recovers its oxygen by absorption from the air. This colouring-matter in its two states of oxidation, Professor Stokes proposes to call *scarlet cruorine* and *purple cruorine.*—*Proceedings of the Royal Society*, vol. xiii. p. 355 (1864).

Mr. Sorby has also published in the ' Quarterly Journal of Science.' No. VI., April 1865, a paper ' On the Detection of Blood Stains by Spectrum-Analysis,' in which he shows how it may be employed with great reliance in cases of the highest judicial importance. These two papers should be consulted.

Blood may be dried by evaporation at a heat of 130° to 140°, and in this state has been transported to the colonies for purifying cane-juice. It is used for making animal charcoal in the Prussian-blue works, and, by an after-process, a decolouring carbon. It is employed in some Turkey-red dye-works. Blood is a powerful manure.

Mr. Pillans, in 1854, took out a patent for the separation of the colouring-matter of the blood, by which he obtained readily—1st, the clot, in a comparatively dry state, comprising hæmatosine, with a portion of serum and all the fibrin; 2nd, a portion of serum, highly coloured with hæmatosine; 3rd, the clear serum.

The blood, in small fragments, is dried on wirework or trays, at a less temperature than will coagulate the hæmatosine, so that, when dry, it may be soluble in water; 110° to 115° is the temperature recommended.

The clear serum is dried and ground and in a fit state to be used as albumen, and may be employed by the printers of textile fabrics for fixing ultramarine blue and other colours, or as a substitute for egg albumen, both in printing colours and in refining liquids.

BLOODSTONE. A very hard, compact variety of hæmatite iron ore, which, when reduced to a suitable form, fixed into a handle, and well polished, forms the best description of burnisher for producing a high lustre on gilt coat-buttons. The gold on china is burnished by the same means.

Bloodstone is a name also applied to the jaspery variety of quartz known as the *heliotrope*, coloured deep green, with interspersed blood-red spots like drops of blood.

BLOOM. The name given to a mass of iron after it leaves the puddling furnace. See Iron.

BLOOMARY. The old iron-furnaces were so called.

BLOWING MACHINE and **FANS.** See Iron, Metallurgy, Ventilation.

BLOWPIPE. (*Chalumeau*, Fr.; *Löthrohr*, Ger.) Jewellers, mineralogists, chemists, enamellers, &c., make frequent use of a tube,—usually bent near the end,—terminated with a finely-pointed nozzle, for blowing through the flame of a lamp, candle, or gas-jet, and producing thereby a small conical flame possessing a very intense heat.

The blowpipe is so extremely useful to the manufacturer and to the miner that a more exact description of the instrument is required.

When we propel a flame by means of a current of air blown *into* or upon it, the flame thus produced may be divided into two parts, as possessing different properties —that of *reducing* under one condition, and of *oxidising* under another.

The *reducing flame* is produced by blowing the ordinary flame of a lamp or candle simply aside by a weak current of air impinging on its outer surface; it is therefore unchanged except in its direction. Unconsumed carbon, at a white heat, giving the yellow colour to the flame, coming in contact with the substance aids in its reduction.

The *oxidising flame* is formed by pouring a strong blast of air into the *interior* of the flame; combustion is thus thoroughly established, and if a small fragment of an oxidisable body is held just beyond the point of the flame, it becomes intensely heated, and, being exposed freely to the action of the surrounding air, it is rapidly oxidised.

The best form of blowpipe is the annexed (*fig.* 144), which, with the description, is copied from Blanford's excellent translation of Dr. Theodore Scheerer's 'Introduction to the Use of the Mouth Blowpipe.'

The tube and nozzle of the instrument are usually made of German silver, or silver with a platinum point, and a trumpet-shaped mouth-piece of horn or ivory. Many blowpipes have no mouth-pieces of this form, but are simply tipped with ivory, or some similar material. The air-chamber A serves in some degree to regulate the blast and receives the stem B, and the nozzle *a*, which are made separately, and accurately ground into it, so that they may be put together or taken apart at pleasure. The point *b* is best made of platinum, to allow of its being readily cleaned, and is of the form shown in the woodcut. When the instrument is used, the mouth-piece is pressed against the lips, or, if this is wanting, the end of the stem must be held between the lips of the operator. The former mode is far less wearying than the latter; and whereas, with the trumpet mouth-piece, it is easy to maintain a continued blast for five or ten minutes, without it it is almost impossible to sustain an unbroken blast of more than two or three minutes' duration. While blowing, the operator breathes through his nostrils only, and, using the epiglottis as a valve, forces the air through the blowpipe by means of the cheek muscles.

Some years since, Mr. John Prideaux, of Plymouth, printed some valuable 'Suggestions' for the use of the blowpipe by working miners. Some portions of this paper appear so useful, especially under circumstances which may preclude the use of superior instruments, &c., that it is thought advisable to transfer them to these pages.

For ordinary metallurgic assays, the common blowpipe does very well. A mere tapering tube, 10 inches long, ¼ inch diameter at one end, and the opening at the other scarcely equal to admit a pin of the smallest kind, the smaller end curved off for 1½ inch to a right angle. A bulb at the bend, to contain the vapour condensed from

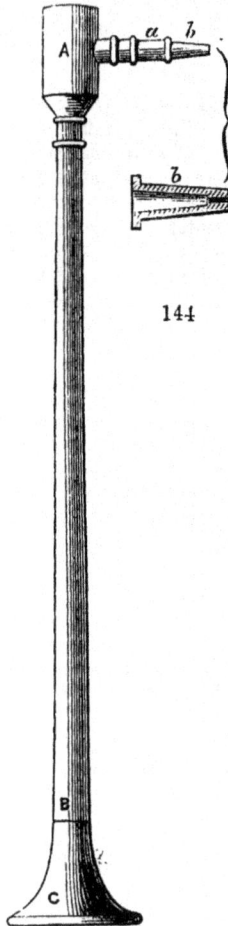

the breath, is useful in long operations, but may generally be dispensed with. In selecting the blowpipe, the small aperture should be chosen perfectly round and smooth, otherwise it will not command a good flame.

A common candle, such as the miner employs under ground, answers very well for the flame.

To support the subject of assay, or 'the assay,' as it has been happily denominated by Mr. Children, two different materials are requisite, according as we wish to calcine or reduce it. For the latter purpose, nothing is so good as charcoal ; but that from oak is less eligible, both from its inferior combustibility and from its containing iron, than that from alder, willow, or other light woods.

For calcination, a very convenient support, where platinum wire is difficult to procure, is white-baked pipe-clay or china-clay, selecting such as will not fuse nor become coloured by roasting with borax.

The supports are conveniently formed by a process of Mr. Tennant. The clay is to be beaten to a smooth stiff body ; then a thin cake of it being placed between a fold of writing-paper, it is to be beaten out with a mallet to the thickness of a wafer, and cut, paper and all, into squares of $\frac{3}{8}$ths inch diameter, or triangles about the same size. These are to be put in the bowl of a tobacco-pipe, and heated gently till dry, then baked till the paper is burnt away, and the clay left perfectly white. They should be baked in a clear fire, to keep out coal dust and smoke as much as possible, as either of these adhering to the clay plates would colour the borax in roasting. A small fragment of the bowl of a new tobacco-pipe will serve instead in the absence of a more convenient material.

A simple pair of forceps (*fig.* 145), to move and to take up the hot assay, may be made of a slip of stiff tin plate, 8 inches long, $\frac{1}{2}$ inch wide in the middle, and $\frac{1}{16}$th inch at the ends. The tin being rubbed off the points on a rough whetstone, the slip is to be bent until they approach each other within $\frac{1}{4}$ an inch and the two sides are parallel ; thus there will be spring enough in the forceps to open and let go the assay when not compressed by the finger and thumb.

145 146

A magnetic needle, very desirable to ascertain the presence of iron, is easily made of the requisite delicacy where a magnet is accessible. A bit of thin steel wire, or a long fine stocking-needle, having $\frac{1}{4}$ inch cut of at the point, is to be heated in the middle that it may be slightly bent there (*fig.* 146). While hot, a bit of sealing-wax is to be attached to the centre, and the point which had been cut off, being heated at the thick end, is to be fixed in the sealing-wax, so that the sharp end may serve as a pivot, descending about $\frac{1}{8}$th inch below the centre, taking care that the ends of the needle fall enough below the pivot, to prevent it overturning. It must be magnetised, by sliding one end of a magnet half a dozen or more times from the centre to one end of the needle, and the other end a similar number of times from the centre of the needle to its other end. A small brass thimble (not capped with iron) will do for the support, the point of the pivot being placed in one of the indentations near the centre of the tap, when, if well balanced, it will turn until it settles north and south. If one side preponderate, it must be nipped until the balance be restored.

A black gun-flint is also occasionally used to rub the metallic globules (first attached, whilst warm, to a bit of sealing-wax), and ascertain the colour of the streak which they give. Thus minute particles of gold, copper, silver, &c., are readily discriminated. A little refined borax and carbonate of soda, both in powder, will complete the requisites.

Having collected these materials, the next object for the operator is to acquire the faculty of keeping up an unintermittent blast through the pipe whilst breathing freely through the nose.

A very sensitive and, for most purposes, sufficiently delicate balance (*fig.* 147, p. 406) was also devised by Mr. Prideaux, of which the following is a description.

The common marsh-reed, growing generally in damp places throughout the kingdom, will yield straight joints, from 8 to 12, or more, inches long; an 8-inch joint will serve, but the longer the better. The joint is to be split down its whole length, so as to form a trough, say $\frac{1}{4}$ inch wide in the middle, narrowed away to $\frac{1}{3}$rd inch at the ends. A narrow slip of writing-paper, the thinner the better (bank-post is very convenient for the purpose), and as long as the reed trough, is to be stuck with common paste on the face of a carpenter's rule, or, in preference, that of an exciseman,—as the inches are divided into tenths instead of eighths ;—in either case observing that the divisions of the inch on the rule be left uncovered by the paper. When it is dry, lines must be drawn the whole length of it, $\frac{1}{8}$th inch apart, to mark out a stripe $\frac{1}{8}$th inch wide. Upon this stripe the divisions of the inch are to be ruled off by means of a small square.

The centre divsion being marked 0, it is to be numbered at every fourth line to the ends. Thus the fourth from the centre on each side will be 10 ; the eighth, 20 ; the twelfth, 30 ; the sixteenth, 40, &c. ; and a slip 10 inches long, graduated into tenths of an inch, will have on each arm 50 lines, or 125 degrees, divided by these lines into quarters. While the lines and numbers are drying, *the exact centre* of the reed-trough may be ascertained, and marked *right* across, by spots on the two edges. A line of gum-water, full $\frac{1}{8}$th inch wide, is then laid with a camel-hair pencil along the hollow, and the paper being stripped from the rule (which it leaves easily), the graduated stripe is cut out with scissors, and laid in the trough, with the line 0 exactly in the centre. Being pressed to the gummed reed, by passing the round end of a quill along it, it graduates the trough from the centre to each end. This graduation is very true, if well managed, as the paper does not stretch with the gum-water after being laid on the rule with the paste.

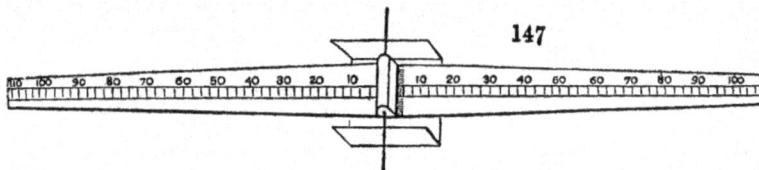

147

A very fine needle is next to be procured (those called *bead*-needles are the finest) and passed through a slip of cork the width of the centre of the trough, about $\frac{1}{4}$th inch square, $\frac{1}{8}$th thick. It should be passed through with care, so as to be quite straight. The cork should then be cut until one end of it fits into the trough, so that the needle shall bear on the edges exactly in the spots that mark the centre, as it is of importance that the needle and the trough be exactly at right angles with each other. The cork is now to be fixed in its place with gum-water, and, when fast dry, to be soldered down on each side with a small portion of any soft resinous cement, on the point of a wire or knitting-needle ; a little cement being also applied in the same manner to the edges of the cork where the needle goes through, to give it firmness, the beam is finished. It may be balanced by paring the edges on the heaviest side : but accurate adjustment is needless, as it is subject to vary with the dampness or dryness of the air.

The support on which it plays is a bit of tin plate (or, in preference, brass plate), $1\frac{3}{8}$ths inch long, and 1 inch wide. The two ends are turned up square $\frac{3}{8}$ths of an inch, giving a base of $\frac{5}{8}$ths of an inch wide, and two upright sides $\frac{3}{8}$ths high. The upper edges are then rubbed down smooth and square upon a Turkey stone, letting both edges bear on the stone together that they may exactly correspond. For use, the beam is placed ovenly in the support, with the needle resting across the edges. Being brought to an exact balance by a bit of writing-paper, or any other substance, placed on the lighter side, and moved toward the end until the equilibrium is produced, it will turn with extreme delicacy, a bit of horsehair, $\frac{1}{8}$th inch long, being sufficient to bring it down freely.

It must not be supposed that any such instrument as this is recommended as in any way substituting the beautiful balances which are constructed for the chemist, and others requiring to weigh with great accuracy. The object is merely to show the miner a method by which he may construct for himself a balance which shall be sufficiently accurate for such blowpipe investigations as it may be important for him to learn to perform for himself. If the suggestions of the chemist who devised the above balance had been carried out, much valuable mineral matter which has been lost might have been turned to profitable account.

The blowpipe is largely used in manufactures, as in soldering, in hardening, and tempering small tools, in glass-blowing, and in enamelling. In many cases the blowpipes are used in the mouth, but frequently they are supplied with air from a bellows moved by the foot, by vessels in which air is condensed, or by means of pneumatic apparatus.

A simple form of regulator for giving a perfectly constant blast has lately been devised by Messrs. Armin, Junge, and Mitzopulos, of Freiburg. The apparatus is thus described : 'A common wide-mouthed bottle is carefully fitted with a caoutchouc cork bored with two holes, into each of which passes a piece of glass tube bent at a right angle. On to one of these tubes is slipped the caoutchouc tube coming from an ordinary caoutchouc bellows, whilst the other is put in communication with the blowpipe nozzle by means of four pieces of caoutchouc tubing joined by three pieces of glass tube, drawn to a fine point at each end. This forms the main peculiarity of the arrangement. When air is forced into the bottle by the blower in jerks, it finds a difficulty in escaping as fast as it comes in, on account of the six fine openings in the glass tubes that it has to pass through on its way from the bottle to the nozzle, and it thus acquires a certain pressure in the bottle, and flows out towards the nozzle as a regular blast. The bottle may be about 6 inches high by $3\frac{1}{2}$ inches wide, with a neck $1\frac{1}{2}$ inch in diameter; but the dimensions are of no great importance. On the whole a somewhat large bottle is better than a small one. The pieces of glass tube we employ are 2 inches long by $\frac{1}{3}$rd inch in diameter. The apparatus will be stronger if instead of a glass bottle a tin cylinder is used, about 4 inches high by 2 inches in diameter, with two tin tubes opening into its top. Small metal cylinders with a fine hole at each end may be used instead of the little glass tubes.'

Many blowpipes have been invented for the employment of oxygen and hydrogen, by the combustion of which the most intense heat which we can produce is obtained. Professor Hare, of Philadelphia, was the first to employ this kind of blowpipe, when he was speedily followed by Clark, Gurney, Leeson, and others. The blowpipe, fed with hydrogen, is employed in many soldering processes with much advantage.

The general form of the 'workshop blowpipe' is that of a tube open at one end, and supported on trunnions in a wooden pedestal, so that it may be pointed vertically, horizontally, or at any angle as desired. Common street gas is supplied through one hollow trunnion, and it escapes through an annular opening, while common air is admitted through the other trunnion, which is also hollow, and is discharged in the centre of the hydrogen through a central conical tube; the magnitude and intensity of the flame being determined by the relative quantities of gas and air, and by the greater or less protrusion of the inner cone, by which the annular space for the hydrogen is contracted in any required degree. See AUTOGENOUS SOLDERING.

BLUBBER. The cellular membrane of the whale, containing the oil. See OIL.

BLUE COPPERAS, or BLUE STONE. The commercial or common names of sulphate of copper. See COPPER, SULPHATE OF.

BLUE GUM. The *Eucalytus globulus* (Lab.), a tree common in Tasmania and South-Eastern Australia, and valuable for its timber and for the gum which it secretes.

BLUE IRON-ORE. See VIVIANITE.

BLUE JOHN. A beautiful variety of fluor spar, found at Tray Cliff, near Castleton, Derbyshire, from which vases and other ornamental articles are wrought. It is now becoming scarce. See FLUOR SPAR.

BLUE LEAD. A name used sometimes by the miners to distinguish galena from the carbonate, or white lead. A variety of galena, to which this name has been applied, and which is pseudomorphous after pyromorphite, has been found at Herodsfoot mine, and Huel Hope in Cornwall, and at some mines in Saxony and France. The specimens from Huel Hope would burn in the flame of a candle like the supersulphide of lead.

BLUE PIGMENTS. The blues of vegetable origin, in common use, are indigo and litmus. The blue pigments of a metallic nature found in commerce are the following:—*Prussian blue;* sesqui-ferrocyanide of iron, called also *Berlin blue; mountain blue*, a carbonate of copper mixed with more or less earthy matter; *Bremen blue,* or *verditer*, a greenish-blue colour obtained from copper mixed with chalk or lime; *iron blue*, phosphate of iron, but little employed; *cobalt blue*, a colour obtained by calcining a salt of cobalt with alumina or oxide of tin; *smalt*, a glass coloured with cobalt and ground.

Molybdenum blue is a combination of this metal and oxide of tin, or phosphate of lime. A blue may also be obtained by putting into molybdic acid (made by digesting sulphuret of molybdenum with nitric acid), some filings of tin, and a little muriatic acid. The tin deoxidises the molybdic acid to a certain degree, and converts it into the molybdous, which, when evaporated and heated with alumina recently precipitated, forms this blue pigment.

Ultramarine is a beautiful blue pigment.

Turnbull's and *Chinese blues* are both double cyanides of iron.

King's blue.—A carbonate of cobalt.

Saxon blue.—A solution of indigo in sulphuric acid.

BLUE VITRIOL. Sulphate of copper. When found in nature, it is due entirely to the decomposition of the sulphides of copper, especially of the yellow copper pyrites, which are liable to this change when placed under the influence of moist air, or of water containing air. See COPPER.

BOG.   The name given to accumulations of peat-earth.   See PEAT.

BOG-BUTTER.   A hydrocarbon compound, like spermaceti, found in the bogs of Ireland.   See ADIPOCERE.

BOG-EARTH.   A soil formed of vegetable fibre and sand.

BOGHEAD COAL, *and other Brown Scotch Cannel Coals.*   The brown cannels are chiefly confined to Scotland, and have been wrought, with the exception of the celebrated Boghead, for the last forty years.   They are found at Boghead, near Bathgate; Rocksoles, near Airdrie; Pirnie, or Methill; Capeldrea, Kirkness, and Wemyss, in Fife.   The first-named coal, about which there has been so much dispute as to its nature, has only been in the market about fourteen years.   It is considered the most valuable coal hitherto discovered for gas- and oil-making purposes; but, strange to say, the middle portion of the Pirnie, or Methill, seam, which was unnoticed for a long period, is nearly as valuable for both purposes.

BOGHEAD.   Amorphous; fracture subconchoidal, compact, containing impressions of the stems of *Sigillaria*, and its roots (*Stigmariæ*), with rootlets traversing the mass. Colour, clove-brown, streak yellow, without lustre; a non-electric; takes fire easily, splits, but does not fuse, and burns with an empyreumatic odour, giving out much smoke, and leaving a considerable amount of white ash. H 2·5.   Specific gravity, 1·2.

According to Dr. Stenhouse, F.R.S., its composition is:—

Carbon	65·72
Hydrogen	9·03
Nitrogen	0·72
Oxygen	4·78
Ash	19·75
	100·00

Dr. Stenhouse's analysis of the ash of Boghead coal (the mean of three analyses), was as follows:—

Silica	58·31
Alumina	33·65
Sesquioxide of iron	7·00
Potash	0·84
Soda	0·41
Lime and sulphuric acid	traces.

Dr. Andrew Fyfe, F.R.S.E., found on analysis that the coal yielded, from a picked specimen, 70 per cent. of volatile matter, and 30 per cent. of coke and ash.   From a ton he obtained 14·880 cubic feet of gas, the illuminating power of which was determined by the use of the Bunsen photometer, the gas being consumed by argands burning from 2½ to 3½ feet per hour, according to circumstances.   The candle referred to was a spermaceti candle, burning 140 grains per hour.

Cubic Feet of Gas per Ton of Coal	Specific Gravity	Condensation by Chlorine in 100 Parts	Durability 1 foot burns	Illuminating Power 1 foot = Light of Candles	Pounds of Coke per Ton of Coal
			Min. Sec.		
14·880	·802	27	88 25	7·72	760

The Pirnie or Methill brown cannel, on examination, gives the following results:—

Specific gravity	1·126
Gas per ton	13,500 feet
Illuminating power	28 candles
Coke and ash	36 per cent.
Hydro-carbons condensed by bromine	20 "
Sulphuretted hydrogen	½ "
Carbonic acid	4¾ "
Carbonic oxide	7¾ "
Volatile matter in coal	65 "
Specific gravity of gas	·700 "

The Boghead coal occurs in the higher part of the Scotch coal-field, in about the position of the 'slaty band' of ironstone; its range is not more than 3 or 4 miles in the lands of Torbane, Inchcross, Boghead, Capper's, and Bathvale, near Bathgate, in the county of Linlithgow. In thickness it varies from 1 to 30 inches, and at the present rapid rate of consumption, it is feared it cannot last many years.

The following section of a pit at Torbane shows that the cannel occurs in ordinary coal-measures, and under circumstances common to beds of coal:—

	Ft.	In.
Boghead house-coal	2	7
Arenaceous shale	6	0
Slaty sandstone	0	7
Shale and ironstone, containing remains of plants and shells	0	10
Cement stone (impure ironstone) . . .	0	4
Boghead cannel	1	9
Fire-clay, full of *Stigmariæ*	0	5
Coal (common)	0	6
Black shale	0	$0\frac{3}{4}$
Coal	0	1
Shale	0	$0\frac{3}{8}$
Coal	0	$0\frac{1}{2}$
Fire-clay	0	$1\frac{1}{2}$
Hard shale	0	3
Thin laminæ of coal and shale	0	$3\frac{1}{2}$
Common coal	0	6
Fire-clay	0	0

One of the chief characters of this cannel is its indestructibility under atmospheric agencies; for whether it is taken from the mine at a depth of fifty fathoms, or at the outcrop, its gas- and oil-yielding properties are the same. Even a piece of the mineral taken out of the drift-deposits, where it had most probably lain for thousands of years, appears to be just the same in quality as if it had been but lately raised from the mine.

In the earth the seam lies parallel to its roof and floor, like other beds of coal; and it is traversed by the usual vertical joints, dividing it into the irregular cubes which so generally characterize beds of cannel. The roof lying above the cement-stone contains remains of *Calamites;* and the ironstone nodules, fossil shells of the genus *Unio.* The floor of the mine contains *Stigmariæ*; and the coal itself affords more upright stems of *Sigillariæ*, and its roots (*Stigmariæ*) and their radicles, running through the seam to a considerable distance, than the majority of coals show. In these respects it entirely resembles the Pirnie or Methill seam. Most cannels afford remains of fish; but in Boghead no traces of these fossils have yet been met with, although they have been diligently sought after.

The roots in the floors, and the upright stems of trees in the seam itself, appear to show that the vegetable matter now forming the coal grew on the spot where it is found. If the mangroves and other aquatic plants, at the present day found growing in the black vegetable mud of the marine swamps of Brasstown, on the west coast of Africa, were quietly submerged and covered up with clay and silt, we should have a good illustration of the formation of a bed of carbonaceous matter showing no structure, mingled with stems and roots of trees showing structure, which is the case with Boghead coal, the structure being only detected in those parts showing evidence of stems and roots, and not in the matrix in which those fossils are contained.

The chemical changes by which vegetable matter has been converted into Boghead cannel will not be here dwelt on; but the chief peculiarity about the seam is its close and compact roof, composed of cement-stone, and shale. This is perfectly water- and air-tight, so much so that, although the mine is troubled with a great quantity of water, it all comes through the floor, and not the roof. This tight covering of the coal has doubtless exercised considerable influence on the decomposing vegetable matter after the latter had been submerged. It is worthy of remark that, above the Pirnie or Methill seam,—the coal nearest approaching Boghead,—a similar bed of impure ironstone occurs.

Away from whin dykes which traverse the coal-field, there are no appearances of the action of an elevated temperature, either upon the coal or its adjoining strata, to give any sanction to the hypothesis, that the cannel has resulted from the partial decomposition of a substratum of coal by the heat of underlying trap, the volatile matters having been retained in what has probably been a bed of shale. First, it must be understood that Boghead cannel, even when treated with boiling naphtha, affords scarcely a trace of bitumen ; and, secondly, when the seam of coal is examined in the neighbourhood of a whin dyke, where heat has evidently acted on it, it is found nothing like cannel, but as a soft sticky substance, of a brown colour, resembling burnt india-rubber. Besides these facts, the seams of coal and their accompanying strata, both above and below the cannel, show no signs of the action of heat, but, on the contrary, exhibit every appearance of having been deposited in the usual way, and of remaining without undergoing any particular alteration.—E. W. B. See CANNEL COAL.

BOGHEAD NAPHTHA (*syn.* Bathgate naphtha), naphtha from the Boghead coal. See NAPHTHA, BOGHEAD.

BOG-IRON ORE is an example of the recent formation of an ore of iron, arising from the decomposition of rocks containing iron, by the action of water charged with carbonic acid. The production of this ore of iron in the present epoch, explains to us many of the conditions under which some of the more ancient beds of iron ore have been produced.

Bog-iron ore is common in the peat bogs of Ireland and other places. See IRON ORES and IRON.

BOG MANGANESE. *Wad,* or earthy manganese. See MANGANESE.

BOGWOOD. The trunks and larger branches of trees dug up from peat bogs. The black oak of the bogs of Ireland, which is so largely employed in the manufacture of ornaments, is so called.

BOHEA. A kind of black tea. See TEA.

BOHEMIAN BOLE. A yellow variety of bole.

BOHEMIAN GARNETS. Garnets belonging to the mineralogical species *Pyrope.* They occur embedded in serpentine at Zöblitz in Bohemia, and also loose in the sands of some of the rivers of Bohemia. These garnets are of a rich dark-red colour, and have been largely employed in cheap jewellery. They are cut and polished in mills worked by water-power, and are mounted by working jewellers at Prague.

BOILED OIL. Linseed oil boiled with litharge, which removes some of its oleaginous parts, and renders the oil more ' drying,' that is, it solidifies more readily.

BOILER. See STEAM BOILER.

BOILER PLATE. Sheets of iron used for making boilers, and now largely employed for constructing railway bridges, ships, tanks, &c. The average resistance of boiler plates is reckoned at 20 tons to the square inch, and the weight which they can carry safely is about 5 tons on the square inch. Riveting is calculated to reduce the strength to a degree corresponding to that of the area which the rivets occupy. Such are the principles by which the Railway Department of the Board of Trade are guided. See IRON.

BOIS DURCI. Finely powdered sawdust, and turnings of hard wood, such as rosewood, ebony, mahogany, and the like, are made into a paste with blood, which is pressed into moulds or formed by dies. It receives a beautiful polish, equal to jet, which it much resembles. This was first introduced to England in 1862 by M. Latry, senior.

BOLE. A kind of clay, often highly coloured by iron. It usually consists of silica, alumina, iron, lime, and magnesia. It is not a well-defined mineral, and, consequently, many substances are described by mineralogists as bole. *Armenian bole* is of a bright red colour. This is frequently employed as a dentifrice, and in some cases it is administered medicinally. *Bole of Blois* is yellow, contains carbonate of lime, and effervesces with acids. *Bohemian bole* is yellowish red. *French bole* is of a pale red, with frequent streaks of yellow. *Lemnian bole* and *Silesian bole* are, in most respects, similar to the above-named varieties. The following analyses are by C. Von Hauer. Capo di Bove—Silica, 45·64 ; alumina, 29·33 ; peroxide of iron, 8·88 ; lime, 0·60 ; magnesia, a trace ; water, 14·27 = 98·72. New Holland—Silica, 38·22 ; alumina, 31·00 ; peroxide of iron, 11·00 ; lime, a trace ; magnesia, a trace, water, 18·81 = 99·03.

BOLETUS. A genus of the mushroom order. See AMADOU.

BOLOGNIAN STONE. A variety of sulphate of baryta, found in roundish masses, which phosphoresces when, after calcination, it is exposed to the solar rays. Bolognian phosphorus was formerly made from this stone. See BARYTA, SULPHATE OF.

BOMBASINE. A worsted stuff mixed with silk ; it is a twilled fabric, of which the warp is silk and the weft worsted.

BOMBYX MORI. The moth to which the silkworm turns. The caterpillar (silkworm) is at first of a dark colour ; but gradually, as with all other caterpillars, it becomes lighter coloured. This worm is about eight weeks in arriving at maturity, during which time it frequently changes its colour. When full grown, the silkworm commences spinning its web in some convenient place. The silkworm continues drawing its thread from various points, and attaching it to others; it follows, there-fore, that after a time the body becomes, in a great measure, enclosed in the thread. The work is then continued from one thread to another, the silkworm moving its head and spinning in a zigzag way, bending the forepart of the body back to spin in all directions within reach, and shifting the body only to cover with silk the part which was beneath it. As the silkworm spins its web by thus bending the forepart of the body back, and moves the hinder part of the body in such a way only as to enable it to reach the farther back with the forepart, it follows that it encloses itself in a cocoon much shorter than its own body; for soon after the beginning, the whole is continued with the body in a bent position. During the time of spinning the cocoon, the silkworm decreases in length very considerably; and after it is completed it is not half its original length: at this time it becomes quite torpid, soon changes its skin, and appears in the form of a chrysalis. The time required to complete the cocoon is five days. In the chrysalis state the animal remains from a fortnight to three weeks: it then bursts its case, and comes forth in the *imago* state, the moth having previously dissolved a portion of the cocoon by means of a fluid which it ejects.

The true silkworm (*Bombyx mori*) is a native of the North of China. Another species, *B. cynthia*, occurs in India.

The late Colonel Sir William Reid reported as follows on the *Bombyx cynthia* :—

' I made several reports on the *Bombyx cynthia* silkworm, which feeds on the castor-oil plant, for the information of the Society of Arts. It had been introduced into Malta from India, and appeared both hardy and wonderfully prolific; yet it failed in Malta in 1855.

' 2. I had, however, previously distributed a great number of eggs, by sending them to Italy, France, and Algeria; and I contrived to watch the accounts of the trials made in those countries. I found that it had spread there, and had been carried to Spain and Portugal, and was creating considerable interest wherever it had been tried.

' 3. I was, therefore, induced to reintroduce it into Malta. At the end of July last, I received a few eggs by post, in a quill, from Paris, and these have multiplied in an extraordinary manner, so that I have not attempted to have them counted. The temperature of the winter season, now December, seems, however, to be affecting them, even in Malta, inasmuch as they grow more slowly than they did in the summer; but, nevertheless, they appear healthy.

' 4. A very interesting paper, on the progress making in different countries in rearing the *Bombyx cynthia*, will be found in the last number of the papers of the French Société d'Acclimation. This paper is by the able President of that Society, M. Geoffroy Saint Hilaire.

' 5. I had, in 1854, successfully sent the insect to the West Indies. The French Society have sent it to Brazil, to the Southern United States, and into Egypt. It is being introduced into Germany, and we are now sending more eggs and worms from Malta to Sicily.

' 6. Experiments are making in France on spinning the silk, which is found to be very fine, very strong, and to take dyes well. In France the cocoons are corded, and afterwards spun, as in Malta. It is said that the chrysalis, on extricating itself from the cocoon, and becoming a moth, does not, as was supposed, cut the thread; and the French have partially succeeded in unwinding the cocoons.

' 7. The great interest I find taken in other countries in the attempts making to naturalise the *Bombyx cynthia*, has induced me to report to you its re-introduction into Malta, with the view of begging you to make this known to the Society of Arts. I enclose an extract from my despatch, dated 7th of July, 1855, which explains the manner in which I successfully sent the insect to the West Indies; and in the same manner it may be easily conveyed from any one country to another. It may be found difficult to preserve the silkworm throughout the winter season, as well as difficult to grow the *Ricinus*, its proper food, in the climate of Europe. The proper climate for the *Bombyx cynthia* is within, or on the borders of, the tropics. But the attempts now making ought not to be the less encouraged on that account, for they are pro-ducing a new raw material for thread and clothing within reach of men of skill and science; and 127,000 cocoons have recently been sent from Algeria to be manufactured in Alsace.

' 8. The extraordinary manner in which the *Bombyx cynthia* multiplies, together with the abundance of food produced for it without culture in warm climates, renders the study of the habits of this insect, and the nature of its cocoons, of considerable importance.

' 9. I send herewith a small sample of the cloth made from the worms reared in Malta. I have the honour to be, Sir,

'Your most obedient humble servant,

'WILLIAM REID, Governor.'

Additional information on the *Bombyx cynthia*, or Eria Silkworm, will be found in the 'Society of Arts' Journal' of June 4, 1858.

Mr. Wells, writing from Grenada, in the West Indies, says of these silkworms forwarded to him by Sir William Reid:—'I have the eighth generation of worms now hatching, having had seven crops of cocoons within the year. These worms multiply one hundredfold in each generation; and there is no doubt of their being easily fed to any amount.' They are fed on the castor-oil plant, *Ricinus communis*, which grows rapidly, can be cultivated without much expense, and yields a good return in its very abundant seeds. See SILK.

BON-BONS. Comfits and other sweetmeats of various descriptions pass under this name. They are manufactured largely in France, and a considerable quantity regularly imported into this country. The manufacture of sweetmeats, confectionery, &c., does not enter so far into the plan of this work as to warrant our giving any special detail of the various processes employed; a general notice will, however, be found under the head of CONFECTIONERY.

Liqueur bon-bons are made in the following manner. A syrup evaporated to the proper consistence is made, and some alcoholic liqueur is added to it. Plaster-of-Paris models of the required form are made; and these are employed, several being fastened to a rod, for the purpose of making moulds in powdered starch, filling shallow trays. The syrup is then, by means of a funnel, poured into these moulds, and there being a powerful repulsion between the starch and the alcoholic syrup, the upper portion of the fluid assumes a spherical form; then some starch is sifted over the surface, and the mould is placed in a warm closet. Crystallisation commences on the outside of the bon-bon, forming a crust enclosing the syrup, which constantly gives up sugar to the crystallising crust until it becomes sufficiently firm to admit of being removed. A man and two boys will make three hundredweights of bon-bons in a day.

Crystallised bon-bons are prepared by putting them with a strong syrup contained in shallow dishes, placed on shelves in the drying chamber, pieces of linen being stretched over the surface, to prevent the formation of a crust upon the surface of the fluid. In two or three days the bon-bons are covered with crystals of sugar; the syrup is then drained off, and the comfits dried.

Painted bon-bons.—Bon-bons are painted by being first covered with a layer of glazing; they are then painted in body colours, mixed with mucilage and sugar.

The French have some excellent regulations, carried out under the 'Préfet de Police,' as to the colours which may be employed in confectionery. These are to the following effect:—

'Considering that the colouring-matter given to sweets, bon-bons, liqueurs, lozenges, &c., is generally imparted by mineral substances of a poisonous nature, which imprudence has been the cause of serious accidents; and that the same character of accidents have been produced by chewing or sucking the wrapping paper of such sweets, it being glazed and coloured with substances which are poisonous; it is expressly forbidden to make use of any mineral substance for colouring liqueurs, bon-bons, sugar-plums, lozenges, or any kind of sweetmeats or pastry. No other colouring-matter than such as is of a vegetable character shall be employed for such a purpose. It is forbidden to wrap sweetmeats in paper glazed or coloured with mineral substances. It is ordered that all confectioners, grocers, dealers in liqueurs, bon-bons, sweetmeats, lozenges, &c., shall have their name, address, and trade, printed upon the paper in which the above articles shall be enclosed. All manufacturers and dealers are personally responsible for the accidents which shall be traced to the liqueurs, bon-bons, and other sweetmeats manufactured or sold by them.'

If similar provisions were in force in this country, it would prevent the use, to an alarming extent, in our cheap confectionery, of such poisonous substances as

Arsenite of copper,	Sulphide of arsenic,
Acetate of copper,	Oxide of lead,
Chromate of lead,	Sulphide of mercury, &c.

The colouring-matters allowed to be used in France are indigo, Prussian blue, saffron, Turkey yellow, quercitron, cochineal, Brazil wood, madder, and the like.

BONES. (*Os*, Fr.; *Knochen*, Ger.) They form the framework of animal bodies, commonly called the skeleton, upon which the soft parts are suspended, or in which they are enclosed. Bones are invested with a membrane styled the periosteum, which is composed of a dense tissue affording glue; whence it is convertible into jelly, by ebullition with water. Bones are not equally compact throughout their whole substance: the long ones have tubes in their centres, lined with a kind of periosteum of more importance to the life of the bones than even their external coat; the flat, as well as the short and thick, bones exhibit upon their surface an osseous mass of a dense nature, while their interior presents a cavity divided into small cellules by their bony partitions.

In reference to the composition of bones, we have to consider two principal constituents : the living portion or the osseous cartilage, called *ossein*, and the inorganic or the earthy salts of the bones.

The osseous cartilage is obtained by suspending bones in a large vessel full of dilute muriatic acid, and leaving it in a cool place at about 50° F. The acid dissolves the earthy salts of the bones without perceptibly attacking the cartilage, which, at the end of a short time, becomes soft and translucid, retaining the shape of the bones ; whenever the acid is saturated before it has dissolved all the earthy salts, it should be renewed. The cartilage is to be next suspended in cold water, which is to be frequently changed till it has removed all the acidity. By drying the cartilage shrinks a little, and assumes a darker hue, but without losing its translucency. It becomes, at the same time, hard and susceptible of breaking when bent, but it possesses great strength.

This cartilage is composed entirely of a tissue passing into gelatine. By boiling with water, it is very readily convertible into glue, which passes clear and colourless through the filter, leaving only a small portion of fibrous matter insoluble by further boiling. This matter is produced by the vessels which penetrate the cartilage, and carry nourishment to the bone. We may observe all these phenomena in a very instructive manner, by macerating a bone in dilute muriatic acid, till it has lost about the half of its salts ; then washing it with cold water, next pouring boiling water upon it, leaving the whole in repose for 24 hours, at a temperature a few degrees below 212° F.

The cartilage, which has been stripped of its earthy salts, dissolves, but the small vessels which issue from the undecomposed portion of the bone remain under the form of white plumes, if the water has received no movement capable of crushing or breaking them. We may then easily recognise them with a lens, but the slightest touch tears them, and makes them fall to the bottom of the vessel in the form of a precipitate ; if we digest bones with strong hot muriatic acid, so as to accelerate their decomposition, a portion of the cartilage dissolves in the acid with a manifest disengagement of carbonic acid gas, which breaks the interior mass, and causes the half-softened bone to begin to split into fibrous plates, separable in the direction of their length. According to Marx, these plates, when sufficiently thin, possess, like scales of mica, the property of polarising light, a phenomenon which becomes more beautiful still when we soak them with the essential oil of the bark of the *Laurus Cassia*. The osseous cartilage is formed before the earthy part. The long bones are then solid, and they become hollow only in proportion as the earthy salts appear. In the new-born infant, a large portion of the bones is but partially filled with these salts ; their deposition in the cartilage takes place round certain invariable *points of ossification*, and begins at a certain period after conception, so that we may calculate the age of the fœtus according to the progress which ossification has made.

Composition of Bones.

	Heintz			Berzelius
	Ox Femur	Sheep	Man Forearm	Human Tooth
Animal matter	30·58	26·54	31·11	28·00
Phosphate of lime	57·67	61·99	59·14	} 64·30
Fluoride of calcium	2·69	2·97	2·23	
Carbonate of lime	6·99	6·92	6·32	5·30
Phosphate of magnesia . . .	2·07	1·58	1·20	1·40

Heintz found that the fixed bases in the bones were sufficient to saturate completely the acids contained in them, so that the phosphate of lime, as well as the phosphate of magnesia, which the bones contain, is composed according to the formula $3RO, PO^5$. Bone phosphate of lime is, therefore, the tribasic or orthophosphate $3CaO, PO^5$ $(Ca^3P^2O^8)$. True bony structure is perfectly free from chlorides and from sulphates, these salts being only found when the liquid pervading the bones has not been completely removed. The bones in youth contain less earthy constituents than those of adults ; and, in advanced age, the proportion of mineral matters increases. Von Biria found more bone-earth in the bones of *birds* than in those of mammals ; he found also the ratio of the carbonate of lime to the phosphate to be generally greater. In the bones of *amphibia*, he found less inorganic matter than in those of mammals and birds; and in the bones of *fishes*, the earthy matters vary from 21 to 57 per cent. The scales of fishes have a composition somewhat similar to that of bone, but they contain phosphate of lime in small quantity only.

In certain diseases (the *craniotabes* in children), the earthy salts fall in the spongy portion of the bone as low as 28·16 per cent. of the dry bone; and in several cases the proportion of earthy matter was found by Schlossberger as low as 50 per cent. At the age of 21 years, the weight of the skeleton is to that of the whole body in the ratio of 10·5 : 100 in man, and in that of 8·5 : 100 in woman, the weight of the body being about 125 or 130 lbs.

The quantity of organic matter in *fossil bones* varies very considerably: in some cases it is found in as large a quantity as in fresh bones, while in others it is altogether wanting. Carbonate of lime generally occurs in far larger quantity in fossil than in recent bones, which may arise from infiltration of that salt from without, or from a decomposition of a portion of the phosphate of lime by carbonic acid or carbonates. Magnesia often occurs in larger quantities in the fossil remains of vertebrated animals than in the fresh bones of the present animal world. Liebig found in the cranial bones excavated at Pompeii a larger proportion of fluoride of calcium than in recent bones; while, on the other hand, Girardin and Preisser found that this salt had greatly diminished in bones which had lain long in the earth, and, in some cases, had even wholly disappeared.

The gelatinous tissue of bones was found by Von Biria to consist of—

	Recent ox bones	Fossil bones
Carbon	50·401	50·130
Hydrogen	7·111	7·073
Nitrogen	18·154	18·449
Oxygen	24·119	24·348
Sulphur	0·216	—

This is the same composition as that of the gelatinous tissues.

In the arts bones are employed by turners, cutlers, manufacturers of animal charcoal, and, when calcined, by assayers, for making cupels. In agriculture, they are employed as a manure. Laid on in the form of dust, at the rate of 30 to 35 cwts. per acre, they have been known to increase the value of old pastures from 10s. or 15s. to 30s. or 40s. per acre; and after the lapse of 20 years, though sensibly becoming less valuable, land has remained still worth two or three times the rent it paid before the bones were laid on. In the large dyeing establishments in Manchester, the bones are boiled in open pans for 24 hours, the fat skimmed off and sold to the candle-makers, and the *size* afterwards boiled down in another vessel till it is of sufficient strength for stiffening the thick goods for which it is intended. The *size* liquor, when exhausted or no longer of sufficient strength, is applied with much benefit as a manure to the adjacent pasture and artificial grass-lands, and the exhausted bones are readily bought up by the Lancashire and Cheshire farmers. When burned bones are digested in sulphuric acid, diluted with twice its weight of water, a mixture of gypsum and acid phosphate of lime is obtained, which, when largely diluted with water, forms a most valuable liquid manure for grass-land and for crops of rising corn; or, to the acid solution, pearl ashes may be added, and the whole then dried up, by the addition of charcoal powder or vegetable mould, till it is sufficiently dry to be scattered with the hand as a top-dressing, or buried in the land by means of a drill.

In France, soup is extensively made by dissolving bones in a steam heat of two or three days' continuance. Respecting the nutritive property of such soup, Liebig has expressed the following strong opinion :—'Gelatine, even when accompanied by the savoury constituents of flesh, is not capable of supporting the vital process; on the contrary, it diminishes the nutritive value of food, which it renders insufficient in quantity and inferior in quality, and it overloads the blood with nitrogenous products, the presence of which disturbs and impedes the organic processes.' The erroneous notion that gelatine is the active principle of soup arose from the observation that soup made, by boiling, from meat, when concentrated to a certain point, *gelatinises*. The jelly was taken to be the true soup until it was found that the best meats did not yield the finest gelatine tablets. which were obtained most beautiful and transparent from tendons, feet, cartilage, bones, &c. This led to an investigation on nutrition generally, the results of which proved that gelatine, which by itself is tasteless, and when eaten excites nausea, possesses no nutritive value whatever.

The following Table exhibits the relation between the combustible animal matter and the mineral substances of bones, as found by different observers ;—

	Organic Portion	Inorganic Portion	Observers
Ox bones . . . {	1	2·0	Berzelius.
	1	2·1	Marchand.
	1	2·0	Berzelius.
Human bones . . {	1	1·8 to 2·3	} Frerichs.
	1	2·0 in mean	
	1	1·6 to 2·2	
	1	1·9 in mean	} Von Biria.
Bird bones . .	1	2·3 to 2·6	

Prior to the use of bones by the turner or carver, they require the oil, with which they are largely impregnated, to be extracted, by boiling them in water and bleaching them in the sun or otherwise. This process of boiling, in place of softening, robs them of part of their gelatine, and therefore of part of their elasticity and contractibility likewise, and they become more brittle.

The forms of the bones are altogether unfavourable to their extensive or ornamental employment: most of them are very thin and curved, contain large cellular cavities for marrow, and are interspersed with vessels that are visible after they are worked up into spoons, brushes, and articles of common turnery. The buttock and shin bones of the ox and calf are almost the only kinds used. To whiten the finished works, they are soaked in turpentine for a day, boiled in water for about an hour, and then polished with whitening and water.

Holtzapffel also informs us that after the turning tool, or scraper, has been used, bone is polished, 1st, with glass-paper; 2nd, with Trent sand, or Flanders brick, with water on flannel; 3rd, with whiting and water on a woollen rag; 4th, a small quantity of white wax is rubbed on the work with a quick motion; the wax fills the minute pores, but only a very minute portion should be allowed to remain on the work. Common bone articles, such as nail- and tooth-brushes, are frequently polished with slaked lime used wet on flannel or woollen cloth. See ' On Bone and its Uses,' by Arthur Aitkin, 'Trans. of Society of Arts,' 1832 and 1839.

Bones have recently been imported into this country, from Australia, in the form of bone-dust tiles, made by crushing the bones and compressing the powder into the form of cakes.

The importance of the trade in bones will be seen from the following statement of *imports* of the bones of animals and fish—not whalebone.

Bones of all kinds (except Whalefins) imported.

	1867 Tons	1868 Tons	1869 Tons	1870 Tons	1871 Tons	1872
Quantity .	246,767	245,120	229,223	215,748	302,079	—
	£	£	£	£	£	
Value .	437,436	430,442	600,019	629,619	659,416	---
				Tons	Tons	Tons
Bones, whether burnt or not for manure .				92,032	94,212	97,778

BONE-BLACK (*Noir d'os*, Fr.; *Knochenschwarz*, Ger.), or *Animal Charcoal*, as it is less correctly called, is the black carbonaceous substance into which bones are converted by calcination in close vessels. This kind of charcoal has two principal applications—to deprive various solutions, particularly syrups, of their colouring-matters, and to furnish a black pigment. The latter subject will be treated of under IVORY BLACK.

The discovery of the antiputrescent and decolouring properties of animal charcoal in general is due to Lowitz, of Petersburg; but their modifications have occupied the attention of many chemists since his time. Kels published, in 1798, some essays on the decolouring of indigo, saffron, madder, syrup, &c., by means of charcoal; but he committed a mistake in supposing bone-black to have less power than the charcoal of wood. The first useful application of charcoal to the purification of raw colonial sugar was made by M. Guillon, who brought into the French markets considerable quantities of fine syrups, which he discoloured by ground wood-charcoal, and sold them to great advantage, as much superior to the *cassonades* (brown sugars) of that time. In 1811, M. Figuier, an apothecary at Montpellier, published a note about animal charcoal, showing that it blanched vinegars and wines with much more energy than vegetable charcoal; and lastly, in 1812, M. Derosnes proposed to employ animal charcoal, in the purification of syrups and sugar-refining. The quantities of bone-black left in the retorts employed by MM. Payen, for producing crude carbonate of ammonia, furnished abundant materials for making the most satisfactory experiments, and enabled these gentlemen soon to obtain ten per cent. more of refined sugar from the raw article than had been formerly extracted, and to improve, at the time, the characters of the lumps, bastards, treacle, &c.

The calcination of bones is effected by two different systems of apparatus; by heating them in a retort similar to that in which coal is decomposed in the gas-works, or in small pots piled up in a kiln. On the second plan, which furnishes the best charcoal, the bones, broken into pieces, are put into small cast-iron pots of the form shown in *fig.* 148, about three-eighths of an inch thick, two of which are dexterously placed with their mouths in contact, and then luted together with loam. The lip of the upper pot is made to slip inside the under one. These double vessels, containing together about fifty pounds of bones, are arranged alongside, and over each other, in an oven like a potter's kiln, till it is filled. The oven or kiln may be either oblong or upright. The latter is represented in *figs.* 149, 150, 151. A is the fire-place or grate for the fuel; c c are the openings in the dome of the furnace through which the flame flows; the divisions of these orifices are shown in *fig.* 151. B is the wall of brick-work. D the space in which the pots are distributed. E is the door by which the workman carries in the pots, which is afterwards built up with fire-bricks, and plastered over with loam. This door is seen in *fig.* 149. F F are the lateral flues for conveying the disengaged gases into the air.

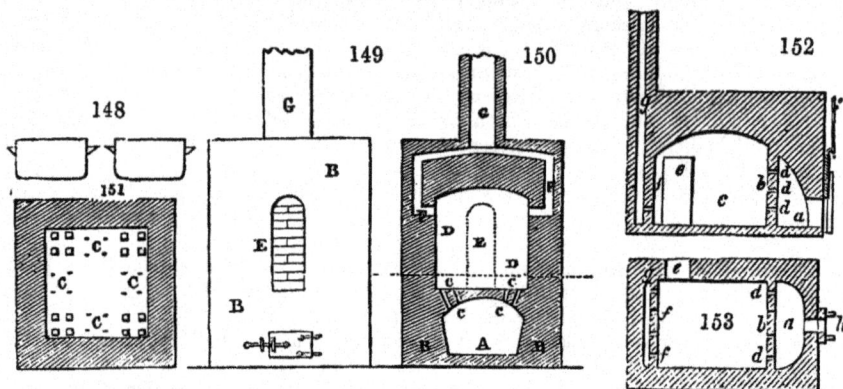

Fig. 152 is a longitudinal section, and *fig.* 153 a ground plan of a horizontal kiln for calcining bones. *a* is the fire-chamber, lying upon a level with the sole of the kiln; it is separated by a pillar *b*, from the calcining hearth *c*. In the pillar or wall, several rows of holes, *d*, are left at different heights; *e* is the entrance door; *f*, the outlet-vents for the gases, vapours, and smoke, into the chimney *g*; *h*, a sliding damper-plate for regulating the admission of the air into the fire in the space *a*.

By this arrangement the offensive emanations are partly consumed, and partly carried off with the smoke. To destroy the smell completely, the smoke should be made to pass through a second small furnace.

The number of pots that may be put into a kiln of this kind depends, of course, upon its dimensions; but, in general, from 100 to 150 are piled up over each other, in columns, at once; the greatest heat being nearest the roof of the kiln, which resembles, in many respects, that used for baking potteryware.

In both kilns the interior walls are built of fire-bricks. In the oblong one, the fiercest heat is near the vaulted roof; in the upright one, near the sole; and the pots, containing the larger lumps of bones, should be placed accordingly near the top of the former and the bottom of the latter. Such a kiln may receive about seventy double pots, containing in the whole thirty-five cwts. of bones.

After the hearth is filled with the pots, and the entrance door is shut, the fire is applied, at first moderately, but afterwards it must be raised, and maintained at a brisk heat for eight or ten hours. The door of the ash-pit and the damper may now be nearly closed, to moderate the draught, and to keep up a steady ignition for six or eight hours longer, without additional firing; after which the doors must be all opened to cool the furnace. When this is done, the brickwork of the entrance-door must be taken down, the kiln must be emptied, and immediately filled again with a set of pots previously filled with bones, and luted together: the pots which have been ignited may, in the course of a short time, be opened, and the contents put into the magazine. But in operating with the large decomposing cylinder retort, the bones being raked out hot, must be instantly tossed into a receiver, which can be covered in air-tight till they are cool.

The bones lose upon an average about one-half of their weight in the calcination. In reference to the quality of the black, experience has shown that it is so much more powerful as a decolouring agent, as the bones from which it was made have been freer from adhering fatty, fleshy, and tendinous matters.

The charcoal is ground in mills with grooved rollers, in order to prevent the formation of dust. The bones are thrown into a long quadrangular box, furnished at its lower aperture with moveable steel cheeks, between which the roller revolves; they are thus coarsely broken up, and the granulation is completed by another pair of bluntly grooved rollers, which can be placed nearer to, or further from, each other at pleasure. The crushed charcoal is collected on sieves, which separate the dust from the grains.

The composition of perfectly dry bone-black of average quality is as follows :— Phosphate of lime, with carbonate of lime, and a little sulphuret of iron, or oxide of iron, 88 parts ; iron in the state of silicated carburet, 2 parts ; charcoal containing about $\frac{1}{15}$th of nitrogen, 10 parts. None of the substances present, except the charcoal, possess separately any decolourising power.

It was formerly supposed that the peculiar absorbing and decolouring power of animal charcoal was only exerted towards bodies of *organic* origin ; but it was found, by Graham, that *inorganic* substances are equally subject to this action; and later experiments have demonstrated that there are few, if any, chemical compounds which altogether resist the absorbing power of charcoal. The action is of a mechanical nature, and in some cases it is sufficiently powerful to overcome chemical affinities of considerable power. It is not confined to charcoal, though pre-eminent in this substance, in consequence of the immense extent of surface which its porous structure presents. The action of charcoal in sugar-refining has been particularly studied by Lüdersdorf. When the defecated saccharine juice is allowed to flow upon a moist and firmly compressed charcoal filter, pure water is the first product that passes through ; but a considerably larger quantity is obtained than was employed for moistening the charcoal. Water is then obtained of a decidedly saline character, which increases in strength, and after this has passed through for some time, a sweet taste becomes perceptible, which gradually increases, and at last entirely masks the saline. This purely sweet fluid continues to flow for some time; after which, the liquid acquires an alkaline reaction from the presence of caustic lime ; it then becomes coloured, the liquor getting gradually darker, till the action of the charcoal ceases. Lime is completely abstracted from lime-water by bone-charcoal; and, according to the experiments of Chevallier, lead-salts are likewise entirely absorbed, the acetate the most readily. It has also been shown by Graham, that iodine even is separated from iodide of potassium. The commercial value of animal charcoal has usually been estimated by its decolouring power on sulphate of indigo ; its absorbent power, which is a property of equal, perhaps of greater importance, may, according to M. Corenwinder, be determined, approximately, by the quantity of lime which a given weight will absorb. For this purpose he employs a solution of saccharate of lime of known strength. An acid liquor is first prepared, composed of 20 grammes of pure oil of vitriol diluted with water to exactly 1 litre. A solution of saccharate of lime is then prepared, by dissolving 125 to 130 grammes of white sugar in water, adding thereto 15 to 20 grammes of quicklime, boiling the liquid, and then filtering to separate the undissolved lime. This solution is prepared of such a nature, that it will be exactly saturated by the same volume of the dilute sulphuric acid. By adding the latter to 50 cubic centimètres of the liquid filtered from the animal charcoal, it is easy to see how many degrees of the burette are required to complete the saturation of the lime. Suppose 35 are required for this purpose, $100 - 35 = 65$, which represent the proportion of lime absorbed by the charcoal : this is, therefore, the number representing the standard, By operating with a burette graduated from the bottom, the degree of the charcoal experimented upon may be read directly.

This decolourising power does not belong alone to bone-black ; different varieties of lignite, or even coal, when well carbonised in close vessels, afford a decolouring charcoal of considerable value. By reducing 100 parts of clay into a thin paste with water, kneading into it 20 parts of tar, and 500 of finely-ground pit-coal, drying the mixed mass, and calcining it out of contact of air, a charcoally matter may be obtained not much inferior to bone-black in whitening syrups.

The restoration of animal charcoal from burnt bones, for the purpose of sugar-refining, has been long practised in France. Mr. W. Parker has made the following process the subject of a patent. The charcoal, when taken from the vessels in which it has been employed for the purposes of clarifying the sugar, is to be thoroughly washed with the purest water that can be obtained, in order to remove all the saccharine matter adhering to it. When the washing process has been completed, the charcoal is laid out to dry, either in the open air or in a suitable stove ; and when perfectly free from moisture, it is to be separated into small pieces, and sifted through a sieve, the wire or meshes of which are placed at distances of about two and a half in every inch. This sifting will not only divide the charcoal into small pieces, but will cause any bits of wood or other improper matters to be separated from it.

The charcoal thus prepared is then to be packed lightly in cylindrical vessels called crucibles, with some small quantity of bones, oil, or other animal matter, mixed with it. The crucibles are then closed by covers, and luted at the joints, leaving no other opening but one small hole in the centre of the cover, through which any gas generated within the vessel when placed in the oven or furnace may be allowed to escape.

The crucibles are now to be ranged round the oven, and placed one upon another, in vertical positions; and when the oven is properly heated, gas will be generated within each crucible, and issue out from the central hole. The gas thus emitted, being of an inflammable quality, will take fire, and assist in heating the crucibles; and the operation being carried on until the crucibles become of a red heat, the oven is then to be closed, and allowed to cool; after which the crucibles are to be removed, when the charcoal will be found to have become perfectly renovated, and as fit for use as before.

A process for the restoration of bone-black, or animal charcoal, was made the subject of a patent by Messrs. Bancroft and MacInnes of Liverpool, which consists in washing the granular charcoal, or digesting it, when finely ground, with a weak solution of potash or soda, of specific gravity 1·06. The bone-black, which has been used in sugar-refining, may be thus restored, but it should be first cleared from all the soluble filth by means of water.

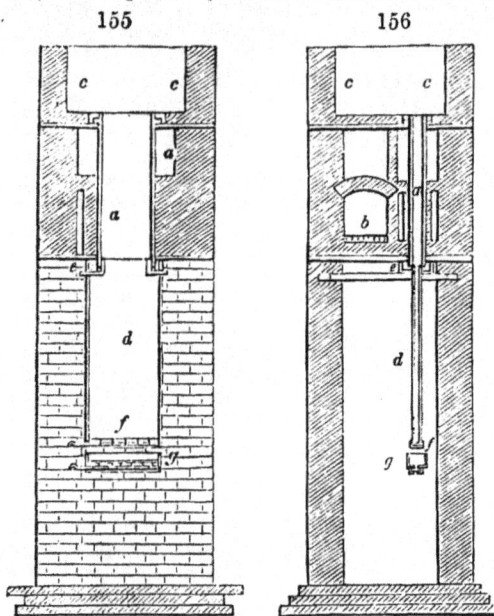

155   156

Mr. F. Parker's method, patented in June, 1839, for effecting a like purpose, is by a fresh calcination, as follows:—

Fig. 155 represents a front section of the furnace and retort; and *fig.* 156 a transverse vertical section of the same. *a* is a retort, surrounded by the flues of the furnace *b*; *c* is a hopper or chamber, to which a constant fresh supply of the black is furnished, as the preceding portion has been withdrawn from the lower part of *a*. *d* is the cooling vessel, which is connected to the lower part of the retort *a* by a sand-joint *e*. The cooler *d* is made of thin sheet-iron, and is large; its bottom is closed with a slide-plate, *f*. The black, after passing slowly through the retort *a* into the vessel *d*, gets so much cooled by the time it reaches *f*, that a portion of it may be safely withdrawn, so as to allow more to fall progressively down; *g* is the charcoal-meter, with a slide door.—H.M.N.

BONE-EARTH. The residue of bones after calcination; it is chiefly phosphate of lime. It finds many uses in the arts.

BONE-LIQUOR. The liquor obtained by distilling bones. It is an impure solution of ammonia—a poor spirit of hartshorn.

BONE-OIL. See DIPPEL'S OIL.

BOOKBINDING 'in all its branches' includes every process by which the sheets as received from the printer (from the pamphlet of a few pages to the folio of enormous size and thickness) are arranged in due order, and the leaves of which each sheet is composed secured and prepared, either simply or elaborately, for the use of the reader. It thus includes every gradation of style and finish, from the stitched and wrappered periodical to the costly and elaborate binding of the most magnificent library.

The sheets of paper on which books are printed are of various dimensions, beginning with the 'pott' and 'foolscap' (the smallest sizes that come from the paper-maker) up to the 'crown,' 'demy,' 'royal,' 'imperial,' 'atlas,' &c. The printer arranges each of his pages so as to occupy, with the required margin, the half, the fourth, the eighth, or the twelfth, and so on down to the forty-eighth, of each sheet, such divisional pages being called respectively folio, quarto, octavo, duodecimo, &c., down to 48mo.; and it will be manifest that as the sheets themselves are larger or smaller from the atlas down to the pott as before stated, so their divisions will vary in proportion, thus, an 8vo. volume may be either a 'foolscap 8vo.,' a 'crown 8vo.,' or a 'demy 8vo.,' &c., and will be larger or smaller accordingly.

The 'gathering' of the sheets that form a volume—that is, the collecting together, in consecutive order into one or more 'gatherings,' of a copy of each of the sheets forming such volumes, is generally done by the printer before they are delivered to the binder. In such cases the first operation at the bookbinder's is that of folding (whether in folio, 4to., or 8vo., &c., as before said). In this operation the margin of the type, and not the margin of the paper, is the guide for the folder, who has to see that the head and sides of the printed matter of each page range or 'register' accurately with those of the opposite page. The work of folding is done by women and girls, who use a bone or ivory folding stick to press the folds of each sheet closely together, and by continued practice the process is so rapidly performed by them, that except in the case of newspapers and other publications where there are enormous numbers of the same sheet requiring no readjustment of machinery, little, if anything, is gained, either in speed, accuracy, or economy, by the use of folding machines, of which various kinds worked by steam-power have been introduced.

When the type of each leaf in a sheet is thus made to coincide it will be almost universally found that the outer edges of some of the leaves project more or less considerably beyond others, so that in order to give the book a neat and regular appearance, even if the edges are not intended to be cut all round, the fore-edge and tail have to be 'trimmed,' that is, the rough and irregularly projecting edges are, after the book is sewn, pared with a knife.

The folded sheets are then 'collated,' that is, examined and laid together in proper consecutive order, in which arrangement the letter or 'signature,' as it is termed, at the foot of the first page of each sheet, and not the general numerical paging of the book, is the collater's guide. If the volume about to be bound has belonging to it plates or maps, printed on distinct paper from that used for the letterpress, each such plate or map is secured by paste to the back edge of its appropriate page of letterpress, or to a special strip of paper termed a 'guard.' Each volume being thus 'folded,' 'collated,' and (if needful) 'placed,' is subjected with others to hydraulic or other pressure to make the leaves lie smoothly and compactly together. The volume is then, if cords are to be used as the cross bands, slightly indented with saw cuts at regular intervals across its back, six such cuts being used for folios, five for quartos, and four or three for smaller sizes. If tape is to be used for the bands, pencil-marks are substituted for the saw cuts.

The book is now ready to be fastened together. The simplest mode of doing this is by stabbing through each volume three or four holes a short distance from its hinder edge, and passing a needle and thread alternately in and out through the holes, securing the ends of the thread together by a knot. A book so fastened ('stitched,' not 'sewn') is of course prevented by the pressure of the thread from opening freely to its back edge, and if the thread is cut or broken at any one part

157

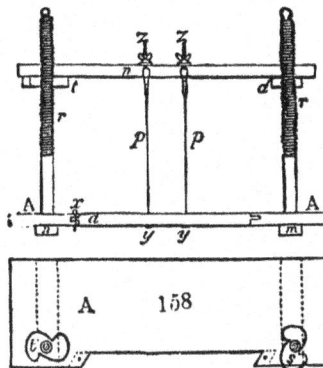

A 158

the whole falls to pieces. This rough and ready process is confined to pamphlets, periodical publications, or some of the commoner school books.

The process of 'sewing' (as distinct from the before-named operation of stitching) is that mostly employed for securing the folded sheets together. For this purpose the sewing press is employed.

Fig. 157 represents the sewing press as it stands upon the table before which the workwoman sits. *Fig.* 158 is a ground plan without the parts *a* and *n* in the former figure. A is the base board supported upon the cross bars *m n* marked with dotted lines in *fig.* 158.

Upon the screw rod *r r, fig.* 157, the nuts *t d* serve to fix the flat upper bar *n* at any desired distance from the base. That bar has a slit along its middle through which the hooks below *z z* pass down for receiving the ends of the sewing cords or tapes (from two or three to six in number according to the size of the volumes under operation) *p p* fixed at *y y* and stretched by the thumbscrews *z z*. The bar *y y* is let into an oblong space cut out of the front edge of the base board and fixed there by a moveable pin *a* and a fixed pin at its other end round which it turns. The cords or bands are fixed at distances and in numbers corresponding to the saw or pencil-marks before named, made in the backs of the folded sheets, and the cross cords become embedded in the saw-marks by the pressure of the sewing thread. This is drawn through the middle of each sheet and turned round each band beginning at the first sheet and proceeding to the last. The first sheet being thus sewn and secured to the bands, the second sheet is laid upon it, the thread carried from the first sheet to the second, and the process is repeated, and so on to the concluding sheet of the volume, the whole being connected together by the cross bands (whether of cord or tape) round which the thread passes, first through one sheet, and then from each sheet to its successor.

A third method of securing the leaves of a book was some years ago introduced by Mr. W. Hancock, namely, by the adhesion of the back edges of each leaf of the book to a coating of caoutchouc and its superimposed lining cloth. In this method, instead of the fold of each sheet or section (consisting of 4, 8, 12, 16, or 24 pages) forming a back through which the needle of the sewer passes, as before described, the whole of the back of the book is cut through by a plough knife or guillotine so as to present a smooth level surface formed of the back edges of the book, which, if separated, would then consist of single detached leaves.

This smooth surface is slightly rasped so as to give greater facility for the adhesion to the edge of each leaf of the caoutchouc, a solution of which is applied in two or three coats, at intervals sufficient to allow each coat to become firmly adhesive. Strips of cloth lining are laid over this, and fastened on with caoutchouc, the outermost strip being so much wider than the back of the book as to form a fly or projecting strip at each side for the purpose of securing the volume to the boards which form, with cloth or leather, the cover of the book. We thus see that, instead of leaves attached by thread at certain points or intervals, each single leaf is agglutinated continuously along the whole length of its back edge to the caoutchouc and cloth lining before described. Books bound in this way open so perfectly flat upon a table without strain or resilience, that they are equally comfortable to the student, the musician, and the merchant. And where a book consists of paper at once thick, tough, and absorbent, the adhesion of each single leaf by its back edge to the caoutchouc coating and lining is generally perfect, and, with careful usage, moderately durable. On the other hand, when the paper composing the book is thin or non-absorbent, the adhesion of each leaf is very uncertain ; and moreover, by frequent use, and especially under the chemical effect of atmospheric and climatic changes, the caoutchouc sooner or later loses its adhesive power over paper of any quality, hardens, cracks, and shrinks, and leaf after leaf becomes more or less insecure and detached. The use of caoutchouc for bookbinding has therefore become far less general than was at one time anticipated, and the needle and thread of the workwoman is still the general medium for connecting the leaves of a book together.

Hitherto we have dealt with the preliminary processes of securing the separate portions of a volume—processes which are common to all kinds of binding, from the simple pamphlet with, or without its paper wrapper, to the most elaborately bound volume in russia or morocco ; except that in the more expensive styles of binding, additional care is taken in the process of sewing ; the thread being more frequently passed through each section, round the cross bands, and from section to section, and more elaborately secured.

The next process is that of inserting the volume into its cover ; and in this, two systems are adopted : one, the original plan of attaching the boards of the cover by drawing the cross cords or bands through holes pierced through each board at its back edge, then fastening the leather or other material used for covering the book over the board, and subsequently adding the lettering and ornament required ; the other that of the more modern 'case-binding.' This is now, from its comparative cheapness and adaptation to the rapid execution of large numbers, the method universally adopted for the great mass of books, as they issue from the publisher's warehouse. We will deal with this last-named process in the first instance. In 'case-binding' the case or cover (generally formed of mill-boards covered with cotton cloth) is made, stamped and lettered with the desired amount of ornament, all complete before it is placed upon the volume. Thus (the exact size of the volume having been first ascertained) the whole process of 'case-making' and 'blocking' can go on simultaneously with or in anticipation of the processes of folding, sewing, and backing up.

The boards used in bookbinding are formed of the pulp obtained from refuse brown paper, old rope, straw, or other vegetable material more or less fibrous; which pulp is pressed into sheets of varying size and thickness, to suit the requirements of the binder; from the sheet scarcely thicker than cartridge paper used for 'limp' bookcovers, to the thick substance now extensively used for books on which a cover with 'bevelled edges' (after the antique style of the old wooden book-covers used by early bookbinders) is prepared.

The size and style of the volume being ascertained, the board-cutter selects his mill-boards accordingly; and having with his shears 'squared,' i.e. cut of at right angles the rough outer edge of two adjoining sides of each board, adjusts the gauge of his cutting-machine to the exact requirement successively of the length and breadth of the volume, until he has completed the tale of 50 or it may be 5,000 pairs of boards for which his order is given. See Board Cutting Machine (*fig.* 159, as manufactured by F. Ullmer).

159

In the meantime, the cloth-cutter in like manner cuts up the corresponding numbers of covers of the dimensions proper for the book. The bookbinders' cloth now so extensively used, is a cotton fabric generally woven in Lancashire, and sometimes dyed and finished there; but these later processes are carried on to a considerable extent, also, in London. The dyed cloth is passed through heated rollers, which being engraved with some grain or pattern, (sometimes in imitation of the grains of russia or morocco leather, sometimes with other patterns) impress the pattern or embossing upon the cloth. A third essential is a supply of a corresponding number of 'hollows.' These are strips of thick paper or of pasteboard, cut to the exact height and thickness required for the book for which the boards and cloth are intended, and which act as gauges for the guidance of the case-makers, and as stiffners for the cloth at the back of the book, between the boards.

These three materials are then passed on to the case-makers: one of whom takes possession of the pile of cloth covers, laid face downwards before him, rapidly passes the glueing brush from the pot of heated and diluted glue standing by his side upon the uppermost piece of the pile, lifts, and passes the glued piece of cloth to his right-hand neighbour, who being provided with the pile of pairs of boards and corresponding hollows, lays, in succession, a board (1), a hollow (2), and a board (3) (*fig.* 160), on the glued surface of the cloth, which is cut of a size sufficient to leave a margin to turn over the edge of the boards and the requisite distance beyond. A narrow space, proportioned to the size and thickness of the volume, is left between the inner edge of each board and the 'hollow,' so as to allow space for the hinge of the case to turn round and be pressed into the ridge which is formed at each side of the back of a volume when prepared for the case.

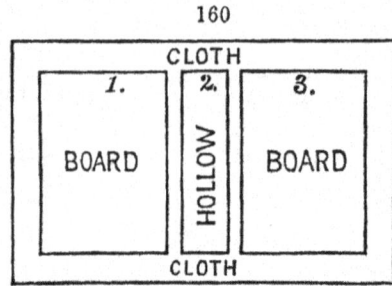

This done, the second case-maker then rapidly and lightly (so rapidly as not to allow the hot glue to soak too much into the cloth and spoil its grain and gloss, and so lightly as not to produce the same defect by too much pressure) passes the palm of his hand or a folding-stick over the cloth, to make it adhere smoothly to the boards and the intermediate hollow, and at once passes each to his right-hand neighbour. The third case-maker in his turn quickly snicks out, with a pair of scissors, the super-fluous cloth at each of the four corners, folds the over-lapping margin of cloth round the edge of the boards and the top and bottom of the hollow, rubs the edges and inner margin smooth with a folding-stick, and each case is then taken by an attendant boy and hung up to dry. This process is soon accomplished, and the batch of cases is next passed on to the blockers.

The blocks or stamps used for lettering and ornamenting the cases of books are of metal, generally of brass, cut in relief, and, besides the letterings, are of various kinds; border frames, bands for the back, corner or centre ornaments, &c.; adapted to the various characters of books, and the tastes of publishers and purchasers. In many instances, special designs, pictorial, emblematical or otherwise, are cut for some particular books; and the number and variety of blocks that accumulate in any large bookbinding establishment thus becomes very great, and absorbs a considerable capital.

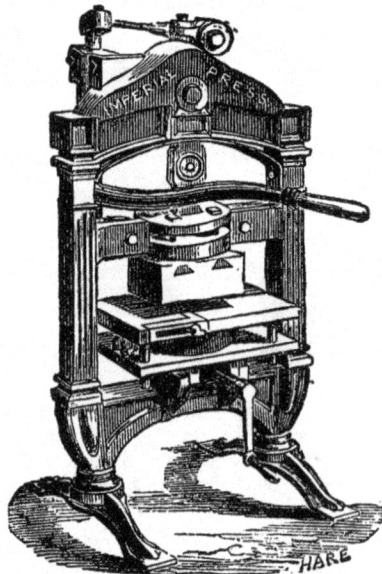

The requisite block, or group of blocks required for the cases in hand being prepared, they are accurately adjusted and secured (with the stamping surface downwards) to the upper bed of an arming press (*fig.* 161, as manufactured by F. Ullmer), which bed is perforated by channels, for the admission of a jet of gas or steam, sufficient to give the required heat to the metal blocks suspended; heat being needful to give distinctness and permanence to the impression on the cloth case. Beneath the stamping block so prepared and suspended, is a table on which has to be fixed a frame or gauge, adjusted to the exact proportions of the case about to be stamped; and the table is then brought by means of regulating screws, to the exact position under the stamping-block, to receive the required impression on the back and sides of each case. The application of a lever, moved either by hand or steam-power, brings the superincumbent and heated block forcibly upon the cloth case; and when the pressure (which has to be carefully adjusted so as not to give too faint an impression on the one hand, or on the other to burn too deeply and injure the fabric and colour of the cloth) the case is withdrawn with the required impression stamped upon it; another is substituted, and the process is repeated throughout the required number of the sort. An impression given simply as above described, is technically termed 'blind blocking,' and is a mere indentation in the cloth case of the pattern of the block applied. When gold or other metal for lettering or ornament is required, the cover of the book has to undergo the previous process of 'laying on' as follows :—

Gold-leaf is laid on a leather cushion and divided by the gentle pressure of a knife-edge into slips of the requisite size, which are then deftly and smoothly lifted by adhesion to a slightly greased pad and transferred from it to the part or parts of the cloth case about to be lettered or ornamented in gold. The case, with the gold-leaf thus laid on, is then subjected to the pressure of the arming-press as in blind blocking; the gold-leaf is pressed by the heated block into the case of the book, which, on being withdrawn from the lower table of the press, is gently wiped with a rag or brushed; this removes the metal-leaf from every unpressed part, leaving the impression of the lettering or ornament clear and distinct.

The cases are then ready to be fixed upon the books to which they belong, and which having been, as before described 'folded, collated, placed and sewn,' and afterwards 'papered' (this last term being given to the pasting of the end papers with a fly-leaf to the beginning and end of each volume) have to undergo the further processes needful to fit them for insertion into the cases. In the first place the edges of each book are either cut at top, tail and fore-edge, or only 'trimmed.' This last operation merely pares down the rough and projecting leaves at the fore-edge and tail nearly to the level of those leaves which present a double or quadruple fold, technically termed 'the bolt,' and leaving the top of the book entirely uncut, so that without reducing the general margin of the book a neat and tolerably uniform edging is presented. The backs of the

162

books are then coated with glue, on which is laid a strip of strong paper, and again over that a lining cloth or webbing of tough but loose and elastic texture, which projects beyond the width of the back so as to form two wings; these, with the projecting ends of the cross-cords or bands and the end papers, form the combined material for securing the book in the case. The back of the book, however, before its insertion in the case, is rounded, either by a peculiar manipulation with the left hand and the use of the hammer in the right hand of the workman, or by the use of the rounding-machine. By this operation a concave surface is presented at the fore-edge of the book corresponding to the convex surface produced by rounding its back, and lastly each volume is tightly nipped (its back slightly projecting beyond the pressure) either between 'backing boards,' or by the jaws of a backing machine (*fig.* 162, as manufactured by F. Ullmer). The whole surface of the back is then hammered and pressed till it spreads out beyond the thickness of the rest of the volume, and a projection is produced along each edge of the back, forming two ridges, which fit into the space before described as being left by the case-makers between each board and the hollow of the case, thus combining to form a hinge and give the needful play to the opening and shutting of the lid of the book.

As before indicated, the end papers, the flap of the lining cloth and the ends of the cords or bands are then pasted to the inside of the case first on one side and then on the other, the projecting ridges of the back being at the same time pressed by the workman into the space left for them between the band and the hollow of the case —the volumes are carefully laid between pressing-boards with their rounded backs put outside the edges of each pressing-board so as to escape the coming squeeze and the pile of boards and books is then subjected to pressure for a needful period, either in an hydraulic or screw-press. After a sufficient space of time and pressure to allow the paste to dry, the press is emptied of its contents, each volume opened and examined to see that it is correctly inserted, and the lot is then ready for delivery to the publisher.

Such, with some variations of detail in different establishments, are the processes by which the myriads of books issued by the large publishing houses throughout the year are bound with great rapidity, at a low price, and in endless varieties of style to suit every taste.

We turn now to the more elaborate and complete style of binding, (technically termed 'extra binding,') which is substantially, with certain modifications, the system adopted ever since the book proper, with its rectangular figure, and its distinct leaves united together at their back edge, superseded the extended sheet or series of sheets which in ancient times were rolled round a cylinder and formed the 'volumen' or roll, from which our term 'volume,' no longer strictly applicable, is derived.

Instead of a case completely fitted and finished being pasted or glued upon the book prepared for it, as previously described, the cover of the book in extra binding is generally fitted on piecemeal, drawn over the boards, and the lettering or ornament added last when the cover has been fitted and attached to the book. The edges of a bound book after being cut round are generally either sprinkled, wholly coloured, marbled, or gilt. In the first, a brush slightly charged with colouring fluid is struck smartly over the edges of the books so as sprinkle them with a uniformly distributed shower of small spots; in the second a sponge or brush dipped in colour is applied to the edges, which are tightly compressed so as not to allow the colour to penetrate the margin of the books; in the third, the edges are applied to colours which by a peculiar process are made to float on water in patterns combined so as to produce a marbled effect, and which are transferred by contact from the surface of the water to that of the book-edge which is afterwards burnished; in the fourth, gold-leaf is laid upon the edges which have been previously coated with a solution of white-of-egg, &c. termed 'glaire,' to which the gold-leaf adheres, and is then burnished with a polishing tool, tipped with agate.

The ends of the cords are then drawn by the 'forwarder' through holes pierced in the boards, near their back edge, unravelled, spread out and hammered down to the level of the board so as to present no unsightly lump under the leather. The leather for the cover is pared round its edges, softened by manipulation and the application of paste-water to make it pliable, and is then pasted evenly and smoothly over the boards and back of the book, worked well into the hinge and round the 'raised bands,' (if there are any), turned neatly over the edges and round the corners, and rubbed down with a folding-stick; 'head-bands' giving a neat and finished appearance and additional security to the turning in of the leather at the back are then added to the top and tail of the book. Sometimes lettering-pieces of a different colour to the rest of the book are used, being pared very thin so as to avoid any unsightly swelling, and pasted and rubbed down on that part of the book which is to receive the lettering. If the book is 'half-bound,' instead of 'whole-bound,' the leather is limited to a strip at the back and a short distance from the back on each side, and to the corners; the sides of the book being covered with either marbled or coloured paper or cloth, and tooled where the last material slightly overlaps the leather back and corners, so as to hide the join. 'Raised bands' are formed of strips of pasteboard or parchment placed at regular intervals across the back of the book, leaving a space termed 'panels' between them, and the pliable leather is stretched and worked over and round the edges of the bands, so as to give to the whole back a neat and uniform appearance.

The 'forwarder' then passes the book on to the 'finisher,' whose duty it is to add the required lettering and ornament.

The tools used by him, whether single letters or figures, or 'pallets' (that is, the title of a book, &c., cut in a single metal block) are mounted on wooden handles, and applied before use to a gas burner, in order to obtain the requisite heat.

If the impression of the tool is intended to be gilt, the finisher lays on gold leaf in a manner similar to that described in case-blocking, and the tool moderately heated is applied, not by an arming press, but by the finisher, on whose steadiness of hand and accuracy of eye the proper and even application of the various tools successively used in lettering or ornament is dependent. Additional pressure is given when needful for the larger tools, by the finisher's leaning his shoulder or chin against the end of the handle to assist the action of his hand. The superfluous gold-leaf is then cleaned off as in case blocking, by a greasy rag or a piece of India-rubber, after which the book is carefully examined, roughnesses smoothed down, and defective workmanship corrected, and a coating of polish or glaize given where required. Lastly, the end papers are pasted down, and after a final examination as to accuracy of lettering and other details, the book, after having a final squeeze to make it lie square and solid, is turned out complete.

The implement generally used by the extra binder for cutting the edges of single books is the plough (*figs.* 163 to 168).

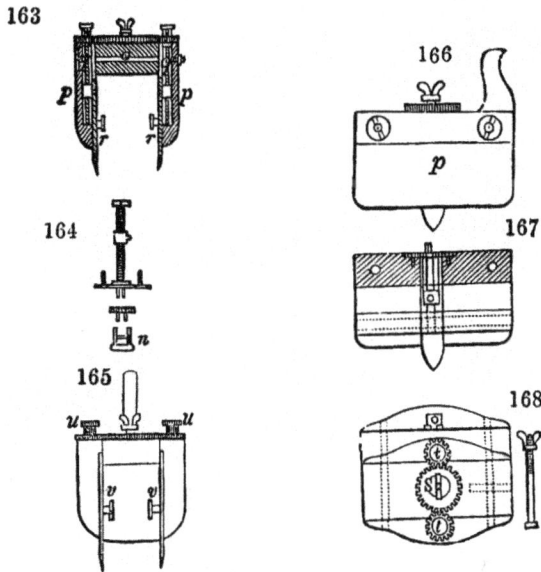

The plough (*fig.* 163) is made to receive two knives or cutters, and which are situated in the plough in the following manner:—The plough is composed of three principal parts—namely, the top, and it two sides. The top, *o*, is made the breadth of the cross piece *a*, and with a handle made fast thereon. The sides, *p p*, are bolted thereto with bolts and nuts through corresponding holes in the top and sides. The figures give inside views and cross sections of the details of the manner in which the cutters and adjustments are mounted. A groove is cut down each cheek or side, in which are placed screws that are held at top and bottom from moving up and down, but, by turning, they cause the nuts upon them to do so; they are shown at *q q*. These nuts have each a pin, projecting inwards, that goes into plain holes made in the top ends of cutters *r r*.

The cutters and the work for causing them to go up and down are sunk into the cheeks, so as to be quite level with their inner surfaces. *Fig.* 164 shows one of these screws apart, how fixed, and with moveable nut and projecting pin. The top of each screw terminates with a round split down, and above it a pinion-wheel and boss thereon, also similarly split. This pinion fits upon the split pin. Above, there is cross section of a hollow coupling cap, with steel tongue across, that fits into both the cuts of the screw pin and pinion boss, so that, when lowered upon each other, they must all turn together. In the middle and on the top of the upper piece, o, the large wheel s, runs loose upon its centre, and works into the two pinion wheels, $t\ t$ (*fig.* 168). The wheel s has a fly nut with wings mounted upon it.

It will now be seen, when the plough is in its place, as at *fig.* 165, that if it be pushed to and fro by the right hand, and the nut occasionally turned by the left, the knives, or cutters, will be protruded downwards at the same time, and these either will or will not advance as the coupling caps, $u\ u$, are on or off.

169

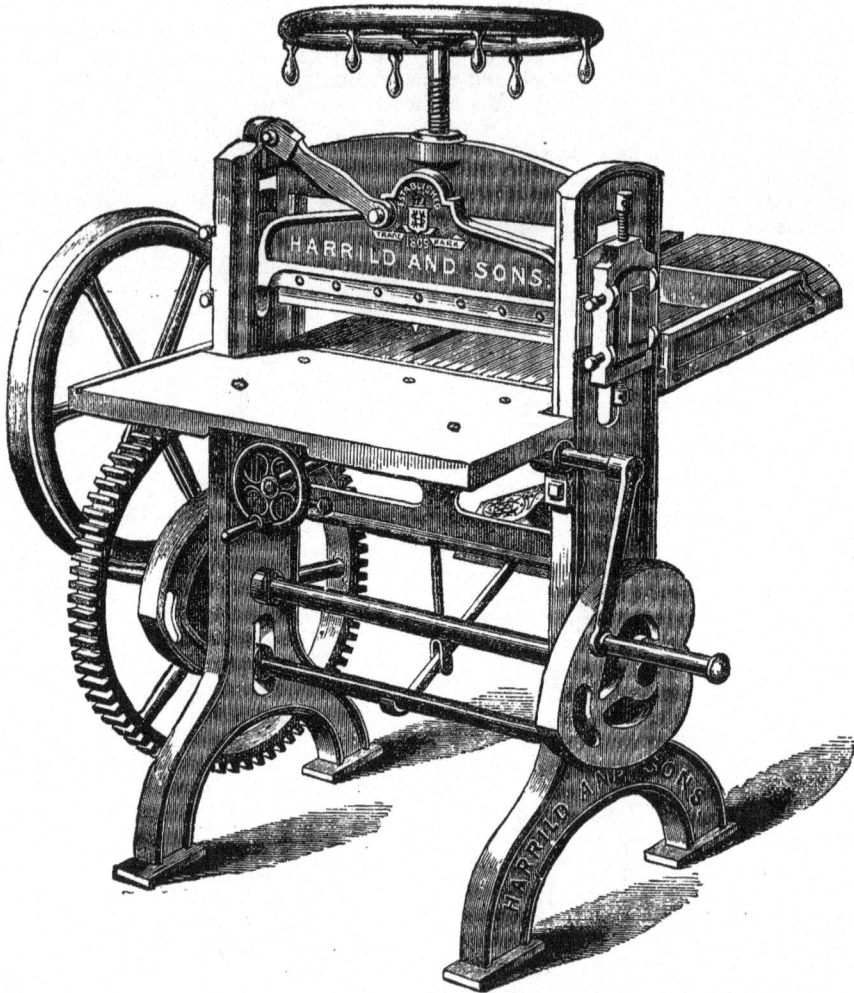

When the edges of a number of copies of the same book have to be cut, the operation is greatly accelerated by the use of Wilson's, or other cutting machines (*fig.* 169), which are adapted for working either by hand or by steam-power.

The cutting machines consist of an iron sliding table fitted with an upright plate at right angles to the surface of the table, against which the backs of the pile of books about to have their fore-edges cut are placed. By means of a turning wheel the fore-edges of the pile of books are then brought in the exact position proper to receive the descending knife-edge. This knife, long enough to reach from side to side of the table, and therefore along the whole range of books placed upon it, is fitted into a frame so as to act on the principle of the guillotine, and either by a directly downward or by a diagonal movement. A few turns of a fly-wheel, worked either by hand or steam-power, bring the heavy pressure of an iron bar upon the pile of books when thus brought into their proper position under the guillotine, by which the pile is squeezed into a firm compact mass, upon which, and simultaneously, the knife-edge is by the same power brought down, and the rough and superfluous fore-edges are at one stroke severed from the rest, leaving a smooth and polished surface on the fore-edges of the books, instead of the rough and uneven one before presented. The position of the pile is then carefully shifted so as to bring in succession the tops and the tails of the pile of books to the like action of the guillotine, and in a very short space of time (varying according to the size and thickness of the volumes operated on) the edges of many hundreds of books are cut smooth and in readiness for the sprinkler, the colourer, the marbler, or the gilder.

BOOKUM WOOD. An Indian wood, used for dyeing red, the produce of the Sappan tree, *Cæsalpinia Sappan*.

BORACIC ACID, or **BORIC ACID.** (*Acide borique*, Fr.; *Borsäure*, Ger.) Composition of the anhydride, BO^3 (B^2O^3); of the crystallised acid, BO^3, $3HO$ ($B^2O^3, 3H^2O$).

The chief sources of this acid and its salts—the borates—are the hot vapours, or *soffioni*, which issue from the ground in certain parts of Tuscany, and are utilised by a process fully described below. In addition to its occurrence in these vapours, boracic acid is found native in a solid state, forming the mineral *Sassoline* or *Sassolite*, so called from Sasso, in Tuscany, the locality in which it was originally discovered by Mascagni. Sassoline is usually found in the form of small white pearly scales, with a soapy feel. Theoretically, the pure mineral should contain 56·4 per cent. of boracic acid (anhydride) and 43·6 of water. Klaproth, in examining the Sassoline of Sasso, found 80 per cent. of boracic hydrate, with 11 per cent. of protosulphate of manganese, and 3 per cent. of sulphate of lime, together with silica, carbonate of lime, and other mechanically-mixed impurities. Sassoline also occurs abundantly in the crater of Vulcano, one of the Lipari Islands, forming a layer on the sulphur and around the fumaroles, or exits of the sulphurous exhalations.

Among the numerous compounds of boracic acid occurring ready formed in nature, the most important are *native borax*, or biborate of soda, and *tincal*, or crude borax : substances fully described under the head of Borax. Of the other native borates, the following are the more interesting species :—

Boracite, a borate of magnesia with chloride of magnesium, containing when pure 62·5 per cent. of boracic acid (anhydride). It crystallises in the cubic system, often in hemihedral or tetrahedral forms, and is remarkable for being pyro-electric—that is, for exhibiting electrical polarity when exposed to a change of temperature. The mineral is further notable for its anomalous optical properties ; thus, a ray of light in passing through a crystal of boracite suffers double refraction, contrary to the general rule that crystals belonging to the cubic system are not capable of thus affecting light. The probable explanation of this anomalous behaviour on the part of boracite is beyond the scope of this article.

Boracite is usually found in association with deposits of rock-salt and gypsum. The mineral occurs crystallised at Lüneburg in Hanover, and at Stassfurt near Magdeburg ; the latter locality also yields a massive boracite called *Stassfurtite*.

Ulexite or *Boronatrocalcite* is a hydrous borate of lime and soda, occurring in white reniform masses, from the size of a hazel-nut to that of a potato, scattered over the dry plains of Iquique, in Southern Peru, and in the Province of Tarapaca, where it is called *tiza*. It is also found in Nova Scotia and in Nevada. A specimen from Peru yielded—boracic acid, 45·46 ; lime 14·32 ; soda, 8·22 ; potash, 0·51 ; sulphuric acid, 1·10 ; chloride of sodium, 2·65 ; sand, 0·32. This analysis was made by Mr. A Dick, in the metallurgical laboratory of the Museum of Practical Geology. The term *Hayesine* was formerly applied to this mineral, but some confusion has arisen in the application of this name. According to Hayes the pure species contained no soda, and was simply a hydrous borate of lime. Mr. David Forbes discovered a borate of lime in the form of white silky flakes suspended in the waters of the hot springs called the Baños del Toro, in the Cordilleras of Coquimbo. The formation of this substance was instructive, as throwing light upon the probable origin of the same compound elsewhere. When the hot vapours, emanating from the neighbouring volcanoes, passed into springs of water highly charged with carbonate of lime, the boracic acid of the vapours combined with the lime to form borate of lime, whilst carbonic acid gas was set free. The term *Bechilite* has been applied by Dana to a borate of lime from Tuscany.

Howlite or *Silicoborocalcite* is a hydrous boro-silicate of lime, containing about 43 per cent. of boracic acid, and occurring in nodular forms in gypsum and anhydrite in Nova Scotia.

Cryptomorphite is a hydrated borate of lime and soda, with 58·5 per cent. of boracic acid, closely related to Ulexite. It has been found in Nevada.

Lardarellite is a borate of ammonia found in the lagoons of Tuscany, and named after the late Count Lardarel—the founder of the Tuscan boracic acid industry.

Lagonite is an earthy borate of peroxide of iron, also found in these lagoons.

In addition to the species noticed above, in which boracic acid forms a main constituent, there are several minerals which contain this acid in subordinate quantity. Thus, boracic acid is present in *Danburite* to the extent of about 28 per cent.; in *Datolite* to about 22 per cent.; in *Tourmaline* in variable proportions up to 12 per cent.; and in *Axinite* it is present in quantity ranging from 2 to 5 per cent. But of all the boracic minerals it is only the borates of soda, lime, and magnesia, which have hitherto been found in sufficient abundance to be economically employed in the preparation of boracic acid and the alkaline borates.

The great supply of boracic acid, however, is derived from the boracic acid lagoons of Tuscany. Before the discovery of this acid, in the time of the Grand-Duke Leopold I., by the chemist Höffer, the fetid odour developed by the sulphuretted hydrogen gas and the disruptions of the ground occasioned by the appearance of new *soffioni*, or vents of vapour, had made the natives regard them as a diabolical scourge, which they sought to remove by priestly exorcisms; but since science has explained the phenomena, the *fumacchi* have become a great boon to the district, and a source of public prosperity.

The hot vapours of the *soffioni* consist of a mixture of permanent gases, condensible vapours, and mechanically-suspended solid particles. Among the usual constituents may be mentioned carbonic acid gas, nitrogen, oxygen, sulphuretted hydrogen, watery vapour, ammonia, sulphate of ammonia, hydrochloric acid, organic matter, and boracic acid. To collect this boracic acid, which is never present in more than very minute quantity, the *soffioni* are enclosed by low walls of coarse masonry, or brick-work, glazed on the inside, and forming a series of circular basins, the diameter and depth of which vary greatly in different works. The larger basins may

170

enclose several distinct vents. A series of these circular basins is arranged in terraces on the side of a hill, as represented in *fig.* 170. A small stream of water, from an adjacent spring, is introduced into the uppermost basin A B, thus forming a small pool or artificial lagoon. By the escape of the hot vapours rising from below,

171

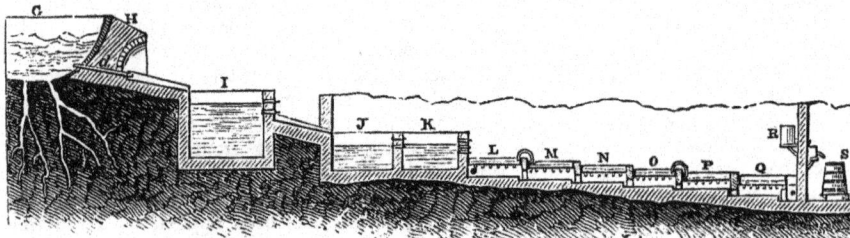

the water of this lagoon becomes more or less agitated and gradually heated, and at the same time impregnated with the boracic acid. After standing for 24 hours in the upper basin A B, the weak solution is run out, through the channel *a* into the second basin C D. Here it takes up another dose of boracic acid, and after 24 hours is run off into the next lower basin E F. After having in this way traversed six or eight of the lagoons, the solution acquires a specific gravity of 1·007, and contains about one-half per cent. of boracic acid. This solution passes from the last basin G H (*fig.* 171) into a series of clarifiers and evaporating vessels, represented in section in *fig.* 171,

172

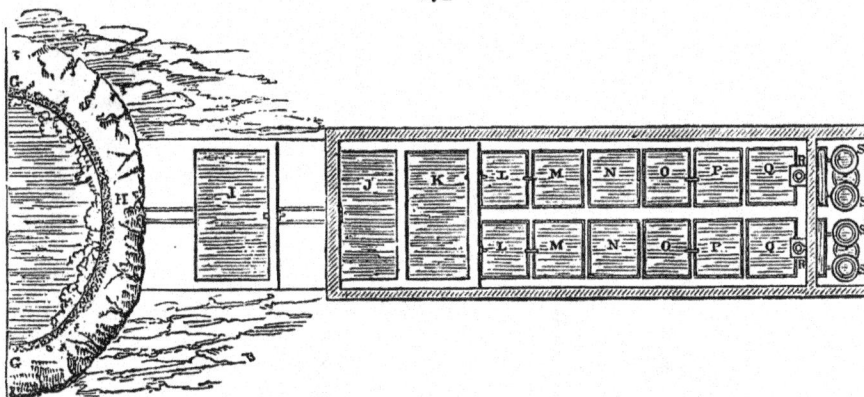

and in plan in *fig.* 172. In the large square brick vessel I, called a *vasco*, the solution deposits much of the mud which it holds in suspension. After subsidence of a great part of its mechanical impurities, the comparatively clear liquor is drawn off into other settling tanks J, K, and thence into a long succession of square leaden evaporating pans, of which half-a-dozen are represented by L, M, N, O, P, Q. The heat for effecting this evaporation was formerly obtained by the combustion of wood, but Count Larderel's capital improvement—an improvement without which the Tuscan *soffioni* could never have been profitably utilized—consisting in dispensing altogether with the use of artificial fuel, and conducting the evaporation by means of the natural heat of the volcanic emanations. Accordingly, jets of steam issuing from the ground are introduced through flues under the evaporating pans, and conducted successively from the lowest to the highest of the series. The solution during its passage through the system of evaporating vessels, which lasts about 62 hours, gradually becomes concentrated, and by the time it reaches the last vessel is sufficiently strong to be passed to the crystallising tubs, s s. *Fig.* 173 represents an improved form of

173

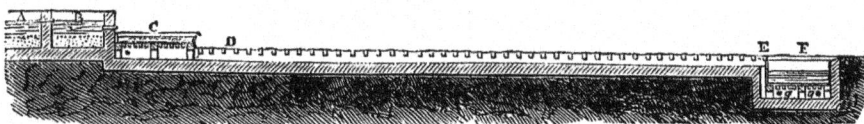

evaporating apparatus, in which the liquid from the *vasco* B passes to a shallow boiler, C, whence it runs slowly over an inclined table of sheet lead, D E, about 150 feet long, and having its surface corrugated so as to form a series of channels through which the solution flows. During its passage, the solution slowly evaporates, by the heat of the *soffioni* introduced below, and finally reaches the vessel F in a sufficiently concentrated form.

174

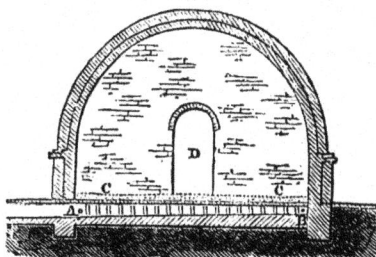

The concentrated solution, obtained by either of these methods of evaporation, is mixed with some of the mother-liquor of the pans, and set to crystallise in the round tubs s s (*figs.* 171, 172, 174), each having a capacity of about 8 cubic feet, and being made of wood, lined with lead. The small crystals on removal are drained in baskets J, at the top of the tub, and while still moist are spread out in a layer on the floor c c of the drying chamber (*fig.* 174), which is heated by steam circulating in a space included between this floor and another floor below.

The boracic acid of the Tuscan lagoons is obtained from nine different works:—Sasso, Larderello, Lervazano, Monte Cerboli, Castel Nuovo, Monte Rotondo, San Frederigo, Lustignano, Lago ; producing 163,855 avoirdupois pounds per month.

The late Count Larderel furnished Mr. W. P. Jervis with the following statement of the production of boracic acid, from the commencement of the works to the year 1859 :—

	Tons	Cwts.			Tons	Cwts.
From 1818 to 1828	521	16	1849		1,043	13
„ 1829 „ 1838	4,870	6	1850		1,043	13
1839	748	13	1851		1,140	0
1840	878	13	1852		1,156	19
1841	886	6	1853		1,208	19
1842	923	15	1854		1,319	7
1843	923	16	1855		1,332	19
1844	923	16	1856		1,427	1
1845	923	15	1857		1,711	4
1846	1,043	13	1858		2,026	10
1847	1,043	13	1859		1,803	18
1848	1,043	13				

Society of Arts' Journal.

Although the boracic acid in the lagoons of Tuscany was discovered in 1777 by Peter Hoeffer, apothecary to the Grand-Duke of Tuscany, until 1818 all the efforts made to render it profitable to obtain it were of the most desultory character, and generally failures. In 1818 Count Larderel established the first works at Monte Cerboli, and used *artificial heat* to effect the evaporation. In 1828 he began to *use the natural heat of the soffioni to evaporate the boracic waters of the lagoons*, effecting thus an enormous saving and greatly extending the works.

The late Professor Graham, in his 'Report on the Chemical Products of the Great Exhibition of 1851,' thus speaks of Larderel's discovery :—

'The preparation of boracic acid by Count F. de Larderel, of Tuscany, was rewarded by a Council medal. Although this well-known manufacture is not recent, having attained its full development at least ten years, still the bold originality of its first conception, the perseverance and extraordinary resources displayed in the successful establishment, and the value of the product which it supplies, will always place the operations of Count de Larderel among the highest achievements of the useful arts, and demand the most honourable mention at this epoch. The vapour issuing from a volcanic soil is condensed, and the minute proportion of boracic acid which it contains (not exceeding 0·3 per cent.) is recovered by evaporation, in a district without fuel, by the application of volcanic vapour itself as a source of heat. The boracic acid thus obtained greatly exceeds in quantity the old and limited supply of borax from the upper districts of India, and has greatly extended the use of that salt in the glazes of porcelain, and recently in the making of the most brilliant crystal, when combined with the oxide of zinc instead of the oxide of lead.'—*Reports of the Jurors of the Great Exhibition of* 1851.

Various hypotheses have been advanced to explain the origin of the boracic acid in the heated vapours of the Tuscan lagoons. Boracic acid is not known in an uncombined state as a constituent of any rock, but it seems likely that the deep-seated rocks whence the vapours issue may contain certain borates—such as boracite—and by the action of hot aqueous vapour on these compounds boracic acid may be eliminated.

The processes of chemical alteration taking place beneath the crater of Vulcano, already spoken of, may, according to the statement of Hoffmann, depend upon conditions very similar to those existing in Tuscany. There, likewise, sulphuretted hydrogen is associated with the boracic acid, and, it would appear in much greater quantity, since the fissures through which the vapour issues are thickly lined with sulphur, which is in sufficient quantity to be collected for sale. A profitable factory is established at the place, which yields daily, besides boracic acid and chloride of ammonium, about 1,700 lbs. of refined sulphur and about 600 lbs. of pure alum.—*Bischof.*

The boracic acid obtained from the waters of the Tuscan lagoons by the process previously described is always more or less impure. M. Payen has given the following as the composition of this crude boracic acid for 100 kilogrammes : —

Pure crystallised boracic acid	74 to 84
Sulphate of ammonia, magnesia, and lime	14 to 8
Sand and sulphur	2·5 to 1·25
Hygroscopic water disengaged at 35° C.	7 to 5·75
Azotic matter, hydrochlorate of ammonia, &c.	2·5 to 1

According to Wittstein, the commercial boracic acid is composed as follows :—

Sulphate of manganese	. . . . . .	a trace
" iron	. . . . . .	0·365
" alumina .	. . . . . .	0·320
" lime	. . . . . .	1·018
" magnesia .	. . . . . .	2·632
" ammonia .	. . . . . .	8·508
" soda	. . . . . .	0·917
" potash	. . . . . .	0·369
Sal ammoniac	. . . . . .	0·298
Silica (in solution)	. . . . . .	1·200
Sulphuric acid (with the boracic)	. . . .	1·322
Crystallisable boracic acid .	. . . . .	76·494
Water	. . . .	6·557

$$\overline{100\text{·}000}$$

To obtain pure boracic acid, the crude commercial product should be converted into borax by saturating its solution with carbonate of soda, and a hot solution of this borax be then decomposed by addition of oil of vitriol, when sulphate of soda is formed, and boracic acid set free. Pure boracic acid crystallises in pearly, white, greasy scales, sparingly soluble in cold water, but dissolving in three times their weight of boiling water, and forming a solution possessing but feebly acid properties. It is more soluble in alcohol, and the solution burns with a characteristic green flame. This flame examined by the spectroscope presents a peculiar system of green bands. At a moderate temperature boracic acid loses part of its water of crystallisation, and forms a compound known as *metaboric acid.* By further heating, the remainder of the water is expelled, and the anhydrous oxide (BO^3) left. This anhydride is readily fusible to a transparent glass of specific gravity 1·83. Many of the borates are also eminently fusible, and hence their value as fluxes. At a higher temperature, boracic anhydride volatilises.

Boracic acid was formerly called *Homberg's sedative salt,* but is not now officinal. It is sometimes used by the druggist to increase the solubility of cream of tartar.

BORACITE. See BORACIC ACID.

BORATE OF LIME. See BORACIC ACID.

BORATE OF SODA. See BORAX.

BORATES. Salts of boracic acid. See ' Watts's Dictionary of Chemistry.'

BORAX. (*Borax,* Fr.; *Borar,* Ger.) Supposed to be the *chrysocolla* of Pliny. In the seventh century, Geber mentions borax; and it was described by Geoffroy and by Baron in the early part of the eighteenth century. Borax is a compound of boracic acid and soda (biborate of soda), found native in Thibet, in China, in Persia, the island of Ceylon, California, and in South America; it has also been found in small quantities in Saxony. The crude product from the former locality was imported into Europe under the name of *tincal.* Tincal was originally brought from a salt lake in Thibet; the borax was dug in masses from the edges and shallow parts of the lake; and in the course of a short time the holes thus made were again filled. The imported tincal was purified from some adhering fatty matter by a process kept a long time secret by the Venetians and the Dutch, and which consisted chiefly in boiling the substance in water with a little quicklime.

Attention has been directed within the last few years to some extraordinary deposits of borax in Borax Lake, California. This lake is a small body of water, forming a narrow arm on the eastern side of Clear Lake, from which it is separated by a low ridge of loose volcanic materials. It is situated about 65 miles N. W. of Suisan Bay, and about 36 miles from the Pacific coast. Borax Lake was first described in 1856, by Dr. Veatch, who detected the presence of borax in the water, and some months afterwards a large bed of crystals of borax was discovered at the bottom. Some of these crystals are microscopic, but others are unusually large, some of the faces measuring from 2 to 3 inches across. They form a layer of variable thickness, intermixed with blue mud at the bottom of the lake, from which they are collected during the dry season. A sample of water from the lake, collected in September 1863, and analysed by Mr. G. E. Moore, contained 2401·56 grains of solid matter per gallon, of which about one-half was chloride of sodium, one-fourth carbonate of soda, and the rest chiefly borax. Indeed, the water contained per gallon 281·48 grains of anhydrous biborate of soda, equivalent to 535·08 grains of crystallised borax. Samples collected from a coffer-dam sunk in the middle of the lake were even richer. The borate of soda has also been found at Potosi, in Peru; and it has been discovered by Mr. T. Sterry Hunt, of the Geological Survey, in Canada, from whose report the following extract is made :—

'In the township of Joly there occurs a very interesting spring on the banks of the Ruisseau Magnenat, a branch of the Rivière Souci, about five miles from the mills of Methot at Saint Croix. The spring furnishes three or four gallons a minute of a water which is sulphurous to the taste and smell, and deposits a white matter along its channel, which exhibits the purple vegetation generally met with in sulphur springs. The temperature of this spring in the evening of one 7th of July was 46° F., the air being 52° F. The water is not strongly saline, but when concentrated is very alkaline and salt to the taste. It contains, besides chlorides, sulphates, and carbonates, a considerable proportion of boracic acid, which is made evident by its power of reddening paper coloured by turmeric, after being supersaturated with hydrochloric acid. . . . The analysis of 1,000 parts of the water gave as follows :—

Chloride of sodium	0·3818
,, potassium	0·0067
Sulphate of soda	0·0215
Carbonate and borate of do.	0·2301
,, of lime	0·0620
,, magnesia	0·0257
Silica	0·0245
Alumina	a trace
	0·7523

'The amount of boracic acid estimated was found to be equal to 0·0279.'

The following is the mode of purifying borax. The crude crystals are to be broken into small lumps, and spread upon a filter lined with a lead grating, under which a piece of cloth is spread upon a wooden frame. The lumps are piled up to the height of 12 inches, and washed with small quantities of caustic soda-lye of 5° B. (specific gravity 1·033) until the liquor comes off nearly colourless ; they are then drained, and put into a large copper of boiling water, in such quantities that the resulting solution stands at 20° B. (specific gravity 1·160). Carbonate of soda equivalent to 12 per cent. of the borax must now be added ; the mixed solution is allowed to settle, and the clear liquid is syphoned off into crystallising vessels. Whenever the mother-waters get foul, they must be evaporated to dryness in cast-iron pots, and roasted, to burn away the viscid colouring matter.

The following process for refining the native Indian borax, or tincal, has been published by MM. Robiquet and Marchand :—

It is put into large tubs, covered with water for 3 or 4 inches above its surface, and stirred through it several times during six hours. For 400 lbs. of the tincal there must now be added 1 lb. of quicklime diffused through two quarts of water. Next day the whole is thrown upon a sieve, to drain off the water with the impurities, consisting, in some measure, of the fatty matter combined with the lime, as an insoluble soap. The borax, so far purified, is to be dissolved in 2½ times its weight of boiling water, and 8 lbs. of muriate of lime are to be added for the above quantity of borax. The liquor is now filtered, evaporated to the density of 18° or 20° B. (1·14 to 1·16 specific gravity), and set to crystallise in vessels shaped like inverted pyramids, and lined with lead. At the end of a few days, the crystallisation being completed, the mother-waters are drawn off, the crystals are detached and dried. The loss of weight in this operation is about 20 per cent.

Borax is sometimes adulterated with alum and common salt : the former addition may be readily detected by a few drops of water of ammonia, which will throw down its alumina ; and the latter by nitrate of silver, which will give with it a precipitate insoluble in nitric acid.

The native boracic acid obtained from the lakes of Tuscany, being manufactured in France into borax, has greatly lowered the price of this article of commerce. When MM. Payen and Cartier first began the business, they sold the crystals at the same price as the Dutch, viz., 7 francs the kilogramme (2⅕ lbs. avoird.); but, in a few years, they could only obtain 2 francs and 60 centimes, in consequence of the market getting overstocked. The mode of making borax from the acid is as follows :—The lake water is evaporated in graduation houses, and then concentrated in boilers till it crystallises. In that state it is carried to Marseilles. About 1,100 lbs. of water are made to boil in a copper, and 1,320 lbs. of crystallised carbonate of soda are dissolved in it by successive additions of about 40 lbs. The solution being maintained at nearly the boiling point, 1,100 lbs. of the crystallised boracic acid of Tuscany are introduced, in successive portions. At each addition of about 22 lbs. a lively effervescence ensues, on which account the copper should be of much greater capacity than is sufficient to contain the liquors. When the whole acid has been added, the fire must be damped by being covered up with moist ashes, and the copper must be covered with a tight lid and blankets, to preserve the temperature uniform. The whole is left in this state during 30 hours; the clear liquor is then drawn off into shallow crystallising vessels of lead, in which it should stand no higher than 10 or 12 inches, to favour its rapid cooling. At the end of three days in winter, and four in summer, the crystallisation is usually finished. The mother-water is drawn off, and employed, instead of simple water, for the purpose of dissolving fresh crystals of soda. The crystals are carefully detached with chisels, re-dissolved in boiling water, adding for each 220 lbs. of borax, 22 lbs. of carbonate of soda. This solution marks 20° B. (specific gravity 1·160); and, at least, one ton of borax should be dissolved at once, in order to obtain crystals of a marketable size. Whenever this solution has become boiling hot, it must be run off into large crystallising lead chests of the form of inverted truncated pyramids, furnished with lids, inclosed in wooden frames, and surrounded with mats to confine the heat. For a continuous business there should be at least 18 vessels of this kind, as the solution takes a long time to complete its crystallisation, by cooling to 30° C. (86° F.) The borax crystals are taken out with chisels, after the liquor has been drawn off and the whole has become cold.

One hundred parts of the purest acid, usually extracted from the lakes of Tuscany, contain only 50 parts of the real boracic acid, and yield no more, at the utmost, than 140 or 150 of good borax.

A considerable saving of expense in manufacturing borax, and a more ready application of the borax to use, has been proposed by Saulter, as follows:—Take about 38 parts of pure crystallised boracic acid, pounded and sifted; mix them well with 45 parts of crystals of carbonate of soda, in powder; expose the mixture upon wooden shelves to heat in a stove-room; and rake it up from time to time. The boracic acid and the alkali thus get combined, while the carbonic acid and water are expelled; and a perfect *dry borax* is obtained.

Borax is an acid borate or biborate of soda, usually crystallised in oblique prisms, with 10 atoms of water. Under certain conditions it may also be obtained in octahedra, containing only half this proportion of water; and by application of heat the whole of the water may be expelled with intumescence. The composition of these three forms of the salt may be thus exhibited:—

Prismatic Borax (NaO, 2BO^3, 10HO).

2 atoms of boracic acid	.	.	.	.	.	70	or	36·6
1 „ soda .	.	.	.	.	.	31	„	16·3
10 „ water	.	.	.	.	.	90	„	47·1

$$191 \qquad 100·0$$

Octahedral Borax (NaO, 2BO^3, 5HO).

2 atoms of boracic acid	.	.	.	.	.	70	or	47·9
1 „ soda .	.	.	.	.	.	31	„	21·2
5 „ water	.	.	.	.	.	45	„	30·9

$$146 \qquad 100·0$$

Anhydrous Borax (NaO, 2BO^3).

2 atoms of boracic acid	.	.	.	.	.	70	or	69·4
1 „ soda .	.	.	.	.	.	31	„	30·6

$$101 \qquad 100·0$$

Borax has a sweetish, somewhat lixivial taste, and affects vegetable colours like an alkali; it is soluble in 12 parts of cold, and in 2 parts of boiling water. It effloresces and becomes opaque in a dry atmosphere; it appears luminous, by friction, in the dark. It melts at a heat a little above that of boiling water, and gives out its water of crystallisation, after which it forms a spongy mass, called calcined borax. The octahedral borax, which is prepared by crystallisation, in a solution of 1·255 specific gravity, kept up at 145° F., is not efflorescent. When borax is ignited, it fuses into a glassy-looking substance.

Dry borax acts on the metallic oxides, at a high temperature, in a very remarkable manner, melting and vitrifying them into very beautiful coloured glasses. On this account it is a most useful re-agent for the blowpipe. Oxide of chrome tinges it of an emerald green; oxide of cobalt, an intense blue; oxide of copper, a pale green; oxide of tin, opal; oxide of iron, bottle green and yellow; oxide of manganese, violet; oxide of nickel, pale emerald green. The white oxides impart no colour to it by themselves. In the fusion of metals, borax protects their surface from oxidisement, and even dissolves away any oxides formed upon them; by which twofold agency it becomes an excellent flux, invaluable to the goldsmith in soldering the precious metals, and to the brazier in soldering copper and iron.

Borax absorbs muriatic and sulphurous acid gases, but no others, whereby it becomes, in this respect, a useful means of analysis.

The strength or purity of borax may be tested by the quantity of sulphuric acid requisite to neutralise a given weight of it, as indicated by tincture of litmus.

When mixed with shellac in the proportion of one part to five, borax renders that resinous body soluble in water, and forms with it a species of varnish.

The applications of borax in the manufacture of enamels, glazes, and of glass, will be noticed in the articles devoted to the consideration of those special industries.

BORING. Whether for the purpose of searching for coal or other minerals, or for obtaining water for the supply of towns or for land irrigation, the importance of boring as a branch of mining science is so important as to command careful consideration in a work of this description.

Under the head of ARTESIAN WELLS, the various physical conditions under which water may be obtained by means of boreholes, have been described. It is now proposed to give an account of the different modes of prosecuting boreholes, and to refer to the purposes, other than the finding of water, for which the science of boring is resorted to.

It may be stated generally, that beyond the question of water supply, the boring of holes is chiefly carried out with the object of proving the existence, or otherwise, of rocks or minerals of more or less value. Whilst in putting down holes for the discovery of water, a simple *hole*, in a firm and durable condition, is all that is required, in the proving of minerals it is very important that the result of the borings should indicate very accurately the character and section of the strata passed through. The extent to which this end has been accomplished will be hereafter referred to.

Boring for water appears to have been in use from the earliest periods, in Egypt and in Asia. In many of the desert tracts there are remains of borings, which served, evidently at one period, to supply the wants of extensive populations which once inhabited those now deserted regions. In the 'Guide du Sondeur,' by M. J. Dégoussée, we find it stated, with reference to China: 'There exists in the canton of Ou-Tong-Kiao many thousand wells in a space of ten leagues long by five broad. These wells cost a thousand and some hundred taëls (the taël being of the value of 6s. 6d.), and are from 1,500 to 1,800 feet deep, and about 6 inches in diameter. To bore these wells, the Chinese commence by placing in the earth a wooden tube of 3 or 4 inches diameter, surmounted by a stone edge, pierced by an orifice of 5 or 6 inches; in the tube a trepan is allowed to play, weighing 300 or 400 lbs. A man mounted on a scaffold, swings a block, which raises the trepan 2 feet high, and lets it fall by its own weight. The trepan is secured to the swing-lever by a cord made of reeds, to which is attached a triangle of wood; a man sits close to the cord, and at each rise of the swing seizes the triangle and gives it a half turn, so that the trepan may take in falling another direction. A change of workmen goes on day and night, and with this continuous labour they are sometimes three years in boring wells to the requisite depth.'

Hand boring.—The surface arrangements usually required for boring by hand, are shown by *fig.* 175. In ordinary practice, a well is first sunk of such a depth that the boring apparatus can be fixed in it; and thus a stage, raised from the surface of the ground, is dispensed with. A stout plank floor, well braced together by planks nailed transversely, and resting on putlocks, forms the stage. In the centre of the floor is a square hole, through which the boring rods pass. The plant required consists of a spring pole A, to assist in giving the necessary motion to the rods when at work, the three legs with pulley blocks, chain, and roller, or windlass for drawing and lowering the rods, and the several lengths of rods required, with the various chisels, pumps, &c.

The borehole is usually commenced by digging a small pit about 6 feet deep, and over this is set up the three legs, with pulley, &c. A few feet of iron tubing are also sometimes inserted at the commencement, to protect the sides of the borehole.

The boring rods are usually from 10 to 20 feet long. The chisel is first inserted, then rods added as the work progresses. At the top of the rods are attached two handles about 4' 0" long, placed at right angles to each other. By means of these the borers work the rods up and down, at the same time giving them a circular motion in order to alter the position of the chisel at each stroke.

As the depth increases, the men at the handles or cross-bar are assisted by means of a pole or lever at the surface; one end being firmly fixed in the ground between two posts, the other being allowed to pass over the hole. From the end of this pole the bore-rods are attached by means of a chain; thus every time the borers strike the chisel, the lever enables them to lift the rods high enough to give the necessary impetus to the rods for the next blow. The chisel is occasionally withdrawn, and a long bucket with a hinged valve at the bottom opening upwards, is attached to the rods, and lowered into the hole. The borers press this down upon the material broken up by the chisel, so that a quantity of *débris* becomes enclosed in the bucket, and is drawn up to the surface. This process is repeated until the hole is made clear, and ready again for the chisel.

The rods are drawn by means of a windlass attached to the three legs, and are un-screwed at every second joint, until the whole of them are drawn out. They have to be again screwed together when they have to be lowered.

175

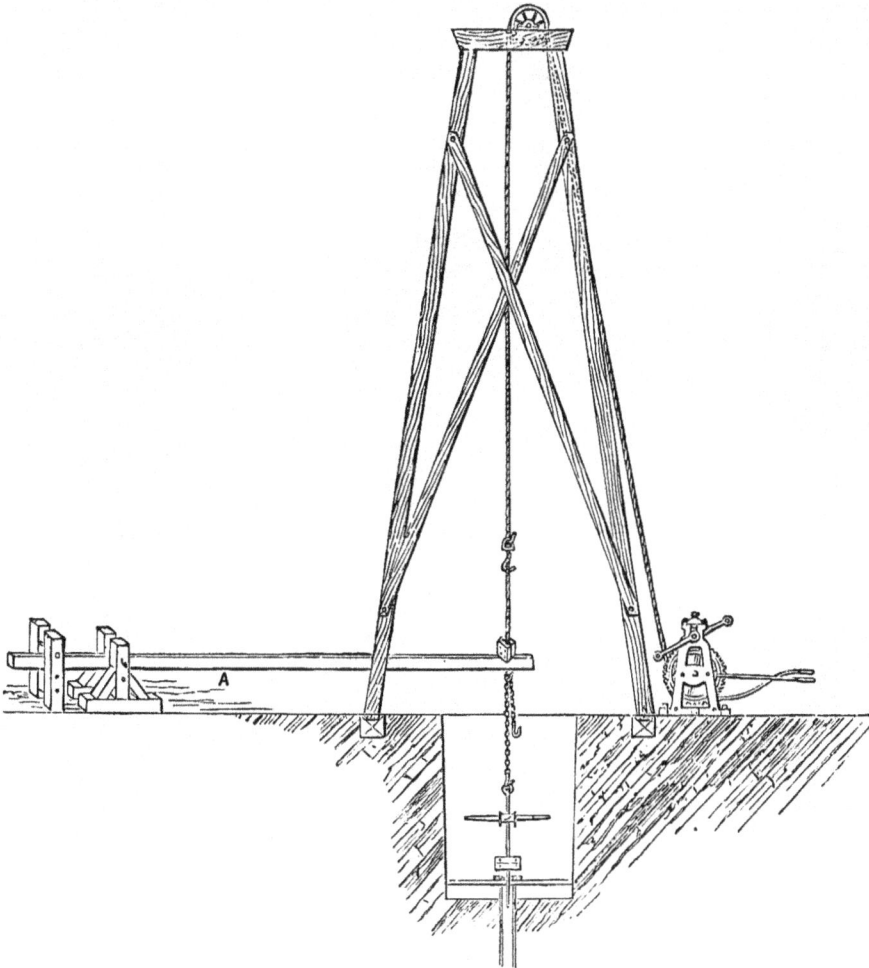

This style of boring is limited to a small depth; the weight of boring rods becomes so great with an increasing depth, that the borers, even when assisted by a lever, are unable to lift them. A depth of about 300 feet may be safely bored in this way.

The nature of strata bored through is ascertained from the material brought up by the bucket; and the borers having constantly hold of the cross-bar, any change of strata is at once indicated by the stroke of the chisel against the various beds met with, being imparted to the hands of the men, who acquire by experience great deli-cacy of touch. A new description of spring has lately been used with the hand-boring machine. This consists of several layers of india-rubber, about 1 inch square, and 2 feet 6 inches long, increasing the number of layers as the weight of rods be-comes greater. Each end of the india-rubber is fixed in strong iron clamps, one attached by a chain to the three legs, and the other coupled to the top of the rods; the elasticity of the india-rubber is thus brought to play upon the motion of the rods.

Horizontal Boring by Hand.—For boring in the sides of mountains, quarries, or other places where long horizontal holes are required, the machine illustrated by *fig.* 176, is sometimes used. The rods, chisels, pumps, &c., are all of the same description as those used for vertical boring, except that they are of somewhat lighter

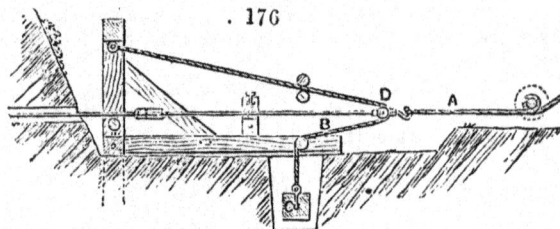

. 176

make. The rods are drawn out of the hole by means of the rope A, the weight C, which hangs in a small pit suspended by the rope B, being raised at the same time. The rope A is then slipped, and the falling weight C drives the rods into the hole again. The rods are kept steady and horizontal by being caused to run over a small roller fixed on the frame, and also by moving in a slide block, adjusted by a screw and nut.

After using the chisel for a short time, the rods are withdrawn, and the pump or scourer introduced to clear away the *débris*, the other work being carried on as with ordinary vertical hand-boring.

Boring by Steam Power.—Where boreholes are required of any considerable depth, and where speed is of importance, hand-labour has been superseded in recent years in a variety of modes; the best of which is probably the system largely adopted in America in searching for petroleum. This machine, which is shown by *fig.* 177, is driven by a small engine, and consists of a lever or wooden beam, connected at one end to a small crank with a reducing slide, by means of which the stroke can be made either short or long.

The chisels used are screwed into a connecting piece, which is attached to an iron-wire rope, and which is constructed with a slide (see *fig.* 34, p. 439), so that after the chisel strikes the bottom of the hole, the top part of the connecting rod slides down, keeping the rope taut in the hole; when again

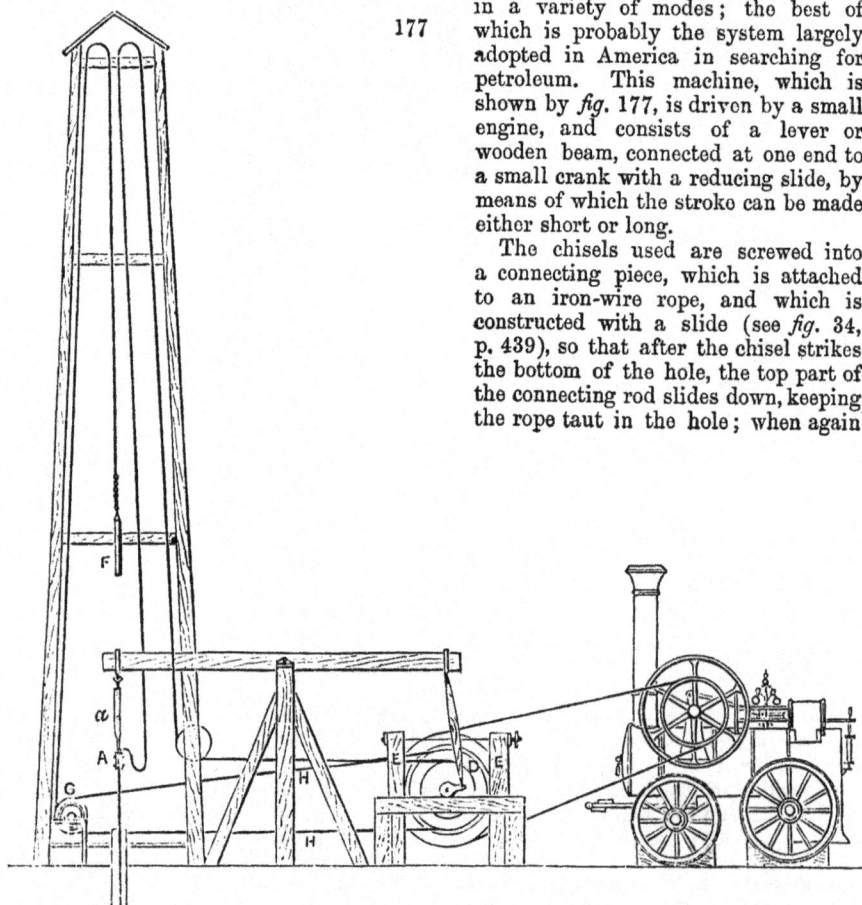

177

lifted up, it rises until it catches the part to which the chisel is connected. This apparatus prevents the rope from becoming slack in the hole when the tool falls.

The chisels employed are of the ordinary description : whilst by hand boring, holes of not more than a few inches diameter can be put down, with this apparatus holes of any diameter to 18 inches can be bored without any difficulty.

The rope is attached to the connecting piece by the clips, and is passed at the top of the hole through strong iron clamps, A, over which it hangs loosely to allow for the upward and downward motion of the boring-tools. The iron clamps are also connected to a screw and slide, *a, fig.* 177, hanging from the end of the wood lever or beam, this screw being used to adjust the length of the rope after it has been attached securely into the iron clamp.

The rope is drawn up by a small drum, D, driven from the same shaft as the crank used for working the beam ; a brake being attached to the drum for the purpose of lowering the chisel and connections into the bottom of the hole. This brake consists of two pieces of timber, E E, which are drawn together by means of a rod and screw.

After the chisel has been at work for a short time, it is drawn up by means of the drum D, and the pump F is then introduced, being lowered by the small drum G, which has also a brake attached. This pump is worked up and down a few times, then drawn up by the wire rope H, driven by the wheel on the main driving shaft.

The engine used is an ordinary portable engine, with a cylinder 9 inches in diameter.

The boring rope is usually $\frac{3}{4}$ inch in diameter, and is covered with tarred hemp rope for protection.

The depth from the surface, and thickness of the various strata passed through is ascertained by observing the wire rope, and by carefully noting the nature of the samples drawn up by the steel pump.

In boring with this machine, a small hole is sometimes kept in advance a distance of about 4 feet, the sides of the hole being removed by the larger chisel, and the pieces thus broken off are brought up by the pump, and kept in sample boxes.

The average rate of boring varies from 10 to 20 feet per day of twenty-four hours. It is usual, whether in boring by hand or steam power, to line the hole from the surface down to the solid strata with tubes ; and should any loose strata, as sand, be afterwards met with, tubes of smaller diameter than those first introduced are put down, this necessarily causing a contraction of the hole, and also of the tools.

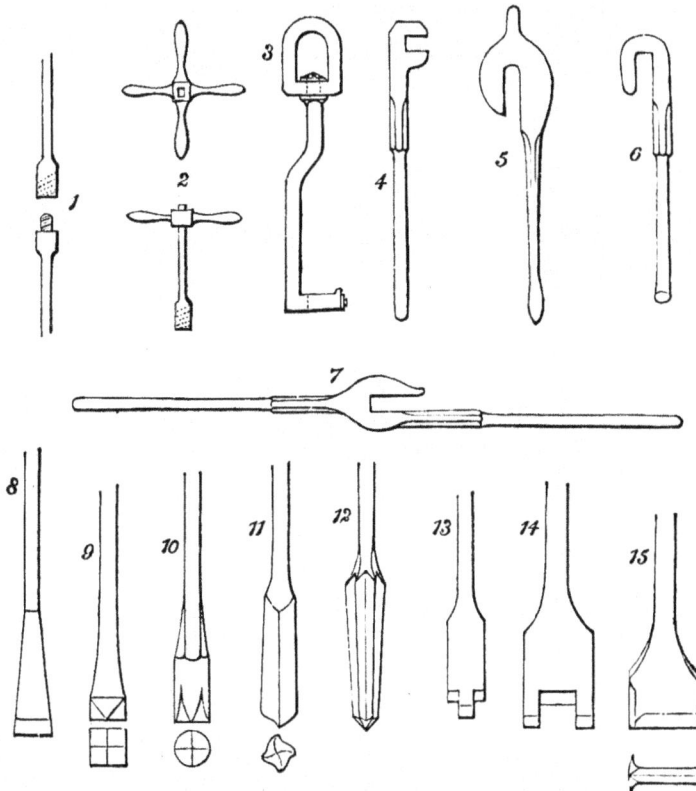

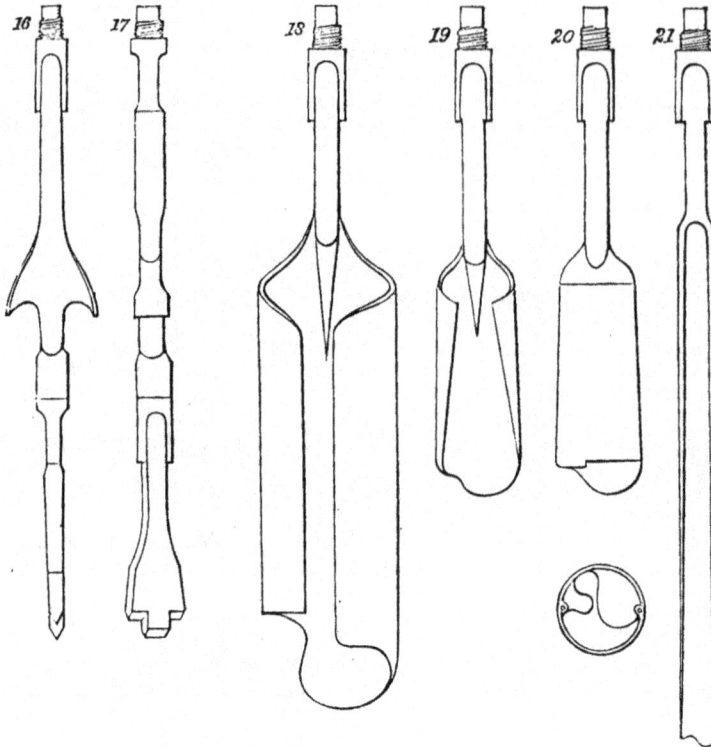

A description may now be given of the various tools used in the two systems of boring referred to :—

Fig. 1 is the joint used for attaching the boring rods together.

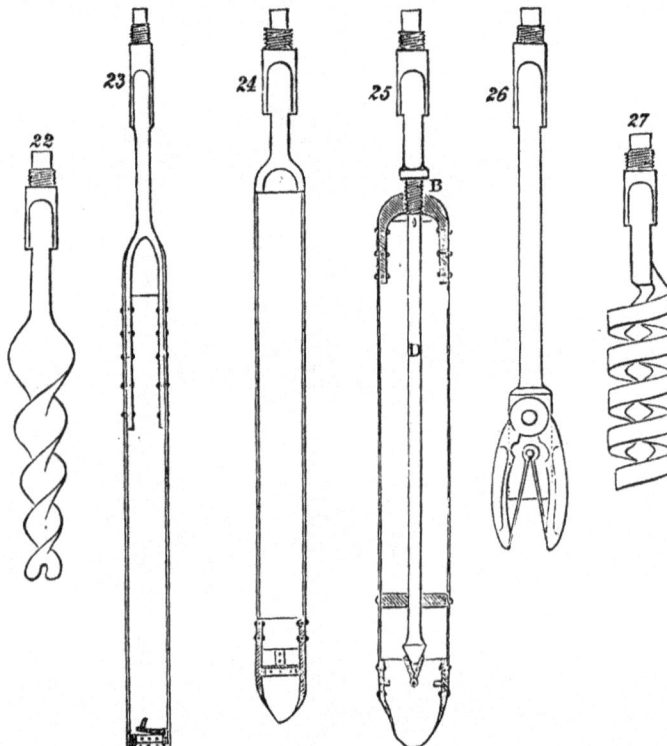

Fig. 2 is the brace-head, or cross-head, with the four handles held by the borers.

Fig. 3 is a catch for raising the rods from the borehole.

Figs. 4, 5, 6, and 7, are spanners, used for screwing the rods together, and holding them steady at the top of the borehole. The shoulders of the rods rest between the claws.

Fig. 8 is the ordinary chisel used for boring.

Figs. 9, 10, 11, and 12, are various forms of chisels used for making the hole cylindrical, and for breaking up hard fragments of rock at the bottom of the hole.

Figs. 13 and 14 are also tools used for the latter purpose.

Figs. 15, 16, and 17, are chisels used for breaking off projections from the sides of the hole: *figs.* 16 and 17 showing two views of the same tool.

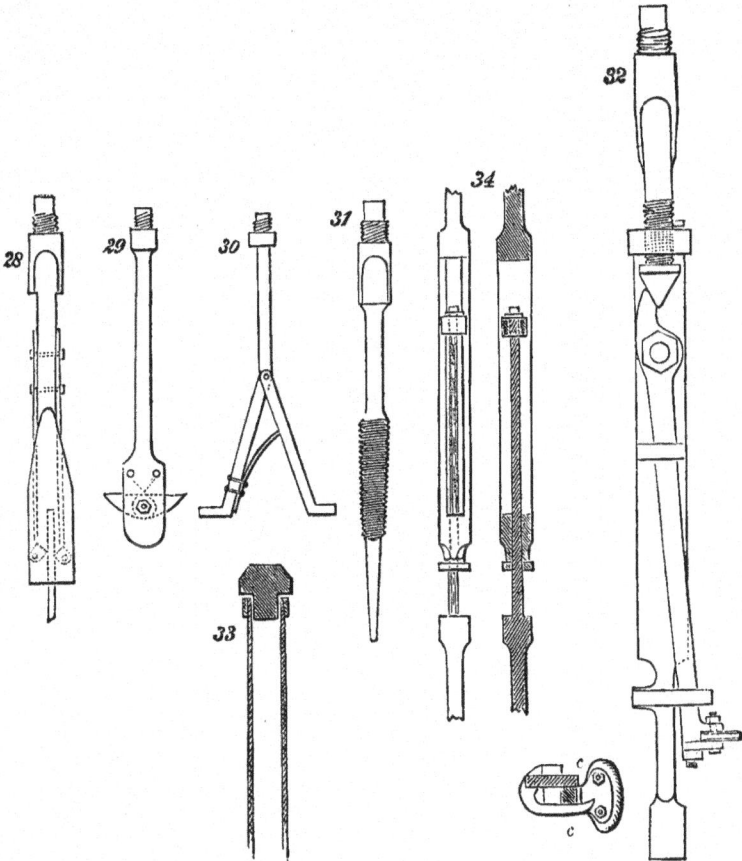

The implements used in extracting *débris* from boreholes are as follow:—

Figs. 18, 19, 20, and 21, are augers or wimbles, used for bringing up argillaceous strata.

Fig. 22 is an auger for boring through clay, generally used in commencing the borehole.

Figs. 23 and 24 are pumps or scourers, for bringing up the *débris* broken up by the chisels.

Fig. 25 is a scourer with valves, which are closed by turning the rods round, the action of the screw B causing the part D to descend.

Fig. 26 is an arrangement of pincers for extracting pieces of rock which are too large to enter the pump.

The instruments employed for *rectifying accidents* are as follow:—

Fig. 27 is a special screw for drawing out broken rods or tools.

Fig. 28 is a spring catch for extracting broken rods.

Figs. 29 and 30 are catches used for extracting broken lining tubes. One of the branches of the appliance shown by *fig.* 30 is fixed, and the other moveable.

Fig. 31 is a screw tap, also used for extracting tubes.

Fig. 32 is a tool used for cutting lining tubes when it is found that they cannot be drawn out all at once. *c* exhibits a plan of the cutter.

Fig. 33 is a plug used for driving down lining tubes.

In some cases it is required after the tubes have been inserted, to recommence boring the hole, and make it of the same size as the outside diameter of the tubes. To accomplish this object several ingenious devices have been designed.

In most of these the chisel intended to form the large diameter of the hole is passed down through the tube flush with the sides of the tool, and when reaching the bottom of the tube it is brought into position in several different ways. In one case, a screw when turned, forces out the cutters. In another, the chisels are pushed out by springs.

Another mode is to attach to the moveable chisels a dry hemp cord, the contraction of which when soaked in water draws up the chisels.

In boreholes of a considerable diameter, a 'free falling' arrangement, as shown by *figs.* 35 and 36, is sometimes adopted. A A are pins, holding in a fixed position two long clutches, which hold the end of the boring rods at E. The disc D is of the same diameter as the hole being put down. When the sliding arms reach the bottom of the stroke, the arrow-head E is caught, and is drawn up to the top of the hole, as shown by *fig.* 35. Immediately the down stroke commences, the resistance against the disc, caused by the water standing in the borehole, causes it to open the clutches and disengage the tool. It will be seen that this apparatus is only applicable where a column of water is present.

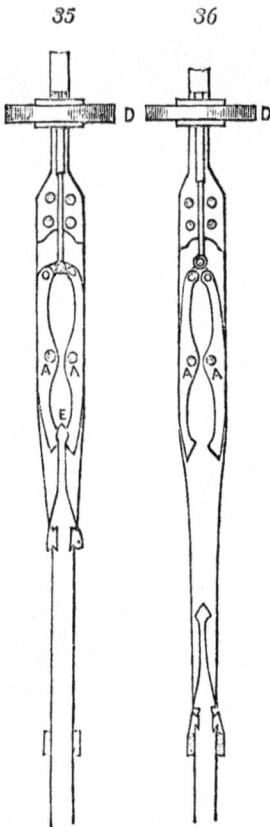

Having now described the tools used in the ordinary modes of Boring, attention may be drawn to various modern improvements in this science.

A method of boring with hollow rods, combined with a force-pump, was introduced about the year 1846 by M. Fauvelle, in order to obviate the necessity of using the shell, the detritus produced by the tool being removed continuously by a downward current of water forced by the pump through the interior of the rod, and rising in the annular included space between the exterior of the rod and the lining tube. In spite of the apparent advantages of this method, namely, the maintenance of a clear face of rock for the cutting tool to work on, and the saving of time due to the abolition of the shell, and the adoption of the method of continuous discharge, it does not appear to have come much into use. Recently, however, a modification in which the discharge of the detrition is effected by an upward current of water through the rod, has been employed to advantage in borings for petroleum in Western Canada.

Fauvelle's system of boring is probably the most simple in existence, and has the power of boring at a quicker speed than other machines. A short description of its mode of working may therefore be desirable.

The machine is driven by engine-power, in the manner shown in *fig.* 178, p. 441.

The boring rods consist of ordinary steam tubing, 2 inches diameter, and jointed together by union boxes. The chisels are welded into short lengths of tubing, small holes being left at the bottom of the tube. Water is forced in at the top of the bore-rods by means of a small force-pump, worked by a crank on a pinion-wheel, which is connected to a larger pinion on the main shaft. The water from this pump is first driven into an air-chamber, and is taken thence by india-rubber tubing to the top of the bore-rods, from which it escapes at the bottom of the rods a few inches above the chisel point. It is forced thence to the surface, carrying with it all the *débris* cut up by the chisel.

This *débris* is caught in pots or settling troughs, and from an examination of these the nature of the strata passed through is ascertained.

Independently of this test, however, the man in charge of the machine constantly has his hands upon the rods, and in this way can tell by the character of the stroke any change of strata, which is at once marked upon the rods.

The boring rods are allowed to have a percussive fall; and are connected by iron clamps to the rope, which passing over a wheel fixed in the shear legs, is fastened to the lever D. An up-and-down motion is imparted to this by the wheel E, which has two blocks or cams fixed in its periphery.

The action of these cams gives two full strokes of the rods for every revolution of the wheel E.

The stroke at commencing a borehole is about 1 foot 3 inches, but as the depth

178

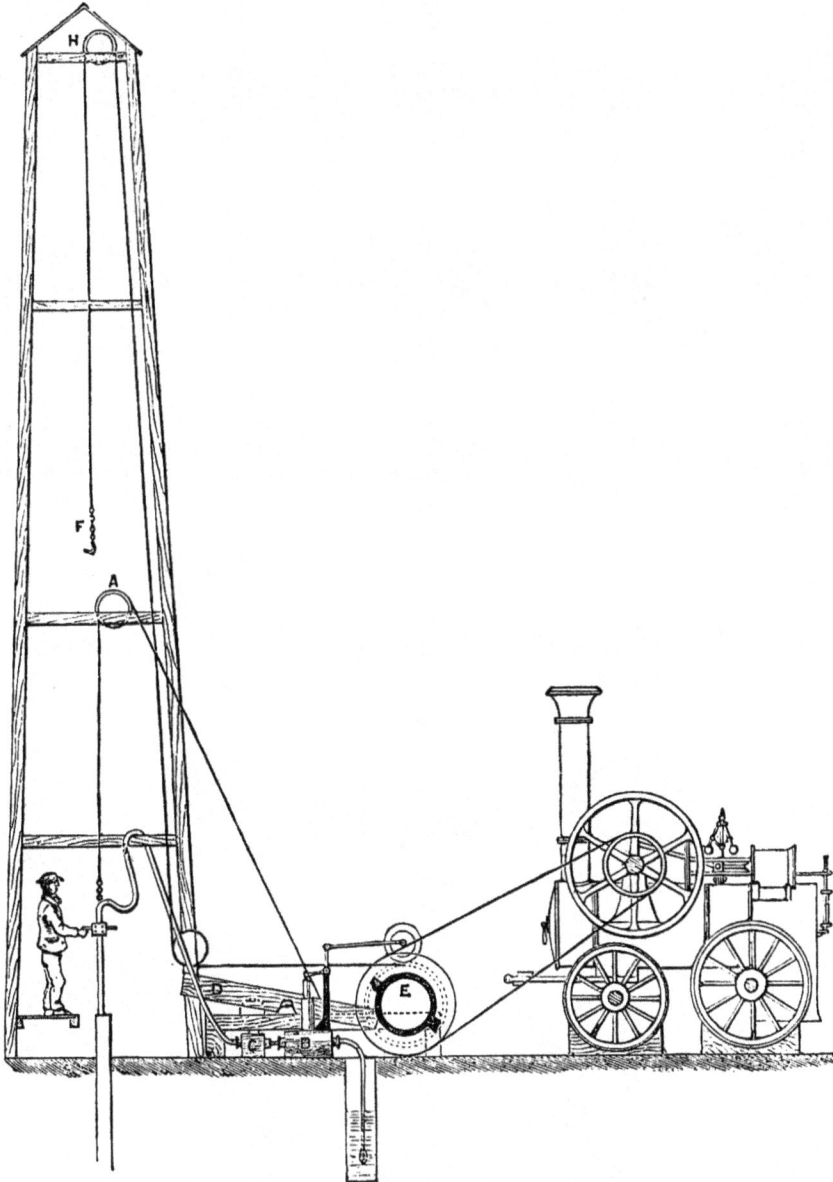

increases, the stroke is shortened by attaching the rope nearer to the centre of the lever.

At a depth of 800 feet this stroke would be not more than a few inches, the weight of rods being sufficient to drive the chisel forward, with a very short stroke.

When the rods have to be drawn for changing the chisel they are attached to the hook F, and are drawn up by means of a small drum on the main shaft to the height of the small wheel H; the first length is then unscrewed and put on one side, the hook F being again lowered, connected to the rods and drawn as above until the whole of the rods are drawn out. There is a brake attached to the drum on the main shaft, which is used for lowering the rods into the hole.

In cases where the strata passed through are of a soft character, tubes are sometimes driven forward as the hole progresses, these at first being about $4\frac{1}{2}$ inches diameter and faced with steel. They are driven forward by a large iron weight, and should the first pipe meet with anything that it cannot drive through, smaller sized tubes are introduced.

The chisel used is about $\frac{1}{8}$th of an inch smaller than the lining tubes.

This machine has bored in chalk a depth of 76 feet in 12 hours.

The Diamond Boring Machine.—In all the modes of boring described above, the borer or drill acts by percussive impact against the face of the strata, producing a volume of powdered rock equal to the solid contents of the borehole. In the diamond machine, invented by M. Leschot, the cutting tool is of a tubular form and receives a uniform rotating motion; the result being the production of a cylindrical core from the rock of the same size as the inner periphery of the tube, showing to great depths the different stratification through which the boring tube passes. The general principles on which the machine is constructed are as follow :—

179

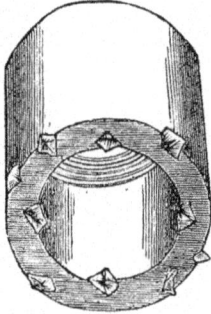

A continuously revolving and progressing boring head, having projecting diamond points, works in combination with a tubular boring bar.

The boring bit (*fig.* 179, is a steel thimble, about 4 inches in length, having two rows of Brazilian black diamonds (such as are used by lapidaries) in their natural rough state firmly imbedded therein, the edges projecting slightly from the outer and inner peripheries respectively. The diamonds in the centre row cut the path of the drill in its forward progress, while those upon the outer and inner periphery of the tool enlarge the cavity around the same and admit the free egress and ingress of the

180

water as hereafter described. As the drill passes into the rock, cutting an annular channel, the portion of stone, encircled by this channel is, when of a compact nature, undisturbed, and the drill rod passing down over it preserves it intact until the solid cylindrical core thus formed is withdrawn with the rods.

The diamonds are placed at intervals of about $\frac{1}{3}$rd of an inch apart both inside and outside the tube, the projection beyond the surface of the metal being not more than $\frac{1}{30}$th of an inch.

The diamond teeth are the only parts of the tool which come in contact with the rock, and their hardness is such that more than 2,000 feet have been drilled by the same points with but little appreciable wear.

The drill rods are made hollow, in order that a volume of water may be conducted

181

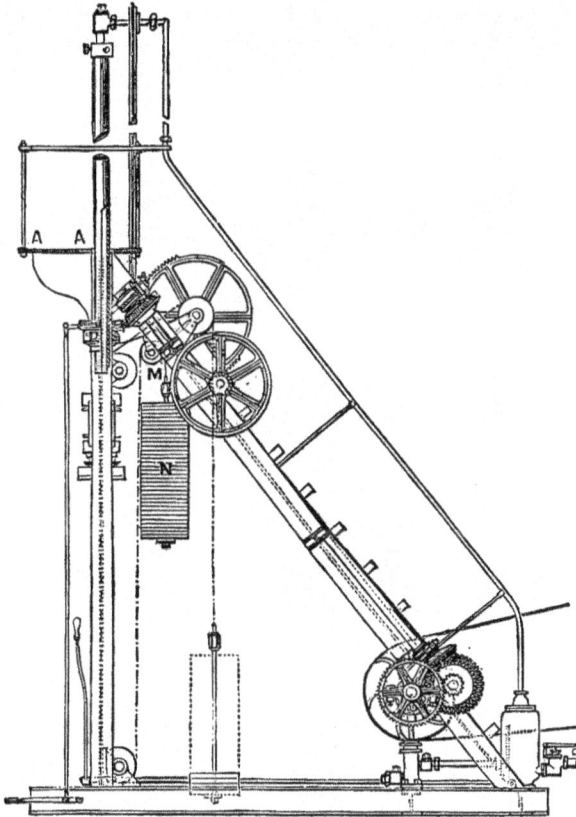

to the boring bit, at once moistening the rock, washing the cuttings away, and preventing the over heating of the diamonds.

The machinery for boring great depths is shown by *fig.* 180, p. 442, and consists of a portable engine having two oscillating 6-inch cylinders with a 6-inch stroke. The boiler is tubular, $3\frac{1}{2}$ feet × 7 feet, and with flues 3 inches in diameter, the steam capacity being about 16 H. P.

The pump P and water hose H are connected by rubber hose with any convenient stream or reservoir of water, and also with the outer end of the drill pipe by similar hose having a swivel joint. Through this hose a stream of water is forced, by M. Fauvelle's system, into the hollow drill rod, from which it only escapes at the bottom of the diamond pointed bit.

The drill rods may be extended to any desirable length by simply adding fresh pieces of tubing. The successive lengths are quickly coupled together by an inside coupling 4 inches long, the drill being held firmly in its place by the chuck G at the bottom of the screw shaft.

The speed of drilling depends chiefly of course upon the character of rock met with : in ordinary rock the drill being fed at the rate of 300 revolutions to the inch—the diamonds cutting the one three-hundredth part of an inch at each revolution, and in marble, hard sandstone, &c., at the rate of an inch for every 200 revolutions.

The progress of the diamond bit or crown does not depend upon the pressure of the rods, which is arranged to be always the same. The diamonds work their way by steady and gentle attrition.

These machines will bore holes from one to three inches in diameter.

The advance per minute in pure Mount Cenis quartz equalled 2½ inches, in granite about 2 inches, and in very hard calcareous dolomite 3 inches.

The diamond machine shown by *figs.* 181 and 182 has lately been perfected by Messrs. Appleby and Beaumont.

The boring bit with diamonds set therein is exactly similar to that used in the machine described, but the boring machinery is of a different description. This machine is worked by an independent engine, and driven by leather or other belts, the circular motion given to the boring rods being conveyed by bevel gear. To this machine appliances are attached for the driving forward of the lining tubes. This is done by means of a series of weights N attached to a chain passing round the wheel M, and connected to the sliding clutch *g*; this is made to press upon the tubes. At the same time an ordinary chisel is attached to the boring rods and worked from the table A A, the rods passing down the centre of the tubes.

182

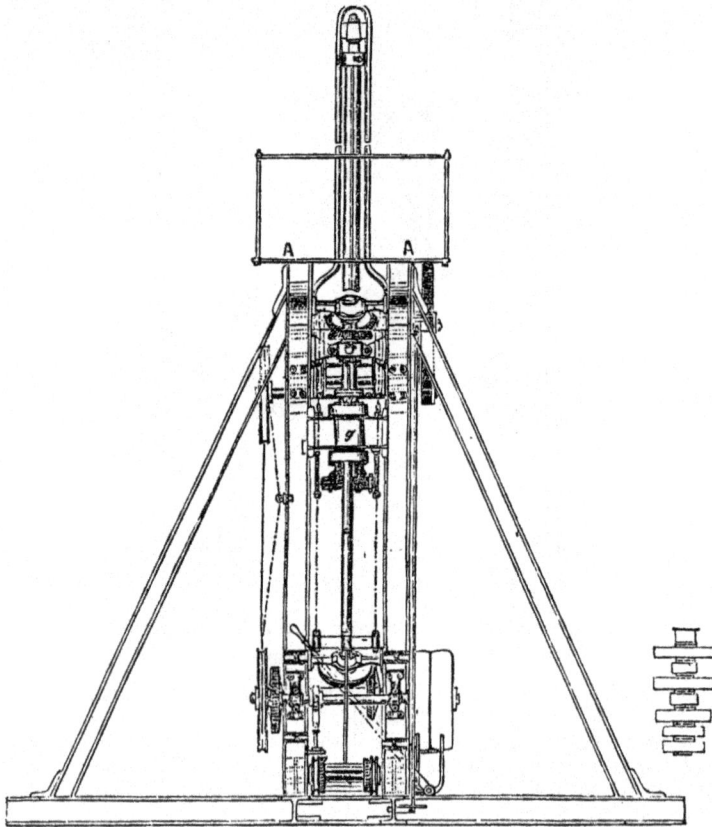

The *débris* is washed out at times by means of the pump fixed upon the machine.

After the lining tubes are made secure and water tight (it being an essential point that all water forced down the boring rods should come up on the *inside* of the lining tubes, so that all washings or indications of change of strata may be at once noticed), the diamond drill is introduced and boring proceeded with in the usual manner.

The rods are drawn by means of a chain passing over shear legs about 45 feet high and wound upon a drum fixed on the machine. The rods are unscrewed in lengths, and placed on one side of the machine.

The rods, by this system, are seldom drawn, except for the purpose of extracting the core made; the core tube being usually about 14′ 0″ long, with a small spring at the bottom for the purpose of retaining the core while drawing the rods. The cores made in these machines are usually from 1 inch to 1½ inch in diameter.

The boring rods are of the best steel, and jointed together by unions or coupling boxes.

In soft strata it is somewhat difficult to obtain a core by the diamond borer, but in boring through hard rocks for which this machine is specially suitable a very perfect core is produced. The best average speed accomplished by this machine in hard rock equals about 50 feet per day of 12 hours.

Mather and Platt's System of Boring.—The Chinese method of boring with ropes, instead of rigid rods, has been tried at different times in Europe, but without any great amount of success; the system of rigid suspension being preferred for working, not only the cutting tool, but also the shell. A very important modification of this principle has, however been introduced by Messrs. Mather and Platt of Salford, who have succeeded in carrying bores of considerable size (8 or 10 inches in diameter) to depths of 1,200 feet and upwards.

In this system, instead of the implements being attached to rods, as in the previous systems, they are suspended by a flat hemp rope about $\frac{1}{2}$ inch thick and $4\frac{1}{2}$ inches broad, such as is commonly used at collieries, and the boring tool and shell pump are raised and lowered as quickly in the borehole as the cages in a colliery shaft.

The flat rope A A, *fig.* 183, from which the boring head B is suspended, is wound upon

183

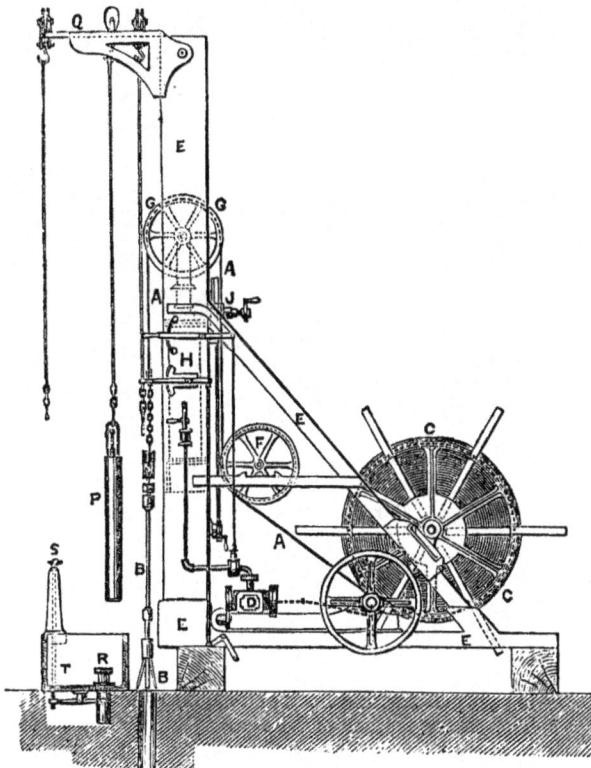

a large drum C, driven by a steam-engine D with a reversing motion, so that one man can regulate the operation with the greatest ease. All the working parts are fitted into a wood or iron framing E, rendering the whole a compact and complete machine. On leaving the drum C, the rope passes under a guide pulley F, and then over a large pulley G, carried in a fork at the top of the piston-rod of a vertical single-acting steam-cylinder H.

This cylinder, by which the percussive action of the boring head is produced, is fitted with a piston of 15 inches diameter, having a heavy cast iron rod 7 inches square, which is made with a fork at the top carrying a flanged pulley.

The boring head having been lowered by the winding drum to the bottom of the borehole, the rope is fixed securely at that length by the clamp J; steam is then admitted underneath the piston in the cylinder H by the steam-valve, and the boring tool is lifted by the ascent of the piston-rod and pulley G; and on arriving at the top of the stroke, the exhaust valve is opened for the steam to escape, allowing the piston-rod and carrying pulley to fall freely with the boring tool, which falls with its full weight to the bottom of the borehole. The exhaust port is 6 inches above the bottom of the cylinder, while the steam port is situated at the bottom; and there is thus always an elastic cushion of steam retained in the cylinder of that thickness for the piston to fall upon, preventing the piston from striking the bottom of the cylinder. The steam and exhaust valves are worked with a self-acting motion by tappets, which are actuated by the movement of the piston-rod; and a rapid succession of blows is thus given by the boring tool on the bottom of the borehole. As it is necessary that motion should be given to the piston before the valves can be acted upon, a small jet of steam is allowed to be constantly blowing into the bottom of the cylinder; this causes the piston to move slowly at first, so as to take up the slack of the rope and allow it to receive the weight of the boring head gradually and without a jerk. An arm attached to the piston-rod then comes in contact with a tappet which opens the steam-valve, and the piston rises quickly to the top of the stroke; another tappet worked by the same arm then shuts off the steam, and the exhaust valve is opened by a corresponding arrangement on the opposite side of the piston-rod. By shifting these tappets the length of stroke of the piston can be varied from 1 to 8 feet in the large machine, according to the material to be bored through; and the height of fall of the boring head at the bottom of the borehole is double the length of stroke of the piston. The fall of the boring head and piston can also be regulated by a weighted valve on the exhaust pipe, checking the escape of the steam, so as to cause the descent to take place slowly or quickly as may be desired.

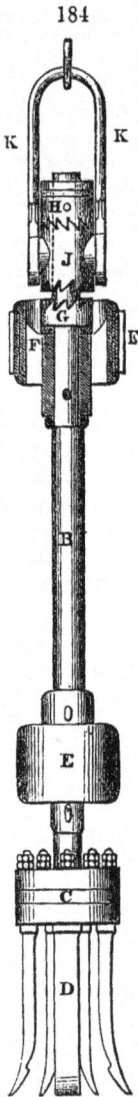

The boring head B *fig.* 184 consists of a wrought-iron bar about 4 inches diameter and 8 feet long, to the bottom of which a cast-iron cylindrical block C is secured. This block has numerous square holes through it, into which the chisels or cutters are inserted with taper shanks so as to be very firm when working, but to be readily taken out for repairing and sharpening. A little above the block C another cylindrical casting E is fixed upon the bar B, which acts simply as a guide to keep the bar perpendicular. Higher still is fixed a second guide F. To effect the rotation of the boring tool, two cast-iron collars G and H are cottered fast to the top of the bar B, and placed about 12 inches apart. The upper face of the lower collar G is formed with deep ratchet-teeth of about two inches pitch, and the under face of the top collar H is formed with similar ratchet-teeth set exactly in line with those on the lower collar. Between these collars and sliding freely on the neck of the boring bar B is a deep bush J, which is also formed of corresponding ratchet-teeth on both its upper and lower faces; but the teeth on the upper face are set half a tooth in advance of those on the lower face, so that the perpendicular side of each tooth on the upper face of the bush is directly above the centre of the inclined side of a tooth on the lower face. To this bush is attached the wrought-iron bow K by which the whole boring bar is suspended with a hook and shackle from the end of the flat rope. The rotary motion of the bar is obtained as follows: when the boring tool falls and strikes the blow, the lifting bush J, which during the lifting has been engaged with the ratchet-teeth of the top collar H, falls upon those of the bottom collar G, and thereby receives a twist backwards through the space of half a tooth; and on commencing to lift again, the bush rising up against the ratchet-teeth of the top collar H receives a further twist backwards through half a tooth. The flat rope is thus twisted backwards to the extent of one tooth of the ratchet; and during the lifting of the tool it untwists itself again, thereby rotating the boring tool forwards through that extent of twist between each successive blow of the tool. The amount of the rotation may be varied by making the ratchet-teeth of coarser or finer pitch. The motion is entirely self-acting, and the rotary movement of the boring tool is ensured with mechanical accuracy. This simple and most effective action taking place at every blow of the tool produces a constant change in the position of the cutters, thus increasing their effect in breaking the rock.

The Shell-Pump, for raising the material broken up by the boring head, is shown in *fig.* 185, and consists of a cylindrical shell or barrel P of cast-iron, about 8 feet long and a little smaller in diameter than the size of the borehole. At the bottom is a clack A opening upwards, somewhat similar to that in ordinary pumps; but its seating, instead of being fastened to the cylinder P, is in an annular frame C, which is held up against the bottom of the cylinder by a rod D passing up to a wrought-iron bridge E at the top, where it is secured by a cotter F. Inside the cylinder works a bucket B, similar to that of a common lift-pump, having an india-rubber disc valve on the top side; and the rod D of the bottom clack passes freely through the bucket. The rod G of the bucket itself is formed like a long link in a chain, and by this link the pump is suspended. The bottom clack A is made with an india-rubber disc which opens sufficiently to allow the water and smaller particles of stone to enter the cylinder; and in order to enable the pieces of broken rock to be brought up as large as possible, the entire clack is free to rise bodily about 6 inches from the annular frame C, as shown in *fig.* 185, thereby affording ample space for large pieces of rock to enter the cylinder when drawn in by the upstroke of the bucket.

185

The general working of the boring machine is as follows :—
The boring head is hooked on to the end of the rope, and lowered to the bottom of the borehole, the rope is then secured by a clamp to prevent it from being drawn off the winding drum. Steam is admitted to the percussion cylinder, and the boring bar kept at work until it has broken up a certain quantity of material in the borehole. After this operation, the steam is shut off, the rope unclamped, and the boring head withdrawn. The shell-pump is next lowered down by the rope, and the *débris* pumped into it by lowering and raising the buckets in the pump about three times, by means of the winding engine, while the pump barrel rests upon the bottom of the borehole. These operations are repeated every fifteen or twenty minutes.

Three men are required to work the machine and sharpen the implements.

Cost of Boring.—It will be understood that the advantage of putting down boreholes, as compared with wells or shafts of large diameter, consists not only in the general convenience in the small size, but also in the relative cost, which may be said to vary according to the area of the perforation, but in an uneven ratio.

The cost of boring shallow holes is naturally much less per foot than the rate of charge for borings at a considerable depth. The general cost of boring by hand or by lever may be taken as follows :—

First	30 feet							1s. per foot.
Second	30 ,,							2s. ,,
Third	30 ,,							3s. ,,
Fourth	30 ,,							4s. ,,

And so on, adding 1s. per foot for each additional 30 feet.

In very hard strata the cost of boring may be taken at 50 per cent. more than the above prices.

The cost of boring by the 'Diamond' machinery amounts to no less than 13s. 6d. per foot for the first 100 feet, and for each additional 100 feet 7s. 6d. per foot is added. The 'Diamond' machinery, however, is capable in hard strata in a day of twelve hours of boring a distance of 50 feet, whereas by hand boring, the average speed in similar rocks cannot be taken at more than 10 feet per day. This refers to a depth of, say 200 feet, but in boring the ordinary system of boring with rods, whether by hand or machinery, where the rods have to be disconnected and the *débris* has to be drawn from great depths, an important element has to be considered. Whilst the weight of the apparatus, consequent upon an increased depth, tends to augment the speed of boring, the drawing, disconnecting, and connecting of great lengths of rods for the purpose of clearing the hole, takes at a depth of about 250 feet really more time than is occupied in the actual boring, and at great depths these processes absorb no less than ⅞ths of the total working time. This serious difficulty is obviated in two systems

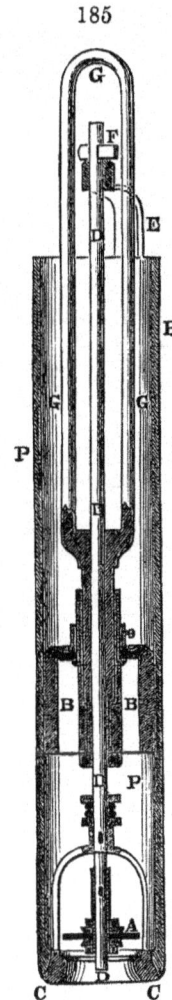

of boring:—1st, the mode supposed to have been originated in China, of using ropes for working the boring tools, in place of rods. This system, which has been successfully carried out in America and elsewhere in the boring for petroleum, as previously described; but the principle has been most thoroughly adapted and re-arranged by Messrs. Mather and Platt. 2nd, by the invention of M. Fauvelle, by means of which the beaten-up rock at the bottom of the borehole, instead of having to be drawn up by rods or ropes, is continuously removed by a current of water forced down the borehole by means of a pump placed at the top.

The foregoing brief reference to certain modes of boring has been made for the purpose of drawing attention to the chief conditions upon which economical boring depends.

On the Application of Boring to the Sinking of Shafts.—The science of boring has recently been applied in a manner, the practical economy of which is of great importance as bearing upon the investment of capital in the sinking of coal-mines through aqueous strata. M. Kind has within the past twelve years in Germany and France put down a number of shafts, varying in diameter from 9 to 14 feet, a considerable distance. These pits have been sunk through strata yielding immense volumes of water, and the whole process has been conducted under water. To enable such shafts to be sunk down to their full depth by shutting off the feeders of waters met with, by means of tubing placed in the shaft, M. Chaudron, a Belgian engineer, came to M. Kind's aid, and by the application of several simple, but ingenious contrivances, hereafter to be described, has succeeded in fixing the necessary tubing under water, and in providing a perfectly efficient joint at the base of the tubing, between the water-bearing and the dry strata.

Of the future coal-fields of England, it is probable that nearly half of the remaining deposit of coal will have to be obtained by sinkings through newer formations than the coal-measures, where very large quantities of water will have to be encountered. This indicates the importance to this country of some economical system of piercing such strata.

The ordinary system of sinking through strata containing large quantities of water has been to provide a large pumping plant, and to pump each feeder of water out as met with, fixing on the rock forming the barrier for each feeder a firmly wedged iron curb, and making it the base of the tubing which is built in segments, such segments

186   187

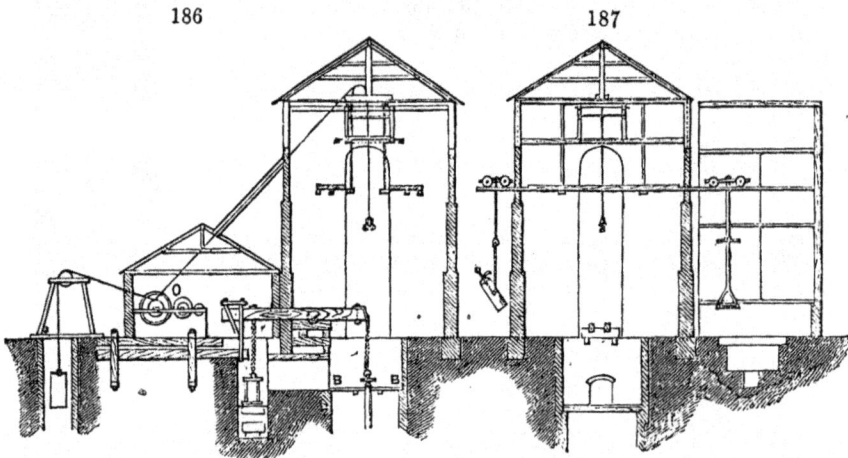

being generally about 4 feet long by 2 feet 9 inches high. The joints between these segments are made secure by means of wooden sheeting wedged tightly. Where the feeders are large, several sets of pumps have sometimes to be introduced into the pit, and the workmen have almost continually to be working in water, and at a great disadvantage. This difficulty, combined with the heavy cost of fuel, cost of buckets and powder, the great liability of accidents to the pumping plant, the cost of fixing the curbs and segmental tubing, and the risk entailed in the large number of joints in the tubing, constitute the chief disadvantages of this system of sinking pits through watery strata.

The Kind-Chaudron system may be briefly described by pointing out the various processes adopted:—

1st. The opening of the mine is commenced by erecting the plant shown by *figs.* 186 and 187, which exhibit two sectional elevations of the surface arrangements required. The general plant consists of the boring machine, this being a cylinder having steam applied to the upper side of the piston only. The piston-rod is attached to one end of a massive beam, to the other end of which the boring tools are suspended. The capstan engine c, is used for lowering and raising the boring tools, and for raising the *débris* made by the boring.

2nd. When the stage B B, on which the borers stand, has been erected, the boring of the pits is commenced. Supposing that the pit to be sunk has a diameter of 13 feet, the first process is to put down a borehole, with a diameter varying from 3 to 5 feet, and the tool used for this hole progresses in ordinary strata, at the rate of about 8 feet per day. When this hole has been put down, say a distance of 60 feet, the larger trepan used for the purpose of making the pit its full size is applied. This instrument is shown by *figs.* 188 and 189 ; it is made of wrought iron, is furnished with 28 teeth or chisels, and weighs about 16 tons. The smaller trepan is of similar design.

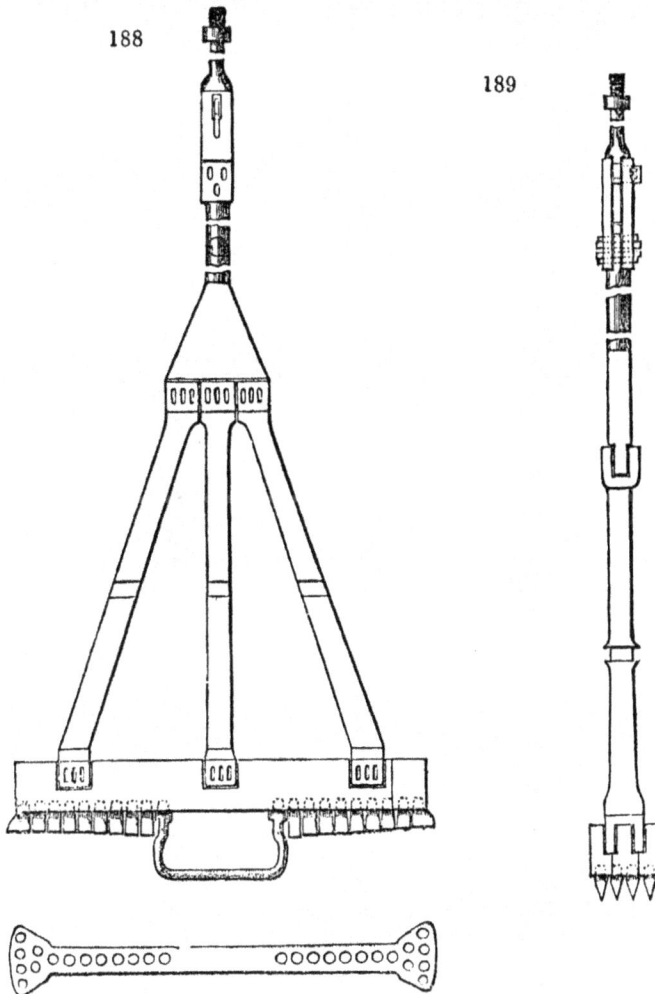

The ordinary speed of the boring when worked by the large trepan may be taken at about 3 feet per day. It will be observed that the faces of the chisels incline to the centre of the pit ; this tends to assist the passing of the *débris* made in the large boring into the cavity formed by the small boring tool, whence it is extracted by the ordinary scourer. This process is continued to the bottom of the aqueous strata, the small borehole being kept about 60 feet in advance of the larger hole. Should broken tools fall into the shaft, the instruments shown by *figs.* 190 and 191 are used, the former, by means of internal teeth, clutches with ease broken bars, &c., having no shoulder, and which cannot be taken hold of by means of the ordinary extractor. *Fig.* 191 is the 'grapin,' used for the purpose of raising broken teeth or other small objects which may have fallen to the bottom of the shaft. This tool has one part sliding into the other, and is lowered with the claws closed. An arrangement of light ropes handled from the surface enables the engineer to work this instrument.

3rd. *Placing the Tubing.*—Instead of being in small segments, the tubing is cast in complete cylinders, about 5 feet high, with inside flanges at both top and bottom, which are turned and faced. The tubing is suspended in the pit by rods, and is lowered down as each new cylinder is added. When the bottom of the water-bearing strata is reached, the arrangement shown by *fig.* 193 is adopted. A sliding *moss-box,* placed inside the base of the tubing, is allowed to rest on the rock floor made for the reception of the tubing, at the point below which no feeders of consequence are expected. The full weight of the tubing resting on this box, causes the moss to protrude at the back, and form a perfectly water-tight joint at the base of the tubing. To render this joint more secure, a few feet of tubing in segments resting upon two strong wedged curbs, are placed in the pit below the *moss-box.*

190   191   192   193

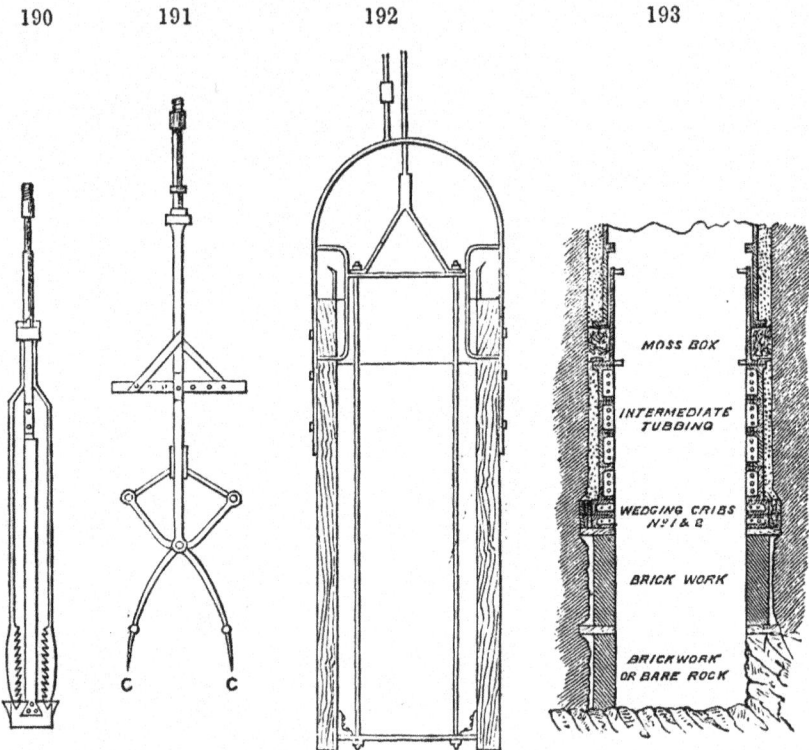

4th. *The Securing of the Rigidity of the Tubing.*—The tubing now, as it were, stands in the pit, resting on the foundation afforded by the moss-box, but without any lateral support. It is secured in its position by means of cement, which is dropped down behind the iron tubing by means of a cement-box with a moveable piston, worked by a rope from the surface. (See *fig.* 192.)

5th. The shaft having now been made secure, the extraction of the water is proceeded with, and the pit is then ready to be sunk either by the ordinary method or otherwise.

The labour and time taken in the changing of the rods becomes so great at considerable depths that the ordinary system of sinking has generally to be resorted to.

Boring in Coal.—An important operation in coal-mines, where explorations have to be made in the direction of old workings, or goofs, which may be holding large quantities of inflammable gas, or water, is *horizontal boring.* In this work only very light rods are used, as the position of the hole makes the strength of the rods a question of secondary importance. The important points to consider are the driving of the hole exactly parallel with the strata, and arranging sufficient holes to render it impossible for the advancing 'heading' to come suddenly upon any old workings or narrow adits. In many cases water of immense pressure has to be bored against. The ordinary mode of boring is shown by *fig.* 194. Here the advancing head, A, may be assumed to be 8 feet wide, and the minimum width of any old headings may be taken at 4 feet. Supposing the pressure anticipated is such that it is only necessary to ascertain the solidity of a thickness of 12 feet of coal on each side of the advancing rod, it is usual to bore three holes, one in the line of the heading, and two flank holes, which can either be driven from the corners, or as shown in the sketch. The flank holes are

194

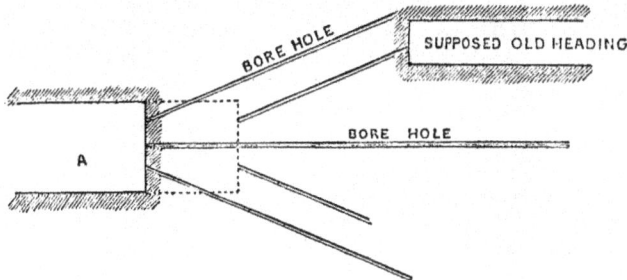

bored at such an angle as will enable them to detect, within a given distance, the presence of any old works which may be in advance of them. Thus it will be seen on *fig*. 194, that the direction of the hole is such that no old head could exist without being discovered by the borers.

Where no extraordinary pressure exists, it is usual for the centre holes to be bored a distance of about 9 yards, after which the heading is advanced, say 3 yards farther, by ordinary mining; hence it will be seen that the use of the centre hole can be continued, while new flank or side holes have to be bored every few yards. The usual size of the holes driven for proving old works is about $1\frac{1}{2}$ inch diameter, and the cost of boring varies from 9*d*. to 2*s*. per yard, according to the length of the hole.

In some cases, where a heavy pressure of water has to be encountered, the rush of water is so rapid, that it is impossible for the borers to stem its progress by means of plugs.

In an important boring conducted under the superintendence of the writer, the arrangement shown by *fig*. 195 was adopted. Here the bore-rod nearest to the handle

195

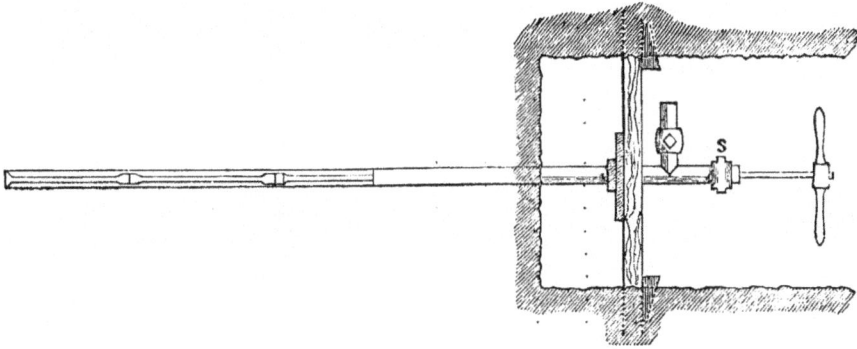

is of turned steel, working through a stuffing-box, s, which is attached to a tube, the end of the tube being wedged tightly into the borehole. Near the stuffing-box is a short elbow, in which is a valve or cock. When the old workings are pricked, and the water is reached, the cock is closed to prevent the occurrence of any serious consequences. About the centre of the tube a disc-bracket is placed, bearing against two beams, one above, the other below the tube, the end of these beams being wedged tightly into the sides of the coal heading. The adoption of this mode not only ensures safety, but conduces to the accuracy with which the hole is driven.

Norton's Patent Well Tubes.—A method of well sinking, patented by Mr. J. L. Norton, of London, by which a supply of water can be obtained in a very short space of time, provided the geological conditions of the part selected for the sinking are favourable, deserves notice.

· The arrangement consists of a wrought iron tube, about 11 feet long and $1\frac{1}{4}$ to 3 inches diameter, terminated at one end by a sharp steel point, and perforated with numerous small holes for a distance of about 2 feet above the point. This tube is driven into the ground by repeated blows from a 'monkey,' or heavy weight, which slides freely on the tube, falling on a shoulder clamped to the lower end of the tube. The monkey is raised by ropes running over a pulley attached to a tripod, which at the same time preserves the upright position of the tube. When the clamp reaches the level of the earth, it is unscrewed and refixed higher up the tube, and the driving is continued as before, additional lengths of piping being added as required. As soon as it is found, by plumbing the tube, that water has been reached, a cleansing pump is screwed to the top of the tube, which brings up the sand and loose earth from the bottom of the tube and immediately around the end of the same, forming a reservoir for the water. Where the water has to be drawn from a sandy soil, a filter is attached to the perforated end of the well-tube, which prevents even the finest sand from being pumped up with the water.

It will be seen at once that this method of obtaining water is not adapted for a rocky country; but for purposes where the water is to be obtained within a comparatively short distance from the surface, and where the strata to be passed through are not of a very hard nature, these wells are very useful, especially as they can be sunk in light soils at the rate of 10 to 12 inches per minute. The quantity of water they can supply must depend upon the yield of the stratum to which they are sunk, but wells of this kind have been known to give a quantity of upwards of 800 gallons per minute.

The greatest depth at which these wells have been used is 120 feet.

Villepique Perforator.—This apparatus consists of two principal parts, namely, a standard or column, and a driving screw with its accessories. The column is formed of stout steel tube, fitted at its lower extremity with a twin claw working on a rocking joint, and at the upper end with a nut fixed inside, in which a screw works, which screw is terminated by a steel point. On this steel tube is a metal clip collar, free to slide from one end to the other, or to revolve around it. This collar can be clamped at any required point. To this collar is attached a malleable iron box, enclosing the mechanism for giving an automatic feed to the screw, and for carrying the driving or main screw. The weight of the whole apparatus is from 50 to 60 lbs. The time required for fixing the perforator in its place is about one minute. The steel augers are mechanically twisted, and have cutting ends to suit the material to be acted on. The following figures are taken from a valuable paper in the 'Transactions of the North of England Institute of Mining and Mechanical Engineers,' vol. xx.

Nature of Material	Diameter of Hole	Depth Bored	Time	Rate per Minute
		inches	min.	
Cleveland ironstone	$1\frac{3}{4}$	18 and 25	2 and 7	
Tough 'Blue Bind'	$1\frac{3}{4}$	$19\frac{1}{2}$	4	Inches 4·87
			min. sec.	
Silkstone coal	2	21	2 18	$9\frac{3}{4}$
Strong stone bind	$1\frac{3}{4}$	22	6 30	$3\frac{1}{2}$
Coal and stone	2	34	4 15	8
Grey shale band	$1\frac{3}{4}$	$13\frac{1}{2}$	1 10	$11\frac{3}{4}$
Iron ball in shale	$1\frac{7}{8}$	6	1 40	$3\frac{1}{2}$
Shale and sandstone	$1\frac{1}{4}$	$12\frac{1}{2}$	1 20	$9\frac{3}{4}$
Magnesian limestone	$1\frac{1}{2}$	$7\frac{1}{2}$	5	$1\frac{1}{2}$
Hard sandstone	2	18	$7\frac{1}{2}$	$2\frac{2}{5}$

Ford's Borer.—A boring machine was invented by Mr. R. G. Ford, of Sandhurst, Victoria, about the year 1868, and patented in England on August 10, 1869. The motion of the tool is reciprocating, and the motive power compressed air, or steam, applied at a pressure of 60 lbs. per square inch. This pressure is constantly exerted on a small annular space in front of the piston, and intermittingly on the whole area of the back of the piston. The ports for the alternate admission of the pressure fluid, and for the exhaust, are opened and closed by a valve, worked by a small piston. The air ports and the movement of the valve are so arranged that the piston cannot strike the front and back of the cylinder.

The rotation of the boring tool is caused by the piston-rod, working a ratchet and paul round a cylinder attached to the front of the working cylinder; and as the piston reciprocates, it carries itself around the cylinder, and makes a complete revolution every twenty-one blows, by which means the machine bores a round hole. The feed is self-advancing, and self-adjustable, effected by the working cylinder being provided with an exterior cylinder, in which it can slide. The motive pressure is constantly tending to propel the working cylinder forward, but is retained by a screw, which is prevented from turning by a paul, which the piston strikes when it makes a full stroke, thus releasing the screw, and permitting the working cylinder to advance forward as the hole increases in depth. The weight of blow which can be struck by this machine is 500 lbs.; number of blows per minute 20 to 600.

The inventor claimed the construction of rock boring machines, in which the piston of the main cylinder distributes and exhausts the motive fluid to and from other cylinders at distinct portions of the stroke. For further particulars and illustration, see Specification No. 2,387, A.D. 1869.

Bergström's Borer.—This machine, used at the Perseberg Mines, near Philipstad, in Sweden, is a modification of that constructed by Schumann, of Freiberg. The machine consists of a cylinder $4\frac{1}{2}$ inches diameter, and a balanced slide valve. The movement of the piston and valve is automatic, the advance of the apparatus is effected by the hand. The length of stroke is 7 inches, cubic inches of air or steam required per stroke 200, or $8\frac{1}{2}$ strokes per cubic foot. Speed from 200 to 350 blows per minute. Pressure required to drive borer, 15 to 20 lbs. per square inch.

Weight of machine, 122 lbs. For additional particulars and illustrations, see paper by C. Le Neve Foster, Miners' Association of Cornwall and Devonshire, 1867.

Sach's Borer.—The lightness, suitability, and economical working of this drill, have induced Prussian engineers to use it somewhat extensively, both in metalliferous mines and collieries. *Fig.* 196 illustrates an arrangement of the drill and stand, employed both in shaft and winze sinking. The cylinder is $2\frac{1}{2}$ inches diameter, borer rod $1\frac{7}{8}$ths inch diameter, back rod 1 inch diameter, valve rod $\frac{3}{8}$ths inch diameter. The valve is a simple plate ; one face being on the portways leading to and from the cylinder, the other retained by a plate carrying the valve arbor. The top of the back rod carries a ring, to which is attached a small rod for rocking the valve-shaft. To this valve-shaft is also attached a horizontal rod, which carries two pauls, one for turning the borer, the other for advancing the cylinder through the medium of a nut travelling on the screw side bar. At a pressure of 25 lbs. per square inch, the borer makes 400 strokes per minute, the length of stroke being 5 inches. The blow pressure is 116 lbs., return pressure 72 lbs. About 45 cubic inches of air or steam are required per stroke, or 38 strokes per cubic foot. The area of steam portway is $\frac{6}{10}$ths of a square inch. The rate of boring per minute in basalt is 3 inches, coal sandstone 3 inches, quartz grauwacke 2 inches, carbonate of iron $1\frac{1}{2}$ inch. One borer requires about one horse-power to drive it.

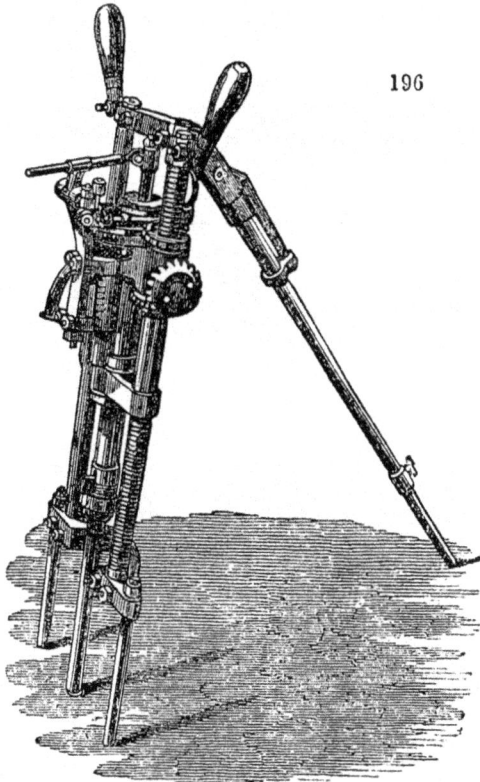

196

Doering's Borer.—This machine is worked by compressed air or steam, at a pressure of about 35 lbs. per square inch. The pressure fluid acts alternately on the front and back of the main piston. The valve for the admission of compressed air, and for the exhaust, is worked by two chambers in the main piston, one of these chambers being always in communication with the main inlet of compressed air, the other chamber in communication with the outer atmosphere. The valve has a separate piston to work it; on the smaller side of the piston a constant pressure of air is maintained, a passage connects the other end of the cylinder, in which the valve-piston works, with a certain point of the main cylinder. The chamber with compressed air passing over this port causes a pressure on the larger area of the valve-piston, which overcomes the constant pressure on the smaller area, and reverses the valve so as to admit compressed air to the opposite end of the main piston. Rotation of the borer is effected by means of a twist bar and ratchet-wheel, the feed or advance is automatic. This machine was employed at Tincroft, and bored 277 holes from the 9th to the 30th of January 1868, or at the rate of 13 holes per 20 hours. In coal sandstone, at 270 strokes per minute, the rate of boring was $1\frac{3}{8}$ths inch per minute. See Specifications of Patents, November 9, 1866, No. 2,922; January 7, 1867, No. 43; June 10, 1867, No. 1,704.

Osterkamp's Borer.—About four years ago, the machine engineer, Osterkamp of Eschweiler, near Aix-la-Chapelle, Prussia, contrived a light-boring machine, with a steam or air-moved valve. He also added a portable stand, with the object of dispensing with the columnar apparatus used in connection with Sach's Borer. The workmen held and directed the machine and also advanced the tool for deepening the hole.

The weight of a cylinder, having a piston-rod $2\frac{6}{10}$ths and piston 3 inches diameter, was 50 lbs. Weight of supporting stand, from 40 to 56 lbs.

This machine bored a hole in coal sandstone $1\frac{1}{2}$ inch diameter, $\frac{8}{10}$ths of an inch deep, in a minute; and in the same time a second hole $\frac{3}{4}$ inch diameter, $1\frac{1}{4}$ to $1\frac{1}{2}$ inch. The speed of the machine at 30 lbs. pressure is about 210 strokes per minute. Length of stroke, 5 inches. Cubic inches of steam or air required per stroke, 40 or 43 strokes per cubic foot. Pressure for blow 135 lbs., for returning piston 75 lbs. For particulars and illustration of Borer, see Specification, No. 1,466, A.D. 1870.

The McKean Rock-drill.—This rock-drill is worked either by steam or compressed air, and can be adjusted to any required position, so that holes may be drilled at any

197

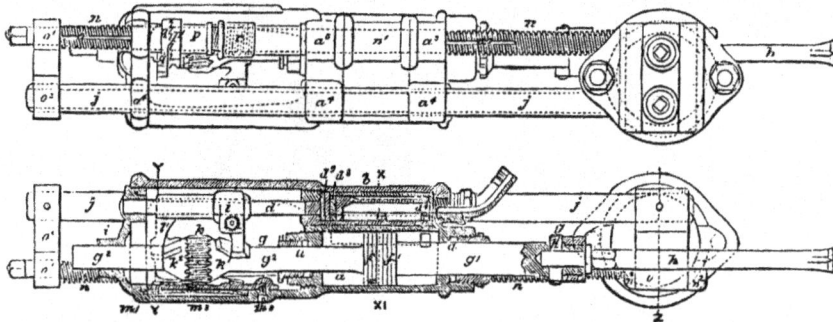

angle, the machine working with equal facility in every direction. The valve is adapted to deliver from 400 to 1,000 blows per minute, while the stroke of the piston and fall of the cutter bar is only $2\frac{1}{2}$ inches or 3 inches; the shock to the cutter bar and piston when striking the rock is cushioned by the steam or air in the cylinder.

The cylinder, valve-chest, and frame for carrying the guides and bearings for the piston, valve-rods and other parts of the machine are cast in one piece. The percussion cylinder is marked *a* and the valve-chest *b*; the valve seating is formed of a small cylinder *c* placed within the valve-chest—situate on one side of the cylinder *a*. The valve *d* is cylindrical, its axis is parallel to that of the piston-rod, and on one side there is formed a projecting curved face d', forming the working part of the valve which alternately covers and uncovers the admission ports *e e*, that extend the whole length of the valve-chest *c*. The exhaust port is formed between the admission ports, and opens into the centre of the cylindrical valve.

The oscillating movement required for actuating the valve is given by the spindle through the key d^3, and the groove. At the bottom of the valve a shoulder d^4 is also formed, fitting tightly in the cylinder. By this means the escape of steam or air is prevented, and sufficient friction is produced to avoid any excessive motion of the valve from the action of the tappets which actuate the spindle. These tappets are shown at *l l'*, where it will be seen that they are attached to a sleeve fastened upon the valve spindle, and at such an angle on each side of the centre line passing through the valve spindle, and piston-rod, that they may be struck by the enlarged portions of the latter k^1 k^2. The piston *f* is formed of steel, in one piece with the piston-rod g^2, and the tool holder g^1. Grooves are formed in the piston, as shown at f', to receive metallic piston-rings. The rod in advance of the piston is of a diameter larger than that at the rear, in order that sufficient strength may be obtained for carrying the cutting bar. The piston-rod g^2 passes through a stuffing box in the cylinder, and takes a bearing at the end of the frame of the drill as shown at i; and as the rod on the front side of the piston also passes through a stuffing box, the chief moving part of the machine is supported at three places in its length. Upon the piston-rod g^2 an enlargement, k^1, k^2, k^3, is made with two conical faces; the valve tappets l l' are in contact with these faces, and the reciprocating motion or the piston-rod imparts to them the necessary motion for actuating the valve. The angle of the tappets can be adjusted at will to regulate the distribution of the steam or air. Between the sloping or conical surfaces of the enlargement of the piston-rod there is a straight length k^3, in which are cut ratchet-teeth in an oblique direction around the surface; these teeth come in contact with a grooved bar m, the grooves m' being cut to correspond with the teeth in k^3. In the frame of the drill is formed a recess, in which a spring m^2 is placed, the centre of the spring pressing against the back of the grooved plate m. At the forward stroke of the piston, the enlargement k^3 pressing against m depresses it, forcing it into the recess; but at the return stroke, the teeth of k^3 engaging in the grooves of m, give it a rotating movement to the piston-rod, piston, and cutter bar, so that a slow and constant turning of the cutter is effected. The amount of rotary motion imparted during each stroke is about one-sixteenth of a revolution.

The automatic feed arrangement for keeping the end of the cutter in contact with the rock consists of a double threaded screw, with a key way in it, as shown, extending from end to end of the machine, the rear bearing being formed by a bracket. On the outside of the cylinder a, two stops o^5 are cast, and between these stops is placed a nut n', which is prevented from turning by being made with a flat side bearing against the outside of the cylinder a. Through this nut the screw n passes; fitting into the ratchet p' is a second ratchet q, with an arm q' that is attached to the tappets l l', which gives a reciprocating motion to the ratchet q, and a constant revolving motion to the sleeve p; the key in which drives the screw, which turns the nut n' and with it the whole drill, whilst the screw n travels freely through the sleeve p. By this means a constant and regular feed is obtained. The end of the screw at o' is, however, made square for the reception of a lever, by which the automatic feed can be replaced by a hand movement. The cutter bar is made adjustable by means of a screw thread and nut, the face of the nut against the key being grooved, so that when it is screwed up tight and the key driven in, there is no possibility of the key shaking loose and the cutter becoming unfastened.

The machine of the size ordinarily used for quarry work or open cutting weighs about 150 lbs. A smaller, and for many purposes a still more convenient form is manufactured, which can be handled by one man.

With a steam pressure of 75 lbs. to the inch, it will drill as a maximum, a $2\frac{1}{4}$-inch hole to a depth of 10 inches per minute in Aberdeen granite; but the average duty may be estimated at from 6 inches to 9 inches per minute, and the number of strokes from 500 to 1,000.

For sinking shafts the machine is mounted on a column placed crosswise in the shaft, and fixed rigidly by the telescopic and screw adjustment above mentioned, from which column any required direction may be readily given to the boring tool, or the drill may be mounted upon adjustable stand or frame, as is designed for quarry and open work.

For driving tunnels where one or more machines may be worked against the face, the machines are mounted upon moveable and adjustable columns, supported upon a carriage moved upon rails.

In reference to this drill Sir George William Denys states as follows:—

(1) Weight of machine without stand, large size $1\frac{1}{2}$ cwt., small do. 1 cwt. (2) Length of drill 38 inches. (3) Diameter of piston 5 inches, length of stroke 2 to 4 inches. (4) Strokes per minute, 500 to 1,000 *ad libitum*. (5) Pressure required 25 to 75, average 50 lbs. (6) Advance of drill, automatic or by hand; but where only one machine is working the hand is preferable, for it obliges the miner to pay attention and see that the drill advances regularly. (7) The nature of the stone varies; we have lime, chert, and grits of every degree of hardness. (8) Diameter of water-wheel 38 feet or 28 feet would have done as well; bucket 4 feet wide; breadth of water trough 2 feet; depth of water varies with the supply from 3 to 8 inches. (9) Compression wet, a half-inch pipe carries the water up the level, and squirts the water with great force into the holes, and keeps them quite clean. (10) Dimensions of level 6 feet high clear of the rails, and about 5 feet wide. (11) The air-pipes are 2 inches in diameter, but I think 1 inch would suffice. (12) The level forehead is now nearly 400 fathoms from the compressor; the ventilation excellent, the air being as good inside the mine as out.

Some special measurements and particulars of this drill are as follow:—Diameter of cylinder 4 inches, piston-rod $2\frac{1}{2}$ inches, diameter of back rod $1\frac{8}{10}$ths inch, area for blow 10 square inches, for return $7\frac{6}{10}$ths square inches, pressure for blow at 50 lbs. per square inch 500 lbs., and for return of piston 380 lbs. Stroke of slide-valve $\frac{1}{4}$ to $\frac{1}{2}$ inch, opening of steam port $\frac{1}{10}$th to $\frac{1}{4}$ inch, length of steam port 6 inches, area of steam port $1\frac{1}{2}$ inch, diameter of steam-pipe $1\frac{1}{4}$ inch, stroke of piston-rod 2 to 4 inches. Turning motion one revolution to sixteen blows. The consumption of steam and air for a 4-inch stroke including portway clearances is about 90 cubic inches, or 19 strokes per cubic foot. See Specifications of Patents, No. 1,104, April 14, 1870, and No. 3,131, Nov. 20, 1870.

The Burleigh Drill in its general arrangements does not differ essentially from some of those which have been described. It has been used in several mines and quarries in this country, and rather extensively in America. See Specification and Illustration of Drill, No. 3,065, A.D. 1866.

The main elements of this drill are the cage, the cylinder, and the piston. The cage is merely a trough, with ways on either side in which the cylinder, by means of a feed-screw and an automatic feed-lever, is moved forward as the drill cuts away the rock.

The piston moves backwards and forwards in the cylinder, and is propelled and operated on substantially like the piston of an ordinary steam-engine. The drill point is attached to the end of the piston-rod, which is a solid bar of steel.

The forward motion of the cylinder in the trough is regulated by an automatic feed, as the rock is cut away.

It is driven by steam or compressed air as a motive power, and with a pressure of 50 lbs. to the inch, strikes from 200 to 300 blows per minute, according to the size of the machine.

The valve used to control the entrance into and egress from the cylinder of the impelling medium is the ordinary **D** or locomotive slide-valve, which is operated by a valve-rod attached to a pivoted piece made sufficiently heavy to possess considerable momentum when put in motion.

The body of the machine is made in one casting, and constitutes the steam or air cylinder and covers and protects most of the feeding and turning mechanism. This body has two wings forming part of a support or carriage, so that the drilling machine may be presented to its work in any direction and at any angle.

The cylinder a has its front end closed by a head c, into which a long stuffing box d is screwed.

To prevent any injurious variation between the amount of the feed and the penetration of the drill, mechanism is introduced which automatically preserves a practical uniformity of feed and penetration. When the feed of the cylinder is in excess of the penetration of the drill, in which case the tappet r does not in the forward stroke of the piston reach and displace the paul—and consequently no feed takes place until the penetration of the drill equals the previous feed or advance of the cylinder. As it may occur when a feed of the cylinder takes place, that the piston on its back stroke might possibly come in contact with the back cylinder head g, a rubber cushion c' is placed against the rear-head u, to act as an elastic cushion to check the back stroke of the piston by impact of the tappet on the piston-rod with the protecting plate facing the cushion.

There are several forms of carriages for mounting drills for tunnel work. That used for the Burleigh drills consists of a trolly on four wheels, with a moveable support, which is actuated horizontally across the trolly and the face of the drift by means of a screw. The hollow bar or stretcher which fixes the carriage when it is in position for work, is held by a moveable support, and fixes itself by means of a screw at the bottom. To this hollow shaft or upright stretcher the drill is attached by a clamp; the drill is raised or lowered by means of a lever, having for its fulcrum a pin in either of the holes in the two bars of iron attached to the moveable support at their bottom ends, and to the hollow shaft at the top ends. When the drill is fixed in position, these bars are allowed to fall back by the removal of the pin at the top which connects them to the hollow shaft.

It is designed to be worked by one man, and may run on rails laid for the purpose.

The compressed air for these machines has been carried through 7·150 feet of an 8-inch iron pipe; and the average difference in pressure at the compressors, and the heading of the tunnel, with an average of six drills in operation, was but 2 lbs. to the inch.

Ingersol's Drill.—This drill, the invention of an American, is entirely automatic in its movements, that is, the borer is turned by a twist bar arrangement, as in Jordan and Darlington's Borer, patented in 1866, while the advance of the tool and movement of the valve are effected by tappet gear, struck by the head of the piston. In connection with this drill, the following particulars have been obtained:—Diameter of cylinder $3\frac{1}{4}$ inches, diameter of piston-rod 2 inches, dimensions of valve portway $1\frac{1}{8}'' \times \frac{3}{8}''$. Length of cylinder in the clear 22 inches, with attachments 39 inches. Pressure of steam required to drive the drill, 45 lbs. per square inch. Length of stroke 6 inches, speed of boring bar 280 strokes per minute, consumption of steam or air, forward stroke 81, backward 64, or together 145 cubic inches. Pressure for blow 373 lbs., for return 231 lbs. Time required to bore $1\frac{1}{2}$ inch hole 1 inch deep in Cornish granite, 30 seconds. Strokes required to bore 1 inch deep, 140. Cubic feet of steam or air, consumed per inch of hole in granite, $11\frac{7}{10}$ths. Advance of machine on screw without change of borer, 18 inches.

Length of stroke necessary to advance borer $5\frac{3}{8}$ths inches. Number of strokes required to make one revolution of tool 10. For illustration, see Specification No. 2,008, A. D. 1872.

Power Jumper.—This machine, the joint invention of Brydon, Davidson and Warrington, consists externally of a long cylinder and valve. The valve and turning gear are automatic; the advance of the tool is performed by hand. The pressure of steam required to work the drill is from 40 to 50 lbs. per square inch, the number of strokes from 300 to 400 per minute. See Specifications No. 3,507 and 3,921, A. D. 1872.

Darlington's Borer, Fig. 198.—The inventor, Mr. Darlington, obtains reciprocatory motion in rock-boring machinery without the intervention of a valve or valvular gear. In one modification a cylinder and motive piston are employed. The cylinder itself has an ordinary inlet portway, a long induction passage, and an outlet portway. The depth and length of the motive piston is proportioned to the position of the several portways, so that the induction and exhaust portways are alternately uncovered by the body of the piston which thus distributes the air or steam. The elastic fluid exerts its force continually against the smaller surface of the piston referred to. This piston, in moving in one direction, first covers the exhaust, then uncovers the induction portway and permits the air or steam to exert its force on the opposite side of the piston, which has a superior area to that on which the pressure is constant. In the return movement which follows, the induction portway is first covered, and immediately afterwards the exhaust is uncovered, releasing the superior area of the piston from the pressure, and allowing the constant pressure on the small area to effect the opposite stroke.

In a second modification, which gives a like action, instead of keeping the fluid pressure continually against the smaller surface of the motive distributing piston, the pressure is alternately admitted to and exhausted from both sides of the piston. To effect this, the piston is made of sufficient length to admit of a groove being turned in it of such a length as to always be in communication with the pressure portway formed about the centre of the length of the cylinder. Two induction passages and two exhaust portways are also formed in the cylinder. The motive piston, in its passage across these said portways, admitting the pressure to one induction portway, communicating with one end of the cylinder, at the same time as it uncovers one exhaust portway and releases the pressure from the opposite end of the cylinder.

Beyond these two modifications of one and the same invention, two other modes of distributing the steam or air have been devised. The objects gained by the foregoing method of obtaining reciprocatory motion for rock-boring and coal-cutting machines are—(1) There is only one working part used in obtaining the motion of the piston, with its rod attached, both being in one solid piece, without any loose or attached part to be destroyed by the effect of rapid reciprocation and percussion. (2) Being enabled to use large portways and passages, which are opened and closed quickly, without having any reference to or being dependent on the movement of a valve, greater rapidity of motion and efficiency of blow are given. (3) Control of speed, weight of blow, and length of stroke given by the machine, and great limit of variation in the range of stroke, total freedom from stoppages due to displacement of valves, as by this arrangement while the pressure is on the piston can never be in equilibrium, but must start at any part of the stroke. (4) Economy in working, as there is no clearance space to be filled with pressure and exhausted to waste at every stroke, the pressure being worked expansively to any degree required. The following are the dimensions of a machine designed to work in ordinary mine levels. Weight of cylinder and piston-rod without frame, 70 lbs; length of cylinder over all 14 inches, diameter of cylinder $3\frac{1}{2}$ inches, speed 1,000 blows per minute, length of stroke from $1\frac{1}{2}$ to 3 inches, cubic inches of air or steam per stroke 34, number of strokes per cubic foot of steam or air 50, weight of blow exclusive of effect due to the weight and momentum of the tool at 30 lbs. pressure per square inch 150 lbs. In this machine the movements are automatic, and completely free from striking gear. For drawings, see Specification No. 1,734, A. D. 1873.

In machine- or hand-boring it is of great importance to employ suitable steel, properly sharpened.

For tough slate of variable hardness the cast steel should be of the very best quality. For hard brittle siliceous rock, steel of slightly inferior brand will afford good working results. The pointing of steel is a matter of great moment, overheating, or a white heat, must be avoided. The borer point should be formed with a hammer, well beaten from red to a black heat; a file, or grinding instrument, ought never to be used. The temper should be established at a dull red heat, the point, if dipped in oil or grease, is said to be toughened, as well as hardened. The hardest temper is indicated by a light straw colour, the softest by blue. The best working

198

temper is considered by some smiths to be just past straw, scarcely red purple; the tool at this colour to be instantly cooled in water.

The proper cutting angle of borers is a subject on which there is a great diversity of opinion, which probably arises from the circumstance that rocks differ even in one and the same mine, and will differ more widely in mines far distant from each other, and also from the fact that smiths do not readily change their practice. But it is self-evident that for soft argillaceous stone the point may be comparatively thin and flat, and that for flinty tough rock it should be well supported by lowness of angle. In machine-drilling, borer points do much more service than in hand-boring. In the former this is due to the uniform conditions of the blow. In the latter the blow is frequently an upset one, its effect being expended mostly on one side of the point. In hand-boring the chisel is almost invariably employed; but with boring machines the 'crown,' and Z or 'set' point is used; the crown for starting a hole, and both the crown and Z for boring in cavernous ground. The Cornish miner is in favour of striking the borer both lightly and quickly. A single handed mallet or hammer weighs 4–5 lbs., a double handed one from 6–8 lbs. Each man gives about 20 blows per minute; the size of steel employed is from $\frac{3}{4}$ to $1\frac{1}{5}$th inch diameter, and when sharpened will present points fully one quarter of an inch wider: that is, a boring bar $\frac{3}{4}$-inch diameter, when sharpened, will cut a hole 1 inch to 1 $\frac{1}{8}$th inch diameter.

Figs. 199, 200, 201 show chisel-point borers; *fig.* 202 a crown borer; and *fig.* 203 a Z borer.

The rate of hand-boring must necessarily depend on the workman, quality of steel, and hardness of rock, also on other minor circumstances. In a shaft 9 × 5$\frac{1}{2}$ feet nine men sunk 15 feet in a period of 26 days of twenty-four hours per day. The average number of holes 1$\frac{1}{4}$ inch diameter bored per shift of eight hours was 3, average depth of each hole 2 feet. During the run of 78 shifts the aggregate depth of the various holes was 468 feet; total cost of removing the ground, 77*l*. The average weight of rock removed per blast was 3$\frac{1}{2}$ cwts. In another shaft the rate of boring per minute, one man striking, was ·17 inch, two men striking ·25 inch. The number of blows required for a hole 30 inches deep was 4,500, number of borers blunted 7; depth bored per borer 4$\frac{1}{2}$ inches. In machine-boring the progress varies chiefly with the rapidity of the blow and toughness of the rock, or from $\frac{1}{2}$ to 6 inches per minute.

The boring machines employed in underground work are best driven by compressed

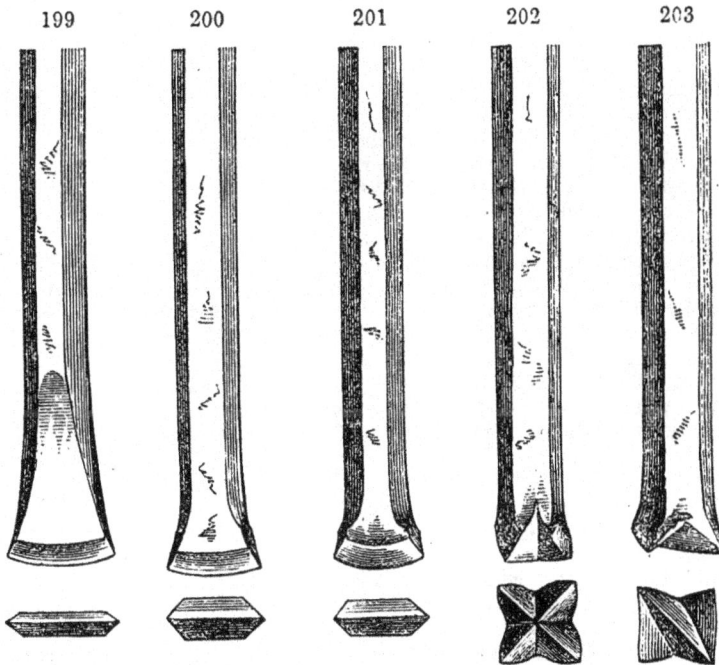

199   200   201   202   203

air. The air-pumps should be well constructed; and the pistons or rams worked in connection with water, with the double object of keeping down the temperature of the air, and expelling into the receiver a volume equal to the cubic contents of the air-pump stroke. Jordan's compressor is a cheap and well-contrived apparatus. Low has also devised an efficient pump; while Ford of Melbourne, and Ångström of Sweden, have produced simple and effective pumps worked in combination with ordinary pump rods.

In order to obtain the full effect of boring machines, the stuff must be removed rapidly after each blast. This object can only be accomplished by employing pneumatic tackles in connection with underground sinks, and having good forwarding ways. The advantages of using machine-borers in mining operations are—(1) Decided economy of time and money; (2) Diminution of the number of skilled miners, who can be advantageously employed in other parts of the mine; (3) Excellent ventilation of shafts, sinks, and levels; (4) Possibility of making the roof, floor, and sides of a level more regular than can be effected by hand-boring; (5) Rate of driving levels or sinking shafts two to four times greater than is practicable by hand-boring.

BORNINE. See TETRADYMITE, OR TELLURIC BISMUTH.

BORNITE. Purple copper ore or Bunt Kupfererz. See COPPER.

It is to be regretted that names so similar as *Bornine* and *Bornite*, both complimentary to Von Born, should have been bestowed upon widely different minerals,

BOROCALCITE. A borate of lime. See BORACIC ACID.

BORON. One of the non-metallic elements; it exists in nature in the form of boracic acid, and as borax, tincal, boracite, borocalcite, &c.

Homberg is said to have obtained boron from borax in 1702; if so, his discovery appears to have been forgotten, since it was unknown, except hypothetically, to the more modern chemists until, in 1808, it was obtained by Gay-Lussac and Thénard, and by Davy in 1808, who decomposed boracic acid into boron and oxygen.

Boron is best obtained from the double fluoride of boron and potassium (BF^3.KF), which is prepared by saturating hydrofluoric acid with boracic acid, and then gradually adding fluoride of potassium. The difficultly soluble double compound thus produced is collected and dried at a temperature nearly approaching to redness. This compound is then powdered and introduced into an iron tube closed at one end, together with an equal weight of potassium, whereupon heat is applied sufficient to melt the latter, and the mixture of the two substances is effected by stirring with an iron wire. Upon the mass being exposed to a red heat, the potassium abstracts the fluorine. The fluoride of potassium may afterwards be removed by heating the mass with a solution of chloride of ammonium, which converts the free potassa into chloride of potassium, and thus prevents the oxidation of the boron, which takes place in the presence of potash; the chloride of ammonium adhering to the boron may be afterwards removed by treatment with alcohol. Boron thus prepared is a dark greenish-brown powder, tasteless, and inodorous; its atomic weight is 11·0.

MM. Wöhler and Deville have, by fusing boracic acid, or amorphous boron, with aluminium, succeeded in obtaining boron in the crystallised state. The form of the boron crystals thus obtained has been the subject of a remarkable enquiry by M. Quintino Sella. They are octahedra, belonging to the pyramidal or square prismatic system. They refract light powerfully, have a specific gravity of 2·68, and seem to be almost as hard as diamond. From the close resemblance of this form of boron to the diamond, it is generally known as *Adamantine* or *Diamond Boron.*

Accompanying this octahedral boron , as it crystallises from its solution in aluminium, are certain copper-coloured six-sided scales, strongly resembling graphite, and hence called *graphitoidal boron.* It has been lately shown, however, that this substance, instead of being an allotropic form of boron, is really a definite compound of boron and aluminium. See BORACIC ACID.

BORONATROCALCITE. A synonym of *Ulexite.* See BORACIC ACID.

BOSJEMANITE. A name given to Manganese Alum. See ALUM, NATIVE.

BOTALLACKITE. An oxychloride of copper found at Botallack Mine, in St. Just, Cornwall.

BOTTLE MANUFACTURE. See GLASS and STONE WARE.

BOUGIE. A smooth, flexible, elastic, slender cylinder, introduced into the urethra, rectum, or œsophagus, for opening or dilating it, in cases of stricture and other diseases. The invention of this instrument is claimed by Aldereto, a Portuguese physician; but its form and uses were first described by his pupil Amatus, in the year 1554. Some are solid and some hollow, some corrosive and some mollifying. They owed their elasticity, as formerly made, to linseed oil, inspissated by long boiling, and rendered dry by litharge. This viscid matter was spread upon a very fine cord or tubular web of cotton, flax, or silk, which was rolled upon a slab, when it became nearly solid by drying, and was finally polished.

Pickel, a French professor of medicine, published the following recipe for the composition of bougies:—Take 3 parts of boiled linseed oil, 1 part of amber, and 1 of oil of turpentine; melt and mix these ingredients well together, and spread the compound at 3 successive intervals upon a silk cord or web. Place the pieces so coated in a stove heated to 150° F.; leave them in it for 12 hours, adding 15 or 16 fresh layers in succession, till the instruments have acquired the proper size. Polish them first with pumice-stone, and finally smooth with tripoli and oil. This process is the one still employed in Paris, with some slight modifications; the chief of which is dissolving in the oil one-twentieth of its weight of caoutchouc, to render the substance more solid. For this purpose the caoutchouc must be cut into slender shreds, and added gradually to the hot oil. The silk tissue must be fine and open, to admit of the composition entering freely among its filaments. Every successive layer ought to be dried in a stove, and then in the open air, before another is applied. This process takes 2 months for its completion, in forming the best bougies called by distinction *elastic bougies*; which ought to bear twisting round the finger without cracking or scaling, and extension without giving way, but retracting when let go. When the bougies are to be hollow, a mandrel of iron wire, properly bent, with a ring at one end, is introduced into the axis of the silk tissue. Some bougies are made with a hollow axis of tinfoil rolled into a slender tube. Bougies are now usually made entirely of caoutchouc, by the intervention of a solution of this substance in sulphuric ether, a menstruum sufficiently cheap in France, on account of the low duty upon alcohol, or of naphtha. There are medicated bougies, the composition of which belongs to Surgical Pharmacy. The manufacture of these instruments of various kinds forms a separate and no inconsiderable branch of industry at Paris. Very superior bougies are now made by the surgical-instrument makers, and by the workers in caoutchouc, in this country.

BOULDER CLAY. The fine laminated clays of the Pleistocene epoch, which immediately overlie the true *Boulder clay* of geologists—so called from the boulders and pebbles interspersed through their mass.

BOULDERING STONE. A name given by the Sheffield cutlers to the smooth flint pebbles with which they smooth down the faces of buff and wooden wheels.

BOURNONITE. A sulphide of antimony, lead, and copper. According to Rammelsberg, sulphur 19·77, antimony 24·34, lead 42·88, copper 13·06. It is found in several parts of Cornwall and Devonshire, and in many of the mining districts of Europe.

BOVEY COAL. A lignite found in large deposits at Bovey-Tracey, in Devonshire, whence its name. See LIGNITE.

BOW PEN. A drawing pen. The parts which hold the ink is formed of two pieces, which are bowed out and adjustable by a screw.

BOWSTRING HEMP. A fibre prepared from the *Sanseviera Zeylanica*. See HEMP.

BOX WOOD. (*Buis*, Fr.; *Buchsbaum*, Ger.) *Buxus sempervirens.*—Two varieties of box wood are imported into this country. The European is brought from Leghorn, Portugal, &c., and the Turkey box wood from Constantinople, Smyrna, and the Black Sea. English box wood grows plentifully at Box Hill, in Surrey, and in Gloucestershire. The English box wood is used for common turnery, and is preferred by brass finishers for their lathe-chucks, as it is tougher than the foreign box, and bears rougher usage. It is of very slow growth, as in the space of 25 years it will only attain a diameter of 1½ to 2 inches. Box wood is used for making clarionets and flutes, carpenters' rules, and drawing scales, and is exclusively employed by the wood engraver. Its sawdust is used for cleaning jewellery. See ENGRAVING ON WOOD.

BRACES. (*Bretelles*, Fr.; *Hosenträger*, Ger.) Narrow fillets or bands of leather or textile fabrics, which pass over the shoulders, and are attached behind and before to the waistbands of trousers, for supporting their weight. Braces are now made of an elastic material, into the structure of which Indian-rubber fibre enters.

BRAHMIN'S BEADS. The seeds of a species of *Elæocarpus*, which are capped with silver and made into necklaces and bracelets.

BRAID. A plaited, twisted or woven trimming.

BRAIDING MACHINE. (*Machine à lacets*, Fr.; *Bortenwerkerstuhl*, Ger.) This being employed, not only to manufacture stay-laces, braid, and upholsterers' cord, but to cover the threads of caoutchouc for weaving brace-bands, deserves a description in this work. Three threads at least are required to make such a knitted lace, but 11, 13, or 17, and even 29 threads are often employed, the first three numbers being

preferred. They are made by means of a frame of a very ingenious construction, which moves by a continuous rotation. We shall describe a frame with 13 threads, from which the structure of the others may be readily conceived. The basis of the

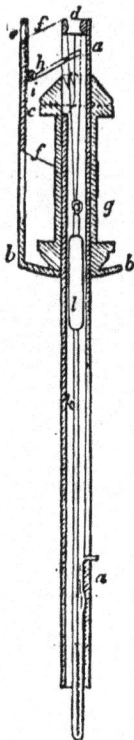

machine consists of four strong wooden uprights, A, *figs.* 204, 205, 206, occupying the four angles of a rectangle, of which one side is 14 inches long, the other side 18 inches, and the height of the rectangle about 40 inches. *Fig.* 204 is a section in a horizontal plane, passing through the line *a b* of *fig.* 205, which is a vertical section in a plane passing through the centre of the machine c, according to the line *c d, fig.* 204. The side x is supposed to be the front of the frame; and the opposite side, Y, the back. B, six spindles or skewers, numbered from 1 to 6, placed in a vertical position upon the circumference of a circle whose centre coincides with that of the machine at the point c. These six spindles are composed—1, Of so many iron shafts or axes D, supported in brass collets E (*fig.* 205), and extended downwards within 6 inches of the ground, where they rest in brass steps fixed upon a horizontal beam. 2, Wooden heads, made of horn-beam or nut-tree, placed, the first upon the upper end of each spindle, opposite the cut-out beam F, and the second opposite the second beam G. 3, Wooden-toothed wheels, H, reciprocally working together, placed between the beam G and the collet-beam E. The toothed wheels and the lower heads for each spindle are in one piece.

206

The heads and shafts of the spindles No. 1 and 6 are one-fifth stronger than those of the other spindles; their heads have five semi-circular grooves, and wheels of 60 teeth, while the heads of the others have only four grooves, and wheels of 48 teeth; so that the number of the grooves in the six spindles is 26, one-half of which are occupied with the stems of the puppets I, which carry the 13 threads from No. 1 to 13.

The toothed wheels, which give all the spindles a simultaneous movement, but in different directions, are so disposed as to bring their grooves opposite to each other in the course of rotation.

K, the middle winglet, triple at bottom and quintuple at top, which serves to guide the puppets in the direction they ought to pursue.

T, three winglets, single at top and bottom, placed exteriorly, which serve a like purpose.

M, two winglets, triple at bottom and single at top, placed likewise exteriorly, and which serve the same purposes as the preceding; *m*, are iron pins inserted in the cut-out beam G, which serve as stops or limits to the oscillations of the exterior winglets.

Now, if by any moving power (a man can drive a pair) rotation be impressed upon the large spindle No. 1, in the direction of the arrow, all the other spindles will necessarily pursue the rotatory movement indicated by the respective arrows. In this case the 13 puppets working in the grooves of the heads of the spindles will be carried round simultaneously, and will proceed, each in its turn, from one extremity of the machine to the opposite point, crossing those which have a retrograde movement. The 13 threads united at the point N, situated above the centre of the machine, will form at that point the braid, which after having passed over the pulley *o*, comes between the two rollers P Q, and is squeezed together, as in a flatting-mill, where the braid is calendered at the same time that it is delivered. It is obvious that the roller P receives its motion from the toothed wheel of the spindle No. 3, and from the intermediate wheels, R, S, T, as well as from the endless screw *z*, which drives at proper speed the wheel W, fixed upon the shaft of the roller P.

The braid is denser in proportion as the point N is less elevated above the tops of the puppets, but in this case, the excentric motion of these puppets is much more sensible in reference to that point towards which all the threads converge than when it is elevated. The threads, which must be always kept equally stretched by means of a weight, as we shall presently see, are considerably strained by the traction occasioned by the constantly excentric movement of the puppets. From this cause, braiding machines must be worked at a moderate velocity. In general, for fine work, 30 turns of the large spindle per minute are the utmost that can safely be made.

The puppet or spindle of this machine, being the most important piece, I have represented it in section, upon a scale one-fourth of its actual size, *fig.* 206. It is formed of a tube, *a*, of strong sheet iron well brazed; *b* is a disc, likewise of sheet iron, from which a narrow fillet *c*, rises vertically as high as the tube, where both are pierced with holes, *d e*, through which the thread *f* is passed, as it comes from the bobbin, *g*, which turns freely upon the tube *a*. The top of this bobbin is conical and toothed. A small catch or detent *h*, moveable in a vertical direction round *i*, falls by its own weight into the teeth of the crown of the bobbin, in which case this cannot revolve ; but when the detent is raised so far as to disengage the teeth, and at the same time to pull the thread, the bobbin turns, and lets out thread till the detent falls back into these same teeth.

A skewer of iron wire, k, is loaded with a small weight, l, melted upon it. The top of this skewer has an eye in it, and the bottom is recurved, as is shown in *fig.* 206, so that supposing the thread comes to break, this skewer falls into the actual position in the figure, where we see its lower end extending beyond the tube a, by about $\frac{1}{4}$ of an inch ; but as long as the thread is unbroken, the skewer k, which serves to keep it always tense during the excentric movement of the puppet, does not pass out below the tube.

This disposition has naturally furnished the means of causing the machine to stop whenever one of the threads breaks. This inferior protrusion of the skewer pushes in its progress a detent, which instantly causes the band to slide from the driving pulley to the loose pulley. Thus the machine cannot operate unless all the threads be entire. It is the business of the operative, who has 3 or 4 under her charge, to mend the threads as they break, and to substitute full bobbins for empty ones, whenever the machine is stopped.

BRAN (*Son*, Fr.; *Kleie*, Ger.) The husky portion of ground wheat, separated by the boulter from the flour. It is advantageously employed by the calico printers, in the clearing process, in which, by boiling in bran-water, the colouring matters adhering to the non-mordanted parts of maddered goods, as well as the dun matters which cloud the mordanted portions, are removed. A valuable series of researches by M. Daniel Kœchlin-Schouch, justified the following conclusions :—

1. The dose of two bushels of bran for 10 pieces of calico is the best, the ebullition being kept up for an hour. A boil for the same time in pure water had no effect in clearing either the grounds or the figures.

2. Fifteen minutes boiling are sufficient when the principal object is to clear white grounds, but in certain cases 30 minutes are requisite to brighten the dyed parts. If, by increasing the charge of bran, the time of the ebullition could be shortened, it would be, in some places, as Alsace, an economy ; because in the passage of the 10 pieces through a copper or vat heated with steam, 1 cwt. of coal is consumed in fuel, which costs from $2\frac{1}{2}$ to 3 francs, while 2 bushels of bran are to be bought for 1 franc.

3. By increasing the quantity of water from 12 to 24 hectolitres with 2 bushels of bran, the clearing effect upon the 10 pieces was impaired. It is therefore advantageous not to use too much water.

4. Many experiments concur to prove that flour is altogether useless for the clearing boil, and that finer bran is inferior for this purpose to the coarser.

5. The white ground of the calicoes boiled with wheat bran is distinguishable by its superior brightness from that of those boiled with rye bran, and especially with barley bran ; the latter having hardly any effect.

6. There is no advantage in adding soap to the bran boil ; though a little potash or soda may be properly introduced when the water is calcareous.

7. The pellicle of the bran is the most powerful part ; the flour and the starch are of no use in clearing goods, but the mucilage, which forms one-third of the weight of the bran, has considerable efficacy, and seems to act in the following way :—In proportion as the mucilaginous substance dissolves the colouring and tawny matters upon the cloth, the husky surface attracts and fixes upon itself the greater part of them. Accordingly, when used bran is digested in a weak alkaline bath, it gives up the colour which it had absorbed from the cloth.

From bran, Péligot obtained 8·0 per cent. of cellulose. Millon succeeded in extracting considerable quantities of glutinous substances from the bran with acetic acid and alcohol. He found in 100 parts, starch, dextrine, and sugar, 50·0 ; sugar, 1·0 ; gluten, 14·9 ; fat, 3·6 ; cellulose, 9·7 ; salts, 5·7 ; water, 13·9 ; and of odorous and resinous matters, 1·2 per cent.

BRANCH COAL. A term applied in Yorkshire to cannel and other kinds of coal, which occurs in layers traversing the ordinary coal of the district. The *branching coal* of South Wales derives its name from the peculiar swelling which takes place in the operation of coking, after which it becomes very light.

BRANDS. Imperfectly carbonised pieces of wood taken from a charcoal heap.

BRANDY. (*Eau de vie*, Fr.; *Branntwein*, Ger.) The name given in this country to ardent spirits distilled from wine, and possessing a peculiar taste and flavour, due to a minute portion of a volatile oil. Each variety of alcohol has an aroma characteristic of the fermented substance from which it is procured ; whether it be the grape, cherries, sugar-cane, rice, corn, or potatoes ; and it may be distinguished even as procured from different growths of the vine. The brandies of

Languedoc, Bordeaux, Armagnac, Cognac, Aunis, Saintonge, Rochelle, Orleans, Barcelona, Naples, &c., being each readily recognisable by an experienced dealer.

Aubergier showed by experiments, that the disagreeable taste of the spirits distilled from the *marc* of the grape is owing to an essential oil contained in the skin of the grape; and found that the oil, when insulated, is so energetic that a few drops are sufficient to taint a pipe of 600 litres of fine-flavoured spirit. See FUSEL OIL.

The most celebrated of the French brandies, those of Cognac and Armagnac, are slightly rectified to only from 0·935 to 1·922 : they contain more than half their weight of water, and come over therefore highly charged with the fragrant essential oil of the husk of the grape. When, to save expense of carriage, the spirit is rectified to a much higher degree, the dealer, on receiving it at Paris, reduces it to the market proof by the addition of a little highly flavoured weak brandy-and-water; but he cannot in this way produce so finely-flavoured a spirit as the weaker product of distillation of the Cognac wine. If the best Cognac brandy be carefully distilled at a low heat, and after distillation the strong spirit be diluted with water to restore it to its original strength, it will be found that the brandy has suffered much in its flavour.

Genuine French brandy evinces an acid reaction with litmus-paper, owing to a minute portion of vinegar; it contains, besides, some acetic ether, and, when long kept in oak casks, a little astringent matter.

The constituents of brandy are *alcohol, water, volatile oil, acetic acid, acetic ether, colouring matter,* and *tannin.—Pereira.*

Pale brandy acquires the slight colour which it possesses from the cask in which it is kept. *Brown brandy* is coloured by *caramel.* Brandy is sold of various strengths, but it is usually about 10 per cent. under proof. The quantities of brandy imported, and its computed value, have been as follow:—

	1867 Proof Galls.	1868 Proof Galls.	1869 Proof Galls.	1870 Proof Galls.	1871 Proof Galls.
Quantity . . .	4,849,832	4,062,885	3,937,266	7,942,965	5,228,568
	£	£	£	£	£
Value	1,376,360	1,309,413	1,249,579	2,153,699	1,895,378

For the last three years the returns are given, showing the quantity retained for home consumption:—

	1870 Proof Galls.	1871 Proof Galls.	1872 Proof Galls.
Imports	9,942,965	5,372,486	3,519,413
Home consumption . .	3,526,132	3,715,675	3,944,725

The duty on brandy was reduced in 1860 to 8*s.* 6*d.* per gallon.

BRANDY, BRITISH. Dr. Ure gave the following formula for its preparation:—Dilute pure alcohol to the proof pitch; add to every hundred pounds weight of it from half a pound to a pound of argol, dissolved in water, a little acetic ether, and French wine vinegar, some bruised French plums, and flavour stuff from Cognac; then distil the spirit with a gentle fire in an alembic furnished with an agitator. British brandies are now sold as pure grain spirits, flavoured and coloured with caramel. See ALCOHOL.

BRASS. (*Laiton, cuivre jaune,* Fr.; *Messing,* Ger.) An alloy of copper and zinc. The brass of the ancients appears, in very early times, to have chiefly consisted of a mixture of copper and tin, and to have consequently, been a species of bronze or bell metal. See ALLOYS.

Brass was formerly manufactured by cementing granulated copper, called *bean-shot,* or copper clippings, with calcined calamine (native carbonate of zinc) and charcoal in a crucible, and exposing them to bright ignition. Three parts of copper were used for 3 of calamine and 2 of charcoal.

James Emerson obtained a patent, in 1781, for making brass by the direct fusion of its two metallic elements, and it is now usually manufactured in this way.

It appears that the best proportion of the constituents to form fine brass is 2 equivalents of copper = 63½ + 1 of zinc = 32·3; or very nearly 2 parts of copper to 1 of zinc.

In the process of alloying two metals of such different fusibilities as copper and zinc, a considerable waste of the latter metal by combustion might be expected; but in reality, their mutual affinities seem to prevent the loss, in a great measure, by the speedy absorption of the zinc into the substance of the copper. Indeed, copper plates and rods are often *brassed* externally by exposure, at a high temperature, to the fumes of zinc, and afterwards laminated or drawn. The spurious gold wire of

Lyons is made from such rods. Copper vessels may be superficially converted into brass by boiling them in dilute muriatic acid containing some tartar and zinc amalgam.

The first step in making brass is to plunge slips of copper into melted zinc till an alloy of somewhat difficult fusion be formed, to raise the heat, and add the remaining proportion of the copper.

The brass of the first fusion is broken to pieces, and melted with a fresh quantity of zinc, to obtain the finished brass. Each melting takes from 8 to 9 hours. The metal is now cast into plates, about 40 inches long by 26 broad, and from one-third to half an inch thick. The moulds were formerly slabs of granite mounted in an iron frame. Granite appears to have been preferred as a mould, because it preserves the heat, whilst, by the asperities of its surface, it keeps hold of the clay lute applied to secure the joinings.

The modern method of making brass, by the direct mixture of the component metals, is largely practised at Birmingham in small square furnaces, built of fire-brick, and measuring from 10 to 12 inches in the side, and about 2 feet in depth. Crucibles of Stourbridge fire-clay, or, rarely, of plumbago, are placed on the iron bars at the bottom of the furnace, and packed round with coke. The ingot copper is first introduced into the crucible, and when this is melted the proper proportion of zinc is cautiously added, the mixture being stirred with an iron poker to ensure union of the metals. As soon as the mixture is thoroughly effected, the crucible is withdrawn, and the molten brass is cast, either into moulds of sand, or into iron ingot moulds, slightly oiled inside, and dusted over with charcoal powder. In the manufacture of the variety of brass called 'Muntz's metal,' an alloy extensively made for sheathing the bottoms of ships, the mixture of metals is generally effected in a reverberatory furnace, instead of in crucibles. See MUNTZ'S METAL.

The cast plates of brass are usually rolled into sheets. For this purpose they are cut into ribands of various breadths, commonly about 6½ inches. The cylinders of the brass rolling mill are generally 46 inches long and 18 inches in diameter. The ribands are first of all passed through the cylinders cold; but the brass soon becomes too hard to laminate. It is then annealed in a furnace, and, after cooling, is passed afresh through the rolls. After paring off the chipped edges, the sheets are laminated, two at a time; and if they are to be made very thin, even 8 plates are to be passed through together. The brass in these operations must be annealed 7 or 8 times before the sheet arrives at the required thickness. These successive heatings are expensive; and hence manufacturers have been led to try various plans of economy. The annealing furnaces are of two forms, according to the size of the sheets of brass. The smaller are about 12 feet long, with a fire-place at each end, and about 13 inches wide. The arch of the furnace has a cylindrical shape, whose axis is parallel to its small side. The hearth is horizontal, and is made of bricks set on edge. In the front of the furnace there is a large door, which is raised by a lever, or chain and counterweight, and slides in a frame between two cheeks of cast-iron. This furnace has, in general, no chimney, except a vent slightly raised above the door, to prevent the workmen being incommoded by the smoke. Sometimes the arch is perforated with a number of holes. The sheets of brass are placed above each other, but separated by parings, to allow the hot air to circulate among them, the lowest sheet resting upon bars of cast-iron placed lengthwise.

The larger furnaces are usually 32 feet long, by 6½ feet wide, in the body, and 3 feet at the hearth. A grate 13 inches broad extends along each side of the hearth, through its whole length, and is divided from it by a small wall, 2 or 3 inches high. The vault of the furnace has a curvature, and is pierced with 6 or 8 openings, which allow the smoke to pass off into a low bell-chimney above. At each end of the furnace is a cast-iron door, which slides up and down in an iron frame, and is poised by a counterweight. On the hearth is a kind of railway, composed of two iron bars, on which the carriage moves with its load of sheets of brass.

These sheets, being often 24 feet long, could not be easily moved in and out of the furnace; but as brass laminates well in the cold state, they are all introduced and moved out together. With this view an iron carriage is framed with bars, which rest on four wheels. Upon this carriage, of a length nearly equal to that of the furnace, are laid the sheets, with brass parings between them. The carriage is then raised by a crane to a level with the furnace, and entered upon the grooved bars which lie upon the hearth. That no heat may be lost, two carriages are provided, the one being ready to put in as the other is taken out; the furnace is meanwhile uniformly kept hot. This method, however convenient for moving the sheets in and out, wastes a good deal of fuel in heating the iron carriage.

The principal places in which brass is manufactured on a large scale, in England, are Bristol and Birmingham, and at Holywell, in North Wales.

At the brass manufactory of Hegermühl, upon the Finon Canal, near Potsdam, the following are the materials of one charge :—41 pounds of old brass, 55 pounds refined copper (*Garkupfer*) granulated, and 24 pounds of zinc. This mixture, weighing 120 pounds, is distributed in four crucibles, and fused in a wind furnace with pitcoal fuel. The waste, upon the whole, varies from 2½ to 4 pounds.

Fig. 209 represents the furnace as it was formerly worked with charcoal; *a*, the laboratory, in which the crucibles were placed. It was walled with fire-bricks. The foundations and the filling-in walls were formed of stone rubbish, as being bad conductors of heat; sand and ashes may be also used; *b*, cast-iron circular grating plates, pierced with 12 holes (see *fig.* 208), over them a sole of loam, *c*, is beaten down, and perforated with holes corresponding to those in the iron discs; *d*, the ash-pit; *e*, the *bock*, a draught flue which conducts the air requisite to the combustion, from a sunk tunnel in communication with several melting furnaces. The terrace or crown of the furnace, *f*, lies on a level with the foundry floor, *h h*, and is shut with a tile of fire-clay, *g*, which may be moved in any direction by means of hooks and eyes in its binding iron ring. *Fig.* 209 the tongs for putting in and taking out the charges, as viewed from above and from the side.

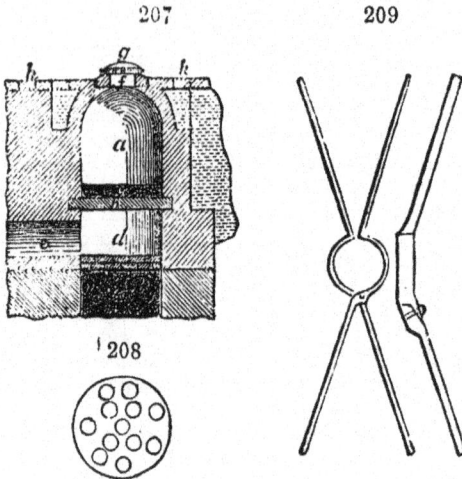

207   209

208

The following description of a Continental brass manufactory, by Dr. Ure, it has been thought advisable to retain, with only a few verbal alterations.

Figs. 210, 211, represent the furnaces more recently constructed for the use of pitcoal fuel; *fig.* 210 being an upright section, and *fig.* 211 the ground plan. In this furnace the crucibles are not surrounded with the fuel, but receive the requisite melting heat from the flame proceeding from the grate upon which it is burnt. The crucibles stand upon seven arches *a*, which unite in the middle at the keystone, *b*, *fig.* 211; between the arches are spaces, through which the flame rises from the grate, *c*; *d*, is the fire door; *e*, a sliding tile or damper for regulating or shutting off the air-draught; *f* an inclined plane, for carrying off the cinders that fall through the grate, along the draught tunnel *g*, so that the air in entering below may not be heated by them.

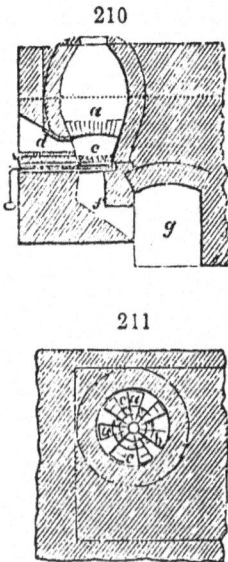

210

211

The crucibles are 16 inches deep, 9½ wide at the mouth, 6½ at the bottom; with a thickness in the sides of 1 inch above and 1½ below; they stand from 40 to 50 meltings. The old brass, which fills their whole capacity, is first put in and melted down; the crucibles are now taken out and charged with the half of the zinc in pieces of from 1 to 3 inches in size, covered over with coal-ashes; then one-half of the copper is introduced; again dust; and thus the layers of zinc and copper are distributed alternately with coal-ashes betwixt them, till the whole charge becomes finally fused. Over all, a thicker layer of carbonaceous matter is laid, to prevent oxidation of the brass. Eight crucibles filled in this way are put into the furnace between the 12 holes of the grate; and over them are laid two empty crucibles to be heated for the casting operation. In from 3½ to 4 hours the brass is ready to be poured. Fifteen English bushels of coals are consumed in one operation; of which six are used at the introduction of the crucibles, and four gradually afterwards.

When sheet brass is to be made, the following process is pursued :—

An empty crucible is taken out of the furnace through the crown with a pair of tongs, and kept red hot by placing it in a hollow hearth surrounded with burning coals; into this crucible the contents of four of the melting pots are poured; the dross is raked out with an iron scraper. As soon as the melting pot is emptied, it is immediately re-charged in the manner above described, and re-placed in the furnace. The surface of the melted brass is swept with the stump of a broom, and then stirred about with the iron rake, to bring up any light foreign matter to the surface, which is then skimmed with a little scraper; the crucible is now seized with the casting tongs, and emptied in the following way :—

The mould or *form* for casting sheet brass consists of two slabs of granite, *a a, figs.* 212, 213. These are $5\frac{1}{2}$ feet long, 3 feet broad, 1 foot thick, and, for greater security,

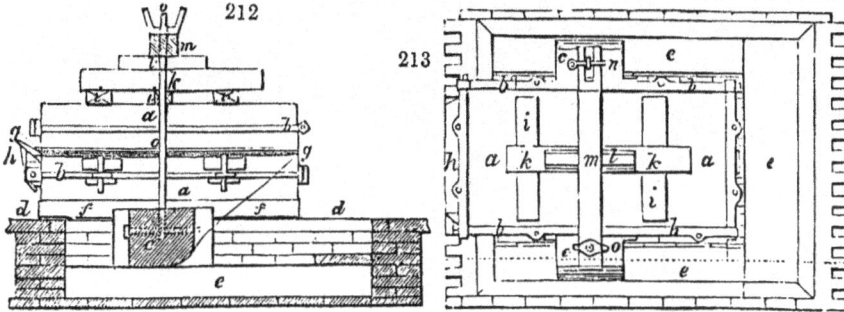

girt with iron bands, *b b*, 2 inches broad, $1\frac{1}{2}$ thick, and joined at the four corners with bolts and nuts. The mould rests upon an oaken block, *c*, $3\frac{1}{2}$ feet long, $2\frac{5}{8}$th broad, and $1\frac{1}{4}$ thick, which is suspended at each end upon gudgeons, in bearing blocks, placed under the foundry floor, *d d*, in the casting pit, *e e*. This is lined with bricks; and is $6\frac{3}{4}$ feet long, $5\frac{1}{2}$ bread, and 2 deep; upon the two long side walls of the pit are laid the bearing blocks which support the gudgeons. The swing blocks are 10 inches long, 18 inches broad, 15 inches thick, and somewhat rounded upon their back edge, so that the casting frame may slope a little to the horizon. To these blocks two cross wooden arms, *f f*, are mortised, upon which the under slab rests freely, but so as to project about 5 inches over the block backwards, to secure an equipoise in the act of casting. *g g* are bars, placed at both of the long sides, and one of the ends, between the slabs, to determine the thickness of the brass plate. Upon the other slab the gate *h* is fastened, a sheet of iron 6 inches broad, which has nearly the shape of a parallel trapezium (lozenge), and slopes a little towards the horizon. This serves for setting the casting pot upon in the act of pouring, and renders it more convenient to empty. The gate is coated with a mixture of loam and hair. The upper slab is secured to the under one in its slanting position by an *armour* or binding. This consists of tension bars of wood, *i, k, l, m*, of the iron bars *n*, (3 to $3\frac{1}{2}$ inches broad, $1\frac{1}{2}$ inch thick, see the top view, *fig.* 213) of a rod with holes and pins at its upper end, and of the iron screw spindle *o*. The mode in which these act may be understood from inspection of the figure. In order to lift the upper slab from the under one, which is effected by turning it round its edge, a chain is employed, suspending two others, connected with the slab. The former passes over a pulley, and may be pulled up and down by means of a wheel and axle, or the aid of a counterweight. Upon each of the two long sides of the slab are two iron rings, to which the ends of the chains may be hooked. The casting faces of the slab must be coated with a layer of finely ground loam; the thinner this is the better.

When calamine is employed, $\frac{1}{2}$ cwt. of copper, $\frac{3}{4}$ cwt. of calamine, and $\frac{1}{3}$rd the volume of both of charcoal mixed, are put into seven crucibles, and exposed to heat during 11 or 12 hours; the product being from 70 to 72 lbs. of brass.

Brass-Plate Rolling.—At Hegermühl there are two re-heating or annealing furnaces, one larger, 18 feet long, and another smaller, $8\frac{1}{2}$; the hot chamber is separated from the fireplace by iron beams, in such a way that the brass castings are played upon by the flames on both their sides. After each passage through the laminating rolls, they are heated anew, then cooled and laminated, until they have reached the proper length. The plates are smeared with grease before rolling.

Fig. 214 shows the ground plan of the furnace and its railway; *fig.* 215, the cross section; and *fig.* 216 the section lengthwise; *a a*, the iron way bars or rails upon the floor of the foundry for enabling the wheels of the waggon to move rapidly backwards and forwards; *b b*, the two grates; *c c*, the ash-pits; *d d*, the fire beams;

e e e, vents in the roof of the hot chamber *f; g, g,* two plates for shutting the hot chamber; *h,* the flue; *i,* the chimney. After rolling, the sheets, covered with black oxide of copper, are plunged for a few minutes into a mother-water from the alum

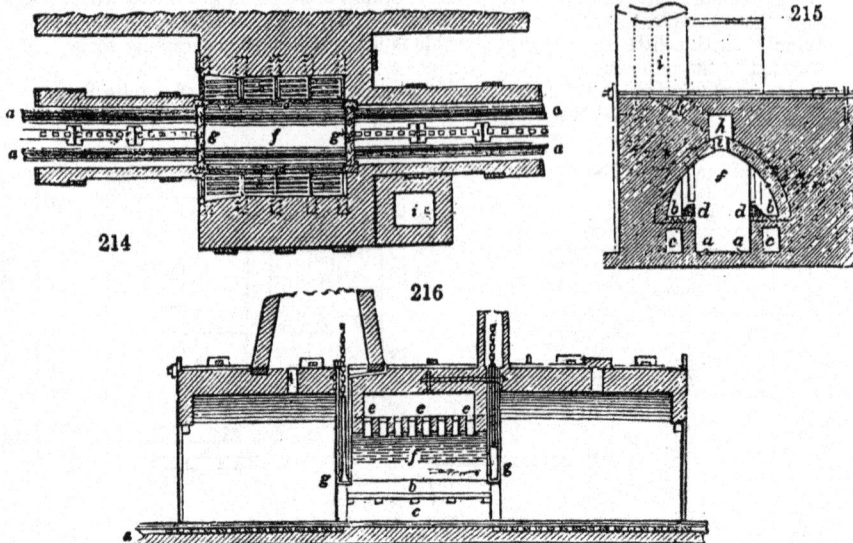

works, then washed in clean water, and lastly, smeared with oil, and scraped with a blunt knife.

For musical purposes, the brass wire of Berlin had acquired great and merited celebrity; but that of Birmingham and of Cheadle is now preferred by foreigners.

The Table on the opposite page, for the compilation of which we are indebted to Mr. Robert Mallet, F.R.S., presents, in a very intelligible form, the chemical and physical conditions of the various kinds of brass.

It is known that common brass, containing from 27·4 to 31·8 per cent. of zinc and from 71·9 to 65·8 per cent. of copper, is not malleable while hot, but that articles of it must be made by casting. As it would be of great advantage in many branches of industry to have an alloy of this kind that could be worked while hot, like malleable iron, the information that such an alloy exists must be welcome to artists.

By melting together 33 parts of copper and 25 parts of zinc, there was a loss of 3 parts, thus making 60 per cent. copper and 40 per cent. zinc. It differs from the English specimens by containing a larger proportion of zinc, and possesses, according to M. Machts, the proprietor of a brass foundry in Hanover, the precious property of malleability in a higher degree than the English specimens.

A piece of 'yellow metal,' similar in colour to this alloy, was found on analysis to contain 60·16 copper and 39·71 zinc, which is the composition of malleable brass. It also showed great density or solidity.

An alloy was prepared by melting together 60 parts copper and 40 parts zinc, which had the following properties:—The colour was between that of brass and tombak, it had a strong metallic lustre, a fine close-grained fracture, and great solidity (density). Its specific gravity at the temperature of 10° C. was 8·44; by calculation it ought only to have been 8·08; thus showing that in the formation of the alloy a condensation must have taken place. Calculation shows that the alloy may be considered as a determinate chemical combination, for the results of the analysis very nearly accord with the assumption that it may be considered as composed of three atoms by weight of copper and 2 atoms by weight of zinc ($3Cu + 2Zn$). The hardness of the alloy is the same as that of fluor spar; it can be scratched by apatite (phosphate of lime), consequently its hardness is $= 4$. The alloy is harder than copper, very tough, and is, in a properly managed fire, malleable; so much so that a key was forged out of a cast rod.

These important properties of this alloy warrant an expectation of its application to many purposes in the arts, and it would appear that they depend on its definite chemical proportions.

We learn some further particulars from the 'Gewerbeverein,' of Lower Austria. The commission obtained from an English specimen 65·03 of copper and 34·76 zinc.

	Chemical Constitution	Composition by Weight per Cent.	Atomic Weight, H=1	Specific Gravity	Fracture[1]	Colour of Fracture	Ultimate Cohesion per Square Inch	Inverse order of Ductility	Order of Malleability at 60°	Inverse Order of Hardness &c.	Inverse Order of Fusibility &c.	Commercial Titles, characteristic Properties in Working, &c.
							Tons					
1	Cu +	100·00 + 0	31·6	8·667	E	Tile red	24·6	8	1	22	15	Copper.
2	10 Cu + Zn	90·72 + 9·28	348·3	8·605	CC	Reddish yellow, 1	12·1	6	13	21	14	Similor, &c. } Several of these are malleable at high temperatures.
3	9 Cu + Zn	89·80 + 10·20	316·7	8·607	FC	Ditto 2	11·5	4	11	20	13	
4	8 Cu + Zn	88·60 + 11·40	285·1	8·633	FC	Ditto 3	12·8	2	10	19	12	
5	7 Cu + Zn	87·30 + 12·70	253·4	8·587	FC	Ditto 4	13·2	9	9	18	11	
6	6 Cu + Zn	85·40 + 14·60	221·9	8·591	FF	Yellowish red, 3	14·1	5	8	17	10	
7	5 Cu + Zn	83·02 + 16·98	190·3	8·451	FC	Ditto 2	13·7	11	2	16	9	Bath metal.
8	4 Cu + Zn	79·65 + 20·35	158·7	8·448	FC	Ditto 1	14·7	7	3	15	8	Dutch Brass.
9	3 Cu + Zn	74·58 + 25·42	127·1	8·397	EC	Pale yellow	13·1	10	4	14	7	Rolled sheet brass.
10	5 Cu + 2 Zn	71·43 + 28·57	222·6	?	...	...	...	...	...	...	...	Normal brass.
11	2 Cu + Zn	66·18 + 33·82	95·5	8·299	EC	Full yellow, 1	12·5	3	6	13	6	British brass.
12	19 Cu + 12 Zn	60·00 + 40·00	988·0	8·200	C	Ditto	1·9	1	3	15	6	Muntz's patent sheathing.
13	Cu + 2 Zn	49·47 + 50·53	63·9	8·230	CC	Ditto 2	9·2	12	5	12	6	German brass.
14	Cu + 2 Zn	32·85 + 67·15	96·2	8·283	CC	Deep yellow	19·3	1	7	10	6	German brass, watchmakers.'
15	8 Cu + 17 Zn	31·52 + 68·48	801·9	7·721	C	Silver white, 1	2·1	0	22	5	5	Very brittle
16	8 Cu + 18 Zn	30·30 + 69·70	834·2	7·836	VC	Ditto 2	2·2	0	23	6	5	Ditto } Too hard to file or turn; lustre nearly equal to speculum metal.
17	8 Cu + 19 Zn	29·17 + 70·83	866·6	8·019	C	Silver grey, 1	0·7	0	21	7	5	Ditto
18	8 Cu + 20 Zn	28·12 + 71·88	898·8	7·603	V	Ash grey, 3	3·2	0	19	3	5	Brittle.
19	8 Cu + 21 Zn	27·10 + 72·90	931·1	8·058	C	Silver grey, 2	0·9	0	18	9	5	Ditto
20	8 Cu + 22 Zn	26·24 + 73·76	936·4	7·882	C	Ditto 1	0·8	0	20	8	5	Very brittle
21	8 Cu + 23 Zn	25·39 + 74·61	995·7	7·443	FC	Ash grey, 4	5·9	0	15	1	5	Barely malleable.
22	Cu + 3 Zn	24·50 + 75·50	128·5	7·449	FC	Ditto 1	3·1	0	16	2	4	Brittle.
23	Cu + 4 Zn	19·65 · 80·36	160·8	7·371	FC	Ditto 2	1·9	0	14	4	3	White button metal.
24	Cu + 5 Zn	16·36 · 83·64	193·1	6·605	FC	Very dark grey,	1·8	0	17	11	2	Brittle.
25	+	0 + 100·00	32·3	6·895	TC	Bluish grey	15·2	13	12	23	1	Brittle zinc.

[1] E, signifies earthy; CC, coarse crystalline; FC, fine crystalline; FF, fine fibrous; C, conchoidal; V, vitreous; VC, vitreo-conchoidal; TC, tabular crystalline.

Elsner analysed a malleable brass, and found it to contain 61·16 copper and 39·71 zinc. These numbers approximate to the composition Cu^3Zn^2 (59·4 per cent. copper and 40·6 zinc).—*Liebig and Kopp's Report.*

The alloy noticed in the preceding paragraphs is identical with that known as 'Muntz's patent sheathing' (see table on preceding page).

The chief properties of value in brass, are its colour, hardness (which is superior to that of copper), and power of taking delicate impressions when cast in a mould.

The malleability of brass varies greatly with its chemical composition, and with the temperature at which it is worked. As a rule, the malleability diminishes with the increase in the quantity of zinc.

The effect of the admixture of foreign metals on brass is somewhat similar to that produced by them in copper. Antimony is most injurious, as it renders the metal brittle and liable to crack at the edges in rolling.

Lead also has a hardening effect on brass, and is useful for all work that requires to be turned or filed; as the addition of about two per cent. causes the turnings to break short, and thus prevents the tool from becoming clogged. The same effect is produced in brass for engraving by the addition of a small quantity of tin.

Brass is apt to undergo a gradual molecular change, especially if subjected to vibration, and thus becomes extremely brittle. Hence, it happens that brass chains used for suspending heavy objects, like chandeliers, occasionally snap without any external violence.

Thin sheet brass may be readily stamped into shape, and in this way ornamental brass objects are now extensively made: the sheet brass being subjected to heavy blows delivered by steel dies. The metal requires, however, to be frequently annealed during the stamping, and the film of oxide which is formed on the surface by the annealing, requires to be removed by dipping in aquafortis; the objects are then washed with water, and lacquered. By varying the strength of the aquafortis, the colour of the brass may be considerably modified.

The surface of brass work requires to be protected from the action of the air, by a coating of a less oxidisable metal, or a resinous varnish or lacquer. The metal is first brought up to a clean face by the process of 'dipping' or immersion into weak nitric acid, whereby the adherent scale or oxide formed during annealing is removed. By varying the strength of the acid employed, and repeating the dipping, the metal may be made to assume a 'matt,' dead, or frosted appearance. After dipping, the metal is washed in water, and dried by imbedding it in hot sawdust. The lacquer, which is an alcoholic solution of shellac, more or less coloured with dragon's blood, according to the tint desired in the finished work, is brushed over the article when in a heated state, and dried over a stove. The colour in the lacquer helps to produce a higher or more golden tint than that due to the metal alone.

Brass work is bronzed in several different ways: the most usual are, immersion in a solution of arsenious acid, in hydrochloric acid, or in bichloride of platinum. The former is chiefly employed for cheap work, such as common gas fittings, while the latter is used for blacking or bronzing telescopes, mathematical instruments, and similar fine work. The effect, in either case, is the production of a film of dark coloured metal on the surface of the brass, namely, arsenic in the former, and platinum in the latter case. This operation is performed after dipping, and before lacquering.

Another method now extensively used, is to apply a coating of a solution of corrosive sublimate (bichloride of mercury) in water, mixed with vinegar. A film of mercury is thus formed on the surface of the brass.

For the method of covering brass with a film of tin, see PIN MANUFACTURE.

BRASS FOIL. Dutch leaf, called *Knitter* or *Rauschgold* in Germany, is made from a very thin sheet brass, beat out under a hammer worked by water-power, which gives from 300 to 400 strokes per minute, from 40 to 80 leaves being laid over each other. By this treatment it may be reduced to leaves not more than $\frac{1}{50000}$th of an inch thick. The metal employed is one rich in copper.

BRASS, YELLOW. The following Table exhibits the composition of several varieties of this species of brass. No. 1 is a cast brass of uncertain origin; 2, the brass of Jemappes; 3, the sheet brass of Stolberg, near Aix-la-Chapelle; 4 and 5, the brass for gilding, according to D'Arcet; 6, the sheet brass of Romilly; 7, English brass wire; 8, Augsberg brass wire; 9, Brass wire of Neustadt-Eberswald, in the neighbourhood of Berlin:—

	1	2	3	4	5	6	7	8	9
Copper .	61·6	64·6	64·8	63·70	64·45	70·1	70·29	71·89	70·16
Zinc . .	35·3	33·7	32·8	33·55	32·44	29·9	29·26	27·63	27·45
Lead . .	2·9	1·4	2·0	0·25	2·86	...	0·28	...	0·20
Tin . .	0·2	0·2	0·4	2·50	0·25	...	0·17	0·85	0·79
	100·0	99·9	100·0	100·00	100·00	...	100·00	100·37	98·60

Tombak, or Red Brass, in the cast state, is an alloy of copper and zinc, containing not more than 20 per cent. of the latter constituent. The following varieties are distinguished :—1, 2, 3, tombak for making gilt articles ; 4, French tombak for sword-handles, &c. ; 5, tombak of the Okar, near Goslar, in the Hartz ; 6, yellow tombak of Paris, for gilt ornaments ; 7, tombak for the same purpose from a factory in Hanover ; 8, chrysochalk ; 9, red tombak from Paris ; 10, red tombak of Vienna.

	1	2	3	4	5	6	7	8	9	10
Copper .	82·0	82	82·3	80	85	85·3	86	90·0	92	97·8
Zinc . .	18·0	18	1·75	17	15	14·7	14	7·9	8	2·2
Lead . .	1·5	3	...	...	...	...	...	1·6		
Tin . .	3·0	1	0·2	3	trace	...	...			
	104·5	104	100·0	100	100	100·0	100	99·5	100	100·0

Mr. Holtzapffel, in his 'Mechanical Manipulation,' has given some very important descriptions of alloys. From his long experience in manufacture, no one was more capable than Mr. Holtzapffel to speak with authority on the alloys of copper and zinc ; and from his work, the following particulars have been obtained :—

The red colour of copper slides into that of yellow brass at about 4 or 5 ounces of zinc to the pound of copper, and remains little altered unto about 8 or 10 ounces ; after this it becomes whiter, and when 32 ounces of zinc are added to 16 of copper, the mixture has the brilliant silvery colour of speculum metal, but with a bluish tint.

The alloys—from about 8 to 16 ounces to the pound of copper—are extensively used for dipping, a process adopted for giving a fine colour to an enormous variety of furniture work. The alloys with zinc retain their malleability and ductility well unto about 8 or 10 ounces to the pound ; after this the crystalline character slowly begins to prevail. The alloy of 2 zinc and 1 copper may be crumbled in a mortar when cold. In the following list, the quantity of zinc employed to 1 lb. of copper is given :—

1 to 1½ oz. gilding metal for common jewellery.
3 to 4 oz. Bath metal, pinchbeck, Mannheim gold, Similor ; and alloys bearing various names, and resembling inferior jewellers' gold.
8 oz. Emerson's patent brass.
10⅖ oz. Muntz's metal, or 40 zinc and 60 copper. 'Any proportions,' says the patentee, 'between the extremes, 50 zinc and 50 copper and 37 zinc and 63 copper, will roll and work well at a red heat.'
16 oz. soft spelter solder, suitable for ordinary brass work.
16½ oz. Hamilton and Parker's patent mosaic gold.

Brass is extensively employed for the bearings of machinery. Several patents have been taken out for compositions varying but slightly. The following, for improvements in casting the bearings and brasses of machinery, appears important :—Mr. W. Hewitson, of Leeds, directs, in his patent, that the proper mixture of alloy, copper, tin, and zinc, should be run into metal or 'chill' moulds, in place of the ordinary moulds. In large castings, it is found more especially that the metals do not mix intimately in cooling, or, rather, they arrange themselves into groups when cast in sand, and the bearings are found to wear out more quickly ; but if the bearings are cast so that the alloy comes in contact with metal, the mixture is more intimate, and the bearings last longer than if cast in dry or green sand moulds.

Mr. Hewitson generally only applies these chill-metal surfaces of the moulds to those parts of a brass, or bearing, that are to receive the shaft or bear the axis of a machine. The chills are preferred of iron, perforated with holes ($\frac{1}{16}$th to $\frac{1}{8}$th inch) for the passage of air or vapours; the surface should be thinly coated with loam, and heated to about 200°.

Fenton's patent metal consists of copper, spelter, and tin: it has less specific gravity than gun-metal, and is described as being 'of a more soapy nature,' by which, consequently, the consumption of oil or grease is lessened.

Many of the patentees of bearing metals assure us, that the metals they now use differ very considerably from the statement in their specifications. Surely this requires a careful examination.

We *exported* of our BRASS MANUFACTURES, in 1864, as follows :—

	Cwts.	£
Brass wire of all sorts, and manufactures of wire	10,950	54,648
Brass tubing	8,077	41,554
Wrought brass of all other sorts, not being ordnance, and not otherwise described	23,646	137,811

In the same year we *imported* :—

	Cwts.	£
Brass manufactures, unenumerated	4,643	49,802
Brass, old, fit only to be re-manufactured	3,085	6,325

BRASS COLOUR, for staining glass, is prepared by exposing for several days thin plates of brass upon tiles in the *leer*, or annealing arch, of the glass house, till they are oxidised into a black powder, aggregated in lumps. This being pulverised and sifted, is to be again well calcined for several days more, till no particles remain in the metallic state, when it will form a fine powder of a russet-brown colour. A third calcination must now be given with a carefully regulated heat, its quality being tested from time to time by fusion with some glass. If it makes the glass swell and intumesce, it is properly prepared; if not, it must be still further calcined. Such a powder communicates to glass greens of various tints, passing into turquoise.

When thin narrow strips of brass are stratified with sulphur in a crucible, and calcined at a red heat, they become friable and may be reduced to powder. This being sifted and exposed upon tiles in a reverberatory furnace for 10 or 12 days, becomes fit for use, and is capable of imparting a chalcedony—red or yellow—tinge to glass by fusion, according to the mode and proportion of using it.

The glassmakers' red colour may be prepared by holding small plates of brass in a moderate heat in a reverberatory furnace till they are thoroughly calcined. When the substance becomes pulverulent, and assumes a red colour, it is ready for immediate use.

Brass colour, as employed by the colourmen to imitate brass, is of two tints—the red or bronze, and the yellow, like gilt brass. Copper filings mixed with red ochre, or bole, constitute the former; a powdered brass, imported from Germany, is used for the latter. Both must be worked up with varnish after being dried by heat, and then spread flat with a camel-hair brush evenly upon the surface of the object. The best varnish is composed of 20 ounces of spirits of wine, 2 ounces of shellac, and 2 ounces of sandarach, properly dissolved. (See VARNISH.) Only so much of the brass powder and varnish should be mixed at a time as is wanted for immediate use. See BRONZE POWDER.

BRASSES, COAL, or **BRASS OF COAL,** or **BRASSEY COAL.** Names given to iron pyrites found in the coal-measures. In 1872 it was estimated that the following quantities were produced and used :—

NORTHUMBERLAND and DURHAM	.	.	.	3,250 tons.
YORKSHIRE	.	.	.	.	.	3,700 ,,
LANCASHIRE	.	.	.	.	.	2,400 ,,
STAFFORDSHIRE	.	.	.	.	.	3,700 ,,

These sulphur ores are employed in Yorkshire, Lancashire, and on the Tyne, in the manufacture of the protosulphate of iron (copperas.) For this purpose they are extended in wide-spread heaps, and thus exposed to atmospheric influences. The result is the conversion of the sulphur into sulphuric acid, which re-uniting with the iron forms the sulphate of the protoxide of iron, which is dissolved out and crystallised. The presence of iron pyrites in coal (Brasses), often gives the tendency to spontaneous combustion. A large number of the ships which are sent from South Wales to Chili, with coals, which are used for smelting the copper ores of that country, take fire when they reach the tropics. This arises mainly from carelessness. In the first place, the coals are not carefully selected. They are bought cheaply, and being small, are put on board the ships, without being washed or picked, and frequently damp. During the voyage, decomposition goes on, and by the time they reach the warmer latitudes, a temperature sufficiently high to occasion actual combustion is produced. By carefully washing the coal and drying it, these casualties might be almost entirely prevented. BRASS is a name given to an iron ore found in the coal-measures of South Wales, which is not a pyritic ore, although for a long period mistaken for it. See COAL BRASS.

BRASSIL. A name given to iron pyrites in Derbyshire, 'a hard substance, and fiery, but yields no metal.'—Hodson, *Complete Derbyshire Miner.*

BRASSING IRON. Iron ornaments are covered with copper or brass by properly preparing the surface, so as to remove all organic matter, which would prevent adhesion, and then plunging them into melted brass. A thin coating is thus spread over the iron, and it admits of being polished or burnished. The electro-magnetic process is now employed for the purpose of precipitating brass on iron. This process was first mentioned in Shaw's 'Metallurgy,' in 1844, where he remarks: 'In depositing copper upon iron, a solution of the cyanide or acetate of copper should be employed. The only value of these salts is, that the surface of iron may be immersed in their solutions without receiving injury by the corrosion consequent upon the deposition of a film of metal by chemical action.' The following solutions are recommended by Dr. Woods, in the 'Scientific American,' for coating iron with copper, zinc, or brass, by the electrotype process:—

To make a *Solution of Copper or Zinc.*—Dissolve 8 ounces (troy) cyanide of potassium and 3 ounces of cyanide of copper or zinc in 1 gallon of rain or distilled water. These solutions to be used at about 160° F. with a compound battery of from 3 to 12 cells.

To prepare a *Solution of Brass.*—Dissolve 1 lb. (troy) cyanide of potassium, 2 ounces of cyanide of copper, and 1 ounce of cyanide of zinc, in one gallon of rain or distilled water; then add two ounces of muriate of ammonia. This solution is to be used at 160° F. for smooth work, and from 90° to 120°, with a compound battery of from 3 to 12 cells. See ELECTRO-METALLURGY.

BRATTICE. The division made in a shaft of a colliery is so called. It is used to ensure an up and a down-cast current of air. Brattices may be also used in any of the levels for the same purpose. They may be of metal, of wood, or tarred canvas. Mining engineers speak of a *natural brattice*, i.e. one independent of any artificial arrangement—when the currents separate naturally in a shaft or a level—and thus produce a natural ventilation.

BRAUNITE. A sesquioxide of manganese, composed when pure of nearly 70 per cent. of manganese, and 30 per cent. of oxygen.

BRAZILIAN ARROWROOT. See ARROWROOT.

BRAZIL NUTS. The hard-shelled fruit of the *Bertholletia excelsa*, which is roundish and about six inches in diameter, contains about two dozen of the elongated wrinkled triangular seeds—these are the 'nuts' of the shops. See PARA NUTS.

BRAZIL WOOD. (*Bois de Pernambouc*, Fr.; *Brasilienholz*, Ger.) This dye-wood gives its name to the part of America whence it was first imported. It has also the names of Pernambuca, Wood of St. Martha, and of Sapan, according to the places which produce it. Linnæus distinguishes the tree which furnishes the Brazil wood by the name of *Cæsalpinia crista*. It commonly grows in dry places among rocks. Its trunk is very large, crooked, and full of knots. It is very hard, susceptible of a fine polish, and sinks in water. It is pale when newly cleft, but becomes red on exposure to the air. The following is a very exact description of the tree producing this wood:—

The *ibiripitanga*, or Brazil wood, called, in Pernambuco, *pao da rainha* (Queen's wood), on account of its being a Government monopoly, is now rarely to be seen within many leagues of the coast, owing to the improvident manner in which it has been cut down by the Government agents, without any regard being paid to the size of the tree or its cultivation. It is not a lofty tree. At a short distance from the ground, innumerable branches spring forth and extend in every direction in a straggling, irregular, and unpleasing manner. The leaves are small and not luxuriant; the wood is very hard and heavy, takes a high polish, and sinks in water; the only valuable portion of it is the heart, as the outward coat of wood has not any peculiarity. The name of this wood is derived from *brasas*, a glowing fire or coal; its botanical name is *Cæsalpinia Brasileto*. The leaves are pinnated, the flower white and papilionaceous, growing in a pyramidal spike: one species has flowers variegated with red. The branches are slender and full of small prickles. There are nine species. See Bell's 'Geography.'

The species *Brasileto*, which is inferior to the *crista*, grows in great abundance in the West Indies. The demand for the *Brasileto*, a few years ago, was so great, owing to its being a little cheaper than the *crista*, that nearly the whole of the trees in the British possessions were cut down and sent home, which Mr. Bell very justly terms improvidence. It is not now so much used, and is consequently scarcer in the English market.

The wood known in commerce as *Pernambuco* is most esteemed, and has the greatest quantity of colouring matter. It is hard, has a yellow colour when newly cut, but turns red by exposure to the air. That kind termed *Lima wood* is the same in quality. *Sapan wood* grows in Japan, and in quality is next the two named above. It is not plentiful, but is much valued in the dyehouse for red of a certain tint; it gives a very clear and superior colour. The quantity of ash that these two qualities of wood contain is worthy of remark. Lima wood, as imported, gives the average of 2·7 per cent., while Sapan wood gives 1·5 per cent.; in both, the prevailing earth is lime. The quantity of moisture in the wood averages about 10 per cent.; that in the ground wood in the market about 20 per cent.

Sapan wood is yielded by *Cæsalpinia Sapan*, and Lima wood by *C. echinata*.

Brazil wood has different shades of red and orange. Its goodness is determined particularly by its density. When chewed, a saccharine taste is perceived. It may be distinguished from red saunders wood by its colouring water, which the latter does not.

BRAZIL WOOD DYES. Boiling water extracts the whole colouring matter of Brazil wood, and if the ebullition be long enough continued, it assumes a fine red colour. The residuum appears black. In this case an alkali may still extract much colouring matter. The solution in alcohol or ammonia is still deeper than the preceding.

The decoction of Brazil wood, called juice of Brazil, is observed to be less fit for dyeing when recent than when old, or even fermented. By age it takes a yellowish-red colour. For making this decoction, Hellot recommends the use of the hardest water; but it should be remarked that this water deepens the colour in proportion to the *earthy* salts which it contains. After boiling this wood reduced to chips, or, what is preferable, to powder, for three hours, this first decoction is poured into a cask. Fresh water is poured on the wood, which is then made to boil for three hours, and mixed with the former. When Brazil wood is employed in a dyeing bath, it is proper to enclose it in a thin linen bag.

Wool immersed in the juice of Brazil wood takes but a feeble tint, which is speedily destroyed; it must therefore receive some preliminary preparations.

The wool is to be boiled in a solution of alum, to which a fourth or even less of tartar is added, for a larger proportion of tartar would make the colour yellowish. The wool is kept impregnated with it, for at least eight days, in a cool place. After this, it is dyed with the Brazil juice with a slight boiling. But the first colouring particles that are deposited afford a less beautiful colour; hence it is proper to pass a coarser stuff previously through the bath. In this manner a lively red is procured, which resists pretty well the action of the air.

Brazil wood is made use of for dyeing silk the colour known as false crimson, to distinguish it from the crimson made by means of cochineal, which is much more permanent.

The silk should be boiled at the rate of 20 parts of soap per cent., and then alumed. The aluming need not be so strong as for the fine crimson. The silk is refreshed at the river, and passed through a bath more or less charged with Brazil juice, according to the shade to be given. When water free from earthy salts is employed, the colour is too red to imitate crimson; this quality is given it by passing the silk through a slight alkaline solution, or by adding a little alkali to the bath. It might, indeed, be washed in a hard water till it had taken the desired shade. They thus become permanent colours. But what distinguishes them from madder and kermes, and approximates them to cochineal, is their re-appearing in their natural colour, when they are thrown down in a state of combination with alumina, or with oxide of tin. These two combinations seem to be the fittest for rendering them durable. It is requisite, therefore, to enquire what circumstances are best calculated to promote the formation of these combinations according to the nature of the stuff.

The astringent principle, likewise, seems to contribute to the permanence of the colouring matter of Brazil wood; but it deepens its hue, and can only be employed for light shades.

To make deeper false crimsons, a dark red juice of logwood is put into the Brazil bath after the silk has been impregnated with it. A little alkali may be added, according to the shade that is wanted.

To imitate poppy or flame colour, an arnotto ground is given to the silk, deeper even than when it is dyed with carthamus; it is then washed, alumed, and dyed with juice of Brazil, to which a little soap water is usually added.

The colouring particles of Brazil wood are easily affected and made yellow by the action of acids.

The colouring particles of Brazil wood are also very sensible to the action of alkalis, which give them a purple hue; and there are several processes in which the alkalis, either fixed or volatile, are used for forming violets and purples. But the colours obtained by these methods, which may be easily varied according to the purpose, are perishable, and possess but a transient bloom. The alkalis appear not to injure the colours derived from madder, but they accelerate the destruction of most other colours.

In England and Holland the wood-dyes are reduced to powder by means of mills erected for the purpose.

The bright fugitive red, called fancy red, is given to cotton of Nicaragua, or peach wood, a cheap kind of Brazil wood. See PEACH WOOD.

The cotton being scoured and bleached, is boiled with sumach. It is then impregnated with a solution of tin (at 5° B., according to Vitalis). It should now be washed slightly in a weak bath of the dyeing wood; and, lastly, worked in a somewhat stale infusion of the peach or Brazil wood. When the temperature of this is lukewarm, the dye is said to take better. Sometimes two successive immersions in the bath are given. It is now wrung out, aired, washed in water, and dried.

M. Vitalis says, that his solution of tin is prepared with two ounces of tin and a pound of aqua regia, made with two parts of nitric acid at 24° B. and three parts of muriatic acid at 22°.

For a rose colour, the cotton is alumed as usual, and washed from the alum. It then gets the tin mordant, and is again washed. It is now turned through the dye-bath, an operation which is repeated if necessary.

For purple, a little alum is added to the Brazil bath.

1. For amaranth, the cotton is strongly galled, dried, and washed.

2. It is passed through the black cask (tonneau noir), till it has taken a strong grey shade. See BLACK DYE.

3. It receives a bath of lime water.

4. Mordant of tin.

5. Dyeing in the Brazil wood bath.

6. The last two operations are repeated.

Dingler has endeavoured to separate the colouring matter of the different sorts of Brazil wood, so as to obtain the same tint from the coarser as from the best Pernambuco. His process consists in treating the wood with hot water or steam, in concentrating the decoction so as to obtain 14 or 15 pounds of it from 4 pounds of wood, allowing it to cool, and pouring into it two pounds of skim milk; agitating, then boiling for a few minutes, and filtering. The dun colouring matters are precipitated by the coagulation of the caseous substance. For dyeing, the decoctions must be diluted with water; for printing, they must be concentrated so that 4 pounds of wood shall furnish only 5 or 6 pounds of decoction, and the liquor may be thickened in the ordinary way. These decoctions may be employed immediately, as by this treatment they have acquired the same property as they otherwise could get only by being long kept. A slight fermentation is said to improve the colour of these decoctions; some ground wood is put into the decoction to favour this process.

Gall-nuts, however, sumach, the bark of birch or alder, renders the colour of Brazil wood more durable upon alumed linen and cotton goods, but the shade is a little darker.

In dyeing wool with Pernambuco Brazil wood, the temperature of the bath should never be above 150° F., since higher heats impair the colour.

According to Dingler and Kurrer, bright and fast scarlet reds may be obtained upon wool, by preparing a decoction of 50 pounds of Brazil wood in three successive boils, and setting the decoction aside for 3 or 4 weeks in a cool place; 100 pounds of the wool are then alumed in a bath of 22 pounds of alum and 11 pounds of tartar, and afterwards rinsed in cold water. Meanwhile, we fill two-thirds with water a copper containing 30 pails, and heated to the temperature of 150° or 160° F. We pour in 3 pailfuls of the decoction, heat to the same point again, and introduce 30 pounds of wool, which does not take a scarlet, but rather a crimson tint. This being removed, 2 pails of decoction are put in, and 30 pounds of wool, which becomes scarlet, but not so fine as at the third dip. If the dyer strengthens the colour a little at the first dip, a little more at the second, and adds at the third and fourth the quantity of decoction merely necessary, he will obtain an uniform scarlet tint. With 50 pounds of Pernambuco, 1,000 pounds of wool may be dyed scarlet in this way, and with the deposits another 100 may be dyed of a tile colour. An addition of weld renders the colour faster, but less brilliant. See WELD.

Karkutsch says the dye may be improved by adding some ox-gall to the bath.

In dyeing cotton, the tannin and gallic acid are two necessary mordants; and the colour is particularly bright and durable when the cloth has been prepared with the oily process of Turkey red.

It is said that stale urine heightens the colour of Brazil dye when the ground wood is moistened with it.

Chevreul obtained the colouring matter from Brazil wood in the following manner : Digest the raspings of the wood in water till all the colouring matter is dissolved, and evaporate the infusion to dryness, to get rid of a little acetic acid which it contains. Dissolve the residue in water, and agitate the solution with litharge, to get rid of a little fixed acid. Evaporate again to dryness; digest the residue in alcohol; filter and evaporate, to drive off the alcohol. Dilute the residual matter with water, and add to the liquid a solution of glue, till all the tannin which it contains is thrown down ; filter again, and evaporate to dryness, and digest the residue in alcohol, which will leave undissolved any excess of glue which may have been added. The last alcoholic solution, being evaporated to dryness, leaves *brazilin*, the colouring matter of the wood, in a state of considerable purity.

BRAZIL. A term given to a hard coal, approaching Anthracite in character, in South Staffordshire.

BRAZILIN and **BRAZILIEN** are two colouring matters which have been separated from Brazil wood, by Chevreul and Preisser. They are probably identical. See Watts's 'Dictionary of Chemistry.'

BRAZING. See SOLDERS and SOLDERING.

BREAD. One of the most important, if not altogether the most important, article of food, unquestionably, is bread; and although rye, barley, oats, and other cereals, are sometimes used by the baker, *wheat* is the grain which is best fitted for the manufacture of that article, not only on account of the larger amount of gluten, or nitrogenous matter, which it contains, and than can be found in other edible grains, but also on account of the almost exact balance in which the nitrogenous and nonnitrogenous constituents exist in that cereal, and owing to which it is capable of ministering to all the requirements of the human frame, and of being assimilated at once and without effort by our organs, whence the name of 'staff of life,' which is often given to it, wheat being, like milk, a perfect food.

Although gluten is one of the most important constituents of wheat, the nutritive power of its flour, and its value as a bread-making material, should not be altogether considered as dependent upon the quantity of gluten it may contain, even though it be of the best quality. Doubtless a high per-centage of this material is desirable, but there are other considerations which must be taken into account; for, in order to become available for making good bread, flour, in addition to being sound and genuine, must possess other qualities beyond containing merely a large amount of gluten. Thus, for example, the *blé rouge glacé d'Auvergne*, which contains hardly 45 per cent. of starch, and as much as 36 per cent. of gluten, though admirably adapted for the manufacture of macaroni, vermicelli, semolina, and other *pâtes d'Italie*, is totally unfit for making good bread ; the flour used for making best white loaves containing only from 13 to 18 per cent. of gluten, and from 60 to 70 per cent. of starch.

Bread is obtained by baking a dough, previously fermented either by an admixture of yeast or leaven, or it is artificially rendered spongy by causing an acid, muriatic or tartaric, to react upon carbonate or bicarbonate of soda, or of ammonia, mixed in the doughy mass ; or, is in Dr. Dauglish's process, which will be described further on, by mixing the flour which has to be converted into dough, not with ordinary water, but with water strongly impregnated with carbonic acid.

Although a history of bread making cannot be given in the present article, a few words on the subject, reproduced from a former edition of this work, will not be deemed uninteresting.

Pliny informs us, that barley was the only species of corn at first used for food ; and even after the method of reducing it to flour had been discovered, it was long before mankind learned the art of converting it into cakes.

Ovens were first invented in the East. Their construction was understood by the Jews, the Greeks, and the Asiatics, among whom baking was practised as a distinct profession. In this art, the Cappadocians, Lydians, and Phœnicians, are said to have particularly excelled. It was not till about 580 years after the foundation of Rome that these artisans passed into Europe. The Roman armies, on their return from Macedonia, brought Grecian bakers with them into Italy. As these bakers had handmills besides their ovens, they still continued to be called *pistores*, from the ancient practice of bruising the corn in a mortar ; and their bakehouses were denominated *pistoriæ*. In the time of Augustus there were no fewer than 329 public bakehouses in Rome ; almost the whole of which were in the hands of Greeks, who long continued the only persons in that city acquainted with the art of baking good bread.

In nothing, perhaps, is the wise and cautious policy of the Roman government more remarkably displayed than in the regulations which it imposed on the bakers within the city. To the foreign bakers who came to Rome with the army from Macedonia, a number of freedmen were associated, forming together an incorporation from which neither they nor their children could separate, and of which even those who married the daughters of bakers were obliged to become members. To this incorporation were entrusted all the mills, utensils, slaves, animals, everything, in short, which belonged to the former bakehouses. In addition to these, they received considerable portions of land; and nothing was withheld which could assist them in pursuing, to the best advantage, their highly prized labours and trade. The practice of condemning criminals and slaves, for petty offences, to work in the bakehouse, was still continued; and even the judges of Africa were bound to send thither, every five years, such persons as had incurred that kind of chastisement. The bakehouses were distributed throughout the fourteen divisions of the city, and no baker could pass from one into another without special permission. The public granaries were committed to their care; they paid nothing for the corn employed in baking bread that was to be given in largess to the citizens; and the price of the rest was regulated by the magistrates. No corn was given out of these granaries except for the bakehouses, and for the private use of the prince. The bakers had besides private granaries, in which they deposited the grain which they had taken from the public granaries for immediate use; and if any of them happened to be convicted of having diverted any portion of the grain to another purpose, he was condemned to a ruinous fine of five hundred pounds' weight of gold.

Most of these regulations were soon introduced among the Gauls; but it was long before they found their way into the more northern countries of Europe. Borrichius informs us that in Sweden and Norway, the only bread known, so late as the middle of the 16th century, was unleaven cakes kneaded by the women. At what period in our own history the art of baking became a separate profession, we have not been able to ascertain; but this profession is now common to all the countries in Europe, and the process of baking is also nearly the same.

The French, who particularly excel in the art of baking, have a great many different kinds of bread. Their *pain bis*, or brown bread, is the coarsest kind of all, and is made of coarse groats mixed with a portion of white flour. The *pain de méteil* is a bread made with rye and barley flour, to which wheat flour is sometimes added also. The *pain bis blanc*, is a kind of bread between white and brown, made of white flour and fine groats. The *pain blanc*, or white bread, is made of white flour, shaken through a sieve after the finest flour has been separated. The *pain mollet*, or soft bread, is made of the purest flour without any admixture. The *pain chaland*, or customers' bread, is a very white kind of bread, made of pounded paste. *Pain chapelé*, is a small kind of bread, with a well-beaten and very light paste, with butter or milk. This name is also given to a small bread, from which the thickest crust has been removed by a rasp. *Pain cornu* is a name given by the French bakers to a kind of bread made with four corners, and sometimes more. Of all the kinds of small bread this has the strongest and firmest paste. *Pain à la reine*, queen's bread, *pain à la Ségovie, pain chapelé*, and *pain cornu*, are all small kinds of bread, differing only in the lightness or thickness of the paste. *Pain de gruau* is a small very white bread made now in Paris, from the flour separated after a slight grinding from the best wheat. Such flour is in hard granular particles.

In England, however, we have but few varieties of bread, the loaves known under the names of *bricks, Coburg, cottage,* and *French rolls*, being all made of the same dough; the only difference is in the *shape* given to them, their various flavours depending on the way in which they are affected by the heat of the oven in the baking. These loaves are crusted all over because they are deposited in the oven separate from each other, or baked in moulds made of tinned iron. The *batch* bread, the more usual variety, is crusted only at the top and bottom, because the loaves, which have a cubic form, touch each other in the oven; those, however, which lie round the oven have a crust on three of their sides. The cottage and French rolls are *generally* made of best flour,—known under the name of *whites*;—but batch bread is made of best flour and of *households*, or flour of second quality, and of *seconds*, which is flour of a third quality—that is, of flour containing more bran than the other kinds just enumerated.

We have also 'rye bread,' which is generally made of nothing else than ordinary wheat flour and bran.

Dr. Ure, in the former edition of this Dictionary, truly remarked, ' The object of baking is to combine the gluten and starch of the flour into a homogeneous substance, and to excite such a vinous fermentative action, by means of its saccharine matter, as shall disengage abundance of carbonic acid gas in it for making an agreeable, soft, succulent, spongy, and easily digestible bread. The two evils to be avoided in baking are, hardness on the one hand and pastiness on the other. Well-made bread is a chemical compound, in which the gluten and starch cannot be recognised or separated, as before, by a stream of water. When flour is kneaded into a dough, and spread into a cake, this cake, when baked, will be horny if it be thin, or if thick, will be tough and clammy; whence we see the value of that fermentative process, which generates thousands of little cells in the mass or crumb, each of them dry yet tender and succulent through the intimate combination of the moisture. By this constitution it becomes easily soluble in the juices of the stomach, or, in other words, light of digestion. It is, moreover, much less liable to turn sour than cakes made from unfermented dough.

'Rye, which also forms a true spongy bread, though inferior to that of wheat, consists of similar ingredients—namely, 61·07 of starch, 9·48 of gluten, 3·28 of vegetable albumen, 3·23 of uncrystallisable sugar, 11·09 of gum, 6·38 of vegetable fibre; the loss upon the 100 parts amounted to 5·62, including an acid whose nature the analyst M. Einhof, did not determine. Rye flour contains also several salts, principally the phosphates of lime and magnesia. This kind of grain forms a dark coloured bread, reckoned very wholesome; comparatively little used in this country, but very much in France, Germany, and Belgium.

'Dough, fermented with the aid either of leaven or yeast, contains little or none of the saccharine matter of the flour, but, in its stead, a certain portion, nearly half its weight, of spirit, which imparts to it a vinous smell, and is volatilised in the oven, whence it might be condensed into a crude, weak alcohol, on the plan of Mr. Hick's patent, were it worth while. But the increased complexity of the baking apparatus will probably prove an effectual obstacle to the commercial success of this project, upon which a few years ago upwards of 20,000l. sterling were foolishly squandered.

'That the sugar of the flour is the true element of the fermentation which dough undergoes, and that the starch and gluten have nothing to do with it, may be proved by decisive experiments. The vinous fermentation continues till the whole sugar is decomposed, and no longer; when, if the process be not checked by the heat of baking, the acetous fermentation will supervene. Therefore, if a little sugar be added to a flour which contains little or none, its dough will become susceptible of fermenting, with extrication of gas, so as to make spongy succulent bread. But since this sponginess is produced solely by the extrication of gas and its expansion in the heat of the oven, any substance capable of emitting gas, or of being converted into it under these circumstances, will answer the same purpose. Were a solution of bicarbonate of ammonia obtained by exposing the common sesquicarbonate in powder for a day to the air, incorporated with the dough, in the subsequent firing it will be converted into vapour, and, in its extrication, render the bread very porous. Nay, if water highly impregnated with carbonic acid gas be used for kneading the dough, the resulting bread will be somewhat spongy. Could a light article of food be prepared in this way, then, as the sugar would remain undecomposed, the bread would be so much the sweeter and the more nourishing. How far a change propitious to digestion takes place in the constitution of the starch and gluten during the fermentative action of the dough has not been hitherto ascertained by precise experiments.

'Dr. Colquhoun, in his able essay upon the art of making bread, has shown that its texture, when prepared by a sudden formation and disengagement of elastic fluid generated within the oven, differs remarkably from that of a loaf which has been made after the preparatory fermentation with yeast. Bread which has been raised with the common carbonate of ammonia, as used by the pastrycooks, is porous no doubt, but not spongy with vesicular spaces, like that made in the ordinary way. The former kind of bread never presents that air-cell stratification which is the boast of the Parisian baker, but which is almost unknown in London. It is, moreover, very difficult to expel by the oven the last portion of the ammonia, which gives both a tinge and a taste to the bread. The bicarbonate would probably be free from this objection, which operates so much against the use of the sesquicarbonate.'—*Ure.*

The conversion of flour into bread includes two distinct operations: namely, the preparation of the dough and the baking. The preparation of the dough, however, though reckoned as one, consists, in fact, of three operations: namely, *hydrating, kneading,* and *fermenting.*

When the baker intends to make a batch of bread, his first care is, in technical language, *to stir a ferment.* This is done, in London, by boiling a few potatoes, in the proportion of 5 lbs. or 6 lbs. of potatoes per sack of flour (which is the quantity we shall assume it is desired to convert into bread), peeling them, mashing and straining them through a cullender, and adding thereto about three-quarters of a pailful of water, 2 or 3 lbs. of flour, and one quart of yeast. The water employed need not be warmed beforehand, for the heat of the potatoes is sufficient to impart a proper temperature (from 70° to 90° F.) to the liquid mass, which should be well stirred up with the hand into a smooth, thin, and homogeneous paste, and then left at rest.

In the course of an hour or two, the mass is seen to rise and fall, which swelling and heaving up is due to carbonic acid, generated by the fermentation induced in the mass, which may be thus left until wanted. In about three hours, this fermenting action will appear to be at an end, and when it has arrived at that stage, it is fit to be used. The ferment, however, may be left for six or seven hours and be still very good at the end of that time, but the common practice is to use it within four or five hours after its preparation. After this the ferment rapidly becomes sour.

The next operation consists in '*setting the sponge.*' This consists in stirring the ferment well, adding thereto about two gallons of lukewarm water, and as much flour as will make, with the ferment, a rather stiff dough. This constitutes '*the sponge.*' It is kept in a warm situation, and in the course of about an hour fermentation again begins to make its appearance, the mass becomes distended or is heaved up by the carbonic acid produced, the escape of which is impeded by the toughness of the mass. This carbonic acid is the result of the fermentation induced under the influence of water, by the action of the gluten upon the starch, a portion of which is converted thereby into sugar, and then into alcohol. A time, however, soon comes when the quantity of carbonic acid thus pent up becomes so great that it bursts through, and the sponge collapses or drops down. This is called the *first sponge.*—But as the fermentation is still going on, the carbonic acid soon causes the sponge to rise again as before to nearly twice its volume, when the carbonic acid, bursting through the mass, causes it to fall a second time; and this constitutes what the bakers call the *second sponge.* The rising and falling might then go on for twenty-four hours; but as the alcoholic would pass into the acetous fermentation soon after the second rising, the baker always interferes after the second, and very frequently after the first sponge. The bread made from the first sponge is generally sweeter; but unless the best flour is used, and even then, the loaf that is made from it is smaller in size and more compact than that which is made with the *second sponge.* In hot weather, however, as there would be much danger of the bread turning sour, if the sponge were allowed to '*take a second fall,*' the first sponge is frequently used. The next process consists in '*breaking the sponge,*' which is done by adding to it the necessary quantity of water and of salt,—the quantity of the latter substance varying from $\frac{1}{2}$ lb. to $\frac{3}{4}$ of a pound per bushel of flour; that is, from $2\frac{1}{4}$ lbs. to $3\frac{3}{4}$ lbs. per sack of flour (new flour, or flour of inferior quality, always requires, at the very least, $3\frac{1}{4}$ lbs. per sack, *to bind it*, that is to say, to render the dough sufficiently firm to support itself while fermenting.) Salt acts, to a great extent, like alum, though not so powerfully. As to the quantity of water to be used, it depends also a great deal on the quality of the flour, the best quality absorbing most; though, as we shall have occasion to remark, the baker too often contrives to force and keep into bread made from inferior flour, by a process called *under baking*, the same amount of water as is normally taken up by that of the best quality. Generally speaking, and with flour of good average quality, the amount of water is such, that the diluted sponge forms about 14 gallons of liquid. The whole mass is then torn to pieces by the hand, so as to break any lumps that there may be, and mix it up thoroughly with the water. This being done, the rest of the sack of flour is gradually added and kneaded into a dough of the proper consistency. This kneading of the dough may be said to be one of the most important processes of the manufacture, since it not only produces a more complete hydration of the flour, but, by imprisoning a certain quantity of air within the dough, and forcibly bringing into closer contact the molecules of the yeast or leaven with the sugar of the flour, and also with a portion of the starch, the fermentation or rising of the whole mass, on which the sponginess of the loaf and its digestibility subsequently depend, is secured. When by forcing the hand into the dough, the baker sees that, on withdrawing it, none of the dough adheres to it, he knows that the kneading is completed. The dough is then allowed to remain in the trough for about an hour and a half or two hours, if either *brewers'* or *German yeast* have been employed in making the sponge;—if, on the contrary, *patent yeast* or *hop yeast* have been used, three or even four hours may be required for the dough to rise up, or, as in technical language, *to give proof.* When the dough is sufficiently '*proofed,*' it is weighed of into lumps, shaped into the proper forms of 4 lbs. 4 oz. each, and exposed for about one hour in an oven to a temperature of about 570° F., the heat gradually falling to 430 or 420° F. The yield after baking is 94 quartern (not 4-lb.) loaves, or from 90 to 92 really 4lb. loaves, as large again as they were when put into the oven in the shape of dough.

The manner in which yeast acts upon the flour—is, as yet, an unsolved mystery, or at any rate an, as yet, unsatisfactorily explained action; for the term 'catalysis,' which has sometimes been applied to it, explains absolutely nothing.

A yeast, or fermenting material, may be prepared in various ways; but only three kinds of yeast are used by bakers: namely, brewers' yeast, or barm,—German yeast, —and patent, or hop yeast.

The most active of these ferments is the first, or brewers' yeast; it is, as is well known, a frothy, thickish material, of a brownish or drab colour, which, when recent, is in a state of slight effervescence, exhales a sour characteristic odour, and has an acid reaction.

When viewed through the microscope, it is seen to consist of small globules of various size, generally egg-shaped. They were first described by M. Desmayières.

The best, and in fact the only, brewers' yeast used in bread-making is that from the ale breweries ; porter yeast is unavailable for the purpose, because it imparts to the bread a disagreeable bitter taste.

German yeast is very extensively used by bakers. It is a pasty but easily crumbled mass, of an agreeable fruity odour, and of a dingy white colour. German yeast will remain good for a few weeks, if kept in a cool place. When in good condition, it is an excellent article ; but samples of it are occasionally seized on bakers' premises, of a darker colour, viscid, and emitting an offensive cheesy odour : such German yeast, being in a putrefied state, is, of course, objectionable.

The so-called '*patent yeast*' is the cheapest and at the same time the weakest of these ferments ; very good bread, however, is made with it, and it is most extensively used by bakers. It is made either with or without hops : when with hops, it is called *hop yeast*, and is nothing more than a decoction of hops to which malt is added while in a scalding hot state ; when the liquor has fallen to a blood heat, a certain quantity of brewers' or German yeast is thoroughly mixed with it, and the whole is left at rest. The use of the hops is intended to diminish the tendency of this solution to become acid.

Potato yeast is a kind of '*patent yeast*' in general use. See YEAST.

The theory of panification is not difficult of comprehension. 'The flour,' says Dr. Ure, 'owes this valuable quality to the gluten, which it contains in greater abundance than any of the other *cerealia* (kinds of corn). This substance does not constitute, as has been heretofore imagined, the membranes of the tissue of the perisperm of the wheat ; but is enclosed in cells of that tissue under the epidermic coats, even to the centre of the grain. In this respect the gluten lies in a situation analogous to that of the starch, and of most of the immediate principles of the vegetables. The other immediate principles which play a part in *panification* are particularly the starch and the sugar ; and they all operate as follows :—

'The diffusion of the flour through the water *hydrates* the starch, and dissolves the sugar, the albumen, and some other soluble matters. The kneading of the dough, by completing these reactions through a more intimate union, favours also the fermentation of the sugar, by bringing its particles into close contact with those of the leaven or yeast ; and the drawing out and laminating the dough softens and stratifies it, introducing at the same time oxygen to aid the fermentation. The dough, when distributed and formed into loaves, is kept some time in a gentle warmth, in the folds of the cloth, pans, &c., a circumstance propitious to the development of their volume by fermentation. The dimensions of all the lumps of dough now gradually enlarge, from the disengagement of carbonic acid in the decomposition of the sugar, which gas is imprisoned by the glutinous paste. Were these phenomena to continue too long, the dough would become too vesicular ; they must, therefore, be stopped at the proper point of sponginess, by placing the loaf lumps in the oven. Though this causes a sudden expansion of the enclosed gaseous globules, it puts an end to the fermentation, and to their growth ; as also evaporates a portion of the water.

'The fermentation of a small dose of sugar is, therefore, essential to true bread making ; but the quantity actually fermented is so small as to be almost inappreciable. It seems probable that in well-made dough the whole carbonic acid that is generated remains in it, amounting to one-half the volume of the loaf itself at its baking temperature, or 212° F. It thence results that less than one-hundredth part of the weight of the flour is all the sugar requisite to produce well-raised bread.

'Although the rising of the dough is determined by the carbonic acid resulting from the decomposition of the sugar, produced by the reaction of the gluten on hydrated or moist flour, considering that the quantity of sugar necessary to produce fermentation does not amount, probably, to more than one-hundredth part of the weight of the flour employed, and perhaps to even considerably less than that,—the saving and economy which are said to accrue to the consumer from the use of unfermented bread (which is bread in which the action of yeast is replaced by an artificial evolution of carbonic acid, by decomposing bicarbonate of soda with muriatic acid, as we said before) is therefore much below what it has been estimated (25 per cent. !) by some writers ; and is certainly very far from compensating for the various and serious drawbacks which are peculiar to that kind of bread, one of which—and it is not the least—is its indigestibility, notwithstanding all that may have been said to the contrary.

'In a pamphlet, entitled, "Instructions for making Unfermented Bread, by a Physician," published in 1846, the formula recommended for bread made of wheat meal is as follows:—

Wheat meal	3 lbs. avoirdupois.
Bicarbonate of soda . .	4⅓ drachms troy.
Hydrochloric acid. . .	5 fluid drachms and 25 minims, or drops.
Water	30 fluid ounces.
Salt	⅔ of an ounce troy.

'Bread made in this manner,' says the author, 'contains nothing but flour, common salt, and water. It has an agreeable, natural taste, keeps much longer than common bread, is *much more digestible*, and much less disposed to turn acid,' &c.

Liebig, in his 'Letters on Chemistry,' very judiciously remarks, 'that the intimate mixture of the saliva with the bread, whilst masticating it, is a condition which is favourable to the rapid digestion of the starch; wherefore the porous state of the flour in fermented bread accelerates its digestion.'

Now, it is a fact, which can be readily ascertained by anyone, that unfermented bread is permeated by fluids with difficulty. It will not absorb water, hence its heavy and clammy feel; nor saliva, hence its indigestibleness; nor milk, nor butter. Unfermented bread will neither make soup, nor toast, nor poultice. When a slice of ordinary bread is held before a bright fire, a portion of the moisture of the bread, as the latter becomes scorched, is converted into steam, which penetrates the interior of the mass, and imparts to it the sponginess so well known in a toast properly made; but if a piece of unfermented bread be treated in the same manner, the steam produced by the moisture, not being able to penetrate the unabsorbent mass, evaporates, and the result is an uninviting slice, toasted, but hard inside and out, and into which butter penetrates about to the same extent as it would a wooden slab of the same dimensions.

'Fermentation,' says Liebig, 'is not only the best and simplest, but likewise the most economical way of imparting porosity to bread; and besides, *chemists, generally speaking, should never recommend the use of chemicals for culinary preparations,* for chemicals are seldom met with in commerce in a state of purity. Thus, for example, the muriatic acid which it has been proposed to mix with carbonate of soda in bread is *always very impure,* and *very often contains arsenic.* Chemists never employ such an acid in operations which are certainly less important than the one just mentioned, without having first purified it.'

In order to remove this ground of objection, tartaric acid has been recommended instead of muriatic acid for the purpose of decomposing the carbonate of soda; but in that way, another unsafe compound is introduced, since the result of the reaction is tartrate of soda, a diuretic aperient, and consequently very objectionable salt, for it is impossible to say what mischief the continuous ingestion of such a substance may eventually produce; and whatever may be the divergence of opinion,—if there be such a divergence,—as to whether or not the constant use of an aperient, however mild, may be detrimental to health, it surely must be admitted that, at any rate, it is better to eschew such, to say the least of it, suspicious materials; and that, at any rate, if deprecating their use be an error, it is an error on the safe side;—after all, a bakehouse is not a chemical laboratory.

Before leaving this question of unfermented bread, we must not omit to speak of a remarkable process invented by Dr. Dauglish, and which has lately excited some attention. Without discussing the value of the idea which is said to have led Dr. Dauglish to invent the process in question, we shall simply describe Dr. Dauglish's method of making bread, and give his own version of its benefits :—

'Taking advantage of the well-known capacity of water for absorbing carbonic acid, whatever its density, in quantities equal to its own bulk, I first prepare the water which is to be used in forming the dough, by placing it in a strong vessel capable of bearing a high pressure, and forcing carbonic acid into it to the extent of say ten or twelve atmospheres' (about 150 to 180 lbs. per square inch); 'this the water absorbs without any appreciable increase in its bulk. The water so prepared will of course retain the carbonic acid in solution so long as it is retained in a close vessel under the same pressure. I therefore place the *flour and salt,* of which the dough is to be formed, also in a close vessel capable of bearing a high pressure. Within this vessel, which is of a spheroidal form, a simply-constructed kneading apparatus is fitted, worked from without through a closely-packed stuffing box. Into this vessel I force an equal pressure to that which is maintained on the aërated water-vessel; and then, by means of a pipe connecting the two vessels, I draw the water into the flour, and set the kneading apparatus to work at the same time. By this arrangement the water acts simply as limpid water among the flour, the flour and water are mixed and kneaded together into paste, and to such an extent as shall give it the necessary *tenacity*. After this is accomplished the pressure is released, the gas escapes from the water, and in doing so raises the dough in the most beautiful and expeditious manner. It will be quite unnecessary for me to point out how perfect must be the *mechanical* structure that results from this method of raising dough. In the first place, the mixing and kneading of the flour and water together, before any vesicular property is imparted to the mass, render the most complete incorporation of the flour and water a matter of very easy accomplishment; and this being secured, it is evident that the gas which forms the vesicle, or sponge, when it is released, must be dispersed through the mass in a manner which no other method—fermentation not excepted—could accomplish. But besides the advantages of kneading the dough before the vesicle is formed, in the manner above mentioned, there is another, and perhaps a more important one, from what it is likely to effect by giving scope to the introduction of new materials into bread making,—and that is, I find that powerful machine-kneading, continued for several minutes, has the effect of imparting to the dough tenacity or toughness. In Messrs. Carr and Co.'s machine, at Carlisle, we have kneaded some wheaten dough for half an hour, and the result has been that the dough has been so tough, that it resembled birdlime, and it was with difficulty pulled to pieces with the hand. Other materials, such as rye, barley, &c. are affected in the same manner. So that by thus kneading, I am able to impart to dough made from materials which otherwise would not make light bread, from their wanting that quality in their gluten which is capable of holding or retaining, the same degree of lightness which no other method is capable of effecting. And I am sanguine of being able to make from rye, barley, oatmeal, and other wholesome and nutritious substances, bread as light and sweet as the finest wheaten bread. One reason why my process makes a bread so different from all other processes where fermentation is not followed is, that I am enabled to knead the bread to any extent without spoiling its vesicular property; whilst all other unfermented breads are merely *mixed*, not kneaded. The property thus imparted to my bread by kneading, renders it less dependent on being placed immediately in the oven. It certainly cannot *gain* by being allowed to stand after the dough is formed, but it bears well the necessary standing and waiting required for preparing the loaves for baking.

'There is one point which requires care in my process, and that is,—the *baking*: as the dough is excessively cold; first, because *cold* water is used in the process; and next, because of its sudden expansion on rising. It is thus placed in the oven some 40° Fahr. in temperature lower than the ordinary fermented bread. This, together with its slow springing until it reaches the boiling point, renders it essential that the *top* crust shall not be formed until the very last moment. Thus, I have been obliged to have ovens constructed which are heated through the bottom, and are furnished with the means of regulating the heat of the top, so that the bread is *cooked through the bottom;* and, just at the last, the top heat is put on and the top crust formed.

'With regard to the *gain* effected by saving the loss by fermentation, I may state what must be evident, that the weight of the dough is always exactly the sum of the weight of flour, water, and salt put into the mixing vessel: and that, in all our experiments at Carlisle, we invariably made 118 loaves from the same weight of flour which by fermentation made only 105 and 106. Our advantage in gain over fermentation can only be equal to the *loss* by fermentation. As there has been considerable difference of opinion among men of science with respect to the amount of this loss—some stating it to be as high as 17½ per cent., and others so low as 1 per cent.— I will here say a few words on the subject. Those who have stated the loss to be as high as 17½ per cent. have, in support of their position, pointed to the extra yield from the same flour of bread when made by non-fermentation, compared with that made by fermentation. Whilst those who have opposed this assertion, and stated the loss to be but 1 per cent. or little more, have declared the gain in weight to be simply a gain of extra water, and have based their calculations of loss on the destruction of material caused by the generation of the necessary quantity of carbonic acid to render the bread light. Starting then with the assumption that light bread contains in bulk half solid matter and half aëriform, they have calculated that this quantity of aëriform matter is obtained by a destruction of but *one* per cent. of solid material. In this calculation the loss of carbonic acid, by its escape through the mass of dough during the process of fermentation and manufacture, does not appear to have been taken into account. All who have been in any way practically connected with bakeries well know how large this loss is, and how important it is that it should be taken into account, that our calculations may be correct.

'One of the strongest proofs that the escape of gas through ordinary soft bread dough is very large arises from the fact, that when biscuit dough, in which there is a mixture of fatty matter, is prepared by my process, about half the quantity of gas only is needed to obtain an equal amount of *lightness* with dough that is made of flour and water only, the fatty matter acting to prevent the escape of gas from the dough. Other matters will operate in a similar manner—boiled flour, for instance, added in small quantities. But the assumption that light bread is only half aëriform matter is altogether erroneous. Never before has there been so complete a method of testing what proportion the aëriform bears to the solid in light bread as that which my process affords. The mixing vessel at Messrs. Carr and Co.'s works, Carlisle, has an internal capacity of ten bushels. When $3\frac{1}{2}$ bushels of flour are put into this vessel, and formed into spongy bread dough, by my process, it is quite full. And when flour is mixed with water into paste, the paste measures rather less than half the bulk of the original dry flour. This will, therefore, represent about $1\frac{3}{4}$ bushel of *solid* matter expanded into 10 bushels of spongy dough, showing in the *dough* nearly 5 *parts aëriform* to 1 solid; and in all instances, if the baking of this dough has not been accomplished so as to secure the loaves to 'spring' to at least *double* their size in the oven, they have always come out heavy bread when compared with the ordinary fermented loaves. This gives the relative proportion of aëriform to solid in light bread at least as 10 to 1, and at once raises the loss by fermentation from 1 to 10 per cent., without taking into account the loss of gas by its passage through the mass of dough.

'Of the quality and properties of the bread manufactured by my process, there will shortly be ample means of judging. I may be allowed, however, here to state, what will be evident to all, that the absence of everything but flour, water, and salt, must render it absolutely pure;—that its sweetness cannot be equalled, except by bread to which sweet materials are superadded;—that, unlike all other unfermented bread, it makes excellent toast; and, on account of its high absorbent power, it makes the most delicious sop puddings, &c., and also excellent poultice. Sop pudding and poultice made from this bread, however, differ somewhat from those made from fermented bread, in being somewhat richer or more glutinous. This arises from the fact of the gluten not having been changed, or rendered soluble, in the manner caused by fermentation; but that this is a good quality rather than a bad one is evident from the fact, that the richer and purer fermented bread is, the more glutinous are the sop, &c., made from it; and the poorer and more adulterated with alum it is, the freer the sop, &c., are of this quality.'

Such then is Dr. Dauglish's plan; and it is impossible to deny that it possesses great ingenuity.

From the fact that, in all his experiments at Carlisle, Dr. Dauglish invariably made 118 loaves from the same weight of flour which, by fermentation, made only 105 or 106, to argue that the *gain over fermentation* can only be equal *to the loss by fermentation*, is to draw a somewhat hasty conclusion; for the gain may be, and is probably due, not to the preservation in the bread of what is generally lost by fermentation, but simply to a retention of water.

It is of course certain that the production of the porosity required in bread produced by the carbonic acid and alcohol evolved by fermentation, entails the loss of a portion of the valuable constituents of the flour, but the amount of that loss should not be estimated, I think, from the proportions which the aëriform bear to the solid matter of the loaf *after it is baked*.

In effect, the fermentation induced in bread differs from that produced at the distillery, in as much as, instead of the fermenting material being sheltered from the air by an atmosphere of carbonic acid, the dough is on the contrary thoroughly permeated by, and retains a considerable quantity of atmospheric air introduced into it by the kneading process, and owing to the presence of which, in fact, the acetous fermentation is carried on to a certain extent, within the dough, simultaneously with the alcoholic fermentations, so that even the 10 parts of aëriform matter to 1 of solid matter in a quartern loaf, are not altogether carbonic acid resulting from the fermentation, but are carbonic acid from that source mixed with the atmospheric air with which the dough is permeated. On the other hand, the aëriform matter thus imprisoned in the dough, expands to at least twice its volume when exposed to the temperature of the oven, and accordingly the bread after breaking becomes as bulky again as the dough from which it was made, and this doubling of the volume being due to the expansion of the gases, and not to the fermentation, bears no proportion whatever to the amount of the sugar of the flour employed in the production of the alcohol and carbonic acid evolved. Moreover, as a quartern loaf, for example, measures about 9 inches by 6·5 inches by 5 inches, making a total of about 292 cubic inches, if we take nine-tenths of that to be aëriform matter, we have 262·8 inches as the aëriform cubic contents of the quartern loaf.

It is ascertained beyond doubt by numerous experiments, that genuine, properly manufactured new bread contains, on an average, 42·5 per cent. of water, and 57·5 of flour, and consequently a quartern loaf weighing really four pounds, would consist of 11,900 grains of water and 16,000 grains of solid matter, 422·5 grains of which are salt and inorganic matter, the rest, 15677·5 grains, being starch and gluten. Now a quartern loaf measuring about 9 × 6·5 × 5 inches gives a total of 292 cubic inches. Assuming with Dr. Dauglish, nine-tenths of that to be aëriform matter, we have 262·8 inches of aëriform cubic contents of a quartern loaf, but as the gases expanded in the dough to double their volume during its being baked into a loaf, we must divide by 2 the 262·8 inches above alluded to, which gives 131·4 as the number of cubic inches of aëriform matter contained in the dough before it went into the oven. Again, assuming with Dr. Dauglish that these 131·4 cubic inches consist altogether of carbonic acid resulting from the fermentation of the flour, they would represent in weight only 62 grains of that gas, and as 1 equivalent = 198 of sugar produces 4 equivalents = 88 of carbonic acid, it follows that, at most, about 140 grains of sugar or solid matter out of the 15677·5 of flour in the quartern loaf would have disappeared, which loss is less than 1 per cent., from which, however, it is necessary to make a considerable reduction, since a large quantity of air is mixed with that carbonic acid, and expanded with it in the oven. Unless, therefore, it can be satisfactorily proved that the unfermented bread manufactured by Dr. Dauglish's process is more nutritious, weight for weight, or more digestible, or possesses qualities which unfermented bread has not, or is sold at a reduced price proportionate to the quantity of water thus locked up and passed off for bread, the benefits and advantages will be all on the manufacturer's side, but the purchasers of the unfermented bread will make but a poor bargain of it.

Of all the operations connected with the manufacture of bread, the most laborious, and that which calls most loudly for reform, is that of kneading. The process is usually carried on in some dark corner of a cellar, where the temperature is seldom less than 60° F., and frequently more, by a man, stripped naked down to the waist, and painfully engaged in extricating his fingers from a gluey mass into which he furiously plunges alternately his clenched fists, heavily breathing as he, struggling, repeatedly lifts up the bulky and tenacious mass in his powerful arms, and with effort flings it down again with a groan fetched from the innermost recesses of his chest, and which almost sounds like an imprecation.

We know, on very good and unexceptionable authority, that a certain large bakery on the borders of a canal actually pumped the water necessary for making the dough directly and at once from the canal, and this from a point exactly contiguous to the dischargings of the cesspool of that bakery! And let us not imagine that this is a solitary instance of horrible filth. The following memoranda recorded by Dr. Wm. A. Guy, in his admirable lecture on 'The Evils of Night-work and Long Hours of Labour,' delivered on Thursday, July 6, 1848, at the Mechanics' Institution, South-ampton Buildings, will serve to illustrate the condition of the bakehouses:—

1. Underground, two ovens, no daylight, no ventilation, very hot and sulphurous.
2. Underground, no daylight, two ovens, very hot and sulphurous, low ceiling, no ventilation but what comes from the doors. Very large business.
3. Underground, no daylight, often flooded, very bad smells, overrun with rats, no ventilation.

After mentioning several other establishments in the same, or even in a worse, condition than those just enumerated, Dr. Guy adds:

'The statements comprised in the foregoing memoranda are in conformity with my own observations. Many of the basements in which the business of baking are carried on are certainly in a state to require the assistance of the Commissioners of Sewers, and to invite the attention of the promoters of sanitary reform.'

If we reflect that bread, like all porous substances, readily absorbs the air that surrounds it, and that, even under the best conditions, it should never, on that account, be kept in confined places, what must be the state of the bread manufactured in such a villanous manner, and with a slovenliness greater than it is possible for our imagination to conceive? What can prove better the necessity of Government supervision than such a fact? The heart sickens at the revolting thought, but after all there is really but little difference between the particular case of the bakery on the border of a canal above alluded to, and the mode of kneading generally pursued, and to which we daily submit.

In the sitting of the Institute of France, on the 23rd of January, 1850, the late M. Arago presented and recommended to the Académie the kneading and baking apparatus of M. Rolland, then a humble baker of the 12th Arrondissement, which, it would appear, fulfils all the conditions of perfect kneading and baking.

'The kneading machine (*pétrin mécanique*) of M. Rolland,' says Arago, 'is extremely simple, and can be easily worked, when under a full charge, by a young man from 15 to 20 years old: the necessity for horse-labour or steam-power may thus be obviated. The machine (*figs.* 217 to 220) consists of a horizontal axis traversing a trough, containing all the dough requisite for one baking batch, and upon which axis a system of curvilinear blades, alternately long and short, are placed in such a manner that, while revolving, they describe two quarters of cylindrical surfaces with contrary curves, so that the convexity of one of these surfaces, and the concavity of the other, is turned towards the bottom of the trough. The axis has a fly-wheel, and is set in motion by two small cog-wheels connected with the handle, as represented in the following figures :—

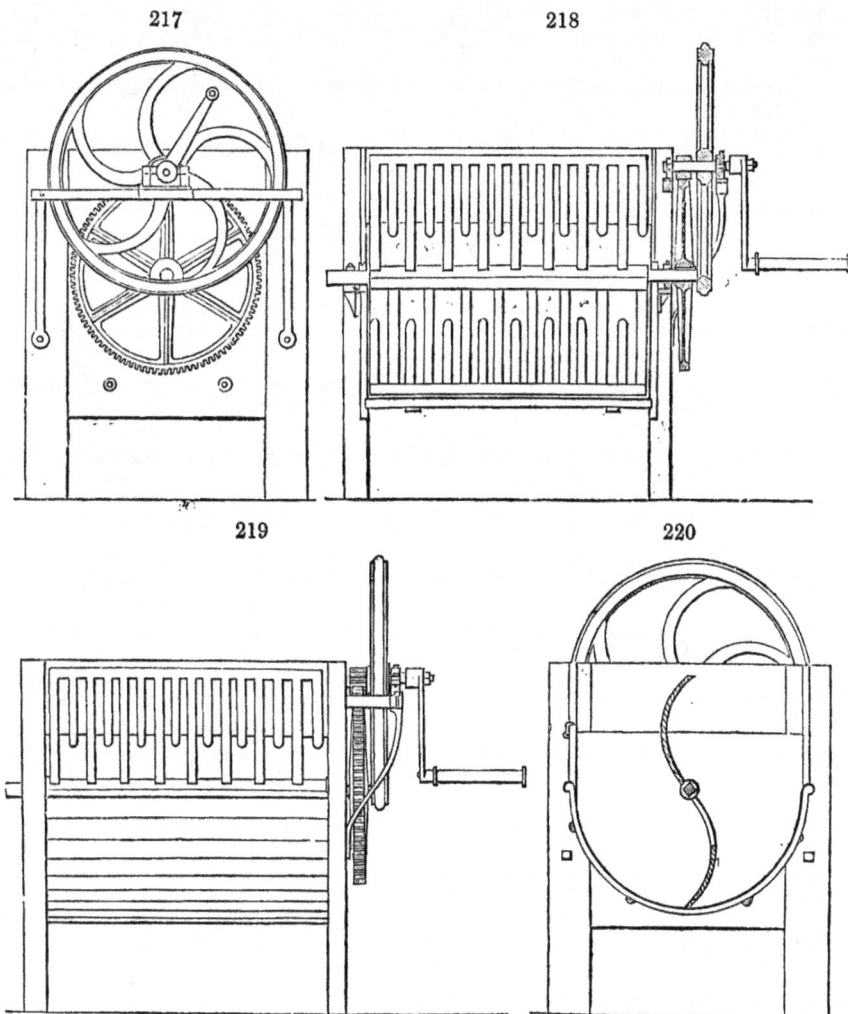

217   218

219   220

The action of the kneading machine is both easy and efficacious. In 20, and if necessary in 15, or even 10 minutes, a sack of flour may be converted into a perfectly homogeneous and aërated dough, without either lumps or clods, and altogether superior to any dough than could be obtained by manual kneading. The time required in kneading varies according to the greater or less density of dough required; and the quantity of dough manufactured in that space of time varies, of course, also with the dimensions of the kneading-trough; for instance, in the trough provided with 16 blades, one sack and a half of flour can be kneaded at once; in that of 14 blades one sack, and in that of 12 blades two-thirds of a sack.

M. Rolland gives the following instructions for the use of the machine, in order to impart to the dough the qualities produced by the operations known in France under the names of *frasage*, *contrefrasage*, and *soufflage*, which we shall presently describe, and to which the bread manufactured in that country mainly owes, in the words of Dr. Ure, 'a flavour, colour, and texture, never yet equalled in London.'

The necessary quantity of leaven or yeast is first diluted with the proper quantity of water, as described before; and in order to effect the mixture, the crank should be made to perform 50 revolutions alternately from right to left.—*Frasage* is the first mixture of the flour with the water. The flour is simply poured into the kneading-trough, or, better still, when convenience permits it, it is let down from a room above through a linen hose, which may be shut by folding it up at the extremity.

Three-fourths only of the flour should at first be put into the trough; the first revolutions of the kneader should be rather rapid, but during the remainder of the operation the turning should be at the rate of two or three revolutions a minute, according to the density of the dough to be prepared. The dough thereby having time to be well drawn out between the blades, and to drop to the bottom of the trough. From 24 to 36 revolutions of the crank will generally be sufficient; but in order to obtain the dough in the condition which the *frasage* would give it in the usual way, it will be necessary to make about 250 revolutions of the crank alternately from right to left, about the same number of turns.

Contrefrasage is the completion of the process of mixing; and, in order to perform that operation, the last fourth part of the flour must now be added, the crank turned 150 revolutions, to wit, 75 turns rather slowly, alternately from right to left, and the remainder at the rate of speed above mentioned.

The operation of *Soufflage* consists in introducing and retaining air in the paste. To effect this, the kneader should be made to perform, during nearly the whole time occupied in the operation, an almost continuous motion backwards and forwards, by which means the dough is shifted from place to place; five revolutions being made to the right, and five to the left, alternately, taking care to accelerate the speed a little at the moment of reversing the direction of the revolving blades.

All these operations are accomplished in twenty or twenty-five minutes.

Of course, the reader should not imagine that these numbers must be strictly followed, they are given merely as a guide indicative of the *modus operandi*.

The kneading being completed, the dough is left to rest for some time, and then divided into lumps, of a proper weight, for each loaf. The workman takes one of these lumps in each hand, rolls them out, dusts them over with a little flour, and puts each of them separate in its *panneton;* he proceeds with the rest of the dough in the same manner, and leaves all the lumps to swell, which, if the flour have been of good quality, will take place at a uniform rate. They are then fit for baking, which operation will be described presently.

Another kneading trough, said to be very effectual, is that for which Mr. Edwin Clayton obtained a patent in August 1830. It consists of a rotatory kneading trough, or rather barrel, mounted in bearings with a hollow axle, and of an interior frame of cast iron made to revolve by a solid axle which passes through the hollow one; in the frame there are cutters diagonally placed for kneading the dough. The revolving frame and its barrel are made to turn in contrary directions, so as greatly to save time and equalise the operation. This double action represents kneading by the two hands, in which the dough is inverted from time to time, torn asunder, and reunited in every different form. The mechanism will be readily understood from the following description:—

Fig. 221 exhibits a front elevation of a rotatory kneading trough, constructed

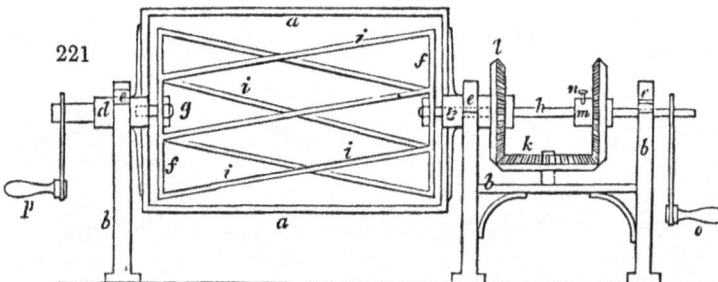

according to improvements specified by the patentee, the barrel being shown in section; *a* is the barrel, into which the several ingredients, consisting of flour, water, and yeast, are put, which barrel is mounted in the frame-work *b*, with hollow axles *c* and *d*, which hollow axles turn in suitable bearings at *e*; *f* is the revolving frame which is mounted in the interior of the barrel *a*, by axles *g* and *h*. The ends of this revolving frame are fastened or braced together by means of the oblique cutters or braces *i*, which act upon the dough when the machine is put in motion, and thus cause the operation of kneading.

Either the barrel may be made to revolve without the rotatory frame, or the rotatory frame without the barrel, or both may be made to revolve together, but in opposite ways. These several motions may be obtained by means of the gear-work, shown at k, l, and m, as will be presently described.

If it be desired to have the revolving motion of the barrel and rotatory frame together, but in contrary directions, that motion may be obtained by fastening the hollow axle of the wheel m, by means of a screw n, to the axle h of the rotatory frame f tight, so as they will revolve together, the other wheels k and l being used for the purpose of reversing the motion of the barrel. It will then be found that by turning the handle o, the two motions will be obtained.

If it be desired to put the rotatory frame f, only into motion, that action will be obtained by loosening the screw n upon the axle of the wheel m, when it will be found that the axle h will be made to revolve freely by means of the winch o, without giving motion to the wheels k, l, and m, and thus the barrel will remain stationary. If the rotatory action of the barrel be wanted, it will be obtained by turning the handle p, at the reverse end of the machine, which, although it puts the gear at the opposite end of the barrel into motion, yet as the hollow axle of the wheel m is not fastened to the axle h by the screw n, these wheels will revolve without carrying round the frame f.

The Hot-water Oven Biscuit-baking Company possesses also a good machine with which 1 cwt. of biscuit dough, or 2 cwts. of bread dough, can be perfectly kneaded in

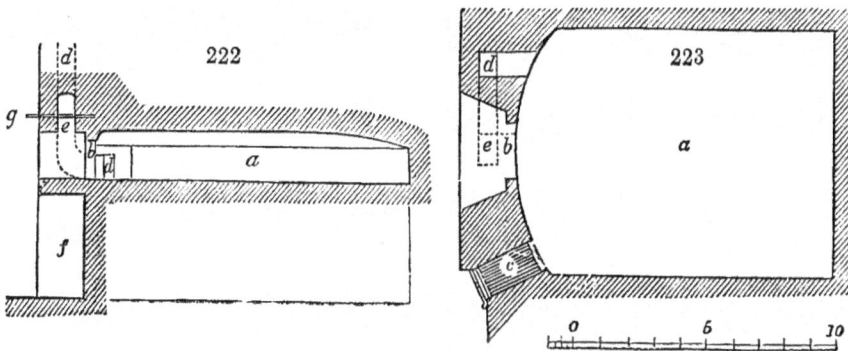

10 minutes. The machine is an American invention, and of extraordinary simplicity, for it is in reality nothing more than a large corkscrew, working in a cylinder, by means of which the dough is triturated, squeezed, pressed, torn, hacked, and finally agglomerated as it is pushed along. The dough as it issues from that machine can at once be shaped into loaves of suitable size and dimensions. A machine capable of doing the amount of work alluded to does not come to more than from 6l. to 7l.; the other forms of kneading machines are likewise inexpensive, so that, in addition to the economy of time which they realise, there does not seem to be any excuse for retaining the abomination of manual kneading.

Among superior and very desirable apparatus for bread-making, there are at any rate three which fulfil the desiderata above alluded to, in the most complete and economical manner. One of them is M. Mouchot's aërothermal bakery; the second is A. M. Perkins' hot-water oven; the third is Rolland's hot-air oven, with revolving floors: all three are excellent.

Before proceeding to explain them, a plan and longitudinal section of an ordinary London baker's oven is given (*figs.* 222 and 223), that the reader may be the better able to judge of the vast improvement realised by the other ovens.

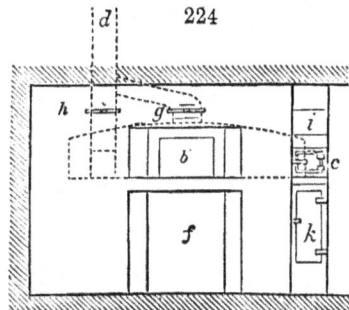

a, the body of the oven; b, the door; c, the fire-grate and furnace; d, the smoke flue; e, the flue above the door, to carry off the steam and hot air, when taking out the bread; f, recess below the door, for receiving the dust; g, damper plate to shut off the steam flue; h, damper plate to shut off smoke flue, after the oven has come to its proper heat; i, a small iron pan over the fire-place c, for heating water; k, ash-pit below the furnace.

Fig. 224 is the front view; the same letters refer to the same object in all the figures.

The flame and burnt air of the fire at *c*, sweeping along the bottom of the oven by the right-hand side, are reflected from the back to the left-hand side, and thence escape by the flue *d*. Whenever the oven has acquired the proper degree of heat, the fire is withdrawn, the flues are closed by the damper plate, and the lumps of fermented dough are introduced.

225

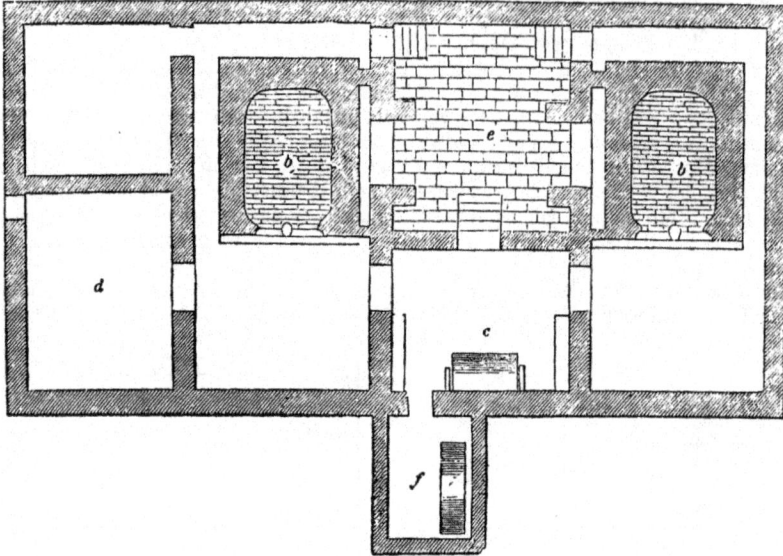

We shall now give a description not only of the oven, but of the improved bakery, *boulangerie perfectionée*, of M. Mouchot.

Fig. 225 is a ground plan of the aërothermal bakehouse : the granaries being in the upper storeys, are not shown here. *b b* are the ovens ; *c*, the kneading machine ; *d*, the place where the machinery is mounted for hoisting up the bread into the store

226

room above ; *e*, a space common to the two ovens, into which the hot air passes ; *f*, the place of a wheel driven by dogs, for giving motion to the kneading machine.

Fig. 226 is a longitudinal section of the oven ; *a*, the grate where coke or even pit-coals may be burned ; *b b*, void spaces which, becoming heated, serve for warming small pieces of dough in ; *c c* are flues for conducting the smoke, &c., from the fire-place ; D, seen in *fig.* 227 (a transverse section through the middle of the oven), is the chimney for carrying off the smoke transmitted by the flues ; E E, void spaces immediately over the flues, and beneath the sole F F, of the oven. By this arrangement the air, previously heated, which arrives from the void spaces B through the flues *c o*,

227

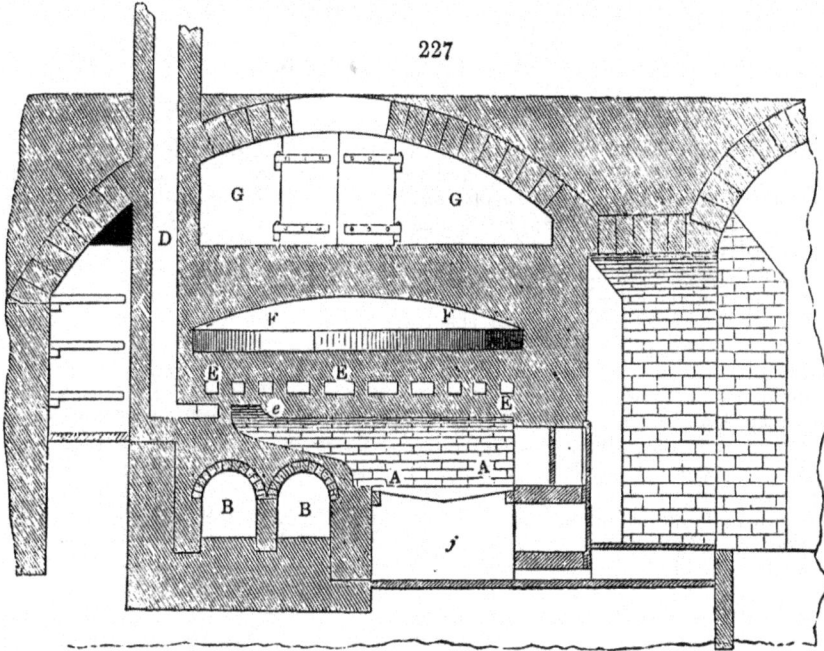

gets the benefit of the heat of the flame which circulates in these flues, and, after getting more heated in the spaces E E, ascends through channels into the oven F F, upon the sole of which the loaves are to be baked or laid. The hot air is admitted into it through the passages *a a*, being drawn from the reservoirs B B B, and also by the passage *d d*, drawn from the reservoirs E E. The sole is likewise heated by contact with the hot air contained in the space E E, placed immediately below it. The hot air, loaded with moisture, issues by the passage *b b*, and returns directly into the reservoir B B. G G, an enclosed space directly over the oven, to obstruct the dissipation of its heat; *g*, vault of the fire-place. *Fig.* 228, the kneading machine, a longitudinal section passing through its axis; P P, the contour of the machine, made of wood, and divided into three compartments for the reception of the dough. The wooden bars *o o* are so placed in the interior of the compartments, as to divide the dough whenever the cylinder is made to revolve. One portion, D, of the cylinder may be opened and laid over upon the other by means of a hinge joint, when the dough and flour are introduced. A, B, C, the three compartments of the machine, two for making the dough, and one for preparing the sponge, called *levain*, or leaven, by the French. *a a* is the pulley which receives its motion from the engine, and transmits it to the cylinder through the pinion *b*, and the spur-wheel *e*; *d d*, the fly-wheel to regulate the motion; *g*, a brake to act upon the fly *d*, by means of a lever *h*; *i*, the pillar of the fly-wheel.

228

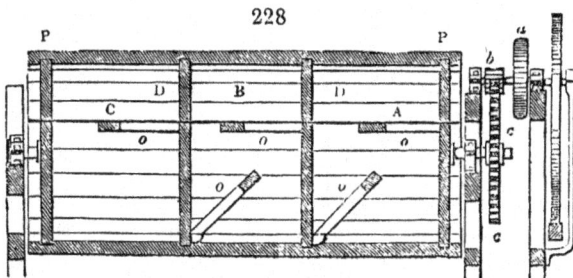

There is a ratchet-wheel counter for numbering the turns of the kneading machine, but it cannot be shown in this view; *n*, cross-bars of wood, which are easily removed when the cylinder is opened; they divide the dough.

Each of the three compartments of the *kneader* (*fig.* 228) is furnished at pleasure with two bars fixed crosswise, but which may be easily removed, whenever the cylinder is opened. These bars constitute the sole agents for drawing out the dough. In a continuous operation, the leaven is constantly prepared in the compartment A; with which view there is put into it—

125 kilogrammes of ordinary leaven or yeast.
  67   ,,   .   .   . flour.
  33   ,,   .   .   . water.
  ———

In all, 225 kilogrammes.

The person in charge of the mechanical kneader shuts down its lid, and sets it a-going. At the end of about seven minutes he hears the bell of the counter sound, announcing that the number of revolutions has been sufficient to call for an inspection of the sponge, in regard to its consistence. The cylinder is therefore opened, and after verifying the right state of the leaven, and adding water to soften, or flour to stiffen it, he closes the lid, and sets the machine once more in motion. In 10 minutes more the counter sounds again, and the kneading is completed. The 450 kilogrammes of leaven obtained from the two compartments are adequate to prepare dough enough to supply alternately each of the two ovens. For this purpose 75 kilogrammes of leaven are taken from each of the two compartments A and A', and placed in the intermediate compartment B. The whole leaven is then $75 + 75 = 150$ kilogrammes; to which are added 100 kilogrammes of flour and 50 of water $= 150$, so that the chest contains 300 kilogrammes. There is now replaced in each of the cavities A and A' the primitive quantity, by adding 50 kilogrammes of flour and 25 of water $= 75$.

The cylinder is again set a-going; and, from the nature of the apparatus, it is obvious that the kneading takes place at once on the leavens A and A', and on the paste B; which last is examined after 7 minutes, and completed in 10 more $= 17$, at the second sound of the counter-bell.

The kneader is opened, the paste on the sides and on the bars is gathered to the bottom by means of a scraper. The whole paste of the chest B being removed, 150 kilogrammes of the leaven are taken, to which 150 kilogrammes of flour and water are added to prepare the 300 kilogrammes of paste destined for the supply of the oven No. 2. These 75 kilogrammes of leaven from each compartment are placed as before, and so on in succession.

The water used in this operation is raised to the proper temperature, viz. 25° or 30° C. (77° or 86° F.) in cold weather, and to about 68° F. in the hot season, by mixing common cold water with the due proportion of water maintained at the temperature of about 160° F., in the basis F, placed above the ovens.

Through the water poured at each operation upon the flour in the compartment B, there is previously diffused from 200 to 250 grammes of fresh leaven, as obtained from the brewery, after being drained and pressed (*German yeast*). This quantity is sufficient to raise properly 300 kilogrammes of dough. As soon as this dough is taken out of the kneader, as stated above, and while the machine goes on to work, the quantity requisite for each loaf is weighed, turned about on the table D, to give it its round or oblong form, and there is impressed upon it with the forearm, or roller, the cavity which characterises cleft loaves. All the lots of dough of the size of one kilogramme, called cleft loaves (*pains fendus*), are placed upon a cloth, a fold of which is raised between two loaves, the cloth being first spread upon a board; which thus charged with 10 or 15 loaves is transferred to the wooden shelves G G, in front of the oven. The whole of them rise easily under the influence of the gentle temperature of this antechamber or *fournil*. Whenever the dough loaves are sufficiently raised here, they are put into the oven, a process called *enfournement* in France; which consists in setting each loaf on a wooden shovel dusted with coarse flour, and placing it thereby on the sole of the oven, close to its fellow, without touching it. This operation is made easy, in consequence of the introduction of a long-jointed gas-pipe and burner into the interior of the oven, by the light of which all parts of it may be minutely examined. The oven first is kept moderately hot, by shutting the dampers; but whenever the thermometer attached to it indicates a temperature of from 300° to 290° C. (572° to 554° F.), the damper or registers are opened, to restore the heat to its original degree, by allowing of the circulation of the hot air, which rises from the lower cavities around the fire-place into the interior of the oven. When the baking is completed, the gas-light, which had been withdrawn, is again introduced into the oven, and the bread is taken out; called the process of *défournement*. If the temperature have been maintained at about 300° C., the 300 kilogrammes of dough, divided into loaves of one kilogramme (2½lbs. avoirdupois), will be baked in 27 minutes. The charging having lasted 10 minutes, and the discharging as long, the baking of each batch will take up 47 minutes. But on account of accidental interruptions, an hour may be assigned for each charge of 260 loaves of 1 kilogramme each ; being at the rate of 6,240 kilogrammes (or 6·75 tons) of bread in 24 hours.

Although the outer parts of the loaves be exposed to the radiation of the walls, heated to 280° or 300° C., and undergo therefore that kind of *caramelisation* (charring) which produces the colour, the taste, and the other special characters of the crust, yet the inner substance of the loaves, or the crumb, never attains to nearly so high a temperature ; for a thermometer, whose bulb is inserted into the heart of a loaf, does not indicate more than 100° C. (213° F.)

Perkins' hot-water oven is an adaptation of that distinguished engineer's stove, which, as is well known, is a mode of heating by means of pipes full of water, and hermetically closed ; but with a sufficient space for the expansion of the water in the pipes. As a means of warming buildings, the invention has already produced the very benefical effects which have gained for it an extensive patronage. There is no doubt but that this novel application entitles the inventor to the warmest thanks of the public. The following figure (229), represents one of these ovens. A, stove ; B, coil of iron pipe placed in the stove ; C C, flow-pipe ; D, expansive tube ; E, oven charged with loaves, and surrounded with the hot-water pipes ; F, return hot-water pipe ; G, door of the oven ; H, flue for the escape of the vapours in the oven ; I, rigid bar of iron supporting the regulating box ; J J, regulating box, containing three

229

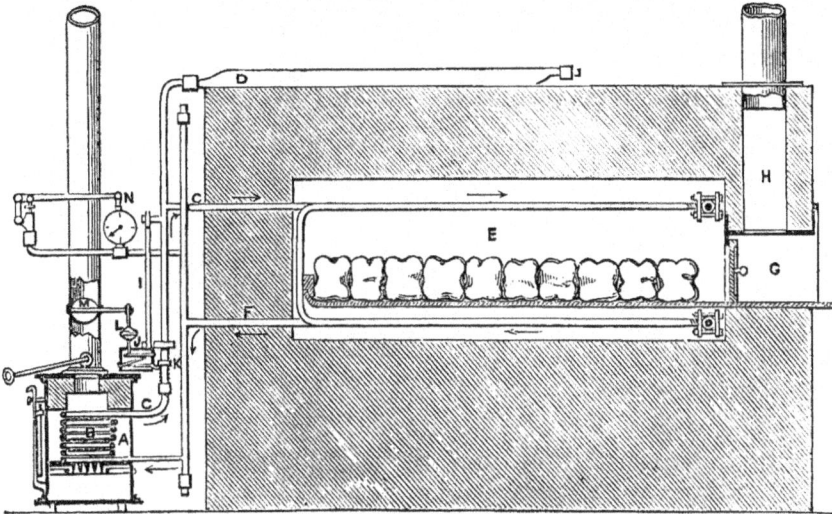

small levers ; K, nut adjusted so that if temperature of the hot-water pipe is increased beyond the adjusted point, its elongation causes the nut to bear upon the levers in the box J, which levers, lifting the straight rod L, shut the damper M of the stove ; N is an index indicating the temperature of the hot-water pipes.

The oven is first built in the ordinary manner of sound brickwork, made very thick in order to retain the heat. Then the top and bottom of the internal surfaces are lined with wrought-iron pipes of one inch external diameter, and five-eighths of an inch internal diameter, and their surface amounts in the aggregate, to the whole surface of the oven. These pipes are then connected to a coil in a furnace outside the oven. The coil having such a relative proportion of surface to that which is in the oven, that the pipes may be raised to a temperature of 550° F., and no more. This fixed and uniform temperature is maintained by a self-regulating adjustment peculiar to this furnace, which works with great precision, and which cannot get out of order, since it depends upon the expansion of the upper ascending pipe close to the furnace acting upon three levers connected with the damper which regulates the draught. The movable nut at the bottom of that expanding pipe being adjusted to the requisite temperature, that precise temperature is uniformly retained. The smallest fluctuation in the heat of the water which circulates in the pipes instantly sets the levers in motion, and the expansion of one thirty-sixth part of an inch is sufficient to close the damper.

It will be observed that if the pipes be heated to 550° F. the brickwork will soon attain the same temperature, or nearly so, and accordingly the oven will thus possess double the amount of the heating surface of ordinary ovens applicable to baking.

The baking temperature of the oven is from 420° to 450° F., which is ascertained by a thermometer with which the oven is provided.

With respect to Rolland's oven, Messieurs Boussingault, Payen, and Poncelet, in their report to the Institute of France; Gaultier de Glaubry, in a report made in the name of the Committee of Chemical Arts to the Société d'Encouragement; and the late M. Arago, represented that oven as successfully meeting all the conditions of salubrity, cleanliness, and hygiène. Wood, coals, ashes are likewise banished from it, and neither smoke nor the heated air of the furnace can find access to it. As in Perkins', the furnace is placed at a distance from the mouth of the oven, but instead of conveying the heat by pipes, as in the hot-water oven, it is the smoke and hot air of the furnace which, circulating through fan-shaped flues, ramifying under the floor and spreading over the roof of the oven, impart to it the requisite temperature. The floor of the oven, on which the loaves are deposited, consists of glazed tiles, and it can thus be kept perfectly clean. The distinctive character of M. Rolland's oven, however, is that the glazed tiles just spoken of rest upon a revolving platform which the workman gradually, or from time to time, moves round by means of a small handle, and without effort.

Figures 230 to 239 represent the construction and appearance of M. Rolland's oven on a reduced scale.

230. Front elevation.	235. Plan of the first floor.
231. Vertical section through the axis of the fire-grate.	236. Plan of the sole.
	237. Plan of the second floor.
232. Ditto, ditto.	238. Plan of the fire-grate and flues.
233. Elevation of one of the vertical flues.	239. Plan of the portion under ground.
234. Suspension of the floors.	

230

When the oven has to be charged, the workman deposits the first loaves, by means of a short peel, upon that part of the revolving platform which lies before the mouth of the oven, and when that portion is filled, he gives a turn with the handle, and proceeds to put the loaves in the fresh space thus presented before him, and so on until the whole is filled up. The door is then closed through an opening covered with glass, and reserved in the wall of the oven, which is lighted up with a jet of gas, or by opening the door from time to time the progress of the baking may be watched; if it appears too rapid on one point, or too slow on another, the journeyman can, by means of the handle, bring the loaves successively to the hottest part of the oven, and *vice versâ*, as occasion may require. The oven is provided with a thermometer, and, in an experiment witnessed, the temperature indicated 210° C. = 420° F., the baking of a full charge was completed in one hour and ten minutes, and the loaves of the same kind were so even in point of size and colour that they could not be distinguished from each other.

The top of the oven is provided with a pan for the purpose of heating the water necessary for the preparation of the dough, by means of the heat which in all other plans (Mouchot's excepted) is lost. The workman should take care to keep always some water in that pan, for otherwise the leaden pipe would melt and occasion dangerous leaks. For this and other reasons, the safest plan, however, would be to replace this leaden pipe by an iron one. The said pan should be frequently scoured, for, if neglected, the water will become rusty and spoil the colour of the bread. Bread baking may be considered as consisting of four operations: namely, heating

231

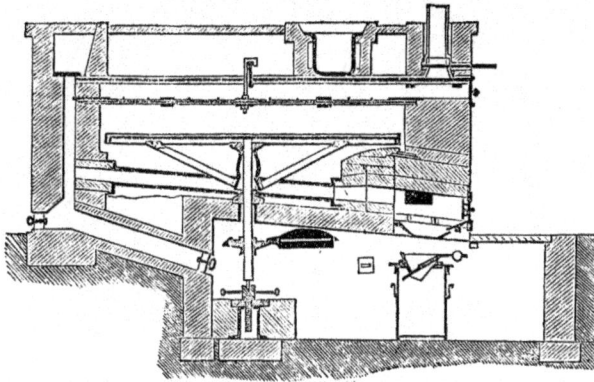

232

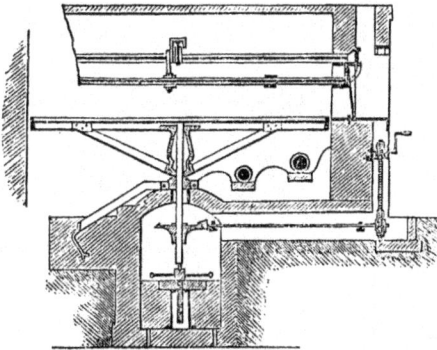

233

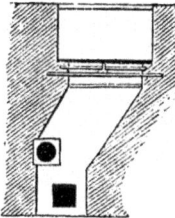

234

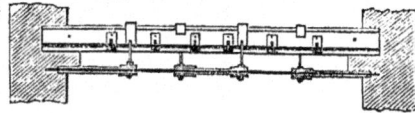

235

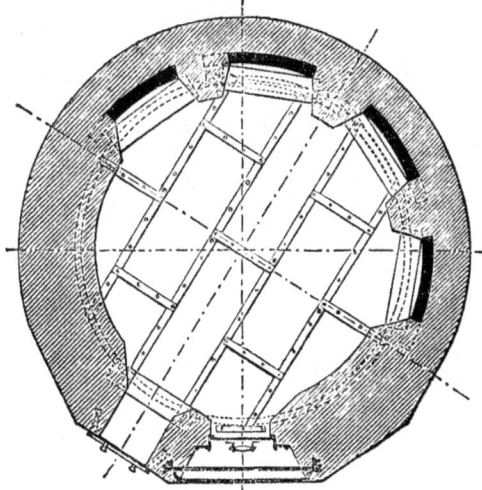

the oven, putting the dough into the oven, baking, and taking the loaves out of the oven. The general direction given by M. Rolland for each of these operations are as follows :—

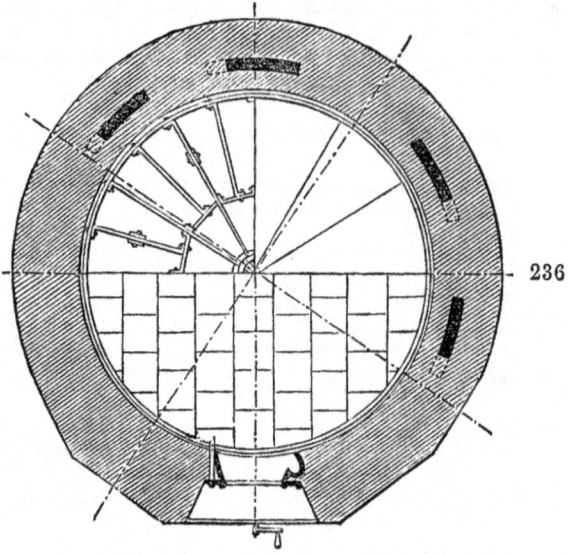

236

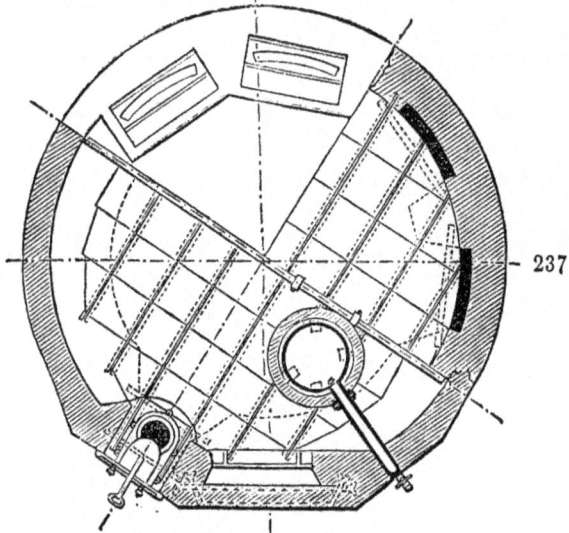

237

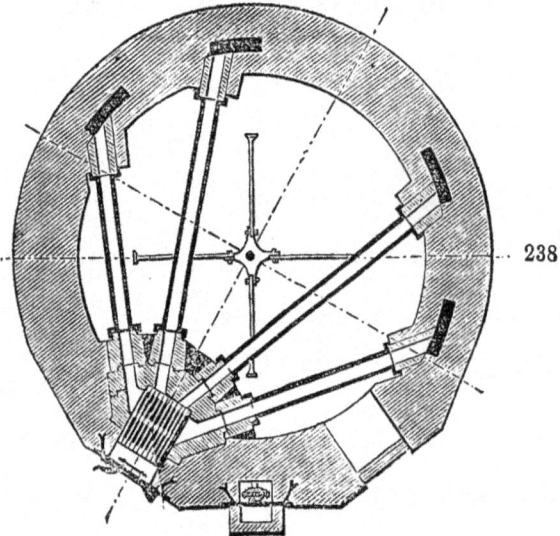

238

In order to obtain a proper heat and one that may be easily managed, it is necessary to charge the furnace moderately and often, and to keep it in a uniform state.

239

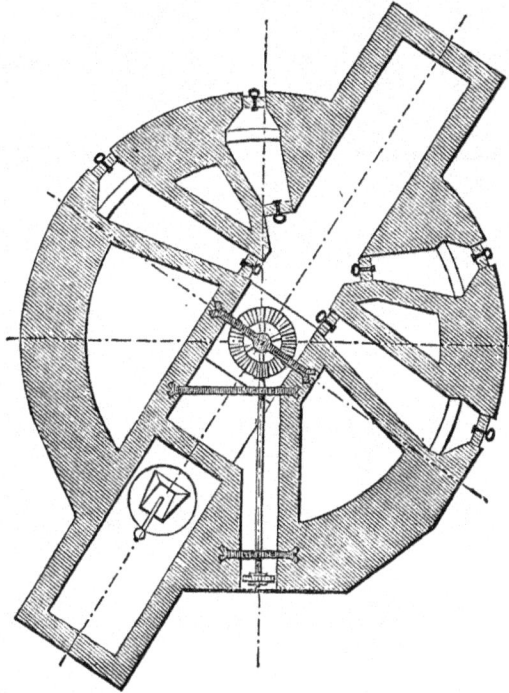

When the fire is kindled, the door should be kept perfectly closed, in order to compel the current of air necessary to the combustion to . pass through the grate, and thence through the flues under and the dome over the oven. If, on the contrary, the furnace door were left ajar, the cold air from without would rapidly pass over the coals without becoming properly heated, and passing in that condition into the flues would fail in raising it to the proper temperature. In order that the flame and heated products of the combustion may pass through all the flues, it is, of course, necessary to keep them clear by introducing into them once a month a brush made of wire, or

240

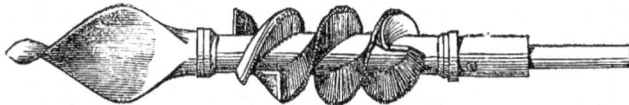

whalebone, or those which are now generally used for sweeping the tubes of marine tubular boilers, and the best of which are those patented and manufactured by Messrs. Moriarty of Greenwich, or How of London. The vertical flues which are built in the masonry are cleared from without or from the pit, according to the nature of the plan adopted in building the oven. These flues need not be cleaned more often than about once in three months.

Sweeping between the floors should be performed about every fortnight.

In case of accident or injury to the thermometers, the following directions, which indeed apply to all ovens, may enable the baker to judge of the temperature of his oven. If, on throwing a few pinches of flour on the tiles of the oven, it remains white after the lapse of a few seconds, the temperature is too low; if, on the contrary, the flour assumes a deep brown colour, the temperature is too high; if the flour turns yellowish, or looks slightly scorched, the temperature is right.

The baking in Rolland's oven takes place at a temperature varying from 410° to 432° F. according to the nature and size of the article intended to be baked. During the baking, the revolving floor is turned every ten or twelve minutes, so that the loaves not remaining in the same place the baking becomes equal throughout.

As to the hot-water oven, a few establishments only have as yet adopted it in England;

one of them is the 'Hot-water Oven Biscuit-baking Company,' on whose premises fancy biscuits only are baked; and another establishment is that of a baker of the name of Neville, carrying on his business in London. With respect to M. Mouchot's system, it is not even known in this country, otherwise than by having been alluded to in one or two technological publications or dictionaries.

The quantity of bread which can be made from a sack of flour depends to a great extent upon the quantity of gluten that the flour of which it is made contains, but the wheat which contains a large proportion of nitrogenous matter does not yield so light a flour as those which are poorer. From a great number of determinations it is found that the amount of gluten contained in the flour to make best white bread ranges from 10 to 18 per cent., that of the starch being from 63 to 70 per cent., the ashes ranging from 0·5 to 1·9 per cent.

In the ordinary plan of bread making, London bakers reckon that 1 sack of such a flour, weighing 280 lbs., will make 94 real 4-lb. loaves (not quartern) of pure genuine bread, although a sack of such flour may yield him 94 or even 95 quartern (not 4-lb.) loaves.[1]

From this account it may be easily imagined that if the baker could succeed in disposing at once of all the loaves of his day's baking either by sale at his shop, or, still better, by delivery at his customers' residences, such a business would indeed be a profitable one commercially speaking, for on that day he would sell from 28 to 34 lbs. of water at the price of bread, not to speak of the deficient weight.

As to those bakers who, by underbaking, or by the use of alum, or by the use of both alum and underbaking, manage to obtain 96, 98, 100, or a still larger number of loaves from inferior flour, or material, their profit is so reduced by the much lower price at which they are compelled to sell their sophisticated bread, that their tamperings avail them but little; their emphatically hard labour yields them but a mere pittance, except their business be so extensive that the small profits swell up into a large sum, in which case they only jeopardise their name as fare and honest tradesmen.

Looking now at the improved ovens, of which we have been speaking merely in an economical point of view, and abstractedly from all other considerations, the profits realised by their use appears to be well worth the baker's attention. But as with the improved ovens the economy bears upon the wages and the fuel, the advantages are much less considerable in a small concern than in a large one. Thus the economy which, upon 12 sacks of flour per week, would scarcely exceed 20 shillings upon the whole, would, on the contrary, assume considerable proportions in establishments baking from 50 to 100 sacks per week.

The richness or nutritive powers of sound flour, and also of bread, are proportional to the quantity of gluten they contain. It is of great importance to determine this point, for both of these objects are of enormous value and consumption; and it may be accomplished most easily and exactly by digesting in a water-bath, at the temperature of 167° F., 1,000 grains of bread (or flour) with 1,000 grains of bruised barley malt, in 5,000 grains, or in a little more than half a pint, of water. When this mixture ceases to take a blue colour from iodine (that is, when all the starch is converted into a soluble dextrine), the gluten left unchanged may be collected on a filter cloth, washed, dried at a heat of 212° F., and weighed. The colour, texture, and taste of the gluten ought also to be examined, in forming a judgment of good flour or bread.

The question of the relative value of white and brown bread, as nutritive agents, is one of very long standing, and the arguments on both sides may be thus resumed.

The advocates of brown bread hold:—

That the separation of the white from the brown parts of wheat grain, in making bread, is likely to be baneful to health;

That the general belief that bread made with the finest flour is the best, and that whiteness is a proof of its quality, is a popular error;

That whiteness may be, and generally is, communicated to bread by alum, to the injury of the consumer;

That the miller, in refining his flour, to please the public, removes some of the ingredients necessary to the composition and nourishment of the various organs of our bodies; so that fine flour, instead of being better than the meal, is, on the contrary, less nourishing, and, to make the case worse, is also more difficult of digestion, not to speak of the enormous loss to the population of at least 25 per cent. of branny flour,

---

[1] It is absolutely necessary thus to establish a distinction between four pounds and quartern loaves, because the latter very seldom indeed have that weight, and this deficiency is, in fact, one of the profits calculated upon; for although the Act of Parliament (Will. IV. c. xxxvii.) is very strict, and directs (sect. vii.) that bakers delivering bread by cart or carriage shall be provided with scales, weights, &c., for weighing bread, this requisition is seldom, if ever, complied with.

There are of course a few bakers whose quartern loaves weigh exactly four pounds, but many are from four to six ounces short.

containing from 60 to 70 per cent. of the most nutritious part of the flour, a loss which, for London only, is equal to at least 7,500 sacks of flour annually;

That the unwise preference given so universally to white bread, leads to the pernicious practice of mixing alum with the flour, and this again to all sorts of impositions and adulterations; for it enables the bakers who are so disposed, by adding alum, to make bread manufactured from the flour of inferior grain to look like the best and most costly, thus defrauding the purchaser and tampering with his health.

On the other side, the partisans of white bread contend, *of course*, that all these assertions are without foundation, and their reasons were summed up as follows in the *Bakers' Gazette*, in 1849:—

'The preference of the public for white bread is not likely to be an absurd prejudice, seeing that it was not until after years of experience that it was adopted by them.

'The adoption of white bread, in preference to any other sort, by the great body of the community, as a general article of food, is of itself a proof of its being the best and most nutritious.

'The finer and better the flour, the more bread can be made from it. Fifty-six pounds of fine flour from good wheat will make seventy-two pounds of good, sound, well-baked bread, the bread, having retained sixteen pounds of water. But bran, either fine or coarse, absorbs little or no water, and adds no more to the bread than its weight.'

And, lastly, in confirmation of the opinion that white bread contains a greater quantity of nutriment than the same weight of brown bread, the writer of the article winds up the white bread defence with a portion of the Report of the Committee of the House of Commons, appointed in 1800, 'to consider means for rendering more effectual the provisions of 13 Geo. III., intituled "An Act for the better regulating the Assize and making of Bread."'

In considering the propriety of recommending the adoption of further regulations and restrictions, they understood a prejudice existed in some parts of the country against any coarser sort of bread than that which is at present known by the name of 'fine household bread,' on the ground that the former was less wholesome and nutritious than the latter. The opinions of respectable physicians examined on this point are,—that the change of any sort of food which forms so great a part of the sustenance of man might for a time affect some constitutions; that as soon as persons were habituated to it, the standard wheaten bread, or even bread of a coarser sort, would be equally wholesome with the fine wheaten bread which is now generally used in the metropolis; but that, in their opinion, the fine wheaten bread *would go farther* with persons who have no other food than the same quantity of bread of a coarser sort.

It was suggested to them that if only one sort of flour was permitted to be made, and a different mode of dressing it adopted, so as to leave in it the fine pollards, 52 lbs. of flour might be extracted from a bushel of wheat weighing 60 lbs., instead of 47 lbs., which would afford a wholesome and nutritious food, and add to the quantity 5 lbs. in every bushel, or somewhat more than $\frac{1}{8}$th. On this they remarked, that there would be no saving in adopting this proposition; and they begged leave to observe, if the physicians are well founded in their opinions, that bread of coarser quality will not go equally far with fine wheaten bread, and increased consumption of wheaten bread would be the consequence of the measure.

From the baker's point of view, it is evident that all his sympathies must be in favour of the water-absorbing material, and therefore of the fine flour; for each pound of water added and retained in the bread which he sells represents this day so many twopences; but the purchaser's interest lies in just the opposite direction.

The question, however, is not, in the language of the Committee of the House of Commons of those days, or of the physicians whom they consulted, whether a given weight of wheaten bread *will go farther* than an equal weight of bread of a coarser sort; nor whether a given weight of pure flour is more nutritious than an equal weight of the meal from the same wheat used in making brown bread. The real question is,—*Whether a given weight of wheat contains more nutriment than* THE FLOUR *obtained from that weight of wheat.*

The inquiry of the Committee of the House of Commons, and the defence of white bread *versus* brown bread, resting as it does, in this respect, upon a false ground, is therefore perfectly valueless; for whatever may have been the opinion of respectable physicians and of Committees, either of those days or of the present times, one thing is certain—namely, that bran contains only 9 or 10 per cent. of woody fibre, that is, of matter devoid of nutritious property; and that the remainder consists of a larger proportion of gluten and starch, fatty, and other highly nutritive constituents, with a few salts, and water, as proved by the following analysis by Millon:—

Composition of Wheat Bran.

Starch	52·0
Gluten	14·9
Sugar . . ·	1·0
Fatty matter	3·6
Woody „	9·7
Salts	5·0
Water	13·8
	100·0

And it is equally certain that wheat itself—the whole grain—does not contain more than 2 per cent. of unnutritious, or woody matter, the bran being itself richer, weight for weight, in gluten than the fine flour; the whole meal contains, accordingly, more gluten than the fine flour obtained therefrom. The relative proportions of gluten in the whole grain, in bran, and in flour of the same sample of wheat, were represented by the late Professor Johnston to be as follows:—

Gluten of Wheat.

Whole grain	12 per cent.
Whole bran	14 to 18 „ „
Fine flour	10 „ „

Now, whereas a bushel of wheat weighing 60 lbs. produces, according to the mode of manufacturing flour for London, 47 lbs.—that is, 78 per cent. of flour, the rest being bran and pollards; if we deduct 2 per cent. of woody matter, and 1½ per cent. for waste in grinding at the mill, the bushel of 60 lbs. of wheat would yield 58 lbs., or at least 96⅔ per cent., of nutritious matter.

It is, therefore, as clear as anything can possibly be, that by using the whole meal instead of only the fine flour of that wheat, there will be a difference of about ⅙th in the product obtained from equal weights of wheat.

In a communication made to the Royal Institute nearly four years ago, M. Mège Mouriès announced that he had found under the envelope of the grain, in the internal part of the perisperm, a peculiar nitrogenous substance capable of acting as a ferment, and to which he gave the name of 'céréaline.' This substance, which is found wholly, or almost so, in the bran, but not in the best white flour, has the property of liquefying starch, very much in the same manner as diastase; and the decreased firmness of the crumb of brown bread is referred by him to this action. The coloration of bread made from meal containing bran is not, according to M. Mège Mouriès, due, as has hitherto been thought, to the presence of bran; but to the peculiar action of cerealin; this new substance, like vegetable casein and gluten, being, by a slight modification, due perhaps to the contact of the air, transformed into a ferment, under the influence of which the gluten undergoes a great alteration, yielding, among other products, ammonia, a brown-coloured matter analogous to ulmine, and a nitrogenous product capable of transforming sugar into lactic acid. M. Mège Mouriès having experimentally established, to the satisfaction of a committee consisting of MM. Chevreul, Dumas, Pelouze, and Peligot, that by paralysing or destroying the action of cerealin, as described in the specification of his patent, bearing date June 14, 1856, white bread, having all the characters of first-quality bread, may be made, in the language of the said specification, 'with using either all the white or raw elements that constitute either corn or rye, or with such substances as could produce, to this day, but brown bread.'

Cerealin, according to M. Mège Mouriès, has two very distinct properties:—the first consists in converting the hydrated starch into glucose and dextrine; the second, which is much more important in its results, transforms the glucose into lactic, acetic, butyric, and formic acid, which penetrate, swell up, and partly dissolve the gluten, rendering it pulpy and emulsive, like that of rye; producing, in fact, a series of decompositions, yielding eventually a loaf having all the characteristics of bread made from inferior flour.

In order to convert the whole of the farinaceous substance of wheat into white bread, it is therefore necessary to destroy the cerealin; and the process, or series of processes, by which this is accomplished, is thus described by M. Mège Mouriès in his specification:—

'The following are the means I employ to obtain my new product:—

'1st. The application of vinous fermentation, produced by alcoholic ferment or yeast, to destroy the ferment that I call "céréaline" existing, together with the fragments of bran, in the raw flour, and which in some measure produces the acidity of brown bread directly, whilst it destroys indirectly most part of the gluten.

' 2ndly. The thorough purification of the said flour, either raw or mixed with bran, (after dilution and fermentation,) by the sifting and separating of the farinaceous liquid from the fragments of bran disseminated by the millstone into the inferior products of corn.

3rdly. The employing that part of corn producing brown bread in the rough state as issuing from the mill after a first grinding, in order to facilitate its purification by fermentation and wet sifting.

' 4thly. The employing an acidulated water (by any acid or acid salt) in order to prevent the lactic fermentation, preserving the vinous fermentation, preventing the yellow colour from turning into a brown colour (the ulmic acid), and the good taste of corn from assuming that of brown bread. However, instead of acidulated water, pure water may be employed with an addition of yeast, as the acid only serves to facilitate the vinous fermentation.

' 5thly. The grinding of the corn by means of millstones that crush it thoroughly, increasing thereby the quantity of foul parts, a method which will prove very bad with the usual process, and very advantageous with mine.

' 6thly. The application of corn washed or stripped by any suitable means.

' 7thly. The application of all these contrivances to wheat of every description, to rye, and other grain used in the manufacture of bread.

' 8thly. The same means applied to the manufacture of biscuits.

' I will now describe the manner in which the said improvements are carried into effect.

' First Instance. *When flour of inferior quality is made use of.*—This description of flour, well known in trade, is bolted or sifted at 73, 74, 75, or 80 per cent. (a mark termed *Scipion mark* in the French War Department), and yields bread of middle quality. By applying to this sort of flour a liquid yeast, rather different from that which is applied to white flour, in order to quicken the work and remove the sour taste of bread, a very nice quality will be obtained, which result was quite unknown to everybody to this day, and which none ever attempted to know, as none before me was aware of the true causes that produce brown bread, &c.

' Now, to apply my process to the said flour (of inferior mark or quality) I take a part of the same—a fourth part, for instance—which I dilute with a suitable quantity of water, and add to the farinaceous liquid 1 portion of beer yeast for 200 portions of water, together with a small quantity of acid or acid salt, sufficient to impart to the said water the property of lightly staining or reddening the test-paper, known in France by the name of *papier de tournesol.* When the liquid is at full working, I mix the remaining portions of flour, which are kneaded, and then allowed to ferment in the usual way. The yeast applied, which is quite alcoholic, will yield perfectly white bread of a very nice taste ; and I declare that if similar yeast were ever commended before, it was certainly not for the purpose of preventing the formation of brown bread, the character of which was believed to be inherent to the nature of the very flour, as the following result will sufficiently prove it, thus divesting such an application of its industrial appropriation.

' Second Instance. *When raw flour is made use of.*—By raw flour, I mean the corn crushed only once, and from which 10 to 15 per cent. of rough bran have been separated. Such flour is still mixed with fragments of bran, and is employed in trade to the manufacture of so-called white flour and bran after a second and third grinding or crushing. Instead of that, I only separate, and without submitting it to a fresh crushing, the rough flour in two parts, about 70 parts of white flour and 15 to 18 of rough or coarse flour, of which latter the yeast is made ; this I dilute with a suitable quantity of water, sufficient to reduce the whole flour into a dough, say, 50 per cent. of the whole weight of raw flour. To this mixture have been previously added the yeast and acid, (whenever acid is applied, which is not indispensable, as before stated), and the whole is allowed to work for 6 hours at a temperature of 77° F. for 12 hours at 68°, and for 20 hours at 59°, thus proportionally to the temperature. While this working or fermentation is going on, the various elements (céréaline, &c.) which by their peculiar action are productive of brown bread, have undergone a modification ; the rough parts are separated, the gluten stripped from its pellicles and disaggregated, and the same flour which, by the usual process, could have only produced deep brown bread, will actually yield first-rate bread, far superior to that sold by bakers, chiefly if the fragments of bran are separated by the following process, which consists in pouring on the sieve, described hereafter, the liquid containing the rough parts of flour thus disaggregated and modified by a well-regulated fermentation,

' The sieve alluded to, which may be of any form, and consist of several tissues of different tightness, the closest being ever arranged underneath or the most forward, when the sieve is of cylindrical or vertical form, is intended to keep back the fragments of bran, which would by their interposition impair the whiteness of bread, and by their weight diminish its nutritive power. The sifted liquid is white, and constitutes the yeast with which the white flour is mixed after being separated, so as to make a dough at either a first or several workings, according to the baker's practice. This dough works or ferments very quickly, and the bread resulting therefrom is unexceptionable. In case the whiteness or neatness of bread should be looked upon as a thing of little consequence, a broader sieve might be employed, or even no sieve used at all, and yet a very nice bread be obtained.

'The saving secured by the application of my process is as follows:—By the common process, out of 100 parts of wheat, 70 or 75 parts of flour are extracted, which are fit to yield either white or middle bread; whilst, by the improved process, out of 100 parts of wheat 85 to 88 parts will be obtained, yielding bread of superior quality, of the best taste, neatness, and nutritious richness.

'In case new yeast cannot be easily provided, the same should be dried at a temperature of about 86° F., after being suitably separated by means of some inert dust, and previous to being made use of it should be dipped into 10 parts of water, lightly sweetened, for 8 to 10 hours, a fit time for the liquid being brought into a full fermentation, at which time the yeast has recovered its former power. The same process will hold good for manufacturing rye bread, only 25 per cent., about, of coarse bran are to be extracted. For manufacturing biscuits, I use also the same process, only the dough is made very hard and immediately taken into the oven, and the products thus obtained are far superior to the common biscuits, both for their good taste and preservation. Should, however, an old practice exclude all manner of fermentation, then I might dilute the rough parts of flour in either acidulated or non-acidulated water, there to be left to work for the same time as before, then sift the water and decant it, after a proper settling of the farinaceous matters of which the dough is to be made; thus the action of the acid, decantation, and sifting, would effectively remove all causes of alteration, which generally impair the biscuits made of inferior flour.

'The apparatus required for this process is very plain, and consists of a kneading trough, in which the foul parts are mixed mechanically, or by manual labour, with the liquid above mentioned. From this trough, and through an opening made therein, the liquid mixture drops into the fermenting tub, deeper than wide, which must be kept tightly closed during the fermenting work. At the lower part of this tub a cock is fitted, which lets the liquid mixture down upon an incline plane, on which the liquid spreads, so as to be equally distributed over the whole surface of the sieve. This sieve, of an oblong rectangular form, is laid just beneath, and its tissue ought to be so close as to prevent the least fragments of bran from passing through; it is actuated by the hand, or rather by a crank. In all cases that part of the sieve which is opposite to the cock must strike upon an unyielding body, for the purpose of shaking the pellicles remaining on the tissue, and driving them down towards an outlet on the lower part of the sieve, and thence into a trough purposely contrived for receiving the waters issuing from the sieve, and discharging them into a tank.

'The next operation consists in diluting those pellicles, or rougher parts, which could not pass through the sieve, sifting them again, and using the white water resulting therefrom to dilute the foul parts intended for subsequent operations. The sieve or sieves may sometimes happen to be obstructed by some parts of gluten adhering thereto, which I wash off with acidulated water for silk tissues, and with an alkali for metallic ones. This washing method I deem very important, as its non-application may hinder a rather large operation, and therefore I wish to secure it. This apparatus may be liable to some variations, and admit of several sieves superposed, and with different tissues, the broadest, however to be placed uppermost.

'Among the various descriptions and combinations of sieves that may be employed, the annexed figures show one that will give satifactory results.

'*Fig.* 241 is a longitudinal section, and *fig.* 242 an end view, of the machine from which the bran is ejected. The apparatus rests upon a cast-iron framing *a*, consisting of two cheeks, kept suitably apart by tie pieces *b*; a strong cross-bar on the upper part admits a wood cylinder *c*, circled round with iron, and provided with a wooden cock *d*. The cylinder *c* receives through its centre an arbor *f*, provided with four arms *e*, which arbor is supported by two cross-bars *g* and *h*, secured by means of bolts to the uprights *i*. Motion is imparted to the arbor *f* by the crank *j*, by pulleys driven by the endless straps *k*, and by the toothed wheel *l*, gearing into the wheel *m*, which is keyed on the upper end of the arbor *f*. Beneath the cylinder *c*, two sieves *n* and *o* are borne into a frame *p*, suspended on one end to two chains *q*, and on the other resting on two guides or bearings *r*, beneath which, and on the crank shaft, are cams *s*, by which that end of the frame that carries the sieves is alternately raised and lowered. A strong spring *u* is set to a shaft borne by the framing *a*, whilst a ratchet wheel provided with a clink allows the said spring,

241   242

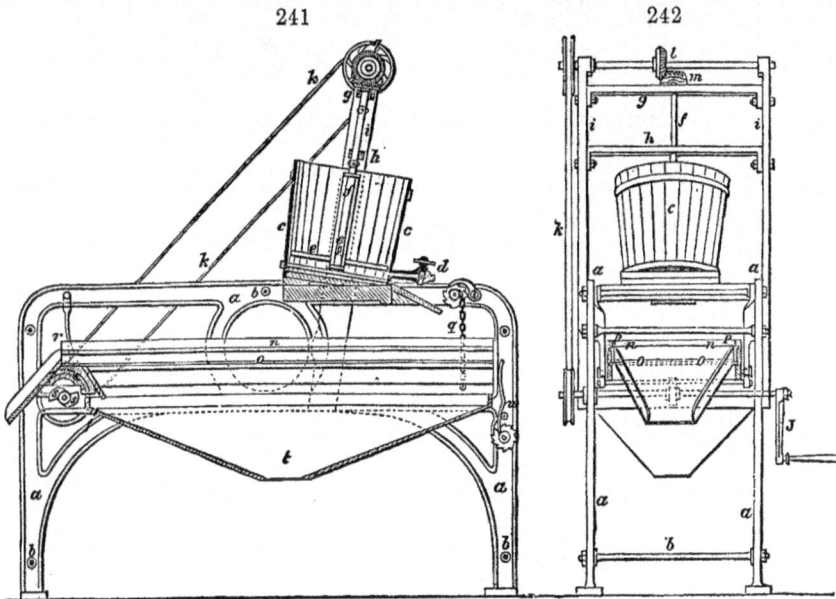

according to the requirements of the work, to give more or less impulse or shaking as the cams *s* are acting upon the frame-sieve carrying the sieve. Beneath the said frame a large hopper *t* is disposed, to receive and lead into a tank the liquid passing through the sieves. The filter sieve is worked as follows :—After withdrawing, by means of bolting hutches, 70 per cent., about, of fine flour, I take out of the remaining 30 per cent. about 20 per cent. of groats, neglecting the remaining 10 per cent., from which, however, I could separate the little flour still adhering thereto, but I deem it more available to sell it off in this state. I submit the 20 per cent. of groats to a suitable vinous fermentation, and have the whole taken into the cylinder *c*, there to be stirred by means of the arbor *f* and the arms *e* ; after a suitable stirring, the cock *d* is opened and the liquid is let out, spread on the uppermost sieve *n*, which keeps back the coarsest bran. The liquid drops then into the second sieve or filter *o*, by which the least fragments are retained ; the passage of the liquid through the filters is quickened by the quivering motion imparted by the cams *s* to the frame carrying the sieve.'

The advantages resulting from such a process are obvious : first, it would appear— and those experiments have been confirmed by the committee of the Académie des Sciences, who had to report upon them—that no less than from 16 to 17 per cent. of white bread of superior quality can be obtained from wheat, which increase is not due to water, as in other methods, but is a true and real one, the Commissioners having ascertained that the bread thus manufactured did not contain more water than that made in the usual way, their comparative examinations in this respect having given the following results :—

Loss by drying in Air.

	Crumb	Crust
Old method	37·8 .	. 12·0 per cent.
New method	37·5 .	. 14·0 ,,
Difference . . .	00·3 .	. 2·0 ,,

Another experiment by Peligot :—

Loss by drying in Air at 248° F.

	Crumb and Crust
New method	34·9 per cent.
Old method	34·1 ,,
Difference	00·8 ,,

Since the enrolment of his Specification, however, M. Mège Mouriès has made an improvement, which simplifies considerably his original process, according to which the destruction of the cerealin, as we saw, was effected by ordinary yeast; that is to say, by alcoholic fermentation. The last improvement consists in preventing cerealin from becoming a lactic or glucosic ferment, by precipitating it with common salt, and not allowing it time to become a ferment. In effect, in order that cerealin may produce the objectionable effects alluded to, it must first pass into the state of ferment, and, as all nitrogenous substances require a certain time of incubation to become so,[1] if, on the one hand, cerealin be precipitated by means of common salt, the glucosic action is neutralised; whilst, on the other hand, the levains being made with flour containing no cerealin—that is to say, with best white flour—if a short time before baking households or seconds are added thereto, it is clear that time will be wanting for it (the ferment) to become developed or organised, and that, under this treatment, the bread will remain white.

The application of these scientific deductions will be better understand by the following description of the process :—

100 parts of clean wheat are ground and divided as follows:

Best whites for leaven	40·0
White groats, mixed with a few particles of bran .	38·0
White groats, mixed with a larger quantity of bran .	8·0
Bran (not used)	15·5
Loss	0·5
	102·0

These figures vary, of course, according to the kind of wheat used, according to seasons, and according to the description of mill and the distance of the millstones used for grinding.

'In order to convert these products into bread,' says M. Mège Mouriès, ' a leaven is to be made by mixing the 40 parts of best flour above alluded to, with 20 parts of water, and proceeding with it according to the mode and custom adopted in each locality. This leaven, no matter how prepared, being ready, the 8 parts of groats mixed with the larger quantity of bran above alluded to, are diluted in 45 parts of water in which 0·6 parts of common salt have been previously dissolved, and the whole is passed through a sieve which allows the flour and water to pass through, but retains and separates the particles of bran. The watery liquid so obtained has a white colour, is flocculent, and loaded with cerealin; it no longer possesses the property of liquefying gelatinous starch, and weighs 38 parts (the remainder of the water is retained in the bran, which has swelled up in consequence, and remains on the sieve). The leaven is then diluted with that water, which is loaded with best flour, and is used for converting into dough the 38 parts of white groats above alluded to; the dough is then divided into suitable portions, and after allowing it to stand for one hour, it is finally put in the oven to be baked. As the operations just described take place at a temperature of 25° C. (=77° F.), the one hour during which the dough is left to itself, is not sufficient for the cerealin to pass into the state of ferment, and the consequence is the production of white bread. Should, however, the temperature be higher than that, or were the dough allowed to be kept for a longer time before baking, the bread produced, instead of being white, would be so much darker, as the contact would have lasted longer. By this process, 100 parts in weight of wheat yield 136 parts of dough, and, finally, 115 parts in weight of bread' instead of 100, which the same quantity of wheat would have yielded in the usual way. This is supposing that the grinding of the wheat has been effected with close set millstones; if ground in the usual manner, the average yield does not exceed 112 parts in weight of bread.

The substances which are now almost exclusively employed for adulterating bread are, water, alone or incorporated with rice, or water and alum : other substances, however, are or have been also occasionally used for the same purpose.

This retention of water into bread is secured by underbaking, by the introduction of rice, of potatoes, and other feculæ, and of alum.

Underbaking is an operation which consists of keeping in the loaf the water which otherwise would escape while baking; it is, therefore, a process for selling water at the price of bread. It is done by introducing the dough into an oven unduly heated, whereby the gases contained in the dough at once expand, and swell it up to the ordinary dimensions, whilst a deep burnt crust is immediately afterwards formed;

[1] Communication of M. Mège Mouriès to the Académie des Sciences, January 1858.

which, inasmuch as it is a bad conductor of heat, prevents the interior of the loaf from being thoroughly baked, and at the same time opposes the free exit of the water contained in the dough, and which the heat of the oven partly converts into steam; while the crust becomes thicker and darker than it otherwise should be, a sensible loss of nutritive elements being sustained, at the same time, in the shape of pyrogenous products, which are dissipated.

The proportion of water retained in bread by underbaking is sometimes so large, that a baker may thus obtain as much as 106 loaves from a sack of flour.

The addition of boiled rice to the dough is also pretty frequently used to increase the yield of loaves; this substance, in fact, absorbs so much water that as many as 116 quartern loaves have thus been obtained from one sack of flour.

From a great number of experiments made with a view to determine the normal quantity of water contained in the crumb of genuine bread, it is ascertained that it amounts, in new bread, from 38 at least to at most 47 per cent.

The quantity of water contained in bread is easily determined, by cutting a slice of it, weighing 500 grains, for example, placing it in a small oven heated, by a gas-burner or a lamp, to a temperature of about 220° F., until it no longer loses weight, the difference between the first and last weighing (that is to say, the loss) indicating, of course, the amount of water.

Alum, however, is the principal adulterating substance used by bakers, *almost without exception, in this metropolis*; as was proved by Dr. Normanby in his evidence before the Select Committee of the House of Commons, appointed in 1855, under the presidence of Mr. W. Scholefield, to inquire into the adulteration of food, drinks, and drugs, which assertion was corroborated and established beyond doubt by the other chemists who were examined also on the subject.

The introduction of alum into bread not only enables the baker to give to bread made of flour of inferior quality the whiteness of the best bread, but to force and keep in it a larger quantity of water than could otherwise be done. We shall see presently that this fact has been denied, and on what grounds.

The quantity of alum used varies exceedingly; but no appreciable effect is produced when the proportion of alum introduced is less than 1 in 900 or 1,000, which is at the rate of 27 or 28 grains in a quartern loaf. The use of alum, however, has become so universal, and the Act of Parliament which regulates the matter has so long been considered as a dead letter, from the trouble, and chance of pecuniary loss which it entails on the prosecutor should his accusation prove unsuccessful, that but few, and until quite lately none, of the public officers would undertake the discharge of a duty most disagreeable in itself and at the same time full of risk.

When alum is used in making bread, one of the two following things may happen: either the alum will be decomposed, as just said, in which case the alumina will, of necessity, be set free as soon as digestion will have decomposed the organic matter with which it was combined; and thus it is presumable that either alum will be re-formed in the stomach, or that, according to Liebig, the phosphoric acid of the phosphates of the bread, uniting with the alumina of the alum, will form an insoluble phosphate of alumina, and the beneficial action of the phosphates will, consequently, be lost to the system; and since phosphoric acid forms with alumina a compound hardly decomposable by alkalis or acids, this may, perhaps, explain the indigestibility of the London bakers' bread, which strikes all foreigners. — *Letters on Chemistry*.

The last defence set up in behalf of alumed bread to be noticed is, that, with certain descriptions of flour, bread cannot be made without it; that by means of alum a large quantity of flour is made available for human food, which, without it, must be withdrawn, and turned to some other less important uses, to the great detriment of the population, and particularly of the poor, who would be the first to suffer from the increase of the price of bread which such a withdrawal must fatally produce.

The process usually adopted for the detection of alum is that known as Kuhlmann's process, which consists in incinerating about 3,000 grains of bread, porphyrising the ashes so obtained, treating them by nitric acid, evaporating the mixture to dryness, and diluting the residue with about 300 grains of water, with the help of a gentle heat; without filtering, a solution of caustic potash is then added, the whole is boiled a little, filtered, the filtrate is tested with a solution of sal-ammoniac, and boiled for a few minutes. If a precipitate is formed it is *not alumina*, as hitherto thought and stated by Kuhlmann and all other chemists, but *phosphate of alumina*,—a circumstance of great importance, not in testing for the presence of alumina, but for the determination of its amount, as will be shown further on, when entering into the details of the modifications which it is necessary to make to Kuhlmann's process.

In a paper read in April 1858, at the Society of Arts, Dr. Odling stated that out of

46 examinations of ashes furnished him by Dr. Gilbert, and treating them by the above process, he (Dr. Odling) obtained, to use his own words, 'in 21 instances, the celebrated white precipitate said to be indicative of alumina and alum, so that had these samples been in a manufactured instead of the natural state—had the wheat, for example, been made into flour—I should have been justified, according to the authority quoted, in pronouncing it to be adulterated with alum. But a subsequent examination of the precipitates I obtained, showed that in reality they were not due to alumina at all. M. Kuhlmann's process, as above described, is possessed of rare merits: it will never fail in detecting alumina when present, and will often succeed in detecting it when absent also. The idea of weighing this *olla podrida* of a precipitate, and from its weight calculating the amount of alum present, as is gravely recommended by great anti-adulteration adepts, is too preposterous to require a moment's refutation.'

In order, however, to render the process for the detection of alum in bread free from objections, the following method is recommended. It requires only ordinary care, and it is perfectly accurate:—

Cut the loaf in half; take a thick slice of crumb from the middle, carefully trimming the edges so as to remove the crust, or hardened outside, and weigh off 1,500 or 3,000 grains of it; crumble it to powder, or cut it into slices, and expose them, on a sheet of platinum foil turned up at the edges, to a low red heat, until fumes are no longer evolved, and the whole is reduced to charcoal, which will require from twenty to forty minutes, according to the quantity; transfer the charcoal to a mortar, and reduce it to fine powder; put now this finely-pulverised charcoal back again on the platinum foil tray, and leave it exposed thereon to a dark cherry-red heat until reduced to grey ashes, for which purpose gas-furnace lamps will be found very convenient. Only a cherry-red heat should be applied, because at a higher temperature the ashes might fuse, and the incineration be thus retarded. Remove the source of heat, drench the grey ashes with a concentrated solution of nitrate of ammonia, and carefully reapply the heat; the last portions of charcoal will thereby be burnt, and the ashes will then have a white or drab colour. Drench them on the tray with moderately strong and pure hydrochloric acid, and after one or two minutes' standing, wash the contents of the platinum foil tray, with distilled water, into a porcelain dish; evaporate to perfect dryness, in order to render the silica insoluble; drench the perfectly dry residue with strong and pure muriatic acid, and, after standing for five or six minutes, dilute the whole with water, and boil; while boiling, add carefully as much carbonate of soda as is necessary nearly, but not quite, to saturate the acid, so that the liquor may still be acid; add as much pure alcohol-potash as is necessary to render it strongly alkaline; boil the whole for about three or four minutes, and filter. If now, after slightly supersaturating the strongly alkaline filtrate with pure muriatic acid, the further addition of a solution of carbonate of ammonia produces, either at once or after heating it for a few minutes, a light, white, flocculent precipitate, it is a sign of the presence of alumina, the identity of which is confirmed by collecting it on a filter, putting a small portion of it on a platinum hook, or on charcoal, heating it thereon, moistening the little mass with nitrate of cobalt, and again strongly heating it before the blowpipe; when if, *without fusing*, it assumes a beautiful blue colour, the presence of alumina is corroborated. If the operator possesses a silver capsule, he will do well to use it instead of a porcelain one for boiling the mass with pure caustic alcohol-potash, in order to avoid all chance of any silica (from the glaze) becoming dissolved by the potash, and afterwards simulating the presence of alumina, though, if the boiling be not protracted, a porcelain capsule is quite available. It is, however, absolutely necessary that he should use *potasse à l'alcohol*, for ordinary caustic potash *always* contains some, and occasionally considerable quantities of alumina, and is totally unsuited for such an investigation. Even *potasse à l'alcohol* retains traces of silica, either alone or combined with alumina; so that for this, and other reasons which will be explained presently, an extravagant quantity of it should not be used.

Lastly, carbonate of ammonia is preferable to caustic ammonia for precipitating the alumina, since that earth is far from being insoluble in caustic ammonia.

The liquor from which the alumina has been separated should now be acidified with hydrochloric acid, and tested with chloride of barium, which should then yield a copious precipitate of sulphate of barytes.

The only precipitate which can, under the circumstances of the experiment, simulate alumina, is the phosphate of that earth, which behaves with all reagents as pure alumina. Such a precipitate, therefore, if taken account of as pure alumina, would altogether vitiate a quantitative analysis if the amount of alum were calculated from it; but the proof that a certain quantity of alum had been used in the bread from which it had been obtained would remain unshaken; since alumina, whether in that state or in that of its phosphate, could not have been found except a salt of alumina —to wit, alum—had been used by the baker. When, therefore, the exact amount of alumina has to be determined, the precipitate in question should be submitted to further treatment in order to separate the alumina; and this can be done easily and rapidly by dissolving the precipitate in nitric acid, adding a little metallic tin to the liquor, and boiling. The tin becomes rapidly oxidised, and remains in the state of an insoluble white powder, which is a mixture of peroxide of tin and of phosphate of tin, at the expense of all the phosphoric acid of any earthy phosphate which may have been present. The whole mass is evaporated to dryness, and the dry residue is then treated by water and filtered, in order to separate the insoluble white powder, and the filtrate which contains the alumina should now be supersaturated with carbonate of ammonia. If a precipitate is formed, it is pure alumina. The white insoluble powder, after washing, may be dissolved in hydrochloric acid, and after diluting the solution with water, the tin may be precipitated therefrom by passing through it a stream of sulphuretted hydrogen to supersaturation, leaving at rest for ten or twelve hours, filtering, boiling the filtrate until all odour of sulphuretted hydrogen has disappeared; an excess of nitrate of silver is then added, and the liquor filtered, to separate the chloride of silver produced, and *exactly* neutralising the filtrate with ammonia; and if a lemon-yellow precipitate is produced, immediately soluble in the slightest excess of either ammonia or nitric acid, it is basic phosphate of silver (3AgO), PhO^5, the precipitate obtained in the first instance being thus proved to be phosphate of alumina. The pure alumina obtained may now be collected on a filter, washed with boiling water, thoroughly dried, and then ignited and weighed. One grain of alumina represents 9·027 grains of crystallised alum.

In testing bread for alum, it should be borne in mind, however, that the water used for making the dough generally contains a certain quantity of sulphates, and that a precipitate of sulphate of barytes will therefore be very frequently obtained, though much less considerable than when alum has been used. Some waters called ' selenitous' contain so much sulphate of lime in solution, that if they were used in making the dough, chloride of barium would afford, of course, a considerable precipitate. For these reasons, therefore, the separation and identification of alumina are the only reliable proofs; because, as that earth does not exist normally in any shape in wheat or common salt otherwise than in traces, the proof that alum has been used becomes irresistible when we find, on the one hand, alumina, and, on the other, a more considerable amount of sulphate of barytes than, except under the most extraordinary circumstances, genuine bread would yield.

Sulphate of copper, like alum, possesses the property of hardening gluten, and thus, with a flour of inferior quality, bread can be made of good appearance, as if a superior flour had been used.

The use of sulphate of copper in bread is said to have originated about 25 or 30 years ago with the bakers of Belgium.

M. Kuhlmann, Professor of Chemistry at Lille, having been called upon several times by the courts of justice to examine, by chemical processes, bread suspected of containing substances injurious to health, collected some interesting facts upon the subject, which were published under the direction of the central council of salubrity of the department du Nord.

For some time public attention has been drawn to an odious fraud committed by a great many bakers in the north of France and in Belgium,—the introduction of a certain quantity of sulphate of copper into their bread. When the flour was made from bad grain, this adulteration was very generally practised, as was proved by many convictions and confessions of the guilty persons. When the dough does not rise well in the fermentation (*le pain pousse plat*), this inconvenience was found to be obviated by the addition of blue vitriol, which was supposed also to cause the flour to retain more water. The quantity of blue vitriol added is extremely small, and it is never done in presence of strangers, because it is reckoned a valuable secret. It occasions no economy of yeast, but rather the reverse. In a litre (about a quart) of water, an ounce of sulphate of copper is dissolved; and of this solution a wine-glassful is mixed with the water necessary for 50 quartern or 4-pound loaves.

Lime water has been recommended by Liebig as a means of improving the bread made from inferior flour, or of flour slightly damaged by keeping, by warehousing, or during transport in ships; and this method, at the meeting of the British Association at Glasgow, in 1855, was reported as having been tried to a somewhat considerable extent by the bakers of that town, and with success; the bread kneaded with limewater, instead of pure water, being of good appearance, good taste, good texture, and free from the sour taste which invariably belongs to alumed or even to genuine bread;— admitting all this to be true, still we should deprecate the use of lime-water in bread, because it cannot be done with impunity; however small the dose of additional matter may be considered when taken separately, it is always large when considered as portion of an article of food like bread, consumed day after day, and at each meal, without interruption. To allow articles of food to be tampered with, under any circumstances, is a dangerous practice, even if it were proved that it can be done without risk, which, however, is not the case; and Liebig himself has said that chemists should never propose the use of chemical products for culinary preparations.

The quantity of ashes left after the incineration of genuine bread, varies from 1·5 at least to at most 3 per cent.; and if the latter quantity of ashes be exceeded, the excess may safely be pronounced to be due to an artificial introduction of some saline or earthy matter.

As to the addition to bread of potatoes, beans, rice, turnips, maize, or Indian corn, which has occasionally been practised to a considerable extent, especially in years of scarcity, it is evident that they are actually permitted under the Act of Parliament, Will. IV. cap. 27. sect. 11.

In his 'New Letters on Chemistry,' Liebig makes the following remarks on the subject:—

'The proposals which have hitherto been made to use substitutes for flour, and thus diminish the price of bread in times of scarcity, prove how much the rational principles of hygiene are disregarded, and how unknown the laws of nutrition are still. It is with food as with fuel. If we compare the price of the various kinds of coals, of wood, of turf, we shall find that the number of pence paid for a certain volume or weight of these materials is about proportionate to the number of degrees of heat which they evolve in burning. . . . . . The mean price of food in a large country is ordinarily the criterion of its nutritive value. . . . . . Considered as a nutritive agent, rye is quite as dear as wheat; such is the case also with rice and potatoes; in fact, no other flour can replace wheat in this respect. In times of scarcity, however, these ratios undergo modification, and potatoes and rice acquire then a higher value, because, in addition to their natural value as respiratory food, another value is superadded, which in times of abundance is not taken into account.

'The addition to wheat flour of potato starch, of dextrine, of the pulp of turnips, gives a mixture, the nutritive value of which is equal to that of potatoes, or perhaps less; and it is evident that one cannot consider as an improvement this transformation of wheat flour into a food having only the same value as rice or potatoes.'

The detection of potato starch, of beans, peas, Indian corn, rice, and other feculæ, which is so easily effected by means of the microscope in flour, is exceedingly difficult, if not impossible, in bread. Bread which has been made with flour mixed with Indian corn is harsher to the touch, and has frequently a slight yellowish colour, and when moistened with solution of potash of ordinary strength, a yellow or greenish-yellow tinge is developed.—The late Dr. A. N. See TOAST, LEAVEN.

We exported in 1871 the following quantities of BREAD and BISCUITS:—

	cwts.
To Russia	2,157
Sweden	2,249
Norway	3,778
Germany	1,967
Holland	10,107
Belgium	9,039
France	194,646
Portugal, Azores, and Madeira	2,353
Italy	7,433
United States,—Atlantic	10,027
Pacific	104
Foreign West Indies	2,424
Peru	1,515
Brazil	3,965
Argentine Confederation	2,219
Channel Islands	4,586
British India:	
Bombay and Scinde	1,611
Bengal	1,499
Ceylon	2,045
British West India Islands and British Guiana	2,296
Other countries	25,027
	291,047

BREAD-FRUIT TREE. (*Artocarpaceæ*, ἄρτος, *bread*; χαρπὸς, *fruit.*) The *A. incisa*, the true bread-fruit tree, is a native of the South Sea Islands, inhabiting such places as are hot and damp. The tree is about twelve inches diameter, and grows to the height of forty feet. The fruit is about the size of a melon, and the seeds are large nut-like bodies. The fleshy receptacle is the valuable part of the fruit. It is very white, and of the consistence of new bread. When washed it becomes excellent food, tasting like wheaten bread, only a little sweeter.

A cloth is made of the fibres of the inner bark; the wood is used for building houses and boats. The leaves are used as towels and table-cloths, and to wrap provisions in. The male catkins serve as tinder, and the juice is employed as birdlime, and to mend the cracks in the water vessels of the natives. See COW TREE, JACK TREE, UPAS TREE.

BRECCIA. An Italian term used for a rock composed of angular fragments of stone, cemented together by an earthy or a mineral substance. It corresponds to the 'brockrans' of the Cumberland miners.

BRECCIATED AGATE. An agate composed of fragments of jasper, bloodstone, &c., cemented by chalcedony.

BREEZES. (*Braise*, Fr.) The dust of coke or charcoal. The coke burner applies this term to the small residual coke obtained in coke burning. The sifted ashes removed from houses is called *breeze*, and sold under that name to brickmakers and others.

BREEZE OVEN. An oven for the manufacture of small coke. Mr. Joseph Davis, of Birmingham, has patented (*Specification*, A.D. 1856, No. 1,425) a breeze oven, many of which are in use in South Staffordshire. The 'thick coal' of South Staffordshire is employed in this oven. The slack is screened, and the finer part is burnt on the grate adjoining the boiler, the remainder is converted into 'breezes.' Mr. Davis's specification will most completely illustrate and explain the character of this oven :—

This invention consists of a coke oven, constructed, arranged, and used as hereinafter described, and illustrated in the accompanying drawings, for the manufacture of the small coke called *breezes*, for economising of heat, and for the suppression or partial suppression of smoke.

243   244

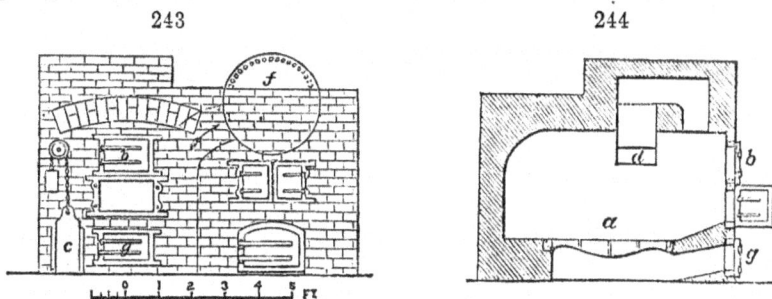

Fig. 243 of the accompanying drawing represents in elevation, *fig.* 244 in vertical section, and *fig.* 245 in plan, a coke oven, combined with the furnace of a steam-boiler, constructed according to this invention.

245

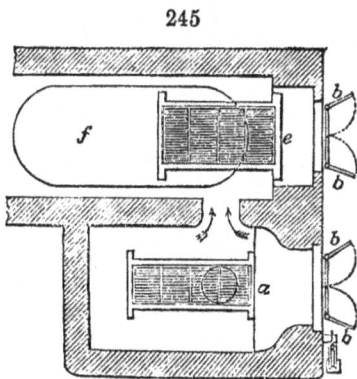

The said coke oven consists of a chamber or furnace, *a*, provided with doors, *b, b*, by which said doors the coal to be coked is introduced and the admission of air regulated. The draught may be further regulated by means of the damper, *c*. The oven, *a*, is also provided with flues, *d*, in which flues dampers may be situated. The heated air and flame from the oven, *a*, may be conducted therefrom either into a stack or chimney, or into the furnace or fireplace, *e*, of a steam-boiler, *f*, or the said heated air and flame may be conducted elsewhere, where they can be applied to heating or other useful purpose. When the flame and heated air from the coke oven, *a*, are conducted into the furnace, *e*, of a steam-boiler, *f*, they may be delivered at or near the bridge of the said furnace, when they will effect the suppression or partial suppression of the smoke from the said furnace. The heat from the coke oven, *a*, also increases the production of steam in the boiler, *f*,

When the coal in the oven, a, has been converted into the small coke, called breezes, the combustion is stopped by the closing of the doors, $b\,b$, damper, c, and the door, g, of the ash-pit; and the breezes are cooled by the introduction of a jet of water into the said oven, the said water being directed upon the breezes; or the said breezes may be withdrawn from the oven in a heated state, and afterwards cooled by water of otherwise. Although I prefer to place the coke oven on the side of the boiler, as represented, yet it may be placed under the boiler, or in any other convenient situation.

Although I have only represented in the accompanying drawing the combination of a coke oven for manufacturing breezes with a steam-boiler, yet the said oven may be combined with any other furnace for the purpose of increasing its heat and suppressing or partially suppressing its smoke; but I believe the nature of my said invention will be sufficiently understood by the description herein given, and illustrated in the accompanying drawing.

The size and form of the ovens may be varied to suit the quantity of breezes to be manufactured, and the particular purposes to which the flame and heated air from the said ovens are to be applied.

BREMEN BLUE and **GREEN.** Pigments containing a basic carbonate of copper with alumina and carbonate of lime. According to one method, blue vitriol (sulphate of copper) is dissolved in 10 parts of water, and a little aquafortis added; the liquid is allowed to stand for a week, and is then filtered; after addition of lime-water, it is precipitated by a solution of pearlash. By Gentele's method, these pigments are prepared from common salt and blue vitriol. A blue or a green colour is produced, according as the pigment is mixed with water or with linseed oil.

BREWING. (*Brasser*, Fr.; *Brauen*, Ger.) The art of making beer, or an alcoholic liquor, from a fermented infusion of some saccharine and amylaceous substance with water.

Figs. 246 and 247 represent the arrangement of the utensils and machinery in a porter brewery on the largest scale, in which it must be observed that the elevation *fig.* 247, is in a great degree imaginary as to the plane upon which it is taken, but the different vessels are arranged so as to explain their uses most readily, and at the same time to preserve, as nearly as possible, the relative position which is usually assigned to each in works of this nature.

The malt for the supply of the brewery is stored in vast granaries or malt-lofts, usually situated in the upper part of the buildings. Of these, we have been able to represent only one, at A, *fig.* 246: the others, which are supposed to be on each side of it, cannot be seen in this view. Immediately beneath the granary A, on the ground-floor, is the mill; in the upper storey above it, are two pairs of rollers (*figs.* 246, 248, and 249), under $a\,a$, for bruising or crushing the grains of the malt. In the floor beneath the rollers are the mill-stones $b\,b$, where the malt is sometimes ground, instead of being merely bruised by passing between the rollers, under $a\,a$.

The malt, when prepared, is conveyed by a trough into a chest d, to the left of b, from which it can be elevated by the action of a spiral screw, *fig.* 250, enclosed in the sloping tube e, into the large chest or bin B, for holding ground malt, situated immediately over the mash-tun D. The mash-tun is a large circular tub with a double bottom; the uppermost of which is called a false bottom, and is pierced with many holes. There is a space of about 2 or 3 inches between the two, into which the stop-cocks enter, for letting in the water and drawing off the wort. The holes of the false bottom, if of wood, should be burned, and not bored, to prevent the chance of their filling up by the swelling of the wood, which would obstruct the drainage: the holes should be conical, and largest below, being about $\frac{3}{8}$ths of an inch there, and $\frac{1}{4}$th at the upper surface. The perforated bottom must be fitted truly to the sides of the mash-tun, so that no grains may pass through. The mashed liquor is let off into a large back, from which it is pumped into the wort-coppers. The mash-tun is provided with a peculiar rotatory apparatus for agitating the crushed grains and water together, which we shall presently describe. The size of the wort-copper is proportional to the amount of the brewing, and it must, in general, be at least so large as to operate upon the whole quantity of wort made from one mashing; that is, for every quarter of malt mashed, the copper should contain 140 gallons. The mash-tun ought to be at least a third larger, and of a conical form, somewhat wider below than above. The malt is reserved in this bin till wanted, and is then let down into the mashing-tun, where the extract is obtained by hot water supplied from the copper G, seen to the left of B.

The water for the service of the brewery is obtained from the well E, seen beneath the mill to the right, by a lifting pump worked by the steam-engine; and the forcing-pipe f, of this pump conveys the water up to the large reservoir or water-back F, placed at the top of the engine-house. From this cistern, iron pipes are laid to the copper G (on the left-hand side of the figure), as also to every part of the establishment where

cold water can be wanted for cleaning and washing the vessels. The copper G can
be filled with cold water by merely turning a cock; and the water when boiled therein,

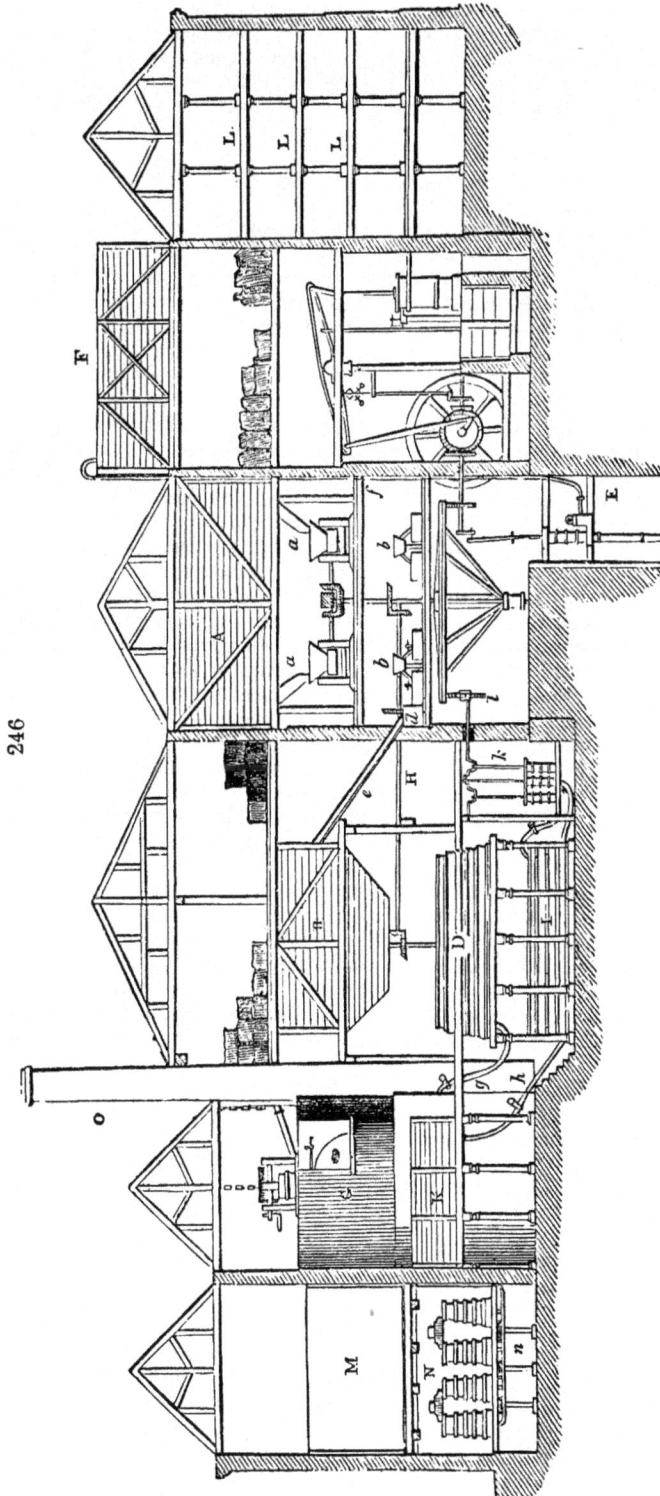

is conveyed by the pipe *g* into the bottom of the mash-tun D. The water is introduced beneath a false bottom, upon which the malt lies; and, rising up through the

holes in the false bottom, it extracts the saccharine matter from the malt; a greater or less time being allowed for the infusion, according to circumstances. The instant the water is drawn off from the copper, fresh water must be let into it, in order to be ready for boiling the second mashing, because the copper must not be left empty for a moment, otherwise the intense heat of the fire would destroy its bottom. For the convenience of thus letting down at once as much liquor as will fill the lower part of the copper, a pan or second boiler is placed over the top of the copper, as seen in *fig.* 252; and the steam rising from the copper communicates a considerable degree of heat to the contents of the pan, without any expense of fuel. This will be more minutely explained hereafter.

During the process of mashing, the malt is agitated in the mash-tun, so as to expose every part to the action of the water. This is done by a mechanism contained within the mash-tun, which is put in motion by a horizontal shaft above it, H, leading from the mill. The mash machine is shown separately in *fig.* 251. When the operation of mashing is finished, the wort or extract is drained down from the malt into the vessel I, called the *underback*, immediately below the mash-tun, of like dimensions, and situated always on a lower level, for which reason it has received this name. Here the wort does not remain longer than is necessary to drain off the whole of it from the tun above. It is then pumped up by the three-barrelled pump *k*, into the pan upon the top of the copper, by a pipe which cannot be seen in this section. The wort remains in the pan until the water for the succeeding mashes is discharged from the copper. But this delay is no loss of time, because the heat of the copper, and the steam arising from it, prepare the wort, which had become cooler, for boiling. The instant the copper is emptied, the first wort is let down from the pan into the copper, and the second wort is pumped up from the under-back into the upper pan. The proper proportion of hops is thrown into the copper through the near hole, and then the door is shut down and screwed fast, to keep in the steam, and cause it to rise up through pipes into the pan. It is thus forced to blow up through the wort in the pan, and communicates so much heat to it, or to water, called *liquor* by the brewers, that either is brought near to the boiling point. The different worts succeed each other through all the different vessels with the greatest regularity, so that there is no loss of time, but every part of the apparatus is constantly employed. When the ebullition has continued a sufficient period to coagulate the grosser part of the extract, and to evaporate part of the water, the contents of the copper are run off through a large cock into the *jack-back* K, below G, which is a vessel of sufficient dimensions to contain it, and provided with a bottom of cast-iron plates, perforated with small holes, through which the wort drains and leaves the hops. The hot wort is drawn off from the jack-back through the pipe *h* by the three-barrelled pump, which throws it up to the coolers L L L; this pump being made with different pipes and cocks of communication, to serve all the purposes of the brewery, except that of raising the cold water from the well. The coolers, L L L, are very shallow vessels, built over one another in several stages; and that part of the building in which they are contained is built with lattice-work or shutter flaps, on all sides to admit free currents of air. When the wort is sufficiently cooled to be put to the first fermentation, it is conducted in pipes from all the different coolers to the large fermenting vessel or gyle-tun M, which, with another similar vessel behind it, is of sufficient capacity to contain all the beer of one day's brewing.

Whenever the first fermentation is concluded, the beer is drawn off from the great fermenting vessel M, into the small fermenting casks or cleansing vessels N, of which there are a great number in the brewery. They are placed four together, and to each four a common spout is provided to carry off the yeast, and conduct it into the troughs *u*, placed beneath. In these cleansing vessels the beer remains till the fermentation is completed; and it is then put into the store-vats, which are casks or tuns of an immense size, where it is kept till wanted, and is finally drawn off into barrels, and sent away from the brewery. The store-vats are not represented in the figure: they are of a conical shape, and of different dimensions, for fifteen to twenty feet diameter, and usually from fifteen to twenty feet in depth. The steam-engine, which puts all the machine in motion, is exhibited in its place on the right side of the figure. On the axis of the large fly-wheel is a bevelled spur-wheel, which turns another similar wheel upon the end of a horizontal shaft, which extends from the engine-house to the great horse-wheel, set in motion by means of a spur-wheel. The horse-wheel drives all the pinions for the mill-stones *b b*, and also the horizontal axis which works the three-barrelled pump *k*. The rollers *a a* are turned by a bevel wheel upon the upper end of the axis of the horse-wheel, which is prolonged for that purpose; and the horizontal shaft H, for the mashing engine, is driven by a pair of bevel wheels. There is likewise a sack-tackle, which is not represented. It is a machine for drawing up the sacks of malt from the court-yard to the highest part of the building, whence the sacks are wheeled on a truck to the malt-loft A, and the contents of the sack are discharged.

The horse-wheel is intended to be driven by horses occasionally, if the steam-engine should fail; but these engines are now brought to such perfection that it is very seldom any resource of this kind is needed.

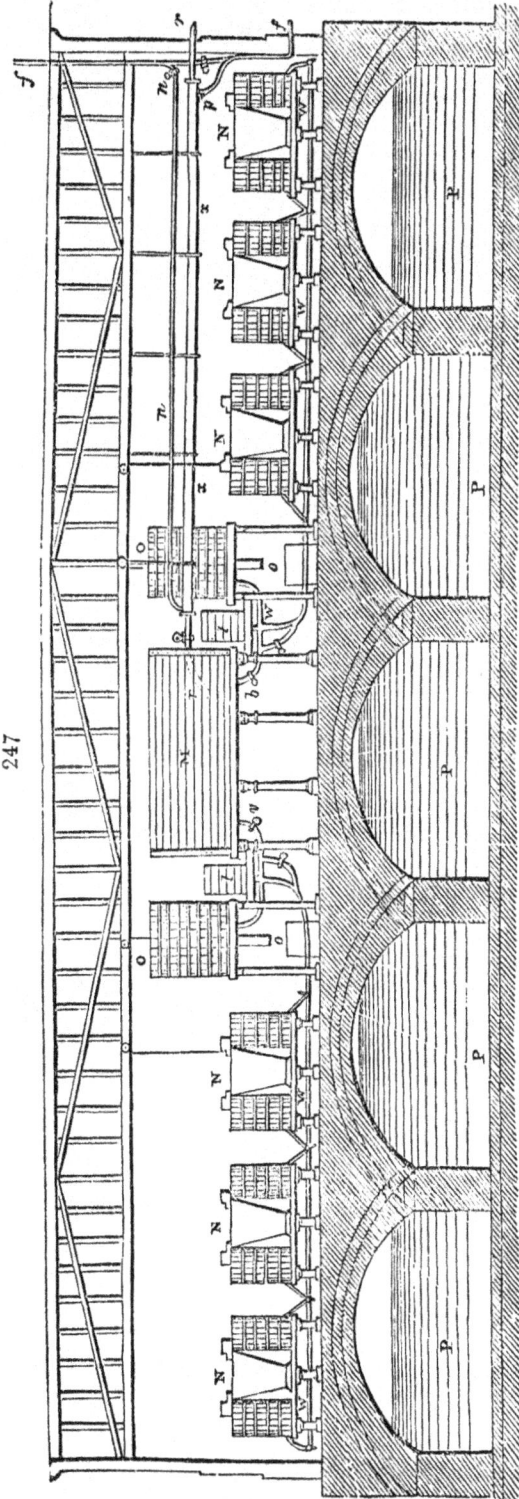

Fig. 247 is a representation of the *fermenting-house* at the brewery of Messrs. Whitbread and Company, Chiswell Street, London, which is one of the most complete in its arrangement in the world: it was erected after the plan of Mr. Richardson, who conducts the brewing at those works. The whole of *fig.* 247 is to be considered as devoted to the same object as the large vessel M and the casks N, *fig.* 246. In *fig.* 247, *r r* is the pipe which leads from the different coolers to convey the wort to the great fermenting vessels or squares M, of which there are two, one behind the other; *f f* represent a part of the great pipe which conveys all the water from the well E, *fig.* 246, up to the water cistern F. This pipe is conducted purposely up the wall of the fermenting-house, *fig.* 247, and has a cock in it, near *r*, to stop the passage. Just beneath this passage a branch-pipe *p* proceeds, and enters a large pipe *x x*, which has the former pipe *r* withinside of it. From the end of the pipe *x*, nearest to the squares M, another branch *n n* proceeds, and returns to the original pipe *f*, with a cock to regulate it. The object of this arrangement is to make all, or any part, of the cold water flow through the pipe *x x*, which surrounds the pipe *r*, formed only of thin copper, and thus cool the wort passing through the pipe *r*, until it is found by the thermometer to have the exact temperature which is desirable before it is put to ferment in the great square M. By means of the cocks at *n* and *p*, the quantity of cold water passing over the surface of the pipe *r* can be regulated at pleasure, whereby the heat of the wort, when it enters into the square, may be adjusted within half a degree.

When the first fermentation in the squares M M is finished, the beer is drawn off from them by pipes marked *v*, and conducted by its branches w w w, to the different rows of fermenting-tuns, marked N N, which occupy the greater part of the building. In the hollow between every two rows are placed large troughs, to contain the yeast which they throw off. The figure shows that the small tuns are all placed on a lower level than the bottom of the great vessels M, so that the beer will flow into them, and, by hydrostatic equilibrium, will fill them to the same level. When they are filled, the communication-cock is shut; but, as the working off the yeast diminishes the quantity of beer in each vessel, it is necessary to replenish them from time to time. For this purpose, the two large vats o o are filled from the great squares M M, before any beer is drawn off into the small casks N, and this quantity of beer is reserved at the higher level for filling up. The two vessels o o are, in reality, situated between the two squares M M; but I have been obliged to place them thus in the section, in order that they may be seen. Near each filling-up tun o is a small cistern t, communicating with the tun o by a pipe, which is closed by a float-valve. The small cisterns t are always in communication with the pipes which lead to the small fermenting vessels N; and therefore the surface of the beer in all the tuns, and in the cisterns, will always be at the same level; and as this level subsides by the working off of the yeast from the tuns, the float sinks and opens the valve, so as to admit a sufficiency of beer from the filling-up tuns o, to restore the surfaces of the beer in all the tuns, and also in the cistern t, to the original level. In order to carry off the yeast which is produced by the fermentation of the beer in the tuns o o, a conical iron dish or funnel is made to float upon the surface of the beer which they contain; and from the centre of this funnel a pipe, o, descends, and passes through the bottom of the tun, being packed with a collar of leather, so as to be water-tight; at the same time that it is at liberty to slide down, as the surface of the beer descends in the tun. The yeast flows over the edge of this funnel-shaped dish, and is conveyed down the pipe into a trough beneath.

Beneath the fermenting-house are large arched vaults, P, built with stone, and lined with stucco. Into these the beer is let down in casks when sufficiently fermented, and is kept in store till wanted. These vaults are used at Mr. Whitbread's brewery, instead of the great store-vats of which we have before spoken, and are in some respects preferable, because they preserve a great equality of temperature, being beneath the surface of the earth.

The kiln-dried malt is sometimes ground between stones in a common corn-mill, like oatmeal; but it is more generally crushed between iron rollers, at least for the purpose of the London brewers.

The Crushing Mill.—The cylinder malt-mill is constructed as shown in *figs.* 248, 249. I is the sloping-trough, by which the malt is let down from its bin or floor to the hopper A of the mill, whence it is progressively shaken in between the rollers B D. The rollers are of iron, truly cylindrical, and their ends rest in bearers of hard brass, fitted into the side frames of iron. A screw E goes through the upright, and serves to force the bearer of the one roller towards that of the other, so as to bring them closer together when the crushing effect is to be increased. G is the square end of the axis, by which one of the rollers may be turned either by the hand or by power; the other derives its rotatory motion from a pair of equal-toothed wheels H, which are fitted to the other end of the axes of the rollers. *d* is a catch which works into the teeth of a ratchet-wheel on the end of one of the rollers (not shown in this view). The lever *c* strikes the trough *b* at the bottom of the hopper, and gives it the shaking motion for discharging the malt between the rollers, from the side sluice *a*. *e e, fig.* 248, are scraper-plates of sheet iron, the edges of which press by a weight against the surfaces of the rollers, and keep them clean.

Instead of the cylinders, some employ a crushing mill of a conical-grooved form, like a coffee-mill upon a large scale.

Fig. 250 is the screw by which the ground or bruised malt is raised up, or conveyed from one part of the brewery to another. K is an inclined box or trough, in the centre of which the axis of the screw H is placed; the spiral iron plate or worm, which is fixed projecting from the axis, and which forms the screw, is made very nearly to

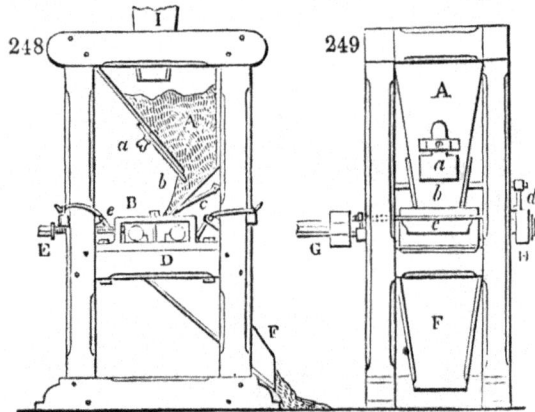

fill the inside of the box. By this means, when the screw is turned round by the wheels E F, or by any other means, it raises up the malt from the box *d*, and delivers it at the spout G.

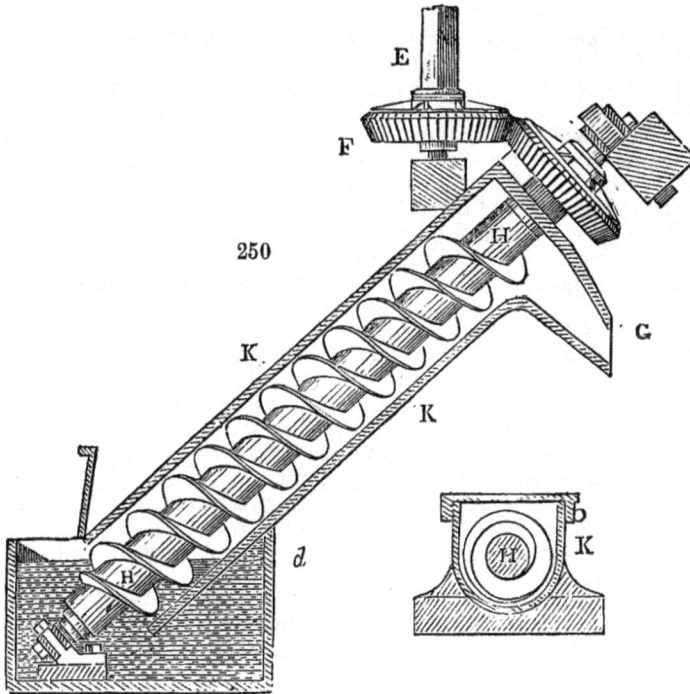

250

This screw is equally applicable for conveying the malt horizontally in the trough K, as slantingly; and similar machines are employed in various parts of breweries for conveying the malt wherever the situation of the works require.

Fig. 251 is the mashing-machine. *a a* is the tun, made of wood staves hooped together. In the centre of it rises a perpendicular shaft *b*, which is turned slowly round

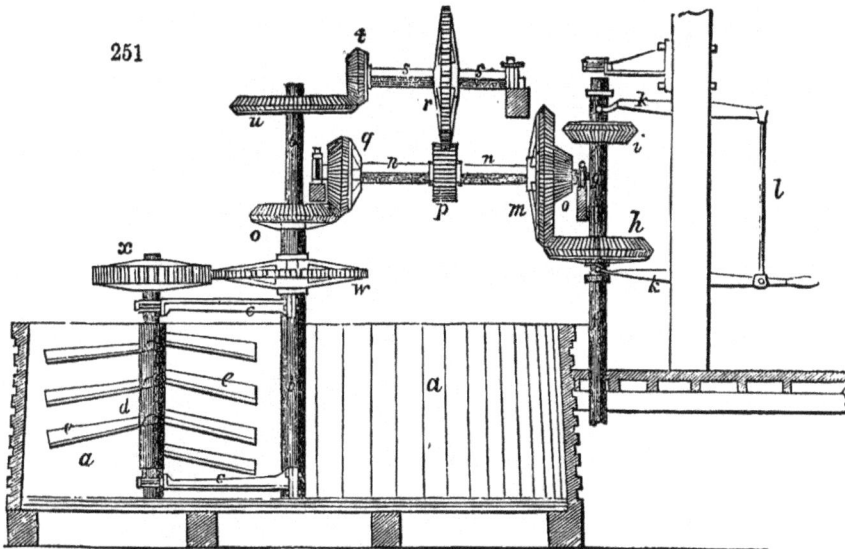

251

by means of the bevelled wheels *t u* at the top. *c c* are two arms projecting from that axis, and supporting the short vertical axis *d* of the spur-wheel *x*, which is turned by the spur-wheel *w*; so that, when the central axis *b* is made to revolve, it will carry the thick short axle *d* round the tun in a circle. That axle *d* is furnished with a number of arms, *e e*, which have blades placed obliquely to the plane of their motion. When the axis is turned round, these arms agitate the malt in the tun, and give it a constant tendency to rise upwards from the bottom.

The motion of the axle *d* is produced by a wheel, *x*, on the upper end of it, which is turned by a wheel, *w*, fastened on the middle of the tube *b*, which turns freely round upon its central axis. Upon a higher point of the same tube *b* is a bevel wheel *o*, receiving motion from a bevel wheel *q*, fixed upon the end of the horizontal axis *n n*, which gives motion to the whole machine. This same axis has a pinion *p* upon it, which gives motion to the wheel *r*, fixed near the middle of a horizontal axle, which, at its left-hand end, has a bevel pinion *t*, working the wheel *u*, before mentioned. By these means, the rotation of the central axis *b* will be very slow compared with the motion of the axle *d*; for the latter will make seventeen or eighteen revolutions on its own axis in the same space of time that it will be carried once round the tun by the motion of the shaft *b*. At the beginning of the operation of mashing, the machine is made to turn with a slow motion; but, after having wetted all the malt by one revolution, it is driven quicker. For this purpose, the ascending-shaft *f g*, which gives motion to the machine, has two bevel wheels *h i*, fixed upon a tube *f g*, which is fitted upon a central shaft. These wheels actuate the wheels *m* and *o*, upon the end of the horizontal shaft *n n*; but the distance between the two wheels *h* and *i* is such that they cannot be engaged both at once with the wheels *m* and *o*; but the tube *f g*, to which they are fixed, is capable of sliding up and down on its central axis sufficiently to bring either wheel *h* or *i* into gear with its corresponding wheel *o* or *m*, upon the horizontal shaft; and as the diameters of *n o* and *i m* are of very different proportions, the velocity of the motion of the machine can be varied at pleasure, by using one or other. *k* and *k* are two levers, which are forked at their extremities, and embrace collars at the ends of the tube *f g*. These levers being united by a rod, *l*, the handle *k* gives the means of moving the tube *f g*, and its wheels *h i*, up or down, to throw either the one or the other wheel into gear.

Figs. 252, 253 represent the copper of a London brewery. *Fig.* 252 is a vertical section; *fig.* 253, a ground plan of the fire-grate and flue, upon a smaller scale: *a* is the close

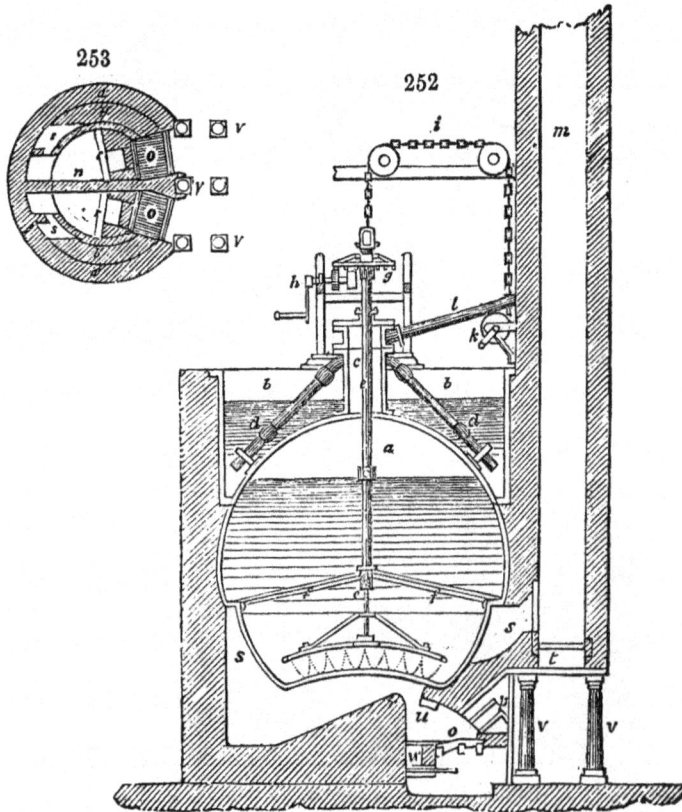

copper kettle, having its bottom convex within; *b* is the open pan placed upon its top. From the upper part of the copper, a wide tube, *c*, ascends, to carry off the steam generated during the ebullition of the wort, which is conducted through four downwards-slanting tubes, *d d* (two only are visible in this section), into the liquor of the pan *b*, in order to warm its contents. A vertical iron shaft or spindle, *e*, passes down through the tube *c*, nearly to the bottom of the copper, and is there mounted with an iron arm, called *a rouser*, which carries round a chain hung in loops, to prevent the hops from adhering to the bottom of the boiler. Three bent stays, *f*, are stretched across the interior, to support the shaft by a collet at their middle junction. The shaft carries at its upper end a bevel wheel *g*, working into a bevel pinion upon the axis *h*, which may be turned either by power or by hand. The *rouser* shaft may be lifted by means of the chain *i*, which, going over two pulleys, has its end passed round the wheel and axle *k*, and is turned by a winch : *l* is a tube for conveying the waste steam into the chimney *m*.

The heat is applied as follows :—For heating the colossal coppers of the London breweries, two separate fires are required, which are separated by a narrow wall of brickwork, *n*, *figs*. 252, 253. The dotted circle *a′ a′*, indicates the largest circumference of the copper, and *b′ b′* its bottom; *o o* are the grates upon which the coals are thrown, not through folding doors (as of old), but through a short slanting iron hopper, shown at *p*, *fig*. 252, built in the wall, and kept constantly filled with the fuel, in order to exclude the air. Thus the low stratum of coals gets ignited before it reaches the grate. Above the hopper *p*, a narrow channel is provided for the admission of atmospherical air, in such quantity merely as may be requisite to complete the combustion of the smoke of the coals. Behind each grate there is a fire bridge, *r*, which reflects the flame upwards, and causes it to play upon the bottom of the copper. The burnt air then passes round the copper in a semicircular flue, *s s*, from which it flows off into the chimney *m*, on whose under end a sliding damper-plate, *t*, is placed, for tempering the draught. When cold air is admitted at this orifice, the combustion of the fuel is immediately checked. There is, besides, another slide-plate at the entrance of the slanting flue into the vertical chimney, for regulating the play of the flame under and around the copper. If the plate *t* be opened, and the other plate shut, the power of the fire is suspended, as it ought to be, at the time of emptying the copper. Immediately over the grate is a brick arch, *u*, to protect the front edge of the copper from the first impulsion of the flame. The chimney is supported upon iron pillars, *v v*; *w* is a cavity closed with a slide-plate, through which the ashes may be taken out from behind, by means of a long iron hook.

We have thus given the general plan and requisites for a brewery on a large scale. We need scarcely say those arrangements will vary in every establishment, according to the requirements and facilities of the locality, and the various modes of operation. The few simple utensils required may be easily recapitulated :—

1. A mill for crushing the malt.
2. An iron pan for heating water.
3. A mash-tun or open tub fitted with a false bottom, a strainer, or with some other means of allowing the wort to run off freely, keeping back the grains.
4. An iron or copper pan for boiling the wort.
5. A shallow vessel or cooler, over which is placed the hop-jack or sieve for straining out the spent-hops.
6. A gyle tun or open tub for commencement of the fermentation.
7. A barrel or cask in which the cleansing is completed.

The first necessity is a plentiful supply of pure water, which it should be the chief aim in all arrangements to render available at the least labour and cost, as on its proper and judicious application greatly depends the regulation of the temperature in the various operations; and the most scrupulous cleanliness in every part is of the utmost importance. The fermenting rooms and store-cellars should be placed below the ground level, for the purpose of attaining a low and equable temperature ; and for this purpose also the double stone fermenting square is highly esteemed. It consists of an inner cubical vessel, containing from fifteen to thirty barrels ; each side formed by one slab of fine slate. This is placed in an exterior square or shell of inferior stone, leaving a space between the inner and outer squares, which can be filled with hot or cold water at pleasure. The inner or fermenting square has a manhole, with a raised rim, in the slab forming the top, on which also are raised four other fine slate slabs, which form a cistern for the expansion and overflow of the beer and yeast during the process of the fermentation, and from which the yeast is readily removed at its close.

The process of brewing may be classed under three heads : the mashing, the boiling, and the fermentation.

For the principle which should guide the brewer in the conduct of these operations, we refer to the article BEER, where it will be seen that the ultimate success of the entire series depends greatly on the regulation of the temperature, the duration, and the proper management of the initial process of malting.

The Mashing.—Upon this very important process information, the result of Dr. A.

Schwarzer's researches, is perhaps the most valuable and precise of the present day, and it would be well if every brewer were familiar with them.

In the *Brewers' Journal*, January 15, 1871, this information is fully detailed, but as the number may not easily be obtainable, it is here reinserted :—

'As a general rule, the larger the quantity of diastase and the greater the heat up to a certain point, the more rapid is the transformation of the gummy portion of the starch into sugar.

'At a temperature of about 167° Fahr., and especially at 177° or 178°, however, a diminution takes place in the action of the diastase, which increases with the further increase of the temperature; and if the heat be raised for a certain time to about 190°, the action of the diastase ceases altogether.

'If also an extract of malt be heated to 190° before the starch is added, a diminution in the action occurs, which is the more determined according to the length of time at which the heat has been maintained.

'The quantity of diastase thus rendered inactive may be ascertained by comparing the action of a certain amount of the overheated extract, with that of a like quantity at the temperature of 145°. Observation must be taken of the time which elapses before all reaction ceases to be exhibited by the iodine test; and the same test must be applied to the action of the extract submitted to the lower temperature.

'Two per cent. of an extract of malt, not weakened by heating, effects the transformation more rapidly than four times that percentage kept at the heat of 178° for one hour, or than twenty per cent. of the same extract maintained for the same period at a temperature of 190°. In the last case scarcely one-tenth of the diastase originally developed in the malt remains in the extract.

'With minute quantities of diastase the action proceeds more rapidly at first with a temperature of 190°, but afterward more slowly than at 145°.

'When the iodine test shows no discolouration, the saccharification is practically terminated, and the continuance of the action of the diastase yields an infinitesimal quantity of sugar.

'If, in one hour, and until the iodine shows no discolouration, fifty per cent. of sugar is formed, and if, during the next three hours, only two per cent. is produced, it is certain that the iodine test shows practically the action is finished.

'The cause of this feeble saccharification after the iodine test ceases to act, does not, however, arise from the exhaustion of the energy of the diastase, because if a new amount of starch be added, it will be rapidly transformed.

'At all temperatures from 167° to 32°, even though employing very different proportions of diastase, from fifty to fifty-three per cent. of sugar is invariably produced from the starch in the extract.

'Admitting that the starch is transformed into an equivalent of sugar, and an equivalent of dextrine, analysis shows that the sugar to be obtained from the extract amounts to 52·6 per cent. of the extract.

'The amount of sugar obtained in practice differs so little from this rate that the small difference may fairly be supposed to arise from errors in the quantities and interruptions in the action of the diastase.

'At temperatures exceeding 167° the quantity of sugar produced falls off in proportion.

'At 190°, after the iodine test ceases to act, the amount of sugar formed in the extract may fall off to twenty-seven per cent.; and even if the extract is heated to that temperature before the addition of the starch gum, and the greatest care be taken to prevent cooling during the experiment, very little change indeed will be observed in the percentage.

'If all these facts be taken into account, it seems certain, that the action of the diastase at temperature below 167° is very different from what it is under greater heats.

'The amount of sugar equal to twenty-seven per cent. which is the minimum value at which the iodine test ceases to exhibit any change, agrees exactly with the transformation of starch into an equivalent of sugar and an equivalent of dextrine.

'A fact deserving of notice is, that between the temperatures of 167° and 190° the difference in the amount of sugar formed is more than twenty per cent.

'In maintaining the extract of malt at 190° for a long period, it is so greatly altered that when the heat is afterward lowered, the amount of sugar is not, or scarcely at all, increased; but if, on the contrary, a solution of starch which contains about twenty-seven per cent. of sugar, be heated to 190°, and afterwards submitted to the action of diastase, not heated and enfeebled at a lower temperature, the percentage may be carried to fifty-two per cent.

'During fermentation, the diastase continues to effect the transformation of starch; and it is not improbable that yeast acts in the same manner as the former.'

With these very important facts before us, it is comparatively easy for the brewer to determine his rule or mode of operation in the process of mashing.

As the heats approaching to 167° tend to detract from the energy of the diastase, such must of course as much as possible be avoided, it being known with equal certainty that when malt-wort is allowed to drop its temperature to a heat approaching 140°, it is liable to acetancy, and more readily so, as the temperature recedes below 140°; about 120° being the most favourable to the change.

Therefore it is advisable that the wort should reach the copper before such a temperature is attained; still further it is ascertained that the value of the desired transformation in the malt-wort is best obtained with a temperature of about 151°, also that saccharification is promoted by agitation, and that the stronger the extract is, the less is the danger of acetification.

Therefore, in the first place, the brewer has to obtain a mash of 151° temperature or thereabouts; but he must do it with liquor as far removed below 167° as possible, and when the goods are thoroughly mashed, 151° of heat should be maintained during their clarification; the wort should then be run from the mash-tun into a copper suitably warmed beforehand, and should then be slowly and carefully heated up to boiling, just by the time the subsequent exhaustion of the malt is completed by the 'sparging.'

In practice the following method will be found extremely easy, and safe in operation:—

Some time before commencing the mash, a sufficiency of boiling water is run into the tun to make it as hot as possible, and immediately before commencing the brewing this hot water is let off again into the underback, or the copper; this being done, the mashing liquor having previously been very carefully prepared, is let into the tun under the false bottom, to the quantity of about one and a half barrels to the quarter of malt, where it arrives at about 164° temperature; when a sufficiency has been let in, the grist is then added and thoroughly mashed, the infusion will then be about 150°, the temperature of reserve mashing liquor has been raised, and when the malt is effectually mashed, a further quantity of about half a barrel per quarter is run in at 166°, and thoroughly mixed up with the mash: the object of the additional liquor is to raise the heat of the mash to about 152°, after which settling and clarification are requisite; this usually occupies about two hours.

The tun having been thoroughly heated before the admission of the mash, it does not abstract the heat from the infusion, either during the operation or when it is completed, but materially assists to maintain the heat for a very considerable time; with a well-protected and covered tun it will do it for four hours if required, without allowing the temperature to drop a single degree.

This is of the greatest importance, for the wort leaves the mash-tun at about 151°; and as it is passed from vessel to vessel is immediately preceded by the hot water from the vessel before it; thus, in turn, each vessel is thoroughly warmed, and we need hardly say most thoroughly cleansed, and being prepared in this way enables the operator to get the wort into the copper before it can fall even to 146° or 147°, leaving the mash in the tun at such heat that all danger of acetification is entirely removed.

As the full value of the mash cannot be obtained by one maceration, recourse is now had to 'sparging,' and to do this properly requires a little careful thought and more careful management.

In the operation of mashing every possible care should be taken that the infused malt—called 'goods'—when drained should lay perfectly level, otherwise the sparging liquor, in running off, will form for itself courses through those portions of the mash that offer the least resistance, and as a consequence some parts of the 'goods' will have treatment in excess of what is desirable, while other portions will be kept with an imperfect sparge.

The liquor for sparging should be of such a heat that it will, on penetrating the 'goods,' raise their temperature gradually from, say 148° or so, to 167° or 168° at the close, this will generally be found sufficient to dissolve out of them all the tractable portions of dextrine, &c. that are of any real value.

It is advisable during the operation to allow the infused malt to drain two or three times that the act of compression may express from them those portions of sweet wort detained in the texture of each individual grain; this will enable the brewer to obtain the whole of the value that is producible from his malt, which may on that account be treated with less pressure in the grinding; care in this latter particular will considerably facilitate all subsequent operations, and give a brilliancy and superior quality to the beer unattainable by other means.

In drawing the wort from the mash-tun, no mechanical means should be neglected that would aid in discharging it clear and bright into the copper, for all flocks and particles of malt that are taken there, very materially interfere with the action and value of the hops upon the wort; but chemical agencies for this purpose should be avoided where possible.

With regard to temperature, the brewer must not only regulate the heat of the water for the first mash by the colour, age, and quality of the malt, whether pale, amber, or brown, but he should also mark the temperature of the atmosphere, as influencing that of the malt, and the absorption of the heat by the utensils employed; remarking that well-mellowed and brown malt will bear a higher mashing heat than pale or newly dried.

The following table of Mashing Heats is by Levesque :—

Table of Mashing Temperatures.

Temp. of the Air	Brown Malt Heat of Mash, 146° to 148° — 6 Firkins per Qr.	Time of Standing	Temp. of the Air	High-dried Heat of Mash, 145° to 147° — 7 Firkins per Qr.	8 Firkins per Qr.	Time of Standing	Temp. of the Air	Amber Heat of Mash, 144° to 146° — 9 Firkins per Qr.	10 Firkins per Qr.	Time of Standing	Temp. of the Air	Pale Malt Heat of Mash, 145° to 145° — 11 Firkins per Qr.	12 Firkins per Qr.	Time of Standing
Fah.		H.M.	Fah.			H.M	Fah.			H.M.	Fah.			H.M.
10	197·00	4·00	10°	189·00	184·00	3·00	10°	178·00	175·00	2·00	10°	172·00	170·00	1·00
15	195·17	4·00	15	187·42	182·59	3·00	15	176·84	173·92	2·00	15	171·00	169·19	1·00
20	193·34	4·00	20	185·84	181·18	3·00	20	175·68	172·84	2·00	20	170·00	168·28	1·00
25	191·51	4·00	25	184·26	179·77	3·00	25	174·52	171·76	2·00	25	169·00	167·37	1·00
30	189·68	4·00	30	182·68	178·36	3·00	30	173·36	170·68	2·00	30	168·00	166·46	1·00
35	187·85	4·00	35	180·10	176·95	3·00	35	172·20	169·60	2·00	35	167·00	165·55	1·00
40	186·02	4·00	40	179·52	175·54	3·00	40	171·04	168·52	2·00	40	166·00	164·64	1·00
45	184·19	4·00	45	177·94	174·13	3·00	45	169·88	167·44	2·00	45	165·00	163·73	1·00
50	182·36	4·00	50	176·36	172·72	3·00	50	168·72	166·36	2·00	50	164·00	162·82	1·00
55	180·53	4·00	55	174·78	171·31	3·00	55	167·56	165·28	2·00	55	163·00	161·91	1·00
60	178·70	3·40	60	173·20	169·90	2·45	60	166·40	164·20	1·50	60	162·00	160·00	0·55
65	176·87	3·20	65	171·62	168·49	2·30	65	165·24	163·12	1·40	65	161·00	159·19	0·50
70	175·04	3·00	70	170·04	167·07	2·15	70	164·08	162·04	1·30	70	160·00	158·28	0·45
Heat of the Tap, 144° to 146°.			Heat of the Tap, 143° to 145°.				Heat of the Tap, 142° to 144°.				Heat of the Tap, 141° to 143°.			

The first column gives the temperature of the air at the time of mashing.

The second column shows the heat of the water, the quantity used, and the resulting heat of the mash—noting, that if the water has been let into the mash-tun at the boiling point, and allowed to cool down, or the vessel has been thoroughly warmed before the commencement of the process, the heat may be taken several degrees lower.

The third column shows the time for the standing of the mash, but this will be modified, as before stated, by the quality of the extract required.

The bulk of the materials used must also enter into the consideration of the temperature, as a large body of malt will attain the required temperature with a mashing heat lower than a small quantity; the powers of chemical action and condensation of heat being increased with increase of volume.

Donovan, speaking of the temperature to be employed in mashing, lays down the following as a general rule :—For well dried pale malt the heat of the first mashing liquor may be, but should never exceed, 170°; the heat of the second may be, 180°; and, for a third, the heat may be, but need never exceed, 185°.

The quantity of water, termed liquor, to be employed for mashing, depends upon the greater or less strength to be given to the beer; but in all cases, from one barrel and a half to one barrel and three firkins is sufficient for the first stiff mashing, but more liquor may be added after the malt is thoroughly wetted.

The grains of the crushed malt, after the wort is drawn off, retain from thirty-two to forty gallons of water for every quarter of malt. A further amount must be allowed for the loss by evaporation in the boiling and cooling, and the waste in fermentation, so that the amount of liquor required for mashing will, in some instances, be double that of the finished beer, but in general the total amount will be reduced about one-third during the various processes.

The following example has been given of the proportions for an ordinary quality of beer :—

Suppose thirteen imperial quarters of the best pale malt be taken to make 1,500 gallons of beer, the waste may be calculated at near 900 gallons, or 2,400 gallons of water will be required in mashing.

As soon as the water in the copper has attained the heat of 160° in summer, or 167° in winter, 600 gallons of it are to be run off into the mash-tun (which has previously been well cleansed or scalded out with boiling water), and the malt gradually but rapidly thrown in and well intermixed, so that it may be uniformly moistened, and that no lumps remain. After continuing the agitation for about half an hour, more liquor, to the amount of 450 gallons, at a temperature of 180°, may be carefully and gradually introduced (it is an advantage if this can be done by a pipe inserted under the false bottom of the mash-tun), the agitation being continued till the whole assumes an equally fluid state, taking care also to allow as small a loss of temperature as possible during the operation, the resulting temperature of the mass being not less than 148°, or more than 152°.

The mash is then covered close, and allowed to remain at rest for an hour, or an hour and a half, after which the tap of the mash-tun is gradually opened, and if the wort that first flows is turbid, it should be carefully returned into the tun until it runs perfectly limpid and clear. The amount of this first wort will be about 675 gallons.

Seven hundred and fifty gallons of water, at a temperature of from 180° to 185°, may now be introduced, and the mashing operation repeated and continued until the mass becomes uniformly fluid as before, the temperature being from 160° to 170°. It is then again quickly covered and allowed to rest for an hour, and the wort of the first mash having been quickly transferred from the underback to the copper, and brought to a state of ebullition, the wort of the second mash is drawn off with similar precaution, and added to it. A third quantity of water, about 600 gallons, at a temperature of 185° or 190°, should now be run through the goods into the mash-tun by the sparging process, or by any means that will allow the hot liquor to percolate through the grains, displacing and carrying down the heavier and more valuable products of the two first mashings. The wort is now boiled with the hops from one to two hours.

By the mashing process before described, the malt is so much exhausted that it can yield no further extract useful for strong beer or porter. A weaker wort might be, no doubt, still drawn off for small beer, or for contributing a little to the strength of the next mashing of fresh malt. But this, we believe, is seldom practised.

The wort is then transferred into the copper, and made to boil as soon as possible, for if it remains long in the underback, it is apt to become acescent. The steam, moreover, raised from it in the act of boiling serves to screen it from the oxygenating or acidifying influence of the atmosphere.

Until it begins to boil, the air should be excluded by some kind of cover.

Dr. Piesse, in 1840, read a paper before the Chemical Society, showing that much extract was left in the malt after brewing, and that it was this matter which was convertible into sugar, which gave its feeding qualities to 'grains.'

It was shown that the malt, after the first wort was drawn off still contained a portion of starch which was not converted into sugar, and that the presence of diastase was necessary to effect this conversion. As diastase is very soluble, there was none of course left in the infused malt.

It is, therefore, recommended by Dr. Piesse, that malt containing diastase should be added to the second wort.

In brewing thirty quarters, I should take twenty-nine quarters for the first mash and add the remaining quarter to the second, by which all the starch, it was contended, would be converted into sugar. To prevent the access of air, which tends to induce acidity, to the wort, it is suggested that a board the size of the back in which it is contained should float on the surface of the fluid. (*Transactions of the Chemical Society*, 1841.)

BRICK. (*Brique*, Fr.; *Backstein, Ziegelstein*, Ger.) A solid rectangular mass of baked clay, employed for building purposes. Brickmaking is exceedingly ancient: the tower of Babel was built with bricks, as we are told in Scripture, and also the city of Babylon. Over the ruins of Babylon, and the sites of the other great cities of the ancient monarchies, we still discover bricks of various kinds. Some are merely sun-dried masses of clay; others are well burnt; and others, again, are covered with a vitreous glaze. The Egyptians were great brick-makers; and the Romans were celebrated for their bricks and tiles, large quantities of them having been employed in the construction of their different military stations in England. Subsequently, the same bricks have at times been used on later structures, as for instance, in St. Alban's Abbey, which contains a large quantity of bricks from ruins of the Roman buildings of Verulamium. The Lollards' Tower of Lambeth Palace, built in 1454, and the older portions of Hampton Court Palace, built in 1514, are good examples of the English brick architecture in mediæval times.

The natural mixture of clay and sand, called *loam*, as well as marl, which consists of lime and clay with little or no sand, are the materials usually employed in the manufacture of bricks.

There are few places in this country which do not possess alumina in combination with silica and other earthy matters, forming a clay from which bricks can be manufactured. That most generally worked is found on or near the surface in a plastic state. Others are hard marls on the coal-measure, New Red Sandstone, and Blue Lias formations. It is from these marls that the blue bricks of Staffordshire and the fire bricks of Stourbridge are made. Marl has a greater resemblance to stone and rock, and varies much in colour; blue, red, yellow, &c. From the greatly different and varying character of the raw material, there is an equal difference in the principle of preparation for making it into brick; while one merely requires to be turned over by hand, and to have sufficient water worked in to make it subservient to manual labour, the fire-clays and marls must be ground down to dust, and worked by powerful machinery, before they can be brought into even a plastic state. Now these various clays also shrink in drying and burning from 1 to 15 per cent., or more. This contraction varies in proportion to the excess of alumina over silica, but by adding sand, loam, or chalk, or (as is done by the London brick-makers) by using ashes or *breeze*—as it is technically called—this can be corrected. All clays burning red contain oxides of iron, and those having from 8 to 10 per cent. burn of a blue, or almost a black colour. The bricks are exposed in the kilns to great heat, and when the body is a fire-clay, the iron unites with a portion of the silica, forming a fusible silicate of protoxide of iron, which melts into an external glaze. Bricks of this description are common in Staffordshire, and, when made with good machinery (that is, the clay being very finely ground), are superior to any in the kingdom, particularly for docks, canal or river locks, railway-bridges, and viaducts. In Wolverhampton, Dudley, and many other towns, these blue bricks are commonly employed for paving purposes. Other clays contain lime and no iron; these burn white, and take less heat than any other to burn hard enough for the use of the builder, the lime acting as a flux on the silica. Many clays contain iron and lime, with the lime in excess, when the bricks are of a light dun colour, or white, in proportion to the quantity of that earth present; if magnesia, they have a brown colour. If iron is in excess, they burn from a pale red, to the colour of cast iron, in proportion to the quantity of that metal.

There are three classes of brick earths :—

1st. Plastic clay, composed of alumina and silica, in different proportions, and containing a small per-centage of other salts, as of iron, lime, soda, and magnesia.

2nd. Loams, or sandy clays.

3rd. Marls, of which there are also three kinds : clayey, sandy, and calcareous, according to the proportions of the earth of which they are composed, viz., alumina, silica, and lime.

Alumina is the oxide of the metal aluminium, and it is this substance which gives tenacity or plasticity to the clay-earth, having a strong affinity for water. It is owing to excess of alumina that many clays contract too much in drying, and often crack on exposure to wind or sun. By the addition of sand, this clay would make a better article than we often see produced from it. Clays contain magnesia and other earthy matters, but these vary with the stratum or rock from which they are composed. It would be impossible to give the composition of these earths correctly, for none are exactly similar; but the following will give an idea of the proportions of the ingredients of a good brick earth: silica, three-fifths; alumina, one-fifth; iron, lime, magnesia, manganese, soda, and potash forming the other one-fifth.

The clay, when first raised from the mine or bed, is, in very rare instances, in a state to allow of its being at once tempered and moulded. The material from which fire-bricks are manufactured has the appearance of ironstone and blue lias limestone, and some of it is remarkably hard, so that in this and many other instances in order to manufacture a good article, it is necessary to grind this material down into particles as fine as possible.

Large quantities of bricks are made from the surface marls of the New Red Sandstone and Blue Lias formations. These also require thorough grinding, but from their softer nature it can be effected by less powerful machinery.—*Chamberlain.*

Recently, some very valuable fire-bricks have been made from the refuse of the China Clay Works of Devonshire. The quartz and mica left after the *Kaolin* has been washed out are united with a small portion of inferior clay, and made into bricks. These are found to resist heat well, and are largely employed in the construction of metallurgical works. See CLAY.

The general process of brick-making consists in digging up the clay in autumn; exposing it, during the whole winter, to the frost and the action of the air, turning it repeatedly, and working it with the spade; breaking down the clay lumps in spring, throwing them into shallow pits, to be watered and soaked for several days. The next step is to temper the clay, which is generally done by the treading of men or oxen. In the neighbourhood of London, however, this process is performed in a horse-mill. The kneading of the clay is, in fact, the most laborious but indispensable part of the whole business; and that on which, in a great measure, the quality of the brick depends. All the stones, particularly the ferruginous, calcareous, and pyritous kinds, should be removed, and the clay worked into a homogeneous paste with as little water as possible.

Mr. F. W. Simms, C.E., communicated to the Institution of Civil Engineers, in April and May, 1843, an account of the process of brick-making for the Dover Railway. The plan adopted is called slop-moulding, because the mould is dipped into water before receiving the clay, instead of being sanded as in making sand-stock bricks. The workman throws the proper lump of clay with some force into the mould, presses it down with his hands to fill the cavities, and then strikes off the surplus clay with a stick. An attendant boy, who has previously placed another mould in a water trough by the side of the moulding table, takes the mould just filled, and carries it to the floor, where he carefully drops the brick from the mould, on its flat side, and leaves it to dry; by the time he has returned to the moulding table, and deposited the empty mould in the water trough, the brickmaker will have filled the other mould for the boy to convey to the floor, where they are allowed to dry, and are then stacked in readiness for being burned in clamps or kilns. The average product is shown in the following Table :—

Force employed	Area of Land		Duration of Season	Produce per Week	Produce per Season
	Roods	Perches	Weeks	Bricks	Bricks
1 moulder . 1 temperer . 1 wheeler . 1 carrier boy 1 picker boy	2	14½	22	16,100	354,200

It appears that while the produce in sand-stock bricks is to that of slop-bricks, in the same time, as 30 to 16, the amount of labour is as 7 to 4; while the quantity of land, and the cost of labour per thousand, are nearly the same in both processes. The quantity of coal consumed in the kiln was at the rate of 10 cwt. 8 lbs. per 1000 bricks. The cost of the bricks was 2l. 1s. 6d. per thousand. The slop-made bricks are fully 1 pound heavier than the sand-stock. Mr. Bennett states that at his brick-field at Cowley, the average number of sand-stock bricks moulded per day was 32,000; but that frequently so many as 37,000, or even 50,000, were formed. The total amount in the shrinkage of his bricks was $\frac{13}{16}$ths of an inch upon 10 inches in length; but this differed with the different clays. Mr. Simms objects to the use of machinery in brick-making, because it causes economy only in the moulding, which constitutes no more than about one-eighth of the total expense.

The principal machines which have been worked for this purpose are three—1st, the pug-mill; 2nd, the wash-mill; 3rd, the rolling-mill.

The pug-mill is a cylinder, sometimes conical, generally worked in a vertical position, with the large end up. Down the centre of this is a strong revolving vertical shaft, on which are hung horizontal knives, inclined at such an angle as to form portions of a screw, that is, the knives follow each other at an angle forming a series of coils round this shaft. The bottom knives are larger, and vary in form, to throw off the clay, in some mills vertically, in others horizontally. Some have on the bottom of the shaft one coil of a screw, which throws the clay off more powerfully where it is wished to give pressure.

The action of this mill is to cut the clay with the knives during their revolution, and so work and mix it, that on its escape it may be one homogeneous mass, without any lumps of hard untempered clay; the clay being thoroughly amalgamated, and in the toughest state in which it can be got by tempering. This mill is an excellent contrivance for the purpose of working the clay, in combination with rollers; but if only one mill is worked, it is not generally adopted, for, although it tempers, mixes, and toughens, it does not extract stones, crush up hard substances, or free the clay from all matters injurious to the quality of the ware when ready for market. This mill can be worked by either steam, water, or horse-power; but it takes much power in proportion to the quantity of work which it performs. If a brick is made with clay that has passed the pug-mill, and contains stones, or marl not acted on by weather, or lime-shells, (a material very common in clays), or any other extraneous matter injurious to the brick, it is apparent from the action of this mill that it is not removed or reduced. The result is this, the bricks being when moulded in a very soft state of tempered material, or mud, considerably contract in drying, but the stones or hard substances not contracting, cause the clay to crack; and even if they should not be sufficiently large to do this in drying, during the firing of the bricks there is a still further contraction of the clay, and an expansion of the stone from the heat to which it is subjected, and the result is generally a faulty or broken brick, and on being drawn from the kilns, the bricks are found to be imperfect.

The clay, being sufficiently kneaded, it is brought to the bench of the moulder, who works it into a mould made of wood or iron, and strikes off the superfluous matter. The bricks are next delivered from the mould, and ranged on the ground; and when they have acquired sufficient firmness to bear handling, they are dressed with a knife, and stacked or built up in long dwarf walls, thatched over, and left to dry. An able workman will make, by hand, 5,000 bricks in a day.

The different kinds of bricks made in England are principally *place bricks*, *grey and red stocks*, *marl facing bricks*, and *cutting bricks*. The place bricks and stocks are used in common walling. The marls are made in the neighbourhood of London, and used in the outside of buildings, they are very beautiful bricks, of a fine yellow colour, hard, and well burnt, and, in every respect, superior to the stocks. The finest kind of marl and red bricks, called cutting bricks, are used in the arches over windows and doors, being rubbed to a centre, and gauged to a height.

Bricks, in this country, are generally baked either in a clamp or in a kiln. The latter is the preferable method, as less waste arises, less fuel is consumed, and the bricks are sooner burnt. The kiln is usually 13 feet long, by $10\frac{1}{2}$ feet wide, and about 12 feet in height. The walls are one foot two inches thick, carried up a little out of the perpendicular, inclined towards each other at the top. The bricks are placed on flat arches, having holes left in them resembling lattice-work; the kiln is then covered with pieces of tiles and bricks, and some wood put in, to dry them with a gentle fire.

This continues two or three days before they are ready for burning, which is known by the smoke turning from a darkish colour to semi-transparency. The mouth or mouths of the kiln are now dammed up with a *shinlog*, which consists of pieces of bricks piled one upon another, and closed with wet brick earth, leaving above it just room sufficient to receive a fagot. The fagots are made of furze, heath, brake, fern, &c., and the kiln is supplied with these until its arches look white, and the fire appears at the top; upon which the fire is slackened for an hour, and the kiln allowed gradually to cool. This heating and cooling is repeated until the bricks are thoroughly burnt, which is generally done in 48 hours. One of these kilns will hold about 20,000 bricks.

Clamps are also in common use. They are made of the bricks themselves, and generally of an oblong form. The foundation is laid with *place brick*, or the driest of those just made, and then the bricks to be burnt are built up, tier upon tier, as high as the clamp is meant to be, with two or three inches of breeze or cinders strewed between each layer of bricks, and the whole covered with a thick stratum of breeze. The fire-place is perpendicular, about three feet high, and generally placed at the west end; and the flues are formed by gathering or arching the bricks over, so as to leave a space between each of nearly a brick wide. The flues run straight through the clamp, and are filled with wood, coals, and breeze, pressed closely together. If the bricks are to be burnt off quickly, which may be done in 20 or 30 days, according as the weather may suit, the flues should be only at about six feet distance; but if there be no immediate hurry, they may be placed nine feet asunder, and the clamp left to burn off slowly.

The following remarks by Mr. H. Chamberlain, on the drying of bricks, have an especial value from the great experience of that gentleman, and his careful observation of all the conditions upon which the preparation of a good brick depends.

'The drying of bricks ready for burning is a matter of great importance, and requires more attention than it generally receives. From hand-made bricks we have to evaporate some 25 per cent. of water before it is safe to burn them. In a work requiring the make of 20,000 bricks per day, we have to evaporate more than 20 tons of water every 24 hours. Hand-made bricks lose in drying about one-fourth of their weight, and in drying and burning about one-third. The average of machine bricks —those made of the stiff plastic clay—do not lose more than half the above amount from evaporation, and are, therefore, of much greater specific gravity than hand-made ones.

'The artificial drying of bricks is carried on throughout the year uninterruptedly in sheds having the floor heated by fires; but this can only be effected in districts where coal is cheap. The floors of these sheds are a series of tunnels or flues running through the shed longitudinally. At the lower end is a pit, in which are the furnaces the fire travels up the flues under the floor of the shed, giving off its heat by the way, and the smoke escapes at the upper end, through a series of (generally three or four) smaller **chimneys or stacks**. The furnace end of these flues would naturally be much more highly heated than the upper end near the chimneys. To remedy this, the floor is constructed of a greater thickness at the fire end, and gradually diminishes to within a short distance of the top. By this means, and by the assistance of dampers in the chimneys, it is kept at nearly an equal temperature throughout. Bricks that will bear rapid drying, such as are made from marly clays or very loamy or siliceous earths, will be fit for the kiln in from 12 to 24 hours. Before the duty was taken off bricks, much dishonesty was practised by unprincipled makers, where this drying could be carried on economically. Strong clays cannot be dried so rapidly. These sheds are generally walled round with loose bricks, stacked in between each post or pillar that supports the roof. The vapour given off from the wet bricks, rising to the roof, escapes. This system of drying is greatly in advance of that in the open air, for it produces the ware, as made, without any deterioration from bad weather; but the expense of fuel to heat these flues has restricted its use to the neighbourhood of collieries. In 1845 attention was turned to the drying of bricks, and experiments carried out in drying the ware with the waste heat of the burning kilns. The caloric, after having passed the ware in burning, was carried up a flue raised above the floor of the shed, and gave off its spent heat for drying the ware. Although this kiln was most useful in proving that the waste heat of a burning kiln is more than sufficient to dry ware enough to fill it again, it was abandoned on account of the construction of the kiln not being good.

'Another system of drying is in close chambers, by means of steam, hot water, or by flues heated by fire under the chambers. I will, therefore, briefly describe the steam-chamber as used by Mr. Beart. This is a square construction or series of tunnels or chambers, built on an incline of any desired length; and at some convenient spot near the lower end is fixed a large steam-boiler, at a lower level than the drying chamber. From the boiler the main steam pipe is taken along the bottom or lower end of the chamber, and from this main, at right angles, runs branch pipes of four inches diameter up the chamber, two feet apart, and at about three feet from the top or arch. From there being so close and shallow a chamber between the heating surface of the pipes and the top, and so large an amount of heating surface in the pipes, the temperature is soon considerably raised. At the top and bottom ends are shutters or lids, which open for the admission of the green ware at the upper end, and for the exit of the dry ware at the lower end of the chamber. Over the steam-pipes are fixed iron rollers, on which the trays of bricks, as brought from the machine, are placed, the insertion of one tray forcing the tray previously put in further on, assisted in its descent by the inclination of the construction. The steam being raised in the boiler flows through the main into those branch pipes in the chamber, and from the large amount of exposed surface becomes condensed, giving off its latent heat. From the incline given to the pipes in the chamber, and from the main pipe also having a fall towards the boiler, the whole of the warm water from the condensed steam flows to the boiler to be again raised to steam, sent up the pipes, and condensed intermittently. The steam entering at the lower end of the chamber, it is of course warmer than the upper end. Along the top end or highest part of the chambers is a series of chimneys and windguards, through which the damp vapour escapes. The bricks from the machine enter at this cooler end charged with warm vapour, and as the make proceeds are forced down the chamber as each tray is put in. Thus, those which were first inserted reach a drier and warmer atmosphere, and, on their arrival at the lower end, come out dry bricks, in about 24 hours, with the strongest clays. In some cases the waste steam of the working engines is sent through these pipes and condensed. Bricks will dry soundly without cracking, &c., in these close chambers, when exposed to much greater heat than they would bear on the open flue first described, or the open air, from the circumstance of the atmosphere, although very hot, being so highly charged with vapour. In practice, these steam-chambers have proved many principles, but they are not likely to become universal, for they are very expensive in erection on account of the quantity of steam-pipes, and involve constant expense in fuel, and require attention in the management of the steam-boiler; but their greatest defect is the want of a current of hot air through the chamber to carry off the excess of vapour faster than is now done. The attaining a higher degree of temperature in these chambers is useless, unless there is a current to carry off the vapour. Why should this piping be used, or steam at all, when we have a large mass of heat being constantly wasted, night and day, during the time the kilns are burning? and after the process of burning the kiln is completed, we have pure hot air flowing, from 48 to 60 hours, from the mass of cooling bricks in the kilns, free from carbon or any impurities; this could be directed through the drying chambers, entering in one constant flow of hot, dry air, and escaping in warm vapour. The waste heat during the process of burning can be taken up flues under the chamber, and thereby all the heat of our burning kilns may be economised and a great outlay saved in steam-pipes, boilers, and attention. It must not be forgotten, also, that so large an atmospheric condenser as the steam-chamber is not heated without a considerable expenditure in fuel. This drying by steam is a great stride in advance of the old flued shed; but practical men must see the immense loss incurred constantly from this source of the spent heat of the burning kilns, and that by economising it, an immense saving will be effected in the manufacture. The kilns are constructed as near the lower end of these chambers as convenient.'

A kiln for attaining the object of the one built in 1846 by Mr. Chamberlain is worked at Epson; but with this difference, that the smoke is consumed. The drying shed is kept quite close, that the hot flues may raise the temperature so high as to dry the ware. In this kiln the heated gases escape from the top, after passing up through the ware, into flues, and are carried to the ground, and thence into the drying shed, which is a very large construction in proportion to the size of the kiln, and holds nearly sufficient ware to fill four kilns. In this shed the heat passes up a hollow wall, about six feet high, and after running through the length of the shed on one side, returns down similar flues on the opposite side of the shed, and is again carried to the kiln, through the bottom of which it passes in two close flues between the three kiln-furnaces, with the exception of small apertures, through which the heat enters to consume the smoke. From these return flues the spent gases rise up a shaft at the end of the kiln. One result of carrying these return flues through the kiln, is the attaining a great draft or suction in the flues to carry off vapour.

The common brick kiln is a rectangular building, generally open, but sometimes arched over. In the side walls and opposite to each other, are built fireplaces, or holes for the insertion of the fuel. The furnaces are formed in the setting of the kiln with unburnt bricks, and above these the kiln is filled as above described. In these kilns, from the raw ware forming the furnace, the flash of the flame, from the fires of the walls, too often vitrefies and destroys the nearest bricks. In the open kiln, as the fire or heat reaches to the top, the fireman soils or earths it down, which throws the draft to another part more backward; and, as it continues to rise, he proceeds with this operation until all the top is earthed in; he then continues the firing until the whole has sunk, by the contraction of the clay in the fire, to the desired depth. The fire-holes are then stopped up with mud, and the kiln is left to cool gradually. If the air were admitted too rapidly while the kiln was at this intense heat, it would cause bricks, made with strong clays, to fly to pieces like glass; it is, in fact, the process of annealing. Cooling too quickly also affects, in many clays, the colour of the bricks.

Temporary kilns are constructed in the country, with unburnt bricks, and called clamps. In Staffordshire, the bricks are burnt in small round kilns, called ovens which hold from 7,000 to 8,000 bricks each; these are burnt from fire in the walls round the ovens, and the raw ware is set in, so as to form a flue from each fire, to direct the flame to the centre. These ovens burn very quickly, and a most intense heat can be obtained in them. Mr. Chamberlain must be again quoted on the burning of bricks :—

'I will now more fully describe a principle of burning which I have had in practice for the last six years, and which I can therefore recommend with great confidence. The great object in brick-making is to attain a sufficient heat to thoroughly burn the ware with as small a consumption of coal as possible; and with nearly an equal distribution of the heat over all parts, so that the whole of the ware, being subjected to the same temperature, may contract equally in bulk, and be of one uniform colour throughout. The advantage is also gained of burning in much less time than in the old kilns, which, on an average, took a week; and the management is so simplified that any man, even though not at all conversant with the manufacture, after he has seen one kiln burnt, will be able to manage another; and the last, though not least, advantage is, that of delivering up to us the waste heat at the ground level, or under the floor of the kiln, to be used in drying the green ware, or in partially burning the next kiln.

' Hitherto the heat has been applied by a series of fireplaces, or flues and openings round the kiln, each exposed to the influence of the atmosphere; and in boisterous weather it is very difficult to keep the heat at all regular, the consequence of which is, the unequal burning we often see. The improvements sought by experimentalists have been the burning the goods equally, and, at the same time, more economically. These are obtained by the patent kilns, as improved by Mr. Robert Scrivener, of Shelton, in the Staffordshire Potteries. The plan is both simple and effective, and is as follows :—A furnace is constructed in the centre of the kiln, much below the floor level, and so built that the heat can be directed to any part of the kiln at the pleasure of the fireman. First, the heat is directed up a tube in the centre to the top of the oven or kiln, and, as there is no escape allowed to take place there, it is drawn down through the goods by the aid of flues in connection with a chimney. Thus, all the caloric generated in the furnace is made use of, and, being central, is equally diffused throughout the mass; but, towards the bottom, or over the exit flues, the ware would not be sufficiently burnt without reversing the order of firing. In order to meet this requirement there is a series of flues under the bottom, upon which the goods are placed, with small regulators at the end of each; these regulators, when drawn back, allow the fire to pass under the bottom, and to rise up among the goods which are not sufficiently fired, and thus the burning is completed. By means of these regulators the heat may be obtained exactly the same throughout; there is, therefore, a greater degree of certainty in firing, and a considerable saving of fuel, with the entire consumption of the smoke. From the fire or draught being under command, so as to be allowed either to ascend or descend through the ware during the time of burning or cooling, the waste caloric can be economised and directed through the adjoining kiln in order to partially burn it, or be used in drying of the raw wares on flues or in chambers. I have found the saving of fuel in these kilns, over the common kiln, 50 per cent.; and to give an idea of the facility with which they can be worked, it is common for my men to fill the kiln, burn, cool, and discharge it in six days.' See KILN.

In France attempts were long ago made to substitute animals and machines for the treading of men's feet in the clay kneading pit; but it was found that their schemes could not replace, with advantage, human labour where it is so cheap, particularly for separating the stones and heterogeneous matter, from the loam. The more it is worked, the denser, more uniform, and more durable, the bricks which are made of it. A good French workman, in a day's labour of 12 or 13 hours, it has been said, is able to mould from 9,000 to 10,000 bricks, 9 inches long, $4\frac{1}{2}$ inches broad, and $2\frac{1}{4}$ thick; but he must have good assistants under him. In many brick-works near Paris, screw presses are now used for consolidating the bricks and paving tiles in their moulds. M. Molerat employed the hydraulic press for the purpose of condensing pulverised clay, which, after baking, formed beautiful bricks; but the process was too tedious and costly. An ingenious contrivance for moulding bricks mechanically is said to be employed near Washington, in America. This machine moulds 30,000 in a day's work of 12 hours, with the help of one horse, yoked to a ginwheel, and the bricks are so dry when discharged from their moulds, as to be ready for immediate burning. The machine is described, with figures, in the 'Bulletin de la Société d'Encouragement,' for 1819.

Mechanical Brick Moulding.—Messrs. Lyne and Stainford obtained, in August 1825, a patent for a machine for making a considerable number of bricks at one operation. It consists, in the first place, of a cylindrical pug-mill of the kind usually employed for comminuting clay for bricks and tiles, furnished with rotatory knifes, or cutters, for breaking the lumps and mixing the clay with the other materials of which bricks are commonly made. Secondly, of two movable moulds, in each of which fifteen bricks are made at once; these moulds being made to travel to and fro in the machine for the purpose of being alternately brought under the pug-mill to be filled with the clay, and then removed to situations where plungers are enabled to act upon them. Thirdly, in a contrivance by which the plungers are made to descend, for the purpose of compressing the material and discharging it from the mould in the form of bricks. Fourthly, in the method of constructing and working trucks which carry the receiving boards, and conduct the bricks away as they are formed.

Fig. 254 exhibits the general construction of the apparatus; both ends of which being exactly similar, little more than half the machine is represented. *a* is the cylindrical pug-mill, shown partly in section, which is supplied with the clay and other materials from a hopper above; *b b* are the rotatory knives or cutters, which are attached to the vertical shaft, and, being placed obliquely, press the clay down towards the bottom of the cylinder, in the act of breaking and mixing it as the shaft revolves. The lower part or the cylinder is opened; and immediately under it the mould is placed in which the bricks are to be formed. These moulds run to and fro upon ledges in the side frames of the machine; one of the moulds only can be shown by dots in the figure, the side rail intervening: they are situated at *c c*, and are formed of bars of iron crossing each other, and encompassed with a frame. The mould resembles an ordinary sash window in its form, being divided into rectangular compartments (fifteen are proposed in each) of the dimensions of the intended bricks, but sufficiently deep to allow the material, after being considerably pressed in the mould, to leave it, when discharged, of the usual thickness of a common brick.

The mould being open at top and bottom, the material is allowed to pass into it, when situated exactly under the cylinder; and the lower side of the mould, when so

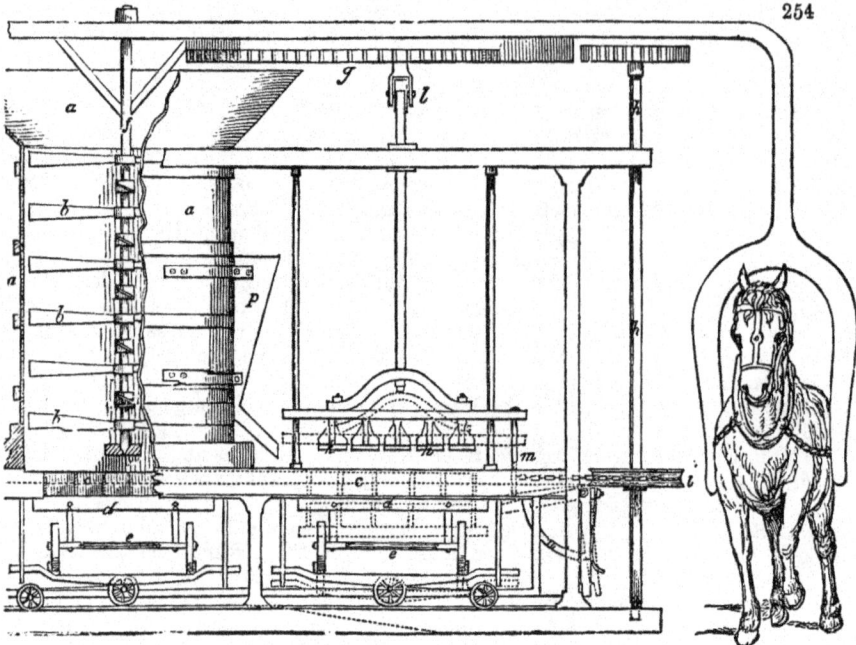

254

placed, it is to be closed by a flat board *d*, supported by the truck *e*, which is raised by a lever and roller beneath, running upon a plain rail with inclined ends.

The central shaft, *f*, is kept in continual rotatory motion, by the revolution of the upper horizontal wheel *g*, of which it is the axis; and this wheel may be turned by a horse yoked to a radiating arm, or by any other means. A part of the circumference of the wheel *g*, has teeth, which are intended at certain periods of its revolution to take into a toothed pinion, fixed upon the top of a vertical shaft *h h*. At the lower part of this vertical shaft there is a pulley *i*, over which a chain is passed that is connected to the two moulds *c*, and to the frame in which the trucks are supported; by the rotation of the vertical shaft, the pulley winds a chain, and draws the moulds and truck frames along.

The clay and other material having been forced down from the cylinder into the mould, the teeth of the horizontal wheel *g*, now come into gear with the pinion upon *h*, and turn it and the shaft and pulley *i*, by which the chain is wound, and the mould at the right hand of the machine brought into the situation shown in the figure; a scraper or edge-bar under the pug-mill having levelled the upper face of the clay in the mould, and the board *d*, supported by the truck *e*, formed the flat under-side.

The mould being brought into this position, it is now necessary to compress the materials, which is done by the descent of the plungers *k k*. A friction-roller *l*, pendant from the under side of the horizontal wheel, as that wheel revolves, comes in contact with an inclined plane, at the top of the shaft of the plungers; and, as the friction-roller passes over this inclined plane, the plungers are made to descend into the mould, and to compress the material; the resistance of the board beneath causing the clay to be squeezed into a compact state. When this has been effectually accomplished, the further descent of the plungers brings a pin, *m*, against the upper end of a quadrant catch-level, *n*, and, by depressing this quadrant, causes the balance-lever upon which the truck is now supported to rise at that end, and to allow the truck with the board *d* to descend, as shown by dots; the plungers at the same time forcing out the bricks from the moulds, whereby they are deposited upon the board *d*; when, by drawing the truck forward out of the machine, the board with the bricks may be removed, and replaced by another board. The truck may then be again introduced into the machine, ready to receive the next parcel of bricks.

By the time that the discharge of the bricks from this mould has been effected, the other mould under the pug cylinder has become filled with the clay, when the teeth of the horizontal wheel coming round, take into a pinion upon the top of a vertical shaft, exactly similar to that at *h*, but at the reverse end of the machine, and cause the moulds and the frame supporting the trucks to be slidden to the left end of the machine; the upper surface of the mould being scraped level in its progress, in the way already described. This movement brings the frction-wheel, *o*, up the inclined plane, and thereby raises the truck, with the board to the under side of the mould, ready to receive another supply of clay; and the mould at the left-hand side of the machine being now in its proper situation under the plungers, the clay becomes compressed, and the bricks discharged from the mould in the way described in the former instance; when this truck being drawn out, the bricks are removed to be dried and baked, and another board is placed in the same situation. There are boxes, *p*, upon each side of the pug cylinder containing sand, at the lower parts of which small sliders are to be opened (by contrivances not shown in the figure) as the mould passes under them, for the purpose of scattering sand upon the clay in the mould to prevent its adhering to the plungers. There is also a rack and toothed sector, with a balance-weight connected to the inclined plane at the top of the plunger-rods, for the purpose of raising the plunger after the friction-roller has passed over it; and there is a spring acting against the back of the quadrant-catch, for the purpose of throwing it into its former situation, after the pin of the plunger has risen.

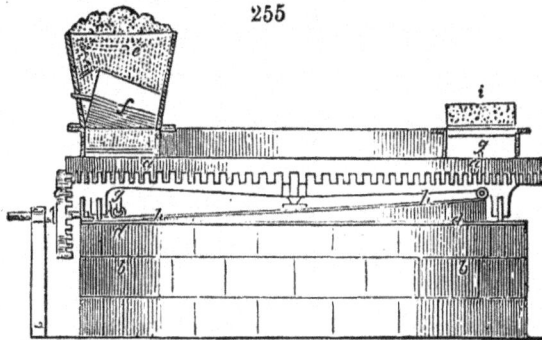

255

An effective machine for brick-making is that patented by Mr. Edward Jones, of Birmingham, in August 1835. His improvements are described under four heads: the first applies to a machine for moulding the earth into bricks in a circular frame-plate horizontally, containing a series of moulds or rectangular boxes, standing radially round the circumference of the circular frame, into which boxes successively the clay is expressed from a stationary hopper as the frame revolves, and after being so formed, the bricks are successively pushed out of their boxes, each by a piston acted upon by an inclined plane below. The second head of the specification describes a rectangular horizontal frame, having a series of moulding boxes placed in a straight range, which are acted upon for pressing the clay by a corresponding range of pistons fixed in a horizontal frame, worked up and down by rods extending from a rotatory crank shaft, the moulding boxes being allowed to rise for the purpose of enabling the pistons to force out the bricks when moulded, and leave them upon the bed or board below. The third head applies particularly to the making of tiles for the flooring of kilns in which malt or grain is to be dried. There is in this contrivance a rectangular mould, with pointed pieces standing up for the purpose of producing air-holes through the tiles as they are moulded, which is done by pressing the clay into the moulds upon the points, and scraping off the superfluous matter at top by hand. The fourth or last head applies to moulding chimney-pots in double moulds, which take to pieces for the purpose of withdrawing the pot when the edges of the slabs or sides are sufficiently brought into contact.

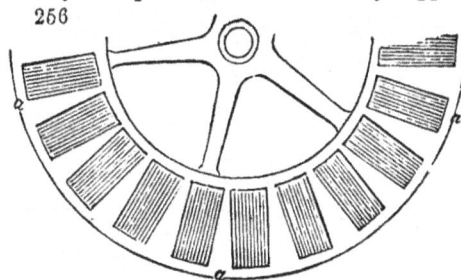

256

Fig. 255 represents, in elevation, the first-mentioned machine for moulding bricks. The moulds are formed in the face of a circular plate or wheel, *a a*, a portion of the upper surface of which is represented in the horizontal view, *fig.* 256. Any convenient number of these moulds are set readily in the wheel, which is mounted upon a central pivot, supported by the masonry *b b*. There is a rim of teeth round the outer edge of the wheel *a a*, which take into a pinion, *c*, on a shaft connected to the first mover; and by these means the wheel *a*, with the moulding boxes, is made to revolve horizontally, guided by arms with anti-friction rollers, which run round a horizontal plate, *a a*, fixed upon the masonry.

A hopper, *e*, filled with the brick earth, shown with one of the moulding boxes in section, is fixed above the face of the wheel in such a way, that the earth may descend from the hopper into the several moulding boxes as the wheel passes round under it, the earth being pressed into the moulds, and its surface scraped off smooth by a conical roller, f, in the bottom of the hopper.

Through the bottom of each moulding box there is a hole for the passage of a piston-rod, g, the upper end of which rod carries a piston with a wooden pallet upon it acting within the moulding box ; and the lower end of this rod has a small anti-friction roller, which, as the wheel a revolves, runs round upon the face of an oblique ring or inclined way, $h\ h$, fixed upon the masonry.

The clay is introduced into the moulding boxes from the hopper fixed over the lowest part of the inclined way h ; and it will be perceived that as the wheel revolves, the piston-rods, g, in passing up the inclined way, will cause the pistons to force the new-moulded bricks, with their pallet, or board, under them, severally up the mould, into the situation shown at i, in *fig.* 256, whence they are to be removed by hand. Fresh pallets being then placed upon the several pistons, they, with the moulds, will be ready for moulding fresh bricks, when, by the rotation of the wheel, a, they are severally brought under the hopper, the pistons having sunk to the bottoms of their boxes, as the piston-rods passed down the other side of the inclined way h.

The second head of the invention is another construction of apparatus for moulding bricks, in this instance in a rectangular frame. *Fig.* 257 is a front elevation of the machine ; *fig.* 258, a section of the same taken transversely. $a\ a$ is the standard frame-work and bed on which the bricks are to be moulded. Near the corners of this standard frame-work, four vertical pillars, $b\ b$, are erected, upon which pillars

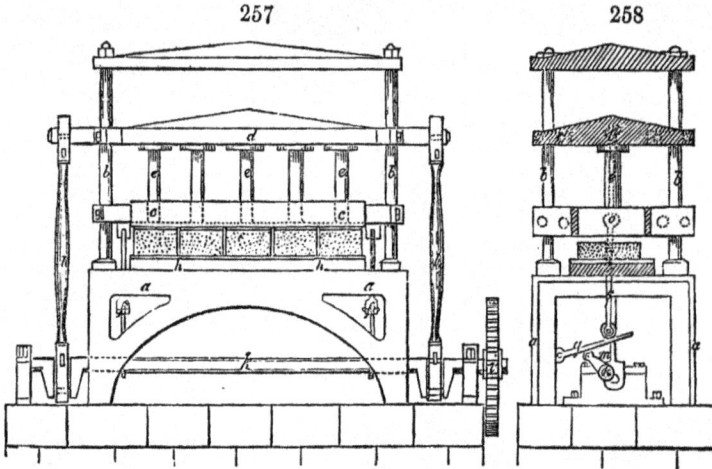

257   258

the frame of the moulding boxes, c, slides up and down, and also the bar, d, carrying the rods of the pistons, $e\ e\ e$. These pistons are for the purpose of compressing the clay in the moulding box, and therefore must stand exactly over and correspond with the respective moulds in the frame c, beneath.

The sliding frame, c, constituting the sides and ends of the moulding boxes, is supported at each end by an upright sliding rod, f, which rods pass through guides fixed to the sides of the standard frame, $a\ a$, and at the lower end of each there is a roller, bearing upon the levers, g, on each side of the machine, but seen only in *fig.* 258, which levers, when depressed, allow the moulding boxes to descend and rest upon the bed or table of the machine $h\ h$.

In this position of the machine resting upon the bed or table, the brick-earth is to be placed upon, and spread over, the top of the frame c, by the hands of workmen, when the descent of the plunger or pistons $e\ e\ e$ will cause the earth to be forced into the moulds, and the bricks to be formed therein. To effect this, rotatory power is to be applied to the toothed wheel i, fixed on the end of the main driving crank-shaft $k\ k$, which on revolving will, by means of the crank-rods $l\ l$, bring down the bar a, with the pistons or plunger $e\ e\ e$, and compress the earth compactly into the moulds, and thereby form the bricks.

When this has been done, the bricks are to be released from the moulds by the moulding frame, c, rising up from the bed, as shown in *fig.* 257, the pistons still remaining depressed, and bearing upon the upper surfaces of the bricks. The moulding frame is raised by means of cams, m, upon the crank-shaft, which at this part of the operation are brought under the levers g, for the purpose of raising the cams and the sliding rods f into the position shown in *fig.* 258.

The bricks having been thus formed and released from their moulds, they are to be removed from the bed of the machine by pushing forward, on the front side, fresh boards or pallets, which of course will drive the bricks out upon the other side, whence they are to be removed by hand.

There is to be a small hole in the centre of each pallet, and also in the bed, for the purpose of allowing any superfluous earth to be pressed through the moulding boxes when the pistons descend. And in order to cut off the projecting piece of clay which would be thus formed on the bottom of the brick, a knife-edge is in some way connected to the bed of the machine, and as the brick slides over it, the knife separates the protuberant lump; but the particular construction of this part of the apparatus is considered to be of little importance, and the manner of effecting the object is not clearly stated in the specification.

Fig. 259 represents Mr. Hunt's machine. The principal parts consist of two cylinders, each covered by an endless web, and so placed as to form the front and back of a hopper, the two sides being iron plates, placed so that when the hopper is filled with tempered clay from the pug-mill, the lower part of the hopper, and consequently the mass of clay within it, has exactly the dimensions of a brick. Beneath the hopper an endless chain travels simultaneously with the movement of the cylinders. The pallet-boards are laid at given intervals upon the chain, and being thus placed under the hopper, while the clay is brought down with a slight pressure, a frame with a wire stretched across it is projected through the mass of clay, cutting off exactly the thickness of the brick, which is removed at the same moment by the forward movement of the endless chain. This operation is repeated each time that a pallet-board comes under the hopper.

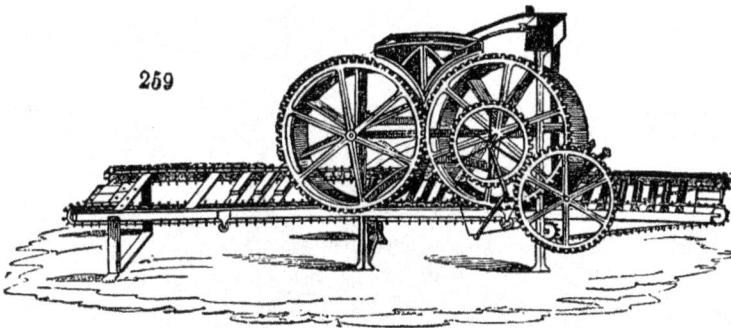

259

There are numerous machines in use for the manufacture of bricks. For the manufacture of perforated bricks, Mr. Beart's machine is the most generally employed. Mr. Chamberlain thus describes it:—' The most universally used die-machine which has been extensively worked up to the present time is Mr. Beart's patent for perforated bricks. This gentleman, who is practically acquainted with these matters, in order to remedy the difficulties I have mentioned in expressing a mass of clay through a large aperture or die, hung a series of small tongues or cores, so as to form hollow or perforated bricks. By this means the clay was forced in its passage through the die into the corners, having the greater amount of friction now in the centre. Still, the bricks came out rough at the edge with many clays, or with what is termed a jagged edge. The water-die was afterwards applied to this machine, and the perforated bricks, now so commonly used in London, are the result. In Mr. Beart's machine, which is a pug-mill, the clay is taken after passing through the rolling-mill, and being fed in at the top, is worked down by the knives. At the bottom are two horizontal clay-boxes, in which a plunger works backwards and forwards. As soon as it has reached the extremity of its stroke, or forced the clay of one box through the die, the other box receiving during this time its charge of clay from the pug-mill, the plunger returns and empties this box of clay through a die on the opposite side of the machine. The result is, that while a stream of clay is being forced out on one side of the machine the clay on the opposite side is stationary, and can, therefore, be divided into a series of five or six bricks with the greatest correctness by hand. Some of these machines have both boxes on one side and the plungers worked by cranks. This machine cannot make bricks unless the clay has previously passed through rollers, if coarse; for anything at all rough, as stone or other hard substance, would hang in the tongues of the die. But the clay being afterwards pugged in the machine is so thoroughly tempered and mixed, the bricks when made cannot be otherwise than good, provided they are sufficiently fired. As to the utility of hollow or perforated bricks, that is a matter more for the consideration of the architect or builder than for the brick-maker. Perforated bricks are a fifth less in weight than solid ones, which is a matter of some importance in transit; but it takes considerably more power to force the clay through those dies than for solid brick-making. In the manufacture of perforated bricks, there is also a royalty or patent-right to be paid to Mr. Beart.'

Mr. Chamberlain's own machine is in principle as follows (*fig.* 260):—The clay is fed into a pug-mill, placed horizontally, which works and amalgamates it, and then forces it off through a mouth-piece or die of about 65 square inches, or about half an inch deeper and half and inch longer than is required for the brick, of a form similar to a brick on edge, but with corners well rounded off, each corner forming a quarter of a 3-inch circle, for clay will pass smoothly through an aperture thus formed, but not through a keen angle. After the clay has escaped from the mill it is seized by four rollers, covered with a porous fabric (moleskin), driven at a like surface speed from connection with the pug-mill. These rollers are two horizontal and two vertical ones, having a space of 45 inches between them; they take this larger stream of rough clay, and press or roll it into a squared block, of the exact size and shape of a brick edgeways, with beautiful sharp edges, for the clay has no friction, being drawn through by the rollers instead of forcing itself through, and is delivered in one unbroken stream. The rollers in this machine, perform the functions of the die in one class of machinery, and of the mould in the other. They are, in fact, a die with rotating surfaces. By hanging a series of mandrels or cores between these rollers, or by

260

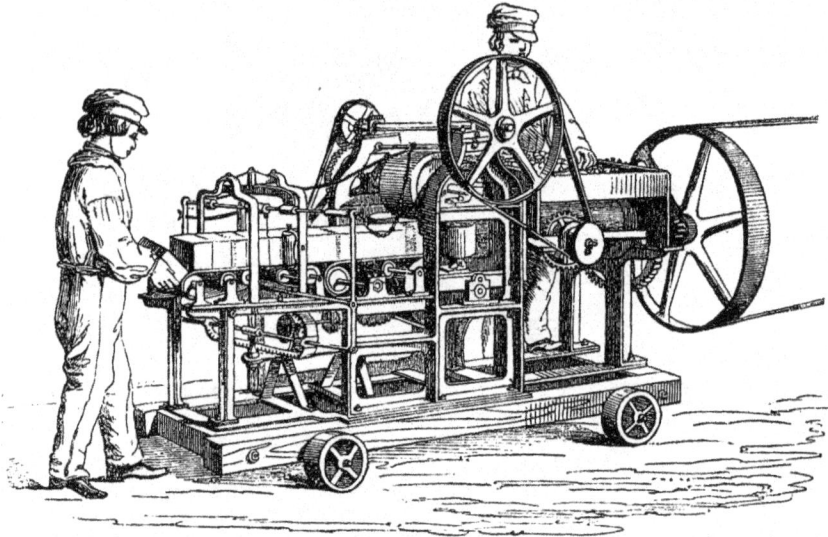

merely changing the mouth-piece, we make hollow and perforated bricks, without any alteration in the machine.

Messrs. Bradley and Craven, of Wakefield, have invented a very ingenious brick-making (*fig.* 261) machine:—

It consists of a vertical pug-mill of a peculiar form, and greatly improved construction, into the upper part of which the clay is fed. In this part of the apparatus the clay undergoes the most perfect tempering and mixing, and on reaching the bottom of the mill, thoroughly amalgamated, is forcibly pressed into the moulds of the form and size of bricks required, which are arranged in the form of a circular revolving table.

As this table revolves, the piston-rods of the moulds ascend an incline plane, and gradually lift the bricks out of the moulds, whence they are taken from the machine by a boy, and placed on an endless band which carries the bricks direct to the waller, thus effecting the saving of the floor room.

The speed of the several parts of the machine is so judiciously arranged, that the operations of pugging, moulding, and delivering proceed simultaneously in due order, the whole being easily driven by a steam-engine of about six-horse power, which, at the ordinary rate of working, will make 12,000 bricks per day; or, with eight-horse power, from 15,000 to 18,000.

In consequence of the perfect amalgamation of the clay, and the great pressure to which it is subjected in the moulds, the bricks produced by this machine are perfect;

and from the stiffness of the clay used, less water has to be evaporated in the drying, thus saving one half the time required for hand-made bricks, and avoiding the risk of loss from bad weather.

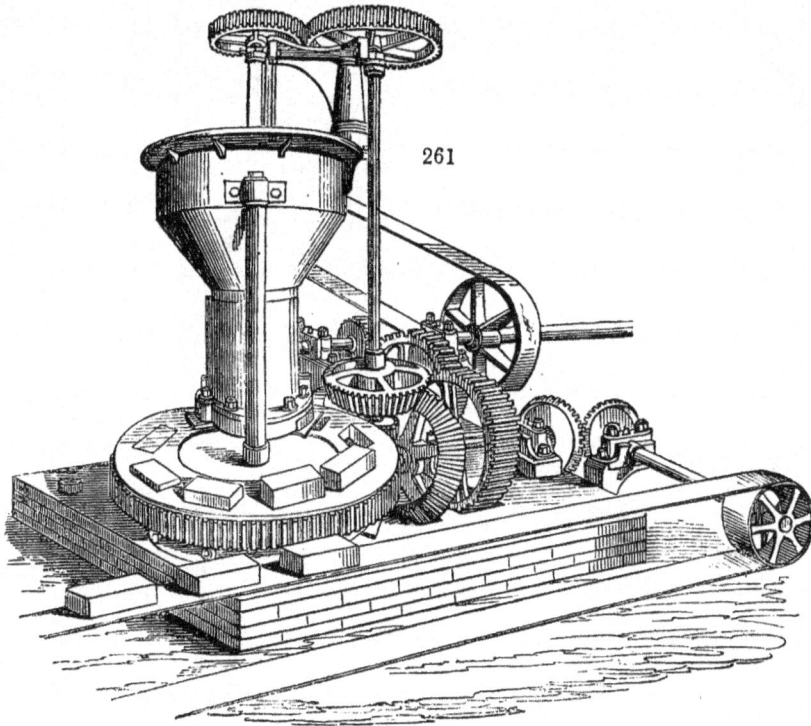

261

The following remarks by Dr. Ure are deserving of attention :—

'The brick kilns and clamps round London and other large cities, which are fired with the breeze rubbish collected from dust-holes that contain the refuse of kitchens, &c., emit, in consequence, most unpleasant effluvia; but brick kilns fired with clean coke or coal give out no gases of a more noxious nature than common household fires. The consideration of this subject was closely pressed upon my attention on being consulted concerning an injunction issued by the Chancellor against a brick clamp in the Isle of Wight, fired with clean coke-cinders from the steam-engine furnace at Portsmouth Dockyard. The bricks, being of the description called sand stock, were of course made in moulds very slightly dusted with sand, to make them fall freely out. The sand was brought from Portsmouth Harbour, and, on being subjected to a degree of heat more intense certainly than it could suffer in the clamp, was thought to give out traces of hydrochloric acid.

'As it is well known to the chemist that common salt strongly ignited in contact with moist sand will emit hydrochloric acid, there was nothing remarkable in the above observation; but I ascertained that the sand with which the moulds were strewed would give out no hydrochloric acid at a heat equal at least to what the bricks were exposed to in a clamp 10 or 12 feet high, and fired at its bottom only with a layer of cinders 3 or 4 inches thick. But I further demonstrated that the entire substance of the brick, with its scanty film of sand, on being exposed to ignition in a suitable apparatus, gave out—not hydrochloric or any other corrosive acid, but ammonia gas. Hence, the allegations that the clamp sent forth a host of acid gases to blight the neighbouring trees were shown to be utterly groundless; on the contrary, the ammonia evolved from the heated clay would act beneficially upon vegetation, while it was too small in quantity to annoy any human being. A few yards to leeward of a similar clamp in full activity, I could perceive no offensive odour. All ferruginous clay, when exposed to the atmosphere, absorbs ammonia from it, and of course emits it again on being gently ignited.'

Floating bricks are a very ancient invention; they are so light as to swim in water; and Pliny tells us that they were made at Marseilles, at Colento, in Spain, and at Pittane, in Asia. This invention, however, was completely lost until M. Fabroni published a discovery of a method to imitate the floating bricks of the ancients.

According to Posidonius, these bricks were made of a kind of argillaceous earth, which was employed to clean silver plate. But as it could not be our tripoli, which is too heavy to float in water, M. Fabroni tried several experiments with mineral agaric, guhr, lac-lunæ, and fossil meal, which last was found to be the very substance of which he was in search. This earth is abundant in Tuscany, and is found near Casteldelpiano, in the territories of Sienna. According to the analysis of M. Fabroni, it consists of 55 parts of siliceous earth, 15 of magnesia, 14 of water, 12 of alumina, 3 of lime, and 1 of iron. It exhales an argillaceous odour, and, when sprinkled with water, throws out a light-whitish smoke. It is infusible in the fire, and, though it loses about an eighth part of its weight, its bulk is scarcely diminished. Bricks composed of this substance, either baked or unbaked, float in water; and $\frac{1}{20}$th part of clay may be added to their composition without taking away their property of swimming. These bricks resist water, unite perfectly with lime, are subject to no alteration from heat or cold, and the baked differ from the unbaked only in the sonorous quality which they have acquired from the fire. Their strength is little inferior to that of common bricks, but much greater in proportion to their weight; for M. Fabroni found that a floating brick, measuring 7 inches in length, $4\frac{1}{2}$ in breadth, and 1 inch 8 lines in thickness, weighed only $14\frac{1}{4}$ oz., whereas a common brick weighed 5 lbs. $6\frac{3}{4}$ oz.

As an experiment, M. Fabroni constructed the powder magazine of a ship of these bricks; the vessel was set on fire, and sank without exploding the powder.

This earth has been found near Clermont, in the Auvergne. Ehrenberg has shown that it is entirely composed of microscopic siliceous shells. Bricks composed of this earth weigh only half as much as the ordinary ones.

Fire bricks are made extensively in the neighbourhood of Newcastle-on-Tyne and at Stourbridge. For the analyses of the clays of which these and others are constructed, see CLAY.

Stone Bricks.—These are manufactured at Neath, in Glamorganshire, and are very much used in the construction of copper furnaces at Swansea. They are usually known as the ' Dinas bricks.'

The materials of which the bricks are made are brought from a quarry in the neighbourhood. They are very coarse, being subjected to a very rude crushing operation under an edge stone, and, from the size of the pieces, it is impossible to mould by hand. There are three qualities, which are mixed together with a little water, so as to give the mass coherence, and in this state it is compressed by the machine into a mould. The brick which results is treated in the ordinary way, but it resists a much greater heat than the Stourbridge clay brick, expands more by heat, and does not contract to its original dimensions. The composition of the three materials is as follows:—

	From Pendreyn	From Dinas	
Silica	94·05	100·	91·95
Alumina, with a trace of ox. iron	4·55	traces	8·05
Lime and magnesia		traces	traces
	98·60	100·	100·00

—Dr. Richardson: Knapp's Technology.

Since the introduction of the Siemens gas-furnace, and the Bessemer process for cast-steel manufacture, into countries which, unlike our own, are not well supplied with fire-resisting materials, great difficulty has been experienced in obtaining bricks of a sufficiently refractory character to withstand the extremely high temperature developed in the melting chamber, as well as the sudden and violent alternations in other parts of the furnace. In order to obviate this difficulty, Mr. Joseph Khern, a well-known Austrian metallurgist, has introduced a plan of manufacturing siliceous bricks, which he describes as being superior to any other refractory material obtained in Austria. The chief ingredient is quartz of the highest possible degree of purity, especial care being taken to reject all such samples as show any admixture of iron or copper pyrites, carbonate of lime, or even mica, or felspar. The quartz so selected is heated in quantities of from 10 to 15 tons, in a Rumford lime-kiln for 10 or 12 hours, till it attains a full red heat, when it is quenched in water; the fragments are then cleaned by a simple jigging process, and subsequently are crushed under a tilt hammer, sufficiently fine to pass through a sieve having 60 holes to the square inch. The hammer weighs $2\frac{1}{2}$ cwts., and is capable of crushing $3\frac{1}{2}$ tons of quartz in 12 hours. Two varieties of clay are used, differing slightly in plasticity; they are prepared by careful weathering, pulverisation under light stamp-heads, and grinding under edge rollers; a final sifting is performed through a sieve of 600 apertures to the inch. The purest quartz is reserved for the first quality of brick, which have to resist the greatest heat; while the second and third class, for less exposed positions, are made chiefly of the remains of bricks which have been already used, ground and sifted afresh. The following are the mixtures employed:—

First class: 16 parts of quartz to 1 plastic clay, or 14 parts of quartz to 1 of leaner clay. Second class: 16 parts of ground bricks of the 1st class, to 1 of clay. Third class: 8 parts of ground bricks of the 2nd and 3rd classes, to 1 of clay.

The latter class are made more with a view to obtain mechanical strength than fire-resisting power.

The materials are mixed together dry, and are thoroughly incorporated by kneading with water, and treading under men's feet; about 18 cubic feet are operated upon at one time. Sufficient water must be added to allow the mixture to be worked into a ball between the fingers without crumbling. The second and third class bricks are formed in open moulds, the stuff being beaten down by a metal rammer of about 4½ lbs. weight; the first class, however, are subjected to a pressure of about 3 tons to the square inch during a period of three quarters of an hour, before they are removed from the moulds. The drying takes place in chambers, through which a current of air passes, at the ordinary temperature in summer, but artificially warmed in winter; the bricks are fit for burning in from 4 to 6 days. The kilns are rectangular chambers, each having two step-grate fireplaces in one of the shorter sides, and a flue communicating with a high chimney at the opposite end. The capacity is about 2,300 or 2,500 bricks. As soon as the kiln is filled, the charging aperture is partly closed, and a gentle fire is kept in the grates, the flue damper being shut. After 36 hours, the charging hole is entirely closed, and the draught is urged by opening the damper inch by inch at intervals, until, at the end of 65 or 70 hours, the whole of the charge has attained a strong white heat. The fires are then removed, the damper is shut down, the grates are filled with sand, and any cracks that may have formed in the kiln are carefully luted up. After standing in this way for 24 hours, the charging place is gradually opened, and in from 36 to 48 hours more, the burnt bricks may be removed.

BRICK CLAY. The familiar term for any clay used in the manufacture of bricks. A good clay for this purpose is a silicate of alumina, combined in various proportions with sand. *Brick clay* is used by geologists in contradistinction to *Boulder clay*.

BRICK EARTH. A marly earth, containing much alumina, largely employed in brick-making.

BRICK KILN. See KILN.

BRICK OIL. This is a relic of old pharmacy: it was prepared by putting red-hot roughly powdered brick into linseed oil. It is no longer used, except by old apothecaries and druggists in remote country towns.

BRICK RED COPPER ORE. See TILE ORE.

BRIDGE. See IRON BRIDGE.

BRIMSTONE. (*Soufre*, Fr.; *Schwefel*, Ger.) SULPHUR.

Our *Imports* of Brimstone for the years ending 1871 were as follows:—

1869		1870		1871	
Quantity Cwts.	Value £	Quantity Cwts.	Value £	Quantity Cwts.	Value £
1,015,329	388,723	1,065,360	386,660	937,049	303,717

BRISTLE. The stiff glossy hair of swine, which grows chiefly on the backs of those animals, both in the wild and the domesticated state. Bristles are used in the manufacture of brushes.

In 1864 our *Imports* of Bristles from Russia were 1,958,112 lbs., valued at 252,923*l*.; from Prussia 59,113 lbs., valued at 7,635*l*.; from Hamburg 207,274 lbs., valued at 26,772*l*.; from Belgium 34,880 lbs., valued at 4,505*l*.; from France 51,859 lbs., valued at 6,699*l*.; from other parts 34,897 lbs., valued at 4,507*l*.: total amount, 2,346,135 lbs., valued at 303,041*l*. In the same year we exported 12,395 lbs. valued at 2,264*l*. The importations for 1872 were:—From Russia, 1,800,933 lbs.; from Germany, 572,727 lbs.; from Holland, 492,921 lbs.; from Belgium, 94,842 lbs.; from France, 60,030 lbs.; and from other countries, 46,642 lbs. The total value being 517,809*l*.

BRISTOL DIAMONDS. Brilliant crystals of quartz, found in the St. Vincent Rocks, near Bristol. They are often cut and polished for ornaments.

BRITANNIA METAL. An alloy of tin with copper and antimony. In the best kinds a little nickel is used. See ALLOYS.

BRITISH GUM. See DEXTRINE.

BRITTLE SILVER-GLANCE. See SILVER ORES.

BRITTLE SILVER ORE. See SILVER ORES.

BRITTLE SULPHURET OF SILVER. See SILVER ORES.

BROAD CLOTH. A fine kind of woollen cloth, which exceeds twenty-nine inches in width. All of less width are known as *narrow cloths.*

BROAD GAUGE. Rails laid wide apart, as on the Great Western Railway and its branches, in contradistinction to the *narrow gauge,* as on all the other railways of the Kingdom. The broad gauge rails are 6 feet apart; the narrow gauge rails 4½ feet.

BROAD LEAF. The *Terminalia latifolia,* a tree, native of Jamaica, the wood of which is used for boards, scantlings, shingles, and staves. It is sometimes mistaken for the almond tree, owing to the shape of its fruit. See TERMINALIA.

BROADSIDE. *A seaman's term*—the full length or side of a ship. *A printer's term*—a full printed page of any sized sheet.

BROCADE. A rich stout silk, formerly much worn by ladies of rank. A name commonly given to any variety of stuff upon which raised flowers are embroidered. The name is also given to a cloth of silk and gold manufactured in Eastern countries.

BROCATELLE. Linsey-woolsey is so called in France. A silk material which is used for lining carriages.

BROCATELLI MARBLE. An artificial marble made from fragments of natural marbles united by means of an artificial cement.

BROCHANTITE. An ore of copper found in this country at Roughton Gill, in Cumberland. It has also been discovered in Siberia, Nassau, and elsewhere. Its composition is sulphuric acid, 17·7; protoxide of copper, 70·3; water, 12·0.

BROCKRAM. A Cumberland miner's term for a *breccia.*

BROMA. A preparation of chocolate.

BROMACETIC ACID.—Obtained by Messrs. Perkin and Duppa. They take a mixture of crystallisable acetic acid and bromine in the proportion of equal equivalents, introduce it into a sealed tube, which is placed in an oil bath and heated to 150° C. The mixture which is nearly colourless, or of a light amber colour, is transferred to a retort, and the excess of acetic acid driven off by heating to 200° C. On cooling, a beautiful white crystalline solid is obtained, which is bromacetic acid, together with hydrobromic acid and bibromacetic acid. The mixed acids are heated to 130° C., carbonic acid passed until the reaction of hydrobromic acid, with nitrate of silver, is no longer evident. Carbonate of lead is then added, the whole heated to 100° C., and allowed to stand for some hours; the liquid filtered off from the crystalline deposit.

The acid thus obtained crystallises in rhombohedra, is exceedingly deliquescent, and very soluble in water or alcohol. It fuses below 100° C., and boils at 208° C. When distilled with acetate of potassium, it gives off acetic acid; when heated with metallic zinc, it yields acetate and bromide of zinc.

It attacks the epidermis powerfully, raising a blister like that produced by a burn. It forms crystallisable salts with most bases, many of which decompose rapidly.

Messrs. Perkin and Duppa have formed the salts of the alkalis and alkaline earths. The lead salt is obtained by neutralising bromacetic acid with oxide of lead, and recrystallising in water, washing the crystalline precipitate with cold water, and recrystallising from water.

The silver salt is obtained by treating bromacetic acid with carbonate of silver, or by adding solution of bromacetic acid to solution of nitrate of silver. It is thrown down as a crystalline precipitate.

Bromacetate of methyl is a colourless mobile liquid, having an aromatic odour; it boils at 144° C. The bromacetate of ethyl boils at 159° C.; that of amyl at 207° C.

By the action of ammonia on bromacetic acid, bromide of ammonium is formed, and glycocol, or a body isomeric with it.

Bibromacetic Acid. Formed when bromine and acetic acid are heated in presence of light, but it is difficult to obtain in large quantities. It is a liquid boiling at 240° C., which is partially decomposed every time it is distilled, evolving hydrobromic acid. It does not solidify at 15° C. It has a very high specific gravity. The silver salt is a crystalline precipitate which is, however, decomposed, by boiling with water, into bromide of silver and a soluble acid.

BROMATES. Compounds of BROMIC ACID with alkalis, alkaline earths, and metals.

BROMIC ACID. A combination of bromine with oxygen, forming bromates.

BROMIC SILVER. See SILVER ORES.

BROMIDES. Compounds of BROMINE with alkalis and metals.

BROMIDE OF SILVER. A salt much used in photography. It is formed by adding a soluble bromide to nitrate of silver, when a white precipitate is produced. See PHOTOGRAPHY.

BROMITE. Native bromide of silver.

BRONZE. (*Bronze,* Fr. and Ger.) A compound metal consisting of copper and tin, to which sometimes a little zinc and lead are added. There is some confusion amongst Continental writers about this alloy; they translate their bronze into the English *brass*.

See, for an example of this, 'Dictionnaire des Arts et Manufactures.' This has arisen from the carelessness of our own writers. Dr. Watson, 'Chemical Essays,' remarks: 'It has been said that Queen Elizabeth left more *brass ordnance* at her death than she found iron on her accession to the throne. This must not be understood as if gun-metal was made in her time of brass, for the term brass was sometimes used to denote copper; and sometimes a composition of iron, copper, and calamine was called brass; and we, at this day, commonly speak of *brass cannon*, though brass does not enter into the composition used for casting cannon.'

Bronze is an alloy of copper and tin.

Brass is an alloy of copper and zinc.

In many instances, we have zinc, lead, &c., entering into the composition of alloys of copper and tin. However this may be, the alloy is called a bronze, if tin and copper are the chief constituents.

This alloy is much harder than copper, and was employed by the ancients to make swords, hatchets, &c., before the method of working iron was generally understood. Most modern archæologists, following the Danish antiquaries, recognise a *bronze age*; that is to say, an epoch of civilisation when bronze was the only metal in general use for cutting instruments, and other useful or ornamental objects. This period is generally held to have been subsequent to the so-called *stone age* and anterior to that of *iron*. Some authorities, however, arguing on metallurgical rather than on archæological grounds, have called this chronology in question, and have maintained that a knowledge of iron must have preceded that of bronze. Be that as it may, it is certain that the use of bronze was general at a very early period in the history of Western civilisation.

The art of casting bronze statues may be traced to the most remote antiquity, but it was first brought to a certain degree of refinement by Theodoros and Rœcus of Samos, about 700 years before the Christian era, to whom the invention of modelling is ascribed by Pliny. The ancients were well aware that by alloying copper with tin, a more fusible metal was obtained, that the process of casting was therefore rendered easier, and that the statue was harder and more durable. It was during the reign of Alexander that bronze statuary received its greatest extension, when the celebrated artist Lysippus succeeded, by new processes of moulding and melting, in multiplying groups of statues to such a degree that Pliny called them the *mob of Alexander*. Soon afterwards enormous bronze colossuses were made, to the height of towers, of which the isle of Rhodes possessed no less than one hundred. The Roman consul Mutianus found 3,000 bronze statues at Athens, 3,000 at Rhodes, as many at Olympia and at Delphi, although a great number had been previously carried off from the last town.

From the analyses of Mr. J. A. Phillips, we learn that most of the ancient coins were bronzes, the quantity of tin relatively to the copper varying slightly. The proportions of copper and tin in many of those coins are given below, the other ingredients being omitted:—

			Copper.	Tin.
A coin of Alexander the Great,	335 B.C.	.	86·72	13·14
„ Philippus V.	. 200 B.C.	.	85·15	11·10
„ Athens	. .	.	88·41	9·95
„ Ptolemy IX.	. 70 B.C.	.	84·21	15·59
„ Pompey	. 53 B.C.	.	74·11	8.56
„ the Atilia family	. 45 B.C.	.	68·72	4·77
„ Augustus and Agrippa,	30 B.C.	.	78·58	12·91

The arms and cutting instruments of the ancients were composed of similar bronzes, as the following proportions, also selected from Mr. J. A. Phillips' analyses, will show:—

				Tin.	Copper.
Roman sword blade, found in the Thames	.	85·70	.	10·02
„ „ „	Ireland	.	91·39	.	8·38
Celtic „ „	Ireland	.	90·23	.	7·50

Layard brought from Assyria a considerable variety of bronze articles, many of them objects of ornament, but many evidently intended for use. Amongst others was a bronze foot, which was constructed for the purpose of support of some kind. This was submitted to the examination of Dr. Percy. It was then found that the bronze had been cast round a support of iron. By this means the appearance of considerable lightness was attained, while great strength was insured. This discovery proves in a very satisfactory manner, that the metallurgists of Assyria were perfectly conversant with the use of iron, and that they employed it for the purpose of imparting strength to the less tenacious metals which they employed in their art-manufactures. This bronze, as analysed in the Metallurgical Laboratory of the Museum of Practical Geology, consists of copper 88·37, tin 11·33.

Examination has shown that all the bronze weapons of the Greeks and Romans were not only of the true composition for insuring the greatest density in the alloy itself, but that these, by a process of hammering the cutting edges, were brought up to the greatest degree of hardness and tenacity.

Before 1542, 'brass ordnance' (*bronze*) was founded by foreigners. Stow says that John Owen began to found brass ordnance, and that he was the first Englishman who ever made that kind of artillery in England.

Bell founding followed. Bell-metal and other broken metal were allowed to be exported hitherto; but it being discovered that it was applied to found guns abroad, 'brass, copper, latten, bell metal, pan metal, gun metal, and shroff metal, are prohibited to be exported.'

Bronze has almost always been used for casting statues, bassi-rilievi, and works which are to be exposed to atmospheric influences. In forming such statues, the alloy should be capable of flowing readily into all the parts of the mould, however, minute; it should be hard, in order to resist accidental blows, be proof against the influence of the weather, and be of such a nature as to acquire that greenish oxidised coat upon the surface, which is so much admired in the antique bronzes, called *patina antiqua*. The chemical composition of the bronze alloy is a matter therefore of the first moment. The Brothers Keller, celebrated founders in the time of Louis XIV., whose *chefs-d'œuvre* are well known, directed their attention towards this point, to which too little importance is attached at the present day. The statue of Desaix, in the Place Dauphine, and the column in the Place Vendôme are noted specimens of most defective workmanship from mismanagement of the alloys of which they are composed. On analysing separately specimens taken from the bas-reliefs of the pedestal of this column, from the shaft, and from the capital, it was found that the first contained only 6 per cent. of tin, and 94 of copper, the second much less, and the third only 0·21. It was therefore obvious that the founder, unskilful in the melting of bronze, had gone on progressively refining his alloy, by the oxidisement of the tin, till he had exhausted the copper, and that he had then worked up the refuse scoriæ in the upper part of the column. The cannon which the Government furnished him for casting the monument consisted of :—

Copper	89·360
Tin	10·040
Lead	0·102
Silver, zinc, iron, and loss	0·498
	100·000

The moulding of the several bas-reliefs was so ill executed, that the chiselers employed to repair the faults removed no less than 70 tons of bronze, which was given them, besides 300,000 francs for their work. The statues made by the Kellers at Versailles were found, on chemical analysis, to consist of :—

	No. 1.	No. 2.	No. 3.	The mean.
Copper	91·30	91·68	91·22	91·40
Tin	1·00	2·32	1·78	1·70
Zinc	6·09	4·93	5.57	5·53
Lead	1·61	1·07	1·43	1·37
	100·000	100·000	100·000	100·000

The analysis of the bronze of the statue of Louis XV. was as follows :—

Copper	82·45	Its specific gravity was 8·482
Zinc	10·30	
Tin	4·10	
Lead	3·15	
	100·00	

The bronzes of France, according to M. L. E. Rivot, contain nearly always four metals, copper, tin, lead, and zinc. They may contain also very small and variable quantities of iron, nickel, arsenic, antimony, and sulphur.

The alloys most proper for bronze to be afterwards struck for medals is composed of from 8 to 12 parts of tin and from 88 to 92 of copper; to which if 2 or 3 parts in the hundred of zinc be added, they will make it assume a finer bronze tint. The alloy of the Kellers is famous for this effect. The metal should be subjected to three or four successive stamps of the press, and be softened between each blow by being heated and plunged into cold water.

The addition of a small proportion of phosphorus has recently been recommended to improve the quality of bronze.

The bronze of bells, or bell-metal, is composed, in 100 parts, of copper 78, tin 22. This alloy has a fine compact grain, is very fusible and sonorous. The other metals sometimes added are rather prejudicial, and merely increase the profit of the founders. Some of the English bells consist of 80 copper, 10·1 tin, 5·6 zinc, 4·3 lead; the latter metal, when in such large quantities, is apt to cause isolated drops, hurtful to the uniformity of the alloy.

The *Tam-tams and Cymbals of Bronze.*—The Chinese make use of bronze instruments forged by the hammer, which are very thin and raised up in the middle; they are called gongs, from the word *tshoung*, which signifies a bell. Klaproth has shown that they contain nothing but copper and tin, in the proportion of 78 of the former metal and 22 of the latter. Their specific gravity is 8·815. This alloy, when newly cast, is as brittle as glass; but being plunged at a cherry-red heat into cold water, and confined between two discs of iron to keep it in shape, it becomes tough and malleable. The cymbals consist of 80 parts copper and 20 tin.

Bronze vessels, naturally brittle, may be made tenacious by the same ingenious process, for which the world is indebted to M. Darcet. Bronze mortars for pounding have their lips tempered in the same way.

Cannon Metal consists of about 90 or 91 copper, and 10 or 9 of tin. From the experiments of Papacino d'Antony, made at Turin, in 1770, it appears that the most proper alloy for great guns is from 12 to 14 parts of tin to 100 of copper; but the Comte Lamartillière concluded, from his experiments made at Douay, in 1786, that never less than 8 nor more than 11 of tin should be employed in 100 parts of bronze.

Gilt Ornaments of Bronze.—This kind of bronze should be easy of fusion, and take perfectly the impression of the mould. The alloy of copper and zinc (brass) is, when fused, of a pasty consistence, does not make a sharp cast, is apt to absorb too much amalgam, is liable to crack in cooling, and is too tough or too soft for the chaser or turner; and if the quantity of zinc was increased, to make the metal harder, it would lose the yellow colour suitable to the gilder. A fourfold combination of copper, zinc, tin, and lead is preferable for making such ornamental bronze articles; and the following proportions are probably the best, as they unite closeness of grain with the other good qualities. Copper 82, zinc 18, tin 3 or 1, lead 1½ or 3. In the alloy which contains most lead, the tenacity is diminished and the density is increased, which is preferable for pieces of small dimensions. Another alloy, which is said to require for its gilding only two-thirds of the ordinary quantity of gold, has the following composition: copper 82·247, zinc 17·481, tin 0·238, lead 0·024.

The antique bronze colour is given to figures and other objects made from these alloys by the following process:—Two drachms of sal-ammoniac, and half a drachm of salt of sorrel, (binoxalate of potash,) are to be dissolved in fourteen ounce measures (English) of colourless vinegar. A hair pencil being dipped into this solution, and pressed gently between the fingers, is to be rubbed equally over the clean surface of the object slightly warmed in the sun or at a stove; and the operation is to be repeated till the wished-for shade is obtained.

The bronze founder ought to melt his metals rapidly, in order to prevent the loss of tin, zinc, and lead by their oxidisement. Reverberatory furnaces have been long used for this operation, the best being of an elliptical form. The furnaces with dome tops are employed by the bell founders, because, their alloy being more fusible, they do not require so intense a heat; but they also would find their advantage in using the most rapid mode of fusion. The surface of the melting metals should be covered with small charcoal or coke; and when the tin is added, it should be dexterously thrust to the bottom of the melted copper. Immediately after stirring the melted mass so as to incorporate its ingredients, it should be poured out into the moulds. In general, the metals most easily altered by the fire, as the tin, should be put in last. The cooling should be as quickly as possible in the moulds, to prevent the risk of the metals separating from each other in the order of their density, as they are very apt to do. The addition of a little iron—in the form of tin plate—to bronze, is reckoned to be advantageous.

One part of tin, and two parts of copper (nearly one atom of tin and four of copper, or more exactly 100 parts of tin and 215 copper), form the ordinary speculum metal of reflecting telescopes, which is of all the alloys the whitest, the most brilliant, the hardest, and the most brittle, The alloy of 1 part of tin and 10 of copper (or nearly one atom of the former to eighteen of the latter), is the strongest of the whole series.

Ornamental objects of bronze, after being cast, are commonly laid upon red-hot coals till they take a dull red heat, and are then exposed for some time to the air. The surface is thereby freed from any greasy matter, some portion of the zinc is dissipated, and the alloy assumes more of a coppery hue, which prepares for the subsequent gilding. The black tinge which it sometimes gets from the fire may be removed by washing it with a weak acid. It may be made very clean by acting upon it with nitric acid, of specific gravity 1·324, to which a little common salt and soot have been added, the latter being of doubtful utility; after which it must be well washed in water, and dried with rags or sawdust.

For the following Table we are indebted to Mr. Robert Mallet, F.R.S., whose investigations in this direction have been most extensive, and as accurate as they are extensive :—

	Chemical Constitution	Composition by Weight per Cent.	Atomic Weight	Specific Gravity	Fracture [1]	Colour of Fracture	Ultimate Cohesion Per Square Inch	Inverse Order of Ductility	Order of Malleability at 60° F.	Inverse Order of Hardness	Inverse Order of Fusibility	Commercial Titles, characteristic Properties in working, &c.
1	Cu	100·00+	31·6	8·667	E	Tile red	24·6	1	2	10	16	Copper.
2	10 Cu+Sn	84·29+ 15·71	374·9	8·561	FC	Reddish yellow, 1	16·1	2	6	8	15	Gun metal, &c.
3	9 Cu+Sn	82·81+ 17·19	343·3	8·462	FC	Reddish yellow, 2	15·2	3	7	5	14	Ditto.
4	8 Cu+Sn	81·10+ 18·90	311·7	8·459	FC	Yellowish red, 2	17·7	4	10	4	13	Gun metal, tempers best.
5	7 Cu+Sn	78·97+ 21·03	280·1	8·728	VC	Yellowish red, 1	13·6	5	11	3	12	Hard mill brasses, &c.
6	6 Cu+Sn	76·29+ 23·71	248·5	8·750	V	Bluish red, 1	9·7	0	12	2	11	Brittle.[2]
7	5 Cu+Sn	72·80+ 27·20	216·9	8·575	C	Bluish red, 2	4·9	0	13	1	10	Brittle.[2]
8	4 Cu+Sn	68·21+ 31·79	185·3	8·400	C	Ash grey	0·7	0	14	6	9	Crumbles.[2]
9	3 Cu+Sn	61·69+ 38·31	153·7	8·539	TC	Dark grey	0·5	0	16	7	8	Crumbles.[2]
10	2 Cu+Sn	51·75+ 48·25	122·1	8·416	VC	Greyish white, 1	1·7	0	15	9	7	Brittle.[2]
11	Cu+Sn	34·92+ 65·08	90·5	8·056	TC	Whiter still, 2	1·4	0	9	1	6	} Small bells, brittle.[2]
12	Cu+2Sn	21·15+ 78·85	149·4	7·387	CC	Ditto 3	3·9	0	8	1	5	
13	Cu+3Sn	15·17+ 84·83	208·3	7·447	CC	Ditto 4	3·1	0	5	1	4	Speculum Metal of authors.
14	Cu+4Sn	11·82+ 88·18	267·2	7·472	CC	Ditto 5	3·1	8	4	14	3	Files, tough.
15	Cu+5Sn	9·68+ 90·32	326·1	7·442	E	Ditto 6	2·7	6	3	15	2	Files, soft and tough.
16	Sn	100·00	58·9	7·291	F	White, 7	2·5	7	1	16	1	Tin.

Bronze, Phosphorised. By carefully dropping phosphorus on melted bronze or copper a product rich in phosphorus is produced. This alloy is claiming much attention, and will be fully treated of under the head of PHOSPHOR BRONZE AND COPPER, which see. See also ALUMINIUM BRONZE.

Bronze Imports are now included under the heads of Brass, Bronze and Metal, Bronzed and Lacquered. Of these articles the following *Imports* are given in 1872 :—

	Cwts.		£
From Germany	679	Value	7,128
„ Holland	536	„	4,718
„ Belgium	303	„	2,317
„ France	4,236	„	44,102
„ United States of America . .	7,848	„	35,331
Other countries	3,773	„	16,179
Total	17,375		109,774

In the same year the *Exportation* of the same metals is given as—
To all countries . . . 1,018 cwts. valued at 5,650*l*.

[1] E signifies earthy ; C C, coarse crystalline ; F C, fine crystalline ; C, conchoidal ; V, vitreous ; V C, vitreous-conchoidal ; T C, tabular crystalline.
[2] All these alloys are found occasionally in bells and specula with mixtures of Zn and Pb.

www.ingramcontent.com/pod-product-compliance
Lightning Source LLC
Chambersburg PA
CBHW081347280326
41927CB00043B/3305